Seventh Edition

BUSINESS AND ITS ENVIRONMENT

David P. Baron
Stanford University

PEARSON

Boston   Columbus   Indianapolis   New York   San Francisco   Upper Saddle River
Amsterdam   Cape Town   Dubai   London   Madrid   Milan   Munich   Paris   Montreal   Toronto
Delhi   Mexico City   São Paulo   Sydney   Hong Kong   Seoul   Singapore   Taipei   Tokyo

2000449

This book is not for sale or distribution in the U.S.A. or Canada

Senior Acquisitions Editor: April Kalal Cole
Editor-in-Chief: Stephanie Wall
Senior Editorial Project Manager: Claudia Fernandes
Editorial Assistant: Bernard Ollila
Director of Marketing: Maggie Moylan
Senior Marketing Manager: Nikki Ayana Jones
Manager, Rights and Permissions: Michael Joyce
Permission Specialist: Brooks Hill-Whilton
Production Project Manager: Thomas Benfatti

Creative Director: Jayne Conte
Cover Designer: Karen Salzback
Cover Art: Shutterstock
Full-Service Project Management: Kiruthiga Anand
Composition: Integra Software Services, Pvt. Ltd.
Printer/Binder: R.R. Donnelley/Willard
Cover Printer: Lehigh-Phoenix Color/Hagerstown
Text Font: 10/12, Times

Credits and acknowledgments borrowed from other sources and reproduced, with permission, in this textbook appear on the appropriate page within text.

Many of the designations by manufacturers and sellers to distinguish their products are claimed as trademarks. Where those designations appear in this book, and the publisher was aware of a trademark claim, the designations have been printed in initial caps or all caps.

Library of Congress Cataloging-in-Publication Data
Baron, David P.
  Business and its environment / David P. Baron. — 7th ed.
    p. cm.
  ISBN-13: 978-0-13-262055-0 (alk. paper)
  ISBN-10: 0-13-262055-3 (alk. paper)
  1. Social responsibility of business. 2. Industrial policy. 3. Commercial law. 4. Business ethics. I. Title.
  HD60.B37 2013
  658.4'08—dc23   2012008787

10 9 8 7 6 5 4 3 2 1

PEARSON

ISBN 10:   0-13-262055-3
ISBN 13: 978-0-13-262055-0

To Mary

BRIEF CONTENTS

PART I Strategy and the Nonmarket Environment 1

Chapter 1 Market and Nonmarket Environments 1
Chapter 2 Integrated Strategy 30
Chapter 3 The News Media and Nonmarket Issues 52
Chapter 4 Private Politics and Social Pressure 74
Chapter 5 Crisis Management 102

PART II Public Politics and Nonmarket Strategy 132

Chapter 6 Nonmarket Analysis for Business 132
Chapter 7 Nonmarket Strategies for Government Arenas 162
Chapter 8 Implementing Nonmarket Strategies in Government Arenas 195

PART III Government and Markets 230

Chapter 9 Antitrust: Economics, Law, and Politics 230
Chapter 10 Regulation: Law, Economics, and Politics 264
Chapter 11 Financial Markets and Their Regulation 291
Chapter 12 Environmental Management and Sustainability 321
Chapter 13 The Investor's Perspective: Renewable Energy 358
Chapter 14 Law and Markets 380

PART IV Global Nonmarket Strategy 417

Chapter 15 The Political Economy of the European Union 417
Chapter 16 China: History, Culture, and Political Economy 448
Chapter 17 Emerging Markets 477
Chapter 18 The Political Economy of India 502
Chapter 19 The Political Economy of International Trade Policy 519

PART V Ethics and Corporate Social Responsibility 557

Chapter 20 Corporate Social Responsibility 557
Chapter 21 Ethics Systems: Utilitarianism 594
Chapter 22 Ethics Systems: Rights and Justice 622
Chapter 23 Behavioral Ethics, Individuals, and Management 659
Chapter 24 Ethics in International Business 681

CONTENTS

List of Cases xxiii

Preface xxvii

About the Author xxxi

Part I Strategy and the Nonmarket Environment 1

Chapter 1 MARKET AND NONMARKET ENVIRONMENTS 1

Introduction 1

The Environment of Business 2

The Role of Management 3

Market and Nonmarket Environments 3

Analysis of the Nonmarket Environment: The Four I's 4

The Nonmarket Environment of the Automobile Industry 5

    Issues 5

    Interests 9

    Institutions 9

    Information 10

Change in the Nonmarket Environment 11

Anticipating Change in the Nonmarket Environment 13

    ■ **EXAMPLE: Graduation Cards 13**

The Nonmarket Issue Life Cycle 14

Summary 15

Cases 16

    The Nonmarket Environment of the Pharmaceutical Industry 16

    The Nonmarket Environment of McDonald's 19

    The Nonmarket Environment of Google 23

Chapter 2 INTEGRATED STRATEGY 30

Introduction 30

Strategy in the Nonmarket Environment 31

    The Importance of Nonmarket Strategy 31

    Competition and Change in the Nonmarket Environment 32

    Strategy and the Nonmarket Issue Life Cycle 32

    Strategies and Borders 33

Integrated Strategy 34

    ■ **EXAMPLE: Google and the Spectrum Auction 34**

    ■ **EXAMPLE: Direct-to-Consumer Advertising and Integrated Strategy in the Pharmaceutical Industry 36**

    Approaches to Integrating Market and Nonmarket Strategies 37

Nonmarket Positioning 38

    ■ **EXAMPLE: eBay's Positioning in Legal Space 38**

    Nonmarket Positioning and Market Strategies 39

    Positioning Spaces 41

    The Perils of Positioning 42

Nonmarket Capabilities and Reputation 42

A Framework for the Analysis of Nonmarket Issues   43
   ■ **EXAMPLE: Citibank and Credit Cards for Undergraduates   45**
Organization of the Nonmarket Strategy Function   46
Summary   46
Cases   47
   Facebook in China?   47
   Personal Watercraft, aka Jet Skis   49

Chapter 3   THE NEWS MEDIA AND NONMARKET ISSUES   52
Introduction   52
The Role of the News Media in Nonmarket Issues   52
Messages and Their Interpretation   54
A Theory of News Media Coverage and Treatment   54
   Intrinsic Audience Interest   55
   Societal Significance   55
   Combining the Perspectives   56
Extending the Theory   57
   Newsworthiness   57
   The Cost of Coverage   58
   Balance and Fairness   58
The Nature of the News Media   59
   News Organizations as Businesses   59
   The Profession   59
   Does the News Media Treat Issues Selectively?   60
   Bias, Accuracy, and Fairness   60
   The Internet and Citizen Journalism   62
Business Interactions with the News Media   62
   The Need for Information   62
   Media Strategies   63
   Responses and Media Vacuums   63
   Media Interviews   64
   Anticipating Issues   64
   Unanticipated Events   65
Recourse in Disputes with the Media   65
   Private Recourse   65
   Recourse to the Law: Defamation and Libel   66
   ■ **EXAMPLE: Procter & Gamble and Neighbor to Neighbor   66**
   Political Recourse   68
Summary   69
Cases   69
   General Motors: Like a Rock? (A)   69
   The News of the World   72

Chapter 4   PRIVATE POLITICS AND SOCIAL PRESSURE   74
Introduction   74
   Private Politics and the Nonmarket Environment   75
   The Evolution of Private Politics   76

Confrontational Private Politics   78

■ **EXAMPLE: Pizza Hut and Health Insurance Reform**   79

Cooperative Private Politics   81

Synergies between Confrontational and Cooperative Private
Politics   83

■ **EXAMPLE: TXU and the Leveraged Buyout**   83

Moderates and Radicals   84

Activist Strategies   *84*

Advocacy Science   85

Target Selection   86

A Generic Strategy of Activists   86

Strategies for Adressing Social Pressure   *87*

Assessment   87

Strategy and Negotiations   88

■ **EXAMPLE: Negotiating with Activists: On Bank**   90

Challenging the Activists   90

Summary   *91*

Cases   *92*

Shell, Greenpeace, and Brent Spar   *92*

Nike in Southeast Asia   *95*

*Anatomy of a Corporate Campaign: Rainforest Action Network
and Citigroup (A)*   *97*

*Anatomy of a Corporate Campaign: Rainforest Action Network
and Citigroup (B)*   *100*

Chapter 5   CRISIS MANAGEMENT   102

Introduction   *102*

The Nature and Causes of Crises   *102*

The Pattern of Crisis Development   *103*

■ **EXAMPLE: PepsiCo and the Syringe Episode**   105

Components of a Crisis Management Program   *107*

Avoidance   108

Preparedness   108

Root Cause Analysis   110

Response   111

Resolution   114

Summary   *115*

Cases   *116*

Mattel: Crisis Management or Management Crisis   *116*

Johnson & Johnson and Its Quality Reputation   *120*

**Part I   Integrative Case: *Wal-Mart: Nonmarket Pressure and Reputation
Risk (A)*   *124***

Part II   Public Politics and Nonmarket Strategy   132

Chapter 6   NONMARKET ANALYSIS FOR BUSINESS   132

Introduction   *132*

*A Framework for the Analysis of Nonmarket Action in Public
Politics*   *133*

Interests and Interest Groups 133
The Amount of Nonmarket Action 134
The Demand for Nonmarket Action 134
The Costs and Effectiveness of Nonmarket Action 135
The Distributive Politics Spreadsheet 136
The Nature of Political Competition 137
Institutions and Institutional Officeholders 139
■ **EXAMPLE: Internet Wine Sales 139**
Moral Determinants of Collective Action 140
Boeing in a Pickle 140
Analysis of Boeing in a Pickle 142
The Nonmarket Issue 142
Distributive Consequences 142
Boeing's Nonmarket Agenda and Objectives 144
The Nature of the Politics 144
Interests and the Demand for Nonmarket Action 144
The Supply Side 145
The Distributive Politics Spreadsheet 146
Institutions and Institutional Officeholders 146
Nonmarket Strategy Formulation 146
The Outcome 148
Summary 149
Appendix A: Nonmarket Action and the Free-Rider Problem 150
Appendix B: The Organization of Congress 152
Cases 157
Tobacco Politics 157
Business versus Business 158
Repeal of the Luxury Tax 160

Chapter 7 NONMARKET STRATEGIES FOR GOVERNMENT ARENAS 162
Introduction 162
Responsible Nonmarket Action 162
Criticisms of Business Nonmarket Action 163
Nonmarket Strategy Formulation 166
Managers and Nonmarket Strategies 166
Implementation 170
Understanding Outcomes 171
Generic Nonmarket Strategies 172
Representation Strategies 172
■ **EXAMPLE: Toshiba and Trade Sanctions 172**
Majority-Building Strategies 174
Informational Strategies 178
Public Officeholders as Targets of Nonmarket Strategies 179
■ **EXAMPLE: China and Most Favored Nation Status 179**
Institutions, Interests, and Strategy Choice 180
Institutions and Responsiveness 180
Interests: Client and Interest Group Politics 181
Summary 182

Appendix A: Condorcet's Paradox and Arrow's Impossibility Theorem   183

Appendix B: The Politics of the Extension of Daylight Saving Time   184

Cases   188

    Federal Express and Labor Organization   188

    Carried Interest Taxation   189

    Wal-Mart and Health Care Policy   192

Chapter 8 IMPLEMENTING NONMARKET STRATEGIES IN GOVERNMENT ARENAS   195

Introduction   195

Lobbying   195

    The Nature of Lobbying   196

    Technical and Political Information   197

    Credibility and Relevance of Information   198

    Access   199

    Bargaining   199

    Timing and Focus   200

    Government Allies   200

    Controls on Lobbying   200

    ■ **EXAMPLE: Michelle Obama and Wal-Mart   201**

Electoral Support   202

    Myths and Realities of Campaign Financing   202

    Election Financing Laws   202

    The Pattern of Campaign Contributions   204

    Purposes of Campaign Contributions   204

Coalition Building   205

    Peak Associations   205

    Trade Associations   206

    Ad Hoc Coalitions   206

    Coalitions and Consensus   206

    ■ **EXAMPLE: Pharmaceutical Politics   207**

Grassroots and Constituency Campaigns   208

    Mobilization   208

    Business Grassroots Campaigns   208

    The Effectiveness of Grassroots Programs   209

Testimony   209

Public Advocacy   210

Judicial Actions   211

Organizing for Nonmarket Effectiveness   212

Developing Nonmarket Capabilities   212

Summary   213

Cases   214

    Internet Taxation   214

    Wal-Mart and Its Urban Expansion Strategy   218

    Responsible Lobbying?   220

Part II Integrative Case: *Amazon.Com and the Amazon Tax*   225

Part III Government and Markets 230

Chapter 9 ANTITRUST: ECONOMICS, LAW, AND POLITICS 230

Introduction 230
Antitrust Law 231
   The Antitrust Statutes 231
   ■ **EXAMPLE: Monopoly** 233
   Exemptions 233
Enforcement of the Antitrust Laws 235
   Government Enforcement 235
   Private Enforcement 237
   Per Se Violations and the Rule of Reason 238
Antitrust Thought 238
   The Structural Approach 239
   The Chicago School 241
   The New IO Approach 243
Examples of the Differences in Antitrust Thought 244
   Vertical Arrangements 244
   Predatory Pricing and Entry Deterrence 246
   Collusion and Price Fixing 247
   Mergers and Merger Guidelines 248
Compliance 250
The Politics of Antitrust 250
Summary 251
Cases 252
   Price Fixing in the Airways 252
   The AT&T and T-Mobile Merger? 253
   The Microsoft Antitrust Case 257

Chapter 10 REGULATION: LAW, ECONOMICS, AND POLITICS 264

Introduction 264
Periods of Regulatory Change 265
The Constitutional Basis for Regulation 266
Regulatory Commissions and Agencies 266
Delegation, Rule Making, Due Process, and Discretion 267
The Nonmarket Environment of Regulatory Agencies 269
   ■ **EXAMPLE: Regulatory Rule Making in the Bush Administration** 270
Explanations for Regulation 271
Market Imperfections 271
   Natural Monopoly 271
   Externalities 272
   Public Goods 273
   Asymmetric Information 274
   Moral Hazard 274
   Allocating Public Resources 276
   Government Imperfections 276
The Political Economy of Regulation 276
   Capture and Rent-Seeking Theories 276
   Fairness 277

Other Public Purposes: Media Ownership Rules   278

Preemption   278

A Political Economy Theory of Regulation   278

■ **EXAMPLE: The Political Economy of Regulation: ATVs**   279

Redistribution and Cross-Subsidization   280

Accomplishing Through Regulation What Cannot Be Accomplished Through Legislation   281

Cost-of-Service Regulation   283

Deregulation   283

Electric Power   283

Auctions   285

Summary   285

Cases   286

Merck and Vioxx   286

Pfizer and Celebrex   288

Enron Power Marketing, Inc., and the California Market   289

Chapter 11   FINANCIAL MARKETS AND THEIR REGULATION   291

Introduction   291

The Formal and Informal (Shadow) Banking Systems   291

The U.S. Regulatory Structure   295

The Federal Reserve System   295

Securities Regulation   295

Credit Card Regulation   296

The Financial Crisis, 2007–2009   296

Mortgage Lending and Subprime Mortgages   296

Financial Crisis Inquiry Commission   298

Causes   299

TARP, Bailouts, and the Stimulus   300

Fannie Mae and Freddie Mac   301

The Dodd-Frank Wall Street Reform and Consumer Protection Act   301

Financial Stability Oversight Council   302

Too Big to Fail   302

The Volcker Rule   302

Derivatives and Swaps   303

Securitization and Excessive Risks   303

Consumer Protection   303

■ **EXAMPLE: Constituency Power**   304

■ **EXAMPLE: Anticipated Consequences—Credit Availability**   304

Compensation   305

Credit Rating Agencies   306

■ **EXAMPLE: Unanticipated Consequences—Experts**   306

Global Capital Requirements Regulation—Basel III   307

Summary   308

Cases   308

Goldman Sachs and Its Reputation   308

Credit Rating Agencies   314

Citigroup and Subprime Lending   318

Chapter 12 ENVIRONMENTAL MANAGEMENT AND SUSTAINABILITY 321

Introduction 321

The Environment and Sustainability 321

Goals and Actions 321

Global Climate Change 322

Policy 322

Tradeoffs 323

Socially Efficient Control of Externalities 324

The Coase Theorem 324

■ **EXAMPLE: The Coase Theorem 325**

Transactions Costs and the Limits of the Coase Theorem 327

Cap-and-Trade Systems 327

Cap-and-Trade Systems to Address Acid Rain 328

Tradable Permits for Sulfur Dioxide and Nitrogen Oxides 329

Global Climate Change and Emissions Trading Systems 330

Kyoto Protocol 331

Emissions Trading in the European Union 332

The Regional Greenhouse Gas Initiative (RGGI) 332

Emissions Trading Within BP plc (British Petroleum) 333

Government Policy 333

The EPA 333

Enforcement 334

Standards Setting and Engineering Controls 335

■ **EXAMPLE: Intel and Project XL 336**

Incentive Approaches 336

Superfund 337

State Policy Initiatives 337

The Political Economy of Environmental Protection 338

The Nature of Environmental Politics 338

Judicial Politics 338

Advocacy Science 338

Distributive Politics 339

Private and Public Politics 340

■ **EXAMPLE: The Equator Principles 340**

Nimby and Private Politics 341

Management of Environmental Protection Issues 342

■ **EXAMPLE: Dow Chemical and Local Environmentalists 344**

■ **EXAMPLE: Mcdonald's and Waste Reduction 345**

■ **EXAMPLE: Environmental Activism at Home Depot 346**

Voluntary Collective Environmental Programs 347

Summary 347

Cases 348

Pacific Gas & Electric and the Smart Meter Challenge 348

Environmental Justice and Pollution Credits Trading Systems 353

Environmentalist versus Environmentalist 356

Chapter 13 **THE INVESTOR'S PERSPECTIVE: RENEWABLE ENERGY   358**

Introduction   358

   Investment Decisions   358

The Environment of Wind and Solar Power   359

   Markets and Government Involvement   359

   Market Signals   360

   ■ **EXAMPLE: Environmentalist Opposition   361**

Economic and Political Rationales for Subsidization   361

   The Costs of Subsidization   362

   Examples   363

   ■ **EXAMPLE: The Market Threat from China   364**

Example: Solyndra, Inc.   365

   Risks and Opportunities Assessment   366

   Market Risks: Prices and Costs   367

   Nonmarket Risks   367

   Distributive Politics Analysis   368

   Implementation   369

   Nonmarket Risks: China   370

   Developments   371

Summary   372

Cases   372

   BrightSource Energy: The Challenges   372

   Silver Spring Networks and the Smart Grid   375

   T-Solar and the Solar Power Market   377

Chapter 14 **LAW AND MARKETS   380**

Introduction   380

The Common Law   381

Property   382

   Bargaining   382

   Incentives and Appropriability   382

Intellectual Property   382

   Intellectual Property Protection   384

   ■ **Patent Wars   385**

   ■ **EXAMPLE: Mickey Mouse Politics and Law   386**

   Trademarks and Trade Secrets   387

Contracts   388

   Enforceability   388

   ■ **EXAMPLE: Genentech and City of Hope   389**

   Breach   390

   Remedies   390

Torts   391

The Product Safety Problem and Social Efficiency   392

Entitlements, Liability, and Social Efficiency   394

   Entitlements and Their Protection   394

   The Assignment of Social Costs and the Choice Between Liability and Regulation   395

Products Liability   396

    The Development of Products Liability Law   396

    Allowable Defenses Under Strict Liability   399

    Preemption   400

    Damages   400

    The Politics of Products Liability   401

Imperfections in the Liability System   403

    ■ **EXAMPLE: Silicone Breast Implants   404**

Summary   406

Cases   407

    California Space Heaters, Inc.   407

    Patent Games: Plavix   409

    Obesity and McLawsuits   411

Part III   Integrative Case: *Spectrum for Wireless Broadband: Old Media Versus New Media   415*

Part IV   Global Nonmarket Strategy   417

Chapter 15   THE POLITICAL ECONOMY OF THE EUROPEAN UNION   417

Introduction   417

The European Union   417

    The Single European Act   418

    The Maastricht Treaty   419

    The Treaty of Lisbon   419

The Institutions of the European Union   420

    The European Commission   420

    The Council of Ministers and the European Council   421

    The European Parliament   422

    The Court of Justice   422

    The European Economic and Social Committee   423

    The EU Legislative Process   423

    The European Central Bank and Monetary Union   424

    Competition Policy   425

    ■ **EXAMPLE: Microsoft and EU Competition Policy   427**

    State Aids and the Common Agriculture Policy   428

    The Social Charter, Social Democracy, and Labor Markets   429

Nonmarket Issues   430

Interests and Their Organization   433

Nonmarket Strategies in the European Union   434

    ■ **EXAMPLE: Pronuptia and Franchising   438**

Summary   439

Cases   439

    The European Union Carbon Tax   439

    The European Union Data Protection Directive (B)   442

    The Euro Crisis   444

Chapter 16 CHINA: HISTORY, CULTURE, AND POLITICAL ECONOMY 448

Introduction 448

Historical Background 448

    Pre-Republican 448

    The Communist Era 450

    The Reform Era 452

Confucianism and Social Explanations 453

    Applications in Society, Politics, and Business 455

The Nonmarket Environment and the Four I's 457

    Institutions and Government 459

    State Institutions 460

    Provincial and Local Governments 462

Business: State-Owned Enterprises, Foreign Direct Investment, and International Trade 462

    State-Owned Enterprises 462

    Foreign Direct Investment 463

    International Trade Policy and WTO Membership 463

    Regulation 464

Continuing Issues 464

    Human Rights 464

    ■ **EXAMPLE: An Intellectual Property Challenge 466**

    Energy and the Environment 468

Summary 469

Cases 470

    Apple and Private Politics in China 470

    Direct Selling in China 471

    Google in China 472

Chapter 17 EMERGING MARKETS 477

Introduction 477

Country Assessment 477

    Individual Freedoms 477

    Economic Freedom 478

    Corruption 478

    Ease of Doing Business 478

    Competitiveness 478

    Political Risk 479

    Sovereign Default Risk 479

    Use of the Measures 479

    Culture 480

Opportunities 480

    Underdeveloped Markets and Business Groups 481

    Opportunity at the Bottom of the Pyramid? 481

    Microfinance 482

    Fair Trade 485

Risk Assessment   487
    Sources and Types of Risks   487
    Festering Anger and Revolution   488
Management in the Nonmarket Environment   492
Summary   493
Cases   493
    Social Entrepreneurship: Banco Compartamos   493
    Social Entrepreneurship: Kiva   495
    Equity Bank of Kenya   496
    MTN Group Limited   498

Chapter 18 THE POLITICAL ECONOMY OF INDIA   502
Introduction   502
Institutions   502
    Government   502
    History and Economic Development   503
    Economic Restrictions   504
Opportunities   505
    Market Opportunities   505
    Business Groups   507
    Patent law   507
    Pharmaceuticals   508
Nonmarket Issues   509
    Corruption   509
    Poverty and Welfare   510
    The Missing Girls   511
Summary   512
Cases   512
    Tesco PLC in India?   512
    Google in India   515
    Advanced Technology Laboratories, Inc.   517

Chapter 19 THE POLITICAL ECONOMY OF INTERNATIONAL TRADE POLICY   519
Introduction   519
The Economics of International Trade   520
    Competitive Theory   520
    Strategic Trade Theory   522
The Political Economy of International Trade Policy   523
    The Dual Nature of the Politics of International Trade   523
    Asymmetries in the Politics   524
International Trade Agreements   525
    The World Trade Organization   525
    General Agreement on Trade in Services (GATS)   526
    Trade-Related Aspects of Intellectual Property Rights (TRIPS)   527
    Agriculture   527

Government Procurement   528

Antidumping, Countervailing Duties, and Safeguards   528

Dispute Settlement   528

The Doha Round of WTO Negotiations   531

Other Trade Agreements   531

U.S. Trade Policy   532

The Structure of U.S. Trade Policy   532

U.S. Trade Law and Its Administration   532

The Political Economy of Protectionism   533

Formal Policies   533

■ **EXAMPLE: Renewable Power and Trade Complaints   534**

Channels of Protection   535

■ **EXAMPLE: Steel Imports and the Nonmarket Campaign   536**

The Political Economy of Market Opening   537

The North American Free Trade Agreement   537

Market Opening Under the Threat of Retaliation   538

Bilateral Free Trade Agreements   539

Summary   539

Cases   540

Cemex and Antidumping   540

Compulsory Licensing, Thailand, and Abbott Laboratories   545

The Airbus and Boeing Trade Disputes   549

Part IV   Integrative Case: *Toys 'Я' Us and Globalization*   552

Part V   Ethics and Corporate Social Responsibility   557

Chapter 20   CORPORATE SOCIAL RESPONSIBILITY   557

Introduction   557

The Trust Gap   557

What Is Corporate Social Responsibility?   558

Milton Friedman's Profit Maximization   559

■ **EXAMPLE: Timberland Company   563**

Compliance with the Law   563

Market and Government Failures and Stakeholders   564

Broader Conceptions of Social Responsibility   566

Perspectives   567

Self-Regulation   568

Corporate Social Responsibility and Corporate Social Performance   568

■ **EXAMPLE: Tuna and Dolphins   569**

A Framework for Understanding Corporate Social Performance   570

Terminology   570

The Setting   570

Motivations for CSP   571

Rewards   573

Summary   574

Empirical Research   574

Corporate Governance   576
   Social Accountability   576
   The Duties of Boards of Directors   577
   Sarbanes-Oxley   578
   Say-On-Pay   578
   The Market for Control   579
Summary   580
Cases   580
   The Collapse of Enron: Governance and Responsibility   580
   Wal-Mart: Nonmarket Pressure and Reputation Risk (B): A New Nonmarket Strategy   586
   Facebook and Online Privacy   588

Chapter 21 ETHICS SYSTEMS: UTILITARIANISM   594
Introduction   594
The Managerial Role of Ethics   594
What Ethics Is and Is Not   595
Personal and Business Ethics   595
Ethics and Individual Interests   596
Ethics, Politics, and Change   596
Casuistry   597
   ■ **EXAMPLE: Saving the Division   597**
The Methodology of Ethics   598
The Relationships Among Moral Philosophy, Ethics, and Political Philosophy   599
Utilitarianism: A Consequentialist System   600
   Utilitarianism and Self-Interest   601
   Aligning Self-Interest with Societal Well-Being   601
   Utilitarianism, Distribution, and Altruism   602
   Summary of the Components of Utilitarianism   602
Utilitarian Duty and the Calabresi and Melamed Principles   602
Act and Rule Utilitarianism   603
   Jointly Determined Consequences   605
   Decision Making in the Face of a Moral Transgression   606
Utilitarianism and Rights   606
Criticisms of Utilitarianism   606
   Philosophical Criticisms   606
   Interpersonal Comparisons of Utility   607
   Identifying Costs and Benefits   608
   The Measurement Problem   608
   The Information Problem   609
Utilitarianism in Application   609
   Categories of Situations   609
   Methodology   610
   ■ **EXAMPLE: Integrity Tests   610**
   ■ **EXAMPLE: Life Insurance Screening for Preexisting Conditions   611**
   ■ **EXAMPLE: Redlining   611**

Summary   612

Cases   613

> *Pricing the Norplant System   613*

> *Gilead Sciences (A): The Gilead Access Program for HIV Drugs   615*

> *Consumer Awareness or Disease Mongering? GlaxoSmithKline and the Restless Legs Syndrome   619*

Chapter 22   ETHICS SYSTEMS: RIGHTS AND JUSTICE   622

Introduction   622

Classification of Ethics Systems   622

Classes of Rights   623

Kantian Maxims or Moral Rules   624

> The Relationship between Maxims and Rights   624

> Intrinsic and Instrumental Rights   625

> ■ **EXAMPLE: Privacy   627**

> Criticisms of Kantian Rights   628

Applied Rights Analysis   629

> Claimed and Granted Rights   629

> A Methodology for Rights Analysis   630

> ■ **EXAMPLE: Life Insurance Screening for Preexisting Conditions   631**

Conflicts Among Rights   631

> Rights and Interests   631

> Prioritization   632

> ■ **EXAMPLE: Integrity Tests   633**

Equal Employment Opportunity   633

> ■ **EXAMPLE: Disparate Impact versus Disparate Treatment   635**

Paternalism   637

Neoclassical Liberalism   637

Categories of Justice Theories   638

> Distributive Justice   638

> Compensatory Justice   639

> Injustice   640

Rawls's Theory of Justice   640

> The Framework for Justice as Fairness   640

> The Principles of Justice   642

> The Role of Incentives   643

> Duty in Rawls's Theory   644

> ■ **EXAMPLE: Clinical Trial Obligations   644**

> Criticisms of Rawls's Theory   645

> ■ **EXAMPLE: Affirmative Action   646**

> Applying the Principles of Justice   647

> ■ **EXAMPLE: Integrity Tests   647**

> ■ **EXAMPLE: Redlining   648**

> ■ **EXAMPLE: Life Insurance Screening For Preexisting Conditions   648**

> Implementing Ethics Principles: Levi Strauss & Company and Global Sourcing   649

Higher Order Standards for Evaluating Ethics Systems   650

Summary 651

Cases 652

   Genetic Testing in the Workplace 652

   Chipotle Mexican Grill and Undocumented Workers 654

   Environmental Injustice? 656

Chapter 23 BEHAVIORAL ETHICS, INDIVIDUALS, AND MANAGEMENT 659

Introduction 659

Behavioral Ethics Experiments 660

   Self-Interest, Altruism, and Fairness 660

   Audience Effects, the Self, and Corporate Social Responsibility 662

   Reciprocity 663

   Behavior in Groups 665

   Implications for the Application of Ethics Principles 666

   Moral Suasion 666

   Conclusions from the Experiments 667

   Extrapolation 668

   Overconfidence in One's Self 668

Managerial Implications 668

The Challenge of Corporate Social Responsibility 670

   ■ **EXAMPLE: Citigroup: Responsibility Under Fire? 671**

   Core Principles and Their Evolution 672

   ■ **EXAMPLE: Johnson & Johnson's "Our Credo" 673**

Sources of Unethical Behavior 673

Summary 674

Cases 675

   Denny's and Customer Service 675

   Insider Trading 677

   Fresenius Medical Care in China 679

Chapter 24 ETHICS IN INTERNATIONAL BUSINESS 681

Introduction 681

International Law and Institutions 681

Cultural Relativism 683

Human Rights and Justice 686

   Slave Labor in Saipan? 686

Operating in Developing Countries 686

AIDS and Developing Countries 687

Responsibility for Working Conditions in Suppliers' Factories 688

   Sweatshops 688

   Private Governance and Self-Regulation: The Fair Labor Association 689

   Company Responses 690

Questionable Foreign Payments and Corruption   *691*

Questionable Payments and Ethics Principles   691

The Lockheed Case   692

A Utilitarian Analysis of Bribery   693

The Foreign Corrupt Practices Act   694

The UK Bribery Act   695

Company Codes   695

Cummins's Practice   696

The OECD Anti-Bribery Convention   698

Summary   698

Cases   699

Google Out of China   699

De Beers and Conflict Diamonds (A)   702

De Beers and Conflict Diamonds (B)   703

Siemens: Anatomy of Bribery   704

Part V   Integrative Case: *Glaxosmithkline and Aids Drugs Policy*   **707**

References   712

Index   724

LIST OF CASES

PART I

Chapter 1

The Nonmarket Environment of the Pharmaceutical Industry   16
The Nonmarket Environment of McDonald's   19
The Nonmarket Environment of Google   23

Chapter 2

Facebook in China?   47
Personal Watercraft, aka Jet Skis   49

Chapter 3

General Motors: Like a Rock? (A)   69
The News of the World   72

Chapter 4

Shell, Greenpeace, and Brent Spar   92
Nike in Southeast Asia   95
Anatomy of a Corporate Campaign: Rainforest Action Network and Citigroup (A)   97
Anatomy of a Corporate Campaign: Rainforest Action Network and Citigroup (B)   100

Chapter 5

Mattel: Crisis Management or Management Crisis   116
Johnson & Johnson and Its Quality Reputation   120

Part I Integrative Case

Wal-Mart: Nonmarket Pressure and Reputation Risk (A)   124

PART II

Chapter 6

Tobacco Politics   157
Business versus Business   158
Repeal of the Luxury Tax   160

Chapter 7

Federal Express and Labor Organization   188
Carried Interest Taxation   189
Wal-Mart and Health Care Policy   192

Chapter 8

Internet Taxation   214
Wal-Mart and Its Urban Expansion Strategy   218
Responsible Lobbying?   220

Part II Integrative Case

Amazon.com and the Amazon Tax   225

PART III

Chapter 9

Price Fixing in the Airways   252
The AT&T and T-Mobile Merger?   253
The Microsoft Antitrust Case   257

Chapter 10

Merck and Vioxx   286
Pfizer and Celebrex   288
Enron Power Marketing, Inc., and the California Market   289

Chapter 11

Goldman Sachs and Its Reputation   308
Credit Rating Agencies   314
Citigroup and Subprime Lending   318

Chapter 12

Pacific Gas & Electric and the Smart Meter Challenge   348
Environmental Justice ion Credits Trading Systems   353
Environmentalist versus Environmentalist   356

Chapter 13

BrightSource Energy: The Challenges   372
Silver Spring Networks and the Smart Grid   375
T-Solar and the Solar Power Market   377

Chapter 14

California Space Heaters, Inc.   407
Patent Games: Plavix   409
Obesity and McLawsuits   411

Part III Integrative Case

Spectrum for Wireless Broadband: Old Media versus New Media   415

PART IV

Chapter 15

The European Union Carbon Tax   439
The European Union Data Protection Directive (B)   442
The Euro Crisis   444

Chapter 16

Apple and Private Politics in China   470
Direct Selling in China   471
Google in China   472

Chapter 17

Social Entrepreneurship: Banco Compartamos   493
Social Entrepreneurship: Kiva   495
Equity Bank of Kenya   496
MTN Group Limited   498

Chapter 18

Tesco PLC in India?   512
Google in India   515
Advanced Technology Laboratories, Inc.   517

Chapter 19

Cemex and Antidumping   540
Compulsory Licensing, Thailand, and Abbott Laboratories   545
The Airbus and Boeing Trade Disputes   549

Part IV Integrative Case   552

Toys 'Я' Us and Globalization   552

PART V

Chapter 20

The Collapse of Enron: Governance and Responsibility   580

Wal-Mart: Nonmarket Pressure and Reputation Risk (B): A New Nonmarket Strategy   586

Facebook and Online Privacy   588

Chapter 21

Pricing the Norplant System   613

Gilead Sciences (A): The Gilead Access Program for HIV Drugs   615

Consumer Awareness or Disease Mongering? GlaxoSmithKline and the Restless Legs Syndrome   619

Chapter 22

Genetic Testing in the Workplace   652

Chipotle Mexican Grill and Undocumented Workers   654

Environmental Injustice?   656

Chapter 23

Denny's and Customer Service   675

Insider Trading   677

Fresenius Medical Care in China   679

Chapter 24

Google Out of China   699

De Beers and Conflict Diamonds (A)   702

De Beers and Conflict Diamonds (B)   703

Siemens: Anatomy of Bribery   704

Part V Integrative Case   707

GlaxoSmithKline and AIDS Drugs Policy   707

PREFACE

The environment of business has interrelated market and nonmarket components. The market environment is characterized by the structure of the markets in which a firm operates and the rules that govern market competition. The nonmarket environment is characterized by the legal, political, and social arrangements in which the firm is embedded. The nonmarket environment determines the rules of the game for the market environment through government policies and public expectations. Just as firms compete in their market environment, they also compete in their nonmarket environment. Nonmarket competition is more complex, however, because that competition includes not only other firms but also activists, interest groups, the public, and government. *Business and Its Environment* is concerned with the interrelationships among the market and nonmarket environments and the effective management of the issues therein. In contrast to a public policy perspective, the approach taken is managerial. That is, it takes the perspective of firms and managers, not of government or the public. It focuses on issues central to the performance of firms, as measured by both shareholder value and conduct in accord with ethics principles and social responsibilities.

The emphasis in the book is on strategy—nonmarket strategy and its integration with the market strategy of a firm. A nonmarket strategy is composed of objectives and a course of action for participating effectively and responsibly in the nonmarket competition on issues arising in the environment of business. The approach taken in the book emphasizes frameworks, principles, and analysis as the foundations for formulating effective and responsible strategies.

The seventh edition of *Business and Its Environment* represents continuity and change. It retains the structure, much of the subject matter, and the conceptual frameworks of the sixth edition. It also retains the strategy orientation and the guidance provided by the normative subjects of ethics and social responsibility. The seventh edition includes chapter cases for class discussion of managerial issues and applications of the conceptual frameworks and institutional material. At the end of each of the five parts of the book are integrative cases on an activist challenge to Wal-Mart, Amazon and the taxation of online sales, spectrum allocation for broadband, globalization, and the pricing of AIDS drugs for developing countries. The seventh edition continues the focus on strategies for improving performance by addressing the challenges in the nonmarket environment and their effects on the market environment. The approach draws on the disciplines of economics, political science, law, and ethics to provide a foundation for strategy formulation and a deeper understanding of the environment of business and nonmarket issues. An integrated perspective strengthens the managerial orientation of the book and also enhances the usefulness of the conceptual materials for other parts of the business curriculum.

NEW TO THIS EDITION

The seventh edition includes four new chapters: Chapter 11, Financial Markets and Their Regulation; Chapter 13, The Investor's Perspective: Renewable Energy; Chapter 18, The Political Economy of India; and Chapter 23, Behavioral Ethics, Individuals, and Management, and three chapters, Information Industries and Nonmarket Issues, The Political Economy of Japan, and Implementing Ethics Systems, from the sixth edition have been deleted. The retained chapters are updated with new conceptual materials and applications. The book also includes 26 new cases for class discussion of timely topics.

- New Chapter 11: Financial Markets and Their Regulation. This chapter examines the financial crisis of 2007–2009, the worldwide recession that followed, and the regulation established in the United States.
- New Chapter 13: The Investor's Perspective: Renewable Energy. This chapter considers the nonmarket environment from the perspective of investors, such as hedge funds, with a focus on opportunities and risks. The renewable power industry in the United States provides the context.
- New Chapter 18: The Political Economy of India. This chapter considers the nonmarket environment of the world's second largest country and a leading emerging market.

- New Chapter 23: Behavioral Ethics, Individuals, and Management. This chapter introduces behavioral ethics through an examination of laboratory experiments that explore issues such as altruism, trust, reciprocity, and cooperation.
- The remaining chapters have been updated on two dimensions. First is the introduction of new conceptual material that brings advances in research into the book. Second is the timeliness of the material to increase student interest and address emerging issues.
- The seventh edition includes 26 new cases on Google (2), Facebook (2), Amazon.com, Johnson & Johnson, News of the World, AT&T and T-Mobile, Goldman Sachs, Pacific Gas & Electric, BrightSource Energy, Apple, Equity Bank of Kenya, Boeing and Airbus, and Chipotle Mexican Grill as well as on industry-wide issues, including credit rating agencies, debit card regulation, spectrum allocation, environmental injustice, insider trading, data protection regulation, the Euro crisis, and renewable power. The new cases address issues in antitrust and regulation, social media, information technology, environmental protection, international business, sustainable energy, and business ethics and responsibility.
- Twenty-five of the cases in the book concern global and international nonmarket issues, and 20 cases deal with environmental and health issues. Each case poses a managerial problem that requires analysis and strategy formulation.

GUIDE TO PARTS

The book is organized in five parts. Part I introduces the nonmarket environment and nonmarket strategy with a focus on issues involving the public, activists, the news media, and crises. Part II is concerned with issues addressed in the context of government institutions and with nonmarket strategies for dealing with those issues. The frameworks developed in this part provide a foundation for Parts III and IV. Part III focuses on the interactions between firms and markets as regulated by government with an emphasis on antitrust, regulation, financial markets, the environment and sustainability, and the law of intellectual property, contracts, and torts. Part IV is explicitly international and provides frameworks for understanding the political economy of countries and the relationships between business and government as a foundation for formulating effective strategies. The European Union, China, India, and emerging markets are considered, and international trade policy is used to bring the policy and strategy issues together. Part V is normative and focuses on ethics and corporate social responsibility. The complexities involved in operating internationally are considered both through conceptual frameworks and cases.

INSTRUCTOR SUPPLEMENTS

At the Instructor Resource Center, www.pearsonhighered.com/irc, instructors can access a variety of print, digital, and presentation resources available with this text in downloadable format. Registration is simple and gives you immediate access to new titles and editions. As a registered faculty member, you can download resource files and receive immediate access to and instructions for installing course management content on your campus server. In case you ever need assistance, our dedicated technical support team is ready to help with the media supplements that accompany this text. Visit http://247.pearsoned.com for answers to frequently asked questions and toll-free user support phone numbers.

The following supplements are available for download to adopting instructors:

- Instructor Resource Manual
- Test Item File
- PowerPoint Presentations

COURSESMART ETEXTBOOK

CourseSmart eTextbooks were developed for students looking to save on required or recommended textbooks. Students simply select their eText by title or author and purchase immediate access to the content for the duration of the course using any major credit card. With a CourseSmart eText, students can search for specific keywords or page numbers, take notes online, print out reading assignments that incorporate lecture notes, and bookmark important passages for later review. For more information or to purchase a CourseSmart eTextbook, visit www.coursesmart.com

ACKNOWLEDGMENTS

I would like to thank David Brady, Christophe Crombez, Daniel Diermeier, Timothy Feddersen, Thomas Gilligan, Daniel Kessler, and Keith Krehbiel for contributing cases to the seventh edition. The Graduate School of Business of Stanford University provided institutional support for the work underpinning this book.

David P. Baron
Stanford, California

ABOUT THE AUTHOR

David Baron has authored over 100 articles and 3 books, one of which is in its seventh edition. His principal research interests have been the theory of the firm, the economics of regulation, mechanism design and its applications, political economy, and nonmarket strategy. His current research focuses on political economy and strategy in the business environment.

David Baron began his academic career at Northwestern University where he taught for 13 years in the Kellogg Graduate School of Management. He joined the Graduate School of Business of Stanford University in 1981. He has also been a visiting professor at the Université d'Aix-en-Provence in France, the Katholieke Universiteit Leuven in Belgium, Harvard University, and the California Institute of Technology. At Stanford, he is the David S. and Ann M. Barlow Professor of Political Economy and Strategy (Emeritus) in the Graduate School of Business. He received a BS from the University of Michigan, an MBA from Harvard University, and a Doctorate in Business Administration from Indiana University. In 2005 he was awarded an honorary doctorate degree by the Katholieke Universiteit Leuven in Belgium.

Professor Baron has taught in the MBA, PhD, and Executive Education programs, receiving the MBA teaching award at Kellogg and the PhD teaching award at Stanford. He has been an innovator in the field of business and its social, political, and legal environment, and is the author of the leading textbook, *Business and Its Environment*, in the field. In 2007 he received the lifetime achievement award from the Aspen Institute.

His research has been supported by the National Science Foundation, Bureau of Health Services Research, Alfred P. Sloan Foundation, and the Citicorp Behavioral Sciences Research Council. He is a Fellow of the Econometric Society and has served on the Board of Editors of the *American Economic Review*, the *Quarterly Journal of Economics*, the *Journal of Economics and Management Strategy*, *Business and Politics*, and *Decision Sciences*.

1

MARKET AND NONMARKET ENVIRONMENTS

INTRODUCTION

Some companies are successful in both their market environment and the social, political, and legal nonmarket environment in which they operate. Google, McDonald's, and Toyota have had continuing success in their markets and have also generally conducted themselves in a manner that has earned the respect of the public and the government. Other companies have had great success in their markets but stumbled before the public and government. Nike became synonymous with athletic footwear, but public concerns about the working conditions in its suppliers' factories tarnished its image and affected its market performance. Wal-Mart, the world's largest company, was targeted by activists, unions, and politicians for its work practices, as well as for depressing wages in the labor market, driving small merchants out of business, and weakening the culture of small towns. Microsoft's market conduct resulted in recurring antitrust judgments in the United States and in the European Union where it was fined € 1.7 billion for antitrust violations and failure to comply with rulings. BP had earned a favorable reputation for its environmental programs, but then it experienced a refinery explosion that killed 15 workers and resulted in criminal fines, and it spilled oil in Prudhoe Bay, Alaska and on the tundra. BP also pleaded guilty to price fixing, paying $303 million in fines. An explosion in 2010 on the Deepwater Horizon oil platform killed 11 workers and resulted in a massive oil spill in the Gulf of Mexico. Citigroup was hit with a series of costly scandals. As a result of its $31 billion acquisition of sub-prime lender Associates First Capital, Citigroup faced private lawsuits for abusive practices, state legislation restricting subprime lending, and fines of $285 million imposed by the Federal Reserve and the Federal Trade Commission. Citigroup also paid $2.8 billion to settle lawsuits for its role in structuring financial instruments for Enron and WorldCom and $735 million for biased securities research. Japan ordered Citigroup to close its private banking business in the country. In addition to the fines and settlements and the damage to its reputation, Citigroup was targeted by activists for its financing of environmentally destructive projects in developing countries. Citigroup repeated its problems with subprime mortgages resulting in write-downs of $40 billion in 2007–2008, the firing of its CEO, and more stringent regulations for mortgage lending. Citigroup was also an aggressive participant in the mortgage-backed securities market, and during the financial crisis it failed and had to be rescued three times by the government.

The problems encountered by Nike, Wal-Mart, BP, Microsoft, and Citigroup originated in their market environments, but the challenges to their operations came from the nonmarket environment. That is, the challenges resulted not from the actions of competitors but instead from the public, interest groups, the legal system, and government. These companies underappreciated the importance of the nonmarket environment and have paid a price for doing so. Even companies that are generally successful in managing in their nonmarket environment face challenges. Google received criticism for tolerating the government-imposed censorship on its Web site in China and eventually relocated its search business to Hong Kong; McDonald's was criticized for contributing to the obesity crisis; Toyota experienced safety problems in the United States that depressed sales. Some companies have changed their strategies as a result of nonmarket pressure. Nike has become a leader in improving the working conditions in its suppliers' factories, and Wal-Mart has implemented an aggressive environmental program and imposed it on its suppliers.

Firms have more control over their fate in the markets in which they operate than they have in their nonmarket environment, but successful companies understand that if they do not manage their nonmarket environment, it will manage them. The long-run sustainability of competitive advantage requires managing effectively in the nonmarket environment. Companies like Google, McDonald's, and Toyota have learned that they can participate both responsibly and effectively in influencing developments in their nonmarket environment.

This book is about managing successfully in the nonmarket environment. The focus is on strategy—nonmarket strategy—and its implementation. That strategy is considered not in isolation but in conjunction with the firm's market or competitive strategy.

This chapter introduces the environment of business, identifies the role of management in the nonmarket environment, and presents a framework for analyzing that environment. The framework is illustrated using the automobile industry as an example. The sources of change in the nonmarket environment are then considered, and a framework for assessing the development of nonmarket issues is presented. Chapter 2 considers the integration of market and nonmarket strategies.

THE ENVIRONMENT OF BUSINESS

The environment of business consists of market and nonmarket components. The market environment includes those interactions between firms, suppliers, and customers that are governed by markets and contracts. These interactions typically involve voluntary economic transactions and the exchange of property. To achieve superior performance, firms must operate effectively in their market environment. They must be efficient in production and responsive to consumer demand. They must anticipate and adapt to change, innovate through research and development, and develop new products and services. Effective management in the market environment is a necessary condition for superior performance, but it is not sufficient.

The performance of a firm, and of its management, also depends on its nonmarket environment. The nonmarket environment is composed of the social, political, and legal arrangements that structure interactions outside of, but in conjunction with, markets and contracts. The nonmarket environment encompasses those interactions between the firm and individuals, interest groups, government entities, and the public that are intermediated not by markets but by public and private institutions. Public institutions differ from markets because of characteristics such as majority rule, due process, broad enfranchisement, collective action, and access by the public. Activities in the nonmarket environment may be voluntary, as when the firm cooperates with government officials or an environmental group, or involuntary, as in the case of government regulation or a boycott of a firm's product led by an activist group. Effective management in the nonmarket environment has become a necessary condition for superior performance just as is effective management in the market environment.

The nonmarket environment has grown in importance and complexity over time and commands increased managerial attention. Nonmarket issues high on firms' agendas include sustainability, global climate change, security, health and safety, regulation and deregulation, intellectual property protection, human rights, international trade policy, antitrust, social pressure from nongovernmental organizations (NGOs) and social activists, news media coverage, social media, corporate social responsibility, and ethics. Although the saliency of particular issues ebbs and flows, nonmarket issues arise sufficiently often to have important consequences for managerial and firm performance. Nonmarket issues, the forces that influence their development, and the strategies for addressing them are the focus of the field of business and its environment. The managerial objective is to achieve superior overall performance by effectively addressing nonmarket issues and the forces associated with them and using nonmarket strategies to unlock opportunities.

Developments in the nonmarket environment affect performance on a number of dimensions. In the automobile industry, emissions and fuel economy standards affect research and development, design, production, pricing, and marketing. Safety regulation and liability standards have similar broad effects. Access to international markets affects competitive strategies involving product design, pricing, and capacity planning. Each of these examples has two components—an underlying issue and its impact on performance. The fuel economy issue, for example, is related to global climate change and security and has broad implications for performance. The focus for management in the nonmarket environment is on how an automobile company can participate effectively and responsibly in the public and private processes addressing these issues. Activity in the nonmarket environment is generally organized around specific issues and is motivated by the impacts of those issues. The regulatory process, for example, focuses on rules to address a specific issue, such as fuel economy standards. Managerial attention thus focuses on specific issues affecting performance, the forces driving those issues, the institutions in whose arenas the issues are addressed, and the participation of firms in shaping the resolution of those issues.

THE ROLE OF MANAGEMENT

Because of its importance for managerial and organizational performance, nonmarket strategy is the responsibility of managers. As illustrated in Figure 1-1, firms operate in both market and the nonmarket environments. Managers are best positioned to assess the impact of their firm's market activities on its nonmarket environment and the impact of developments in the nonmarket environment on market opportunities and performance. Management thus is responsible for formulating and implementing nonmarket as well as market strategies.

Firms typically deal with nonmarket issues in proportion to their potential impacts on performance. Managers are in the best position to assess those impacts and to formulate strategies to address the issues. Managers also participate in the implementation of nonmarket strategies. They may address the public on issues, communicate with the media, testify in regulatory and congressional proceedings, lobby government, participate in coalitions and associations, serve on government advisory panels, meet with activists, negotiate with interest groups, partner with NGOs, and build relationships with stakeholders.

Successful management requires frameworks for analyzing nonmarket issues, principles for reasoning about them, and strategies for addressing them. These frameworks, principles, and strategies enable managers to address issues in a systematic manner and guide their firms successfully and responsibly in their nonmarket environments. In formulating nonmarket strategies, managers may draw on the expertise of lawyers, communications specialists, Washington representatives, and community relations specialists. Managers, however, ultimately must evaluate the quality of the advice they receive and combine it with their own knowledge of the market and nonmarket environments. Most firms have found that managers must be involved in all stages of their efforts to address nonmarket issues.

MARKET AND NONMARKET ENVIRONMENTS

As illustrated in Figure 1-1, the market and nonmarket environments of business are interrelated. A firm's activities in its market environment can generate nonmarket issues and change in its nonmarket environment. That change may take the form of government actions, such as legislation, regulation, antitrust lawsuits, and international trade policies. Similarly, the actions of interest groups and activists may force a firm to change its market practices. As an example of the market origins of nonmarket issues, in the 1990s lower real gasoline prices and changing consumer demand resulted in sport utility vehicles (SUVs) and light trucks capturing half the light-vehicle market in the United States. This reduced average fuel economy and, in conjunction with the global climate change and security issues, generated renewed pressure to increase fuel economy standards, with proposals to double the standard between 2011 and 2025.

Nonmarket issues and actions also shape the market environment. Higher fuel economy standards affect virtually all aspects of automobile design and manufacturing and the competitive advantages of automakers. The market environment is also shaped by the actions of interest and activist groups and the public support for their causes. The *Exxon Valdez* oil spill increased environmental pressure on firms through liability for damages, more stringent regulations, and direct public pressure. The boom in the real estate and home construction markets in the 2000s

FIGURE 1-1 The Environment of Business

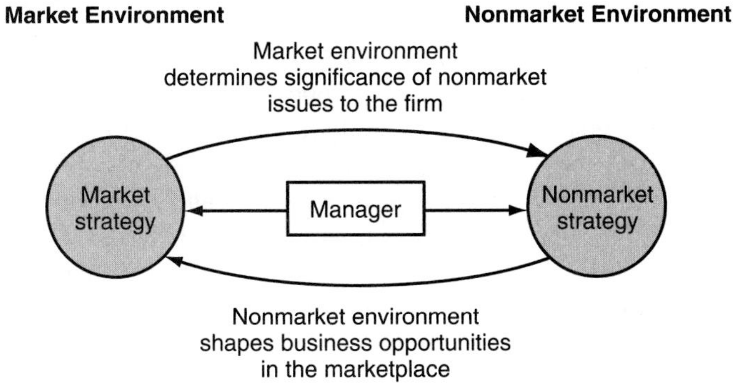

Market Environment   **Nonmarket Environment**

Market environment
determines significance of nonmarket
issues to the firm

Market strategy — Manager — Nonmarket strategy

Nonmarket environment
shapes business opportunities
in the marketplace

was spurred by lax mortgage lending standards and aggressive lending and was fueled by the rapid growth of mortgage-backed securities. Housing prices began to fall in 2007, resulting in a financial and economic crisis that required a government bailout of many banks and mortgage lenders. The crisis and abuses by mortgage lenders and financial institutions led to public pressure on government to strengthen regulation of the financial sector, resulting in the most substantial changes since regulation was first imposed in the 1930s.

Both the market and nonmarket environments of business are competitive. In the market environment, firms compete through their market or competitive strategies. In the nonmarket environment, legislation, regulation, administrative decisions, and public pressure are the result of competition involving individuals, activists, interest groups, and firms. In the market environment, strategies are intermediated by markets, whereas in the nonmarket environment, strategies are intermediated by public and private institutions, including legislatures, courts, regulatory agencies, and public sentiment. Just as the market environment of business changes and competitive advantage evolves, the nonmarket environment changes and the issues on a firm's nonmarket agenda evolve.

The nonmarket environment should thus be thought of as responsive to the strategies of firms and other interested parties. Those strategies can affect market opportunities. Robert Galvin (1992), who led Motorola for over three decades, described the company's approach to its nonmarket environment as "writing the rules of the game."[1]

> The first step in any defined strategy is writing the rules of the game honorably and fairly in a manner that gives everyone a chance with predictable rules. Our company has started industries. We have helped write standards. We have helped write trade rules. We have helped influence policies. We have helped write national laws of countries where we have engaged, always in a respectful way. We have never taken for granted that the rules of the game would just evolve in a fashion that would make for the greatest opportunity…. With the right rules of the game, one's opportunity for success is enhanced.

Galvin's point is not that companies dictate the rules of the game but rather that those rules are shaped by the strategies of firms and other interested parties and by the governing institutions. Companies and their leaders can shape those rules by participating responsibly in the public and private processes that address market and nonmarket issues. This participation can affect the market environment of firms and the opportunities available to them as well as the nonmarket environment and the issues firms will face in the future.

ANALYSIS OF THE NONMARKET ENVIRONMENT: THE FOUR I'S

The nonmarket environment of a firm is characterized by four I's:

- Issues
- Interests
- Institutions
- Information

Issues are the basic unit of analysis and the focus of nonmarket action. Using the agricultural biotechnology industry as an example, the central nonmarket issues have been the formulation of regulatory policies for bioengineered foods and the public reaction to those foods. Interests include the individuals and groups with preferences about, or a stake in, the issue. The principal interests are the agricultural biotechnology companies, the interest groups and activists concerned about biotechnology issues, and the public.

Institutions are defined by Douglass North (1990) as "the rules of the game in a society… that shape human interactions," and these institutions provide arenas in which interests seek to influence the outcomes on issues. Government institutions include entities such as legislatures and regulatory agencies. Nongovernmental institutions include those such as the news media that provides information to society as well as public sentiment composed of societal expectations and norms of behavior that arise from ethics and culture. The Environmental Protection Agency, the Department of Agriculture, the Food and Drug Administration, and Congress are

---

[1]See Yoffie (1988a, 1988b) for analysis of aspects of this strategy.

the principal public institutions in whose arenas agricultural biotechnology issues are addressed. The public sentiment about bioengineered foods is influenced by market forces as well. As the prices of agricultural products and foods rose in the late 2000s, some consumers and firms that had shunned bioengineered foods began to change their policies in response to their lower prices resulting from higher productivity and resistance to crop damage.

Information pertains to what the interests and institutional officeholders know or believe about the issues and the forces affecting their development. In the case of agricultural bio-technology, information pertains to the risks associated with individual products and with the technology itself. The public acceptance of bioengineered crops and animals is influenced by both scientific knowledge and concerns about the unknown and can differ across countries and cultures. Information is provided by firms, activists, government institutions, and the media.

The task for management is to formulate and implement strategies that effectively address the nonmarket issues recognizing that other interests are also choosing and implementing strategies. These strategies compete in the context of institutions in which information plays an important role. Each firm and industry has a set of issues that it must address, and these issues constitute its nonmarket issue agenda. Associated with each issue are the institutional arenas in which the issue will be addressed, the interests likely to be involved, and the information available. Many issues on a firm's nonmarket agenda require issue-specific strategies, and the analysis of the associated interests, institutions, and information provides a foundation for strategy formulation, as considered in Chapter 2.

The nonmarket environment of the automobile industry is used next to illustrate the four I's framework. The chapter cases on the pharmaceutical industry, McDonald's, and Google provide opportunities to characterize the issues, interests, institutions, and information in their nonmarket environments and to consider the development of the issues.

THE NONMARKET ENVIRONMENT OF THE AUTOMOBILE INDUSTRY

This section identifies selected issues facing the automobile industry and then identifies the interests, institutions, and information associated with them.

Issues

FUEL ECONOMY REGULATION 2012–2016 (UNITED STATES) The Department of Transportation (DOT) and the Environmental Protection Agency (EPA) issued new regulations for fuel economy and GHG emissions for model years 2012–2016, with standards set based on the physical footprint of a vehicle, so fuel economy standards were higher for small cars than for large cars. The standards were intended to achieve an average fuel efficiency for cars and light trucks of 35.5 mpg in 2016 compared to the 27.5 mpg fleet average in place since the 1970s.

FUEL ECONOMY REGULATION 2017–2025 (UNITED STATES) With the fuel economy standards set through 2016, DOT and the EPA proposed 2025 standards in the range from 47 to 62 mpg. The Sierra Club and other NGOs supported the Freedom from Oil campaign that sought to reduce carbon emissions. The campaign targeted the automakers and appealed to the public to write President Obama in support of a 60 mph fuel economy standard. The administration, federal regulators, and regulators from California then began bargaining with the automakers, the United Auto Workers (UAW) union, and environmental groups. The outcome was a standard of 54.5 mpg. To soften the strong opposition by automakers, large footprint vehicles were given more time to meet the standards, but Asian automakers objected.

FUEL ECONOMY REGULATION (CHINA) In 2003 the State Council of China chose a weight-based system for fuel economy standards for automobiles, vans, and SUVs. By 2009 China's average fuel economy was 35.8 mpg, and it set a standard of 42.2 mpg for 2015. The standards were developed by the Automotive Technology and Research Center and were issued by the State Council.

FUEL ECONOMY REGULATION (EUROPEAN UNION) As part of its Kyoto Treaty obligations, the European Union (EU) had adopted a voluntary fuel economy standard of 140 grams of carbon dioxide per kilometer, but the industry failed to meet the standard. Under strong pressure from environmental groups, the European Commission proposed a mandatory standard of 120 grams for 2012. The European Parliament asked for a less aggressive standard to ease the burden on automakers, and the Commission relented, setting the standard at 130 grams for automobiles with an additional 10 grams to be achieved through more efficient tires, improved air conditioners, and cleaner fuels. The European Automobile Manufacturers Association warned that the requirements would "lead to a loss of jobs and relocation of production outside the EU."[2]

GASOLINE TAX   The U.S. federal gasoline tax was $0.184 per gallon, and General Motors CEO Dan Akerson called for a $1 a gallon tax, saying it would be better for the environment than the proposed fuel economy standards being discussed for the 2017–2025 period. He said, "There ought to be a discussion of the cost and benefits" of the alternatives.[3]

SAFETY STANDARDS   The National Highway Traffic Safety Administration (NHTSA) proposed a safety standard that would effectively require all cars, light trucks, and busses to have rear-view cameras by 2012. The regulator estimated that half the estimated 228 deaths and 13,000 injuries a year from "back over" crashes could be avoided at an estimated annual cost to the industry of between $1.9 billion and $2.7 billion.[4]

TRAFFIC SAFETY   Traffic fatalities plummeted in 2009 to 33,963, down 22 percent from 2005 levels. Part of the explanation was the severe recession that reduced the miles driven, and campaigns against drunk driving led by Mothers Against Drunk Driving (MADD) and other NGOs may have helped. In addition, safety features such as side air bags mandated by the National Highway Traffic Safety Administration (NHTSA) had helped reduce fatalities.

DISTRACTED DRIVING   NHTSA released data indicating that distracted driving accounted for 16 percent of traffic deaths and 20 percent of injuries in 2009. These were believed to be underestimates, since in many accidents drivers do not admit that they were using mobile devices and the police rarely investigate.[5] After her mother was killed in a collision by a man using a mobile phone, Jennifer Smith founded FocusDriven, patterned after MADD, to make distracted driving as socially unacceptable as drunk driving.[6]

SAFETY RECALLS   Toyota experienced a series of alleged safety problems with an array of its vehicles, leading to the recall of 11 million vehicles beginning in September 2009. The problem that attracted the most attention was unintended acceleration in which a vehicle suddenly accelerated. Toyota corrected slipping floor mats and sticky gas pedals and paid $49 million in fines for its delayed response to the problems.[7]

SAFETY REGULATION   Some persons involved in unintended acceleration accidents claimed that Toyota's electronically controlled accelerator was a fault. Toyota investigated and concluded that the accelerator system was not faulty, but the claims continued. NHTSA hired a testing firm to conduct tests of Toyota's electronic acceleration system, and the study concluded that there was no defect and the most likely explanation for unintended acceleration was driver error.

PRODUCTS LIABILITY/TORTS   Toyota was subject to numerous lawsuits filed by trial lawyers on behalf of people claiming to have been injured by unintended acceleration.[8] In the first case to go to trial, a federal court jury held for Toyota in a lawsuit filed by a New York doctor who alleged that a defect in the electronic throttle system or the floor mats in his Scion caused the car to crash into a tree. The jury foreman stated, "We weighed all the evidence and came to the

---

[2]*New York Times*, February 8, 2007.
[3]*Detroit News*, June 7, 2011.
[4]Press release, National Highway Traffic Administration, December 3, 2010.
[5]*Economist*, April 16, 2011.
[6]Ibid.
[7]*San Jose Mercury News*, December 21, 2010.
[8]In the United States trial lawyers typically received one-third of any settlement or court award.

conclusion that there was not a defect with the automobile." A Toyota spokesperson said the case "clearly demonstrates a plaintiff's inability to identify, let alone prove the existence of, an alleged electronic defect in Toyota vehicles that could cause unintended acceleration."[9]

FRANCHISE AGREEMENTS   In a class-action lawsuit, an Ohio county court ordered Ford to pay $2 billion to 3,000 truck dealers that claimed that the company had breached its franchise agreements with them.[10] Ford had used a Competitive Price Assistance program that dealers claimed resulted in dealers paying different prices for the same vehicle, which they claimed transferred profits from the dealers to the automaker. Ford appealed the decision.

INTERNATIONAL TRADE   The United States Trade Representative (USTR) urged Congress to ratify the Korea–U.S. Free Trade Agreement (KORUS), which had the support of the American Automotive Policy Council, representing Chrysler, Ford, and GM. In 2010 Korea exported 515,646 automobiles to the United States, and the United States exported 16,659 to Korea.[11] KORUS generated opposition from fiscal conservatives in Congress representing taxpayers because the Obama administration included $1 billion for trade adjustment assistance for displaced workers in the bill before Congress.

TARIFFS (CHINA)   The European Union, Canada, and the United States filed a formal complaint with the World Trade Organization (WTO) regarding China's average 15 percent tariff on automobile parts. In 2009 the WTO ruled in favor of the petitioners, and China restructured its tariffs to comply with the ruling.

TRADE DISPUTE   In February 2011, Argentina president Chritina Kirchner withdrew automatic import licenses on a number of products from Brazil. In May newly elected Brazilian president Dilma Rousseff retaliated by withdrawing automatic import licenses for automobiles manufactured in Argentina. Eighty-five percent of Argentinean auto exports were to Brazil. The secretaries of industry for the two countries agreed to resolve the dispute in the context of the Mercosur (Common Market of the South) trade agreement.[12]

DISASTER RELIEF   Japan approved financial aid to its auto parts manufacturers, some of which had been hit hard by the March 11, 2011, earthquake and tsunami. The Japan Auto Parts Industry Association was in discussions with the Development Bank of Japan over details for the $640 million fund for part manufacturers in Iwate, Miyagi, and Fukushima prefectures.[13]

BANKRUPTCY RELIEF   The U.S. government provided $80 billion in Troubled Asset Relief Program funds to the automobile industry in conjunction with the bankruptcies of Chrysler and General Motors, and the government reported that it expected to recoup all but $14 billion.[14] Critics argued that the cost was much greater because of tax breaks given to the companies and that the funds had largely gone to support the UAW and other favored creditors.[15]

EMISSIONS   California had been granted authority to set more stringent auto emissions standards than those set by the federal government, and in 2011 the California Air Resources Board was preparing to mandate that 5.5 percent of new car sales in the state by 2018 have zero emissions, which effectively required the cars to be electric. The proposal was opposed by the Association of Global Automakers, which included Honda, Nissan, and Toyota.[16] The Alliance of Automobile Manufacturers, which included Chrysler, Ford, and General Motors as well as some non-U.S. auto companies, also opposed the California initiative.

---

[9]*New York Times*, April 2, 2011.
[10]Ford sold its medium and heavy duty truck business in 1998.
[11]*St. Petersburg Times*, July 4, 2011.
[12]*Wall Street Journal*, May 25, 2011.
[13]*Wall Street Journal*, May 31, 2011.
[14]Ford did not request government funds and did not go bankrupt. Canada also provided funds to support Chrysler, and Fiat bought a minority interest, which it increased to a majority interest in 2011.
[15]David Skeel, *Wall Street Journal*, June 6, 2011
[16]*Wall Street Journal*, June 11–12, 2011.

SUBSIDIES   The electric car market was bolstered by a federal tax credit of up to $7,500 depending on the size of the battery for the purchase of an eligible electric car.[17] Some states waived their sales tax on electric vehicles, and the California legislature provided a rebate of up to $5,000. A California buyer of a $109,000 Telsa roadster could receive $12,500 in rebates and tax credits. Funds for the costly subsidy programs were jeopardized by the financial woes of states and the federal budget reductions.

INTELLECTUAL PROPERTY   In 2007 Telsa Motors applied for a "Telsa" trademark in the European Union, but the application was opposed by Telsa Holding of the Czech Republic. After 3 years and a settlement with Telsa Holding, Telsa Motors filed an amended application with the Office for Harmonization in the Internal Market to resolve the conflict. Sixty percent of Telsa's sales were in Europe.

LOCAL PROTESTS   Tata Motors announced its Nano, the people's car, in 2008, but was quickly forced to move its planned production plant because of protests in West Bengal by farmers and local politicians claiming that Tata had obtained the land for the plant at unfairly low prices. Tata relocated the plant to Gujarat state, delaying the introduction of the Nano.

RIGHTS   Women are prohibited from driving in Saudi Arabia under the country's interpretation of the Wahhabi version of Sunni Islam. Using Facebook, Twitter, and YouTube, Manal al-Sharif called for women to defy the ban and drive on June 17, 2011. The protesting women also organized Saudi Women for Driving, which circulated a petition on Change.org's Web site calling for Subaru to leave the country.[18] Within a month over 57,000 people had signed the petition.

GOVERNANCE   Volkswagen, which is 50.7 percent owned by Porsche, 20 percent by the German state of Lower Saxony, and 17 percent by Qatar Holding LLC, had the goal of being the largest automobile manufacturer in the world by 2018. It had grown through cost reductions, including lowering its labor costs, and plant expansions in Slovakia and the United States. To gain additional bargaining power with the company, Volkswagen's labor unions led by IG Metall announced that they would purchase up to 3 percent of the company's stock. Labor representative Bernd Osterloh said, "We want Volkswagen's staff in the future to be able to exert its influence at shareholder meetings..."[19]

UNION BARGAINING   In 2007 and on the brink of failure, General Motors and the UAW negotiated a labor contract allowing a two-tiered wage scale under which new workers would be paid $14 an hour, about half that of workers already employed. With sales increasing in 2011, GM announced that it would spend $2 billion in factory improvements, recall 1,300 laid off workers, and hire additional workers at $14 an hour. A two-tiered wage structure was anathema to the UAW, and the union made it clear that in the 2011 contract bargaining, it wanted to get back some of the concessions it had made in the past.

CONSUMER INFORMATION   The DOT and the EPA unveiled new labels to be affixed to new cars and trucks giving not only the familiar miles per gallon but also the estimated annual fuel cost and the 5-year savings or additional fuel cost compared to the average vehicle. With support by environmental groups, the agencies planned to give vehicles letter grades from A to D for their fuel efficiency, but the auto companies objected strongly and the EPA found that consumers were confused by the grades thinking that they were given for overall vehicle quality. Dan Becker, director of the Safe Climate Campaign of the Center for Auto Safety, complained, "It is deeply disappointing that the Obama administration abandoned" the idea.[20]

NEWS MEDIA   Electric carmaker Telsa Motors sued the British Broadcasting Corporation in London for its "Top Gear" program's report in which Jeremy Clarkson said, "Although Telsa

---

[17]The federal tax credit scale was set so that the 16-kwh battery Chevrolet Volt qualified for the full rebate.

[18]Subaru was targeted because it was "progressive" and had marketed its cars to women. *The Gazette* (Montreal), June 23, 2011.

[19]*Wall Street Journal*, June 9, 2011.

[20]*Wall Street Journal*, May 20, 2011.

says it will do 200 miles, we worked out that on our track it would run out after 55 miles, and if it does run out, it's not a quick job to charge it up again."[21] Telsa also said in its defamation lawsuit that the report showed a Telsa roadster being pushed into a hanger even though it had not run out of power. Telsa stated that the report "grossly misled potential purchasers of the Roadster."[22]

Interests

Interests include those who have a stake in an issue and the organizations they form. U.S., Asian, and European automobile companies have interests that are opposed on some issues, such as the unionization of the auto plants, and aligned on others such as the state regulation of carbon dioxide emissions. Other interests with direct economic stakes in these issues are car buyers and employees. Some interests are well organized, as in the case of workers represented by the UAW and IG Metall, and others, such as car buyers, are unorganized.

Interests also include special interest, activist and advocacy groups, and other NGOs. Special interest groups pursue issues because of the benefits that accrue to their members, as in the case of the trial lawyers' association. Watchdog groups monitor the activities of firms and call those activities to the attention of the media, government, and public. Advocacy groups, such as the Sierra Club, represent the interests of individuals, such as those affected by pollution. Activist groups can take direct action against firms to force them to change their policies or can appeal to the public for support in the cases of FocusDriven and Saudi Women for Driving.

The organized and unorganized interests are listed in Table 1-1.[23]

Institutions

The market and nonmarket environments in Figure 1-1 include activities that take place both within and outside formal institutions. The principal government institutions are legislatures, the executive branch, the judiciary, administrative agencies, regulatory agencies, and international institutions such as the WTO. These institutions both establish rules and serve as arenas in which interests compete to influence those rules. The nonmarket environment includes the set of laws established by these institutions, as well as regulations, such as safety standards, established by

---

TABLE 1-1 Organized and Unorganized Interests

Organized Interests	Unorganized Interests
Automakers	Car Buyers
American	Tax Payers
European	Public
Asian	Nonunion Workers (foreign automakers in the United States)
United Auto Workers	West Bengal Farmers
IG Metall	
Trial Lawyers	
NGOs	
Sierra Club	
Center for Auto Safety	
MADD	
Saudi Women for Driving	
FocusDriven	

---

[21]Top Gear has been the BBC's top-rated show for a decade and has a worldwide audience of 350 million viewers. *San Jose Mercury News*, March 31, 2011.
[22]*San Jose Mercury News*, March 31, 2011.
[23]Not all relevant interests are listed.

administrative and regulatory agencies. The nonmarket environment also includes the comon, or judge-made, law of torts, which governs the liability system in the United States.

Institutions can also be established by private parties. Such institutions include markets, arbitration mechanisms, and voluntary agreements. The nonmarket environment also includes nongovernmental institutions such as the news media, social media, and public sentiment. As considered in Chapter 3, the news media plays an important role in informing those in the nonmarket environment about issues, but it also serves as an institution. That is, firms, other interests, and NGOs attempt to communicate to the public through the news media. NGOs and other organizations increasingly use the social media to communicate with their supporters and the public.

A nonmarket issue can be addressed in several institutional arenas. The U.S. Department of Transportation addresses the distracted driving issue through regulations and public information campaigns, whereas FocusDriven uses the social and news media to build support and influence drivers and the public more broadly.

Institutions are not unitary bodies. Congress is composed of two chambers and 535 members who represent constituencies with varied interests. Institutions also have internal structures that affect how nonmarket issues are addressed. Congress acts by majority rule, has a committee system, and follows a complex set of procedures for enacting legislation. Understanding the workings of these institutions, their procedures, and the forces that operate within them is essential for successful management in the nonmarket environment. Managers must also be familiar with the mandates, agendas, and procedures of regulatory agencies, such as NHTSA and the EPA, and the standards used by the courts in rendering judgments about their actions.

Some institutions are specific to an individual country, whereas others represent a set of countries. The institutions in whose arenas the nonmarket issues for the automobile industry are addressed are categorized in Table 1-2.

Information

Information refers to what interests and institutional officeholders know about an issue, the consequences of alternative courses of action, and the preferences of those concerned with the issue. Issues are often contested because interests have conflicting preferences regarding their resolution, as in the case of the proponents and opponents of a CO_2 emissions standard of 120 grams per kilometer in the European Union. Issues can also be contested because interests have different information. Auto companies may have superior information about the preferences of car buyers for higher fuel economy vehicles, and environmentalists may have superior information about the extent of public concern about climate change. Organizations such as the National Academy of Sciences as well as universities play an important role in providing scientific assessments of issues such as fuel economy and auto safety but science is not always conclusive.

TABLE 1-2 Institutions

United States	International	Global
Presidency	European Union	World Trade Organization
Congress	Commission	Kyoto Treaty
USTR	Parliament	News Media
Department of Transportation	China	Social Media
NHTSA	State Council	
Environmental Protection Agency	Ministry of Industry—Brazil and Argentina	
Courts—Federal	Saudi Arabia Law	
Courts—State	Mercosur	
State Legislatures	KORUS	
California Air Resources Board	Courts—United Kingdom	

Information is also frequently at the heart of strategies for addressing nonmarket issues. Lobbying, for example, involves providing information to officeholders about the likely consequences of policy alternatives. Information provision is also important in regulatory rule making because of the complexity of most regulatory issues and because agencies are required to develop a record supporting their actions. Information can also be an instrument of nonmarket competition. On the issue of sharply higher fuel economy standards for 2017–2025, the government estimated that the cost of a car would increase between $770 and $3,500, and the industry estimated that the cost increase would be $6,000 or more.[24] The Alliance of Automobile Manufacturers estimated that a standard of 62 mph sought by California would cost the United States 220,000 jobs.

Information can be important to the progress of issues. The regulation requiring rear-view cameras was spurred by the media attention given to the tragedy of a child being run over in his own driveway. Information can also lead to the resolution of issues. The mounting scientific evidence about climate change and the high gasoline prices led to agreement on the new fuel economy labels on new vehicles.

CHANGE IN THE NONMARKET ENVIRONMENT

The nonmarket environment changes as issues are resolved, current issues progress, and new issues arise. This section focuses on the origins of issues and the forces that give rise to them. The following sections address the anticipation of nonmarket issues and their progression and resolution.

Nonmarket issues originate from both external forces and a firm's own actions. Most changes in the tax law originate in response to ideas that capture a degree of political support. However, the issue of eliminating the investment tax credit, which had been a component of U.S. tax policy for over 20 years, arose in part because of political action by service industries that viewed the credit as a subsidy to capital-intensive industries. The issue of automobile safety regulation arose from an automobile accident and articles by two young policy activists. The issue of a possible health risk from the electromagnetic field generated by high-voltage electricity transmission lines arose from a small-scale inferential study linking power lines to leukemia in children. As the varied origins of these issues indicate, managers must be sensitive to the sources of nonmarket issues—even those such as possible health risks from the electromagnetic field generated by transmission lines—that initially seem remote or even far-fetched.

Nonmarket issues have five basic sources:

- Scientific discovery and technological advancement
- New understandings
- Institutional change
- Interest group activity
- Moral concerns

Scientific discovery and technological advancement can produce fundamental changes in both the market and nonmarket environments. In the market environment, they create opportunities for new products and processes, new applications of existing knowledge, and the foundations for future discoveries. They also give rise to nonmarket issues. Measurements suggesting that the earth was warming spawned issues ranging from higher fuel economy standards to the deforestation of tropical rain forests. The discovery of an ozone hole above the Antarctic confirmed theories of ozone depletion and propelled a number of nonmarket issues ranging from the elimination of CFCs to measures to reduce the incidence of skin cancer. When the theory of ozone depletion was initially advanced, DuPont was pressured to stop producing CFCs. DuPont argued that there was yet no evidence that CFCs actually caused ozone depletion and pledged in a public advertisement that it would cease production if scientific evidence showed a relationship. Recognizing the importance of the issue, DuPont worked on developing a substitute for CFCs. When a National Academy of Sciences study concluded that there was a causal link, DuPont announced the next day that it would immediately cease production, and it had a substitute ready.

---

[24]*Wall Street Journal*, July 19, 2011.

Nonmarket issues can also arise from new technology and scientific uncertainty. The spectacular success of the cellular telephone industry was interrupted one day when a man called the *Larry King Live* television talk show and claimed that his wife had died from brain cancer caused by extensive use of a cellular telephone. Earlier in the day, a CEO of a major corporation had announced that he had brain cancer, and the previous day a CEO of another major corporation had died of brain cancer. The call and speculation that the CEOs might have been heavy users of cellular telephones caused a panic. The stock prices of the nation's largest cellular telephone company and the largest manufacturer of cellular telephones dropped by over 5 percent. Fears were calmed by statements of government officials that there was no scientific evidence linking cellular telephones to cancer. The industry pledged to conduct additional research into whether radio-frequency radiation emitted by the telephones was harmful. The promise of research to fill the gap in scientific information reassured cellular telephone users, and the growth in demand resumed. The U.S. Federal Communications Commission concluded that there was no scientific evidence of a link between cell phone use and cancer, but the issue received renewed attention when in 2011 a panel of scientists assembled by the World Health Organization reviewed the published research and concluded that cell phone use was "possibly cancerous."[25] A study from Denmark released later in the year found no evidence of cancer, although it did not study heavy users.

Nonmarket issues also arise from changes in understandings. The environmental movement brought to the attention of the public damage to the natural environment and the associated health risks. Renewed confidence in markets and the failure of socialist economic systems spurred a wave of privatization in both developed and developing countries. Increasing evidence of the economic benefits of international trade led not only to further reductions in trade barriers through the WTO but also to market integration in North America through the North American Free Trade Agreement (NAFTA) and in the European Union through the Single European Act. Antitrust policy and enforcement changed substantially during the 1980s as a consequence of new understandings about the effects of the competitive practices of firms. Changes in the membership of the Supreme Court during the 1980s and the understandings the new members brought with them resulted in changes in affirmative action policies. A Bangladesh economist, Muhammed Yunis, recognized that the lives of poor people would be improved by providing small loans at modest interest rates to replace borrowing from money lenders. Concerns about the working conditions in factories in developing countries resulted in firms such as Nike and Adidas assuming responsibilities for the working conditions.

Issues also become salient because groups organize to advance their own interests. Interest groups formed around the issue of extending daylight saving time and worked for nearly a decade to obtain an extension A less visible campaign led to a further extension in 2007. The growth and developing effectiveness of the American Association of Retired Persons led it to push for congressional enactment of a catastrophic illness insurance plan, only to have a grassroots revolt among its members lead to repeal of the act before it had taken effect. Consumer groups took political action over abusive financial market practices, resulting in the establishment of the Consumer Financial Protection Bureau in 2011. Interest groups can also block change, as in the case of the auto industry and higher fuel economy standards, which remained unchanged for more than two decades.

Nonmarket issues also arise because of institutional actions. A Supreme Court decision in 1988 supported a new theory of "fraud on the market," under which a firm could be held liable if its stock price fell significantly when the firm's projections of future earnings had been favorable. This provided incentives for trial lawyers to file class action lawsuits against high-technology companies when their naturally volatile stock price fell. No evidence of fraud was required to file a lawsuit, and filing allowed the lawyers to conduct discovery and depose company executives. To avoid the costs and disruptions of discovery and depositions, and the subsequent costs of a trial, many companies settled the lawsuits even though they expected to win. Settlements totaled nearly $7 billion. Viewing the practice as extortionary and the lawsuits as frivolous, companies backed federal legislation granting a safe harbor for forward-looking projections, and Congress enacted the statute over President Clinton's veto.

Change in the nonmarket environment also comes from market forces. In the mid-1990s, new markets associated with the Internet, wireless systems, and integrated services resulted in a

---

[25]The WHO panel gave the radio frequency magnetic fields of cell phones the same rating it had given to coffee.

restructuring of the telecommunications industry, including mergers, acquisitions, and strategic alliances. Congress then struggled with legislation to lift the archaic restrictions on competition left over from the era of regulation. The demand for mobile communications technology and social media led automakers to equip cars with devices ranging from GPS navigation systems to handless communications systems to onboard televisions. Those market forces contributed to the issue of distracted driving, which accounted for a growing share of traffic fatalities and injuries.

Nonmarket issues also arise because of heightened moral concerns. Privacy concerns associated with the Internet resulted in both self-regulation by Internet service providers and Web sites and calls for new legislation. In the European Union, privacy concerns led to strong legislation on the handling and use of personal information on the Internet. Moral concerns were also raised about subprime lending to borrowers who did not qualify for bank loans, leading to regulations to limit predatory lending. Moral concerns about the spread of AIDS in developing countries and the suffering of its victims resulted in pressure on pharmaceutical firms to lower their prices for AIDS drugs.

ANTICIPATING CHANGE IN THE NONMARKET ENVIRONMENT

The effectiveness with which a firm and its managers address nonmarket issues depends on their approach to the nonmarket environment. One approach is to respond to nonmarket issues only when they are strong enough to force the firm to act. A second approach emphasizes limiting the extent of the damage once the firm has been challenged by an issue. A third approach is anticipatory and is intended to prepare the firm to take advantage of opportunities as they arise and address issues before they become problems. A fourth approach is proactive with the firm and its managers not only anticipating nonmarket issues but also acting to affect which issues arise and how they will be framed. This approach recognizes that nonmarket issues and their development are affected by the way business is conducted. The fourth approach is the most effective, but it requires considerable sensitivity to the sources of nonmarket issues and how they progress. A fundamental step in anticipating nonmarket issues is to view the potential issue or business practice from the perspective of others who might be concerned about it, as the graduation cards example illustrates.

EXAMPLE   Graduation Cards

Graduation represents an important market for the greeting card industry. In its preparation for the college graduation season, Hallmark Cards was considering the array of cards it would market. Cards could reflect a variety of themes, but two traditionally popular ones were transition and celebration. One transition was coming of legal drinking age, and Hallmark was considering cards featuring alcoholic beverages. Alcoholic beverages were also associated with celebration, so the cards would draw on two themes. One card being considered had a photo of a Budweiser can with a small cherubic character saying, "You're graduating?" Another card portrayed a beer and eggs breakfast on graduation day, and a third suggested a robe large enough to cover two champagne bottles.

Graduation cards are bought by friends and relatives of the graduate, and it is from their perspective that the cards must be considered—for both their market and nonmarket potentials. The proposed cards were intended for the college graduation market, and virtually all those recipients would be of legal drinking age. College students, however, were not the only ones graduating. Twice as many students graduate from high school each year, and they are not of legal drinking age.

Some parents and relatives could view the cards as promoting alcoholic beverages and contributing to underage drinking and to drunk driving. Parents and others concerned about underage drinking provided the potential for a nonmarket reaction to the cards.

The next step is to assess whether people concerned about the cards are likely to act in the nonmarket environment. Some parents and relatives will be concerned about the cards, but they are dispersed and most have limited means of generating a nonmarket issue. Some, however, participate in organizations such as the Parent Teacher Association (PTA) and MADD that are experienced in dealing with nonmarket issues, know how to attract the news media to bring an issue to the attention of the public, and hence know how to put it on a firm's agenda. This does not mean that a nonmarket reaction is certain, but it certainly is possible.

Hallmark chose to market the cards, and the reaction was swift. MADD activists began to pressure store owners to stop selling the cards, and the media picked up the story. Faced with public criticism, Hallmark withdrew the cards from the market and subsequently decided not to produce graduation cards with a reference to alcoholic beverages.

THE NONMARKET ISSUE LIFE CYCLE

The progression of nonmarket issues can be understood in terms of a life cycle. The nonmarket issue life cycle relates the stage of development of an issue to its impact on a firm.[26] This is not a theory, since it does not provide an explanation for how or why an issue develops or a basis for predicting its likely development. In particular, it does not identify the causal factors that govern an issue's progress. The life cycle concept is useful, however, because it identifies a pattern and serves as a reminder that issues with simple origins can garner support, propelling them through a series of stages and resulting in significant impacts. Issues do not, however, have a life of their own. Instead, their progression is governed by the attention they receive from interests and institutions.

Nonmarket issues can progress through five stages: (1) issue identification, (2) interest group formation, (3) legislation, (4) administration, and (5) enforcement. As an issue progresses through its life cycle, its impact on the firm tends to increase. As the impact increases, management's range of discretion in addressing the issue correspondingly decreases. The impact may take the form of government actions such as regulation or changes in public sentiment that limit the alternatives available to management.

To illustrate the nonmarket life cycle, consider the issue of automobile safety regulation. The progression of the issue is illustrated along the horizontal axis in Figure 1-2, and the vertical axis represents the impact on automobile manufacturers. In the 1950s, automobile safety was viewed primarily as a function of road conditions and the driver's skill. In 1957, as Congressman Kenneth Roberts of Alabama and his wife were returning from their honeymoon, their car was rear-ended. Both were injured, but their well-packaged glass and china wedding presents in the backseat were undamaged. Roberts recognized that an ignored dimension of the auto safety issue was the vehicle itself and how safely it contained its passengers.

Roberts held congressional hearings on the issue, but no action resulted. In 1959 two articles on the issue were published. A young attorney named Ralph Nader published an article on automobile safety that focused on automobile design. A young official in the Department of Labor, Daniel Patrick Moynihan, published an article arguing for a broader perspective on the automobile safety issue. Interest group activity began to develop, and the media was attracted to the issue, particularly when it was revealed that General Motors had hired a private detective to investigate Nader. In 1962 the issue entered the legislative stage when the General Services Administration (GSA) issued a standard for brake fluid. Legislation was introduced in Congress and, after considerable deliberation and intense politics, the Motor Vehicle Safety Act of 1966 was enacted. The act established NHTSA, which was given administrative rule-making authority to establish mandatory automobile safety standards.

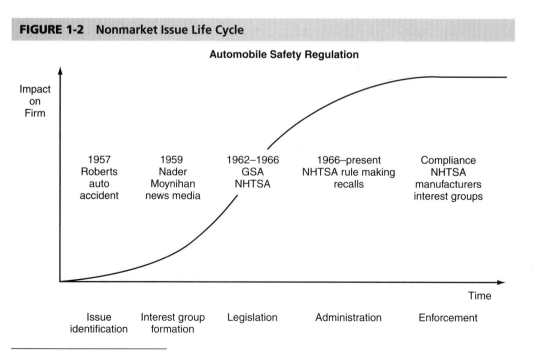

FIGURE 1-2 Nonmarket Issue Life Cycle

---

[26]The life cycle concept was originated by Ian Wilson while at General Electric.

The enforcement phase for auto safety regulation has been multifaceted. Auto manufacturers test their models extensively, not only for compliance with regulations but often to exceed government standards. NHTSA continues to mandate new standards such as rear-view cameras, enforces the regulations, and obtains recalls of vehicles. Advocacy groups such as the Center for Auto Safety monitor both the industry and the enforcement activities of NHTSA. Safety regulations are also enforced through the courts as a result of lawsuits filed by individuals and trial lawyers.

Nonmarket issues that complete their life cycles do not always result in more restrictions on business, as evidenced by the issue of airline deregulation. Economists analyzing the performance of airlines regulated by the Civil Aeronautics Board (CAB) concluded that regulation was inducing inefficiencies and increasing costs. The issue attracted attention because of the large differences between the fares of the CAB-regulated airlines and airlines such as Southwest that operated only intrastate routes and hence were not subject to CAB regulation. Regulatory oversight hearings brought additional attention to the issue and planted the seeds of legislative action. These developments coincided with increased public criticism of economic regulation and decreased confidence in government. As congressional and executive branch attention increased, the issue entered the legislative stage. When economist Alfred Kahn was appointed to head the CAB, he moved quickly to take administrative action to deregulate the industry, which spurred the legislative process. The result was legislation that eliminated the economic regulation of the domestic airline industry. After transferring some of its other functions to other government agencies, the CAB ceased to exist. Similar concerns about the economic consequences of surface transportation regulation resulted in the elimination of the Interstate Commerce Commission, the first federal regulatory agency.

Not all nonmarket issues, of course, garner enough support to pass through all five stages, and many do not survive the legislative stage. The fact that an issue does not pass through all the stages does not mean that it has no impact. The attention an issue receives can produce change even in the absence of institutional action. The consumer movement has not progressed as far as its supporters had hoped, and Congress had not passed major consumer legislation since 1976. Despite the consumer movement's failure to achieve new legislation, it resulted in many significant changes in business practices. Furthermore, interest groups and NGOs are active in advocating for consumer interests. The financial crisis of 2007–2009 led to legislation establishing the first new consumer regulatory agency since the 1970s.

SUMMARY

The field of business and its environment is concerned with issues in the nonmarket environment that have potentially important effects on organizational and managerial performance. Managers are in the best position to understand how the firm's market activities give rise to nonmarket issues and to assess the significance of nonmarket issues for market strategies and overall performance. Managers thus have the responsibility for addressing nonmarket issues and use both nonmarket and market strategies to achieve superior performance.

The nonmarket environment of a firm is characterized by four I's: issues, interests, institutions, and information. As indicated by the example of the automobile industry, nonmarket issues have important implications for firms and their market and nonmarket performance. Nonmarket issues may be identified externally or by management and may arise from scientific discovery, new understandings, interest group activity, institutional change, and moral concerns. Because these factors change over time, the nonmarket environment and a firm's nonmarket issue agenda evolve.

Management must not only deal effectively with nonmarket issues but must also anticipate issues and take proactive steps to address them. Many nonmarket issues pass through stages—issue identification, interest group formation, legislation, administration, and enforcement. This pattern serves as a reminder that issues evolve, even seemingly minor issues can have substantial effects, and the impact increases as issues move through the stages of their life cycles. Not all nonmarket issues pass through all five stages, however, and some, such as deregulation, result in fewer rather than more restrictions. The progress of an issue is shaped by the actions of firms and other interests and by the characteristics of the institutions in whose arenas the issue is addressed.

ORGANIZATION OF THE BOOK

This book is organized in five parts, and cases for discussion are provided in each chapter. An integrative case is provided at the conclusion of each part. Part I introduces the nonmarket environment, the nonmarket issues firms face, and the factors, including activist and NGO pressures, the news media, and public sentiment, that affect the development of those issues. The focus is on the formulation of strategies for addressing nonmarket issues and the integration of those strategies with market strategies. Part II considers issues addressed in the context of government hired institutions with an emphasis on legislatures. The substantive focus is on conceptual frameworks for analyzing nonmarket issues, understanding government institutions, and formulating effective strategies for addressing those issues. The frameworks developed in this part provide a foundation for Parts III and IV. Part III focuses on the interactions between government and markets with an emphasis on antitrust, regulation, environmental protection, and court-adjudicated law. Part IV is explicitly global and provides frameworks for understanding the political economy of countries and the relationships between business and government. The European Union, China, India, and emerging markets, and international trade policy is used to bring the policy and strategy issues together. Part V is normative and focuses on the social responsibilities of firms and the guidance that ethics provides. Ethics systems and reasoning are the centerpieces of Part V, and the applications focus on corporate social responsibility in domestic and international contexts.

CASES

The Nonmarket Environment of the Pharmaceutical Industry

U.S. spending on pharmaceuticals increased by 19 percent to $131.9 billion in 2000, the fifth consecutive year of increases above 13 percent. Expenditures were expected to top $150 billion in 2001. The expenditures reflected the importance of drugs as health care therapies and the continuing discoveries of new treatments as a result of the industry's research and development efforts. A study by a research center supported by the pharmaceutical industry reported that the cost of developing a new drug had increased from $231 million in 1987 to $802 million in 2000 (in inflation-adjusted dollars). The expenditures also reflected high prices, heavy marketing expenditures, and high profits. These factors attracted the attention of government officials, activists, and advocacy groups.

Public Citizen, a consumer activist organization, published a report arguing that the pharmaceutical industry exaggerated the cost of developing new drugs.[27] The Pharmaceutical Research and Manufacturers Association (PhRMA) hired Ernst & Young to evaluate the Public Citizen report.[28] Ernst & Young criticized the report and concluded that the pharmaceutical industry paid a higher percentage of its revenues as taxes than all other industries in the United States. Critics responded that the tax payments were large because the industry's profit margins were so high.

In a study based on the annual reports of nine pharmaceutical companies, Families USA reported that eight of the companies spent more than twice as much on marketing as on research

and development. Six of the companies had net incomes that exceeded their research and development expenditures. Families USA also reported that prices for the 50 most prescribed drugs for seniors had increased at twice the rate of inflation.

PhRMA replied, "The Families USA 'study' condemns the pharmaceutical industry for being a success at developing medicines upon which millions of patients depend. When the pharmaceutical industry does well, patients do even better. Because the pharmaceutical industry is profitable, Americans have the best chance in the world of getting the cure for Alzheimer's, cancer, diabetes or AIDS."[29]

One reason pharmaceutical profits were high was that the brand-name companies faced buyers that controlled only small shares of the market. One fear of the brand-name companies was that buyers would join together and use their bargaining power to drive prices down. Maine had passed a law empowering the state to negotiate prices and purchase prescription drugs for its residents. PhRMA filed a lawsuit against the state, and a federal court issued a preliminary injunction preventing the state from implementing the law. The Court of Appeals, however, reversed the lower court decision.

The state of Florida passed new legislation to use its purchasing power for drugs included under Medicaid, the federal program administered by the states that funded medical care for the poor. Florida included in its formulary—the list of drugs for which reimbursement would be provided—only those drugs for which the manufacturers agreed to pay rebates to the state beyond the rebates required by Medicaid. Rather than give in to the pressure, Pfizer reached an agreement with the

---

[27]Public Citizen, "Rx R&D Myths: The Case Against the Drug Industry's R&D 'Scare Card,' " Washington, DC, July 2001.
[28]Ernst & Young, LLP, "Pharmaceutical Industry R&D Costs: Key Findings about the Public Citizen Report," August 8, 2001.

[29]www.phrma.org.

state under which its prescription drugs were included in the formulary without any price discount. Instead, Pfizer agreed to pay for nurses to monitor tens of thousands of patients to make sure they took their medications and had checkups on a regular basis. PhRMA had a different response to Florida's program. It filed a lawsuit arguing that federal law required that all prescription drugs be available to Medicaid recipients unless a drug had been shown to have no therapeutic benefits.

Florida also adopted a counter-detailing program in which pharmacists employed by the state visited doctors to encourage them to prescribe generic drugs rather than the higher-priced brand-name drugs.[30] The pharmacists provided a "report card" to each doctor indicating the doctor's Medicaid prescriptions record.

On a regular basis the news media carried articles on developments in the pharmaceutical industry. Since the fortunes of companies depended on the results of clinical trials and the FDA's drug approval decisions, the business press covered the FDA closely. The business press also covered patent extension decisions and the progress of patent infringement cases. Congress and the Bush administration had pharmaceutical issues high on their agenda, resulting in media coverage of legislative and regulatory reform issues. The nonbusiness media also covered the industry, focusing more on the impact of drugs—and their prices—on consumers.

The media was also concerned about the sponsorship of research and clinical testing. Pharmaceutical companies financed research in universities and hospitals and typically retained the intellectual property rights to the resulting discoveries. The scientific and medical press had become concerned about the implications of this trend for the integrity of their publications. The British journal *Nature* required authors to disclose any financial interests related to the studies they published in the journal.

Journals were also concerned about the symmetry of what was published. Pharmaceutical companies were hesitant to disclose negative research results that might undermine products. The *New England Journal of Medicine,* the *Journal of the American Medical Association,* and other journals adopted a policy to force pharmaceutical companies that sponsored clinical research to allow researchers to publish unfavorable as well as favorable results.

Judges had also become concerned about links between expert witnesses and the pharmaceutical industry. Some judges required expert witnesses to disclose their financial connections to the industry.

In an unprecedented action, Blue Cross of California, a unit of WellPoint Health Networks, filed a Citizen Petition with the FDA to switch from prescription-only to over-the-counter (OTC) status three second-generation antihistamines—Allegra, produced by Aventis; Claritin, produced by Schering-Plough; and Zyrtec, marketed in the United States by Pfizer. This would benefit consumers because the second-generation antihistamines were nonsedating, whereas the 100 first-generation antihistamines sold on the OTC market were sedating. A switch would put the second-generation antihistamines under considerable price pressure.

In January 2001, Schering-Plough's third-generation antihistamine Clarinex was approved for sale in the European Union, and in the same month the FDA issued an "approvable" letter for the drug indicating that there were no outstanding clinical or scientific issues. The FDA, however, withheld approval because of quality control problems in Schering-Plough's New Jersey and Puerto Rico manufacturing facilities. Public Citizen had put pressure on the FDA by writing to the Secretary of Health and Human Services, citing consultants' reports on the production facilities and FDA warning letters to Schering-Plough.

Public Citizen also asked the Secretary of Health and Human Services to undertake criminal prosecution of Schering-Plough. A study by Public Citizen concluded that the probable cause of 17 deaths was asthma inhalers sold without the active medication albuterol. In 1999 and 2000 Schering-Plough had recalled 59 million inhalers because advocacy groups had raised concerns about them. A Schering-Plough spokesperson said that 5,000 people a year died from asthma and that there was "no evidence that a patient was ever harmed by an inhaler subject to any recalls." He added that "every inhaler returned to the company by a patient claiming injury and alleging the canister lacked active ingredient has been tested and found to contain active ingredient."[31]

The pricing and marketing of prescription drugs was of concern to state and federal law enforcement agencies. Twenty pharmaceutical companies were under investigation for price reporting practices associated with the sale of drugs to Medicaid and Medicare. One focus of the investigation was the reporting of high wholesale prices while providing deep discounts to doctors. This increased the doctor's margin, providing incentives to prescribe the drugs.

In 1997 the FDA had revised its regulations, allowing direct-to-consumer (DTC) advertising of prescription drugs. Schering-Plough and other pharmaceutical companies began to advertise directly to consumers through television, radio, and print. The advertisements gave a toll-free number to call for information, referred to magazine advertisements where warnings were given, and instructed viewers to "ask your doctor." The marketing strategy was to induce consumers to ask their doctors for the drug by brand name. The strategy proved to be very successful, pushing Claritin sales to $2.5 billion in the United States. In 2000 Merck spent $161 million on DTC advertising for Vioxx, which was more than Budweiser spent advertising its beers. PhRMA explained that DTC advertising helped educate consumers and involve them more in their own health care.

The National Institute for Health Care Management, a research institute funded by Blue Cross Blue Shield, reported that DTC advertising had increased from $700 million in 1996 to $2.5 billion in 2000 and that the increase was concentrated in 50 drugs. The institute also reported that the increase in pharmaceutical spending was due to an increase in prescriptions written and not to price increases. PhRMA explained, "We have an epidemic of undertreatment of serious illnesses in the United States."[32]

[30]Marketing of drugs directly to doctors is referred to as detailing.

[31]*Wall Street Journal,* August 10, 2001.
[32]*New York Times,* November 11, 2001.

The American Medical Association (AMA) took an interest in the DTC advertising issue. The AMA supported the objectives of educating patients and involving them in their own health care but was concerned that the doctor–patient relationship could be strained when patients asked for a drug by brand name. An AMA ethics committee stated, "Physicians should resist commercially induced pressure to prescribe drugs that may not be indicated. Physicians should deny requests for inappropriate prescriptions and educate patients as to why certain advertised drugs may not be suitable treatment options...."[33] In 2001 the AMA wrote to the Senate Commerce Committee stating, "Our physician members have expressed concern about the impact that direct-to-consumer advertising has on the physician/patient relationship and on health care costs." The AMA asked the committee to direct the FDA to study the impact of DTC advertising. The FDA began a review.

DTC advertising also attracted the attention of activist and advocacy groups. The Prescription Access Litigation Project filed a lawsuit against Schering-Plough claiming that its advertising of Claritin was deceptive and boosted demand and the price of the drug. Some policy specialists observed that if DTC advertising were restricted, consumers would simply turn to the Internet for information on prescription drugs.

The Commission of the European Union (EU) proposed a fast-track approval process for new drugs. The objective was to reduce the approval time from 18 months to 9 to 12 months, which would be faster than the approval time of 14 months in the United States. The Commission also proposed a relaxation of restrictions on DTC advertisements, but not broadcast advertising, for treatments of certain diseases, including diabetes, AIDS, and asthma.

In 2001 Bayer withdrew its newly introduced and fast-selling cholesterol-lowering drug Baycol because over 50 deaths were associated with its use. The drug had been approved in the United Kingdom, and other EU member states had adopted that decision. Responsibility for monitoring the safety of the drug, however, was unclear. The European Agency for the Evaluation of Medical Products said it had little role in safety because it had not participated in the licensing. The recall brought home to the European governments the confusion in drug safety regulation and the poor communication among the member states. The Medicines Control Agency of Germany faulted Bayer for not having disclosed problems earlier.

Post-marketing monitoring of drugs was also an issue in the United States. One concern was the rapid adoption of drugs as a result of aggressive marketing by the brand-name pharmaceutical companies. This meant that if there were side effects not identified in the clinical testing, problems could be extensive.[34] *BusinessWeek* called for an independent body like the National Transportation Safety Board to investigate problems with drugs.

Many developing countries faced an AIDS crisis, and the cost of the cocktail of drugs used to treat AIDS was beyond their means. South Africa used its Medicines Act to threaten the pharmaceutical industry with compulsory licensing and parallel imports of AIDS drugs. Thirty-nine international pharmaceutical companies filed a lawsuit against the South African government but later dropped the lawsuit and agreed to substantial price reductions.[35]

PhRMA opposed the practice of deep discounts for drugs for developing countries because it contributed to "parallel trade." Parallel trade was the importation of drugs by developed countries that had been exported with deep discounts to developing countries. The industry argued that parallel trade resulted in the importation of adulterated and counterfeit drugs or drugs that had been improperly stored and handled and thus imposed a safety risk on the importing country. A bill introduced in Congress, however, would authorize pharmacies and wholesalers to purchase prescription drugs that had been exported from the United States.

Brazil faced high costs of purchasing AIDS drugs and negotiated price reductions with several drug companies, but Roche refused to offer a substantial reduction. Brazil then announced that it would issue a license to a Brazilian company to produce a generic version of Roche's drug.[36] Roche conceded and reduced the price to Brazil by an additional 40 percent.

The protection of intellectual property rights was an important issue for the brand-name pharmaceutical companies. The industry supported the World Trade Organization (WTO) and its enforcement of the TRIPS (Trade-Related Aspects of Intellectual Property Rights) Agreement. The United States filed a trade complaint with the WTO against Brazil for its law allowing compulsory licensing for drugs not manufactured in the country.

The pharmaceutical industry criticized India for restrictions on imports of pharmaceuticals and for encouraging a domestic industry that copied drugs under patent. A 1972 Indian law allowed companies to copy a patented drug if they used a different manufacturing process. Pharmacists prescribed much of the drugs in India, and the drug companies competed for their attention. Brand-name companies began offering gifts to pharmacists if they prescribed the company's drugs, and Indian companies began to provide bonuses of free drugs. GlaxoSmithKline provided color television sets to pharmacists who met certain targets.

Patents provided the most important protection for intellectual property in the pharmaceutical industry. The patent on Schering-Plough's Claritin was scheduled to expire in December 2002, and with the FDA and in Congress the company sought without success to extend the market exclusivity. To delay the entry of competitors, Schering-Plough filed a patent infringement lawsuit against 10 generic pharmaceutical companies, claiming that their versions of Claritin would, when ingested, necessarily produce a metabolite on which Schering-Plough held a patent. The courts had not upheld this "metabolite defense," but neither had they rejected it. At a minimum, the lawsuit could delay entry of the generics.

To resolve a lawsuit, Schering-Plough reached a settlement with Upsher-Smith Laboratories and American

---

[33]American Medical Association, "E-5.015 Direct-to-Consumer Advertisements of Prescription Drugs," www.ama-assn.org.
[34]See the Chapter 10 cases, *Merck and Vioxx* and *Pfizer and Celebrex.*

[35]See the Part V integrative case, *GlaxoSmithKline and AIDS Drug Policy.*
[36]The Brazilian constitution allowed the country to violate a patent in the case of abusive practices.

Home Products regarding their generic versions of K-Dur. Schering-Plough paid $60 million to Upsher-Smith, which then agreed not to market its drug. Upsher-Smith had received a 180-day exclusivity period as a result of being the first company to develop a generic version, so other companies could not market their generic drugs during that period. In April 2001, the Federal Trade Commission voted unanimously to file civil charges challenging the agreement as a violation of the antitrust laws.

In addition to using patent infringement defenses, brand-name pharmaceutical companies used FDA rules to stave off generics. The patent on Bristol-Myers Squibb's blockbuster diabetes drug Glucophage expired in September 2000, and the company had initially been successful in staving off the generics by inducing patients to switch to two new versions of the drug that were not chemically equivalent to Glucophage.

Based on new clinical tests, the FDA had approved Glucophage as safe for children, and Bristol-Myers received exclusive rights until 2004 for use by children. A 1994 FDA rule required that labels must contain dosage and use information for children, but generics could not include such information on their labels because Bristol-Myers had exclusive rights to the data. The dilemma for the FDA was that its rule technically might block all generic versions of Glucophage. The dilemma had delayed the FDA approval of 14 generic versions for months, and Bristol-Myers was prepared to file a lawsuit if the FDA required provision of dosage and use information.

Medicare did not provide prescription drug benefits, and only about one-third of the elderly had prescription drug insurance coverage. Congress wanted to provide prescription drug benefits under Medicare, but Democrats in Congress sought

to provide roughly twice the coverage supported by the Bush administration. The pharmaceutical industry had opposed the legislation based on concerns that it would increase buyers' bargaining power relative to the pharmaceutical companies.

In response to congressional attempts to provide prescription drug coverage under Medicare, the Bush administration reached an agreement with pharmacy-benefits managers (PBMs) to negotiate drug discounts with pharmaceutical companies. The pharmaceutical companies opposed the plan because of the price pressures it would create. Two pharmacy associations, the National Association of Chain Drug Stores and the National Community Pharmacist Association (NCPA), filed a lawsuit to block the drug discount plan. The pharmacists opposed the plan because they feared being forced to shoulder the discounts.

The pharmacists were also concerned about direct competition from PBMs. In attempting to lower pharmaceutical expenditures, PBMs had begun to operate mail-order prescription refill services, making them direct competitors to the independent pharmacists. The NCPA, with 25,000 members nationwide, responded by launching a campaign to pressure state governments to increase their regulation of PBMs. The PBMs argued that the NCPA campaign was intended to increase its members' profits. ▪

Preparation Questions

1. Characterize the issues, interests, institutions, and information in the environment of the pharmaceutical industry.
2. Which issues will be addressed in which institutional arenas, and which interests will be active on those issues?
3. Where are these issues in their life cycles?

The Nonmarket Environment of McDonald's

McDonald's, the world's largest restaurant chain with 30,000 restaurants in 118 countries serving 46 million customers daily, faced a host of nonmarket issues in the early 2000s.

OBESITY

The body mass index (BMI) of Americans increased throughout the twentieth century, and the proportion of people considered obese increased from 15 to 31 percent from 1980 to 2000.[37] Sixty-four percent of American adults were overweight or obese. Interest in the obesity issue intensified after the release in February 2004 of a report by the Centers for Disease Control and Prevention estimating that 400,000 deaths annually were caused by obesity-related illnesses compared to 435,000 deaths caused by tobacco. The Surgeon General estimated that health care costs resulting from obesity were $117 billion annually.

Economists studied the increase in the BMI and concluded that it was due to several factors. Calorie intake had increased about 10 percent, and the strenuousness of work had decreased. Moreover, technological change had substantially reduced the relative cost of food, leading people to eat more.

In contrast to the economists, activists blamed fast food and the failure to provide nutritional information about menu items. Trial lawyers sought a new mass tort after their success in litigation against tobacco companies and saw obesity as an opportunity. Professor John Banzhaf, a law professor at George Washington University, who advised trial lawyers in obesity lawsuits against McDonald's, said, "A fast-food company like McDonald's may not be responsible for the entire obesity epidemic, but let's say they're 5 percent responsible. Five percent of $117 billion is still an enormous amount of money."[38] The first two obesity lawsuits had been dismissed.[39]

---

[37]Cutler, Glaeser, and Shapiro (2003) concluded that demographic changes did not explain the increase in obesity.

[38]*Time,* August 3, 2003.
[39]See the Chapter 14 case, *Obesity and McLawsuits,* for more information on the issue.

THE CHEESEBURGER BILL

The restaurant and food industries argued that obesity was a matter of individual responsibility and lobbied Congress for protection from obesity lawsuits. In 2004 the House quickly passed the Personal Responsibility in Food Consumption Act, dubbed the cheeseburger bill, on a 276–139 vote. The bill provided protection from obesity and weight-based lawsuits unless the weight gain was due to the violation of a state or federal law. Author of the bill Ric Keller (R-FL) said, "We need to get back to the old-fashioned principles of common sense and personal responsibility and get away from this new culture where everybody plays the victim and blames other people for their problems."[40] James Sensenbrenner (R-WI) was more direct, stating that "fat people should 'look in the mirror' and that parents need to monitor children's eating habits to make sure that 'little Johnny' doesn't become 'big Johnny.'"[41] House Speaker Dennis Hastert (R-IL) commented, "We as Americans need to realize that suing your way to better health is not the answer. Trial lawyers need to stop encouraging consumers to blame others for the consequences of their actions just so they can profit from frivolous lawsuits against restaurants."[42]

Referring to the cheeseburger bill, Representative James McGovern (D-MA) argued, "It protects an industry that doesn't need to be protected at this particular point and we're dealing with a problem that doesn't exist. The problem that does exist is that we have an obesity problem in this country."[43] Neil Barnard, president of the Physicians Committee for Responsible Medicine, commented, "[The bill] is an unsavory attempt to protect corporate profits at the expense of American health. The bill strips the public of its right to seek any redress against food manufacturers for their contribution to the obesity crisis, and the related epidemics of heart disease and diabetes."[44]

The restaurant industry backed the Common-Sense Consumption Act, the state version of the cheeseburger bill, which would shield restaurants and food processors from obesity liability. As of mid-2004 the cheeseburger bill had been introduced in 23 state legislatures, and eight states had enacted it.

FILMMAKING ACTIVISM

The news media extensively covered the fast-food and obesity issue, and the issue became the subject of films. McDonald's was the target of a 98-minute film, *Super Size Me,* by filmmaker Morgan Spurlock. Spurlock ate only at McDonald's for 30 days, gained 25 pounds, and received warnings from doctors about his health. "Spurlock's approach was undeniably extreme. He supersized his meals whenever a counter worker made the offer, and ordered everything on the menu at least once. He also stopped exercising. As a result he was often eating twice as many calories a day as he needed. And as any nutritionist will tell you, it only takes an extra 100 calories a day to gain 10 pounds a year."[45]

In response to Spurlock's film, the Competitive Enterprise Institute (CEI) supported preparation of a film by Soso Whaley in which for two 30-day periods she ate only at McDonald's. She lost 18 pounds by controlling her calorie intake. The CEI stated, "Whaley's documentary project, focusing on personal responsibility, obesity, and public health, is taking on the increasing victim mentality being fostered by public health activists and the dishonest bashing of the fast food industry."[46]

MEAL AND MENU NUTRITION INFORMATION

The public attention to the obesity issue led to the introduction of the Menu Education and Labeling Act (MEAL) in the House and the Senate. The so-called McMenu bills applied to chains with 20 or more locations operating under one trade name. The Senate bill required disclosure "in a statement adjacent to the name of the food on any menu...the number of calories, grams of saturated fat plus trans fat, and milligrams of sodium contained in a serving of the food..."

The participants in the news conference accompanying the bill submission were Senator Tom Harkin (D-IA), Representative Rosa DeLauro (D-CN), and Margo Wootan, nutrition policy director of the Center for Science in the Public Interest (CSPI). Harkin said, "So many people are getting suckered into these supersized gimmicks because they are led to believe that bigger is better value. But if you continue to choose supersized, the odds are you will be supersized." Wootan said, "People have good nutrition information in the supermarkets, but people can only guess what they're eating at chain restaurants."[47] The National Restaurant Association, representing 870,000 restaurants with 11.7 million workers, opposed the "one-size-fits-all" and "pre-packaged" MEAL bill. The Association observed, "When Americans do dine out at one of the nation's 870,000 restaurants they find a wide variety of venues, menu items, and portion sizes—meeting customers' demands for choice, value and flexibility, as well as their tastes and dietary needs."[48]

HEALTHY LIFESTYLES

As a result of the concern about obesity, McDonald's suspended its promotion of supersize meals and developed a "healthy lifestyles" program, initially offering additional items, including fruit and salads. In April 2004 the company launched a Lifestyles Platform to address obesity and physical well-being. The Platform included new food choices and ordering options such as the "Go Active" adult Happy Meal, education and easily accessible nutrition information, and physical activity, including the distribution of 15 million Stepometers and walking/fitness booklets. In 2004 it announced that by the end of the year it would introduce a new "core menu" and phase-out supersize options.

The CSPI continued to focus on McDonald's. In response to McDonald's announcement that it would add salads and healthy meals to its menu, Executive Director Michael F. Jacobson declared, "Consumers have good reason to be skeptical

[40]The Daily Buzz, www.foodservice.com, March 11, 2004.
[41]Ibid.
[42]Associated Press Online, March 10, 2004.
[43]Ibid.
[44]The Daily Buzz, www.foodservice.com, March 9, 2004.
[45]*San Francisco Chronicle,* April 21, 2004. The film included John Banzhaf, who commented that the documentary would result in more lawsuits.

[46]Competitive Enterprise Institute, Washington, DC, April 15, 2004.
[47]Copley News Service, November 24, 2003.
[48]U.S. Newswire, November 5, 2003.

about the company's latest promises, since the company broke its promise to reformulate its trans-fat-laden cooking oil. By frying in partially hydrogenated vegetable oil, McDonald's recklessly promotes heart disease among its consumers."[49]

CHILDREN'S ADVERTISING

Advertising to children had long been of concern to children's advocates and members of Congress, which had restricted advertising on children's television programs. McDonald's promoted its trademark golden arches on Barbie dolls and backpacks, and some schools had McDonald's days for lunch. McDonald's also used plastic toy promotions often timed with the release of a movie. "'It seems very clear it's a breach of duty,' says John Banzhaf... 'Schools get paid a kickback for every sugary soft drink or burger sold.'"[50] Professor Walter Willett of Harvard University's School of Public Health said, "The vast majority of what they sell is junk.... We don't sell children guns, alcohol or drugs, but we do allow them to be exploited by food companies."[51]

OBESITY IN THE WORKPLACE

McDonald's also faced obesity issues in the workplace. A 6 feet 1 inch, 420-pound man was offered a job as a cook but was told that he could not begin work until his specially ordered uniform with a 54-inch waistband arrived. After waiting 4 months for the uniform he filed a lawsuit against McDonald's alleging violation of the Americans with Disabilities Act (ADA).[52] The ADA did not prohibit discrimination based on appearance, but some plaintiffs argued that they were not hired or not treated fairly because employers wrongly concluded that they had a disability. A 5 feet 1 inch, 320-pound woman had filed a lawsuit on this theory. In 1997 the U.S. Court of Appeals ruled that "obesity, except in special cases where the obesity relates to a physiological disorder, is not a 'physical impairment.'"

ACRYLAMIDE

Researchers in Sweden detected the chemical acrylamide in a variety of foods but particularly in carbohydrates cooked at high temperatures. The researchers specifically mentioned french fries from McDonald's and Burger King. Researchers in other countries, including those at the Food and Drug Administration (FDA), confirmed the findings. Activists, including the CSPI, argued that the concentrations of acrylamide exceeded the EPA and WHO standards for water. Author Steven Milloy countered that in the study on which the EPA based its drinking water standard, the lowest concentration at which rats had a significant increase in cancer was 500 micrograms per kilogram of body weight.[53] Milloy stated that for a 154-pound man this was equivalent to 35,000 micrograms, which would require eating 486 large servings of McDonald's

french fries every day for life. He added, "Acrylamide hysteria is nothing more than a convenient, if not cynical, tactic of CSPI to advance its anti-fun food agenda."[54]

The issue of consumer warnings regarding acrylamide resurfaced in California in April 2004. The Safe Drinking Water and Toxic Enforcement Act required a public notice for substances "known to the state to cause cancer, birth defects or other reproductive harm." In 1990 California had declared acrylamide, which was used in treating sewage water, to be such a substance. The concern was for workers who produced or worked with acrylamide. Private attorneys filed lawsuits to force the state to require fast-food companies to warn the public. The state began conducting studies to determine if there was any danger to people.

MAD COW DISEASE

In December 2003 the first case of mad cow disease documented in the United States was detected in Washington state in a downer (immobile) cow that had been purchased from Canada.[55] The FDA immediately began an informational campaign, as did the beef industry and the food and restaurant industries, to assure the public that there was no threat to humans. The National Cattlemen's Beef Association (NCBA) had been preparing for such an event by providing information to the public on beef safety.

McDonald's, which did not buy meat from downer cattle nor cattle parts that could carry the disease, stated that the recall of beef by the federal government had "absolutely no connection whatsoever to McDonald's or our suppliers." McDonald's had dealt with the issue of mad cow disease in a number of other countries and had used that experience to prepare for such an event in the United States. McDonald's posted on its Web site a letter to its customers and also distributed copies to customers in its restaurants. McDonald's reported that its sales were not affected.

Critics of the FDA and U.S. Department of Agriculture (USDA) continued to sound the alarm, and the media reported their claims, but no one seemed to pay attention. The CSPI criticized the actions of the USDA, stating that "consumer protection has certainly fallen short." Concerned about the ban on American beef imposed by a number of countries, the USDA set up an international panel to assess the situation. The panel recommended that the United States adopt stronger standards, consistent with international standards, and stated that more cases were likely in the future and that the present case should not be viewed as an "imported case." The NCBA criticized the recommendation as not taking into account the steps the United States and Canada had taken since 1989 to reduce the likelihood of BSE.

ANTIBIOTICS AND GROWTH HORMONES

Human health concerns had been raised about the possible development of antibiotic resistance in humans as a result of the use of antibiotics in food animals. Recognizing the importance

---

[49]Press Release, CSPI, April 15, 2004.
[50]*New York Times,* August 3, 2004.
[51]Ibid.
[52]During this period, McDonald's sold the restaurant to a franchisee who was unaware of the employment offer (*New York Times,* August 4, 2003).
[53]See Milloy (2001).

[54]Steven Milloy, "French Fry Scare," www.cato.org. Americans ate 28 pounds of potato chips and french fries a year on average.
[55]Mad cow disease is bovine spongiform encephalopathy (BSE), and in humans it is known as variant Creutzfeldt-Jakob disease (vCJD).

of antibiotics for both human and veterinary medicine, McDonald's developed a policy based on the principle that "All users of antibiotics, including those who supervise use in animals and those who supervise use in humans, must work to sustain the long-term efficacy of antibiotics for human and veterinary medicine."[56] McDonald's established Sustainable Use Guiding Principles to govern their use. In the absence of a specific disease or likely threat of a specific disease, "antibiotics belonging to classes of compounds approved for use in human medicine" were to be phased out.

McDonald's, the environmental group Environmental Defense, and Elanco Animal Health joined together to create the Antibiotics Coalition. "By working together, McDonald's and Environmental Defense have leveraged the company's purchasing power to reverse the trend of antibiotics overuse in animal agriculture. McDonald's new policy demonstrates that reducing antibiotic use is both feasible and affordable."[57]

In 2000 McDonald's began phasing out growth-promoting antibiotics in Europe, and by the end of 2001, it had eliminated all such antibiotics in its suppliers' chicken feed. Antibiotics in the fluoroquinolone class were discontinued in the United States in 2001. In 2003 it announced that use of growth-promoting hormones would be phased out by all its suppliers.

ANIMAL WELFARE

McDonald's was targeted by People for the Ethical Treatment of Animals (PETA) and other animal welfare groups over the treatment of food animals. In response McDonald's adopted new standards for its beef suppliers, including minimum space standards for cattle in feedlots. McDonald's market power quickly led feedlot operators to meet the standards, bringing about change in the entire industry. Standards were also set for animal transport and care.

In 2000 PETA distributed "Unhappy Meals" boxes similar to the boxes used for Happy Meals. Each box contained a doll resembling Ronald McDonald with a bloody butcher's knife in his hand. McDonald's pledged to improve the welfare of chickens, and PETA suspended its campaign.[58]

Change began when the USDA hired Dr. Temple Grandin, a professor at Colorado State University who researched animal welfare, to evaluate the conditions in 24 meat-processing plants.[59] Her report startled the government and the industry. She documented substantial, and unnecessary, animal suffering. In 1997 McDonald's decided to visit Grandin and was impressed by her scientific, quantitative approach to evaluating the slaughter of animals. "We went to Colorado State and saw her, and it was magic. She pitched her program, and we thought it was perfect."[60] Grandin demonstrated how she "measured animal behavior and conditions, how she paid attention to animal vocalizations, how she studied their responses to electric prods, how she cataloged their adaptations

to various conditions."[61] McDonald's adopted new standards based on Grandin's research and imposed them on its suppliers.

In response to pressure from McDonald's and other large customers, the United Egg Producers (UEP), which represented virtually all egg producers in the United States, developed an "animal care certified" logo that retailers could carry on their egg cartons. To qualify, producers had to file monthly reports and have an on-site compliance audit annually. Adele Douglass, former director of the American Humane Association, commented, "What the UEP has done is incredible. They've moved a whole industry forward." Paul Shapiro, of Compassion Over Killing, however, said, "What the UEP is trying to do is increase space minimally to prevent an inevitable legislative ban on cages. We find animal abuse is the norm in the egg industry and not the exception. These hens never see daylight, never touch earth, and never even flap their wings."[62]

DEFAMATION

In 2001 Carmen Calderón complained to the public health agency in Chile that her son had come down with food poisoning after eating in a McDonald's restaurant. McDonald's filed a $1.25 million lawsuit against Calderón, seeking an apology for what it viewed as an unsubstantiated claim.

THE ENVIRONMENT

McDonald's established an environmental policy pertaining to natural resources, rain forests, sustainability, and waste management. It refused to purchase beef from "rainforest or recently deforested rainforest land." McDonald's also participated in the European Union's Greenlights Programme and the U.S. Green Lights program to reduce electricity use in its restaurants. In Denmark McDonald's opened the first HFC/CFC-free restaurant. Minister of the Environment Hans Chr. Schmidt said, "Today McDonald's is showing how companies can make a difference by setting new standards for environmental performance.... It's a good day for the environment."[63] Greenpeace claimed credit for forcing McDonald's to open the restaurant.

SUPPLIERS

As a result of concerns in the 1990s about the treatment of workers in overseas suppliers' factories, McDonald's developed a Code of Conduct for Suppliers. The code covered employment practices pertaining to the use of prison and forced labor, child labor, working hours, compensation, nondiscrimination, and the workplace environment. McDonald's refused to do business with suppliers that did not abide by the code and reserved the right to conduct unannounced inspections of suppliers' facilities.

FRANCHISEES

By 2000 McDonald's was the largest employer in Brazil and was named employer of the year by *Exame* magazine. The economic downturn and the rise of the U.S. dollar, however,

[56]McDonald's Global Policy on Antibiotic Use in Food Animals, www.mcdonalds.com.

[57]PR Newswire, June 19, 2003.

[58]Associated Press Online, March 24, 2002.

[59]www.grandin.com.

[60]*International Herald Tribune,* June 26, 2003.

[61]Ibid.

[62]The Business Press/California, March 31, 2003.

[63]McDonald's Corporate Press Release, January 16, 2003.

squeezed McDonald's franchisees. In response McDonald's purchased hundreds of franchises, and by 2003 only 184 of 582 restaurants in Brazil were owned by franchisees. The remaining franchisees filed a lawsuit against McDonald's alleging that it squeezed them by overcharging for rent and opening too many restaurants.[64]

VEGETARIANISM

A 2000 Roper poll commissioned by the Vegetarian Resource Group found that 6 percent of girls and 2 percent of boys between 6 and 17 years never eat meat. "Janet Carr, nutrition director at Remuda Ranch, a clinic for women with bulimia and anorexia in Wickenburg, Arizona, says about 25 percent of her teen clients classify themselves as vegetarians. 'Can someone be a healthy vegetarian? I would say yes, absolutely, but it's a difficult challenge, you have to put a lot of effort into it,' Carr says."[65] The National Cattlemen's Beef Association began a marketing campaign aimed at 8- to 12-year-old girls emphasizing beef as a source of protein, iron, and B_{12}, of which the USDA indicated young girls did not get nearly enough.

BRAND NAME ATTRACTIONS

In April 2003 two incendiary devices failed to ignite at a Chico, California, McDonald's where Animal Liberation Front (ALF) activists had written "Meat is Murder" on the restaurant. The next day, firebombs exploded at a McDonald's and an Arby's in Albuquerque, New Mexico. The Earth Liberation Front (ELF) produced a videotape, "Igniting the Revolution," that featured McDonald's as a target. "Wherever they are, McDonald's are a legitimate target for people who want to protect the earth. McDonald's is a symbol of international animal abuse and environmental destruction," said Rodney Coronado, who had spent 4 years in prison for a firebombing in 1992.[66] Directions on building firebombs were available on the ALF and ELF Web sites. ■

Preparation Questions

1. Characterize the four I's.
2. What is the time frame of each issue?
3. Which issues should have the highest priority?
4. What overall strategy should McDonald's adopt for dealing with these nonmarket issues?

The Nonmarket Environment of Google

Google had become extraordinarily popular because of the efficiency of its search engine, and that popularity grew through its applications. The key to its financial success was the placement of advertisements tailored to the search queries of a user. Its strategy had three components: search, ads, and apps. Google's objective was "to organize the world's information and make it universally accessible." Its motto was "Don't be evil."

Accompanying Google's success and growth was an expanding set of nonmarket challenges. Some of these challenges came from competitors, some from producers of complementary products, some from content producers, and some from NGOs and the public.

PRIVACY

It was inevitable that Google would become public enemy number one to privacy activists. Google appointed Peter Fleischer as global privacy counsel with responsibility for encouraging Googlers to build privacy into new products early in the development process. He also worked for more uniformity in privacy laws across countries so that the company would not have to deal with differing laws and regulations.

More important, however, was the evolving concept of privacy. Fleischer observed, "The ability to retain and find information, once it's public, means that the whole concept of privacy is changing and might be irreversible."[67] In September 2007 Fleischer spoke to a United Nations audience and said,

"The ultimate goal should be to create minimum standards of privacy protection that meet the expectations and demands of consumers, businesses and governments." Marc Rotenberg of the Electronic Privacy Information Center (EPIC) commented, "Google, under investigation for violating global privacy standards, is calling for international privacy standards. It's somewhat like someone being caught for speeding saying there should be a public policy to regulate speeding."[68]

Some privacy issues were as amusing as serious. Mary Kalin-Casey of Oakland, California tried Google's Street View and went to the apartment building she lived in and managed. She zoomed in and saw her cat Monty sitting in the window of her apartment. She quickly wrote on a blog, "The issue that I have ultimately is about where you draw the line between taking public photos and zooming in on people's lives. The next step might be seeing books on my shelf. If the government was doing this, people would be outraged." The news media picked up on the story and raised the privacy issue. Google responded that "Street View only features imagery taken on public property. This imagery is no different from what any person can readily capture or see walking down the street."[69]

Google Earth was blocked by the government of Bahrain because it allowed people to see the private homes and royal palaces of the ruling Khalifa family. Mahmood al-Yousif, who had encouraged citizens to post photos of the properties, said, "Some of the palaces take up more space than three or four villages nearby and block access to the sea for fishermen.

---

[64]*Wall Street Journal,* October 21, 2003.
[65]*Morning Call,* May 23, 2003.
[66]Associated Press State & Local Wire, April 28, 2003.
[67]*San Francisco Chronicle,* December 30, 2007.

[68]*Washington Post,* September 15, 2007.
[69]*New York Times,* June 1, 2007.

People knew this already. But they never saw it. All they saw were the surrounding walls." The Khalifa family was Sunni, and the majority Shias lived in the villages to which al-Yousif referred.[70]

The Federal Trade Commission (FTC) issued draft rules on Internet privacy principles and sought comments. Pam Dixon, who headed the World Privacy Forum, campaigned for a binding "do not track" list similar to the "do not call" list that blocks telemarketers. The Network Advertising Initiative allowed consumers to opt out of data collection by the 20,000 Web sites that participated in the Initiative.[71] The FTC draft sought to cover a much broader set of Web sites and preferred that the advertising industry exercise self-regulation rather than require government regulation. Jules Polenetsky, the chief privacy officer for AOL, said, "The industry needs to get together and formally push out the appropriate set of rules." He said that the FTC action "will provide the much-needed push to help crystallize emerging best practices across the industry."[72] Shortly before the FTC action, Ask.com became the first search engine to allow users to opt out of collection of their queries. Congress announced plans for hearings on Internet privacy for early 2008.

ACQUISITION OF DOUBLECLICK

In 2007 Google made a $3.4 billion merger offer for DoubleClick. In 2000 DoubleClick had been involved in an explosive privacy conflict when it had acquired a company that collected data on catalog purchases and planned to combine that data with browsing data. Privacy advocates and government officials complained, and bowing to both private and public political pressure, DoubleClick pledged not to combine any databases that contained personally identifiable information.

The merger required approval by the FTC and also the attorneys general of the states. In addition, approval was required by other countries in which the two companies operated, most importantly the European Union.[73] Microsoft objected to the acquisition, stating that it would "substantially reduce competition in the advertising market on the Web." Microsoft general counsel Bradford Smith stated, "By putting together a single company that will control virtually the entire market ... Google will control the economic fuel of the Internet."[74] CEO Eric Schmidt replied, "We've studied this closely, and their claims, as stated, are not true." AT&T complained, "We think antitrust authorities should take a hard look at this deal and the implications. If any one company gets a hammerlock on the online advertising space, as Google seems to be trying to do, that is worrisome."[75] Both Microsoft and AT&T had been defendants in major antitrust cases. Scott

Cleland, president of the consulting firm Precursor, established a Web site, googleopoly.net.

A subcommittee of the Senate Judiciary Committee on antitrust held hearings on the proposed acquisition in September, and David Drummond, chief legal officer for Google, said the two companies were "complementary businesses." The subcommittee chair and the ranking Republican member, however, wrote to the FTC stating that the proposed merger "raises very important competition issues in a vital sector of the economy" and "raises fundamental privacy concerns worthy of serious scrutiny." Microsoft testified in opposition to the acquisition.

DoubleClick's history tied the privacy issue to the competition issue. The New York State Consumer Protection Board urged federal regulators to reject the merger unless the companies were prevented from tracking and storing information on Web surfing by consumers. Executive Director Mindy Bockstein warned that if data were misused it "could seriously harm the privacy rights of consumers."[76] EPIC, the Center for Digital Democracy, and the U.S. Public Interest Research Group filed a formal request with the FTC to investigate the planned merger and its potential for privacy infringement. They complained that the merger "would impact the privacy interests of 233 million Internet users in North America." EPIC complained that combining Google's tracking search inquiries and DoubleClick's cookies that track browsing would be a privacy concern. DoubleClick explained that the cookies were owned by its clients and that would not change with an acquisition. Nicole Wong of Google said, "EPIC utterly fails to identify any practice that does not comply with accepted privacy standards. Nothing about the proposed acquisition of DoubleClick changes our commitment to these privacy principles."[77]

Privacy was generally not an antitrust issue, however, although it was under the purview of the FTC. In December the FTC voted 4–1 to approve the acquisition. Drummond wrote, "It is telling that while our competitors tried hard to come up with theories of how our customers and partners could be harmed by the deal, those customers and partners did not agree with those theories."

Prior to filing for approval in the European Union (EU), Google declared that the merger "poses no risk to competition and should be approved." Upon filing, the European Commission conducted an initial investigation and concluded that the two companies were "the leading providers" of online advertising space and services. The Commission then began an in-depth investigation and subsequently approved the acquisition.

EUROPEAN UNION PRIVACY REGULATIONS

Privacy concerns in the European Union led the data-protection officers of the member states to examine Google's data storage practices. EU law required data holders to store an individual's data only as long as necessary.[78] For example, companies were allowed to store data for a limited period in case a customer

[70]*Financial Times*, November 25, 2006.

[71]*Los Angeles Times*, December 21, 2007.

[72]*New York Times*, December 21, 2007.

[73]Within weeks of Google's announcement of the deal other companies rushed to acquire ad placement companies. Yahoo paid $680 million to acquire the rest of Right Media, the advertising agency WPP paid $649 million for 24/7 Real Media, and Microsoft paid $6 billion for aQuantive, whose Atlas unit competed with DoubleClick (*New York Times*, May 29, 2007).

[74]*Los Angeles Times*, August 6, 2007.

[75]*New York Times*, April 16, 2007.

[76]*San Jose Mercury News*, May 10, 2007.

[77]*San Francisco Chronicle*, April 21, 2007.

[78]See the Chapter 15 case, *The European Union Data Protection Directive (B)*.

returned a purchase and wanted a refund. Google also argued that retaining data was important to efforts to fight hackers. Privacy advocates, however, remained concerned. London-based Privacy International reported that of the 2,000 complaints it received in 2006, 96 percent were about Google and its data retention policies. An EU Data Retention Directive was to take effect on September 1 and would limit retention to 24 months for ISPs and telephone companies, but it was not clear whether the directive pertained to search engines.

An advisory panel for the data protection officers wrote to Google asking it to justify its retention policy, and Google entered into discussion with them.[79] Google pointed out that after data had been stored for a time, it made the queries anonymous. The officers as well as Internet users remained concerned, and the planned acquisition of DoubleClick added to the concern. BEUC, the largest consumer group in Europe, objected to the acquisition by writing to the European Commission advisory panel arguing that a merger threatened the privacy of EU residents. It wrote, "Never before has one single company had the market and technological power to collect and exploit so much information about what a user does on the Internet. The unprecedented and unmatched databases of user profiles…appear also to be clear violations of users' privacy rights."[80]

After additional criticism regarding its retention of search query data, Google announced in June that it would retain the data only for 18 months. Nicole Wong explained, "We have decided to make this change with feedback from privacy advocates, regulators worldwide and, of course, our users."[81] Google's Peter Fleischer stated, "Retention of logs data is critical to our ability to operate and improve our services and to provide adequate security for our users. We believe we can still address our legitimate interests in security, innovation, and anti-fraud efforts with this shorter period."[82] London-based Privacy International had given Google the lowest privacy rating of any major company, and Fleischer replied, "We were disappointed with the report because it is full of numerous inaccuracies."[83]

In May 2008 Peter Hustinx, the EU's chief data protection officer, warned Google that if it introduced Street View in the EU it would have to comply with the data protection directive.

SPECTRUM AUCTION

Television broadcasters were required to convert their broadcasts to digital signals in 2009. Since digital broadcasting used less of the electromagnetic spectrum than analog broadcasting, the FCC planned to auction a block in the 700 megahertz (MHz) band of the spectrum. This band could be used to offer nationwide wireless broadband service.[84]

Mobile operators had restricted both the hardware devices and software that consumers could use on their networks. Google viewed a wireless service as a computer service rather than a telephone service, as current mobile services viewed it. Also, Google was developing a wireless telephone and wanted the phone to be usable on the network of whichever firm won the spectrum block. Google also wanted any nationwide wireless broadband network to be open to all software applications and any compatible devices, which would be a major departure from current FCC policy.

Google launched a nonmarket campaign to influence the FCC's design of the auction. Its strategy was unconventional. It made an offer to the FCC to bid at least $4.6 billion for the C block but only if the spectrum license met four conditions. One condition was that the spectrum be open to any device. A second condition was that it be open to any software application. A third condition was that the operator of any network be required to lease portions of the spectrum at wholesale rates. The fourth was that new networks would have to be mutually compatible. Each of these conditions would reduce the value of the spectrum to the winning bidder, which explained Google's pledge of a minimum bid.

Google's offer was supported by public interest groups as well as high-tech firms, including Yahoo, Intel, eBay's Skype, and Frontline Wireless, an investment fund headed by former FCC commissioner Reed Hundt and backed by Silicon Valley venture capitalists. The *Wall Street Journal*, however, in an editorial was critical of Google and its audacity: "[Google] wants to make sure it can continue to free-ride on your broadband subscription bills, even in the mobile world. It wants to make sure it won't have to share the proceeds of its massive search and advertising dominance with suppliers of network capacity."[85] A *Fortune* article was titled "Don't Be Arrogant. How Google is starting to act like your garden-variety monopoly."[86]

The FCC was responsive to Google's position, and its draft rule included Google's first two conditions but not the requirement to lease portions of the spectrum at wholesale rates. The FCC's final rules included a minimum auction price of $4.6 billion, and if that price were not met, the open access provisions would be dropped and another auction conducted.

When the FCC announced its draft auction rules, Google praised the rules but said that they did not go far enough. The Cellular Telecommunications Industry Association called it "Silicon Valley welfare."[87] AT&T said, "This is an attempt to pressure the U.S. government to turn the auction process on its head by ensuring only a few, if any, bidders will compete with Google. If Google is serious about introducing a competing business model into the wireless industry, Chairman Martin's compromise proposal allows them to bid in the auction, win the spectrum, and then implement every one of the conditions they seek."[88] Verizon was equally critical. "Google's filing

---

[79]*New York Times*, May 26, 2007.

[80]*San Jose Mercury News*, July 5, 2007.

[81]*New York Times*, March 15, 2007.

[82]*New York Times*, June 13, 2007.

[83]Ibid.

[84]The 700 megahertz spectrum was ideally suited for wireless transmission, since signals could penetrate buildings and cover greater distances, requiring fewer towers.

[85]Editorial, *Wall Street Journal*, July 18, 2007.

[86]*Fortune*, August 20, 2007.

[87]Ibid.

[88]*New York Times*, July 21, 2007.

urges the FCC to adopt rules that force all bidders to implement Google's business plan—which would reduce the incentives for other players to bid," said executive vice president Thomas J. Tauke.[89]

INTELLECTUAL PROPERTY

Google had an aggressive view of the intellectual property rights of others. Its vision of "organizing the world's information" required access to the content produced by others. Google did not use material from a media source that requested that it not do so, but in the absence of such a request it used the material. Lee Bromberg, a partner at Bromberg & Sustein, explained, "What characterizes Google is its very aggressive approach to copyright law. My own view, as someone who often defends intellectual property, is that in every area where Google has pushed it has been over the line, but it has an interesting carrot-and-stick approach. The carrot is your content gets to be displayed to Google's vast army of users, which increases rather than diminishes its commercial value to you. The stick is that it says it is just going to access your content as part of the plan to control and organize our knowledge, and that it is up to you to opt out. Well, you can't burden the copyright holder with an obligation to demand their content is not used."[90]

GOOGLE BOOKS

Google announced that it would digitize the book collections of the University of California, Harvard University, Oxford University, the University of Michigan, Stanford University, and the New York Public Library. Google planned to provide short excerpts in response to queries about a book, and this required the company to scan and store the entire book. Google argued that since it would only provide snippets of a book in response to queries it represented fair use under the copyright laws.

Google's Book Search Library Project drew immediate fire from publishers and from the company's competitors. The Association of American Publishers and the Authors Guild filed a copyright-infringement lawsuit against Google. The president of the World Association of Newspapers, Gavin O'Reilly, said, "If you subscribe to the Ten Commandments, Google operated with only nine, leaving out 'thou shall not steal.'"[91] Google had a different view from traditional media. Eric Schmidt had said that Google had a "genuine disagreement" and that the media had to show that its content had value. "That's often a difficult conversation."[92]

Google News

In 2007 Google began to supplement its News service by inviting, on an experimental basis, individuals and organizations that had been mentioned or quoted in an article to offer comments attached as a link on the story page. Journalists and editors were also allowed to attach comments. Google individually checked

and verified the identity of those providing the comments but did no editing. The company was generally praised for allowing rebuttals and comments. The executive editor of Washingtonpost.com, Jim Brady, said, "It's a typical Google idea: It's an interesting concept, and I'm not sure how they're going to do it technically, but because it's Google, it's worth watching."[93] Some news pages allowed anyone to post comments on articles or to link to blogs.

Google News found opposition in Europe. A Belgian court found Google guilty of copying copyrighted content without permission and fined the company for each day it had violated the copyright. Google said, "We believe that Google News is entirely legal. We only ever show the headlines and a few snippets of text and small thumbnail images. If people want to read the entire story they have to click through to the newspaper's Web site." The lawsuit was filed by Copiepresse, which represented 18 European publications. Copiepresse said, "Today we celebrate a victory for content producers. We showed that Google cannot make profit for free from the credibility of our newspaper brands, hard work of our journalists and skill of our photographers."[94] The decision by the Belgian court was significant because the copyright laws in European countries were quite similar, and Agence France-Presse had filed lawsuits in France and the United States against Google. Google defied the Belgian court, which had ordered it to publish the court's ruling in the case. Google announced that it would appeal both the decision and the order.

Google also took the copyright issue to the content providers. The Computer and Communications Industry Association, which included Google and Microsoft as members, filed a complaint with the Federal Trade Commission alleging that the warnings used by content providers were misrepresenting the law. The warning for Major League Baseball was "...the accounts and description of this game may not be disseminated, without express written consent." The Association stated that the warnings "materially misrepresent U.S. copyright law, particularly the fundamental built-in First Amendment accommodations which serve to safeguard the public interest" and had a "chilling effect" on users who were deterred from legitimate uses.[95]

U.S. GOVERNMENT ENFORCEMENT

Google was also on the other side of intellectual property protection issues. The U.S. government sought to enforce the Child Online Protection Act, which was intended to stop child pornography by imposing criminal penalties on individuals with Web sites containing material harmful to minors. The government asked for data on search queries that it could use to develop filtering technology to identify predators and purveyors of child pornography. America Online, Microsoft's MSN, and Yahoo complied with the request, but Google refused and continued to do so after the government issued a subpoena for the data. It told the Department of Justice,

[89]Ibid.
[90]*The Independent*, October 11, 2006.
[91]*Sunday Times*, March 11, 2007.
[92]Ibid.

[93]*Wall Street Journal*, August 8, 2007.
[94]*New York Times*, February 14, 2007.
[95]*Wall Street Journal*, August 1, 2007.

"Google's acceding to the request would suggest that it is willing to reveal information about those who use its services. This is not a perception Google can accept. And one can envision scenarios where queries alone could reveal identifying information about a specific Google user, which is another outcome that Google cannot accept."[96]

The government had asked Google for a random sample of 1 million Web addresses and a week's search requests, with any information that could identify the user removed. The Department of Justice then took Google to court to force it to provide the information. In the court hearing the government substantially scaled back its request, and the judge ordered Google to provide 50,000 random Web addresses. The judge also ruled that providing the requested 50,000 random search queries could harm Google through a loss of goodwill among its users.[97]

TRADEMARKS

American Airlines filed a lawsuit against Google for selling search terms like "American Airlines" to other firms for advertising. Google responded, "We are confident that our trademark policy strikes a proper balance between trademark owners' interests and consumer choice."[98] Other companies also complained about competitors' ads appearing when users searched on their name. In 2006 Google was successfully sued in France by Louis Vuitton and agreed to remove all ads for a Louis Vuitton search. In the United States Geico had filed a similar lawsuit, but the companies settled the lawsuit before the court had reached a final verdict. In a case filed by Perfect 10 about posting thumbnail images, the Ninth Circuit Court of Appeals ruled, "We conclude that the significantly transformative nature of Google's search engine, particularly in light of its public benefit, outweighs Google's superseding and commercial use of the thumbnails in this case."[99]

GOOGLE HEALTH

Google assigned a team to develop Google Health, which proclaimed on a prototype Web page, "At Google, we feel patients should be in charge of their health information, and they should be able to grant their health care providers, family members, or whomever they choose, access to this information. Google Health was developed to meet this need."[100] Earlier in the year Microsoft had acquired Medstory, which provided software to manage health care information.

GOOGLE TELEPHONE

Eric Schmidt commented on the opportunities for ads on wireless telephones: "What's interesting about the ads in the mobile phone is that they are twice as profitable or more than the non-mobile phone ads because they are more personal." He also said, "We are partnering with almost all of the carriers and manufacturers to get Google search and other Google applications onto their devices."[101] Google also announced an open source mobile phone platform called Android that could be used to develop new wireless services.

YOUTUBE

Google acquired YouTube in 2006 for $1.65 billion. YouTube was subject to intellectual property complaints because users posted pirated videos and broadcasts. Google was protected by the 1998 Millennium Copyright Act that provided a "safe harbor" to Internet sites that promptly removed copyrighted material in response to a complaint from the holder. The act, however, did not require the site operator to actively search to determine if material posted violated a copyright. Google investigated the complaints it received. Critics, however, were not satisfied.

YouTube was also subject to censorship. When a posting contained a trailer for an as-yet unreleased film by a Dutch lawmaker that was critical of Islam, Pakistan shut down YouTube by directing all traffic to a "black hole" where all content was discarded. A routing error, however, resulted in most of the world's access to YouTube to disappear for several hours.

TOLLS

Google and other Internet sites feared that ISPs would begin to impose a "congestion charge" on users that occupied large amounts of capacity when using broadband services. The possibility of such charges posed a risk for YouTube, where users uploaded and downloaded videos. Paul Gallant with Stanford Group Company observed, "Google sees network owners as potentially coming between it and its customers, so they realize how critical Washington was to their long-term game plan. Google is still nowhere near the Bells and cable [television] when it comes to lobbying, but it does have a real cachet that can make up some of the gap."[102]

Google advocated "net neutrality" and sought laws to require ISPs to treat all Internet traffic alike. This meant that users would not be differentiated by how much Internet capacity they used.

DISCRIMINATION

In 2004 Google fired its director of engineering, Brian Reed, because he was "slow." Reed filed a California age discrimination lawsuit against Google, but the trial judge dismissed the lawsuit. Reed appealed the dismissal, and the Sixth Circuit Court of Appeals in California ruled that sufficient evidence had been presented to justify the case going to trial. Google appealed the ruling, and in 2008 the California Supreme Court agreed to consider Google's appeal.

CORPORATE SOCIAL RESPONSIBILITY

Environmental Practices

Google decided to influence attitudes and policy toward the environment. "We want to leverage our assets and influence

[96]*International Herald Tribune*, January 21, 2006.
[97]*San Francisco Chronicle*, March 18, 2006.
[98]Reuters, August 20, 2007.
[99]*Washington Post*, May 17, 2007.
[100]*New York Times*, August 14, 2007.
[101]*Wall Street Journal*, August 2, 2007.
[102]*Washington Post*, July 30, 2007.

the world beyond the computer. We are going to argue in public to change attitudes on a number of things. The first one is energy standards," said Urs Holzle of Google.[103]

With a motto of "Do no evil" Google was concerned about the environmental impact of the energy used by its hundreds of thousands of computers. The company pledged to become carbon neutral and announced a project backed by hundreds of millions of dollars to reduce the cost of renewable energy by 25–50 percent. Its objective was to produce a gigawatt of electricity at a cost below the cost of producing electricity from coal. Larry Page predicted that the goal could be reached within a matter of "years, not decades."[104]

Philanthropy

When it went public, Google pledged to contribute 1 percent of its assets, 1 percent of its profits, and employee time to philanthropy. In 2008 Google fulfilled its pledge by establishing Google.org, or DotOrg in Google-speak, that was unusual in its structure. It was established as for-profit so that it could invest in start-ups and form partnerships. For-profit status, however, meant that taxes had to be paid on contributions from Google to the organization and on any earnings. The organization selected five initiatives: helping communities identify and deal with potential pandemics before they could spread, supporting public services information in developing countries, aiding medium-sized businesses in developing countries, developing renewable energy at a cost less than coal, and speeding the commercialization of a car capable of getting 100 miles per gallon. DotOrg invested $10 million in closely held eSolar, Inc.

Indigenous Peoples

Google joined with the Surui tribe of Brazil's Amazon jungle in a project to provide satellite images of its reservation so that the tribe could identify illegal logging and mining. Megan Quinn of Google explained, "If you look at the Surui land today in Google Earth, you'll see their island of healthy green rainforest is surrounded almost completely by clear-cut, barren land. The stark contrast at their boundary is dramatic, and conveys vividly what is at stake."[105]

CHINA

Human Rights

Using servers located in the United States, Google began offering a Chinese-language version of Google.com in 2000, but the site was frequently unavailable or slow because of censoring by the Chinese government. Google had a significant share of searches in China, but it lagged behind the market leader Baidu.com. Google concluded that it was imperative to host a Web site from within China, but Google had to decide how to deal with the censorship imposed by the Chinese government.

As a result of an extensive debate within the company, cofounder Serge Brin explained, "We gradually came to the realization that we were hurting not just ourselves but the Chinese people."[106] Google decided to offer a site, Google.cn, but without features that allowed users to provide content. Google offered neither e-mail nor the ability to create blogs, since user-generated material could be seized by the Chinese government. This avoided Google putting individuals in jeopardy of being arrested. Because it would be required by Chinese law to censor search results associated with sensitive issues, Google decided to place a brief notice at the bottom of a search page when material had been censored, as it did in other countries such as France and Germany, which ban the sale of Nazi items. Google planned to exercise self-censorship and developed a list of sensitive items by consulting with third parties and by studying the results of the Chinese government's Internet filtering. Senior policy counsel Andrew McLaughlin stated, "In order to operate from China, we have removed some content from the search results available on Google.cn, in response to local law, regulation or policy. While removing search results is inconsistent with Google's mission, providing no information (or a heavily degraded user experience that amounts to no information) is more inconsistent with our mission."[107] Representative Tom Lantos (D-CA) asked during a congressional hearing, "Can you say in English that you are ashamed of what you and your company...have done?"

New York City's comptroller, who managed the city's pension plans that held $338 million of Google shares, announced that he would submit a shareholder proposal with the SEC for voting at the company's annual shareholder meeting. The proposal stated, "Technology companies in the United States have failed to develop adequate standards by which they can conduct business with authoritarian governments while protecting human rights."[108] The New York State Pension Funds also qualified a shareholder resolution demanding that the company not host Web sites in countries that restricted Internet usage.

In its competition with Baidu.com Google invested in Tianya.cn, a Chinese Web site that allowed users to connect with each other and answer one another's questions. The Web site would use Google technology. This Web site seemed to raise new risks that Google had sought to avoid.

The next phases of Google's operations in China are considered in the Chapter 16 case *Google in China* and the Chapter 24 case *Google Out of China*.

Online Video

China's State Administration of Radio, Film, and Television and the Ministry of Information Industry clarified its rules for video-streaming, allowing companies such as Youku and

---

[103]*Financial Times*, June 20, 2007.
[104]*Chicago Tribune*, November 28, 2007.
[105]*Sydney Morning Herald*, July 10, 2007.
[106]*San Jose Mercury News*, March 3, 2006.
[107]*New York Times*, January 25, 2006.
[108]*San Jose Mercury News*, May 2, 2007.

Tudou to "re-register and continue operations" if they were currently in compliance with the law. Although the regulations issued in early 2008 were not entirely clear, they appeared to require new companies to be owned or controlled by the government. This appeared to block Google's YouTube. The government reiterated its prohibition against pornography and material that "promoted violence or other serious illegal business."[109]

MICROSOFT AND VISTA

When Microsoft rolled out its new Vista operating system, Google recognized that it disadvantaged Google's search engine by only using Microsoft's search engine for queries entered by right clicks and pane windows.[110] Microsoft argued that it was easy to set the selection for the search engine. To get leverage over Microsoft, Google sought to intervene in the court responsible for the enforcement of the federal antitrust consent decree with Microsoft, which was to expire in November 2007.[111] The Department of Justice and Microsoft had reached a compromise regarding aspects of Vista. In an amicus brief Google told the court that it could provide information useful to the court and said that it was concerned that despite the compromise Microsoft would not eliminate its anticompetitive conduct. Google asked that the consent decree be extended. Google also lobbied in state capitals, arguing that its applications were unfairly discouraged in Vista. In 2007 Microsoft relented and made several changes that made it easier to conduct searches with non-Microsoft search engines.

MICROSOFT AND YAHOO

In 2008 Microsoft made a $44.6 billion unsolicited offer for Yahoo. CEO Steve Ballmer argued that a merger would create a viable number two competitor to Google's advertising placement business. Google senior vice president David Drummond raised antitrust concerns in writing on the company's blog, "Could Microsoft now attempt to exert the same sort of inappropriate and illegal influence over the Internet that it did with the PC? While the Internet rewards competitive innovation, Microsoft has frequently sought to establish proprietary monopolies—and then leverage its dominance into new, adjacent markets." Google CEO Eric Schmidt reportedly called Jerry Yang of Yahoo to offer support in opposing the offer. Commentators speculated, however, that moves such as Yahoo outsourcing its advertising placement to Google could run into antitrust problems of their own by reducing competition. The antitrust subcommittees in both the House and Senate indicated they would hold hearings if Yahoo agreed to the merger, providing Google an opportunity to take its case to Congress, as Microsoft had done in Google's acquisition of DoubleClick. ▪

Preparation Questions

1. Identify the four I's for Google's nonmarket environment.
2. Where are the issues in their life cycles?
3. How should Google deal with the host of privacy issues associated with its applications? How should it deal with the risk of intellectual property lawsuits? How do these affect new product development and acquisitions?
4. Does Google's size affect its antitrust risk?
5. What issues are associated with the launch of Google Health?
6. What issues might arise in Google's ownership of Tianya.cn?
7. How should Google interact with Microsoft?

[109]*Wall Street Journal*, February 6, 2008.
[110]In 2005 Google had outbid Microsoft to be the primary search service for AOL. Google paid $1 billion and obtained a 5 percent share of AOL.
[111]See the Chapter 9 case, *The Microsoft Antitrust Case*.

2 INTEGRATED STRATEGY

INTRODUCTION

A business strategy has both market and nonmarket components. A market strategy is a concerted pattern of actions taken in the market environment to create value by improving the economic performance of a firm. A nonmarket strategy is a concerted pattern of actions taken in the nonmarket environment to create value by improving overall performance. A firm that decides to enter a country that has open markets relies primarily on a market strategy. A firm that decides to enter a country that has erected trade barriers needs a nonmarket strategy in addition to a market strategy. An effective business strategy integrates these two components and tailors them to the firm's market and nonmarket environments as well as to its capabilities.[1]

Market and nonmarket strategies focus on the pursuit of opportunity and advantage in the face of market and nonmarket competition with the objective of achieving superior performance. In this book, performance is considered on two dimensions. Initially, it is measured by the value created for the firm's owners. Then, in Part V the objective is broadened using concepts of corporate social responsibility and ethics.

This chapter focuses on nonmarket analysis and strategy and their integration with their market counterparts. As illustrated in Figure 2-1, effective management in the nonmarket environment requires conceptual frameworks for (1) analyzing nonmarket issues and the broader environment, (2) formulating effective strategies for addressing those issues, (3) integrating those strategies with market strategies, and (4) positioning the firm in its nonmarket environment. The strategy concept is introduced first, and the integration of market and nonmarket analysis and strategy formulation are considered using a Google example. Strategic positioning

FIGURE 2-1   Management and Integrated Strategy

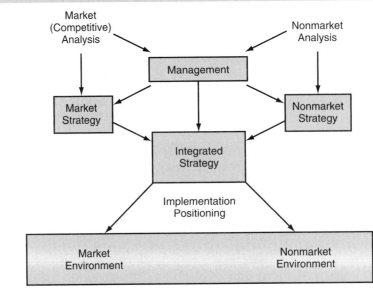

[1]This material is adapted from Baron (1995b). Copyright © 1995 by the Board of Regents of the University of California. Reprinted from the *California Management Review*, Vol. 37, No. 2. By permission of The Regents.

in the nonmarket environment is then considered and illustrated using the example of eBay. Nonmarket analysis is then considered, and a framework for analysis is presented and illustrated using an example involving Citibank.

STRATEGY IN THE NONMARKET ENVIRONMENT

The Importance of Nonmarket Strategy

The importance of a nonmarket strategy is related to the control of a firm's opportunities, as illustrated in Figure 2-2. Opportunities can be controlled by government at one extreme and markets at the other extreme. Nonmarket strategies are more important the more opportunities are controlled by government and are less important, but often still important, when opportunities are controlled by markets. In some industries, such as consumer electronics and computer software, government exercises relatively little control over firms and their activities. In contrast, government exercises considerable control over pharmaceuticals and local telecommunications services. The automobile industry is somewhere in between. One important role of nonmarket strategy is to unlock opportunities controlled by government, as illustrated by the strategies of firms to deregulate the telecommunications industry. Another important role of nonmarket strategy is to avoid the control of opportunities by government, as in the case of self-regulation by companies on Internet privacy protection.

Over time, industries can move along the control dimension. In many countries the government had controlled telecommunications services through ownership of a monopoly supplier. In the pursuit of improved performance, many of these countries privatized their telecommunications firms and replaced ownership with regulation and competition. In the United States the regulation of telecommunications has been progressively replaced by market competition, with long-distance and mobile services being the most extensively controlled by markets and local service the least. The Internet has been at the right in Figure 2-2, but nonmarket issues such as privacy, taxation of electronic commerce, and protection of intellectual property have made nonmarket strategy of increasing importance, as considered in Chapter 14.

In addition to government and markets, two other factors affect opportunities. First, opportunities can be controlled by private politics, which includes actions such as protests, boycotts, and public criticism by activist, advocacy, and interest groups, as well as public sentiment regarding business. The more intense is private politics, the more important is nonmarket strategy, as

FIGURE 2-2   Nonmarket Strategy and the Control of Opportunities

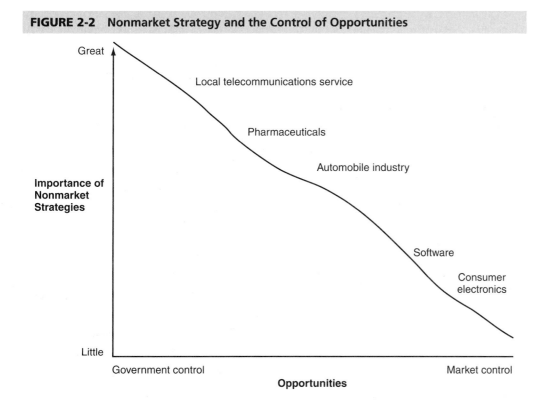

FIGURE 2-3   Nonmarket Strategy and Private Politics

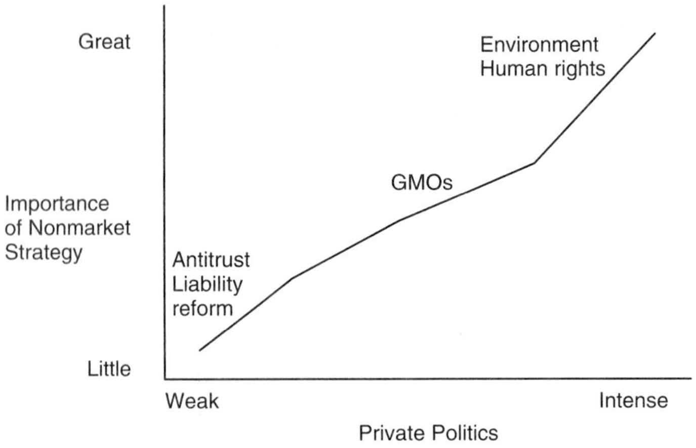

illustrated in Figure 2-3. Issues such as the environment, sustainability, human rights, privacy, health, and safety attract private politics, as considered in Chapter 4. In contrast, issues such as intellectual property protection, liability reform, and antitrust seldom attract private politics but are the subject of public politics. Issues such as the use of genetically modified organisms in food attract intense private politics in Europe but less in the United States.

Second, opportunities can be affected by moral concerns, which can require restraint. Part V of the book provides principles to guide firms and their managers in reasoning about moral concerns and broader social responsibilities and whether a firm should self-regulate. For example, before the issue became salient, Levi Strauss & Co. used moral principles in formulating a policy governing working conditions in its overseas suppliers' factories, as discussed in Chapter 23.

Competition and Change in the Nonmarket Environment

Market strategies typically take the nonmarket environment as given and focus on the competitive positions of firms in the industry, the threats from substitutes and potential entrants, and the bargaining power of suppliers and customers.[2] When a firm looks ahead, however, neither the market nor the nonmarket environments can be viewed as static. Moreover, change depends importantly on the strategies a firm, its competitors, and other interests use to influence those environments.

When a firm chooses a market strategy, that strategy competes with the strategies of other participants in the market. Similarly, when a firm chooses a nonmarket strategy, that strategy competes with the strategies of other firms, interest groups, and activists. That competition shapes the nonmarket environment and often the market environment as well. The nonmarket environment thus should be thought of as competitive, as is the market environment. Nonmarket competition focuses on specific issues, such as a proposal to increase U.S. fuel economy standards, as well as systemic issues, such as intellectual property protection. A broader set of participants is typically present in the nonmarket environment than in the market environment, so a firm often has a more complex strategy problem in the nonmarket environment. Nonmarket strategy is essential because in its absence competitors in the nonmarket environment will influence the outcome of issues and shape the rules of the game to their advantage.

Strategy and the Nonmarket Issue Life Cycle

Timing can be crucial to the success of a nonmarket strategy. Using the life cycle concept from Chapter 1, Figure 2-4 identifies strategies as a function of the stage at which a firm begins to address a nonmarket issue. The firm has more flexibility and a wider range of alternatives the earlier it addresses an issue. If an issue is addressed at the issue identification stage, strategies can be directed at affecting the development of the issue. The firm may also be able to frame the

---

[2]See Porter (1980); Oster (1999); Besanko, Dranove, Shanley, and Schaefer (2009); and Saloner, Shepard, and Podolny (2001).

FIGURE 2-4   Nonmarket Issue Life Cycle and Strategies

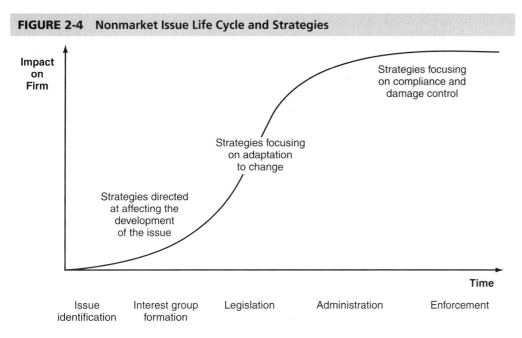

issue prior to interest group formation. Levi Strauss was one of the first companies to address the issue of working conditions in its suppliers' overseas factories, and the policies it developed kept it out of the line of attack by activists.

If a firm addresses the issue once interest groups have formed and the issue is in the legislative stage, the firm has less flexibility and its range of alternatives is narrower. Nike was late in addressing the issue of working conditions at its suppliers' factories in Asia, and it became a target for activists and their antisweatshop campaign, as considered in Chapter 4. Nike found itself in the position of reacting to the nonmarket strategies of others rather than shaping the development of the issue. Its opportunity to participate in the resolution of the nonmarket issue was largely limited to the enforcement stage. Nike's nonmarket strategy involved damage control, followed several years later by an effort to become a leader in ensuring good working conditions.

Strategies and Borders

Bartlett and Ghoshal (1989) characterize market strategies as multidomestic (multinational), international, and global. A global market strategy is one in which "products and strategies are developed to exploit an integrated unitary world market." Global market strategies often focus on achieving cost advantages through global-scale operations, as exemplified by Honda's early strategy of selling the same motorcycles in all the markets it entered. In the nonmarket environment, examples of global strategies are (1) working for free trade globally, (2) applying universal ethics principles, and (3) implementing the same environmental standards in all countries.

An international strategy centers on transferring the parent company's expertise to foreign markets. eBay, for example, took its online auction service to other countries, with mixed success. International strategies are specific applications of distinctive competences in other countries.

For many nonmarket issues, a global or international nonmarket strategy may not be successful because strategies must take into account the institutions in whose context the issues are addressed, the organization of interests, and other country-specific factors. In France, Yahoo! was quickly met with a lawsuit because World War II Nazi items were auctioned on its U.S. Web site. French law prohibits buying or selling Nazi items. Yahoo! refused to ban the items because it was legal to sell them in other countries, including the United States. In contrast, eBay designs its online auction venues in strict accord with the laws of each country in which it operates. As it expanded globally, Facebook faced the challenge of dealing with government censorship in China and in numerous other countries. Many nonmarket issues have a strong domestic component, so nonmarket strategies are more likely than market strategies to be multidomestic when issues, institutions, and interests differ across countries.

The success of a multidomestic strategy requires issue-specific action plans tailored to the institutions and the organization of interests in individual countries. Examples of nonmarket issues that require a multidomestic approach include tax policy, antitrust policy, safety regulation, pharmaceuticals approval, intellectual property rights enforcement, and environmental regulation. Although there are common principles, such as information provision as the key to effective lobbying, that underlie the strategies used to address these issues, differences in the institutions across countries typically require country-specific strategies. In the United States lobbying focuses on Congress and its committees. In Japan lobbying focuses more on the bureaucracy and political parties and their leaders. In the European Union, lobbying focuses on the Commission and the Directorates-General as well as on national institutions as a means of influencing the Council of Ministers. In Germany, lobbying occurs through peak business and labor associations and their chambers, as well as directly by individual firms and their interactions with the bureaucracy and political parties.

INTEGRATED STRATEGY

An effective market strategy is necessary for successful performance, but it is seldom sufficient. An effective nonmarket strategy is rarely sufficient, but for most firms it is necessary for success. Market strategies serve the objective of superior performance by developing and sustaining the competitive advantage required to take advantage of market opportunities. Nonmarket strategies serve the objective of superior performance by participating effectively and responsibly in the public processes that affect the control of opportunities. The performance of a firm also depends on how well its nonmarket strategy is integrated with its market strategy. Because firm performance is the responsibility of management, managers are responsible for both market and nonmarket strategies and for their integration, as illustrated in Figure 2-1.

Nonmarket strategies can be used to shape the market environment in which a firm operates. In the boxed example "Google and the Spectrum Auction," Google sought to open wireless communication to its applications and to reduce the bargaining power of the dominant carriers AT&T and Verizon Wireless. Google formulated a nonmarket strategy to seize an opportunity provided by the switch of television broadcasts from analog to digital transmission that freed spectrum for new uses. Its nonmarket strategy was integrated with its market strategy of providing an open access operating system for wireless communication that would accommodate applications including its AdSense advertisement placement technology, which generates the bulk of its revenue and profits.

EXAMPLE   Google and the Spectrum Auction

The Strategic Challenge

Google's core strategy centered on providing information to people, and it wanted mobile device users to have the widest possible access to the Internet. Google's primary source of revenue was advertising placements using its AdSense technology, and it wanted the opportunity to place ads on wireless devices. CEO Eric Schmidt explained, "There are at least 4 billion mobile phone users in the world today, and there are more mobile phones worldwide than there are Internet users of landline phones. Getting people access to information is Google's core mission and mobile phones have to be part of that."[1] He also commented on the opportunities for ads on wireless telephones: "What's interesting about the ads in the mobile phone is that they are twice as profitable or more than the nonmobile phone ads because they are more personal."

Google faced two challenges in the United States. The first was to develop a technology that allowed new applications to be developed for mobile phones. The second was

the control of mobile networks by the two dominant carriers, AT&T and Verizon. Those carriers restricted the devices that ran on their networks to those they and their partners sold and also restricted the applications that could be run. For example, Verizon did allow Google's Web Search bar on its phones. Moreover, if new technology and new applications for using the Internet via mobile devices created added value for users, the mobile phone carriers were in a position to capture the profits through their charges for access to their networks. Google's goal was a nationwide network with open access for mobile devices in which users could choose their devices and apps. This required breaking the grip of the wireless carriers.

Integrated Strategy

Google's integrated strategy had market and nonmarket components. In the nonmarket environment Google had an opportunity. Television broadcasters were scheduled to end analog transmission and convert to all-digital transmission in February 2009. This would free frequencies on the so-called

---

[1]*Network World*, November 8, 2007.

C block of the spectrum that could be used to develop a new nationwide mobile network. These frequencies were ideal for wireless service because the signals could easily penetrate buildings and carried long distances, requiring fewer transmission towers. As it had done in the past, the Federal Communications Commission (FCC) planned to auction the frequencies.[2] Google had the resources to bid for the spectrum and develop its own mobile network, but doing so did not fit its mission or capabilities. A better outcome would be for whichever company or consortium that won the spectrum auction to build an open network. The incentives, however, for the bidders were to restrict access to increase their ability to capture value from customers, applications developers, and advertisers. Google wanted the FCC to require the winner to build an open network and better yet to require access to be provided at wholesale prices to resellers. This would further weaken the control of the dominant carriers.

Google made a proposal to the FCC for an open access requirement for the C block and pledged to bid at least $4.6 billion for that block if the spectrum license met four conditions. One was that the spectrum be open to any device. The second was that it be open to any software application. The third condition was that the operator of any network be required to lease portions of the spectrum at wholesale rates. The fourth was that any new networks would have to be mutually compatible. Each of these conditions would reduce the value of the spectrum to the winning bidder, which explained Google's pledge of a minimum bid. Although Google pledged to bid for the C block, its preferred outcome was that another carrier win the auction.

In the market environment Google developed an operating system, named Android, in conjunction with the Open Handset Alliance (OHA) that Google had formed with 33 other companies. In contrast to the wireless operating systems of Microsoft, Research in Motion, Palm, and Symbian (used by the largest handset maker Nokia), Android provided an open platform for software and equipment developers to develop their own applications independent of any requirements of mobile network operators or phone manufacturers. Google released Android in November 2007 to give developers an "early look" at the operating system. The key for Google was Internet access with search capabilities that could attach Google's AdSense technology. In addition, the company could produce a GPhone that would operate with Android and any applications. Google refused to reveal whether it planned to introduce a GPhone, but Andy Rubin, director of mobile platforms, said, "if you were to build a GPhone, you'd build it out of this [Android] platform."[3]

Android was released in a bare-bones form relying on third-party developers for specific applications. Serge Brin,

Google president of technology, said, "The best applications [for the Android platform] are not here yet. That's because they're going to be written by you and by many other developers."[4] Google offered $10 million in prizes for the best applications. Fabrizio Capobianco, CEO of Funambol, speculated that Google planned to capitalize on Android's "location-aware capabilities."[5]

Dylan Schiemann, CEO of SitePen, assessed the significance of Android: "The mobile carriers always want to control everything, but they're showing signs of backing off on that. Carriers have enjoyed a long period where they've controlled what you put on a phone, and what they've charged you for what you put on your phone. If the Android platform works, it could change that dynamic."[6]

In its auction design, the FCC required Google's first two conditions for an open network. In the auction Verizon Wireless bid $4.74 billion for the nationwide C block, topping the only other bid of Google. Verizon Wireless paid a total of $9.5 billion for spectrum in the FCC auction and announced that it would launch a new open wireless network in 2010. Users could soon have the opportunity to choose their own devices, apps, games, ringtones, graphics, and so on. Commenting on Google not having to build its own wireless network, Gregory L. Rosston, a former FCC official, said, "Now they can just spend $1 million a year on a law firm to ensure Verizon lives up to the openness requirement."[7]

Google was delighted to lose. Richard Whitt of Google said, "Although Google didn't pick up any spectrum licenses, the auction produced a major victory for American consumers. We congratulate the winners and look forward to a more open wireless world."[8]

Phase II of Its Nonmarket Strategy

Google then began the second phase of its nonmarket open access strategy. It wrote to the FCC with a proposal to unlock the white spaces—the spaces between the spectrum licensed to individual broadcast television channels. Google maintained that only 5 percent of the TV white spaces were used, and hence capacity was available for high-speed mobile services. Google further proposed that unlicensed users be allowed to use the white spaces, whereas only licensed devices were allowed on the spectrum recently auctioned. Google also proposed using spectrum-sensing technology that would allow the government to interrupt service in an emergency. Google, along with Philips Electronics, Intel, Dell, and Microsoft, was a member of the White Spaces Coalition, but the proposal was made only by Google.

---

[2]The C block would be made available in Europe in 2010 and in South Korea in 2012.

[3]*Network World*, November 8, 2007.

[4]*Network World*, November 13, 2007.

[5]Ibid.

[6]*Network World*, November 8, 2007.

[7]*New York Times*, April 4, 2008.

[8]*RCR Wireless News*, March 24, 2008.

Nonmarket strategies focus on issues that affect the opportunities of a firm, its positioning in its market and nonmarket environments, and the sustainability of its capabilities and reputation. A nonmarket strategy consists of objectives and a plan of action to address the issues on a firm's agenda, and that strategy must be tailored to the institutions in whose arenas the issues will be addressed. That strategy must also anticipate the strategies of other interests, including those aligned with and those opposed to the interests of the firm. Part II of this book develops these components in the context of government institutions.

Both market and nonmarket strategies have the objective of superior performance and focus on securing market opportunities and addressing threats to those opportunities. Synergies can be present between market and nonmarket strategies, and the overall business strategy is more effective the more those synergies can be exploited. A synergy is present if a nonmarket action increases the return from a market action or, conversely, a market action increases the return from a nonmarket action. Google's nonmarket strategy focusing on an open network using the C block and opening the whitespaces unlocked opportunities for the deployment of its Android operating system, which within 3 years became a leading platform for mobile devices and applications along with Apple's system.

The boxed example "Direct-to-Consumer Advertising and Integrated Strategy in the Pharmaceutical Industry" illustrates how a nonmarket strategy can both unlock an opportunity that market strategies can then exploit and protect those opportunities once unlocked. The nonmarket strategy of the industry convinced the Food and Drug Administration (FDA) that advertising in the broadcast media would improve public health by educating consumers about the availability of treatments. This led to products such as Claritin, Rogaine, and Viagra becoming household names. The rapid expansion of "lifestyle" drugs brought criticism to the industry, requiring a nonmarket strategy to defend the opportunity to advertise to consumers in the broadcast media.

EXAMPLE   Direct-to-Consumer Advertising and Integrated Strategy in the Pharmaceutical Industry

The pharmaceutical industry had traditionally marketed prescription drugs directly to doctors using detail (sales) forces, whereas over-the-counter drugs were advertised directly to consumers using the print and broadcast media. The industry recognized that advertising prescription drugs directly to consumers through the broadcast media could generate additional demand by increasing consumer awareness of the availability of treatments. This could also generate demand for as yet unrecognized or untreated maladies and could shift some patients to patented drugs from over-the-counter drugs, as in the case of antihistamines. Since patented drugs provided profit margins of 90 percent or so, the opportunities for profits were huge. Although the long-run impact of direct advertising in the broadcast media was difficult to predict, the potential seemed almost unlimited. If successful, the advertising could alter the market strategies used by pharmaceutical companies, since the return on research and development would be increased on drugs that could be directly advertised to consumers. Direct advertising of patented drugs to consumers, however, was limited to the print media by FDA regulations.

Unlocking this potential opportunity required an integrated strategy, the first component of which was a nonmarket strategy directed at the FDA. The industry lobbied the FDA on the direct advertising issue using the theme that

better informed consumers would improve public health. The FDA eventually concurred, and in 1997 allowed direct-to-consumer (DTC) advertising of prescription drugs in the broadcast media.

The second component was to explore the potential of DTC advertising. Pharmaceutical companies began to advertise directly to consumers on television and radio. The advertisements typically gave a toll-free number to call for information, referred to magazine advertisements where warnings were required, and instructed viewers to "ask your doctor." The marketing strategy was to induce consumers to ask their doctors for the drug by brand name. This strategy proved to be very successful. Schering-Plough reportedly spent $322 million on advertisements for Claritin in 1998 and 1999, and U.S. sales reached $2.5 billion in 2000.[1] A 2001 survey by *Prevention Magazine* found that 72 percent of the respondents recalled an advertisement for Claritin.

The increased return on drugs that could be advertised through the broadcast media had several implications for market strategies. One was that the incentives for drug development were altered in favor of drugs that could be effectively advertised, as in the case of lifestyle drugs. Another implication was the reexamination of approved drugs, including those whose patents had already expired, that could be used for other indications that could be advertised through the broadcast media. A third implication was that new "diseases" or maladies could be identified and promoted to consumers.

---

[1]Stephen S. Hall, "Prescription for Profit," *New York Times Magazine*, March 11, 2001.

GlaxoSmithKline's (GSK) Requip (ropinirole) had earlier been approved for the treatment of Parkinson's disease, and when doctors began to prescribe it for patients complaining of a restless sensation in their legs, GSK recognized an opportunity. GSK obtained FDA approval for low dosages for treating the restless sensation, and upon approval began promoting the drug for a new malady—restless legs syndrome (RLS). With heavy DTC advertising, sales of Requip jumped.[2]

Criticism of DTC advertising in the broadcast media began to mount as the advertisements became pervasive. The American Medical Association was concerned that consumers would pressure doctors to obtain unneeded prescriptions. The Prescription Access Litigation Project filed a lawsuit against Schering-Plough claiming that its advertising of Claritin was deceptive, boosted demand and increased the price of the drug. Richard Kravitz of the University of California at Davis said of RLS, "Physicians don't know much about it and may be wanting to follow the path of least resistance and prescribe a medication for a condition that a patient might not have."[3] Some physicians and health-care specialists referred to the promotion of drugs for an underappreciated malady as "disease-mongering,"

defined as the "corporate-sponsored creation or exaggeration of maladies for the purpose of selling more drugs."[4] The Senate held hearings on DTC advertising.

The criticism required a nonmarket strategy by the pharmaceutical companies. The companies lobbied Congress and attempted to respond to the critics. The Pharmaceutical Research and Manufacturers Association explained the rationale and success of DTC advertising.[5]

> A study released by *Prevention Magazine* … found DTC advertising "is an extremely effective means of promoting both the public health and prescription medicines"…. More importantly, the survey found that DTC advertising prompted an estimated 21.2 million Americans to talk to their doctors about a medical condition or illness they had never discussed with their physicians before. In other words, millions of people who had previously suffered in silence were encouraged to seek help.

DTC advertising in the broadcast media was preserved, but the threat of restrictions remained, requiring continued monitoring of the nonmarket issue.

---

[2]See the Chapter 21 case *Consumer Awareness or Disease Mongering? GlaxoSmithKline and the Restless Legs Syndrome.*
[3]*Washington Post*, May 30, 2006.

[4]*BusinessWeek*, May 8, 2006.
[5]www.phrma.org.

Approaches to Integrating Market and Nonmarket Strategies

One approach to developing an integrated strategy is to incorporate nonmarket strategy formulation into the process of developing a market strategy. For example, regulation pertaining to who may provide services, as in telecommunications, could be incorporated into the analysis of the rivalry among incumbent firms and potential new entrants. The drawback to this approach is that the institutions in which regulatory policies are established are quite different from markets, so the nature of the analysis is different. Moreover, in markets only the parties that transact play a role, whereas in nonmarket institutions a wide range of interests are enfranchised to participate.

Market and nonmarket strategies could also be viewed as separate. Just as market analysis focuses on competitive forces, nonmarket analysis can focus on assessing threats (such as those arising from government, interest groups, and activist pressures) and on unlocking market opportunities. Viewing nonmarket issues as a separate force, however, risks missing the interrelationships between market and nonmarket issues and the complementarities between strategies to address those issues.[3]

The most effective means of integrating market and nonmarket strategies is to incorporate both into the business strategy process. That is, market and nonmarket strategies should be chosen together in addressing forces in the market and nonmarket environments.[4] The nonmarket strategy component then focuses on specific nonmarket issues that affect market threats and opportunities and on nonmarket actions as complements to market actions.

For some companies such as those in the pharmaceutical industry, integrated market and nonmarket strategies are a conscious part of everyday management. For other companies strategy formulation is periodic but nevertheless when market strategies must be developed, nonmarket strategies should be developed at the same time. For example, in 2012 Facebook had to formulate a market strategy for entering the Chinese market, which already had several

---

[3]Gale and Buchholz (1987) discuss the relationship between political strategies and Porter's (1980) five forces. Yoffie (1987) characterizes strategies by the approach taken to political issues.
[4]Baron (1997a, 1999, 2001) provides formal models of integrated strategies and a nontechnical presentation in (1996).

successful social networking companies. The principal nonmarket issues associated with entering the market were how to deal with censorship required by the Chinese government and how to protect user data sought by the government. The chapter case *Facebook in China?* considers the strategy formulation challenge for Facebook.

Because nonmarket strategies must be tailored to the specific issues, interests, institutions, and information in the nonmarket environment, there is no short list of generic nonmarket strategies. Moreover, the nonmarket agenda of a firm is in part set externally in the environment rather than by the firm, and strategies must attend to that agenda. The chapter case *Personal Watercraft aka Jet Skis* provides an opportunity to evaluate market and nonmarket strategies and the effectiveness of their integration in the face of nonmarket forces.

NONMARKET POSITIONING

Firms strategically position themselves in the markets in which they operate, focusing on the benefits to customers and costs to the firm.[5] They also strategically position their products in attribute space, both in an absolute sense and relative to rival products. Positioning is a foundation for market or competitive strategy because it can be a source of competitive advantage.

Just as firms position themselves in their market environments, they also position themselves strategically in their nonmarket environments. Positioning provides a foundation for nonmarket strategy and can enhance a market strategy and its integration with a nonmarket strategy. Nonmarket positioning also affects the set of issues and challenges a firm faces, including challenges from activist and interest groups, governments, and competitors.[6] Market positioning also affects the set of nonmarket issues a firm encounters. Nike, the Gap, and other footwear and apparel manufacturers positioned themselves as design and marketing companies and sourced their products from independent contractors, primarily in Asia. The working conditions in the contractors' factories, however, generated a host of nonmarket challenges for the firms.

Nonmarket positioning should be a conscious choice rather than dictated by a firm's market positioning or by those in its environment. Too often firms find themselves in a position they wish they had avoided. A firm may find itself confronted by protests over its environmental practices, disadvantaged by a regulatory action, or exposed to avoidable liabilities. Alternatively, a firm may benefit from having established a relationship of trust with a regulatory agency, joined with an environmental group to resolve a wildlife habitat problem, or provided expertise to a congressional committee addressing a complex issue in patent protection. Not only is nonmarket positioning important for avoiding problems and attracting benefits, it also provides a platform on which both market and nonmarket strategies can be constructed. Nonmarket positioning thus should be a strategic choice just as positioning a product in attribute space is a strategic choice. The eBay example illustrates this choice.

EXAMPLE   eBay's Positioning in Legal Space

eBay, the market leader in person-to-person online auctions, had over 30 million members in its trading community and hosted 5 million auctions on a given day. The company had carefully positioned itself relative to state and federal laws, and that positioning shielded it from certain liabilities. In turn, the scope of its activities was influenced by that shield. eBay provided a venue for online auctions, and unlike an offline auction house, it did not review the listings of items posted by sellers, see the items auctioned, or verify their authenticity. It also did not participate in the transaction, other than to charge fees for each listing and item sold. eBay was not an agent of either the seller or the buyer.

A critical issue for eBay was whether it could be held liable for the listings provided by sellers or for postings on its bulletin boards. The Communications Decency Act (CDA) of 1996 shielded an Internet service provider (ISP) from liability for what was said or written on an Internet site, whereas an Internet content provider could be liable for postings. eBay positioned itself as an ISP, thus receiving protection under the CDA. That positioning, however, meant that eBay had to

---

[5]See Besanko, Dranove, Shanley, and Schaefer (2009); Saloner, Shepard, and Podolny (2001); and Porter (1980, 1985).
[6]The contributors in Aggarwal (2001) consider positioning of firms in Asia, although most of the analysis focuses on market positioning.

be careful not to provide content, such as commenting on the authenticity of items listed for sale. Instead, eBay provided links to Internet sites where members could obtain opinions, authentication, and grading of items ranging from coins to Beanie Babies to comic books.

Offline auction houses were regulated by state laws, and eBay carefully avoided the jurisdiction of those and other state laws. eBay argued that it was similar to the newspaper classified ads rather than an offline auction house. eBay also positioned itself relative to violations of the law by the buyers and sellers on its site. A small number of sellers engaged in fraud, others sold items that violated copyrights, and others sold banned items. eBay monitored its site for possible fraud, as did members of its trading community. For example, eBay used shill-hunter software to identify shill bidding rings, and community members reported possible shill bidders.

Although eBay monitored for fraud, it did not monitor for copyright violations because doing so might make it liable for any infringing items it failed to find. A federal Court of Appeals decision in *Fonovisa, Inc. v. Cherry Auctions, Inc.* held that a swap meet owner was liable for copyright violations because pirated recordings were sold on its venue.[1] The Court ruled that the owner had the ability to monitor its site for illegal items and failed to do so. eBay could monitor its site for possible copyright violations, but with nearly 1 million new listings a day, complete monitoring was virtually impossible.

The Digital Millennium Copyright Act of 1998 (DMCA) clarified the monitoring issue by stating that Web sites could be liable if they monitored for intellectual property infringements and failed to find an infringing item. A site, however, had a safe harbor if it did not monitor, provided that it removed violating items when notified by a copyright holder. eBay had already implemented such a program, referred to as VeRO (verified rights owners). Monitoring was performed by the copyright holders, who asked eBay to remove infringing items. eBay assisted the copyright holders by creating a system in which VeRO members could query on key words and automatically receive e-mail notification of any listing with those key words.

This did not satisfy the Business Software Alliance (BSA), which developed a model code requiring Internet sites to prescreen listings for copyright violations. Even though Amazon.com agreed to the code, eBay refused to do so. It subsequently began restricted monitoring by examining only what was within the "Four Corners" of a seller's listing and dropping from its site items so identified as infringing a copyright. eBay

believed that the CDA provided protection from liability if it relied solely on the listing provided by the seller.

Intellectual property law provided little protection for eBay's database. In a 1991 decision, *Feist Publications, Inc. v. Rural Telephone Service Co.,* 499 U.S., 340, the U.S. Supreme Court held that "facts," even if collected through "sweat and effort," remained in the public domain. Earlier court decisions had held that databases were protected by copyright under the "sweat of the brow" doctrine. This doctrine prevailed despite 1976 amendments to the Copyright Act that required a degree of creativity or originality for compilations of data to receive copyright protection. In *Feist* the court affirmed the originality and creativity requirement and stated that "all facts—scientific, historical, biographical and news of the day … are part of the public domain available to every person."

Bidders' Edge, an auction aggregator, used a robot to copy all of eBay's auction listings and make them available to users of its Web site. Bidders' Edge argued that the listings were compilations of facts and hence under *Feist* were not protected by copyright. eBay chose not to attempt to meet the creativity test, since by doing so it would risk being viewed as an Internet content provider and being subject to other litigation. eBay was successful in protecting its database from robotic searches by relying on trespass law.

By either good fortune or considerable foresight, eBay had also positioned itself well in another part of legal space. A competitor, BidBay, entered the online auction market with a logo and cover page that closely resembled eBay's. In addition to the similarity of its name, BidBay's cover page used the same color scheme, location of the company name and menu bar, search window, and category list as did eBay. In intellectual property law, the most defensible trademarks are those that are "arbitrary and fanciful." An eBay attorney explained, "eBay is a completely coined name. It means nothing."[2] eBay filed a trademark infringement lawsuit against BidBay, which agreed to change its name.

Nonmarket environments can differ across political jurisdictions. In July 2011, the European Court of Justice ruled in a lawsuit filed by L'Oreal that eBay played an "active role" in its Web site and hence was responsible for violations of trademarks when fake goods were sold on its Web site. The Court also ruled that the fact that eBay did not promote the fake goods did not absolve it of responsibility for removing fake items from its Web site or disabling access to the fake goods.[3]

---

[1] For the text of the ruling, see http://www.law.cornell.edu/copyright/cases/76_F3d_259.htm

[2] *San Jose Mercury News,* July 31, 2001.
[3] *Financial Times,* July 13, 2011.

Nonmarket Positioning and Market Strategies

Nonmarket positioning is influenced by a firm's market strategy. Starbucks Coffee has cultivated a particular market segment and established an image of social awareness and concern. It stated that "contributing positively to our communities and environment" is "a guiding principle of the company's mission." This positioning was appealing to a clientele of socially aware, higher income consumers and contributed to Starbucks' cachet. Starbucks backed this image with action. For example, in conjunction with Conservation International it financed Mexican farmers to grow coffee beans in the forest shade so that land would not be cleared for agricultural purposes.

As they do in the market environment, some firms attempt to differentiate themselves in their nonmarket environment. Starbucks and Patagonia have done so by their commitment to social responsibility. Many firms have made commitments to environmental protection, and Gilead Sciences made a commitment to make its leading AIDS drugs accessible to low-income countries.[7]

Frequently, firms seek cover rather than visibility in their nonmarket environment so that their activities are obscured from the view of the public. Pharmaceutical companies often prefer the anonymity of working through the Pharmaceutical Research and Manufacturers Association (PhRMA) to taking action themselves. Moreover, in implementing nonmarket strategies, pharmaceutical companies prefer to work behind the scenes, focusing on relationship building and lobbying rather than more visible activities.

One role of nonmarket strategy is to level the playing field for the implementation of a market strategy. Mattel as well as other toy companies found lead in the paint on some of their branded toys produced in China, resulting in a crisis in which millions of units were recalled.[8] To restore confidence in its brands, Mattel began testing all its toys for lead, putting the company at a cost disadvantage. In addition, toy manufacturers had a collective reputation that was tarnished by the safety issue. To level the playing field and strengthen the reputation of the industry, Mattel and other leading toymakers sought government-mandated safety testing of toys. Similarly, once Nike had become a leader in improved working conditions in its suppliers' factories, it sought through nonmarket leadership to have its competitors match its performance to close the cost gap.

One benefit of nonmarket positioning can be the opportunity to work with NGOs to address nonmarket issues. A number of companies have turned to environmental groups both to find better solutions to problems and to solidify their nonmarket positioning. Conservation International (CI) works with "environment-friendly companies" to find innovative solutions to their environmental problems. In 2001 CI and Ford, which provided $25 million of funding, launched the Center for Environmental Leadership in Business to engage the private sector. The Center worked for positive environmental changes with programs in agriculture and fisheries, energy and mining, forestry, and travel and leisure.

Nonmarket positioning can also affect the set of issues a firm faces. As the eBay example indicates, positioning can affect the legal liabilities to which a firm is exposed. Nonmarket positioning can also affect the likelihood of targeting by activists and interest groups. A company with a demonstrated commitment to the environment faces less risk of criticism by environmental groups. ExxonMobil had quite a different stance, opposing the Kyoto Protocol, and environmental activists launched a boycott of Esso gas stations in Europe.

A favorable position in the space of public sentiment can be quickly lost, however. As discussed in Chapter 1, an explosion at a BP refinery in Texas cost the lives of 15 workers, and a blowout on the Deepwater Horizon oil platform in the Gulf of Mexico killed 11 workers and produced a massive oil spill. BP's favorable position was gone, and recovery would be difficult.

In contrast to the rest of the oil industry, BP had supported the Kyoto Protocol and joined the Pew Trust's climate change program—the Business Environmental Leadership Council—that requires members to implement a voluntary carbon emissions reduction program. BP also had joined the International Climate Change Partnership, the World Resources Institute, the Energy and Biodiversity Initiative, the Papua Conservation Fund, and the Climate, Community, and Biodiversity Alliance. In addition, the BP Conservation Program provided conservation grants in 58 countries. BP made substantial investments in solar energy and implemented an aggressive, voluntary CO_2 reduction program in cooperation with the environmental group Environmental Defense. To establish credibility with the public, Environmental Defense published audited inventories of the company's emissions. BP also

---

[7]See the Chapter 21 case *Gilead Sciences (A): The Gilead Access Program for HIV Drugs.*

[8]See the Chapter 5 case, *Mattel: Crisis Management or Management Crisis?*

used product design in reducing pollution. Five years before federal regulations were to take effect, BP marketed a gasoline that contained 80 percent less sulfur than ordinary premium gasoline.[9]

Positioning Spaces

Nonmarket positioning takes place in three interrelated spaces: public sentiment, political (lawmaking and rule making), and legal (enforcement of existing laws and regulation).

POSITIONING IN THE SPACE OF PUBLIC SENTIMENT   Public sentiment is determined by the diverse interests, viewpoints, and preferences of the individuals in a society. Public sentiment toward a company or industry can affect the public's response to a company's actions and whether social pressure is directed at the company. Favorable public sentiment can not only allow a company to avoid nonmarket issues, but also affect its reception in the market place. Chrysler and General Motors had to be bailed out by the government, whereas Ford avoided bankruptcy during the financial crisis and recession. Some car buyers favored Ford, and the company had more credibility with the public and government. Gilead Sciences made its AIDS drugs accessible to low-income countries, which gave the company a more favorable position in the space of public sentiment than those of pharmaceutical companies that had balked at making their drugs accessible.

POSITIONING IN POLITICAL SPACE   Lawmaking and rule making take place in political space, where the formal rules of the game are made. Positioning in political space can affect the opportunity to participate effectively in lawmaking and rule-making processes.

Because of the importance of nonmarket issues to the profitability of the industry, the pharmaceutical industry has developed a position of strength in political space. The industry has positioned itself by building relationships with members of Congress and the executive branch. This positioned the industry well for the politics and negotiations over health care reform in 2009 and 2010. Major pharmaceutical companies were invited to the bargaining table, and the reforms were favorable to the industry, leading it to support the health care reform legislation. In contrast, the generic pharmaceutical companies were not invited to the bargaining table.

In the mid-2000s, Google recognized that its absence from Washington had given its rivals such as Microsoft, Yahoo, and the telecommunications companies an advantage in legislative and regulatory arenas. It first used its record as an innovator and its cachet to educate members of Congress and regulators on Internet applications, mobile devices, and innovation. It then began developing a Washington office to provide information on government concerns and initiatives. This positioned Google well in its efforts for spectrum opening and open networks. Similarly, in 2011 Facebook recognized its disadvantage in Washington relative to companies like Google, and it followed a strategy similar to Google's to better position itself in political space. President Obama joined Mark Zuckerberg at Facebook's headquarters for an open forum available on Facebook's Web site, and Facebook opened a Washington office.

POSITIONING IN LEGAL SPACE   Positioning in legal space affects not only the liabilities to which a company is exposed but also a company's market and nonmarket strategies. eBay's positioning as an ISP provides protection in the United States under the CDA, but it also means that the company is limited in its ability to provide content on its Web site.

In legal space, patents provide the most important protection for intellectual property for many industries, and perhaps nowhere are patents more important than in the pharmaceutical industry. The pharmaceutical industry regularly seeks stronger patent protection and was successful in obtaining a 6-month patent extension for approved drugs that were subsequently tested for use by children.

Microsoft had taken an aggressive approach to its markets and largely ignored its legal environment, as considered in the Chapter 9 case *The Microsoft Antitrust Case*. In contrast to Microsoft's approach to its antitrust environment, Cisco Systems has sought to avoid antitrust problems and fix potential problems before they develop. Its positioning begins with respect for government officials and with a commitment to invest in relationships with antitrust enforcers

---

[9]The gasoline earned BP sulfur emissions credits that it could use or sell. Emissions credits are considered in Chapter 12.

so that potential problems can be fixed before they lead to a lawsuit. Cisco also works to educate antitrust enforcers about high-technology industries and stands ready to provide technical expertise to regulators. Cisco makes regular assessments of its antitrust status and looks for early warning signs of potential problems. Part of their legal positioning is training their personnel to avoid antitrust problems and actions that might lead to problems. Sales representatives at Cisco receive antitrust training and are told to avoid aggressive competitive language that might be construed as anticompetitive.

The Perils of Positioning

Positioning is intended to improve overall performance by affecting the set of issues a firm faces and by providing a foundation for both market and nonmarket strategies. Positioning can at times, however, be perilous. Starbucks' positioning in the space of public sentiment and its 15,000 outlets, have made it a convenient arena for a variety of activists seeking to appeal to its clientele as well as to the company itself. Activists were concerned with the working conditions in coffee-producing plantations and targeted Starbucks despite its considerable efforts to support coffee-producing families and protect the environment. Anarchists and antiglobalization activists protesting the Seattle World Trade Organization meeting laid siege to a Starbucks store.

Starbucks' positioning also created expectations about its business practices, and activists demanded more from the company than it was willing to provide. In conjunction with demonstrations at the Republican national convention in 2004, several hundred demonstrators protested Starbucks' business practices, including its opposition to unionization, and also used Starbucks stores as a site for antiglobalization protests. Starbucks was slow to adopt Fair Trade coffee because of concerns about coffee quality. The activist group Global Exchange sought to speed the adoption of Fair Trade coffee and had to select a target company for a campaign. It chose Starbucks rather than major coffee roasters because it was viewed as a soft target because of its commitment to social responsibility.

In addition, Starbucks' positioning attracted activists who sought to promote causes with no connection to the company. Local activist groups in Seattle targeted Starbucks to attract attention and media coverage to their causes with the hope that the company would take up their cause. Opponents of the use of recombinant bovine growth hormone had picketed Starbucks to pressure it to stop using milk produced from cows treated with the hormone. Starbucks had agreed to stop using such milk, but the protests resumed the following year to try to force Starbucks to be more aggressive in promoting the cause.

NONMARKET CAPABILITIES AND REPUTATION

Just as firms create value by developing market capabilities, firms develop nonmarket capabilities to add value. Nonmarket capabilities take several forms. One is expertise in dealing with government, the news media, interest and activist groups, and the public. Another is knowledge of the procedures and functioning of the institutions in whose arenas nonmarket issues are resolved. A reputation for responsible actions earned with governments, stakeholders, and the public also constitutes a nonmarket capability.

These nonmarket capabilities can give a firm a nonmarket advantage.[10] Nonmarket capabilities generate value as a function of how costly it is for market and nonmarket rivals to replicate them and for competitors, activists, and interest groups to dissipate them. As part of its business policy Wal-Mart was the largest corporate contributor to charities. Most of its contributions were made locally where its stores were located, and employees played a role in choosing the recipients. This approach to charitable giving strengthened local communities and increased employee job satisfaction. It also helped relieve concerns about the company's impact on local competitors. This component of its overall strategy was effective in the small towns that were the focus of its market strategy, but when it came to opening stores in urban areas, the approach was insufficient.

As indicated in Chapter 1, Wal-Mart was criticized by activists, unions, and politicians for allegedly depressing wages and driving small merchants out of business. In a public referendum,

---

[10]See Prahalad and Hamel (1990) for a discussion of core competencies.

voters in Inglewood, California defeated a proposal to change a zoning requirement to allow Wal-Mart to build a superstore. The criticism not only damaged its reputation but also threatened its expansion strategy, as considered in the Chapter 8 case *Wal-Mart and Its Urban Expansion Strategy*. Wal-Mart belatedly began to develop nonmarket capabilities and improve its reputation. It began an advertising campaign featuring employees telling how happy they were working for Wal-Mart. It also opened a Washington office to develop better relationships with the federal government, sponsored PBS and NPR programs, and started a fellowship program for minority journalism students. It worked with environmental groups to develop an aggressive environmental protection and energy conservation program, and it imposed it on its suppliers. The broader set of challenges and actions by Wal-Mart are addressed in the Part I integrative case *Wal-Mart: Nonmarket Pressure and Reputation Risk (A)*.

Some capabilities must be developed internally, and some can be contracted for externally. Firms can hire outside legal counsel, public affairs experts, ethicists, and lobbyists. For example, Wal-Mart hired Washington lobbyists to represent its interests. The principal nonmarket capabilities that cannot be replicated, however, are knowledge, expertise, and skills of a company's managers in addressing nonmarket issues. Members of Congress are more interested in speaking with the company's CEO or local store managers than with a Washington lobbyist. The better the CEO and other managers understand the issues, interests, and institutions that comprise the nonmarket environment, the more effective they will be in developing and implementing nonmarket strategies.

The value of a nonmarket capability also depends on the effectiveness of a firm's allies in addressing nonmarket issues. On many issues, a firm's market rivals are its nonmarket allies, as when an issue affects firms in an industry in a similar manner. Consequently, industry members frequently work through a trade association or an ad hoc coalition to implement nonmarket strategies. In markets, firms are prohibited by antitrust laws from colluding. In the nonmarket environment, the law generally allows firms to join forces to formulate and implement nonmarket strategies. Pharmaceutical companies thus work through PhRMA on issues such as patent policy that affect companies in a similar manner.

An important nonmarket asset is a reputation for responsible actions and principled behavior. In lobbying, for example, providing incorrect or strategically biased information can harm a reputation and impair future lobbying. Reputations, however, are ultimately established, and destroyed, by actions. Many firms invest in their public reputations just as they invest in their market reputations for service or quality. A reputation can be durable if sustained by actions consistent with it. Reputations, however, can be fragile and quickly tarnished. Johnson & Johnson has a guiding tenet *Our Credo* that places patients and the public first. It developed a widely applauded reputation for its swift and effective response in the Tylenol product tampering that caused seven deaths in Chicago. The company neglected its nonmarket capability, however, and by 2010 it was embroiled in an extensive product quality crisis that badly damaged its reputation, as addressed in the Chapter 5 case *Johnson & Johnson and Its Quality Reputation*. A tarnished reputation is difficult to rebuild, as BP, ExxonMobil, Nike, and Johnson & Johnson have learned.

A FRAMEWORK FOR THE ANALYSIS OF NONMARKET ISSUES

Nonmarket issues are typically complex and require conceptual frameworks to guide analysis and strategy formulation. This section presents such a framework and illustrates its use with an example involving Citibank. In this framework the unit of analysis is the nonmarket issue. The initial step involves generating strategy alternatives. Managers must exercise creativity in generating alternatives beyond those that immediately suggest themselves. For example, to spur the use of mobile devices, Google proposed opening the C-band of the radio spectrum and the white spaces of the television for the development of open networks for mobile devices. As an alternative to higher fuel economy standards, General Motors advocated a tax on carbon fuels as a means of addressing the global climate change issue.

Once alternatives have been identified, they can be evaluated in three stages—*screening, analysis,* and *choice,* as illustrated in Figure 2-5. In the screening stage, alternatives that are contrary to the law, widely shared ethics principles, or a well-evaluated company policy are eliminated. In the case of the automobile industry, an alternative involving noncompliance with mandatory NHTSA safety standards would be screened out. Several automobile companies,

FIGURE 2-5   Framework for the Analysis of Nonmarket Issues

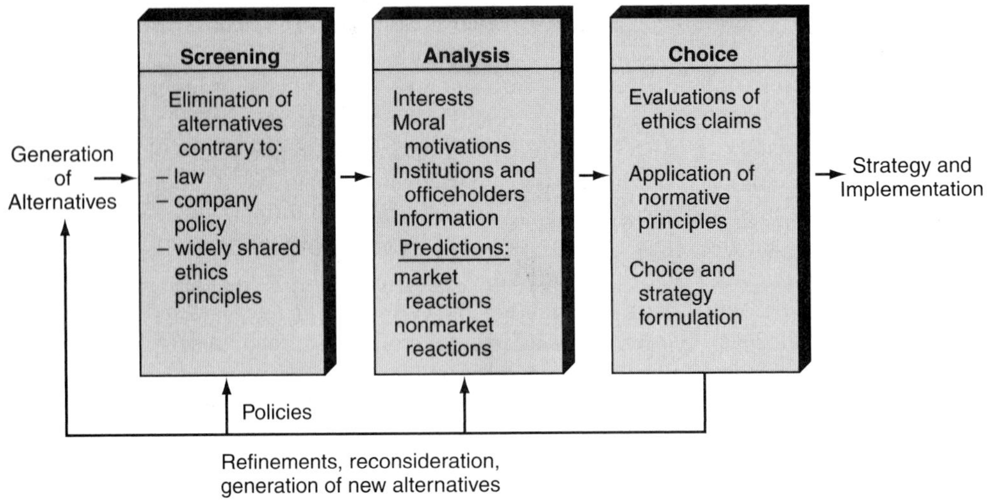

however, have routinely paid a fine, as provided for by law, for not meeting fuel economy standards.

The alternatives that remain after the screening stage are then analyzed to predict their likely consequences. The analysis stage is based on the methods of economics, political science, and other social sciences and focuses on predicting the actions of interests and the consequences of alternative strategies. For example, pharmaceutical companies had to predict how strong the opposition to their direct-to-consumer advertising in the broadcast media might be. Prediction focuses on interests, institutions and their officeholders, and information and takes into account the likely actions of the other interested parties. The analysis stage also considers moral motivations of nonmarket behavior and how others evaluate the firm's actions.

The alternatives are evaluated and a choice made in the third stage. On issues that do not involve significant moral concerns, choice is based on the interests of the firm and its stakeholders. The objective is typically value creation, taking into account the impact of alternatives on stakeholders who are important to sustainable performance. If the issue involves significant moral concerns, normative principles pertaining to well-being, rights, and justice are to be applied, as considered in Part V of this book.

In the nonmarket environment, moral claims about rights are frequently made. Some rights are "granted" in the sense that the government or moral consensus has both established them and clearly assigned the associated duty to respect them. When the duty has not been clearly assigned or the right itself has not been established by government or through moral consensus, the right is said to be "claimed." Granted rights are to be used to screen out alternatives in the first stage, whereas claimed rights are to be evaluated in the choice stage. For example, there is a general consensus that firms should not exploit children. There may be disagreement, however, about what constitutes exploitation, as in the case of advertising children's toys on Saturday morning television.[11]

The process illustrated in Figure 2-5 is intended to yield specific strategies—concerted sets of actions to be taken by identified individuals or business units—and policies that guide managers in addressing market and nonmarket issues. Those policies can be stated as rules to be followed or as principles to be used in reasoning about what to do in a particular situation. For example, the banks subscribing to the Equator Principles use those principles in the first stage to screen out alternatives and in the third stage to decide whether to fund a project.

The framework presented in Figure 2-5 is to be viewed as dynamic. The evaluations in the choice stage and the consequences of the choices made provide a basis for learning, refinement of strategies, and improved methods of analysis.

---

[11]See Hamilton (1998) for a study of the political economy of TV violence and children.

EXAMPLE   Citibank and Credit Cards for Undergraduates

In 1987 Citibank decided to offer Visa and MasterCard credit cards to undergraduate college students. Its objective was to develop an early relationship with individuals likely to be frequent users of the cards once they joined the workforce. To assess the creditworthiness and future earnings potential of an applicant, Citibank used several indicators. For students who were not employed or worked only on a part-time basis, it used their undergraduate major as one measure of creditworthiness. According to Bill McGuire, a spokesman for Citibank, "using the major [is] a good indicator of future earning potential and of students' ability to pay debt."[1]

Application of the Framework

First Stage: Screening

The nonmarket issue is whether it is acceptable to use students' undergraduate majors as a basis for issuing credit cards. The first stage of the framework involves determining whether use of an applicant's undergraduate major is contrary to the law, widely shared ethics principles, or company policy. Use of undergraduate major as a predictor of creditworthiness is neither illegal discrimination nor a violation of the Equal Credit Opportunity Act. Similarly, individuals do not have a granted right to have a credit card, and moral consensus on using an applicant's undergraduate major is not evident. The use of undergraduate major thus passes the screening stage.

Several moral claims, however, remain to be considered in the subsequent stages of the analysis. As some people claim, should everyone have a right to credit with that right withdrawn only upon failure to make the required payments? Could access to credit bias a student's choice of a major? Instead of resolving these questions in the screening stage, the framework calls for their resolution in the choice stage following the second-stage analysis.

Second Stage: Analysis

The second stage of the framework focuses on predicting consequences of alternatives not only for Citibank but also for others. The anticipated market consequences are lower credit losses and higher usage than if Citibank did not use the undergraduate major. Although many lower income people are good credit risks because they match their purchases to their income, people with higher incomes are more likely to have higher credit card usage. Based on similar considerations, Citibank had instituted the Citidollars program, which operated like a frequent-flyer program, providing discounts on products based on credit card usage.

The possible nonmarket consequences of using undergraduate major are more difficult to quantify than the market consequences, but that does not mean that they are less important or that managers cannot reason about them. Failure to anticipate the consequences of nonmarket behavior is a frequent cause of failed managerial decisions. Citibank's use of undergraduate major is a case in point.

The first questions in the analysis are whether people are likely to become aware of Citibank's policy and, if so, whether they would be motivated to take action. The law requires that a person denied credit be notified of the reasons for the denial. Those denied will be disappointed, and some will be angry. That anger could be based on self-interest, but some students could be concerned about the principle underlying Citibank's policy. Some might believe on moral grounds that creditworthiness should be based on credit history and the ability to pay rather than on undergraduate major or likely future earnings. Others might believe that basing creditworthiness on undergraduate major could distort students' choices of majors and ultimately of professions. Some might be concerned that Citibank's practices could induce lying by students who might falsely report their majors to increase their chances of receiving a credit card.

The predictive focus is on whether nonmarket action might be expected, what form that action might take, and what impact it might have. Indeed, Citibank contributed directly to the nonmarket action and to the issue becoming public. At the University of California–Berkeley, a Citibank canvasser, who had set up a table at the student union to take applications, was asked by a reporter from the student newspaper if it were true that some students were being rejected as a result of their major. "The canvasser advised her to fill in the credit application by listing business administration or electrical engineering as her major, instead of English."[2]

The next step is to predict whether the issue will become public. Students have a variety of means of making an issue public, ranging from bringing it before the student government to complaining to university administrators to organizing demonstrations. The most effective way to call attention to the issue is to attract the news media. How likely the media is to cover this issue can be assessed using the theory presented in the next chapter. In brief, the media finds claims of discrimination and unfairness to be newsworthy. Furthermore, students know how to make the issue more newsworthy by organizing protests and taking symbolic actions. This does not imply that protests can be expected on most college campuses, but a manager should ask how many protests are necessary to attract the news media. The answer may be "one."

This analysis does not predict that the issue will inevitably become public, but it does indicate that it might. Citibank, however, need not abandon the use of undergraduate major simply because of the possibility of a nonmarket action. Most of the public would never learn of the issue, and many of those who do might believe that Citibank's policy was appropriate. Those who view the use of undergraduate major as inappropriate, however, are the concern.

With regard to immediate effects, few students had a business relationship with Citibank that they could end

---

[1]*Peninsula Times Tribune*, March 20, 1988. The following is the application of the framework to the Citibank example and is not Citibank's analysis.

[2]*Peninsula Times Tribune*, March 20, 1988.

(Continued)

(Continued)

in protest. Nor, due to the costs of switching banks, were they likely to be able to persuade any significant number of Citibank customers to withdraw their business. The immediate market consequences were thus likely to be small. The effect on future business, however, might be more significant. Some students might choose not to deal with Citibank in the future. Furthermore, Citibank's recruiting on college campuses might be affected, either through boycotts or other direct action. At Berkeley, student protesters demanded that Citibank be barred from recruiting on campus as a result of the issue. In addition, Citibank's reputation could be affected by a controversy. Certainly, Citibank management could be embarrassed by protests and media coverage.

The Outcome

The issue became public through student protests at Berkeley, and the national news media was quickly attracted to the issue, providing critical coverage. As the pressure mounted, Citibank announced that it was abandoning use of a student's undergraduate major. Had Citibank analyzed the situation as called for by Figure 2-5 and been sensitive to the types of concerns—in particular the moral motivations of nonmarket action—that can result from a market strategy, it could have avoided a situation that at a minimum was an embarrassment. The Chapter 11 case *Citigroup and Subprime Lending* provides another example.

ORGANIZATION OF THE NONMARKET STRATEGY FUNCTION

During the 1970s several companies formed strategic planning departments to assist management in developing long-range market strategies. These staff departments were typically attached to, but separate from, top management, which proved to be the cause of many failures. Similarly, several companies formed issues management groups to identify and address nonmarket issues. That experiment also produced failures, particularly when the group focused on societal issues rather than on specific issues affecting the firm's performance.[12]

Wartick and Rude (1986) analyzed the problems experienced by issues management groups in eight firms.[13] They identified four conditions necessary for success:

- Top management must support and be involved in the effort.
- Field units and relevant staff departments must be involved.
- The issues management unit must fill a void in the managerial decision-making process.
- Results must come from the effort.

The perspective taken in this book is that there should be no void for an issues management unit to fill. That is, the responsibility for addressing nonmarket issues should reside with operating managers and not with a separate staff unit.

Management rather than staff now formulates a firm's market strategy, and the same is true for nonmarket strategies. Managers must be involved because they are in the best position to assess the consequences of nonmarket factors for market strategies and overall performance. The nonmarket environment is often more complex than the market environment, however, because public institutions are complex and a larger set of interests participate. Successfully addressing a nonmarket issue may require expertise in the law, government institutions, and public communication. In such cases, managers may need the advice of specialists. Managers must, however, be able to evaluate the advice they receive. To do so, they need to be as knowledgeable about the relevant nonmarket issues as they are about the markets in which the firm operates. Because managers operate continuously in their market environment and often only on an episodic basis in their nonmarket environment, frameworks such as that in Figure 2-5 can be particularly helpful in structuring analysis and strategy formulation.

SUMMARY

A business strategy must be congruent with the capabilities of a firm and the characteristics of its environment—both market and nonmarket. Just as the environment has two components, a business strategy has both market and nonmarket components, and these components must

---

[12]Littlejohn (1986) describes the issues management activities of Monsanto and Gulf Oil.
[13]Also see Sigman and McDonald (1987).

be integrated. The nonmarket component is of greater importance when the opportunities of a firm are controlled by government, challenged by private politics, or involve moral concerns. Nonmarket strategies can be directed at competitive forces or at unlocking opportunities blocked by the nonmarket environment. Because strategies depend on the issues, interests, institutions, and information that characterize the nonmarket environment, they are more likely to be multidomestic than global. Nonmarket strategies are based on capabilities such as the knowledge and experience of managers in addressing nonmarket issues and the reputation of the firm for responsible actions. Nonmarket capabilities can be developed, and their development is part of an overall business strategy.

Positioning in the nonmarket environment provides a foundation for strategy and hence is a strategic choice of the firm. Positioning can attract opportunities and affect the set of issues the firm faces. Positioning takes place in legal, political, and public sentiment spaces. eBay's positioning in legal space has shielded it from certain liabilities and responsibilities. The brand-name pharmaceutical companies have established a strong position in political space, and Starbucks has established a position of social awareness and social responsibility in the space of public sentiment. Positioning can also generate risks as Starbucks has learned.

Most companies focus on those nonmarket issues with a potentially significant impact on performance. Addressing nonmarket issues in an effective manner is aided by frameworks that organize analysis, reasoning, and strategy formulation. The framework illustrated in Figure 2-5 is composed of three stages: screening, analysis, and choice. The screening stage rules out those alternatives that are contrary to the law, company policy, or ethical consensus. The analysis stage focuses on the prediction of nonmarket actions and their likely consequences. The choice stage involves evaluating those consequences and any ethics claims and making choices based on those evaluations. The results of the choice stage are strategies for addressing the issue and policies that can be used to guide managers in the screening stage for future issues.

CASES

Facebook in China?

INTRODUCTION

Seventy percent of Facebook's 500 million users were outside the United States, and Facebook was available in 70 languages. Facebook had started a Chinese language version in 2008, but it functioned poorly because of government censorship.[14] Access to Facebook was completely blocked by the Chinese government in 2009, which not only deprived the company of access to a market with as many Internet users as it had on its Web site, but it also provided an opportunity for competitors in China to grow and flourish. Facebook had not paid much attention to China as is managed its spectacular growth, but that changed in 2010.

FACEBOOK'S PERSPECTIVE ON CHINA

In a speech at Stanford University in the fall of 2010 CEO and founder Mark Zuckerberg said that Facebook was trying to decide on the "right partnerships that we would need to do in China to succeed on our own terms. Before we do anything there, I'm personally spending a lot of time studying it and figuring out what I think the right thing to do is. It's such an important part of the world. I mean, how can you connect the

whole world, if you leave out a-billion-six people?"[15] He also said, "I don't want Facebook to be an American Company— obviously, we are in America—but I don't want it to be this company that just spreads American values all across the world....For example, we have this notion of free speech that we really love and support at Facebook, and that's one of the main things we're trying to push with openness. But different countries have their different standards around that....My view on this is that you want to be really culturally sensitive and understand the way that people actually think."[16] Zuckerberg revealed that he was studying Mandarin for an hour a day.

Zuckerberg also said that Facebook would first enter Japan, South Korea, and Russia and then turn its attention to China. He said, "Our theory is that if we can show that we as a western company can succeed in a place where no other company has, then we can start to figure out the right partnerships we would need to succeed in China on our own terms."[17] The company had opened offices in Brazil, India, and Singapore, and opened one in Hong Kong in February 2011.

In December 2010 Zuckerberg traveled to China and visited Baidu, the leading search company, Internet

---

[14]Chapter 16 presents information on China, and the Chapter 16 case *Google In China* and the Chapter 24 case *Google Out of China* provide information on censorship of the Internet.

[15]*Wall Street Journal*, December 23, 2010.
[16]*Wall Street Journal*, June 10, 2011.
[17]*The Guardian*, December 21, 2010.

company Sina, and China Mobile, the largest telecommunications company and government owned.

THE CHINESE MARKET

The Chinese market had matured quickly with a set of highly successful companies which were formidable competition for new entrants. Renren.com was a close approximation to Facebook and the most popular social networking site. Sina offered a micro-blogging service Sina Weibo similar to Twitter, and Tencent offered Twitter-like services with its QQ instant messaging service being particularly popular. Other popular social networking sites were Kaixin001, 51.com, and Douban. Kai Lukoff, co-founder of ChinaMetrix in Shanghai, however, said, "Chinese developers love Facebook" because it is generous in its arrangements with developers.[18] Blogger Zhang Wen wrote, "If you put your Facebook page on your name card, you'll look cool and well-connected to a global community, not just stuck in China."[19]

On the occasion of the opening of its Hong Kong office Blake Chandlee, Facebook vice-president for commercial development in Asia, Latin America, and emerging markets, said, "We're growing all over the world and the Asian region is a big, big part of it." He added, "Mobile is the future of our business, especially in markets like Asia and Latin America." He also said, "We have nothing to announce about what we're doing or not doing. There are a number of areas around the world where we have gaps. There are lots of reasons why I don't want to talk about China. Today, Facebook is available in Chinese in a number of different dialects. We always want all users around the world to have access to Facebook. In some places they do, some places they don't, whether it be temporarily or permanently."[20]

CENSORSHIP

The Chinese government had blocked Facebook, YouTube, and Twitter since the riots in Urumqi province in 2009. The government feared collective action that could impact social stability and government control, and social media provide a coordination mechanism for collective action, as was evident in the so-called "Arab Awakening" in 2011. When asked where the next uprising would occur, Egyptian activist Wael Ghonim, said, "Ask Facebook." Facebook director of international communications Debbie Frost said, "We've witnessed brave people of all ages coming together to effect a profound change in their country. Certainly, technology was a vital tool in their efforts, but we believe their bravery and determination mattered most."[21]

The Chinese social media Web sites had well-developed relations with the Chinese government and practiced self-censorship based on informal guidance from the government. Foreign companies operating in the country also practiced self-censorship or faced disruptions in their services.

The Chinese government also required Internet companies to turn over to the government personal data on persons who register domain names in the country.[22] This had caused GoDaddy.com to stop registering domain names in China. Robin Li, co-founder of Baidu, said, "Socialism with Chinese characteristics drives the development of the Chinese Internet."[23]

Arvind Ganesan of Human Rights Watch provided his interpretation of censorship in China, "The underlying intent is, if you're engaging in political speech, we want to know who's engaging in it and what Web site is behind it. This is a way the Chinese government can send a chilling message to people that they shouldn't speak freely online. It is forcing us companies to be both the censor and the spy on behalf of the Chinese government."[24] Rebecca MacKinnon, an expert on Chinese censorship, commented, "This is part of the Chinese conundrum. The government requires companies to police and censor most of the Internet for it. I find it hard to see exactly how [Facebook] would organize their business in China in such a way that would insulate them from these problems that nobody else has managed to avoid."[25] Chinese activists had written to Facebook complaining that the company had taken down their page "Never Forget June Fourth," the day the Tiananmen Square protest began. Facebook said the group had set up the wrong kind of page.[26]

Facebook lobbyist Adam Conner commented on Facebook's challenges in countries, "Maybe we will block content in some countries, but not in others. We are occasionally held in uncomfortable positions because now we're allowing too much, maybe, free speech in countries that haven't experienced it before." Facebook refused to elaborate on Conner's comments, but Frost said, "Right now we are studying and learning about China but have made no decisions about if, or how, we will approach it."[27]

Conner's comment sparked a reaction both among NGOs and in Congress. Kenneth Roth, executive director of Human Rights Watch, wrote to Zuckerberg urging "that, as you work to define the terms of your entry, you do not collude with Chinese authorities in censoring political speech or helping them retaliate against Facebook users who want to benefit from the openness and connectivity Facebook provides."[28] Roth expressed particular concern over Facebook's requirement that users register their real names where "authorities have a history of identifying and jailing internet users for political speech, …." He asked Facebook to give users in China "some form of online anonymity." He also asked how Facebook would operate if it formed a partnership with Baidu and how it would deal with Chinese government attempts to censor "domestic and global

[18]*Straits Times*, December 24, 2010.
[19]Ibid.
[20]*South China Morning Post*, February 9, 2011.
[21]*Wall Street Journal*, April 20, 2011

[22]The information required included "a color, head and shoulders photograph and other business identification, including a Chinese business registration number and physical, signed registration forms." *Washington Post*, March 25, 2010.
[23]*San Jose Mercury News*, July 10, 2011.
[24]*Washington Post*, March 25, 2010.
[25]*San Jose Mercury News*, July 10, 2011.
[26]*The Guardian*, December 21, 2010.
[27]*Wall Street Journal*, April 20, 2011.
[28]Kenneth Roth, Letter to Mr. Mark Zuckerberg, May 10, 2011, www.hrw.org.

content." The Committee to Protect Journalists also criticized Facebook for requiring users to register with their real name. Michael Anti, an independent journalist in China, had his Facebook account deactivated in 2011 because he had used another name to establish the account.[29]

The Global Network Initiative, which includes as members NGOs, university schools and centers, and financial and consulting companies, had been founded in 2008 by three Internet companies, Google, Microsoft, and Yahoo, and provided principles and implementation guidelines for firms operating in countries that restrict speech and expression.[30] No other Internet companies had joined, and Google withdrew from China in 2010, moving its servers to Hong Kong.[31] A Facebook spokesperson Andrew Noyes, commented, "As Facebook grows, we'll continue to expand our outreach and participation, but it is important to remember that our global operations are still small, with offices in only a handful of countries."[32]

Bill Bishop, a media entrepreneur in Beijing, said, "It is inevitable that to comply with Chinese laws they or their partner are going to have to turn over data. The day that happens they should expect a call from Congress."[33] Facebook was already under fire from Congress on privacy issues, and Representatives Joe Barton (R-TX) and Edward Markey (D-MA) had written to Facebook demanding an explanation for allowing outside Web sites to obtain personal information from users with their permission.[34] In an editorial the *Washington Post* warned that Facebook could "become another bearer of the double standard of Western companies in China such as Yahoo and Microsoft."[35]

THE CHALLENGE

Facebook wanted to enter the Chinese market, but the question was how. It could enter on its own, acquire a Chinese Internet company, or partner with a company such as Baidu that did not have its own social networking service. An important part of its market strategy, would be how to deal with the nonmarket challenges it would face in China, including censorship and demands to provide information on users to the Chinese government. In addition to choosing its market and nonmarket strategies for entering China, the company had to prepare for the inevitable criticism and pressure it would face from the U.S. government and NGOs. ■

Preparation Questions

1. Should Facebook enter the Chinese market on its own and develop its own relations with the Chinese government?
2. Should Facebook join with Baidu in a joint venture that would be managed by Baidu? Might the government make demands on Facebook regarding its Web sites outside China?
3. Other countries also censor Internet services, although not as broadly or continuously as China. Should Facebook develop a global policy governing how it deals with censorship before it enters the Chinese market?
4. If it enters China, should it allow users to be anonymous? Should it join the Global Network Initiative?
5. What strategy should Facebook use to deal with the pressure it will face in the United States?

Personal Watercraft, aka Jet Skis

Personal watercraft, popularly known as water bikes or jet skis, are vessels powered by a jet pump with engines up to 135 horsepower and capable of reaching speeds of over 60 mph. Jet skis skyrocketed in popularity during the 1990s with sales reaching $1.2 billion in 1996, accounting for 37 percent of the boats sold in the United States. The average jet ski cost $6,328 in 1996, and over a million were in operation. The leading producer with nearly half the market was Bombardier, based in Montreal, producer of Sea Doo personal watercraft. Other producers included Polaris Industries, Kawasaki, and Yamaha. Despite, or perhaps because of, their popularity jet skis were under attack from several quarters.

Safety concerns resulted from the speed of jet skis and from some of their operating characteristics. One characteristic was that they were nearly impossible to control when an operator lost hold of the throttle. A study published in the *Journal of the American Medical Association* reported that injuries associated with personal watercraft increased dramatically with an estimated 12,000 people treated in hospital emergency rooms in 1995, including four fatalities. The study also indicated that the accident rate for personal watercraft was substantially higher than for regular motorboats. In California, jet skis accounted for 55 percent of boating injuries but only 18 percent of registered boats. The industry responded that surveys had shown that the average personal watercraft was used more per year than larger boats, making the accident rates "roughly comparable" to water skiing. Kawasaki stated, "More fatalities are routinely recorded for kayaking and canoeing." The National Transportation Safety Board had begun a study of jet ski safety, and a number of states and interest groups were pressuring the U.S. Coast Guard to examine jet ski accidents.

John Donaldson, executive director of the Personal Watercraft Industry Association, said, "This is just a recreational activity—it's fun. It's not a firearm....It's not a proven health risk like cigarettes." Pat Hartman of Polaris Industries said that jet skis were "as safe as the driver. It's like a loaded gun. If it's in the wrong hands, it's not safe."

[29]*New York Times*, March 28, 2011.
[30]www.globalnetworkinitiative.org.
[31]See the Chapter 24 case *Google Out of China*.
[32]*New York Times*, March 7, 2011.
[33]*The Guardian*, April 21, 2011.
[34]*Wall Street Journal*, April 20, 2011.
[35]*Washington Post*, April 24, 2011.

EPA regulations set new hydrocarbon and nitrogen oxide emissions standards for boats, and those standards would become more stringent each year until 2006 when a 75 percent reduction in emissions would have been achieved. The standards were applied on a "corporate average" basis that required all of a company's certified engines, on average, to achieve the standards. This allowed greater flexibility to manufacturers. The Earth Island Institute, an environmental activist group, criticized the EPA regulations as too weak.

The California Air Resources Board had begun a study to determine if jet skis should be regulated for their emissions. Other state and local agencies in California began to examine jet ski operations as a source of MTBE, a gasoline additive that reduced automobile emissions but could contaminate water supplies. The Northern California Marine Association expressed concern about the effect of a boating ban on recreation and the businesses that serviced boating. Administrative Director Mary Kirin Velez said, "Our whole emphasis is on getting the governor to give a waiver to let the oil companies produce gasoline without using MTBE."[36]

Local environmental groups also took up the cause. The Bluewater Network organized a public demonstration in San Francisco comparing jet skis with two-stroke and four-stroke engines. The two-stroke engine left an oily residue in the water, whereas the four-stroke engine left no apparent residue. Russell Long, director of the Bluewater Network, called jet skis "America's No. 1 water polluter....We don't want to take away anyone's Jet Ski. Our focus is the new ones that haven't been built yet."[37]

Two-stroke engines used gasoline mixed with oil, and critics argued that the fuel did not burn completely. In four-stroke engines the lubricating oil was kept separate from the combustion compartment.[38] Two-stroke engines, however, delivered more power and faster acceleration. Two-stroke engines had been banned in motorcycles because of their emissions. The Tahoe Regional Planning Agency voted to ban two-cycle engines from Lake Tahoe to reduce water pollution. The EPA issued regulations taking effect in 1999 that required fuel injection, which would substantially reduce pollution.

In addition to water pollution, homeowners and others complained of the noise made by personal watercraft. Mark Desmeules, director of Maine's Natural Resources Division, referred to jet skis as "the Ninja bikes of the water." He added, "That's why there is such a public outcry—the ability of just one of them to degrade the quality of the natural experience for so many people."[39] Vermont responded by banning jet skis from lakes with less than 300 acres. Legislation introduced in Minnesota would have banned personal watercraft on lakes with less than 200 acres, but opposition by the Jetsporters Association of Minnesota led to defeat of the bill. Jim Medema of the International Jet Sports Boating Association said, "The vote sent a clear message to those that would discriminate against PWC owners. We want to ensure that Minnesotans can continue to ride their PWC safely and responsibly without any unfair restrictions that do not apply to other boaters."

The National Park Service, an agency of the Department of the Interior, was considering regulations that would allow individual park superintendents to designate personal watercraft usage areas. The regulations were supported by over 100 conservation organizations, including the American Canoe Association, the National Parks and Conservation Association, and the Earth Island Institute. The International Jet Sports Boating Association opposed the regulations. Both sides urged their members to write to the secretary of the interior. Mark Speaks of Yamaha Motors said, "I have not read a study that personal watercraft are particularly annoying to wildlife. I don't know why they would be more annoying to wildlife than any other boat."[40]

Local governments also were addressing personal watercraft issues. For example, the city council of Evanston, Illinois, recommended that PWC operators be charged permit fees twice as high as for other boats. The Illinois Department of Natural Resources notified Evanston that such fees were discriminatory and that it could lose state grants if they were imposed.

The industry implemented several nonmarket strategies to address the issues it faced. Industry members had formed the Personal Watercraft Industry Association (PWIA), which acted on behalf of industry members in public arenas. "Where conflict exists, the PWIA seeks to support resolution through the careful balancing of the interests of all parties, including PWC and other boat operators, swimmers, fishermen, paddlesports enthusiasts, environmentalists, and shoreline residents or recreationists."[41]

At the state level the PWIA developed model legislation intended to make waterways safer and to reduce conflicts. Twenty-six states enacted regulations based on the model legislation, which included a minimum age requirement of 16 years for operators, defined and restricted unsafe operation, prohibited night time operation, required that operators and passengers wear personal flotation devices, required operators of personal watercraft equipped with engine shutoff lanyards to use them, prohibited tow lines, and required safety instruction.[42] Mandatory instruction had been required in Connecticut since 1989 and was credited with keeping accidents down. The PWIA supported state legislation such as that in North Carolina that would prohibit nighttime use and increase the minimum age to 16 unless the person was between 12 and 16 and had an adult onboard or had taken a boat safety course.

Manufacturers' Web sites provided instructions on watercraft safety, rules of the road, and self-tests on operation safety. Jet skis came with a videotape, booklets, and warning labels on the watercraft. Web sites for jet skis also provided an environmental guide, including instructions to fuel and clean watercraft engines away from the water and shore. Operators

[36]*San Jose Mercury News*, February 14, 1998.
[37]*San Francisco Chronicle*, March 26, 1997.
[38]*The Wall Street Journal*, February 18, 1998.
[39]*San Francisco Chronicle*, December 30, 1997.

[40]Ibid.
[41]Yamaha Web site, www.yamaha-motor.com.
[42]Yamaha Web site. Many states, for example, had no age requirement to operate a personal watercraft.

were also instructed to avoid bird habitats and shallow waters where the watercraft could stir up sediment.

Legislative and regulatory activity took place at the federal, state, and local levels as well as in special jurisdictions such as the Tahoe Regional Planning Agency. The PWIA Web site provided tracking information on legislative and regulatory activity at each of these levels. Manufacturers also encouraged watercraft owners to take political action on issues pertaining to jet skis. Bombardier asked owners to contact their government entities to learn about possible legislative and regulatory action and also provided advice about how to participate effectively in public processes. It recommended that individuals ask their legislators about any restrictions being considered, identify key legislators including committee chairpersons, and ask about hearings schedules. Bombardier also provided guides for effective testimony; for example, "When testifying at the hearing, thank the legislators for the opportunity to make your views known, and state your position on the issue in a clear and concise manner. Be prepared to answer questions, and do not be confrontational or react defensively."

In response to the criticisms, manufacturers made changes in their watercraft in an attempt to reduce complaints and regulatory pressure. Bombardier announced that all its 1999 Sea-Doo models would include sound reduction technologies adapted from the automotive industry. The technologies included a new muffler, new composite parts that reduced noise levels, and a resonator that suppressed certain frequencies. Bombardier announced that the sound pressure level had been reduced by 50 percent on one of its models.

One strategy of the industry was to lend jet skis to government agencies, and in 1997 nearly 2,000 were on loan to game wardens, search and rescue teams, firefighters, and police and sheriff departments. Mary Ann Anderson, who had led the fight against jet skis in the San Juan Islands of Washington, said, "What they are doing is very ironic—producing a machine that needs to be highly regulated because of the way it is built and the power involved in it. Then they give this product to law enforcement, which are supposed to be policing them. It's ridiculous."[43]

The issues associated with jet skis were similar in some regards to those of snowmobiles in the 1970s. Bombardier and Polaris also manufactured snowmobiles and along with other manufacturers had taken measures, such as developing trails, to defuse criticism by landowners. Bombardier credited the strategy of loaning snowmobiles to law enforcement agencies and search and rescue teams as helping gain their acceptance. As public acceptance increased, the market for snowmobiles continued to grow. ▪

Preparation Questions

1. Identify the issues, interests, institutions, and information associated with jet skis.
2. How have the jet ski manufacturers used market and nonmarket strategies to address the issues they face?
3. Should the jet ski manufacturers join the National Marine Manufacturers Association, which represents power boat manufacturers?
4. Should the jet ski industry seek to be included in the same regulatory category as power boats, or should it seek to have its own regulatory category, for example, with respect to no-wake zones?
5. What nonmarket strategy should a company such as Bombardier adopt? How should it be integrated with its market strategy?

---

[43]*San Francisco Chronicle*, December 30, 1997.

3 | THE NEWS MEDIA AND NONMARKET ISSUES

INTRODUCTION

The news media plays an important role in society by providing information to the public about matters affecting people's lives and the society in which they live. The news media also plays an important role in identifying nonmarket issues and stimulating action that affects their progress. The news media finds business of interest, and with stories instantly transmitted worldwide by the broadcast media and the Internet, a firm's actions are in the eye of the media and under the scrutiny of interest groups, activists, and government. Phil Knight, chairman and CEO of Nike, stated in Nike's 1996 annual report, "Yet no sooner had the great year ended than we were hit by a series of blasts from the media about our practices overseas." As this comment suggests, many companies dread media coverage of their nonmarket issues and have had to develop a capability for interacting with the media.

The essential role the news media plays in a democracy is accompanied by a responsibility to provide information in an accurate and unbiased manner so that individuals can formulate their own conclusions about issues. News organizations, however, face incentives, including those provided by profits, and pressures from competition among news organizations. Similarly, journalists face incentives associated with career and professional advancement. These incentives and pressures complicate the fulfillment of that responsibility. The news media itself is a diverse collection of organizations, including television, radio, Internet services, blogs, social media, newspapers, magazines, and journals, and each faces its own set of challenges.

This chapter considers the role of the news media in the development of nonmarket issues. To analyze that role, a theory of media coverage and treatment is presented. The theory provides a basis for anticipating the impact of news coverage on the progress of issues through their life cycles. The news media as an institution is then considered, focusing on the business and professional incentives that motivate news organizations, their editors, and journalists. Finally, approaches to interacting effectively with the news media are presented, including recourse in the event of a dispute.

THE ROLE OF THE NEWS MEDIA IN NONMARKET ISSUES

In Chapter 1 the news media was identified as one of the institutions in whose arena nonmarket issues are addressed. Indeed, Cater (1959) referred to the news media as the "fourth branch" of government, formalizing Thomas Carlyle's 1841 description of British statesman Edmund Burke's characterization of journalists as the "Fourth Estate."[1] Editors and journalists are the "officeholders" of the institution. In addition to serving as an arena in which nonmarket issues are addressed, the news media plays an important role in identifying nonmarket issues and placing issues on the agendas of firms. Media coverage can

- Alert the public, activists, interest groups, and government officeholders to nonmarket issues.
- Raise concerns about the policies and practices of firms.
- Provide information about the likely effects of alternative courses of action.
- Reduce the costs of collective action.
- Enhance a nonmarket strategy by conveying information provided by a firm or interest group.
- Represent interests and principles consistent with the news media's perception of its role in society.

Interest groups and activist organizations, as well as government officeholders, are prepared to act on a variety of issues, and media coverage can inform them and spur action. Media coverage can also make a message widely known among the public and thereby reduce the cost of collective action. An interest group such as a union or trial lawyers may seize the opportunity created by media coverage of an event to further their

---

[1]Quoted in Sparrow (1999, p. 5).

interests. Media coverage can also provide an opportunity for a politician to advance an issue, represent constituents affected by it, or claim credit for addressing it.[2]

Nonmarket entrepreneurs outside of public office have developed strategies for attracting media coverage to call attention to issues, influence the public, and stimulate private and public politics. As considered in Chapter 12, environmental groups use the annual release of the EPA's Toxic Substances Inventory to hold press conferences to name the nation's largest polluters and call for more stringent environmental standards. Similarly, Greenpeace is effective in using media coverage to advance the issues on its agenda, as illustrated by the Chapter 4 case *Shell, Greenpeace, and Brent Spar.*

A striking example of the role the news media can play in an activist group's strategy was provided by the Natural Resources Defense Council's (NRDC) campaign against Alar, a chemical used to make apples ripen more uniformly and stay crisp when stored. In a policy study, "Intolerable Risk: Pesticides in Our Children's Food," the NRDC argued that Alar increased the risk of cancer in children and called for a ban on its use. To advance its position through the media, the NRDC hired Fenton Communications. After the media campaign, David Fenton described the strategy.[3]

> Our goal was to create so many repetitions of NRDC's message that average American consumers (not just the policy elite in Washington) could not avoid hearing it—from many different media outlets within a short period of time. The idea was for the "story" to achieve a life of its own, and continue for weeks and months to affect policy and consumer habits. Of course this had to be achieved with extremely limited resources....
>
> It was agreed that one week after the study's release, [Meryl] Streep and other prominent citizens would announce the formation of NRDC's new project, Mothers and Others for Pesticide Limits. This group would direct citizen action at changing the pesticide laws, and help consumers lobby for pesticide-free produce at their grocery stores.
>
> The separation of these two events was important in ensuring that the media would have two stories, not one, about this project. Thereby, more repetition of NRDC's message was guaranteed.
>
> As the report was being finalized, Fenton Communications began contacting various media. An agreement was made with *60 Minutes* to "break" the story of the report in late February. Interviews were also arranged several months in advance with major women's magazines like *Family Circle, Women's Day,* and *Redbook* (to appear in mid-March). Appearance dates were set with the *Donahue Show,* ABC's *Home Show,* double appearances on NBC's *Today Show* and other programs....
>
> In addition, we arranged for Meryl Streep and Janet Hathaway of NRDC to grant 16 interviews by satellite with local TV major market anchors....
>
> In the ensuing weeks, the controversy kept building. Articles appeared in food sections of newspapers around the country. Columnists and cartoonists took up the story. *McNeil/Lehrer,* the *New York Times,* and *Washington Post* did follow-up stories; as did the three network evening programs and morning shows. Celebrities from the casts of *L.A. Law* and *thirtysomething* joined NRDC for a Los Angeles news conference.

This episode illustrates the responsiveness of the media to an issue such as pesticide use and the media's role in stimulating nonmarket action that can advance an issue through its life cycle. Media coverage made the NRDC's message widely known, leading to demands by the public to ban Alar. Not only did the NRDC orchestrate newsworthy events, but it also timed them to extend the media attention. This was despite the weak scientific basis for NRDC's claims.[4]

This example is not intended to suggest that it is easy to use the media in a nonmarket strategy. The news media guards its independence and is careful to avoid being used as part of a nonmarket strategy. However, when an issue is of interest to viewers and readers, the news media has incentives to cover it. That coverage can serve the interests of activists, interest groups,

---

[2]See Cook (1989) and Graber (2000).
[3]*Wall Street Journal,* October 3, 1989.
[4]See the Chapter 3 case *The Alar Episode* in the fifth edition of this book.

public officeholders, or companies. The Alar episode serves as a reminder of the potential effect of media coverage on the progress of an issue. Addressing the issue then is considerably more difficult.

MESSAGES AND THEIR INTERPRETATION

Because of the importance of the news media, firms and their managers must anticipate which issues will attract media coverage and how the media will treat them. Figure 3-1 illustrates the role of the media in informing the public and facilitating nonmarket action. Issues and events are observed by the media, which then decides whether to cover them and how to treat those it covers. Coverage and treatment provide messages to which readers and viewers are exposed and on which interest groups, politicians, firms, and others form their perceptions and base their actions. Those actions can themselves be newsworthy, attracting further coverage and giving the issue a life of its own.

The messages provided by the news media are interpreted in a variety of ways depending on individuals' prior information, beliefs, and preferences. Even though the interpretation of messages can vary, their impact can be systematic and hence important. In a series of laboratory experiments, Iyengar and Kinder (1987) investigated the agenda-setting role of the news media and the ways in which news stories affected viewers' attitudes toward issues and political leaders. Their research indicated that viewers attached greater importance to an issue after seeing news coverage of it. They also found that news coverage primes viewers by affecting "what springs to mind and what is forgotten or ignored."[5] These agenda-setting and priming effects are important to both the development of nonmarket issues and management's efforts to address them.

A THEORY OF NEWS MEDIA COVERAGE AND TREATMENT

To assess the role of the news media in nonmarket issues, a theory is needed for the process shown in Figure 3-1 in which the media observes issues and events and chooses whether to cover them and how to treat those it covers. The unit of analysis is the issue, and the theory is intended to explain and predict coverage and treatment. Treatment may take several forms:

- A straightforward presentation of facts and description of events
- An interpretation of the facts and events
- An exploration of their potential significance and ramifications
- Advocacy of a course of action

Advocacy is in principle, but not always in practice, to be restricted to the editorial page.

A variety of explanatory variables could be used in a theory of media coverage and treatment, but in the interest of parsimony only two are considered—the intrinsic audience interest in the

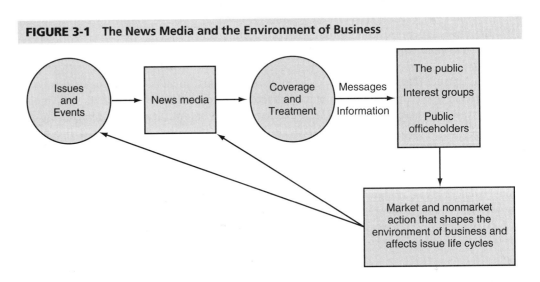

FIGURE 3-1   The News Media and the Environment of Business

---

[5]Iyengar and Kinder (1987, p. 114).

issue and its societal significance as perceived by the news media. As indicated in the previous section, audience interest and societal significance may themselves be influenced by media coverage and treatment.

Intrinsic Audience Interest

The audience interest perspective begins with the observation that coverage and treatment decisions by news media are influenced by revenue and hence audience considerations. Subscription and advertising revenues are based on circulation and ratings, and the objective is to attract an audience by covering issues of interest to readers and viewers and treating those issues in a manner that will hold their attention. From this perspective, predicting which issues the media will cover requires determining which issues are of intrinsic interest to readers and viewers. Similarly, predicting the treatment an issue will receive requires determining what attracts and holds their attention. The principal predictions of the intrinsic audience interest perspective are that (1) coverage increases with audience interest, and (2) treatment will be chosen to appeal to and retain an audience.

Assessing intrinsic audience interest in issues such as international trade policy, product safety, environmental protection, and working conditions in overseas suppliers' factories generally lies in the realm of judgment rather than measurement. A product safety issue centering on a hazard to consumers attracts an instant audience, as in the case of lead in paint on children's toys, as considered in the Chapter 5 case *Mattel: Crisis Management or Management Crisis.* In contrast, many international trade issues have limited audience interest due to their complexity and their indirect effects on people. Environmental issues matter to many people, so environmental stories have a natural audience. Moreover, the more proximate the consequences, the more intense the audience interest.

Societal Significance

The societal significance perspective views coverage and treatment as a reflection of the news media's perception of the significance of an issue to society. This perspective reflects the news media's role in serving democracy by providing information citizens need. Veteran journalist Edwin Newman (1984, p. 19) said, "We in the news business help to provide the people with the information they need to frame their attitudes and to make, or at any rate to authorize or ratify, the decisions on which the well-being of the nation rests." Louis H. Young (1978), former editor-in-chief of *BusinessWeek,* stated, "Reporters see themselves as guardians of the public's right to know." Applied to business issues, he described an incident involving a company's board of directors meeting and explained, "The magazine's position was—and is—that what the directors ate or drank was their business; but when they considered replacing the chief executive of a company it was the business of stockholders, both present and future."

A duty to provide information to the public places the news media in a watchdog role, and that role frequently is an adversarial one. Louis Banks, former managing editor of *Fortune,* noted, "The editorial mind-set is influenced by the periodic—and important—feats of investigative reporting or crisis coverage that bring out the natural adversarial aspects of the business-media relationship and reassure the media about their watchdog, top-dog role."[6]

The societal significance perspective emphasizes issues important to the social fabric and to tensions in that fabric. Two similar events will receive quite different coverage if one has a racial dimension and the other does not. Similarly, issues that have a human cause are more likely to be covered. Two similar health risks associated with food products will receive different coverage if one involves a man-made risk and the other a natural risk. The societal significance perspective also emphasizes forerunners of changes in the social fabric, particularly when moral concerns are raised. An issue such as the responsibility of U.S. companies for the working conditions in the factories of their overseas suppliers has societal significance, as Nike painfully learned.[7]

The societal significance perspective can be summarized as follows. The news media has a special role in a democracy and is assigned, or has assumed, the duty of serving the people's right to know about issues important to the fabric of society. In the United States this duty

---

[6]*Fortune,* October 14, 1985, p. 207.
[7]See the Chapter 4 case *Nike in Southeast Asia.*

is recognized in the First Amendment, which protects the news media in its role of providing information to people. The greater the media's perception of an issue's societal significance, the more likely it is to be covered. Also, the greater the perceived societal significance, the more likely the treatment will be characterized by advocacy consistent with the media's vision of an informed democracy. Issues high on the societal significance dimension include health, safety, environmental protection, human rights, security, and social justice.

Combining the Perspectives

Combining these two perspectives provides a theory of news coverage and treatment as a function of intrinsic audience interest and the media's assessment of the societal significance of the issue. In this theory, treatment depends more on societal significance than on audience interest, whereas coverage depends more on audience interest.

Figure 3-2 illustrates the predictions of the theory, which are refined in the next section. The theory predicts that issues low on both the audience interest dimension and the societal significance dimension will receive little coverage. Most routine business news is in this category as are regulation and antitrust, and coverage usually is limited to the business press. Deregulation of the electric power or telecommunication industry has an important impact on economic efficiency, but economic deregulation has neither high audience interest nor high perceived societal significance. Furthermore, economic deregulation is complex and thus difficult for the media to explain or for readers or viewers to understand. The treatment of such issues tends to be factual, objective, and balanced.

Issues that are high on the audience interest dimension but low on the societal significance dimension include the weather and natural disasters, sports, and entertainment. These issues receive considerable coverage and are generally treated in a factual manner with relatively little advocacy.

Issues low on the audience interest dimension but high on the societal significance dimension include income distribution, foreign policy, and much of politics. Such issues are likely to receive only moderate coverage because of their limited audience interest. Their treatment,

---

FIGURE 3-2   Theory of Media Coverage and Treatment

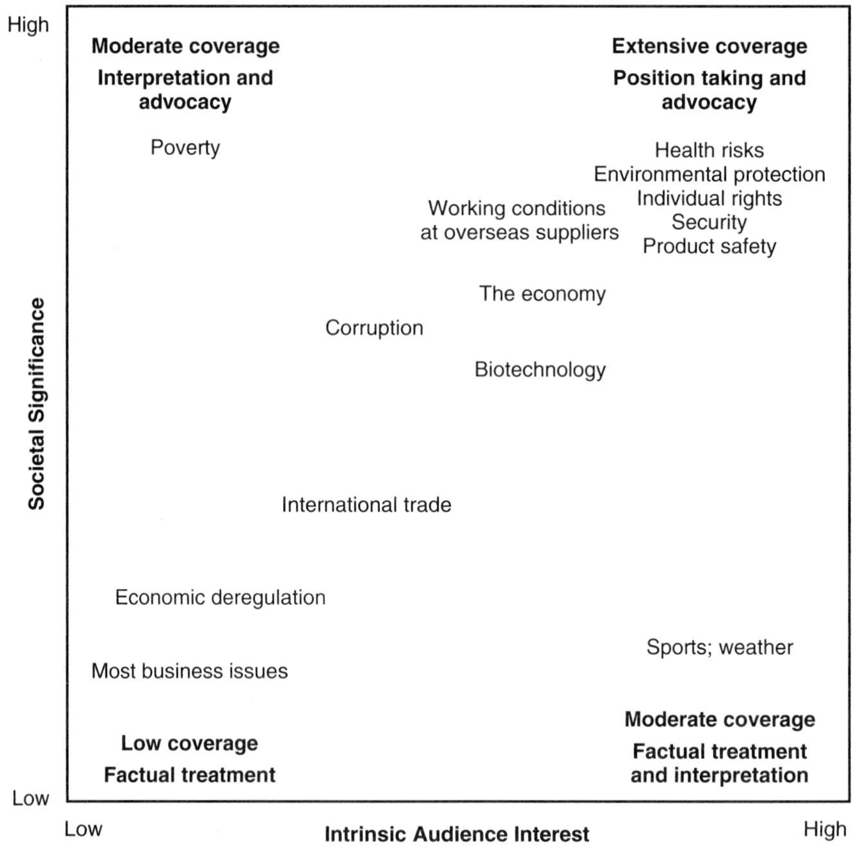

however, may involve a degree of position taking or advocacy. The working conditions in overseas factories are a distant issue for most readers and viewers, but when activists and unions framed it as a human rights issue, it received considerable coverage reflecting its high societal significance as perceived by the media. In its role as a protector of the public's right to know, the news media may advocate a course of action. Treatment of the issue, for example, frequently used the term "sweatshops."

Issues high on both the intrinsic audience interest and societal significance dimensions receive extensive coverage, and their treatment may involve both factual reporting and advocacy. These issues include health, safety, security, environment, human rights, and both natural and man-made crises. A health risk, particularly the protection of society from such a risk, is high on both the audience interest and the societal significance dimensions. Consequently, the Alar issue received considerable coverage, and its treatment reflected the media's perceived duty to warn the public. The media covered the events organized by the NRDC because those events made the story more appealing to audiences. The coverage conveyed the NRDC's message, and by implication the media's treatment advocated that precautions be taken and the government regulate Alar.

Coverage and treatment can differ between the print and broadcast media, between the *New York Times* and the *New York Post,* and Fox News and MSNBC. Moreover, over time issues may change their location in the audience interest–societal significance space. Over the past three decades issues involving health risks and environmental protection have moved to the upper right in Figure 3-2. Similarly, the issue of working conditions in overseas factories was propelled toward the upper right in the 1990s.

This theory of news media coverage and treatment is based on two sufficient conditions—societal significance and intrinsic audience interest. Other features of stories, such as visual effects, human interest, confrontation, and controversy, are also important. The theory is extended along these dimensions in the next section.

EXTENDING THE THEORY

Newsworthiness

The concept of newsworthiness extends the intrinsic audience interest and perceived societal significance dimensions. An issue is more newsworthy if it has a degree of immediacy or urgency. The massive television coverage of a natural disaster such as the earthquake, tsunami, and nuclear power plant meltdown in northern Japan results in part because it is a breaking story. The risk to life and property makes it urgent. The burning of Amazon Basin rain forests has less urgency, but its link to global climate change makes it more immediate than it would otherwise be. A groundwater contamination issue has a greater degree of urgency if there is a possible threat to health, as in the case of hydraulic fracking for natural gas.

An issue is more newsworthy if it has a human interest dimension with which the audience can identify, as in stories about victims of injustice, accidents, or natural disasters. A story is also more interesting if it is told by someone involved in the issue rather than by a correspondent. In an era of remote channel changers, television producers are reluctant to air a "talking head" segment with a correspondent telling a long and complex story. When the story is told by those involved, however, the result is often more than just an eyewitness account, since the participants have an opportunity to make judgments about the issue or advocate action.

An issue often is more newsworthy if it involves a celebrity. The NRDC was correct in thinking that Meryl Streep would attract coverage for the Alar issue. Similarly, the news media may choose to cover an issue because it is entertaining, or it may add an entertainment dimension to the story. Particularly for television, an issue is more newsworthy if it has visual appeal.

A story is more newsworthy if it involves confrontation or controversy. An environmental issue is more newsworthy if it contains allegations that apple growers are creating hazards for an unsuspecting public. A story is more newsworthy if it ties to an issue such as health with high intrinsic audience interest. In particular, linking Alar to the health of children not only provided a human interest dimension but also demonstrated that the news media was fulfilling its role by protecting the public's right to know. A common approach to developing confrontation and controversy in a story is to have each side tell its version of the issue. This provides balance, but it also highlights the controversy.

In contrast, stories about ideas are often difficult to write and present, particularly for a medium such as television. Stories about ideas provide limited opportunities for drama, human interest, or visual effects. The media thus may not give as much coverage to issues centering on ideas as they might merit in terms of their societal significance. To explain why the national news media was slow to cover the savings and loan crisis that cost the economy tens of billions of dollars, Ellen Hume wrote: "It was all too complicated and boring to interest many mainstream journalists. Regulatory changes—such as the accounting tricks and reduced capital requirements that helped paper over the first phase of the savings and loan crisis in the early 1980s—weren't big news…. When asked why TV hadn't covered the crisis much even after it made headlines in 1988, the president of NBC News, Michael Gartner, observed that the story didn't lend itself to images, and without such images, 'television can't do facts.' "[8] Hume added that as the issue developed, the victims (the depositors) did not complain because their deposits were federally insured. Controversy and conflict were absent. Media interest subsequently increased as the magnitude of the crisis became evident and as malfeasance was revealed.

The Cost of Coverage

News coverage depends on the costs of obtaining information and producing a story. Costs include assigning journalists to stories and beats, maintaining bureau offices, getting reporters to where the stories are breaking, and providing editorial and administrative support. Once journalists are assigned to a story and are on location, the marginal cost of coverage is reduced and the media is more likely to use stories from that source. As Edwin Newman (1984, p. 29) stated, "What is news on television often depends on where your reporters and cameramen are. If you keep people at the White House, you will be tempted to use stories from there, if only for economic reasons…. If you send reporters and camera crews on a trip with the secretary of state, you tend to use what they send back. If you staff a story day after day, you will have it on the air day after day."

Both the costs of obtaining information and budget pressures have forced most media organizations to rely increasingly on low-cost sources of information such as interest groups, government agencies, and businesses rather than developing the information firsthand. Firms and interest groups thus are frequently sources of the information the news media needs to present stories. These sources often strategically provide information, and journalists may end up relying on what their sources claim about facts rather than gathering those facts directly.[9] Brooks Jackson, a Cable News Network correspondent and former *Wall Street Journal* reporter, observed, "We usually depend on governmental institutions or groups like Common Cause or Ralph Nader or General Motors or somebody to make sense out of all this data for us."[10]

Balance and Fairness

Journalism standards and editorial controls require that a story be accurate and the treatment be balanced and fair. Accuracy involves not only verifying facts but also ensuring that the story as presented portrays the situation correctly. Balance requires presenting both sides of an issue, which often involves providing an opportunity for the various sides to present their views on the issue. Fairness involves not only ensuring that those involved in an issue have an opportunity to present their views but that a person or subject is not presented or treated in an unjust manner. The latter is particularly relevant on those issues high on the societal significance dimension on which the media may take an advocacy position.

With the growth of cable television and the Internet the number and variety of news programs, blogs, and postings have increased and their nature has changed. The annual report "The State of the News Media" funded by the Pew Charitable Trusts concluded,

> A growing pattern has news outlets, programs, and journalists offering up solutions, crusades, certainty and the impression of putting all the blur of information in clear order for people. The tone may be just as extreme as before, but now the other side is not given equal play. In a sense, the debate in many venues is settled—at least for the host.[11]

---

[8]Ellen Hume, "Why the Press Blew the S&L Scandal," *New York Times,* May 24, 1990.

[9]Baron (2005) provides a theory of strategic provision of information by sources.

[10]Quoted in Ellen Hume, "Why the Press Blew the S&L Scandal," *New York Times,* May 24, 1990.

[11]www.stateofthemedia.org/2007.

THE NATURE OF THE NEWS MEDIA

News Organizations as Businesses

In the United States, news organizations are owned by for-profit companies, so profit is a primary objective. ABC is owned by Walt Disney, CBS by Viacom, NBC by General Electric, and Fox by the News Corporation. As profit-oriented firms, news media companies are interested in attracting readers and viewers, since subscription and advertising revenue depend on audience size. Reuven Frank (1991, p. 222), former president of NBC News, said "The product of commercial television is not programs. If one thinks of making goods to sell, the viewers are not the customers, those who buy the product. Advertisers buy the product, pay money for it. Programs are not what they buy, what they pay for is audience, people to heed their messages. The bigger the audience, the more they pay…."

News organizations are in a highly competitive industry. They compete not only against other companies in the same medium but also across media. Competition has intensified with the rise of Internet news organizations that exploit synergies with broadcast news organizations. Competitive pressures have increased the importance of attracting an audience.[12] Competitive pressures also mean that there are strong incentives to be first with a breaking story, which can affect accuracy.

Young (1978, p. 2) offered a perspective on the implications:

> As more organs of the media are owned by large corporations, whose prime interest is financial, the journalistic principles of a publication can be compromised by—or dissipated in—the business needs. The demand [is] for more circulation, more advertising, and more profit. To achieve these, the media will cater to populist—meaning antibusiness—fears and prejudices, entertain instead of enlighten, pander instead of lead. They reduce big issues to oversimplified personality battles, because both people and disputes make good reading and viewing.

This statement is surely too strong, but it indicates the tension between the incentives to attract an audience and the standards of the journalism profession. The chapter case *The News of the World* provides an opportunity to consider the incentives of a media organization and its reporters.

The Profession

Media decisions are made by people who choose careers in journalism. Journalists are younger, better educated, and more liberal than the American public. A survey by the American Society of Newspaper Editors (ASNE) found, "At the bigger papers, 61 percent of newsroom respondents described themselves as Democrats (or leaning toward Democrat) and only 10 percent as Republicans (or leaning toward Republican)."[13] In 1992, 89 percent of the Washington journalists surveyed voted for Bill Clinton and 7 percent for George H.W. Bush. Sixty-one percent of the journalists rated themselves as liberal or liberal to moderate and 9 percent as conservative or conservative to moderate.[14] Editors were more evenly balanced in their orientation and political preferences.

A widely shared perspective among journalists is that they are serving the public. Some journalists joined the profession in the wake of Robert Woodward and Carl Bernstein's triumph in the Watergate affair. Not only had journalists succeeded in uncovering illegal activity, but their work led to the resignation of a U.S. president. Journalists seek the "scoop that will echo around the world."

Writing before Watergate, Epstein (1973, p. 219), who studied the operations of network television news programs, addressed journalists' views of their role and power.

> Privately almost all network correspondents expressed a strong belief in their ability to effect change in public policy through their work, if not as individuals, then certainly as a group. Some considered their self-perceived political powers "frightening" and "awesome," while others merely depicted them as a necessary part of the political process.

---

[12]The sametype of competitive and performance pressures are present in government-owned media. Küng-Shankleman (2000) provides an analysis of the BBC and CNN as businesses in their market and nonmarket environments.
[13]ASNE, Chapter "Characteristics of the Respondents." www.asne.org.
[14]Povich (1996, p. 137).

Journalism is governed by standards enforced by news media organizations and professional associations.[15] A journalist is trained to present the who, what, where, when, and why of a story. Journalistic judgments, however, can lead to quite different treatments of stories. As an example, the Institute of Medicine, a unit of the National Academies of Science, released a report on the health effects of indoor mold and moisture. On May 26, 2004, the headline in the *Wall Street Journal* read, "Indoor Mold Linked to Problems Such as Asthma and Coughing," the headline in the *San Jose Mercury News* read, "Report: Mold seen as irritant, but not as bad as feared," and the *New York Times* headline read, "Panel Finds Mold in Buildings Is No Threat to Most People."

Journalists seek professional attainment, recognition, and reward. A necessary condition for attainment is that a journalist's work be published or aired and have an impact. Journalists thus have strong incentives to present stories that will pass editorial scrutiny and be sufficiently newsworthy that editors will print or air them. Stories must also be read or viewed, so journalists seek to make their stories engaging. Making stories engaging, however, can result in inaccuracies, bias, and in some cases fabrication. The chapter case *General Motors: Like a Rock? (A)*, considers such a situation.

Does the News Media Treat Issues Selectively?

The news media may not cover every issue under the same criteria. Most issues are treated under controls and editorial standards. On some issues, however, the media takes an advocacy approach, suspending the standards of fairness and balance. Epstein (1973, p. 233) wrote that

> controls tend to be disregarded when executives, producers and correspondents all share the same view and further perceive it to be a view accepted by virtually all thoughtful persons. News reports about such subjects as pollution, hunger, health care, racial discrimination, and poverty fall in this category. On such consensus issues, correspondents are expected by executives openly to advocate the eradication of the presumed evil and even put it in terms of a "crusade," as a CBS vice-president suggested with respect to the pollution issue. At times, however, what are assumed to be commonly held values turn out to be disputed ones in some parts of the country; and when executives are apprised of this (by affiliates and others), the usual "fairness" controls are applied to the subject.

There is certainly consensus on preferring less to more pollution, but often the issue, as in the case of global climate change, is how much reduction in emissions is warranted by the cost and how that cost is to be distributed. On these dimensions, considerable disagreement exists.

In the wake of the firing of Jayson Blair for the fabrication of stories, the *New York Times* created the position of public editor devoted "to receiving, investigating, and answering outsiders' concerns about our coverage." Public editor Daniel Okrent described his conclusions about the coverage of social issues: "And if you think *The Times* plays it down the middle on any of [the social issues], you've been reading the paper with your eyes closed…. [It is] quite another thing to tell only the side of the story your co-religionists wish to hear. I don't think it's intentional when *The Times* does this. But negligence doesn't have to be intentional…. *Times* editors have failed to provide the three-dimensional perspective balanced journalism requires."[16] Okrent referred to *The Times'* coverage as "cheerleading," and his assessment is consistent with Epstein's observation about perceived "consensus issues." The publisher of *The Times* described its consensus viewpoint as "urban."

Bias, Accuracy, and Fairness

The public widely views the media as biased. A survey by the ASNE (1999) revealed that 78 percent of the public believed that there was bias in news reporting.[17] There was little consensus,

---

[15]The Poynter Institute provides information on journalistic ethics: www.poynter.org. Codes of ethics and responsibilities for journalists can be found at www.asne.org/ideas/codes.

[16]*New York Times,* July 25, 2004.

[17]Groseclose and Milyo (2005) found "a very significant liberal bias" in the news media. Eighteen of the 20 news outlets studied were found to be more liberal than the average U.S. voter and "closer to the average Democrat in Congress than to the median member of the House of Representatives." Their methodology required no judgments about which media outlets were liberal or conservative or the degree of bias. They simply counted the number of citations a news publication made to each of 50 think tanks and computed a score by comparing those citations to citations of those think tanks in speeches by members of Congress. The positions of Congress members on a left–right scale were determined using a statistical procedure based on rankings by interest groups.

however, on the nature and direction of the perceived bias. The ASNE wrote, "The public appears to diagnose the root causes of media bias in two forms. First (and at best), bias is a lack of dispassion and impartiality that colors the decision of whether or not to publish a story, or the particular facts that are included in a news report and the tone of how those facts are expressed. Second (and at worst), they see bias as an intent to persuade."

Public confidence in the news media has declined for the past two decades as "The State of the News Media" found. The report stated, "since the early 1980s, the public has come to view the news media as less professional, less accurate, less caring, less moral, and more inclined to cover up rather than correct mistakes."[18] The Edelman Trust Barometer surveys people in 23 countries, and they consistently rank the media last in trustworthiness among business, government, NGOs, and media.

Most nonmarket issues involving business are complex, and the ability to present that complexity and achieve accuracy, balance, and fairness differs considerably among media organizations. Some newspapers and magazines can present complex stories in a comprehensive manner and in enough detail to provide accuracy and balance. Television, however, may not be well suited to presenting complex stories, in part because of the brief time that can be allocated to a story. As Epstein (1980, p. 127) stated, "This enforced brevity leaves little room for presenting complex explanations or multifaceted arguments." As importantly, the need to retain viewer interest requires that a story be attractive and entertaining. The desire to develop human interest and controversy in a limited time slot can lead to sacrifices in balance and accuracy. Qualification and complexity, even when written into a story, may be edited out to provide time for other stories. Many complaints by business executives about television news coverage are due to the simplification needed to fit a story into a restricted time slot. Distortion in a story thus could result from simplification rather than bias.

Because journalists write for the audience and not for the protagonists in a story, the protagonists may view a story as not giving sufficient attention or credence to their side. The difference between the objective of providing information to the public and the subject's desire for a favorable portrayal can lead to a perception of bias.

The treatment of an issue, particularly when advocacy journalism is practiced and editorial controls are suspended, can put firms in a difficult position. News coverage of fires due to the use of space heaters may involve the victims telling of their plight and demanding that the manufacturer and the government take action. Given the framing of the issue, manufacturers may have considerable difficulty providing information about the safety features already incorporated, the possibility that the victims may have misused the heaters, and the measures taken to reduce the likelihood of misuse. The fact that no space heater can be perfectly safe reduces the credibility of such explanations.[19]

Media coverage can also be alarmist, which can put firms in a difficult position. The media coverage in the Alar episode was alarmist, as was coverage of the outbreak of SARS in 2003. Health scares are frequently fanned by the media because "fear sells," but the media can also exercise restraint. Michael Fumento, writing in the *Washington Post,* commented on the media's restraint in the coverage of the first case of mad cow disease in the United States:[20]

> Part of the explanation for the paucity of panic, though probably only a minor one, may be that there's no cause for it—and even the media know this…. Watching the British over the last decade may also have helped us keep our heads level…. The United Kingdom's top BSE official said in 1996 that as many as half a million Britons would die from the bad beef, while an estimate in the *British Food Journal* a year earlier pegged potential deaths at as many as 10 million…. A 2001 study in *Science* magazine estimated the number [of cases] will probably top out at 200.

Sales at McDonald's and other restaurants in the United States were largely unaffected by the case.

Cost pressures on news organizations, journalists' incentives to have stories aired or published, deadlines and space constraints, and competitive pressures can result in inaccuracies in

---

[18]www.stateofthemedia.org/2007.
[19]See the Chapter 14 case *California Space Heaters, Inc.*
[20]*Washington Post,* January 18, 2004.

stories. Cost pressures, for example, led some news organizations to shift some fact-checking responsibilities to their reporters. This resulted in a number of serious violations of professional standards. News organizations responded by strengthening their internal controls. CNN, for example, established an internal watchdog office, the Journalistic Standards and Practices office. Cost and competitive pressures, however, work against stronger internal controls. The chapter case *The News of the World* considers an episode of unprofessional and illegal behavior at a British tabloid.

The Internet and Citizen Journalism

The sources of information about nonmarket issues and the firms affected by them have broadened substantially with the expansion of the Internet. Seventy percent of users report that they access news online, although the percent using online services daily is considerably lower, according to surveys by the Pew Research Center. The sources have also diversified with the advent of blogs and social media. Usage varies with age, with young people relying more on the Internet for news than other sources. A survey of high school students by the Knight Foundation indicated that nearly a third of the respondents viewed blogs as news sources, although only 10 percent viewed blogs as trustworthy compared to 45 percent for television news.

The rise of blogs and social media allows citizens to be journalists, and many use the Internet to comment on nonmarket issues affecting business developments. With information and commentary passed along on the Internet instantly, the media environment of firms has become more complex. Moreover, the public exposure to corporate actions has expanded. Social activists and NGOs use the Internet and social media to communicate with supporters, broaden support for their causes, and challenge companies, as considered in Chapter 4.

Companies have also begun to use blogs and other online forums to disseminate information and communicate with stakeholders, journalists, and the public. These formats can be used to answer questions about the conduct of the company, counter critics, and supply additional information on issues beyond what the mainstream media and blogs report. Companies also use these forums to correct mistakes by the news media or to present another side to a story. Journalists increasingly use such information in the stories they write. These forums can also be used in times of crisis to communicate with the public, as considered in Chapter 5.

BUSINESS INTERACTIONS WITH THE NEWS MEDIA

Business concerns with media coverage and treatment stem from several factors. First, few companies like their activities to be publicly scrutinized. Second, the media guards its independence and in particular does not serve as a public relations arm of firms. Third, the desire for balance and the incentive to develop controversy to make stories appealing often gives critics of the company an opportunity to deliver their message to the public. Fourth, some executives agree with Louis Young that the media caters to antibusiness sentiments. Fifth, particularly in the case of television interviews, the control of the editing process gives the media the opportunity to select the parts of an interview that make the best story, and those may not be the parts business wants to have aired. Sixth, media treatment almost always results in oversimplification, precluding the presentation of a full account of a company's side of the story. Because of these concerns many firms have developed capabilities for interacting with the media.

In interacting with the media, managers should be both cautious and realistic in their expectations. In a case against ABC's *Primetime Live,* Court of Appeals judge Richard Posner wrote, "Investigative journalists well known for ruthlessness promise to wear kid gloves. They break their promise, as any person of normal sophistication would expect. If this is 'fraud,' it is a kind against which potential victims can easily arm themselves by maintaining a minimum skepticism about journalistic goals and method."[21]

The Need for Information

Many business issues are newsworthy, and frequently only business has the information that can serve as the basis for a story. This provides firms with an opportunity to develop a relationship

---

[21]*New York Times,* July 13, 1998.

with news organizations in which they provide the information needed in exchange for stories that will be fair and balanced. As one prominent journalist commented, "We need access [to information] and sources can trade on access." Many firms sustain those relationships through their forthrightness and the credibility of the information they provide. Many firms have professionalized their interactions with the media by employing communications specialists and by giving their managers media training. Business interactions with the media are also broadening as more managers interact with the media.

Media Strategies

Media strategies guide interactions with the media and communication with stakeholders and the public. Evans (1987, pp. 84–87) identified six elements of an effective media strategy:

- The unusual is usual.
- Emphasize the consistency of business and the public interest.
- Remember your audience.
- Communicate through the press.
- The medium is the message.
- Establish credibility—not friendship.

A firm's interactions with the media should be tailored to the audience. In interacting with the media the firm is speaking not just with the journalist but, more importantly, with the audience. The information presented thus should be directed at the likely audience. In the case of an issue that will be covered only by the business press, the information should be tailored for a knowledgeable audience. If the audience is broader, the information should be accessible to the layperson.

For most nonmarket issues the interests of a firm are consistent with some aspect of the public interest or at least with the interests of stakeholders. Emphasizing the effects of the issue not on profits but on stakeholders can be effective, as can pointing out that the practice in question is consistent with the public interest. In interviews, managers thus should not only answer questions but also take the opportunity to make affirmative statements about the firm's practices.

The development of relationships of confidence is easier with the business press than with the general media because of the business press's greater need for information and because it typically assigns journalists to regular beats. The journalist then has an incentive to develop expertise and a relationship with the firm, and the resulting stories may be more accurate and balanced. If a journalist demonstrates an understanding of the industry and the issues, a firm may choose to release its information first to him or her as a reward.

Developing relationships with journalists from the more general news media, particularly television, is often more difficult because fewer journalists are assigned to business beats. For those journalists, the incentive to develop expertise on the business issues can be weak. A journalist assigned to an issue high on the social significance dimension—products with a health risk to children, for instance—may not have expertise on the issue. In such cases it is particularly important for a company to communicate effectively with the journalist and the audience and not leave a media vacuum for others to fill.

Responses and Media Vacuums

On many issues—particularly those that may generate nonmarket action—business prefers to avoid media coverage. One tempting strategy is not to comment to the media in the hope that no story will appear. If it seems likely that the story will appear anyway, a "no comment" strategy can be risky. Especially on issues that are high on the societal significance dimension, the media may take an advocacy approach either directly or indirectly by airing the allegations of others. Leaving a vacuum that the firm's critics can fill with their side of the story can often be more damaging than having the firm tell its side of the story, even if that story is not fully compelling. Providing facts and demonstrating concern, even if the facts are not all favorable to the firm, can narrow the space in which critics can maneuver.

Just as media a vacuum is generally unwise attacking critics is usually not a good strategy, since it can create a second story that can prolong an issue. After a half-time employee of Électricité de France wrote a book criticizing French corporations for their rigid social norms and urging French workers to adopt "calculated loafing" and to "spread gangrene through the system from inside," her employer sent her a letter calling her before a disciplinary hearing. The letter was given to the news media, and coverage of the episode caused sales of the book to skyrocket.[22]

Many firms have concluded that there are some media representatives or programs with which it is better to not talk. Many will not talk with investigative journalism programs such as *60 Minutes* because of concerns about how they and their firm will be portrayed. They prefer a statement such as "The company refused to comment" to risking an interview from which the editors will extract a 15-second clip to be interspersed among interviews with the critics of the firm.

Media Interviews

Because of its importance in the development of nonmarket issues, managers frequently grant interviews to the media and are called on to speak to the public. Media training is customary in many firms, and a communications consulting industry has developed to support that training. Many firms also provide guidelines for their managers in dealing with journalists. The Hewlett-Packard Company's guidelines are presented in Figure 3-3.

Perhaps the best advice for media interviews was given by the publisher of a major newspaper. He said that when dealing with the press, there were three cardinal rules. The first is "Tell the truth." The second is "Tell the truth." The third is "Always remember the first two." A pragmatic version of the publisher's cardinal rules was provided by a judge who said, "Always tell the truth—it's easier to remember." Answering truthfully is always a good policy, but simply responding to questions is not. Managers must be prepared to make affirmative points when responding to an interviewer's questions and seize opportunities to tell the company's side of the story.

When asked to appear for a television interview, some business executives ask to go on live so that their comments cannot be edited. Stations, however, typically will not agree to an unedited interview. The interviewee thus is often advised to answer questions in a manner that makes them difficult to edit. Sometimes a firm may ask the reporter to submit questions in advance, but that request is usually rejected. When agreeing to an interview, some firms find it prudent to audiotape or videotape the interview. Taping the interview provides a record of what transpired and can be useful if a dispute with the media arises. Taping may also caution journalists to be careful about what they write or broadcast. When agreeing to an interview, it is important to recognize that at times the media may already have the story in the can and may be seeking an interview to develop controversy.

Anticipating Issues

Many firms attempt to educate the media about important issues in their nonmarket environment. Some go further and attempt to communicate directly with the interest groups that are likely to

---

FIGURE 3-3 Hewlett-Packard Company Media Guidelines

Hewlett-Packard Company's Twelve Guides for Conducting a Media Interview

- Assume everything you say is "on the record."
- Speak in plain English.
- State your main point or conclusion first.
- If you don't understand a question, say so.
- If presented with a "laundry list" of questions, identify the one question you are responding to before answering it.
- Don't hesitate to repeat an answer.
- Volunteer information to make your points and to give perspective.
- Use anecdotes and illustrations involving people.
- Have fun doing the interview, without being flippant, of course.
- Don't be afraid to admit mistakes.
- Don't expect the editor to clear the story with you before it is published.
- Never, never, never stretch the truth.

---

[22]*New York Times,* August 14, 2004. Corinne Maier, *Bonjour Paresse,* Éditions Michalon, Paris, 2004.

be concerned with issues. To the extent that it can anticipate an issue, a firm is better positioned if it has laid the groundwork to deal effectively with the issue as it progresses through its life cycle.

When a nonmarket issue can be anticipated, the theory of the news media can be used to assess whether the issue is likely to be covered and, if so, the type of treatment it is likely to receive. For those stories that will be covered only by the business press, a firm can hope, and in many cases expect, that the journalist has a degree of expertise in the subject matter of the story. If, in addition, the issue is low on the societal significance dimension, the firm may need to do little more than provide the media with facts along with its side of the issue.

A broader set of news organizations is likely to be attracted to issues that are high on the societal significance dimension, making interactions with the media more complex. Such issues may also attract or be initiated by activist groups or NGOs, as in the case of Alar. These groups can be expected to advance their side of the issue through their own media strategy. The Alar episode was more orchestrated than most, but the point is clear. Interest and activist groups can orchestrate events to advance their causes both in a planned manner and in response to an issue brought to their—and the public's—attention by the media.

When media coverage of an issue can be anticipated, the firm has the opportunity to prepare. Preparation includes gathering the relevant information about the issue and its context and assigning a spokesperson to interact with the media. Preparation also includes evaluating the messages likely to be conveyed by the media and its sources. As discussed in the context of Figure 3-1, the messages are a function not only of the coverage and treatment given to the issue but also of the information the audience already has. Individuals, interest groups, and politicians may evaluate a story in different ways. Some may consider the story in terms of their own self-interest, whereas others may look at it in terms of broader principles. These varied evaluations can result in market and nonmarket actions that affect the progress of the issue and cause change in the firm's environment.

Unanticipated Events

Because events such as environmental accidents can occur, firms should have a routine to follow in the event of a breaking story. For serious matters firms should have a crisis management plan, as considered in Chapter 5. If the issue is one that need not be made public—embezzlement, for example—the first decision is whether to release the information to the news media or attempt to keep it confidential. The latter can be successful in many cases, but leaks occur more often than most managers think.

If the incident is public, the first step is to gather as much information as possible as quickly as possible. There is little that can damage a firm more than having others uncover information that management itself does not have. An accurate record-keeping system that, for example, keeps track of the toxic wastes generated by a plant and where they are disposed can be essential. Having the facts readily accessible not only allows the firm to be in the position of being the best source of information for the media but also provides a basis on which management can develop a strategy for addressing the underlying issue. In implementing a strategy, it is also often wise for the firm to speak with a single voice. The spokesperson must have all the information on the issue so as not to be blindsided and to better anticipate the story's likely development.

RECOURSE IN DISPUTES WITH THE MEDIA

Private Recourse

The subjects of news coverage at times perceive stories to be incomplete, inaccurate, or unfair. Some take actions ranging from writing to the editor to correct inaccuracies to initiating legal action. Firms may also take economic measures against the media by, for example, withdrawing advertising in response to a story that management believes has misrepresented the facts. The Procter & Gamble example describes one such case. When neither economic measures nor legal action is warranted, companies can bring concerns about a story to the attention of the media. Some firms make a practice of notifying editors about their concerns, with the objectives of improving future stories and establishing a reputation for being ready to act.

The news media is governed by professional standards, and journalists and editors develop and maintain reputations for professionalism. Organizations such as the Society of Professional

Journalists, Sigma Delta Chi, and the ASNE work to foster high professional standards and ethics in journalism. Media organizations discipline their correspondents, editors, and managers who violate professional standards. Correspondents may be suspended, reassigned, or fired for violations. In the chapter case *General Motors: Like a Rock? (A)*, NBC took disciplinary actions when it was revealed that its *Dateline* producers and correspondents had used a model rocket engine to ignite a fire during a test collision of a GM truck. NBC reassigned the correspondent and fired the producer of the *Dateline* segment. The senior producer and the executive producer of *Dateline* resigned, and Michael Gartner, president of NBC News, also resigned. NBC created the position of ombudsman to supplement its professional standards and to review segments produced for its news programs as well as programs such as *Dateline*.

Recourse to the Law: Defamation and Libel

Defamation is a branch of torts pertaining to false statements made to a third party that damage a person's reputation.[23] The category of "person" includes not only humans but legal entities such as corporations. Defamation takes the form of either libel or slander. Libel pertains to statements

---

EXAMPLE   Procter & Gamble and Neighbor to Neighbor

Neighbor to Neighbor, an activist group located in San Francisco, opposed U.S. support for the government in El Salvador and called for the end of military aid to that country. The group claimed that coffee growers in El Salvador financed death squads with money obtained from exporting coffee to the United States. From the group's perspective, U.S. coffee companies that imported Salvadoran coffee beans were supporting the death squads.

Neighbor to Neighbor took its message to the American public by placing advertisements in the *New York Times,* the *New London Day* (Connecticut), and *The Progressive* magazine. The group also advocated a consumer boycott of U.S. coffee brands. The best-selling U.S. brand was Folgers, produced by the Procter & Gamble Company (P&G). To generate support for the boycott, the group produced a 30-second television commercial that it planned to air on several television stations. The commercial, narrated by Ed Asner, named only Folgers and showed an upside-down coffee cup dripping blood.[1] The inscription on the cup read "Seal of Salvadoran Coffee," and Asner said, "The murderous civil war in El Salvador has been supported by billions of American tax dollars and by the sale of Salvadoran coffee.... Boycott Folgers. What it brews is misery and death."[2]

Of the 30 television stations approached by Neighbor to Neighbor, all but two rejected the commercial. After reviewing it for taste and content, investigating its content, and obtaining legal advice on the possibility of libel suits, the CBS affiliate WHDH-TV in Boston broadcast the commercial twice in May 1990. Seymour L. Yamoff, president

and general manager of WHDH-TV, stated, "The information on this particular commercial is correct.... We screen them for accuracy, libel, slander and 'Do they meet a standard of fairness?'" He also stated that the station had never broadcast such "issue advertisements" other than in election campaigns, and he could not recall any such advertisement being aired in Boston during the 20 years he had lived there.

P&G was shocked by the commercial. It purchased coffee from 30 countries, and less than 2 percent of its supply came from El Salvador. P&G was one of the largest television advertisers and provided advertising revenue of $1 million annually to WHDH-TV. That represented nearly 2 percent of the station's advertising revenue. The revenue from broadcasting the Neighbor to Neighbor commercial totaled less than $1,000.

P&G decided to withdraw its advertising from WHDH-TV and threatened to withdraw its advertising from any other station that broadcast the ad. WHDH-TV hired a *Washington Post* reporter, Scott Armstrong, to conduct an inquiry into the commercial. In the draft of his report, he concluded "that certain conclusions ... were not substantiated."[3] As a result of the report, WHDH-TV adopted a new policy: "Any public-issue commercials submitted to the station in the future will be broadcast only after the truth of their claims has been determined."[4] "A P&G spokesman said, 'We were satisfied that WHDH had on further review concluded that certain representations in the anti-Folgers ad were not substantiated and ... it was an appropriate time to resume advertising on that station.'"[5] As a result of a peace accord between the government and rebels in El Salvador in March 1992, the boycott was called off.

---

[1] The print advertisements had mentioned other coffee brands in addition to Folgers.

[2] *Boston Globe,* December 12, 1990. A similar commercial calling for a boycott of Hills Brothers Coffee was aired on the West Coast where Hills Brothers had its largest market share.

[3] *Boston Globe,* December 12, 1990.
[4] Ibid.
[5] Ibid.

---

[23] A tort is a civil wrong that damages a person or property.

that are either written or broadcast, whereas slander pertains to statements that are spoken. A finding of slander requires a showing of actual damages, but a finding of libel generally does not require such a showing. Defamation cases are governed by state law and the common law. Defamation cases generally center on statements made in public, but in *Dun & Bradstreet v. Greenmoss Builders,* 472 U.S. 749 (1985), Greenmoss Builders was awarded $350,000 when Dun & Bradstreet issued an erroneous credit report. Thus, defamation more generally applies to a statement made to a third party.

A defendant in a defamation suit has several possible defenses, which fall into the categories of "truth" and "privilege." A defendant always has the defense that what was said, written, or broadcast was the truth. In some U.S. states truth constitutes an absolute defense, whereas in others it may be subject to limitations such as those arising from laws on privacy. For example, in some states it is illegal to disclose that someone has been convicted of a crime or has a disease.

The courts exercise judgment in assessing a truth defense. In 1990, 20 Washington State apple growers filed suit against CBS and the NRDC seeking $250 million in damages, alleging that the *60 Minutes* segment on Alar had led to a panic among consumers that cost the state's growers $150 million in sales. A federal district judge dismissed the suit because the plaintiffs had not shown that the broadcast was false. The judge stated, "Even if CBS's statements are false, they were about an issue that mattered, cannot be proven as false and therefore must be protected."[24] CBS had argued that its story was based on an EPA report, and the judge stated, "A news reporting service is not a scientific testing lab, and these services should be able to rely on a scientific Government report when they are relaying the report's contents."[25]

A degree of privilege is provided to the media by the First Amendment, which extends protection but does not provide an absolute defense. In *New York Times v. Sullivan,* 376 U.S. 254 (1964), the Supreme Court delineated a standard of proof required of plaintiffs in a defamation lawsuit.[26] The ruling requires plaintiffs who are "public figures" to show that the statement in question was made with actual malice—that is, either with knowledge that it was false or with "reckless disregard" for whether it was true.[27] Being careless or sloppy with the facts is not sufficient for a finding of libel. In a complex case, the court attempts to balance the rights of the plaintiff with the rights of the media as provided by the First Amendment. Although plaintiffs win some libel suits against the media, the media is generally successful in the United States in defending itself given the protection provided by the Constitution and Supreme Court rulings.

The rationale for the standard enunciated in *Sullivan* is that although persons retain rights to privacy, they lose a degree of privateness when they participate in "public" activities. The publicness of a plaintiff is not restricted to public officeholders but also pertains to private citizens who voluntarily appear in public. A corporate executive who makes public speeches or testifies in public hearings may be held to be a public figure in a defamation suit. Thus, a corporate plaintiff in a defamation suit may have to meet the standard of proof delineated in *Sullivan.*

To illustrate the application of this standard, in 1981 anchorman Walter Jacobson of CBS's Chicago television station WBBM stated in a commentary that Brown & Williamson Tobacco Corporation was trying to lure young people to its Viceroy cigarette by using a marketing strategy that related the cigarette to "pot, wine, beer, and sex." Jacobson based his commentary on a Federal Trade Commission (FTC) study that reported that a Brown & Williamson advertising agency had hired a consultant who had proposed such a strategy. The FTC study, however, did not indicate that Brown & Williamson had adopted the consultant's recommendations. Indeed, Jacobson's assistant had told him prior to the broadcast that the company had rejected the proposed strategy. In spite of having been so informed, Jacobson made his commentary. The jury concluded that Jacobson made a statement that he knew to be false and held for

---

[24]*Auvil v. CBS "60 Minutes,"* 836 F. Supp. 740 [E.D. Wash.].

[25]*New York Times,* September 15, 1993.

[26]This case arose when supporters of Martin Luther King placed an advertisement in the *New York Times* describing the activities of the Alabama police. The advertisement contained "several minor inaccuracies and exaggerations" (Schmidt, 1981), and an Alabama jury found that the supporters and the newspaper were guilty of defamation under state law. The Supreme Court viewed a standard requiring complete accuracy as conflicting with the First Amendment's protection of freedom of the press.

[27]If the plaintiff proves actual malice, the court presumes there is actual damage, relieving the plaintiff of the burden of proving damages.

Brown & Williamson. The jury awarded $3 million in compensatory damages and $2 million in punitive damages against CBS and WBBM and $50,000 in punitive damages against Jacobson. A federal judge reduced the compensatory damages to $1, but the Court of Appeals reinstated $1 million in compensatory damages. The decision was appealed to the Supreme Court, which allowed the Court of Appeals decision to stand.

A relatively untested aspect of the law pertains to information posted on the Internet. Such postings can be widely disseminated and could form the basis for a defamation lawsuit. Online service providers could also be the potential subject of a lawsuit if they played a role in maintaining a bulletin board or exercising editorial control over postings or access. The Communications Decency Act of 1996 provides a degree of protection to Internet service providers, and that law has protected eBay against defamation and other lawsuits, as indicated in Chapter 2. No case has yet reached the Supreme Court to clarify the application of the law, but the Court of Appeals ruled that AOL was not liable for postings on its Web site.

Libel laws differ considerably across countries. In the United Kingdom libel cases have been easier for plaintiffs to win in part because defendants do not have the protection of *Sullivan*. In the 1980s McDonald's filed a libel suit against Greenpeace volunteers in the United Kingdom who had distributed leaflets criticizing the company's policies. In the longest trial in UK history the court ruled in favor of McDonald's and ordered the volunteers to pay £60,000. The court, however, soundly criticized McDonald's and its practices.[28] The episode, known as McLibel, attracted widespread public attention, support for the volunteers, and hostility toward McDonald's. In a complaint against the UK government for stifling their rights to criticize a company, the volunteers took their case to the European Court of Human Rights in Strasbourg, which in 2005 ruled in favor of the volunteers.

The UK considered changing its libel laws to make it more difficult for plaintiffs to win lawsuits and to stop libel tourism. In one case, a Saudi Arabian businessman filed a libel suit against an American author over a book that had sold only 23 copies in the United Kingdom.[29] The media in the UK had had enough and lobbied the three principal political parties for a change in the law, which all three parties supported. In addition to curbing libel tourism the draft legislation provided greater protection for the media for stories that were true. The legislation was supported by free speech activists, but some argued that it did not go far enough to protect the media. Some favored protection such as that provided by *Sullivan*. Independently of the legislative initiative, the courts were reining in libel tourism. In 2011 a UK court dismissed a lawsuit filed in London by a Ukrainian billionaire against a Ukrainian newspaper.[30] Prior to the legislative effort, as discussed in Chapter 1, a Telsa Motors filed a defamation lawsuit in the UK against *On the Road* for an unfavorable story on the Telsa roadster's battery life.

Political Recourse

The First Amendment provides protection to the news media, and *Sullivan* strengthens that protection in the case of public figures. Commercial speech, however, receives less protection. Although the apple industry failed to obtain relief in the courts, the Alar episode generated considerable sympathy for the industry. The American Feed Industry Association (AFIA), a trade association, seized the opportunity and hired a law firm specializing in food and drug issues to draft a model "food-disparagement bill" for introduction in state legislatures. The model bill would change state libel laws to provide a cause for action against a party that made "disparaging statements" or disseminated "false information" about the safety of a food product. Steve Kopperud, senior vice president of AFIA, said, "There has been long-standing frustration … that an activist organization, for the price of a full-page ad in *USA Today,* can say whatever it wishes to scare the public."[31] Thirteen states enacted versions of the model bill, which became known as "veggie-libel" laws. Critics of these laws argued that they placed the burden of proof on defendants to demonstrate conclusive scientific evidence, which they argued was a standard that would stifle free speech.

---

[28]The volunteers appealed, but their appeal was rejected. A description of the case can be found at www.mcspotlight.org/case. A documentary film, *McLibel,* of the episode was produced and widely circulated.

[29]*New York Times,* March 21, 2011.

[30]Ibid.

[31]Marianne Lavelle, *National Law Journal,* May 5, 1997.

SUMMARY

The news media is a major source of information for those in the nonmarket environment. It alerts the public, activists and NGOs, public officeholders, and interest groups to nonmarket issues and the activities of firms. Those interested in advancing an issue may attempt to use the media as a component of their nonmarket strategies. Although the media guards its independence, it may at times find components of those strategies to be newsworthy, as in the Alar episode.

Because the news media plays an important role in the development of nonmarket issues, managers must assess which issues the media is likely to cover and the treatment those issues are likely to receive. The theory of coverage and treatment predicts that the news media will cover issues with intrinsic audience interest or perceived societal significance. Stories are more likely to be newsworthy if they have broad audience interest, immediacy, human interest, controversy and conflict, and, for television and the Internet, visual appeal. Societal significance pertains to the media's role as a protector of the public's right to know. In this role, the media may at times engage in advocacy by making judgments or supporting particular policies.

The media needs information for its stories, and on many issues business is the best and least-costly source of information. Firms thus have an opportunity to develop relationships with journalists who cover business issues on a regular basis. Managers may be called on to interact with the media, and to prepare for those interactions, they need to be fully informed about the issue in question as well as about the likely audience.

Business issues are often complex and may be difficult for television and the general media to cover. Although the media applies standards of accuracy, fairness, and balance to a story, it has incentives to make the story appealing to the audience and therefore may overemphasize conflict and controversy. It may also simplify a story to fit a time slot, a space limit, or a dead-line. Many of the complaints about news coverage of business result from oversimplification.

The news media is both a business and a profession. Media companies are motivated by profit considerations, and journalists have career interests. Editorial controls govern conduct, and journalists are guided by professional standards. A tension, however, exists between those standards and corporate and individual incentives, as the *The News of the World* chapter case indicates.

The subjects of media stories frequently believe that they were unfairly treated or that a story was inaccurate or biased. One means of recourse is a defamation lawsuit, but such lawsuits are typically costly and difficult to win. The standard under which a case is judged is important to its eventual outcome. For a public figure, the standard is articulated in *New York Times v. Sullivan*. This standard provides considerable protection for the media because a public figure must show actual malice and a "reckless disregard" for the truth.

Some critics have called for restraints on the news media. Despite its lapses and occasional abuses, the news media plays an essential role in a democracy, and the imperfections in the coverage and treatment of stories may be the cost borne for the benefits provided. As Thomas Jefferson wrote, "Were it left to me to decide whether we should have a government without newspapers or newspapers without a government, I should not hesitate to prefer the latter."[32]

CASES

General Motors: Like a Rock? (A)

In 1992 the General Motors Corporation struggled through rocky management shake-ups and its third consecutive year of red ink. If any silver lining could be found in GM's financial cloud, it was its line of pickup trucks. Large pickups were one of GM's few profitable products from its ailing North American operations. Sales of Chevy and GMC full-size pick-ups exceeded half a million in 1991. Greater expectations for 1992 and 1993 coincided with a beefed-up marketing campaign centering on the theme "Like a Rock." However, as events unfolded, GM management found itself between a rock and a hard place.

In 1992 the Center for Auto Safety (CAS) petitioned NHTSA to recall some 5 million Chevrolet and GMC full-size pickup trucks. The CAS claimed that more than 300 people

---

had died in side-impact accidents involving the trucks. Unlike most other pickups, GM class C/K pickups built during the years 1973–1987 were equipped with twin "side-saddle" gasoline tanks positioned outside the main frame rails. In 1987 GM made a design change in its trucks and brought the tanks inside the frame.

The CAS petition was not the first sign of a potential problem in GM's pickups. For years GM had managed to avoid the eye of the media by fighting on a case-by-case basis as many as 140 fuel tank-related lawsuits. Most were settled out of court with settlements occasionally exceeding $1 million. Throughout these legal proceedings, GM steadfastly defended the overall safety of its trucks. GM regularly pointed out that the NHTSA standard called for crashworthiness at 20 mph, and its pickups easily met that standard. In the 1970s GM regularly tested its trucks with side-impact crashes at 30 mph. In the mid-1980s it increased its internal standard to 50 mph. That fires sometimes broke out in the highest speed tests was not disputed but rather was viewed by GM as evidence that it was pushing its tests to the limit in an effort to make its trucks safer.

Data and interpretations concerning the relative safety of GM trucks were mixed. According to NHTSA, GM's side-saddle trucks were 2.4 times as likely as Ford's to be involved in deadly side-impact crashes. According to the Insurance Institute for Highway Safety—a research group supported by insurance companies—the GM trucks might be slightly more prone to fire than similar models built by Ford and Chrysler, but they could be far safer in certain kinds of accidents. This conclusion, according to GM, suggested a need for a broader and more appropriate criterion of safety—that of overall crashworthiness. At least one large database on accidents indicated that in terms of the overall probability of a fatal accident, GM trucks were marginally safer than their competitors.

In November 1992, NBC's *Dateline* aired a 15-minute segment entitled, "Waiting to Explode?" Its focus was the GM series C/K pickup trucks. In preparation for the segment, the NBC news crew hired three "safety consultants" to assist in conducting two crash tests of GM pickups on a rural Indiana road on October 24. Each test simulated a side-impact crash by using a tow truck to push a Chevy Citation along the road into a pickup. The pickup was parked on the road perpendicular to the oncoming car, which slammed into the pickup's passenger side. A minute-long videotape of the tests was aired, and correspondent Michele Gillen stated that the tests were "unscientific." In the first of the tests, Gillen stated that the car was moving at about 40 mph. The truck was jolted significantly, but no fire ensued. In the second test, a fire broke out at a speed stated to be 30 mph. In the broadcast one safety consultant described the fire as "a holocaust."

After the nationally televised broadcast that reached approximately 11 million viewers, GM officials examined the NBC test segment in slow motion. Suspicions arose. GM wrote to NBC almost immediately, stating that the show was unfair and requesting NBC's test data. NBC refused to comply. In a follow-up contact, GM asked NBC to allow it to inspect the pickups. On January 4 the producer of *Dateline* told GM the

vehicles were "junked and therefore are no longer available for inspection."

In the meantime, 32-year-old Pete Pesterre, editor of the magazine *Popular Hot Rodding,* had been pursuing some suspicions of his own. He was intimately familiar with GM trucks. He had owned four of them and once was involved in a side-impact crash from which he emerged unscathed. After Pesterre wrote an editorial criticizing the *Dateline* segment, a reader from Indiana called Pesterre and informed him that he knew a Brownsburg, Indiana, firefighter who was at the scene of the NBC crash tests. When the Brownsburg Fire Department is on assignment, as it was the day NBC staged the crashes, its firefighters customarily videotape the action for subsequent use in training. GM contacted the fire chief, who provided a copy of the tape. Similarly, GM learned that an off-duty sheriff's deputy was on site and had also videotaped the tests. GM also acquired his tape.

To analyze the tapes (including NBC's), GM called on its Hughes Aircraft subsidiary to deploy digital-enhancement techniques for sophisticated frame-by-frame analysis. These investigations revealed that NBC had been less than precise about both the sequence and speeds of the two tests. The first test conducted was the second test aired. The GM/Hughes analysis suggested the actual speed was 39 mph instead of the 30 mph stated in the *Dateline* segment.[33] This test yielded the so-called holocaust. In the other test NBC claimed a speed of 40 mph, but GM/Hughes concluded the speed was 47 mph. No fire occurred in this test.

Another revelation came from the audio portion of the firefighter's tape. After the first test—which, although slower, did produce a fire—the firemen were noticeably unimpressed with the outcome. It was clear that the fire was confined to the grass, short lived, and not life endangering. One firefighter laughed, and one said, "So much for that theory."

Meanwhile, GM was able to locate and acquire the two wrecked Citations and the two wrecked pickups. The recovered pickups were sent to GM's plant in Indianapolis where workers discovered a model rocket engine in the bed of one truck. Inspections of the bottom of the truck uncovered flare marks and remnants of duct tape in two places where GM's video analysis had curiously shown both smoke and fire in frames prior to impact in the crash. Additional inspection of tapes and photographs fueled suspicions that a detonator or starter device had been wired to the rocket engine.

GM officials wanted to examine the trucks' fuel tanks but they had been stripped from the trucks. GM immediately went to court seeking a restraining order to bar one of the NBC consultants from disposing of the fuel tanks. Days later, through his attorney, GM learned that the consultant had given the tanks to a neighbor. Eventually GM obtained the tanks.

Having obtained the pickups and the tanks, GM identified and contacted the trucks' previous owners. From the

---

[33]The 9 mph is important because energy is a function of the square of the velocity. To be precise, $e = .5MV^2$, where e is kinetic energy, M is mass, and V is velocity.

owner of the truck that was struck and caught fire, GM learned that the gas cap was nonstandard. The owner had lost gas caps several times and in the last instance obtained one that did not fit correctly. GM also strongly suspected that the tank had been "topped off" with gasoline prior to the test. (Tanks are designed with five gallons of excess space to make topping off impossible with properly functioning fuel pumps.) GM sent the gas tank of the truck to an X-ray lab and a metallurgist to test whether, as NBC correspondent Gillen claimed, the tank was punctured and therefore was responsible for the fire. According to the experts, it was not punctured. GM had therefore amassed considerable data that supported a different theory about the crash results and the *Dateline* segment. The pieces of the puzzle were as follows:

- A possibly topped-off tank
- A faulty fuel cap in the truck involved in the fiery accident
- Rocket engines that flared prior to impact
- Footage indicating that the fire was confined primarily to grass and did not engulf the cab of the pickup
- Fuel tanks that, contrary to NBC claims, had not been punctured

Additionally, GM conducted background checks on NBC's "safety experts" and learned the following:

- The consultant referred to by NBC as "vice president of the Institute for Safety Analysis" had no engineering background but was a former stock-car driver with a BA in Asian studies.
- The second consultant worked as a "safety consultant" for trial lawyers and had worked as a consultant for ABC News in seven segments on auto safety. He majored in industrial design but did not complete college.
- The third was from the Institute for Injury Reduction, a nonprofit organization that tests products for plaintiffs' attorneys. He had no college degree but studied Japanese and had a diploma in Korean from the U.S. Government's Defense Language School.

On Monday, February 1, 1993, GM's executive vice president and general counsel, Harry Pearce, presented these findings to GM's board of directors. When asked how the directors responded, Pearce said, "They were shocked."

In January, GM had sent yet another letter to Robert Read, the *Dateline* producer, this time detailing GM's specific findings. Read responded without informing either NBC President Robert Wright or NBC News President Michael Gartner. In a subsequent letter to Read dated February 2, GM carbon-copied Wright and Gartner, finally bringing the case to

the attention of top NBC officials. NBC management responded by having its top public relations advisers and NBC General Counsel Richard Cotton draft a letter from Gartner to GM. The letter asserted three separate times that the NBC story was entirely accurate. "NBC does not believe that any statements made … were either false or misleading … the *Dateline* report was and remains completely factual and accurate."[34]

On February 4, 1993, an Atlanta jury awarded $101 million in punitive damages and $4.2 million in compensatory damages to the parents of a 17-year-old boy killed in a fiery death in a GM C/K pickup. The parents had argued that the placement of the fuel tank outside the frame of the pickup made it vulnerable to puncturing during a collision. GM's defense in the trial had been that the boy had died instantly during the collision which, the GM attorney argued, occurred at such a high speed that the death could not be blamed on the truck's design.

On Friday, February 5—the morning after the verdict in the liability case and a few days before a scheduled press conference by the CAS—GM management had a weekend to consider some delicate strategic options. One major option was to file a defamation suit against NBC. Defamation was the communication (e.g., by journalists) to a third party (e.g., viewers) of an untrue statement of fact that injures the plaintiff (GM). A second major option was to go public with the information it had developed on the *Dateline* segment. With the liability verdict and its aftermath fresh in the news, GM would be taking a significant risk in drawing still more attention to its pickups. Said one Wall Street analyst, "A successful rebuttal won't make anybody go out and buy trucks. The publicity [of an aggressive defense by GM and an attack on GM's critics] can't do anything but harm GM."[35] This perspective reflected the rule of thumb that "any news is bad news" when it involves a major company, a less than perfectly safe product, and a high level of public sensitivity toward product safety. ▪

Preparation Questions

1. From GM's perspective, what are the nonmarket issues? What are their sources? Where are they in their life cycles?
2. Should GM fight the *Dateline* issue as a matter of principle? Why or why not?
3. What kind of media coverage should GM anticipate over the next week? Does GM have any control or influence over this situation?
4. Should GM file a defamation suit and/or go public with its findings about the *Dateline* segment?
5. In the position of Mr. Gartner at NBC, what would you have done upon receiving GM's letter and findings?

---

[34]*Wall Street Journal*, February 11, 1993.

[35]*Wall Street Journal*, February 8, 1993.

The News of the World

INTRODUCTION

The Sunday tabloid *The News of the World* died on July 10, 2011. The newspaper had the largest readership in the United Kingdom with a circulation of 2.8 million and was profitable, but its reporters had for years hacked into the cell phones of prominent UK residents, paid police for information for stories, and possibly committed other questionable acts. The demise of the newspaper began as the rival newspaper *The Guardian* reported information about *The News of the World* based on its own investigative journalism, and the scandal spread as far as Prime Minister David Cameron and Rupert Murdock, CEO and chairman of the News Corporation, owner of *The News of the World*. The attention paid to the case exploded when it was revealed that reporters had hacked into the cell phone of a missing 13-year old girl who had been kidnapped and later was found murdered. The revelations led to arrests, grilling of Rupert Murdock and his son James by a committee of Parliament, resignations of several former editors of the newspaper, extensive investigations and litigation, and possible criminal charges. The Federal Bureau of Investigation (FBI) in the United States began an investigation of the News Corporation newspapers. As the scandal grew Murdock closed the paper. The full story would only be known as investigations were completed and cases prosecuted, and this case presents the issues as of mid-2011.

BACKGROUND

Rupert Murdoch was the son of an Australian newspaperman, Oxford educated, and later became an American citizen. He had built the News Corporation into a global media empire, and although newspapers represented only 3 percent of the company's profits, they were of special interest to him. News Corporation was highly successful, although in recent years performance had slipped, and the 80-year-old Murdoch had been criticized for making some questionable acquisitions. For example, News Corporation paid $5.6 billion for the *Wall Street Journal* in 2007 and was forced to write off half the investment within 2 years.

The News of the World was owned by News International, which also owned the weekday *Sun*, and News International was owned by the News Corporation, which also owned *The Times* of London and the *Sunday Times*. The News Corporation also owned Sky News, 39 percent of satellite TV broadcaster British Sky Broadcasting (BSkyB), and had made a £12 billion offer for the rest of BSkyB.

James Murdoch was CEO of BSkyB and Deputy COO of News Corporation with responsibilities for Europe and Asia, and he had headed of News International during the late 2000s. The 38-year-old was believed to be the heir apparent in the News Corporation.

The Murdoch newspapers were powerful in the UK, and executives interacted frequently with government officials. Tim Bale, a political scientist at the University of Sussex, said, "British politicians had gotten the idea, rightly or wrongly, that they couldn't win an election without the endorsement of Murdoch and his newspapers."[36] Newspapers in the UK typically had a partisan orientation, with the Murdoch papers being conservative and *The Guardian* being left-leaning.

News Corporation officials traveled in high company. Rupert Murdoch had frequently visited the previous prime minister Gordon Brown at Number 10 Downing Street, the residence and office of the Prime Minister. Murdoch also had visited newly elected prime minister David Cameron on his second day in office. Rebekah Brooks, CEO of News International and former editor of the *Sun*, was a favorite of Murdoch's and also was highly visible in London society. Brooks was also a friend of Prime Minister Cameron.

THE SCANDAL AS OF JULY 2011

The beginning of the scandal was *The News of the World* article that revealed details of the knee surgery on Prince William. The royal family had never released any information on the knee problem or the surgery and suspicions arose that the cell phones of the staff of the royal family had been hacked. Scotland Yard investigated, leading to the arrest and imprisonment in 2007 of royal editor Clive Goodman and a private investigator Glenn Mulcaire, who was under contract to *The News of the World*. Both had signed confidentiality agreements and remained silent about the case.[37] Scotland Yard viewed the case as closed. *The News of the World* said that the case was the result of a single "rogue reporter" (Goodman), whom the newspaper had fired. In 2011 it was revealed that News International continued to pay the legal fees for Goodman and Mulcaire.

Goodman protested the firing and filed a wrongful termination lawsuit against the newspaper, arguing that hacking by reporters was widespread. News International hired a law firm to investigate the situation, and the firm issued a carefully worded and narrowly framed letter stating that the hacking appeared to be confined to Goodman. As the scandal began to unfold in 2011 News International hired Lord Ken Macdonald, a former head of public prosecutions, to reexamine the evidence. He stated that clear evidence of criminality was "blindly obvious" after a review of "three to five minutes."[38] Five former reporters for the Sunday tabloid *The People* said there was frequent hacking in the newsroom in the late 1990s and early 2000s. One said, "I don't think anyone quite realized the criminality of it."[39]

When Mulcaire was arrested in 2006, the police seized his detailed notes on his investigations. When the scandal began to unfold in 2011, the police reexamined the notes and found evidence of widespread hacking of celebrities and government officials with some 4,000 names appearing in the notes.[40] The most incendiary case was the hacking of the cell phone of a 13-year-old girl who was missing and feared

---

[36]*Economist*, July 18–24, 2011.
[37]Scotland Yard is a term used to refer to the Metropolitan Police Service.
[38]*New York Times*, July 21, 2011.
[39]Ibid.
[40]Mulcaire was the subject of 37 lawsuits alleging hacking, and more were likely.

kidnapped. The inbox on the phone was full, and the hackers deleted messages so that new messages could be received. This gave false hopes to the parents that she was still alive. She was later found murdered.

The *News* also settled for £725,000 a privacy violation lawsuit filed by Gordon Taylor, head of the soccer union in the UK, even though no story was ever written.[41] Details of the case were never revealed, but the amount paid was far beyond what was typically paid to settle privacy lawsuits. James Murdoch, who was head of News International, approved the payment and later said that he had been advised that the settlement was reasonable, since the company was likely to lose in court and the cost could be as high a £1 million.[42]

As more privacy violation cases were filed in 2010, James Murdoch said, "the company immediately went to look at additional records" and turned the information over to the police.[43] He said he had been given bad advice and had been told that the hacking was the work of a single reporter.

A select committee of Parliament took up the case and held hearing in July. In his testimony Rupert Murdoch expressed outrage and said he was the right man for the job of cleaning house. He stated, "I feel that people I trusted—I don't know who, on what level—have let me down, and I think they have behaved disgracefully, and it's for them to pay. And I think, frankly, that I'm the best person to see it through."[44]

In the hearing the Murdochs denied knowledge of the hacking and payments to the police, and James Murdoch stated that his understanding had been that the hacking was the work of a single reporter. Within a few days of their testimony three News International executives stated that there were inaccuracies in the Murdochs' testimony.

The scandal led Brooks to resign, and the following day she was arrested by Metropolitan Police on suspicion of hacking and making corrupt payments to police. In 2003 when Brooks was the editor of the *Sun* she told the same Parliament committee, "We have paid the police for information in the past." In 2011 she clarified her statement saying it was based on a "widely held belief." In the UK an arrest is the first step in a criminal investigation and charges often are not filed against the individual arrested.[45] None of the 10 people arrested was charged with a crime, and all were quickly released. Brooks was held for 12 hours.[46]

After Prime Minister Cameron expressed concerns about News Corporation acquiring the rest of BSkyB, the company withdrew the offer. The UK regulator Ofcom, which was responsible for licensing, began an investigation into whether News Corporation met the "fit and proper" standard for a broadcast license.

Cameron had hired Andy Coulson, former editor of *The News of the World*, as his communications director on the recommendation of Chancellor of the Exchequer George Osborne. Coulson had resigned as editor of the *News* in 2007 after the conviction of Goodman and Mulcaire. With the scandal threatening to taint the prime minister, Coulson resigned.

The scandal also reached Scotland Yard. In addition to the allegations of police officers being paid for information for stories and of possible bribery, Scotland Yard had hired as a public relations advisor Neil Wallis, a former editor of *The News of the World*. Because of the allegations of police corruption and the hiring of Wallis, the Metropolitan Police Commissioner Sir Paul Stephenson resigned, as did assistant commissioner John Yates.

After the scandal had erupted, News Corporation announced an internal investigation that it said would be independent and have powers to compel employees to provide information. The company was quickly criticized for not having hired an outside law firm with no ties to the company to conduct the investigation, as several other companies had done in other cases.

In May 2009 the *Daily Telegraph* scooped the other UK newspapers, breaking a story on the misuse by MPs of their parliamentary expenses accounts for personal purposes. Several MPs resigned as a result of the revelations. Rupert Murdoch was reportedly irritated because a stolen disc containing the expense records had been offered to both the *The Sun* and *The Times of London* for $450,000. Upon the advice of a News International lawyer both papers rejected the offer. The lawyer later left the company.[47] ■

Preparation Questions

1. What incentives led reporters at *The News of the World* to hack into cell phones and pay police officers for information for stories? Were these likely widespread practices in the industry at the time?
2. Should the News have tried to keep the lawsuits from the 2000s quiet?
3. In 2011 should News Corporation have hired an outside firm to conduct an independent investigation?
4. What should News Corporation have done as the scandal unfolded and what should it do now?
5. Should Rupert Murdock resign?

---

[41]In 2010 the *News* also apparently settled for £1 million a lawsuit by Max Clifford, a public affairs consultant (*Economist*, July 16, 2011).

[42]*New York Times*, July 20, 2011.

[43]Ibid.

[44]Ibid.

[45]In contrast, in the United States arrests are typically quickly followed by the filing of charges.

[46]Former News International chairman Les Hinton had become publisher of the *Wall Street Journal*. He resigned as information about the scandal was revealed.

[47]*New York Times*, July 27, 2011.

4 | PRIVATE POLITICS AND SOCIAL PRESSURE

INTRODUCTION

On July 27, 2011 the *Wall Street Journal* carried a story under the headline "Under Pressure, McDonald's Adds Apples to Kids Meals," and the *New York Times* headlined "McDonald's Trims Its Happy Meal—Bowing to Its Critics, Company Adds Fruit and Reduces Fries." The company had come under intense social pressure stemming from the efforts of health officials, NGOs, and first lady Michelle Obama to combat obesity among children. "In May, more than 550 health professionals and organizations called on McDonald's to stop marketing 'junk food' to children and to retire Ronald McDonald...."[1] Marion Nestle, a professor of nutrition at New York University, called the changes by McDonald's a sham and said, "They're going to get huge publicity for this—an ounce less of French Fries. I'm not impressed."[2] The NGO Center for Science in the Public Interest commented, "McDonald's is not giving the whole loaf, but it is giving a half or two-thirds of a loaf."[3] The Center was representing a woman who had filed a lawsuit against the company for including toys in its Happy Meals. McDonald's had announced that it was reducing the calories, fat, and sodium and including apple slices in its Happy Meals, but it refused to stop including toys.

In addition to pressure from individuals and NGOs, McDonald's also faced actions by government. San Francisco had passed an ordinance prohibiting including toys with meals unless both a fruit and a vegetable were included in the meal, and New York City was considering a similar measure. Federal regulators had also proposed standards for meals for children aged 2–17, including limits on calories, sodium, sugar, and fat.

Jan Fields, president of McDonald's USA, said the company was not going to retire Ronald McDonald and that toys are "the most fun part. That's what makes it happy."[4] But, the company was bowing to social pressure and self-regulating in the hope of avoiding greater restrictions on the conduct of its business. She added, "From a business standpoint, it is something we need to do to protect that business."[5]

The social pressure McDonald's faced had two sources. The first was the government and the threat of legislation or regulation. The interests concerned with the issue of childhood obesity attempted to influence public policy through government institutions such as Congress and the Food and Drug Administration. This activity is referred to as *public politics*, since it takes place in the areas of government institutions. Public politics is the focus of Parts II and III of this book.

The second source was the criticism directed at McDonald's claiming that fast food contributed to childhood obesity and that enticing children with toys was instrumental in causing children to frequent McDonald's restaurants. This form of social pressure was directed not at government but directly at McDonald's, and the resolution of the issue, to the extent that it can be resolved, takes place outside the arenas of government institutions. This social pressure is the result of *private politics*, which is the subject of this chapter. Private politics focuses on changing the behavior of private economic agents not through government action but through social pressure and the threat of harm to the business.

Private politics is frequently led by NGOs and social activists, many of whom have concluded that more progress toward their goals can be achieved by targeting economic agents directly rather than by working through government. Issues that attract private politics include the environment, health, human rights, and social justice, and firms often exercise self-regulation on these issues. Private politics is strategic, with firms, interest groups, NGOs, and activists choosing and implementing strategies to influence the outcome of an issue. These strategies are deployed in the space of public sentiment, and the competition between these strategies determines the outcome. The success of a private politics strategy depends on support from at least a

---

[1] *Wall Street Journal*, July 27, 2011.
[2] *New York Times*, July 27, 2011.
[3] Ibid.
[4] *Wall Street Journal*, July 27, 2011.
[5] Ibid.

portion of the public. Those challenging a firm through private politics often have an advantage in this competition because of the greater trust the public has in NGOs relative to business.

The "trust gap" between NGOs and companies favors the NGOs. The GlobeScan "Trust in Institutions" surveys covering 14 countries consistently found NGOs ranked highest in trust compared to the United Nations, large local companies, national governments, and global companies, in that order. For 2005 the difference between the percentage of those surveyed responding "Trust" in the institution and the percentage responding "No Trust" was +29 for NGOs and −15 for global companies.[6] The Edelman Trust Barometer for 2011 surveyed 5,025 people in 23 countries on their trust in NGOs, business, government, and the media. Overall 61 percent responded that they had trust in NGOs compared to 56 percent who had trust in business. For the United States, the responses were 55 percent and 46 percent, respectively.[7]

Private politics can be motivated by self-interest as well as by broader concerns. In some cases it arises because an individual becomes concerned about an issue, as in the instance in Chapter 1 of the person who telephoned Larry King and said that his wife had died from brain cancer caused by radiation from heavy use of a cellular telephone. More often, private politics originates from interest groups, as when U.S. labor unions act to demand higher wages and improved working conditions in the overseas factories supplying the apparel and footwear industries, where union members were losing jobs because of imports. Similarly, unions helped create and fund the organizations that led the campaign against Wal-Mart, as considered in the Part I integrative case *Wal-Mart: Nonmarket Pressure and Reputation Risk (A)*. Private politics is most frequently initiated by activists, advocacy groups, and NGOs that serve the interests of others in addition to the interests of their members. The causes these individuals, interest groups, and NGOs pursue are important components of the nonmarket environment, and the issues on their agendas are frequently thrust onto the agendas of firms. Understanding their concerns, organization, and strategies is essential for formulating effective strategies to address the issues they raise and the pressures they generate.

Private Politics and the Nonmarket Environment

Private politics can shape the nonmarket environment in several ways. First, those initiating private politics can identify issues about which management either is unaware or has not understood as important to others, as in the case of the possible health risks from cellular telephone radiation. Similarly, the actions of Greenpeace calling attention to Shell UK's plan to sink the oil storage platform, Brent Spar, in the North Atlantic generated intense private politics in Europe even though the plan had been approved by the UK government.[8] Oil companies now involve stakeholders and NGOs as well as governments in developing disposal plans for oil platforms. The issues these groups raise and the concerns they express may point in the direction of more effective and responsible management.

Second, social activists and NGOs can affect the organization of interests by forming watchdog and advocacy groups and by mobilizing people to work for causes. These groups have been instrumental in advancing the causes of environmental protection, health and safety protection for consumers, and civil and human rights. These organizations are an increasingly important component of the nonmarket environment.

Third, the social pressure these groups exert can affect the institutional configuration of the nonmarket environment. In public politics their actions have led to new laws, expanded regulatory authority, court orders, legislative oversight activities, and executive branch initiatives. These groups were the prime movers behind the creation of the Environmental Protection Agency and the Consumer Products Safety Commission, and organized labor worked for the creation of the Occupational Safety and Health Administration. In private politics, activists have spurred the formation of private governance organizations such as the Fair Labor Association and the Forest Stewardship Council, which govern the private regulation of labor practices in overseas apparel and footwear factories and in timber harvesting and forest management, respectively. This private regulation has been growing as an alternative to government regulation.

---

[6]www.globescan.com/rf_ir_first.htm.
[7]www.edelman.com/trust/3011/uploads/Edelman\%20Barometer\%20Global\%20Deck.pdf
[8]See the chapter case *Shell, Greenpeace, and Brent Spar.*

Fourth, individuals, interest groups, and activists provide information that influences public and private politics. Rachel Carson's *Silent Spring* spurred the environmental movement by calling attention to the harmful effects of DDT. Activists at the Earth Island Institute spurred a public outcry and boycotts of tuna products when they produced a film showing dolphins drowning in nets used to catch tuna, as considered in Chapter 20.[9]

The news media and social media play a major role in disseminating this information, and an important component of private politics strategies is to attract media coverage, as illustrated by the campaign against the apple-ripening chemical Alar discussed in Chapter 3.

The Evolution of Private Politics

Private politics led by social activists has evolved over the past several decades. During the 1970s and 1980s activists primarily focused on public politics, seeking legislation and regulation to compel firms to change their practices. Activists were often disappointed by the slow progress made working through government, and some adopted a different strategy. They decided to directly challenge companies to force them to change their practices. The activists turned to corporate campaigns that deployed confrontational tactics to pressure their target companies. These campaigns were directed at the companies whose behavior the activists wanted changed. The chapter cases *Shell, Greenpeace, and Brent Spar* and *Nike in Southeast Asia* center on corporate campaigns led by Greenpeace and labor unions and human rights NGOs, respectively. Corporate campaigns were frequently successful when they targeted companies with a reputation or brand equity that could be harmed by the media attention given to the campaigns and the activists' claims.

Social activists, however, found that corporate campaigns had limits because they could not gain leverage over many companies. To stop the harvesting of old growth timber, activists targeted timber companies, but most of them did not have branded products or a public face that could be harmed by the pressure of a campaign. By the 1990s activist groups recognized that not only was it difficult to obtain change through government but corporate campaigns had limits as well. Some activists innovated with a different strategy. To stop the harvesting of old growth timber, they targeted not the timber companies themselves but the markets in which they operated. The activists turned their attention to the retailers that sold lumber made from old growth timber. Retailers such as Home Depot and Lowe's had a public face and brand equity that could be harmed by confrontational campaigns, and they were more responsive to the social pressure than were the timber companies. The retailers then pressured the timber companies. These market campaigns were able to reach where corporate campaigns had had only limited success. Market campaigns are directed at the components of the value chain that are most susceptible to harm from a successful campaign.

Commenting on the boycott campaign against ExxonMobil for its stance on climate change, Paul Gilding, former head of Greenpeace International, said, "The smart activists are now saying, 'OK, you want to play markets—let's play.' [Lobbying government] takes forever and can easily be counter-lobbied by corporations. No, no, no. They start with consumers at the pump, get them to pressure the gas stations, get the station owners to pressure the companies and the companies to pressure governments. After all, consumers do have choices where they buy their gas, and there are differences now. Shell and BPAmoco (which is also the world's biggest solar company) both withdrew from the oil industry lobby that has been dismissing climate change."[10]

Michael Brune, executive director of Rainforest Action Network (RAN), which had innovated with market campaigns, said, "Companies were more responsive to public opinion than certain legislatures were. We felt we could create more democracy in the marketplace than in the government."[11] Democracy in the marketplace means that citizen consumers express in markets their views on the performance of firms. If they object to logging in old growth forests, they can impose their will on the logging companies by refusing to buy old growth products. Moreover, they can refuse to buy from retailers, such as Home Depot, that purchased old growth lumber, and they could support demonstrations and protests against the retailers. RAN conducted an

---

[9]Putnam (1993) provides an analysis of the boycott of H. J. Heinz over the killing of dolphins in conjunction with tuna fishing.

[10]*New York Times,* June 2, 2001.

[11]Brune subsequently became executive director of the Sierra Club.

effective campaign against Home Depot, which agreed to stop buying lumber made from old growth timber, and then turned its attention to Lowe's and Kinkos. Both agreed to stop selling products made from old growth timber.

Corporate and market campaigns use similar confrontational tactics. The activist makes a demand on a company to change its practices and explicitly or implicitly threatens the company with harm if it does not do so. If the company does not accept the demand and change its practices, the activist launches a campaign against it intended to harm it directly or indirectly through the markets in which it operates. The tactics used in the campaign are considered in more detail later in the chapter, but they can involve civil disobedience, media attacks, boycotts, and actions intended to damage reputations and brands. Many of these tactics are similar to those used by labor unions, but private politics led by activists differs from union campaigns in two important ways. First, unlike labor unions, social activists are not linked to their target by a market and hence have no direct market power over their target. Second, labor unions engage in public politics by delivering votes, election campaign volunteers, and campaign contributions.

A second innovation in private politics came in the 1990s when some NGOs began to adopt a cooperative rather than a confrontational approach in which they worked with companies to reduce threats to the environment, protect human rights, and improve social welfare. Gwen Ruta of the Environmental Defense Fund (EDF) commented on the change, "At the time, it was heresy to say that companies and NGOs could work together; now it is dogma, at least for the Fortune 500."[12] By the late 2000s cooperative engagements between companies and NGOs were common. The *Financial Times* in conjunction with Dalberg Global Development Advisors surveyed 445 companies that engaged in long-term partnerships with NGOs or public agencies.[13] The companies were asked to evaluate the NGOs and United Nation's agencies on the dimensions of accountability, adaptability, communication, and execution. EDF ranked second among global organizations. EDF accepts no corporate funds but has been criticized by some social activists, "who asked why firms as rich as Wal-Mart and KKR [Kohlberg Kravis Roberts] should be the ultimate recipients of their charity."[14] In response to the criticism, social activists point to the results of their cooperation. Wal-Mart has adopted a green strategy and imposed it on its suppliers, and KKR has improved the energy efficiency of the companies in its portfolio by $160 million through its collaboration with EDF.

The demand for cooperative engagements was spurred by the success of market campaigns. Market campaigns posed a social pressure threat for a new set of firms such as retailers and banks that in the past had not been threatened by social activism. Market campaigns thus brought a whole new set of companies into play and thrust activist-led social pressure onto their nonmarket agendas. Moreover, the targeted companies often were not doing any direct harm to the environment or causing social bads and felt abused by claims that they were causing harm, even indirectly. Most of these firms were new to confrontational private politics and found that the brand equity and corporate reputations that they had so carefully built in the marketplace were not shields against social pressure but instead attracted social pressure. Their strength in the marketplace made them vulnerable and hence attractive targets for market campaigns. By the 2000s many of these companies sought an alternative, and cooperative social activists and NGOs provided that alternative.

The scope of social activism and private politics also increased during the 1990s. The development of the Internet provided better communication between social activists and the public and between social activists and the volunteers who participated in campaign activities. The Internet also strengthened fundraising. The Internet thus allowed more effective corporate and market campaigns to be conducted. At the same time, the public politics efforts of social activists and NGOs were meeting with less success as business interests became more skilled at opposition public politics. In addition, shifts in public sentiment gave the Republicans a majority in the House of Representatives in 1994, which made it more difficult to pursue a social agenda through public politics.[15]

---

[12]*Economist*, June 5, 2010.

[13]www.ft.com/reports/philanthropy2007

[14]*Economist*, June 5, 2010.

[15]Brulle and Jenkins (2010, pp. 84–85) present data on pro-environmental success in the House of Representatives. From 1989 through 1993 the average success percentage was over 70, whereas from 1994 through 2003 (the end of their data period) it was 30.

Private politics social pressure became the preferred instrument of many activists, and with the increased social pressure firms began to seek shelter. Some NGOs saw an opportunity to make progress toward their agendas by working with rather than against firms, and firms sought shields against the confrontational activists. Cooperative engagements became more common.[16]

Confrontational Private Politics

Confrontational campaigns typically focus on a social issue such as the emissions of toxic substances in a particular region, workers' rights in factories in developing countries supplying developed countries, the rights of indigenous peoples in mining areas, animal rights, conflict minerals, rainforest conservation, predatory lending, or the opening by Wal-Mart of superstores selling groceries. Social issues can cut across product market lines. The issue of animal testing, for example, affects the cosmetics and pharmaceutical industries as well as laboratories in universities. The lines of business of a firm determine the scope of the social pressure the firm could face. A mining company may face social pressure over conflict minerals, rainforest conservation, the rights of indigenous peoples, and toxic emissions.

Activists organize corporate and market campaigns to advance the issues on their agendas, and a frequent component of a campaign is a boycott. Some boycotts are more symbolic than real, but many attract media and public attention. Boycotts against such companies as Starkist Tuna, General Electric, the Walt Disney Company, Nike, Shell, Citigroup, Boise Cascade, and Coca-Cola have attracted national and international attention. The Walt Disney Company was the subject of several boycotts. The National Hispanic Media Coalition organized a boycott because of Disney's record in hiring Hispanics. The Southern Baptist Convention organized a boycott to protest Disney's decision to extend employee benefits to gay and lesbian domestic partners. International labor groups called for boycotts of Disney toys because of the working conditions in the factories of its Asian suppliers. The Texas State Board of Education sold 1.2 million Disney shares to protest violence and sexually explicit movies produced by its Miramax Films subsidiary. The Immune Deficiency Foundation called for a boycott of Disney because of its movie *Bubble Boy,* and civil rights groups called for a boycott because of a racially offensive promotion on a radio station owned by Disney.

In the early 1990s General Electric came under attack for its operation of nuclear weapons facilities. A boycott and other pressures were directed at the company by the United Methodist Church, Physicians for Social Responsibility, and INFACT, an activist group that had led the campaign against Nestlé for its marketing of infant formula in developing countries. INFACT produced a documentary film, *Deadly Deception: General Electric, Nuclear Weapons and the Environment,* that won an Academy Award for best documentary in 1992. The award provided the filmmaker an opportunity to criticize General Electric in her acceptance speech, which was broadcast worldwide. Physicians for Social Responsibility claimed that its campaign against General Electric caused physicians to switch purchases of $43 million of medical equipment, such as magnetic resonance imaging machines, from General Electric to other suppliers. General Electric denied that the campaign had any effect, but in 1993 it sold its aerospace division, which included its nuclear weapons business.

Boycott targets may also be chosen because of opportunity. Greenpeace used the occasion of the 2000 Olympics in Australia to launch a boycott of Coca-Cola, which was an official sponsor of the Olympics. The objective was to stop the company from using hydrofluorocarbons (HFCs) as a refrigerant in its dispensing machines. Greenpeace Australia produced a downloadable poster under the caption "Enjoy Climate Change" depicting Coke's family of polar bears worriedly sitting on a melting ice cap. Greenpeace urged the public to download the posters and paste them on Coke machines. Coca-Cola conceded quickly. Jeff Seabright, vice-president for environment and water resources for Coca-Cola, explained, "Our reputation is important to us. So rather than become defensive, we asked what we can do."[17]

Activist and interest groups often use both private and public politics strategies, as the Pizza Hut example illustrates.

---

[16]Government also initiated voluntary programs, particularly in the area of environmental protection. See Prakash and Potoski (2006).

[17]*Business Week*, March 12, 2007.

EXAMPLE   Pizza Hut and Health Insurance Reform

In the summer of 1994, Congress was occupied with Clinton administration proposals to change the health care system. Interest group activity was intense. In July the Health Care Reform Project, an interest group formed by a coalition of organizations led by labor unions, released a report attacking Pizza Hut and McDonald's for providing less health care coverage for their employees in the United States than they provided in other countries.[1] The group sought mandatory employer-provided health insurance and universal coverage. To publicize its campaign, the group held a press conference and placed full-page advertisements in the *New York Times* and the *Washington Post.* The headline read "No Matter How You Slice It … Pizza Hut Does Not Deliver the Same Health Benefits in America as It Does in Germany and Japan." The group also produced a commercial it planned to show on four New York and Washington television stations. Showing a young man delivering a pizza by bicycle, the commercial said that Pizza Hut provided health coverage for all its employees in Germany and Japan, "but for many workers in America, Pizza Hut pays no health insurance. Zero." Neither the advertisement nor the commercial mentioned McDonald's. The strategy of the interest groups was coordinated with one of their allies in Congress, Senator Edward Kennedy (D-MA), chairman of the Senate Labor Committee, who appeared at the press conference and asked, "What do they have against American workers?" He announced plans to hold committee hearings the next week on the issue and asked Pizza Hut and McDonald's to appear.

Under attack, Pizza Hut first addressed the immediate problem of the television commercial. Its Washington law firm wrote to the television stations pointing out its concerns with the commercial. The letter stated, "If you cause to be broadcast any statement to the effect that Pizza Hut does not offer health care coverage for its employees in the United States, the company will regard that false broadcast as having been made with knowledge of falsity or in reckless disregard of falsity."[2] This thinly veiled threat of a libel lawsuit caused the television stations not to broadcast the advertisement.

Pizza Hut then sought to explain more fully the underlying issue and defend its policies. It indicated that health care coverage was not provided for part-time, hourly employees for the first 6 months of employment, although employees could purchase a basic plan for $11 a month. After 6 months the company paid for a modest supplement to that insurance. Pizza Hut had 120,000 employees who worked 20 hours a week or less, and most of them had health care coverage through their families. Moreover, few part-time workers remained on the job for 6 months. Pizza Hut also explained that health care coverage was mandatory in Germany and Japan and was one of the reasons a pizza that sold for $11 in the United States sold for $19 in Germany and $25 in Japan. Pizza Hut claimed that the cost of a pizza would increase by 10 percent if the plan supported by the interest groups and Senator Kennedy were adopted.

Pizza Hut also had allies in Congress, and its home state senators, Robert Dole (R-KS) and Nancy Kassenbaum (R-KS), defended the company. Speaking on the floor of the Senate, Senator Dole said, "I don't know what company or industry will next be attacked by the White House, the Democratic National Committee or their allies, but from the arguments they use, I know they like their pizzas with a lot of baloney."[3]

Pizza Hut CEO Allan S. Huston appeared before Senator Kennedy's committee and defended the company's record and practices. Choosing to let Pizza Hut take all the heat, McDonald's declined to appear. Committee staffers placed a Big Mac, fries, and a soft drink on the table in front of the empty chair provided for McDonald's CEO. Senator Kennedy attacked the companies for "an unacceptable double standard."

Shortly afterward, the Clinton administration's health care reform efforts collapsed in disarray, and the Health Care Reform Project closed its doors. Although Pizza Hut had incurred only minor harm, the issue of health care coverage for part-time workers was unlikely to go away. The issue had attracted considerable media attention because of the societal significance of health issues and the attention being given to health care reform. Moreover, organized labor and other interest and activist groups, as well as some members of Congress, would continue to raise the issue—perhaps with different tactics.

---

[1]Health Care Reform Project, "Do As We Say, Not As We Do," Washington, DC, July 1994.

[2]*New York Times,* July 16, 1994. See the section "Recourse to the Law" in Chapter 3 for the explanation for this language as a basis for a libel lawsuit.

[3]*New York Times,* July 24, 1994.

Do campaigns and boycotts have an effect on either the performance of firms or on their policies? Nearly all targets state that a boycott had no significant effect on their performance, yet some customers do stop purchasing the products of a boycott target. A boycott of Mitsubishi Electric organized by RAN led Circuit City to stop carrying Mitsubishi televisions. The loss of a large retailer could not have helped Mitsubishi sales. Some boycotts have been found to have significant effects. Chavis and Leslie (2008) found that the sale of French wines in the United States decreased significantly as a result of the informal boycott resulting from France's opposition to the invasion of Iraq in the aftermath of September 11. The question thus is better posed in terms of the magnitude of the effect on company performance.

Several studies have measured the stock price performance of companies that were the target of a boycott relative to the stock price performance of companies not subject to a boycott. The empirical evidence is largely inconclusive.[18] Moreover, the effects can depend on the nonmarket issue. Epstein and Schnietz (2002) studied the effect on the stock prices of firms identified as "abusive" by the antiglobalization demonstrations at the 1999 Seattle World Trade Organization meeting. Firms that were identified as environmentally abusive experienced a statistically and economically significant decrease in their share prices, whereas the share prices of firms identified as abusive of human rights were unaffected. Despite the varying evidence, most firms are concerned about the possibility of a boycott not only because of possible lost sales but also because the public attention, frequently under the scrutiny of the media, could harm their brands as well as their reputations and public images.

RAN does not attempt to organize boycotts because it believes that it is too difficult to demonstrate to a target the effect of a boycott. Instead, in its campaigns RAN focuses on the public face and brand equity of its targets. The goal is to call attention to objectionable practices of the target, casting doubt on the public face the company has created through its public relations and advertising. RAN primarily targets consumer-facing companies with branded products so that consumers can take individual actions against the target. In the chapter case *Anatomy of a Corporate Campaign: Rainforest Action Network and Citigroup (A)(B),* RAN conducted an aggressive campaign against Citigroup, focusing on its public face, and some consumers cut up their Citibank credit cards and some students pledged not to do business with Citigroup.

Activists have been vocal opponents of agricultural biotechnology, causing delays in new products and increased costs. The strength of activist groups varies across countries. The opposition to agricultural biotechnology has remained moderate in the United States as more products have been brought to market without the harmful effects claimed by their critics. Opposition to agricultural biotechnology, however, remains strong in much of Europe. Because of private politics, a major Swiss pharmaceutical company located biotechnology units just over the French border and connected those units by pipeline to its plant just inside Switzerland. In effect, the plant lies on both sides of the border with the biotechnology processes located in France.

The Health Care Reform Project campaign against Pizza Hut and McDonald's involved private politics by the Project members and public politics led by its allies in Congress. Both components of the strategy were directed not at initiating or passing legislation but instead were intended to pressure the companies to provide more health care benefits to their part-time employees. A decade later, a related campaign was launched against Wal-Mart as considered in the Part I integrative case *Wal-Mart: Nonmarket Pressure and Reputation Risk (A).*

In 2003 the AIDS Healthcare Foundation (AHF) launched a public and private politics campaign against GlaxoSmithKline (GSK) to force the company to make its AIDS drugs accessible to developing countries.[19] AHF asked investors, including CalPERS, to pressure GSK to lower its drug prices for developing countries. It filed a lawsuit in the United States challenging GSK's patent on AZT, the first antiretroviral drug. It also filed a complaint in South Africa challenging GSK's pricing practices and a lawsuit in California alleging that GSK engaged in false advertising of its AIDS drugs. AHF lobbied the California state government to put pressure on GSK and its pricing policies. AHF organized protests and demonstrations against GSK in the United States and barred company personnel from its AIDS outpatient facilities in the United States.

Which companies are most susceptible to social pressure and boycotts? Figure 4-1 identifies characteristics of companies, their products, and their operating environment that make them

---

[18]Davidson, Worrell, and El-Jelly (1995) found that the announcements of 40 boycotts between 1969 and 1991 resulted in a statistically significant decrease in the share price of the targets. Friedman (1985), Pruitt and Friedman (1986), and Pruitt, Wei, and White (1988) found evidence that boycotts significantly reduced the market values of target firms. Koku, Akhigbe, and Springer (1997), however, found that the market values of 54 target firms increased significantly. Teoh, Welch, and Wazzan (1999) found no significant effect of the boycott of South Africa on either U.S. firms or on shares traded on the Johannesburg Stock Exchange. Friedman (1999), Manheim (2001), and Vogel (1978) have studied individual boycotts in more detail.

[19]See the Part V integrative case *GlaxoSmithKline and AIDS Drug Policy.*

FIGURE 4-1 Susceptibility to Private Politics

- Products
  - consumer products
  - products with low switching costs
  - a brand name that can be damaged
- Operating environment
  - activities that produce harmful externalities
  - operating in an interest group-rich environment
  - multinational/global operations—issues can spill over to other units and countries
  - operating in developing countries
- Organization
  - a decentralized organization, so that external effects, including intracompany, are not naturally considered

susceptible. A consumer products company is susceptible because consumers can take action by switching to competing products. This is easiest when switching costs are low, as in the case of gasoline, tuna, or televisions. A company with a brand name is also susceptible because customers can punish it by not buying other products it sells. General Electric experienced this even outside its consumer product lines.

A company whose activities produce harmful externalities such as pollution or a health hazard could be subject to protests from those affected or from advocacy groups that support them. Operating in an interest group-rich environment, as in Europe or the United States, provides a ready set of groups that can initiate private politics. Also, multinational companies must be concerned about the effects of operations in one country that are of concern to interest groups and activists in other countries. Operations in developing countries may encounter fewer organized interest and activist groups, but groups in developed countries closely monitor activities in developing countries. Shell learned this from its decision not to intervene when the Nigerian government executed nine activists, including a Nobel Peace Prize nominee, who were protesting environmental degradation from oil fields operated by Shell. The organization of a company can also increase susceptibility. In a highly decentralized company such as Shell, a subsidiary in one country may not take into account or even be aware that its activities can spur private politics affecting subsidiaries in other countries.

The effectiveness of private politics social pressure depends on a variety of factors, four of which are identified here. The first is the social value achieved by causing a potential target to change its practices, as in the mitigation of a negative externality or improvement in the working conditions in suppliers' factories in developing countries. The second is how tough the potential target is, where toughness depends on the cost of changing its practices. The third is how vulnerable a potential target is, where vulnerability can depend on brand equity or reputation that could be harmed by a campaign. The fourth is the extent to which potential targets take into account the social value of a change in their practices when making their decisions; that is, the extent to which they accept social responsibilities. The characteristics identified in Figure 4-1 can be used in the chapter cases *Shell, Greenpeace, and Brent Spar* and *Nike in Southeast Asia* to identify why the campaigns were successful.

As an example of susceptibility to confrontational social pressure, pharmaceutical companies producing prescription drugs can be difficult to harm, whereas consumer products companies may be quite vulnerable. Friedman (1999) studied animal rights campaigns against cosmetics companies and pharmaceutical companies and found that virtually all the campaigns against cosmetics companies succeeded in halting animal testing, whereas all the campaigns against pharmaceutical companies were unsuccessful. Cosmetics companies had brand equity that could be damaged and had many rivals to which consumers could switch, whereas switching costs for prescription drugs are high and most drugs are not sold under the company's name.

Cooperative Private Politics

NGOs with expertise may be able to adopt a cooperative strategy. An NGO could help a firm identify the benefits and costs from changing its environmental practices, as in the case of EDF working with McDonald's to reduce behind-the-counter waste and packaging,[20] or provide expertise as in the case of EDF working with BP to develop an internal carbon-trading system. An NGO could also help firms develop an externally legitimate policy.[21] For example, several NGOs worked with the U.S. timber industry to develop a sustainability policy implemented through the Sustainable Forestry Initiative (SFI). The SFI has a more moderate set of sustainability standards than those of the Forest Stewardship Council (FSC), which more radical activists wanted the timber firms to join. NGOs also worked with four major banks to develop the Equator Principles that govern project finance. Gwen Ruta (2010, p. 189) explained EDF's approach: "To put its ideas into action, EDF works with unexpected allies: corporations, fishermen, landowners, and others who have a stake in the outcome. With a 20-year history of uncommon partnerships, EDF seeks to bring about lasting change not through confrontation, but through constructive engagement with powerful market leaders." The cooperative NGO thus can use its expertise to help the target discover the consequences of a change in practices, where ex ante neither the NGO nor the target knows the specific benefits that might be discovered. It can also help design an externally legitimate policy that governs the change in practices of the target, where legitimacy pertains to the confidence the public and other NGOs have that the firm will fully implement the policy.[22] Certification by the NGO is one way that external legitimacy is granted.

A firm could adopt its own policy or participate in an industry program to address a social issue, but frequently these efforts lack legitimacy and do little to reduce social pressure. Some industry programs are viewed by NGOs as greenwashing or as part of an advertising or public relations program. Conroy (2007, pp. 178–179) explained the legitimacy problem of the Council for Responsible Jewellery Practices (CRJP), established to address the conflict minerals issue.

> No social or environmental NGO participated in the development or governance of the CRJP, nor in the development of the code of practice. NGOs were simply asked to provide comments on documents drafted by CRJP. As a result, the organization suffered from the same fundamental lack of credibility as other industry-led attempts to take control of reputational risk management …
>
> NGOs were also concerned that there was no threshold or basis for entry into CRJP. Members were not required to demonstrate any commitment to standards or best practices. The only requirements for membership were that a company was active in the jewelry industry, was willing to pay a fee, and had expressed a commitment to some relatively vague language regarding social, environmental, and ethical performance…

Before, during, and after CRJP's founding, NGOs hammered away at the lack of an entry threshold for CRJP and the lack of any real NGO role.

Conroy notes that CRJP subsequently joined with NGOs in a new cooperative initiative, the Initiative for Responsible Mining Assurance, to address the concerns raised by the NGOs.

External legitimacy could involve the certification of a change in the target firm's practices as in the case of the timber industry. For certification to provide external legitimacy, the activist must have a degree of expertise to be able to judge the extent to which the change in practices accomplishes the activists' goals. External legitimacy improves the standing of the firm with the public, reduces social pressure, and makes the target less attractive to a confrontational activist because there is less that can be accomplished through a campaign.

Firms may have their own expertise but have difficulty establishing external legitimacy on their own because of an absence of trust by the public and a lack of transparency about their operations. A firm could recognize that a change in its practices would be rewarded by consumers, but it may lack a mechanism to assure skeptical consumers that it has actually changed its practices. The public cannot observe the change in practices nor know the costs and benefits associated with alternative changes that could have been made. A cooperative engagement can allow an activist to observe the firm's alternatives and certify for the public that the change

---

[20]McDonald's Corporation–Environmental Defense Fund, Waste Reduction Task Force, 1991 (April), "Final Report," available at www.environmentaldefense.org.

[21]GreenBiz.com listed 10 prominent NGOs that work with companies on their environmental practices. www.greenbiz.com/print/35540

[22]The activist could also have expertise in the sense of knowing better the attitude of the public and how likely the public is to respond to or reward a change in practices by the firm.

has been made while not revealing specific information to the public and competitors. This can also help create markets. For example, a company could develop a green product, but consumers could be skeptical about whether the product was actually green. Certification by an NGO that has the expertise to verify that the product is green can give consumers confidence and thereby create a market for the product. For example, the Sierra Club has endorsed Clorox's Green Works products.

Cooperative and confrontational strategies can leave activist groups on opposite sides of an issue. Forest products are certified by independent third parties to have come from forests managed with certain social, environmental, and conservation practices. Competing certification systems have been established. The FSC was supported by RAN, Greenpeace, the Sierra Club, and other NGOs. SFI was developed by the timber industry in cooperation with Conservation International and the Nature Conservancy. The groups backing the FSC criticized the SFI as letting the fox guard the henhouse.

Synergies between Confrontational and Cooperative Private Politics

Most companies prefer cooperation to confrontation when faced with private politics social pressure. Indeed, the threat from confrontational private politics is one factor leading to the increase in cooperative engagements between companies and NGOs. That is, confrontational private politics creates a demand for engagements with cooperative activists, and that demand is greater the greater is the threat. Radicals may create a greater demand than do moderates. Kert Davies (2010, p. 200) of Greenpeace stated, "[Greenpeace's] reputation for radical actions positions it particularly well to play the bad cop that can drive a target organization to partner with groups that seem more middle-of-the-road in orientation,...." Because of the synergy between confrontational and cooperative private politics, cooperative NGOs may participate or support the campaigns of confrontational NGOs to strengthen the demand for cooperative engagements. The greater that demand, the more bargaining power the cooperative NGO has to obtain greater changes from its corporate partners in cooperative engagements. The boxed example illustrates the leverage that social pressure from confrontational activists can give cooperative activists. The social pressure against the construction of the coal-fired power plants drove TXU and the private equity firms seeking to acquire it into a cooperative engagement with EDF and NRDC.

EXAMPLE   TXU and the Leveraged Buyout

TXU was a major Texas power producer that made two major strategic decisions in 2007. First, because of strong economic growth in Texas it planned a major expansion in its power generation capacity. Since coal-fired plants were by far less costly than natural gas or nuclear plants, TXU announced that it would build 11 coal-fired power plants. Second, the company entered into an agreement to sell itself to the private equity firms KKR and Texas Pacific Group, which would take the company private. The price was $45 billion, the largest ever for a leveraged buyout.

The announced capacity expansion generated intense social pressure from social activists and NGOs that opposed the use of coal and argued that the company should develop renewable power sources. The social activists and NGOs also took their case to the arenas of public politics, where they intervened in the regulatory approval process for the plants. They also sought to stop the plants in the Texas legislature and in Washington. Their objective was to force the company to cancel plans for all 11 coal-fired power plants. The private and public politics threatened to derail both the capacity expansion and the leveraged buyout.

Former EPA Administrator William K. Reilly was a senior advisor to the Texas Pacific Group and had witnessed the power of confrontational private politics coupled with public politics. He advocated an engagement with cooperative NGOs. The private equity companies contacted EDF and NRDC and sat down in private to work out an agreement.[1] EDF and NRDC both wanted the coal-fired plants cancelled, and EDF had been a vocal critic in Texas. The threat from the confrontational NGOs and from public politics gave EDF and NRDC bargaining power. The companies reached an agreement in which the number of coal-fired power plants was reduced from 11 to 3, and the companies pledged to invest in alternative energy sources.[2] The endorsement of the agreement by EDF and NRDC provided external legitimacy to the deal and may have facilitated regulatory approval.

---

[1]*Business Week*, March 12, 2007.
[2]See Krill (2010, p. 220).

Moderates and Radicals

Some NGOs are operated by self-proclaimed radicals and others by moderates, such as those at EDF. Davies (2010, p. 196) of Greenpeace wrote,

> According to reports from Greenpeace staff of conversations with people at companies it has targeted, corporations may have a greater fear of its campaigns than those of other organizations because of the strong connotation of the Greenpeace brand. Thus some of the negative perceptions of the organization may actually serve to support its cause, upholding Machiavelli's proposition that it is better to be feared than loved, when campaigning against corporations. Indeed, the notion that NGOs often can be more effective by imposing harms rather than offering benefits is consistent with the economics literature,

To the extent that radical activists conduct more intense confrontational campaigns than do moderate activists, the greater is the demand for cooperative engagements and the greater is the bargaining power of the NGOs participating in those engagements. That is, the tougher is the bad cop, the more leverage the good cop has. Most companies prefer to cooperate with moderate rather than radical NGOs.

Some activists have developed both cooperative and confrontational capabilities. For example, in Europe Greenpeace uses its confrontational strategy and also cooperates with firms as in the case of the deployment of the refrigeration technology it developed to replace CFCs and HFCs. Spurred in part by the campaign by Greenpeace Australia, Coca-Cola along with PepsiCo, Unilever, and McDonald's participated with Greenpeace in the Refrigerants Naturally initiative. Gerd Leipold, head of Greenpeace International, said, "We've shifted from just pointing out the problems to pushing for real solutions. When congratulations are deserved, we offer them."[23]

Companies do interact with the more radical NGOs and social activists, as well as with moderates. DuPont employs Paul Gilding as a consultant. DuPont CEO Charles O. Holliday commented, "We work with our enemies."[24] Working with enemies does not mean, however, conceding to their demands. Scott Noesen, director of sustainable development for Dow Chemicals, said, "Our job is not to please or convince the activists. The best we can do is set meaningful targets and report on our successes and failures."[25]

ACTIVIST STRATEGIES

Activists choose nonmarket strategies just as firms do. They seek to pressure firms to change their practices, and although some have a large membership that could be mobilized for action against a target, most have limited resources and a small membership base. Activists thus face a collective action problem, and a campaign serves as a coordinating mechanism for those with concerns about the practices of firms. The news media and the social media play a central role by providing information about the issue, the firm's practices, and the target. Activists often take out advertisements in newspapers and magazines as part of their attempt to inform the public, but they also rely on "earned" media—that is, media coverage of the campaign itself. Information provision is intended to both harm the target and create a degree of common knowledge and informal coordination among members of the public to mitigate a free-rider problem; that is, eliciting participation by the public. The chapter case *Anatomy of a Corporate Campaign: Rainforest Action Network and Citigroup (A)(B)* illustrates RAN's approach to influencing a target.[26]

Direct pressure is applied by calling attention to the activities of a company as in the Citigroup case. Activists often refer to this strategy as "naming and shaming." The objective of shaming is to harm the target firm by damaging its brand, its reputation, or the morale of its

---

[23]*Business Week*, March 12, 2007.
[24]Ibid.
[25]Ibid.
[26]Baron and Diermeier (2007) provide a formal theory of activist campaigns and firms' nonmarket strategies.

employees. During the campaign against sweatshops, Nike concluded that the criticisms of the company had made its advertising and marketing people more cautious and less creative.

The information provided by activists is typically not verifiable by the public, but it can have credibility because of the trust gap. The trust gap can create an asymmetry between the effectiveness of NGOs and firm strategies. Because the public tends to trust NGOs more than firms, negative information provided by an NGO can have more impact on the development of an issue than can information provided by the target. Using the terminology of Chapter 3, one negative message by an NGO can offset several positive messages by a firm. Thus, not only can the reputation of a firm be harmed by an activist, but it can be difficult to repair the damage. That is, the trust gap can mean that the firm receives little credit for the good it does.

Pressure can be applied through centralized and decentralized activities. The campaign against Pizza Hut was centralized through labor unions. As an example of a decentralized strategy, the Emergency Planning and Community Right-to-Know Act requires the federal government to publish annually the Toxics Release Inventory, which lists for every plant in the country the emissions of over 300 possibly hazardous chemicals. Using data from the Inventory, the NRDC holds an annual press conference and releases a study of the nation's biggest polluters. The Inventory and the media coverage alert local community groups to the emissions in their areas. Local groups, using private politics, then pressure firms in their areas to reduce their emissions. Partly as a result of these activities, several major companies, including DuPont and Dow Chemical, have reduced emissions below the levels required by EPA regulations.

The Internet has helped activists coordinate their actions and mount their campaigns on a broader and more decentralized basis. Carol Browner, former head of the Environmental Protection Agency during the Clinton administration and former director of the White House Office of Energy and Climate Change Policy in the Obama administration, said, "Environmental groups have become truly sophisticated in using the Web to move information to millions of people literally overnight, and to attack companies on a global scale."[27] The coordinated antiglobalization protests against international institutions that began in 1999 in Seattle against the World Trade Organization and continued against the International Monetary Fund, World Bank, and G-8 are ample evidence. The Internet has also become important in fundraising for NGOs, as the success of the activist organization MoveOn demonstrated. MoveOn wanted to raise $25,000 to take out an issue advertisement and sent out an appeal on the Internet. It received $400,000, launching the Internet as an important source of activist funding. Social media can be as powerful by coordinating the actions of people with shared interests.

Activist groups also use their standing before courts, legislatures, and administrative organizations to petition, sue, and advocate action. Environmental legislation and certain health and safety legislation were written to give citizens the right to petition regulatory agencies for action and sue those agencies if they fail to act. Many groups utilize litigation to force action by the target or to generate bargaining power. Activists also use shareholder rights as a component of their strategies and campaigns. The most common tactic is to question the company at its annual meeting, and a more formal approach is to file a shareholder resolution with the Securities and Exchange Commission. Shareholder resolutions are filed on a variety of issues, including human and animal rights, diversity, community issues, the environment, and product-specific issues.[28] These resolutions are rarely successful but are part of a private politics strategy to put pressure on a company and its reputation.

Advocacy Science

A frequently used strategy of activists is to conduct a policy study or scientific investigation to call attention to an issue. Even when it involves only secondary sources, this practice of "advocacy science" can advance the activists' cause. As in the Alar case considered in Chapter 3, a study can attract the media, and hence the public, which adds a degree of credibility to the claims of the activists. It can also attract sympathetic politicians, who can provide support, introduce

---

[27]*New York Times,* September 9, 2001.
[28]See Rehbein, Waddock, and Graves (2004) for a study of shareholder resolutions and the objectives of the groups filing the resolutions.

bills, and hold hearings at which activists can testify. Advocacy science is most effective if it can be coordinated with other actions to prolong attention to the issue and provide a series of newsworthy events.

Target Selection

An important component of a private politics campaign is the selection of a target. Activists typically seek to change practices in an industry, but targeting an individual firm rather than an industry is preferred because the threat of harm is concentrated. Activists sometimes target "worst offenders." For example, environmental activists concluded that ExxonMobil was the most obstinate opponent of measures to address global climate change. As a result, European activists led a boycott of Esso products. In contrast, hoping that they will be responsive, activists sometimes target companies, such as Starbucks, that have positioned themselves as socially responsible and environmentally friendly. Argenti (2004, pp. 110–111) explained the decision by the activist organization Global Exchange to target Starbucks to sell fair trade coffee: "Truly socially responsible companies are actually more likely to be attacked by activist NGOs than those that are not …. Our interviews with Global Exchange suggested that Starbucks was a better target for the fair trade issue because of its emphasis on social responsibility, as opposed to a larger company without a socially responsible bent." Starbucks had revealed itself as a soft target.

Finally, in response to a boycott intended to force Starbucks to demand reform of the Seattle police department, a Starbucks spokesperson commented, "We are not an activist or a political organization. When people say that we should do more than take money from the community, we do give back. What we are willing to do is to help invigorate the community by providing jobs, supporting educational and philanthropic programs for youth, and it hurts us when a small group of people decide that we need to be doing something else, which happens to be on their agenda."[29]

Several empirical studies have attempted to identify the characteristics of firms that make them more likely to be targeted. Using data on environmental campaigns Lenox and Eesley (2009) found that large firms, firms with greater toxic emissions, and firms that are more advertising intensive are more likely to be targeted. They also found that campaigns against larger firms and firms with higher emissions are more aggressive, and the target was more likely to concede to the activist demands the higher the emissions.[30] King and Soule (2007) studied the firms targeted in social and union protests and concluded "that protestors tend to target large, weakly performing firms. Firms that have been targeted by protestors in the past are more likely to be protested against in the future." Rehbein, Waddock, and Graves (2004) found that the firms with worse environment performance and product-related concerns had a higher probability of being targeted with a shareholder resolution. Hendry (2006) conducted interviews with five environmental NGOs and concluded that larger firms and firms closer to the consumer are more likely to be targeted, as are firms with a greater environmental impact. These studies are consistent with the factors identified in Figure 4-1.

Activists also target individuals in both their personal and professional roles. Attention typically focuses on those perceived as influential and possibly influenceable. RAN directed attention to Citigroup CEO Sandy Weill by putting his picture in advertisements and on posters, and schoolchildren sent him valentines asking him to stop Citigroup's financing of environmentally destructive projects. Pro-choice demonstrators participating in the National Organization of Women's nationwide boycott picketed Domino's Pizza outlets, claiming that the chain opposed abortion rights. Although Domino's Pizza had no policy on abortion, its owner, Thomas S. Monaghan, had made a personal contribution of $50,000 to the Committee to End Tax-Funded Abortions.

A Generic Strategy of Activists

Figure 4-2 characterizes a generic strategy used by many activist groups in advancing the issues on their agendas. This characterization draws on the role of the media in informing the public about issues, as considered in Chapter 3. The activist group first identifies an issue such as health

---

[29]*Los Angeles Times,* June 26, 2001.
[30]For a broader set of campaigns Eesley and Lenox (2006) report results consistent with their study of environmental campaigns.

FIGURE 4-2   Activists' Generic Strategy

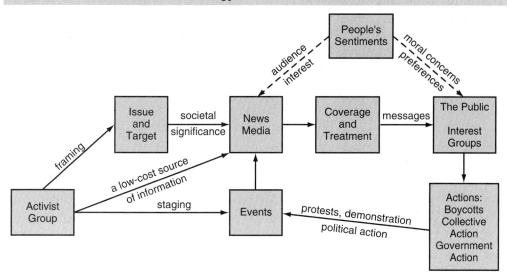

insurance or fuel economy and selects a target such as Pizza Hut or Ford. The activist group may have a first-mover advantage and be able to frame the issue by identifying its societal significance and the company's role in the issue. The audience interest in an issue is determined by people's sentiments, and those sentiments may be based on moral concerns, as in the case of workers without health care insurance. To attract the news media, the activists may orchestrate events. The activists also seek to become a low-cost source of information for the journalists. For example, Greenpeace has photographers and camera crews that broadcast its actions worldwide. When media coverage is difficult to attract, some activist groups take out advertisements in newspapers. Activists increasingly rely on the social media to provide and transmit information and to coordinate activities.

People's responses to this strategy depend on their sentiments and concerns about the issue. The hope of the activists is that individuals and interest groups will take action in the form of protests, boycotts, and collective action, which may attract further news media coverage. In addition, government officials may be attracted to the issue. Greenpeace's actions in the chapter case *Shell, Greenpeace, and Brent Spar* attracted the support of motorists, labor unions, and government officials. The basic strategy of the activists is to frame the issue to attract the interest of the public and the media and induce people and government officeholders to take actions that give the issue a life of its own. The Chapter 16 case *Apple and Private Politics in China* concerns a challenge to Apple from an environmental campaign.

STRATEGIES FOR ADDRESSING SOCIAL PRESSURE

Assessment

Because the nonmarket environment is populated by interest and activist groups, firms must develop approaches to dealing with these groups. Figure 4-3 highlights several basic steps successful companies have taken. First, a company must assess its positioning and any possible

FIGURE 4-3   Addressing the Activist Environment

- Identify the relevant interest groups and activist organizations in your market and nonmarket environments.
- Understand their agenda, preferences, and capabilities.
- Understand the broader public support for their agenda.
- Consult with them on important issues; a number of companies have established regular forums for exchanging information and views.
- Cooperate when that is beneficial.
- Fight when you are right and can win—but be careful.

private politics challenges to that position. This assessment begins by answering the question of what is demanded of the firm by the activists and, more importantly, by the public. A firm like McDonald's has a major public presence, making it the subject of a wide set of demands, as identified in the Chapter 1 case *The Nonmarket Environment of McDonald's*. The demands made on an investment banking firm or consulting firm are much more limited.

The next step is to assess vulnerability to a private politics campaign. This involves assessing not only the firm's own vulnerability but also the vulnerability of those in its value chain. The determinants of vulnerability are identified in Figure 4-1 and are the same as those used by activists in selecting their targets.

It is also important to assess the extent of public support for the activists' agendas. This depends on the issue as well as the public. Agricultural biotechnology meets stronger opposition in Europe than in the United States, and in the United States milk from cows treated with BST has stronger opposition than bioengineered soybeans. A number of firms have established forums with activist groups for exchanging information and viewpoints on issues. Firms generally prefer to interact with cooperative activists and avoid those that emphasize confrontation. Some interactions can lead to cooperative efforts to resolve problems, as in the McDonald's and EDF project discussed later in the chapter. On some issues, however, firms fight the activists when they are confident that they are both right and can win the fight. In some cases, such as that of Nike and Disney, firms have underestimated the resolve of activists and the force of social pressure.

If a company is potentially vulnerable, the next step is to consider whether it is possible to forestall a possible campaign through self-regulation, by working with cooperative NGOs, or by making public commitments to new policies. Interacting with a cooperative NGO can provide benefits, particularly when the group has expertise. When it considered establishing oil operations in Iran, Shell met with Amnesty International to discuss how it might handle human rights matters in the country.

On some issues companies view an NGO as part of the solution. This has become common on environmental issues in particular, as considered in Chapter 12. When partnering with an NGO, firms frequently prefer science-based NGOs with reputations for working with companies. EDF, Conservation International, and the World Wildlife Fund are frequent partners of companies. In some cases the formation of new organizations may be warranted. Staples joined with NatureServe, Conservation International, and the Nature Conservancy to form the Forest and Biodiversity Conservation Alliance. Major global banks worked with Conservation International to develop the Equator Principles.

When a firm is challenged by an activist group or NGO, the specific issues of concern must be evaluated. The frameworks developed in the previous chapters may be used to assess the challenge. Management should assess where the issue is in its life cycle and how rapidly it is progressing. Often the issues generated by activists and interest groups are early in their life cycles, and thus firms have an opportunity to affect their progress. The next step involves identifying other potentially interested parties and assessing how likely they are to become active on the issue. As indicated in Figure 4-2, activists may attempt to bring the issue to the attention of the public and government officials through media strategies. The theory of the media presented in Chapter 3 can be used to assess how the media is likely to cover and treat the issue. Assessing the effectiveness of alternative strategies is often difficult when the issue is the subject of media and public attention, and that attention may advance an issue quickly through its life cycle. In the case of a boycott, the firm must assess whether customers and the public are likely to be aware of the issue and sympathetic to the position of the activists. Sympathy, however, does not necessarily translate into action, so the likelihood that individuals will actually respond must be assessed.

Strategy and Negotiations

Determining the most effective strategy requires understanding the nature and strength of the activists, the concerns that motivate them, the likelihood of media coverage, the likely support for the issue among consumers and the public, how much harm the activist could cause, how central the issue is to their agenda, and whether they are led by professionals or amateurs. Professionals are more difficult to co-opt, but they may be more practical as well. With limited resources, activists and interest groups must determine which issues to address, and they may abandon an issue that appears to be unwinnable or requires too much of their available resources.

When confronted with private nonmarket action, a natural reaction is to be defensive. A better response is to evaluate the claims and demands made by the activists and determine whether they have merit. In some cases a firm may conclude that the activist's position is correct. RAN targeted Kinko's as part of its Old Growth Campaign, and within a few weeks received a letter from Kinko's stating that RAN's demands were consistent with Kinko's environmental policies. In disbelief, RAN called Kinko's to argue for its demands. Kinko's was surprised, since its letter stated that it agreed with RAN—Kinko's would stop sourcing supplies from old growth forests.

McDonald's faced a major solid-waste disposal problem, and when invited by EDF to discuss the problem, it accepted. The result was a voluntary working arrangement with EDF to develop an action plan that included waste reduction, recycling, and substitute packaging. The arrangement provided McDonald's with fresh ideas for addressing its waste disposal problem. This cooperative project is considered in more detail in Chapter 12, which also considers a cooperative project between Federal Express and EDF.

If the interactions with an activist group reach the point of bargaining over the resolution of the issue, a firm must assess the benefits and costs of alternative resolutions. It is also important to determine how an agreement will be monitored and how misunderstandings that might subsequently develop will be resolved. A firm must also assess whether its competitors will follow suit or whether the playing field will become uneven. Many firms prefer that the playing field be level with their competitors adopting the same policies for dealing with the issue.

An important component of a strategy for addressing a private politics campaign is to shore up the support of a firm's employees, some of whom may be sympathetic with the demands made by the activists. In its Old Growth Campaign, Weyerhaeuser was targeted by RAN after Boise Cascade had agreed to stop harvesting old growth timber. After an initial demonstration in Seattle and speaking at Weyerhaeuser's annual meeting, RAN paused its campaign as it prepared for a series of actions against the company later in the year. During the pause, Weyerhaeuser published in its employee newsletter a lengthy interview with the executive responsible for sustainable forestry and for meeting with RAN. She explained the company's position and also warned of the actions that might be taken against the company. The objective was to protect employee morale by explaining the extensive steps the company was already taking to protect forests and manage them in an environmentally sound manner.

Negotiations with activists can be voluntary, as in the case of McDonald's decision to join with EDF to address solid-waste problems. In many cases, however, the objectives of the activists and the interests of the company are in conflict. In such cases, negotiations between the activists and the company may be required to resolve the issue. Often negotiations take place in the presence of social pressure. In the OnBank boxed example the activists had a one-shot opportunity—the required approval by the Federal Reserve Bank—to extract concessions from the bank. This made it relatively easy for the bank to "buy off" the activists, and because the bank had a strong incentive to resolve the issue and complete the merger, an agreement could be reached. In the chapter case *Anatomy of a Corporate Campaign: Rainforest Action Network and Citigroup (A)(B)*, RAN and Citigroup did not have a one-shot opportunity, and the negotiations were lengthy.

In cases where the stakes are high and monitoring of the firm's actions is difficult, the parties may require more than a simple agreement. To resolve issues of working conditions in factories in Southeast Asia, activists and footwear and apparel companies formed a private regulatory organization, the Fair Labor Association (FLA), to monitor working conditions in suppliers' factories. The FLA is considered in more detail in Chapter 24, but in brief it is a private governance organization established to assure that its standards for working conditions are met. The FLA has no enforcement powers, but it has informational powers stemming from its authority to inspect the working conditions in overseas factories and release its findings to the public.

To monitor its agreement with Home Depot, RAN used local volunteers. With some training, it is possible to distinguish between lumber from old growth trees and that from younger trees. Volunteers then walked through Home Depot aisles visually checking the lumber and reporting to RAN on their findings. RAN's only enforcement mechanism, however, was the threat to relaunch its campaign against the company.

EXAMPLE   Negotiating with Activists: On Bank[1]

In response to charges that some financial institutions limited lending in inner-city neighborhoods, Congress enacted the Community Reinvestment Act (CRA). The CRA required federally chartered banks to lend in the communities in which their depositors lived. The Home Mortgage Disclosure Act (HMDA) required banks to report their mortgage lending by census tract. When two banks announced a merger, activist groups frequently seized the opportunity to challenge the merger. The groups asserted that the merging banks had not complied with the CRA, and they backed that assertion with data on mortgage lending by census tract filed in compliance with the HMDA.[2]

OnBank announced it would acquire another local bank, Merchants National Bank & Trust. When an inner-city resident's application to refinance his mortgage was rejected by OnBank, he turned to a community organization. The organization examined OnBank's lending record and found that it had seldom made loans in the community, had no branches in the inner city, and refused to participate in the city's Syracuse Housing Partnership. Merchants, however, had four branches in the inner city, participated in the Housing Partnership, and made significantly more loans in the inner city. Community organizations feared that the acquisition might result in

Merchants operating as OnBank did. The community organizations began a letter-writing campaign to state and federal regulators calling attention to OnBank's lending record. OnBank countered with data showing that its record compared favorably with other banks in the state of New York. OnBank received endorsements from local organizations such as the United Way and the Urban League.

The community organizations gave OnBank a list of 26 concerns and proposed that they and the bank meet. The two sides met to discuss the issues, but the bank was unwilling to conclude an agreement. Meanwhile, OnBank was negotiating with state regulators, and when the state approved the acquisition, the community groups protested and attracted considerable media coverage. The acquisition still required approval by the Federal Reserve Bank, and the protests led to a second meeting at which regulators were present as observers. Little progress was made until the bank agreed to participate in a number of smaller working groups to address specific issues. The smaller groups made rapid progress, and with a threat of direct action against the bank and federal approval still pending, the bank and the community organizations reached an agreement to increase lending in the inner city.[3] The threat of direct action against the bank, the required regulatory approval, and the reporting of lending data by census tract provided the opportunity to pressure OnBank and obtain lending commitments.

[1]This example is based on an article in the *Wall Street Journal,* September 22, 1992.

[2]In response to complaints by banks the CRA was relaxed in 2005 for banks with assets under $1 billion.

[3]This process is repeated throughout the nation when bank mergers are planned.

Challenging the Activists

The demands made in a campaign often are unreasonable or too costly to meet, and firms resist or fight back. Some firms decide that they will agree to disagree with the activist and bear whatever pressure the activist can muster. The movement to market campaigns reflected the ability of companies to withstand the social pressure from corporate campaigns without incurring long-term harm. Companies that do not have the characteristics listed in Figure 4-1 may choose to bear the social pressure.

The target of a campaign may also fight back. This may involve filing a lawsuit against the activist organization. BP, for example, filed a lawsuit against Greenpeace as a result of its boarding a drilling rig under tow to an exploration location. BP was able to name as defendants the individuals who organized the boarding, and Greenpeace quickly ended its campaign.[31] A lawsuit, however, carries the risk of creating a second media story, as in the McLibel example presented in Chapter 3.

When targeted by RAN, Boise Cascade wrote to all of RAN's donors and to the Internal Revenue Service challenging its tax status. This only generated sympathy for RAN and its cause, and Boise Cascade subsequently conceded to RAN's demands. Many firms, when opposing an activist campaign, choose not to attack the activist group but instead provide information about the issues in question in the hope of weakening public support for the campaign. A target may invest in reputation management by providing positive information about its record and making sure that employees are on board. Targets may also develop an alternative organization. The

[31]The rig was not the Brent Spar.

timber industry established the Sustainable Forest Initiative to implement forest management standards that were more practical and less costly than those of the activist-backed Forest Stewardship Council.[32]

In some cases, a firm may change the boundaries of the organization. PETA and other animal rights organizations campaigned against pharmaceutical companies to stop animal testing of their products. Some of those companies farmed out their testing to independent companies, such as Huntingdon Life Sciences, which became the subject of an intense and at times violent campaign by activists opposed to animal testing. Stop Huntingdon Animal Cruelty (SHAC) also targeted pharmaceutical companies that used Huntingdon. SHAC picketed the homes of Chiron executives, including sending a hearse to the house of a Chiron executive to pick up her very-alive body. Environmental extremists also bombed Chiron's facilities. In 2004 the FBI arrested seven people for violence against Huntingdon and Chiron.

Activists and NGOs have been criticized for being both "unelected" and unaccountable. They do not stand for election to allow the public to express its evaluation of their performance. They do not have to abide by governance requirements, such as Sarbanes-Oxley, considered in Chapter 20, that apply to firms. Some opponents of activists support applying Sarbanes-Oxley to NGOs and nonprofits. Activists and NGOs could be accountable to the public, government, their members, and financial supporters. SustainAbility, Ltd., a London consulting firm, published a report (2002), "The 21st Century NGO: In the Market for Change," asking for greater public accountability.

SUMMARY

Private politics takes place outside the arenas of government institutions and typically involves the use of social pressure to cause a firm to change its practices. Private politics is often led by activist organizations and other NGOs that attempt to advance issues on their agendas through direct pressure and offers of collaboration. Activists play an important role in the nonmarket environment because they can (1) alert management to issues of concern to the public, (2) affect the organization of interests, (3) lead to changes in institutions, and (4) provide information to the public and government officials.

Private politics strategies of activists are frequently integrated with public politics strategies. A private politics strategy may be composed of target selection, actions to attract the media, and efforts to develop public support. These strategies may involve advocacy science, policy studies, and media strategies to bring issues to the attention of a broader public. Activist organizations employ a variety of strategies to advance the issues on their agendas. Some focus on confrontation, whereas others cooperate with companies. The objective of confrontation is to shine the spotlight of public attention on a firm with the hope that social pressure will be generated and cause the firm to change its practices. Cooperative activists provide expertise to help companies improve their social and environmental practices or provide external legitimacy that allows companies to credibly demonstrate their improved practices to consumers and the public. These strategies are often complemented using public politics as a lever to encourage negotiations on the issue.

In dealing with activist organizations, firms take a number of approaches. Some ignore the issues and the activists in the hope that their interest will wane or that they will fail to generate broader support. Many negotiate directly with the activists, as in the OnBank case. Others collaborate with cooperative activists to find a solution to the identified problems, as in the case of McDonald's and EDF. When a firm believes that its practices are appropriate or that the activist group is weak, it may oppose the activists. Most firms, however, prefer to negotiate rather than become engaged in a protracted confrontation that could attract the attention of the media, the public, and government officials.

---

[32]See Sasser, Prakash, Cashore, and Auld (2006) for an analysis of why U.S. timber firms participate in the SFI rather than the FSC.

CASES

Shell, Greenpeace, and Brent Spar

The North Sea was a mature petroleum province where several facilities had already been abandoned or were approaching the ends of their useful lives. There were about 400 offshore petroleum platforms in the North Sea, about half of which were in the United Kingdom sector. The removal of platforms was governed by a variety of international regulatory principles. According to the guidelines of the International Maritime Organization, any installation in shallow waters had to be completely removed and dismantled on land. A substantial portion (about 50 in UK waters) of the current installations, however, were in deeper water, and if approved, could be disposed of at sea. According to the British interpretation of international conventions and guidelines as well as UK legislation, operators had to submit their preferred disposal option, the Best Practical Environmental Option (BPEO), for government approval. Each such case for disposal then was individually considered on its merits. If the platforms were disposed of at sea, any remains had to be left at least 55 meters below the surface. Proposals had to be well documented and include a review of the options considered. The costs of abandonment were to be borne by the field licensee. Part of the cost (50–70 percent) was tax deductible.

ROYAL DUTCH/SHELL

The Royal Dutch/Shell Group of Companies was a multinational holding of service and operating companies engaged in various branches of the oil, natural gas, chemicals, coal, and related businesses throughout the greater part of the world.[33] The parent companies, Royal Dutch Petroleum Company (domiciled in The Netherlands) and "Shell" Transport and Trading Company, plc (domiciled in the United Kingdom), did not themselves engage in operational activities. There were about 295,000 shareholders of Royal Dutch and some 300,000 of Shell Transport. Royal Dutch and Shell Transport owned the shares in the Group Holding Companies, Shell Petroleum NV (The Netherlands), Shell Petroleum Company Limited (United Kingdom), and Shell Petroleum Inc. (USA). These Group Holding Companies held all Group interests in the operating companies, such as Shell UK and Shell Germany (Deutsche Shell AG). The management of each operating company, although bound by common standards, was fairly independent in its decision making and was responsible for the performance and long-term viability of its own operations. It could, however, draw on the experience and expertise of other operating companies.

By most international standards Royal Dutch/Shell was one of the most successful companies in the world. It was the largest corporation in Europe and the third largest in the world. In recent years Royal Dutch/Shell was Europe's most profitable company. Since 1992, however, it had been in the process of restructuring. One reason was that its return on capital lagged behind its main competitor, Exxon. According to C. A.

J. Herkstroeter, president of the Group, the process of restructuring, although encouraging, was not yet satisfactory in terms of return on capital employed. Group companies had about 106,000 employees in 1994 (down from 117,000 in 1993). Its net income in 1994 was £4,070 million (up 36 percent from 1993), its return on capital was 10.4 percent (up from 7.9 percent from 1993), and its debt-to-capital ratio was 16.7 percent (down from 17.8 percent in 1993).

THE ISSUE—DISPOSAL OF LARGE OFFSHORE PETROLEUM FACILITIES

The Brent Spar was a cylindrical buoy, 463 feet high and weighing about 14,500 tons. Between 1976 and 1991 it was used as an oil storage facility and tanker loading buoy for the Brent field (which along with Brent Spar was 50 percent owned by Esso AG, a unit of Exxon Corporation). In 1991 a review concluded that the necessary refurbishing of the facility was economically unjustifiable. Brent Spar was thus decommissioned in September 1991. Shell UK, one of the operating companies of the Royal Dutch/Shell Group, considered several disposal options. These options were evaluated according to engineering complexity, risk to health and safety of workforce, environmental impact, cost, and acceptability to the British authorities and other officially designated parties. The latter included government bodies such as the Scottish National Heritage and the Joint Nature Conservancy Committee, as well as "legitimate users of the sea" (as specified in the 1987 Petroleum Act), mainly fishermen's associations and British Telecom International.[34]

Two options survived the initial screening process: horizontal onshore dismantling and deepwater disposal. The former consisted of the rotation of the buoy to the horizontal, transport to shore, and onshore dismantling. The latter involved towing the structure to a deepwater disposal site in the Northeast Atlantic and sinking the platform. The study commissioned by Shell UK concluded that deepwater disposal dominated on the grounds of engineering complexity, risk to health and safety of the workforce, and cost (about £11 million versus £46 million). Both alternatives were acceptable to the other parties consulted.

With respect to possible environmental impacts, the study concluded that both options were equally balanced. Whereas the environmental impact was expected to be minimal for both options, horizontal dismantling (due to its considerably higher engineering complexity) would involve an increased potential for mishaps that, if one were to occur in shallow inshore water, could have a significant impact on other users of the sea. In addition, a research team at the University of Aberdeen recommended deep-sea disposal. Consequently, Shell UK proposed deepwater disposal as its BPEO to the British Department of Energy, the relevant

---

[33]Royal Dutch Petroleum Company, Annual Report, 1994.

[34]Rudall Blanchard Associates Ltd. (for Shell UK Exploration and Production), Brent Spar Abandonment BPEO, December 1994.

regulatory agency. In mid-February 1995 the British Energy minister, Tim Eggart, announced that Shell's BPEO was accepted. The European governments were informed about the decision and were given 3 months to protest the decision. Although some of the European governments, including Germany, were generally critical of deep-sea disposal, no government officially protested, and so Shell UK scheduled the towing of Brent Spar to the disposal site in the North Atlantic for mid-June.

GREENPEACE

Founded in 1971, Greenpeace had grown to be the world's largest environmental group. It had about 3.1 million contributors worldwide and a budget of about $140 million. Offices were located in 30 countries with a full-time staff of about 1,200. In addition, Greenpeace owned four ships, a helicopter, and modern communications equipment. It could also draw on a wide network of thousands of volunteers. In 1994 Greenpeace was forced to cut its budget by about 10 percent and dismiss more than 90 staff members because of a drop in contributions mainly due to Greenpeace USA's opposition to the Persian Gulf War. The Greenpeace offices were fairly independent but coordinated their decisions through Greenpeace International, located in Amsterdam. Greenpeace strongholds were in Germany, the Netherlands, and the United States.[35]

One of the largest and most active Greenpeace sections was in Germany. Greenpeace e.V. (Germany) had about 120 full-time staff members, a budget of roughly $50 million, and could rely on over 500,000 enlisted volunteers.[36] Its German headquarters and the North Sea logistic centers were located in Hamburg. Greenpeace enjoyed high acceptance and popularity among the German public and had frequently captured center stage through spectacular actions, which was reflected in donations that reached a record in 1994. Greenpeace Germany alone contributed over 40 percent of the total budget of Greenpeace International. Recently, Greenpeace Germany had also been active in developing alternative solutions to environmental problems.

One of Greenpeace's principal strategies was to attract the public's attention through high-profile, confrontational actions, which were covered by Greenpeace photographers and film crews. "We try to keep it simple," said Steve D'Esposito, an American who was executive director of Greenpeace International. "One, we raise environmental awareness. Two, we want to push the world toward solutions, using the most egregious examples. The whole point is to confront; we try to get in the way. Confrontation is critical to get coverage in the press or to reach the public some other way."[37]

THE BRENT SPAR PROTESTS

After being informed about Shell UK's plans concerning Brent Spar in summer 1994, Greenpeace commissioned a policy study to consider the arguments for deep-sea disposal. The study concluded that total removal and not deep-sea disposal should be adopted as the BPEO, especially from the viewpoint of the environment.[38] By March, Greenpeace had devised a plan to board the Brent Spar. To win public support through television coverage, Greenpeace acquired satellite communications and video equipment.

On April 30, 1995, 14 Greenpeace activists from the United Kingdom, the Netherlands, and Germany landed on the Brent Spar by boat. They were joined by a group of nine journalists who with Greenpeace filmed the incident and broadcast it by satellite. After a 3-week occupation, the group was expelled by Shell. Although the UK media gave little coverage to the Greenpeace campaign, German television extensively broadcast footage of soaked activists. Harald Zindler, head of the section Campaigns of Greenpeace Germany, who organized the Brent Spar landing, recalled, "We were very happy when Shell decided to clear the platform. It portrayed Shell as an unresponsive and inconsiderate big business."[39] In response to the media coverage, expressions of outrage and protest in Germany and the Netherlands grew. Members of all German political parties and the German minister of the environment, Angelika Merkel, condemned Shell's decision to dump the rig in the deep sea. On May 22, the worker representatives on Shell Germany's supervisory board expressed "concern and outrage" at Shell's decision to "turn the sea into a trash pit."[40]

Under pressure, executives of Shell Germany met with Jochen Lorfelder of Greenpeace, who argued that 85 percent of German motorists would participate in a boycott. He told Shell that "in the four weeks it would take to tow the Brent Spar to its dumping site, Greenpeace would make life a nightmare for Shell." The chairman of Shell Germany explained that Shell UK's studies indicated that deep-sea disposal was the best alternative for the environment. Lorfelder answered, "But Joe Six-Pack won't understand your technical details. All he knows is that if he dumps his can in a lake, he gets fined. So he can't understand how Shell can do this."[41]

On June 7 Greenpeace activists again landed on the Brent Spar but were soon expelled. The next day the Fourth International North Sea Conference began in Esbjerg, Denmark. One of the main topics was the disposal of petroleum facilities. Germany introduced a proposal that would rule out any disposal at sea. Norway, France, and the United Kingdom, however, blocked the proposal.[42] In the meantime, calls for an informal boycott of Shell by German motorists were mounting. Proponents included members of all German political parties, unions, motorists' associations, the Protestant Church, and the former chief justice of the German Constitutional Court, Ernst Benda.

In its media campaign, Greenpeace successfully appealed to the German enthusiasm for recycling. In their homes many

---

[35]*Frankfurter Allgemeine Zeitung,* June 12, 1995.

[36]Interview with Harald Zindler, Greenpeace Germany, August 11, 1995.

[37]*New York Times,* July 8, 1995.

[38]Simon Reddy (for Greenpeace International), "No Grounds for Dumping," April 1995.

[39]Interview, August 11, 1995.

[40]*Wall Street Journal,* July 7, 1995.

[41]Ibid.

[42]Accepted proposals of this conference were nonbinding.

Germans separated garbage into bags for metal, glass, paper, chemicals, plastic, and organic waste. Harald Zindler pointed out the appeal of Greenpeace's strategy to the general public: "The average citizen thinks: 'Here I am dutifully recycling my garbage, and there comes big business and simply dumps its trash into the ocean.'" Greenpeace always tried to keep its message simple and connect it to the public's everyday experiences and values.

Despite the mounting protests and another attempt by Greenpeace to board the rig, Shell began towing the Brent Spar to its dumping site on June 11 as scheduled. During the following week the boycott of German Shell gas stations was in full swing. Sales were off 20–30 percent[43] and in some areas up to 40 percent.[44] The mayor of Leipzig banned city vehicles from using Shell gasoline. Boycotts also spread to the Netherlands and Denmark. During the G7-summit at Halifax, Canada, German Chancellor Helmut Kohl criticized Shell and the British government for persisting with the proposed deep-sea dumping. Two days later a firebomb exploded at a Shell gas station in Hamburg.

Shell had used high-powered water cannons to keep a Greenpeace helicopter from approaching the Brent Spar, but on June 16, two Greenpeace activists again succeeded in landing on the rig by arriving before the water cannons had been turned on. They managed to stay on Brent Spar while the rig was being towed to its chosen disposal site. On June 19, the German economics minister, Guenther Rexrodt, announced that his ministry, too, would join the boycott. During this period the German public received inconsistent messages from Shell. Although Shell Germany suggested that the project could be halted, Shell UK refused to stop the towing. Meanwhile in the United Kingdom, Prime Minister John Major was repeatedly attacked in Parliament but refused to reconsider the government's decision to approve Shell's proposal.

SHELL'S CLIMBDOWN

After a meeting of the Royal Dutch/Shell Group's managing directors in The Hague on June 20, Christopher Fay, chairman of Shell UK, announced that Shell would abandon its plans to sink the Brent Spar. Fay stressed that he still believed that deep-sea disposal offered the best environmental option but admitted that Shell UK had reached an "untenable position" because of its failure to convince other governments around the North Sea.[45] Shell UK would now attempt to dismantle the platform on land and sought approval from Norwegian authorities to anchor the Brent Spar temporarily in a fjord on the Norwegian coast.

The decision was received with joy by environmentalists and with an angry response by the British government. John Jennings, chairman of Shell Transport, apologized in a letter to the British Prime Minister. A variety of public relations experts criticized Shell's handling of the protests and its decision to abandon its original plans. Mike Beard, former president of the Institute of Public Relations, commented, "They failed to communicate the benefits of the course they believed to be right;

they lost what they believed to be their case; and now they're having to defend something they don't consider to be defensible."[46]

In response, Dick Parker, production director of Shell Expro, defended the company's decision not to involve environmental interest groups like Greenpeace: "Greenpeace does not have formal consultative status under the guidelines set out for an offshore installation proposal. Other bodies who represent a wide range of interests or who are accountable to their members are part of the process, and we consulted them."[47] Following the decision to halt the project, Shell started an advertising campaign admitting mistakes and promising change.

AFTERMATH

In the June 29 issue of *Nature*, two British geologists at the University of London argued that the environmental effects of Shell UK's decision to dump the Brent Spar in the deep sea would "probably be minimal." Indeed, the metals of the Brent Spar might even be beneficial to the deep-sea environment. Disposing of the Brent Spar on land could pose greater risks to the environment.[48] Robert Sangeorge of the Switzerland-based Worldwide Fund for Nature said, "Deep-sea disposal seemed the least harmful option." He called the Brent Spar episode "a circus and sideshow that distracted from the big environmental issues affecting the world."[49] In response, however, a spokesperson for Shell UK reiterated that the company would stick to its decision to abandon deep-sea disposal.

The Brent Spar remained anchored in Erfjord, Norway. After an independent Norwegian inspection agency, Det Norske Veritas, had surveyed the contents of the Brent Spar, some doubts arose about Greenpeace's estimates of the oil sludge remaining on Brent Spar. Shell had previously estimated that the Spar contained about 100 tons of sludge. Greenpeace had estimated 5,000 tons. On September 5, Greenpeace UK's executive director, Lord Peter Melchett, admitted that the estimates were inaccurate and apologized to Christopher Fay. Shell UK welcomed the apology and announced its intention to include Greenpeace among those to be consulted in its review of options and the development of a new BPEO.[50] ■

Preparation Questions

1. From Shell UK's perspective, what was the issue in this case, and where was it in its issue life cycle?
2. In which institutional arenas was this issue addressed? Which interests were active on this issue?
3. Evaluate Shell UK's decision process in choosing a BPEO. Could it have effectively communicated its rationale for deep-sea disposal to the public? Was Shell UK right in abandoning its initial plan? How should Shell have managed the Brent Spar disposal? From the perspective of

[43]*Wall Street Journal*, July 7, 1995.
[44]*Wirtschaftswoche*, June 22, 1995.
[45]*Financial Times*, June 21, 1995.

[46]*Financial Times*, June 23, 1995.
[47]Shell UK (Sarah James, ed.), "Brent Spar," July 1995.
[48]E. G. Nisbet and C. M. R. Fowler, "Is Metal Disposal Toxic to Deep Oceans?" *Nature* 375:715, June 29, 1995.
[49]*Wall Street Journal*, July 7, 1995.
[50]*Financial Times*, September 5–9, 1995.

a major multinational corporation such as Royal Dutch/ Shell, what strategy should be adopted to participate in, influence, and prepare for the development of this or similar issues? In what way, if any, might the organization structure of Shell have contributed to the Brent Spar debacle? Should the management of issues such as the disposal of the Brent Spar be centralized?

4. How did Greenpeace view this issue? What were its objectives and strategy? Why was it able to win the public

opinion war? Could Greenpeace use the estimated costs of deep-sea and on-land disposal to its advantage? Why was Shell unable to explain its position and reasoning to the public?

5. Why did the German government not protest Shell's plan before the boycott? Why did the German government oppose deep-sea dumping? Why did the British government approve Shell's BPEO?

6. What should Shell UK do now about the Brent Spar?

Source: This case was prepared by Daniel Diermeier from public sources, including materials supplied by the Shell Petroleum Co. Ltd. (London, UK) and Greenpeace e.V. (Hamburg, Germany), as well as an interview with Harald Zindler, head of the section Campaigns (Bereichsleiter Aktionen) of Greenpeace Germany. Copyright © 1995 by Daniel Diermeier. All rights reserved. Reprinted with permission.

Nike in Southeast Asia

Phil Knight, chairman of the board and CEO, opened Nike's 1996 annual report with an account of the record revenues of $6.5 billion. One paragraph later, though, he added: "Yet no sooner had the great year ended than we were hit by a series of blasts from the media about our practices overseas." Nike had been widely criticized by labor and human rights groups over the working conditions and wages at its suppliers' factories in Asia. The media followed developments closely as revelations of sweatshops in the United States added to the public interest in Nike. *Doonesbury* likened Nike factories to Dickensian sweatshops.

Sourcing shoes from low-wage countries in Asia had been one of the foundations of the company's strategy. Nike had never owned a factory in Asia; instead the company contracted production from independent companies. Shoes and apparel thus were manufactured in independently owned and operated factories, and Nike took ownership of the product only when it left the factory. The factories were mostly owned by Korean and Taiwanese companies with whom Nike maintained long-term relationships.

In 1997 Nike bought the bulk of its shoes from China, Vietnam, and Indonesia. As the company's visibility increased, so did the scrutiny of its practices. Nike had to deal with allegations of subcontractors running sweatshops marked by poor working conditions, worker abuse, and below-subsistence wages. Shoes that sold for up to $140 were manufactured by workers earning about $2 a day in such countries as Vietnam and Indonesia.

Nike had contracts with a dozen factories in Indonesia in 1997, employing around 120,000 people. Both Nike's South Korean and Taiwanese manufacturing partners had come to Indonesia to take advantage of the low labor costs. In Nike audits, several incidents involving Korean and Taiwanese plant managers had been reported. The workers considered some managers too strict, or even abusive, shouting at or striking workers, or issuing punishments considered excessive for bad work or tardiness. In one case, a worker had to run laps around the factory because the shoes she assembled had defects.[51] Nike insisted that managers who were found to be abusive be

transferred or removed. Employees and union activists from the Union of Needletrade, Industrial and Textile Employees (UNITE) in the United States confirmed that Nike's audits had been effective; at the Nikomas plant; for example, a security guard who hit a worker had been quickly fired by the owners.[52]

Underpayment of wages had led to several cases of unrest at Nike's Indonesian contract factories. In April 1997 workers at PT HASI staged a mass strike and protest. They demanded to be paid the new basic minimum monthly wage of 172,500 rupiah ($71.37), excluding allowances, that went into effect on April 1. A representative of the workers said that the company had included their "attendance" allowance in their basic wage, which meant that their minimum wage had actually stayed at last year's levels. The *Jakarta Post* quoted the personnel manager of the company as saying that because of its financial situation, it had been given permission by the manpower ministry to delay paying the 1997 minimum wage.

About 10,000 of the 13,000 workers at the factory marched 6 miles to the district parliament to demand the increase. Later in the week they burned cars and ransacked the factory's offices. The company then agreed to pay the minimum wage without including allowances for attendance, overtime, transport, holiday pay, and meals.[53] Nike claimed that its contract factories paid more than what most laborers would earn in other jobs. "We turn away more prospective employees than we could hire," Knight commented. "It sounds like a low wage and it is. But it's a wage that's greater than they used to make."[54]

In Vietnam, Nike's footwear plants had been under attack by both workers and media since 1996 when a 29-year-old Korean forewoman at the Sam Yang factory lined up 15 female Vietnamese workers and beat them around the face with an unfinished shoe because she was angered by the quality of their work. Workers staged an immediate strike, and the forewoman was fired the same day. Later, she was found guilty

---

[51]"Sweatshops Haunt U.S. Consumers," *BusinessWeek,* July 29, 1996.

[52]Ibid.

[53]"Workers Win Pay Raise at Nike Plant in Indonesia," *Reuters Asia-Pacific Business Report,* April 23, 1997.

[54]"Protests as Nike CEO Addresses Stanford Students." *San Francisco Examiner,* April 30, 1997.

in a Vietnam court of "humiliating" workers.[55] In another incident a Taiwanese manager from the Pao Chen factory forced 56 slow workers to run laps until a dozen fainted. The manager was sentenced to 6 months in prison for physically abusing workers.[56]

The monthly minimum wage at foreign-owned factories in Vietnam was $45 in 1997, compared with about $20 per month at state-owned factories. The Nike contract factories were believed to pay the minimum wage, but some had been accused of paying workers less than this in the first 3 months of employment, which was illegal.

When it came to average per-capita income, cost of living, and the value of workers' benefits, statements from Nike and claims from human rights groups such as the Vietnam Labor Watch (VLW) differed. Although Nike said that the annual per-capita income in areas where Nike factories were located was $200, VLW claimed it was $925. A *San Jose Mercury News* investigation found the average to be $446 in the areas where 14 of the 15 factories were located. According to Nike, most workers saved enough of their salary to send money home to their families. VLW interviewed 35 workers, and none said they could save money. The *Mercury News* found that 12 of 24 workers could save money. Nike claimed that workers received free health care, whereas the VLW said workers' health insurance was deducted from their paychecks. The *Mercury News* found that employers, by law, deducted and contributed 1 percent of employees' salaries to government medical insurance.[57]

Nike had its first "Code of Conduct" for its contract factories in 1992, after the initial criticism of its labor practices in Asia. In a Memorandum of Understanding signed by all Nike contractors, the contractors were required to comply with all local government regulations, including those on occupational health and safety. Nike banned the use of forced labor, and required environmental responsibility, nondiscrimination, and equal opportunity practices. The rights of association and collective bargaining were to be guaranteed. Nike's production managers, who were stationed at the factories, monitored working conditions on a daily basis. Enforcement was not a problem according to Nike; many factories produced exclusively for Nike, which gave the company tremendous leverage. Beginning in 1994 Nike hired the Indonesian office of the international accounting firm Ernst & Young to monitor the plants for worker pay, safety conditions, and attitudes toward the job. The auditors were to pull workers off the assembly line at random and ask them questions that the workers would answer anonymously. In September 1997 Nike severed contracts with four factories in Indonesia that did not pay workers the minimum wage. This was the first time Nike had fired contractors for noncompliance with its code of conduct.

In 1996 Nike established a Labor Practices Department to monitor subcontracted manufacturing facilities and upgrade conditions for factory workers around the world. The creation of the department was "a further step in Nike's ongoing commitment to have products made only in the best facilities with the best working conditions in the sports and fitness industry." Specific emphasis would be on Indonesia, China, and Vietnam.[58]

Nike had long promised independent monitoring of its factories, and in February 1997 it hired Andrew Young, civil rights activist and former U.S. ambassador to the United Nations and mayor of Atlanta, to review its labor practices. The appointment received a mixed reception; Nike and Young emphasized his independence, but critics claimed he was hired to promote the company's image.

Young's report was released in June 1997 and called conditions in Nike's overseas factories comparable with those in U.S. factories. The report stated, "The factories that we visited which produce Nike goods were clean, organized, adequately ventilated and well lit …. I found no evidence or pattern of widespread or systematic abuse or mistreatment of workers in the twelve factories." The Young report did not specifically address the wage issue, which Young considered too complex and beyond the capacity of his firm. Phil Knight said, "We will take action to improve in areas where he suggests we need to improve. For although his overall assessment is that we are doing a good job, good is not the standard Nike seeks in anything we do."[59] When the Young report was released, Nike took out full-page advertisements in major papers summarizing the key recommendations from the report.

The report was immediately criticized by human rights and labor groups. Thuyen Nguyen, director of VLW, noted that Young spent only 10 days visiting factories in China, Vietnam, and Indonesia; his tours were conducted by management, and he talked to workers through Nike interpreters. "Workers are not about to complain in front of the boss, especially in authoritarian countries where workers labeled troublemakers can be fired and jailed," wrote Nguyen.[60] Medea Benson, director of the human rights group Global Exchange, said, "I think it was an extremely shallow report. I was just amazed that he even admitted that he spent 3 hours in factories using Nike interpreters and then could come and say he did not find systematic abuse."[61]

In a letter to Phil Knight, a coalition of women's groups including the National Organization of Women, the Ms. Foundation for Women, the Black Women's Agenda, and the Coalition of Labor Union Women wrote, "While the women who wear Nike shoes in the United States are encouraged to perform their best, the Indonesian, Vietnamese, and Chinese women making the shoes often suffer from inadequate wages, corporal punishment, forced overtime, and/or sexual harassment."[62] Fifty-three members of Congress wrote to Phil Knight

[55]"Culture Shock: Korean Employers Irk Vietnamese Workers," *Far Eastern Economic Review*, August 22, 1996.
[56]"Nike Aide in Vietnam Convicted," *Wall Street Journal*, June 1997.
[57]"Nike's Fancy Footwork in Vietnam," *San Jose Mercury News*, June 25, 1997.

[58]"Nike Establishes Labor Practices Department," Canada NewsWire, October 3, 1996.
[59]*New York Times*, June 25, 1997.
[60]"Report on Nike Work Force Glossed over Issues," Thuyen Nguyen. Letter, *New York Times*, June 30, 1997.
[61]*New York Times*, June 25, 1997.
[62]*New York Times*, October 20, 1997.

accusing Nike of "ruthlessly exploiting" workers. Knight invited the Congress members to visit the factories.

The criticism and actions against Nike also occurred at the local level. Protesters distributed leaflets at a Nike-sponsored event at Stanford University where Phil Knight had received his MBA.

Five months after Andrew Young's report, the heat was turned up further when an audit by Ernst & Young, initially intended for Nike's internal use, was leaked to the media. The report revealed unsafe conditions at the Tae Kwang Vina Industrial Ltd. Factory in Vietnam, including chemical levels 6–177 times that allowed by Vietnamese regulations. The audit also stated that dust in the mixing room was 11 times the standard and that a high percent of the employees had respiratory problems. Major problems detailed in the report were the unprotected use of dangerous materials, poor air quality, and overtime-law violations. Over 75 percent of the workers in the factory were said to suffer from respiratory problems. Nike said that the shortcomings in the audit had been addressed.

The publicity surrounding labor practices was worrisome to Nike management. In some regions around the world, surveys showed that the bad publicity had affected consumers' perceptions of Nike. Consumers were used to considering Nike a leader in its field, but here the company was stumbling. Bob Wood, vice president of U.S. marketing, stated, "It's obviously not good. It's something that we're really concerned about, but we haven't noticed any literal decline in demand or sell-through of our products because of it."

Knight admitted that Nike had been ill prepared for the media offensive. "Our communications staff is woefully inadequate to deal with this problem right now," he explained. "Our

Washington, DC, office essentially is one guy, and he's always dealt essentially with the [international] trade, with the quota issues." In 1997 Nike's public relations department had a staff of approximately 10 people. According to Knight, "They should probably have fifty people in there, but they have to be the right people, and organized right." Martha Benson, a Nike spokesperson in Asia, explained, "We are about sports, not Manufacturing 101."[63]

Phil Knight could not have been more sure that Nike was a force for positive change in Asia. "Whether you like Nike or don't like Nike, good corporations are the ones that lead these countries out of poverty," he said in an interview. "When we started in Japan, factory labor there was making $4 a day, which is basically what is being paid in Indonesia and being so strongly criticized today. Nobody today is saying, 'The poor old Japanese.' We watched it happen all over again in Taiwan and Korea, and now it's going on in Southeast Asia." ▪

Preparation Questions

1. How serious are the criticisms of the practices in the factories of Nike's suppliers in Indonesia and Vietnam? Are Nike's sales likely to be hurt by the criticisms and the actions of activists?

2. How effectively has Nike addressed the sequence of episodes? Was hiring Andrew Young wise?

3. What, if anything, should Nike do about the wages paid in its suppliers' factories in Asia? Is Phil Knight right in saying that companies like Nike can "lead countries out of poverty"?

4. How should Nike deal with the inevitable continued scrutiny its practices will receive?

Anatomy of a Corporate Campaign: Rainforest Action Network and Citigroup (A)

Citigroup, the world's largest project finance bank, provided financing for extractive projects such as mining, logging, and oil exploration. Some of these projects took place in developing countries and in rain forests and other endangered ecosystems. In 2000 the Rainforest Action Network (RAN) launched its Global Finance Campaign with Citigroup as the target. The goal was to convince Citigroup, and eventually all lenders, to stop financing destructive activities in endangered ecosystems.

Project finance referred to the financing of long-term industrial (e.g., pulp and paper mills), public service, and infrastructure (e.g., telecommunications) projects. The cash flows generated by a project were used to repay the debt financing.[64]

Creditors did not have recourse to the project companies (contractors) for failure to repay the debt—only to a project's

specific assets, rights, and interests, which served as collateral for the funding. Most project finance deals were highly leveraged with project companies providing 20–40 percent of the required funds as equity. Typically, a lead bank arranged a project's financing and then opened the deal to participation by other banks and investors. The project finance market peaked in 2000, when $379 billion was funded globally.

EXTRACTIVE PROJECTS AND RAIN FORESTS

Environmental NGOs (nongovernmental organizations) had historically targeted logging and mining companies directly. In the late 1990s, however, some environmental activist organizations, such as RAN, began to focus on the commercial banks financing extractive industries. The objective was to cut off funding for projects that led to the destruction of rain forests in developing countries. Through project finance, revolving credit facilities, or general corporate loans, many banks funded the extraction of timber, wood pulp, wood chip, and oil, in addition to open-pit mining for ores and land clearing

[63]*Wall Street Journal,* September 26, 1997.
[64]Michelle Chan-Fishel, "Project Finance Trends: Key Players, Regions, and Sectors," Friends of the Earth–US, September 22, 2003.

for cattle farming, all of which contributed to the destruction of rain forests.

Tropical rain forests received between 4 and 8 meters of rain a year. Rain forests covered only 2 percent of the Earth's surface, yet they housed about half of the world's 5–10 million plant and animal species. According to the National Academy of Sciences, a 4-square-mile area of rain forest typically housed 1,500 species of flowering plants, 750 of trees, 125 of mammals, 400 of birds, 100 of reptiles, 60 of amphibians, and 150 of butterflies. Drugs for cancer treatment, heart problems, arthritis, and birth control came (in some cases exclusively) from rain forest plants. Rain forests also held years and years of carbon buildup in their vegetation. When this vegetation was burned or cut and left to decay, the carbon was released as CO_2. CO_2 released in this manner was the second largest factor contributing to the greenhouse effect.

The primary rain forests in India, Bangladesh, Sri Lanka, and Haiti had been destroyed. By 1985, 55 and 45 percent, respectively, of the Philippines' and Thailand's rain forests had been destroyed. According to the National Academy of Sciences, over 50 million acres of rain forest were destroyed a year.

THE RAINFOREST ACTION NETWORK

RAN was founded in 1985 with the mission of protecting tropical rain forests and the human rights of people living in them. RAN used tools such as citizen protests, media, nonviolent civil disobedience, and publications to bring awareness to the issues and pressure governments, corporations, and lending institutions. RAN had about two dozen employees, all in the United States, organized in three departments: operations, development (fundraising), and campaigns. RAN had a full-time media specialist who interacted with the news media and participated in campaign planning. Within the campaigns department, RAN typically had a campaign manager for each campaign and used an organizing staff of about five to support whichever campaign was active at the time.

In the mid-1990s RAN changed its focus from public policy to the private sector with the objective of changing the practices of companies with environmentally destructive practices. RAN executive director Michael Brune said, "Companies were more responsive to public opinion than certain legislatures were. We felt we could create more democracy in the marketplace than in the government."

RAN'S GLOBAL FINANCE CAMPAIGN

Selecting a Target

In late 1999 RAN was concluding a successful 2-year campaign (led by Brune) targeting Home Depot, which had agreed to end by 2003 the sale of wood from endangered forests. For the Global Finance Campaign, RAN planned to use a model similar to the one used for Home Depot—target a large, brand-oriented, U.S.-based multinational company that had a strong retail presence, was a leader in its industry, and had a key role in facilitating the destruction of old growth forests and supporting

extractive industries. Because RAN was a small organization with the goal of shifting the practices of entire sectors, not just individual companies, it relied on the ripple effect of targeting a market leader.

One company stood out as the best target—Citigroup, the world's largest bank. Citigroup was the leading global, emerging market project finance bank and the leading developing country project finance bank. Citigroup also had a key role in a number of specific projects that alarmed RAN, such as the Camisea pipeline in Peru (Citigroup was the financial advisor on the project but did not directly fund it) and the Chad-Cameroon pipeline under construction by ExxonMobil, Chevron, and a consortium of central African oil companies.[65] In researching Citigroup's involvement, RAN relied on data from Dealogic's ProjectWare, a database of project finance deals.

In 2000 Citigroup had net income of $13.5 billion on revenues of $111.8 billion and had customers in over 100 countries and territories. Citigroup's activities included global consumer banking, global corporate and investment banking, global investment management and private banking, and investment activities. Citigroup's global consumer group offered banking, lending, investment services, and credit cards to customers in over 50 countries and territories. The global consumer group reported core net income of $5.3 billion on $30.4 billion of revenues in 2000.[66]

Citigroup had a public image and a brand to protect (in particular, its large consumer banking operation and credit card business), which made it an attractive target. Ilyse Hogue, RAN's campaign manager for the Global Finance Campaign, said:

> Citigroup had poured $100 million into its brand image, most recently on its "Live Richly" marketing campaign, which was predicated on the notion that "there is more to life than money." We saw a company that was investing a lot in making the public believe that they operated in line with common social values. Part of Citi's vulnerability was the juxtaposition of what it articulated to the public with what we saw on the ground from Citi's finance activities.

RAN began the campaign expecting it to last up to 5 years but hoping to win in 3 years. RAN dedicated three staff members, including Hogue, full time to the Global Finance Campaign.

RAN had such limited resources and Citigroup was such a large target that many people thought RAN could not win the campaign. RAN believed, however, that Citigroup's vulnerability was its sensitivity to public opinion, so exploiting that vulnerability by publicizing Citigroup's environmental practices became the heart of RAN's strategy.

---

[65]For years RAN had developed relationships with allies (e.g., other NGOs, indigenous federations, and others) on the front lines of the affected areas. These allies kept RAN apprised of project developments and enabled it to track the projects and their financing.

[66]Citigroup Inc. 2000 Annual Report.

RAN's Strategy during the First Two Years of the Campaign[67]

In developing its strategy, RAN drew heavily on past campaigns and consulted with allies that had interacted with Citigroup and were interested in helping. RAN dubbed Citibank the "World's Most Destructive Bank" and on April 13, 2000 wrote to Citigroup CEO Sandy Weill, asking the company to recognize its role in, and take action to address, the destruction of the world's old growth forests and the acceleration of climate change. As with most of RAN's campaigns, this introductory letter presented the issues and a set of demands. Five days later a group of RAN campaigners addressed the board of directors and Sandy Weill at Citigroup's annual meeting, voicing their concerns in front of a room of shareholders. On April 19, Citigroup agreed to meet with RAN to discuss its connection with the fossil fuel and forest industries. Citigroup, however, took no action to address the issues.

After Citigroup's annual meeting, RAN organized a 3-day strategic brainstorming session, attended by about 20 ally organizations, to generate ideas, increase awareness, and spur interest in the campaign. Some of RAN's strategies included shareholder resolutions, high-profile media attention, paid advertisements, Days of Action with student networks, disruptions of Citibank branches, and other nonviolent civil disobedience (e.g., banner hangs). Hogue believed the media was one of the best arrows in RAN's quiver when going after a target's brand image.

In September 2000 RAN launched the campaign on college campuses, encouraging a boycott of Citigroup credit cards and job recruitment. Many of RAN's actions were designed to call the public's attention to the campaign objectives and attract media coverage, which was essential to informing the public. In October, RAN organized a Day of Action that included demonstrations in which participants cut up their Citibank credit cards and closed their Citibank accounts. In December, carolers gathered at Citigroup's headquarters and sang "Oil Wells" to the tune of "Jingle Bells." The campaign also targeted Sandy Weill. For Valentine's Day 2001, Weill received hundreds of valentines, asking him to show the Earth some love and stop funding rain forest destruction. April 2001 saw the second Day of Action, with 80 actions in 12 countries on 5 continents. The actions included hanging banners, marches, and leaving symbolic piles of wood chips and oil at Citibank branches. Also in April, 500 schoolchildren sent drawings to Weill asking him to stop funding rain forest destruction. In October, an oil pipeline under construction in an Ecuadorian cloud forest reserve was obstructed by dozens of indigenous women and children. Students across the United States gathered at local Citibank branches, bringing pledges from 12,000 students who refused to do business with the "#1 funder of global warming." In February 2002 students at 60 U.S. colleges participated in a National Student Week of

Action, which included demonstrations as well as telephone calls and letters delivered to Citigroup.[68]

Much of RAN's media attention was "earned"—media coverage that RAN did not pay for, such as press coverage of Days of Action or articles written about the Global Finance Campaign. In addition, RAN paid for a number of advertisements in various newspapers and magazines criticizing Citigroup and challenging it to take leadership in protecting the environment.

Enlisting students was important to the success of the campaign, and RAN found that students at many universities were eager to participate. To mobilize student groups, RAN campaigners traveled to campuses to spur interest in the campaign. In addition, RAN hired organizers from Green Corps, an organization that trained young environmental activists to become future leaders. Green Corps had historically been politically aggressive but had not promoted the use of civil disobedience. Green Corps organizers were hired on a short-term basis and saturated campuses—educating students, organizing Days of Action, and establishing groups (or relationships with existing student groups) with which RAN could coordinate.

Students at Columbia University, through SEEJ (Students for Environmental and Economic Justice), played a significant role in the campaign over time. Citigroup had a substantial presence at Columbia—it had an affinity agreement with Columbia, and Citigroup's logo appeared on student identification cards. Nearly 4,000 Columbia students opened accounts with Citibank each year.[69]

RAN's ability to gain the support of young people, such as college students, was critical in getting Citigroup's attention. Many students refused Citibank credit cards as a result of the campaign and wrote letters to Citigroup to that effect. Hogue said, "Cards issued to college students are kind of a gateway drug, in Citigroup's mind. If Citigroup breeds brand loyalty by issuing credit cards to young people, then Citigroup has their business for college loans, mortgages, their kids' college, and retirement."

During the first 2 years of the campaign, RAN met frequently with Citigroup to discuss the issues—the difficulty was getting any real response or action from Citigroup. RAN was clearly frustrated by the lack of progress.

Response from Citigroup

Citigroup had assigned its vice president of community relations to interact with RAN, although she initially delegated day-to-day communications with RAN to others. Community relations typically dealt with issues like community reinvestment and partnering with Habitat for Humanity. As the campaign wore on,

---

[67]www.ran.org.

[68]During campaign activities, no activists were injured or served jail time. However, there were many arrests of RAN staff, students, concerned citizens, and volunteers. Arrests sometimes led to fines or community service, but most charges were dropped.

[69]"SEEJ Members Influence Citigroup Corporate Agenda," *Columbia Daily Spectator*, February 3, 2004.

the vice president, who had a long tenure at Citigroup and was highly respected, began to develop expertise on project-finance and environmental issues.

After 2 years of campaign activity and regular meetings with RAN, Citigroup had to decide what to do about the RAN campaign. ∎

Preparation Questions

1. Identify the issues, interests, institutions, and information characterizing this nonmarket situation.
2. Was it strategically wise for RAN to launch a campaign on project finance? Can RAN realistically expect to affect project finance, which is provided by banks around the world?
3. Was Citigroup a good or bad target for RAN? Why not focus on the project contractors themselves?
4. Is Citigroup vulnerable to such a campaign? What harm can RAN impose on Citigroup, and how serious is that harm?
5. What should RAN do next in its campaign? Should it abandon the campaign? Should it accept a symbolic agreement with Citigroup and turn its attention elsewhere?
6. What action, if any, should Citigroup take in light of the RAN campaign?

Source: This is an abridged version of a case written by Research Associate Erin Yurday, Cornell MBA 1998, under the supervision of Professor David P. Baron. This case would not have been possible without the help of Mike Brune and Ilyse Hogue of Rainforest Action Network. Copyright © 2004 by the Board of Trustees of the Leland Stanford Junior University. All rights reserved. Reprinted with permission.

Anatomy of a Corporate Campaign: Rainforest Action Network and Citigroup (B)

The Rainforest Action Network (RAN) launched its campaign against Citigroup in April 2000 with the objective of forcing Citigroup to recognize and take responsibility for its role in rain forest destruction through its financing. After two challenging years, RAN believed that the campaign was gaining momentum, but RAN was still meeting with Citigroup personnel who had little real authority. Ilyse Hogue, campaign manager for the Global Finance Campaign, said, "We were convinced that no one inside Citigroup with any decision-making ability was paying attention to us." RAN was at a low point in the campaign. Outside developments then suddenly put the spotlight on corporate governance and Citigroup. RAN took advantage of the opportunity and stepped up the pressure beginning in the summer of 2002.

ENRON

In July 2002, following Enron's bankruptcy, billions of dollars of deals that Citigroup had structured for Enron came into question. Some of these deals made the funds flowing into Enron look like energy trades instead of loans. The funds were off balance sheet, hiding part of Enron's debt burden from ratings agencies, investors, and creditors. Some of the transactions also made Enron's core energy trading activities look as if they were generating more cash than they actually were.[70]

JACK GRUBMAN

Coinciding with the Enron news was more bad news for Citigroup. Criticism of Jack Grubman, the star telecom analyst of Citigroup's Salomon Smith Barney, had been growing for some time—complaints focused on biased research resulting from his dual roles as investment banker and analyst. One example was Grubman's upgrade of AT&T from "neutral" to "buy" in 1999. At the time of the upgrade, AT&T was preparing a multibillion-dollar stock offering, and Salomon was seeking a lead role in the underwriting. Reports suggested that Weill, an AT&T board member, nudged Grubman to reassess AT&T. New York State Attorney General Eliot Spitzer and the National Association of Securities Dealers began investigating.[71]

Much of the Enron and Grubman related news was reported on July 22 and 23, 2002. On the 22nd, Citigroup's stock closed at $32.04, down 11 percent from the previous day's close. On the 23rd, Citigroup's stock fell another 16 percent, closing at $27.

STEPPING UP THE PRESSURE IN THE GLOBAL FINANCE CAMPAIGN[72]

RAN had considered Citigroup a good target because of its pride in its brand name and its sensitivity to public opinion. Now that Citigroup had been implicated in the Enron and Grubman scandals, RAN stepped up the pressure.

A national Day of Action was planned for November 6, 2002, with 40 different actions, including a demonstration at Citigroup's headquarters by New York University students. On November 13, a full-page advertisement appeared in the *New York Times* with the headline, "Did you know that someone is using your Citigroup credit card without your authorization?" Later that month, activists blockaded all the Citibank branches in San Francisco's financial district using U-locks, kryptonite chains, and concrete-filled barrels. Activists in New York, Washington D.C., and Miami locked themselves to the doors of Citibank branches, shutting them down. In December, over 2,500 letters and pictures from children across the United States were delivered to Weill, asking him to stop funding global warming and forest destruction.

---

[70]See the Chapter 20 case *The Collapse of Enron.*

[71]Charles Gasparino, "The Stock-Research Pact: How Settlement Train Kept on Track," *Wall Street Journal*, December 23, 2002; Charles Gasparino, "Spitzer Staff Gathers Salomon E-Mails Criticizing Grubman," *Wall Street Journal*, July 16, 2002.

[72]www.ran.org.

In January 2003, RAN launched a "Hometown Showdown," a 2-month campaign in New York City, which included visiting Citibank branches, plastering posters around the city, and organizing student groups. The campaign got personal in January 2003 when activists visited Greenwich, Connecticut, where Weill lived, and plastered grocery stores with "Wanted" posters with Weill's picture. The protesters delivered campaign information to Weill's neighbors and son. In February, at a Citigroup-sponsored parade in Hartford, Connecticut in which Citigroup employees carried red umbrellas with the slogan "On the Move," protestors appeared, holding a banner that read, "Citi: On the Move in the Wrong Direction. #1 in Rainforest Destruction."

In March, former Treasury Secretary Robert Rubin, a Citigroup executive and board member, was speaking at the Columbia Business School when students disrupted him. Other students hung a banner reading, "Rubin and Citigroup: Partners in Environmental Crime." According to an article in the *Columbia Daily Spectator*, at the lecture, a student asked Rubin, "How can you justify funding the pipeline in Ecuador?" Rubin replied that the pipeline was not a Citigroup project. The student asked again, "Is it not true that you're funding the pipeline?" Moments later, Rubin replied, "Yes, we are funding it."[73]

Also in March 2003, Weill arrived at Cornell University, his alma mater, to a festive rally and a banner reading, "Sandy Weill, Class of '55, Make Us Proud: Stop Funding Destruction." RAN president and founder Randy Hayes was invited to speak on these issues by a Cornell student group the night before Weill's speech. Hayes then accompanied the students into the speech and offered to debate Weill on the issues. In April a television commercial aired in New York City featuring Susan Sarandon, Ed Asner, Daryl Hannah, and Ali McGraw cutting up their Citigroup credit cards and showing graphic footage of the environmental damage from projects financed by Citigroup. RAN claimed that 20,000 Citigroup credit cards were cut up as a result of the campaign.

NEXT STEP

By the spring of 2003, RAN believed that Citigroup was vulnerable from the Enron and Grubman scandals and the stepped-up campaign. Citigroup had kept RAN at a distance for 3 years by holding regular meetings but never progressing from discussions to negotiations. Citigroup knew that RAN was planning protests at Citigroup's upcoming April 15, 2003 annual meeting, marking the 3-year anniversary of RAN's initial contact with Citigroup. ▪

Preparation Questions

1. What damage, if any, is the RAN campaign doing to Citigroup?
2. Is RAN acting responsibly in campaigning against project financing? In its campaign tactics?
3. How vulnerable is Citigroup as a result of the Enron and Grubman scandals?
4. What should Citigroup anticipate next? What, if anything, should it do? Should it begin serious negotiations with RAN?
5. If Citigroup were to agree to negotiate, which agreements should RAN be prepared to accept and which to reject? What enforcement mechanism for the agreement should RAN seek?

Source: This case was written by Research Associate Erin Yurday, Cornell MBA 1998, under the supervision of Professor David P. Baron. This case would not have been possible without the help of Mike Brune and Ilyse Hogue of the Rainforest Action Network. Copyright © 2004 by the Board of Trustees of the Leland Stanford Junior University. All rights reserved. Reprinted with permission.

[73]"SEEJ Members Influence Citigroup Corporate Agenda," *Columbia Daily Spectator*, February 3, 2004.

5 | CRISIS MANAGEMENT

INTRODUCTION

Crises happen even to firms that take measures to avoid them. Acts of nature and random events occur. Most crises involving businesses, however, have a degree of human involvement and at least the possibility that the firm was responsible for the crisis occurring. Human involvement could be on the part of the firm as in the case of the *Exxon Valdez* oil spill, a villain outside the firm as in the case of Tylenol laced with cyanide, or innocent persons in the case of patients experiencing side effects of a prescription drug. Crises require immediate attention and can have lasting effects on brands and the reputations of companies. Crises can also alter the operating practices of firms and industries. Medicines have tamper-resistant packaging, new oil tankers have double hulls, warnings on many prescription drugs are stronger, disclosure of pharmaceutical clinical trial results is broader, and postmarketing testing is conducted on some drugs.

Many firms, even those that have not experienced a crisis, have taken measures to reduce the likelihood of a crisis, formulated management preparedness plans, and developed crisis response plans. Wal-Mart had studied weather forecasts and projected the likely path of Hurricane Katrina and had delivered to its stores and distribution centers in the Gulf Coast states supplies that would be needed by people in the event of a disaster. When the hurricane struck, Wal-Mart was ready with portable generators, bottled water, and other needed items. In many cases, however, a crisis is difficult to forecast, but nevertheless firms can prepare for the types of crises that might develop and be ready to respond.

This chapter addresses crisis management and its components: avoidance, preparedness, root cause analysis, response, and resolution. The focus is on crises that directly affect a firm's stakeholders and the broader public. The conceptual frameworks developed in the previous chapters provide the foundation for effective crisis management, and approaches specific to crisis management are introduced, particularly those associated with crisis response and communication.[1]

THE NATURE AND CAUSES OF CRISES

A crisis is a situation in which harm to people or property either has occurred or is imminent. A crisis typically is unexpected, can escalate quickly, and can damage a firm's operating performance, its reputation, and the credibility of management. A crisis often requires action under time pressure, so management must act with a sense of urgency. A crisis can attract the media and private politics actors. Moreover, the public may sympathize with those who were harmed, particularly if they were unsuspecting or unsophisticated. Many crises develop quickly, as in the case of Tylenol poisoning, but some fester for extended periods. The protests against Nike for alleged sweatshop conditions in the factories of its overseas suppliers continued for several years.[2]

Tylenol In 1982, seven people died from Tylenol capsules injected with cyanide. The crisis was identified when the Chicago medical examiner and fire department found that victims had in common the use of Tylenol. To prevent any further loss of life, Johnson & Johnson issued a nationwide recall of 31 million Tylenol capsules at a cost of $100 million. CEO James Burke personally appeared on television to explain the recall and answered questions at a news conference. The company's strong and rapid response and the evidence that the tampering had taken place in retail stores and not in the manufacturing process relieved Johnson & Johnson of responsibility.[3] Sales of Tylenol recovered quickly once the product was reintroduced. The company was acclaimed for its quick action in an uncertain situation in which lives were at risk, and its handling of the crisis strengthened the company's reputation for quality. By the late 2000s, however, quality

---

[1]Diermeier (2011) provides an insightful and comprehensive coverage of reputation and crisis management.

[2]See the Chapter 4 case *Nike in Southeast Asia*.

[3]The Tylenol bottles were found to have been purchased in a small number of stores, and the batch numbers of the bottles quickly led police to conclude that the tampering had occurred in the stores. The killer has never been found.

problems developed at several Johnson & Johnson plants and the company faced a new crisis described in the chapter case *Johnson & Johnson and Its Quality Reputation.*

Exxon Valdez   The 1989 grounding of the *Exxon Valdez* and the accompanying spill of 11 million gallons of crude oil created an environmental crisis, and Exxon's response escalated the crisis.[4] Exxon responded by moving a team from Houston to Valdez, Alaska, in 20 hours and was prepared to spray a chemical dispersant on the oil as called for in its oil spill procedures. For 2 days the Coast Guard prevented Exxon from doing so to run tests on the dispersant, and then a delay of an additional 2 days resulted because of bad weather that grounded aircraft. Exxon revealed that the captain of the tanker was sleeping at the time of the grounding. Reports circulated that the captain, who had been assigned to the *Exxon Valdez* after completing alcohol rehabilitation, was drunk. Exxon was viewed by many people as directly responsible and in the eyes of many people as negligent. As considered later, the company's communication to the public provoked more criticism, and the damage to the company's reputation continues today.

Société Génerale   Although the specifics and timing are difficult to predict, some crises have a positive probability of developing. Rogue traders have caused billions of dollars of losses to financial markets firms, and firms engaged in financial services and commodities and currency trading have developed procedures and systems to control trading risks. Société Génerale, a leading financial services group in the euro zone, was proud of its control system, yet in 2008 a 31-year-old securities trader in France was revealed to have evaded the controls for 3 years, taking €50.4 billion in positions in European stocks. Unwinding the positions resulted in a loss of €4.9 billion, and forced the bank to quickly sell €5.5 billion in new shares to remain viable.

Goldman Sachs   Goldman Sachs was the most profitable of the former investment banks and was a major player in the mortgage-backed securities business that contributed to the financial crisis. Goldman Sachs profits suffered less than other banks during the crisis, since it had reduced its exposure to mortgage-backed securities at the same time it continued to design and sell the securities to customers. The bank was also found to have allowed an outside investor to provide advice on the selection of mortgages to back new securities to be issued, and those securities were chosen because the investor believed they would fail. The investor planned to short the new securities, which Goldman marketed without informing customers of the investor's role. The Securities and Exchange Commission filed a lawsuit against Goldman and private lawsuits followed. The Chapter 11 case *Goldman Sachs and Its Reputation* provides more information.

BP   An explosion at BP's Texas City, Texas, refinery in 2005 killed 15 workers and injured another 170 people. The company had been warned of safety problems, and cost-cutting due to budget pressures may have led the company to delay dealing with the problems. The accident resulted in the company pleading guilty to criminal charges, paying fines, and facing liability lawsuits. The accident severely damaged BP's reputation—the company prided itself on its environmental and social responsibility programs—and dissipated public trust in the company.

BP in the Gulf of Mexico   In April 2010 a methane gas explosion on the Deepwater Horizon drilling platform under contract to BP killed 11 workers and resulted in an oil spill 20 times the size of the *Exxon Valdez* spill. The well was capped nearly 3 months later after several unsuccessful attempts, and a relief well was completed in September, ending the threat. The government shut down the fishing industry in the Gulf, and other economic activities were also affected. BP established a $20 billion fund to compensate victims for economic and other losses, and the company lost over half its market value. The extent of the ecological damage was unclear, and the Gulf Coast beaches were open for business the following summer.

THE PATTERN OF CRISIS DEVELOPMENT

Crises often have a pattern that can be conceptualized using the life cycle framework introduced in Chapter 1. Adapted for crisis management, the stages are identification, escalation, intervention, and resolution. The Chapter 4 case *Shell, Greenpeace, and Brent Spar* provides an

---

[4]The oil spill was the largest in the United States at the time but was exceeded by 21 other spills in other countries.

opportunity to identify the stages of development of a crisis resulting from Shell's plans to sink an obsolete oil storage vessel in the North Sea.

The first stage in the life cycle of a crisis is *identification*. A crisis may result from a single event or from a series of developments over time. The subprime mortgage crisis of 2008 was the result of risky home mortgages issued over a period of several years that resulted in widespread defaults when the economy slowed. A crisis can also result from a single event such as an accident, as in the case of Exxon officials who received a call from the captain of the *Exxon Valdez* that the ship had "fetched up hard aground" and was "leaking some oil." Some crises are revealed directly to the public whereas others are identified from inside the company. The Tylenol crisis was identified by a medical examiner and the fire department whose investigations identified the link between two deaths that were then traced to Tylenol capsules. The crisis at Société Générale was identified internally and became public when the company notified law enforcement officials and regulators of its findings.

Some crises have unusual causes and come as a considerable surprise, as the Perrier example indicates.

PERRIER AND BENZENE   Perrier mineral water, produced by Source Perrier S.A. of France, is a mixture of natural spring water and a gas obtained from wells near the source at Vergeze. The gas from the well is basically carbon dioxide but contains a number of other elements, including benzene and hydrogen sulfide. Benzene is a suspected carcinogen, and hydrogen sulfide is the gas that smells like rotten eggs. To remove the benzene and the hydrogen sulfide, Source Perrier used carbon filters and relied on the smell of hydrogen sulfide to know when to change the filters. Trouble developed when Perrier switched to gas from a new well that contained a lower concentration of hydrogen sulfide. Workers then did not change the filters as often as needed to remove the benzene, and traces of benzene were left in the bottled mineral water. Routine tests in the United States disclosed benzene, and although the amounts were believed not to constitute a health hazard, the public was concerned and the media covered the issue extensively. Perrier initially dismissed the benzene reports, but after the disclosure, distributors in Japan, the Netherlands, and Denmark recalled the water. Perrier decided to issue a worldwide recall.

The second stage is *escalation*. Some crises explode as a result of media coverage, government actions, or company actions. In some cases, such as that of the *Exxon Valdez*, the crisis is exacerbated by the actions of the company, and in other cases the company's response quickly resolves the issue as in the case of the Tylenol poisonings. Other crises develop more slowly as in the case of side effects of drugs that are revealed through post-marketing surveillance and reports from hospital emergency rooms.

An important factor influencing the development of the public phase of a crisis is media coverage. Often media coverage begins before the firm can act, and hence the firm is forced into a reactive mode. Particularly in a reactive situation, communication with stakeholders, the public, and government through the media can be crucial to dealing with the crisis. A crisis and the accompanying media coverage can also lead to action by activists and NGOs as well as by government regulators. Congress is often interested in crises and can respond with legislation, as the chapter case *Mattel: Crisis Management or Management Crisis* indicates. Media coverage in a crisis can put a firm's reputation and brand equity at risk.

The effect of the media on the development and severity of a crisis can be assessed using the frameworks presented in Chapter 3. Greater media coverage can be expected when the issue at the core of the crisis is viewed as important to society and when the potential audience is large. Environmental degradation is an important societal issue and is of interest to a broad segment of society. Moreover, environmental issues often have a visual aspect that is attractive to media coverage. Although no deaths or human injuries resulted from the *Exxon Valdez* spill, media broadcasts showing dead birds, otters, and fish covered with oil shaped the public's assessment of the incident and made Exxon's task more difficult. In the BP oil spill in the Gulf of Mexico, people could watch in real time the oil gush from the damaged well and spread in the Gulf. The media can also be in an advocacy mode, which can be to the detriment of the firm in the crisis. In some cases the media can also uncover information that can be helpful to the firm and calm a crisis.

Chapter 3 focuses primarily on institutionalized media, but with the Internet anyone can assume the role of the media. Disgruntled consumers, activists, and employees can post messages on blogs and videos on YouTube and other sites. These postings can identify, accelerate, or cause a crisis. The Internet also provides an opportunity for firms to communicate with stakeholders as well as its critics. A number of firms and their executives maintain blogs to communicate with the media and the public.

A particularly difficult situation for many companies is when fact and perception differ. In 1991 drivers of Audi 5000 cars claimed that the car suddenly accelerated resulting in accidents. The media extensively covered the issue, and trial lawyers took the cases to the courts. Audi sales were decimated by the crisis. The company knew that its cars did not suddenly accelerate and that the accidents were most likely due to drivers stepping on the gas pedal when they intended to step on the brake pedal. Scientific tests later confirmed that the car was not responsible. In 2010 Toyota also experienced an unintended acceleration crisis, some of which was due to improperly installed floor mats and poor positioning of the gas pedal. Drivers also claimed that the electronic accelerator system was faulty and took their cases to court. Toyota knew, and subsequent tests confirmed, that the electronic accelerator system did not cause unintended acceleration. The damage had been done, however.

Intervention involves actions by the company or government to deal with the crisis and provide assistance to victims. These actions include communication with stakeholders, the public, and government as well as substantive measures to resolve the crisis and lessen the likelihood that a similar crisis will occur in the future.

Some crises are more innocent but nevertheless serious, as the "PepsiCo and the Syringe Episode" example indicates. Even when a crisis is due to fraud, an intentional hoax, or a simple mistake, it is essential for the company to intervene by communicating with the public and cooperating with law enforcement, regulatory, and public health officials. Particularly in a situation in which a company is certain that the claims are false, it is best to turn to law enforcement and regulatory authorities.

EXAMPLE   PepsiCo and the Syringe Episode[1]

On June 9, 1993, Earl and Mary Triplett of Tacoma, Washington, returned from a vacation and decided to have a late-night snack. Earl poured part of a Diet Pepsi into a glass for Mary, and he drank the rest of the contents with a straw. When he went to bed, he put the Diet Pepsi can in the sink. The next morning the Tripletts were surprised to find a syringe and needle in the can. Neither had been injured, but they alerted authorities, and the local media reported the incident. After a second report the next day in the Seattle area, the Federal Drug Administration (FDA) warned Diet Pepsi drinkers in four western states served by the Alpac Corporation, the regional bottler for PepsiCo, to empty the contents of cans into a glass before drinking it.

The two incidents led to national news reports of possible product tampering and were quickly followed by a rash of other reports of incidents. Approximately 50 incidents of objects found in soft drink cans were reported in 23 states, mostly Pepsi products. No injuries were reported.

PepsiCo faced the issue of whether to recall products already on store shelves, cease production, or take other action. The company was confident that it was virtually impossible for a syringe or other object to get into a can. Craig A. Weatherup, president of PepsiCola North America, said, "It is 99.99 percent assured that nothing is happening in the facilities themselves, in the plants. It's literally, physically impossible."[2] When cans enter a bottling plant, they

are covered by sheets, bound with straps, and checked for damage and quality. When they are ready for the bottling process, the straps are removed, and the cans are checked to see that they are empty. When the cans are ready to enter the bottling process, the sheets are removed and the cans are turned upside down and rinsed inside with water. The cans are then turned upright and filled by machines at a speed of 650–2,000 cans a minute. The filled cans proceed immediately to a seamer and are capped. The product is then inspected and packaged. A can is upright and open for less than 1 second.

PepsiCo inspected all its canning lines and examined its plant records searching for evidence of problems. It also investigated the origins of the cans reported in the incidents. Weatherup said, "These cans were produced at very different plants, some six months ago, some six weeks ago, some six days ago. And therefore there's no correlation between the complaints, when these cans were produced or where they were produced."[3] PepsiCo officials were confident that no tampering had taken place and that the syringes had gotten into the cans after they had been opened. PepsiCo concluded that a product recall was not warranted.

The FDA investigated the claims of objects found in Pepsi products in Washington and found no relation between the two incidents. Neither drink was contaminated. Roger Lowell, a district FDA director, said that the acidity of the soft drink would likely kill any bacteria or virus. FDA

---

[1]This case was prepared from public sources by David P. Baron. Copyright © 1994 by the Board of Trustees of the Leland Stanford Junior University. All rights reserved. Reprinted with permission.

[2]*New York Times,* June 19, 1993.
[3]Ibid.

(Continued)

(*Continued*)

Commissioner David E. Kessler stated, "It is simply not logical to conclude that a nationwide tampering had occurred." The FDA's investigation could find no pattern in the reports. They were spread around the country and involved a variety of types of containers produced by different bottlers, in some cases months apart. The FDA had sophisticated forensic techniques, and investigators were unable to confirm even one case of tampering. On June 14 the FDA decided not to issue a recall of Pepsi products.

When FDA Commissioner Kessler telephoned Weatherup on the evening of June 14, both knew that the claims of tampering were false. PepsiCo still had to deal with the public concerns. The company staffed telephone banks to answer consumer concerns and reassured its bottlers and distributors. The company also decided to produce a video of the canning process and sent it up by satellite on June 15. Bottlers and distributors were also concerned, and PepsiCo sent them information by fax twice a day. Some bottlers took steps of their own. The Buffalo Rock Company, a Pepsi bottler in Birmingham, Alabama, opened its plant to TV news crews.

Even though the claims appeared to be either hoaxes or hysteria, PepsiCo still faced a communications challenge. The company had to decide who would present the company's views to the public, and Weatherup was chosen because of his knowledge of the bottling process. On the evening of June 15, Weatherup and Kessler appeared on *Nightline* to defend the decision not to recall Pepsi products. Kessler knew that an arrest of a Pennsylvania man was imminent, and his assurance that there was no public danger helped calm public concerns. He also observed that in 1984 a single case of alleged tampering with Girl Scout Cookies resulted in 487 reports, none of which was ever verified. Weatherup then made appearances on *The MacNeil/Lehrer NewsHour*, the *Larry King Show*, and all three network news shows and morning news programs. He also made himself available for interviews by satellite. He urged consumers "to rely on their common sense and good judgment" and stated that no one had been injured and no contaminated drinks had been found. He assured the public that a syringe could not possibly have found its way into a can.

PepsiCo also faced the problem of reassuring retailers that pulling its products from their shelves was unwarranted. After Synthia Smith of San Jose, California, reported finding a syringe in a can of caffeine-free Pepsi, Safeway pulled Pepsi products from the store where she had bought it. The next day the store replaced the product with a batch from a different bottler. Debra Lambert, a spokeswoman for Safeway, said that there had been no appreciable decrease in Pepsi sales. She said, "Business was brisk after the product was replaced. People seem to be seeing it as a hoax." San Jose police searched Smith's home and found another syringe similar to the one she had reported finding in a Pepsi can. Her husband was a diabetic, and a recommended means of disposing of a syringe used for an insulin injection was to place it in an empty can.

An Aurora, Colorado, woman claimed to have found a syringe in a Pepsi can she opened at the supermarket checkout counter. A supermarket surveillance camera showed her taking an object out of her purse and placing it in the can she had just purchased and opened. She then showed it to the checkout person who saw a syringe in the can and reported it to the store manager. On June 17 PepsiCo released a videotape it had prepared in which Weatherup narrated the events in the supermarket surveillance tape of the woman. Weatherup said his purpose was to "tell you what really happened."

The FBI arrested several people who had reported finding objects in Pepsi cans, local police arrested several others, and several others recanted their claims. Some of those arrested apparently had hoped to extort a cash settlement from PepsiCo. Product tampering hoaxes are not uncommon. In February 1993 the FBI had arrested Douglas John Knight after he deposited a $350,000 check extorted under FBI surveillance after he threatened to tamper with Pepsi products. In March 1993 Bobby Jo Johnson of Oklahoma City was convicted on charges of tampering with a Pepsi can.[4]

After the FBI had made over 20 arrests and the tampering claims had stopped, PepsiCo ran full-page advertisements in a dozen national newspapers, and bottlers ran advertisements in 300–400 local papers explaining the hoax and thanking customers for staying with its products. Weatherup stated: "We'd like to thank the millions of Americans who have stood behind us. We're eager to put this incident behind us. Consumer safety and product integrity are of utmost importance to us. We know that the American people, in their good sense and extraordinary fairness, will continue to support us as we go forward. It's time to get on with business."[5]

---

[4]Federal law against filing false tampering charges provides for a maximum penalty of 5 years in prison and a fine of $250,000.
[5]Pepsi news release, Somers, N.J., June 18, 1993.

In some cases a potential crisis can be dissipated and die a natural death. Reports surfaced that McDonald's put worms in its hamburgers. Repeated denials by the company helped calm anxieties among customers, but founder Ray Kroc put the issue to rest by stating, "We couldn't afford to grind worms into our meat. Hamburger costs a dollar and a half a pound, and night crawlers six dollars."[5] Other absurd crises can fester. Periodically, Procter & Gamble is subjected to rumors that its moon and stars logo is a sign of devil worship. Despite their absurdity the rumors have persisted over several decades. In other cases the crisis can have more substantial consequences, even if it is a hoax or fraud, as illustrated in the Wendy's example.

---

[5]*Time*, 1992.

WENDY'S In 2005 the media extensively covered the story of a woman who found a human finger in her chili at a Wendy's restaurant in San Jose, California. Wendy's explained that it was impossible for the finger to have gotten into its chili because of the process by which it was prepared and packaged. Moreover, any restaurant employee who had lost a finger would have reported it to the company and sought medical treatment. Nevertheless, sales at Wendy's restaurants dropped as a result of the incident and the media coverage.

The police and the local news media began to investigate the incident, and the investigations revealed that the woman had a history of questionable actions that had led to her arrest on several occasions. She had also filed lawsuits evidently intended to shake down companies, including a fast-food company. The police arrested her and her boyfriend for attempting to extort Wendy's. The police found that the finger had been taken by her boyfriend from the site of an accident where he worked, and she had put the finger in her chili. Both the woman and her boyfriend were charged with fraud, convicted by a jury, and sentenced to prison.

Resolution involves turning the crisis into a manageable nonmarket issue. This may be accomplished by eliminating any further potential for harm, assuring the public and the media that the crisis has passed, or compensating those harmed. Source Perrier subsequently changed its procedures to regularly test the gas for chemical contaminants and reported that no benzene had been detected since the change. Resolution can also involve moving the crisis into the institutions of government. After the recall, the Tylenol crisis resided in the hands of law enforcement officials and the FDA.

The aftermath can persist long after the crisis has ended. A crisis involving a rogue trader leads to more costly and stringent internal controls in banks. Reputation damage can also persist, as in the case of Exxon. More stringent regulation can result as in the case of testing toys for lead. Frequently, when the crisis involves harm to people or damage to property, lawsuits follow. Trial lawyers represent victims and file lawsuits on their behalf. The lawyers typically receive one-third of any settlement or judgment and thus have strong incentives to pursue cases.

Even those crises in which a company had no responsibility can have a lingering effect on a company and its reputation. More people recall that a customer found part of a human finger in her chili at a Wendy's restaurant than recall that the woman planted the finger there in an attempt to extort a settlement from the company.

COMPONENTS OF A CRISIS MANAGEMENT PROGRAM

Crisis management has five components: avoidance, preparedness, root cause analysis, response, and resolution. The timing of these components and the pattern of crisis development are depicted in Figure 5-1. The Brent Spar episode in Chapter 4 is a good example of a company without a crisis management plan to deal with the private politics that erupted over its disposal plan.

FIGURE 5-1 Crisis Management and the Crisis Life Cycle

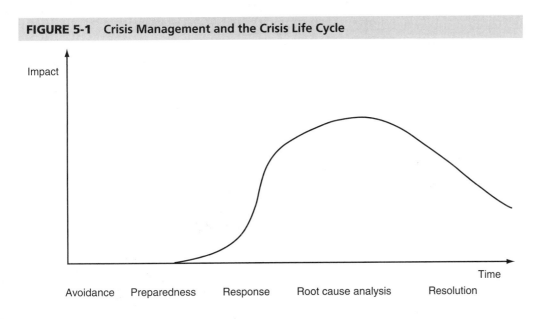

Avoidance

The most important component of a crisis management program is avoidance, and the next most important component is preparedness. The best approach to crisis management is to reduce the likelihood of a crisis developing, and an important precursor to doing so is an assessment of its internal risks and the exposure of the company in its nonmarket environment.

One aspect of an avoidance strategy is auditing. One type of audit focuses on risks and their causes. This is also the first step in developing measures for reducing risks that can damage the performance of the firm. Audit findings must be acted upon. In 2005 prior to the refinery explosion, a BP health and safety report had warned that the refinery would "likely kill someone in the next 12–18 months."[6] The risk assessment should also include an assessment of the risk of litigation and regulatory actions.

Another type of audit focuses on reputation risk. This audit assesses the potential impacts of a crisis on the stakeholders of the firm and its reputation with them, the public, and government. Reputations are difficult to evaluate in terms of both their importance and the extent to which they can be damaged by a crisis and a company's response to it. A reputation for responsible management can be important in the marketplace, in relations with business partners, and with respect to groups and institutions in the nonmarket environment. Activists, NGOs, regulators, and legislators give additional scrutiny to firms with bad reputations.

Reputations are built by actions, through products, and by policies to which a firm adheres. Reputations are strengthened and maintained by conduct that accepts responsibility for actions and that benefits stakeholders and respects the public trust. Reputations are also strengthened by openness, forthright conduct, and transparency.

Reputations are harder to build than they are to dissipate. Johnson & Johnson had developed a strong reputation not only for its handling of the Tylenol crisis but also for tangible concern for its stakeholders. The company put this reputation at risk by letting its manufacturing quality slip, as the chapter case indicates. Not only did Johnson & Johnson harm its reputation with consumers, but the FDA increased its scrutiny of the company and finally put under its supervision the production facilities at Johnson & Johnson's McNeil consumer products subsidiary.

Many firms appear to overestimate the strength of their reputation and the protection it might provide. Many people are skeptical of firms and their motives and have a low level of trust in business. This can make a reputation fragile and easily damaged. A crisis, accident, or scandal can severely strain a reputation, and failure to respond in a responsible manner can result in damage that is difficult to repair. Moreover, years of reputation building can be dissipated quickly. BP's reputation as an environmentally and socially responsible company was severely damaged. In addition to the refinery explosion, leaks in a pipeline in Alaska spilled oil in Prudhoe Bay and on the tundra and price fixing in the propane market called into question its credibility, as well as the quality of its management. The 2010 explosion on the Deepwater Horizon and the resulting oil spill put another nail in the coffin of BP's reputation.

A firm may be thought of as having a reputation or trust account that reflects the aggregate effect of its past actions and conduct. The balance in the trust account is increased by how effectively it operates its business and manages its interactions with stakeholders, the public, and government. The balance is decreased by crises, illegal acts, and public criticism of its conduct. Negative events can be more powerful than positive events. The public remembers negative events more than positive events, and hence one negative event can wipe out trust built by several positive events. This asymmetry is important to recognize and makes effective crisis management imperative.

Preparedness

An essential part of preparedness is organization. Firms susceptible to a crisis need a crisis management team that can be mobilized quickly and can substantively address the root cause of a crisis. Exxon was prepared for one dimension of an oil spill crisis—it had a cleanup plan. It was unprepared, however, for the public component of a crisis—that is, expressing remorse,

---

[6]*Wall Street Journal*, March 14, 2008.

assuming responsibility for the incident, interacting with the local residents, and dealing with the media and government.

In most cases a company wants one spokesperson who can speak for the company with a single, consistent voice. The spokesperson must be continuously informed about the facts of the situation and new developments. Two considerations are important in selecting the spokesperson. First, the person should be effective in communicating with the public and in interacting with the media. Second, the person should be knowledgeable about the central factors involved in the crisis. PepsiCo chose a person knowledgeable about the bottling process, which was at the center of the crisis. Peter S. Goodman writing in the *New York Times* stated, "Many analysts say BP erred in putting its message in the hands of its CEO, Tony Hayward. Inclined toward pinstriped suits, Mr. Hayard found himself in coastal communities in the American South where shrimpers donned stained coveralls in pursuit of a catch now polluted by his company's gushing inventory. His words of regret were delivered with a British accent, and he complicated his task with a series of tin-eared utterances."[7] BP later chose a senior executive, who had been raised in Mississippi, to head the company and its efforts to deal with the crisis.

The other aspect of organization is policies that help team members as well as others to act effectively in response to developments. Exxon's cleanup procedures involved the quick application of a dispersant to reduce the environmental damage from a spill. Johnson & Johnson had operated under a long-established mission statement, "Our Credo," presented in Chapter 23, that emphasizes the primacy of serving its stakeholders. The chapter case raises the issue of whether that mission statement had been compromised by profit pressures.

In addition to policies, some firms engage in scenario exercises in which they explore the range of crises that could develop. Firms also earmark resources that can be mobilized if a crisis occurs. This can involve physical resources such as those to contain an oil spill or deal with a fire or explosion. It also can involve the identification of outside contractors that can provide assistance or experts whose advice can be quickly obtained.

An important part of preparedness is organizational learning. Some firms encounter crises frequently enough that they have an opportunity to refine and develop their approach to crisis management and improve their preparedness. In the Wal-Mart and Hurricane Katrina example that follows, the company had experienced enough hurricanes that it had developed statistical data on the items people bought in anticipation of a hurricane and after it had struck. McDonald's had experienced crises resulting from mad cow disease in the United Kingdom and other European countries and had learned from those experiences. When the first case of mad cow disease was reported in the United States, it was prepared to act. It assured the public that its beef was safe and described the measures it took to avoid animals that might have the disease. Sales were unaffected.

Insurance against the cost of a crisis can also be purchased. Insurance is offered for natural disasters, industrial accidents such as fires, and liability for product injuries. More innovative insurance is also offered. XL Insurance offers food-and-drink product contamination insurance, which also covers product recalls. Insurance coverage is available for oil and chemical spills, political risks, and foreign direct investments. Insurance, however, only compensates for direct harm done to the insured and does not help manage in a crisis situation nor does it compensate for damage to a firm's reputation or its brand equity.

PREPAREDNESS: WAL-MART AND HURRICANE KATRINA With over 3,300 stores in the United States, Wal-Mart was experienced in dealing with crises of many types, including hurricanes. Analysis of its sales data revealed that prior to a hurricane people stocked up on items ranging from bottled water to generators, and after a hurricane had struck they bought chain saws and cleaning supplies. Wal-Mart operated an Emergency Operations Center in its headquarters and had begun tracking a storm in the Caribbean when it was upgraded to tropical depression status, some 6 days before it struck the Gulf Coast as Hurricane Katrina. Using forecasts from the National Weather Service and private meteorologists, the company projected the path of the storm. Wal-Mart initially sent supplies to its stores in Florida where the storm was projected to hit. To keep its stores operating, Wal-Mart used its truck fleet to deliver back-up generators, fuel,

---

[7]*New York Times,* August 22, 2010.

and dry ice. When the storm crossed the tip of Florida without causing much damage, Wal-Mart turned its attention to the Gulf Coast. With the aid of its meteorologists it projected landfall just east of New Orleans and immediately began sending generators and supplies to its distribution centers in the Gulf region.[8] Wal-Mart also sent a "loss-prevention" team to protect its stores from looting.

As the devastation from the hurricane and flooding became evident, Wal-Mart delivered $3 million of supplies to residents and relief and rescue personnel and donated $17 million in cash to relief organizations. Stores gave away clothing, food, and pharmaceuticals to desperate local residents, and truck drivers remained in the area hauling relief supplies to where they were needed. The company set up mini Wal-Marts in the backs of trucks, in tents, and remaining buildings to distribute free items such as food, water, clothing, and other essentials. Some Wal-Mart stores were used as shelters and headquarters for police and the National Guard. The mayor of Kenner, Louisiana, said, "The only lifeline in Kenner was the Wal-Mart stores. We didn't have looting on a mass scale because Wal-Mart showed up with food and water so our people could survive. The Red Cross and FEMA need to take a master class in logistics and mobilization from Wal-Mart."[9] When the hurricane hit, 126 Wal-Mart stores were forced to close because of lost power, storm damage, or flooding, but within 2 weeks all but 13 stores were operating and 97 percent of their employees were back at work or had been offered jobs elsewhere in Wal-Mart stores.

Root Cause Analysis

The first step in developing an effective response is to analyze the crisis. This is straightforward for many companies. Wal-Mart was accustomed to dealing with the impacts of hurricanes, having dealt with four in the year before Hurricane Katrina. Toyota understood that the floor mats were a problem when they became dislodged, and it also knew that its electronic accelerator system was not responsible for unintended acceleration. In contrast, Tokyo Electric Power was uncertain about the extent of damage to the nuclear reactors in Fukishima and was also uncertain about how to contain the radiation and to prevent a meltdown of the reactors' cores.

When analysis is not straightforward, the four I's identified in Chapter 1 provide the starting point. This requires identifying the issues involved in the crisis. In the Tylenol crisis the issues were the likely tampering but more importantly the possibility of further harm to consumers. Information was incomplete, since the company had no idea how many capsules had been laced with cyanide. Nor did the company know whether capsules were poisoned outside the Chicago area. The relevant institutions were the FDA and the court of public sentiment that would assess the company's handling of the crisis. The interests were primarily the consumers who were potentially at risk, in addition to Johnson & Johnson's shareholders and employees.

A second step is root cause analysis, which has the objective of identifying the causes of the crisis. This provides the basis for resolution of the present crisis, avoidance of future crises, and preparedness for crises that do result. In the Société Génerale case the root cause was flaws in the supervision and control system used to monitor trades. The bank quickly fixed the flaws, and it also continued to search for accomplices. The root cause in the BP refinery accident crisis was cost-cutting that had led to unsafe working conditions, and the Gulf of Mexico crisis may also have been due to cost-cutting. For Tokyo Electric Power the root cause was a back-up cooling system that relied on power from the electricity grid, which had been knocked out by a once-in-a-hundred-years event. The root cause in the *Exxon Valdez* crisis was a failure by the tanker crew and captain to follow procedures. In the Pepsi crisis it was clear to the company and the FDA that the incidents were hoaxes or fraud.

The root cause in the Tylenol crisis was product tampering, and as that became clear and the product recall progressed, Johnson & Johnson was absolved from responsibility. Nevertheless, product tampering remained a concern, and companies improved their packaging to make tampering more difficult and easier for consumers to detect if it had occurred. The root causes are multiple, but incentive compensation systems and inadequate controls and monitoring

---

[8]Some other companies such as Home Depot also used their distribution systems to provide relief items.
[9]*Fortune*, October 3, 2005.

are important causes. One root cause of the subprime mortgage crisis was the incentives for mortgage brokers and lenders to issue mortgages to unqualified borrowers to collect fees up front, coupled with the opportunity to package mortgages and sell portfolios to investors who were either unable to assess their riskiness or relied on the reputation of the sellers.

In the early 1990s Denny's restaurants were revealed to have discriminated against African American customers, resulting in lawsuits and widespread media attention.[10] The company identified the root cause as insensitivity to discrimination and a lack of training of employees. The company implemented an extensive training program and created opportunities for minorities to advance within the company. Several years later Denny's was ranked as the best company for minorities to work.

Response

Response includes actions to resolve the crisis, deal with the root cause, and communicate with stakeholders, the public, and government. The appropriate action depends on the root cause and the specifics of the situation. In the Tylenol crisis the principal concern was whether additional bottles with cyanide-laced capsules could be on retailers' shelves or in consumers' medicine cabinets. With the guidance of "Our Credo" it was clear that Johnson & Johnson had to recall Tylenol, but whether the risks were confined to the Chicago area was unclear. The only way to be sure of eliminating further harm was to issue a nationwide recall.

In the Pepsi crisis the root cause was not product tampering, and neither people nor property were at risk of harm. No recall was needed, but PepsiCo still had to decide whether a recall was needed to reassure consumers. Since no deaths or injuries had been reported, PepsiCo's challenge was to communicate effectively with consumers and to work with government to end the crisis.

EFFECTIVE AND INEFFECTIVE COMMUNICATION Communication and rectification are the two principal components of crisis response. Since crises often develop quickly, information is often incomplete and speculation and rumors can fly. Even when information is complete or the crisis self-evident, it is important to communicate effectively with those affected as well as the public more broadly. A large industry of communications specialists is available to provide advice on effective communication, and firms have developed their own capabilities. As considered in Chapter 3, many firms provide media relations training for their executives.

Communication with stakeholders can be crucial. PepsiCo faxed information twice a day to its bottlers and distributors to keep them abreast of the developments. Companies also need to communicate with employees who may be concerned about the role of their employer in the crisis. When Denny's identified the root cause of the discrimination, it began training its employees and also produced a television advertisement in which its servers and restaurant managers pledged to provide good service to all customers.

Companies also have to communicate with the public, and this communication often takes place through the media and blogs. Interacting with journalists is considered in Chapter 3, and communication with journalists in a crisis is guided by the same principles. The difference is the time pressure resulting from the crisis and the possibility that the firm may not know the origins or causes of the crisis. Johnson & Johnson's first hint of a possible crisis came from an inquiry by a reporter covering the medical examiner's suspicions about the poisonings.[11]

In some crises the government can play an important role in communicating with the public, but the firm often has better information than the government, making cooperation with government essential. PepsiCo worked with the FDA to assure the public that no product tampering had occurred. Choosing a spokesperson knowledgeable about the root cause of the crisis can be important, particularly when the cause and nature of the crisis are complex. As already mentioned, PepsiCo chose as its spokesperson an executive who was knowledgeable about the bottling process.

The messages conveyed can be crucial to resolving the crises and protecting the reputation of the company. Communication specialists advocate messages that are truthful, sincere, and express concern for those affected. If people have been harmed, messages should express

---

[10]See the Chapter 23 case *Denny's and Customer Service.*
[11]Fink (2002).

concern and sympathy for the victims, and, if appropriate, pledge aid to the victims. Because stakeholders and the public may be suspicious of the company as a result of the crisis, messages should be transparent and reassuring. For example, a message could be that the company is taking all possible steps to ensure that further harm does not result and that the problem does not reoccur. Credibility of the company and spokesperson are important, particularly when the company has a trust deficit. Some people assume the worst when a crisis erupts, and some people are suspicious of communication by businesses because of the incentives to protect the profits of the firm rather than to attend to those harmed by the crisis. For some people perception becomes reality.

BP CEO Tony Hayward provided a striking example of what not to say when communicating with the public and with victims of the explosion and oil spill. In an interview, he said, "The Gulf of Mexico is a very big ocean. The amount of volume of oil and dispersant we are putting into it is tiny in relation to the total water volume." A few days later he said, "the environmental impact of this disaster is likely to have been very, very modest."[12] Even if this were true, the perception created by media coverage of oil gushing from the well, the actions of the federal government, and the alarms sounded by environmentalists was quite different, and Hayward's statements were met by disbelief. One effective communication approach is to express personal sorrow for the harm incurred by victims. In apologizing to the victims, Hayward said, "We're sorry for the massive disruption it's caused to their lives. There's no one who wants this thing over more than I do. I'd like my life back."[13] Mentioning the disruption in his life after pointing to the disruption in the lives of the victims seemed to belittle the victims. Hayward received further criticism when he went on vacation to watch a yacht race in which his boat was racing—while oil continued to gush into the Gulf of Mexico. Senator Richard Selby (R-AL) said, "That yacht should be here skimming and cleaning up the oil."[14] BP then took a more effective approach. It aired advertisements in which its employees on the Gulf Coast talked about what they and the company were doing to help the environment and the victims.

In addition to communicating with stakeholders and the public, a firm in crisis must also communicate with government agencies. In the Tylenol crisis Johnson & Johnson worked with local governments and the FDA. Mattel lobbied Congress for new legislation mandating testing for lead in paint on toys. After the company was raked over the coals in congressional hearings, Lucas van Praag, Goldman Sachs' head of corporate communications, said, "One of the things we've learned is it may be perfectly legal but if it's too complicated to explain to ordinary, rational people, then maybe it's a business we ought not be in."[15] Communication may also be addressed to financial analysts, business partners, suppliers, dealers, and others in the firm's value chain.

The effectiveness of messages can be enhanced if they are corroborated by messages from independent sources. In some cases the media can play this role, and in others the government assumes this role. The FDA corroborated PepsiCo's message that the syringe could not have been put in the can during the bottling process. Similarly, police and medical examiner reports revealed that the poison in Tylenol capsules had been injected after the bottles were on retailers' shelves.

Systematic evidence on the effectiveness of crisis communication is difficult to come by, and some researchers have turned to laboratory experiments. Uhlmann, Newman, Brescoll, Galinsky, and Diermeier (2008) conducted an experiment in which 126 corporate executives evaluated three responses to a hypothetical crisis involving finding lead in paint on a toy. One response emphasized engagement and a pledge to investigate the incident and take appropriate action. A second response was defensive, challenging the independent investigation that had been conducted and stating that the company's safety procedures were effective. The third response

---

[12]*New York Times,* August 22, 2010. Kenneth R. Fineberg, the government-appointed administrator of the $20 billion relief fund for victims of the oil spill said that the Gulf of Mexico would be largely restored to pre-spill conditions by the end of 2012. (*New York Times,* March 3, 2011) Feinberg, who had served as special master of the September 11 Victims Compensation Fund and as overseer of executive compensation for companies that received bailout funds during the financial crisis, was criticized by a number of environmentalists for his statement.

[13]*New York Times,* August 22, 2010.

[14]*The Sunday Telegraph,* June 20, 2010.

[15]*New York Times,* August 22, 2010.

was "No comment." The executives were asked to evaluate the company, and the engagement message yielded a significantly more favorable evaluation than the other two, which had comparable evaluations. This study suggests that the message itself can affect the public's evaluation of the company and perhaps its reputation and brand equity.

Exxon   Exxon's communication with the public was ineffective at best. Immediately after the oil spill, an Exxon official accepted responsibility for the cleanup. Exxon also took out advertisements in 100 newspapers and magazines for "An Open Letter to the Public" from chairman Lawrence Rawl stating, "I want to tell you how sorry I am that this accident took place. We at Exxon are especially sympathetic to the residents of Valdez and the people of the state of Alaska." Rawl also appeared on television giving the same message. Later, in a statement to the press, the company said,

> The *Exxon Valdez* spill was an accident, a bad one. But accidents can happen to anyone. If Exxon's rules and regulations governing conduct aboard ship had been followed, the accident would not have occurred. If Exxon had been permitted to follow the cleanup plan immediately, the effects of the spill would not have been as extensive.[16]

Several messages conveyed in these statements drew criticism. First, the statements characterized the episode as an accident, but many observers viewed Exxon as having caused the oil spill. Second, Exxon seemed to blame the captain and crew, and the spill was clearly their fault, but Exxon was responsible for their conduct. Third, taking responsibility for the cleanup was not enough. Extensive media coverage showed not only the oil in the bay and on shore, but the public also saw repeated images of otters and sea birds covered in oil, some of which were dead and others in jeopardy. No cleanup could restore the lost wildlife and the damage to their habitat. Moreover, skeptics worried about whether the natural environment could ever recover from the spill. Fourth, the livelihood of fishers and other businesses in Prince William Sound were jeopardized. Fifth, although Exxon had been delayed by the Coast Guard from beginning its cleanup, placing blame on the government appeared to be an attempt to shift responsibility. Nor was it clear to the public that if Exxon had been able to implement its cleanup procedures immediately, the damage would have been significantly mitigated.[17] Sixth, although Exxon expressed sympathy for the residents of Valdez, it did little to aid them in the days after the spill. Within a year of the oil spill, Exxon had voluntarily compensated the people affected by the spill, but that was not sufficient to overcome the adverse effects of the media coverage and its earlier communication with the public. Residents subsequently filed a lawsuit for compensation for private harm.

What Might Exxon Have Done?   Exxon was in a difficult position and appears to have been more concerned with potential liability and possible punitive damages for the oil spill than with its reputation. Whether the risk to the company's reputation was more serious than the liability risk is not clear, but Exxon likely could have reduced its reputation risk, and perhaps avoided being labeled a pariah by many people, if had responded differently. Given the seriousness of the situation and the intense media and public attention, how effective any communication could have been remains speculative.

Exxon repeatedly referred to the oil spill as an accident, but it was not an accident caused by nature but by its employees. The company accepted responsibility for the cleanup but it did not apologize. Apologizing and acknowledging responsibility for the spill, as well as for the cleanup, likely would have helped the company communicate more effectively. Exxon also could have expressed remorse for its role rather than just expressing sympathy. It also could have acknowledged the harm to animal life and to the livelihood of local residents who depended on the Sound. Tangible actions, such as establishing a private fund for dealing with wildlife habitats and for compensating fishers who depended on the Sound, might have spoken louder than words. Moreover, top management could have gone to the scene to represent the company, talk with residents, and assure the public and government officials about the cleanup. Exxon was

---

[16]*New York Times,* May 3, 1989. Quoted in Tyler (1997).

[17]Exxon had initially said that if it had been allowed to use the dispersant, 50 percent of the oil could have been contained. Exxon later said that the containment would have been 35 percent. *Anchorage Daily News,* March 24, 1989.

undoubtedly correct not to discuss whether the ship's captain had been drinking, since that was a factual matter to be addressed in court.

CONCERNS ABOUT LIABILITY In formulating a strategy for addressing a crisis, a firm must consider both its exposure to liability and its response to stakeholders and the public. Advice from legal counsel is essential, but managers should not underestimate the cost of reputation damage and harm to a brand that can result from an inadequate response.

Did Exxon's public statements, expressions of concern, and cleanup actions reduce its potential liability? The prior question is whether the harm from a liability judgment would exceed the harm from the additional reputation damage to the company if it had changed its approach to communicating with the public. Hindsight indicates that Exxon's reputation remains tainted by the *Exxon Valdez* episode, exposing the company to greater public and private politics pressure. Reputation damage is difficult to value, however.[18] Resolution of the litigation occurred 19 years after the oil spill.

It is not at all clear that the verdicts would have been different if Exxon had apologized and accepted responsibility for the episode and the conduct of the captain and crew. Trials involve discovery that results in the revelation of information, and witnesses can describe events. The failure to apologize or to admit responsibility thus may have had little effect on the outcome of litigation. Firms, however, rarely admit negligence, since that can provide the basis for punitive damages, as considered in Chapter 14. If the captain of the *Exxon Valdez* was drunk and asleep when the ship went aground, he and Exxon could have been found negligent. The Supreme Court has begun to cap the ratio of punitive damages to compensatory damages, but nevertheless those damages can be large.

The litigation record is now complete, and Exxon's assessment of the litigation risk at the time might have been different from what hindsight reveals. A jury acquitted the captain of criminal charges. Exxon faced five criminal charges and pleaded guilty to three lesser charges and paid a $25 million fine. In addition to $2.1 billion in cleanup costs, Exxon paid $900 million in compensatory damages and several hundred million dollars to local fishers, for a total cost of $3.4 billion. A jury also awarded Alaskan residents $5 billion in punitive damages, but an appeals court ruled that the award was excessive and cut the award to $2.5 billion. Exxon appealed to the Supreme Court, and in 2008 the Court reduced the award to $507 million.

Resolution

The Tylenol crisis was resolved when no further deaths resulted and law enforcement authorities concluded that the tampering had been the work of a person who had opened the packages, removed and opened the bottles, injected cyanide, put the bottles back in the packages, and resealed them. Once that became clear, Johnson & Johnson reintroduced Tylenol with new packaging, and sales quickly recovered to pre-tampering levels. One lesson from this episode is that the problem should be fixed before the firm begins to resume its normal marketing activities.

As the *Exxon Valdez* episode indicates, some crises, and their effects, can persist. The reputation damage to Exxon continues, and for many people the company remains a symbol of irresponsibility. Many crises are difficult to resolve because of continued attention from the media, NGOs, politicians, and trial lawyers. BP attempted to resolve one aspect of its refinery explosion crisis by negotiating a settlement with the Department of Justice. BP pleaded guilty to a felony violation of the Clean Air Act and paid a fine of $50 million. In 2008 the settlement was questioned by Representative John Dingell (D-MI), who asked whether BP "executives have culpability, and should have been held to account?"

The PepsiCo example illustrates effective management in a crisis situation. Even though the company knew that reports of objects found in its cans were false at best and fraud at worst, it had to reassure consumers and the public of the safety of its products. The company knew that the FDA had responsibility for food safety and would be investigating the reports. This was a boon to PepsiCo, since the FDA would likely corroborate its statements that it was impossible for these objects to get into a can. To demonstrate this, PepsiCo uploaded film of its bottling process showing the speed of the operation and showing that a can was upright and uncapped for

---

[18]Exxon had profits of $40.6 billion in 2007—the largest ever of any U.S. company.

less than 1 second. As mentioned, one of its bottlers opened its plant to TV crews so that they could film the can filling process. PepsiCo also kept its bottlers informed of developments and the steps it was taking to deal with the crisis. Copycats continued to report objects in Pepsi cans, but the reports of arrests for filing false reports ended the copycatting.

A HARDBALL RESPONSE In 2007 the government of Thailand issued compulsory licenses for the production of drugs used in the treatment of cancer, heart conditions, and AIDS. The licenses allowed generic drug makers in India and elsewhere to produce drugs whose patents had not expired. Abbott Laboratories held the patent on one of the drugs, which was an important second-line treatment for AIDS. (See the Chapter 19 case *Compulsory Licensing, Thailand, and Abbott Laboratories*.)

Abbott chose a hardball response. The company announced that it was withdrawing all its applications for registering new drugs in Thailand, including an important new version of its AIDS drug that required no refrigeration. Abbott's decision was widely criticized by AIDS activists and public health officials. The criticism damaged not only Abbott's reputation but also that of the pharmaceutical industry more broadly. Few if any pharmaceutical companies would have responded as Abbott did. Whether the response improved Abbott's bargaining power with the government of Thailand or other governments that might issue compulsory licenses remains unclear.

Because of Abbott's actions the French AIDS activist group Act Up–Paris launched a cyber attack in which between 500 and 1,000 activists in 12 countries participated in an International Day of Action to overload Abbott's Web site during a 4-hour period, halting online sales. In response, Abbott filed a lawsuit in a French criminal court alleging that the group had violated two articles of French criminal law. Abbott was again widely criticized by AIDS activists and NGOs for filing the lawsuit, adding to the reputation damage.[19]

SUMMARY

Crises happen. They are typically unexpected, often escalate quickly, and frequently are characterized by uncertainty about their cause and likely developments. Even though their occurrence may be difficult to anticipate and their development hard to predict, firms can improve their crisis management through planning and preparation.

Crises have patterns that progress through stages. Some crises are identified within a firm, but many are identified outside the firm by consumers, business partners, or government. Crises can escalate quickly, particularly when the media covers the developments. How a crisis develops depends on the intervention of not only the firm but often government as well. In cases involving safety and health, natural disasters, or environmental damage, government agencies have expertise and can be an important source of information and action. Government can typically mobilize resources and deploy them where they are needed. Firms and government agencies often work together in resolving a crisis. Crises pass, but their effects can continue in the form of changes in management practices, new government regulations, or increased public scrutiny of the performance of firms.

Crisis management is intended to anticipate the possibility of a crisis and be prepared to respond effectively if one develops. The most important component of crisis management is avoidance; that is, reducing the probability that a crisis will occur. This can involve audits of risks and reputations to assess exposure and changes in management practices to reduce the likelihood of a crisis. Preparedness involves organization as well as identifying resources to be mobilized in the event that a crisis occurs. When a crisis occurs, a firm must respond appropriately and communicate effectively with those involved as well as with the public and government. A response requires identifying the root cause of the crisis so that its effects can be contained and future crises avoided. A response also requires action to provide relief to those affected and steps to ensure that more are not affected. Effective communication can involve acceptance of responsibility, an apology to those affected, expression of concern for those affected, and assurance that the problem is being addressed and will not reoccur. Government agencies can play an important role in communicating with the public, identifying the source of the crisis, and helping address

---

[19]Abbott subsequently dropped the lawsuit.

its effects. Once a crisis has been resolved, a firm must reassess its crisis avoidance measures and its preparedness.

The chapter case *Mattel: Crisis Management or Management Crisis* presents a case in which lead was found in the paint on Mattel toys. The case proceeds in chronological stages that allow the formulation of responses and strategies as the crisis unfolds. *Johnson & Johnson and Its Quality Reputation* concerns a series of quality problems that jeopardized the company's reputation. Crises are also present in the following cases: *Shell, Greenpeace, and Brent Spar* (Chapter 4), *Goldman Sachs and Its Reputation* (Chapter 11), *Obesity and McLawsuits* (Chapter 14), *Merck and Vioxx* (Chapter 10), *Pfizer and Celebrex* (Chapter 10), and *Denny's and Customer Service* (Chapter 23).

CASES

Mattel: Crisis Management or Management Crisis

INTRODUCTION

In late 2006 and early 2007 a number of imports from China were found to pose health risks. In the most serious case the deaths of 200 people in Haiti and Panama were linked to syrup from China containing the chemical diethylene glycol used in antifreeze. British Airways withdrew Chinese toothpaste from its in-flight pouches because of the presence of the chemical. Large quantities of imported dog food were found to contain the chemical melamine, resulting in death and injury to as many as 4,000 pets. An investigation by the Chinese government found that two suppliers had intentionally used melamine to save money and increase the protein content. The U.S. Food and Drug Administration (FDA) banned the importation of certain seafoods from China because of contamination. Representative Bart Stupak (D-MI) commented, "While I am pleased that the FDA realizes the danger these Asian and Chinese seafood imports pose to the American people, I am concerned that it requires congressional prodding of the FDA to take the steps necessary to keep American consumers safe."[20] No serious injuries or fatalities were reported in the United States.

Safety and health concerns were not limited to food. In November 2006 the retailer Target recalled 200,000 Kool Toyz action figures because of lead contamination and sharp edges. On June 13, 2007 RC2 Corporation recalled 1.5 million of its Thomas & Friends toy trains because of high lead levels in the paint. RC2 quickly fired both the company producing the trains and the paint vendor but did not disclose their names. Some 8,000 toy factories in China employed 3 million people and produced most of the world's toys. Approximately 80 percent of the toys sold in the United States were made in China.

China was at first defensive. It banned two shipments of food from the United States and even released a statement that an FDA regulation allowed diethylene glycol in toothpaste. The FDA stated that its regulation allowed as an additive polyethylene glycol, not diethylene glycol. China subsequently announced that it was strengthening its food safety regulations and ordered 180 food plants to close. It also said inspectors had uncovered 23,000 violations of food safety regulations. The *China Daily* reported finding industrial chemicals in foods ranging from candy to seafood to pickles and biscuits. In July a high-ranking official of China's Food and Drug Administration was sentenced to death for corruption and approving counterfeit drugs.

With safety concerns about imports from China on the minds of readers, on July 26, 2007 the *New York Times* carried a feature article on the precautions Mattel, the world's largest toymaker, took to ensure the safety of its toys. In contrast to other toymakers Mattel owned the factories in China where its most popular toys, such as Barbie dolls and Hot Wheels cars, were made. Those factories accounted for half the company's sales with the rest coming from toys manufactured under contract, often by suppliers with long-term relationships with the company. Mattel also operated a testing laboratory in Shenzhen, China where employees tested products for safety, including possible misuse of the toys. Jim Walter, a Mattel vice president, said, "We are not perfect; we have holes. But we're doing more than anyone else." Professor S. Prakash Sethi of the City University of New York, who regularly conducted inspections of Mattel suppliers' factories, said, "Mattel is the gold standard."[21]

Mattel had strict requirements for its contract suppliers, which were subject to inspections by independent auditors. Products were tested at the factory and supplies were tested at the door. The *New York Times* article stated, "Elisha Chan, the director of product integrity and corporate responsibility, is charged with guarding against dangerous defects like lead-based paint. Suppliers are closely monitored, he says, and sending in fake or tainted supplies is a ticket to losing the contract with Mattel. And some vendors have, says Mr. Chan." The article also stated, "Many Western companies operating in China do not test their raw materials, even though suppliers are

---

known for substituting cheaper materials to pad their profits." Dane Chamorro with the consultancy Control Risks commented, "This is very common. The samples you get are always fantastic; but once they rope you in they can cut back. And a lot of Chinese companies will do anything to cut costs."[22] Lead paint, for example, reportedly cost from 30 to 60 percent less than paint without lead.

Other commentators placed the blame on the Western companies that pressured their suppliers to keep costs down and meet tight deadlines. Dara O'Rourke, a professor at the University of California, Berkeley, stated, "There is a lot of scapegoating China, but I would argue that this was caused by a system that is designed to push down costs and speed up delivery."[23]

On July 30, after the RC2 and Target recalls, the Sierra Club wrote to 10 companies stating that it would file a lawsuit against them if within 60 days they did not file a report with the Environmental Protection Agency (EPA) on their lead-tainted products. The letter claimed that the companies were required to report to the EPA under the Toxic Substances Control Act. A Target spokesperson stated, "We have no indication that Target has violated any EPA laws relating to this matter."[24] The action by the Sierra Club was part of a broader campaign by activists, NGOs, and public health officials against products containing lead, which in large enough quantities can cause brain damage, organ failure, and death.

MATTEL, INC.

In 2000 Mattel had a loss of $431 million on sales of $4.566 billion. To turn the company around, Mattel hired CEO Robert A. Eckert from Kraft Foods. Eckert sold off a number of product lines to focus on toys, and by 2006 the company had net income of $593 million on sales of $5.650 billion. Its principal brands in addition to Barbie and Hot Wheels were American Girl and Fisher-Price. Mattel made *Fortune* magazine's 100 best companies to work for in 2008, ranking 70th.

In the 1980s Mattel began to build factories in China, and by 2007 it owned 12 factories there.[25] During Eckert's tenure Mattel consolidated its remaining production among a smaller set of suppliers in China, but it continued to rely on 30–40 suppliers with whom it had long-term relationships. Those suppliers had, however, over time used subcontractors which were not under Mattel's supervision. Since 1996 suppliers' factories had been subject to a code governing working conditions, and factories were subject to inspection by an independent organization.

Mattel claimed not to squeeze its suppliers and had a policy of paying extra for materials that were safe, including lead-free paint. Thomas A. Debrowski, head of worldwide operations, said, "We insist that they continue to use certified paint from certified vendors, and we pay for that, and we're perfectly

willing to pay for that."[26] Mattel had 200 employees in China responsible for training and supervising suppliers, but those employees were not stationed permanently at the factories of the suppliers.

THE CRISIS

The first hint of a crisis came from France. The French retailer Auchan had hired Intertek, a large testing company, to test the toys it stocked. On June 6 Intertek found high levels of lead in the paint on some Mattel toys. Mattel intercepted the shipment to France and did not report the problem immediately because the items were not being sold in the United States.

The incident led Mattel to undertake an internal investigation, which found lead in the paint of a number of its toys. Mattel traced the products back to the Lee Der Industrial Company with headquarters in Hong Kong and factories on the mainland, including the city of Foshan. Lee Der was founded in 1993 by Xie Yuguang and Zhang Shuhong, who managed the factory in Foshan. Zhang was respected by employees, and the company treated its employees fairly, paying overtime and paying on time. Zhang was known to provide workers with iced tea and fruit on hot summer days as well as for lending money out of his own pocket to employees who needed an apartment or other assistance.[27]

Further investigation revealed that a Mattel-certified paint supplier, Dongxing New Energy Company, had run out of yellow pigment and arranged on the Internet to buy 330 pounds of powder from a local company, Dongguan Zhongxin Toner Powder Factory, that was not certified by Mattel. Dongguan Zhongxin had provided fake documentation on the powder certifying its quality. Neither the powder nor the paint was tested, although Lee Der had testing equipment at its factory in Foshan.

Mattel had to determine whether to announce a voluntary product recall or to have the Consumer Product Safety Commission (CPSC) decide whether to recall the toys. The CPSC would have to investigate, but the CPSC was understaffed and was required to satisfy procedural requirements before it could order a recall. A voluntary recall by Mattel would be faster and could be coordinated with the CPSC, which was required to monitor the progress of any nationwide recall. If Mattel decided on a voluntary recall, it had to decide whether to recall only those items known to be contaminated or to issue a broader recall in case other batches of products also were contaminated. Mattel also had to decide whether to make public the source of the problem and name the contractors involved and whether to fire them. It also would have to notify retailers to stop selling the product and communicate with consumers for the return of contaminated products already purchased.

Mattel also had to assess whether its current policies and procedures were sufficient to ensure safety. In addition to procedures such as factory audits and inspections, technology could be used to mitigate certain risks. For example,

[22]Ibid.
[23]*New York Times*, September 21, 2007.
[24]*Wall Street Journal*, July 30, 2007.
[25]Mattel closed its last factory in the United States in 2002. Approximately 65 percent of its toys were manufactured in China, with some production in Indonesia and Mexico.
[26]*New York Times*, August 29, 2007.
[27]*Los Angeles Times*, August 24, 2007.

it conducted tests at its testing laboratories, but it could also deploy testing equipment to individual factories, as it had done in its factory in Tijuana, Mexico. A handheld device for detecting heavy metals had recently been developed and could provide a first-level screening. Mattel also had to anticipate how the product safety issue might evolve in the next few months.

What should Mattel do?

THE DECISION AND AFTERMATH

Mattel decided to voluntarily recall the toys but delayed the recall until it could put up a Web site with information for retailers and consumers about how to return the products, according to David Allmark, general manager of Fisher-Price. On August 2 Mattel issued a voluntary fast-track recall in cooperation with the CPSC. The recall covered 83 toys with 1.5 million units worldwide, of which 967,000 were in the United States, two-thirds of which had not yet reached retailers' shelves. The recall was broader than needed, but the company sought to err on the side of caution. Mattel also announced that it was reviewing its procedures for ensuring product safety. Eckert said, "We apologize to everyone affected by this recall, especially those who bought the toys in question. We realize that parents trust us with what is most precious to them—their children. And we also recognize that trust is earned. Our goal is to correct this problem, improve our systems, and maintain the trust of families that have allowed us to be part of their lives by acting responsibly and quickly to address their concerns."[28] In a video posted on Mattel's Web site Eckert said, "I can't change what has happened in the past, but I can change how we work in the future." Eckert mentioned that he had four children. Videos mocking the company quickly appeared on YouTube, including one involving a character called "Tickle Me Lead-Mo."[29]

In its announcement of the recall Mattel explained the source of the problem, naming Lee Der and its supplier. Lee Der suspended production at the factory in Foshan, but on August 6 Zhang received a new order from Mattel which would allow the factory to resume production. He called the production manager and told him to tell the workers to report for work. On August 7 he learned that Mattel had disclosed the name of his company as having produced the recalled toys. Two days later China's Administration of Quality Supervision and Inspection and Quarantine banned Lee Der from exporting. The next day Zhang closed the factory and told the production manager to start selling the equipment. Zhang then hanged himself in the factory.

"'After the recall was announced, the company flew a delegation to China to meet with manufacturers,' said a Mattel spokesperson last week. Factory owners were asked to gather in a room where Jim Walter, Mattel's senior vice president of worldwide quality assurance, reiterated basic safety standards. The attendees were required to sign a new safety contract. 'They needed to reaffirm what they had agreed to in previous years,' said the spokesperson."[30] Walter explained, "The

message was very clear. If you cannot do these things, please let us know. No problem, but you won't be doing business with us."[31]

THE CRISIS: PHASE II

During a conference call with Mattel supervisors in Hong Kong on the safety issue, one of the supervisors received a call from the testing laboratory in Shenzhen reporting that lead had been found in the paint of a toy car known as "Sarge," based on a character in Disney's movie *Cars*. The cars were made by Hong Kong–based Early Light Industrial Company, which had supplied Mattel for 20 years and was owned by Francis Choi, one of Asia's wealthiest persons. Early Light had outsourced the painting to another company, Hong Li Da, which unknown to Early Light purchased paint from an unauthorized supplier. The lead paint problem was detected by Early Light, and Choi said, "We informed Mattel immediately."

What should Mattel do?

THE DECISION AND AFTERMATH

On August 14 Mattel issued another voluntary fast-track recall of 436,000 Sarge die-cast vehicles. Mattel credited detection of the problem to its reemphasis to suppliers of its standards, along with expanded testing. Mattel announced the lead paint had come from Hong Li Da and that Early Light Industrial was not responsible for the problem.

At the same time Mattel voluntarily recalled 18.2 million toys worldwide with small, powerful magnets that could come loose. This supplemented a November 2006 recall. The company stated that it had "implemented enhanced magnet retention systems in its toys across all brands."[32] Mattel made it clear that the problem was due to its own design error and not to problems with its suppliers. The day before the recall Mattel had begun an advertising campaign designed to assure consumers of its commitment to product safety.

Jim Walter also announced strengthened procedures the company was implementing. The procedures had three components. First, every batch of paint was required to be tested. Second, production controls were strengthened and unannounced factory inspections were increased. Third, every production run of finished toys was tested. Mattel also announced that it had met with all its suppliers to make certain that they fully understood the new procedures. It began to use the hand-held device for initial screening for heavy metals.

Some parents had purchased lead detection kits to test their children's toys. The CPSC reported in August that the kits were unreliable, producing both false positives and false negatives.

On September 4 Mattel voluntarily recalled worldwide 850,000 units of 11 products made in China because of "impermissible levels of lead." The products were in the Barbie and Fisher-Price brands. Mattel said that the recall was the result of "the company's ongoing investigation of its toys manufactured

---

[28]Mattel, Inc. press release, August 2, 2007.

[29]*Wall Street Journal*, August 15, 2007.

[30]*Wall Street Journal*, August 14, 2007.

[31]*New York Times*, August 15, 2007.

[32]Mattel, Inc. press release, August 14, 2007.

in China ....,"[33] On October 25 Mattel recalled 55,550 units of one product sold in Canada, Ireland, the United Kingdom, and the United States because of "impermissible levels of lead." Mattel identified the supplier in China and the subcontractor. Mattel was cooperating with the CPSC.

Some small U.S. companies that produced their toys in the United States seized the opportunity to promote their use of lead-free paint. Whittle Shortline Railroad proclaimed its products as "100 percent kid-safe," and owner Mike Whitworth said, "We are little bitty, but we are taking some leaps and bounds here. Actually, we have seen about a 40 percent jump [in sales] since late June."[34]

One remaining issue was what to do with the recalled product. Most consumers never returned recalled products, although RC2 reported that 60 percent of its Thomas & Friends toy trains had been returned. Rachel Weintraub, director of product safety at the Consumer Federation of America, described the issue, "The first step is the product is recalled. The second step is the manufacturer gets some of the product back. And the third step is: What happens next?"[35] Recalled toys could legally be sold in other countries if the recall was voluntary. The EPA required testing of recalled products and a disposal plan for recalled products containing lead. Concentrations above 5 ppm required special disposal procedures. Otherwise, the products could be disposed of in landfills.

THE SCOPE OF THE CRISIS

The recalls by Mattel and other companies put pressure on the Chinese government and its export-driven industries. The government was sensitive to criticism, particularly as it was racing to complete preparations for the 2008 Olympic Games. Moreover, Mattel's product recalls had resulted in thousands of Chinese workers losing their jobs. China Labor Watch, a worker rights organization based in New York, seized the opportunity and released a report alleging brutal conditions and illegal practices in toy factories in China.[36]

The State Council of China released a report in August stating that 85 percent of its food exports passed quality inspections, up from 78 percent a year earlier. The State Council also announced that it had established a cabinet-level committee headed by Vice Prime Minister Wu Yi to improve the quality and safety of products made in China.

Mattel was concerned about its relationship with the Chinese government. After the waters had calmed somewhat, Mattel sent Debrowski to China to apologize. Debrowski said that Mattel's recalls over lead paint were "overly inclusive" and that the larger recall involving magnets was due to a design error by Mattel and not to Chinese manufacturers. Debrowski's apology caused an uproar in the United States where Mattel was accused of kowtowing to China and the suppliers on which it relied. Senator Charles Schumer (D-NY) said, "It's like a

bank robber apologizing to his accomplice instead of to the person who was robbed. They're playing politics in China rather than doing the right thing."[37] A Mattel spokesperson explained that Debrowski had apologized to the Chinese people as customers, as Mattel had apologized in other countries.

The crisis quickly moved into government arenas. Hearings were held in the United States, and the European Union took up the issue led by the consumer affairs commissioner Maglena Kuneva and members of the European Parliament. Dwight Justice of the International Trade Union Confederation said, "Companies are not afraid of being punished if they don't apply standards in factories in China." Critics called for mandatory testing of products, but Anne Starkie-Alves, head of the Toy Industries of Europe association, warned about the volume of imports and said of current practices, "I think there are very good systems in place."[38] Peter Mandelson, commissioner for international trade, warned about inaction, "If the EU doesn't take defensive measures when they are justified, we will risk encouraging a backlash against China's trade growth. Given the mood in Europe, the burden of proof is shifting to China to demonstrate that it is trading fairly and that its goods are safe."[39]

In Senate hearings Mattel CEO Eckert apologized to Congress and pledged that the company was changing its practices to prevent safety problems. He announced that the company was now testing each batch of products for lead and requiring all its suppliers to buy only from authorized vendors. Mattel, along with other U.S. toy manufacturers, called for mandatory testing by independent laboratories. Toys 'Я' Us complained that information provision about recalls needed to be improved, so that retailers would not unknowingly continue to sell recalled products. Senators called for stronger measures including possible criminal prosecution for selling dangerous products.

Hearings were also held in the House, which in December approved a bill that would reduce the allowable lead content in consumer products, strengthen the CPSC, and improve the tracking of recalled products. Safety activists said the bill did not go far enough and supported a stronger bill reported by committee in the Senate. The Senate bill would increase the maximum fine from $1.8 million to $100 million and allow state prosecutors to enforce the federal law, but the Senate delayed acting on the bill.

MANAGEMENT CRISIS?

In November 2007 *Consumer Reports* discovered lead in Mattel's Fisher-Price blood-pressure cuff in its toy medical kit and alerted the attorney general of Illinois, which had standards more stringent than federal standards. Illinois regulators tested the product and found that the lead content of the plastic cuff was 4,500–5,900 ppm. Although there was no federal standard for lead in plastic, the lead content was roughly eight times the federal standard for lead in paint. Mattel also had tested the

---

[33]Mattel, Inc. press release, September 4, 2007.

[34]*New York Times,* August 15, 2007.

[35]*New York Times,* December 22, 2007.

[36]"Investigations on Toy Suppliers in China: Workers are still suffering," August 2007. www.chinalaborwatch.org.

[37]*New York Times,* September 21, 2007.

[38]*New York Times,* September 15, 2007.

[39]*New York Times,* September 18, 2007.

product and found "higher than anticipated" lead levels. A Mattel spokesperson stated that the product met both U.S. federal and European Union safety standards for lead in plastic. In August Toys 'Я' Us had recalled vinyl baby bibs and offered refunds to consumers because some of the bibs had lead in the plastic. The lead in the bibs was revealed by testing at independent laboratories sponsored by the *New York Times* and a California environmental group. The lead concentrations did not exceed federal standards, but they exceeded Toys 'Я' Us' own standards, resulting in the recall. The company said the bibs posed no health risk unless they were so worn that pieces could break off and be swallowed by a child. Toys 'Я' Us spokesperson Julie Vallese said, "Parents shouldn't be alarmed."[40]

In December Mattel recalled the toy medical kit but only in Illinois and notified retailers that it was accepting the return of the toys. Mattel did not make a public statement about the return. Consumers could also return the toys, and Mattel gave instructions on the Internet. It was not clear that there was any risk from the lead, since sucking on the plastic was unlikely to release the lead, according to scientists.

As a result of Mattel's limited recall, in December Representative Elijah Cummings (D-MD) wrote to Mattel asking it to stop using lead in its products. In January Mattel responded by reporting that 70 percent of the products in question had been returned. This response did little to calm the critics. On January 29, 2008, 56 members of Congress wrote to Mattel expressing concern for the lack of action by the company. The letter stated, "We challenge you to live up to your words and set a standard for the entire industry by completely eliminating the use of lead in all the children's products manufactured by Mattel."

What should Mattel do? ▪

Source: This case was prepared from public sources by Professor David P. Baron. Copyright © 2008 by the Board of Trustees of the Leland Stanford Junior University. All rights reserved. Reprinted with permission.

Johnson & Johnson and Its Quality Reputation

We believe our first responsibility is to the doctors, nurses and patients, to mothers and fathers and all others who use our products and services. In meeting their needs everything we do must be of high quality.

Johnson & Johnson, "Our Credo"

It makes me question their quality control. It makes me wonder if they have the parents' best interest and the children's best interest at heart.

Mark Mandel, father of a 21-month-old daughter and a microbiologist at the Feinberg School of Medicine at Northwestern University.[41]

INTRODUCTION

Johnson & Johnson had grown rapidly over the past two decades with sales of $62 billion, after-tax profits of $12.2 billion, and 115,000 employees in 2009. The company was composed of more than 250 separate business units that allowed for innovation while providing internal risk diversification. The company emphasized earnings growth and had recorded earnings increases for 94 consecutive quarters until the first quarter of 2009.[42] CEO William C. Weldon explained, "If you have 250 grains of sand and 240 are going up and 10 are not doing so well, it really doesn't affect you. It's really the magic of decentralization that allows things to work at Johnson & Johnson."[43]

Johnson & Johnson was widely acclaimed for its handling of the Tylenol product tampering that resulted in the poisoning deaths of seven people in 1982. The company pulled all Tylenol off the shelves worldwide at a reported cost of $100 million, and police and fire officials in Chicago concluded that someone had opened the product packages in the stores and inserted the poison. CEO James E. Burke appeared on television several times to reassure the public that everything possible was being done to avoid further harm. The company was guided by its "Our Credo."

Johnson & Johnson had a strong reputation for product quality, but its commitment to quality conflicted with cost pressures. According to a story in *Fortune* magazine, a number of current and former employees maintained that cost pressures may have compromised quality control in the 2000's.[44] By the end of the decade quality control at Johnson & Johnson had become a public issue.

CHILDREN'S TYLENOL

In 2009 Johnson & Johnson discovered a possible problem with Children's Tylenol produced in its McNeil Consumer Healthcare plant in Fort Washington, Pennsylvania. McNeil said the problem posed no safety hazards but nevertheless represented a quality defect. The company regularly tested all the ingredients for its healthcare products and on April 14, 2009 tests revealed the presence of *Burkholderia cepacia* bacteria in raw materials used in the production of children's and infant's Tylenol. The bacteria were not a threat to healthy people but can cause serious respiratory illness in people with chronic respiratory problems or weakened immune systems.[45]

None of the contaminated raw material was used in production, but some product had been made from the same batch in which the bacteria had been found. The product was tested, and no bacteria were found. McNeil continued to ship the product made from the batch of raw materials.

---

[40]*New York Times*, August 18, 2007.
[41]*New York Times*, May 3, 2010.
[42]*New York Times*, September 29, 2010.
[43]Ibid.

[44]Mina Kimes, "Why Johnson & Johnson's Headache Won't Go Away," *Fortune*, September 6, 2010.
[45]*Wall Street Journal*, September 29, 2010.

As a result of an inspection the FDA cited the company for violating good manufacturing practices on June 4, 2009, and the company stopped shipping the product made from the batch of raw materials. McNeil faced the issue of what to do with the product on retailers' shelves and in consumer's homes. McNeil decided to find out how much product was on retailers' shelves so that it could determine the kind of action to take. A Johnson & Johnson staffer wrote in an email, "We may want to see if our sales group can do some discreet store visits to assess what is out there for a few stores across the country."[46] Johnson & Johnson hired a contractor Inmar, Inc. to make the assessment, and Inmar hired WIS International to help in the assessment.[47]

On July 30, 2009 McNeil decided to recall the outstanding product and began to work with the FDA on the details of a voluntary recall.[48] On August 21, 2009 McNeil began a recall from wholesalers, although the public was not notified. The company notified doctors of the recall on September 18, 2009 and 6 days later posted a recall notice on its Web site for consumers.[49]

THE PHANTOM RECALL

In 2008 McNeil discovered that it had produced Motrin with less strength than stated on the label and the package and that two lots failed to dissolve properly. Rather than recall the product, McNeil decided in 2009 to hire contractors to purchase as much of the product as possible. A contractor was hired to visit 5,000 stores at a cost of $487,500. The buyers were to act as "regular customers" and were instructed that "THERE MUST BE NO MENTION OF THIS BEING A RECALL."[50] One memorandum stated, "Do not communicate to store personnel any information about this product." Another stated, "Just purchase all available product."[51] Johnson & Johnson spokeswoman Bonnie Jacobs later explained, "Given that there was no safety risk, the objective was to remove the affected product from a unique distribution channel, mainly convenience stores and gas stations with as little disruption and consumer confusion as possible."[52] She also said that the memoranda were prepared by the contractor and not by McNeil. Commenting on the revelation of the "phantom recall," Allan Coukell, director of the Pew Prescription Project, commented, "It's fairly shocking— the idea that if there was a quality problem, they'd try to bring the product back instead of being transparent."[53]

THE FORT WASHINGTON PLANT

Inspections at McNeil's Fort Washington, Pennsylvania plant identified 20 manufacturing problems. On April 30, 2010 McNeil recalled 140 million bottles of Children's Tylenol, Motrin, Benadril, and Zyrtec, stating that the recall was made because of manufacturing deficiencies and not because of adverse health effects.[54] Four million bottles were on retailers' shelves, and 136 million bottles had been purchased by consumers. The company had approximately 70 percent of the infant and children's market. Johnson & Johnson's head of consumer products Colleen Goggins apologized "to the mothers and fathers and caregivers for the concern and inconvenience."[55] There were no reported illnesses or deaths associated with the products.

Deborah M. Autor of the FDA said "The findings are serious …. We had concerns about the company's failure to investigate and correct quality problems."[56] Johnson & Johnson temporarily closed the Fort Washington plant to improve manufacturing processes and quality. The FDA began a criminal investigation of the company.

CONGRESS TAKES AN INTEREST

House Oversight committee Chairman Edolphus Towns (D-NY) and ranking Republican Darrell Issa (R-CA) held a hearing into Johnson & Johnson's conduct in May 2010. Towns said to Goggins, "I have become deeply concerned about your company. It paints a picture of a company that is deceptive, dishonest and willing to put the health of children at risk." Goggins replied, "There was never any intent to deceive or hide anything." Representative Eleanor Holmes Norton (D-DC) asked whether the delay in reporting was a "cover up." In prepared testimony Goggins said, "Reports of possible adverse events, for example, are reported to the FDA quickly."[57] When asked about the phantom recall, Goggins said, "I can't tell you right now what they were instructed to do or not, sir."

With a bottle of Children's Tylenol on the table Issa stated, "It is a moral outrage for a company specifically marketing its products for children to allow a culture of neglect and irresponsibility to taint the medicines that parents and physicians trust to help children get well." Deputy FDA Commissioner Joshua M. Sharfstein stated, "From what we know, we don't have evidence of children who had serious problems because of quality problems."

Weldon remained silent for the first several months of the evolving events before appearing on CNBC. The House held a second hearing on September 30, 2010, and Weldon testified. He accepted "full accountability" for the quality problems, and lamented that "children do not have access to our important medicines." At the hearing Issa asked Weldon, "Does Johnson & Johnson oversee its divisions properly, or do they have too much autonomy? Does the big name—Johnson & Johnson—mean quality, or do you have to judge each division separately?" In prepared testimony Weldon said, "From Johnson & Johnson's perspective, our response to this issue was the most responsible it could possibly be." He said that the

---

[46]Ibid.

[47]Ibid. Inmar provides assistance and services to pharmaceutical companies in retrieving medicines that have been recalled.

[48]The FDA does not have the authority to force a recall of the product, but the FDA can ask the producer to issue a voluntary recall.

[49]*Wall Street Journal*, September 29, 2010.

[50]*Los Angeles Times*, May 28, 2010.

[51]*New York Times*, June 12, 2010.

[52]Ibid.

[53]*Washington Post*, May 28, 2010.

[54]Recalls are posted on www.mcneilproductrecall.com. Earlier in 2009 Johnson & Johnson had recalled bottles of children's medications because of a musty odor. FDA regulations require a company to report consumer complaints within three days, but Johnson & Johnson waited a year.

[55]*Los Angeles Times*, May 28, 2010.

[56]*Washington Post*, May 5, 2010.

[57]*New York Times*, May 28, 2010.

company had a standard and held all its companies to that standard. Weldon also commented on the phantom recall, "McNeil should have handled this differently. We made a mistake." Referring to the recall of children's Tylenol Issa said, "That failure will mar Johnson & Johnson's image for many, many years." Weldon said the "episode was not a model for how I would like to see Johnson & Johnson companies approach problems with defective product when they arise."

BABY PRODUCTS IN CHINA

In March 2010 the NGO Campaign for Safe Cosmetics released test results on Johnson & Johnson baby products, such as shampoos and soaps, sold in China, alleging that nearly half the products tested contained formaldehyde and 1,4-dioxane, which are classified as possible carcinogens by U.S. regulators. A large supermarket chain responded by taking some Johnson & Johnson products off the shelves, and a woman complained that her baby developed a rash from Johnson & Johnson's Baby Bedtime Oil. Johnson & Johnson (China) explained that the rash was most likely caused by an allergy and not related to a quality problem. China's General Administration of Quality Supervision, Inspection and Quarantine tested 31 batches of 26 Johnson & Johnson products and found only one with 1,4-dioxane and in concentration 3.27 ppm.[58] Wu Dong, director of Johnson & Johnson's market research center commented, "The amount is like three drops of water in a whole swimming pool. The 1,4-dioxane is widely seen in our daily goods, such as tomatoes, fresh shrimp and coffee. Shrimp contain 20 to 30 ppm."[59] Consistent with an earlier Johnson & Johnson statement, he explained that the 1,4-dioxane found was a result of processing, "It is like adding oil, salt when cooking cabbage. Some byproducts could be formed during cooking."[60] The U.S. industry association The Personal Care Product Council said, "The levels of the two chemicals the group reportedly found are considered to be 'trace' or extremely low, are well below established regulatory limits or safety thresholds, and are not a cause for health concern."[61] In a statement Johnson & Johnson said, "The trace levels of certain compounds found by the Campaign for Safe Cosmetics can result from processes that make our products gentle for babies and safe from bacteria growth ... and all our products meet or exceed the regulatory requirements in every country where they are sold."[62] The company said, "We are disappointed that the Campaign for Safe Cosmetics has inaccurately characterized the safety of our products, misrepresented the overwhelming consensus of scientists and government agencies that review the safety of ingredients, and unnecessarily alarmed parents." He Qiaomei, a mother from Guangzhou, said, "The manufacturer should be brought to justice."[63] The U.S. Consumer Product Safety Commission stated, "The presence of 1,4-dioxane, even as a trace contaminant, is cause for concern." There were no U.S. standards for 1,4-dioxane and formaldehyde in personal care products in the United States.

OTHER QUALITY PROBLEMS

Johnson & Johnson operated a joint-venture plant with Merck in Lancaster, Pennsylvania that produced Mylanta, Pepcid, and other products. In July 2010 Johnson & Johnson received a subpoena from a grand jury inquiring into quality control problems. The FDA had received complaints from consumers who found maximum strength Pepcid in regular-strength bottles and mint-flavored tablets in a berry-flavored bottle.[64] There was no risk of harm to consumers from the quality control problems at the Lancaster plant, but FDA inspectors identified a variety of problems at the plant.

Johnson & Johnson also recalled products produced in its Las Piedras, Puerto Rico plant after the FDA found that a chemical used in treating wooden pallets caused a musty smell in the products. Spokeswoman Jacobs said that the FDA had been notified of the issue and that the company planned to retrieve the product. The FDA, however, wanted the company to issue a recall. Neisa M. Alonso, an FDA investigator and recall coordinator in Puerto Rico, wrote, "It seems that your company is doing a recall even though you are calling it a 'retrieval.' The agency's position is that your company should do a voluntary recall of the product since it appears that you are already doing a recall of the product."[65] In July 2010 McNeil issued a voluntary recall of 21 lots of Benadryl, Children's Tylenol, Motrin, and two adult strength Tylenol products.

In August 2010 Johnson & Johnson's Vision Care unit recalled 100,000 boxes of 1-Day Accue TruEye soft contact lenses sold in six Asian and 19 European countries because of reported pain and stinging.

JOHNSON & JOHNSON REMEDIATION

McNeil developed a plan to correct the quality control problems. On February 5, 2010 McNeil president Peter McNeil wrote to the FDA stating that the company "recognizes the seriousness of this situation and has identified this corrective action plan as our top priority .... We are confident that this corrective plan provides the approach necessary to identify and implement systemic actions that will improve and enhance our quality processes and systems while addressing the concerns raised by the FDA."[66]

Johnson & Johnson's CEO Weldon announced that chief quality officers would be appointed for each of its divisions. On CNBC Weldon stated that, "We want to ensure nothing like this happens again." Weldon referred to the McNeil unit as an "outlier" and said that the problems were isolated to that unit.

In August 2010 Johnson & Johnson announced that it would "create a single framework for drug, medical device and consumer healthcare units."

[58]BBC Monitoring Asia Pacific, March 22, 2009.
[59]Ibid.
[60]Ibid.
[61]BBC Monitoring Asia Pacific, March 17, 2009.
[62]Ibid.
[63]Chinadaily.com.cn, March 17, 2009.

[64]Washington Post, July 24, 2010.
[65]New York Times, June 12, 2010.
[66]New York Times, March 18, 2010.

CLOSING

Referring to the cost of the series of events, Jim Purtow, a partner at the consulting firm PRTM, commented, "The return on investment equation has just changed dramatically. Look at the cost for a company if you get into FDA issues—the potential fines, the cost of remediation, the actual loss of product sales, all that consumer good will lost—it's a huge amount."[67]

Despite the media coverage of Johnson & Johnson's travails, a consumer survey of 1,042 people in July 2010 revealed that Tylenol scored higher on customer loyalty and intent to purchase than its principal rival Advil.[68] ■

Preparation Questions

1. What may have been the cause of the quality problems at Johnson & Johnson?
2. How much harm has likely been caused to Johnson & Johnson?
3. How should Johnson & Johnson have handled the quality problems? Does it matter whether there is a health risk? What does "Our Credo" require?
4. What should Johnson & Johnson do in China about the claims of the Campaign for Safe Cosmetics?
5. Should quality control at Johnson & Johnson be centralized?

---

[67]*New York Times*, September 29, 2010.
[68]*Wall Street Journal*, September 29, 2010.

PART I

Wal-Mart: Nonmarket Pressure and Reputation Risk (A)

It's time for Wal-Mart to understand that their company practices run counter to the very values that make this country great—fairness, opportunity, and equality.

Senator Edward Kennedy

Some well-meaning critics believe that Wal-Mart stores today, because of our size, should, in fact, play the role that is believed that General Motors played after World War II. And that is to establish this post–World War middle class that the country is proud of …. The facts are that retail does not perform that role in this economy.

H. Lee Scott, CEO Wal-Mart

INTRODUCTION

By 2005 the company founded by Sam Walton operated over 5,482 stores in 16 countries and employed 1.3 million associates in the United States, making it the second largest employer after the federal government. For fiscal 2005 net income was $11.2 billion on sales of $312.4 billion, compared to $10.3 billion and $288 billion, respectively, in fiscal 2004. An estimated 100 million customers shopped at Wal-Mart stores. Wal-Mart's stock price, however, had languished over the past several years. Wal-Mart had an inward focus emphasizing its two key constituencies—its customers and its associates. Sam Walton had believed that dealing with the public was a waste of time and saw little need to be concerned with a broader constituency.

When Wal-Mart became the largest U.S. company in sales in 2002, it began to attract increased attention. Its expansion into the grocery business, however, was a precipitating event. Wal-Mart entered the grocery business in 1988, and its presence grew with the expansion of its supercenters. By 2002 it had become the largest grocery chain and was larger than Safeway and Albertson's combined. In 2003–2004 in Southern California, Safeway, Albertsons, and Kroger supermarkets locked out their union employees, demanding that they make wage and benefit concessions so that the supermarkets could be more competitive with Wal-Mart. After 4 months the union conceded, agreeing to lower wages and benefits for new workers. The unions were threatened and decided to attack Wal-Mart directly. They redirected their efforts from attempting to organize Wal-Mart employees to private and public politics and formed activist organizations to attack the company and its reputation.

Wal-Mart was criticized for providing low wages and inadequate health care benefits, driving small merchants out of business, damaging the culture in small towns, harming the environment, and violating workers' rights. A series of incidents attracted attention, and a number of lawsuits were filed against the company alleging violations of labor laws, discrimination, and poor working conditions in overseas factories supplying the company. Wal-Mart also became a focus of the media. It had been the subject of 950 articles a week in 2001, but by 2004 it was the subject of 2,165 articles a week. Many of those articles were critical of the company's practices and repeated the allegations of the company's critics.

As the nonmarket pressure on Wal-Mart intensified, some observers linked the pressure to its stock price. Wal-Mart's stock price had fallen by 27 percent since 2000, when H. Lee Scott became CEO. Lisa Featherstone, writing on Salon.com, argued that Wal-Mart's low stock price was due "to what they call 'headline risk,' which is Wall Street-speak for bad press. That lagging stock price may become a critical pressure point for activists pressuring Wal-Mart to change its ways."[69] By its silence in the face of criticism Wal-Mart had left a vacuum that its critics were more than happy to fill.

CEO Scott commented, "Over the years, we have thought that we could sit in Bentonville, take care of customers, take care of associates, and the world would leave us alone. It just doesn't work that way anymore."[70] Members of the board of directors asked for a reputational audit of the company. Wal-Mart concluded that a focus solely on customers and associates was no longer viable and that a nonmarket strategy was needed to address its critics and change its deteriorating reputation. That strategy required engagement with its environment as well as addressing the private and public politics the company faced.

Central to any nonmarket strategy was reducing the threat to its reputation by countering the nonmarket opposition it faced and by better positioning the company in its broader environment. A nonmarket strategy also had to be synergistic with the company's market strategy. For example, Wal-Mart wanted to attract higher-income customers who would purchase bigger-ticket items.[71] Higher-income customers were thought to be more sensitive to the issues raised by the company's critics.

MARKET STRATEGY

Wal-Mart's market strategy was based on low prices backed by efficiency. Growth was a key component of its business strategy, and initially the company had focused on small towns and the suburbs of large cities. As those markets became saturated, Wal-Mart sought other ways to grow sales and profits. It revised its market strategy and entered new geographic markets and expanded the offerings in its existing stores. The principal remaining markets were in urban areas in the United States and in other countries. Wal-Mart announced that it would add between 555 and 600 stores globally in 2006, including 270 to

---

[69]*Wall Street Journal*, August 16, 2005.
[70]*Wall Street Journal*, July 26, 2005.
[71]Target Stores had achieved higher per store growth than Wal-Mart in part by appealing to higher-income shoppers.

280 supercenters compared to 266 opened in 2005. CEO Scott said, "We could be three or four times bigger in the U.S."[72] Wal-Mart, however, had experienced local opposition to store openings in Chicago, Los Angeles, and New York City.

The second component of Wal-Mart's growth strategy was expanding its offerings. The company had entered the automotive service market, sold pharmaceuticals, and sold jewelry. It began selling groceries for two reasons. One was a cost advantage relative to supermarkets. The other was to attract higher-income customers who would also shop for higher margin electronic and other products. Wal-Mart also sought to offer banking and other financial services in its stores, but it had been blocked in several attempts. Its latest attempt was a pending application to form an industrial bank in Utah. On a trial basis the company began to provide health care through in-store clinics.

A central pillar of Wal-Mart's business model was to avoid unionization, and it had successfully defeated numerous attempts to organize its workers.[73] When employees at a store began to solicit signatures to request a union certification vote, the company would send a team of labor experts to the store to organize opposition to the drive. Management held mandatory associates' meetings to provide anti-union information. One message was that rather than pay union dues to hire someone to speak for them, associates could speak directly to management to address any problems. The company provided "I can speak for myself" buttons to employees.

Another pillar of its market strategy was its workforce. Despite the criticisms of Wal-Mart for low wages and inadequate benefits, people were eager to work for the company. One reason was the opportunity for advancement, provided in part by the growth in the number of its stores. CEO Scott said, "At Wal-Mart you can, without a high school degree, start as a cart pusher in the parking lot and end up being a regional vice-president."[74] Wal-Mart stated that "Nationally, more than 9,000 hourly associates were promoted into management jobs last year, and two-thirds of our store management started their careers with Wal-Mart in hourly positions."[75]

Eleven thousand people applied for the 400 jobs at a new store in Oakland, California in 2005. The average wage paid in the Bay Area was $10.82 an hour. Melvin Brown, 52, who had applied for a job, said, "I think this is a good place to work. It seems like everybody gets along well with everybody."[76] "Lisa Jackson, 34, a Wal-Mart employee for nine years, working as a cashier, truck unloader, and overnight stock clerk, is now a manager of the electronics department at the new Oakland store. 'I love my job,' Jackson said. 'I like the people, and I love what I do.'"[77] Wendall Chin, coalition director for the Alameda County Central Labor Council said, "Wal-Mart is one of the largest employers in the world—they have to be a model for the society they are promoting. If they don't provide a decent lifestyle, it's scary....It's not just about jobs. It's (having) a good job that you can raise a family on."[78]

PRIVATE POLITICS

Opposition to its geographic expansion in the United States developed quickly, led by local NIMBY groups, unions, and organizations aligned with unions. Some of its product line extensions also met with opposition from interest groups potentially threatened by the extensions. Wal-Mart also came under fire for a number of its operating practices. For example, it contracted with custodial firms to clean its stores, and some of those firms employed illegal immigrants. In 2003 Immigration and Naturalization Service agents raided 60 Wal-Mart stores and arrested 245 illegal immigrants working for 12 contractors. Wal-Mart's contracts with the custodial firms prohibited them from employing illegal workers, but critics claimed that Wal-Mart knew that illegal workers were used. Wal-Mart settled a government lawsuit for $11 million and agreed to establish stricter controls to ensure that contractors hired legally eligible workers.[79] The company denied that it knew that illegal workers were used.

In addition to criticism for specific issues such as contractors employing illegal workers, Wal-Mart faced a well-organized and well-financed set of campaigns. The campaigning organizations were backed by the unions that had tried and failed to organize Wal-Mart workers and that were threatened by its product extensions, particularly the sale of groceries. In 2005 the Service Employees International Union (SEIU) provided funding to establish Wal-Mart Watch to campaign against the company. The SEIU pledged $1 million to finance the campaign and supported a staff of 36 in Washington, D.C. The Union of Food and Commercial Workers (UFCW) had failed to organize Wal-Mart employees and suspended its organizing efforts. It established an Internet-based organization, WakeUpWalMart.com, and supported a staff of six in Washington, D.C. The organization carried the campaign to the Internet, and over 160,000 people signed up to participate in the campaign.

The campaigns were headed by Democrat operatives who had worked on presidential campaigns. WakeUp Wal-Mart was led by Paul Blank, former political director for Howard Dean's presidential campaign, and Chris Kofinis, who worked on the campaign to draft Wesley Clark. The media team for Wal-Mart Watch was led by Jim Jordan, former director of the John Kerry campaign, and Tracy Sefl, a former Democratic National Committee aide who was responsible for press reports about President Bush.[80] MoveOn.org, which financed political campaigns, led the public and governmental aspects of the campaign.

A documentary film, *Wal-Mart: The High Cost of Low Price*, by Robert Greenwald, extended the campaign to theaters. Wal-Mart viewed the film as inaccurate and misleading and produced a short film pointing out the factual errors.

[72]*Wall Street Journal,* October 26, 2005.

[73]Other large retailers such as Home Depot and Target were also nonunion.

[74]*Business Week,* October 3, 2005.

[75]*San Jose Mercury News,* September, 2004.

[76]*San Francisco Chronicle,* August 17, 2005.

[77]Ibid.

[78]Ibid.

[79]The 12 contractors pleaded guilty to criminal charges and paid $4 million in penalties.

[80]*The New York Times,* November 1, 2005.

Wal-Mart promoted a favorable film, *Why Wal-Mart Works & Why That Makes Some People Crazy,* by Ron Galloway. A press release said, "The riveting documentary explores why Wal-Mart is one of the greatest success stories in business history, how it improves the lives of individual working Americans and their communities, and the social pathology behind the escalating attacks on the company by special interest groups."[81] Wal-Mart challenged Mr. Greenwald to show both films side-by-side.[82]

One criticism of Wal-Mart was that it harmed the culture of small towns by driving small merchants out of business through its low prices. Commentators noted that other companies such as Home Depot, Lowe's, and Zales also drove small merchants out of business but did not face the same criticisms. Another criticism focused on the health care benefits available to its part-time and full-time employees. Unions and their allies also complained that Wal-Mart's low wages depressed the wages of workers in other companies. Ironically, the greatest beneficiaries of Wal-Mart's business strategy were low-income consumers who benefited from its low prices.

In December 2004 six unions announced an unusual campaign against Wal-Mart. The $25 million campaign was not directed at organizing workers but at publicizing its claim that Wal-Mart was depressing wages and benefits. The unions argued that now that Wal-Mart was the largest U.S. company it had an obligation to be a model for other companies, as General Motors had been decades earlier.[83] Greg Denier of the UFCW said, "This isn't a campaign, this is a movement. There's no precedent for this. It's a movement to confront the reality of Wal-Martization. No other company has ever had the global economic impact that Wal-Mart has."[84] A Wal-Mart spokeswoman responded, "You need to ask one question: Is it fair to ask American consumers to pay higher prices to subsidize a relatively small pocket of individuals just because they are making the most noise."[85]

In April 2005, 50 groups, including unions, environmental groups, and community organizations, joined together to work through the Center for Community and Corporate Ethics with the objective of forcing Wal-Mart to change its practices. The Center was formed with $1 million from the SEIU. Andy Grossman, executive director of the coalition and former executive director of the Democratic Senatorial Campaign, said, "We're focusing on Wal-Mart because of the huge impact it has on each of the different parts of American life it touches. They do provide goods at the lowest price, but that sometimes comes at a high cost to society."[86] Carl Pope, executive director of the Sierra Club, said, "We recognize that we are much more likely to win the battle against a giant like Wal-Mart if we act on multiple fronts. You don't want to challenge Wal-Mart just on health care or just on the environment or just on sex discrimination. You want to pressure them on all three. This is an assault on a business model. We're not trying to shut Wal-Mart down."[87]

In solidarity with the lead unions, on August 10, 2005 members of the National Education Association and the National Federation of Teachers picketed Wal-Mart stores and held rallies at schools in 34 cities in 24 states to protest Wal-Mart practices. The "Send Wal-Mart Back to School" campaign was supported by WakeUpWalMart.com and was initiated by the UFCW.[88] The teachers urged parents not to buy their children's school supplies at Wal-Mart. Although the members of the teachers unions repeated the usual allegations about low wages and benefits, their true motivation may have been closer to home. Wal-Mart had long had a commitment to education, providing $45 million in scholarships and grants to teachers, but it also supported policies that were anathema to the teachers unions.[89] One protesting teacher complained that the Walton Family Foundation had contributed to school-voucher campaigns and supported tax credits for families sending their children to private schools. Don Dawson, a math teacher, said, "We don't solve problems in public education by taking money away. We can't afford to go backwards."[90]

The UFCW and the SEIU also joined with the community activist group ACORN to form the Wal-Mart Workers Association to work for better conditions for Wal-Mart employees. Wade Rathke of ACORN explained, "We are building something that's never been seen; it's neither fish nor fowl. We're focusing on Wal-Mart because it is the largest employer in the area—and in the whole nation—and is setting standards that affect communities and employment relations across the nation."[91] The association intended to engage Wal-Mart on issues relating to working conditions. For example, some employees complained that Wal-Mart reduced the number of hours they could work. Wal-Mart explained that it used an algorithm to determine how large a staff was needed at various times in the month.

The UFCW in conjunction with WakeUpWalMart.com sponsored full-page advertisements on November 14, 2005 under the heading "Wal-Mart vs. America." The ad stated: "You Decide":

Wal-Mart's America vs. Our America

600,000 workers without company health care vs. Affordable health care

2 million women suing for discrimination vs. Equal pay for equal work

---

[81]Business Wire, November 17, 2005.

[82]*New York Times,* November 1, 2005.

[83]After World War II General Motors and the United Auto Workers reached collective bargaining agreements that promised gains in real income to workers regardless of the state of the economy or the company's profitability. The real income of workers rose sharply, and the agreements became the pattern for the automobile industry. Nelson Lichtenstein, "Wal-Mart's Bargain with America," *San Jose Mercury News,* September 12, 2004.

[84]*New York Times,* December 11, 2004.

[85]Ibid.

[86]*New York Times,* April 3, 2005.

[87]Ibid.

[88]*San Jose Mercury News,* August 11, 2005.

[89]See www.walmartfacts.com. Wal-Mart made over $170 million in charitable donations in 2004. Most of the donations were made to local community organizations chosen by local store employees.

[90]*San Jose Mercury News,* August 11, 2005.

[91]*New York Times,* September 3, 2005.

Repeated child labor law violations vs. Protecting children

Poverty-level wages vs. Living wages

Corporate special interest lobbyists vs. The American people

WakeUpWalMart commissioned Zogby International to conduct a national survey of people's attitudes toward Wal-Mart. The poll revealed that "56 percent of Americans agreed with the statement 'Wal-Mart was bad for America. It may provide low prices, but those prices come with a high moral and economic cost.' In contrast, only 39 percent of American adults agreed with the opposing statement, 'I believe Wal-Mart is good for America. It provides low prices and saves consumers money every day.'"[92]

WakeUpWalMart carried the campaign to a higher level. The group recruited 65 ministers to sign a letter to CEO Scott. The letter stated, "Jesus would not embrace Wal-Mart's values of greed and profits at any cost, particularly when children suffer as a result of those misguided values."[93] In a break of solidarity Tracy Sefl of Wal-Mart Watch replied, "What would Jesus do, indeed. I think he would say the ad was a mistake. We heard from numerous supporters who were offended."[94] Wal-Mart spokesperson Sarah Clark commented, "To us, these are both campaigns directed by union leadership intended to criticize a company trying to help working families. There are well-meaning critics out there. These two organizations don't fall into that category."[95]

PUBLIC POLITICS

The unions and other critics of Wal-Mart saw little hope for action by the federal government, but the states provided some hope. In a move intended to put pressure on the governor, the California state legislature passed a bill requiring an "economic impact" statement for any new store with at least 130,000 square feet, 20,000 types of items, and more than 10 percent of sales from nontaxable goods. The only type of store that would meet those conditions was a Wal-Mart supercenter that sold groceries. The bill had been backed by the California Labor Federation. The governor vetoed the bill, and the state legislature was unable to override the veto.

One opportunity for Wal-Mart's critics lay in pressures on state budgets from the rising cost of Medicaid, the federally mandated, but state-funded, health care program for low-income individuals. The pressures had increased because of rising health care costs and federal welfare reform. "The expansion of Medicaid to cover the working poor has fundamentally broadened the nation's safety net and changed the lives of low-wage workers in the USA. It also has put enormous strain on federal and state finances and made taxpayers the health insurance provider for millions of workers at Wal-Mart, McDonald's and other low-wage employers .... 'People who left welfare went into jobs paying $5.15 to $7.15 an hour,' says Michael Paxton, the county's [Washington County, Ohio] welfare director.

'Medicaid and food stamps and child care assistance make it possible for people to work at low wages' .... Many workers choose Medicaid over insurance offered by their employers because it is less expensive. Wal-Mart workers pay $273 a month for the company's family medical coverage and get fewer benefits than Medicaid."[96]

In April 2005 Wal-Mart Watch ran a full-page ad alleging that Wal-Mart wages forced thousands of its employees to use food stamps and Medicaid for health care. In the internal memo leaked to the media, a Wal-Mart vice-president wrote that 5 percent of its associates were on Medicaid compared to 4 percent nationally and that 46 percent of the children of Wal-Mart's associates were uninsured or on Medicaid.

Regardless of Wal-Mart's impact on state Medicaid expenditures, many states had incurred large increases in their health care expenditures, putting pressure on state budgets. Unions recognized this burden and devised a strategy to appeal to state governments. The AFL-CIO developed a model bill to be introduced in state legislatures, and their efforts were directed at over 30 states. The Maryland General Assembly passed the bill, popularly known as the Wal-Mart bill, which required all employers in the state with 10,000 or more employees to spend at least 8 percent of their sales on medical benefits for their employees or pay the difference into the state's health insurance program. Only four companies had 10,000 employees, and Wal-Mart was the only one to which the law would apply. The Republican governor vetoed the bill, but the heavily Democrat state legislature overrode the veto.[97] The governor had said that the law would chill business activity in the state. Wal-Mart had announced that it would build a distribution center on the Maryland Eastern shore employing up to 1,000 workers, and legislators from the region feared that the company would switch the distribution center to another state. Referring to the unions, a Wal-Mart lobbyist said, "They have a power we can't match, and we worked this bill very hard."[98] Bills had been introduced in 12 states.

The override in Maryland spurred new efforts in states such as California. Wal-Mart had 70,000 employees in California, and another 68 companies had 10,000 or more employees. The state legislature earlier had passed a bill requiring the disclosure of the names of all companies with 25 or more employees receiving public health care, as under Medicare. The governor vetoed the bill, and it was not overridden.

ISSUES

Wal-Mart faced a number of additional issues, some of which arose from its product extensions and some from its operating practices.

Groceries

By 2005 Wal-Mart had 1,866 supercenters selling groceries. Supermarkets bore the brunt of Wal-Mart's expansion.

---

[92]WakeUpWalMart press release, December 1, 2005.
[93]Wall Street Journal, January 11, 2006.
[94]Ibid.
[95]Ibid.

[96]USA Today, August 2, 2005.
[97]Overriding a veto in Maryland required a 60 percent vote of each chamber of the legislature.
[98]New York Times, January 13, 2006.

Albertson put itself up for sale, and Winn-Dixie announced plans to cut 22,000 jobs, or 28 percent of its workforce.

In response to the unions and their allies, Wal-Mart quoted a columnist for the *Sacramento Bee*, who studied the conflict with the UFCW and wrote, "So for the sake of 250,000 grocery store clerks and baggers and their employers, the other 35 million people in this state are asked to agree to pay billions of dollars more than they ought to for the necessities of life and to deprive themselves of choices that could make their lives better. You don't have to be a Wal-Mart shopper to see that this is not a bargain that makes sense."[99]

Banking

At the beginning of 2005 Wal-Mart announced that it would issue a Wal-Mart Discovery credit card in cooperation with GE Consumer Finance. The credit card would have no fee and give 1 percent cash back. Wal-Mart also had bank branches of its partners in 1,000 of its stores, and it had begun a venture with SunTrust that would place co-branded money centers in stores. Wal-Mart was on the road to realizing its objective of offering financial services to its customers.

In 2005 Wal-Mart filed an application with the Federal Deposit Insurance Corporation (FDIC) for permission to open an industrial bank in Utah, also known as an industrial loan corporation, to process the credit and debit card transactions from its stores. Federal law prohibited a nonfinancial institution from engaging in banking, but an industrial bank was not classified as a bank under federal law. An industrial bank was state-chartered and regulated and was supervised by the FDIC. Wal-Mart's objective was to process its 140 million transactions a month at lower cost. Other companies, including American Express, Daimler-Chrysler, General Electric, Merrill Lynch, Toyota, and Target Corporation operated industrial banks in Utah, and Berkshire Hathaway had applied to establish one. General Electric and Target used their banks to issue commercial credit cards.

The FDIC extended its comment period on Wal-Mart's Utah application to 2 months, since in contrast to the maximum of six comments received on a typical application more than 1,100 comments were received on the Wal-Mart application. In response to the application, a coalition formed to oppose Wal-Mart. The coalition included the Independent Community Bankers of America, the National Grocers Association, National Association of Convenience Stores, and the UFCW. Local banks feared that Wal-Mart would open branch banks in its stores. Wal-Mart Watch also filed a petition with 11,000 signatures opposing the application.[100] WakeUpWalMart launched an Internet-based campaign against the application. The FDIC announced it would hold a public hearing on the application.

In-Store Health Care

Wal-Mart had provided pharmacy departments in its stores for years, and a natural extension was to provide health care.

Federal law prohibits "self-referrals" which prohibits pharmacies from operating clinics, so Wal-Mart partnered with InterFit Health and other providers to open clinics in its stores in several states. CVS, Target, Rite-Aid, Brooks Eckerd Pharmacy, and Costco also planned to open clinics in their stores. The clinics provided basic diagnostic services and medical care by nurse practitioners. The clinics were drop-in, and prices were low. The clinics were also open long hours corresponding to pharmacy hours.

Unionization

Employees at two Wal-Mart stores in Canada had voted for a union, but the union members had failed to negotiate a contract with Wal-Mart and later voted to decertify the union. Employees also voted for a union at a store in Quebec. That store had been operating at a loss, and Wal-Mart decided to close it. The UFCW–Canada filed a complaint with the Quebec labor relations board. The board found against Wal-Mart, concluding that the closing of the store was not "real, genuine and definitive," since Wal-Mart could reopen the store because it had a long-term lease on the building and had not found another tenant for it.[101]

Unions had repeatedly tried to organize workers at Wal-Mart stores in the United States. Every attempt had failed. In 2004 butchers at a store in Texas voted 7–3 for a union, and Wal-Mart responded by switching to prepackaged beef, eliminating the position of butcher. In 2005 the National Labor Relations Board ruled that employees of Wal-Mart Tire and Lube Express in Loveland, Texas could hold a union election. The campaign for an election was led by one employee, supported by the UFCW, who was able to obtain signatures of a majority of the employees to request an election. The employees, however, voted 17–1 against the union. The union alleged that the employees were intimidated and appealed the election result. A National Labor Relations Board examiner found in favor of Wal-Mart and recommended that the election be certified. Debbie Moore, a former union member who now worked for Wal-Mart and along with her co-workers had voted 19–0 against a union in another election, explained her vote, "Right now, in this day and era, I don't think I need a union to pay for anybody to protect me."[102]

Store Openings

Wal-Mart's strategy of opening stores in urban areas met with protests in Chicago, Los Angeles, and New York. The opposition was led by unions and their allies and in some cases by local NIMBY groups. In Chicago one store application was rejected and another approved. Voters in one Los Angeles suburb rejected a change in zoning laws that would have allowed the construction of a Wal-Mart supercenter, and the company abandoned plans to open a store in Queens.

Alderwoman Emma Mitts, who represented a West Side ward in Chicago, explained her support for the opening of a

---

[99]*New York Review of Books,* April 7, 2005. The columnist reported that he was not a Wal-Mart shopper.
[100]*New York Times,* October 15, 2005.

[101]*New York Times,* September 20, 2005. The board did not examine Wal-Mart's explanation that the store was closed because it was losing money.
[102]*Wall Street Journal,* August 15, 2005.

Wal-Mart store in her ward: "For a lot of people, this will be their first job of any kind. This is where they'll learn that in the world of work, you have to show up on time, you have to look good, you have to be helpful and courteous. Our young people are going to learn how to stock shelves, how to answer customers' questions, how to make change. Don't underestimate what it will mean to our community to have a place where young people can learn skills like these."[103]

Environment

In 2001 Wal-Mart reached a settlement with the Environmental Protection Agency and the Department of Justice for violations of the Clean Water Act in 17 locations. Wal-Mart agreed to implement a $4.5 million environmental management plan and pay a $1 million civil fine.[104] In 2004 Wal-Mart paid a $3.1 million civil fine for storm water violations at 24 construction sites.

The Coalition of Tri-Lakes Committees in Colorado opposed the opening of Wal-Mart stores. It argued that although MTBE was no longer used in Colorado, "fuel from other states such as California that still allow use of MTBE could be brought here by visitors to the state. MTBE from gasoline that leaks from vehicles on the Wal-Mart parking lot could be washed off by storm water and could contaminate the surrounding environment and groundwater."[105]

Wal-Mart was also criticized for the footprint of its stores and parking lots, which reduced green spaces and wetlands and contributed to urban sprawl. The company was also criticized for generating disposal problems from in-store restaurants and for the solid waste disposal problem generated by the packaging of the products it sold. The company also generated substantial greenhouse gases, particularly from its huge truck fleet.

Health Care Benefits

Critics claimed that Wal-Mart failed to provide company health care benefits for 900,000 of its workers. Wal-Mart reported that 48 percent of its employees were covered by its health insurance plans, compared to the national average of 67 percent and in retailing 46 percent.[106] Wal-Mart provided no retiree medical benefits.

In response to its critics, in 2005 Wal-Mart offered a low-cost health insurance plan with monthly premiums 40 percent lower than its other plans. The new plan had a $1,000 deductible after three visits to a doctor and three generic prescriptions. The premiums were $23 a month for a single worker, $37 for one parent and children, and $65 a month for two parents and children. In its first year the plan attracted 53,000 current and new employees, including 31,000 who switched from other Wal-Mart plans.[107] The company also offered a health insurance plan for $11 a month designed for employees with low health care needs. Unions continued to criticize Wal-Mart for not providing an affordable health care plan for employees with higher health care needs.

In October 2005 an incendiary internal Wal-Mart memorandum to the board of directors was leaked to the media. The memo primarily focused on reducing health care costs. Wal-Mart's benefits costs had increased from $2.8 billion to $4.2 billion 3 years later. Its associates were also aging more rapidly than the population. M. Susan Chambers, vice president for benefits, called for hiring healthier employees as a means of reducing costs.[108] To discourage unhealthy associates and job applicants, she suggested designing "all jobs to include some physical activity (e.g., all cashiers do some cart-gathering)."[109] She also suggested offering educational benefits in an attempt to attract younger, and presumably healthier, employees. She defended her memo stating, "This is not about cutting. This is about redirecting savings to another part of their benefit plans."[110]

Wages

Wal-Mart maintained that its wages and benefits were high relative to retailing in general and to comparable firms. Critics claimed that Wal-Mart, because of its size, should provide wages and benefits high enough to support a family with a single wage-earner. "If Wal-Mart spent $3.50 an hour more for wages and benefits of its full-time employees, that would cost the company $6.5 billion a year. At less than 3 percent of its sales in the United States, critics say, Wal-Mart could absorb these costs by slightly raising its prices or accepting somewhat lower profits."[111]

Wal-Mart's Susan Chambers wrote that "the cost of an associate with seven years of tenure is almost 55 percent more than the cost of an associate with one year of tenure, yet there is no difference in his or her productivity. Moreover, because we pay an associate more in salary and benefits as his or her tenure increases, we are pricing that associate out of the labor market, increasing the likelihood that he or she will stay with Wal-Mart."[112]

In response to a critical book review in the *New York Review of Books*, Wal-Mart took out a two-page ad "to set the record straight." The company reacted to a critique "so riddled with mistakes and blinded by ideology that it offered a fundamentally erroneous view of the way we do business and the contributions we make to thousands of communities."[113] In response to the criticism that Wal-Mart wages were too low to

[103]*New York Times,* July 6, 2004.

[104]EPA News Release, June 7, 2001.

[105]www.coalitiontlc.org/wal-mart.htm.

[106]Henry J. Kaiser Family Foundation. *Wall Street Journal,* December 3–4, 2005.

[107]*Wall Street Journal,* December 3–4, 2005.

[108]WellPoint, a large health care insurer, reported that 7 percent of its customers accounted for 63 percent of its medical costs (*Wall Street Journal*, October 27, 2005).

[109]"Supplemental Benefits Documentation," Board of Directors Retreat FY06, Wal-Mart Stores, Inc.

[110]"Supplemental Benefits Documentation," Board of Directors Retreat FY06, Wal-Mart Stores, Inc.

[111]*New York Times,* May 4, 2005,

[112]"Supplemental Benefits Documentation," Board of Directors Retreat FY06, Wal-Mart Stores, Inc.

[113]*New York Review of Books,* April 7, 2005.

support a family, the company pointed out that only 7 percent of its associates were single wage earners supporting a family and that its average wage was nearly twice the minimum wage. The ad pointed out that "74 percent of its hourly associates were full-time compared to 20–40 percent at comparable retailers, which meant that Wal-Mart provides considerably more health care benefits than do comparable retailers, who typically do not provide benefits for part-time workers. In contrast, Wal-Mart offers health care benefits to part-time as well as full-time associates."

The Labor Research Association (LRA) used Costco as an example of a successful retailer that paid higher wages than Wal-Mart.[114] The LRA claimed that Costco paid $16 an hour, compared to $12 a hour at Sam's Club, and that 82 percent of Costco's employees were covered by its health plans. Many Costco employees were represented by unions, and their wage and benefits agreements served as the reference point for the rest of Costco's employees.

Employment Practices

Wal-Mart had experienced a number of challenges to its employment practices. In 2005 it paid $135,540 to settle Department of Labor charges that workers under the age of 18 had operated dangerous equipment such as chain saws and cardboard balers. An internal audit by Wal-Mart revealed numerous instances in which minors worked too late at night or during school hours.

Wal-Mart also was sued by three former employees who alleged that the company had shaved time off their payroll records when they failed to punch in after a meal break or failed to punch out at the end of a shift. The lawsuit was spurred by a newspaper article mentioning the practice. Plaintiffs' attorneys sought class-action status for the lawsuit.

A group of employees in California filed a lawsuit, which was granted class-action status, alleging that they had been denied compensation for lunch breaks not taken as required by California law. The law required a 30-minute, unpaid lunch and dinner break. Wal-Mart claimed that the employees had failed to file for the pay on a timely basis. A jury awarded the workers $57 million in compensatory damages and $115 million in punitive damages. Wal-Mart said that hourly employees "did take substantially all of their meal periods" and planned to appeal the decision. Scott Brink, a Los Angeles attorney who represents employers in labor issues, said, "California has the most stringent and Byzantine wage and hour laws in the country. Wal-Mart has found itself caught, apparently, on some of these very technical wage and hour laws that are peculiar to California."[115] Wal-Mart revised its practices and now "sends alerts to cashiers when it is time for their meal breaks."[116] A lawsuit in Pennsylvania on the same issue was granted class-action status in 2006.

Discrimination

In 2001 six women employees filed a lawsuit against Wal-Mart alleging that they were paid less than men with comparable qualifications and were not promoted at the same rate as men. Witnesses for the plaintiffs provided evidence that women were paid between 5 and 15 percent less than men, and a federal judge in San Francisco granted class-action status to the lawsuit to cover 1.6 million current and former workers. Wal-Mart denied the allegations and appealed the decision to grant class-action status. Wal-Mart's lead attorney stated, "The judge has precluded Wal-Mart from arguing that certain individuals should not be part of the class, that there were reasons they might have received less pay or were passed over for promotion."[117] The U.S. Ninth Circuit Court of Appeals agreed to hear Wal-Mart's appeal.

Activists also regularly introduced shareholder resolutions at Wal-Mart's annual meeting on issues ranging from executive compensation to environmental reporting. One resolution sponsored by the National Council of Women's Organizations called on the company to have more than two women on its 14-person board. The company urged shareholders to vote against the resolutions, and they did so by votes of at least 80 percent.

Wal-Mart began using a "mapping" process on its Web site to suggest other DVDs of "similar interest" to buyers of DVDs. A blogger noticed that buyers of DVDs such as *Charlie and the Chocolate Factory* and *Planet of the Apes* were referred to movies with African American themes such as *Martin Luther King: I Have a Dream/Assassination of MLK*. The movies were also linked to *Home Alone* and *The Powerpuff Girls*. Within 2 minutes the story was up on Crooks and Liars and hundreds of comments followed. Wal-Mart responded quickly by changing the process and apologizing, stating that the process had malfunctioned.

Wal-Mart did not extend health care benefits to domestic partners unless required by state law. It, however, updated its ethics code to prohibit discrimination against "immediate family members" including domestic partners in certain states that had changed their laws on domestic partnerships and civil unions.

Working Conditions in Suppliers' Overseas Factories

In 2005 the International Labor Rights Fund filed a lawsuit in California state court alleging sweatshop conditions in the factories of Wal-Mart contractors in five countries. The lawsuit claimed that Wal-Mart's code of conduct represented a legal obligation to the workers in its suppliers' factories. Wal-Mart responded that it employed 200 inspectors who made 12,000 monitoring visits in 2004. If violations of its policies were found, the contractors were required to correct the problems or were discontinued. In 2004 1,200 factories were suspended for at least 90 days for violations, and 108 were permanently banned. Wal-Mart said that the Labor Rights Fund had "a history of presenting opinions as fact" and had ties to the

---

[114]The LRA "provides research and educational services for trade unions." LRA Online, "The Costco Challenge: An Alternative to Wal-Martization." July 5, 2005.
[115]*San Francisco Chronicle,* December 23, 2005.
[116]Ibid.

[117]*Los Angeles Times,* August 6, 2005.

UFCW.[118] Four of the workers represented in the lawsuit were California supermarket workers who claimed they suffered lower wages and benefits because of low prices made possible by violations of Wal-Mart's code.

Critics demanded that Wal-Mart agree to unannounced and independent inspections rather then use its own inspectors. Apparel and footwear companies that participated in the Fair Labor Association (FLA) were subject to inspections by independent organizations certified by the FLA.

HURRICANE KATRINA

In the aftermath of hurricane Katrina that devastated New Orleans and the Gulf Coast, city, state, and federal agencies floundered in providing essential relief. In contrast Wal-Mart had anticipated the threat and was prepared. When Katrina was upgraded to storm category, Wal-Mart began to plan for an emergency. It stocked its stores with supplies people would need if the storm struck, and it established staging areas that were stocked with items such as generators and bottled water.[119] After the hurricane struck, Wal-Mart donated $17 million for the relief effort, provided $3 million of supplies to relief workers and displaced citizens, and made vacant buildings available for relief agencies.

Newspapers published a photograph of a line of Wal-Mart trucks loaded with relief supplies for New Orleans being blocked by FEMA officials.[120] On "Meet the Press" the president of Jefferson Parish, outside New Orleans, said that if "the American government would have responded like Wal-Mart has responded, we wouldn't be in this crisis."[121] *Fortune* published a four-page article on the relief provided by local store managers and the company under the headline "The Only Lifeline Was the Wal-Mart."[122]

Preparation Questions

1. Identify the primary issues facing Wal-Mart. Should Wal-Mart have been able to anticipate the issues it now faces?

2. Which interests are opposed to Wal-Mart and what are their costs of organizing for nonmarket action? Which interests are aligned with Wal-Mart and what are their costs of organizing for nonmarket action?

3. In which institutional arenas will the issues be resolved? What role will government institutions play?

4. How effective has Wal-Mart's strategy been in addressing the pressures on the company? How will the likely resolutions of these issues affect Wal-Mart's ability to execute its market strategy?

5. Should Wal-Mart stop its opposition to the unionization of its associates?

6. Should Wal-Mart agree to independent inspections of its suppliers' factories?

7. Should Wal-Mart select its employees based on their expected health care costs? Should it include physical work in every job?

8. What should Wal-Mart do about the environmental pressures it faces? Should it undertake environmental initiatives?

9. What should Wal-Mart do in the aftermath of the Wal-Mart bill in Maryland? Should it switch its distribution center to another state? What should it do about similar bills in other states?

10. Should Wal-Mart make concessions to improve the chances for approval of its industrial bank application in Utah? For example, should it pledge not to open branch banks?

11. As the largest private-sector employer in the United States, should Wal-Mart be a model or should it straightforwardly serve its principal constituents—its associates and customers?

---

[118]*New York Times,* September 16, 2005.
[119]*Wall Street Journal,* September 12, 2005.
[120]*New York Times,* September 14, 2005.
[121]*San Jose Mercury News,* September 7, 2005.
[122]*Fortune,* October 3, 2005.

6 NONMARKET ANALYSIS FOR BUSINESS

INTRODUCTION

This chapter presents frameworks for analyzing political and nonmarket action on issues addressed in government institutions. The frameworks provide the foundation for strategy formulation and implementation in Chapters 7 and 8, respectively. Although the focus is on public politics—the competition among interests in the arenas of government institutions—the approach also applies to private politics, as considered in Chapter 4. The approach is presented in the context of U.S. institutions, but, as indicated in Part IV of the book, it is also applicable to settings outside the United States. The approach is illustrated using a case involving Boeing and tax benefits on foreign leasing.

The perspective here is that the nonmarket actions taken by diverse, pluralistic interests in the context of government institutions determine the outcomes of nonmarket issues characterized by public politics. The study of individual interests and the manner in which they are transformed into nonmarket action thus is one foundation for the analysis of nonmarket issues. In public politics nonmarket action is transformed into outcomes through government institutions—legislatures, administrative agencies, regulatory agencies, courts, and international accords. The characteristics of these institutions are the other foundation of nonmarket analysis. Because these institutions structure the nonmarket actions of individuals, firms, and interest groups, the approach presented here is referred to as *structured pluralism*.

Structured pluralism is illustrated in Figure 6-1 in the context of the issues, interests, institutions, and information that characterize the nonmarket environment. The nonmarket issue is the unit of analysis. The actions of the pluralistic interests concerned with the issue compete in the arenas of government institutions. Those institutions have structures and procedures under which their officeholders consider alternatives for resolving the issue. The officeholders have preferences derived from their policy interests and, through the constituency connection, the interests of their constituents. Information comes from two sources. First, research and public policy analysis provide technical information about the likely consequences of alternative policies. Second, interest groups provide politically relevant information to institutional officeholders. The outcome of this process is a public policy to address the issue.

FIGURE 6-1 Structured Pluralism

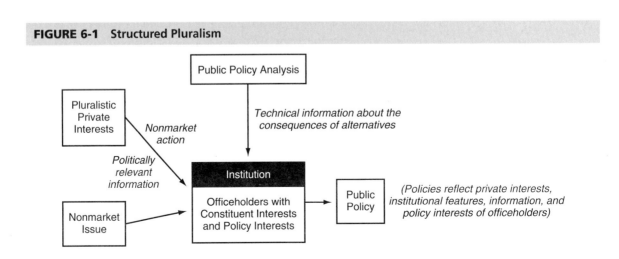

A FRAMEWORK FOR THE ANALYSIS OF NONMARKET ACTION IN PUBLIC POLITICS

Interests and Interest Groups

The term *interests* has a dual use in nonmarket analysis and strategy formulation. One refers to those individuals, firms, and organizations with a stake in an issue. The other refers to the magnitudes of their stakes. Interests in the first usage are the actors (as in interest groups), and interests in the second usage are the stakes of the actors, which provide incentives for nonmarket action.

The framework begins with an assessment of incentives. Stakes may be distributive or moral. Most issues have *distributive consequences*, as measured by benefits and costs, surpluses and rents, or profits and losses. In the chapter case *Tobacco Politics*, interests ranging from tobacco farmers to convenience stores to advertising agencies estimated the effect on their sales and profits of a proposed excise tax. Issues may also involve *moral concerns*. In the chapter case *Repeal of the Luxury Tax*, the motivation of some backers of the luxury tax was moral rather than distributive, that is, the rich should contribute more to fund government programs. The moral determinants of nonmarket action are often more difficult to assess than the distributive consequences, but on some issues they are as important.

Incentives, whether distributive or moral in origin, can cause an individual, firm, union, NGO, or activist group to become active on an issue. They may act on their own, but they may also organize, coordinate, and mobilize for collective action. Interest groups form among individuals and organizations with aligned interests. A necessary condition for formation of an interest group is that the benefits from collective action exceed the costs of organization. Interest groups may organize around a single issue, such as a reduction in credit card swipe fees as in the chapter case *Business versus Business*. High-tech companies, public accounting firms, and other firms formed an ad hoc coalition to coordinate their actions to obtain uniform national standards for securities fraud lawsuits. Interest groups may also be organized by a political entrepreneur who mobilizes the common interests of dispersed individuals, by a trade association that represents firms in an industry, or by a labor union that represents the interests of workers. Although interest groups form because of an alignment of interests, they are sustained by the fruits of their efforts.

Interest groups can also have aligned interests that lead them to act in parallel rather than jointly. The Daylight Saving Time Coalition and the RP Foundation Fighting Blindness both worked to extend daylight saving time, although the former represented business interests and the latter represented individuals afflicted with night blindness. Aligned interests also allow specialization. Environmental interest groups engage in a wide range of nonmarket activities, and many focus on particular issues or strategies. The Sierra Club has a broad agenda, the Wilderness Society focuses on open lands, and Greenpeace uses confrontation to draw attention to environmental issues.

In some cases an interest group may be successful in having the government establish an agency through which its interests can be served. The Small Business Administration, the Department of Agriculture, and the Export-Import Bank are examples of such agencies. Members of Congress interact directly with interest groups and have established means of responding to their interests—the agriculture and small business committees of both chambers are examples. Environmental interest groups, however, repeatedly have sought without success a cabinet department for environmental protection.

Constitutions and laws grant rights to individuals and organizations to pursue their interests and to protect those interests from the actions of others. U.S. trade law gives firms, labor unions, and communities the right to seek relief from imports. Similarly, wilderness groups exercise their rights before the courts to block the use of public lands for solar farms. Whatever their motivation, interest groups have become skillful in putting pressure on elected and administrative officeholders through direct action, their standing before the courts and regulatory agencies, and their rights to participate in governmental processes. The chapter case *Tobacco Politics* provides an opportunity to assess the interests involved in the tobacco issue.

The Amount of Nonmarket Action

From the perspective of structured pluralism, a principal driver of public policies is the nonmarket action taken by interests. That nonmarket action includes activities such as lobbying, grassroots and other forms of constituent activity, research and testimony, electoral support, and public advocacy.

The supply-and-demand framework from economics can be used to assess the amount or quantity of these activities. The demand side pertains to the benefits associated with nonmarket action on an issue, and the supply side pertains to the cost of taking, or supplying, nonmarket action. An increase in the benefits results in more nonmarket action, and an increase in the costs results in less nonmarket action. One component of the nonmarket strategy of a firm is thus to increase the benefits for the interests on its side of an issue and decrease the benefits of the opposing interests on the other side of the issue. A second component is to reduce the cost of nonmarket action for the interests on its side of the issue through, for example, the formation of an interest group or coalition.

The demand for nonmarket action is characterized by three factors. One is the aggregate benefits to the interests on one side of an issue. The second is the per capita benefits for an individual interest, such as a taxpayer, firm, or union. The third factor is alternative means, referred to as substitutes, for achieving the benefits by, for example, turning to a different institutional arena or by changing a market strategy.

The cost of nonmarket action has three components. The first includes the costs of organizing for collective action. The second includes the direct costs of undertaking nonmarket action, such as the cost of lobbying, maintaining a Washington office, or preparing testimony, as considered in Chapter 8. The third component is the effectiveness of nonmarket action, which depends on the size of the interest group and its coverage of legislative districts. The following sections consider the demand and supply of nonmarket action in more detail.

The Demand for Nonmarket Action

The demand for nonmarket action is derived from the distributive consequences of an alternative, such as a bill before Congress. For firms, those consequences are reflected in sales, profits, and market value. Employee interests are measured in terms of jobs and wages. For consumers, the distributive consequences are measured in terms of the prices, qualities, and availability of goods and services.

The demand for nonmarket action depends on the *aggregate benefits* for an interest. In the Boeing example, the aggregate benefits to taxpayers from eliminating the tax breaks on foreign leasing exceeded the aggregate benefits to Boeing from preserving the tax breaks. In the daylight saving time example in Chapter 7, the benefits to firms stemmed from the increase in demand for their products, and those benefits were greater when the extension of daylight saving time was longer. In the chapter case *Repeal of the Luxury Tax*, builders of yachts and their employees would benefit because repeal would shift outward the demand curve for yachts.

Aggregate benefits are important indicators of the demand for nonmarket action. In many cases, however, the *per capita benefits* are a better measure of the incentive to take nonmarket action, since individual interests compare their potential benefits to the cost of participation. If the benefits are substantial and concentrated, the per capita benefits can be high, and those who benefit will have an incentive to act. The per capita benefits for Boeing as a company were $200 million a year from preserving the tax breaks on foreign leasing. The per capita effect of lower swipe fees on credit and debit cards was huge for large retailers, credit card companies, and card issuers.

If the aggregate benefits are widely distributed rather than concentrated, the per capita benefits can be small, providing little incentive for nonmarket action. Although the aggregate benefits to taxpayers from eliminating tax breaks on foreign leasing were larger than the benefits to Boeing, the per capita benefits for an individual taxpayer were very small. Individual taxpayers generally take little nonmarket action because their per capita benefits are typically exceeded by their costs of taking action. In some cases, however, nonmarket action can occur even when benefits are not large on a per capita basis. Proposition 13, a public referendum in California that reduced property taxes, resulted from political entrepreneurship that allowed individuals to lower their property taxes by simply casting enough votes.

On some issues the benefits from nonmarket action can be obtained through other means, referred to as *substitutes*. The benefits from nonmarket action are lower when there are other means of generating them, and the closer these substitutes come to replicating the benefits, the smaller are the incentives to act. Substitutes may be available in the market environment or in the nonmarket environment. In the luxury tax case, current yacht owners could keep their old yachts rather than buy new ones, and buyers of new yachts could register them offshore. On an issue such as unitary taxation—the taxation of corporate profits on a worldwide basis by a state—a foreign electronics firm considering where to locate a new U.S. subsidiary has an incentive to support the repeal of California's unitary taxation law. That firm, however, has available the market substitute of locating its subsidiary in Oregon, which repealed its unitary taxation law. The alternative of avoiding unitary taxation by locating in Oregon reduces the benefits from, and hence lowers the firm's incentives for, taking nonmarket action to change the California law.[1]

An example of a public substitute is pursuing an objective in a different institutional arena. In the chapter case *Tobacco Politics*, farmers had a substitute to opposing the tobacco settlement. They could seek government subsidies to compensate them for reducing their acreage in tobacco and transitioning to other crops. In the case of Internet wine sales, the wineries sought state legislation to allow direct interstate sales of wine to consumers. A substitute in the six states that allowed intrastate but not interstate direct sales was to file lawsuits seeking equal treatment for interstate direct sales. If a lawsuit succeeded, the demand for new legislation in that state would be reduced.

The Costs and Effectiveness of Nonmarket Action

The amount of nonmarket action also depends on cost, or supply, considerations. One cost is associated with identifying, contacting, motivating, and organizing those with aligned interests. If the number of affected individuals or groups is small, the *costs of organizing* are likely to be low. When the number is large, those costs can be high. Taxpayers are costly to organize because they are numerous and widely dispersed, whereas pharmaceutical companies are relatively easy to organize. The costs of organization can be reduced by associations and standing organizations. Labor unions, the Sierra Club, and business groups such as the National Federation of Independent Business reduce the cost of organizing for nonmarket action.

The greater the cost of organizing, the more serious the *free-rider problem*, as considered in Appendix A. If the number of potential members of a group is small, the benefits from one additional participant can be significant enough to justify that member's participation. Furthermore, as indicated in Appendix A, when groups are small, punishment and exclusion are easier to apply to those who free ride. If the group is large, a potential participant may conclude that joining in collective action will have little effect on the outcome and hence may decide to free ride. Interest groups attempt to reduce the free-rider problem by bundling together nonmarket action and services for their members. Many industry associations collect market data that they make available only to their members. The Sierra Club publishes a magazine and also arranges trips for its members. The free-rider problem also can be mitigated when interests expect to address a series of nonmarket issues, since they then have longer-run incentives.

Another component of the cost of organizing is mobilizing interest group members to deliver collective nonmarket action. Members may be mobilized on an ad hoc basis to address a particular issue. In the chapter case *Business versus Business*, convenience store owners flew to Washington to lobby for lower credit card swipe fees. Members may also be represented by a formal organization that can monitor issues and act when the interests of the group can be served. In addition to this readiness function, formal organizations monitor the progress of issues through their life cycles. Trade and professional associations, unions, the National Federation of Independent Business, and environmental groups provide these functions.

EFFECTIVENESS   *Effectiveness* refers to the impact of a given level of nonmarket action on the outcome of an issue. Effectiveness depends on several factors, including the number of members of an interest group and their geographic distribution. Those members are constituents of legislators. For a firm, potentially relevant constituents are its stakeholders—shareholders, employees, suppliers, distributors, and in some cases customers.

---

[1]Under pressure from a number of countries, California revised, but did not eliminate, its unitary taxation law. In 1994 the Supreme Court upheld the law allowing the taxation of profits on a unitary basis.

Numbers   There are few automobile manufacturers, but they have many employees, extensive dealer organizations, many suppliers, and millions of customers. The Sierra Club has 1.3 million members and supporters, and the National Federation of Independent Business has over 600,000 member firms. The greater the *number* of members of an interest group, the greater is its potential effectiveness, but the costs of organizing and mobilizing those members can be high. In addition, members may have an incentive to free ride.

Coverage   Particularly for issues addressed in legislative arenas, the effectiveness of nonmarket action depends on the geographic location of interest group members. Nonmarket strategies based on the constituency connection between voters and their representatives are more effective the greater the number of political jurisdictions covered by the group. Although small businesses do not have the resources of large businesses, they are politically effective because they are numerous and located in every political jurisdiction. Automobile assembly plants are concentrated in a relatively small number of congressional districts, but the *coverage* of the auto companies' dealer and supplier networks is extensive. General Motors CEO Rick Wagoner attended the national auto dealers convention in 2008 to enlist participation of dealers and generate coverage of state political jurisdictions to address state greenhouse gases emissions regulations. Wagoner explained why dealers were important in implementing General Motor's strategy at the state level, "Dealers are very effective in the political process because we don't have a plant in every state. We have dealers in every state."[2] The greater the coverage by the members of an interest group, the more effective is its nonmarket action.

Resources   A nonmarket strategy must be financed, and the greater the *resources* available to an interest group, the greater the set of activities that can be funded. Financial resources fund research, lobbying, legal services, grassroots campaigns, and the group's administrative staff. The greater a group's stake in an issue, the greater are the resources that potentially can be contributed to a nonmarket strategy. Pharmaceutical companies have ample resources, and when the stakes are high, as for the issue of reimportation of drugs or Medicare coverage of prescription drugs, substantial resources are allocated to nonmarket action. The members of the Sierra Club also have ample resources, but their willingness to contribute to the Club's nonmarket campaigns is more limited. The free-rider problem can limit the funds available for nonmarket action.

Supply Side Summary   Supply side considerations imply that the costs of organizing interests are high when the costs of identifying and mobilizing those with common interests are high. These costs are also high when the free-rider problem is more prevalent and fewer means are available to mitigate it. Nonmarket action is more effective when the group has more members, their resources are greater, and it has more extensive coverage of legislative districts. A strategy that reduces the costs of collective action or increases effectiveness will increase the impact of the group's nonmarket action.

The effectiveness of nonmarket action also depends on the actions others take on an issue. A grassroots political campaign in which members of an interest group contact their congressional representatives can be quite effective. If, however, an interest group on the other side of the issue responds by mounting its own grassroots campaign, the effectiveness of the first campaign will be reduced. Consequently, the assessment of the benefits from nonmarket action must take into account the likely actions of opposing interest groups. In many cases there are synergies between the actions of groups with aligned interests, even when those actions are independent. In the daylight saving time case, the independence of the actions of business and the RP Foundation Fighting Blindness increased the effectiveness of the other's nonmarket action.

The Distributive Politics Spreadsheet

The analysis of the demand and supply sides can be summarized in a spreadsheet as presented in Figure 6-3 for the Boeing example. The distributive politics spreadsheet pertains to a specific alternative, such as a bill to revoke the tax benefits on foreign leasing, or more generally to a particular change from the status quo. The spreadsheet is organized in terms of the interests that would benefit from the adoption of the alternative, and hence support it, and the interest groups that would be harmed by the alternative, and hence oppose it. The top panel of the spreadsheet pertains to the supporting interests and the bottom panel to the opposing interests. The

---

[2]*San Jose Mercury News,* February 10, 2008.

spreadsheet is intended to summarize rather than substitute for the analysis of the benefits and costs of nonmarket action.

The demand side information summarized in the spreadsheet for each interest includes the available substitutes, the aggregate benefits, and the per capita benefits for individual members of the interest group. The supply side information includes the number of members, their coverage of political jurisdictions, their resources, and their costs of organizing for nonmarket action, including any free-rider problems.

The information summarized in the spreadsheet provides the basis for predicting the nonmarket action likely to be generated by the interests. This prediction then is used in conjunction with institutional characteristics to assess the likely outcome of the issue and to formulate strategies to influence the outcome. The Boeing example illustrates the link between the analysis summarized by the spreadsheet and strategy formulation.

Institutions are not included in the spreadsheet because they are viewed as arenas in which the nonmarket actions of interests are deployed, as discussed in the next section. The institutional officeholders who decide the fate of the nonmarket alternative are also not included in the spreadsheet, since they are regarded as part of the institution.

THE NATURE OF POLITICAL COMPETITION

The nonmarket actions of interests may be viewed as competing in an institutional arena. Their actions, coupled with the characteristics of the institution and its officeholders, determine the outcome of the competition. The outcome may be a win for one side and a loss for the other. The ratification of the North American Free Trade Agreement (NAFTA) was a win for business and consumers and a loss for organized labor. In other cases, the outcome may be a compromise influenced by all the competing interests. In the daylight saving time example in Chapter 7, the outcome was in the center of the distribution of preferences of members of Congress, whose preferences reflected the interests of their constituents.

Building on the work of Lowi (1964), Wilson (1980) categorized the nature of political competition on an issue as a function of the concentration or dispersion of the benefits and costs from an alternative.[3] Although this categorization focuses on the nature of the politics and not on the outcome, it is useful for distinguishing among types of competition and provides a context for formulating strategies, as considered in Chapter 7.

The Wilson–Lowi matrix presented in Figure 6-2 pertains to the benefits and harm from a nonmarket alternative, such as the enactment of a bill, relative to the status quo. The columns of

FIGURE 6-2 Nature of Political Competition: Wilson–Lowi Matrix

Benefits from Enacting the Nonmarket Alternative

	Concentrated	Widely Distributed
Concentrated	Interest Group Politics	Entrepreneurial Politics (Converse of Client Politics)
Widely Distributed	Client Politics (Converse of Entrepreneurial Politics)	Majoritarian Politics

Harm from Enacting the Nonmarket Alternative

Qualifications: 1. Magnitudes of costs and benefits
2. Costs of organizing and effectiveness of nonmarket action

---

[3]Heckathorn and Maser (1990) provide a reformulation of Lowi's typology from a transactions cost perspective.

the matrix correspond to those interests that would benefit from the alternative relative to the status quo. The rows of the matrix correspond to interests that would be harmed by the alternative relative to the status quo. The benefits or harm are said to be *concentrated* if the per capita effects are high. If the per capita effects are low, they are said to be to be *widely distributed*. Eliminating the tax breaks for foreign leasing would concentrate harm on Boeing and a few other exporters. The increased tax revenue was widely distributed among taxpayers. On some issues the benefits (or harm) may be widely distributed across interests, yet some benefits (or harm) may be concentrated for some specific interests. Interests with concentrated effects have a stronger incentive to take nonmarket action, whereas interests with widely distributed effects have weaker incentives.

If both the benefits and the harm are concentrated, both supporters and opponents have incentives to act. If, in addition, their costs of nonmarket action are low, interest groups will be active on both sides of the issue. The resulting competition, as indicated in the Wilson–Lowi matrix, takes the form of *interest group* politics. The outcome is then largely determined by the amounts and effectiveness of the nonmarket action generated by the interests on each side of the issue. Legislation that pits business against labor is typically characterized by interest group politics. International trade policy, which often finds business opposed by labor unions and environmentalists, is also characterized by interest group politics.

When the consequences from an alternative are widely distributed, the incentives to take nonmarket action are weak. When this is the case for both the interests who would benefit and those who would be harmed by the alternative, the political competition is said to be *majoritarian*. The outcome then is determined by the preferences of a majority. The politics of Social Security are majoritarian because each individual benefits from Social Security but is also taxed to support it, albeit by different amounts. The politics of the extension of daylight saving time were at one level majoritarian, since everyone was affected.

When the benefits from an alternative are concentrated and the harm is widely distributed, the interests that benefit have stronger incentives to take nonmarket action than do those who incur the harm. The competition then takes the form of *client* politics with the beneficiaries working to become the clients of the institutional officeholders—that is, to have the officeholders serve their interests. In client politics, the beneficiaries face little risk of opposition from the other side. Firms seeking a subsidy for ethanol used in motor fuels engage in client politics. The extension of daylight saving time had a component of client politics because some benefits were concentrated on businesses and the harm was widely distributed among individuals on the western edges of time zones where it would be dark when they awakened.

When the benefits are widely distributed and the harm is concentrated, those bearing the harm have a stronger incentive to take nonmarket action than do the beneficiaries. Wilson refers to this situation as *entrepreneurial* politics, since if the alternative is to be adopted over the status quo, an entrepreneur is needed to mobilize or represent those with widely distributed benefits. A member of Congress, an activist, or a business leader can be a nonmarket entrepreneur. The elimination of tax breaks in the Boeing example involved entrepreneurial politics, since the benefits were to taxpayers and the harm was borne by exporters.

In terms of the concentration and distribution of benefits and harm, entrepreneurial politics is the opposite side of the coin from client politics. On which side of the coin the political competition is located depends on the alternative in question. In entrepreneurial politics, benefits from the alternative are widely distributed, whereas the harm from the alternative is concentrated. This favors the status quo, and for the alternative to be adopted a political entrepreneur is needed to mobilize the interests with widely distributed benefits. In client politics the benefits to the interest groups supporting the alternative are concentrated and the harm to those supporting the status quo is widely distributed, so other things being equal, the alternative is favored over the status quo.

One strategy of interests is to attempt to change the nature of the politics of an issue. The politics of the extension of daylight saving time was basically majoritarian because everyone would be affected by an extension. Although a majority of people likely preferred the extension, their benefits were widely distributed. Some benefits, however, were concentrated, and those beneficiaries worked to change the politics from majoritarian to client through collective action. The Daylight Saving Time Coalition, representing business, and the RP Foundation Fighting Blindness, representing those suffering from night blindness, reduced the costs of nonmarket action for the beneficiaries. Those opposing the extension were unable to organize effectively and unable to prevail against the better organized supporters of an extension.

The Internet wine sales example illustrates the application of the Wilson–Lowi matrix, and the chapter case *Repeal of the Luxury Tax* provides an opportunity to assess the nature of the political competition and to identify which interests will be active on the issue.

Institutions and Institutional Officeholders

Although the Wilson–Lowi matrix identifies some of the important characteristics of the politics of a nonmarket issue, it does not provide a complete theory of the outcome. Free-rider problems, the coverage of political jurisdictions, and the effectiveness of nonmarket strategies affect the

---

EXAMPLE   Internet Wine Sales[1]

The Twenty-first Amendment to the Constitution ended prohibition and also gave the states the right to regulate the sale of alcohol. All but three states adopted a three-tier system in which producers (tier one) sold to distributors (tier two) who sold to retailers (tier three) and then to the consumer. This system made interstate direct sales of alcoholic beverages illegal.

Over the past decades the number of wineries increased 500 percent to 2,700, most of which were family-owned "cottage businesses" shipping fewer than 25,000 cases a year. During the same period the number of distributors (wholesalers) decreased from 5,000 to 400.

The development of the Internet made possible an online market in wine with the potential to broaden the availability of wines, benefiting both consumers and wineries. Online retailers quickly appeared. Direct sales from wineries to consumers, however, would bypass distributors, costing them significant business. The distributors sought a ban on direct sales, and the wineries sought specific permission for direct sales. By 2003, 26 states allowed direct sales, and 24 states banned direct sales, including five states in which a direct sale was a felony.[2] In Virginia rival bills backed by the two sides were introduced in the state legislature. This example considers the demand and supply of nonmarket action and the political competition in Virginia.

The principal interests were consumers, wineries, retailers, and distributors.[3] Consumers had a large aggregate stake, but their per capita stakes were small. Moreover, they were costly to organize, particularly in light of the free-rider problem. Consumers could not be expected to be active on this issue, although their interests could be represented by the wineries or by political entrepreneurs in state government. The wineries were organized primarily through the Wine Institute in California and Wine America. The 50 largest wineries accounted for 95 percent of the wine sales in the United States, and their wines generally had broad distribution. The smaller wineries had limited access to interstate markets, so their interests in direct sales were strong. Their per capita

states were high, and they were already organized, so their costs of nonmarket action were low. The effectiveness of their action, however, was limited because most of the wineries were out of state and hence were not natural constituents of Virginia legislators. Fortunately for the wine industry, Virginia also had wineries, providing some direct coverage of state legislative districts. The out-of-state wineries, however, had a degree of political effectiveness because they could represent the interests of Virginia consumers. Five wine industry associations and centers formed Free the Grapes to represent the interests of consumers and the wineries. Retailers of wine would be harmed by Internet wine sales, and their interests were aligned on this issue with those of the distributors. The distributors were represented by the Wine and Spirit Wholesalers of America, and Southern Wine and Spirits took the lead role. The distributors had large stakes and were well organized, and their costs of acting were low.

In terms of the Wilson–Lowi matrix, consider first the bill to specifically allow direct sales. The harm would be borne by the retailers and distributors, and that harm was concentrated. Consequently, the nature of the politics was either interest group or entrepreneurial. The principal beneficiaries of direct sales would be consumers, and if they were the only interest benefiting, the politics would be entrepreneurial. The wineries could be viewed as representing the interests of consumers in entrepreneurial politics, but they had their own interests and were the ones to take nonmarket action. The politics thus were primarily interest group with some elements of entrepreneurial politics. Consider next the alternative of a ban on direct sales. The benefits from a ban would accrue to the retailers and distributors, so the politics were either client or interest group. Again, if only consumer interests were present, the politics would be client, but the presence of the organized wineries made it interest group politics, again with some elements of client politics.

The nature of the politics does not predict the outcome, which requires a more fine-grained analysis of the demand, supply, and effectiveness of nonmarket action. The Boeing example provides such an analysis. In Virginia consumers and the wineries won. Direct sales by out-of-state wineries were allowed with a permit, but wineries were required to remit taxes and ship their wines by a common carrier registered with the state.

---

[1]This example is based on Wiseman and Ellig (2004).

[2]The legal strategies and court decisions pertaining to direct shipments are considered in Chapter 14.

[3]In Virginia retail sales of liquor but not wine were through state Alcohol Beverage Control stores.

nature and the intensity of the politics, but outcomes also depend on the institutions that deal with the issue. This chapter and Chapters 7 and 8 consider issues addressed in legislative institutions and particularly the U.S. Congress. Appendix B provides information on Congress and the legislative process. The characteristics of Congress, such as the committee structure and the legislative process, can be important. The position taken by a cabinet agency or the president can also be important.

Since an institution provides an arena in which interests deploy their nonmarket strategies, the preferences of those who hold offices in the institution can affect the outcome. Officeholders may support an interest group or work to advance their own policy agendas. They may attempt to influence other officeholders or trade their vote on an issue of lesser importance for the vote of another officeholder on a more important issue. Legislators, however, are constrained by both their duty to represent their constituents and their desire to be reelected. One means of determining how legislators are likely to vote on a political alternative is to examine the interests of their constituents and how those interests depend on the alternative in question. The implications of this constituency connection for strategy formulation are developed further in Chapters 7 and 8.

MORAL DETERMINANTS OF COLLECTIVE ACTION

On some issues, moral concerns motivate individuals and groups to take nonmarket action. Moral concerns based on considerations of well-being, rights, and social justice are the subject of Part V of this book, and only a brief discussion of these concepts is presented here. Assessing how individuals with various moral concerns view a nonmarket alternative can be difficult. The equally difficult task is determining how many people have a particular moral concern and how likely they are to act either in the arenas of government institutions or through private politics.

Because moral concerns can differ among individuals, nonmarket competition can take place on moral dimensions, as in the cases of abortion and genetically modified organisms. Just as one would not expect all physicians to perform abortions, neither would one expect all people of goodwill to agree on issues regarding genetically modified organisms, working conditions in the factories of foreign suppliers, or drug testing of employees. The difficulty in predicting when moral concerns will lead to nonmarket action is due not only to the different concerns of individuals but also the conviction with which those concerns are held can differ.

Despite these difficulties, managers must attempt to understand the moral motivations of individuals and interest groups and the strategies they are likely to employ. A church group concerned about a corporation's marketing activities in developing countries may use a private politics strategy that is quite different from the strategy of exporters seeking a higher lending authorization from the Export-Import Bank. The exporters may use low-profile strategies such as lobbying and coalition building. The church group may initiate shareholder resolutions, pressure institutional investors, and demonstrate to attract the attention of the news media and government officeholders. As considered in Chapter 11, some consumers felt they were deceived by credit card companies and subjected to unfair charges. Their complaints had both distributive and moral motivations, and members of Congress sought to represent their interests and concerns in the context of the Dodd–Frank financial reform legislation.

BOEING IN A PICKLE

Since 1962 the investment tax credit had provided incentives for capital investment through credits deducted from a firm's tax liability. By the 1980s, however, a number of companies were incurring operating losses and had no tax liability to which the credits could be applied. With the nation in a recession, Congress passed the Economic Recovery Tax Act (ERTA) of 1981 to stimulate economic activity. ERTA allowed companies with losses to purchase capital equipment and "sell" the investment tax credit to a profitable company that could use the credit to reduce its taxes. Thus, a steel company with operating losses could obtain a new rolling mill by having a lessor take title to the mill and then lease it back to the steel company. The lessor would receive the investment tax credit plus the tax benefits from accelerated depreciation, and the lease payments by the steel company would be lowered by the amount of those benefits.[4] ERTA thus restored the incentives for capital investment of those companies with operating losses.

Prior to ERTA many foreign sales were made under lease arrangements designed to capture the investment tax credit. A U.S. lessor would purchase capital equipment from a U.S. manufacturer, take the investment tax credit and the tax benefits from accelerated depreciation, and lease the equipment to a foreign customer. The tax benefits were then shared among the three participants in the transaction. Commercial aircraft had frequently been sold through these leasing arrangements. Investment tax credits were available for aircraft purchased by a U.S. lessor and leased to a foreign airline if the aircraft were used substantially in regular service to the United States. The "substantially" condition involved a modest number of landings on U.S. territory in a year.

Foreign leasing inadvertently became an issue because of the way ERTA was written. Its language allowed tax-exempt entities to make the same type of lease arrangements a steel company or a foreign airline could make. In addition, ERTA allowed the sale and leaseback of assets already owned by a firm or a tax-exempt entity. Tax-exempts thus could sell an existing asset to a lessor, who would take the investment tax credit and the accelerated depreciation benefits and lease the asset back to the tax-exempt at a price reflecting the tax benefits.

The number of tax-exempt entities that could benefit from such leasing was enormous. Every municipality, museum, school district, university, library, nonprofit corporation, and government entity could use it. The pace of leasing by tax-exempts began to accelerate in 1983, and the federal government became alarmed about the potential loss of tax revenues, particularly because of the record federal budget deficit and the sluggish economy. In addition, several leasing plans attracted media attention. Bennington College announced plans to sell its campus to alumni and then lease it back, with the alumni passing back to the college the tax benefits allowed by ERTA. The Navy planned to lease 13 cargo ships instead of purchasing them, with the "purchaser" of the ships taking the investment tax credit and the depreciation benefits and passing back to the Navy a portion of the tax benefits in the form of a price reduction. Transactions such as the Navy's and sale-and-leaseback transactions such as that planned by Bennington College were clearly contrary to the intent of ERTA.

The House Ways and Means Committee had drafted ERTA, and members of that committee had a vested interest in its original intent. Representative J. J. (Jake) Pickle (D-TX), a ranking member of the committee, was determined to eliminate the abuses of ERTA. His idea was that those who were exempt from taxes should not receive tax benefits. This was expressed as, "People who don't pay taxes should not get tax breaks."[5] This slogan was quickly interpreted to include foreign lessees, since foreign firms do not pay U.S. taxes. U.S. exporters that had used leasing for foreign sales suddenly faced the risk of losing the tax benefits on which they had relied.

In May 1983 Representative Pickle introduced a bill, H.R. 3110, that would deny the investment tax credit and accelerated depreciation benefits to tax-exempts and to foreigners who leased assets from U.S. lessors.[6] Hearings were held 2 weeks later, and H.R. 3110 was passed by the Ways and Means Committee on July 27. Floor action in the House was scheduled for the end of October. Senators Robert Dole (R-KS) and Howard Metzenbaum (D-OH) introduced a similar bill in the Senate.

At the then-current volume of leasing, the Department of Treasury estimated that the bill would increase tax receipts by $1.65 billion per year, with foreign leasing accounting for $570 million. Approximately $300 million of the $570 million was attributable to Boeing, which used leasing for nearly half its foreign sales of 747s.[7] The other exporters affected included oil drilling rig manufacturers, producers of containers for ocean shipping, and other aircraft manufacturers.

---

[4]The economic efficiency rationale for this provision of ERTA was that it would equalize marginal tax rates across firms and thus lessen distortions in the pattern of capital investment. The political pressure from industries unable to use the investment tax credits was undoubtedly the impetus for the provision, however.

[5]*Fortune,* September 19, 1983, p. 52.

[6]Straight-line depreciation would be allowed on foreign leasing.

[7]In 1983 the 747 was the only Boeing aircraft still in production that was certified for transoceanic flights. The 767 was not yet certified because of a Federal Aviation Administration's (FAA) administrative rule that permitted transoceanic crossings by twin-engine aircraft only if there remained no more than 60 minutes flying time from an acceptable airport. Approval was later granted, allowing the 767 to make transoceanic flights.

In 1983 the 747's only competitors were the DC-10 and the Airbus A300. The A300's range did not allow it to make transoceanic flights, so many observers believed that the 747 had little foreign competition for flights to the United States. The DC-10 had a smaller capacity than the 747 but a similar range. McDonnell-Douglas was rumored to be phasing out the DC-10 because of lagging sales.

Boeing maintained that it was locked in a fierce competitive struggle with the highly subsidized Airbus, a consortium of four European companies supported by their home governments. According to Boeing, foreign airlines used their wide-bodied aircraft on many routes that involved a trade-off between long legs and short hops. For some foreign airlines, the A300 was a substitute for the 747, according to Boeing. An airline that operated routes in Asia as well as a route to the United States could fly 747s on the U.S. route and A300s on the Asian route, with a series of hops if necessary. Alternatively, it could use 747s on the Asian routes and fly each aircraft on the U.S. route sufficiently often to qualify for the leasing tax benefits. Boeing thus argued that elimination of the tax benefits on foreign leasing would result in a loss of U.S. exports. Critics of foreign leasing, however, maintained that Boeing would not lose sales because it faced no competition. Furthermore, if sales would be lost, then U.S. taxpayers must be subsidizing foreigners. Representative Pickle wanted such subsidization stopped.

One means by which Airbus was subsidized was through government export financing at below-market interest rates. To compound Boeing's problem, the U.S. Export-Import Bank (Eximbank) had recently stopped providing subsidized export financing for 747s. This decision reflected the Eximbank's limited lending authorization and its conclusion, strongly criticized by Boeing, that the 747 faced no effective competition.[8]

In addition to Pickle's bill, hearings were scheduled before the Senate Finance Committee, chaired by Senator Dole, for the end of September. Neither senator from the state of Washington was a member of the Finance Committee, and Republican Slade Gorton was in his first term in the Senate. Longtime Senator Henry Jackson had died in August 1983 and had been replaced by the former Republican governor Daniel Evans, who was in the process of campaigning to retain his seat in the November special election.

Boeing's problem was how to deal with the challenge posed by Representative Pickle's bill.

ANALYSIS OF BOEING IN A PICKLE

The Nonmarket Issue

The issue of eliminating the tax benefits on leasing by tax-exempt and foreign entities arose suddenly as a result of the rapid increase in leasing by tax-exempts. The potential loss of tax revenue for the federal government was large, and the issue advanced quickly to the legislative stage of its life cycle. Although the politics of the issue were basically distributive, the sale-and-leaseback deals on existing assets by tax-exempts constituted abuse of ERTA's intent because those deals neither created jobs nor stimulated economic growth. The tax abuse coupled with the record federal budget deficit meant that the issue was likely to advance quickly through the rest of its life cycle. The dilemma for Boeing was that its leasing was threatened by the actions of the tax-exempts.

The following analysis illustrates the approach presented in this chapter.[9] The analysis is intended to develop an understanding of the politics of the issue and the relative strengths of the interests involved. This provides a basis for making judgments about the likely outcomes and therefore about strategy.

Distributive Consequences

The demand for nonmarket action depends on the value of the associated tax benefits. The investment tax credit ranged up to 10 percent and represented a cash inflow for the entity holding title to the asset. The value of the accelerated depreciation was the present value of the difference in the tax liability between accelerated and straight-line depreciation. On a sale of a $100 million 747, the tax benefits threatened by Pickle's bill were approximately $20 million,

---

[8]The Eximbank had limited lending authority, requiring it to support those sales where its financing would have the greatest incremental effect on exports. See Baron (1983) for an analysis of Eximbank financing.
[9]This is not a description of Boeing's analysis.

composed of a $10 million investment tax credit and approximately $10 million due to accelerated depreciation. At a sales rate of ten 747s a year, Boeing's tax benefits at stake were approximately $200 million.[10]

Although the magnitude of the tax benefits from foreign leasing is straightforward to estimate, the distribution of those benefits is more complex. A foreign leasing transaction involves three parties: the aircraft manufacturer, the foreign lessee, and the U.S. lessor. The share of the tax benefits captured by each party depends on the competitiveness of the aircraft and leasing markets. The leasing industry includes large banks, some insurance companies, and several leasing companies. Because of the substantial number of potential lessors, competition would be expected to leave them with competitive profits. That is, the aircraft manufacturer and the lessee can choose among a number of lessors, which should drive down their share of the benefits to competitive levels. The bulk of the benefits thus should accrue to the aircraft manufacturer and the foreign airline.[11]

The distribution of the tax benefits between the manufacturer and the airline depends on whether other aircraft are close substitutes for the 747 for the route configuration of the airline. Indeed, each airline can be considered individually, since sales result from negotiations between the airline and aircraft manufacturers. For an airline for which there is no substitute for the 747, Boeing is in the position of a monopolist and captures the tax benefits. For example, consider a foreign airline that is willing to pay no more than $100 million for a 747. With foreign leasing Boeing can make the following arrangement. It can sell the 747 to a lessor for $125 million, with the lessor taking the 20 percent tax benefits of $25 million and leasing the aircraft to the foreign airline for $100 million. If the Pickle bill were enacted, Boeing would reduce its price to $100 million, retain the sale, and no jobs would be lost. Boeing would, however, have lost $25 million as a result of the Pickle bill.

If there were some degree of competition from the A300, the tax benefits from leasing would be shared between the foreign airline and Boeing. If the A300 were a close substitute, the foreign airline might capture all the benefits. In that case, the elimination of the tax benefits would result in the loss of sales and jobs. U.S. taxpayers in that case would be subsidizing the foreign airline. In other cases Boeing and the airline would each capture a share of the tax benefits.

The Eximbank apparently concluded that the 747 faced little competition and that Boeing captured the bulk of the tax benefits from its financing, so eliminating Eximbank support for the 747 sales would have little impact on the number of aircraft sold or on Boeing workers. Representative Pickle and his staff came to the same conclusion. Even if there were a degree of competition, Representative Pickle and the other supporters of the bill had an attractive issue. If there was competition and foreign airlines captured a portion of the benefits, then U.S. taxpayers were subsidizing foreign airlines that competed with U.S. airlines. If there was little competition and Boeing captured the benefits, U.S. taxpayers were subsidizing a large, profitable company. Boeing was in a pickle.

Boeing maintained that foreign leasing allowed it to make sales that otherwise would be lost to Airbus and that Pickle's bill would cost jobs at both Boeing and its suppliers. In its testimony before the Senate Finance Committee, Boeing could expect to be asked why it could not lower its price to avoid losing sales if the tax benefits were eliminated. Boeing could also expect to be asked if the tax benefits on foreign leasing subsidized the foreign airlines that competed with U.S. airlines.

To assess the impact of the Pickle bill, Boeing must determine if there are any public or private substitutes for the leasing. One obvious private substitute is to lower its price, which is possible, since Boeing is far down the learning curve on an aircraft that it had been producing for nearly 20 years. The other possible private substitute is to arrange for foreign lessors to make the lease arrangements, taking advantage of their own domestic tax laws. Other countries, however, did not have investment tax credits, so even if foreign lessors financed Boeing's exports, the tax

---

[10]The difference between this figure and the Treasury estimate of $300 million is that the Treasury was reporting the tax collections reflecting the accelerated depreciation during the first years after the sale. The $200 million is a present value that takes into account the lower depreciation in later years.

[11]If the lessors captured a substantial share of the tax benefits, Boeing could establish its own financing subsidiary as McDonnell-Douglas had done. That would permit Boeing to realize the depreciation tax benefits but not the investment tax credit.

benefits would be much lower. The Eximbank was unlikely to reverse its withdrawal of financing for 747s, so that public substitute was not a realistic alternative. The U.S. government was unlikely to subsidize a profitable company.

This analysis suggests that Boeing is likely to be capturing most, or at least a substantial share, of the tax benefits. If the tax benefits were lost through Pickle's initiative, except for some airlines for which the A300 was a close substitute, Boeing would retain the bulk of its sales by reducing its prices. Boeing thus stood to lose profits but probably few aircraft sales as a consequence of the Pickle bill—at least that was the conclusion reached by Representative Pickle, the Ways and Means Committee, and the Eximbank.

Boeing's Nonmarket Agenda and Objectives

Boeing had several issues on its nonmarket issue agenda, including Eximbank policy, U.S. pressure on Airbus and its parent countries, antitrust concerns in the U.S. aircraft industry, the high value of the dollar, the Reagan administration's increased defense spending from which it expected to benefit, and the media and public criticism being directed to defense contractors. The actions the company took on the foreign leasing issue could affect its ability to deal with the other issues.

Choosing an objective is a central component of a nonmarket strategy, and Boeing could pursue the following objectives:

1. Defeat of the Pickle bill
2. An exemption for job-creating leases consistent with the intent of ERTA
3. An exemption for job-creating export leases consistent with the intent of ERTA
4. An exemption for its own leases
5. Grandfathering of current orders
6. A phaseout of the tax benefits on foreign leasing

The best outcome for Boeing would be the defeat of Pickle's bill, but there is considerable support for the bill, and it is likely to pass in some form.[12] Objective 2 is consistent with the original intent of ERTA, but a substantial tax loss would remain because tax-exempts would still be able to use leasing for new projects although not for sale-and-leaseback deals. This objective is unlikely to be achievable. Objective 4 singles out Boeing without any particular justification, and so it, too, is unlikely. Therefore, Boeing's primary objective should be 3, with 5 and 6 as contingent objectives in the event that an exemption for job-creating export leases cannot be obtained. This objective means that the interests of other exporters are aligned with Boeing's interests, whereas the tax-exempts are opposed to Boeing's interests.

The Nature of the Politics

The principal beneficiaries of the Pickle bill are taxpayers and those who would benefit from lower interest rates if the federal budget deficit were reduced.[13] These benefits are widely distributed and small on a per capita basis. The harm resulting from Pickle's bill is concentrated among tax-exempts, exporters of capital goods that use lease financing, and lessors. In the framework of the Wilson–Lowi matrix, the politics of Pickle's bill are entrepreneurial, and Pickle is the entrepreneur. This issue is attractive to a politician because it involves good government—the elimination of a tax abuse—and the entrepreneur can claim credit for it. Boeing's objective, however, is not to defeat the Pickle bill, which was expected to pass, but instead is to obtain an exemption for job-creating export leases. The relevant alternative thus is the exemption, and using the Wilson–Lowi matrix again, Boeing, the other exporters, and lessors are clients with concentrated benefits from an exemption with widely distributed costs for taxpayers.

Interests and the Demand for Nonmarket Action

Boeing accounts for over half the tax benefits associated with foreign leasing, so the other exporters have smaller stakes in the issue than Boeing has. Employees, suppliers, shareholders,

---

[12]One indication of this was that the Senate bill was introduced by Senators Dole and Metzenbaum, who were from different parties and had quite different positions on many issues. Their support signaled that this was not a partisan issue.
[13]U.S. airlines that competed with foreign airlines would also benefit to the extent that the foreign airlines captured some of the tax benefits.

and local communities that depend on the exporters would also benefit from an exemption to the extent that sales would be lost. The lessors are likely to earn competitive profits on foreign leasing and have only a weak incentive to take action on the issue.[14] Since a relatively small number of firms is affected, general business associations such as the Chamber of Commerce and the National Association of Manufacturers are unlikely to be active on the issue.

The tax-exempts have a strong demand for nonmarket action in opposition to the Pickle bill. They also oppose an exemption for export leases because if the exemption fails, Boeing would then join them in opposing the Pickle bill. Although the impact on any one tax-exempt is small compared with the impact on Boeing, in the aggregate their demand is great. Many tax-exempts are already squeezed by federal budget reductions and the recession. Furthermore, they have few, if any, substitutes for replacing the tax benefits. Collectively, their demand is very high.

The interests of taxpayers are opposed to those of Boeing and the tax-exempts. The benefits to taxpayers from the Pickle bill correspond to the additional tax receipts, which would contribute to a lower federal budget deficit and hence lower interest rates and increased economic activity.

The Supply Side

The affected exporters not only are few in number but also are geographically concentrated. Boeing's affected employment, if it lost sales, would be in Seattle. Oil drilling rig exporters are concentrated on the Gulf Coast, and container manufacturers are few in number. The exporters thus have poor coverage of congressional districts, even though they have considerable resources. Boeing has a supplier network whose coverage is extensive, and it could attempt to organize its suppliers for nonmarket action. Boeing, however, may not want to mobilize its suppliers in a grassroots campaign because the overt use of political pressure by a defense contractor could attract media attention and result in a backlash.

The tax-exempts are numerous, their coverage of congressional districts is virtually complete, and many of their leaders and supporters have access to members of Congress. Although they have few resources, they have the ability to deliver considerable nonmarket pressure. To assess their strategy, it is useful to distinguish between those tax-exempts that already have a leasing deal in hand or in the planning stages and those that do not. Those who will benefit from leasing in the future are as yet unidentified, so it is difficult to mobilize them for nonmarket action. The former group, however, has identifiable benefits and a strong incentive to organize and act.[15] Their benefits, however, can be protected by simply grandfathering existing deals. Grandfathering would allow Pickle and Dole to avoid constituency pressure while preventing further drains on the Treasury.

Taxpayers are numerous, have complete coverage of congressional districts, and have large resources. They are costly to organize, however, and given their low per capita benefits, cannot be expected to be active on this issue. Their interests are represented by a political entrepreneur, Representative Pickle.

Boeing's ability to generate effective nonmarket action on this issue is limited. It could attempt to mobilize its shareholders, but most are unlikely to contact their representatives on a complex issue such as this. Furthermore, a letter from Boeing stressing the urgency of this issue could cause some of them to sell their shares. Boeing employees have a demand for nonmarket action if aircraft sales would be lost, but Boeing's claim of lost sales is offset by the arguments of the Eximbank and the Ways and Means Committee. Employees' costs of organizing are low. Their coverage of congressional districts, however, is limited to the Seattle area. Consequently, their nonmarket action is likely to have only a limited effect, although their unions could represent them. Similarly, the communities potentially affected by the bill are geographically concentrated. Boeing could obtain coverage of congressional districts by mobilizing its suppliers. Their demand for nonmarket action varies considerably as a function of their volume of

---

[14]No lessor testified in the House hearings on the Pickle bill, although one association of lessors involved primarily in domestic leasing sent a letter that was entered into the hearing record.

[15]Some of the groups testifying were the National Housing Rehabilitation Association; American Federation of State, County, and Municipal Employees; YMCA; National Conference of Black Mayors; Municipal Finance Officers Association; Bennington College; and the Preservation Alliance of Louisville and Jefferson County.

747 subcontracts, but in all likelihood enough suppliers could be mobilized to supply a moderate amount of nonmarket pressure. As a defense contractor, however, Boeing is cautious about taking high-profile actions.

The Distributive Politics Spreadsheet

Figure 6-3 presents a distributive politics spreadsheet summarizing this analysis. The conclusion from this analysis is that the supporters of an exemption for job-creating export leases are unlikely to be able to generate a substantial amount of nonmarket action. Attention should thus be directed to the contingent objectives of grandfathering and phasing out the tax benefits.

Institutions and Institutional Officeholders

Although Congress is the institutional arena in which this issue was contested, the executive branch was also interested in the budget consequences. A White House working group had begun meeting to develop measures to curb the leasing by tax-exempts.

Boeing might have been able to enlist the support of executive branch agencies concerned with exports. The Department of Commerce and the U.S. Trade Representative were potential supporters. The Department of the Treasury had stated that the additional tax receipts from eliminating the tax benefits on export leasing were not as important as the exports potentially at risk, but the Treasury could not be expected to work on Boeing's behalf.

Boeing's best hope was to have an exemption for job-creating export leases incorporated into the Senate Finance Committee's bill. Success in the Finance Committee would likely mean success on the Senate floor. If the committee did not provide an exemption, the chances of having an exemption amendment adopted on the Senate floor were slim, given the limited coverage of Boeing and the other exporters. Obtaining an exemption through a floor amendment in the House would be difficult because the Rules Committee would have to give the bill an open rule or a modified rule that allowed the amendment. Ways and Means bills sometimes receive a closed rule that prohibits amendments, and Representative Pickle would certainly seek one. There was little hope of successfully introducing an amendment in the House, once the bill had been passed by the Ways and Means Committee.

The likelihood that the Pickle bill would pass in the House meant that if Boeing were successful in obtaining an exemption in the Senate, it would have to preserve that exemption in a conference committee. The contingent objective of grandfathering current orders might be a reasonable compromise to achieve in conference. Pickle would be among the House conferees.

The key institutional actor was Senator Dole. Although Boeing had a major facility in Wichita, much of the work there in 1983 was on defense contracts. The Senator had won with nearly two-thirds of the vote in the last election and was electorally safe. His current policy interest was in reducing the federal deficit, and his personal objectives were to become Senate majority leader and position himself for a possible run for the presidency. To achieve the first objective, he had to avoid offending his Senate colleagues, who were under pressure from their constituents to preserve leasing deals for tax-exempts in their states. Dole could easily accommodate them and still be fiscally responsible simply by grandfathering their deals already in progress. The bill then would have clear sailing through the Senate.

The final opportunity for Boeing then would be the president. It was unlikely that he would veto this bill, which promoted fiscal responsibility, since he had been berating Congress for its unwillingness to cut spending. If a veto were likely, Congress had ways to protect the bill. One was to consolidate the Pickle bill with other pending tax legislation the president wanted passed. That could insulate the leasing provisions from a veto.

Nonmarket Strategy Formulation

For a nonmarket strategy to be successful on an issue characterized by client politics, the client must demonstrate to enough members of Congress that either their constituents would benefit from an exemption or their own policy interests would be served. Given the belief that the 747 faced little competition, it would be difficult to demonstrate either that many jobs would be preserved by an exemption or that the trade deficit would be significantly affected. Indeed, the pressure on Congress came from the tax-exempts, and members were busy working to protect their constituents' deals. A client can attempt to build a coalition, but in this case there were only

FIGURE 6-3 Distributive Politics Spreadsheet

Alternative being analyzed: Exemption for job-creating exports

Supporting Interests

| Interests | Demand Side — Benefits from Supporting an Exemption | | | Supply Side — Ability to Generate Nonmarket Action | | | | Prediction |
	Substitutes	Aggregate	Per Capita	Numbers	Effectiveness — Coverage	Resources	Cost of Organizing	Amount of Nonmarket Action
Boeing Company	lower price	large	large	small	little	large	small	moderate
• shareholders	sell shares	large	small	large	extensive	large	very high	little
• employees	few	large	substantial	large	little	limited	very low	little
• suppliers	other business	substantial	moderate	substantial	extensive	moderate	high	moderate
Communities								
• Boeing	few	substantial	considerable	small	little	small	low	little
• suppliers	few	moderate	moderate	considerable	extensive	small	high	limited
Oil rig mfgrs.	lower price	moderate	small	few	little	moderate	low	little
Container mfgrs.	lower price	moderate	small	few	little	moderate	low	little
Lessors	other loans	moderate	moderate	small	little	large	low	little

Opposing Interests

| Interests | Demand Side — Benefits from Opposing an Exemption | | | Supply Side — Ability to Generate Nonmarket Action | | | | Prediction |
	Substitutes	Aggregate	Per Capita	Numbers	Effectiveness — Coverage	Resources	Cost of Organizing	Amount of Nonmarket Action
Taxpayers	none	large	very small	huge	complete	huge	very high	little
Tax-exempts	none	substantial	substantial	large	extensive	small	low	large

a few potential coalition members (the other exporters and the lessors), and their coverage of congressional districts was very limited.

Boeing's best strategy was to provide information through lobbying arguing that export leases created jobs in a manner consistent with the objectives of ERTA. In doing so it could distinguish between its lease transactions and sale-and-leaseback transactions that did not create jobs. Boeing could also emphasize its importance in lowering the U.S. trade deficit. The trade deficit, however, was of much less concern to members of Congress than the budget deficit. Boeing could also challenge as inflated the Treasury estimate of the increase in tax revenues from eliminating the tax benefits on foreign leases.

Members of Congress were uncertain about Boeing's claims about the effects on sales and jobs, so Boeing could enlist the aid of some of its customers, such as Singapore Airlines, to attest to the impact of this legislation on their orders. In the upcoming hearings, senators, however, were likely to ask if Boeing could not lower its price to retain sales. This would reduce Boeing's profits, but few in Congress were concerned about lower profits for a quite profitable company.

Boeing could argue to the members of the Finance Committee that it faced unfair competition from a highly subsidized Airbus and that eliminating the tax benefits on foreign leasing would place it at a further disadvantage. This argument, however, had not stopped the Eximbank from ending its financing of 747s. Moreover, Congress preferred to try to stop unfair competition than to subsidize U.S. firms. Furthermore, all U.S. exporters were complaining about losing sales because of the high value of the dollar.

In pursuing its objectives, Boeing could enlist the aid of the congressional delegation from the state of Washington. The House delegation was small, however, and the senators had little seniority. Senator Evans was spending much of his energy campaigning for election in November, and Senator Gorton was in his first term. Neither was on the Senate Finance Committee. Boeing thus had relatively weak representation in Congress, and few other members were likely to view Boeing as their client.

Because of the other issues on its nonmarket issue agenda and because of the sensitivity of overt political activity by a defense contractor, Boeing generally prefers to maintain a low profile. Using suppliers for a grassroots campaign would have too high a profile for this issue.[16] A grassroots program involving employees would also be high profile and would likely have been insufficient to attain Boeing's primary objective given the limited coverage of congressional districts.

Boeing's best nonmarket actions were lobbying and coalition building. Lobbying the Senate Finance Committee was essential. Boeing would be able to address the complexity of the issue in its discussions with key committee members and their staffs. It could also discuss its contingent objectives and the importance of protecting orders already in hand. In its lobbying, Boeing should stress the effects of lost sales on its suppliers and on its own operations and employees. The cost of lobbying was low compared with the potential consequences, and Boeing should use its executives in the lobbying.

Boeing could form a coalition with other firms that used leasing to finance exports, or it could coordinate its nonmarket activities with them. McDonnell-Douglas, oil drilling rig manufacturers, container manufacturers, engine manufacturers, and a few other exporters had incentives to act, although the aggregate effect on them was smaller than on Boeing. These companies were relatively few in number and had relatively poor coverage of congressional districts. The same was true of lessors, so there was a mismatch between their demand for nonmarket action and their ability to supply nonmarket pressure.

Boeing should, of course, modify its market strategy by developing alternative means of financing foreign sales.

The Outcome

The Pickle bill had strong support from members of Congress who wanted to stop the tax abuse and the drain on tax revenues. As is clear from the previous analysis, exporters were unable to generate sufficient nonmarket pressure to stop the Pickle bill. The bill was

---

[16]Boeing undoubtedly wanted to avoid media attention because the political entrepreneur had the better side of this issue. A large, profitable company seeking to preserve tax benefits—or subsidies, as its critics called them—had the potential for unfavorable media treatment, which could hurt a defense contractor. Defense contractors were being criticized because of cost overruns and excessive charges.

incorporated in the Deficit Reduction Act of 1984. The final provisions eliminated the tax benefits for both tax-exempts and foreign leases, but the current projects of many of the tax-exempts were grandfathered. Straight-line depreciation was allowed for foreign leases, but the depreciation period had to extend for the life of the asset or 125 percent of the lease term. The other tax benefits were phased out over several years. Grandfathering was provided for wide-body aircraft, containers, and drilling rigs. The provision for Boeing read: "The amendments in this section shall not apply with respect to any wide body, 4-engine commercial passenger aircraft used by a foreign person or entity if (i) on or before November 1, 1983 the foreign person or entity entered into a written binding contract to acquire such aircraft, and (ii) such aircraft is placed into service before January 1, 1986." Boeing thus achieved its contingent objectives.[17]

SUMMARY

The analysis of nonmarket and political action has two foundations—interests and institutions. Interests can arise from distributive consequences and moral concerns. Distributive consequences can be assessed in terms of the benefits and costs from an alternative. The moral determinants of nonmarket action are based on considerations of well-being, rights, and social justice.

Interests give rise to a demand for nonmarket action, and that demand depends on the private and public substitutes available. The incentive to act depends on the per capita benefits, and if the aggregate benefits are high but the per capita benefits are low, incentives for nonmarket action can be weak.

The costs of nonmarket action are of three types. The first is the cost of organizing interests and joining together for collective action. The second is the direct cost of implementing a nonmarket strategy. The third is associated with the effectiveness of a given amount of nonmarket action. If the number of affected interests is small, the costs of organization are likely to be low. The larger the number of affected interests, the more likely they are to encounter the free-rider problem. The effectiveness of nonmarket action depends on the number of people affected, their resources, and their coverage of legislative districts. The paradox of collective action is that while effectiveness increases with the number of interests affected and with their coverage of legislative districts, dispersed groups often have low per capita benefits and high costs of organization, resulting in little nonmarket action. The analysis of the benefits and costs of taking nonmarket action can be summarized in the distributive politics spreadsheet.

The nature of political competition depends on the relative concentration and dispersion of the benefits and harm from enactment of a nonmarket alternative. The categories of client, interest group, entrepreneurial, and majoritarian politics characterize the nature of the political competition, but the outcome depends on additional factors, including the characteristics of the institutions in whose arenas the competition takes place.

The Boeing case indicates the complexity of even a relatively straightforward issue. It also illustrates the difference between the demand for nonmarket action and its supply. Taxpayers had low per capita benefits relative to their costs of taking nonmarket action and thus had to be represented by a political entrepreneur. The tax-exempts had benefits that exceed their costs, so they were active. Boeing and other exporters had a high demand for nonmarket action and low costs of organizing, but their effectiveness was limited by a lack of coverage of congressional districts. As a defense contractor, Boeing preferred a low-profile strategy to avoid compromising its effectiveness on other issues. Boeing's best political strategy was to lobby using the message that sales and jobs would be lost. The best that Boeing was able to achieve, however, was a phaseout of the benefits and the grandfathering of orders in hand.

---

[17]The case *Leasebacks by Tax-Exempt Entities* in the fifth edition of this book considers a second episode in the foreign leasing saga.

Nonmarket Action and the Free-Rider Problem

THE BENEFITS AND COSTS OF NONMARKET ACTION

Pluralist theories predict that common interests, such as those that result from a potential increase in industry profits, lead to nonmarket action consistent with those interests. These demand-side theories draw implications about nonmarket activity directly from the interests of individuals and firms. Olson (1965), however, argued that such theories ignore the costs of taking nonmarket and collective action. Those costs are an important determinant of the effectiveness of those with common interests.[18] The higher those costs, the lower the nonmarket action taken, and therefore the less effective are those with common interests.

Taxpayers have a common interest in lower taxes, and consumers have a common interest in lower prices. With some exceptions, neither taxpayers nor consumers have been particularly effective in public politics, in part because their costs of organizing for collective action are high relative to the per capita benefits they would receive as a result of that action.[19] The (per-capita) benefits for an individual consumer from eliminating sugar import quotas are outweighed by the costs of taking nonmarket action. Large groups thus may have a high demand for political action, but their costs of acting can also be high. Common or aligned interests therefore do not translate directly into nonmarket success but instead are mediated by the costs of nonmarket action.

THE FREE-RIDER PROBLEM AND COLLECTIVE ACTION

The costs of nonmarket action can be reduced through *collective action*. On many nonmarket issues, a firm's interests are aligned with those of other firms, customers, or suppliers. With an alignment of interests, collective action is possible. Outcomes of nonmarket issues, however, often have the property of a public good in the sense that they pertain to everyone, regardless of whether they contributed to obtaining the outcome. For example, working to decrease swipe fees on credit card transactions benefits all retailers regardless of whether they contributed to obtaining the decrease.[20] When the benefits from nonmarket action accrue to those who do not contribute, a *free-rider problem* may be present.[21]

Consider an industry composed of n small firms. Suppose that nonmarket action by any one firm costs that firm c and yields benefits b for each of the n firms in the industry, for a total benefit of nb. For example, participation by an individual retailer increases the likelihood that swipe fees will be decreased, which is a public good for the firms in the industry. Whenever $nb > c$, the firms in the industry are better off in the aggregate if an individual firm participates in the collective action. Consequently, it is collectively rational for all firms to contribute to the nonmarket action when $nb > c$.

What is collectively rational, however, may not be individually rational. An individual firm has an incentive to contribute to the collective action only if the cost c it incurs is less than the benefits it receives from its own participation, and those benefits are only b. Consequently, if $c > b$, an individual firm has no incentive to participate even though its participation produces collective benefits nb to the industry that exceed its costs c.[22] The firm then prefers to free ride on the efforts of the other firms, since doing so saves it the cost c and it loses only the benefits b from its own contribution. Each firm has an incentive to free ride, and the possibility of collective action is in doubt. The free-rider problem thus is present when $b < c < nb$.[23] The characteristic of such dilemmas is that what is collectively rational is not individually rational.

The larger the number of potential participants, the more serious is the free-rider problem. Large groups such as consumers and taxpayers often have difficulty overcoming this problem. The Consumer Federation of America, for example, has no individual members, but instead its members are other organizations. Large groups thus must develop other means to induce participation. Some groups form associations to reduce the cost of nonmarket action. Some groups encourage participation by providing selective benefits that can be denied to those who do not participate. The largest organized interest group in the United States is AARP (American Association of Retired Persons), which has a membership of over 30 million. AARP is politically active on a variety of issues of concern to its members, and it attracts members in part by providing selective benefits to them. AARP, for example, offers its members discount prices on pharmaceuticals and supplemental health insurance, as well as discounts on travel and accommodations.

Labor unions also face a free-rider problem in obtaining contributions from members to undertake nonmarket activities. The unions have solved this collective action problem by obtaining legislation that requires mandatory dues from everyone in a collective bargaining unit, and those dues can be used

---

[18]See Moe (1980) and Hardin (1982).

[19]This does not mean that the interests of consumers and taxpayers are not reflected in political outcomes. Their interests can be represented by a government officeholder, who can claim credit for having done so, or by an NGO such as the Consumer Federation of America or the National Taxpayers Union.

[20]The swipe fee issue is considered in the chapter case *Business versus Business*.

[21]See Shepsle and Boncheck (1997) for an introduction to collective action.

[22]If $c < b$, each individual firm benefits sufficiently from its own participation to act on its own, so there is no collective action problem. Large retailers such as Wal-Mart and Target had an incentive to work for lower swipe fees.

[23]The free-rider problem is a special case of a prisoners' dilemma. In a prisoners' dilemma each player has a dominant strategy, and if each plays that strategy the outcome is worse for both than is the outcome if both were to choose a different strategy.

for nonmarket action as well as supporting candidates in federal and state elections.[24]

One possibility for resolving the free-rider problem and other social dilemmas is cooperation in which the parties take into account not only the consequences for themselves but for the other parties as well. Cooperation in this sense is mutual altruism. In the context of the free-rider problem, each firm would participate at a cost c and receive nb in benefits—provided that all others participated. If a firm agrees to participate, however, it has an incentive to defect from the cooperative agreement. This would save the firm c and its benefits would be reduced by only b, which is less than c. The temptation is thus to free ride on the participation of others. Indeed, if a firm harbors some doubt about whether others will participate, not participating becomes even more compelling. Such doubts can lead to no participation by any firm.

This reasoning suggests that free-rider problems are difficult to resolve, yet many are resolved. Resolution often occurs because the free-rider problem is repeated rather than encountered only once. In that case, players have a stake in the future, and the set of strategies that players can employ is much broader. A player can, for example, reward or punish another player for the choice made in the previous round, and the expectation of punishment such as exclusion for failure to participate can induce participation. In employing these strategies, the players do not take into account the interests of the other party in their reasoning about how to play, so altruism is not involved. This resolution of the free-rider problem is thus noncooperative rather than cooperative.

Behavior generated by repeated play can be supported by the creation of an institution to punish deviations from the mutually beneficial actions. The World Trade Organization was created to lower trade barriers for the mutual benefit of its members and has a dispute resolution and punishment mechanism to deal with violations of its trading rules.[25] Similarly, firms that repeatedly take nonmarket action on issues on which their interests are aligned may be able to solve the free-rider problem by forming an association that acts on the behalf of its members on a series of issues and can monitor free riding. Retailers have formed a number of trade associations, including the Retail Industry Leaders Association and the Merchants Payments Coalition, that were active in the swipe fee case.

---

[24]Union members can file a statement each year to take back the portion of their dues that would otherwise go to electoral support.

[25]The World Trade Organization is considered in Chapter 19.

The Organization of Congress

The Congress is bicameral. The House of Representatives is composed of 435 voting members serving 2-year terms and elected from districts with approximately the same population.[26] The 10 largest states account for half the members, whereas Alaska, Delaware, Montana, North Dakota, South Dakota, Vermont, and Wyoming have only one representative each. House districts are reapportioned after each census, and as a result of the 2010 census, the West and the South gained seats at the expense of the Northeast and the Midwest. The Speaker is the presiding officer of the House and is selected by the majority party and elected by the entire House.

Each of the 50 states has two senators, serving staggered 6-year terms. States with a small population thus have relatively more weight in the Senate, and states with large populations have relatively more weight in the House. The vice president presides over the Senate and has a vote in case of a tie.

The Constitution specifies neither how the chambers are to be organized nor how they are to conduct their business. Over time, they have developed their own formal and informal organizational structures and procedures. The formal organization is found in the committee structure and the legislative process. The informal organization is found in the party organization within the chambers. Each party elects a leader, whips, a secretary of the party conference, and heads of policy and steering committees. The primary responsibility of the whips is to generate party discipline on those issues on which the party has taken a position. Although parties and the party organization of Congress are important, members have considerable latitude in their voting, and party discipline is not the rule.

THE LEGISLATIVE PROCESS

During the 111th Congress (2009–2010), 6,562 bills were introduced in the House and 4,054 in the Senate, yet only a few hundred were enacted.[27] Most bills are written by members of Congress, and bills originating in the executive branch (the Presidency) are introduced by a member of the president's party. Many bills are introduced with little expectation that they will even be considered, and some are introduced to appeal to interest groups or constituents. When submitting a bill, a member will often seek cosponsors, but cosponsorship does not commit a member to support the bill if it comes to the floor for a vote. The number of cosponsors also does not necessarily translate into votes because interest group activity often intensifies with the submission of a bill and can result in some members changing their positions.

Figure 6-4 illustrates the legislative process.[28] When a bill is introduced, it is referred to a committee. The committee can then consider the bill or, in the case of most bills, take no action on it. A bill is usually considered first by a subcommittee, which, by a majority vote, sends it to the full committee. A subcommittee cannot, however, effectively block a bill that a committee majority wishes to consider because the committee can consider the bill directly. Much of the substantive legislative work in Congress is done in committees, including amending and rewriting ("marking up") bills.

When a bill receives a majority vote in committee, it is ready to be scheduled for consideration on the floor of the chamber. In the House the bill goes to the Rules Committee, which assigns an amendment rule that governs floor consideration. The Rules Committee may assign a restrictive rule, which specifies or restricts the amendments that can be offered, or an open rule, which places no restrictions on the amendments that may be offered on the floor. Amendments on the floor, however, are governed by a standing rule of the House that prohibits nongermane amendments.[29] Little true debate actually takes place, and many speeches on the floor are made to appeal to constituents.

The legislative process in the Senate is similar to that in the House except that all bills are technically considered on the floor under an open rule. In practice, however, the Senate operates under unanimous consent agreements (UCAs) specifying which amendments are to be considered on the floor. These agreements are negotiated under the auspices of the Senate leadership. An objection to a UCA by any senator prevents it from taking effect.

Senate rules allow members to speak on the floor for an unlimited time, and senators opposed to a bill can speak continuously (a filibuster), thus preventing a vote on a bill. Cloture can be invoked by a vote of 60 senators, preventing any member from speaking for more than an hour and precluding nongermane amendments. The minority party in the Senate frequently uses a filibuster to extract concessions from the majority or at times to kill a bill. A filibuster thus makes it more difficult to change the status quo.[30]

Before a bill can be enacted, it must be passed by both chambers in identical language. The bills passed by each chamber seldom have the same language or substantive provisions and must be reconciled before they are sent to the president. Conference committees composed of representatives of each chamber and selected by the majority party leadership are

---

[26]Representatives from the District of Columbia, American Samoa, Guam, Northern Mariana Islands, Puerto Rico, and the Virgin Islands are members of the House but do not have a vote.

[27]Any legislation pending at the end of a Congress dies.

[28]Smith, Roberts, and Vander Wielen (2009) provide detailed information on Congress, the legislative process, and congressional procedures. For additional information see Schickler, Lee, and Edwards (2011).

[29]On a majority vote, the House may waive any of its rules.

[30]See Krehbiel (1996) and Brady and Volden (1998) for theories of gridlock and Krehbiel (1998, 1999) for a theory in which filibusters and vetoes play an important role.

FIGURE 6-4 How a Bill Becomes a Law

This graphic shows the most typical way in which proposed legislation is enacted into law. There are more complicated, as well as simpler, routes, and most bills never become law. The process is illustrated with two hypothetical bills, House bill No. 1 (HR 1) and Senate bill No. 2 (S 2).

Bills must be passed by both houses in identical form before they can be sent to the president. The path of HR 1 is traced by a solid line, that of S 2 by a broken line. In practice most bills begin as similar proposals in both houses.

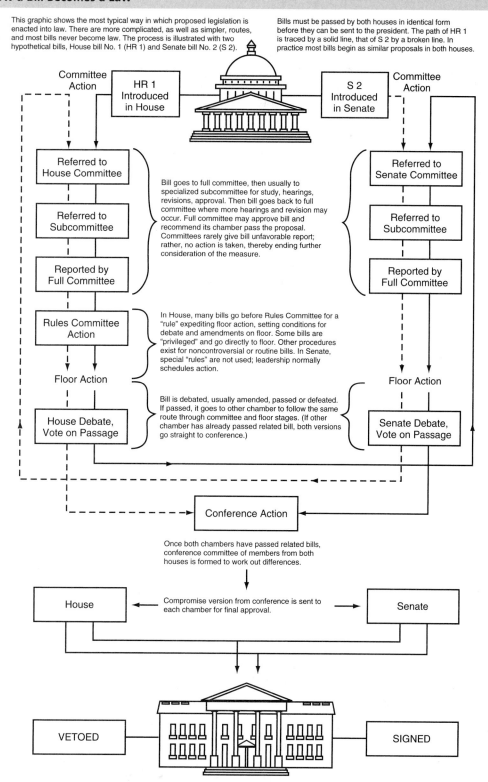

Committee Action

HR 1 Introduced in House

S 2 Introduced in Senate

Committee Action

Referred to House Committee

Referred to Senate Committee

Bill goes to full committee, then usually to specialized subcommittee for study, hearings, revisions, approval. Then bill goes back to full committee where more hearings and revision may occur. Full committee may approve bill and recommend its chamber pass the proposal. Committees rarely give bill unfavorable report; rather, no action is taken, thereby ending further consideration of the measure.

Referred to Subcommittee

Referred to Subcommittee

Reported by Full Committee

Reported by Full Committee

Rules Committee Action

In House, many bills go before Rules Committee for a "rule" expediting floor action, setting conditions for debate and amendments on floor. Some bills are "privileged" and go directly to floor. Other procedures exist for noncontroversial or routine bills. In Senate, special "rules" are not used; leadership normally schedules action.

Floor Action

Floor Action

Bill is debated, usually amended, passed or defeated. If passed, it goes to other chamber to follow the same route through committee and floor stages. (If other chamber has already passed related bill, both versions go straight to conference.)

House Debate, Vote on Passage

Senate Debate, Vote on Passage

Conference Action

Once both chambers have passed related bills, conference committee of members from both houses is formed to work out differences.

House

Compromise version from conference is sent to each chamber for final approval.

Senate

VETOED

SIGNED

Compromise bill approved by both houses is sent to the president, who can sign it into law or veto it and return it to Congress. Congress may override veto by a two-thirds majority vote in both houses. Bill then becomes law without president's signature.
Source: Congressional Quarterly, *Guide to Congress*, Washington, D.C., 1989

usually used to reconcile major legislation.[31] Members of both parties from the committee that reported the bill plus the authors of principal amendments are typically appointed to the conference committee. Conference committees are important because the conferees have to bargain when the bills passed by the two chambers differ substantially. Thus, conference committees are often the focus of political activity. If the conferees from the two chambers agree on common language, the bill is returned to the floor of each chamber for a final passage vote. If approved by both chambers, it is sent to the president for signature or veto.

A bill passed by Congress becomes law when the president signs it or when Congress overrides a presidential veto on a vote of two-thirds of the members of each chamber. When a bill is passed while Congress is still in session, the president must act on the bill within 10 days or it automatically becomes law. If Congress is no longer in session, the president can choose not to act on the bill, and then it dies.[32] The authority to veto legislation gives the president considerable power.

Because legislation can be stopped at a number of points in the legislative process, it is more difficult to enact than to stop legislation. To be enacted, a bill must clear a number of hurdles. Committees represent an important hurdle, which gives power to the committees and their chairs. A majority of the members of the parent body can circumvent any hurdle that a chairperson or committee might erect, however.

COMMITTEES

Most of the work of Congress is done in committees, and each chamber chooses its own committee structure. The House has 21 and the Senate has 16 standing committees, each of which has several subcommittees. Each chamber may also have select and special committees, and there are four joint committees.

Committees have policy jurisdictions, but those jurisdictions can overlap when issues cut across formal boundaries. In the House, for example, the regulation of an agricultural pesticide could be under the jurisdiction of the Agriculture Committee as well as committees with environmental jurisdictions. Committees thus can battle over jurisdictions and hence over influence on legislation.

Government expenditures are governed by a complex process requiring both an authorization and an appropriation. The House Agriculture Committee or the Armed Services Committee may authorize expenditures for an agricultural subsidy program or a new weapons system, but the funds for those programs are provided by the Appropriations Committee. The process is designed to have the authorization committee act first, with the Appropriations Committee then providing funding no greater than the amount authorized. In recent Congresses authorization committees have begun to require program funding at particular levels. Since the 1990s the budget process has involved complex bargaining between the president and Congress over both the budget and the funding of individual programs.

Authorization committees have the responsibility for writing legislation and reauthorizing programs with fixed expiration dates. In addition to their legislative roles, authorization committees have oversight responsibilities. Committees attempt to influence the policies of regulatory and administrative agencies by holding hearings and threatening legislative or budgetary action.

Committee membership is proportional to a party's representation in the chamber, and party conferences assign their members to committees. Newly elected legislators give a ranking of their committee preferences, and the party conferences do their best to assign members to the committees they have requested. Members of the House generally serve on two standing committees, and some also serve on select or joint committees. In the Senate, each member serves on several committees. Members accumulate committee-specific seniority, and the members of each committee are ranked by seniority within their party. Seniority is usually not transferable if the member changes committees. Because committee and subcommittee chairs are generally selected according to seniority and because chairpersons have strategic positions, members do not frequently change committees. Remaining with the same committee also gives members an incentive and an opportunity to develop expertise in its policy jurisdiction.

The chairs of committees and subcommittees are chosen by the majority party. When the Republicans captured a majority in the House in 2011, all chairs changed from Democrats to Republicans.

Approximately half of the House majority party and virtually all the Senate majority party are chairs of a committee or subcommittee. Committee chairs are selected by a party conference, and incumbents generally retain their chairs. Occasionally, however, a chair is replaced. When they became the majority party in the House in 1995, the Republicans passed over several more senior members in selecting committee chairs. Committee chairs traditionally have chosen the chairs of their subcommittees. In addition to their role as the first stage of legislative activity, subcommittees have the opportunity to hold hearings to direct public attention to issues and provide interest groups with a forum to advance their interests.

COMMITTEE AND PERSONAL STAFFS

Members of Congress each have a personal staff that includes a chief, a press secretary, legislative assistants, and administrative assistants. The staff keeps the member informed about legislation, hearings, and other developments and also serves as an important link between members and their constituents and interest groups. A substantial portion of staff time is devoted to providing constituents with services such as assisting with lost Social Security checks, assisting with immigration problems, and interacting with government agencies. The staff also responds to constituents' letters on issues.

---

[31]Instead of convening a conference, Congress often uses the procedure of amendments between the chambers to reconcile differences between bills. As in the daylight saving time example presented in Chapter 7, one chamber can simply adopt the language of the other's bill. A bill may go through several iterations of amendments between the chambers before common language is reached.

[32]This is called a pocket veto.

Committee staffs have shown a similar pattern. The committee staff is directed by the chair of the committee and, at quiet times, may serve as an adjunct to his or her personal staff. The committee staff is important in drafting legislation, marking up bills, and interacting with interest groups. For firms, trade associations, unions, and other interest groups, the staff represents an important point of access to the legislative process and to information about the committee's activities. The majority party is allocated a substantially larger number of committee staff positions than the minority party.

LEGISLATORS AND THEIR CONSTITUENTS

Whatever are their personal policy objectives, legislators must be reelected to have a continuing opportunity to achieve those objectives. Legislators thus vote on bills based on two considerations—their reelection incentives and their policy preferences.[33] Elected representatives thus are responsive to the preferences of their constituents not only because they have a duty to represent them but also because they want to be reelected. To enhance the reelection of incumbents, some states have gerrymandered their congressional (and state legislature) electoral districts so that few of their districts are competitive.

An electoral constituency includes voters, campaign volunteers, and providers of campaign resources. The reelection motive gives legislators an incentive to be attentive to the interests of those likely to vote. It also gives them an incentive to develop a personal constituency by providing services to constituents. Mayhew (2004) refers to this as the *constituency connection*. The reelection motive may also provide an opportunity for interest groups with electorally important resources to influence the behavior of legislators.

Mayhew characterized members of Congress as exhibiting two types of behavior: *credit claiming* and *blame avoidance*. Credit claiming is the practice of claiming credit for legislative or oversight activity that is in the interest of constituents. Blame avoidance involves distancing oneself from unpopular events, policies, or positions that might provide an opportunity for an electoral challenger. Because it is difficult for most constituents to know the actual effectiveness, or in some cases even the position, of a legislator, credit claiming may go beyond actual accomplishments. Interest groups, however, monitor legislators and often have a good idea of their effectiveness.

PARTIES

Political parties are important in legislative politics, yet legislators have a considerable degree of independence from party positions and party leaders. In Congress, parties attempt to maintain discipline in voting in committees and on the floor. On issues important to their constituents, however, members often depart from the party position.

Parties in the United States are relatively weak compared to parties in many other countries, particularly those countries with a parliamentary system of government. One reason is that in the United States nominations for elected office are controlled locally rather than by a national party. In addition, issues important to voters are often local rather than national, which allows members to develop local, personal constituencies to improve their reelection prospects. This personal vote is developed through district work, directing federal funds to the district, and constituent service. Parties are also relatively weak in the United States because most campaign contributions are made directly to candidates rather than to parties, which gives members a further degree of independence.

THE PRESIDENCY AND THE EXECUTIVE BRANCH

The president has a range of powers—some granted by the Constitution, some delegated by Congress, and some derived from public support.[34] The Constitution assigns to the president the right to veto legislation as well as certain powers in foreign affairs. Congress has delegated to the president the authority to negotiate treaties and trade agreements. The president also has authority in certain administrative areas, as granted by legislation. President Reagan had a substantial impact on regulatory rule making through his executive authority. In 1981 he issued an important executive order requiring a cost–benefit analysis of new regulations proposed by executive branch agencies. When President Clinton took office, he modified the order, requiring a review of costs and benefits only for major regulatory rule making. President Bush strengthened the role of the office that reviews regulations.

The president also appoints, with the consent of a majority of the Senate, the heads of cabinet departments, the members of regulatory and other commissions, and the top levels of executive branch agencies. The executive branch thus is responsive to the policy objectives of the president. The executive branch agencies and cabinet departments have influence not only on the administration of laws but also on policy formation through their expertise and their ability to develop policy proposals.

One of the most important powers of the president is the responsibility, with the consent of a majority of the Senate, to appoint members of the federal judiciary. In addition to deciding individual cases, the judiciary interprets the Constitution and federal statutes. The precedents established by court decisions have lasting effects. Through their appointments, the Reagan and (George H. W.) Bush administrations changed the Supreme Court from one with a liberal and judicial activist orientation to one with a more conservative orientation reflecting judicial restraint.

The president submits an annual budget to Congress. Although Congress may make any changes it chooses, the

---

[33]See Fiorina (1989) and Mayhew (2004) for analyses of congressional behavior.

[34]The president can be removed from office only through impeachment by the House and a trial in the Senate. Andrew Johnson and Bill Clinton have been impeached, but neither was convicted.

president, through pressure, bargaining power, and the veto, has considerable influence over the final product. The budget process is typically characterized by intense bargaining between the Office of Management and Budget and the congressional leadership.

In reasoning about political behavior, it is important to recognize that the absence of certain behavior does not mean that it is not important. For example, presidents cast relatively few vetoes, even when the president and Congress are from different parties. The infrequency of vetoes does not, however, mean that the veto is unimportant. The threat of a veto causes Congress not to pass some legislation that it would otherwise pass and causes it to modify legislation that it does pass so as to avoid a veto.

Tobacco Politics

The tobacco industry has long been an economic juggernaut. By one estimate, as of 1998 tobacco accounted for 500,000 jobs and generated up to $170 billion in revenue annually in the United States—an amount approximately equal to the gross domestic product of Columbia.[35] Tobacco was grown in 20 states and was one of the most successful cash crops. Renewed efforts to regulate tobacco were fueled by new reports on the effects of secondhand smoke, such as one claiming that smoking accounted for as many as 400,000 deaths annually.

The federal government's efforts to control tobacco and cigarette advertising can be traced to 1954, when Representative John Dingell (D-MI) proposed a bill banning interstate advertising of tobacco products and alcoholic beverages. Although Representative Dingell's proposal did not succeed, in 1970 President Nixon signed a bill banning cigarette advertising on radio and television. In the 1980s several additional measures were passed that restricted smoking, including a ban on smoking on domestic airline flights. The 1990s saw further action taken against the tobacco industry, with legislation enacted to limit tobacco advertising and ban smoking in federal buildings.

Throughout this period, antismoking advocates portrayed the tobacco industry as an all-powerful, evil empire that held lawmakers in its hip pocket. Antismoking advertisements in the late 1990s claimed that tobacco companies consciously targeted teenagers in their advertising campaigns in the hope of recruiting and addicting the nation's youth. The threat to the tobacco industry and its beneficiaries increased significantly in November 1997, when S.1415, the National Tobacco Policy and Youth Smoking Reduction Act, was introduced by Senator John McCain (R-AZ).

PROVISIONS OF THE ACT

S.1415 was an outgrowth of an agreement reached on June 20, 1997, known as the Tobacco Resolution. The agreement between the major tobacco companies, state attorneys general, and class action lawyers provided the tobacco industry with protection from future punitive damages lawsuits and set caps on damage payments in exchange for a substantial per-pack tax increase and lump-sum damages payments.[36] Overall, the bill would constitute a significant increase in the regulatory role of the federal government with respect to the tobacco industry. As proponents of the bill portrayed it, the bill required tobacco companies to pay $506 billion over 25 years to cover health care expenses related to smoking. The mechanism for funding this transfer was a $1.10 excise tax on the price of each pack of cigarettes. The bill also provided block grants to states to deal

with medical costs stemming from tobacco use. In return for the tax increase, the liability of tobacco companies would be capped at $6.5 billion per year.

In addition to the monetary and legal provisions, the bill also restricted tobacco advertising and promotion. Tobacco companies would be prohibited from advertising on billboards, in public arenas, and on the Internet. In an attempt to reduce underage smoking, human or cartoon characters such as R. J. Reynolds's "Joe Camel" were to be banned from advertising campaigns. Companies also would not be allowed to sell items of clothing bearing their brand name, provide gifts to customers, sponsor public events, or pay for product placements in television programs or movies. Advertisements could no longer use phrases such as "low tar" or "light" that would imply that a given cigarette brand was less dangerous than another brand.

Other provisions would affect the regulation and distribution of tobacco. The Food and Drug Administration (FDA) would have the power to regulate nicotine like a drug, including, with the consent of Congress, the power to ban it altogether. Retail stores would have to apply for licenses to sell tobacco, and tobacco companies would have to disclose all corporate documents about their product, which would then be placed in a national depository for public use.

INTERESTS

In addition to the tobacco companies, other interests would be affected. Trial lawyers for plaintiffs in individual and class action lawsuits would receive a financial windfall. To avoid the public fallout and demands for accountability associated with the payment of extremely large fees, the bill created a payment mechanism whereby three "arbitrators" representing lawyers and tobacco companies would determine the actual payment figures. In addition, tobacco companies agreed to provide the class action lawyers, who were instrumental in the agreement, an annuity of up to $500 million a year.[37]

State attorneys general who had filed state lawsuits wanted S.1415 to pass for two reasons. The first was to recover damages associated with smoking that could be used to cover state Medicaid expenses. The second and more subtle reason was the expectation of political gains from public sentiment for helping to pass what was being promoted as a major blow against the tobacco industry.

Foremost among the bill's supporters were dozens of antismoking groups, including the Coalition on Smoking OR Health, Americans for Nonsmokers' Rights, Action on Smoking and Health (ASH), Airspace, The BADvertising Institute, Smoke*Screen, the National Center for Tobacco-Free Kids, Effective National Action to Control Tobacco (ENACT), the American Heart Association, and the American Lung Association.

Wholesalers would be hurt by the per-pack excise tax provision because of the way the tax was to be collected.

---

[35]The $170 billion estimate is from Alan Greenblat, "Growing Ranks of Cigarette Tax Critics Invigorate Big Tobacco's Lobbying Effort," *Congressional Quarterly Weekly Report*, May 16, 1998, p. 1306. Bulow and Klemperer (1998), however, report that retail sales of cigarettes were only $50 billion, which suggests that the $170 billion figure includes multiplier effects.

[36]Bulow and Klemperer (1998) provide an excellent overview of the provisions of the resolution.

[37]Bulow and Klemperer (1998).

Wholesalers would have to extend credit to many retailers, and the book value of wholesalers' inventory would be higher, resulting in higher insurance costs and "shrinkage" (theft). In estimating the damage at $367 million over 5 years, the American Wholesalers Marketers Association's spokeswoman, Jacqueline Cohen, explained, "Your shrinkage will grow."[38]

Cigarette-only stores would benefit under the proposed legislation because they would be exempt from point-of-sale promotional restrictions that would affect other retailers. Some of these stores were "adult bookstores."

Convenience stores would be hurt by the excise tax and the registration requirements. Convenience store cigarette sales accounted for approximately 40 percent of U.S. cigarette sales, and cigarettes alone comprised 20 percent of the average convenience store's total business.[39] A 1997 Department of Agriculture study confirmed the suspicion that many of these stores would likely not survive price and distribution reforms such as those included in S.1415.

The National Association of Convenience Stores, an international trade association, represented almost 3,300 convenience store operators, petroleum marketers, and suppliers, with 63,000 convenience stores around the world. In 1996 the convenience store industry posted $151.9 billion in sales.[40]

Grocery chains would also be hurt, since tobacco companies currently paid $2 billion annually in slotting fees to obtain prime placement for their products. Grocery retailers were organized in a number of associations, including the Food Marketing Institute (FMI)—a trade organization of over 100 grocers, including Giant-Eagle, Dominick's, Piggly-Wiggly, Safeway, and Tom Thumb. The FMI's annual trade show hosted over 35,000 representatives from the supermarket industry. Additionally, the National Grocers Association had a membership of 2,060 and a budget of $5 million. It had food retailer members in 50 states and also included 60 wholesale food distributors.

The advertising industry would also be affected. By one account, tobacco advertisements and promotions totaled $5 billion, and the provisions of S.1415 chipped away at virtually every advertising approach used by firms.[41] Although print advertisements only generated $20 million in revenue,

the prohibition on billboard advertising would eliminate $290 million in revenue. Point-of-purchase displays would also be prohibited and would reduce retailer revenues from slotting fees. The American Association of Advertising Agencies, with membership of 6 percent of the 13,000 U.S. agencies, accounted for 75 percent of advertising revenue in the United States.[42]

Tobacco farmers naturally opposed S.1415, but a 1997 Department of Agriculture study found that the preponderance of jobs attributed to tobacco were in the retail and wholesale trade—not in farming per se. Furthermore, the bill as drafted was sensitive to farmers' concerns, providing transition payments for them. Meanwhile, the foreign market for cigarettes continued to grow.

Concert promoters would be rocked by the expected loss of underwriting, which was dependent on prominent displays of advertisements. Likewise, organizers of golf tournaments would be driven to find alternative sources of underwriting revenue, while the net proceeds for tennis promoters would decline.

Not even universities escaped the reach of tobacco politics. By one estimate as many as 70 percent of university portfolios included tobacco stock, and some portfolio managers began to contemplate alternative investment strategies due to heightened public antitobacco sentiment and/or reduced profitability of tobacco firms. Harvard and Johns Hopkins had already divested, and Yale's board of trustees considered selling $16.9 million of tobacco stock from its $6 billion portfolio. ▪

Preparation Questions

1. For each of the following groups, assess the likelihood that it will engage in nonmarket action on S.1415, and identify the specific cost and/or benefit characteristics underlying your assessment: smokers, tobacco companies, tobacco farmers, trial lawyers, antismoking groups, cigarette-only stores, grocery stores, convenience stores, advertising agencies, concert and event promoters, and universities.

2. Using the Wilson–Lowi matrix, what kind of politics best characterizes the activity surrounding McCain's bill?

3. Assess the prospects for coalition formation.

4. What outcome do you predict for the bill and why?

Business versus Business

Businesses are on the opposite sides of a variety of issues. In 2010 retailers sought to reduce the fees they paid on credit and debit card sales and faced off against the card companies and the banks that issue the cards. The institutional arena was Congress.

Retailers were estimated to pay $48 billion annually for "swipe fees" on credit and debit card purchases, according to the Nilson Report. Debit cards accounted for somewhat less than half the amount, but the cards were growing rapidly in popularity. Retailers sought to reduce the swipe fees paid when customers used the cards for payments. The swipe fees included network fees that were paid by merchants to Visa and MasterCard and interchange fees of $15.8 billion that were paid

---

[38]Greenblat (1998).

[39]Greenblat (1998).

[40]www.cstorecentral.com/public/nacs/rf05.htm.

[41]Greenblat (1998). Data provided by Bulow and Klemperer (1998); Table 10, however, suggests that all tobacco marketing expenses are treated as advertising expenses in the $5 billion figure. Most marketing expenses are promotional allowances such as price cuts for distributors and coupon and retail value-added promotions, neither of which would be prohibited by the bill.

---

[42]Some legal scholars believed the advertising provisions in S.1415 would be subject to court challenges on grounds of violating the First Amendment.

by retailers to the issuers of the debit cards, primarily banks such as JPMorgan Chase. The interchange fees amounted to $19.7 billion in 2009, and averaged 1.63 percent of the transaction amount which was much higher than the costs of processing a check.

The opportunity for retailers was the Obama administration's financial reform initiative. The House passed its version of the bill, which included a provision to regulate interchange fees, with the Federal Reserve as the regulator. The Senate version of the bill incorporated an amendment authored by Senator Dick Durbin (D-IL) that included the regulation of network fees as well. The shares of Visa fell by 9.9 percent and MasterCard fell by 8.6 percent when the Durbin amendment passed.[43] The share prices of the largest card issuers, Citigroup, Bank of America, and JPMorgan Chase, which had debit card usage of $550 billion in 2009, fell between 2.3 and 3.1 percent. Visa stated, "We hope Congress sees today's amendment for what it is—an attempt by retailers to increase their profits at the expense of consumers."[44]

Lobbying on the Durbin amendment was intense, and after it passed, attention turned to the conference committee that would reconcile differences between the House and Senate bills. Large card issuers such as JPMorgan Chase lobbied intensely against the regulation. The card companies argued that reducing the interchange fees would result in higher charges for consumers. The banks argued that any reductions in interchange fees would require them to raise fees on other services and reduce rewards programs. Noah Hanft, general counsel of MasterCard explained, "We continue to have concerns that the ultimate outcome of this legislation would be the passing of merchant acceptance costs to consumers at a time when Americans can least afford it."[45]

The banks also argued that any reductions in fees would go into the profits of retailers rather than the pockets of consumers. Ken Clayton of the American Bankers Association said, "We kind of view this as a direct transfer from the consumers' pockets to retailers' bottom lines. Who ends up feeling the burden from this? Financial institutions lose a revenue stream that allows them to offer other services to low-income consumers."[46]

The retailers were equally active. Home Depot stated, "Any relief as it pertains to these fees will give Home Depot the ability to reduce our cost of doing business …. Such benefits are likely to include lower prices and investment in the business to better serve customers."[47] Scott Mason of Lowe's Companies said, "Every dollar we pay the credit-card companies is a dollar we can't pass on to consumers or use to hire employees. Literally you are talking about hundreds of millions of dollars."[48] Eric Hausman of Target Corporation said, "They do cost us hundreds of millions of dollars—an expense we

cannot control—and become part of the cost of goods sold, which many people do not realize."[49]

The conferees eliminated the regulation of network fees, and the shares of Visa and MasterCard increased by 5.0 percent and 4.3 percent, respectively. The House and Senate conferees failed to agree on a rule for interchange fees, but instead mandated a study to be conducted and a deadline to act. The language in the conference agreement directed the Federal Reserve to limit the interchange fee to a level that was "reasonable and proportional" to the actual costs of processing transactions. The agreement gave the Federal Reserve 9 months to study the issue and set a limit on the fees.[50] John Emling, a lobbyist representing the Retail Industry Leaders Association, said, "We have the data ready and we have the right people ready to go to the Fed, and we've had an ongoing dialogue with the Fed."[51]

Retailers would also be allowed to offer discounts to people who paid in cash, but the discounts could not depend on the issuer of the card that would otherwise have been used. Merchants were also allowed to run their debit card transactions on two networks, so a transaction paid with a MasterCard debit card could be processed on VisaNet. These provisions gave merchants greater bargaining power relative to the card issuer.

The Federal Reserve was required to issue a final rule by April 21, 2011, and in advance it issued a proposed rule that would cap the swipe fee at $0.12. The average charges under the current system were $0.44, so the card issuers would lose huge amounts of revenue. The Boston Consulting Group estimated that card issuers would lose $9 billion in revenue because of the Durbin Amendment and another $16 billion because of the Federal Reserve's anticipated rule making and the Credit CARD Act of 2009.[52]

Banks with assets less than $10 billion were exempted from the regulation, but even though their fees were exempt, credit unions and community banks were concerned about competitive forces. The Fed's proposed rate generated renewed political activity by small community banks, which argued that they would be forced by competitive pressures to meet the $0.12 rate. The banks said this would force them to raise fees on depositors' accounts or reduce the financial products they offer. In response the Financial Institutions and Consumer Credit subcommittee of the House Financial Services Committee held a hearing on the Fed's rate setting. In testimony Federal Reserve Chairman Ben Bernanke said, "It is possible the exemption will not be effective in the marketplace." Sheila Bair, Chairman of the Federal Deposit Insurance Corporation said, "I think the likelihood of this hurting community banks and requiring them to increase fees they charge for accounts is much greater than any tiny benefits retail

---

[43]*Financial Times*, May 15, 2010.

[44]Ibid.

[45]*Wall Street Journal*, June 22, 2010.

[46]Ibid.

[47]Ibid.

[48]Ibid.

[49]Ibid.

[50]The requirements were included in the Dodd-Frank Wall Street Reform and Consumer Protection Act.

[51]*New York Times*, June 27, 2010.

[52]*Wall Street Journal*, February 8, 2011.

customers maybe get from any savings." Senator Durbin said that Chairman Bernanke was "just basically wrong."[53] The Fed announced that it was reserving judgment about the final rule until all the comments received had been considered.

When the proposed rule was announced, the card issuers and banks added a new dimension to the issue in arguing that the Dodd–Frank Act directed it to set a swipe fee that was limited to the "reasonable and proportional" cost of transactions but the Fed had ignored debit card fraud which cost the card issuers and banks $1.4 billion in 2009.[54] The banks also claimed that the reductions in swipe fees would benefit large retailers rather than the small retailers that the reduction in swipe fees was supposed to benefit. John P. Buckley Jr. of the Gerber Federal Credit Union, told a congressional subcommittee, "I am appalled that our members will shoulder tremendous financial burden and still be on the hook for fraud loss while large retailers receive a giant windfall at the hands of the government."[55] The banks referred to a comment made by a Home Depot executive that the company would gain $35 million from the reduction.

The retailers countered with a fly-in by convenience store owners who complained that high swipe fees hurt their competitiveness. "'These fees are stunting business growth and hurting efforts to hire more workers and expand operations,' Douglas Kanter, a lobbyist for the Merchants Payments Coalition, a retailer trade group, said recently."[56]

Preparation Questions

1. Which interest group, the retailers or the card companies and card issuers, is the stronger? How important are the small banks and credit unions that issue cards?
2. Will a lower swipe fee be passed on to consumers or captured by retailers?
3. Will small banks and credit unions be forced by competition to lower their charges?
4. Is the Federal Reserve likely to reconsider its proposed rule? Which interest group will have the greatest influence on its decision?
5. What strategy should the card companies and the large bank issuers use at this point?

Repeal of the Luxury Tax

In 1990 Congress, with the acquiescence of the Bush administration, enacted legislation imposing a 10 percent federal luxury tax on the sale of furs and jewelry costing more than $10,000, automobiles costing more than $30,000, boats costing more than $100,000, and aircraft costing more than $250,000 (except for aircraft used at least 80 percent for business). Effective in 1991, the tax was applied to the difference between the price and the tax base, so the tax on a $1,000,000 yacht was $90,000. The luxury tax was a component of the Deficit Reduction Act of 1990 and was viewed not as a significant source of additional revenue but as a symbol that the rich should bear a larger share of the tax burden. The tax yielded $251 million in 1991 and $146 million in the first half of 1992 with the vast majority coming from the sale of automobiles.

As the economy slowed, sales of boats costing at least $100,000 began to decrease, falling from 16,000 in 1987 to 9,100 in 1990. In 1992 after the luxury tax was imposed, only 4,200 boats were sold. Sales of boats 35 feet or longer fell from 1,300 in 1989 to 400 in 1991, with sales revenue falling from $2.5 billion to $800 million. Employment in the industry decreased from 600,000 to 400,000 in 1993. Hatteras Yachts of New Bern, North Carolina, experienced a 50 percent decrease in sales and was forced to lay off 1,000 of its 1,800 employees. Viking Yacht of New Gretna, New Jersey, was forced to cut its workforce to 65 people. Yacht manufacturers from Minnesota, Wisconsin, Maine, Connecticut, and Florida experienced similar declines. As one potential customer who decided to stick

with his current yacht rather than purchase a new one said, "I don't care how much you spend for a boat, $190,000 in taxes is ludicrous."[57] Some purchasers of yachts registered their boats in the Bahamas and the Cayman Islands to avoid the luxury and state sales taxes. The National Marine Manufacturers Association and its members blamed the collapse of the market on the luxury tax.

The light aircraft industry was also hard hit, as were the other industries subject to the tax. Jaguar auto sales fell by 55 percent, and the company decided to rebate the luxury tax of over $3,000 to customers.

The luxury tax had been enacted by inserting it in a large tax bill during conference committee deliberations, and opponents had little opportunity to oppose it. Once in place and its effects were realized, opposition mounted. "The purpose [of the tax] was to tax the rich and their toys," said Republican Senator John H. Chafee of Rhode Island, a big boat-building state. "What it really did was hurt the toymakers."[58] Senator Robert Dole (R-KS) of Kansas, where light aircraft manufacturers were located, said, "A lot of middle-class people are losing their jobs."[59]

Opponents of the tax pressured Congress and the Bush administration, and Senator Dole introduced a bill to repeal the tax. The repeal bill was included in a more comprehensive bill, but Congress was unable to reach agreement on the package. Opponents saw another opportunity in the spring of 1993 as President Clinton pushed for a deficit reduction package that

[53]Ibid.
[54]*New York Times,* March 8, 2011.
[55]Ibid.
[56]Ibid.
[57]*BusinessWeek,* August 3, 1993.
[58]Ibid.
[59]*Wall Street Journal,* June 12, 1991.

would include increases in personal and corporate income taxes in addition to an energy tax. ▪

Preparation Questions

1. Use supply-and-demand analysis to identify the incidence of the luxury tax for producers and consumers. Summarize your analysis in a distributive politics spreadsheet.

2. Are the consumers or producers of luxury goods more likely to be politically active on this issue? Why?

3. Are the interests of U.S. automobile manufacturers aligned with those of yacht builders?

4. What is the nature of the politics of this issue?

5. Are the opponents of the luxury tax likely to be successful?

NONMARKET STRATEGIES FOR GOVERNMENT ARENAS

INTRODUCTION

For many firms and industries the rules of the game are established by legislation. For 65 years the Glass-Steagall Act imposed walls between the banking, insurance, and securities industries, and after decades of effort by industry members the act was repealed in 1999 by the Gramm-Leach-Bliley Act. The Telecommunications Act of 1996 opened telecommunications markets but left some barriers to entry in certain segments of the market. Congress has regularly passed legislation imposing a moratorium on any new taxes on the Internet.

Companies and other interests use nonmarket strategies to participate effectively and responsibly in nonmarket issues addressed by legislative institutions. The First Amendment to the Constitution grants to persons, including companies, the right to free speech and the right to petition government. Business and other interests thus have the right to participate in government processes, and that participation requires effective strategies. This chapter considers the strategy process, presents generic nonmarket strategies, and provides examples. The integration with market strategies is addressed through the chapter cases. The context is U.S. institutions, but the approach is also applicable to other countries, as indicated in Part IV of the book.

Strategy formulation in the nonmarket environment differs in a number of ways from its counterpart in the market environment. First, nonmarket issues attract a broader set of participants than those involved in markets. Second, important components of nonmarket strategies are implemented in public view, which requires sensitivity to the concerns of that broader set of participants. Third, the logic of collective and individual nonmarket action is different from the logic of market action. Fourth, in the nonmarket environment issues are not resolved by voluntary agreements as in markets but in most cases by government institutions with the power to set and enforce the rules of the game. In their strategy formulation and implementation, companies and other interests must ensure that their strategies are not only effective but also responsible. In the framework for the analysis of nonmarket issues presented in Figure 2-5, nonmarket strategies must be evaluated for responsibility in both the screening and the choice stages.

This chapter first considers the issue of responsible nonmarket action and the legal basis for business participation in government policy processes. Then, a perspective on understanding the outcomes of nonmarket issues is presented to provide a foundation for strategy formulation. The process of nonmarket strategy formulation is developed with a focus on strategic assets. Three basic strategies are then presented and illustrated with examples. A representation strategy is based on the constituency connection between voters and their representatives and involves directing constituent pressure to government officeholders. A majority building strategy involves building a majority to support or oppose legislation and focuses on pivotal legislators. Informational strategies focus on the strategic provision of technical and political information to officeholders. These generic strategies are then related to the nature of nonmarket competition as considered in Chapter 6. Implementation of nonmarket strategies is the subject of Chapter 8.

RESPONSIBLE NONMARKET ACTION

In the long run, a firm has influence on nonmarket issues to the extent that its interests are aligned with those of people. In the short run, however, firms and such other interests as labor unions and activists can have greater influence. An important issue thus is the appropriateness of interests attempting to influence public decisions. In addressing this issue, an analogy to markets is useful. In market competition, a firm that faces little competition has market power that enables it to restrict output and raise its price. Society has two responses to such a situation. First, it may rely on market forces. A high price can attract entrants to the industry and provides incentives to develop substitute products that can reduce the market power of the incumbent firm. Second, society may control the exercise of market power through, for example, antitrust or regulation, considered in Chapters 9 and 10, respectively.

In nonmarket competition, society also has two responses to the exercise of nonmarket power. First, it can rely on countervailing influences from opposing interests to mitigate that power. The pluralism of competing interests can be effective in limiting power, but participation can be asymmetric because of the free-rider problem and other costs of organizing and taking nonmarket action. In some cases, advocacy groups can represent the interests of those with high costs, and watchdog groups can alert the public and government officeholders, thereby limiting the exercise of nonmarket power. Second, society can control the exercise of nonmarket power or require disclosure of nonmarket actions. For example, corporations are prohibited from making contributions to federal election campaigns, and contributions by a political action committee (PAC) are strictly limited and must be publicly reported. In addition, actions such as hiring a lobbyist and holding ex parte meetings with regulators require public disclosure. These responses to the exercise of nonmarket power, however, leave a substantial gray area in which firms must exercise judgment, and at times restraint, to ensure that nonmarket strategies are responsible and do not exceed the limits of public acceptability. The Chapter 8 case *Responsible Lobbying?* addresses these concerns.

Criticisms of Business Nonmarket Action

BUSINESS OBJECTIVES AND THE PUBLIC INTEREST   One criticism of nonmarket action by business is that it can be contrary to the public interest. What is in the public interest, however, is often the subject of fundamental disagreement. For example, the antidumping laws that impose duties on imported goods sold at lower prices than in the exporting country are viewed by economists as harmful to consumers and the economy. Yet, antidumping laws have been in place for over 80 years in the United States, have been adopted by most countries, and are allowed by the World Trade Organization agreements. Firms, labor unions, interest groups, and governments use the antidumping laws against foreign imports, even though that may be contrary to some conceptions of the public interest.

From a pluralist perspective, the public interest is identified by the interests of individuals and groups in the context of political institutions. The public interest thus can be advanced by business participation, since the interests of firms are ultimately the interests of those who have a stake in their performance, including shareholders, employees, retirees, customers, suppliers, and the communities in which they operate.

Firms have the right to participate in political processes irrespective of the particular interests they represent. In *First National Bank of Boston v. Bellotti,* 435 U.S. 765 (1978), the Supreme Court held that the First Amendment protects the right of corporations to make expenditures and participate in the political competition on a state ballot proposition. The Bank of Boston had challenged a Massachusetts law prohibiting a corporation from making expenditures to influence the vote on public referenda that did not "materially" affect the corporation. The Supreme Court held that the Bank of Boston's right under the First Amendment derived less from its right to speak than from the public's right to hear what others have to say. The court stated that freedom of speech "embraces at least the liberty to discuss publicly and truthfully all matters of public concern without previous restraint or fear of subsequent punishment ...." In addition, the court ruled that a state could not single out a set of entities, such as corporations, because of the interests they represent. The court stated that the prohibition in the Massachusetts law was "an impermissible legislative prohibition of speech based on the identity of the interests that spokesmen may represent in public debate over controversial issues ..."

Two years later, the Supreme Court overturned a ruling by the Public Service Commission of New York that had prohibited Consolidated Edison from including messages about public issues in its billing envelopes.[1] The court held that the prohibition was an impermissible restriction on speech. In *Pacific Gas & Electric Co. v. Public Utilities Commission of California,* 475 U.S. 1 (1986), the Supreme Court ruled that a company cannot be compelled to include messages from other groups in its billing envelopes. The California Public Utilities Commission (PUC) had ordered Pacific Gas & Electric to include an insert from a consumer group with its bills. The

---

[1]*Consolidated Edison Company v. Public Service Commission of New York,* 199 S. Ct. 2326 (1980).

Supreme Court held that a corporation cannot be forced to associate with ideas to which it objects any more than can an individual. The majority opinion stated that the PUC order "discriminates on the basis of the viewpoints of the selected speakers and also impermissibly requires appellant to associate with speech with which appellant may disagree ... that kind of forced response is antithetical to the free discussion that the First Amendment seeks to foster."

The rights accorded corporations by the First Amendment can also override certain restrictions imposed by legislatures. In *Eastern Railroad Conference v. Noerr Motor Freight,* 365 U.S. 127 (1961), the Supreme Court ruled that collective nonmarket action, such as joint lobbying to influence government, does not violate antitrust laws against collusion because the First Amendment grants the right to petition government. Firms thus have the right to form and participate in coalitions and associations to conduct nonmarket activity.[2]

UNWARRANTED POWER In *Austin v. Michigan Chamber of Commerce,* 494 U.S. 652 (1990), the Supreme Court upheld a Michigan law that prohibited corporations from making independent expenditures on behalf of a candidate.[3] Justice Thurgood Marshall, writing for the majority, referred to "the corrosive and distorting effects of immense aggregations of wealth that are accumulated with the help of the corporate form." In his dissent, Justice Antonin Scalia wrote, "The fact that corporations amass large treasuries is not sufficient justification for the suppression of political speech unless one thinks it would be lawful to prohibit men and women whose net worth is above a certain figure from endorsing political candidates." These opinions reflect disagreement about whether a corporation has the same freedom of speech as a person and whether its resources pose a threat to democratic processes.

The criticism that business has unwarranted power also arises because some interests may not participate due to their high costs of taking action. Other interests thus are necessarily "overrepresented." Corporate participation in political activities, however, can give voice to people whose interests might otherwise be unrepresented. Just as unions represent their members, corporations can give voice to their stakeholders.[4] Firms represent the interests of their shareholders and pensioners when they act to increase shareholder value. Similarly, firms often represent the interests of employees and suppliers on issues affecting sales, which determine employment and purchases from suppliers. In the Chapter 8 case *Wal-Mart and Its Urban Expansion Strategy,* the company's interests were aligned with those of the prospective employees who would be hired if its stores were approved by the Chicago city council. Firms may also represent the interests of customers. In the Part II integrative case, Amazon represents the interests of its customers when it opposes state efforts to tax online sales.

Often, the nonmarket power of business is controlled because it is naturally divided. Business differs from many single-interest groups because business interests are often fragmented, leaving firms on opposite sides of issues. U.S. automobile manufacturers and auto dealers were on the opposite sides of the enactment of lemon laws. American exporters interested in opening foreign markets to domestic goods oppose protectionist measures because they are concerned about retaliation by other countries. Generic and brand-name pharmaceutical companies are on opposite sides of many issues, including patent enforcement and market exclusivity. In the Chapter 6 case *Business versus Business,* retailers opposed credit card companies and issuers over the level of credit card swipe fees. Because business interests on many issues are fragmented, so is business power.

Business nonmarket power is also checked by the power of other interest groups. There are many well-funded environmental groups, and they have been effective in advancing their agendas through both public and private politics. Activist groups also serve as a check on business power. The news media and the social media play an important role in monitoring the nonmarket activities of business and other interest groups.

---

[2]The protection of the First Amendment does not extend to "sham" organizations. See also *Mine Workers v. Pennington,* 381 U.S. 637 (1965), and *California Motor Transport Co. v. Trucking Unlimited,* 404 U.S. 508 (1972). The Noerr-Pennington doctrine may not apply to nongovernmental legislative bodies such as standard-setting bodies; see *Allied Tube & Conduit Corp. v. Indian Head,* 486 U.S. 492 (1988).

[3]An independent expenditure is made directly, for example, by taking out an advertisement supporting a candidate rather than through a candidate's campaign organization.

[4]See Hirschman (1970) for an analysis of the voice issue.

Business interests can also be aligned with activist groups. Shaffer and Ostas (2001) studied the enactment of state automobile lemon laws. Prior to the enactment of the laws, car buyers could seek recourse in the case of a lemon by filing a lawsuit under warranty law. The defendant in a lawsuit was generally the auto dealer that sold the car, since the automobile manufacturer was shielded by a privity rule that limited a consumer's ability to sue down the supply chain to the producer. Lemon laws were pushed by consumer and activist groups, yet the enactment of these laws was due more to the support automobile dealers. The lemon laws in most states shifted responsibility from auto dealers to auto manufacturers, and the 25,000 dealerships located in every congressional district worked hard for the laws. On this issue auto dealers' interests were aligned with those of consumer and of activist groups.

The abstract ability to exercise power is also not the same as its actual use. Business Political Action Committees (PACs) could make their campaign contributions on a partisan basis, but instead they contribute to both Democrats and Republicans. In contrast, labor PACs contribute almost exclusively to Democrats. Business may also exercise self-restraint on the use of its power. In the example presented in Chapter 6, because of its broader nonmarket agenda, Boeing did not mobilize its supplier network to oppose restrictions on the tax treatment of leasing to foreign customers. Similarly, an increasing number of companies do not have PACs.

THE POSSIBILITY OF MANIPULATION   A third criticism of business nonmarket activity goes beyond interests and power and focuses on manipulation. Manipulation can take two basic forms. One involves misrepresentation or activities that play on ignorance, fear, or biases. As considered in Chapter 8, providing false or misleading information rarely is beneficial in the long run. An example is the tobacco company CEOs swearing in a congressional hearing that they believed that cigarette smoking was not addictive. Enron consistently misrepresented information about its financial condition and the propriety of its financing deals, as considered in the Chapter 20 case *The Collapse of Enron*. In the framework for nonmarket analysis presented in Chapter 2, nonmarket strategies with these characteristics are to be rejected in the screening stage.

The second form involves exploiting institutional features. For example, a company may exploit a gray area or a loophole in the law that it knows will be closed by the government. Long-Term Capital, a darling of the financial services industry until its collapse in the 1990s, was found by a federal court to have engaged in illegal tax-beneficial deals that were without economic substance. In the Chapter 10 case *Enron Power Marketing and the California Market* the company exploited flaws in the design of the California electricity market and was accused of price manipulation.

As another example, to induce pharmaceutical companies to bring generic drugs to market quickly when a patent on a drug expired, Congress passed a law granting a 6-month exclusivity period to the first company to bring a generic drug to market. Pharmaceutical companies with drugs whose patents were about to expire responded with "authorized generics" in which the companies contracted with generic drug makers to bring authorized copies of the patented drugs to market, thereby reducing the incentives of other generic drug companies to enter the market. In the context of the framework in Chapter 2, strategies that exploit institutional features are to be evaluated in the screening stage to determine whether they are responsible.

The distinction between participation in and manipulation of public processes can be a fine one. In 1984 Johnson & Johnson, the maker of Tylenol, the best-selling nonprescription pain reliever, faced a new competitive challenge when the Food and Drug Administration (FDA) allowed the nonprescription sale of the drug ibuprofen, an antiarthritis drug previously available only by prescription. Upjohn estimated that within 2 years ibuprofen would garner 10–15 percent of the $1.3 billion pain-reliever market. Bristol-Myers planned to market Upjohn's ibuprofen under the brand name Nuprin, and American Home Products planned to market its version under the brand name Advil.

To counter this competitive challenge, Johnson & Johnson filed a lawsuit against the FDA challenging the sufficiency of the warnings on ibuprofen labels as well as the procedures under which it had approved the nonprescription sale. The suit alleged that the FDA had authority over the advertising only of prescription drugs, not over-the-counter drugs. Johnson & Johnson claimed injury by the alleged improper approval, stating that it would have a "direct and immediate impact" on Tylenol sales. Bristol-Myers responded, calling the suit "an arrogant and unconscionable effort by Johnson & Johnson to keep an important new drug off the nonprescription pain-relief market."[5]

By 1989 the tables had turned as American Home Products, which makes Anacin as well as Advil, asked the FDA to require drugs containing acetaminophen to include in their labels a warning about possible kidney damage from extended use.[6] The objective was to handicap the market leader, Tylenol, which has acetaminophen as its principal ingredient. The tables turned further in 1994 as American Home Products filed suit against Syntex and its marketing partner Procter & Gamble, charging that their FDA-approved advertising for their recently approved pain reliever Aleve involved "unwarranted and unsubstantiated claims." Were the Johnson & Johnson and American Home Products' actions responsible uses of the companies' standing before the FDA and the courts, or did they involve manipulative use of institutional procedures? The Chapter 14 case *Patent Games: Plavix* considers another set of strategies used by pharmaceutical companies.

NONMARKET STRATEGY FORMULATION

Managers and Nonmarket Strategies

Because of the importance of nonmarket issues for the performance of firms, responsibility for formulating nonmarket strategies ultimately rests with management. From the lower levels of a firm, nonmarket issues often are seen as regrettable complications that reduce autonomy and create headaches. The higher managers are in an organization, however, the more likely they are to appreciate that the progress of these issues can be affected by the firm's participation. They are also more likely to be involved in the formulation and implementation of nonmarket strategies.

Most managers address nonmarket issues on an episodic rather than a continual basis. They thus need parsimonious frameworks for formulating effective and responsible strategies. Much of the task of strategy formulation involves bringing together the approach to nonmarket analysis presented in Chapter 6, institutional knowledge, and the analysis of the nonmarket environment developed in Part I of this book. The following sections present this approach and provide examples.

As indicated in Figure 7-1, the nonmarket strategy of a firm competes in institutional arenas against the strategies of other interests. The outcome of this competition often involves

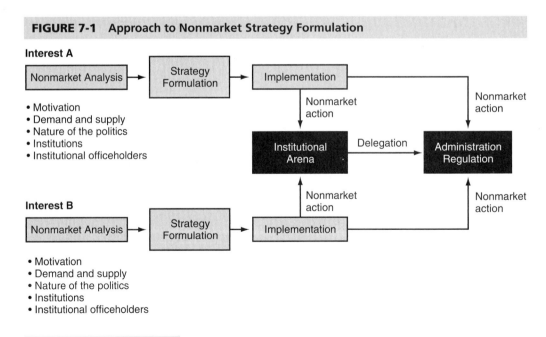

FIGURE 7-1   Approach to Nonmarket Strategy Formulation

Interest A

Nonmarket Analysis → Strategy Formulation → Implementation

• Motivation
• Demand and supply
• Nature of the politics
• Institutions
• Institutional officeholders

Nonmarket action → Institutional Arena — Delegation → Administration Regulation

Nonmarket action

Interest B

Nonmarket Analysis → Strategy Formulation → Implementation

• Motivation
• Demand and supply
• Nature of the politics
• Institutions
• Institutional officeholders

Nonmarket action

Nonmarket action

---

[5]The suit failed, and ibuprofen was marketed on a nonprescription basis beginning in 1985.

[6]The basis for the submission was a May 1989 study by the National Institute of Environmental Health Sciences that suggested that daily use of drugs containing acetaminophen for over a year could cause kidney damage. This possibility was confirmed in a study reported in 1994 in the *New England Journal of Medicine.* In 2011 Johnson & Johnson reduced the maximum daily dose of Extra Strength Tylenol from 4,000 milligrams to 3,000 milligrams.

the delegation of administrative responsibility to an agency or a regulatory commission. For example, the interest group competition over the specifics of the Dodd-Frank Financial System Reform Act was intense in 2010, and Congress delegated most of the details of the reforms to the regulatory agencies as considered in Chapter 11. The interest group competition over the details was as intense as it was for the act itself, resulting in delays in implementation. Nonmarket strategies thus focus both on the initial institutional arena in which an issue is addressed and on the subsequent delegation to administrative or regulatory agencies. The foundation for those strategies is nonmarket analysis.

NONMARKET ANALYSIS   Nonmarket analysis forms the basis for effective strategies. Building on Part I and Chapter 6, nonmarket analysis includes the following components:

- Assessing the characteristics of the issue and where it is in its life cycle
- Identifying the interests affected by the issue
- Assessing motivations and incentives
- Analyzing the likely demand for and supply of nonmarket action
- Assessing the nature of the politics of the issue
- Identifying the institutional arenas in which the issue will be addressed
- Assessing institutional characteristics
- Identifying the relevant institutional officeholders and their constituent and policy interests

If the issue is primarily distributive, the Wilson-Lowi matrix (Figure 6-2) provides a first step in assessing the nature of the competition. To predict the likely outcome, the demand for and costs of generating nonmarket action must be assessed to determine which interests are likely to participate and their effectiveness. The distributive politics spreadsheet (Figure 6-3) provides a format for summarizing this analysis. If the issue has moral dimensions, the likelihood of morally motivated nonmarket action must be assessed.

OBJECTIVES   The specification of objectives is an essential component of a nonmarket strategy not only because objectives focus attention but also because they affect which interests will be aligned with and against a firm. In the example in Chapter 6, the objective of seeking an exemption for job-creating export leases put Boeing on the opposite side of the issue from the tax-exempt organizations. Contingent objectives must also be specified and pursued in case the primary objectives cannot be achieved. The primary objective may be the defeat of a legislative proposal, but if the proposal is likely to pass in some form, a more realistic objective is to seek wording that lessens its impact, provides alternative means of compliance, or allows time to adjust. In the chapter case *Wal-Mart and Health Care Policy*, breaking with the retail industry, Wal-Mart chose to support the Obama administration's call for an employer mandate. The choice of objectives is a central feature of the chapter case *Carried Interest Taxation*.

SELECTION OF INSTITUTIONAL ARENAS   In which institutional arenas nonmarket issues are addressed is typically determined by the forces that put the issues on the firm's agenda. Boeing had no alternative but to address the foreign leasing issue in Congress. In some cases, however, a firm has the opportunity to choose the institutional arena. A firm injured by unfair foreign competition can file a petition for relief under a number of sections of U.S. trade law. As considered in Chapter 19, the section selected determines the process and the institutions that will govern it. The processes differ—some are administrative, whereas others encourage negotiations with the other countries involved. In the Chapter 19 case *Cemex and Antidumping*, Cemex, the Mexican company that has become the world's third largest cement producer, sought to overturn an antidumping order in the institutional arenas of the International Trade Commission, the International Trade Administration, the U.S. Court of International Trade, the General Agreement on Tariffs and Trade, the North American Free Trade Agreement, and finally Congress. Similarly, high-tech companies addressed the issue of frivolous securities fraud lawsuits first in the courts, then in Congress, then in a state referendum, and finally back in Congress.

Firms may also pursue an objective at either the federal or the state level. In the Chapter 8 case *Internet Taxation*, opponents of Internet sales taxes worked at the state level to stop new taxes and worked at the federal level to impose a moratorium on new taxes. The states began to impose taxes in the 2010s, and Amazon fought the taxes on a state-by-state basis, as considered in the Part II integrative case *Amazon.com and the Amazon Tax*. Firms seeking protection from hostile takeovers had little success in Congress or with the Securities and Exchange Commission, so they turned their attention to the states. Pennsylvania enacted a law that made it more difficult to acquire firms incorporated there. Business has had only limited success at the federal level in its attempts to reform the liability system, but it has had success at the state level.

NONMARKET STRATEGY CHOICE   Strategies are the link between objectives and the specific actions taken to achieve them. When there is competition among interests, as in the case of interest group politics, the effectiveness of a strategy depends on the strategies of others active on the issue. Strategy formulation thus is not a linear process but instead involves adjustments that take into account the strategies of other interests as well as the progress of the issue through its life cycle. One aspect of the strategy challenge therefore is to anticipate the strategies of other participants. The chapter case *Carried Interest Taxation* considers such a situation.

One basic principle underlying strategy formulation in interest group politics is that the weight of nonmarket action for and against an alternative affects the outcome. Therefore, a strategy should increase the benefits to those with aligned interests and reduce their costs of taking nonmarket action. For example, a firm may reduce the costs of participation for its employees, suppliers, and customers. Conversely, a strategy could reduce the opposing side's incentives to take nonmarket action. Identifying substitutes, for example, can reduce the incentives to oppose the objective sought. As discussed in Appendix B, the Daylight Saving Time Coalition (DSTC) effectively eliminated opposition by the National Association of Broadcasters by including in the legislation a provision asking the Federal Communications Commission to authorize AM radio stations to begin broadcasting before sunrise. In the Boeing example, opposition from tax-exempt organizations was reduced by grandfathering those deals already under way. In the Chapter 8 case *Wal-Mart and Its Urban Expansion Strategy,* Wal-Mart sought a way to reduce the opposition by unions.

The nonmarket strategies available to firms are the same as those available to other interest groups, but their appropriateness and effectiveness can differ. Activists often rely on high-profile campaigns to attract the attention of the media and the public. Such strategies are seldom effective for business and, if undertaken, may embroil the firm in a highly visible controversy that constrains its ability to act on other issues. The set of effective nonmarket strategies for firms thus is often smaller than the set of strategies used by other interests.

UNILATERAL AND COALITION STRATEGIES   A firm may have a choice between forming a coalition or acting unilaterally to address an issue. If the issue could increase industry demand, the firms in the industry have aligned interests. Such issues are best addressed at the industry level through an ad hoc coalition or an industry association. Even if the firms in an industry address an issue collectively, an individual firm may choose to supplement the industry strategy.

An industry strategy potentially suffers from two problems: the incentive to free ride and the heterogeneity of interests. In the Part II integrative case online retailers collectively opposed the collection of sales taxes on online sales, but most retailers chose to free-ride on the efforts of Amazon.com.

On many issues the interests of firms in an industry differ. The greater the heterogeneity of their interests, the more difficult it is to form a coalition. In addition, firms may have different views about the best strategy. As the AIDS pandemic grew, the pharmaceutical industry came under nonmarket pressure to increase the availability of AIDS drugs to developing countries that lacked the means to pay for them. An industry response was precluded by the fact that only a few companies had AIDS drugs. Those companies sought to address the issue jointly, but Pfizer objected to the preferential pricing approach of the other companies. Pfizer broke ranks and provided its drug at no cost.

NONMARKET ASSETS   Firms and interest groups build their strategies on nonmarket assets. Access to institutional officeholders is an important asset to be developed and maintained. Access to members of Congress is a necessary condition for effective lobbying. That access can be based on the constituency connection, campaign contributions, or a reputation for providing reliable information. Some firms obtain access by hiring former government officials or retaining well-connected advisors and consultants. Some firms attempt to develop personal relationships between their managers and government officeholders.

In the chapter case Wal-Mart supported an employer mandate and sought a seat at the bargaining table as the Obama administration worked to build support for its reform. Opposition to the opening of Wal-Mart stores in cities had stalled its urban expansion strategy, but in 2011 it found an opening by joining with First Lady Michelle Obama to bring fresh and nutritious foods to "food deserts, " as considered in Chapter 8.

The reputation of the firm and its top management is also an important asset. The success of Intel has been due both to its leading-edge technology and respect for its leaders. Reputation also depends on how responsible are the nonmarket actions of the firm and its managers. Actions that are deceptive, manipulative, or represent an abuse of power can quickly damage a reputation and depreciate its value. Government officeholders as well as interest and activist groups can have long memories.

The costs of collective action are a significant obstacle to nonmarket action, so any means of lowering those costs represents an important asset. A trade association reduces the costs of collective action, particularly for industries with many firms and for issues on which it is important to present a common rather than a fragmented position. The U.S. timber industry responded to the sustainability movement by developing within its industry association its own sustainability standards.

When seeking legislation, it is often effective for the firms in the industry to adopt a common position. When an industry seeks to defeat legislation, a fragmented position may be more effective by revealing to officeholders a wider set of contentious dimensions and adverse consequences of the legislation.

THE RENT CHAIN   An important nonmarket asset is the alignment of the firm's interests with those of constituents of government officeholders. The value of this asset depends on the number of people affected, their resources, and their coverage of political jurisdictions. A large employment base or an extensive supply or distribution network is a potentially important asset. In the Part II integrative case, Amazon.com used its affiliates as a component of its strategy to stop state taxation of online sales. The value of the asset increases as its coverage of political jurisdictions broadens, since greater coverage provides a broader base for lobbying and grassroots activities. Automobile dealers represent an important nonmarket asset of the automobile industry because they are numerous, have substantial resources, and provide extensive coverage of congressional districts. This asset, however, can be a liability when interests are not aligned, as in the case of the enactment of lemon laws.

Porter (1985) introduced the concept of a value chain that identifies the stages of a firm's operations in which value is created for its owners. Nonmarket strategies are also directed at creating value, and the *rent chain* is the analogous concept.[7] The underlying principle of the rent chain is that the greater the rents affected by a nonmarket issue, the greater are the incentives to take nonmarket action to obtain or protect those rents. The rent chain represents a basis for influence in the nonmarket environment, particularly in the context of distributive politics.

A rent is a surplus. In the long run the rent of a firm equals its profit, but in the short run a rent can differ from profit because of sunk costs. Rents are also earned by the factors of production. Employees earn a rent if their wages and benefits are higher than what they could earn in alternative employment. When jobs are threatened by a nonmarket issue, employees have an incentive to act to protect their rents. Labor unions are thus one of the strongest supporters of protectionist measures when the jobs of their members are threatened by imports. The United Steel Workers and steel producers joined to seek quotas on imports, as considered in Chapter 19. Rents can also be earned by distributors, retailers, and customers, which can motivate them to take nonmarket action. Rents are thus a fundamental source of incentives for nonmarket action.

A firm's rent chain includes those stakeholders that benefit from their interactions with the firm. When a nonmarket alternative, for example, would increase the demand for a firm's products, the employees and suppliers benefit in addition to shareholders. Interests are then aligned along the rent chain, and there is the potential for collective action. Because rents are earned by the factors of production—in supply chains, in the channels of distribution, and by customers—the rent chain is larger than the value chain. The relationship between the rent chain and the value chain is illustrated in Figure 7-2. To the extent that jobs, supply contracts, alliance relationships, and communities are affected, the firm has an additional basis for

---

[7]This concept is developed in more detail in Baron (1995a).

FIGURE 7-2 The Rent Chain

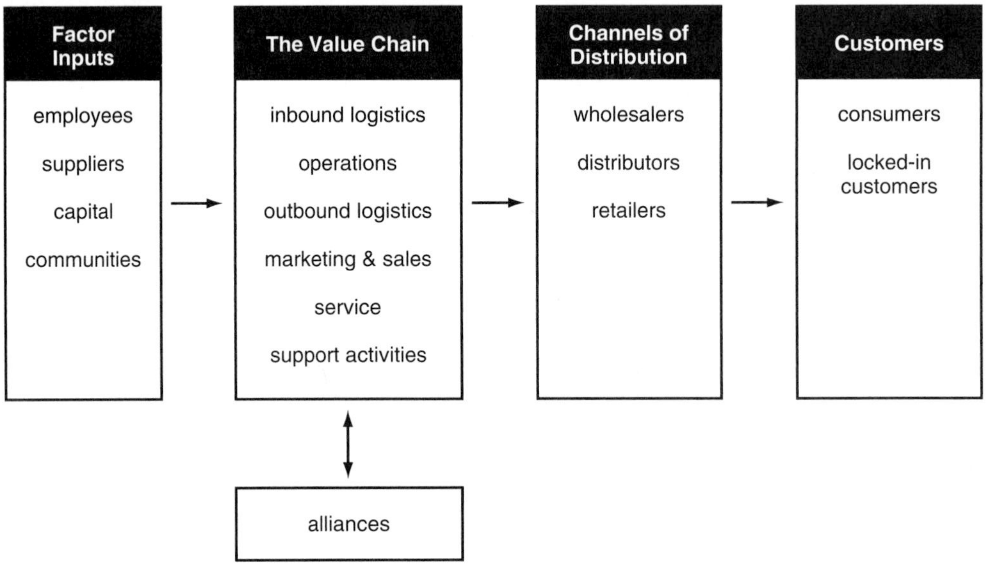

Factor Inputs	The Value Chain	Channels of Distribution	Customers
employees	inbound logistics	wholesalers	consumers
suppliers	operations	distributors	locked-in customers
capital	outbound logistics	retailers	
communities	marketing & sales		
	service		
	support activities		

alliances

appealing to government officeholders. Grassroots strategies are based on the rent chain, and lobbying also draws strength from information about the effects of alternatives on the rents of constituents.

The rent chain provides two types of strategic advantage. First, it can provide enfranchisement, giving the firm the right, or opportunity, to participate in public processes. Many U.S. pharmaceutical firms believed it was important to locate facilities in Japan to be able to participate effectively in the regulatory and consultative processes that set drug prices. In a country where market opportunities are controlled by government regulation and where administrative directives are pervasive, locating a portion of the rent chain in that country can be important for obtaining access to legislators and regulators. Second, a rent chain can provide the basis for generating nonmarket action through the constituency connection. Toshiba's strategy, considered later in the chapter, included such a component.

The rent chain can also be mobilized on issues outside governmental institutions. In 1992 Wal-Mart was the subject of a critical story on NBC's *Dateline,* alleging that some of the company's Asian suppliers used child labor. The story also raised concerns about whether Wal-Mart's Buy America program for creating jobs by sourcing products in the United States was being compromised. In response to the allegations, several of Wal-Mart's suppliers, including large companies such as General Electric Lighting and smaller companies such as Brinkman Corporation and Cheyenne Lamps, took out advertisements in newspapers with headlines, "We Support Wal-Mart's Buy America Program."

Implementation

Implementation of nonmarket strategies pertains to the selection of specific actions and the assignment of tasks to organizational units and individual managers. This can involve designating managers to lobby in Washington, undertaking a grassroots strategy, hiring a Washington law firm to provide technical advice on a legislative issue, or forming an ad hoc coalition. The specifics of strategy implementation are considered in Chapter 8.

Strategies are implemented over time, so contingent strategies should be developed. This is particularly important because the nonmarket competition on an issue may move from one institutional arena to another. In the context of Figure 7-1, a firm that fails to achieve its objective in a legislature arena may continue its nonmarket activity before the administrative agency to which responsibility has been delegated. If unsuccessful at that stage, the firm may take the issue to an administrative or judicial arena. In the Chapter 14 case, *Obesity and McLawsuits,* McDonald's and the fast-food industry took actions in the judicial arena, Congress, and state legislatures.

UNDERSTANDING OUTCOMES

In formulating a nonmarket strategy to be implemented in an institutional arena, it is helpful to have a theory about how the institution makes decisions. The Boeing example in Chapter 6 provides a theory of outcomes based on the strength and effectiveness of interests. The Boeing example involved a complex set of alternatives based on whether jobs were created. Some issues have a simpler set of alternatives that can be arrayed on one dimension. For example, the alternatives may be the budget for a government program, the stringency of an environmental standard, or the patent duration for pharmaceuticals. The alternatives in the example considered in Appendix B were the number of weeks of daylight saving time. If (1) the alternatives are one-dimensional, (2) the legislative process is open so that all alternatives can be considered, and (3) voters have a most-preferred alternative, or ideal point, and prefer alternatives closer to rather than farther from that ideal point, then the outcome is the median of the ideal points. The median ideal point will receive at least a majority of votes against any alternative to either its left or its right. That is, including the median, there is a majority of voters on one side or the other that will defeat any other alternative. The logic of the median voter theorem is developed further in the daylight saving time example.

The median voter theorem is powerful because it is only necessary to know voters' ideal points and not their entire preference ordering over alternatives. Moreover, if the median ideal point is known, it is not necessary to know the exact location of the ideal points of other voters.

The median voter theorem is an important tool for analyzing legislative outcomes in an open process: that is, a process in which any alternative can be proposed. If the issue under consideration is one-dimensional and the ideal points of the members of a legislature can be estimated, the outcome can be predicted. Moreover, strategies can focus on pivotal legislators who could change the median and hence the outcome.

Arrow (1963) has shown that there is no consistent mechanism that can predict outcomes for a general set of alternatives in more than one dimension and for any set of preferences voters can have. Appendix A explains this result. This means that the median voter theorem does not extend to alternatives with more than one dimension, but related results suggest that outcomes are likely to be close to the intersection of the medians on each dimension.

Legislators' ideal points are not directly observable, but information on them can be inferred from their voting records. Interest groups analyze roll-call votes on issues on their agendas and provide scores for each member of Congress. The League of Conservation Voters provides ratings based on how members of Congress voted on environmental issues. Similarly, Americans for Democratic Action (ADA) (a very liberal group), the Chamber of Commerce (COC) (a more conservative group), and the American Federation of State, County and Municipal Employees (AFSCME), a union with 1.3 million members, provide ratings based on issues important to them.[8] These ratings are used by analysts as an indicator of the relative location of the ideal points of members of Congress on various policy dimensions. Following are the 2010 ratings for the current Senate minority leader Mitch McConnell (R-KY), House minority leader Nancy Pelosi (D-CA), Senate majority leader Harry Reid (D-NV), and Speaker of the House John Boehner (R-OH).[9]

	Americans for Democratic Action	Chamber of Commerce	League of Conservation Voters	AFSCME
Mitch McConnell (R-KY)	0	100	0	8
Nancy Pelosi (D-CA)	95	40	100	100
Harry Reid (D-NV)	75	18	100	92
John Boehner (R-OH)	0	100	0	0

[8]For each member of Congress, the *Almanac of American Politics 2012* (Barone and McCutcheon, 2011) presents ratings by the following organizations: League of Conservation Voters, Americans for Democratic Action, Chamber of Commerce, AFSCME, Information Technology Industry Council, National Taxpayers Union, Club for Growth, Family Research Council, American Civil Liberties Union, and American Conservative Union. Each group selects a different set of issues on which to score members, so the ratings are not directly comparable. Similarly, the issues differ from year to year, so intertemporal comparisons are problematic.

[9]The ratings for the two chambers are not directly comparable because the two chambers do not always have roll-call votes on the same issues. The data for Representative Pelosi are for 2006, since as Speaker of the House she did not vote during the 2009–2010 Congress.

These ratings indicate that both McConnell and Boehner are conservative (low ADA scores) and responsive to business concerns (high COC scores), Reid and Pelosi are liberals (high ADA scores) and responsive to union interests (high AFSCME scores), and McConnell and Boehner are not responsive to environmental issues, whereas Reid and Pelosi are.

GENERIC NONMARKET STRATEGIES

Three generic nonmarket strategies are *representation, majority building,* and *information provision.* These strategies are not mutually exclusive but instead can be used together when there are synergies. Representation strategies are based on the consequences of alternatives for constituents of government officeholders. The Toshiba example and the Chapter 6 case, *Repeal of the Luxury Tax,* involve representation strategies. These strategies may involve the mobilization of a rent chain and may include a grassroots campaign, coalition building, and public advocacy, as considered in Chapter 8.

Majority building strategies focus on developing the needed votes in a legislature to enact or defeat a bill. A majority building strategy can build on a representation strategy, as when the rent chain is mobilized in districts of pivotal legislators. The chapter case, *Federal Express and Labor Organization,* involves majority building strategies.

Informational strategies focus on providing information to government officeholders. Informational strategies can be coupled with representation and majority-building strategies, as when a firm lobbies to provide information in conjunction with a grassroots strategy involving the mobilization of its rent chain. Informational strategies are important in the chapter case *Carried Interest Taxation.*

Representation Strategies

A representation strategy is based on the connection between elected officeholders and their constituents. Because members of Congress are interested in reelection, they are interested in serving their constituents. A firm's stakeholders are constituents, so a firm has an opportunity to build support for its objectives by representing stakeholders' interests. It may go further by mobilizing them for nonmarket action. Automakers represent the buyers of SUVs and light trucks when they seek fuel economy standards based on the "footprint" of the vehicle. Pharmaceutical companies represent the interests of patients who benefit from their drugs when they work with patient advocacy groups to obtain fast track approval of new drugs.

When its attempts to overturn U.S. antidumping duties were unsuccessful, Cemex established a production base in the United States. It acquired a cement plant in Texas and built ready-mix plants in the Southwest. This gave the company a rent chain and constituent base on which it could deploy a representation strategy to obtain relief from the duties. Its U.S. operations were geographically concentrated, however, limiting its coverage of congressional districts. To overcome its coverage deficit, Cemex formed an alliance with the 180,000 member National Association of Home Builders (NAHB). Their legislative objective was an amendment to U.S. trade law to allow the Department of Commerce to temporarily suspend antidumping duties in times of shortage of a good.[10] The coalition deployed a representation strategy, but it was countered by a representation strategy of the U.S. cement producers, and the status quo prevailed. In response, Cemex then acquired the largest independent U.S. cement company, expanding both its value chain and its rent chain.

EXAMPLE   Toshiba and Trade Sanctions

The U.S. Department of Defense observed that Soviet Union submarines were operating more quietly than in the past, making tracking more difficult. A Pentagon investigation revealed that Soviet propeller technology had improved substantially, possibly due to the sale of highly sophisticated milling equipment to the Soviet Union by the Toshiba Machine Company of Japan. Any such sale would be in violation of the regulations of the Coordinating Committee for Multilateral Export Controls (CoCom), an international agreement that prohibited the export to communist countries of technology that could improve their military capability.

---

[10]The European Union has such a provision in its international trade laws, and suspensions are allowed under GATT.

When a U.S. newspaper reported the Pentagon investigation in March 1987, the Japanese Ministry of International Trade and Industry (MITI) shrugged off the report. U.S. pressure, however, eventually led MITI to investigate. MITI found that the Toshiba Machine Company had twice sold milling machines to the Soviet Union in violation of both CoCom regulations and Japanese law. This machinery could have enabled the Soviets to improve their propeller technology. Toshiba Machine Company was 50.1 percent owned by the Toshiba Corporation (referred to as Toshiba hereafter), which reportedly was unaware of the illegal sales. The MITI investigation also revealed that Toshiba Machine had falsified export documents to qualify for export licenses and that the trading company Wako Koeki had illegally arranged for computer software for the milling machines to be supplied by Kongsberg Vaapenfabrik, a government-owned Norwegian defense contractor.

The uproar in the United States was immediate. Several consumer boycotts of Toshiba products were reported, and members of Congress smashed Toshiba products on the lawn of the Capitol. A $1 billion sale of Toshiba laptop computers to the U.S. Department of Defense came under fire. Some U.S. companies canceled purchase agreements with Toshiba, and others were noticeably nervous about dealing with it.

Political entrepreneurs were eager to represent constituents angry over the sale of the milling machines. In mid-June the House passed a nonbinding resolution calling on the Department of State to seek compensation from Japan for damages. Bills barring Toshiba sales to the Defense Department and banning all Toshiba imports to the United States for a period of 2 to 5 years were speeding through Congress. Legislatively imposed sanctions seemed a certainty.

STRATEGY FORMULATION Toshiba's problem was characteristic of client politics. Because sanctions seemed inevitable, the relevant status quo was that sanctions would be imposed, and Toshiba's objective was to limit them. On the other side of the issue, the costs from opposing a reduction in the sanctions were widely distributed rather than concentrated on identifiable interest groups. Pressure for sanctions came from the public and from entrepreneurs in Congress, who wanted to prevent further illegal sales to the Soviet Union and to claim credit for doing so.

To limit the sanctions, Toshiba adopted a multifaceted strategy that addressed the threat of sanctions and the concerns the incident had caused.[11] The facets included putting its house in order and directly addressing the political issue in the United States. In Japan, Toshiba's strategy had two components. The first was to ensure that no further illegal sales were made by any of its subsidiaries or affiliated companies. The second was to work with the government to ensure that other Japanese companies would also comply with CoCom regulations.

In the United States reaction to the sales did not distinguish between the Toshiba Machine Company and the Toshiba Corporation. Toshiba Machine had U.S. sales of $100 million. Toshiba, with U.S. sales of $2.6 billion, was a much more visible target. One component of Toshiba's strategy was to direct attention to the Toshiba Machine Company. This involved providing information about the relative independence of Toshiba Machine and the fact that Toshiba had been unaware of the sales. A second component of its strategy was to protect Toshiba Machine's business in the United States. The fact that Toshiba Machine had production plants and hence stakeholders in the United States allowed Toshiba to argue that sanctions would hurt constituents. A third component of its strategy was to attempt to place time limits on any sanctions and allow exceptions for certain exports such as spare parts and specialized products, particularly those used for defense purposes. Furthermore, Toshiba sought to grandfather sales agreements already signed. A final component of Toshiba's U.S. strategy was to focus attention on the future rather than on the past. Toshiba emphasized the measures it was taking to ensure that such violations would not happen again.

STRATEGY IMPLEMENTATION To implement its strategy, Toshiba took a number of steps in Japan and the United States. Both Toshiba and the Japanese government acted to put their own houses in order. In an act of contrition, the chairman as well as the president of Toshiba resigned their positions. Toshiba increased by 80 its staff responsible for verifying compliance with export regulations. MITI announced that it would increase its surveillance of exports, strengthen penalties for violations, and contribute more to the support of CoCom's secretariat in Paris. MITI also offered to provide the U.S. Department of Defense with the same milling machines that had been sold to the Soviet Union so that it could develop improved submarine detection devices. The Japanese government hurriedly prepared strengthened laws on CoCom compliance.

Toshiba's strategy in the United States was implemented on a broad scale, reportedly at a cost of $30 million. It took out full-page advertisements apologizing for its actions and pledged

---

[11]The account presented here is based on public sources and does not necessarily reflect the reasoning of Toshiba executives. Instead, the presentation is intended to analyze Toshiba's strategy and its implementation.

not to make any further illegal sales. In other quarters Toshiba attempted to assure its critics that it was taking steps to prevent further violations.

Toshiba mounted a major lobbying campaign. To obtain access to Congress and the executive branch, it hired several former government officials, including the former chairman of the House Budget Committee, a well-known Republican lawyer who had served in the Nixon administration, a lobbyist who had served in the Nixon White House, and a former deputy U.S. trade representative.

Toshiba used its rent chain in a grassroots strategy by bringing to Washington the managers of many of its U.S. operations. It also flew a number of its suppliers and customers to Washington to impress on Congress the harm to U.S. interests that harsh sanctions would cause. Toshiba's employment of 4,200 people in the United States provided a link between possible sanctions and constituents' jobs. For example, Toshiba had a microwave oven plant in Tennessee and was able to enlist the governor to write to each member of the state's congressional delegation warning that retaliatory measures directed at Toshiba could have a direct impact on over 600 employees in the state. Even potential employment provided a basis for generating political action. The governor of Indiana, who had been working to attract a Toshiba facility to his state, asked the Indiana congressional delegation to oppose sanctions.

Toshiba had little difficulty enlisting the support of its customers, many of whom relied on its products. The Electronic Industries Association argued that over 4,000 jobs held by employees of Toshiba's customers were threatened by the sanctions. Some 40 companies, including Apple and Honeywell—importers of Toshiba printers and semiconductors, respectively—opposed the proposed sanctions. Toshiba suppliers also rallied to its defense. Toshiba was able to enlist other allies as well. In a letter to the House Armed Services committee chairman, an assistant secretary of defense wrote that Japan was "succeeding in punishing the guilty, establishing stronger controls, and funding antisubmarine warfare programs which will help the United States and Japanese navies."[12]

THE OUTCOME The sanctions eventually imposed against Toshiba were considerably less severe than initially expected, and Toshiba's nonmarket strategy was given considerable credit for the outcome. The sanctions included a ban on imports by Toshiba Machine and Kongsberg for 3 years and a ban on any sales to the U.S. government for the same period. The parent company in Japan was also banned from sales to the U.S. government for the same period. However, exceptions were provided for products necessary for national security, spare parts, servicing and maintenance, and for those items already under contract.

Majority-Building Strategies

VOTE RECRUITING A majority is required to enact legislation, or in the case of a presidential veto, two-thirds of the members of both the House and the Senate are required to overturn the veto. Conversely, to defeat legislation a blocking majority of votes is required or, in conjunction with a veto, one-third of the members of the House or Senate is required. Strategies directed at legislatures focus on building a majority for or against an alternative.[13] The chapter case, *Wal-Mart and Its Urban Expansion Strategy* concerns building a majority in the Chicago city council for permission to open two stores.

A key component of a majority-building strategy is *vote recruitment.* Votes are recruited by interest groups and by public officeholders. For example, the majority and minority leaders in the House and Senate recruit votes on some issues by providing favors to legislators. Similarly, the president frequently recruits votes by providing favors to members of Congress. President Clinton used this approach to recruit votes of congressional Democrats for the North American Free Trade Agreement.

Votes may be recruited by interest groups through a variety of means. One is in conjunction with a representation strategy based on the constituency connection. Votes can also be recruited through vote trading. A legislator who has strong preferences on issue A and does not care about issue B may be willing to trade her vote on B for a vote on A of another legislator who

---

[12]*The New York Times,* March 14, 1988.
[13]Baron (1999) introduces the concepts of majority building and vote recruitment strategies for client and interest group politics.

has strong preferences on B. Consequently, an interest group with allies in the legislature may be able to enlist them in vote trading and recruiting.

Votes are also recruited by providing politically valuable support for a legislator. This could involve pledges of electoral support or endorsements by constituency groups such as those in a firm's rent chain. Other means include assisting in voter mobilization and supplying volunteers as practiced by labor unions, providing endorsements and advertisements as used by the Sierra Club and other environmental interest groups, and campaign contributions. There is little evidence that campaign contributions influence congressional voting, and the caps on contributions are very low. Campaign contributions are thus better thought of as developing access to members of Congress for the purpose of lobbying, as considered in Chapter 8. Support also includes opportunities for legislators to claim credit for serving the interests of their constituents.

PIVOTAL VOTERS   A vote recruitment strategy focuses on *pivotal voters*—those most likely to switch the outcome between victory and defeat.[14] To identify the pivotal voters in a vote recruitment strategy, consider an issue for which the alternatives can be arrayed on a line. Consider a 101-member legislature that operates under simple (50 percent) majority rule and is considering two alternatives, $a = 60$ and $b = 30$, as depicted in Figure 7-3. Also suppose that the preferences of each legislator are represented by the distance of an alternative from her ideal point—the outcome she most prefers.[15] To simplify the exposition, assume that legislators' ideal points are uniformly distributed along the line in Figure 7-3 with the legislator the farthest to the left having ideal point 0 and the legislator farthest to the right having ideal point 100. The median legislator is denoted by m and has an ideal point at 50. Since alternative a is closer to m than is alternative b, the median legislator prefers a.

Consider client politics in which an interest group prefers b to a. The first step in a vote recruitment strategy is to identify the pivotal voters. The pivotal voter is indifferent between a and b and is the one with an ideal point at 45, which is the midpoint between a and b, as illustrated in Figure 7-3. In the absence of a vote recruitment strategy by the interest group, alternative a would be enacted on a vote of 56 to 45, assuming that the indifferent voter (45) votes with the majority. Consequently, for alternative b to win, the interest group and those in the legislature who prefer b to a must recruit six votes. That is, the 45 legislators with ideal points to the left of 45 will vote for b regardless of whether the interest group recruits them; they are natural allies of the interest group on this issue, and consequently, only six additional votes are needed to form a majority for b.[16] Any six legislators who would vote for a are pivotal, but the interest group prefers to recruit those votes that are least costly. The least-costly votes are of those legislators who only mildly prefer a to b. These are the legislators with ideal points between (and including) 45 and 50. The focus of a vote recruitment strategy is thus on these six legislators.

There is no reason to recruit legislators with ideal points from 51 through 100. First, their votes are not needed to pass b. Second, recruiting their votes would be more costly because they prefer a to b more strongly than the legislators with ideal points between 45 and 50. Using the same logic, recruiting the vote of legislator $m = 50$ is more costly than recruiting the vote of legislator 45, because m prefers a to b more strongly than does legislator 45. Consequently, greater support or a more valuable vote trade must be provided to m than to legislator 45.

FIGURE 7-3   Majority Building and Pivotal Voters

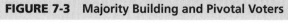

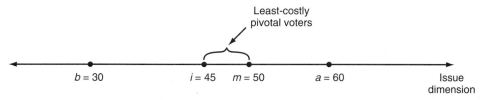

---

[14]A formal theory of vote recruitment in client politics is presented in Snyder (1991).

[15]The preferences of legislators can be assessed based on the characteristics of their constituents and their past voting record using the interest groups ratings discussed earlier in the chapter.

[16]If the interest group and its allies in the legislature are uncertain about the preferences of legislators, they may want to recruit more than six votes as insurance.

MULTIPLE PIVOTS   The U.S. legislative process is more complicated than the example just considered because it has multiple pivots. First, it is a bicameral system, which requires that both the House and Senate pass a bill in identical language before it can become law. To enact legislation, it may be necessary to recruit pivotal voters in both chambers. To defeat legislation, however, it is only necessary to build a majority in one of the two chambers, so other things equal it is easier to defeat than to enact legislation. Second, senators can filibuster a bill, and cloture—stopping the filibuster and proceeding to a vote—requires the votes of 60 senators. Third, the president can veto a bill, and overriding the veto requires two-thirds of both the House and Senate.[17] Institutions in other countries also have multiple pivots. In Japan, a two-thirds vote in the lower house of the Diet is required to enact legislation when the upper house opposes a bill. The Council of Ministers of the European Union operates with qualified majority rule, which requires a supermajority of votes to approve legislation. The Chapter 15 case *The European Union Carbon Tax* involves a pivot at the qualified majority, and the chapter case *Federal Express and Labor Organization* involves a pivot at the majority needed to overcome a filibuster.

MULTIPLE PIVOTS, PUBLIC AND PRIVATE POLITICS, AND SELF-REGULATION   To illustrate the importance of multiple pivots, consider a simplified version of the institutional structure in the United States as depicted in Figure 7-4. Consider a unidimensional policy space corresponding to the stringency of environment regulation of firms in an industry with legislators' ideal points arrayed from 0 to 100 in one unit increments. Suppose that the agenda is open, so all legislators can make a policy proposal. The two relevant pivots are the filibuster pivot $f = 40$ (in the Senate) and the veto override pivot $v = 67$, whose vote is required to override a presidential veto when the president has an ideal policy to the right of 67.[18] Consider first a status quo between f and v and a policy proposal to the right of the status quo. Any policy to the right of 40 would be blocked by a filibuster by the 41 legislators with ideal points from 0 to 40. Similarly, any policy to the left of the status quo would be vetoed by the president and an override would be blocked by the 34 legislators with ideal points between 67 and 100. The interval between 40 and 67 is referred to as the *gridlock interval*, since a status quo in the interval cannot be changed by public politics.

If a legislator such as a committee chair had agenda power, however, she could obtain a policy inside the gridlock interval. Consider the top panel of Figure 7-4. Suppose that the status quo, the current environmental practices in the industry, is $q = 32$ and the committee chair has an ideal policy of 47. The committee chair could propose the policy $x = 47$, and it would not be

FIGURE 7-4   Public Politics, Private Politics, and Self-Regulation

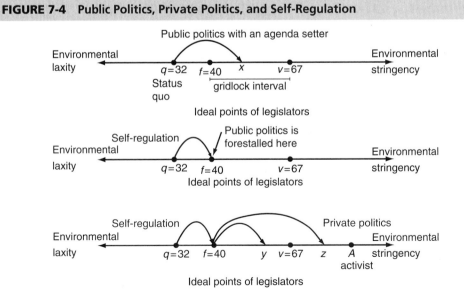

filibustered since legislator 40 prefers a policy of 47 to 32. The policy 47 would be approved by all legislators that prefer 47 to 32, and the president also prefers it and would sign the bill.

To illustrate strategy choice, consider the middle panel of Figure 7-4. To prevent the committee chair from proposing $x = 47$ and having the legislature approve it, the firms can *self-regulate* to the filibuster pivot $f = 40$. With practices at f government cannot adopt more stringent regulations to the right because 41 legislators would block the regulations. Self-regulation thus can forestall public politics.

Private politics, however, can still affect the firms. Public politics requires majorities to enact new legislation, whereas in private politics minorities can prevail. Moreover, minorities can achieve outcomes that majorities in public politics cannot achieve. Consider the bottom panel in Figure 7-4 with the firms having self-regulated to f and an activist with an ideal environmental policy located at A to the right of the gridlock interval. An activist could mount a private politics campaign against the firms, and since private politics does not require a majority, it is not bound by the status quo interval. If the campaign succeeds, the firm could be forced to adopt environmental practices in the interior of the gridlock interval, as illustrated by the policy y, or if the campaign is very successful, outside the interval at z. Private politics thus can go where public politics cannot.

COMPETITION AND MAJORITY BUILDING The vote recruitment strategy considered in the context of Figure 7-3 involves only one interest group and thus corresponds to client politics, where opposing interests have weak incentives to take nonmarket action. This strategy is also used in interest group politics in which the opposing interest group has already implemented its strategy and the interest group supporting b has the last move. For example, in the chapter case *Federal Express and Labor Organization,* organized labor deployed its strategy by enlisting its allies in the Senate to undertake a filibuster against a bill sought by Federal Express. Given that organized labor had already deployed its strategy, Federal Express was in the situation depicted in Figure 7-3.

When two interest groups are actively competing, majority building becomes more complicated. Suppose that interest group G_a supports the status quo a and group G_b supports alternative b. Because G_b seeks to overturn the status quo, it naturally moves first. If it attempts to build a majority by recruiting votes, the opposing interest group can recruit a majority among any of the legislators to preserve the status quo. For example, if in the context of Figure 7-3 G_b were to recruit the votes of legislators 45 through 50, group G_a could counter either by attempting to recruit those same legislators or by attempting to recruit voters to the left of 45 who only mildly prefer b to a. Consequently, group G_b must employ a *majority protection* strategy that may require recruiting more than the minimal number of pivotal voters. That is, group G_b may have to recruit a supermajority of voters and provide them with sufficient support to protect each majority against the strategy of the opposing interest group.[19]

AGENDA SETTING If the legislative process is open so that legislators can easily offer amendments, and if there is no vote recruitment, the winning alternative is typically centrally located among the preferences of legislators, as in the daylight saving time example in Appendix B. That is, in an open process the median voter theorem provides the basic prediction of the outcome. If interests can recruit pivotal voters, the outcome can be moved, as considered in the context of Figure 7-3.

If the legislative process is relatively closed and a committee's bill, for example, is protected from amendments by a restrictive rule, strategic agenda setting is possible. In the European Union the Commission is the principal agenda setter, and under some legislative procedures amendments by the European Parliament are difficult to make. The committee in the first example and the Commission in the second are agenda setters. Nonmarket strategies often focus on agenda setters.

Agenda-setting strategies focus first on recruiting the agenda setter and then on building support for the alternative on the agenda. Consider Figure 7-3, and suppose that the status quo is a. Also, initially assume that there are no interest groups attempting to recruit votes. If the agenda setter has an ideal point at 30, it can place the alternative $c = 41$ on the agenda and a majority will

---

[19]Groseclose (1996) and Groseclose and Snyder (1996) present theories of competitive vote recruitment.

vote for it against the status quo a. To see this, note that the pivotal voter $m = 50$ just prefers $c = 41$ to $a = 60$. Consequently, an interest group on the left with an agenda-setter ally with ideal point 30 can obtain $c = 41$ without having to recruit any votes.[20]

The ability of an agenda setter to use the status quo to its advantage is mitigated to the extent that there is vote recruitment competition between interest groups. A strategy that involves agenda setting is thus more likely to be effective in client politics. An agenda setter's power is also limited by the ability of others to offer amendments or counterproposals. When amendments are freely allowed, the median voter theorem is applicable, and in the absence of vote recruitment the outcome is likely to be centrally located.

Informational Strategies

Information is a politically valuable resource. Information enables officeholders to better serve their constituents and pursue their policy interests. Interest groups thus employ informational strategies in an attempt to influence outcomes. Informational strategies are based on the superior information an interest group has about, for example, the consequences of alternatives for constituents. Thus, a necessary condition for an informational strategy to be effective is that the interest group is better informed about some aspect of the issue than are government officeholders. Informational strategies typically involve providing information favorable to the firm or interest group. That is, firms advocate "their side of the issue" as in a court where lawyers advocate the side of their clients. Officeholders understand this and take the advocacy into account in updating their beliefs. Even though it may be provided strategically, the information can be beneficial to the officeholder.

The strategic provision of information is the principal component of lobbying, testimony in legislative or regulatory proceedings, and public advocacy. To implement an informational strategy through lobbying, an interest group may invest in obtaining access to legislators or administrative officials. Influence thus often has two stages. The first involves obtaining access, and the second involves the strategic provision of information. In public processes such as those of many regulatory agencies, interests have due process rights to participate in the process and provide information. In legislative institutions, however, access to a pivotal legislator is not guaranteed and may have to be developed. A firm's rent chain can provide access through the constituency connection.

Lobbying involves the strategic provision of two types of information—*technical* and *political*. Technical information pertains to the likely consequences of alternatives. Political information pertains to the effects of alternatives on the constituents of officeholders. Political information is often provided in conjunction with representation and majority building strategies. Both technical and political information may be provided strategically—advocating the outcome sought by the interest. This may involve the strategic advocacy of a position, the choice of methodologies that generate data and conclusions favorable to an interest, or the emphasis on favorable, and deemphasis on unfavorable, information. Some informational strategies are counteractive—that is, they are undertaken to counter the information provided by an opposing interest.

Information must be credible to have an effect. Credibility can be established in several ways. First, the information may be verifiable in the sense that the officeholder or her staff can check its validity. Second, if it is not verifiable, information can be credible if the group's interest is aligned with the interests of the officeholder. That is, the officeholder can rely on the information the interest group provides because she knows that the interest group would not provide the information unless it wanted her to act on it. A member of Congress whose constituents have strong environmental preferences may rely on the information provided by the Sierra Club. Third, if an interest group and the officeholder have divergent preferences, the information provided can be credible if it is confirmed by information provided by a nonaligned or opposing interest. This information need not be identical to provide confirmation. Fourth, an interest may commission a study by an organization that has a degree of independence. Studies are frequently used to bolster advocacy. Credibility is considered in more detail in Chapter 8.

---

[20]Viewing the alternative placed on the agenda as a function of the status quo, note that a more extreme status quo allows the agenda setter to obtain an outcome closer to his or her ideal point. For example, if the status quo were 70, the agenda setter could place the alternative $c = 31$ on the agenda and it would pass. If the status quo were 80, however, the agenda setter would put the alternative $c = 30$ on the agenda, since that is its ideal point.

A concern about informational strategies is whether an interest is legally or morally obligated to provide information that it prefers not to disclose. Unless there is specific legislation or regulation compelling the provision of information, a firm is generally not legally obligated to provide such information. It would be illegal, however, for a pharmaceutical company to withhold data on the safety of an approved drug, and it would be immoral, and probably illegal, to make false claims about a product's performance. It is both allowed and commonplace, however, for interests to advocate their side of an issue or to provide estimates based on methodologies likely to provide answers favorable to their side. A common example is a trial in which the plaintiff and the defendant provide expert witnesses who reach different conclusions regarding an issue. In executive and legislative institutions, the same type of advocacy takes place. Some pharmaceutical companies, however, have been accused of withholding clinical test results that failed to demonstrate that a drug was an effective treatment for a health condition. This issue is the subject of the Chapter 10 case *Merck and Vioxx*.

Public Officeholders as Targets of Nonmarket Strategies

In public politics, nonmarket strategies are ultimately directed at government officeholders, who are often in a collective decision setting such as a legislature or a regulatory commission. These officeholders have duties to their institution and to their constituents. The constituency connection provides a basis for developing allies among legislators. Allies are legislators who see the firm's interests as consistent with their own. Some allies may support bills that benefit the firm, whereas others may simply be willing to listen to the firm's position on an issue.

The interests of officeholders may also depend on career concerns. Those career concerns include reelection, running for higher office, advancement in a bureaucracy, and employment after government service. Because of career concerns, most officeholders are risk averse and wary of taking actions that risk their advancement or jeopardize their electoral prospects.

When officeholders seek to avoid risk, the status quo is often favored. An interest group seeking to preserve the status quo can thus adopt a strategy emphasizing the uncertainty inherent in the issue. This may involve counteractive lobbying that calls into question the information provided by the proponents of a change from the status quo. Another strategy that is often effective is raising new dimensions of the issue. Toshiba, for example, emphasized the importance of its products to U.S. defense contractors. In the chapter case *Carried Interest Taxation* private equity and venture capital firms emphasized the uncertain effect on economic growth of the taxation of carried interest. Through its informational lobbying Boeing attempted to emphasize the uncertainty about the consequences of failing to renew China's MFN status, as indicated in the example.

Conversely, an interest that seeks to change the status quo should focus on reducing uncertainty about the consequences of the change. In the Chapter 6 case *Repeal of the Luxury Tax*, yacht builders provided specific information about the loss of jobs caused by the luxury tax. Such information must be credible, and its corroboration by other interests contributed to the repeal of the tax.

EXAMPLE China and Most Favored Nation Status

Prior to China's admission into the World Trade Organization (WTO), the United States had annually extended most favored nation (MFN) status to China. Congress had refused to grant permanent MFN status because of human rights concerns, disclosures that China had supplied missiles and chemical weapons technology to Iran, and revelation that it had attempted to gain influence in the United States through illegal campaign contributions. In 1997 the extension was in trouble in Congress.

Boeing, the largest U.S. exporter, was involved in intense market competition with Airbus, based in France and three other countries, for a $4 billion sale to China. China was expected to purchase an estimated $140 billion of aircraft over the next 20 years. In early April at the United Nations human rights conference in Geneva, the United States voted for a resolution to condemn China, whereas France voted against the resolution, causing it to fail. With President Chirac of France scheduled to visit China in May, Boeing faced a considerable challenge to obtain the sale.

Larry S. Dickenson, vice president of international sales for Boeing, noted the advantage France had obtained through

(*Continued*)

(Continued)

its vote on the human rights motion: "When President Chirac arrives in Beijing in a few weeks, I am sure he will be rewarded for that stance."[1] When President Chirac arrived in China, the government announced that it would purchase 30 Airbus aircraft valued at $1.5 billion. China's Premier Li Peng explained the decision to buy from Airbus: "They do not attach political strings to cooperation with China."[2] The president of Boeing's commercial aircraft business, Ronald Woodard, said, "The Chinese just bought 30 Airbus planes to reward Europe for not punishing human rights. The Europeans love the fight over MFN."[3]

Boeing and other U.S. firms, such as the Ford Motor Company, used informational and representation strategies in support of both MFN and China's admission into the WTO. Representative Todd Tiahrt (R-KS), who had worked for Boeing for 14 years, said he talked with Boeing lobbyists "once a week, sometimes daily. They never fail to bring [MFN] up."[4]

The information provided by Boeing and other companies pertained to the effects on the companies, their stakeholders, and the constituents of members of Congress, as well as to broader consequences. Dickenson identified the long-term seriousness of the matter: "If we lose the opportunity to get China into a rule-based organization like the WTO now, it will take us another five years to get back to the spot we're in today."[5] He added, "I told [Congress] about Airbus, Chirac's visit, what was likely to happen. I told them the realities: that every time there's a blip in U.S.-China relations, it helps our foreign competitors."[6]

---

[1]*New York Times,* April 29, 1997.
[2]*BusinessWeek,* June 16, 1997.
[3]Ibid.
[4]Ibid.
[5]*New York Times,* April 29, 1997.
[6]*Wall Street Journal,* June 24, 1997.

Analysis

In this case, Boeing could provide information on (1) the likelihood that sales would be lost, (2) the profits that would be affected if sales were lost, (3) the effects on its, and its suppliers' stakeholders, (4) future sales that might be jeopardized, and (5) the effects on the competitive positions of Airbus and Boeing. Some of this information was soft in the sense that an officeholder would be unable to verify its accuracy and completeness. In particular, the information in (1), (4), and (5) was to varying degrees soft and difficult to evaluate. Other information, such as that in (3), was hard in the sense that the officeholder could understand the data by inspection; for example, Boeing could identify the aircraft it was offering to China, the current subcontractors, and the possible lost sales. Because Boeing had superior information, it had an opportunity to advocate its position strategically. This could involve emphasizing favorable information and remaining silent about unfavorable information. It could also involve emphasizing worst-case scenarios, such as the maximum number of jobs that could be lost, or utilizing data that presented its side of the issue in a favorable manner. Boeing, however, had a lengthy nonmarket agenda and interacted regularly with Congress and the executive branch. It thus had an incentive to build and maintain a reputation for providing reliable information.

Informational strategies can be integrated with broader nonmarket strategies including those of other interests. The major companies with business at risk in China divided lobbying responsibilities. Boeing lobbied representatives from Alabama, Kansas, and Washington, and General Motors lobbied representatives from Georgia, Michigan, and Texas. The companies also backed grassroots organizations that supported continuation of MFN status. Boeing backed the Kansas Alliance for U.S.-China Trade, which had grown to include 120 member companies that did business with China. Similarly, in California 350 companies participated in the Coalition for U.S.-China Trade. MFN was granted.

INSTITUTIONS, INTERESTS, AND STRATEGY CHOICE

Institutions and Responsiveness

The choice among the three generic nonmarket strategies depends on the interests involved with the issue and the institutions in whose arenas the issue will be addressed. The significance of institutional arenas for strategy is illustrated in Figure 7-5. Institutions can be arrayed in terms of their political responsiveness to constituent interests. Institutions that are highly responsive to constituent interests are legislatures and the presidency, or more generally institutions whose officeholders are directly elected. In contrast, the courts are not very politically responsive but instead make their decisions based on the Constitution, statutes, and case law precedents. Regulatory and administrative agencies are somewhere in between, depending on their policy domain and mandate. The figure provides more detail on the responsiveness of the institutions.

In politically responsive institutions success depends more on the ability of interests to supply nonmarket action, and in less politically responsive institutions success depends more on the provision of technical information. For judicial institutions, informational strategies, and particularly strategies that provide technical information and legal argument, are most effective. In legislative arenas representation strategies are more important, since they can be based on the constituency connection. Informational strategies that provide political information about the impact of a bill on constituents, for example, are often used in conjunction with representation strategies in politically responsive institutions.

FIGURE 7-5   Institutions and Responsiveness

Institutions		
Courts	Regulatory Administrative	Congress Presidency

← Less   *degree of political responsiveness*   more →

To what are the institutions responsive?

Constitution	statutes and mandate	Constituents
due process	due process	interest groups
Statutes	interests with standing	policy agenda
the record	court review	(administration)
Precedents	congressional and	congressional
Ideology	executive pressure	committee agendas

The choice of a nonmarket strategy for issues addressed in regulatory or administrative agencies depends on their political responsiveness. An agency with a narrow mandate such as the International Trade Commission (ITC; see Chapter 19) is less politically responsive than is an agency with a broad mandate such as the Environmental Protection Agency (EPA). Representation strategies tend to be more effective in the EPA than in the ITC. Similarly, the Department of Justice and Federal Trade Commission are closer to the courts than are the Department of Commerce and United States Trade Representative.

Interests: Client and Interest Group Politics

The choice among nonmarket strategies is related to the nature of the politics of an issue, as characterized in the Wilson-Lowi matrix presented in Chapter 6. In client politics the benefits are concentrated on the clients, whereas harm is widely distributed. Because the opposition is not active in client politics, the client interest group usually adopts a low-profile strategy outside the view of the public. Lobbying and information provision are typically the centerpieces of such a strategy. The information is often political—about the constituents who would benefit from the alternative sought by the client or about how that alternative would serve the policy interests of the officeholder. In a legislative arena the strategy frequently focuses on both majority building and agenda setting with a particular focus on committees. In conjunction with a majority build-ing strategy, a firm may use a high-profile strategy of organizing and mobilizing its stakeholders and those of other interests into a coalition that can take coordinated action and improve the coverage of legislative districts. The Daylight Saving Time Coalition's strategy of adding candy manufacturers by including Halloween in the extension is an example.

The danger in a behind-the-scenes nonmarket strategy in client politics is that watchdog groups and opponents in the legislature will shine light on the activities of the client. The label often given to client relationships is "special-interest" politics, and many members of Congress seek to avoid such politics. Clients thus often wrap their objectives and messages in the rhetoric of the public interest.

Interest group politics usually involves more visible strategies. A high-profile strategy could include public advocacy and grassroots activities. Firms engaged in interest group politics also use lobbying and coalition building. The formation of the Daylight Saving Time Coalition was important in achieving an extension that had for many years been stalled in Congress. Informal alignments of interests can also be important, as in the case of the Coalition and the RP Foundation Fighting Blindness.

If a coalition seeks new legislation, its chances of success are enhanced if its allies are able to restrict the opportunities of others to amend the proposal in ways that could split the coalition. This can at times be accomplished by incorporating the desired legislation in a larger bill to give it a degree of protection. Representative Pickle incorporated his bill ending the tax benefits for tax-exempts and foreign leasing into a larger tax bill. In the chapter case *Federal Express and Labor Organization,* the company and its allies were successful in having a provision inserted in a bill in conference committee, after which no amendments were allowed.

Competition between interest groups gives more importance to pivotal legislators, often increasing the cost of vote recruitment in majority building strategies. Providing substitutes for opposing interests can be effective in reducing their incentives and conserving the resources of the interest group and its allies. The Daylight Saving Time Coalition supported pre-sunrise authorization for radio stations to eliminate their opposition. The cost of a vote recruitment strategy can also be reduced by proposing compromises.

When a firm is on the side of dispersed benefits in entrepreneurial or majoritarian politics, a number of strategies are available. One is to identify pockets of interests that can be organized and mobilized. The basic politics of the extension of daylight saving time was majoritarian, but there were pockets of interests—convenience stores, recreation and sporting goods firms, candy makers, and nursery firms—that could be organized. This transformed the politics from majoritarian to client politics. A second strategy is to identify other aligned interests, as in the case of the Daylight Saving Time Coalition and the RP Foundation Fighting Blindness. A third strategy is to seek a nonmarket entrepreneur who can either organize those with dispersed benefits or represent them from within the government institution. To the extent that an entrepreneur is able to mobilize dispersed interests, the potential of collective action can be realized. Particularly when interests are not well informed about an issue, a nonmarket entrepreneur can alert those interests and provide information on the possible consequences of the issue. Pharmaceutical companies use this approach in mobilizing patient advocacy groups that benefit from particular drug therapies.

SUMMARY

Nonmarket action by firms as well as other interests must meet standards of responsibility. Firms have the constitutional right to speak on issues and to petition government, and those actions should be forthright and transparent. The nonmarket power of firms is often controlled by the differences in their interests. In addition, the power of business is often limited by the actions of groups such as organized labor, NGOs, and social activists. Firms must avoid the temptation to manipulate public processes and should exercise restraint in the gray area between manipulation and the acceptable exercise of their rights.

The formulation of nonmarket strategies is the responsibility of managers, and the strategy process has as components:

- Nonmarket analysis (Chapter 6)
- Specification of primary and contingent objectives
- Selection of institutional arenas
- Strategy formulation
- Development and utilization of nonmarket assets, including the rent chain
- Implementation (Chapter 8)

The principal nonmarket strategies used by firms are representation, majority building, and information provision. Representation strategies are based on the link between the firm's rent chain and an officeholder's constituents. Majority-building strategies involve building a majority in support of or in opposition to a legislative alternative. These strategies focus on pivotal legislators and agenda setters. Informational strategies involve the strategic provision of technical and political information as in advocacy and are often used in conjunction with representation and majority-building strategies.

The choice among strategies depends on the relevant institutions and other involved interests. Institutions can be arrayed in terms of their political responsiveness. Representation strategies are used for politically responsive institutions such as Congress and the presidency. Strategies involving the provision of technical information are associated with less politically responsive institutions including the courts and some regulatory and administrative agencies. Strategies involving the provision of political information are often used in conjunction with representation strategies. In legislatures, majority-building strategies are often supported by representation and informational strategies.

The nature of the politics also affects strategy choice. In client politics firms face no direct opposition, and firms typically prefer low-profile strategies implemented through lobbying. In interest group politics firms may be forced to adopt a higher profile strategy to counter the opposition. In client politics majority-building strategies are relatively straightforward to formulate, but in interest group politics a firm may need not only to build a majority but also to protect that majority from the majority-building strategies of those on the other side of the issue.

Condorcet's Paradox and Arrow's Impossibility Theorem

In one of the most important accomplishments in the social sciences, Kenneth Arrow (1963) demonstrated that it is generally impossible to design institutions that aggregate the possible preferences that individuals might have to make a social choice in a manner consistent with a set of reasonable conditions. This impossibility theorem has a variety of implications for public institutions and hence for strategies for addressing nonmarket issues.

Arrow asked whether it is possible to design institutions that, using the preferences of individuals, can select social alternatives or public policies in a manner consistent with a minimal set of conditions that any institution should possess. Those institutions include simple majority rule, a strong executive system in which an executive has veto power over a majority-rule legislature, and a parliamentary system in which a government continues in office until the next election or until it loses a vote of confidence. To illustrate this result, the institution of simple (50 percent) majority rule is used.

Suppose there are three individuals (1, 2, and 3) and three social alternatives (A, B, and C). Suppose also that the preferences of the individuals are as given in Figure 7-6, where, for example, individual 1 prefers A to B, B to C, and C to A. When each alternative is paired against each of the other alternatives under majority rule, A defeats B by a vote of 2 to 1, B defeats C by a vote of 2 to 1, and C defeats A by a vote of 2 to 1. Each alternative thus defeats one alternative but is defeated by another. Majority rule thus is incapable of choosing an alternative. That is, majority rule cannot aggregate the preferences of these individuals to select a social alternative.

This paradox, due to Condorcet (1785), illustrates the fundamental problem Arrow examined. Arrow showed that for any institution satisfying certain reasonable conditions, there is some configuration of individual preferences such that the institution yields no consistent choice, as in the *Condorcet paradox.*[21]

AGENDAS

One implication of Arrow's impossibility theorem is that in an actual institution there may be an opportunity to act strategically. for example, with the preferences in Figure 7-6, suppose that individual 1 is the agenda setter and can specify the order in which a legislature will vote on the three alternatives. Suppose individual 1 sets the agenda in Figure 7-7 in which A is first voted against C and then the winner is voted against B. In their voting, the three individuals will recognize that in the second stage the winner of the first vote will be voted against B, so the outcome will be B if C is the winner of the first vote and will be A if the winner of the first vote is A. These winners are denoted by the circled alternatives in Figure 7-7. Consequently, the first vote is actually a vote between an outcome of A and an outcome of B. Both individuals 1 and 3 prefer A to B and thus will vote for A rather than C on the first vote. Then, on the second vote, 1 and 3 will vote for A over B, yielding A as the winner. The agenda setter in this case obtains the alternative that he or she most prefers. It is straightforward to show that the other two possible agendas formed from the three alternatives yield B and C as the outcomes.

This example should not be interpreted as implying that agendas are regularly manipulated. An agenda setter who acts against the preferences of a majority can always be replaced. Instead, the example indicates that a simple institutional structure, in this case an agenda, can result in a consistent social choice.[22] That choice depends on which agenda is used, and hence there are incentives for strategic behavior. This also implies that institutional positions with agenda-setting authority are important.

FIGURE 7-6 Condorcet's Paradox

Individual's Preference Ordering		
1	2	3
A	B	C
B	C	A
C	A	B

FIGURE 7-7 A Voting Agenda

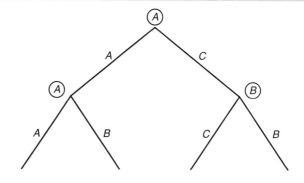

The Politics of the Extension of Daylight Saving Time

Since the Uniform Time Act was enacted in 1966, daylight saving time had begun on the last Sunday in April and lasted 6 months until the last Sunday in October.[23] Bills to extend daylight saving time were introduced in Congress beginning in 1976, and the battle for an extension lasted for 10 years, concluding in 1986 with a 3-week extension to the first Sunday in April. The forces that led to the extension are representative of those present on many nonmarket issues affecting business.

Two contrasting approaches can be taken to explain the extension. The public interest perspective predicts that the alternative that best serves the public will be adopted. In this case, the public interest would select the extension that yielded the greatest differences between aggregate benefits and costs. This perspective was first advanced in 1784 when Benjamin Franklin argued to the French that they could save 96 million candles per year from an extra hour of daylight.[24] During World Wars I and II the United States adopted daylight saving time, and in World War II it lasted for 3½ years. During the oil crisis of 1973–1974, the United States extended daylight saving time as a means of saving energy. The waning of the oil crisis and protests from parents who objected to their children having to walk to school in the early morning darkness led to the elimination of the extension. Subsequently, the Department of Transportation (DOT) estimated that the extension during the oil crisis saved 6 million barrels of oil. The extension of daylight saving time in 1986 occurred at a time when energy savings were considered less important. A variety of business interests benefitted from an extension including recreation and retail businesses. In addition the RP Foundation Fighting Blindness, representing people afflicted with night blindness, was an important participant in the nonmarket competition.

The second approach focuses on the nonmarket competition resulting from the actions of those whose interests are affected by the length of daylight saving time. For most nonmarket issues it is better to view nonmarket action as arising from the interests of individuals, firms, and groups than to view nonmarket outcomes as the result of the pursuit of the public interest. This does not mean that public policy analysis has no effect on the outcome of political activity. Often it does. Even in those cases, however, public policy analysis should not be viewed as the determinant of the outcome of the nonmarket activity. Instead, public policy analysis is better viewed as providing information about the consequences of alternatives for the various interests affected.

In the case of the extension of daylight saving time, Congress was the relevant institution and lobbying was the principal action of the proponents and opponents of an extension. To predict the outcome of the nonmarket competition, the first step is to use the framework presented in this chapter to understand the effectiveness of the interests. The second step is to understand how the institution resolves the competing interests and their actions. In this case, the median voter theorem provides the understanding. The third step is to identify the design of effective nonmarket strategies for firms and other interests given the characteristics of the relevant institutions and their decision-making processes and procedures.

THE LEGISLATIVE HISTORY OF THE EXTENSION

In 1976 the Senate passed a bill extending daylight saving time to 8 months and 1 week, but the House did not act. In 1981 the House passed a bill providing for a shorter extension, but the Senate did not act. In 1983 the House rejected an extension. Finally, in 1985 the light at the end of the tunnel began to appear. Representative Edward J. Markey (D-MA), chairman of the Subcommittee on Energy Conservation, introduced a bill that would extend daylight saving time to the third Sunday in March and the first Sunday in November. The Subcommittee approved the bill by voice vote. The Energy and Commerce Committee, however, approved an amendment by Howard C. Nielson (R-UT) that moved the starting date back 2 weeks to the first Sunday in April. Approving the amended bill by voice vote, the committee sent it to the full House, which approved it by a 240 to 157 vote in October 1985.

In July 1985 Senator Slade Gorton (R-WA) introduced a bill extending daylight saving time, but opposition by senators from rural and Midwestern states led by Senators Wendell Ford (D-KY) and J. James Exon (D-NE) blocked the bill in the Commerce Committee. With the committee gates closed, Senator Gorton introduced his extension bill as a rider to an authorization bill for fire prevention and control programs. The amendment provided the same starting date as the House bill, but to recruit additional votes Gorton removed the 1-week extension in the fall. By a 36 to 58 vote the Senate defeated a motion to table the amendment and then by voice vote adopted the amendment and the bill. The House and Senate thus had both passed extensions of daylight saving time, but the measures were not identical. Rather than convene a conference to reconcile the bills, the House chose to enact the Senate bill. An authorization bill for fire prevention and control had been working its way through the House, and on June 24, 1986, the House, by unanimous consent, agreed to drop the 1-week extension in November and adopted the Senate bill.

THE POLITICS OF DAYLIGHT SAVING TIME

The politics of daylight saving time can be understood as a competition between those interests favoring and those opposed to an extension. Congress was the institutional arena for that

---

[23]States retained the right not to adopt daylight saving time. The dates had been chosen because the weather was generally similar at the beginning and end of the period.

[24]*Fortune*, November 12, 1984, p. 147.

competition. Senator Ford characterized the differences in interests as "any Kentucky mother who has sent a first-grader out to catch a bus on a dark, misty April morning takes a dim view about … electricity that might be saved on the East and West coasts and the number of afternoon tennis games that might be played here in Washington."[25]

The effects of an extension were broadly distributed, and at the beginning of the nonmarket competition in 1976, interests were poorly organized and their strategies only loosely coordinated. The status quo prevailed. The benefits to a number of groups, including recreation and business interests, were substantial, however, so interest groups had an incentive to form.

An extension of daylight saving time would affect a wide array of economic activity. As James Benfield, a lobbyist who served as executive director of the Daylight Saving Time Coalition (DSTC), explained, "Here's a way to increase economic activity by doing nothing more than changing the time on your wrist …. We are simply fine-tuning our use of time to adjust for daily life patterns and to translate those patterns into dollars for business."[26] An extension would shift the demand curve outward for a variety of goods. The Barbecue Industry Association estimated that an extension would increase the sales of briquettes by $56 million and starter fluid by $15 million. The Kingsford Company was an active supporter of the extension, and its parent company Clorox helped fund the DSTC. Bob Lederer of the American Association of Nurserymen stated, "When daylight saving time comes, people think spring and they start buying plants. And if daylight saving comes earlier, people will buy a lot more plants."[27] The Sporting Goods Manufacturers Association estimated that golfers would spend $7 million more on clubs and balls and would play 4 million more rounds of golf a year. Expenditures for tennis balls and rackets could increase by $7 million per year. Hardee's estimated that an extension would increase sales by an average of $800 per week per store. The Southland Corporation estimated that daylight saving time could increase sales at its 7-Eleven stores by $30 million annually. Pamela Sederholm, a spokesperson for 7-Eleven, said, "Women shop in daylight hours at a 7-Eleven. They go to supermarkets when it's dark." 7-Eleven also helped fund the DSTC.

Benfield conceived the idea of including Halloween in the extension to bring the candy industry into the DSTC.[28] Candy makers were interested in an additional hour of daylight on Halloween because some parents would allow their children to extend their trick-or-treating. Those candy companies were represented by the Chocolate Manufacturers Association, National Candy Brokers Association, and the National Confectioners Association. Representative Markey said, "This small step could make trick-or-treating for young children a much safer experience."[29] The deletion of the fall extension by Senator Gorton was a substantial blow to the candy interests— as well as to children.

Firms measured the impact of an extension in terms of their sales and profits. Increased sales also mean that customers benefit. Similarly, increased sales mean an increase in employment. The difference between the incentives of a firm (or its shareholders) and the incentives of customers and employees is both in the magnitude of their benefits and the cost of taking nonmarket action. Firms have relatively low costs of taking nonmarket action and thus may act when those with higher costs would not act. Customers and future employees typically are widely dispersed, costly to organize, and have incentives to free-ride, so they would not be expected to be active on the daylight saving time issue. Their interests, however, were represented by the firms that benefited from an extension. Thus, an important consequence of the participation of firms in nonmarket activity is that they often represent the interests of those who might otherwise not be represented due to high costs and low per-capita benefits. Firms regularly inform members of Congress of the jobs that would be created and other benefits that would accrue to their constituents.

An important factor in political competition is the alignment of interests among dissimilar groups. An interest group with a strong incentive to support the extension of daylight saving time was the RP Foundation Fighting Blindness, which had 400,000 members who suffered from retinitis pigmentosa and other eye diseases that caused night blindness. Although their interests were not directly economic, as were those of 7-Eleven and Kingsford, they had an incentive to support an extension just as business had. The fact that individuals with night blindness were disadvantaged could, however, be more compelling to some members of Congress than the economic interests of firms, customers, and employees.

On most issues, there are opposing interests, and one nonmarket strategy is to provide substitutes to reduce the adverse consequences to those opposed to the issue. The National Association of Broadcasters, for example, opposed the extension. Although most of the 2,450 AM radio stations licensed to operate only in the daytime had a PSA (presunrise authorization) that allowed them to begin broadcasting with reduced power at 6:00 A.M., nearly 450 did not have a PSA.[30] For many of these stations the most profitable advertising time was the morning commute hours, and profits would be reduced by an extension that would add an hour of broadcast time in the evening and eliminate an hour in the morning. This opposition was relatively easy to accommodate because adjustments in authorizations for AM radio stations were virtually costless to the supporters of the extension. As Benfield argued, the Federal Communications Commission (FCC) could extend the broadcast time in the morning. The amendment offered by Senator Gorton contained a provision allowing the FCC to make appropriate adjustments in broadcast authorizations.

In other instances there may be no means of satisfying opponents. Some Christian fundamentalists opposed the extension because they viewed it as contrary to God's will. Some Orthodox Jews opposed the extension because their morning prayers cannot begin earlier than 45 minutes before sunrise, and the length of the prayers might make them late for work.

---

[25]*Congressional Quarterly Weekly Report*, May 24, 1986, p. 1177.

[26]*Fortune*, November 12, 1984, p. 150.

[27]Ibid., pp. 150–151.

[28]He was successful in expanding the coalition from 4 members in 1983 to 16 in 1985.

[29]*Congressional Quarterly Weekly Report*, May 4, 1985, p. 839.

[30]*Congressional Quarterly Weekly Report*, May 24, 1986, p. 1177.

A number of other groups also opposed the extension.[31] Some parents opposed it because their children would have to go to school in the dark. This was more of a problem on the western edges of time zones.[32] Some farmers objected to the extension, and their interests were represented by a number of members of Congress. Representative Thomas A. Daschle (D-SD) said, "The time shift would hurt farmers, particularly the estimated 30 percent who hold second jobs and who would have less daylight to perform morning chores." Even more important, he said, was the safety threat to "children who would wait in the dark for school buses as early as 6:30 A.M."[33] These interests were represented by organizations such as the PTA and the American Farm Bureau.

THE ROLE OF INFORMATION

One feature of political competition is the provision of information about the consequences of political alternatives. The DOT and the National Safety Council reported that the extension of daylight saving time would not significantly increase the risk to schoolchildren. Opponents of the extension attacked DOT's accident data from the 1974 to 1975 extension and argued that it was insufficient to warrant any conclusion. In 1986 the DOT countered when Secretary Elizabeth H. Dole wrote to Senate majority leader Robert Dole (R-KS) stating that DOT studies concluded that an extension "would reduce traffic deaths nationwide by a minimum of 22, injuries by a minimum of 1,525, and societal costs from auto accidents by a

minimum of $28 million [annually] ... with possible savings being as much as twice as large."[34]

The impact of such facts is difficult to determine, but whatever their significance, politics is not primarily a competition among facts. Politics is better viewed as a competition of interests, and information is important to the extent that it helps identify the relationship between political alternatives and their consequences for those interests. Through the efforts of the DSTC, many legislators learned of the benefits to businesses and their constituents. Complaints from farmers, parents, and others provided information that led Representative Daschle and Senators Exon and Ford to oppose an extension.

AN ANALYTICAL CHARACTERIZATION OF THE POLITICS OF DAYLIGHT SAVING TIME

The next step in the analysis is to move from interests to outcomes. In the case of daylight saving time, the median voter theorem provides that step. The alternatives before Congress can be summarized by the length of daylight saving time, as measured by the number of weeks constrained by beginning and ending on a Sunday. The principal alternatives are displayed in Figure 7-8. The status quo q is farthest to the left, and Representative Markey's bill, denoted by m, is farthest to the right.

Because of the constituency connection, members of Congress were concerned about the interests of their constituents. Particularly in states and districts at western edges of a

---

FIGURE 7-8 Median Voter Theorem and Daylight Saving Time

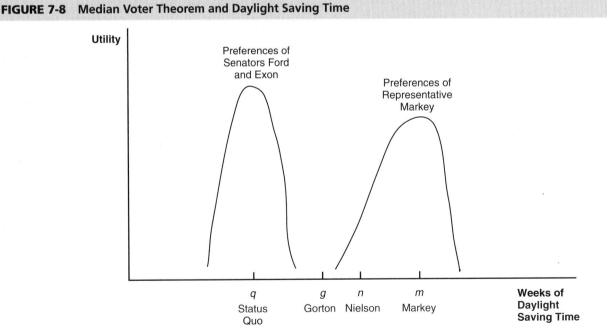

---

[31]Some opposition defied logic. Representative Thomas F. Hartnett (D-SC) asked "how big the mushrooms are going to be with that extra hour of daylight in the evening" (*Fortune,* November 12, 1984, p. 150).

[32]DOT estimated that dawn would be, on average, at 6:48 A.M. but would occur at 7:00 A.M. on the western edges of time zones.

[33]*Congressional Quarterly Weekly Report,* May 4, 1985, p. 839.

[34]*Congressional Quarterly Weekly Report,* May 24, 1986, p. 1177. Sood and Ghosh (2007) estimated that the extension of daylight saving time significantly reduced crashes for vehicle occupants and crashes involving pedestrians.

time zone, pressure from farmers and parents of school-age children outweighed the pressure from the supporters of the extension. Senators Ford and Exon, then, can be thought of as preferring a length of daylight saving time at, or perhaps to the left of, the status quo. This is illustrated in Figure 7-8 by a preference function with a peak at their most preferred length, their ideal point, and declining the farther an alternative is from that point.[35] The preferences of Representative Markey, whose district was on the eastern edge of a time zone, are also illustrated in Figure 7-8. Indeed, each member of Congress can be thought of as having preferences of a similar form.

If the House had only two alternatives, q and m, representatives would simply vote for their preferred alternative. The alternatives were not restricted, however, because the legislative process was open and a bill with any number of weeks of daylight saving time could be proposed. Legislators could thus introduce alternatives they preferred to either q or m. For example, an alternative to the right of q and to the left of the median would be preferred to q by all those representatives with ideal points to the right of the median plus some of those to the left. It thus would defeat q on a majority vote. Indeed, the only alternative that could not be defeated in this manner by some other alternative is the median of the ideal points of the legislators. That is, any other alternative would receive fewer than half the votes against the median. Hence, the median is the majority-rule winner. In the House, Representative Nielson's amendment n to the Markey bill was closer to the median and was preferred by a majority to both q and m.

In the Senate Commerce Committee Senators Ford and Exon were successful in preserving the status quo against Senator Gorton's bill g. Senator Gorton, however, was able to attach his bill as a rider to an authorization bill. A majority of the Senate preferred g to q, as reflected by the 36 to 58 vote defeating the motion to table g. The fact that Senator Gorton's proposal provided a week less of daylight saving time than the Nielson amendment may indicate that Gorton believed that n was farther from the median of the ideal points in the Senate.

The House and the Senate had thus passed extensions that were preferred to the status quo, but before an extension could become law, the two chambers had to reconcile the two bills. Bargaining between the chambers resulted in the House agreeing to g, which was enacted.[36]

---

[35]Daschle's district was also at the western edge of a time zone, whereas Gorton's state was at the eastern edge.

[36]In 2005 Congress again extended daylight saving time effective in 2007. Daylight saving time now begins the second Sunday of March and ends the first Sunday of November. The public policy explanation for the extension was energy savings, but as *ABC News,* July 26, 2005, headlined, "Are Golf, Shopping Behind Daylight Saving Time?" The Sporting Goods Manufacturing Association and the National Association of Convenience Stores were principal sources of funding for the DSTC.

CASES

Federal Express and Labor Organization

Historically, labor relations for the Federal Express Corporation had been governed by the Railway Labor Act (RLA), which required that unions attempting to organize the employees of a company must do so nationally. Federal Express had operated as an "express company" under the RLA. Organized labor, however, claimed that a bill enacted in 1995 subjected Federal Express to labor organization under a different law, the National Labor Relations Act (NLRA), which allowed unions to organize workers locally. Avoiding unionization was a key element of Federal Express's market strategy. Of its 110,000 domestic employees, only its 3,000 pilots were unionized.[37] Because local organization was usually easier for a union than national organization, Federal Express wanted Congress to pass new legislation that would clearly place its labor practices under the RLA.

Federal Express's nonmarket objective was to have a Senate ally attach a relatively small amendment (a "rider") to a much larger bill (a "vehicle"). The legislative vehicle in this instance was the annual authorization bill for the Federal Aviation Administration, which was regarded as a "must-pass" measure. The substantive aim of the rider was to remove the jurisdictional ambiguity associated with the status quo by clearly making Federal Express's labor relations subject to the RLA.[38] Although minor in comparison with the larger bill, the amendment would have attracted attention and opposition if offered outright on the Senate or House floors, so Federal Express deferred to the judgment of one of its Senate allies who successfully negotiated for insertion of the amendment in the conference committee. When the bill and rider came back to the Senate for a vote on final passage, however, senators aligned with organized labor decided to mount a fight. They sought to block the vote on final passage of the conference report (and hence the bill) unless and until the rider were dropped. They began a filibuster.

To stop the filibuster (i.e., to invoke cloture) and thereby move to certain passage of the bill and the rider, Federal Express and its supporters in the Senate had to build a majority of at least 60 votes. Suppose that supporters were willing to trade votes or other support of varying value to recruit the needed votes to stop the filibuster. Let the status quo q denote the current ambiguous labor jurisdiction, and let the conference committee bill b denote unambiguous RLA jurisdiction. Along with the filibuster pivot f (the 41st ideal point) in the Senate, these points are identified in Figure 7-9.

Assume that each senator has a symmetric utility function, so that his or her preference for q or b is determined by the relative distances from his or her ideal point to q and b. For convenience, assume also that the shapes of senators' utility functions are symmetric and that their ideal points are uniformly distributed (equally spaced) over the line as shown. The median senator's ideal point is shown as m, and Federal Express's allies have ideal points on the right side of the spectrum. Finally, assume that if the support provided or votes traded are sufficiently valuable, a senator will vote for b. Remember, however, that Federal Express supporters do not want to trade more votes or provide more support than is necessary. ■

Preparation Questions

1. Which senators will not receive support or vote trades and why not?
2. Which senators will receive support or vote trades and why?
3. Which senator will receive the most valuable support or vote trades and why?
4. Does it make a difference if an opposing group (say, the AFL-CIO) were simultaneously working to offset the efforts of Federal Express and its legislative allies by implementing its own vote recruitment strategy?

FIGURE 7-9 Federal Express and Labor Organization

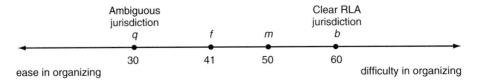

Source: This case was prepared by Professors David P. Baron and Keith Krehbiel for the purpose of illustrating theories of vote recruitment. Although it is based on an actual legislative history, it is not intended to suggest that Federal Express dealt with this nonmarket issue in this manner. Copyright © 1997 by the Board of Trustees of the Leland Stanford Junior University. All rights reserved. Reprinted with permission.

---

[37]"This Mr. Smith Gets His Way in Washington," *New York Times*, October 10, 1996.

[38]Public laws cannot mention private companies explicitly. Therefore, the language that accomplished this task was necessarily opaque. The provision simply inserted the term "express company" into the Railway Labor Act of 1926. The term had been stricken—some claimed accidentally—from the law in 1995 when Congress eliminated the Interstate Commerce Commission, which had regulated surface transportation.

Carried Interest Taxation

INTRODUCTION

Congress threatened to increase from 15 percent to 35 percent the tax rate on the income of partners in private equity firms, venture capital firms, and some real estate and oil and gas partnerships. Partners in these firms received a share, typically 20 percent but as high as 30 or 40 percent for some elite firms, of the gain on investments above a predetermined high water mark, with the remainder going to the limited partners and outside investors. The 20 percent economic interest in the venture typically was greater than the partners' investment of their own capital, so the economic interest did not represent a return on capital. Their economic interest was preferred to as carried interest or "sweat equity" as some in the industry referred to it. Carried interest was currently treated as a long-term gain and taxed at the long-term capital gains rate of 15 percent. Legislation passed by the House of Representatives would treat carried interest as ordinary income, which was taxed at a 35 percent rate.

Victor Fleischer, a law professor at the University of Illinois–Chicago, testified in a congressional hearing, "This quirk in the tax law is what allows some of the richest workers in the country to pay tax on their labor at a low rate."[39] On his blog Harvard University economics professor Greg Mankiw quoted economist and columnist Paul Krugman, who had asked, "why does Henry Kravis pay a lower rate on his management fees than I pay on my book royalties?" Mankiw answered, "In both cases, a person (investment manager, author) is putting in effort today for a risky return at some point in the future. The tax treatment should be the same in the two cases."[40]

Douglas Lowenstein, president of the Private Equity Council, argued, "The proposal would undo decades of established partnership tax law and create a new standard that reserves capital gains rates only for those with the wherewithal to invest equity into an enterprise. Congress should not raise private equity taxes by 130 percent and create the risk that some of the benefits of this economic activity could be discouraged. Partners 'who invest their time and effort to add value to an asset they own' are rightfully paying the lower capital gains rate on the resulting investment profits."[41]

BACKGROUND

Some critics of the current tax treatment, including unions, were opposed to private equity firms because jobs were frequently eliminated when acquired firms were restructured. Other critics cited the extremely high incomes of private equity firm partners. Stephen A. Schwarzman, a co-founder of the Blackstone Group, earned $684 million in 2006 and held a $3 million birthday party that included entertainment by Martin Short and Patti LaBelle. Blackstone went public in June 2007 with a market capitalization of $33 billion, and Schwarzman's

share was valued at $7.5 billion. The bill to increase the tax on carried interest was introduced in the House the day after Blackstone went public.

Senator Gordon Smith (R-OR) chided his colleagues, "It seems to me we were brought to this hearing because of the extravagant lifestyle of one person."[42] The legislative threat, however, was not due to extravagance but to a flaw in the personal income tax law and a "pay as you go" pledge by congressional Democrats. The flaw was the adjusted minimum tax (AMT) which threatened an additional tax burden on 23 million taxpayers. In 1968 the AMT had been enacted to make certain that wealthy individuals could not avoid personal income taxes. The flaw was that the income at which the AMT took effect was not adjusted for inflation. If Congress did not act, the AMT exemption income would fall from $62,550 in 2006 to $45,000 in 2007 for taxpayers filing joint returns with the average increase in taxes estimated at $2,000 per taxpayer. Most members of Congress viewed the AMT as unneeded and a political hazard and wanted it eliminated.

In 1990 Congress adopted a "pay as you go" rule in a bipartisan effort to reduce the budget deficit. Congress began to waive the rule in the late 1990s, and in 2002 the Republican-controlled Congress allowed the provision to expire.[43] When the Democrats won majorities in both chambers in 2006, they resurrected the "pay as you go" provision to demonstrate their fiscal responsibility in light of what they claimed was uncontrolled spending by the Republican Congress.[44] The rule required that any tax revenue lost from the reduction or elimination of the AMT be made up by increases in revenue from other taxes.

LEGISLATION

Charles Rangel (D-NY), the new chairman of the House Ways and Means Committee, introduced major tax reform legislation in the form of the Tax Reduction and Reform Act of 2007. The $796 billion (over 10 years) bill provided for the permanent repeal of the AMT and a reduction in the corporate profits tax rate from 35 percent to 30.5 percent.[45] To make up the lost revenue, the bill would tax carried interest at 35 percent and impose a 4 percent surtax on individual incomes above $150,000 and $200,000 for couples filing a joint return.[46] The bill would also eliminate a special tax rate for manufacturers, disallow for tax purposes the use of the LIFO accounting method for inventories, and disallow certain deductions associated with untaxed foreign profits.

---

[39]*International Herald Tribune*, September 22, 2007.

[40]http://gregmankiw.blogspot.com, July 19, 2007.

[41]*Daily Deal/The Deal*, October 26, 2007.

[42]*Los Angeles Times*, September 19, 2007.

[43]*Wall Street Journal*, November 9, 2007.

[44]Waiving the rule required a majority in the Senate and in the House both a majority and approval by the Democrat leadership. (*Wall Street Journal*, November 9, 2007)

[45]Rangel argued that the U.S. corporate income tax was too high and hurt U.S. competitiveness.

[46]The surtax on high-income filers was estimated to increase tax revenues by $634 billion over 10 years.

Democrats called the bill the "mother of all tax revisions," and Republicans labeled it the "mother of all tax hikes," since the "pay as you go" rule required that the lost tax revenue be made up by tax increases. The business community generally applauded the provisions eliminating the AMT and reducing the corporate tax rate, but opposed the tax increases.

The Bush administration opposed any increase in taxes. Secretary of the Treasury Hank Paulson argued that a tax increase would "hurt the ability of our businesses and workers to compete in a global economy. The proposed new surtax on individual income would burden millions of small businesses, and undermine job creation."[47] Representative Jim McCrery (R-LA), ranking minority member of the Ways and Means Committee, said that Rangel was exploiting the AMT to "lock Congress into a system where we are guaranteed to raise taxes by $3.5 trillion over 10 years. That will hurt our nation's competitiveness and cost us American jobs."[48]

THE CARRIED INTEREST PROVISION

The higher tax on carried interest would raise $25.7 billion over 10 years. The director of the Congressional Budget Office, Peter R. Orszag, testified: "Most economists would view at least part, and perhaps all, of the carried interest as performance-based compensation for management services … rather than a return on financial capital invested by that partner." Alan Auerbach, a University of California–Berkeley economics professor, estimated that the proposed tax increase on carried interest would likely not decrease the assets of pension plans by more than two basis points a year nor raise the cost of partnerships by more than 20 basis points a year. He stated, "If half of the tax increase were shifted to investors, this tax burden would imply a reduction of at most around 2 basis points in the annual return of these pension funds' assets, and quite possibly less."[49]

The private equity industry had anticipated the threat to the tax treatment of carried interest and had begun hiring experts and lobbyists. Private equity firms spent $5.5 million on hired lobbyists in the first 6 months of 2007. Blackstone paid Ogilvy Government Relations $3.74 million during the first half of 2007.[50] Over 20 lobbying firms were working for the industry, and the industry hired former members of Congress and Clinton administration officials to lobby against the tax increase. Peter G. Peterson of Blackstone and David M. Rubenstein of the Carlyle Group had personally lobbied members of Congress. Lisa McGreevy, chief lobbyist for the Managed Funds Association, said, "I have already done more than 250 meetings on the Hill and have the swollen feet to prove it."[51]

Money managers also contributed to congressional campaigns with hedge funds contributing $4.4 million with 77 percent going to Democrats. Venture capital firms contributed $6.3 million with a majority going to Democrats, according to *Congressional Quarterly*.[52] Some staffers for members of Congress warned that the intense lobbying by the private equity industry was creating enemies on the Hill. According to the *Financial Times*, the Private Equity Council and the Managed Funds Association "tend to blame each other for black eyes to the industry's reputation."[53]

Bruce Rosenblum, managing director of the Carlyle Group and chairman of the Private Equity Council composed of Blackstone, Carlyle, and nine other firms, testified that "Another possible consequence is that U.S. firms will become less competitive with foreign PE firms, and even foreign governments with huge investment war chests. As governments the world over are striving to make their tax systems more competitive to attract foreign capital and challenge U.S. dominance, this Congress is considering a proposal that would go in the opposite direction."[54]

The U.S. Chamber of Commerce echoed this position. The Chamber stated that the tax increase on carried interest would affect 15.5 million Americans in 2.5 million partnerships.[55] Russell Read, chief investment officer of CalPERS, which had a $17.5 billion stake in private equity, said referring to a tax increase, "My personal expectation is that this will be a factor. How large it will be is really difficult to know."[56] CalPERS took no position on the issue of the taxation of carried interest nor did the National Conference on Public Employee Retirement Systems (NCPERS). NCPERS had initially opposed the tax increase on carried interest but withdrew its opposition because "a majority of our members do not share that opinion."

Others were also active. The Real Estate Roundtable wrote to members of Congress and testified in hearings. Adam Ifshin, president of DLC Management, a real estate development firm, testified before the House Ways and Means Committee, stating in written testimony, "The bill presents a barrier to entry for those who bring the ideas, the know-how, and the effort to those with money to invest. Development and redevelopment in many communities would suffer, no question about it."[57]

In September 2007 the Access to Capital Coalition was formed by a group of minority and women money managers with the financial backing of the Private Equity Council. Willie E. Woods Jr. stated, "The present carried interest policy has been essential to attracting top talented minorities and women to the industry as independent firms and fund managers. Its elimination, consequently, would have the unfortunate effect of impeding this great progress."[58]

The business opposition to the tax increase on carried interest was not unanimous. Leo Hindrey Jr., managing partner

[47]*Financial Times*, October 26, 2007.

[48]*Daily Deal/The Deal*, October 26, 2007.

[49]*Pensions and Investments*, September 17, 2007.

[50]Blackstone was also fighting a bill that would ban the listing on stock exchanges of partnerships that pay no corporate income tax (*Financial Times*, November 1, 2007). Another provision would tax such firms at the corporate tax rate of 35 percent.

[51]*Financial Times*, November 1, 2007.

[52]*New York Times*, November 2, 2007.

[53]*Financial Times*, November 1, 2007.

[54]*Pensions and Investments*, September 17, 2007.

[55]*Los Angeles Times*, September 7, 2007.

[56]Ibid.

[57]Ifshin had testified on behalf of the Real Estate Roundtable and the International Council of Shopping Centers, many of which are organized as partnerships. *Washington Post*, September 7, 2007.

[58]*Washington Post*, September 7, 2007.

of InterMedia Partners LP, a private equity firm, stated in testimony before the House Ways and Means Committee, "A tax loophole the size of a Mack truck is right now generating unwarranted and unfair windfalls to a privileged group of money managers, and, to no one's surprise, these individuals are driving right through this $12 billion-a-year hole. Congress, starting with this committee, needs to tax money management income—what we call carried interest—as what it is, which is plain old ordinary income."[59] William D. Stanhill, founding partner of Trailhead Investors in Denver, stated in testimony, "I don't think it's fair for … teachers and firefighters to subsidize special tax breaks for me and other venture capitalists. Or for private equity and hedge fund managers."[60] He also stated that a higher tax rate would not affect venture capital, "We get ample compensation, financial and psychic, for the work we do and the risks we take."[61]

Warren Buffett supported a tax increase. Referring to when he ran an investment partnership, he said, "I was managing money for other people … believe me, it's an occupation. I believe you should tax people on carried interest."[62] Earlier in June he had told a gathering of 400 venture capitalists and money managers gathered to raise funds for Senator Hillary Clinton (D-NY), "The 400 of us [here] pay a lower part of our income in taxes than our receptionists do—or do our cleaning ladies, for that matter. If you're the luckiest 1 percent of humanity, you owe it to the rest of humanity to think about the other 99 percent."[63]

In October the Service Employees International Union staged a protest against the Carlyle Group with a street theater depicting executives such as David Rubenstein as "Fat Cat Tycoons." For Halloween the union repeated the performance, including a protester dressed as "Sugar Daddy David Rubinstein" who handed out candy to mock lobbyists.[64]

Professor Fleischer commented, "The Private Equity Council has done a great job using sound bites to shape the debate. It started out as a debate about the tax rates that wealthy fund managers pay. Now it's about whether tax reform would hurt pensioners, minorities, and destroy capitalism as we know it."[65]

In September venture capitalists gathered for lunch in Palo Alto, California, and Mark Heesen of the National Venture Capital Association (NVCA) warned the group that "We are in a true battle." The NVCA sought to distance itself from the money management firms. Emily Mendell of the NVCA stated, "We are making distinctions between the long-term nature of venture capital investment versus the shorter-term economics that the other funds employ. We have a unique argument—we don't do arbitrage, we don't do financial engineering, we make assets from nothing. We build companies." Ted Schlein, a partner at Kleiner Perkins Caufield & Byers and chairman of

NVCA, said, "If Congress is serious about promoting a competitiveness and innovation agenda and supporting new energy technologies, then it should be extremely thoughtful before it passes legislation which will discourage investments in the startups and small businesses that are key players in these arenas." Jonathan Silver, a venture capitalist with Core Financial Partners, stated in testimony before the House Ways and Means Committee, "Early-stage companies would be harder to form and fund, reducing the overall number of venture-backed companies and hurting the lifeblood of our entrepreneurial ecosystem."[66]

LEGISLATIVE DEVELOPMENTS

The Senate was considering a bill to increase the tax on carried interest only for private equity firms that went public. Blackstone wrote to Senator John Kerry (D-MA) that the bill under consideration by the Senate Finance Committee would increase the Group's taxes by $525 million a year and partners' taxes by $175 million and would reduce its market capitalization by $10.5 billion. Senator Kerry had compared "private equity executives with other entrepreneurs who risk their own capital and therefore merit special tax treatment."[67] Senator Charles Schumer (D-NY) planned to introduce a bill that would increase taxes on all partnerships in addition to those generating carried interest.

On an 88–5 vote the Senate passed its own tax bill, which eliminated the ATM for 19 million taxpayers, reducing their taxes by $51 billion. The Senate, however, opposed any tax increase and waived the "pay as you go" rule. Senate Majority Leader Harry Reid (D-NV) had decided not to push the tax on carried interest because Republicans had threatened a filibuster and Democrats would be unable to invoke cloture and bring the bill to a vote. Senator Barack Obama (D-IL) issued a statement in response: "If there ever was a doubt that Washington lobbyists don't actually represent real Americans, it's the fact that they stopped leaders of both parties from requiring elite investment firms to pay their fair share of taxes, even as middle-class families struggle to pay theirs."[68]

Rangel's tax reform bill was bogged down because of its complexity, and needing to deal with the AMT issue so that the Internal Revenue Service could prepare the 2007 tax forms and tax refunds would not be delayed, Rangel introduced a bill to provide a 1-year fix. The $76 billion bill would freeze the AMT for 1 year, extend some popular tax credits for families, and increase the tax on carried interest.[69] On November 1 on a 22–13 vote the Ways and Means Committee passed the bill, and the full House approved it within a week on a 216–193 vote. After the committee vote, Lowenstein of the Private Equity Council said, "We are disappointed with

[59]*Pensions and Investments,* September 17, 2007.
[60]Ibid.
[61]*International Herald Tribune,* September 22, 2007.
[62]*Financial Times,* November 15, 2007.
[63]Ibid.
[64]*Mergers and Acquisitions Journal,* December 1, 2007.
[65]*New York Times,* October 3, 2007.

[66]*International Herald Tribune,* September 22, 2007.
[67]*Financial Times,* August 25, 2007.
[68]*Mergers and Acquisitions Journal,* December 1, 2007.
[69]The freeze was designed to keep the number of taxpayers subject to the AMT at the same level as in 2006. The income level was set at $66,250 for joint filers and $44,350 for single filers. The tax credits were detailed in *Accounting Today,* December 17, 2007.

the committee's actions today, and we will continue to oppose legislation to change the tax treatment of carried interest. We remain hopeful that in the end this legislation will not be enacted into law."[70]

With time fleeting, the House and Senate conferred and agreed to the House freeze on the AMT but dropped the tax increase on carried interest, sending the bill to President Bush for his signature.

Lisa McGreevy of the Managed Funds Association commented, "This issue is definitely still on the table and will stay there until major tax reform is passed." ■[71]

Preparation Questions

1. Evaluate the strategy used by the private equity industry to deal with the threatened increase in taxes on carried interest.

2. Should the venture capital industry join with the private equity industry, or should it separate from the private equity industry? That is, is it better for the venture capital industry to join with the private equity industry in a broad coalition to defeat higher taxes on carried interest, or should the venture capital industry pursue, either as a primary or a contingent objective, an objective such as taxing as ordinary income carried interest associated with money management and private equity but not taxing carried interest on venture capital investments associated with creating jobs?

3. Now that Rangel's legislative effort failed, will the carried interest issue go away?

4. If the tax on carried interest were increased, what would be the effect on the private equity and venture capital markets? How should firms in those industries adjust their market strategies?

5. Formulate a strategy for the venture capital industry to deal with the carried interest taxation issue.

Wal-Mart and Health Care Policy

On June 30, 2009, Wal-Mart executive vice president Leslie Dach went to the White House to deliver a letter to President Obama's Chief of Staff Rahm Emanuel in which the company announced its conditional support for mandatory health insurance provided by companies. The letter was signed by Wal-Mart CEO Mike Duke, Andrew W. Stern, president of the Service Employees International Union (SEIU), and John D. Podesta, who headed the Obama administration's transition team and was head of the Center for American Progress, a liberal policy organization. The letter stated, "We are for an employer mandate which is fair and broad in its coverage, but any alternative to an employer mandate should not create barriers to hiring entry level employees. We look forward to working with the Administration and Congress to develop a requirement that is both sensible and equitable. Support for a mandate also requires the strongest possible commitment to rein in health care costs. Guaranteeing cost containment is essential."

The SEIU had been at war with Wal-Mart for years.[72] It had attempted without success to organize Wal-Mart employees and, given its failure and its inability to get Congress to act, decided to conduct a private politics campaign against the company. In 2005 it provided $1 million to create and staff Wal-Mart Watch, an NGO that campaigned against the company for years.

In 2006 Wal-Mart developed a new nonmarket strategy.[73] It had presaged its strategy in 2005 when it called on Congress to increase the minimum wage.[74] It also broadened its health insurance offerings and reduced the waiting time before an employee became eligible. By 2009 53 percent of its employees were insured through the company, up from 46.2 percent 3 years earlier. The average for the retail industry was 45 percent. The company estimated that 94 percent of its employees had health insurance through the company, a spouse, parents, or Medicaid, which covered 36,000 of its 1.4 million employees.

Then-CEO Lee Scott began meeting with Andrew Stern of the SEIU in late 2006, and gradually relations between the company and the union improved. The SEIU continued to fund Wal-Mart Watch, which relentlessly criticized the company, but the staff of the activist group decreased from 40 to 10 in 2009. Wal-Mart had opened a war room in 2005 to address the barrage of criticism it faced, but closed it 2 years later as it embarked on its new strategy. The company and the SEIU joined to call for affordable health care for all by 2012.

One objective of Wal-Mart's new health insurance strategy was to obtain a seat at the table as the Obama administration, Congress, and various affected interest groups bargained over the configuration of a new health care policy. The pharmaceutical industry had initiated this strategy by pledging cost reductions of $80 billion over 10 years, and hospitals pledged cost reductions of $155 billion over 10 years. "Everybody is now trying to get their seat on the train," said Emanuel.[75]

---

[70]*Los Angeles Times*, September 2, 2007.

[71]*Financial Times*, November 1, 2007.

[72]See the Part I integrative case *Wal-Mart: Nonmarket Pressure and Reputation Risk (A)* and the Chapter 20 case *Wal-Mart: Nonmarket Pressure and Reputation Risk (B): A New Nonmarket Strategy.*

[73]Ibid.

[74]Wal-Mart pays significantly above the minimum wage, so an increase would have little effect on the company. It would, however, affect many small retailers that pay the minimum wage, making them less competitive.

[75]*New York Times*, July 1, 2009.

In a scathing editorial the *Wall Street Journal* criticized Wal-Mart's support for an employer mandate and more generally for going along with the Obama administration's desire "to transfer the choices about [health care] coverage to government from consumers." The *Journal* explained why businesses like Wal-Mart were participating, "Businesses are going along with this and other gambits in part because of a prisoners' dilemma. They're terrified of being shut out of the Democratic health negotiations lest they get stuck with the bill." The *Journal* more generally criticized big businesses for "trying to buy protection or some political reprieve …. Yet the political class is simply pocketing these concessions and demanding more, hastening the day when government controls most U.S. health dollars."[76]

The National Retail Federation (NRF), which represented 1.6 million retail establishments employing 24 million people and with sales of $4.6 trillion, was shocked by Mal-Mart's support for an employer mandate.[77] Two weeks after the announcement the NRF swung into action. NRF CEO Tracy Mullin wrote to its members, "When Wal-Mart sent a letter to President Obama two weeks ago supporting government mandates on businesses as a part of reform, the retail industry was astonished. Seeing the company in lock-step with the unions on this issue was troubling to say the least. Although the move may provide a short-term public relations boost to Wal-Mart, it could have long-lasting, devastating consequences to retailers throughout the country. This stunning turn of events left NRF with a decision to make. We could stand idly by and allow Wal-Mart to tip the scales on the health care debate, cower and release an innocuous statement that would neither support nor condemn their decision, or stand up for all retailers and come out swinging."[78] The NRF sent a letter to the chair and ranking minority member of the House Ways and Means Committee expressing strong opposition to the House health care reform bill. The letter stated, "Employer mandates of any kind amount to a tax on jobs. We can think of few more dangerous steps to take in the middle of our present recession."[79] NRF executives and lobbyists intensified their efforts in Washington, speaking with members of Congress about the health care reform alternatives under consideration. NRF executives also worked the media, appearing on television news shows and meeting with reporters.

Neil Trautwein of the NRF said, "We have been one of the foremost opponents to an employer mandate. We are surprised and disappointed by Wal-Mart's choice to embrace and employer mandate in exchange for a promise of cost savings."[80] He added that an employer mandate was "the single most destructive thing you could do to the health-care system shy of a single-payer system" and "would quite possibly cut off the economic recovery we all desperately need." Wal-Mart spokesperson David Tovar responded, "We know that others may have a different opinion, but we believe that we have taken a pro-business position. The present system is not sustainable."[81] Costco CFO Richard Galanti commented that Wal-Mart probably believed it was "going to be dragged into providing coverage one way or another, and might as well drag everyone else in retailing along with them."[82] Over 90 percent of Costco's employees were enrolled in the company's health care plan. Costco's employees were unionized.

A central concern about the Obama administration's health care reform was how costly the expanded insurance coverage sought by the administration would be and how it would be financed. The administration claimed that health care costs to those currently with health insurance could be lower with widespread coverage. The administration also pledged that any health care bill would contain the growth in health care costs.

MARKET EFFECTS

As a retailer Wal-Mart faced competition from other domestic firms, including large firms such as Target and Costco and numerous small retailers. Many small retailers did not offer health insurance to their employees, and an employer mandate would directly increase their costs. An employer mandate thus would hit most other retailers harder than Wal-Mart. Moreover, Wal-Mart was one of the few retailers that had weathered the recession well.

The cost of mandatory insurance would be incurred by employers, but health insurance and other benefits were part of the total compensation of an employee. In a perfectly competitive economy the cost to the employer of mandatory employer-provided health care coverage would be borne entirely by employees through lower wages. In a less competitive economy the cost would be shared between the employee and the employer, with the employer bearing some portion of the cost. For some marginal firms the additional cost could force them out of business.

Len Nichols of the New America Foundation described an employer mandate as "essentially a tax on low-wage labour."[83] He favored an individual mandate that required people to have health insurance just as people are required to have automobile insurance. The Chamber of Commerce, which represents 3 million businesses, opposed an employer mandate.

Wal-Mart recognized the potential effect on small businesses. The letter delivered stated, "Not every business can make the same contribution, but everyone must make some contribution. We are for an employer mandate which is fair and broad in its coverage, …."

Recognizing the impact, congressional leaders were discussing a lower requirement for small businesses. Congress had provided exemptions for small businesses on a number of regulatory measures.

[76]*Wall Street Journal*, Editorial, "Everyday Low Politics," July 2, 2009.
[77]Wal-Mart was not a member of the NRF.
[78]Tracy Mullin, NRF, July 13, 2009.
[79]Steve Pfister, NRF, Letter to Congressmen Charles Rangel and Dave Camp, July 9, 2009.
[80]*Wall Street Journal*, July 1, 2009.
[81]*Wall Street Journal*, July 14, 2009.
[82]Ibid.
[83]*The Economist*, July 11, 2009.

Under the current health care system Wal-Mart faced rising medical insurance costs and higher wages to the extent that employees had their own coverage if for no other reason than U.S. health care expenditures have been increasing at a 6 percent rate annually. Rising health care costs affected all employers, so the competitive positions in a domestic industry would not be greatly affected. The rising costs, however, were borne by the company and its employees and passing higher costs on to consumers would reduce demand. Cost containment thus was likely more important to Wal-Mart than was a government mandate. ■

Preparation Questions

1. What is the likely effect of an employer mandate on Wal-Mart's competitiveness relative to other retailers? Are small retailers likely to be exempted?
2. Is an employer mandate a tax on low-wage labor?
3. How likely is it that Congress and the Obama administration can contain the cost of health care?
4. Should Wal-Mart have joined with the SEIU and the Center for American Progress? Identify the reasoning that led Wal-Mart to this decision. Do you find any fault in that reasoning?

8

IMPLEMENTING NONMARKET STRATEGIES IN GOVERNMENT ARENAS

INTRODUCTION

Nonmarket strategies must be implemented effectively, and conversely, the effectiveness with which strategies can be implemented affects the choice among them. For example, implementing an informational strategy as considered in Chapter 7 requires access to government officeholders, the development of politically relevant information, lobbying, and possibly public advocacy. If access cannot be obtained or politically relevant information cannot be developed, an informational strategy is unlikely to be effective. Strategy formulation and implementation thus are necessarily intertwined. This chapter considers the following implementation activities: (1) lobbying, (2) electoral support, (3) coalition building, (4) grassroots and constituency campaigns, (5) testimony, (6) public advocacy, and (7) judicial actions.

Nonmarket issues often receive media and public attention, and that attention can shape and accelerate nonmarket activity. An important decision is whether a firm's nonmarket strategy should be high or low profile. A low-profile strategy emphasizes behind-the-scenes activities such as lobbying and is intended to reduce the chances of a reaction from opposing interest groups, public, or government officeholders. Most companies prefer low-profile strategies. A high-profile strategy involves more visible activities, including grassroots campaigns, public advocacy, and broad-scale lobbying. Whether a nonmarket strategy is implemented in a high- or low-profile manner depends on the nature of nonmarket competition, as considered in Chapters 6 and 7. In opposing higher fuel economy standards, the auto industry initially used a high-profile strategy to raise public concerns about safety, cost, and choice and a low-profile strategy to build a coalition of firms and unions that would be harmed by higher standards. By 2007 the high-profile strategy was no longer viable, and the industry began cooperating with government and relied on lobbying.

LOBBYING

Lobbying is a central component of most representation and informational strategies. Lobbying is the strategic communication of *politically relevant information* to government officeholders. That information may be provided to the president, a governor, executive branch officials, members of Congress or state legislatures, their staff, and committee staff. Lobbying also occurs at regulatory and administrative agencies, where it often takes place in ex parte meetings. Lobbying requires access, and access may be obtained through the constituency connection, campaign contributions, and personal relationships. In contrast to public advocacy and testimony before congressional committees, lobbying typically takes place behind the scenes.

Firms and other interests spend much more on lobbying than on any other implementation activity. According to data compiled by the Center for Responsive Politics, companies, unions, and other organizations spent $3.5 billion in 2010 on registered lobbying in Washington, D.C.[1] In addition, these interests spent substantial amounts on lobbying not subject to reporting requirements.

Lobbying expenditures by sector are reported in Table 8-1, and not surprisingly, the largest expenditures are in sectors in which government policy and regulation are important. This is consistent with Figure 2-2, which relates the importance of nonmarket strategies to the control of opportunities by government versus markets. As discussed in a later section, the pattern of lobbying expenditures is quite different from the pattern of campaign contributions. Business emphasizes lobbying, whereas labor unions emphasize election campaign contributions. For example, General Electric spent $253.0 million on lobbying from 1989 to 2011, whereas its political action committee donated $15.2 million to election campaigns over that period. The lobbying expenditures by individual companies vary with their nonmarket agendas. No unions were among

---

[1] www.opensecrets.org/influence.

TABLE 8-1 Lobbying Expenditures	
	2010 (millions)
Misc. business*	$577
Health	521
Finance, insurance, & real estate	475
Communications/electronics	369
Energy and natural resources	450
Transportation	244
Ideology/single issue	153
Defense	146
Agribusiness	121
Construction	53
Labor	47
Lawyers and Lobbyists	37
Total	$2,205

Note: *Includes business associations, retailing, miscellaneous manuacturers, chemicals, etc.

Source: Center for Responsive Politics, www.opensecrets.org/lobby

the top 20 spenders on lobbying for the 1989–2010 period or for 2010, but 10 of the top 15 election donors were unions. The trial lawyers who are aligned with organized labor were also among the top 15. The top three companies in 2010 lobbying expenditures were Pacific Gas & Electric, General Electric, and Federal Express.

Lobbying also takes place at state and local levels. Lobbying expenditures in California totaled $272 million in 2006, as reported by the Center for Public Integrity.

The Nature of Lobbying

Lobbying is important because of the large number of bills under consideration; for example, over 5,000 bills may be introduced in the House in a session. Members necessarily know little about many of the bills, so they have a demand for information. Conversely, in some cases members will check with lobbyists to determine whether the draft language of a bill is acceptable to them—that is, whether the interest group the lobbyist represents will support or at least not oppose it. This serves as a useful barometer of the political support or opposition a bill is likely to receive.

The scope of lobbying has broadened considerably over the past two decades. This broadening has had four components. First, managers have become more active participants in lobbying, just as they have become more deeply involved in formulating nonmarket strategies. Second, the professional lobbying industry has grown substantially as more interests participate in public policy processes. Third, the professional lobbying industry has become increasingly specialized with firms focusing on mobilizing constituents, grassroots lobbying, and research and technical services as well as the more traditional functions of monitoring government, providing access, and communicating information. Fourth, on majoritarian issues such as health care policy that affect large numbers of people, lobbying coordinated with advocacy through the mass media has become more common.

Lobbying is strategic in the sense of advocating one's position or countering the information provided by the other side. Analogous to a court trial, an interest advocates its side of an issue, and interests on the other side of the issue advocate their positions. Lobbying is also strategic in the sense that it is targeted to influential or pivotal officeholders and timed to the stages of the institutional process governing the issue. Lobbying does not involve threats or coercion and should not involve false information. Crying wolf and making false claims rarely is effective in the long run. Members of Congress and their staffs have heard such claims before and can have long memories.

Executives are often effective lobbyists because members of Congress and other government officials want to hear about a firm's concerns from the people in charge. A busy member of Congress will more often meet with a CEO or other high-ranking manager than with a representative of the firm's Washington office. High-level managers also have better knowledge of the firm's activities than do professional lobbyists and thus can be more specific. They also can make commitments that others cannot.

Technical and Political Information

Lobbying conveys two types of information: technical and political. Technical information consists of data and predictions about the consequences of alternative policies. In the chapter case *Internet Taxation* both supporters and opponents of the taxation of online sales provided technical information on the effects on the economy and on the tax revenue lost by states. In the Boeing and foreign leasing example in Chapter 6 Boeing provided technical information about the sales it could lose if the tax benefits on foreign leasing were reduced.

Political information pertains to the impact of an alternative on the constituents or policy interests of an officeholder. In the chapter case *Wal-Mart and its Urban Expansion Strategy* the company emphasized the number of jobs that would be created if its new store application were accepted. To support their lobbying, many firms develop data on their rent chains, including the number of employees and the supply contracts in each congressional district. This enables the firm to tell members of Congress how much business in their districts could be affected by a legislative proposal. The task of the lobbyist is to provide information that links the interests of the firm with those of legislators.

As an example of political information, consider the 1986 attempt to eliminate the tax credit for employing disadvantaged youths. The Treasury had estimated that eliminating the credit would increase tax collections by nearly $500 million a year, helping to reduce the federal budget deficit. One of the largest employers of youth, and thus one of the largest recipients of the tax credit, was the fast-food industry. The lobbying message of Pizza Hut was that the tax credit was an employment program that served constituents and was consistent with the public objective of providing opportunities for disadvantaged youth. The members of the tax-writing committee understood that Pizza Hut would benefit from retention of the tax credit, but they also understood that Pizza Hut's interests were aligned with those of the disadvantaged. The tax credits were retained.

When lobbying Congress, information should be provided at several levels, as illustrated in Figure 8-1. The CEO or other high-ranking managers may directly lobby a member of Congress with access facilitated by a professional lobbyist or government affairs professional. In addition to lobbying at the top, lobbying also takes place at the level of the member's personal staff and the staff of the relevant committees. The staff is the eyes and ears of the member, and

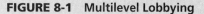

FIGURE 8-1   Multilevel Lobbying

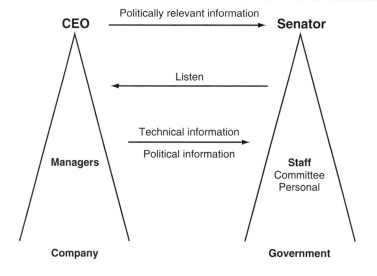

providing information to a key staffer may be as effective as meeting with the member. Technical information and detailed policy studies are best presented to the staff rather than the member. Political information can also be presented to the staff, which is generally quite knowledgeable and well equipped to evaluate such information.

The following are principles of effective lobbying:

- Know the institutional arenas in which the issue is addressed (e.g., Congress works through committees).
- Look for alignments of interests and explore opportunities to build coalitions.
- Time lobbying to the stages of the institutional decision-making process. (Lobby committee members, then pivotal floor members in advance of a floor vote.)
- Target key officeholders.
- Know the officeholder's interests and goals and frame messages accordingly.[2]
- Respect the officeholder and staff; in most cases they are intelligent and savvy.
- Educate but don't just talk. Listen to the officeholder and staff for information about their interests and concerns and for strategic advice about process, the preferences of other officeholders, and so on.
- Make straightforward presentations. Members of Congress are busy, understand politics well, and can see beyond window dressing. (Managers and professional lobbyists often leave a detailed written statement with members or their staff.)
- Explore compromises or concessions that might help resolve officeholders' concerns.
- Give credit to the officeholder.
- Establish access and maintain continuing relationships for the future (e.g., meet with committee staff even if there is no pending issue). Don't wait until there is a crisis.

Credibility and Relevance of Information

Information provided through lobbying must be both credible and relevant. Credibility requires an established reputation, self-evident data and analysis, or corroboration by others with different interests. A firm may have developed a reputation for providing technical information or for being a reliable predictor of the effects of legislative alternatives on the constituents of a government officeholder. Lobbying information that is backed by data and studies is generally more effective. Even if information is soft and cannot be backed by conclusive data, lobbying can be effective when the interests of the firm and the government officeholder are aligned, as in the Pizza Hut and youth employment example. Firms operating on the Internet used this alignment in conveying information about the possible effects of online taxes on growth, entrepreneurship, and employment. Information can also be credible if it can be corroborated by information provided by a party with opposing or nonaligned interests. The automakers' information about the relation between safety and vehicle size was corroborated by studies by the Insurance Institute for Highway Safety and by universities and was supported by a report by the National Academy of Sciences.

Politically relevant information is something that is not known to the government officeholders and their staffs; that is, "Tell me something I don't already know." Consider an issue that threatens the business of a firm. Officeholders understand that firms are interested in profits, and information about the effect on profits is unlikely to be effective. For example, a regulatory issue that would lower the profits of all firms in an industry could still leave a level playing field. If, however, a firm can credibly demonstrate that constituents will be hurt, firms will fail, or jobs will be lost or new businesses not started, the message can be effective. The messages of the opponents of Internet taxation focused on this.

The provision of technical and political information through lobbying is consistent with the pluralism perspective that public policies are determined by a competition of interests in the arenas of government institutions. Better information provided to officeholders then results in policies that in principle better serve the interests of citizens. This process can be subverted by the provision of false or manipulated information. As considered in Chapter 7, providing such information is irresponsible. Moreover, false or manipulated information is often exposed, which can damage

---

[2]Information on members of Congress and governors is provided in the *Almanac of American Politics 2012,* Barone and McCutcheon (2011).

a reputation and reduce the effectiveness of future nonmarket strategies. In addition, lobbying that is too aggressive could cause a backlash, as in the chapter case *Responsible Lobbying?*

Access

Congressional decentralization in the early 1970s gave additional autonomy to subcommittees and thereby increased the number of influential positions substantially. Successful lobbying thus requires more than developing relationships with a few powerful committee chairpersons. A firm that interacts with Congress on a variety of issues must maintain access to several committees and their relevant subcommittees. Lobbying typically focuses on members who hold strategic positions, such as a committee or subcommittee chair, and members who may be able to enlist the support of others. On many issues, lobbying executive branch agencies can also be important. The Department of the Treasury, for example, can have a significant effect on the outcome of a tax issue through its expertise in predicting the revenue effects of alternatives. The Department of Commerce is often a willing advocate of business interests. On a trade issue, lobbying may target the Office of the U.S. Trade Representative in addition to members of Congress. These agencies do not have direct constituents as does a member of Congress, so technical information is relatively more important than political information, although the latter is important to their political principals in Congress and the White House.

Members of Congress and executive branch officials have only limited time to meet with lobbyists and must allocate access. Those who have access possess an important asset. The key to continued access is the ability to provide politically valuable resources. Those resources include information about the effects of political alternatives on constituents, technical information pertaining to the likely consequences of alternatives, and information about the support that can be mustered for or against an alternative. Those resources also include electoral support, endorsements, and campaign contributions. Former officeholders are frequently useful in providing contacts, access, and expertise. Public Citizen reported that 43 percent of the members who left Congress from 1998 to 2005 became registered lobbyists.

Federal Express, which faces a continuing set of issues addressed in Congress, has developed access through a variety of means. As Doyle Cloud, vice president of regulatory and government affairs, explained, "We have issues constantly in Washington that affect our ability to deliver the services our customers demand as efficiently as possible."[3] In 2010 Federal Express spent $25.6 million on lobbying, including outside lobbying firms. Using outside firms is common, particularly for their contacts and established relationships with government officials. Federal Express also had on its board of directors Howard H. Baker Jr., former Republican Senate majority leader, and George J. Mitchell, former Democratic Senate majority leader.

Bargaining

On some nonmarket issues a company or an industry association may engage in explicit or implicit bargaining with a committee chair in Congress, an administrative agency, or the White House. In the health care reform legislation adopted in 2010 the pharmaceutical industry bargained with the White House over cost reductions. The deal struck reflected the bargaining power of the two sides. The Obama administration sought price reductions on pharmaceuticals, and its implicit threat was that Congress could seek large reductions and would allow the re-importation of drugs from countries such as Canada. The bargaining power of the pharmaceutical industry was the very real threat that it would launch a Harry-and-Louise style advertising campaign against health care reform, as had been successfully used to defeat the health care reform effort in the Clinton administration.

In setting fuel economy standards for 2025 the Detroit-three automakers bargained with the White House, resulting in an almost doubling of the mileage standards. Chrysler and General Motors were in a weak bargaining position because they had been bailed out by the government during the financial crisis, and the public would likely have reacted negatively to strong opposition from the industry.

---

[3]*New York Times,* October 12, 1996.

Timing and Focus

Lobbying should be timed to the stages of the legislative process. Some interests begin early and work with members of Congress in drafting new legislation. At the subcommittee or committee stage, the appropriate focus is the committee members, particularly the chair and ranking minority member. When legislation is being drafted or marked-up, lobbying often focuses on the committee staff who do the drafting. Because majority rule governs the committee process, lobbying is also directed at those who are likely to be pivotal, as considered in Chapter 7. Larry Whitt, vice president of Pizza Hut, explained, "We focus on those on the fence."[4] Lobbying for support on the floor requires a broader effort and again focuses on pivotal members. The Chapter 7 case *Federal Express and Labor Organization* focuses on pivotal legislators.

On an issue in conference committee, the focus is on the conferees. In the case of the tax credit for employing disadvantaged youth, the House bill provided a 2-year extension, whereas the Senate bill provided a 3-year extension. Having been successful in both chambers, Pizza Hut turned its attention to the conference committee. Peyton George, a lobbyist for Pizza Hut, stated, "I've figured out my list of who will be the conferees, and I'm trying to maintain contact with every one of [them]."[5]

Government Allies

The effectiveness of lobbying can be enhanced by developing allies in Congress. The Semiconductor Industry Association (SIA) encouraged the formation of the Congressional Support Group, a caucus composed of senators and representatives who worked to support the SIA's legislative agenda. Because many SIA members were headquartered in California, the California congressional delegation also represented its interests. Having allies in government can make a difference in the outcome of a nonmarket competition. Not all expressions of support by members of Congress, however, are credible. For example, in response to constituent or interest group pressure, members of Congress may introduce or cosponsor bills they know will not pass.

Executive branch officials may also act as allies if doing so will help them further their agency's policy objectives. The Department of Commerce may support a firm seeking to open a foreign market to U.S. goods and may take a position opposing a bill supported by organized labor.

Allies can come in many forms as the boxed example indicates. Whether this helps Wal-Mart open stores in urban areas remains to be seen (see the chapter case *Wal-Mart and Its Urban Expansion Strategy*).

Controls on Lobbying

The First Amendment to the Constitution establishes the right to petition government, so lobbying is a relatively unregulated activity. The principal law governing lobbying is the Lobbying Act of 1946. In *United States v. Harriss,* 347 U.S. 612 (1954) the Supreme Court interpreted the act as pertaining only to the direct lobbying of Congress by a hired lobbyist. Therefore, activities that involve a firm's own managers and Washington representatives are not considered lobbying under the law, although Washington representatives of firms may be required to register. The act also does not cover public relations and grassroots political activities or consultants and advisors.

Recent legislation has focused on disclosure. Lobbyists are required to register with the clerk of the House and the secretary of the Senate. They must file quarterly reports listing the issues and bills on which they are lobbying, the positions they support, how long the lobbying is likely to take, and details about how their efforts are funded. Corporate executives that lobby, however, are not required to register.

In 1995 with unanimous votes by both the House and Senate, Congress passed the Lobbying Disclosure Act, which requires lobbyists to report the fees they receive as well as their expenditures. The act also requires registration of those who lobby the executive branch

---

[4]*Peninsula Times Tribune,* February 23, 1986.
[5]*Wall Street Journal,* June 25, 1986.

EXAMPLE   Michelle Obama and Wal-Mart

In his 2007–2008 presidential campaign Barack Obama was asked after a speech to a union audience if he would shop at Wal-Mart. He said, "I won't shop there."[1] Shortly after moving into the White House, Michelle Obama took up the cause of childhood obesity. Her campaign, the Partnership for a Healthier America, had several components such as exercise and healthier eating. In January 2011 Wal-Mart announced that it would save customers $1 billion a year on fresh fruits and vegetables and would reformulate its Great Value line of foods with less salt and sugar added. At a Washington media event, Michelle Obama said, "When 140 million people a week are shopping at Wal-Mart, then day by day and meal by meal, all these small changes can start to make a difference."[2]

A major problem in bringing fresh foods to people who might otherwise turn to fast foods was the absence of supermarkets in many communities. The Department of Agriculture defined a "food desert" as a low-income area where one-third of the population or 500 people, whichever was smaller, lived more than one mile from affordable food.[3] Some 23.5 million people were estimated to live in food deserts. In a meeting at the White House hosted by Michelle Obama, Wal-Mart and other companies, including Walgreens

and SuperValu, announced plans to reach 9.5 million of those people. Wal-Mart planned to open or expand 275–300 stores selling fresh and affordable food by 2016. Michelle Obama said to the companies, "With your commitments today, you all are showing us what's possible. This isn't some mysterious issue that we can't change. We know the answer. It is right here."[4] Leslie Dach, Wal-Mart executive vice president, said, "Her leadership causes companies like ours to go back and ask questions that challenge ourselves."[5] Wal-Mart had fared better than other retailers during the recession, but its same store sales had fallen, and its customers were demanding more fresh foods.

Wal-Mart also announced that it was contributing $25 million for summer youth programs across the country, including $625,000 for Washington, D.C., where it planned to open four stores. In contrast to several other cities the mayor of Washington, D.C., asked Wal-Mart to open a fifth store in an underserved community. City council member Michael A. Brown said, "Everyone can't afford to shop at Harris Tweeter or Whole Foods."[6]

When asked about candidate Obama's statement that he would not shop at Wal-Mart, presidential press secretary Robert Gibbs said, "Lots has happened since 2007."[7]

[1]*Toronto Star*, February 26, 2011.
[2]Ibid.
[3]For rural areas the distance was 10 miles.

[4]*New York Times*, July 21, 2011.
[5]*Washington Post*, July 21, 2011.
[6]*Washington Times*, February 23, 2011.
[7]*Washington Post*, January 21, 2011.

and the staffs of Congress members. This provision was estimated to have increased the number of registered lobbyists by a factor of 3–10. In 2010 there were 12,967 registered lobbyists who actually lobbied in Washington, according to the Center for Responsive Politics.

Laws as well as House and Senate rules prohibit gifts to members of Congress, including dinners and privately paid travel to conventions and events.[6] Laws prohibiting gifts also cover executive branch officials. In 1997 Tyson Foods pleaded guilty to providing the secretary of agriculture in the Clinton administration with $12,000 of illegal gratuities. Tyson paid a criminal fine of $4 million and costs of $2 million. The Robert Mondavi winery hosted a visit by the secretary that included wine and dinner. The $187 for the wine and $207 for the dinner for the secretary and his friend resulted in $150,000 in civil penalties for the winery, including paying for a public education program on bribery and gratuity laws.

The Ethics in Government Act of 1978 addressed the "revolving door" of officials who leave government service and then lobby their former employers. The act restricts the contacts of former executive branch officials and regulators with their former agencies for a 2-year period and former members of Congress and congressional staff from lobbying Congress for 1 year after their terms in office end.[7] The law also prohibits officials who were involved in international trade or negotiations from lobbying their former offices for 1 year.

The interactions of business and other interest groups with regulatory agencies are limited by ex parte requirements. Public notice of meetings with regulatory officials is required unless all interested parties are present.

[6]Senate rules allow gifts or meals up to $50 and up to $100 from any individual.
[7]The prohibition extends to 2 years in areas for which they had primary responsibility.

ELECTORAL SUPPORT

Electoral support focuses on providing electorally important resources to candidates. Unions and some interest groups endorse candidates, provide campaign workers, staff get-out-the-vote campaigns, align with political parties, contribute to campaigns, and fund political advertising for and against candidates. Most businesses refrain from these activities because of concerns that some stakeholders would object. Business spends much more on lobbying than on electoral resources, and its contributions to charities dwarf both. Corporate campaign contributions were approximately $300 million in the late 1990s, compared to lobbying expenditures of $3 billion and charitable contributions of $35 billion.[8] This section considers the myths and realities of corporate campaign contributions, the legal context for campaign contributions, the pattern of contributions, and the role of contributions in corporate nonmarket strategies.

Myths and Realities of Campaign Financing

A popular impression about campaign financing is that huge amounts of money are involved, contributions buy favor from officeholders, and corporations provide the bulk of the funding. These are largely myths. Ansolabehere, de Figueirdo, and Snyder (2003) studied campaign finance and were left with quite different conclusions. Despite the popular impression, campaign expenditures by all candidates for federal office have not grown relative to the size of the economy, although expenditures in real terms have increased. For the 2009–2010 election cycle, campaign spending in all federal elections was approximately $3.6 billion, and for the 2007–2008 cycle, which included a presidential election, spending was $5.3 billion. Spending for all state elections for 2009–2010 was $3.9 billion. Expressed as a percent of GDP, expenditures decreased during the twentieth century until the campaign financing reforms in the mid-1970s and have been essentially constant since then except for substantial increases in spending on presidential campaigns. The bulk of the contributions are made by individuals. Moreover, the number of PACs declined 12 percent since 1988, and only 60 percent of the Fortune 500 firms had a PAC.

In the 2009–2010 election cycle slightly more than half the total dollars spent in federal elections went to Democrats, and in the 2007–2008 election cycle 57 percent went to Democrats. For the presidency, the Obama campaign spent $730 million on the 2008 election, and the McCain campaign spent $333 million. PAC contributions represented 36 percent, 19 percent, and less than 1 percent of contributions to House, Senate, and presidential races, respectively. For the 2009–2010 election cycle 70.4 percent of the campaign contributions by the top 20 PACs went to Democrats and 29.6 percent to Republican candidates.[9]

Empirical studies show little effect of campaign contributions on congressional voting, and despite examples suggesting the contrary, contributions seem to have little effect on policy. Moreover, if contributions did buy favor from elected officials, business would be expected to contribute up to the campaign limits. Average PAC contributions to campaigns, however, were $1,700 compared to a limit of $10,000 for primary and general election campaigns. Moreover, few corporate PACs contributed the maximum. Ansolabehere, de Figueirdo, and Snyder asked the rhetorical question, "Why is there so little money in politics?" Their conclusion is that there is not more money in campaigns because money has little direct effect on policy.

A second question then is why companies contribute at all. The conclusion of Ansolabehere, de Figueirdo, and Snyder was that contributions are a form of consumption or entertainment for the executives of the contributing companies. As indicated by the decline in the number of PACs, fewer companies are finding the entertainment worth the cost. Most companies that do make campaign contributions make them to gain access to members of Congress for lobbying.

Election Financing Laws

Federal election financing is regulated by the Federal Election Commission (FEC) under the Federal Election Campaign Act (FECA), as amended in 1974. Corporations are prohibited by the Tillman Act of 1907 from making contributions to the federal election campaigns of candidates. Contributions by unions were prohibited in 1943. State campaign contribution laws can vary

---

[8]Milyo, Primo, and Grosclose (2000).
[9]The numbers reflect the prominance of labor unions in the top 20 PACs.

substantially from federal law. In California, corporations may make direct contributions to state election campaigns.[10]

At the federal level, corporations, labor unions, trade and professional associations, and groups of individuals may form multicandidate PACs for the purpose of soliciting contributions and distributing them to candidates or expending them independently in election campaigns.[11] A major turning point for PAC activity was a 1976 FEC ruling that employees as well as shareholders could contribute to corporate PACs. Most contributions to corporate PACs are now made by employees, primarily management, and contributions must be voluntary.[12]

Unions collect funds for political contributions through dues, but members cannot be forced to contribute to the union's political activities. The Supreme Court has held that individuals may not be compelled to support political positions they oppose. Applied to unions, this means that members and covered nonmembers can be forced to pay only that fraction of the dues used for collective bargaining purposes.[13]

Campaign financing law distinguishes between expenditures in electoral campaigns and contributions to those campaigns. In *Buckley v. Valeo,* 424 U.S. 1 (1976), the Supreme Court ruled that any limit on campaign expenditures threatens the freedoms of speech and association and thus violates the First Amendment. This decision also overturned state laws limiting campaign spending.[14] As a result of this decision, candidates are not restricted in their personal expenditures. In 2000 Jon Corzine spent $60.2 million of his own funds to win a Senate seat by 3 percent of the vote. Hillary Clinton raised $40.8 million to finance her 2006 New York Senate race.

Although expenditures are not limited, limits on contributions to candidates' campaigns have been upheld by the Supreme Court. The court reasoned that such limits represent less of an abridgment of First Amendment rights than limits on expenditures.[15] Contributions to a candidate's campaign are called *hard money* contributions and are strictly limited, as indicated in Table 8-2.

Violations of campaign contribution regulations can lead to substantial penalties. A prominent lobbyist was convicted of making illegal campaign contributions to the same secretary of agriculture mentioned previously and was fined $150,000 and ordered to write an essay on the election laws. The essay was distributed to the members of the American League of Lobbyists.[16]

In 2002 Congress enacted the Bipartisan Campaign Reform Act (McCain-Feingold) to restrict fundraising and spending by political party committees outside federal limits and to restrict issue ads mentioning candidates. The FEC, however, did not ban "527" groups, which spent nearly $600 million in 2009–2010 election cycle at the federal and state level.

In 2010 the Supreme Court in *Citizens United v. Federal Election Commission* (558 U.S. 08-205 (2010)) overturned a 1990 decision that had limited independent expenditures in

TABLE 8-2 Hard Money Contribution Limits (2007–2008)

Contributor	To Candidate Committee (per election)	To National Party (per year)	To State and Local Parties	To PAC or Other Political Committee	Aggregate Total
Individual	$2,500*	$30,800*	$10,000	$5,000	$117,000*
PAC	$5,000	$15,000	$10,000	$5,000	None

Note: *Amounts are adjusted for inflation in odd years.

[10]For information on state contribution limits, see www.ncal.org/programs/legismgt.about.ContriLimits.htm.

[11]The FEC designates six categories of PACs: corporate, labor, nonconnected, trade/membership/health, cooperative, and corporation without stock. The organization and operation of PACs are discussed by Handler and Mulkern (1982).

[12]See Sabato (1984) for a study of PACs. See www.opensecrets.org and www.fec.gov for data on campaign contributions.

[13]In 1998 the Supreme Court held that federal labor law permitted dues collected from nonunion workers in the private sector to be used only for collective bargaining purposes. In 1986 it had made a similar ruling for public employees. In 1991 the Court extended this principle in ruling that public employee union members cannot be forced to support lobbying and other political activities.

[14]In 1998 the Supreme Court declined to review this decision.

[15]Independent expenditures on campaigns were held to be immune to restrictions in *FEC v. National Conservative Political Action Committee,* 470 U.S. 480 (1985), but in *FEC v. Massachusetts Citizens for Life,* 479 U.S. 238 (1986) the Supreme Court stated that restrictions on expenditures by for-profit corporations would be upheld.

[16]*New York Times,* September 29, 1998.

elections and a 2003 decision that had upheld parts of the McCain-Feingold that restricted spending by corporations and unions.[17] For the majority Justice Anthony M. Kennedy wrote, "If the First Amendment has any force, it prohibits Congress from fining or jailing citizens, or associations of citizens, for simply engaging in political speech." The Court upheld the disclosure requirements of McCain-Feingold. Kennedy wrote, "Disclosure permits citizens and shareholders to react to the speech of corporate entities in a proper way." Critics of the decision claimed that it would transform elections, whereas others doubted that corporations would rush in with independent expenditures because of the possible reaction by consumers, employees, and shareholders.

The Pattern of Campaign Contributions

Campaign contributions are an important aspect of electoral politics, if not of nonmarket strategies of business. PAC contributions constitute, however, a relatively small percent of campaign financing. Corporations accounted for 35 percent of total PAC contributions in the 1997–1998 election cycle.[18]

PAC contributions are primarily made to incumbents, reflecting the need for access for lobbying. Corporate PACs contribute slightly more to Republicans than to Democrats, whereas labor PACs contribute almost exclusively to Democrats.[19] The largest PACs contributing to candidate campaigns are mainly not corporate but are formed by realtors, beer wholesalers, trial lawyers, unions, and auto dealers. Of the top 20 PAC contributors in the 2009–2010 election cycle, only three were corporations—Honeywell International, AT&T, and Boeing—and only one business association, the American Bankers Association, was included in the top 20.

Many PACs have higher independent expenditures on issues than contributions to candidate campaigns. In the 2009–2010 congressional election cycle the PACs with the greatest total expenditures were American Crossroads, Crossroads Grassroots Policy Strategies, the American Federation of State, County, and Municipal Employees, and the Club for Growth. The objective of many of the largest spenders is to affect election outcomes rather than to seek access.

Purposes of Campaign Contributions

Campaign contributions are made for three basic purposes. The first is to affect the outcomes of elections, the second is to obtain access to present or future officeholders, and the third is to obtain services. Most contributions by individuals are made for the first purpose, as are the contributions by labor unions. Business, however, takes a more pragmatic approach and tends to make contributions to those most likely to win, largely for the purpose of facilitating access for lobbying. The fact that a high percentage of contributions are made to incumbents reflects this. As former Senator Rudy Boschwitz (R-MN) commented, "All they're [corporate PACs] doing is buying a bunch of access and playing the damn thing like a horse race. They don't do it philosophically. They do it on who's going to win."[20] The role of campaign contributions in providing access was explained in a deposition by former Senator Alan Cranston (D-CA) in the "Keating five" ethics inquiry: "The only thing I will grant is that the person who makes a contribution has a better chance to get access than someone who does not. All senators know you may get ten, twenty, thirty, fifty phone calls a day, people trying to reach you, and you cannot answer all those phone calls. So you answer those from those whose names you recognize and who you think you have some obligation to at least hear out."[21]

An access theory of campaign contributions predicts that the more valuable the services the candidate can provide, the more an interest group will be willing to contribute. This suggests that access to those members of Congress who hold strategic positions should be more valuable than access to those members who do not. In particular, it implies that senior members, and particularly the chairs of committees and subcommittees, should receive more contributions than

[17]The federal ban on corporate contributions to federal election campaigns was not affected by the decision.

[18]Milyo, Primo, and Groseclose (2000).

[19]Organized labor also provides substantial in-kind support in addition to campaign contributions. Unions provide volunteer workers who staff phone banks, ring doorbells, deliver campaign materials, and help register voters.

[20]*New York Times,* September 26, 1988.

[21]*New York Times,* November 30, 1990.

other members.[22] The data support this prediction. Similarly, members of the committees that deal with legislation affecting an industry may receive contributions from the firms in those industries. In addition, this theory predicts that the bulk of contributions are made to incumbents. In part this reflected the incumbency advantage, and in part it reinforced that advantage.

Studies by Hall and Wayman (1990) and Wu (1994) indicate that another purpose of campaign contributions is to develop allies and encourage them to work for legislation that both the member and the contributor support. Thus, campaign contributions could affect legislative outcomes by mobilizing congressional efforts on behalf of legislation rather than by directly affecting the votes of the recipients.

Many companies would like not to make political contributions but believe that they are caught in a prisoners' dilemma. That is, if no other interest group were to make contributions, an interest group that made a contribution could be important to the candidate and access would be more likely. Conversely, if many firms and interest groups contribute, a noncontributor might be at a disadvantage, possibly suffering a loss of access. Contributing, then, could be a dominant strategy, resulting in a situation in which all interest groups contribute, with their contributions then counteracting each other's contributions, yielding little or no benefits. All could be better off not contributing.

COALITION BUILDING

Coalition building is an important component of many nonmarket strategies. Coalitions are the principal means of forging a majority from a collection of minorities. Business coalitions are of three types: peak organizations, trade associations, and ad hoc coalitions. Peak associations emphasize issues that affect more than one industry, trade associations represent a single industry, and ad hoc coalitions tend to be issue specific. Trade associations and individual firms also participate on issues addressed by peak organizations and trade associations, respectively.

Many of the most effective coalitions are ad hoc and issue specific, as in the case of the Daylight Saving Time Coalition. Some are not formal coalitions but instead are alignments of interests, as in the case of the Daylight Saving Time Coalition and the RP Foundation Fighting Blindness considered in Chapter 6.[23] At times, two interest groups may find themselves working on the same side of one issue and opposite sides of another. Automobile manufacturers, dealers, and the United Auto Workers (UAW) opposed increases in fuel economy standards, but the automakers and the UAW were on opposite sides of the North American Free Trade Agreement, and automakers and dealers were on opposite sides of lemon laws as discussed in Chapter 7.

Peak Associations

Peak, or umbrella, organizations include firms from a number of industries and thus represent a range of interests. In the United States these organizations include the U.S. Chamber of Commerce, the National Association of Manufacturers, the Business Roundtable, the American Business Conference, the National Federation of Independent Business, and the National Small Business Association, among others. These organizations support issues such as liability reform, tax reductions, trade liberalization, and regulatory reform. The heterogeneity of the interests of their members and their desire to maintain a reasonable internal consensus, however, limits the scope of the issues on which they act. Consequently, most companies do not rely solely on peak organizations to represent their interests but instead participate in trade associations and often take independent nonmarket action.[24]

As an example of an umbrella organization, the Chamber of Commerce is the oldest general business organization in the United States and has a budget of $150 million. The Chamber focuses on tax, labor, trade, and regulatory issues, and on other issues of importance to small businesses. An important source of strength for the chamber is its 3,000 state and local chambers, which give it complete coverage of congressional districts. To generate political pressure, it organized over 2,700 Congressional Action committees, composed of local businesspeople who have personal contacts with members of Congress. The chamber also had a public interest

---

[22]See Kroszner and Stratmann (1998) for a study of financial services PACs and their contributions to committees.
[23]See Salisbury (1992) for an analysis of interest group alignments.
[24]Peak organizations are more important in other countries. The *Keidanren* in Japan and the peak organizations in Germany and other European countries are quite influential.

lobby, the Grassroots Action Information Network, that conducted grassroots campaigns. The Chamber's National Chamber Alliance for Politics provided electoral support to candidates.

The National Federation of Independent Business (NFIB) focuses on the concerns of small business. The influence of small business should not be underestimated. Although individual small businesses may have limited resources, collectively their resources are large. The NFIB, for example, has 600,000 members and offices in Washington and every state capital. It has been effective in lobbying and mobilizing small firms by reducing their cost of participation in collective action. The NFIB worked effectively for President George W. Bush's tax cut plan. About 85 percent of NFIB members pay their business taxes through their individual tax returns, and the tax plan allowed the immediate expensing of an additional $75,000 of equipment. Small business has also been effective in obtaining exemptions from certain regulations. Its effectiveness is strengthened by the access provided by the small business committees in the House and Senate.

Trade Associations

Trade associations serve a variety of market and nonmarket functions.[25] Market functions include the collection of market and industry statistics, the development of technical standards, and in some cases research. Nonmarket functions center on reducing the cost of collective action, particularly by reducing the costs of information acquisition. Trade associations monitor legislative activity, regulatory rule-making activities, and administrative actions. They also reduce the cost of lobbying, grassroots programs, and other political strategies. Small firms are more likely than large firms to rely on trade associations.

The Pharmaceutical Research and Manufacturers Association (PhRMA), with a 2004 budget of $150 million, allocated $72.7 million for lobbying Congress, $4.9 million for lobbying the FDA, and $48.7 million for advocacy aimed at state governments. Funds were also allocated to fight a union-led campaign for lower drug prices in Ohio, support policy research, hire economists to discuss pharmaceutical issues, oppose the Canadian discount drug system, fund public advocacy, and foster ties with minority congressional caucuses and medical organizations.[26]

Ad Hoc Coalitions

Ad hoc coalitions are interests that join together on specific nonmarket issues. High-tech companies, public accounting firms, underwriters, and others that had been subjected to frivolous securities fraud lawsuits formed the Uniform Standards Coalition to work for federal legislation requiring security fraud lawsuits to be filed in federal rather than state courts. The Coalition was successful, and after legislation was enacted in 1999, the Coalition disbanded.

Although firms in the same industry are often aligned on issues, they may be opposed on some nonmarket issues. In 1992 British Airways announced it would invest $750 million in USAir, forming a global alliance. Robert L. Crandall, chairman of American Airlines, criticized the investment on the grounds that the arrangement provided the United Kingdom increased access to the U.S. market, while U.S. airlines remained restricted in their access to the U.K. market. Crandall was subsequently joined by the CEOs of United Airlines, Delta Air Lines, and Federal Express. USAir countered their lobbying with a grassroots letter-writing campaign by its employees, but the relentless lobbying by the four airlines caused British Airways to cancel the investment and alliance.[27]

The alignment of interests on some issues can be broad. The clean air legislation pending in Congress during the 1980s led to the formation of the Clean Air Working Group, which included 2,000 businesses and trade associations. Aligned with the group were labor unions representing auto, construction, and other workers. This allowed the opponents of stringent legislation to speak from a relatively unified position on the 1990 amendments to the Clean Air Act.

Coalitions and Consensus

The alignment of interests not only affects who participates in a coalition but also the bargaining within a coalition. When interests are closely aligned, bargaining is relatively easy because

---

[25]See Lynn and McKeown (1988) for an analysis of trade associations.
[26]*New York Times,* June 1, 2003.
[27]The following year British Airways invested $340 million in USAir, but by 1996 the alliance had disintegrated.

disagreements are likely to be small. On an issue where interests are poorly aligned, the bargaining can be more complex and lengthy.

On some issues, disagreements among members of a coalition may be irreconcilable. In 1999 eBay and eight other Internet service providers, including Amazon.com, America Online, DoubleClick, and Yahoo!, formed NetCoalition.com. The coalition's mission was to serve as "the collective public policy voice of the world's leading Internet companies...." Within a few months, however, the collective voice split over the issue of database protection. eBay backed legislation to protect its databases, and other members backed rival legislation that, according to eBay, would provide little if any protection. eBay withdrew from the coalition.

Jet ski or personal watercraft (PWC) manufacturers faced a host of nonmarket issues related to safety, pollution, noise, and disruption of fishing, canoeing, and other water sports. One strategy used by the PWC manufacturers was to argue that any new regulations on jet skis should also apply to boats. The purpose was to force boat manufacturers to oppose the new regulations. PWC manufacturers and boat producers belonged to the National Marine Manufacturers Association (NMMA), which worked against the proposed regulations. Genmar, the world's largest independent boat manufacturer, however, objected to being aligned with the PWC manufacturers and quit the NMMA in protest.[28]

Trade associations can be effective on those nonmarket issues that have similar impacts on their members. In those cases a trade association can effectively speak with one voice before congressional committees, regulatory agencies, and executive branch agencies. As the jet ski example indicates, however, on matters that affect members quite differently, consensus may not be possible. The pharmaceutical politics example illustrates this even in the case of an industry with seemingly homogeneous interests.

EXAMPLE   Pharmaceutical Politics

The Food and Drug Administration (FDA) requires extensive laboratory and clinical testing that can take from 5 to 10 years or more, and tens of millions of dollars, before a new drug was approved for sale. Because a drug is patented before testing begins, a new drug might have only a few years of patent protection before generic drug manufacturers can introduce a chemically identical drug. The companies retained some protection because generic drugs also had to be tested, which could take up to 5 years to complete even though their active ingredients were chemically identical to those in the already approved drugs. Furthermore, a federal appeals court had ruled that testing by a generic drug manufacturer could not begin until the patent on the original drug had expired.

The Generic Pharmaceutical Industry Association (GPIA) sought legislation requiring the FDA to establish simplified approval procedures for generic drugs, requiring proof only that a generic drug was biochemically identical to an already approved drug. Legislation to expedite the approval of generic drugs was introduced in both the House and the Senate, and it received considerable support. Changes in the generic drug approval process would have a major impact on the brand-name drug companies because patents on over 150 drugs with annual sales of $4 billion either had recently expired or were about to expire.

The Pharmaceutical Manufacturers Association (PMA), representing the makers of brand-name patented drugs,

opposed the legislation, arguing that the revisions in FDA testing requirements would reduce their incentives to develop new drugs.[1] This, it was argued, would result in fewer drugs being discovered, which in turn would reduce the quality of health care.

The PMA sought outright defeat of the legislation. Once it became apparent that this objective could not be realized, it reached a compromise in negotiations among the GPIA and the chairpersons of the cognizant congressional committees. The compromise would extend patent protection for certain brand-name drugs and speed the approval process for generic drugs.

Consensus on the compromise could not be sustained within the PMA, however. Eleven companies were furious with the compromise and succeeded in having the head of the PMA and its chief lobbyist fired. The CEOs of the companies, including American Home Products, Hoffman-LaRoche, and Merck, then lobbied intensely over the next few weeks to strike from the compromise bill the provision that would speed the approval of generic drugs.[2] Their efforts failed, however, and they were only able to obtain a provision pertaining to exclusive-marketing rights for nonpatented drugs.

---

[1]The PMA was later renamed the Pharmaceutical Research and Manufacturers Association (PhRMA).
[2]*Dun's Business Month,* January 1986, p. 36.

---

[28]The Genmar chairman stated, "I am convinced the PWC industry will ultimately force new regulations and restrictions on the boating industry that will cause irreparable damage to us all due to their product's potential dangers and the abuse of our lakes and rivers." (Genmar press release, November 19, 1997.) See the Chapter 2 case *Personal Watercraft aka Jet Skis.*

GRASSROOTS AND CONSTITUENCY CAMPAIGNS

Grassroots campaigns are based on the connection between constituents and their elected representatives. Grassroots campaigns are often a component of a broader representation strategy and are often tactical in nature. Labor unions, community interest groups, environmental groups, the National Rifle Association, and many other interest groups engage in grassroots nonmarket activity intended to demonstrate the breadth and intensity of their members' interests on issues.[29] Beginning in the 1980s, firms and industries adopted this strategy and applied it effectively to issues on their nonmarket agendas. The grassroots campaign by Toshiba (Chapter 7) was effective because it revealed the potential costs to employees, suppliers, and customers. Grassroots campaigns have become sufficiently common that a grassroots lobbying industry has developed to organize the campaigns. The industry includes firms that, for example, translate data by postal zip codes into congressional districts. This allows shareholder, retiree, supplier, and customer lists to be organized by district to target members of Congress. PacifiCare organized patients by congressional district. Grassroots activity has also become increasingly specialized. Some political consulting firms now provide "grass-tops" services: they recruit prominent citizens to lobby their representatives or senators on issues. Grassroots strategies are high-profile and many companies prefer low-profile strategies.

Mobilization

Members of interest groups and stakeholders of firms must be mobilized for effective grassroots action. Mobilization involves providing information to stakeholders on the significance of an issue and helping to reduce the costs of participation. Letter-writing campaigns are the least expensive grassroots activity. They are also difficult to implement because constituents often are unwilling to spend the time to write a letter or send a telegram. Volume can be generated through the use of preprinted letters, postcards, or e-mail, but recipients know that postcards generally do not reflect the same intensity of preferences as handwritten letters. Although handwritten letters have a greater impact than postcards, there is a trade-off with volume. Some congressional offices sort and count mail by issue and distinguish between letters and postcards. Others, however, just weigh the postcards. In a survey of congressional staff Lord (2000) found that letter writing and telephone calls had the greatest effect and petitions and mass-mailing responses the least effect.

A more effective means of demonstrating grassroots preferences is to have constituents go to Washington or a state capital to lobby. Labor unions developed this tactic by organizing "bus-ins" in which busloads of union members converged on Washington to lobby and engage in other political activities. "Fly-ins" are the modern counterpart of bus-ins. Industry members frequently organize fly-ins often using industry associations to coordinate activity. In the Chapter 6 case *Business versus Business* convenience stores organized a fly-in to work for lower swipe fees on credit and debit card purchases.

Grassroots activities may be directed at government officeholders, as in the case of a fly-in, or they may be directed at constituents. The former are components of informational strategies and are a form of lobbying. The latter are components of representation strategies and are intended to develop public support for an alternative. The Internet has become an important force in generating constituent grassroots actions such as letter writing and e-mailing members of Congress. The activist organization MoveOn.org sent out an e-mail appeal for $25,000 to pay for an advertisement, and it received $400,000 in response.

Business Grassroots Campaigns

A business grassroots strategy involves corporate stakeholders as identified by the rent chain. These stakeholders can include employees, shareholders, retirees whose pensions depend on company performance, franchisees, suppliers, and in some cases customers. Not all constituencies are equally easy to organize and mobilize, however.[30] Shareholders may be mobilized to some extent, but alerting them to a potentially serious issue may cause them to sell their shares.

To the extent that their interests on an issue are aligned with those of the firm, employees may be relatively easy to include in a grassroots program. Mobilizing employees can generate

---

[29]See Fowler and Shaiko (1987) for an analysis of the grassroots activities of environmental organizations.
[30]See Keim (1985) and Baysinger, Keim, and Zeithaml (1985) for an analysis of corporate grassroots programs.

criticism, however. In the last days of the Clinton administration's attempt to restructure the U.S. health care system, IBM asked its employees to oppose bills mandating employer-provided health insurance. Some employees complained about the request, and IBM was publicly criticized for changing its practice of not involving employees in political issues.

More recently, however, companies have begun to embrace grassroots strategies involving employees. International Paper encourages employees to write their representatives on policy issues and may recommend a candidate to employees requesting such information.[31] Cigna urged its employees to write members of Congress on tort reform legislation in 2004. Some firms also take positions on ballot initiatives and referenda. Silicon Valley firms urged their employees to vote no on Proposition 211 that would make it easier for plaintiffs to win securities fraud lawsuits.

Suppliers and customers are frequently mobilized when their rents are affected. The grassroots campaign organized by Toshiba to weaken sanctions resulting from its illegal sales relied heavily on its U.S. production base, its suppliers, and its customers. Toshiba's U.S. production provided a link between possible sanctions and jobs at its suppliers. Similarly, Toshiba had little difficulty enlisting the support of its customers, many of whom depended on its products.

The Effectiveness of Grassroots Programs

The effectiveness of a grassroots program depends on the supply-side factors considered in Chapter 6 as well as on the credibility of the program itself. The larger the number of participants in a grassroots program and the more extensive their coverage of political jurisdictions, the more effective it is likely to be. These factors determine the amount of pressure that can be transmitted through the constituency connection. This pressure, however, must be credible. The following two examples, both of which involved attempts to defeat legislation, illustrate the credibility dimension of a grassroots campaign.

Legislation was introduced in Congress to require financial institutions to withhold taxes on the interest and dividend income of savers and trust fund beneficiaries. Supporters of the proposal included Treasury officials and members of Congress concerned with the federal budget deficit. In addition to the considerable administrative expense to financial institutions, the legislation would reduce the short-term cash flow to savers and beneficiaries, who would receive lower quarterly payments as taxes were withheld. The financial institutions were in a position to mobilize a dispersed constituency of savers to oppose the bill. Their grassroots campaign generated over 22 million letters and postcards, and the interest-withholding issue died.

In 1987 the Pharmaceutical Manufacturers Association campaigned against the adoption of a catastrophic illness program for the elderly. Pharmaceutical companies were concerned that federal budget pressures would lead to the substitution of generic for brand-name drugs and perhaps to price controls, or reimbursement limits, on drugs. The PMA hired a political consulting firm to conduct a $3 million grassroots campaign opposing the program. Even though the campaign generated over 100,000 contacts between constituents and members of Congress, it was largely ineffective. Congress members knew that their constituents did not understand the program under consideration. Moreover, it may have worsened relations with members of Congress. As Senator Lloyd Bentsen (D-TX) said, "I know the difference between grassroots and Astroturf."

In his survey of congressional staff Lord (2000) found that corporate constituency activity was relatively more effective in influencing how members of Congress voted on legislation, and professional and executive lobbying were relatively more important in influencing the content of legislation. The effect of constituency actions was greater in the House than the Senate presumably because members of the House face elections every 2 years. Among the corporate constituents, employee contacts with staff and members had the largest effect.

TESTIMONY

Companies testify before regulatory agencies, congressional committees, administrative agencies, and courts. In a regulatory setting, testimony is important not only because the information presented can affect regulatory decisions but also because it creates a record that may serve as

---

[31]*Wall Street Journal,* September 3, 2004.

a basis for judicial review. Many regulatory rulings are challenged in the courts, and the courts will at times consider both substantive and procedural challenges to a ruling. Testimony thus not only must stand up to cross-examination during a hearing, but it should also provide a basis for a possible court action.

Congressional hearings serve a variety of purposes ranging from issue identification to information provision. A hearing provides an opportunity to present a position that may be backed by a policy study conducted by a firm, association, or coalition. Testimony of firms and interest groups, however, is often preceded by lobbying, so for many members of Congress hearings provide little new information.

Hearings are not always held to obtain information. Some are held to generate publicity and mobilize support for a particular position. For example, trial lawyers and consumer groups have opposed liability reform, and one of their tactics is to bring accident victims to congressional hearings to testify against limits on liability awards. Hearings can also be managed to promote the side of the issue supported by the committee chair. Testimony on the chair's side of an issue may be scheduled in the morning so that television stations will be able to prepare the story and edit the tape in time for the evening news. Testimony on the other side may be scheduled late in the afternoon, when it is too late for the evening news. By the next day, that testimony is often too old for television. Hearings thus can provide a stage on which a committee chair can play out a story to advance a policy interest or cater to constituents.

Stephen Breyer (1982, pp. 317–340), now a Supreme Court justice, gave a detailed description of the 1974 oversight hearings on regulation of the airline industry. Breyer, who then served on the committee staff, characterized the hearings as "drama" to be orchestrated. In preparation for hearings, the committee staff prepared a script that included an opening statement for the chair and a set of questions to ask each witness. Because the chair already knew much of what the witness would say, the chair was able to direct the dialogue. Breyer also discussed the tactics used by members of Congress in their questioning of witnesses. One tactic was to ask a zinger—a question whose only possible answer would support the Congress member's own position. For instance, in the foreign leasing example in Chapter 6, Representative Pickle asked the general manager of Boeing, "Are we not subsidizing the competition of our own [international airlines]?"[32]

PUBLIC ADVOCACY

On some issues, particularly those characterized by majoritarian politics, firms use public advocacy to communicate directly with the public. The health care industry demonstrated the effectiveness of mass communication with its "Harry and Louise" advertisements, raising alarms about the Clinton administration's plans to restructure the health care industry. The ads turned the public against the administration's plan, contributing to its collapse.

During the political activity on the Clinton administration's health care restructuring proposal, pharmaceutical firms concerned about possible price controls and mandated rebates adopted a nonmarket strategy that included a communication component. The industry's basic strategy was to emphasize the discovery of new drugs and the incentives needed for research and development. The industry association added "Research" to its name and undertook lobbying and public advocacy with the message that the discovery of new drugs would be jeopardized by price controls.

Several major pharmaceutical companies also formed a coalition, Rx Partners, that conducted media tours in 65 cities and hosted a series of breakfasts for members of Congress. Individual firms also took action. Several companies conducted public education campaigns similar to those of Rx Partners. Bristol Myers held 350 meetings with community groups and lobbied extensively in Congress. Several companies conducted advertising campaigns that emphasized the discovery of new drugs. They also stressed the beneficial therapeutic value of existing drugs, which, invariably, some member of Congress or a relative had used. As the threat of price controls dissipated, the industry turned to advertisements containing personal testimony on the benefits of pharmaceuticals. The Obama administration had learned from this episode and took a quite different approach to its health care reform initiative.

---

[32]Hearing, Committee on Ways and Means, House of Representatives, Washington, D.C., June 8, 1983, p. 212.

JUDICIAL ACTIONS

Judicial actions pertain not only to those cases in which a firm finds itself the defendant but also to those in which it initiates legal action as a component of a nonmarket strategy. Judicial actions are taken in state and federal courts, which are governed by statutory and common law. Judicial actions are also taken in quasi-judicial arenas, such as those of regulatory and administrative agencies, which are governed by administrative law. Judicial strategies are used to enforce rights, obtain damages for breach of contract, and address unfair competitive practices under the antitrust laws. Many firms aggressively protect their intellectual property by filing patent and copyright infringement lawsuits, as considered in Chapter 14.

Rambus, Inc., a chip designer, has used litigation as a means of forcing companies to pay it royalties on its patents. It has filed numerous lawsuits in the United States and other countries against companies it claimed had used its patented designs in memory chips. In 2008 it won a court case that allowed it to obtain $133.4 million from Hynix Semiconductors and to pursue lawsuits against Nanya Technology, Micron Technology, and other chip manufacturers, which could result in royalty income between $700 million and $10 billion. Rambus' share price increased 39 percent after the verdict. Rambus continued its litigation strategy with a lawsuit against Hynix Semiconductors and Micron seeking $12 billion in damages.

Lawsuits are also used to deter competitors from taking certain actions and to caution the media or regulatory or administrative agencies. Firms frequently file lawsuits against regulatory agencies, alleging an inadequate basis in the record for their rule making. General Motors filed suit against the Department of Transportation because of its preliminary decision to recall GM pickup trucks with side-mounted gas tanks.[33] The secretary of transportation backed down and did not order a recall. On the other side, environmental and activist groups often file lawsuits against agencies for not adequately enforcing the law.

A judicial strategy can also be used to open markets. The coalition working for the direct to consumers sale of wine via the Internet used litigation to overturn protectionism by states. Florida, Michigan, New York, North Carolina, Texas, and Virginia allowed intra-state direct sales by wineries within their states but prohibited interstate direct sales. The coalition filed lawsuits to overturn the ban, but the Court of Appeals upheld the ban.[34] The Supreme Court agreed to hear an appeal by the coalition, and in *Heald v. Engler*, 594 U.S.460 (2005), the Supreme Court overturned the Court of Appeals and ruled that the Constitution does not allow the discriminatory treatment of intrastate and interstate direct shipment of wine.

Judicial action, particularly in the courts, can be costly. The Department of Justice's antitrust lawsuit against AT&T took 8 years before it was settled out of court with the breakup of the Bell system. It is estimated to have cost AT&T $360 million and the government $15 million.[35] In arenas governed by administrative law, cases, such as petitions to the International Trade Commission for relief from injury by imports, often proceed more expeditiously and at lower cost because of legislatively imposed time limits. Although lawsuits can be extremely costly, awards can also be high. As a fledgling company, MCI successfully sued AT&T on antitrust grounds, and its award was used to finance its expansion. MCI also filed a number of other lawsuits against both AT&T and the FCC seeking the opportunity to provide expanded telecommunications services. The lawsuits helped open the telecommunications market to competition.[36]

Regulatory and administrative law channels may be used for a variety of purposes, including protecting rights, handicapping a competitor, or gaining a direct advantage. When the FDA attempted to streamline its rules for approving generic drugs, the brand-name pharmaceutical companies filed lawsuits challenging its authority to do so. Thwarted in this administrative channel, the generic drug companies took their cause to Congress, as the "Pharmaceutical Politics" example indicates.

---

[33]See the Chapter 3 case *General Motors: Like a Rock? (A).*
[34]See Wiseman and Ellig (2004).
[35]Shipper and Jennings (1984, p. 115).
[36]MCI merged with Sprint.

ORGANIZING FOR NONMARKET EFFECTIVENESS

Firms that expect to be involved in issues addressed in government arenas must anticipate rather than simply react to developments. Consequently, they need to organize and be prepared for action. It is essential to monitor issues, and for many firms this means full-time representation in Washington and in the capitals of key states. For other firms, associations can be a cost-effective means of providing intelligence. Many large firms also have a government affairs department that provides expertise and monitors the development of issues. A department may include lawyers, communications experts, former government officials, lobbyists, and analysts.

Washington offices serve as the eyes and ears of firms. They provide information on developing issues and are a locus of expertise about issues, institutions, and officeholders. Because nonmarket issues are often episodic in nature, firms on occasion engage the services of political consulting firms, Washington law firms, or public relations firms. Similarly, lobbyists may be hired for a specific issue. The size of a firm's permanent staff thus is determined relative to the cost and effectiveness of outside alternatives.

Because lobbying is the centerpiece of most companies' interactions with government, most employ lobbyists who are either political professionals or experienced managers responsible for presenting the company's concerns to government officials. Their responsibilities typically include maintaining relationships with members of Congress, executive branch officials, and government agencies. Access is a necessary condition for lobbying, so many firms make a practice of maintaining contact with those members of Congress in whose districts they have their operations and with the committees that regularly deal with issues on their nonmarket agendas. Firms also provide training for their managers who are involved in nonmarket issues. That training often emphasizes sensitivity to the possible public reaction to the firm's activities and the development of personal skills for participating effectively in government arenas.

DEVELOPING NONMARKET CAPABILITIES

Companies develop capabilities for implementing nonmarket strategies. Google's most important nonmarket capability was the credibility it had earned from its success in Internet technology and applications. The public and governments listened when Google spoke not because of its market power but because of its success. More was required, however, to deal with the myriad of issues it faced and those that would arise in the future. In 2005 it opened an office in Washington with one employee, a lawyer responsible for intellectual property issues. Alan Davidson of Google commented, "Washington and its policy debates are important. We can't ignore them."[37] As Google's nonmarket agenda grew, its executives began to make Washington a regular stop on their trips. Its executives testified before Congress on expanding the number of highly educated workers allowed to immigrate to the United States and on the future of videos on the Internet. Google also was dealing with the human rights and censorship issue, intellectual property, and telecommunication regulation regarding possible Internet capacity policy.

As the number of nonmarket issues it faced grew, it decided to develop its nonmarket capability and to do it by building on its technology expertise. It increased its staff in Washington and began interacting with members of the government. Adam Kovacevich of its Washington office explained, "We're trying to approach government in a 'Googley' way—some things we're doing are traditional and some aren't."[38] One approach was to show members of Congress and their staffers how they could use Google applications in their constituency activities and election campaigns. Jamie Brown, a Google lobbyist, explained, "The vast majority of my time is spent educating people about the company and its economic footprint." One of her principal activities was to conduct "Google 101" seminars to educate congressional staffers about the company. Robert Boofstin of Google said, "We're more and more under the microscope. It would be disingenuous to say we weren't trying to have influence with decision makers and people who try to influence them."[39]

---

[37]*Washington Post,* June 20, 2007. See the Chapter 1 case, *The Nonmarket Environment of Google,* and the Chapter 16 case, *Google in China.*
[38]*San Jose Mercury News,* June 2, 2007.
[39]*Wall Street Journal,* July 20, 2007.

In July 2007 YouTube and CNN hosted a debate among Democratic presidential candidates. Google took the opportunity to demonstrate its products to the candidates' campaign staffs. Google argued that its ads were a cost-effective way to reach voters. Google also created a space called "You Choose" on YouTube where presidential candidates could post videos.

Google also established NetPAC, a political action committee, and explained, "We started this NetPAC in order to be able to support officeholders and candidates who share our vision of promoting and preserving the Internet as a free and open platform for information, communication and innovation. Google has thrived thanks to the opportunities of the free market so we believe it is important to look at policymakers as they make decisions that impact our users and business."[40]

Google sought to emphasize policy over politics and opened its Public Policy Blog to advocate its policy positions.[41] "We're seeking to do public policy advocacy in a Googley way. We want our users to be part of the effort," explained Andrew McLaughlin. Google, however, did not attempt to enlist its users in a grassroots campaign on its behalf for any of the issues on its agenda.

SUMMARY

Firms and interest groups have broad nonmarket portfolios. Lobbying is essential in addressing issues in legislative, regulatory, and administrative arenas. Lobbying involves demonstrating to officeholders that the interests of their constituents or their own policy interests are aligned with those of the firm and its stakeholders. Providing politically relevant information to officeholders is at the heart of effective lobbying. That information may be technical or political, and relevant to the constituents or policy interests of officeholders. Lobbying often focuses on committees and their staffs. Testimony in hearings is related to lobbying and can be coordinated with it. Access to policymakers is necessary for lobbying. It can be attained through the constituency connection, personal relationships, former government officials, and in some cases campaign contributions. Lobbying remains a relatively unregulated activity.

Corporate electoral support primarily involves campaign contributions, since firms rarely endorse candidates. These contributions are typically made to obtain access to members of Congress and otherwise seldom play a major role in the nonmarket strategies of most firms.

Coalition building is an important component of many nonmarket strategies. Firms participate in peak organizations, trade associations, and ad hoc coalitions. Peak organizations address general business issues rather than industry-specific matters. Trade associations are important, particularly for issues that pertain to a specific industry. Ad hoc coalitions address specific issues and often bring together interests that may not be aligned on other issues. When members of a coalition have heterogeneous interests, the maintenance of the coalition requires effort, and its activities are determined through internal bargaining. Many firms supplement coalition activities with their own individual nonmarket strategies.

Grassroots campaigns are based on the rent chain and are designed to influence legislators through the constituency connection. Firms and interest groups often organize and mobilize their constituents for grassroots activities, including letter-writing and visiting Washington for personal lobbying. The effectiveness of these activities depends on their credibility as well as on their scale. Grassroots campaigns are often coordinated with public advocacy. Public advocacy is used to inform both the public and those involved in policymaking processes.

Judicial strategies are implemented both in the courts and in regulatory arenas governed by administrative law. These strategies can be effective but can also be expensive.

Most large firms are organized to address nonmarket issues in government institutions. That organization may involve a Washington office, professional lobbyists, a government affairs department, associations and coalitions, and management training. This organization supports but does not substitute for management involvement in nonmarket strategy formulation and implementation.

---

[40]*The Guardian*, October 24, 2006.

[41]http://googlepublicpolicy.blogspot.com.

CASES

Internet Taxation

On May 10, 2000, the House of Representatives passed H.R. 3709, the "Internet Non-Discrimination Act," by a resounding majority of 352–75. The bill provided a 5-year extension of an existing moratorium on new Internet taxes that was due to expire in 2001.[42] The bill had been embraced by a diverse coalition of consumer groups, Internet users, and high-tech companies that argued that the imposition of taxes on electronic commerce would slow both the development of the Internet and the growth in the U.S. economy.

In the Senate intense lobbying by a diverse set of interests caused Senator John McCain (R-AZ), chairman of the Commerce Committee, to cancel a hearing on a bill to make the tax moratorium permanent. When questioned about the cancellation, McCain said the topic of Internet taxes was "incredibly complex [and had] not been nearly fleshed out enough."[43] At the same time the legislation stalled in the Senate, the solidarity of the high-tech community on the Internet taxation issue began to slip. In a June hearing before the Joint Economic Committee, Intel Chairman Andy Grove argued for applying sales taxes to transactions on the Web, saying that he felt there was no "justification" for the online tax advantage. At the same hearing, Hewlett-Packard CEO Carly Fiorina warned that "to apply the current system of taxation to the online world would be disastrous." She, however, criticized those opposed to any Internet taxes, saying that such a stance was "unrealistic."[44] A new report by the General Accounting Office (GAO) estimated that state and local governments stood to lose anywhere between $300 million and $3.8 billion in sales tax revenue in 2000.[45]

PRECEDENTS AND MAIL-ORDER SALES

The controversy surrounding Internet taxation resulted from court decisions that exempted from taxes mail-order sales to out-of-state residents. In two landmark court cases, *National Bellas Hess v. Department of Revenue of the State of Illinois* (386 U.S. 753, 1967) and *Quill v. North Dakota* (504 U.S. 298, 1992), the U.S. Supreme Court concluded that requiring mail-order merchants to calculate, collect, and remit the appropriate tax to the appropriate authorities would constitute an undue burden because of the approximately 35,000 state and local tax rates in effect. The Court decided that merchants were only required to collect sales taxes from customers that resided in a state where the merchant had a "nexus." A nexus, loosely defined, was a physical presence, such as an office or retail outlet.

The Supreme Court decisions effectively absolved merchants of their responsibility for tax collection on out-of-state sales, but responsibility for the remittance of the tax remained for consumers. Most states required the remittance of "use" taxes for goods bought from out-of-state vendors. The rate of these use taxes was usually identical to the state sales tax rates for goods sold within the state. It was the responsibility of individual consumers to report to their state government how much tax they owed and pay accordingly. Use taxes provided governments with a legal basis to collect revenue on out-of-state purchases, but such collection rarely occurred. Compliance was very low, as most consumers were unaware that they were required to pay the use tax. Few states attempted to collect from individual consumers.[46] Although the inability to collect use taxes on catalog sales had not led to new tax legislation, the rise of the Internet significantly changed perceptions about the scale of purchases potentially free from state and local taxes. As more transactions migrated to the Web, state and local governments feared a substantial erosion of their tax bases.[47]

Fears of dwindling revenues were accompanied by the concerns of offline Main Street merchants who felt that the tax advantage of online stores gave them a significant advantage. These issues led to the introduction of bills in several state legislatures, all of which were aimed at providing some form of tax collection on online sales, at least from their own residents. Online merchants, however, argued that they had to bear delivery costs, which, as with catalog sales, offset the tax exclusion. The online merchants also argued that they did not use state resources other than for delivery and hence should not be required to fund state services.

While state and local governments were clamoring for action, the federal government was effectively putting on the brakes. The Internet Tax Freedom Act (ITFA), introduced in Congress by Representative Christopher Cox (R-CA) and Senator Ron Wyden (D-OR), was passed as part of the Omnibus Appropriations Act of 1998. Placing a 3-year moratorium on new Internet taxes, the ITFA also created the Advisory Commission on Electronic Commerce to study issues related to the taxation of the Internet and to recommend to Congress by April 2000 an appropriate tax policy.

The Advisory Commission consisted of 19 members, 8 from industry and consumer groups, 8 from state and local

---

[42]The existing moratorium prohibited the imposition of "multiple and discriminatory" taxes on electronic commerce. These taxes included those that subjected buyers and sellers to taxation in multiple states and localities, as well as taxes on goods specifically sold over the Internet by companies that did not have brick-and-mortar counterparts in the state. Discriminatory taxes included taxes imposed on Internet sales but not on catalog sales. The moratorium also prohibited the federal government from imposing taxes on Internet access or electronic commerce generally.

[43]*Wall Street Journal,* June 22, 2000.

[44]*Atlanta Journal and Constitution,* June 8, 2000.

[45]*Report to Congressional Requesters,* "Sales Taxes: Electronic Commerce Growth Presents Challenges; Revenue Losses Are Uncertain," United States General Accounting Office, June 2000.

[46]States that took measures to collect use taxes met with little success. Several states, such as New Jersey, had a separate line for use taxes on residents' income tax forms. In 1997 less than 1 percent of New Jersey residents reported use taxes. (Robert J. Cline and Thomas S. Neubig, 1999, "Masters of Complexity and Bearers of Great Burden: The Sales Tax System and Compliance Costs for Multistate Retailers," Technical Report, Ernst and Young Economics Consulting and Quantitative Analysis.)

[47]All states except Alaska, Delaware, Montana, New Hampshire, and Oregon had a sales tax.

government, and 3 from the Clinton administration. Early in its deliberations the Commission separated into three camps. One camp, including executives such as C. Michael Armstrong of AT&T and Theodore Waitt of Gateway, was in favor of taxing electronic commerce, provided that an equitable collection mechanism could be devised. A second group included representatives of state and local governments and was prepared to support any tax regime that would allow recovery of revenues lost to electronic commerce. A third group, represented by Governor James Gilmore (R-VA) and Grover Norquist of the Americans for Tax Reform, opposed any taxes on online commerce.[48]

The Commission considered a variety of alternatives ranging from no taxes to a flat tax on all electronic transactions. One alternative considered would keep the current tax system intact but would require credit card companies to act as trusted third parties in collecting use taxes from consumers and remitting them to the relevant governments.[49] While the Commission was studying the tax options, new measures were being introduced in Congress to address the Internet tax question. Wyden and Cox introduced new legislation asking the World Trade Organization to consider a permanent global moratorium on Internet taxes. Senator McCain introduced legislation to make the ITFA tax moratorium permanent. On the other side of the aisle Senator Ernest Hollings (D-SC) introduced legislation mandating a uniform 5 percent tax on all remote sales, including Internet and mail-order transactions.

As the April deadline approached, the Advisory Commission was unable to reach a consensus for "official" recommendations, which required the agreement of 13 members. An agreement could not be achieved because the members representing the Clinton administration and state and local governments abstained on necessary votes, arguing that the Commission had been subverted by industry interests and was not operating with the consensus of the relevant stakeholders.[50] Congressional leaders urged the Advisory Commission to make unofficial policy recommendations nonetheless. Among the unofficial recommendations was an additional 5-year extension on the existing tax moratorium, which was quickly incorporated into the pending Internet Non-Discrimination Act.

INTERESTS AND THEIR STAKES

Online consumers were, not surprisingly, opposed to the Internet taxes. According to one poll, 57 percent of Internet users took tax rates into account when making purchasing decisions.[51] Similarly, 75 percent of online consumers reported that they would be less likely to purchase goods online if they were required to remit taxes for their purchases. Furthermore, large-sample statistical studies indicated that taxing online sales could reduce online purchases by as much as 30 percent.[52]

Many members of the high-tech community opposed online taxes, arguing that instituting taxes on the Web would chill the growth of the Internet in at least two ways. First, if taxes were imposed, consumers might choose not to shop online, constricting the Web's expansion. The demand for many companies' products and services was directly proportional to how many people were using the Web. Second, executives argued that the high costs associated with collecting and remitting use taxes under the current system would lead to the death of many online firms. The possibility of chilling the Internet's expansion and the high compliance costs led most high-tech companies to support an extended moratorium. They argued that given time more consumers would experiment with, and gain confidence in, online commerce, and during the moratorium some solution might be developed to handle the burdensome compliance costs. Recent research had supported this infant industry argument for an extension of the tax moratorium.[53] Many high-tech leaders viewed the Internet as an essential component of the infrastructure of both business and society, and its public goods characteristics warranted as extensive an expansion of the Internet as possible.

Among the groups that voiced opposition to "discriminatory" taxes (i.e., taxes that targeted online products but had no catalog or telephone-order counterparts) was the Information Technology Association of America (ITAA), which represented over 26,000 companies, including Compaq, IBM, MCI-Worldcom, and Microsoft. The American Electronics Association represented over 3,000 companies in the high-tech and electronics industry and also opposed new Internet taxes.

To counter the advocates of online taxes, companies formed several ad hoc coalitions. The Global Business Dialogue on Electronic Commerce was a consortium of several major companies, including Disney, Hewlett-Packard, and IBM, and was co-chaired by America Online CEO Steven Case and Time-Warner CEO Gerald M. Levin.

Another ad hoc coalition, the Internet Tax Fairness Coalition (ITFC), was formed by 11 companies and associations. ITFC was "committed to ensuring that any taxation imposed on electronic commerce not thwart the development of the Internet marketplace."[54] Mark Nebergall of the ITFC also stressed fairness: "In order to achieve a true 'level playing field,' remote merchants must enjoy the simplicity and predictability of sales tax collection and remittance enjoyed by brick-and-mortar stores. Otherwise, the burden on remote sellers amounts to a competitive advantage for merchants deciding to stay out of electronic commerce." The ITFC also argued that virtually all sectors of the U.S. economy, including state and municipal governments and Main Street businesses, had benefited from the growth of the Internet. Furthermore, there was currently no efficient technology to collect taxes under the

---

[48]*New York Times,* September 13, 2000.

[49]*Washington Post,* October 4, 1999.

[50]*Washington Post,* March 22, 2000.

[51]*Atlanta Journal and Constitution,* July 2, 2000.

[52]Goolsbee (2000) also argued that the implementation of online current use taxes would lead approximately 20–25 percent of the current consumer base not to shop online.

[53]Goolsbee, ibid. For a discussion of other research on these topics, see Wiseman (2000).

[54]The members were America Online, Charles Schwab, Cisco Systems, First Data Corporation, and Microsoft, as well as the American Electronics Association, Information Technology Association, Investment Company Institute, Securities Industry Association, and Software and Information Industry Association.

present tax system. The ITFC argued that any hasty decision on Internet taxation could hinder the country's economic growth.

Opposing the tax moratorium were conventional brick-and-mortar businesses that viewed the tax advantage to online retailers as unfair competition and injurious to their business. The National Retail Federation (NRF) represented retailers ranging from small independent shops to major department stores. Representing shopping centers was the International Council of Shopping Centers, which had 38,000 members. An ad hoc coalition was formed specifically to address the Internet tax question. The E-Fairness Coalition, composed of several interest groups and major retail firms, including the International Council of Shopping Centers, the American Booksellers Association, Tandy/Radio Shack, and Wal-Mart, claimed to represent over 350,000 retail outlets. It consistently argued for a "level playing field" where "customers [were] treated fairly regardless of where they [chose] to shop."[55]

State and local governments strongly favored some form of Internet sales taxation. Arguing that online commerce would lower their tax revenues by as much as $20 billion a year by 2002, state governors had begun pressuring their representatives in Washington. The governors were represented by the National Governors Association (NGA), a national lobbying organization representing the interests of the 50 states. A counterpart to the NGA was the National Council of State Legislatures (NCSL), which represented state legislatures.

City and county governments had voiced their opposition to any tax-moratorium extension.[56] City governments were organized primarily through the U.S. Conference of Mayors, which represented approximately 1,100 cities with populations of at least 30,000. Eighteen thousand smaller cities and towns were represented by the National League of Cities. In legislative matters the National Association of Counties represented over 1,800 counties, covering almost 75 percent of the U.S. population.

The June report by the GAO added to the concerns of state and local governments. The GAO estimated that they would lose sales tax revenue up to $3.8 billion in 2000 and up to $12.4 billion in 2003. A University of Tennessee study estimated the sales tax loss at $20.1 billion in 2003. The GAO also estimated that the losses in 2003 would be $20.4 billion if the taxes not collected on mail-order catalog and telephone sales were included.

CONGRESSIONAL ACTIVITY

Any legislation on Internet taxation implicitly dealt with interstate commerce and hence was referred to the cognizant committee in each chamber of Congress. Under the Rules of the House, the Judiciary Committee, chaired by Henry Hyde (R-IL), had jurisdiction over all legislation dealing with "interstate compacts generally," which included Internet taxation. The Standing Rules of the Senate assigned matters dealing with interstate commerce to the Commerce, Science and Transportation Committee, chaired by Senator McCain. During his bid for the

Republican presidential nomination McCain had come out in favor of a permanent moratorium on all Internet sales taxes.

Congress faced other vexing taxation issues created by technological change. State and local governments imposed taxes of between $4 and $7 billion on telephone usage, but with the growth of cellular telephone usage the state and local governments faced the question of which tax rates applied to cell phones. In July 2000 Congress resolved the issue by enacting legislation specifying that the applicable taxes were those for the address to which the bill was sent. Exceptions were made for corporations that provided cellular telephones to their employees, allowing the company to designate the area code in which the phone was registered as the location for taxation. Lisa Cowell, executive director of the E-Fairness Coalition, commented, "A lot of politicians have stopped hiding behind this bogeyman of 'it can't be done' because no one knows where the customer is."[57]

While the Internet Non-Discrimination Act had sailed through the House without serious complications, the procedural differences between the House and the Senate raised possible problems for the moratorium extension. Any senator could filibuster the bill, which if cloture were not invoked, would likely kill the bill, since the Senate had important pending legislation remaining. One senator, in particular, had voiced opposition to an extended moratorium and had proposed an alternative scheme to remedy the problem of multiple and conflicting tax jurisdictions. Senator Byron Dorgan (D-ND) proposed that online sellers be required to collect and remit use taxes at point of sale, and states could join a "compact" to collect and distribute tax revenues. To join the compact, states would have to adopt uniform definitions of taxable products and have a flat use-tax rate for the entire state. As of June 2000, several states had announced their participation in this "streamlined sales tax project," an NGA initiative to create uniformity in tax laws so as to facilitate online collection. Working with the NGA, the NCSL organized a tax project to simplify state sales taxes. Wal-Mart was one of five retailers that volunteered to test a pilot technology to distinguish among the myriad of state and local tax laws. If successful, the program would be a major step toward making taxation of online sales practical.

STATE ACTIVITY: CALIFORNIA

Legislative activity at the state level complicated the movement toward a uniform federal solution for the tax issue. In August 2000 the California state legislature passed legislation requiring Internet merchants with brick-and-mortar stores in California to collect sales taxes on purchases made online by California residents. If enacted, Barnesandnoble.com and Borders.com would have to collect taxes on purchases made by California consumers, since they had retail outlets in California even though their Internet businesses were housed outside California.[58] Barnesandnoble.com and Borders.com claimed

[55]www.e-fairness.org.
[56]*Chicago Sun Times,* July 24, 2000.

[57]*New York Times,* July 19, 2000.
[58]Amazon.com did not have a nexus in California and thus did not collect taxes from California residents. It collected state sales taxes in its home state of Washington.

that their online companies were separate from their brick-and-mortar companies and hence were not affected by the nexus principle. Borders.com, however, directed customers to a Borders store if they wanted to return a book. Although proponents of the bill hailed it as a "fair and square measure," other parties, such as the American Electronics Association, argued that California was trying to "shoehorn e-commerce business into an old tax system that doesn't make any sense."[59] As the legislation arrived on Governor Gray Davis's desk, observers wondered what its enactment might mean for the future of electronic commerce and state tax autonomy.

INTERNATIONAL ACTIVITY

International developments were also complicating U.S. attempts to resolve the Internet taxation issue. The 1999 Human Development Report of the United Nations made a formal recommendation to impose a $0.01 "bit tax" for every 100 e-mails sent between users. The tax would raise an estimated $70 billion a year for underdeveloped countries. Both the Clinton administration and Congress urged the WTO to impose bans on the bit tax and similar Internet-specific taxes. Embracing the sentiments of the Clinton administration, at its Seattle meeting in December 1999 the WTO decided to extend for 2 years an existing moratorium on Internet taxes, effectively striking down the bit tax proposal.

Other international organizations were also weighing in on the tax question. In October 1998 the 29-nation Organization for Economic Cooperation and Development (OECD) proposed the Ottawa Taxation Framework Conditions. In the hope of developing a uniform taxation scheme for online commerce, the Ottawa Conditions envisioned a tax plan that was economically neutral, efficient, simple, fair, and flexible.[60] The conferees agreed that any taxation scheme should levy taxes on goods based on where they were consumed rather than where they were produced. The flexible nature of Internet commerce, however, raised difficult questions about how to determine where, precisely, goods purchased online were consumed.[61] The OECD established several industry and government working groups to examine these issues in more detail. The United States and the European Union (EU) used the OECD as a forum for their negotiations on Internet taxation.

Most EU member states imposed a value-added tax (VAT) on electronically delivered goods and services supplied by EU companies to EU residents. In June 2000 the EU Commission proposed extending the VAT to non-EU companies, despite the existing WTO moratorium. Specifically, the proposal required any firm selling more than €100,000 worth of electronic goods into the European Union to be registered with one of the 15 member states' tax authorities and charge that state's rate. The VAT rates of the EU member states varied from 15 percent in Luxembourg to 25 percent in Denmark and Sweden. The VAT accounted for approximately 40 percent of the tax revenue of the EU member states and financed the entire EU budget.[62]

The Commission was heavily criticized by the United States for acting unilaterally despite continued negotiations within the OECD. Stuart Eizenstat, Undersecretary of the Treasury Department, argued that the proposal "if implemented, could well hinder the development of [the] global medium of [electronic] commerce." Similarly, Andy Grove came out against the VAT, calling it "e-protectionism."[63] Implementation issues also arose as to how such taxes would be collected, as well as whether the necessary unanimous endorsement of all member states of the European Union could be expected. Mark Bohannon of the U.S.-based Software and Information Industry Association called the Commission report "fatally flawed" because it was impossible to determine where a customer in cyberspace resided.[64]

COMPANIES

A variety of companies would be directly affected by an Internet tax, and others would be indirectly affected. A tax would have a major impact on Amazon.com, the largest online retailer. A sale to a customer in California saved the customer the sales tax of approximately 8 percent, and a sale to a Texas customer saved 8.5 percent.[65] The tax savings helped compensate for delivery costs, which were paid by the customer. Despite not facing sales taxes, Amazon.com lost $207 million before special equity arrangements on sales of $578 million in the quarter ending June 20, 2000.

Amazon.com had worked behind the scenes to oppose any Internet taxes. Its perspective was revealed in its commentary on the California bill to impose taxes on sales by those online companies that claimed that their Internet companies were separate from their brick-and-mortar stores. "Paul Misener, vice president for global public policy at Amazon.com, said he does not see any need to tax Internet sales in general since so many state and local governments are running surpluses right now. 'We really have to see the problem first,' he said. 'This is almost a solution in search of a problem.' Misener added that if online sales are taxed, it should be at a lower rate than off-line transactions because sales made over the Internet 'use fewer state and local resources.' Amazon opposes the... bill because it does not recognize this principle, even though the bill would affect one of the company's biggest competitors: Barnesandnoble.com."[66]

Cisco Systems, the leading supplier of servers for the Internet, supported the Internet Non-Discrimination Act because state governments were running surpluses and

[59]*San Francisco Chronicle,* August 31, 2000.

[60]OECD Committee on Fiscal Affairs, "Implementing the Ottawa Taxation Framework Conditions," June.

[61]*Financial Times,* "Plan for Taxing Internet Commerce Outlined," October 9, 2000.

[62]In contrast, sales taxes accounted for approximately 25 percent of the tax revenue of U.S. states and none of the federal government's tax revenue. The VAT systems in Europe were less complicated than the sales tax systems across the U.S. states.

[63]*BusinessWeek,* June 26, 2000.

[64]*New York Times,* September 30, 2000.

[65]Customers in the state of Washington were required to pay the sales tax.

[66]*San Jose Mercury News,* September 12, 2000.

"the often-confusing tax rules of 7,500 separate jurisdictions could severely impede development of this rapidly expanding medium for global trade, investment, and communication. State and local governments should use an extended moratorium period to simplify their existing, complex tax structures."[67]

Cisco worked on the Internet taxation issue primarily through the Internet Tax Fairness Coalition and the American Electronics Association. Katrina Doerfler of Cisco, testifying on behalf of the American Electronics Association, articulated five principles for any legislation on Internet taxation. "One, impose no greater tax burden on electronic commerce than other traditional means of commerce. Two, support simplicity in administration. Three, retain and clarify nexus standards. Four, avoid new access taxes on the Internet. And, five, consider tax issues in a global context."[68] ▪

Preparation Questions

1. How would the market strategy of Amazon.com be affected by the application of state and local sales taxes to online sales?
2. How would the market strategy of Cisco Systems be affected by the application of state and local sales taxes to online sales?
3. How much influence are the various interests identified in the case likely to have on the issue of Internet taxation?
4. Are there any interests not identified in the case that are likely to be active on this issue? Will they be able to overcome the free-rider problem?
5. What is likely to be the outcome of the Internet Non-Discrimination Act?

Source: This case was written by Alan Wiseman under the supervision of Professor David P. Baron. Copyright © 2000 by the Board of Trustees of the Leland Stanford Junior University. All rights reserved. Reprinted with permission.

Wal-Mart and Its Urban Expansion Strategy

Wal-Mart was the world's largest corporation with sales of $256 billion, a $9 billion profit, and 1.3 million associates, as it called its employees. Wal-Mart was the most admired company in *Fortune*'s annual survey. In addition to its traditional merchandise Wal-Mart had expanded to sell pharmaceuticals and groceries. In the United States its strategy had been to locate in small towns and suburban areas. Only 38 of its 3,000 stores were located in cities with populations of at least 1,000,000. With attractive sites in its traditional areas becoming scarce, Wal-Mart embarked on an urban expansion strategy. The company had 53 Wal-Mart and Sam's Club stores in the Chicago metropolitan area, but none in the city itself. In 2004 Wal-Mart sought approval to build two stores in Chicago.[69] The stores would employ 600 workers.

Wal-Mart's market strategy emphasized low prices, low costs, an efficient distribution system, bargaining power over suppliers, helpful salespeople, and opportunities to advance as the company opened new stores. Although the company paid low wages, those wages were comparable to those paid by its competitors such as Target and K-Mart. Wal-Mart provided health insurance to its employees after 1,000 hours of employment. Wal-Mart also employed many elderly workers who were eligible for Social Security and Medicare.

Wal-Mart had experienced a host of labor incidents that generated criticism. In late 2003 Immigration and Customs Enforcement agents raided several Wal-Mart stores, taking into custody 200 undocumented workers employed by custodial service companies that cleaned the stores. It was also revealed that some Wal-Mart employees had been forced to punch out and continue working, and some minors had worked too many

hours. Wal-Mart was also criticized for refusing to sell some magazines and CDs and concealing parts of the covers of some magazines. The media reported that in high-crime areas Wal-Mart had a policy of locking night shift employees in the building to prevent "shrinkage" from theft. In many cases there was no one with a key to unlock the doors in the case of an emergency, and employees had to call a store manager to have the doors unlocked. Employees could use the emergency exits, but Wal-Mart had made it clear they were not to do so except in a true emergency such as a fire. Some employees said that they had been told that they would be fired if they used the emergency exits. Wal-Mart was also named in the largest-ever class-action lawsuit on behalf of 1.6 million women alleging job discrimination in promotions.

Activists and union leaders criticized Wal-Mart for its low wages and because its low prices put pressure on other companies, including small retailers. Wal-Mart became a political symbol as Democratic presidential primary candidates Howard Dean and Richard Gephardt criticized the company for its health benefits. Wal-Mart had become a symbol of low pay and was accused of driving down wages across the country.

Wal-Mart had a history of opposing unionization, and its employees had rejected unions on a number of occasions. John Bisio, a Wal-Mart spokesperson, explained that the reason "our associates haven't wanted third-party representation is because they have faith in the company, and it provides them with tremendous opportunity."[70]

In Southern California supermarkets faced increased competition from Wal-Mart superstores that sold groceries. To remain competitive, the supermarkets sought to require their employees to bear a share of their health care insurance costs. The United Food and Commercial Workers (UFCW) struck Kroger, Albertsons, and Safeway for 5 months before agreeing to have employees share in the insurance costs.

---

[67]www.cisco.com/warp/public.

[68]Hearings, House Committee on the Judiciary, Subcommittee on Commercial and Administrative Law, June 29, 2000.

[69]Wal-Mart stated that it had no current plans to sell groceries in the proposed new stores.

[70]*New York Times,* May 6, 2004.

Earlier in the year Wal-Mart had sought to open a 60-acre shopping center in Inglewood, California, but local opposition led the city government to reject the changes in zoning rules needed for the project to go ahead. Wal-Mart then campaigned to put the matter before the voters, but in a public referendum voters rejected it by a 60–40 vote.

THE CHICAGO STORES

Wal-Mart planned to open stores on the sites of a closed Ryerson Tull steel facility on the south side and a recently closed Helene Curtis plant on the west side. Both communities were poor and largely African American.

The opposition to Wal-Mart in Chicago was led by the Chicago Workers' Rights Board, which represented a coalition of labor, religious, and civic groups. At a rally an economist from the University of Illinois at Chicago predicted that Wal-Mart's entry would cost more jobs than it would create. He said, "As a rule, Wal-Mart squeezes more sales out of each man hour, so they can generate the same dollars out of fewer workers. So, you'll have a net loss."[71] The unions focused on the specific threat. "The Chicago Federation of Labor has made three demands of the retailing behemoth it called 'Public Enemy No. 1': that Wal-Mart agree not to sell groceries at any of its Chicago stores to avoid driving down the wages of its supermarket competitors, that the company remain neutral in any union-organizing campaign, and that it pays its Chicago employees a 'living wage.' "[72]

Elizabeth Drea of the UFCW said, "Wal-Mart has a well-documented history of violating workers' rights and devastating communities with its predatory practices."[73] She added, "Wal-Mart usually comes in and pays the minimum wage, which forces all other workers' wages downward. That means there's a long-term impact many people may not be willing to explore."[74]

The NGO Good Jobs First produced a study reporting that Wal-Mart had received over $1 billion in state and local tax subsidies during its decades-long expansion. The study was financed in part by the UFCW.[75] A Wal-Mart spokeswoman responded that in the past decade "Wal-Mart has collected $54 billion in sales taxes, paid $4 billion in local property taxes, and paid $192 million in income and unemployment taxes to local governments." "It looks like offering tax incentives to Wal-Mart is a jackpot investment in local government," she said.[76]

Mark Brown, writing in the *Chicago Sun-Times,* said, "Of course, if Chicagoans prefer to keep their tax dollars closer to home, they can shop at Target or Lowe's or Home Depot or any of numerous other discount retail stores operated with non-union workers, all of which have opened new locations in the city in recent years without a peep from organized labor that I can recall…. Labor's main concern seems to be in protecting its workers in the grocery business, because some Wal-Mart stores operate full-service groceries, although the company says that's not part of its initial plan here."[77]

Alderwoman Emma Mitts, who represented the West Side ward in which a store would be located, explained her support for the stores: "For a lot of people, this will be their first job of any kind. This is where they'll learn that in the world of work, you have to show up on time, you have to look good, you have to be helpful and courteous. Our young people are going to learn how to stock shelves, how to answer customers' questions, how to make change. Don't underestimate what it will mean to our community to have a place where young people can learn skills like these."[78] She estimated that the unemployment rate in her ward was 60 percent. In response to the criticisms of Wal-Mart, Mitts said, "We want to take the worst retailer in the world, the worst, as they say, and make it the best. But you know something? To make them the best, you've got to have them inside."[79]

Wal-Mart's average hourly compensation for its associates in the Chicago area was $10.77, which it argued was not low relative to small retailers or large retailers, including Home Depot and Target. "Opponents cited a February 2004 report from U.S. Representative George Miller (D-CA), a senior member on the House Committee on Education and the Workforce, which says that the average Wal-Mart employee nationally earns $8.23 an hour, below the average supermarket employee's wage of $10.35 an hour."[80] Bisio said, "As far as having an impact on the overall economy, if you talk to the Chambers of Commerce in any town where we're present, they'll tell you that we not only create jobs, but we also help attract revenues for ourselves and neighboring retailers, which generates taxes that pay for law enforcement jobs and roads and everything else."[81]

Alderman Howard Brookins Jr., in whose South Side ward the Ryerson Tull facility was located, said, "I don't understand any opposition. Target and Home Depot aren't unionized and they're in the city."[82] Brookins added, "When [Wal-Mart] said they were interested in coming, there was interest from other businesses. Restaurants such as Red Lobster and Applebee's, that weren't interested in coming into the inner city before, signed onto the project."[83]

After Wal-Mart opened a store in Los Angeles, local merchants did not experience the disaster critics had predicted. "'The traffic is definitely there. We're seeing more folks,' says Harold Liecha, a cashier at Hot Looks, a nearby clothier…. But the larger picture is that many [shops] that were there before the big discounter arrived are still there. There are new jobs now where there were none. And a moribund mall is regaining vitality. In short, Wal-Mart came in—and nothing bad happened."[84]

---

[71]*Columbia Chronicle* via U-Wire, May 17, 2004.

[72]*Chicago Sun-Times,* May 26, 2004.

[73]*USA Today,* May 26, 2004.

[74]*Columbia Chronicle* via U-Wire, May 17, 2004.

[75]Good Jobs First also lobbied for a living wage.

[76]*New York Times,* May 24, 2004.

[77]*Chicago Sun-Times,* May 6, 2004.

[78]*New York Times,* July 6, 2004.

[79]*New York Times,* May 6, 2004.

[80]*Columbia Chronicle* via U-Wire, May 17, 2004.

[81]*New York Times,* May 6, 2004.

[82]*Crain's Chicago Business,* April 5, 2004.

[83]*Columbia Chronicle* via U-Wire, May 17, 2004.

[84]*BusinessWeek,* May 10, 2004.

Wal-Mart had worked to build support for the stores in both the communities and Chicago more broadly. Approval of each store required 26 votes from the 50-member city council, and the council usually deferred to the wishes of the relevant alderman. This, however, was not business as usual, and despite support from Mayor Richard Daley, the city council postponed a vote on the stores.

Mr. Bisio observed, "In Chicago, you have to be willing to step out of your so-called comfort zone and what you're used to doing. We recognize that there are experiences there that are different from other places. Organized labor is very strong there. We know we're going to be subject to great scrutiny, and we really want to adhere or conform to the spirit of how things are done in Chicago."[85] ■

Preparation Questions

1. Should Wal-Mart give up on entering Chicago?
2. If not, should it agree to the demands of the Chicago Federation of Labor?
3. What should it do to build a majority in the city council?
4. Formulate an integrated strategy for Wal-Mart's urban expansion.

Source: This case was prepared from public sources by Professor David P. Baron. Copyright © 2004 by David P. Baron. All rights reserved. Reprinted with permission.

Responsible Lobbying?

Our goal is about cervical cancer prevention, and we want to reach as many females as possible with Gardasil. We're concerned that our role in supporting school requirements is a distraction from that goal, and as such have suspended our lobbying efforts.

Dr. Richard M. Haupt, Merck, February 20, 2007

Caution: Too much lobbying may result in an overdose of suspicion. Push too hard and you may experience political acid reflux.

Ellen Goodman, *Boston Globe,* March 1, 2007

INTRODUCTION

In 1965 a German doctor, Harald zur Hausen, received a postdoctoral fellowship at the University of Pennsylvania where he first conjectured that cervical cancer was caused by a virus.[86] Subsequently, the human papilloma virus (HPV) was identified as the cause of cervical cancer. HPV was transmitted only through sexual activity, often had no visible symptoms, and was generally eliminated by the body's immune system. Nevertheless, the Food and Drug Administration estimated that worldwide there were 470,000 new cases of cervical cancer a year and 233,000 deaths a year. In the United States there were 9,710 new cases and 3,700 deaths a year. Treatment for cervical cancer cost the Medicare system $1.7 billion a year, and private insurance paid more. Karen Lustgarten of Planned Parenthood said, "Cancer prevention is preferable to cancer treatment at any age."[87]

Approximately 80 percent of all cervical cancers were caused by HPV types 16, 18, 31, and 45.[88] In 2006 Merck received FDA approval for the first vaccine, Gardasil, for HPV. Gardasil protected against types 16 and 18, which accounted for 70 percent of cervical cancers and 90 percent of genital warts. Gardasil was highly effective for women who had not been infected and less effective for women who had HPV.

Merck priced the vaccine at $360 for the three injections and was also working on programs for the use of Gardasil in developing countries at much lower prices. Analyst Steve Brozak of W.B.B. Securities projected sales of Gardasil at $1 billion a year and billions more if states mandated vaccination.[89] Sales in 2006 were $235 million.

Prior to FDA approval, Merck began to develop a market for Gardasil. It launched an intensive campaign to get states to make vaccination mandatory for girls entering middle school. The campaign generated a backlash against mandatory vaccination, and Merck suspended its campaign. Merck had to reflect on its failure and decide what to do next.

In 2005 Merck had sales of $22 billion and profits of $4.6 billion. The company, however, was fighting on a case-by-case basis hundreds of thousands of lawsuits on its painkiller drug Vioxx, which the company had withdrawn from the market in 2004. The company had established a reserve of $970 million for Vioxx litigation expenses. Merck's biggest drug, Zocor, had lost patent protection in 2006, and another of its major drugs, Fosamax, would lose patent protection in 2008.

GARDASIL AND APPROVALS

The technology used in Gardasil was developed in 1993 by CSL Limited of Australia, which discovered how to make tiny shells that would lead the body's immune system to attack HPV. The National Cancer Institute and Medimmune, Inc. began working to develop a vaccine, and Medimmune later licensed its technology to GlaxoSmithKline.

Dr. Kathrin Jansen of Merck also began working on a vaccine in 1993, and Merck licensed the technology from CSL in 1995. Jansen conceived of using a yeast to make the shells. Merck had a large library of yeast that had been developed for

---

[85]*New York Times,* July 6, 2004.
[86]He received the 2008 Nobel Prize in Medicine for his discovery.
[87]*Palm Beach Post,* February 20, 2007.
[88]Over 100 types of HPV had been identified.

[89]Associated Press, January 30, 2007.

research on a hepatitis-B vaccine, and Jansen and Merck yeast experts succeeded in developing ways to grow large quantities of the shells. This research provided the foundation for Gardasil.[90]

Gardasil was approved on June 8, 2006, for protection against HPV types 16 and 18 for cervical cancer and against HPV 6, 11, 16, and 18 for precancerous lesions and genital warts for women 9–26 years. Gardasil was also approved for use in a number of other countries including Mexico, Australia, Canada, and Brazil. The European Agency for the Evaluation of Medicinal Products approved the vaccine in October 2006 for the 25 member nations of the European Union.

The Centers for Disease Control (CDC) Advisory Committee on Immunization Practices recommended that women between 9 and 26 years of age be vaccinated against HPV and that vaccinations be given at ages 11 and 12 before girls became sexually active.[91] Vaccination was intended not only to protect the person vaccinated but also to reduce the likelihood of transmission of HPV. Gardasil was endorsed by the American Academy of Pediatrics, which stopped short of recommending mandatory vaccinations.[92]

HPV was primarily transmitted through sexual activity. A CDC survey of physicians revealed that 46 percent would vaccinate 10–12-year-olds and 89 percent would vaccinate 16–18-year-olds. Some 11 percent believed that vaccination might increase sexual behavior.[93] A survey of pediatricians published in the *Journal of Adolescent Health,* however, reported that "half the pediatricians expect parents to resist vaccinating their child against any sexually transmitted infection. About 42 percent expect parents to fret that immunization may lead to riskier sexual behaviors, and fully 70 percent said they expect safety concerns about the HPV vaccine to weigh on parents' decision to immunize children."[94]

The CDC Advisory Committee also voted to add Gardasil to the federal program that pays for vaccines for low-income children up to 18 years of age. This vote was important because private insurers would then cover the vaccination. WellPoint, Incorporated, one of the largest private health insurers, announced that it would provide coverage.

Gardasil was effective in stopping cervical cancer among those who did not have HPV, but its effectiveness in the 9–26 age group would be lower because many of the women already had HPV. A study of "female students at Rutgers University in New Jersey found that 26 percent were already infected with HPV when they arrived as freshmen. The rate was 60 percent after 3 years of college."[95]

Merck had tested Gardasil on boys ages 9–15 for prevention of genital warts and head and neck cancer, and additional tests were underway. Merck had not yet sought FDA approval for Gardasil for males. Initial testing had shown that

it was likely to be effective for the prevention of genital warts. Although Gardasil had only been approved for females, doctors could prescribe the drug for males. Insurance plans, however, were not required to cover prescriptions for males, since the drug had not been approved for them.

GlaxoSmithKline (GSK) was close behind Merck in developing an HPV vaccine. A 2004 article published in the medical journal *Lancet* reported successful tests of its vaccine Cervarix. By 2006 GSK had tested its vaccine on 16,000 women worldwide and had Phase III clinical trials under way on 35,000 women in 25 countries. The company had submitted a marketing application with the European Agency for the Evaluation of Medicinal Products in March 2006 and planned to submit an application to the FDA for marketing approval in the spring of 2007. One Phase III study showed that Cervarix was 100 percent effective for women 9–55 years of age. GSK estimated that the market for HPV vaccines could reach $7.5 billion within a few years.

The CDC issued a publication, *Human Papillomavirus: HPV Information for Clinicians,* for health care professionals. In the publication the CDC wrote, "Although this vaccine offers a promising new approach to the prevention of HPV and associated conditions, this vaccine will not replace other prevention strategies, such as cervical cancer screening.... Vaccine providers should notify vaccinated females that they will need regular cervical cancer screening as the vaccine will not provide protection against all types of HPV that cause cervical cancer." Pap tests introduced in the 1950s had reduced the death rate from cervical cancer by 70 percent, and a new DNA-based test for HPV had recently been approved by the FDA.[96]

MARKET DEVELOPMENT

While conducting Phase III trials, Merck began wrestling with the issues surrounding the marketing of its vaccine. The issues centered on public acceptance, mandating the vaccine, and obtaining reimbursement from the government and private insurers. Merck also knew that Medimmune and GlaxoSmithKline, among others, were working on vaccines.

In anticipation of the approval of Gardasil, Merck began developing the market. In 2005 it provided financial support for a public education campaign, *Make the Connection,* established in 2005 by the Cancer Research and Prevention Foundation and Step Up Women's Network.[97] The campaign featured the Web site www.maketheconnection.org and included a series of educational events in 15 cities beginning in September 2005. The campaign also included television "public service announcements" similar to the direct-to-consumer advertisements used by pharmaceutical companies. The announcements featured Kimberly Elise and Elizabeth Röhm,

---

[90]The National Cancer Institute and Medimmune used host cells from butterfly caterpillars, but scaling to large quantities proved difficult.

[91]A booster shot might be required 5 to 10 years after the vaccination. Merck was monitoring women who had been vaccinated.

[92]*Wall Street Journal,* April 16, 2007.

[93]*Wall Street Journal,* May 17, 2006.

[94]*Wall Street Journal,* November 30, 2005.

[95]*Wall Street Journal,* November 21, 2002.

---

[96]The Pap test was developed by Cornell University pathologist George Papanicolaou. Precancerous lesions identified by a Pap test were typically surgically removed.

[97]The Cancer Research and Prevention Foundation, founded in 1985, provided grants for cancer prevention, education, and prevention programs. Step Up Women's Network, founded in 1998, focused on strengthening community resources for women and girls.

who discussed cervical cancer and urged the viewers to contact their doctors. The campaign asked women to make a commitment to talk to their doctors about cervical cancer. For each commitment Merck pledged to contribute $1, up to a maximum of $100,000, to the Cancer Research and Prevention Foundation for cervical cancer programs.

Merck lobbied extensively at the state level in support of mandatory vaccination and conducted a television advertising campaign for Gardasil. "It aired TV ads featuring young girls skipping rope while reciting the slogan, 'I want to be one less' woman to battle the disease." The ads stated that Gardasil "'may help protect you' from HPV strains 'that may cause 70% of cervical cancer.'"[98]

Merck also worked with Women in Government to promote vaccination in line with the CDC Advisory Committee's recommendation. Women in Government was formed in 1988 for elected women in state governments and focused on public policy issues, particularly those affecting women. One of those issues was preventing cervical cancer. In 2004 it launched its "Challenge to Eliminate Cervical Cancer Campaign." President Susan Crosby said, "Cervical cancer can be our first victory in the war on cancer. By ensuring that women are educated about this disease and the virus that causes it, and that they have access to preventive technologies, regardless of socioeconomic status, we can ensure that no more women die of this preventable disease."[99]

Women in Government released a study, "Partnering for Progress 2007: The 'State' of Cervical Cancer Prevention in America," that evaluated the states on their performance on cervical cancer incidence and mortality. The study concluded that the states that performed best were those that provided reimbursement for HPV testing. Women in Government also concluded that vaccinations were an essential part of the campaign to eliminate cervical cancer. Crosby said, "To truly achieve this goal, we must make FDA-approved HPV vaccines available to all age-appropriate girls and women. That is what our recommendations, including the middle school entry requirement, are designed to do."[100] More specifically, the organization's policy recommendation regarding "School Entrance Requirements" was, "States should require cervical cancer/HPV vaccination for girls to enter middle school, in conjunction with other adolescent vaccines required at this time, and should allow parents to opt out in accordance with states' existing exemption allowances (e.g., medical, religious and/or philosophical)."[101]

Women in Government held an "HPV & Cervical Cancer Summit" in Washington, D.C., and conducted activities in all the states. The organization held dinners and meetings on HPV and cervical cancer in a number of major cities in the United States. "In early January [2007], Women in Government held a conference for some 60 state legislators in Marco Island, Fla., paying for their airfare and hotel rooms. One of the speakers was Christine Baze, a pop singer and cervical-cancer survivor.

As she performed songs on the piano, Ms. Baze told the story of her battle with the disease and said she wished a vaccine had been available to her. Ms. Baze says Women in Government paid her a $2,500 fee and covered her travel and lodging. She says she didn't receive any money from Merck for the appearance, but the company has paid her $7,500 to speak at three other events."[102]

Women in Government received contributions from Merck, GlaxoSmithKline, and Digene, which had developed the first FDA-approved test to detect HPV DNA.[103] Merck's Deborah Alfano sat on Women in Government's business council in 2006. The organization posted model legislation on its Web site.

According to the National Conference of State Legislatures, bills to mandate, fund, or educate the public about HPV and cervical cancer had been introduced in 34 state legislatures.[104] Many of the bills were introduced by members of Women in Government, and many of the bills requiring mandatory vaccinations included an opt out provision for religious or moral reasons.

Merck used a combination of traditional lobbying and a public information and advocacy approach relying on television advertisements. It increased its budget for lobbying in states like Texas.

Merck was not the only company to work with health advocacy groups to raise awareness of HPV and cervical cancer and its treatment. The Partnership to End Cervical Cancer, a 20-member coalition of medical, public health, and NGOs plus GlaxoSmithKline and Digene Corporation, stated, "Comprehensive vaccination programs work—as we've seen with the significant reduction or elimination of smallpox worldwide and measles in the Western Hemisphere. Today, the Partnership is making the commitment to play a leadership role in the campaign to end as much of cervical cancer as can be prevented with these vaccines and screening in this country."[105] GSK provided financial and administrative support for the partnership.

Digene had worked to educate women and governments about the importance of testing for HPV and began a direct-to-consumer television advertising campaign in 2006 to this effect. It expanded the campaign to more cities in 2007. Digene also provided support to the Academy for Educational Development and the Coalition of Labor Union Women for their 5-year campaign to reduce cervical cancer.

STATE ACTIONS

Health care programs, and particularly mandated vaccinations, were the responsibility of the states. In some states health departments were responsible for public health programs such as vaccination programs. The New Hampshire Health Department decided to provide the vaccine to girls under 18 at no cost,

---

[98]*Wall Street Journal,* April 16, 2007.
[99]Women in Government, press release, September 21, 2006.
[100]PR Newswire, September 12, 2006.
[101]Women in Government, September 12, 2006.

[102]*Wall Street Journal,* April 16, 2007. Baze spoke at the 2006 HPV & Cervical Cancer Summit.
[103]At least 25 of the 81 sponsors were pharmaceutical companies. www.womeningovernment.org/home/support_ sponsors.asp.
[104]www.ncsl.org/programs.health/HPVvaccine.htm.
[105]PR Newswire, September 13, 2006.

and the governor of South Dakota announced a similar program. In most states legislation was required to provide the funds for such programs or to require mandatory vaccination.

A bill introduced in the Florida legislature would require vaccination of girls of age 11 or 12 before they could enroll in a public or private school. Parents were allowed to opt out their children after having received information on cervical cancer. Virginia was moving more rapidly than other states, and the legislature had passed a mandatory vaccination bill. The governor was reviewing the opt out provision before deciding whether to sign the bill.

In Texas Governor Rick Perry issued an executive order requiring that girls entering the sixth grade as of 2008 be vaccinated against HPV.[106] For those not covered by insurance he also ordered that the vaccine would be free for girls ages 9 to 18 and covered by Medicaid for women from ages 19 to 21. Krista Moody, a spokesperson for the governor, explained, "The governor believes we should protect as many young women as possible—rich and poor, insured and uninsured—while maintaining parents' rights to opt their daughters out of receiving the vaccine."[107]

CRITICS

As the public and organized private groups became aware of Merck's efforts to promote and secure a first-mover advantage for Gardasil, and particularly mandatory vaccination, criticism grew. The criticism focused not only on Merck's efforts but also on the wisdom of mandatory vaccination and whether a state should wait until more evidence of side effects had accumulated.

Critics in Texas claimed that Governor Perry's action was the result of cronyism. Dawn Richardson, president of Parents Requesting Open Vaccine Education, said, "He's circumventing the will of the people. There are bills filed. There's no emergency except in the boardroom of Merck, where this is failing to gain the support they had expected."[108]

Merck had contributed $6,000 to Perry's election campaign. Perry's former chief of staff, Mike Toomey, was a lobbyist, one of whose clients was Merck, and Representative Dianne Delisi, the state director of Women in Government, was the mother-in-law of Perry's current chief of staff. Delisi had met in September with the governor's budget director for an "HPV Vaccine for Children Briefing," according to her calendar. She had also met with Toomey three times, and two other Perry staffers had met with a Merck lobbyist.[109] The wife of Perry's former chief of staff was a nurse who had promoted health and spoken at a Women in Government conference on cervical cancer.[110] Cathie Adams of the Texas Eagle Forum commented, "We have too many coincidences. I think that the voters of Texas would find that very hard to swallow."[111]

Public criticism of Governor Perry's order grew, and the Texas legislature held a hearing on the order and began considering rescinding it. The state House of Representatives voted 118 to 23 to rescind the governor's order, but the Senate took a different approach by passing a bill that prevented the state from mandating vaccinations before 2011. The House approved the bill on a 132 to 2 vote.[112]

A bill to mandate vaccination began hearings in California in March 2007 and was met with skepticism. Opponents of the bill said the California children would be "guinea pigs" and that parents rather than the state should make the decision about vaccinations for a virus that was transmitted by sexual activity.

Criticism of the vaccine had begun with some conservative Christian groups claiming it would encourage premarital sex. Stephen Cable, president of Vermont Renewal, echoed a theme of a number of conservative organizations, "To think that an 11-year old would be forced to take this vaccine, based on the assumption they'll be sexually active, it's more than annoying…. There are a lot of parents who haven't heard about this (legislation). When they do, the hair will be standing up on the back of their necks."[113] "In recent weeks, opposition to state mandates has grown among parents who want the freedom to make such a medical decision on their own, and who are worried about exposing their children to the unforeseen side effects of a new vaccine. Physicians and consumer advocates have also questioned the need to immunize young girls against a disease that is no longer very prevalent in the U.S. and doesn't develop until much later in life."[114] A spokesperson for the Center for Medical Consumers stated, "Parents should be concerned that the only company that makes this vaccine is pushing behind the scenes for mandatory laws."[115]

Mandating the vaccine also drew fire from family values groups. The Minnesota Family Council said a mandate "undermines abstinence and excuses premarital sex. It's not dealing with a contagious disease that someone can get in public. It's specifically resulting from a particular behavior."[116]

State senator Janet Greenip of Maryland opposed legislation mandating the vaccine stating, "The vaccine is very important, but I'm reluctant to make it mandatory. If it is good, people will do it."[117] Dr. Mark Myers, executive director of the National Network for Immunization Information, however, cautioned, "A lot of us are concerned that if you allow people to opt out of one vaccine, they will opt out of other vaccines that are due at the same time."[118]

One concern raised was whether Gardasil had been sufficiently tested in very young girls. Of those tested only 1,184 were preteen girls. The National Vaccine Information Center, an organization formed by parents concerned about the harm from vaccines, reported that through the end of 2006, 385 adverse events had been reported associated with the use of Gardasil.

---

[106]Texas had not mandated two other vaccines approved in recent years for meningitis and whooping cough.
[107]*New York Times,* March 14, 2007.
[108]Associated Press, February 3, 2007. The citizens group had worked for opt out provisions for other vaccines.
[109]Associated Press, February 22, 2007.
[110]*New York Times,* February 17, 2007.
[111]Associated Press, February 22, 2007.

[112]*New York Times,* April 26, 2007.
[113]Associated Press, February 22, 2007.
[114]*Wall Street Journal,* February 21, 2007.
[115]*Wall Street Journal,* February 7, 2007.
[116]*Pioneer Press,* February 22, 2007.
[117]Associated Press, January 19, 2007.
[118]*New York Times,* February 17, 2007.

The CDC stated that the adverse events were not a cause for concern. When the FDA approved Gardasil, it ordered Merck to track a number of 11- and 12-year-olds in a postmarketing study scheduled to be completed in 2009. The FDA action requiring a postmarketing study was common.

The Health Information National Trends Survey (HINTS) conducted by the National Cancer Institute collected data from 3,000 women between the ages of 18 and 75. Only 40 percent had heard of HPV and fewer than half were aware of the connection to cervical cancer. A study of 645 adults by the Annenberg National Communication Survey found that 56 percent had heard of HPV and 42 percent had heard about a vaccine. The respondents were asked to read three statements about the vaccine and asked if they would get vaccinated. When the statement stated that the vaccine protected against cervical cancer, 63 percent of the women indicated that they were "very likely" or "somewhat likely" to get vaccinated, compared to 43 percent when the statement said it protected against cervical cancer and a sexually transmitted infection.[119]

Critics contended that Merck's lobbying campaign was intended to obtain mandatory vaccination before GlaxoSmithKline's vaccine for HPV was approved. Vera Hassner Sharav, a critic of pharmaceutical companies, called the HPV vaccine campaign the "Help Pay for Vioxx" losses campaign.[120]

Cathie Adams, president of the Texas Eagle Forum, commented on the relationship between Women in Government and Merck, "What it does is benefit the pharmaceutical companies, and I don't want the pharmaceutical companies taking precedent over the authorities of parents." Referring to Merck's lobbying campaign, she said, "It's corrupt as far as I'm concerned."[121]

In February two women legislators in Minnesota removed their names from sponsorship of a school-mandated vaccine. The Minnesota Medical Association called for the appointment of a scientific advisory board to study whether the vaccine should be mandated. Minnesota already required vaccination for hepatitis B, which is sexually transmitted.

Debbie Halvorson, the majority leader of the Illinois Senate, said she would continue to work for a mandatory vaccination. She said, "If the people out there are thinking that Merck is doing all this, and pushing our buttons, they need to just step away. The fact that I'm doing what I'm doing has nothing to do with Merck." Halvorson had had a hysterectomy as a result of human papilloma virus.[122]

CLOSING

Margaret McGlynn, Merck president for vaccines, responded to critics of its lobbying campaign by stating, "Each and every day that a female delays getting the vaccine there is a chance she is exposed to human papilloma virus."[123] Merck spokesperson Janet Skidmore said, "What we support are approaches that achieve high immunization rates. We're talking about cervical cancer here, the second-leading cancer among women."[124] Patti Stinchfield, an immunization expert in Minnesota and a member of the CDC's vaccine advisory committee, commented, "It's hard to argue against a vaccine that prevents cervical cancer in your sisters and aunts and mothers. That's where the argument goes if you want to argue against this vaccine."

In response to the criticism, Merck's Dr. Haupt commented on the views of medical organizations and public health officials, "They believe the timing for the school requirements is not right. Our goal is to prevent cervical cancer. Our goal is to reach as many females as possible. Right now, school requirements and Merck's involvement in that are being viewed as a distraction to that goal."[125] Merck suspended its lobbying but indicated that it would continue its educational efforts directed at health officials and legislators.

Dr. Joseph A. Bocchini, chairman of an American Academy of Pediatrics committee on infectious diseases, said, "If the public had enough experience with the vaccine and had enough knowledge about HPV, the question about whether to get the vaccine or give it to their daughters wouldn't be an issue."[126] Dr. Bocchini praised the decision by Merck to stop its lobbying campaign for school-mandated vaccinations. He said that the focus should be on educating parents.[127]

In April an article in the *Wall Street Journal* questioned the efficacy of mandatory vaccination, suggesting that it would be better to rely on Pap screening. In May researchers published an article in the *New England Journal of Medicine* analyzing 12,167 women 3 years after vaccination. Whereas Gardasil was 98 percent effective for women who had never been infected by HPV, it was only 44 percent effective when women who had previously been infected were included. Gardasil was only 17 percent effective in preventing precancerous lesions.[128] ▣

Preparation Questions

1. What was Merck's motivation for its market development strategy?
2. Were the components of its market development strategies responsible?
3. Should Merck have been able to anticipate the opposition that developed to its strategy?
4. Should it have suspended its lobbying for mandatory vaccinations? In which circumstances and under what conditions should it resume its lobbying?
5. Design a marketing program for the use of Gardasil for males.

Source: This case was prepared by David P. Baron based on public sources. Copyright © 2008 by the Board of Trustees of the Leland Stanford Junior University. All rights reserved. Reprinted by permission.

[119]*Cancer Vaccine Week,* December 4, 2006.
[120]*New York Times,* February 17, 2007.
[121]Associated Press, January 30, 2007.
[122]*New York Times,* February 21, 2007.

[123]*New York Times,* February 17, 2007.
[124]Associated Press, January 30, 2007.
[125]*New York Times,* February 21, 2007.
[126]*New York Times,* February 17, 2007.
[127]*Wall Street Journal,* February 21, 2007.
[128]*Wall Street Journal,* May 10, 2007.

PART II

Amazon.com and the Amazon Tax

INTRODUCTION

As a result of a Supreme Court decision pertaining to catalog sales, Amazon.com and other online retailers were not obligated to collect state and local sales taxes on their online sales unless they had a physical presence or "substantial nexus," such as an office or a retail outlet, in the state. Most states required their residents to pay a use tax on items purchased in other states. For some items such as an automobile, which had to be registered in the state, it was easy to collect the use tax. But, for online purchases few customers paid the tax. Brick-and-mortar retailers had attempted without success to convince Congress to overturn the Supreme Court decision and require online retailers to collect sales taxes.[129]

Customers found Amazon.com attractive because of the convenience of online shopping and also because they could avoid sales tax which could be as high as 9 or 10 percent. Both gave Amazon a competitive advantage relative to brick-and-mortar stores, and the substantial nexus decision gave it a competitive advantage over other online sellers such as Barnes & Noble, Home Depot, and Wal-Mart that had a physical presence in nearly all states. The competitive advantage also affected how Amazon organized its business. It had an incentive to locate warehouses in states without a sales tax, as well as where shipping costs determined where a warehouse should be located. The company placed ownership of the warehouse with a subsidiary, so that Amazon itself had no physical presence in the state. Amazon also had affiliates in each state that placed Amazon links and advertisements on their Web sites and received a payment for each Internet user directed to its site. During the so-called Great Recession of 2007–2009 and its aftermath, online retailers thrived relative to other retailers as cost-conscious consumer flocked to the Internet. Sales of online merchants increased by 4.8 percent, whereas sales at brick-and-mortar retailers decreased by 9.1 percent during the recession.[130] The rise of price comparison Web sites also aided Amazon relative to online retailers that were obligated to collect sales taxes. Amazon's sales increased by 40 percent in 2010 to $34 billion, and in the fourth quarter sales were $13 billion. Its sales had broadened, and media products represented less than half of its sales.

The recession caused tax collections by states to drop sharply, resulting in large budget deficits in many states. The states eyed the sales tax revenue lost because of online sales as an opportunity to reduce their deficits and sought ways to force online retailers to collect the tax. The Supreme Court ruling provided protection for online retailers without a nexus in the state, but the concept of a nexus provided an opportunity. New York enacted a law, widely referred to as the "Amazon law," that defined an affiliate as a sales agent and declared that the presence of sales agents in the state constituted a nexus. Several other states followed New York's lead, and others such as Texas decided that a warehouse owned by an Amazon subsidiary was a nexus and sent Amazon a bill for back taxes. Other states contemplated similar laws. Amazon faced the challenge of both defending the status quo at the federal level and dealing with the state initiatives. The state initiatives posed the immediate threat. The Alliance for Main Street Fairness which backed Internet sales taxation had turned its attention from Congress to the states and took out full-page newspaper advertisements featuring excerpts from local newspapers advocating taxation of online sales. The Alliance was backed by big-box retailers including Wal-Mart, Target, Best Buy, Sears, and JC Penny.

BACKGROUND

The Supreme Court held in *Quill Corp. v. North Dakota*, (504 U.S. 298, 1992) that the Commerce Clause of the Constitution prevented a state from requiring a mail-order company to collect sales tax on purchases by residents unless the company had a physical presence, or substantial nexus, in the state, since collections would be burdensome and impede interstate commerce. Online retailers relied on this decision to avoid collecting sales taxes in states where they did not have a nexus.

Most states had both sales and use taxes. Residents of a state that purchase items outside the state were required to pay to their resident state its sales tax applied to the purchase price. Few residents paid the use tax. Of the 50 states only Alaska, Delaware, Oregon, Montana, and New Hampshire had no sales tax, although Delaware has a gross receipts tax. Amazon collected sales taxes on purchases by residents only in Washington, Kansas, Kentucky, and North Dakota, where it had sales operations, and in New York while it appealed a court decision.

The National Conference of State Legislatures estimated that uncollected sales taxes on online and mail-order sales were $8.6 billion in 2010. A University of Tennessee study estimated that uncollected taxes on Internet sales would be more than $11 billion by 2012. However, a study by Navigant Economics for NetChoice, an association including as members eBay, Expedia, Oracle, Overstock.com, and Yahoo, estimated the tax loss at only $4 billion a year.[131] The California Board of Equalization, the tax collecting agency of the state, estimated that in 2010 the state lost $1.15 billion in uncollected sales taxes from online shopping and catalog sales. Of that amount $795 million was from consumers with the rest from businesses.

There were approximately 7,500 jurisdictions in the United States that imposed a sales tax, and online and catalog retailers argued that the complexity associated with applying the tax rates to each purchase would be overly burdensome, particularly to small retailers. A group of 23 states participated

---

[129]See the case *Internet Taxation* in Chapter 8.
[130]www.foxnews.com, June 19, 2011.
[131]Congress Daily/A.M., July 30, 2010.

in the Streamlined Sales Tax Governing Board to simplify and harmonize sales taxes across the states. Twenty advisory states also participated, but the complexity of the task was considerable. The group had to decide issues such as "whether a Twix bar is a cookie and exempt from sales taxes or a candy that isn't exempt."[132] Scott Peterson, executive director of the group, said, "I think we're soon getting to a point where Congress will have to enact a law giving states authority to require out-of-state online retailers to collect local sales taxes."[133] Mary Osaka, spokesperson for Amazon, said, "We are not opposed to collecting sales tax within a constitutionally permissible system applied even-handedly."[134]

THE THREATS FROM THE STATES

The tax laws affected Amazon's organization, its location decisions, and its strategy more broadly. Amazon located its warehouses based in part on shipping costs and in part on tax considerations. For tax purposes Amazon had incentives to locate in states in which it necessarily had a physical presence, which had no state sales tax, and where sales were relatively low as in the case of a state with a small population. Where shipping costs dictated the location of a warehouse as in the case of Texas, Amazon had established a subsidiary to own the warehouse under an "entity isolation" strategy, allowing the company to claim that the warehouse was not a nexus.[135] Amazon maintained that a nexus was necessarily something that sold products, whereas a warehouse only shipped products. Amazon's warehouses were located in its headquarters state of Washington and in Texas and several other states. Amazon supported its marketing through arrangements with "affiliates"—Web sites on which Amazon advertised and paid the affiliate for each user directed to Amazon's Web site.

States began to counter Amazon's strategy by rewriting their laws to designate affiliates and warehouses owned by a subsidiary as nexuses. Amazon responded not only by contesting the state laws but also by removing the newly designated nexuses.

NEW YORK

New York was the first state to enact an Amazon law. The 2008 law stated that a remote vendor, that is, Amazon, that enters into an agreement with a resident who refers customers to the vendor and receives in exchange a commission is an "in-state vendor." By this definition Amazon's New York affiliates made it an in-state vendor that was required to collect the sales tax on sales to New York residents. The implicit claim was that Amazon had a substantial nexus in the state, and hence was not protected by *Quill*. Amazon filed a lawsuit challenging the law, but collected the state sales tax as it contested the law in the courts. Lower state courts upheld the law, and Amazon appealed their decisions.

COLORADO

Colorado took a somewhat different approach to collecting taxes on online sales. It required online sellers to notify Colorado customers on each transaction that they owed sales and use tax and to provide them with a year-end statement of their purchases. The law enacted in 2010 also required the online retailer to provide the state department of revenue with a statement summarizing the online purchases of each customer with a Colorado shipping address and the amount of their purchases. The online retailer could avoid the notification and reporting requirements if it collected and remitted the sales tax. Amazon responded quickly to the enactment of the law by severing its relationships with its Colorado affiliates. In an e-mail to its Colorado affiliates Amazon wrote, "We and many others strongly opposed this legislation ..., but it was enacted anyway. There is a right way for Colorado to pursue its revenue goals, but this new law is a wrong way."[136] Governor Bill Ritter Jr. responded, "Amazon has taken a disappointing—and completely unjustified—step of ending its relationship with associates. While Amazon is blaming a new state law for its action, the fact is that Amazon is simply trying to avoid compliance with Colorado law and is unfairly punishing Colorado businesses in the process." Former affiliate Brad Feld wrote, "[T]he many small businesses and solo entrepreneurs who make money off of Amazon's affiliate program just lost a revenue stream (which, by the way, is used to employ people and pay states taxes)."[137] The local activist group ProgressNow Colorado called for a boycott of Amazon "until Amazon.com stops using Coloradans as pawns."[138]

Rebecca Madigan, director of the Performance Marketing Association of affiliates, said, "States say they are doing this to generate revenue. But these laws won't achieve this objective because the states won't get the sales tax once online retailers such as Amazon drop their affiliates. At the same time, there will be a reduction in state income tax paid by affiliates as they lose revenue from Amazon. Logic is on our side."[139]

Closing affiliate programs was believed to have little effect on Amazon and other large online retailers. Jonathan Johnson, president of Overstock.com which had also severed ties with its affiliates, said, "We ended them in New York, Rhode Island and North Carolina, and it hasn't hurt our sales. People like to find coupons and deals from affiliate members. If they don't find them from a Los Angeles- or San Bernardino-based affiliate marketer, they'll find them from someone in Dallas or San Antonio."[140] Ken Rockwell, who operated an affiliate Web site, commented on the pending legislation in California which he said would cost him 90 percent of his income: "I happen to be in California, but I can do what I do if I move to Tahiti or the south of France."[141]

Barnes & Noble saw an opportunity and invited former Amazon affiliates in states with "e-fairness legislation" to

[132]*DallasNews.com*, April 14, 2010.
[133]Ibid.
[134]*Washington Post*, May 2, 2010.
[135]The subsidiary was named Amazon.com KYDC LLC. (*Wall Street Journal*, August 2, 2011)

[136]*Washington Times*, March 23, 2010.
[137]Ibid.
[138]Ibid.
[139]*The Times* (London), March 17, 2011.
[140]*Los Angeles Times*, February 27, 2011.
[141]Ibid.

operate through BN.com. Barnes & Noble wrote in its invitation, "If Amazon doesn't want you, we do!" It explained that because it has stores in every state it would collect the sales tax so customers would not "have to worry about being hassled or persecuted by state tax auditors."[142]

The Direct Marketing Association filed a lawsuit claiming that the law was unconstitutional under *Quill*. A judge imposed a temporary injunction on application of the law because of privacy concerns.

NORTH CAROLINA

North Carolina had passed an Amazon tax, and Amazon terminated its affiliate program in the state. The state Department of Revenue decided to try to collect back taxes on Amazon's sales and asked the company to provide it information about purchases by product category by residents dating back to 2003.[143] Amazon refused on privacy grounds and filed a lawsuit in federal court to block the request. The company argued, "Customers who fear that their purchases will not be private are less likely to purchase books, movies, music or other items that might be personal, sensitive or controversial."[144] North Carolina responded stating that the lawsuit was "misleading." Amazon quoted from the Department of Revenue order that asked for "all information for all sales to customers with a North Carolina shipping address."[145]

The privacy issue attracted the attention of the American Civil Liberties Union (ACLU). Executive Director Jennifer Rudinger said, "Consumers have reasonable expectation of privacy and a First Amendment right to read, hear or view a wide range of popular or unpopular expressive materials without their choice being subjected to unnecessary government scrutiny. [The] demands threaten to have a major chilling effect on future consumers' expressive choices."[146] ACLU attorney Aden Fine stated, "The state of North Carolina, like all other governmental entities, is not entitled to know what citizens are reading, listening to or watching."[147] The ACLU joined Amazon in the case. The Electronic Frontier Foundation also was concerned about the government possibly using data that was collected for a different purpose. Legal director Cindy Cohn said, "We need to strengthen the law that when we collect information for one purpose, it isn't used for another."[148] Federal judge Marsha Pechman ruled for Amazon.

TEXAS

Texas faced a large budget deficit for 2011 and was in the midst of devising means of reducing it when state comptroller Susan Combs after an administrative review determined that Amazon's warehouse constituted a nexus. She sent Amazon a bill for $269 million for back taxes for online sales. She commented, "It's a time-honored custom not to pay taxes. A lot of people try not to, but it's up to the state to make sure that there's tax fairness."[149]

Amazon responded by announcing that it was closing its Texas warehouse and cancelling its plans to expand in Texas. The closing cost 119 employees their jobs. The company wrote to its Texas employees, "We were planning to build additional facilities and expand in Texas, bringing more than 1,000 new jobs and tens of millions of investment dollars to the state, and we regret the need to reverse course."[150] Dave Clark of Amazon wrote to employees explaining, "Despite much hard work and the support of other Texas officials, we've been unable to come to a resolution with the Texas Comptroller's office."[151]

After Amazon announced it was closing its warehouse, spokesperson Allen Spelce of the comptroller's office said, "We regret losing any business in the state of Texas. But our position hasn't changed: If you have a physical business presence in the state of Texas, you owe sales tax."[152] Texas governor Rick Perry disagreed. He said, "The comptroller made that decision independently. I would tell you, from my perspective, that's not the decision I would have made."[153]

OTHER STATES

Amazon terminated its business relationships with affiliates in Rhode Island even before its Amazon tax became law. The company explained, "This bill would take effect immediately upon enactment—either by the governor's signature or an override of his veto."[154] Amazon also ended its business arrangements with affiliates in Hawaii in anticipation of the state passing an Amazon tax. Amazon explained to its affiliates, "We were forced to take this unfortunate action in anticipation of actual enactment because of the uncertainty and timing of a veto, and the possibility that a veto would be overridden."[155] Connecticut also enacted an Amazon tax, and Amazon immediately severed ties with affiliates in the state.

Undeterred by Amazon's strategy Illinois enacted an Amazon tax in March 2011 as a step in dealing with its massive budget deficit. Amazon immediately terminated its contracts with its 9,000 affiliates in the state. Rebecca Madigan of the Performance Marketing Association, which represented affiliates, stated that the Illinois affiliates generated revenue of $611 million and paid $18 million in taxes in 2009.[156] Commenting on the Amazon tax in Rhode Island, she said. "We're seeing small businesses being hit. They are the collateral damage through all of this legislation, which inaccurately classifies affiliate marketers as sales agents rather than advertising channels."[157] Paul Misiner, Amazon vice president, said,

---

[142]*Wall Street Journal*, February 15, 2011.

[143]*Washington Post*, May 2, 2010.

[144]*New York Times*, May 3, 2010.

[145]*Wall Street Journal*, April 22, 2010.

[146]*Washington Post*, May 2, 2010.

[147]*Washington Times*, August 20, 2010.

[148]*New York Times*, May 3, 2010.

[149]*New York Times*, March 14, 2011.

[150]*The Times* (London), March 17, 2011.

[151]*Wall Street Journal*, February 11, 2011.

[152]*Dallas News.com*, February 11, 2011.

[153]*DallasNews.com*, February 12, 2011.

[154]*Wall Street Journal*, June 30, 2009.

[155]*Wall Street Journal*, July 1, 2009.

[156]*Wall Street Journal*, March 11, 2011.

[157]*Wall Street Journal*, June 30, 2010.

"These new tax laws affecting affiliates are supported by the national retailing chains that covet the affiliate advertising programs of their competitors."[158]

The Virginia legislature took up the issue of an Amazon tax based on designating affiliates as constituting a nexus. Chris Manns had successfully built a price comparison Web site CheapestTextbooks with 10 employees and was an Amazon affiliate, receiving income for customers referred to Amazon. He testified that he would have to move out of the state if he were cut off by Amazon. The bill to impose an Amazon tax died, but the sponsor promised to reintroduce it next year.[159]

Amazon had planned to open warehouses in South Carolina and Tennessee with the warehouses owned by subsidiaries. Amazon insisted on a tax exemption in Tennessee. An exemption from the collection of the state sales tax in South Carolina had expired, and Amazon sought assurances that it would not be required to collect the tax. A spokesperson for the South Carolina governor said, "The governor is taking a hard look at the issues surrounding Amazon. Economic development and job creation are two of her highest responsibilities and priorities, and while the governor wants to make sure we keep promises made to companies, she also wants to make sure we are being fair to the companies we already have in the state."[160]

CALIFORNIA

California's Democrat-controlled legislature passed an Amazon law in 2010, but it was vetoed by Republican governor Arnold Schwarzenegger. In 2011 Assemblywoman Nancy Skinner reintroduced an Amazon tax bill based on the New York bill stating, "Out-of-state online retailers designed their business model to avoid collecting sales tax. This puts our Main Street businesses, which play by the rules, at a competitive disadvantage. It's not fair to hurt California businesses that are struggling to keep their doors open."[161] Rosemary Rodd, who owned a professional audio store, said, "We get people who come in here and try the thing out and talk to my people about what works best for them. Then they buy it on the Internet and tell me, 'I'm a musician. I'm broke. The $200 I saved was just too much.'"[162] Democrat Betty Yee, a member of the State Board of Equalization, said, "I've gone into Home Depot, and it's practically empty. It's like one big showroom now. Consumers go in and touch and feel and test products, and then they go home and order online from out of state."[163] The bill was backed by the California Retailers Association. Barnes & Noble vice president Gene DeFelice said, "We are at a serious competitive disadvantage."[164] The Direct Marketing Association representing online retailers opposed the bill. eBay complained that the bill would force out-of-state sellers to collect taxes on sales to California residents, imposing a heavy

burden on small sellers. David London of eBay said, "Tax barriers that block small business from using the Internet will stifle job growth, reduce competition for retail giants and undermine entrepreneurial small businesses trying to spur economic growth."[165] Rebecca Madigan representing 25,000 online affiliates in California said, "Out-of-state advertisers will simply stop advertising on the California websites to avoid having to collect California sales tax."[166]

With a new Democrat governor taking office in 2011 and an enormous state budget deficit, the tax bill received new life. The legislature passed the bill and the governor signed it. As in the laws adopted by other states, affiliates were designated as constituting a physical presence. Amazon had 10,000 affiliates in California, and another 2,000 online retailers in the state were estimated to have 15,000 affiliates. The bill contained two provisions specifically directed at Amazon. One provision let the state collect sales tax from an online retailer that either itself or through a subsidiary develops products sold by the retailer. This would potentially cover Amazon's subsidiary A2Z Development Centers Inc. that had an office in Studio City that handled online advertising and Lab126 in Cupertino that developed Kindle book readers. The other provision, known as a "long-arm statue," allowed the state to determine which businesses were responsible for collecting sales taxes.[167] Yee said, "The world of commerce has changed so must that physical presence does not necessarily mean having a brick-and-mortar physical location."[168] A spokesperson for Governor Jerry Brown explained, "Our stance is simple: thousands of brick-and-mortar businesses in California follow the law and collect sales tax every day. We expect Amazon to do the same."[169]

Upon enactment of the law, Amazon severed ties with its affiliates, as did Overstock.com and hundreds of other online retailers. In an e-mail Amazon wrote, "We oppose this bill because it is unconstitutional and counterproductive. It is supported by the big-box retailers, most of which are based outside California, that seek to harm the affiliate advertising programs of their competitors."[170] Affiliate Ken Rockwell said, "This is not good for anybody, and it affects the companies who pay me. It seems like the government is messing with something that it really doesn't understand. A lot of people make a few dollars here and there by being affiliates, and they really need the money."[171]

One alternative for Amazon was to file a lawsuit against the state in an attempt to block the law, and another was to move its subsidiary and lab out of the state. Amazon could also join with other online retailers and the former affiliates and attempt to reverse the state's action in the legislature. The online sales tax bill was passed during a budget emergency in

[158]*Wall Street Journal*, March 17, 2011.
[159]*Washington Post*, May 2, 2010.
[160]*New York Times*, March 14, 2001.
[161]*Los Angeles Times*, February 27, 2011.
[162]Ibid.
[163]*Los Angeles Times*, December 9, 2010.
[164]*Los Angeles Times*, January 20, 2011.

[165]*Los Angeles Times*, February 27, 2011.
[166]*Los Angeles Times*, January 20, 2011.
[167]To accommodate eBay the bill also had a provision exempting out-of-state sellers with less than $500,000 in sales. eBay complained that many of its sellers had sales in excess of the exemption limit. *Wall Street Journal*, June 30, 2011.
[168]*Wall Street Journal*, August 3, 2011.
[169]*New York Times*, July 12, 2011.
[170]*San Jose Mercury News*, June 30, 2011.
[171]Ibid.

the state, and as the economic recovery sputtered, state tax collections remained uncertain. The economy in California lagged behind the rest of the country, and the unemployment rate was higher than the national average.

Another alternative for Amazon was to turn to the voters. California had a citizens' initiative process in which signatures could be collected to put a measure prohibiting online taxes on the ballot for a direct vote. Approximately 434,000 signatures would be required, and Amazon had hired an in-state consultant for advice on the initiative alternative. Amazon vice president Paul Misener explained, "At a time when businesses are leaving California, it is important to enact policies that attract and encourage business, not drive it away." He called the possible ballot initiative "a referendum on jobs and investment in California."[172] He added, "Californians deserve a voice and a choice about jobs, investment and the state's economic future."[173]

In response, a group of NGOs set up a Web site and called for a boycott of Amazon. Jessica Lehman of Community Resources for Independent Living said, "If Amazon.com won't contribute to California, then we won't contributed to Amazon.[174]

As an alternative to a contentious ballot initiative, Amazon made an unusual offer to the state of California. It offered to build five distribution centers, employing 7,000 in the state if the state would impose a moratorium on its online sales tax collection until 2014. The moratorium would provide time for Congress to enact a federal law to deal with online sales taxation. The unemployment rate in the state was 2 percent higher than the national average of 9.1 percent.

Preparation Questions

1. How serious is the threat of an online sales tax to Amazon? How would sales be affected if Amazon were required to collect sales taxes in all states? How would profits be affected?
2. What overall nonmarket strategy is Amazon using to deal with the sales tax issue? What is its relation to its market strategy?
3. Is Amazon acting responsibly in terminating its relationships with associates in states that enact an Amazon tax?
4. Should Amazon have closed the warehouse in Texas?
5. What should Amazon do in California? Should it continue with the ballot initiative? Was its moratorium proposal wise?
6. What strategy should Amazon adopt to address the online sales tax issue at the federal level?

[172]*New York Times*, July 12, 2011.
[173]*New York Times*, July 14, 2011.
[174]*San Jose Mercury News*, August 16, 2011.

9

ANTITRUST: ECONOMICS, LAW, AND POLITICS

*People of the same trade seldom meet together, even for merriment
and diversion, but the conversation ends in a conspiracy against the
public or in some contrivance to raise prices.*

—AdamSmith, 1776

INTRODUCTION

Antitrust policy is an amalgam of social policy, economics, law, and administrative practice.[1] Antitrust policy had its origins in the populist movement of the 1870s when a number of states enacted statutes to regulate economic activity and control the exercise of economic power. At the federal level, this movement led to the Interstate Commerce Act of 1887, which provided for federal regulation of interstate commerce, and the Sherman Act of 1890, the first federal antitrust statute. These acts resulted from political pressure by farmers and others concerned about railroad cartels, the railroads' pricing practices, and the distribution of power between farmers and railroads. The laws thus represent both social and economic policy.

As social policy, the antitrust laws express concern about concentrations of economic power and the potential for abuse inherent in that concentration. This parallels the concern about the concentration of political power and the preference for its dispersion in the electorate and among the institutions of government. Just as the Constitution controls political power through checks and balances among the branches of government and through popular elections, antitrust policy focuses on controlling economic power.

Antitrust policy also reflects economic policy. The basic objective is to protect competition and by doing so to benefit consumers. Antitrust thus is concerned with the structure of markets, the conduct of market participants, and the resulting performance of those markets. Protecting competition does not mean protecting competitors; vigorous competition can result in firms being driven from the market. Moreover, practices that may appear to be anticompetitive must be evaluated in terms of their effects on consumers. Antitrust economics has both a theoretical and an empirical component. Theory has been an indispensable guide for reasoning about the relationships among structure, conduct, and performance. Empirical research has provided evidence about those relationships.

Antitrust law includes statutes and the court decisions interpreting those statutes. The principal federal statutes are the Sherman Act, the Clayton Act of 1914, and the Federal Trade Commission Act of 1914. These acts are broadly worded, employing such terms as *monopolize, restraint of trade,* and *unfair practices.* This has required the courts to interpret the acts in the context of the specifics of individual cases.[2] Antitrust law is thus both statutory and interpretive. It is also the subject of politics as interest groups, politicians, and public policy specialists attempt to influence the law.

Although there have been few major changes in the antitrust statutes in recent years, antitrust has not been static. Change comes from its administration and enforcement. At the federal level, public enforcement is provided by the Antitrust Division of the Department of Justice (DOJ) and the Federal Trade Commission (FTC). During the 1980s the DOJ and the FTC made significant changes in antitrust policy through their merger guidelines, which revised the policies governing federal enforcement. Similarly, enforcement

---

[1]The antitrust policies of the European Union are considered in Chapter 15.
[2]See Carp and Stidham (2001) for information on the U.S. federal courts.

policies on vertical restraints of trade changed considerably. During the 1990s the pace of antitrust enforcement increased substantially. The antitrust laws, however, are enforced less by government than by private litigants—often by one firm filing a lawsuit against another. Over 90 percent of the lawsuits filed under the federal antitrust laws are brought by private litigants. Consequently, decisions made by courts on cases brought by private litigants cause antitrust law to evolve, even when there is no legislative or government enforcement activity.

Much of the recent evolution of antitrust law, and of antitrust policy more broadly, has resulted from changing economic and legal thought about markets, business strategies, and performance. This thought has a coherence and perspective not necessarily found in the historical record of court decisions, and it has shaped a number of recent decisions. Three approaches, or schools of thought, to reasoning about antitrust are considered in this chapter.

The traditional or structure-conduct-performance school focuses on the structure of industries and on conduct that may foreclose opportunities or diminish competition. In the 1970s new understandings of the functioning of markets and the nature of competition were developed by the Chicago school of economics; these understandings had a major impact on antitrust enforcement and court decisions.[3] More recently, industrial organization economists have challenged some conclusions of the Chicago school by considering more closely the implications of informational asymmetries, repeated encounters, and strategic interactions among market participants. This perspective has qualified a number of the conclusions of the Chicago school.

These understandings of the purpose of antitrust policy and its appropriate application are particularly important in the United States because of the adversarial nature of judicial proceedings. Both plaintiffs and defendants have incentives to make the best cases they can and to use whatever new understandings support their sides. Consequently, new theories and empirical evidence quickly can find their way into court proceedings. Hearing these arguments, judges make decisions that can be influenced by how compelling the theories are, in addition to the facts of the case, empirical evidence, and legal precedents.

Antitrust policy has broad implications for management. Firms must conform to the law, but in many cases and for many practices, there is a considerable gray area in which the requirements of the law are unclear or untested. Similarly, because antitrust law evolves, a practice that once was allowable under the law may no longer be legal, and practices that were once illegal may now be legal. Legal counsel is essential when issues or practices may have antitrust implications. Managers, however, must have an understanding of antitrust law, enforcement practices, and antitrust thought, since they must recognize when a policy or practice may raise antitrust concerns.

The purpose of this chapter is to introduce antitrust law and thought, the forces that have shaped antitrust policy, and the forces that may shape its future development. The next section introduces the principal antitrust laws and discusses their enforcement, both by the government and private litigants. The following section considers the two rules under which antitrust lawsuits are tried: a rule of reason and a per se rule. The three schools of antitrust thought are then introduced and applied to vertical arrangements, predatory pricing, collusion and price fixing, and mergers. The antitrust guidelines used by the DOJ and FTC to review mergers are then considered. The effects of antitrust decisions on market opening are discussed, and the politics of antitrust is considered.

ANTITRUST LAW

The Antitrust Statutes

The principal antitrust statutes, excerpts from which are presented in Figure 9-1, have remained largely intact for almost 100 years. Section 1 of the Sherman Act pertains to unreasonable *restraints of trade* with a focus on joint conduct. Section 2 focuses on unilateral conduct and proscribes attempts to monopolize or to maintain a *monopoly*. The Sherman Act thus pertains to the reality of monopoly and restraints of trade and to the process of obtaining or maintaining a monopoly.

The Clayton Act goes further by addressing potentially anticompetitive actions. The Clayton Act contains terms such as "may be" and "tend to," which address monopolization and

---

[3]Much of the theory was developed by economists and legal scholars at the University of Chicago.

FIGURE 9-1 Excerpts from the Antitrust Statutes

Sherman Act

Section 1. Every contract, combination in the form of trust or otherwise, or conspiracy, in restraint of trade or commerce among the several States, or with foreign nations, is hereby declared to be illegal …. Every person who shall make any contract or engage in any combination or conspiracy hereby declared to be illegal shall be deemed guilty of a felony …

Section 2. Every person who shall monopolize, or attempt to monopolize, or combine or conspire with any other person or persons, to monopolize any part of the trade or commerce among the several States, or with foreign nations, shall be deemed guilty of a felony …

Clayton Act

Section 2. (a) That it shall be unlawful for any person engaged in commerce … to discriminate in the price between different purchasers … where the effect of such discrimination may be substantially to lessen competition or tend to create a monopoly in any line of commerce, or to injure, destroy or prevent competition … nothing herein contained shall prevent differentials which make only due allowance for differences in the cost of manufacture, sale, or delivery …

Section 3. That it shall be illegal for any person [to enter an arrangement] … on the condition … that the lessee or purchaser thereof shall not use or deal in the goods … of a competitor or competitors, where the effect … may be to substantially lessen the competition or tend to create a monopoly in any line of commerce.

Section 7. That no corporation engaged in commerce shall acquire, directly or indirectly, the whole or any part of the stock or other share capital … where in any line of commerce in any section of the country, the effect of such acquisition may be substantially to lessen competition, or tend to create a monopoly.*

Federal Trade Commission Act

Section 5. (a)(1) Unfair methods of competition in commerce, and unfair or deceptive acts or practices in commerce, are hereby declared unlawful.**

*As amended by the Celler-Kefauver Act of 1950.
**As amended by the Wheeler-Lea Act of 1938.

restraints in their incipiency. The Federal Trade Commission Act goes beyond the other two acts by prohibiting unfair methods of competition and *unfair or deceptive acts*. The broad language employed leaves considerable room for interpretation and thus a substantial role for the courts.[4]

The Sherman Act does not provide for private lawsuits, but Section 4 of the Clayton Act states "that any person who shall be injured in his business or property by reason of anything forbidden in the antitrust laws may sue therefore in any district court of the United States …." This allows private parties to bring lawsuits for practices that are illegal under either the Sherman Act or the Clayton Act. Section 4 also provides for treble damages. Section 7 of the Clayton Act prohibits mergers that may substantially lessen competition or create a monopoly.

The Robinson-Patman Act of 1934 strengthened Section 2 of the Clayton Act's prohibition of price discrimination. The Robinson-Patman Act was intended to protect small businesses and merchants from their larger competitors, which were able to obtain lower prices on their supplies. Small grocers, for example, sought protection from supermarkets, which used their greater buying power to obtain lower prices. Critics of the Robinson-Patman Act claim that it causes firms to be wary of price competition, resulting in higher prices for consumers. Proponents, however, contend that it is necessary to prevent small firms from being driven out of business, which would increase concentration and lessen competition.

Practices that come under the antitrust laws are classified as horizontal or vertical. A *horizontal* practice is one that involves activities in the same industry. A merger, for example,

---

[4]See Areeda and Kaplow (1997), Areeda and Hovenkamp (2004), and Gavil, Kovacic, and Baker (2008) for comprehensive treatments of antitrust law and Spulber (1989) and Viscusi, Vernon, and Harrington (2005) for the economics of antitrust.

EXAMPLE   Monopoly

In basic economic theory a monopoly is present when a firm has a dominant position in a market and can restrict its output thereby increasing the price consumers pay. In some markets, however, a monopoly may be the inevitable result of competition. For example, if there are benefits from standardization, competition can drive the market to concentrate on a single standard. If that standard is proprietary, as in the case of Microsoft's Windows operating system, a monopoly results. A monopoly achieved as a result of market forces combined with a superior product is not illegal, since consumers can benefit from the competition to become the standard and from the development of a superior product.

Monopoly is the subject of Section 2 of the Sherman Act. In *United States v. Aluminum Co. of America*, 148 F2d 416 (2d Cir 1945), Judge Learned Hand formulated a two-step procedure for deciding monopolization cases under Section 2.[1] The first step is to determine if the defendant has a monopoly. The second step is to determine if the monopoly was willfully acquired or unreasonably maintained or if it was the result of "superior skill, foresight and industry."

[T]he offense of monopoly … has two elements: (1) the possession of monopoly power in the relevant market and (2) the willful acquisition or maintenance of that power as distinguished from growth or development as a consequence of a superior product, business acumen, or historical accident.

Having a monopoly thus is not illegal, as in the case of a firm that becomes a monopoly through a superior product with which others are unable to compete. Willful monopolization or maintenance of a monopoly through anticompetitive practices is illegal.

For example, the online person-to-person auction market tipped to eBay, which had over 80 percent of the market. Similarly, Microsoft had over 90 percent of the personal computer operating system market. Having such monopolies is not illegal if they were achieved through superior performance and characteristics of the market. Maintaining a monopoly using anticompetitive practices is illegal, as is using a monopoly position in one market to attempt to monopolize another related market. In the chapter case *The Microsoft Antitrust Case*, the DOJ alleged that Microsoft used anticompetitive practices to maintain its monopoly in the personal computer operating system market and used that monopoly to attempt to monopolize the Internet browser market.[2]

[1] Early cases broke up the oil [*Standard Oil Co. v. United States*, 221 U.S. 1 (1911)] and tobacco [*United States v. American Tobacco Co.*, 221 U.S. 106 (1911)] monopolies.

[2] Monopolization cases are rarely filed. The most recent case prior to the Microsoft case was against IBM for monopolization of the computer industry. That case was filed on the last day of the Johnson administration in 1969 and later dropped by the Reagan administration.

is horizontal if the two firms operate in the same industry. Horizontal arrangements include monopolization, predatory pricing, price fixing, bid rigging, the allocation of customers, and group boycotts. The concern with horizontal arrangements is that they may increase market power, leading to lessened competition and higher prices.

Vertical practices are those involving firms in a supply arrangement or a channel of distribution. Vertical practices include the allocation of territories by a manufacturer among distributors or retailers, refusals to deal, exclusive dealing arrangements, resale price maintenance, reciprocal arrangements, and tying. Vertical practices also include the merger of a manufacturer and a supplier or distributor. Figure 9-2 provides brief definitions of the principal practices of concern under the antitrust laws.

Exemptions

A number of exemptions from the antitrust laws are provided. The Norris-LaGuardia Act of 1932 strengthened the statutory exemption the Clayton Act provided to unions. The economic activities of labor unions taken in their own interest, such as strikes, are protected. Exemptions are also provided for agricultural cooperatives and for certain activities of industries, such as insurance, that are regulated by government.[5] Exemptions for joint export trading activities are also provided under the Webb-Pomerene Act of 1918 and the Export Trading Company Act of 1982. A partial antitrust exemption was established for joint research and development ventures

[5] The exemption for the insurance industry is provided in the McCarron-Ferguson Act, and the exemption for agricultural cooperatives is provided by the Capper-Volstad Act of 1922.

FIGURE 9-2   Arrangements and Practices Subject to Antitrust Scrutiny

Horizontal

Horizontal merger—A merger is horizontal if it involves two firms in the same industry. A horizontal merger comes under Section 7 of the Clayton Act and under Section 2 of the Sherman Act, if it would create a monopoly.

Horizontal price fixing (collusion)—Horizontal price fixing includes explicit or implicit agreements to control prices in an industry or with respect to a product. Horizontal price fixing comes under Section 1 of the Sherman Act.

Monopoly—Concerted efforts to monopolize come under the purview of Section 1 of the Sherman Act, and the unilateral attempt to monopolize comes under Section 2 of the Sherman Act.

Price discrimination—Price discrimination involves charging customers different prices that are not justified by cost differences of serving those customers. Price discrimination comes under Section 2 of the Clayton Act, as amended by the Robinson-Patman Act.

Vertical

Boycotts and refusals to deal—A manufacturer refuses to sell to a distributor or a retailer. If two or more parties agree to refuse to deal with another party, it is a boycott. These practices are considered under Section 1 of the Sherman Act.

Exclusive dealing—A manufacturer grants another firm an exclusive right to distribute or market a particular product. Exclusive dealing comes under Section 3 of the Clayton Act.

Exclusive territory—A manufacturer grants an exclusive territory to a seller, and no other seller is permitted to sell in the territory. Exclusive territories come under Section 1 of the Sherman Act.

Resale price maintenance—A manufacturer requires a retailer to sell only at a price at least as high as a price it specifies. Such cases come under Section 1 of the Sherman Act.

Tying—Tying is the practice of bundling one product with another. For example, Mercedes-Benz requires its dealers to carry only Mercedes-Benz parts.* Tying arrangements come under Section 3 of the Clayton Act and Section 1 of the Sherman Act.

Vertical integration—Vertical integration involves the joining together, in terms of a merger or venture, of firms at various stages of a production process or channel or distribution. A vertical merger comes under Section 7 of the Clayton Act.** A vertical contract that forecloses or restrains competition comes under Section 3 of the Clayton Act.

Conglomerate

Conglomerate merger—A conglomerate merger involves two firms that do not operate in the same industries either as competitors or as part of a channel of distribution or supply. Conglomerate mergers come under Section 7 of the Clayton Act. The concern in the case of a conglomerate merger is the elimination of a potential competitor.***

*The DOJ dropped its antitrust suit against Mercedes-Benz because it concluded that a tying arrangement could only be anti-competitive if it is based on horizontal market power.
**See *Brown Shoe Co. v. U.S.*, 294 (1962), in which the Supreme Court invalidated the merger between Brown Shoe and the G. R. Kinney retail chain.
***See *Federal Trade Commission v. Procter & Gamble Co.*, 368 U.S. 568 (1967).

and for certain insurance pools. Exemptions can also be provided by specific legislation, as in the Soft Drink Interbrand Competition Act considered later in the chapter.

Baseball never had a statutory exemption from the antitrust laws but was protected by a 1922 Supreme Court decision, which had been upheld in subsequent decisions because the courts believed that it was the role of Congress, not the courts, to change the antitrust status of baseball.[6] In 1998 Congress modified the antitrust exemption by no longer exempting labor agreements, but a partial exemption continues.

---

[6]See *Federal Baseball Club of Baltimore v. National League of Professional Baseball Clubs*, 259 U.S. 200 (1991), *Toolson v. New York Yankees, Inc.*, 346 U.S. 356 (1953), and *Flood v. Kuhn*, 407 U.S. 258 (1972).

ENFORCEMENT OF THE ANTITRUST LAWS

Government Enforcement

Both the DOJ and the FTC have the authority to enforce the Sherman and Clayton Acts, but only the FTC can enforce the Federal Trade Commission Act.[7] Their dual enforcement responsibilities led the DOJ and the FTC to reach an interagency liaison agreement in 1948. As a result of the agreement, cases are allocated primarily by industry and secondarily by the nature of the complaint.[8] For example, the DOJ has enforcement responsibility for computer software and the FTC for semiconductors, so the DOJ filed the antitrust lawsuits against Microsoft and in 2008 the FTC began a formal investigation of Intel. Most enforcement activities are civil rather than criminal, and only the DOJ can bring criminal charges under the antitrust laws. Bringing criminal charges requires a grand jury indictment, and the standards of proof are higher than in a civil case.

In criminal cases the available penalties are fines and imprisonment. In civil cases injunctive relief can be granted, contracts dissolved, and business units ordered divested. Fines cannot be imposed in civil cases except to compensate the government for actual damages when it is a purchaser of goods and services. The courts not only decide cases but also approve consent decrees, such as that which split AT&T into seven regional operating companies and a residual AT&T. The DOJ can enforce the antitrust laws only through lawsuits filed in federal courts, but the FTC has authority to issue orders directly. The FTC can also seek injunctions in federal court, for example, to block a proposed merger.[9]

The FTC is an independent commission with five commissioners appointed, subject to Senate confirmation, by the president to 7-year terms. It can initiate its own investigations of practices it believes may violate the antitrust laws. As a consequence of an investigation, the FTC may negotiate a consent decree with a firm. If a firm refuses to agree to a consent decree, the FTC can continue the case through an administrative law procedure. A hearing is held before an administrative law judge, who issues an opinion and recommendation for action. The case is then decided by a majority vote of the commission. As penalties, the FTC can issue cease and desist orders that have the effect of injunctions against the activity in question. If a firm violates an order, the FTC can impose fines. Both the orders issued by the FTC and the court decisions in cases brought by the DOJ can be appealed to the U.S. Court of Appeals.

A consent decree is an agreement reached by the litigants under the sanction of a court. It does not involve a judicial determination and hence does not signify a violation of the law. A consent decree generally involves restrictions on the actions of the defendant. It binds only the consenting parties and does not set a precedent for other cases. A consent decree may remain in effect indefinitely and requires the agreement of the plaintiff, the defendant, and the court to lift or modify it. In 1997 a federal court lifted a 1956 consent decree that had restricted IBM's sales and service practices on its mainframe and mid-range computers. The judge concluded that IBM's market power "has substantially diminished."

The Hart-Scott-Rodino Antitrust Improvements Act of 1976 amended Section 7 of the Clayton Act to enhance the enforcement of the antitrust laws pertaining to monopolization and restraint of trade through mergers.[10] Hart-Scott-Rodino requires pre-merger notification to the DOJ and the FTC of plans to merge and the submission of data by the merging companies. In 2009, 1,726 mergers were reported to the DOJ and FTC under Hart-Scott-Rodino. The FTC and DOJ revised the notification requirements in 2011.

The DOJ and FTC decide which agency will review a merger based on "expertise and experience." A merger cannot be completed for 30 days, and during this period the agencies can require the firms to submit information about the market effects of their merger. For example, the firms may be required to submit information about their market shares in the market segments in which they both participate. In 2001 the Hearst Corporation agreed to pay a $4 million fine

---

[7]Technically the FTC has no authority to enforce the Sherman Act, but in practice, it does. The courts have held that practices violating the Sherman Act constitute "unfair" methods of competition under Section 5 of the Federal Trade Commission Act.

[8]See Shugart (1990, p. 947).

[9]See Clarkson and Muris (1981) for an analysis of FTC policy and enforcement. See Weaver (1977) for a study of FTC enforcement policy and Elzinga and Briet (1976) for a study of antitrust policies.

[10]See Federal Trade Commission (1990).

for failure to produce key documents as required by Hart-Scott-Rodino. If the DOJ or FTC decides that there are grounds to challenge the merger, it seeks a preliminary injunction. In most cases, this convinces the firms to abandon their plans to merge. The chapter case *The AT&T and T-Mobile Merger?* concerns a DOJ review of a planned merger.

The 1974 Antitrust Procedures and Penalties Act classified as felonies violations such as price fixing and increased the allowable fines. Fines against corporations can be as high as $10 million per count in criminal cases. Individuals, including managers of corporations, can be fined up to $350,000 and can be imprisoned for up to 3 years. Since 1990 the federal government has been able to collect treble damages. Federal sentencing guidelines enacted in 1991 allow fines to be based on the amount of business affected, in addition to other factors. In 1999 Roche Holdings, BASF, and Rhone-Poulenc (now Aventis) pleaded guilty to criminal price fixing in vitamins, and Roche paid $500 million in fines and BASF $225 million. Rhone-Poulenc paid no fine in exchange for cooperating with the government. The chapter case *Price Fixing in the Airways* considers a price-fixing case.

The Robinson-Patman Act prohibits price discrimination not justified by cost differences in serving customers. In addition to a cost difference defense, a firm can defend itself by arguing that the price discrimination was necessary to meet competition. The Clayton Act assigns the burden of proof in a price discrimination case to the plaintiff to show that there has been discrimination. Given a prima facie case, the defendant has the burden to show that the discrimination was justified, for example, by cost differences.[11] During the past 25 years the DOJ and the FTC have effectively stopped enforcing the Robinson-Patman Act because of their view that it stifles competition. Private antitrust lawsuits continue to be filed.

The DOJ and the FTC have also stopped enforcing the prohibition against resale price maintenance, although private lawsuits continue. Resale price maintenance pertains to restrictions imposed by manufacturers on the prices that can be charged by retailers. In the 1930s small retailers sought protection from price competition by having manufacturers establish minimum resale prices. States passed "fair trade laws" that required retailers to sell at the prices specified in contracts signed with manufacturers. The Miller-Tydings Act of 1937 allowed states to exempt price maintenance agreements from coverage under Section 1 of the Sherman Act as long as there was competition from other brands. The McGuire Act extended this to nonsigners of resale price contracts. In 1975 Congress repealed the Miller-Tydings and the McGuire Acts and withdrew the states' authority for fair trade laws.

The explanation for the lack of government enforcement of the resale price maintenance and price discrimination provisions of the antitrust laws is found in the changing schools of antitrust thought considered later in the chapter. To indicate the type of case to which the DOJ and the FTC objected, Cuisinart was found to have violated the antitrust laws by requiring sellers of its food processors to maintain a minimum retail price. Cuisinart held a dominant share of the market for food processors at the time the lawsuit was filed, but its share was largely due to its having developed the original product. Cuisinart had no fundamental horizontal market power, since entry into the food processor market was easy. Furthermore, the high minimum price established by Cuisinart stimulated entry, which quickly eroded its market share. Prices fell substantially when entry occurred. The resale price agreement, if it had continued, would likely have had little effect on the market for food processors. To clarify its policy, in 1985 the DOJ issued revised guidelines indicating that it would not investigate vertical accords when a firm has less than a 10 percent market share. A market share above 10 percent could lead to an investigation.

In spite of the lack of enforcement against certain vertical arrangements, federal enforcement of the antitrust laws is active. During the 1990s the pace of federal antitrust enforcement accelerated considerably. In part this was due to the increase in merger activity, but vigorous enforcement of price-fixing and other antitrust violations also occurred. In 1998 three former Archer Daniels Midland executives, including the son of the chairman of the board, were sentenced to 2–3 years in prison for price fixing of lysine and citric acid. An FBI videotape of a price-fixing meeting is available from the DOJ.[12]

---

[11]A prima facie case is one that needs no further demonstration.

[12]The videotape is available from the U.S. Department of Justice, Antitrust Division, Freedom of Information Act Unit, 325 Seventh Street, NW, Suite 200, Washington, D.C., 20530.

In 1998 the DOJ filed an antitrust case against Visa and MasterCard alleging that their prohibitions preventing banks from issuing other credit cards such as Discover and American Express was exclusionary. The district court found against Visa and MasterCard and ordered them to allow banks to issue other cards. The companies appealed, but the Court of Appeals upheld the lower court decision. The companies then appealed to the Supreme Court, which rejected the appeal, opening a $1.3 trillion market to American Express and Morgan Stanley's Discover card. Private lawsuits were filed after the decision.

Although the federal antitrust agencies are usually successful in obtaining at least a consent decree in the cases they bring, companies do win cases. In 1994 in a case brought by the DOJ alleging that General Electric had engaged in price fixing for industrial diamonds, the judge ruled that the DOJ had presented insufficient evidence and dismissed the case without requiring the company to present a defense.

Private Enforcement

Most antitrust cases are the result of private lawsuits.[13] The number of private antitrust suits filed in federal courts increased beginning in the early 1960s and peaked at over 1,600 in 1977, declining to 570 in 1997. From 2006 to 2008 the number of private antitrust lawsuits averaged about 1,000 a year and decreased sharply during the recession.[14] The decline was a function of a number of factors, including Supreme Court decisions that made it more difficult for plaintiffs to prevail in cases involving vertical restraints and predatory pricing. Court decisions have also raised the evidentiary threshold for a court to consider a case. Firms also instituted compliance programs that contributed to the decrease.

Most antitrust lawsuits are brought under the Sherman Act, and cases pertaining to vertical arrangements represent a somewhat higher percent of the total than those pertaining to horizontal practices. Of the total cases in their study, Salop and White (1988) found that 36.5 percent were filed by competitors and 27.3 percent by dealers. Most cases are settled to avoid the cost of litigation. AMD, the second largest producer of microprocessors, had filed four antitrust cases against Intel, the largest producer of microprocessors. In 2009 Intel paid $1.25 billion to AMD to settle all the outstanding lawsuits by the two companies.

The treble damages provision of the Clayton Act provides strong incentives for a private party to file an antitrust lawsuit. If a suit is filed against a firm by the DOJ, private parties often follow with private lawsuits. For example, the DOJ action against British Airways in the *Price Fixing in the Airways* chapter case was followed by a private class action lawsuit. A court decision for the government is interpreted by the courts as providing a prima facie case against the defendant, greatly increasing the likelihood that private lawsuits will be decided in favor of the plaintiff. In the vitamin price-fixing case, private class action lawsuits were filed against seven drug companies. The companies settled the lawsuits for $1.1 billion. The companies also reached a $340 million settlement with state attorneys general, bringing the total fines in the United States to $2.2 billion.

In 1996 Wal-Mart and other retailers filed an antitrust lawsuit against Visa and MasterCard, which had imposed an "honor-all-cards" policy on merchants, requiring them to accept debit cards if they accepted Visa and MasterCard credit cards. The merchants alleged that this was illegal tying under Section 1 of the Sherman Act and also that Visa and MasterCard were attempting to monopolize the debit card market in violation of Section 2 of the Sherman Act. As the case was going to trial in 2003 a settlement was reached in which Visa paid $2 billion and MasterCard $1 billion to the merchants and agreed to revise their policies and reduce their charges for debit cards.[15]

Treble damages are understandably controversial. Their proponents argue that they provide an important incentive for private enforcement. Critics contend that treble damages provide an incentive to challenge the practices of competitors, thereby making firms reluctant to compete on a number of dimensions, including price.

---

[13]Viscusi, Vernon, and Harrington (2000, p. 68) report that approximately 90 percent of antitrust lawsuits filed in U.S. courts during the 1970s and 1980s were private. See also White (1988).

[14]These numbers include an increasing share of private class action lawsuits, many of which were duplicative as trial lawyers competed to be chosen as lead counsel by the courts.

[15]The lawyers for the plaintiffs asked for fees of $600 million, but the judge reduced the amount to $220 million.

Private lawsuits can have significance beyond their impact on the parties involved. When a private antitrust case is tried and appealed, higher court decisions can establish a precedent that is then followed by courts in similar cases. Many of the important interpretations of the antitrust statutes and the precedents followed by the courts have come from private lawsuits.

Per Se Violations and the Rule of Reason

The courts have held that there are some sufficiently egregious acts that on the face of it violate the antitrust laws. These acts are said to be *per se* illegal, and the only defense allowed is that the defendant did not commit the act. The Supreme Court established this rule in *Northern Pacific Railroad Co. v. U.S.,* 356 U.S. 1 (1958), stating, "There are certain agreements or practices which because of their pernicious effect on competition and lack of any redeeming virtue are conclusively presumed to be unreasonable and therefore illegal without elaborate inquiry as to the precise harm they have caused or the business excuse for their use."

In contrast, other cases are considered by the courts under a *rule of reason.*[16] Under this rule, a restraint of trade, for example, is illegal if it is unreasonable. Per se violations are presumed to be unreasonable. The rule of reason was needed because much of the language of the antitrust laws is too sweeping and a literal interpretation would be harmful to competition and efficiency. Section 1 of the Sherman Act, for example, might be interpreted as prohibiting supply contracts because they restrain the opportunities for others. Similarly, combinations such as partnerships might otherwise be held to be in violation of the Sherman Act. The DOJ case against Visa and MasterCard for exclusionary practices was tried under a rule of reason.

A defendant has two defenses under a rule of reason. The first is the same as under a per se rule—the defendant did not commit the act in question. The second is that, although the defendant committed the act, it was not unreasonable to do so. The burden of proof is on the plaintiff to show that it is unreasonable. In evaluating whether an act is unreasonable, courts look to its purpose and effect. In the case of vertical arrangements, the stimulation of interbrand competition is a purpose the courts recognize. In evaluating the effect of an act, the courts examine whether it restrains or promotes competition and whether it is the least restrictive means of achieving the purpose. A court may hold for the plaintiff if either the purpose or the effect is unreasonable.

The courts do not decide which rule is applicable on a case-by-case basis but instead hold that certain practices are per se illegal and others are not. Presently, price fixing, output restraints, and the allocation of customers among competitors are per se violations of the antitrust laws. Some practices that in the past were considered per se offenses are now considered under the rule of reason. For example, in 1997 the Supreme Court ruled that maximum price resale maintenance, where a manufacturer sets a maximum price that retailers may charge, is not per se illegal and is to be considered under a rule of reason.[17] In 2007 the Supreme Court extended this to minimum resale price maintenance on the grounds that it could stimulate interbrand competition.

A variety of arrangements and practices have come under the scrutiny of the antitrust laws, as indicated in Figure 9-2. A treatment of each of these requires more space than is available, so the following sections focus instead on antitrust thought and on the application of that thought in the areas of vertical restraints, predatory pricing, collusion, and mergers.

ANTITRUST THOUGHT

Antitrust policy, enforcement practices, and court decisions are influenced by the prevailing schools of thought about the purposes of antitrust policy and the likely consequences of specific practices. The *structural* or *structure-conduct-performance school* of thought prevailed into the 1970s, when it was confronted with the understandings of the *Chicago school.* The

---

[16]The rule of reason was first articulated by the Supreme Court in *Standard Oil Co. of New Jersey v. United States,* 221 U.S. 1 (1911), which broke up the Standard Oil Trust. A judicial rule is a standard of interpretation for a law that is ambiguous in the absence of that interpretation.

[17]*State Oil Company v. Khan,* 522 U.S. 3; 118 S.Ct. 27 S.

Chicago, or law and economics, school viewed the objectives and principles of antitrust policy differently, particularly with regard to vertical arrangements. It has had considerable influence on legal education, the courts, and the enforcement activities of the DOJ and FTC beginning with the Reagan administration. In addition, the courts have adopted many understandings of the Chicago school, and several Chicago school scholars have been appointed to the federal judiciary.

In the 1990s antitrust practice and policy were influenced by the work of industrial organization (IO) economists, who focused on new considerations such as network externalities and compatibility and on new theories of oligopoly that take into account the strategic interactions among market participants in imperfectly competitive markets. This *new IO* approach challenges some of the understandings of both the structural and the Chicago schools. The new IO approach is a collection of theories rather than a unified perspective from which broad conclusions can be drawn. Furthermore, courts have only cautiously embraced its theories, in part because of the complexity and subtle reasoning involved. Nevertheless, it represents an important force in antitrust thought. These three approaches agree on many points but differ on others. Figure 9-3 contrasts the approaches.

The Structural Approach

From the perspective of social and economic policy, government intervention in markets is intended to improve economic performance and further the social objective of limiting economic power. From this perspective, concentrations of economic power should be checked, just as political power is checked. Because economic power can result in the unfair treatment of competitors and consumers, government has a responsibility to protect citizens, competitors, and society from the presence, and the abuse, of economic power. Antitrust policy and regulation are the principal public instruments for checking that power.

The structural approach views the performance of markets as determined by the conduct of market participants, which is largely determined by the structure of the market, such as the number of competitors and barriers to entry. This approach takes as its starting point the economic theories of monopoly and perfect competition. Perfect competition serves as the standard for evaluating an industry, and monopoly is its antithesis. Monopolistic pricing can be characterized by the generalized Lerner index, given by

$$\frac{p - mc}{p} = \frac{1}{n\varepsilon}$$

where p is price, mc is marginal cost, n is the number of firms in the industry, and ε is the price elasticity of demand.[18] The left side of the index is the percentage markup on price; for a monopoly ($n = 1$), the markup equals one divided by the elasticity of demand. As the number of firms increases, the markup decreases and price approaches marginal cost, which is the case of perfect competition. Market power is thus the ability to command a price above marginal cost and that power is greater the smaller the number of firms in an industry, other things equal. In the chapter case *AT&T and T-Mobile Merger?* the DOJ considered the effects of reducing the number of mobile wireless carriers.

The structural approach thus views economic power as a function of the number of firms in the industry or, correspondingly, their market shares. The smaller the number of firms, the more likely they are to restrict output to raise prices and worsen the performance of a market. The focus of antitrust policy thus should be on the structure of the industry, and industries with substantial *concentration*—a substantial market share held by a small number of firms—should be regarded with suspicion. The structural approach finds support for this conclusion in empirical studies that show a positive correlation between industry concentration and profitability, as predicted by the Lerner index.

Improving performance in the market requires dealing with industry structure as well as the conduct of market participants. Remedies for antitrust violations should include

---

[18]This relation is derived from a Cournot model of oligopoly.

FIGURE 9-3 Structural, Chicago School, and New IO Perspectives

Dimension	Structural	Chicago School	New IO
• Purpose of antitrust policy	Social and political as well as economic objectives.	Economic objectives—efficiency with a focus on prices.	Economic objectives; static and dynamic efficiency.
• View of markets	Markets are fragile and prone to failure.	Markets are resilient; market imperfections can be addressed through incentives.	Most markets are resilient, but some have imperfections such as network externalities; strategic behavior can limit efficiency.
• What is needed	Government to protect society from economic power.	Competition is the best protector of consumers and economic efficiency.	Competition is the best protector of consumers, but government intervention can be required.
• Perspective on consumers	Need to protect consumers from others and from themselves; e.g., unfair practices.	Consumers are responsible for their own decisions and will protect themselves.	Consumers can protect themselves when they have choices.
• Requirements for markets to function efficiently	Protect competitors to prevent monopoly; avoid foreclosing opportunities for competitors.	Conditions for perfect competition are sufficient but not necessary.	Both innovation and competition are required for efficiency; dynamic efficiency is important.
• Relationship between the number of competitors and market performance	More competitors mean more competition.	Competition can be effective with only a few competitors.	Competition can be effective with a small number of competitors.
• Entry	High barriers to entry reduce efficiency; potential entry may not limit the power of incumbent firms.	Few barriers to entry; barriers are due to the efficiency of incumbent firms; potential entry limits the economic power of incumbents.	Barriers to entry can be present; e.g., from the economies of standardization.
• Sources of economic power	Market power derives from horizontal power and from vertical arrangements.	Market power can only arise from horizontal power.	Market power derives from horizontal factors but can be extended through vertical arrangements and strategic behavior.
• Collusion	Increases profits, so firms can be expected to collude.	Is difficult for firms to enforce and thus is unlikely.	Is possible with repeated encounters.
• Where is collusion most likely	In concentrated markets.	In industries with government regulation or protection.	In industries with repeated encounters and easy monitoring, as well as in regulated and protected industries.
• Interpretation of the relationship between concentration and profits	Positive correlation indicates that more concentration reduces market efficiency and increases profits.	Positive correlation is more likely due to lower costs of larger firms.	Positive correlation can be due to lower costs, market power, or strategic opportunities.
• Relevant market for antitrust scrutiny should be	Defined narrowly so that pockets of concentration can be detected and addressed.	Defined broadly to include substitutes and imports.	Defined broadly to include substitutes and imports.
• Conclusion about antitrust	Proscribe many practices as per se offenses.	Judge business practices in terms of their effects on efficiency and prices; use the rule of reason.	Judge business practices in terms of impact on present and future competition; use rule of reason except for egregious practices such as price fixing.
• Values underlying the perspective	Efficiency and fairness; government protection.	Economic efficiency; individual choice and responsibility.	Economic efficiency; individual and collective responsibility.

breaking up monopolies, ordering the divestiture of business units, requiring tight standards for mergers, and requiring the licensing of technologies. Because a larger number of firms correlates with more competition and lower prices, the more firms in the industry the better. To ensure that there are enough firms for vigorous competition, it may be desirable to protect firms from their rivals, particularly from predatory behavior or from unfair advantages such as not being able to purchase inputs at low prices (as reflected in the Robinson-Patman Act).

The Lerner index implies that market power arises from horizontal considerations. Market power can also result from vertical arrangements in channels of distribution, as when a manufacturer requires a distributor or retailer to maintain a minimum price, carry only the manufacturer's replacement parts, or sell only within a specified territory. From the perspective of the structural approach, it is important to avoid foreclosing opportunities for competitors, since competition would then be less vigorous. Vertical arrangements thus should be viewed with suspicion because they can foreclose opportunities for competitors and increase economic power.

The economic power of the incumbent firms in an industry can be checked by entry into the industry. The structural approach thus is concerned about possible *barriers to entry*. Barriers to entry are said to include such factors as technological advantages, advertising and brand names, and capital requirements. Because of barriers to entry and economic concentration, the structural approach often views markets as fragile. Government thus has a role in helping markets function more efficiently.

When there are barriers to entry and economic power is concentrated in a relatively small number of firms, incumbent firms may have an opportunity to collude. The structural approach views collusion as more likely the more concentrated the industry. Collusion can take the form of price fixing among firms in an industry or in a channel of distribution. Empirical research finding a positive correlation between concentration and profitability could reflect collusion. This provides another rationale for focusing on concentrated markets.

Because economic power harms consumers through higher prices, the structural approach holds that markets should be viewed narrowly to identify market segments in which economic power is present. Similarly, it is important to keep market opportunities open. Consequently, restraints of trade and market foreclosures should be limited to those that are absolutely necessary, and antitrust should proscribe practices that foreclose opportunities or restrain competition. Many of those practices should be per se illegal.

In summary, the structure-conduct-performance paradigm views market performance as following from conduct, which follows from the structure of markets. Antitrust policy thus should be concerned about concentration, barriers to entry, possible collusion, and exclusionary practices. Antitrust enforcers should closely scrutinize market structure for economic concentration, market foreclosures, and restraints of trade. Antitrust remedies should include structural as well as conduct remedies.

The Chicago School

The Chicago school views the objective of antitrust policy as economic efficiency, which may be understood in its simplest form as the maximization of producers' plus consumers' surplus. Since economic efficiency depends on the level of prices, the focus is on the prices consumers pay. Thus, a price equal to marginal cost is efficient, whether it results from a perfectly competitive market or a monopolistic industry in which price is held down by the threat of entry. The focus of the Chicago school is on performance—the prices in markets—rather than on the structure of markets.[19] The Chicago school recognizes the potential for horizontal market power and its abuse but believes that competition, not government, is the best protector of consumers and the best promoter of economic efficiency.

Perfect competition is the ideal, but the conditions for perfect competition—many firms, a homogeneous product, technologies available to all firms, and symmetric information—are viewed as sufficient but not necessary for economic efficiency. Competition can be

---

[19]See Posner (1976) for an analysis of antitrust policy from the Chicago school perspective.

efficient even with few firms in an industry since, given the opportunity, firms will compete vigorously.

The Chicago school is skeptical about the nature and scope of barriers to entry. Claimed barriers such as advertising, brand-name advantages, and capital requirements are unlikely to be true barriers. Capital markets are viewed as efficient, so investors will provide capital for ventures that have prospects for at least a market rate of return. Barriers to entry are likely to be due to the cost advantages of incumbent firms, and the inability of a potential entrant to raise capital could be due to efficiency advantages of incumbent firms. Thus entry may be limited not by structural barriers but by economic efficiency. Indeed, incumbent firms are those that have already survived competition.

The positive correlation between industry concentration and profitability that the structural approach views as reflecting the exercise of economic power could, according to the Chicago school, result from the greater efficiency of those firms that have survived the competitive process. Furthermore, larger firms may have lower costs because of economies of scale. Their markups thus could be higher but their prices lower than if the firms in the industry were smaller. That is, if as firms become larger their costs decrease and competition is present to force prices down, consumers benefit. The firms could also benefit despite lower prices because they have lower costs. Consequently, both markups and profits could increase with concentration, yet higher concentration could result in lower prices for consumers.

The Chicago school also views collusion among firms as unsustainable because of the difficulties in monitoring and enforcing collusive agreements. Colluding firms have a strong incentive to cheat on an agreement by, for example, making secret discounts to customers to increase sales. A collusive agreement may have the structure of a prisoners' dilemma in which each firm finds it in its interest to cheat on the agreement. Unless there is a clear mechanism for monitoring the agreement, collusion is likely to be unsustainable.

From the Chicago school's perspective, collusion is most likely to be sustainable when there is government protection or regulation. Government regulation that precluded entry into the airline and trucking industries was viewed as having resulted in implicit collusion, with much of the rents captured by labor rather than by firms. Consistent with this perspective, during the Reagan administration the DOJ pressed its antitrust case against AT&T because it believed that regulation was inhibiting competition and technological progress. The DOJ, however, dropped its antitrust case against IBM because whatever market power IBM might have had was being dissipated by the rapid technological change in the computer industry.

Because barriers to entry are low and collusion is difficult to sustain, competition—both existing and potential—can be expected. Because it is the performance of the market that is important, the rule of reason should be used by courts in judging practices under the antitrust laws. Correspondingly, few practices should be per se illegal. In particular, vertical restraints are harmful only if the firm has horizontal market power, which should be assessed for its consequences for prices.

In assessing horizontal power the relevant market should be defined broadly. Both present and potential competition should be considered because either can hold prices down. The relevant market also includes not only the product in question but also close substitutes for it. The definition of the relevant market should also include imported as well as domestic products. In the case of capital goods, the relevant market should include the market for used goods. In the case of a commodity such as aluminum, it should include the scrap and recycling markets as well as aluminum produced directly from bauxite

In summary, the Chicago school views the objective of antitrust policy as economic efficiency and views competition as the best means of achieving efficiency. Perfect competition is not the only means of achieving efficiency, however, as competition among a few firms can be sufficient to drive prices down to marginal costs. Barriers to entry are viewed with skepticism and collusion is viewed as difficult to sustain, so market forces should correct most attempts to restrain trade. Furthermore, the relationship between profitability and concentration may be due to costs that decrease with the size of firms rather than to the exploitation of market power. Because the objective is economic efficiency, the focus of antitrust policy should be on performance, and the market in which that performance is assessed should be viewed broadly.

The Chicago school does not conclude that conduct such as vertical arrangements should be legal. Instead, it concludes that vertical arrangements could be pro-competitive rather than anticompetitive. Hence, they should not be per se illegal but rather should be considered under a rule of reason. This allows firms to use those practices that stimulate competition and enhance efficiency but also allows successful prosecution of practices that harm efficiency.

The New IO Approach

The new IO approach to antitrust is derived from the economics of modern industrial organization. This approach rejects the static equilibrium approach taken by the Chicago school and focuses on the opportunities for strategic behavior not initially considered by the Chicago school.[20] For example, even when firms act in a noncooperative manner, implicit collusion could result from repeated interactions among market participants and could be sustained by expectations that cheating would be met by punishment by other market participants. Similarly, interactions over time may allow firms to develop a reputation for a particular mode of behavior, such as price cutting in response to entry into a market, that can deter potential entrants.

The possibilities for such strategic behavior are greater when there is incomplete information about factors important to the strategy choices of a firm. A potential entrant may have incomplete information about the costs of incumbent firms and thus may be reluctant to commit the capital required for entry, since it could turn out that the incumbent firms actually had costs lower than anticipated. Furthermore, incumbent firms may be able to deter entry by signaling that they have low costs when they actually have high costs.

The new IO approach is also concerned with the potential for anticompetitive behavior in markets characterized by network externalities and where compatibility and standardization are required. For example, the benefits from standardizing software development on a small number of platforms, such as Microsoft's Windows operating system, can result in the development of market power for the suppliers of the platforms. Similarly, network effects are important in businesses ranging from Internet commerce to credit cards to residential real estate. In addition to supply-side incentives for larger networks, there may also be demand-side increasing returns. This generates incentives to compete to develop the largest network, and the winner then has an "essential facility" and hence market power. Moreover, the owner of an essential facility may be able to use it to thwart innovation or block alternative technologies that provide the potential for competition. The threat to Microsoft's dominance of the desktop operating systems market from the Internet and the Java programming language was alleged by the DOJ to have led to anticompetitive practices.

As summarized in Figure 9-3, the new IO perspective on antitrust focuses on the objectives of static and dynamic efficiency; thus, it is concerned not only about the performance of markets at a point in time but also about innovation and incentives to develop new products and processes. Most markets are viewed as resilient, although some markets have imperfections such as those due to network externalities. Therefore, although competition and ensuring choice among products are the best protectors of consumers, government intervention may be warranted to ensure that standardization on a particular technology does not lead to market abuse and that incentives and opportunities for innovation are not thwarted. Most markets can be efficient even if there is only a small number of competitors, provided that barriers to entry are low, but otherwise markets may require scrutiny. For example, switching costs and the efficiencies from standardization can make it difficulty for a firm with a new technology to enter a market dominated by an incumbent. Easy entry thus cannot be assured.

The new IO perspective agrees with the Chicago school that market power derives from horizontal considerations but holds that it can be extended through vertical arrangements. For example, the DOJ alleged that Microsoft attempted to extend its market power to the Internet by bundling its Internet browser with its operating system and giving its browser away for free.

The new IO perspective acknowledges that competition with only a few firms can be efficient in a one-time encounter, but it also recognizes that repeated encounters provide an opportunity for implicit collusion. Collusion is more likely the better each firm can monitor the actions of their competitors. The price-fixing cartels in vitamins, lysine, and citric acid are evidence of the ability of firms to collude. The positive empirical relationship between concentration

---

[20]See Holt and Scheffman (1989) for a discussion of this approach and its implications for antitrust.

and profits thus could be due to lower costs or to collusion and market power. In examining the likelihood that market power will impair static and dynamic efficiency, the new IO perspective views the relevant market as broadly defined.

With respect to antitrust enforcement and policy, the new IO perspective concludes that business practices should be evaluated in terms of their effects on static and dynamic efficiency under the rule of reason except in egregious situations such as price fixing. Individuals can protect themselves when choice is available in the market, but government intervention can be warranted when choice and innovation are stifled through exclusive practices and the exercise of market power.

The new IO approach concludes that there are situations in which firms can employ anticompetitive strategies, as in the case of products that exhibit network externalities or have compatibility and standardization characteristics, as well as when implicit collusion can be supported by repeated encounters. The new IO approach has not at this point presented a comprehensive theory of antitrust economics, however. Instead, the approach is a collection of theories about behavior under particular structural and informational conditions.

The three schools of thought have narrowed their differences over time as each has acknowledged certain of the insights from the other schools of thought. The following section illustrates some of the consequences as well as remaining differences.

EXAMPLES OF THE DIFFERENCES IN ANTITRUST THOUGHT

Vertical Arrangements

The principal area in which the structural and Chicago schools differed was in regard to vertical arrangements. These arrangements take a variety of forms, but most involve restrictions imposed by a manufacturer on the sale or distribution of its products. Because most of these arrangements involve the foreclosure of a market opportunity or a restraint of trade, a number of vertical practices had been held by the courts to be per se illegal. Economic understandings developed by the Chicago school, along with a Supreme Court required to interpret laws containing imprecise and general language, changed the law on vertical arrangements. Many of the vertical arrangements that had been per se illegal during the 1970s are now considered under a rule of reason. Furthermore, the courts have upheld the use of many of the previously illegal vertical arrangements. These changes have occurred in the absence of new legislation.

Vertical price restrictions had been per se illegal since the Supreme Court decision in *Dr. Miles Medical Co. v. John D. Park & Sons,* 220 U.S. 373 (1911). Nonprice vertical restrictions were not per se illegal, however, until the decision in *U.S. v. Arnold Schwinn & Co.,* 388 U.S. 365 (1967). In *Schwinn,* the Supreme Court decided that vertical nonprice restrictions on the resale of goods, such as territorial restrictions, restrictions on customers served, refusals to deal, and exclusive dealerships, were per se illegal.

The Chicago school found little logic in the court's reasoning, since from its perspective a vertical arrangement could be harmful to competition only if there was horizontal market power. That is, vertical arrangements do not create market power but can extend market power, for example, from a dominant market position. Indeed, vertical arrangements generally are viewed as tolerable unless there is horizontal market power. When that power is present, vertical arrangements should be judged under a rule of reason.

In reasoning about vertical arrangements, the Chicago school distinguished between *interbrand* and *intrabrand* competition. Intrabrand competition refers to competition between sellers of the same brand, as in the case of two Toyota dealers competing against each other. Those dealers also compete against the sellers of other makes of automobiles—interbrand competition. If interbrand competition is vigorous so that a manufacturer does not have horizontal market power, restrictions on intrabrand competition will have little impact on the efficiency of the market.

Moreover, vertical arrangements that restrict intrabrand competition can make interbrand competition more efficient by, for example, strengthening dealer networks. Competition among stronger networks holds down prices, and stronger dealer networks can reduce costs and better serve consumers on the nonprice dimensions of sales. Restrictions on intrabrand competition can also reduce transactions costs in a firm's channels of distribution, as Williamson (1975) emphasized.

In addition, the Chicago school argued that competition does not take place only on price. Many products require the provision of information to enable consumers to use the product effectively. Also, many products must be supported with service, both at the time of purchase and later. To provide information and customer service, manufacturers establish dealer networks. The networks, however, are often plagued by a free-rider problem. Customers can visit a dealer to obtain information and then buy online or from a discount store that offers neither information nor service. Customers then are free riding on the information provided by the licensed dealers. This weakens the dealer network, resulting in less information being provided to consumers. Consumers then may make less-informed decisions, reducing economic efficiency. Indeed, one reason dealers charge a higher price than discount stores is that they must have a margin adequate to cover the costs of a well-trained sales staff and a service facility.

In *Continental TV v. GTE Sylvania,* 433 U.S. 36 (1977), the Supreme Court, influenced by this reasoning, changed the precedent established in *Schwinn.* The court held that nonprice vertical restraints should be considered under a rule of reason. GTE Sylvania, a producer of television sets, had experienced declining sales. By the beginning of the 1960s it had only 1–2 percent of the U.S. market. Sylvania distributed its television sets through both company-owned and independent distributors, which supplied retailers. In an attempt to increase its sales, Sylvania changed its method of distribution by eliminating its distributors and selling directly to franchised retailers. Sylvania also required its retailers to sell only from a specified location. This provision allowed Sylvania to control the number of retail outlets in an area. The objective of the changes was to attract a smaller but stronger group of retailers that would have the incentive to promote Sylvania TV sets. The franchised dealers could sell other brands and were not restricted in the prices they could charge.

The change proved successful. Dealers promoted Sylvania sets, increasing its market share to 5 percent by 1965. In 1965 Sylvania decided to authorize a new retailer in San Francisco. Continental TV, a Sylvania dealer there, protested and asked permission to sell Sylvania TVs in Sacramento. Sylvania refused, and Continental decided to sell them there anyway. Sylvania then refused to sell to Continental. Continental sued, and the federal district court, following *Schwinn,* held in its favor. The Court of Appeals reversed the decision and ordered a retrial on the grounds that it did not believe that *Schwinn* was applicable in this case. Continental appealed, and the Supreme Court took the case as an opportunity to reconsider whether vertical arrangements such as the one in question should be per se illegal.

The Supreme Court concluded that "Per se rules of illegality are appropriate only when they relate to conduct that is manifestly anticompetitive." As indicated in *Northern Pacific,* such conduct must have a "pernicious effect on competition" and have no "redeeming virtue." In considering whether this was true of the practice in *Sylvania,* the court found that "The market impact of vertical restrictions is complex because of their potential for a simultaneous reduction in intrabrand competition and stimulation of interbrand competition ...." The court then held that a vertical restriction could not be said a priori to have a pernicious effect on competition or to have no redeeming virtue. Hence, nonprice vertical arrangements were not per se illegal. The court pointed to the possible redeeming virtues, stating:

> New manufacturers and manufacturers entering new markets can use the restrictions in order to induce competent and aggressive retailers to make the kind of investment of capital and labor that is often required in the distribution of products unknown to the consumer. Established manufacturers can use them to induce retailers to engage in promotional activities or to provide service and repair facilities necessary to the efficient marketing of their products. Service and repair are vital for many products, such as automobiles and major household appliances. The availability and quality of such services affect a manufacturer's good will and the competitiveness of his product. Because of market imperfections such as the so-called "free rider" effect, these services might not be provided by retailers in a purely competitive situation ...

The Supreme Court affirmed the decision of the Court of Appeals and thus changed the per se rule of illegality for vertical practices to a rule of reason, reversing what had served as law for the previous 10 years. Since *Sylvania,* most nonprice vertical restrictions have been considered under a rule of reason. The new IO perspective generally agrees with this result, as does the structural perspective.

The Supreme Court followed the *Sylvania* decision with two decisions extending the applicability of the rule of reason in nonprice vertical arrangements. In *Monsanto Co. v. Spray-Rite Service Co.,* 465 U.S. 752 (1984), the court held that terminating a price-cutting dealer after complaints from several other dealers was not a per se violation. In *Business Electronics Corp. v. Sharp Electronics Corp.,* 485 U.S. 717 (1988), the court held that terminating a dealer relationship because another dealer had complained about its price cutting was not a per se violation unless there had been an agreement between the manufacturer and the complaining retailer. The rationale for these decisions was again that the practices could have the redeeming virtue of strengthening the dealer networks and stimulating interbrand competition and thus should be tried under a rule of reason.

Predatory Pricing and Entry Deterrence

The traditional perspective on predatory pricing is that a firm can drive a competitor out of a market by cutting prices below the competitor's costs. A firm with deep pockets can bear the short-term losses from the price cutting, and once the weaker rival is forced from the market, it can set higher prices to recoup its losses. The standard used to determine if a firm is engaging in predatory pricing is whether price is below marginal cost. Marginal cost is not easy for a court to measure, however, so a standard such as average variable cost is often used as the proxy.[21]

The Chicago school's criticism of this view of predatory pricing focused on its aftermath. Suppose a firm were to engage in predatory pricing and successfully drove a competitor out of the market. Could it then set a higher price than prior to the predation? The answer depends on whether there are barriers to entry in the industry. If there are not, and the Chicago school is skeptical about the presence of barriers to entry, then raising the price will simply attract new entrants. This will force the price down, and the predation will have been for naught. Recognizing this, a firm will not engage in predatory pricing in the first place.

If there were high barriers to entry, a firm could exercise market power. The principal barrier to entry recognized by the Chicago school is due to the sunk costs of incumbent firms. Even those sunk costs, however, are not a long-run deterrent to entry because once an entrant has entered the market, its costs are also sunk, and the incumbent firm no longer has a reason to price below long-run costs. The entrant will anticipate this and not be deterred from entering. Also, if an incumbent firm has sunk costs, a competitor already in the market is also likely to have sunk costs. Prices thus would have to be cut below short-run marginal costs to drive out that competitor.[22]

Even if predatory pricing were possible, it may not be desirable to drive a smaller competitor from the market. An industry leader would have to incur losses on a larger volume of sales. Predation in this case might not be in the interest of an industry leader, even if there were barriers to entry.

The conclusion of the Chicago school is that predation is unlikely to be successful, so it will not be attempted. The price cutting observed in markets is instead likely to be the result of competition rather than of predation. Applying antitrust law to alleged predation thus would discourage firms from competing on price, resulting in higher prices.

Research from the new IO perspective, however, casts some doubt on these conclusions. One theory of potential entry is based on the recognition that a potential entrant may not know if an incumbent firm has a cost advantage. Because of this incomplete information about the incumbent's costs, the incumbent may be able to signal that it has low costs, even though its costs are actually high. The incumbent can do this by setting a price equal to the average of what a low-cost and a high-cost incumbent firm would choose. This pricing strategy can deter some entry that would be desirable from the perspective of economic efficiency.[23]

Another theory developed from the new IO perspective indicates that an incumbent firm may have an incentive to engage in predatory pricing in several geographic or product markets

---

[21]See Areeda and Turner (1975).

[22]This argument would not hold if an incumbent had a known cost advantage over a competitor or a potential entrant. The incumbent then could set a price just low enough that the potential entrant would stay out of the market. In this case, the threat of potential entry limits the incumbent firm's ability to increase its price but does not necessarily force the price down to the cost of the most efficient producer.

[23]See Milgrom and Roberts (1982) for a development of this theory.

so as to develop a reputation as a "tough" competitor, thus discouraging entry by new firms in other markets.[24] The development of such a reputation hinges on potential entrants' incomplete information about, for example, the costs of the incumbent firm. A reputation for toughness, then, may deter entry into a market even if no real barriers to entry are present. In the supermarket industry Safeway developed a reputation as a tough competitor, which, according to some economists, deterred entry in some local markets.

Whatever the appropriate economic theory of predatory behavior, antitrust scrutiny of price cutting poses a serious concern. In practice it is difficult to distinguish between vigorous price competition and predatory pricing. Even in a competitive industry, prices can rise and fall in response to shifts in demand, and when entry occurs, prices will adjust as other firms change their outputs or exit the industry. Applying antitrust law in situations in which prices are being cut could stifle price competition. For example, new entrants may set low prices to build market share and utilize their capacity efficiently. Precluding an incumbent firm from responding to those prices would restrain competition and possibly prevent output from being produced at the lowest possible cost.

As an example, in the chapter case *The Microsoft Antitrust Case,* the court did not conclude that Microsoft's decision to give away its Internet Explorer browser for free was anticompetitive, even though that decision was a major blow to its rival Netscape, which was forced to set its price to zero. Pricing Internet Explorer at zero, which is its marginal cost, is economically efficient. The court concluded that a price of zero benefited consumers, and the competition to win in the browser market stimulated substantial improvements in browser quality, also benefiting consumers. Pricing at zero in this case was not predatory.

Collusion and Price Fixing

All schools of thought agree that collusion and horizontal price fixing are anticompetitive, and the DOJ has vigorously prosecuted price fixing and obtained large fines, criminal convictions, and prison sentences for those found guilty. The schools, however, disagree about how likely it is that collusive arrangements can be sustained.

The structural perspective on collusion and price fixing is that firms will collude when possible, so tight antitrust supervision is necessary. The Chicago school, however, points to historical evidence indicating that cartels broke down as a result of cheating by their own members. Furthermore, the larger the number of firms required to collude, the more difficult it is to prevent cheating. For collusion to be sustained, the colluders must have a means of detecting cheating, as in the case of bidding on government contracts when the bids are publicly reported. In the chapter case *Price Fixing in the Airways* cheating was easier to detect because trans-Atlantic airfares were publicly posted.

The new IO approach, however, reaches the conclusion that collusion and price fixing are easier to sustain than suggested by the Chicago school. Moreover, the number of convictions obtained provides evidence that price fixing is not rare. Because firms in the same industry will be in competition over time, they have a broad set of strategies that could sustain explicit or implicit collusion.[25] A firm that believes that another firm is cheating on an implicit agreement to maintain high prices can punish that firm by lowering its own price. If the second firm is confident that the first firm indeed has an incentive to punish any perceived cheating, the second firm could have no incentive to cheat in the first place. The threat of punishment in repeated encounters thus can, in principle, enforce high prices even when there is neither an explicit agreement nor communication among the firms. Price-cutting thus could be a means of punishing deviations from implicit collusion rather than an indication of either vigorous competition or predation.

In the chapter case *Price Fixing in the Airways,* British Airways and Virgin Atlantic fixed fuel surcharges on passenger flights, and airlines carrying cargo across the Pacific also fixed prices. The number of airlines involved was small, so coordination was not difficult. The

---

[24]See Kreps and Wilson (1982) for a development of this theory.
[25]Green and Porter (1984) present and empirically test this theory.

price fixing continued for 2 years and was revealed as a result of a leniency program of the Office of Fair Trade in the United Kingdom. The program provides leniency for a company that reports price fixing to the authorities. Virgin Atlantic and Lufthansa reported the price fixing on Atlantic and Pacific cargo fares, respectively. The airlines said that the price fixing had occurred at lower levels in the company, and when brought to the attention of higher-level management, the leniency program provided incentives to report the price fixing to authorities.[26]

Mergers and Merger Guidelines

Mergers can create horizontal market power or restrain competition in supply or distribution channels. The passage of the Celler-Kefauver Act in 1950 decreased the number of mergers, but when the Reagan administration took office in 1981, it signaled that it did not view mergers with the same hostility as had prior administrations. Indeed, mergers were viewed as potentially beneficial to efficiency and competition. Mergers can yield cost efficiencies and synergies that benefit consumers. Mergers can also remove ineffective management and eliminate inefficient cross-subsidization of one line of business by another.

To provide guidance to firms about when it was likely to initiate an antitrust investigation, the DOJ issued revised merger guidelines in 1982.[27] The FTC issued similar guidelines, and in 1992 the agencies jointly issued updated guidelines. Those guidelines were subsequently updated in 1997 and 2010.[28] The guidelines reflect both structural and Chicago school perspectives by identifying where market power may be present and whether it can be exercised. The guidelines also reflect the new IO perspective with respect to the dynamics of competition. In contrast to the structural perspective, the guidelines do not assume that market power automatically will be exercised. Market power is viewed as a horizontal concept, and nonhorizontal mergers, either vertical or conglomerate, that do not affect market concentration are not necessarily a threat to competition. Nonhorizontal mergers are a concern only to the extent that they have horizontal consequences, such as eliminating a potential entrant.

The merger guidelines identify collusion as the means to the exercise of market power. The exercise of market power requires a restriction of output to increase prices and profits. Since the smaller a firm's market share the more it has to restrict output to achieve a given price increase, unless a firm has a dominant market position, collusion must be the means to the exercise of market power. In accord with the Chicago school's perspective, the greater the number of firms that would have to collude to restrict output, the more likely collusion is to break down. Collusion is easier the more homogeneous the product, since then there is only one dimension of competition that must be monitored under an explicit or implicit collusive arrangement. Collusion is more difficult when products are differentiated and substitutes are available in the relevant markets and is easier when repeated encounters provide an opportunity to punish cheating on the collusive arrangement.

In its definition of the relevant market, the DOJ and FTC focus on "economically meaningful" markets. These are defined in terms of products and geographic areas in which a firm could restrict output and thereby increase price above prevailing levels. To do so, a firm would have to have horizontal market power. Assessing market power involves consideration of substitute products, since an attempt to raise prices may cause consumers to switch to a substitute. It also takes into account imports and the resale market for durable goods.

A merger can result in improved efficiency, and in 1997 the FTC issued a revision to the merger guidelines. The FTC identified the potential efficiencies from a merger and stated that the efficiencies considered should be net of the efficiencies that would have been realized in the absence of a merger. The FTC also stated that any efficiency claims must be verifiable and substantiated. It also stated that efficiencies would likely carry little weight if the merger were to create a monopoly or near-monopoly.

---

[26]The European Union also has a leniency program under which the first firm receives 100 percent leniency, the second 50 percent, and the third 30 percent.

[27]Ordover and Willig (1983) provide an evaluation of the DOJ merger guidelines.

[28]Department of Justice and Federal Trade Commission, Horizontal Merger Guidelines, Washington, DC, August 19, 2010.

To assess the potential for achieving price increases in the case of horizontal mergers, the DOJ and FTC use the Herfindahl-Hirschman Index (HHI) to measure concentration in an industry. The HHI is defined as the sum of the squares of the market shares of firms, or

$$\text{HHI} = \sum_{i=1}^{n} s_i^2,$$

where n is the number of firms in the industry and s_i is the market share of the ith firm expressed as a percent. The HHI is zero for a perfectly competitive industry and is 10,000 for a monopoly. If two firms with 10 percent market shares merge, the HHI increases by 200. For an industry with 10 firms with equal market shares, the HHI is 1,000, and for an industry with two firms with 30 percent shares and eight firms with 5 percent shares, the HHI is 2,000.

The DOJ and FTC view markets as unconcentrated if the HHI is below 1,500, moderately concentrated if the HHI is between 1,500 and 2,000, and concentrated if it is above 2,500. Mergers of two firms in an unconcentrated market ordinarily are not opposed nor are mergers that increase the HHI by less than 100. In moderately concentrated markets, mergers that increase the HHI by more than 100 "often warrant scrutiny." In highly concentrated markets mergers that increase the HHI between 100 and 200 also "often warrant scrutiny." An increase of more than 200 is presumed to "enhance market power," and the merger is likely to be opposed unless there is "pervasive evidence" to the contrary.

The use of the HHI requires identification of the relevant market for determining market shares. In 2007 Whole Foods Market, the largest marketer of natural and organic groceries, sought to acquire the second largest firm, Wild Oats Markets, for $565 million. The FTC investigated the proposed merger and concluded that it would reduce competition and increase prices of premium natural and organic food. The FTC sought a preliminary injunction in federal courts to prevent the firms from merging. The companies argued that there was no distinctive market for natural and organic groceries and that the relevant market was broad, since Safeway, Wal-Mart, and others also sold those groceries. The judge agreed with the companies that the relevant market was larger than the premium grocers, and denied the request for a preliminary injunction. The FTC filed an appeal of the judge's decision, and the court of appeals reversed the lower court decision, ruling that the relevant market was "premium and natural organic supermarkets" as used by the FTC. The Court of Appeals sent the case back to the district court for reconsideration.

After the rejection of the injunction, the district court had permitted the acquisition to go forward, and Whole Foods had already consolidated and integrated Wild Oats stores and distribution facilities. The district court and the FTC were now left with the question of whether and how they should unring the bell. The FTC and Whole Foods subsequently reached a settlement in which the company sold 13 existing stores and the leases and assets on 19 stores that had been closed. The FTC stated that the settlement substantially restored competition in 17 markets.

In addition to the structural factors involving market concentration, the antitrust agencies take into account technological change and the rate of innovation in an industry. In an industry that experiences rapid technological change, a large market share of merging companies may be of little concern because market share can be won or lost relatively quickly. Similar reasoning led to dropping the government's antitrust suit against IBM.

The antitrust enforcement agencies frequently negotiate with merging companies under the "fix-it-first" approach in which areas of antitrust concern are fixed prior to a merger being consummated. For example, in 2004, after initially opposing it, the FTC approved the merger of Nestlé and Dreyer's Grand Ice Cream after potentially anticompetitive features had been fixed. Dreyer's sold three of its brands, and Nestlé sold its U.S. distribution assets. Similarly, in 1996 the FTC required Ciba-Geigy and Sandoz to sell part of their gene-therapy technology as a condition for their merger to form Novartis.

Mergers are a result of the market strategies of companies, and their success can require support by nonmarket strategies. In 2011 Deutsche Telecom decided not to make further investments in the U.S. wireless market and agreed to sell its subsidiary T-Mobile USA to AT&T, the second largest wireless company, for $39 billion. A merger of the two companies required approval by the Federal Communications Commission for the transferal of spectrum licenses and of the DOJ, since the horizontal merger would increase the concentration in an already highly concentrated industry. AT&T deployed a broad nonmarket strategy in an attempt to gain approval from the two agencies, as considered in the chapter case *AT&T and*

T-Mobile Merger?. Opponents of the merger also deployed nonmarket strategies in an attempt to stop the merger.

Mergers often come under the jurisdictions of other countries. The European Union approved the AOL Time Warner merger with the stipulation that Bertelsmann AG withdraw from a joint venture in Europe in which AOL's CompuServe and Vivendi SA participated. In 2001 the United States approved a merger between General Electric and Honeywell after the companies agreed to some minor fixes. The European Union, however, rejected the merger, causing the companies to abandon their merger plans. This decision is considered in more detail in Chapter 15.

COMPLIANCE

Compliance with the antitrust laws involves both procedures and policy. Firms provide training and guidance to employees who may encounter situations in which antitrust concerns are present. For example, in its "Standards of Business Conduct," Hewlett-Packard provides guidance on trade practices (vertical arrangements), price discrimination, unfair practices, and competitor relations (horizontal practices). Cisco Systems requires employees to watch an antitrust primer on its Web site. Companies with dominant market positions restrain their competitive practices and language. Cisco and Intel do not use the term leveraging, as in "leveraging from a dominant position."

A firm may find itself in a situation in which a contemplated practice falls in an area in which the antitrust laws and the court decisions interpreting them are unclear or changing. In addition to seeking the advice of counsel, the firm should examine whether the purpose of its practice is anticompetitive. In *Sylvania* the court held that the policy of territorial restrictions served the purpose of stimulating interbrand competition. In such a case a firm should use a practice that is the least restrictive in achieving the desired purpose. On retrial the court acquitted GTE-Sylvania because it concluded that the practice of terminating a dealer that violated its policy was the least restrictive means of achieving the intended purpose of strengthening its dealer network. Hewlett-Packard's policy on terminating relationships is cautious despite the decisions in *Sylvania, Monsanto,* and *Sharp*: "Terminating relationships with customers can lead to litigation. It is therefore important that the decision to terminate be made carefully and for valid business reasons. HP's Legal Department should be consulted before terminating any such relationship without the customer's consent. Possible termination of one customer's contract should not be discussed with another customer."[29]

THE POLITICS OF ANTITRUST

Antitrust policy has important distributive as well as efficiency consequences for firms and consumers, so it is the subject of nonmarket action.[30] In the 1970s the FTC adopted an aggressive posture and initiated several new investigations, some of which were directed at such politically influential industries as insurance and funeral homes. The resulting political pressure on Congress led it to pass the Federal Trade Commission Improvements Act of 1980, which reined in the FTC.[31] The framework for nonmarket analysis presented in Part II of this book provides the basis for analyzing the politics of antitrust policy.

Most proposed changes in the antitrust laws fail because of the intensity of the ensuing politics and the complexity of the issues. In 1986 the Reagan administration proposed amending Section 7 of the Clayton Act (which deals with mergers) by replacing "may be" and "tend to" with "significant probability." It also proposed relaxing merger standards for firms that had been injured by foreign competition. Because of a concern that private antitrust lawsuits were being used to stifle competition, the administration proposed eliminating treble damages except for price-fixing violations. The FTC and the Reagan administration also proposed that the FTC authority over unfair advertising be eliminated, because the term *unfair* was too vague to be enforced. None of these initiatives was successful.

---

[29]Hewlett-Packard Company, "Standards of Business Conduct," Palo Alto, CA, 1989.
[30]See Shugart (1990) for a perspective on antitrust and interest group politics.
[31]See Weingast and Moran (1983),Moe (1985), and Wilson (1989, Chap. 13) for differing perspectives on the relationship between the FTC and Congress.

Democrats in Congress have also sought revisions in the antitrust laws, attempting to counter DOJ and FTC decisions to stop bringing lawsuits for certain vertical restraints. They attempted to revise the standards established by the Supreme Court in *Monsanto* and *Sharp* involving nonprice vertical arrangements. In 1991, for example, the Senate passed a bill that would make it easier to win cases against retail price maintenance practices. Both activist groups and discounters who had been cut off by manufacturers backed the bill, arguing that consumers were injured by the nonprice arrangements. They were opposed by manufacturers and specialty retailers, who viewed vertical arrangements as promoting interbrand competition. The bill failed.

The politics of antitrust also manifests itself in legislative action seeking exemptions or providing for affirmative defenses in antitrust lawsuits. For decades the soft drink industry had been organized around exclusive territories for its distributors. Soft drink manufacturers produced syrup, which was sold to bottlers that were allowed to distribute the soft drink only in a specified geographic area. In 1971 the FTC issued complaints against seven national-brand soft drink syrup manufacturers, including Coca-Cola, PepsiCo, Seven-Up, and Canada Dry. The complaints charged that exclusive territorial distributorships were illegal vertical restraints of trade. With the strong support of the National Soft Drink Association, in 1972 a bill was introduced in the Senate to permit exclusive territorial arrangements for soft drink manufacturers.

The FTC complaint was resolved in 1978 when the FTC ruled that the exclusive distributorships were anticompetitive. The decision was appealed and was still before the courts when Congress finally acted. After 10 years of effort, the soft drink manufacturers and their bottlers succeeded in 1980 in obtaining an effective antitrust exemption. The Soft Drink Interbrand Competition Act provided protection from antitrust lawsuits if soft drinks were in "substantial and effective competition." Despite opposition by the DOJ, the bill passed the Senate on an 86 to 6 vote, passed the House on a voice vote, and was signed by President Carter.[32]

SUMMARY

The principal antitrust laws are the Sherman Act, the Clayton Act, and the Federal Trade Commission Act. The Sherman Act pertains to monopolization and restraints of trade. The Clayton Act addresses monopolization and restraints of trade in their incipiency and provides the basis for government authority over mergers. The act also restricts price discrimination. The Federal Trade Commission Act prohibits unfair competition and unfair and deceptive acts.

Both the DOJ and the FTC have enforcement responsibilities for the Sherman and Clayton Acts, but only the FTC can enforce the FTC Act. Considerable enforcement of the antitrust laws occurs through private lawsuits, most of which are filed by one firm against another. Private lawsuits are encouraged by the prospect of treble damages.

Antitrust enforcement and court decisions are influenced by schools of thought about the role of antitrust policy and the likelihood of adverse economic consequences from business practices. The structural approach is based on the structure-conduct-performance paradigm and focuses on the structure of industries and on practices that may foreclose opportunities for competitors. The Chicago school focuses on economic efficiency and consumer prices and views markets as both resilient and the consumer's best protection. Both the structural approach and the Chicago school view horizontal market power as a concern but differ about how likely collusion is and how substantial are barriers to entry. The Chicago school concludes that most practices should be considered under a rule of reason, whereas the structural approach supports a broader application of the per se standard. The new industrial organization perspective emphasizes the strategic interactions among competitors that can result from repeated interactions and asymmetric information. These strategic interactions have the potential to sustain implicit collusion and limit entry into industries. This perspective also focuses on factors such as network externalities and standardization that can provide the basis for anticompetitive practices.

These schools of thought have influenced the thinking of government antitrust officials and judges. In the case of vertical arrangements and resale price maintenance, the courts reversed

---

[32]The case *The Malt Beverage Interbrand Competition Act* in Baron (1996) considers the beer industry's unsuccessful attempt to obtain similar protection.

earlier decisions in holding that those practices are no longer per se illegal but are to be considered under a rule of reason. Certain arrangements that enhance interbrand competition but harm intrabrand competition have been held by the courts to be legal under the antitrust laws.

The DOJ and FTC have applied revised guidelines to the surveillance of mergers. The guidelines are based both on industry structure and on the likelihood that market power can be exercised. The government has used a fix-it-first approach to reduce the anticompetitive effects of mergers that otherwise would produce efficiencies.

Antitrust policy has important distributive consequences and so is the subject of considerable political activity. The complexity of the issues, however, makes significant legislative changes in the antitrust laws difficult to achieve.

CASES

Price Fixing in the Airways

Crude oil prices increased rapidly in the 2004–2006 period, and the increase in fuel costs placed a burden on airlines. Airlines began to add "fuel surcharges" to air fares, adding a new instrument of price competition. British Airways (BA) contacted Virgin Atlantic Airways and began discussing the situation in 2004, and the discussions resulted in increases in the surcharge from £5 to £60 on return trans-Atlantic flights over the next 2 years. Virgin's legal department subsequently notified the United Kingdom's Office of Fair Trading (OFT) that the two firms had colluded to fix the fuel charges. Virgin was taking advantage of a "leniency policy" included in the Competition Act of 1998, that provides immunity to firms that reveal illegal competitive activities. The objective of the leniency policy was to provide an incentive to disclose wrongdoing. In response to Virgin's disclosure BA admitted guilt and established a £350 million reserve for fines. Two BA executives resigned as a result of the price fixing. The European Union was also conducting an investigation of the price fixing and could levy substantial fines.

BA cooperated fully with the OFT, and stated that its policy was "to conduct its business in full compliance with all … the laws." As a result of its investigation in 2007 the OFT fined BA £121.5 million, the largest civil penalty it had ever imposed.[33] Simon Williams, director of cartel operations for the OFT, said, "Had BA not made admissions and cooperated from the outset, they would have been fined many millions of pounds more … tens of millions of pounds."[34] Philip Collins, the head of the OFT, said the fine would "send an important message … about our intention to enforce the law."[35] Ryanair CEO Michael O'Leary commented, "The fuel surcharges levied by British Airways and Virgin Atlantic are just their latest price-fixing scam. The flag-carriers have been price fixing for years …."[36] Ryanair had not added fuel surcharges.

A few hours after the OFT announced the fine, in a case filed by the U.S. Department of Justice, a court imposed a $300 million fine on British Airways, the second largest fine ever imposed in a DOJ case. The fine also covered a separate case in which British Airways and Korean Air Lines admitted to fixing prices and surcharges on air cargo flights.[37] Korean Air Lines was also fined $300 million, and Qantas paid $61 million. The price-fixing conspiracy was exposed by Lufthansa AG, and Lufthansa and Virgin were notified that restitution would be required for customers even though the companies were conditionally accepted into the DOJ "corporate leniency" program. William W. Mercer of the DOJ said, "When British Airways, Korean Air and their co-conspirators got together and agreed to raise prices for passenger and air-cargo fares, American consumers and businesses ended up picking up the tab for their illegal conduct."[38] Craig Kelly, a lighting manufacturer in Sydney, complained, "We just missed out on contracts of upwards of a million dollars because of price. It could very well have been the cartel margin that Qantas was ripping us off that was enough to push us over the edge and lose the contract."[39]

In addition to the fines by the antitrust authorities the airlines faced the likelihood of class action cases in the United States on behalf of customers who were overcharged because of the price fixing. Michael Hausfeld, a U.S. attorney, said he would be filing a representative action lawsuit in the UK to give consumers "the opportunity to recover that which was robbed from them."[40] British AIrways CEO Willie Walsh said, "I want to reassure our passengers that they were not overcharged. Fuel charges are a legitimate way of recovering costs."[41] Walsh also stated, "The activities that went on were in breach of the law and fines were established in accord with the guidelines. They could have been as high as $850 million but we cooperated

---

[33]The maximum fine allowable under European Union law was 10 percent of sales.
[34]Reuters, August 1, 2007.
[35]*The Economist*, August 4, 2007.
[36]*Daily Mail*, August 4, 2007.

[37]The investigation involved authorities in the United States, the United Kingdom, South Korea, and elsewhere. The fine was composed of $200 million for cargo flights and $100 million for passenger flights.
[38]*Wall Street Journal*, August 2, 2007.
[39]*Daily Telegraph* (Australia), January 17, 2008.
[40]*Guardian,* August 18, 2007. In the United Kingdom a "representation action" under the OFT law is the counterpart of a class action lawsuit.
[41]*Wall Street Journal*, August 2, 2007.

fully with the investigation, which was the right thing to do."[42] Walsh blamed the price fixing on "a very limited number of individuals within British Airways."[43]

In 2008 British Airways and Virgin Atlantic Airways reached a $200 million settlement in a class action lawsuit filed in federal court in the United States alleging price fixing on fuel surcharges. The plaintiff's law firm also had filed a separate class action lawsuit alleging price fixing on trans-Pacific routes. ▪

Preparation Questions

1. What were the incentives that led the airlines to fix prices?
2. Show how a leniency program can put price fixers in a prisoners' dilemma.
3. What procedures should be put into place to ensure that employees do not engage in price fixing?
4. How hard is it to conceal price fixing?

The AT&T and T-Mobile Merger?

This transaction is all about consumers. It's about keeping up with consumer demand. It's about having the capacity to drive innovation and competitive prices for consumers.

Randall Stephenson,
CEO and President, AT&T Inc.[44]

Beware of habitual monopolists bearing gifts ...

The Economist, March 24, 2011

INTRODUCTION

In March 2011 Deutsche Telekom decided to invest no further in the 4G rollout in the competitive U.S. wireless market and agreed to sell for $39 billion its T-Mobile USA subsidiary to AT&T, the second largest wireless carrier in the United States. T-Mobile was the fourth largest wireless carrier, and the acquisition and merger of the two companies would increase AT&T's U.S. market share to over 40 percent, putting it ahead of Verizon Wireless, a 50–50 joint venture of Verizon Communications and Vodafone.

AT&T argued that the merger was necessary to give it the 700 MHz spectrum it needed to provide 4G LTE service, the future of wireless communication.[45] With the additional spectrum and infrastructure resulting from the merger, AT&T said it would be able to serve 97 percent of the population and double its existing geographic coverage. The company also said that the merger would allow it to realize substantial efficiencies from the combined assets of the two companies. AT&T was also acquiring spectrum from Qualcomm.

The acquisition and merger required approval by federal agencies. The Federal Communications Commission (FCC) had to approve any transfer of spectrum licenses and communications authorizations from T-Mobile to AT&T. The merger could also be challenged by the Department of Justice (DOJ),

since even before the acquisition and merger the market was highly concentrated. AT&T was confident that the merger would be approved. "If the merger fails to gain approval then AT&T will pay T-Mobile a $3 billion breakup fee, transfer over some AWS spectrum it doesn't need for its LTE deployment, and grant them a roaming agreement at a value agreeable to both parties."[46] AT&T sought to justify the merger to the antitrust authority on efficiency grounds. It also deployed a nonmarket strategy in support of the merger.

Prior to announcing the merger, AT&T had enlisted support from NGOs, the Communications Workers of America (CWA) union, and companies and venture capitalists in Silicon Valley. Their endorsements supported AT&T's political and efficiency arguments in favor of the merger. The opponents of the merger also deployed nonmarket strategies to counter AT&T's strategy and influence the government agencies with authority over the merger. Both Houses of Congress held hearings on the merger, and the FCC and DOJ demanded extensive data for review of the merger. AT&T was ready with a contingent nonmarket strategy intended to address any antitrust and regulatory concerns that might be raised.

THE U.S. WIRELESS MARKET

Verizon was the largest wireless provider with 38 percent of the market followed by AT&T, Sprint, and T-Mobile. With the acquisition of T-Mobile, AT&T would have approximately a 44 percent market share, but market shares varied considerably across local markets. Demand for wireless service had skyrocketed with the introduction of smartphones that allowed users to connect to the Internet, transmit data, and download videos and movies. Innovation was rapid, and technological innovation was expected to continue. AT&T argued that the merger would allow it to roll out a nationwide 4G LTE network more quickly than it otherwise could, which would not only meet rapidly increasing customer demand but encourage further innovation. Critics, however, argued that the merger would cement the Verizon and AT&T duopoly and control innovation to the advantage of the companies.

---

[42]*Sunday Telegraph,* August 3, 2007.
[43]*USA Today,* August 2, 2007.
[44]Randall Stephenson, Testimony, House Committee on the Judiciary, Subcommittee on Intellectual Property, Competition, and the Internet, May 26, 2011.
[45]LTE stands for Long-Term Evolution, which is a form of 4G network. AT&T included both LTE and HSPA+ as 4G networks, as did other carriers. Verizon was rolling out LTE faster than AT&T. AT&T explained that LTE required more testing of the new technology. (Computerworld, May 26, 2011).

[46]Taylor Wimberly, androidandme.com, March 20, 2011.

T-Mobile had been losing customers. In the third quarter of 2010 it lost 60,000 customers, in the fourth quarter 2010 318,000, and in the first quarter of 2011 471,000. Sprint reported that it lost 100,000 wireless subscribers in the second quarter of 2011, and its share price fell 40 percent during the market plummet in August. Verizon and AT&T had retained their market shares.[47]

Capacity for 4G LTE networks could be expanded in several ways. First, capacity including spectrum could be acquired from another company, as in the T-Mobile acquisition and the purchase from Qualcomm. Second, additional cells could be built or higher cell towers could be used. Network architectures using picocells and femtocells, small wireless base stations, or cells within a cell could also be used to expand capacity. New technologies also held promise for the future but were not presently available.

As evidence of competition in the industry, AT&T cited the growth of Leap Wireless and MetroPCS Communications, which offered prepaid wireless communications. Wireless service was also provided by 100 companies serving rural markets, and several prominent regional carriers, such as US Cellular and Cellular South, also provided service. High-speed wireless was, however, limited in rural areas because of the low population density.

As its WiMax offerings faltered, Clearwire announced plans for a $600 million 4G LTE network but faced the task of finding the funds. Speculation centered on an acquisition of Clearwire by Sprint, which already held a 54 percent stake in the company, or funding provided by cable companies Comcast and Time Warner.[48] LightSquared planned to build a nationwide 4G LTE network but had not yet received permission to enter the market.

A substantial component of the cost of operating a wireless network was access, which was increasing provided by backhaul carriers. Paul Schrieber of Sprint said, "a third of the expense to run a cellular site goes to purchasing special access for backhaul connections." He added, "Sprint typically has to commit to five-year contracts with its large rivals to get the best rates, with the pricing structured to discourage looking at alternative suppliers."[49] Brocade defined backhaul as: "Wireless backhaul is the part of the network that carries voice and data traffic in the [Radio Access Network] from the mobile xStation to the mobile operators' core network."[50] In August 2011 the FCC opened a large block of spectrum for wireless backhaul, which would support the development of 4G networks.

AT&T and Verizon provided backhaul as did companies such as FiberTower, TTM, and Zayo, primarily using microwave and fiber technologies.[51] The need for backhaul capacity was driven by the rapid growth in wireless data transmission and mobile Internet and video, which required high bandwidth.

AT&T'S NONMARKET STRATEGY

AT&T's basic strategy was to present a strong case to the FCC and DOJ justifying the merger. The company argued that the regulators should consider the merger on a market-by-market basis. In May the FCC asked AT&T for detailed information on market share, geographic coverage, spectrum licenses, and any capacity constraints. In response, it flooded the Department of Justice with 1.2 million files.

CEO Randall Stephenson presented the company's basic argument that despite the concentration in the market the efficiencies that would result from the merger and the increased innovation would outweigh any competitiveness concerns. He said, "Our two companies have very complementary assets, which means that combining them will create much more service-enhancing network capacity—the equivalent of the spectrum—than the two companies could have done separately. That, in turn, means more room for growth and innovation, fewer dropped and blocked calls, and a faster, more reliable mobile Internet experience."[52] AT&T stated that the merger would allow it to save $10 billion in "avoided purchases and investments" and $10 billion in call center and billing costs.[53]

AT&T worked to enlist support from government officials, interest groups, and NGOs. The FCC was the focus of the strategies of proponents and opponents of the merger, since it was more responsive to influence activities than was the Department of Justice, as illustrated in Figure 7-5 in Chapter 7.

AT&T was able to obtain the support of 26 governors and 77 mayors for the merger.[54] The company also lined up support from NGOs, several of which filed statements in support of the merger. The NGOs were criticized in newspaper editorials, and Hilary Shelton, senior vice president for policy and analysis of the NAACP, responded in a letter to the editor. She wrote, "For 12 years, the NAACP has monitored corporations on workers' rights, diversity and community reinvestment. Throughout these evaluations, AT&T has demonstrated a commitment to livable wages, meaningful benefits, diversity in its use of contractors and professional development opportunities for its racially and ethnically diverse work force. T-Mobile has failed to provide adequate protection to its employees and has undermined all attempts to unionize."[55] AT&T was listed as a contributor of "$1 million or more" on the NAACP Web site. Bowing to criticism, the Gay and Lesbian Alliance Against Defamation (GLAAD) withdrew its support for the merger and wrote the FCC that it was now taking a "neutral position."[56] The Minority Media and

---

[47]*Wall Street Journal*, June 23, 2011.

[48]*Washington Post*, August 19, 2011.

[49]*Wall Street Journal*, May 25, 2011.

[50]Brocade, "Technical Brief: Next-generation Wireless Backhaul Solutions." See also Fujitsu, "Understanding Mobile Wireless Backhaul."

[51]Backhaul providers also included large companies such as Ericsson and Alcatel-Lucent.

[52]Randall Stephenson, Testimony, House Committee on the Judiciary, Subcommittee on Intellectual Property, Competition, and the Internet. May 26, 2011.

[53]*Los Angeles Times*, September 1, 2011.

[54]One governor supporting the merger was Bobby Jindal (R-LA). AT&T was a sponsor of his wife's charity the Supriya Jinday Foundation. *Washington Post*, June 1, 2011.

[55]*New York Times*, July 15, 2011.

[56]Daily Deal/The Deal, July 13, 2011.

Telecommunications Council, an advocacy group for the interests of minorities that had never taken a position on a merger, came out in support of it. In a filing with the FCC, the Council's executive director David Honig wrote, "In a democratic society, the nation simply cannot afford to guess wrong and see the digital divide widen. In today's digital age, access to high-speed Internet is no longer a luxury—it is a necessary predicate of first-class citizenship, and thus it is a fundamental right for all Americans."[57] Ellen Miller, executive director of the Sunlight Foundation, commented, "They've curried favor with organizations who, whether through direct or indirect expectations, will go to bat for them. That's what a sophisticate lobby does, and AT&T is among the best at this in Washington."[58]

Self-interest drove many of the supporters of the merger. AT&T was the only wireless provider whose workers were represented by a union, whereas T-Mobile and Sprint had successfully fought unionization. With AT&T and Sprint the only possible acquirers of T-Mobile, the CWA support for the merger was immediate. CWA president Larry Cohen said, "in contrast to AT&T's strict neutrality policy with respect to union organizing and positive partnership with CWA, Sprint has a long history of hostility to union organizing and workers' rights."[59] He also stated, "Sprint has outsourced up to 70 percent of its customer contact workforce to places like the Philippines, India, and Mexico. Sprint is the only U.S. wireless company that outsources network management, ... AT&T and its unions, by comparison, recently negotiated the return of 3,000 DSL-related customer service jobs to the United States, ..."[60] Union support led to 77 Democrats in the House endorsing the merger.[61]

Cohen wrote in *USA Today*, May 20, 2011, "This merger promises to bridge the digital divide and will, if regulators insist on guarantees of date certain buildout and mapping that is monitored."[62] He stated that Deutsche Telekom had made it clear that it would not invest further in the company, and the only other possible buyer was Sprint which did not have the financial resources to acquire T-Mobile.

To solidify CWA support, AT&T pledged to include the T-Mobile workers in the union's bargaining unit. The union would add 23,000 new members to the 43,000 AT&T wireless workers already represented without having to go through a representation election. Through growth in AT&T wireless and several acquisitions, CWA representation had increased from 9,300 to 43,000 within a decade. In 2011 the union was under pressure from Verizon Communications, which sought extensive concessions in pensions, sick days allowed, and health care contributions from workers in its wireline business. In August 45,000 members of the CWA and the International Brotherhood of Electrical Workers went on strike against Verizon in opposition to any concessions.

AT&T traveled to Silicon Valley to line up support from companies and venture capitalists with a stake in wireless. The company met with 10 large companies and received endorsements for the merger from Facebook, Microsoft, and Yahoo.[63] Facebook and other companies filed a statement with the FCC in which they said, "Many policy related efforts will not be able to quickly address near term capacity needs. The FCC must seriously weight the benefits of the merger and approve it."[64] AT&T also met with 20 venture capitalists, and received endorsements from Kleiner Perkins Caufield & Byers and Sequoia Capital. Matt Murphy, a partner at Kleiner, said, "A key part of any user experience is how responsive the app is, and that requires low latency, and I don't want us to be in a situation where we don't have the kind of networks we need to make these applications perform as best as they possibly can."[65]

THE OPPOSITION

SprintNextel, which was the first company to roll out a nationwide 4G network, vigorously opposed the merger. CEO Daniel R. Hesse stated, "We urge the Department of Justice and the FCC to take a hard look at this transaction and to weigh carefully the irreparable harm to competition, innovation, and customer choice against the purported benefits of combining two overlapping businesses."[66] He argued that with the purchase of spectrum from Qualcomm, AT&T could serve rural areas and more customers without the spectrum from T-Mobile. Hesse also complained about backhaul fees, "Sprint must pay more than $2 billion a year in backhaul fees to its competitors, AT&T and Verizon earn enormous profits from their control over backhaul. By controlling the availability and price of backhaul, AT&T and Verizon are also able, to a large degree, to control their competitors' costs and quality of service."[67]

The merger was also opposed by the 100 wireless carriers that belonged to the RCA—The Competitive Carriers Association. The carriers primarily served rural areas covering 80 percent of the area of the United States. In testimony before a Senate subcommittee Victor H. Meena, president and CEO of Cellular South and chairman of the RCA, criticized the merger on the grounds of creating a dominant duopoly, dominance of the 700 MHz band and deployment of "essentially proprietary LTE networks and devices that work only on their spectrum," and unwillingness to sign roaming agreements with local service companies.[68] Leap Wireless and MetroPCS also opposed the merger, citing the increased concentration in the industry.

The Computer and Communications Industry Association (CCIA), which includes Microsoft as a member, strongly opposed the merger for fear that it would stifle competition and delay the

[57]Daily Deal/The Deal, May 31, 2011.
[58]*Washington Post*, June 1, 2011.
[59]Larry Cohen, Testimony, Senate Committee on the Judiciary, Subcommittee on Antitrust, Competition Policy, and Consumer Rights, May 11, 2011.
[60]Ibid.
[61]Daily Deal/The Deal, July 28, 2011.
[62]*USA Today*, May 20, 2011.

[63]*Wall Street Journal*, May 19, 2011. Microsoft had a smartphone partnership with Nokia using its Windows 7 operating system.
[64]*Wall Street Journal*, June 8, 2011.
[65]Ibid.
[66]Daniel R. Hesse, Testimony, Senate Judiciary Committee, Subcommittee on Antitrust, Competition Policy and Consumer Rights, May 11, 2011.
[67]Ibid.
[68]Victor H. Meena, Testimony, Senate Judiciary Committee, Subcommittee on Antitrust, Competition Policy and Consumer Rights, May 11, 2011.

rollout of advanced technology. Ed Black, president and CEO of the CCIA, called it "the most brazen merger proposal in history" and "a clear violation of the relevant antitrust rules."[69] He added, "To believe that [regulators] would approve a merger that would give AT&T 45% of the market, especially when they have a duopoly in the wireline market, is very difficult to believe."[70]

Consumers Union expressed concerns about the merger, stating, "There is a great deal of data and evidence that this transaction will lead to a highly concentrated market, which will likely lead to higher prices and less choice for consumers."[71] Parul P. Desai, policy counsel of the Consumers Union, addressed the market concentration issue. "As of 2008, the FCC estimated the HHI to be 2,848, which already exceeds both the DOJ (2,500 HHI) and FCC (2,800 HHI) definition of a heavily concentrated market …. It has been estimated that this acquisition will increase the national HHI by an additional 650–700 points, which means that scrutiny over the proposed acquisition should be increased, with a presumption that the acquisition will enhance market power."[72] Desai also complained that special access "rates continue to be a barrier to entry and growth for smaller and regional carriers." The Yankee Group, a research and consulting firm, reported that the concentration in 17 of the 27 largest metropolitan areas would "jump dramatically" as a result of the merger.[73]

Sprint Nextel broadened its strategy by going to the states. Several states had statutes allowing their public utility commission to review mergers of wired telecommunications companies, and although it was not clear that they could stop a wireless merger, they could express an opinion about it. Sprint wrote to the California Public Utility Commission (PUC) urging it to begin an investigation of the merger. The PUC subsequently decided to do so, and froze its 30-day review rule to allow an extended investigation. The PUC observed that the merger would give AT&T a 47 percent wireless market share in the state. All the other states declined to oppose the merger with the exception of West Virginia which was still reviewing it. An AT&T spokesperson responded, "Spint's letter [to the PUC] merely reiterates substantially the same unfounded accusations it has been peddling to the press, to Congress, and to the FCC. We're confident that the FCC and DOJ, after a full review of the facts, will determine that the transaction will be good for consumers, for workers, and for the economy."[74]

After holding hearings on the merger Senator Herb Kohl (D-WI), chairman of the Subcommittee on Antitrust, Competition Policy and Consumer Rights of the Judiciary Committee, wrote to Attorney General Eric Holder and FCC chairman Julius Genachowski stating, "I have concluded that this acquisition, if permitted to proceed, would likely cause substantial harm to competition and consumers, would be contrary to antitrust law and not in the public interest, and therefore should be blocked by you agencies."[75] The ranking Republican member of the subcommittee Michael S. Lee (R-UT) was more cautious, asking for a "careful review" of the merger.

A group of seven NGOs, including the Consumers Union, the National Hispanic Media Coalition, and the Future of Music Coalition, wrote to the FCC chairman asking for public hearings on the merger. The group said, "The AT&T/T-Mobile merger proposal deserves the commission's highest level of scrutiny and consideration."[76]

Companies and NGOs opposed to the merger formed the No Takeover Project. The Project set up a Web site and used Facebook to spread its message and urge people to write their governors and state attorneys general.

AT&T'S CONTINGENT STRATEGY

In July AT&T asked to submit new economic data to the FCC, and the FCC stopped the clock on its review of the merger. Jay Schwartzman of the opposition Media Access Project commented, "It suggests that AT&T's initial showing was deemed inadequate. It indicates it's going to take longer and that AT&T is going to have a stiffer burden to meet in justifying this merger to the FCC."[77] AT&T's strategy, however, was to propose a fix-it-first plan to relieve potential concerns about concentration in particular markets. It had all along argued that the merger should be evaluated on a market by market basis, and this positioned it to propose a fix-it plan to relieve concentration in particular markets. An AT&T spokesperson said, "As we said on the day we announced the merger with T-Mobile USA, we anticipate there will be some divestitures, as we have had in past mergers, but any speculation about the amount of divestitures is premature."[78] The asset sales could include the sale of some of the 9,200 stores the two companies had, since a number of them were proximate. CoStar Group, which tracks commercial properties, reported that 41 percent of AT&T stores had a T-Mobile store within a mile.[79]

In addition, AT&T proposed selling assets and spectrum licenses in selected markets. To manage the asset sales the company hired Bank of America-Merrill Lynch. The fix-it-first plan was viewed as attractive by small wireless carriers that saw an opportunity to acquire spectrum and licenses. Leap Wireless CFO Walter Berger expressed interest in any divested assets, and Braxton Carter, CFO of MetroPCS, also saw the possibility of acquiring divested spectrum or customers.[80]

In a blunder, lawyers for AT&T filed an unredacted copy of a letter with the FCC for posting on a public Web site rather than a letter with confidential information redacted. The unredacted letter was quickly taken off the Web site, but it had been noticed. According to the *Wall Street Journal*, "The full version says that AT&T had considered and rejected plans to expand the network to 97% of the U.S. at a cost of $3.8 billion."[81]

[69]The Deal/Daily Deal, May 24, 2011.
[70]Ibid.
[71]Parul P. Desai, Testimony, House Committee on the Judiciary, Subcommittee on Intellectual Property, Competition, and the Internet. May 26, 2011.
[72]Ibid.
[73]*Los Angeles Times*, August 11, 2011.
[74]Daily Deal/The Deal, May 20, 2011.
[75]Herb Kohl, Letter, June 30, 2011.
[76]Daily Deal/The Deal, June 29, 2011.
[77]*Wall Street Journal*, July 21, 2011.
[78]*Wall Street Journal*, August 12, 2011.
[79]*Wall Street Journal*, June 23, 2011.
[80]*Wall Street Journal*, May 18, 2011.
[81]*Wall Street Journal*, August 25, 2011.

Preparation Questions

1. How effective is AT&T's strategy? What else should AT&T do?
2. How effective is the opposition?

3. Is the concentration issue likely to be decisive?
4. Should the merger be approved?

The Microsoft Antitrust Case

At a 1995 meeting with Intel, Microsoft's chairman and CEO Bill Gates said, according to an Intel executive, "This antitrust thing will blow over. We haven't changed our business practices at all."

On May 18, 1998, the U.S. Department of Justice (DOJ) together with 19 state attorneys general filed an antitrust action against Microsoft Corporation under Sections 1 and 2 of the Sherman Act (the Act). The DOJ complaint was filed to restrain anticompetitive conduct by Microsoft, the world's largest supplier of computer software for personal computers (PCs), and to remedy the effects of its alleged past unlawful conduct.

The DOJ specifically alleged four violations of the Act:

1. *Microsoft engaged in "unlawful exclusive dealing and other exclusionary agreements"* (Section 1 of the Act). The DOJ contended that Microsoft's agreements requiring other companies not to license, distribute, or promote non-Microsoft products, or to do so only on terms that materially disadvantage such products, and its agreements with PC manufacturers restricting modification or customization of the PC boot-up sequence and screens "unreasonably restrict competition." The DOJ claimed that "the purpose and effect of these agreements are to restrain trade and competition in the Internet browser and PC operating system markets."

2. *Microsoft engaged in "unlawful tying"* (Section 1 of the Act). The DOJ viewed the Windows operating systems and Microsoft's Internet Explorer browser as separate products—they were sold in different markets, their functions were different, there was separate demand for them, and they were treated by Microsoft and other industry participants as separate products. The DOJ claimed that it was socially "efficient for Microsoft not to tie them and/or to permit [PC manufacturers] to distribute Windows 95 and Windows 98 without Microsoft's Internet browser software." The DOJ argued that "Microsoft had tied and plans again to tie its Internet browser to its separate Windows operating system, which has monopoly power." The "purpose and the effect of this tying are to prevent customers from choosing among Internet browsers on their merits and to foreclose competing browsers from an important channel of distribution."

3. *Microsoft illegally maintained its monopoly of the PC operating systems market* (Section 2 of the Act). The DOJ contended that Microsoft "possesses monopoly power in the market for PC operating systems" and claimed that Microsoft had maintained that power through anticompetitive conduct.

4. *Microsoft attempted to monopolize the Internet* (Section 2 of the Act). The DOJ claimed that Microsoft had targeted Internet browsers because they had the potential to facilitate the development of products to compete with its Windows operating system and thereby "erode Microsoft's Windows operating system monopoly." Microsoft allegedly engaged in a "course of conduct, including tying and unreasonably exclusionary agreements," for the purpose of obtaining a "monopoly in the Internet browser market."

THE 1995 CONSENT DECREE

The DOJ also sought to show that Microsoft remained dismissive of a long-running antitrust investigation, even after Microsoft had signed a consent decree with the DOJ in 1995. The DOJ had filed an action against Microsoft under Section 2 of the Sherman Act for "unlawfully maintaining its monopoly in the market for PC operating systems." The complaint alleged, among other things, that Microsoft had engaged in anticompetitive agreements and marketing practices directed at PC manufacturers, and the consent decree restricted those practices.

In 1997 the DOJ filed a complaint against Microsoft alleging that it had violated the consent decree. In response, Judge Thomas Penfield Jackson, in whose court the 1998 antitrust case was also tried, issued a preliminary injunction requiring Microsoft to offer Windows independently of Internet Explorer. In July 1998 a federal Court of Appeals overturned Judge Jackson's order, stating that the courts should not be "second guessing the claimed benefits of a particular product design." This ruling gave Microsoft an argument to use in the 1998 case. It could argue that consumers benefited from the integration of Internet Explorer and the Windows operating system.

MICROSOFT'S POSITION

Microsoft maintained that because of the nature of the industry it did not have a monopoly in the PC operating systems market nor could it become a monopoly in the Internet browser market, despite its market shares in these markets.

According to Microsoft the rapid change in technology and in the business environment did not allow a single company to establish and maintain a monopoly. Microsoft also argued that antitrust law definitions, such as a monopoly identified by market share, did not apply to the software market as they did to traditional markets. Since it could not be categorized as a monopoly, Microsoft contended that its business conduct, even if as depicted by the DOJ, did not amount to unlawful conduct. Microsoft also rejected many of the DOJ's factual claims regarding its actual conduct and intent. For example, Microsoft argued that Windows and Internet Explorer were integrated to provide consumers with a superior product.

Microsoft also argued that its competitors employed strategies similar to its own. Moreover, the fact that firms with little market power used the same competitive strategies suggested that there were efficiencies associated with those practices. Although competitive strategies identical to those of a dominant firm were likely to be harmless when used by firms with little or no market power, when used by a firm with substantial market power, the efficiency benefits of those strategies could be outweighed by their anticompetitive effects.

THE TRIAL

An industry's economics are key in any antitrust case and in particular in the Microsoft case. The DOJ proved at least some of its alleged "course of conduct" factual claims with credible clarity, so the court's decision focused on fundamental economic issues rather than on factual controversies. The trial consisted of two phases. The first was a decision by Judge Jackson on the facts of the case and the specific allegations made by the DOJ. If Judge Jackson found for the DOJ, the second phase would focus on remedies for the illegalities.

THE DOJ'S CASE

The DOJ's complaint was based on a set of factual claims, which together were intended to establish Microsoft's "unlawful course of conduct." The first determination by the court was the relevant market. The judge ruled that Intel-based desktop operating systems constituted the relevant market.

The DOJ sought to demonstrate the following:

- Microsoft possessed monopoly power in the market for PC operating systems (OS). Its Windows operating system was used on over 80 percent of all Intel-based PCs, the dominant type of PC in the United States. More than 90 percent of all new Intel-based PCs were shipped with a pre-installed version of Windows. PC manufacturers had no commercially reasonable alternative to Microsoft's operating systems for their PCs.
- Barriers to entry in the market for PC operating systems were high. One of the most important barriers stemmed from network effects and was due to the number of software applications that must run on an operating system to make it attractive to end users. End users wanted a large number of applications, and because Windows was the dominant operating system, most applications were

written to run on Windows. It would be prohibitively expensive to create an alternative operating system to run the programs that ran on Windows.

- Consequently, the most significant potential threat to Microsoft's operating system monopoly was not from existing or new operating systems but from new software products that could support, or themselves become, "platforms" to which applications could be written and which could be used on multiple operating systems. The specific threat to Windows was from Internet browsers and the Java programming language.

THE THREAT OF INTERNET BROWSERS AND JAVA

The DOJ cited Microsoft CEO Bill Gates as saying in May 1995 that the Internet posed a serious potential threat to Microsoft's Windows operating system. Mr. Gates warned his executives:

A new competitor "born" on the Internet is Netscape. Their browser is dominant, with a 70 percent usage share, allowing them to determine which network extensions will catch on. They are pursing a multi-platform strategy where they move the key API [applications programming interface] into the client [the browser] to commoditize the underlying operating system.

The DOJ asserted that Internet browsers posed a competitive threat to Microsoft's operating system monopoly in two basic ways.

- If application programs could easily be written to run on multiple operating systems, competition in the market for operating systems could be revitalized. The combination of browser technology and the Java programming language developed by Sun Microsystems for writing software that would run on any operating system threatened one of the key barriers to entry protecting Microsoft's operating system monopoly. Browsers represented the most significant vehicle for the distribution of Java technology to end users. Microsoft recognized that the widespread use of browsers could increase the distribution and use of Java and hence threaten Microsoft's operating system monopoly.
- A browser was itself a "platform" to which many applications were being written. Instead of writing software to run on Windows, software developers could write to the browser platform. Since the browser would run on any operating system, software applications would be decoupled from the operating system. PC companies thus could use other operating systems on their computers.

The DOJ presented documents and e-mail messages indicating that Microsoft regarded Java as a key threat. A Microsoft document said that it was a "strategic objective" for Microsoft to "kill cross-platform Java" by expanding the "polluted Java market"—Microsoft's altered version of Java. A senior Microsoft executive identified Java as "our major threat" in an e-mail and added that Netscape's Internet browser was Java's "major distribution vehicle."

MICROSOFT'S ALLEGED RESPONSE TO THE THREAT

Microsoft embarked on an extensive campaign to market and distribute its own browser, Internet Explorer (IE). Microsoft executives had described this campaign as a "jihad" to win the "browser war." The DOJ acknowledged that continued competition on the merits between Navigator and Internet Explorer would result in greater innovation and the development of better products at lower prices. The DOJ alleged, however, that Microsoft was unwilling to compete on the merits. The DOJ cited Microsoft's Christian Wildfeuer writing in February 1997 that Microsoft concluded that it would "be very hard to increase browser share on the merits of IE four alone. It will be more important to leverage the OS asset to make people use IE instead of Navigator."

The DOJ alleged that Microsoft engaged in anticompetitive conduct to halt this threat.

- One measure was to develop a polluted version of Java that would run on the Windows OS but not on other operating systems. This could force a recoupling of software applications to Windows.
- A second step was to bundle IE with Windows and provide it free. To bundle IE with Windows, Microsoft removed IE from the Add/Delete menu so that neither PC manufacturers nor users could delete it.
- The DOJ argued that providing IE at no additional cost to PC manufacturers that preloaded Windows or to users who purchased Windows constituted predatory pricing. The alleged intent was to drive Netscape, which charged $10–$15 to PC manufacturers who preloaded it, out of the market. Netscape was forced to provide Navigator for free, eliminating much of its revenue.
- The DOJ also alleged that giving away IE for free represented illegal leveraging from its operating system monopoly in an attempt to monopolize the browser market.
- The DOJ alleged that Microsoft provided discounts to PC manufacturers that agreed not to preload Navigator. Microsoft was said to "take $7.50 off the unit price of Windows if PC makers agree to carry a 'Windows' logo on their machines and submit to certification by Microsoft's labs."[82] Microsoft maintained that price discounts to PC makers were not favoritism to reward them for not carrying rival products but instead were volume discounts.
- Microsoft's contracts with PC manufacturers were alleged to be exclusionary. While not prohibiting PC manufacturers from preloading Navigator, the contracts were written to discourage the use of rival products. Contracts restricted the ability of PC manufacturers to modify the start-up sequence and desktop. Microsoft also allegedly required PC manufacturers to favor its products and threatened to terminate their license to use Windows if they failed to do so. The DOJ produced documents from Compaq and depositions of its executives indicating that Compaq might have taken the Netscape Navigator icon

off its desktops and chosen Internet Explorer because of fear of retaliation by Microsoft. Microsoft pointed to depositions by Compaq executives stating that Microsoft had never objected to the Navigator icon appearing on the desktop. Microsoft had objected when Compaq planned to delete the Internet Explorer icon.
- Microsoft was alleged to have illegally tied IE to Windows by not giving original equipment manufacturers (OEMs) and consumers the opportunity to purchase one without the other. Tying occurs when a firm conditions the purchase (or license) of one product on the purchase (or license) of another product. Pro-competitive reasons for tying include cost savings and quality control (it could be easier to identify the source of quality problems with a tied sale than if the products were sold separately). Tying could, however, be an anticompetitive leveraging practice if it foreclosed competition in network markets.
- Microsoft allegedly withheld APIs from software developers that threatened its products.
- Microsoft built incompatibility into its products. For example, when Microsoft's Real Media player was installed, RealNetwork's media player would not work.[83]

MICROSOFT'S DEFENSE

Microsoft challenged the government's witnesses and sought to support its own fundamental line of argument. Microsoft argued that it did not have monopoly power, any apparent monopoly power could quickly be dissipated in a dynamic industry, its behavior and practices were not abusive and were similar to standard practices in the industry, and consumers were not harmed but instead benefited from its practices. As the defendant Microsoft did not have to prove its arguments but instead needed only to raise substantial doubt about the DOJ's allegations.

Microsoft witnesses argued that the relevant market was not operating systems but was much broader and included the Internet and handheld computers, for neither of which Microsoft had a dominant position. Microsoft argued, for example, that it was not a monopolist, since it faced competition from Sun's Java programming language and Internet browsers.

Microsoft argued that if it had monopoly power in operating systems, it would have charged a much higher price for Windows. A government witness countered that all that the price charged for Windows indicated was "that Microsoft is not maximizing its short-run profits."

Many economists viewed pricing IE at zero as economically efficient, since the marginal cost of producing an additional copy of IE was essentially zero. Moreover, consumers benefited from competition in browsers, since improvements in browser quality resulted from the competition. A government witness, however, testified that it would be difficult to determine the exact standard for concluding that a price for Internet Explorer was predatory, but the fact was that Microsoft charged a "zero price" and had spent $100 million a year since 1995 developing IE.

---

[82]*Wall Street Journal*, March 1, 1999.

[83]Microsoft was able to eliminate the source of the incompatibility.

Microsoft executives denied allegations of coercive behavior and argued that consumers benefited from its innovations. Paul Maritz, senior group vice president, testified, "Ironically, the very thing that makes Windows valuable to computer manufacturers, software publishers and customers … is now under attack in this lawsuit. The popularity of Windows, owing entirely to Microsoft's efforts to innovate, evangelize and license the software cheaply to promote wide distribution, is derided as monopoly."

Much of Microsoft's defense was directed at countering the testimony of government witnesses. A considerable portion of that testimony centered on recollections of and notes taken at private meetings between Microsoft and companies such as Apple, Intel, and Netscape. Microsoft witnesses provided different interpretations of what had transpired at the meetings than had the government's witnesses. Paul Maritz, for example, testified that Microsoft opposed Intel's development of software because that software was second-rate and that Microsoft had withheld software support for Intel's MMX microprocessor because of overzealous intellectual property claims by Intel. Maritz also denied that he had ever told an Intel executive that Microsoft would "cut off Netscape's air supply." He also said that Microsoft's reluctance to continue producing software for Apple's Macintosh was due to concerns that Apple might fold.

Microsoft also denied that it had harmed Netscape through exclusive arrangements with and financial incentives to PC makers and Internet service providers. A Microsoft attorney stated, "Whatever those arrangements were, whatever measure of exclusivity they created for a period of time, Netscape was able to gain a substantial number of new users. There was no foreclosure of consumer choice."[84]

A Microsoft executive testified that it had not attempted to undermine Java. The DOJ, however, produced a memo from Bill Gates stating that he was "hardcore about NOT supporting" Java. When the executive tried to explain what Gates meant, the judge abruptly cut him off, stating that it was abundantly clear what Gates meant.

Microsoft's direct testimony was attacked effectively by DOJ lead attorney David Boies. The *Wall Street Journal* wrote, "Microsoft's defense is in disarray and its executives and economist have been battered so badly on the witness stand that the judge has questioned key elements of the Redmond, Wash., software giant's case."[85] The *New York Times* referred to the trial as "a humbling courtroom experience" for Microsoft.[86] *Fortune* said, "We're seeing Microsoft's defense go down in flames."[87] Microsoft countered that the DOJ's attacks amounted to showmanship and that the case would be decided on the facts and the law.

One major faux pas for Microsoft occurred in Senior Vice President James Allchin's testimony. Allchin showed videotape produced by Microsoft that purported to show "performance degradations" in the Windows 98 operating system when Internet Explorer was removed from the system. The videotape

had been produced to challenge the testimony of a government witness that Internet Explorer could be removed from the Windows operating system without any significant performance degradation. The government consultants who reviewed the videotape noticed that the title bar displayed the words "Internet Explorer" even though the Microsoft narrator said it had been removed. Allchin maintained that the computer shown was the one from which its browser had been removed. Two days later Microsoft admitted that the videotape was prepared in a studio and showed a number of different computers to simulate its claims about performance degradation. Microsoft then prepared new videotape that observers said showed that the system without Internet Explorer performed well, although applications requiring a browser, of course, did not work.

DEVELOPMENTS OUTSIDE THE COURTROOM

Two developments occurred during the trial that lent support to Microsoft's argument that the market was constantly changing and monopoly power was a transient phenomenon at most. In November 1998 AOL announced that it would acquire Netscape for $4.2 billion and form an alliance with Sun Microsystems. Microsoft asserted that the deal fundamentally changed the industry's landscape and that it therefore was sufficient grounds for the DOJ to drop the lawsuit. DOJ witnesses such as William Harris, chairman and CEO of Intuit Corporation, stated that they did not view the new alliance as an industry shift that would diminish Microsoft's dominance.

Microsoft also asserted that Linux, a free UNIX operating system, posed a potential threat to Windows because several of Microsoft's chief competitors were writing software to run on it. On March 1, 1999, Oracle, Intel, Dell, and Hewlett-Packard all announced substantial investments in Linux, and IBM announced greater offerings of computers using Linux. Although Linux had several million devotees around the world, it held an insignificant share of the operating system market. A DOJ expert witness firmly rejected the proposition that it threatened Windows: "Whatever role Linux may have, it is not expected to constrain the monopoly power of Microsoft …. If you truly believe this product is going to constrain Microsoft's market share, then run, don't walk, to your broker and sell Microsoft stock short."

REMEDIES

If the court found against Microsoft, the next issue would be which remedies to impose. Many companies in the industry, including rivals of Microsoft, were fearful that the cure imposed could be worse than the disease. The principal fear was that some form of government supervision or oversight of the industry would be imposed that would impede innovation and technological change.

Possible remedies were classified as behavioral or structural. Behavioral remedies sought to eliminate the abusive conduct and exclusionary practices without altering Microsoft's control of the Windows operating system. Structural remedies focused on eliminating Microsoft's Windows operating system monopoly either by breaking up the company or by replicating the source of its power through the creation of clones. Behavioral

[84]*New York Times,* February 28, 1999.

[85]*Wall Street Journal,* February 18, 1999.

[86]*New York Times,* February 28, 1999.

[87]*Fortune,* March 1, 1999.

remedies were favored by those who worried that breaking up Microsoft's monopoly could lead to multiple industry standards that would impede the development of software applications. Many commentators and industry members, however, were skeptical that behavioral remedies would be sufficient to curb Microsoft's alleged monopoly power and abusive conduct. Opposition to behavioral remedies resulted not only from skepticism about their effectiveness but also because such remedies would require supervision or regulatory oversight of the industry. Most industry members and economists feared any supervision or oversight of a dynamic industry with rapid product development and obsolescence.

Most behavioral remedies under discussion focused on breaking Microsoft's hold on PC manufacturers that resulted from its licensing agreements for Windows. A number of PC manufacturers had sought more flexible licensing agreements, and under antitrust scrutiny Microsoft had recently granted some leeway.

Behavioral remedies could include stopping Microsoft from using exclusive contracts prohibiting PC manufacturers from offering other Internet browsers. Another behavioral remedy would be to require Microsoft to publish its "most-favored customer" prices and make those prices available to all OEMs. This would reduce the likelihood that Microsoft could punish an OEM by not offering it a discount available to other OEMs. More generally the court could impose a pricing "transparency" policy under which Microsoft would set fixed prices for its products. A third behavioral remedy would require Microsoft to publish the APIs, or software hooks, required to write software for the Windows operating system. This would address the alleged strategy of releasing APIs in stages or selectively to favored software developers.

In February 1999 the 1,400 member Information Industry Association (IIA), of which Microsoft was a member, presented a report to the DOJ urging it to "seriously consider" structural remedies.[88] The structural remedy preferred by the IIA was to break Microsoft into three standalone companies. One would have the Windows operating system, including the CE and NT systems. Another would have Microsoft's software business, and the third would have its Internet and electronic commerce businesses.

An alternative structural remedy was to break Microsoft into three to five clones, referred to as "Baby Bills," each of which would have Microsoft's source codes for Windows and its other products. A related proposal was to auction the Windows code and brand name to several companies. These remedies would introduce competition and break the alleged monopoly power of Microsoft. The IIA report, however, concluded that this type of remedy could be harmful if it led to multiple technical standards.

THE TRIAL COURT: CONCLUSIONS OF LAW AND FINDINGS OF FACT

On April 3, 2000, Judge Jackson ruled that Microsoft had violated the Sherman Act. Microsoft's conduct was found to have violated the Sherman Act not because of the practices themselves, many of which were standard in the industry, but because they were used by a monopolist to maintain its monopoly. As conclusions of law, he found that the relevant market was "Intel-based PC operating systems" and that Microsoft had a monopoly. The judge concluded that Microsoft's conduct had a "significant exclusionary impact." He also concluded that "middleware [Navigator and Java] threatened to demolish Microsoft's coveted monopoly power" and that Microsoft engaged in a "deliberate assault upon entrepreneurial efforts …." He cited Microsoft's efforts in the OEM channel to stifle innovation, including tactics such as requiring the installation of IE and bundling proprietary software. The former constituted illegal tying of one product with a monopoly product, which he concluded was in effect a per se violation of the Sherman Act. The latter constituted "exclusionary behavior in the IAP [Internet access provider] channel," which also constituted a violation of Section 1 of the Sherman Act.

The judge also concluded that Microsoft's behavior was as a whole "predacious" and cited providing IE for free and offering promotional inducements to bundle it with other offerings. In addition, he concluded that Microsoft used its control of technical information (APIs) to induce Internet service vendors to distribute the so-called "polluted" version of Java. Judge Jackson also found that although Microsoft had used exclusionary contracts, such as inducing Compaq not to distribute Navigator, those contracts "did not ultimately deprive Netscape of the ability to have access to every PC worldwide to offer an opportunity to install Navigator." These exclusive contracts thus were not themselves sufficient to constitute a violation of Section 1.

JUDGE JACKSON'S REMEDIES

At the conclusion of the trial Judge Jackson urged the DOJ and Microsoft to reach a settlement of the case. In a highly unusual move he appointed a distinguished U.S. Court of Appeals judge, Richard Posner, to convene the parties and seek a settlement. Efforts to reach a settlement, however, failed.

On June 7, 2000, Judge Jackson ordered both structural and behavioral remedies in response to his findings that Microsoft had violated the Sherman Act. The remedies largely followed those recommended by the DOJ and the 19 state attorneys general. Jackson's decision was notable in that it took an arguably hostile tone toward the company. He stated that Microsoft was "unwilling to accept the notion that it broke the law" and that it had "proved untrustworthy in the past."

The structural remedy involved breaking Microsoft into two separate companies. One, referred to as "ops," would have Microsoft's operating systems business, including Windows 2000, Windows ME, and Windows CE. The other, referred to as "apps," would have all other lines of business, including software applications (e.g., Microsoft Office, Exchange, IE) and Internet services (e.g., MSN, Hotmail, Expedia, CarPoint). Microsoft was ordered to submit to the court a plan for creating the two companies. The breakup would be complete at the management level with a "firewall" between the two companies.

---

[88]The initial draft reportedly recommended structural remedies, but lobbying by Microsoft led to the wording "seriously consider."

In addition to the structural remedy, Judge Jackson's ruling included a set of behavioral remedies intended to restore viable competition in the operating system and applications markets. The behavioral remedies were to last for 10 years and pertained to Microsoft's conduct with respect to customers and rivals. In response to allegations that Microsoft had illegally tied IE to the Windows operating system, Judge Jackson ruled that Microsoft must allow OEMs to remove any applications from the operating system. OEMs could modify the start-up sequence and desktop, including removing Microsoft icons, and would be given 30 days' notice before Microsoft could terminate a Windows license. Microsoft would have to license operating systems products under uniform conditions with the exceptions of volume discounts. Microsoft would be prohibited from interfering with any non-Microsoft middleware, discriminating against a hardware or software company for using non-Microsoft products, favoring Microsoft over non-Microsoft products, or linking licenses to the use of Microsoft products. Microsoft would also be required to continue to offer the previous version of its Windows OS when it introduced a new version. This was intended to limit Microsoft's ability to force migration.

To ensure the "interoperability" of software and hardware, Judge Jackson ordered Microsoft to allow hardware, software, and computer makers access to technical information and developers to view the "relevant necessary portions" of code. This included all APIs and portions of the OS code. The APIs and code would be available only in a "secure facility."

THE COURT OF APPEALS DECISION

Microsoft appealed the decision and in its appeal attacked the conduct of Judge Jackson for statements made outside of the courtroom. Microsoft asked that he be removed from the case. On June 28, 2001, the U.S. Court of Appeals issued a unanimous decision affirming some of the trial court's conclusions, vacating some of its orders, and remanding some to a different district court for resolution.

In its most important ruling the Court of Appeals vacated the order breaking Microsoft into two separate companies. In doing so the Court observed that divestiture had traditionally been reserved for firms that had grown through acquisition and merger, but the Court left the door open for a divestiture order. The District Court was ordered to reconsider the appropriateness of divestiture and whether there was a sufficient relationship between the maintenance of monopoly and the illegal conduct to warrant the full structural remedy of divestiture. The Court of Appeals also ordered the district court to hold full evidentiary hearings on appropriate remedies.

The Court of Appeals concurred with Judge Jackson's conclusion about monopoly power: "We uphold the District Court's finding of monopoly power in its entirety." This conclusion was important not only for the present case, but also because in private antitrust cases the plaintiffs would not have the burden of proving that Microsoft had monopoly power.

The Court of Appeals concurred that Microsoft's conduct violated the Sherman Act. First, its license restrictions on OEMs were found to be anticompetitive. Second, the exclusion of IE from the Add/Remove program of Windows so that a user could not remove IE was found to be a violation of Section 2. The Court stated, "Microsoft failed to meet its burden of showing that its conduct serves a purpose other than protecting its operating system monopoly." The Court also held that Microsoft developed a polluted version of Java that would run only on Windows, and this "conduct is exclusionary, in violation of Section 2 of the Sherman Act."

The Court of Appeals reversed without remand Judge Jackson's conclusion that Microsoft attempted to monopolize the browser market. The Court stated that the Department of Justice had not properly defined the relevant market nor established that there were barriers to entry.

Judge Jackson had concluded that the tying or bundling of IE with Windows was in effect a per se violation of Section 1 of the Sherman Act. The Court of Appeals, however, concluded that per se analysis was inappropriate and remanded the issue to the District Court to be considered under a rule of reason.

The Court of Appeals also strongly criticized the conduct of Judge Jackson and disqualified him from the case. The court found "no evidence of actual bias" but concluded that "the trial judge engaged in impermissible ex parte contacts by holding secret interviews with members of the media and made numerous offensive comments about Microsoft officials in public statements outside the courtroom, giving rise to an appearance of partiality." Consequently, the court vacated the remedies ordered by Judge Jackson and on remand assigned the case to a different trial judge to be assigned by random draw. The new judge would determine the remedies.

The headline of the front page article of the *Wall Street Journal* on the day after the Court of Appeals decision was "With Its Old Playbook, Microsoft Is Muscling into New Web Markets: Using Aggressive Bundling, It Roils High-Tech World with Windows Overhaul."

THE SETTLEMENT AND NEXT STAGE

Claiming victory, the DOJ did not appeal the decision. Microsoft, however, appealed the decision and Judge Jackson's findings of fact, but the Supreme Court refused to consider the appeal. Faced with a complex and potentially lengthy case dealing both with tying and remedies, District Court Judge Colleen Kollar-Kotelly appointed a mediator to attempt to settle the case. In November the DOJ and Microsoft reached a settlement. The state attorneys general engaged in brief negotiations with Microsoft, obtaining some potentially important changes in the settlement. In a highly unusual development, however, nine state attorneys general refused to accept the settlement. Thomas F. Reilly, attorney general of Massachusetts, said, "There is no question in my mind that Microsoft will use this agreement to crush the competition, and they will have the imprimatur of the U.S. government to do it."[89] Kelly Jo MacArthur, general counsel for RealNetworks, said, "This is a reward, not a remedy. This agreement allows a declared illegal monopolist to determine, at its sole discretion, what goes into the monopoly operating system in the future."[90] She

---

[89]*New York Times*, November 6, 2001.
[90]*Wall Street Journal*, November 5, 2001.

was referring to Microsoft integrating its Media Player into Windows XP, in effect giving it away for free just as IE had been integrated into Windows without charge. Scott McNealy, CEO of Sun Microsystems, asked, "Does anyone think this settlement is going to change Microsoft's behavior? These guys are unfettered."[91] Michael Morris, senior vice president and general counsel of Sun Microsystems, said, "I think everybody who isn't a Microsoft vassal understands, and has been saying, this is the most bizarre, pointless, ridiculous antitrust settlement that anyone could have possibly imagined. It doesn't even pass the red face test."[92] In a more dispassionate statement professor David Yoffie and research associate Mary Kwak, co-authors of *Judo Strategy,* referred to the settlement as "a spectacular victory for Microsoft."

Microsoft chairman Bill Gates said the case had "a profound impact on me personally and on our company" and "we will focus more on how our activities affect other companies." He added, "While the settlement goes farther than we might have wanted, we believe that settling this case now is the right thing to do to help the industry, and the economy, to move forward."[93] CEO Steve Ballmer observed that during the lawsuit "our industry didn't rise to support us the way we might have supposed as an industry leader."[94] Bill Gates said that Microsoft was "committed to becoming a better industry leader."

U.S. assistant attorney general Charles A. James, who headed the antitrust division of the DOJ and negotiated the settlement, said, "The settlement will promote innovation, give consumers choice and provide computer manufacturers and the industry with more certainty as they go forward in marketing their products. This consent decree will remedy the problems that were caused by Microsoft's unlawful conduct, prevent the recurrence of those problems and restore competition in the software industry."[95] Observers speculated that Mr. James was eager to settle the case to remove uncertainty from the economy in the wake of the September 11 terrorist attacks.

The terms of the settlement were as follows:

- Microsoft can integrate any product into Windows.
- PC makers can hide any Microsoft feature, and Microsoft cannot restrict or retaliate against any PC maker that installs non-Microsoft software.
- Microsoft must license Windows on the same terms to all PC makers and must publish its prices on a Web site.
- Microsoft must share certain technical information for middleware, both for desktop systems and server software

for the Internet, with software developers. Microsoft retains all intellectual property rights but must license that property to allow PC makers and software developers to exercise their rights under the agreement. Microsoft cannot retaliate against any software developer.

- Microsoft must appoint an internal compliance officer to ensure that its executives and board members understand the terms of the settlement.
- A three-person technical committee, with one member appointed by Microsoft, one by the DOJ, and one by agreement of both parties, was established to determine which parts of the software code need to be released to competitors, to monitor compliance, and to hear complaints. The committee has no enforcement authority but can inform Microsoft and the courts of serious complaints, possibly leading to a court enforcement hearing.
- The consent decree extended for 5 years, and if Microsoft willfully and systematically violated the terms, it would extend for an additional 2 years.

Judge Kollar-Kotelly set two tracks for the case. On the first track, under the Tunney Act a 90-day review period began in which the judge must decide if the settlement is in the public interest. The public and the parties in the case could make comments. In this track the DOJ and Microsoft would be on the same side in defending the settlement. On the second track to resolve the case pursued by the nine remaining states, the judge scheduled hearings on remedies to begin March 11, 2002.

In 2002 both Sun Microsystems and Netscape/AOL filed private antitrust lawsuits against Microsoft. ∎

Preparation Questions

1. Should the DOJ have brought an antitrust case against Microsoft?
2. Does the evidence indicate that Microsoft violated the Sherman Act?
3. Did Microsoft's conduct benefit consumers?
4. Were Judge Jackson's remedies appropriate? Should a structural remedy be used?
5. Were the terms of the settlement appropriate? Sufficient?
6. What, if anything, should be done with Microsoft's operating system monopoly and its dominance in other software applications?

[91]*New York Times,* November 5, 2001.
[92]*San Jose Mercury News,* November 3, 2001.
[93]*New York Times,* November 3, 2001.
[94]*Wall Street Journal,* November 5, 2001.
[95]*New York Times,* November 5, 2001.

10

REGULATION: LAW, ECONOMICS, AND POLITICS

INTRODUCTION

Markets and property rights are the centerpieces of the free enterprise system. Markets allow people to exchange goods and services, and property rights allow them to gain from trade. Markets also provide information by establishing prices that reflect the cost of society's resources used to produce goods and services. Under some conditions, however, markets may not function efficiently, inhibiting gains from trade. When there are market imperfections, government intervention in markets could improve their efficiency. This intervention can be the responsibility of the judiciary, as in the case of antitrust law enforced through the courts, or it can be the responsibility of regulatory agencies responsible for particular markets or imperfections. Regulation is government intervention in economic activity using commands, controls, and incentives. Both regulation and judicial enforcement are based on legislatively enacted statutes. This means that regulation can be used for purposes other than making markets more efficient. Regulation is thus a political as well as an economic instrument.

Regulation takes place through a public process that is relatively open and allows participation by interested parties. In contrast to antitrust, regulation is not implemented through judicial institutions but instead by independent commissions and agencies of the executive branch. The courts, however, have played an important role in interpreting regulatory statutes, assessing their constitutionality, and ensuring that regulatory decisions satisfy due process requirements.

Regulatory decisions and rule-making proceedings are extremely important to many firms, industries, and interest groups. Kerwin (1994, p. 194) reported a survey of 180 interest groups that found that two-thirds of the groups saw participation in regulatory rule making as at least as important as lobbying Congress.

Regulation includes a broad set of interventions:

- Controlling prices (retail electric power, local telephone service)
- Setting price floors (crops, minimum wages)
- Ensuring equal opportunity (banning discrimination in employment)
- Regularizing employment practices (overtime)
- Specifying qualifications (occupational licensure)
- Providing for solvency (financial institutions, insurance, pension plans)
- Controlling the number of market participants (broadcast licenses, taxi medallions)
- Limiting ownership (media, airlines)
- Requiring premarketing approval (toxic chemicals, pharmaceuticals)
- Ensuring product safety (pharmaceuticals, toys, food)
- Mandating product characteristics and technology (automobile safety standards)
- Establishing service territories (local telephone service)
- Establishing performance standards (automobile emissions standards)
- Controlling toxic emissions and other pollutants (sulfur dioxide emissions trading)
- Specifying industry boundaries (insurance, banking)
- Allocating public resources (spectrum allocations)
- Establishing technical standards (telecommunications interconnections)
- Controlling unfair international trade practices (antidumping)
- Mandating disclosure and restricting terms (credit cards)
- Providing information (labeling)
- Rationing common pool resources (fisheries)
- Protecting consumers (credit regulation)
- Controlling risks (equity in derivatives)

As this list indicates, regulation is a broad subject and often specific to particular industries, products, and conditions. The focus of this chapter is the nature of regulation. Two principal perspectives are considered—one based on the correction of market imperfections and the other based on the political economy of regulation. The institutional focus is on regulation administered by government agencies and commissions with applications to electric power and the use of auctions. Financial market regulation is considered in Chapter 11, environmental regulation in Chapter 12, renewable power incentives and regulation in Chapter 13, and the regulation of international trade in Chapter 19.

The next section identifies periods of regulatory activity in the United States, and the following section considers the constitutional basis for regulation. Regulatory agencies and the regulatory process are then discussed. The nonmarket environment of regulatory agencies is considered with an emphasis on external influences on agencies. The economic rationale for correcting market imperfections is presented, including natural monopoly, externalities, public goods, asymmetric information, and moral hazard. The broader political economy of regulation is then considered along with the distributive objectives of regulation. The chapter concludes with an analysis of deregulation in the electric power industry.

PERIODS OF REGULATORY CHANGE

The United States has experienced four major periods of regulatory change. The first occurred during the populist era of the late 1800s as a result of nonmarket action by interest groups. Farmers succeeded in establishing regulatory bodies at the state level to control the market power of grain elevators and railroads. This was extended to the federal level with the passage of the Interstate Commerce Act in 1887, which established the Interstate Commerce Commission (ICC) with the authority to regulate railroad rates. In the same tradition, legislation was enacted early in the twentieth century to shore up regulatory and antitrust powers that had been narrowly construed by the courts.[1]

The second period was the progressive era and the New Deal. Regulation was extended to labor markets and to industries, including electric power, food, pharmaceuticals, trucking, air transport, securities, and communications. Much of this regulation was industry specific and focused on pricing, entry, and conditions of service.

The third period, which began in the 1960s and accelerated in the 1970s, brought social regulation. In contrast to the earlier regulation that focused on the economic regulation of industries, social regulation addressed externalities and hazards. Regulation was extended to consumer products, the environment, and the workplace. The new social regulation differed substantially from the regulation of earlier periods, since it cut across industries. This changed the nature of the politics of regulation. In economic regulation, the politics had been dominated by industry interests, as when the railroads used ICC regulation to limit competition from the emerging interstate trucking industry. The new social regulation brought to the politics of regulation a new set of interest groups, including safety and health activists and environmentalists.

The fourth period brought economic deregulation to several industries, including electric power, natural gas transmission, telecommunications, air transport, and surface transportation. Public policy analysts, regulators, and executive branch officials recognized that instead of keeping prices low, regulation often led to higher costs and higher prices. Beginning in the 1970s several regulatory systems were dismantled, and market forces were substituted to improve economic efficiency. In some industries, such as electric power and telecommunications, economic regulation has steadily been replaced by market competition. The deregulation movement also led to the substitution of market-like mechanisms, such as auctions and the trading of pollution permits, for regulatory control and allocation procedures. On January 1, 1996, the first federal regulatory agency, the Interstate Commerce Commission, closed its doors.

The past five decades have witnessed two quite different regulatory movements. The social regulation that began during the 1960s has expanded at the same time as deregulation has occurred in a number of industries. Although few regulatory agencies have been created in recent years, the authority of some existing social regulatory agencies such as the Environmental

---

[1]See McCraw (1981) for the history of regulation. The Sherman Antitrust Act was enacted in the same era.

Protection Agency has expanded. Economic regulation has moved in the other direction as markets and competition have been substituted for government controls. These two movements have come together as market-like mechanisms have been substituted for some social regulation, as in the case of the trading of pollution allowances considered in Chapter 12.

THE CONSTITUTIONAL BASIS FOR REGULATION

Government regulation can be traced to the 1100s when the English monarchy began to contract with private parties for the provision of services. The monarchy granted rights-of-way to stage lines and in return retained the authority to regulate services and prices. Private property committed to a public use thus became subject to government controls. This contractual relationship between the state and a firm provided the basis for the evolution of regulatory authority through the common law (considered in Chapter 14).

The U.S. Constitution not only provides the authority for regulation but also limits its application. Section 8 of Article I of the Constitution gives Congress the power "To regulate Commerce … among the several States …." The Fifth Amendment to the Constitution limits this power by stating, "No person shall be deprived of life, liberty, or property, without due process of law; nor shall private property be taken for public use without just compensation." The Fourteenth Amendment extends the due process protection to actions taken by the states.

Many of the legal principles of regulation in the United States have come from court decisions that draw on the common law. The common law doctrine that private property committed to a public use could be regulated was extended to property that was "affected with a public interest." In *Munn v. Illinois,* 94 U.S. 113 (1877), the Supreme Court upheld an Illinois statute regulating the prices charged by grain elevators, which in the state constitution had been declared "public warehouses." The court cited the English common law principle that when "affected with a public interest, [private property] ceases to be *juris privati* only …. Property does become clothed with a public interest when used in a manner to make it of public consequence, and affect the community at large. When, therefore, one devotes his property to a use in which the public has an interest, he, in effect, grants to the public an interest in that use, and must submit to be controlled by the public for the common good …." In this sweeping statement, the court established the government's right to regulate private property. However, the court went on to warn: "We know that this is a power which may be abused; but there is no argument against its existence. For protection against abuses by the legislatures the people must resort to the polls, not to the courts." In upholding minimum price regulation of milk sold in grocery stores, the Supreme Court in *Nebbia v. New York,* 291 U.S. 502 (1934) ruled that the same principle applied to enterprises not affected with a public interest. The government's authority to regulate is thus extremely broad.

The Fifth and Fourteenth Amendments, however, place limits on regulation.[2] In *Smith v. Ames,* 169 U.S. 466 (1898), the Supreme Court held that "What a company is entitled to ask is a fair return upon the value of that which it employs for the public convenience."[3] This established the right of public utilities to obtain a fair return on their capital and led to cost-of-service regulation. The due process provisions of the Constitution are also important factors in structuring regulatory processes, as considered later in the chapter.

REGULATORY COMMISSIONS AND AGENCIES

The principal federal regulatory agencies are listed in Figure 10-1. Regulatory agencies are of two basic forms—independent commissions and executive branch agencies. Independent commissions include the Federal Communications Commission, Federal Trade Commission, Federal Reserve System, International Trade Commission, Federal Energy Regulatory Commission, Securities and Exchange Commission, National Labor Relations Board, Consumer Products Safety Commission, and Nuclear Regulatory Commission. The Federal Communications Commission, for example, has five commissioners appointed by the president and confirmed by the Senate. They serve 5-year terms, and no more than three commissioners may be from the

---

[2]The "takings" clause in the Fifth Amendment has been the subject of political and legal activity intended to require public compensation for the loss of value due to regulations such as zoning and environmental protection.
[3]See also *Federal Power Commission et al. v. Hope Natural Gas Co.,* 320 U.S. 591 (1944).

FIGURE 10-1 Principal Federal Regulatory Agencies and Commissions

Federal Reserve System (1913)
Federal Trade Commission (1914)
International Trade Commission (1916) (formerly the Tariff Commission)—considered in Chapter 19
Federal Energy Regulatory Commission (1930) (formerly the Federal Power Commission)
Food and Drug Administration (1931) [HHS]
Securities and Exchange Commission (1934)
Federal Communications Commission (1934)
National Labor Relations Board (1935)
Federal Aviation Administration (1948) [DOT]
Federal Maritime Commission [1961]
Equal Employment Opportunity Commission (1965)—considered in Chapter 22
Environmental Protection Agency (1970)—considered in Chapter 12
National Highway Traffic Safety Administration (1970) [DOT]
Consumer Product Safety Commission (1972)
Occupational Safety and Health Administration (1973) [DOL]
Nuclear Regulatory Commission (1975) (formerly the Atomic Energy Commission)
Consumer Financial Protection Bureau (2011)

Source: Congressional Quarterly, *Federal Regulatory Directory*, 7th ed., Washington DC, 1994.

Note: The cabinet departments in which agencies are located are shown in brackets.

same political party. Most commissions make decisions through majority-rule voting and formal rule-making procedures.

Agencies typically have a single administrator appointed by the president or a cabinet secretary. Most executive branch regulatory agencies are located in a cabinet department, as in the case of the Federal Aviation Administration, National Highway Traffic Safety Administration (NHTSA), Occupational Health and Safety Administration, and Food and Drug Administration (FDA). The Environmental Protection Agency is an independent executive branch agency not housed in a cabinet department.[4] The Consumer Financial Protection Bureau considered in Chapter 11 is funded by the Board of Governors of the Federal Reserve System.

Most states also have regulatory commissions and agencies. Considerable economic activity such as local telephone and electricity service is regulated by the states and not the federal government. Most states also have regulatory agencies to deal with environmental, occupational safety, and health issues. As indicated in Chapter 12, federal law delegates the implementation of certain federal regulations to the states. States, for example, are responsible for developing implementation plans for achieving clean air standards.

DELEGATION, RULE MAKING, DUE PROCESS, AND DISCRETION

Article I, Section 1 of the Constitution grants Congress the sole power to enact laws. It does not authorize Congress to delegate policymaking to agencies. Yet regulatory agencies promulgate rules, establish policies, and resolve disputes. Prior to 1935 courts held that the delegatee was simply making a determination in the implementation of a law enacted by Congress. In 1935 the Supreme Court overturned as unconstitutional two delegation provisions of the National Industrial Recovery Act. Since then, the courts have not overturned a congressional delegation.[5] Instead, the courts have sought to ensure that the exercise of any delegated authority is consistent with the constitutional protections of the Fifth and Fourteenth Amendments and the common law doctrine of consistency.

Congress also was concerned about the exercise of agency powers and enacted the Administrative Procedure Act (APA) of 1946 to provide for public notice and comment prior to agency action. Agencies also adopt their own rule-making procedures in a manner consistent with the APA. Under the APA, agencies can use either a formal or an informal rule-making

---

[4]For a description of the regulatory agencies, see Congressional Quarterly (2009).
[5]See Mashaw and Merrill (1985, pp. 2–5).

process.[6] The informal model of rule making requires publishing in the *Federal Register* a Notice of Proposed Rule Making (NPRM) and a request for the submission of comments. The agency may also hold public hearings on the proposed rule. The agency next reviews the comments received, revises the rule, and publishes it in the *Federal Register* with an effective date at least 30 days in the future. Under the formal model, the agency employs a quasi-judicial process involving hearings conducted by an administrative law judge, the presentation of evidence, and the cross-examination of witnesses. A formal record of the proceedings is kept and may be reviewed by the courts. Appearances may be made and testimony given by any interested party. The authorizing statutes of some agencies also prescribe public hearings for certain types of actions. Under this model, the agencies are restricted by ex parte rules against having contacts with interested parties outside the proceedings.[7]

The APA grants parties the right to sue for judicial review of an agency action. One basis for that review is the failure to follow the procedures required for an action. This is review under the framework of *procedural due process*. If an agency fails to follow APA procedures or procedures it has established, the courts can overturn the agency's decision.

The courts also review regulatory actions for whether they are *arbitrary* or *capricious*. The basic concerns are whether an action exceeds the scope of the mandate of the regulatory agency and whether it has a basis in the record of evidence the agency has.[8] The APA [Section 706(2) (A)] requires that agency actions not be "arbitrary, capricious, an abuse of discretion, or otherwise not in accordance with law." An important procedural due process decision pertained to the bases for changing a regulatory rule. NHTSA began rule-making proceedings on air bags in 1967. In 1977, the first year of the Carter administration, it promulgated a rule requiring new automobiles to be equipped with a passive restraint system—either an air bag or automatic seat belts. The Reagan administration opposed the rule, and the new administrator of NHTSA revoked it in October 1981. The revocation was based not on new information but rather on a reevaluation of the previous record. The administrator concluded that because auto manufacturers planned to use seat belt systems that were easily detachable, the benefits from the rule would not justify the costs. The insurance industry, one of the principal interest groups that had worked for the passive restraint rule, filed a lawsuit challenging the revocation, and the case reached the Supreme Court.[9] The court ruled that the revocation was arbitrary and capricious because NHTSA had failed to develop new evidence to justify a change in the rule.[10]

The courts also review regulatory actions for *substantive due process* when there is a constitutional issue present. Regulatory decisions thus are required to bear a relationship to a proper public purpose under the Constitution. In *Nebbia,* the Supreme Court stated:

> So far as the requirement of due process is concerned, and in the absence of other constitutional restriction, a state is free to adopt whatever economic policy may reasonably be deemed to promote public welfare, and to enforce that policy by legislation adapted to its purpose …. If the laws passed are seen to have a reasonable relation to a proper legislative purpose, and are neither arbitrary nor discriminatory, the requirements of due process are satisfied …. With the wisdom of the policy adopted, with the adequacy or practicality of the law enacted to forward it, the courts are both incompetent and unauthorized to deal.

The courts have traditionally been reluctant to substitute their judgments for those of a legislature.[11]

Rule making is the most important activity of most regulatory agencies. Agencies must follow the procedures specified in the APA and in their authorizing statutes. Interested parties not only participate in both formal and informal rule-making proceedings, but they also

---

[6]See Kerwin and Furlong (2010), and Breyer (1982, pp. 378–381). Magat, Krupnick, and Harrington (1986) and Owen and Braeutigam (1978) consider the administrative processes of regulation.

[7]See Mashaw and Merrill (1985, pp. 470–476).

[8]See Mashaw and Merrill (1985, pp. 318–385).

[9]*Motor Vehicles Manufacturers Assn. v. State Farm Insurance Co.,* 463 U.S. 29 (1983).

[10]For the majority, Justice Byron R. White wrote, "We have frequently reiterated that an agency must cogently explain why it has exercised its discretion in a given manner, and we affirm this principle again today." See Mashaw and Merrill (1985, pp. 343–354).

[11]See Edley (1990) for a treatment of administrative law and judicial review.

attempt to influence agency actions outside those proceedings. Contacts with firms and other interests generally must be disclosed in advance through ex parte notification requirements, which contributes to the relative openness of regulatory processes. Lobbying and other forms of information provision are the principal approaches to influencing agency decisions in addition to participation in formal rule-making procedures.

THE NONMARKET ENVIRONMENT OF REGULATORY AGENCIES

Regulatory agencies operate in a complex environment, and even "independent" regulatory commissions are subject to a variety of influences, as illustrated in Figure 10-2. Commissioners and administrators of regulatory agencies are appointed by the president, and most require Senate confirmation. The appointment of regulators can have an important impact on regulatory policy and practice, as the discussion of the deregulation of the airline industry in Chapter 1 indicates. When President Carter sought to deregulate the surface transportation industries, he needed a majority of pro-deregulation commissioners on the ICC. When his appointment of the chairman gave the pro-deregulation side a 4–3 majority, with four seats vacant, he chose not to fill the vacancies. The ICC then began to deregulate. The executive branch can also influence regulatory commissions through the policy expertise of cabinet agencies. The president thus has a number of instruments to influence regulatory agencies, particularly those in the executive branch.

The president also exercises considerable influence through the review of regulations. President Carter issued an executive order requiring analysis of all new regulations and established the Regulatory Analysis Review Group to review those analyses. Shortly after taking office, President Reagan issued Executive Order 12291, which required that "regulatory action shall not be undertaken unless the potential benefits to society from the regulation outweigh the potential costs to society." The order required regulatory agencies to prepare a Regulatory Impact Analysis for any proposed rule.[12] The Office of Management and Budget (OMB) reviewed the agencies' analyses and could request changes. The order was an important tool in the Reagan and George H. W. Bush administrations' efforts to limit regulation. When he took office, President Clinton modified President Reagan's order by restricting the reviews by OMB's Office of Information and Regulatory Affairs (OIRA) to "significant" regulations and by requiring that OMB take into account "qualitative" as well as quantitative measures of costs and benefits. OMB estimated that the benefits from the regulations reviewed by OMB ranged from $96 billion

FIGURE 10-2   Influences on Regulatory Agencies

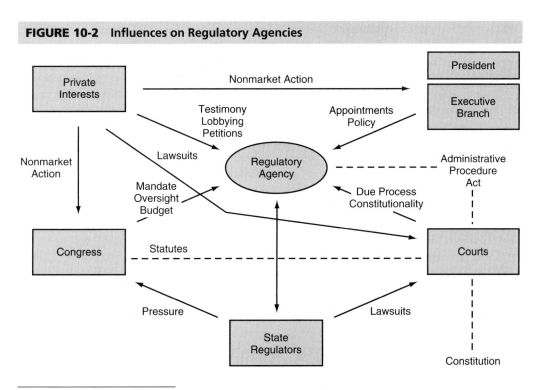

---

[12]See Weidenbaum (2004, p. 171).

EXAMPLE   Regulatory Rule Making in the Bush Administration

The George W. Bush administration set out to make regulation less burdensome and to apply better data and science to the analysis of regulatory rules. The Data Quality Act required regulatory agencies to set standards for the quality of their scientific studies, including the quality not only of the data but also of the analysis of the data. OIRA played the lead role in the evaluation of proposed new rules and modification of existing rules.

As examples of the changes, the Bush administration relaxed costly requirements for hospital emergency rooms that had led a number of hospitals to close their emergency rooms. At the urging of the U.S. Conference of Mayors, the EPA revised brownfields regulations to allow the sale of contaminated sites to private parties that would assume cleanup responsibilities. In response to a surge in lawsuits pertaining to eligibility for overtime pay, the administration put into place new rules under the Fair Labor Standards Act that required mandatory overtime for an additional 1.3 million workers but allowed employers to decide whether employees earning between $23,660 and $100,000 were administrators and hence not eligible for overtime. Unions claimed that this threatened the overtime pay of 6 million workers. Under the Clean Air Act the EPA proposed a system of tradable mercury permits to achieve reductions in mercury pollution.[1] New rules issued under the Endangered Species Act counted hatchery-raised salmon as well as wild salmon in determining whether a species was endangered. Following complaints by the governors of western states, the administration revised rules issued in the final days of the Clinton administration prohibiting logging and other activities in "roadless areas" of national forests. Under the new rules governors of states could ask the Forest Service for permission to authorize logging.

---

[1]Tradable permit systems are considered in Chapter 12.

---

to $484 billion and the costs ranged from $40 billion to $46 billion.[13] The influence of the president on specific rules is indicated by the example.

Congress exercises considerable influence over regulatory agencies through its budgetary and oversight authority. Congressional influence also comes from its ability to revise and block changes in statutes. The Reagan administration attempted to deregulate in the area of social regulation, but the congressional oversight committees with responsibilities over the regulatory agencies joined with interest groups to oppose those efforts. For example, the Reagan administration sought to eliminate the Consumer Products Safety Commission (CPSC), but Congress refused.

Congress has power over regulatory agencies because it writes their legislative mandates and reauthorizes those agencies whose statutes require it. In contrast to the statutes establishing economic regulation that use broad terms such as "the public interest," the statutes establishing social regulation often have very detailed language. For example, the reauthorization bill passed in 1990 required the CPSC to establish safety standards for automatic garage door openers.[14] Congress also can include provisions in budget appropriations bills that prevent regulatory agencies from spending any funds on particular programs or regulatory initiatives. For example, in the 1990s Congress prohibited the Department of Energy from spending on any new rule making on energy efficiency standards.

Congress and its committees also provide oversight of regulatory agencies and can pressure regulators through oversight hearings in which regulators can be called to task for their actions. Members of Congress also frequently call or write regulatory agencies asking for explanations of agency actions. The agencies always answer.

Federal regulatory agencies can also be influenced by state regulatory agencies. The National Association of [state] Regulatory Utility Commissions strongly criticized Congress for imposing a moratorium on new energy efficiency standards. State regulatory commissions also make their interests known to their state's congressional delegation and may file lawsuits against federal regulatory agencies.

Private interests affect regulatory agencies directly through their participation in hearings and other regulatory proceedings and indirectly through pressure on Congress and the executive branch. The statutes for some regulatory agencies give citizens rights to petition for action. Private interests also lobby regulatory agencies, although ex parte contracts with regulators must be disclosed in advance. Private interests also often take their cases to the courts. Activists file lawsuits to force regulators to enforce what the activists see as the agency's mandate. Firms frequently appeal regulatory decisions. Fox Television successfully appealed an FCC order blocking the acquisition of local television stations. The courts have a considerable influence on

---

[13]OMB, Report to Congress on the Costs and Benefits of Federal Regulations, March 12, 2007.
[14]*Congressional Quarterly Weekly Report,* October 27, 1990.

regulation, reviewing regulatory actions for constitutionality and for consistency with statutes. As considered in Chapter 12, many of the rules promulgated by the EPA are appealed.

EXPLANATIONS FOR REGULATION

Two theories have been offered to explain where regulation is and is not imposed. The first is the theory of market failures or imperfections, which predicts that regulation will be instituted to correct market imperfections. The second political economy theory predicts that regulation is provident in response to pressure from interest groups. The regulation of the prices charged by grain elevators that gave rise to *Munn v. Illinois* allowed farmers, rather than grain elevators, to capture the profits from the sale of their crops. The same interests were important in the passage of the Interstate Commerce Act and the Sherman Antitrust Act. The market imperfections perspective is grounded in economic theory, and the next section examines five types of market imperfections: natural monopoly, externalities, public goods, asymmetric information, and moral hazard.[15] The following section then considers political economy explanations for regulation.

MARKET IMPERFECTIONS

Natural Monopoly

A monopoly is natural if one firm can produce a given set of goods at lower cost than can any larger number of firms. A *natural monopoly* results when costs are decreasing in the scale of output or in the scope of the set of goods a firm produces. The classical theory of natural monopoly predicts that a monopolist will restrict its output, raising its price above marginal cost. The restriction of output causes economic inefficiency because some consumers who are willing to pay the cost of the resources required to satisfy their demand are prevented from doing so by the restricted output and higher prices. This inefficiency is referred to as a *deadweight loss* (DWL), since an opportunity to achieve economic gains is forgone.

The case of a monopoly is illustrated in Figure 10-3, which presents a demand curve (*D*) and the monopolist's average cost (*AC*) and marginal cost (*MC*) curves. The marginal and

FIGURE 10-3 Monopoly and Deadweight Loss

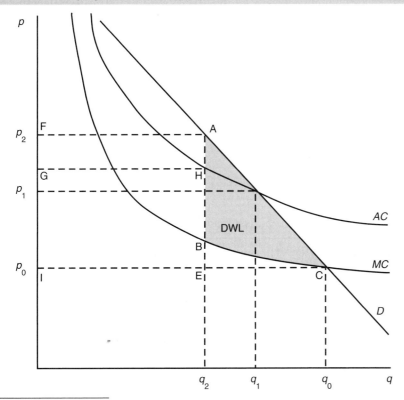

[15]See Breyer (1982, Ch. 1), Spulber (1989), and Viscusi, Vernon, and Harrington (2005) for discussions of the nature of market imperfections.

average cost curves are decreasing because of economies of scale. A monopolist exercises its market power by restricting its output to the point q_2 at which marginal revenue (not shown) equals marginal cost, resulting in a price p_2 that is above average and marginal costs. The profit of the firm is the difference between the price p_2 and average cost multiplied by the quantity q_2; that is, profit is the area FAHG. *Consumer surplus* is the area under the demand curve above the price p_2. A deadweight loss results because there are consumers who are willing to purchase the product at a price lower than p_2 but above the marginal cost of producing it. These units are the difference between q_0 and q_2, and the deadweight loss is the shaded area ABC.

In the case of a natural monopoly, economic theory recommends that government set price equal to marginal cost, or p_0, so that all consumers who are willing to pay the incremental cost of the resources expended to satisfy their demand will purchase the good. Lowering the price to p_0 has two effects. The first is the elimination of the deadweight loss because output expands from q_2 to q_0. The second is a pure transfer from the firm to consumers consisting of the profit FAHG and the area GHEI, which represents a gain in consumer surplus and a loss of profit from lowering the price from p_2 to p_0.

In the presence of decreasing costs, however, pricing at marginal cost does not provide sufficient revenue to cover the total cost of the firm. Total costs could be covered by a government subsidy financed by taxes. This alternative is generally opposed, however, because taxes distort the activity on which they are levied and subsidies weaken the incentives of the monopolist to be responsive to consumer demands. Consequently, either regulated prices are set equal to average costs, denoted p_1 in Figure 10-3, or costs are covered through fixed charges, such as monthly charges. For example, under cost of service regulation consumers pay usage-independent monthly charges to cover the fixed costs of electric power plants, including a fair rate of return on capital.

Before concluding that regulation is warranted in the case of a natural monopoly, two questions must be answered. The first is whether there are any natural monopolies. If there are, the second is whether significant economic efficiency would be gained by regulation. With respect to the first question economies of scale and scope certainly exist over some sets of goods and services, but these economies may be exhausted at output levels that allow more than one supplier to be in the market. Empirical studies indicate, for example, that the large electric power plants in the United States have exhausted the achievable economies of scale. Moreover, advancements in gas turbine generators have resulted in highly efficient power generation at much smaller scales. A natural monopoly can also result if having more than one supplier would result in an uneconomical duplication of facilities. Local electricity distribution systems within cities may remain a monopoly to avoid duplicate sets of distribution wires. This rationale does not apply in telecommunications, however, since cable television and wireless communications systems provide alternatives to local wire connections. A monopoly could also result from network effects and standardization, as found in the Chapter 9 case *The Microsoft Antitrust Case* with respect to personal computer operating systems.

If there is a natural monopoly, it does not necessarily follow that there is substantial economic inefficiency. First, if entry into the industry is easy, the threat of potential competition may limit the extent to which an incumbent monopolist will restrict its output. Second, a monopolist may choose to use nonlinear pricing, involving fixed charges and a low unit price; that is, a price near p_0. This can both increase profits and benefit consumers. Third, if there are a number of possible suppliers of a monopoly service, competitive bidding for the right to be the monopolist can be used to lower the supply price and increase economic efficiency. Similarly, an alternative to the regulation of the electric power industry is for communities to own the local distribution system and solicit bids from power companies for the supply of electricity.[16] As considered in the section on deregulation, industries such as electric power and telecommunications had been subject to price regulation based on a natural monopoly rationale. Competition, however, continues to replace regulation in these industries, not only improving pricing but also inducing more efficient production.

Externalities

Externalities are of two types. A pecuniary externality is present when the actions of one economic agent affect other economic agents through changes in the prices of goods and services.

---

[16]See Joskow and Schmalensee (1983) and White (1997) for an assessment of the potential for competition in electric power.

When a firm builds a plant, its demand for labor can drive up the wage rate in the local labor market, unless labor is perfectly elastically supplied. This pecuniary externality does not result in economic inefficiency because the wage rate in the labor market is determined by the forces of supply and demand. Thus, a pecuniary externality does not provide a rationale for regulation.

Pecuniary externalities do, however, affect rents and hence may motivate nonmarket action. The oil shocks of the 1970s increased prices dramatically, and politicians responded by enacting a complex regulatory system to lower the price of oil so as to reduce the rents of the owners of U.S. crude oil reserves. The price controls, however, both dampened the incentive to find new domestic crude oil and stimulated the demand for oil, resulting in increased oil imports. The resulting inefficiency was sufficiently costly that crude oil price regulation was eliminated by the early 1980s.[17] The increases in oil prices in 2007–2008 and 2010–2011 did not result in price controls or new regulation.

The second type of externality is nonpecuniary and occurs when an action of one economic agent directly affects the preferences or production opportunities of another economic agent. An individual who drives an automobile generates pollution that both is unhealthy and affects visibility. Similarly, one firm's waste disposal site may pollute another's water supply. These externalities result in a divergence of private costs from social costs. Economic inefficiency results unless agents take into account the full social costs of their activities. Externalities provide an efficiency rationale for regulation to align private and social costs, as considered in Chapter 12 on environmental protection. Energy-efficiency regulation of household appliances may be warranted because burning carbon-based fuels to generate electricity causes externalities in the form of pollution and the release of gases that contribute to global climate change. Energy-efficiency regulation is, however, only a second-best form of regulation, as considered in Chapter 12 in the context of incentive-based systems for environmental protection.

Public Goods

A *public good* is one whose consumption by one person does not reduce its availability for others. When a person consumes a private good such as an apple, it is not available for consumption by others. When a person consumes a good such as national defense or a radio broadcast, however, the amount of the good available for consumption by others is not diminished. For a private good, economic efficiency requires that the marginal utility from consumption equals the price of the good, or, more correctly, that the marginal rate of substitution of one private good for another equals the ratio of their prices. Since a public good is available to all economic agents in a quantity undiminished by their consumption, economic efficiency requires that the sum of the marginal utilities of all individuals equal the price of the public good.[18] Many public goods are "local" in the sense that at some point adding more people diminishes the amount of the good available for others due to congestion, as in the case of a bridge at rush hour.

For some public goods, such as national defense, bridges, and roads, government provision is customary. Government provision, however, does not imply that a good has the characteristics of a public good. Many goods, such as public housing, food stamps, and soil-bank programs, are provided by government to redistribute income rather than because they are public goods. Also, public goods can be supplied by the private sector. Radio and television broadcasts are provided by private enterprises subject only to noneconomic regulation. Similarly, the government privatized its Landsat satellite system, which provides data and photographs of the earth's surface.

A fundamental problem with either private or public provision of public goods centers on the "revelation of preferences." If those who benefit from a public good are asked to pay for it based on how much they value it, people may understate their valuations so as to free ride on the payments of others. Because of the free-rider problem, public provision may be warranted. This, however, does not resolve the problem of determining the public's aggregate valuation of the good and thus whether it should be supplied in the first place. If individuals could be excluded from consuming the public good, the revelation and free-rider problems could

---

[17]See Breyer (1982, pp. 164–171) and Kalt (1981) for analyses of the inefficiency resulting from crude oil price regulation.

[18]In this sense, an externality is also a public good (or bad), since the efficient provision of goods involving externalities requires that the sum of the marginal utilities and disutilities from its supply be equated to its marginal cost.

be resolved—at least in principle. For example, preventing satellite dish owners from obtaining television programming not broadcast over the air induces customers to pay for Direct TV and the Dish Network.

Asymmetric Information

A market imperfection can also result from *asymmetric information.* If people have different (private) information at the time they act, markets may not perform efficiently, even when there are advantageous trades that could be made. Akerlof (1970) considered the case of a used car market in which each seller knows the true value of the car she wants to sell, but the buyers know only the probability distribution of the values of the cars that might be offered for sale. For each used car there is a potential buyer who is willing to buy it, but a buyer cannot through casual inspection determine the true value of any particular used car offered for sale. All the buyer knows is that a car might be a lemon, might be high quality, or might be somewhere in between.

Because a potential buyer does not know the true value of any particular car, the maximum amount the buyer is willing to pay is the average of the values of those cars that will be offered for sale. Potential sellers with high-quality cars find that the amount buyers are willing to pay is less than the value of their cars. They thus will not offer their cars for sale. Buyers recognize this and understand that the only cars that will be offered for sale will be those of low quality. The average value of those low-quality cars is low, however, so buyers will be willing to pay only a low amount. The low amount buyers are willing to pay again means that the potential sellers of cars at the high end of the remaining range will not offer their cars for sale. Buyers will then be willing to pay even less for any car offered for sale. The market thus may collapse with no sales being made. This is clearly inefficient, because for every used car there is a buyer who is willing to buy it if its true value were known.

This phenomenon, known as *adverse selection,* also occurs when sellers have incomplete information about customers. Insurance, in principle, is to provide coverage for individuals with similar risk characteristics. When those characteristics cannot be readily observed, people with quite different risks can be placed in the same pool. High-risk individuals have an incentive to buy insurance, which can drive up the price of insurance and cause some low-risk individuals not to buy insurance. Insurance companies respond to this adverse selection by requiring a physical examination for life insurance and basing auto insurance rates on observables such as accident and traffic citation histories and the number of years of driving experience.

When market participants have incomplete information and acquiring information is costly, the mandatory provision of information through regulation may be warranted. Regulation may not be warranted in all situations involving asymmetric information, however. Information has value, so there is a demand for it. In the used car example, a potential buyer may take the car to a mechanic for inspection. More generally, individuals may invest in information acquisition or hire agents who are more knowledgeable than they are. On the supply side, manufacturers can offer warranties to signal to consumers that their products are of high quality.[19] Some dealers, for example, offer warranties on their used or pre-owned cars.

Information, however, can remain undersupplied when it is in the self-interest of its possessor not to supply it. Manufacturers are understandably reluctant to release negative information about their products because doing so may reduce demand, in which case consumers may not be adequately informed about hazards. The chapter case *Merck and Vioxx* concerns the issue of how much and when information should be released about clinical drug trials, and the chapter case *Pfizer and Celebrex* asks if Pfizer should withdraw Celebrex from the market based on the available information. Similarly, an employee may be incompletely informed about possible health and safety hazards in the workplace. In such situations, regulation could be warranted. The liability system, considered in Chapter 14, however, is an alternative to regulation.

Moral Hazard

Moral hazard refers to inefficient actions induced by policy instruments that cause people not to bear the full consequences of their actions. In the case of medical care, fully insured individuals have an effectively unlimited demand for medical care, since they bear none of the cost of

---

[19]See Spence (1973) for the seminal work on signaling.

the care they receive. In addition, individuals may not have the proper incentive to take socially efficient preventive measures because they know that the cost of any illness or accident will be covered by insurance. For example, federally funded flood insurance encourages people to live in areas prone to flooding and can lead to socially inefficient location decisions.

Regulation is one response to moral hazard problems, but regulation can also cause moral hazard problems, making the regulation itself less effective. In a controversial article Peltzman (1975) argued that automobile safety regulation induced drivers to take more risks, thus reducing the effectiveness of mandatory safety standards. Peterson and Hoffer (1994) studied data on automobile personal injury and collision insurance claims from 1989 to 1991 and for each model compared data for those vehicles with an air bag to those with no air bag. Their data indicated that the number of accident claims was systematically higher for the identical automobile model with air bags than those without an air bag. Although these results were consistent with Peltzman's argument, they could be due to higher-risk drivers being more likely than lower-risk drivers to choose automobiles with air bags.

As an example of moral hazard, the 1986 Emergency Medical Treatment and Active Labor Act (EMTALA) requires all hospitals that both participate in Medicaid and have an emergency room to provide a medical screening evaluation to anyone who comes to their emergency room and to stabilize a patient's condition if there is a medical emergency. The rules implementing EMTALA also require that physicians be on call to treat a wide array of conditions in emergency rooms. Patients were also granted the right to sue the hospital. Uninsured individuals who could not pay began using emergency rooms for their health care, imposing a heavy cost burden on hospitals. Moreover, doctors began to refuse to be on call because they could be exposed to fines or a lawsuit. The response of an increasing number of hospitals, particularly those in low-income areas, was to close their emergency rooms. In 2003 and 2004 six hospitals in the Los Angeles area closed their emergency rooms to avoid the costs of EMTALA. The regulation had induced behavior that may have reduced rather than expanded the availability of emergency care.

Moral hazard can also occur within a firm. To increase the incentives for individuals to report corporate wrongdoing, federal laws allow a whistle-blower to receive 10–30 percent of any judgment won in court. In response to such laws, companies have instituted internal disclosure and ethics systems to reduce the likelihood of wrongdoing and encourage the reporting of suspected wrongdoing at an early stage. Moral hazard results because the reward provided by the federal law encourages employees to avoid the companies' internal control systems, wait for sufficient evidence to accumulate, and then go directly to the public authorities. This makes the internal systems less effective in stopping wrongdoing.

In industries in which cost-of-service pricing and rate-of-return regulation are used, cost increases are passed on to consumers. The incentive for the firm to hold down costs is thus weakened. This is a form of moral hazard because the firm does not bear the full consequences of the higher costs that result from its own decisions.

The principal means of dealing with this market imperfection is to structure incentives so that the moral hazard is taken into account in decision making. In the case of medical insurance, copayments can be required and reimbursement limits imposed. Moral hazard can also be addressed by monitoring the behavior of individuals to increase the likelihood that they take proper care. Imposing fines for not wearing a seat belt is an example of monitoring. Moral hazard is also reduced by breaking the link between cost increases and the prices charged for services, as in price cap regulation used in some states for local telecommunications services.

Markets can also resolve some potential moral hazard problems. A common problem in markets is the incentive for sellers to shirk on the quality of the goods or services they sell. For example, if quality can be observed only through use, a seller may have an incentive to shirk. If, however, consumers can sully the reputation of the firm by informing other consumers that the firm shirked on quality, shirking can be reduced or eliminated. The cost of harming a reputation has been dramatically reduced by the development of social media. Consumers can follow the strategy of purchasing from the firm as long as its reputation for producing high-quality products is unsullied and not purchasing from it if its reputation is ever sullied. If the potential gain from future sales is sufficiently great, the firm will have no incentive to shirk on quality.[20]

---

[20]See Kreps (1990) for an exposition of this theory.

Allocating Public Resources

The radio spectrum is a common resource that is allocated by government agencies. In 2008 the mobile wireless communication revolution was beginning, but it was clear to some companies that the potential was enormous. A possible bottleneck was the limited electromagnetic spectrum available for wireless communication. The FCC was preparing for the conversion from analog to digital television transmission scheduled for June 2009, and Google saw an opportunity. Analog transmission required unoccupied spectrum, referred to as white spaces, between the television channels to avoid interference, but with digital television transmission the unoccupied spectrum was no longer needed. This spectrum was ideal for wireless communication because it carried long distances and could penetrate buildings. Google proposed to the FCC that the white spaces be made available on an unlicensed basis for use in wireless communication, and it launched a campaign to support its proposal. Along with Philips Electronics, Intel, Dell, and Microsoft, Google formed the White Spaces Coalition to advance the cause. Google campaigned for its proposal with a November 2008 presentation, "White Spaces: Access to the Future." The FCC saw the proposal as consistent with its objective of supporting the growth of wireless communication, and in late 2008 voted to make the white spaces available for unlicensed use.

Protests about the technical requirements for the allocation quickly mounted from a variety of sources. Broadcasters complained that the new wireless communication could interfere with their broadcasts and with their use of wireless microphones. Wireless microphones were used by news reporters, entertainers, sports announcers, and church ministers. Dolly Parton urged the FCC to halt the allocation. The FCC suspended its 2008 decision and sought a solution to the problems. To advance the white spaces opening, in 2009 Microsoft commissioned a study by Perspective Associates that concluded that making the white spaces available for Wi-Fi would result in $3.9–$7.3 billion per year in new economic activity over the next 15 years.[21] The FCC's solution included developing a database of available digital signals that could be used to find an available channel on which to transmit. The database would be updated daily. The FCC also developed engineering specifications for devices so that they would not interfere with broadcasts. To accommodate wireless microphones, two channels on the low range of the spectrum were made available in each market. The technical changes were sufficient to satisfy the opposition, and the FCC voted unanimously to provide the white spaces for unlicensed use. The next phase of the efforts to provide spectrum for wireless communication was to seek the reallocation of unused television channels, as considered in the Part III Integrative case *Spectrum for Wireless Broadband: Old Media versus New Media*.

Government Imperfections

Market imperfections in many cases warrant government regulation. In some cases, however, regulation may be a cure that is worse than the disease. Wolf (1979, p. 138) argues that government intervention to deal with a market imperfection or failure may itself be subject to a "nonmarket failure."[22] He argues that the market failure "rationale provides only a necessary, not a sufficient, justification for public policy interventions. Sufficiency requires that specifically identified market failures be compared with potential nonmarket failure associated with the implementation of public policies ..."

Market imperfections are thus only a necessary condition for regulation to improve economic efficiency. Regulation is not perfect, and even well-intentioned regulation can in some instances worsen the performance of markets. In addition, regulation is not always intended to correct market imperfections but instead can be the result of political forces that serve objectives other than economic efficiency. The next section considers the political economy of regulation.

THE POLITICAL ECONOMY OF REGULATION

Capture and Rent-Seeking Theories

One theory of economic regulation is that it is initially imposed to address a market imperfection, but through interaction with the firms they regulate, regulators begin to see the firms'

---

[21]TECHWEB, September 24, 2009.
[22]See also Wolf (1988).

problems as their own. Regulation then evolves over time to serve the interests of regulated firms in addition to, or instead of, the goal of economic efficiency.[23] This *capture* theory predicts that regulation initially will be found where there are market imperfections and over time will evolve to serve the interests of the regulated industry.

Observing that much of the economic regulation of industries increased costs and generated profits for firms, Chicago school economists provided a different explanation for where regulation would be found. Their focus was not on market imperfections but on the ability of interest groups to obtain regulation through political pressure. From this perspective, regulation is demanded by interest groups and supplied through the political process.[24] Regulation thus was not established to address market imperfections and then captured but instead was established to benefit politically effective interests. Once established, regulation continued to serve those interests. From this *rent-seeking* perspective, the railroads in the nineteenth century sought regulation to support their cartel agreements, which were plagued by defections and cheating. Similarly, regulation in the airline and trucking industries was sought in part to serve the interests of incumbent firms by limiting entry and passing on cost increases through higher regulated prices. This perspective and the supporting empirical evidence provided the impetus for the deregulation of a number of industries.

Regulation is also supplied in response to the demands of interest groups other than business. This is clearest in the context of social regulation where, for example, environmental groups successfully overcame agricultural interests in obtaining the regulation of pesticides and where organized labor succeeded in obtaining workplace safety and health regulation. During the early 1990s consumer complaints about basic cable television prices led Congress to establish price regulation over the veto of President Bush.

Firms also seek federal regulations to avoid individual states imposing different regulations. Appliance manufacturers sought uniform energy-efficiency standards across the states to avoid having to produce different models for different states. Some Internet service and content providers supported federal Internet privacy standards to preclude the enactment of disparate state standards. Companies also seek regulation to level the playing field by requiring competitors to meet the same standards they meet. When McDonald's decided to implement a no-smoking policy in its company-owned restaurants, it sought uniform federal regulation to impose a no-smoking policy on all restaurants. The large toy companies such as Mattel and Hasbro sought mandatory testing for lead in paint on children's toys so that other companies would not free ride on the safety reputation they built through their own testing.

Fairness

Regulation is also used to accomplish fairness goals. This can involve policies such as lifeline rates for telephone service for low-income people and the provision of aid such as food stamps. Fairness can also be sought in cases in which consumers do not or cannot easily take precautions. During the financial crisis the practices of financial services companies became a center for attention. Some consumers found themselves burdened by high interest payments on their borrowing on credit cards.[25] In some cases consumers had poorly understood the terms under which the cards were issued, and in other cases there were undisclosed practices. For example, for some consumers who had credit card balances at two different interest rates, such as an introductory rate and a standard rate, payments were applied to the balance with the lower interest rate. In other cases, when a cardholder exceeded a prespecified limit and a penalty rate was applied, that rate was applied to all balances and not just to future borrowing. Moreover, consumers complained not only that some terms of the credit card use were undisclosed but also that some disclosures were difficult to understand. Consumers complained to members of Congress and to regulators, and their advocates such as the Consumer Federation of America campaigned for restrictions on card issuers. Regulators had the authority to restrict or ban many of the practices that generated complaints, but fearing that the regulators would not go far enough, members of Congress introduced legislation to restrict the practices.

---

[23]See Bernstein (1955) and Quirk (1981).

[24]See Stigler (1971), Posner (1974), and Peltzman (1976).

[25]This occurred at the same time as the subprime loan crisis that caused many borrowers to lose their homes.

Other Public Purposes: Media Ownership Rules

Regulation can also be used for other public purposes. For example, the Federal Communications Commission (FCC) has traditionally been fearful that concentrations of ownership in the news media might stifle the full reporting of news or restrict the diversity of views expressed. To support diversity objectives and avoid concentrations of ownership, the FCC had promulgated media ownership rules that restricted the number and type of media outlets that could be owned by the same company. Over time the structure of the media industry changed as a result of the growth of television and the decline of newspapers and the advent of the Internet as a source of news. These changes required that the media rules be reexamined. This generated intense nonmarket action with some companies seeking to preserve the status quo and others seeking changes that would benefit themselves.

In 2008 FCC chairman Kevin Martin again sought to promulgate new media rules to accomplish two objectives. One was to strengthen newspapers whose circulation and advertising revenue had been declining. The other was to limit the power of the largest cable company, Comcast Communications. Martin voted with the other two Republican members of the FCC to relax the newspaper-broadcast cross-ownership rule that applied to the 20 largest media markets. The new rule would allow a company to own both a newspaper and either a television station or radio station if there were at least eight other independent sources of news. If the company was a television station, it could not be one of the four largest in the market. This relaxation benefited newspapers, but the newspapers complained that the revision was so minor that it would have little effect on market developments.

Martin joined with the two Democrat members of the FCC to limit further acquisitions of cable companies by large cable providers, the largest of which was Comcast with nearly 30 percent of the market. By a 3–2 vote the FCC issued a rule that prohibited any company from owning cable systems serving more than 30 percent of the market nationally. This rule making followed a number of other actions that restricted the practices of cable systems and accelerated the provision of video services by telephone companies.

The two rules were criticized by all sides. A group of 25 senators notified Chairman Martin that they would lead a legislative effort to revoke any media rules the FCC promulgated. The new media rules also found their way to the courts.

Preemption

A major regulation issue is whether a decision by a federal regulatory agency preempts lawsuits in state courts. The Food and Drug Administration has the responsibility for approving drugs and medical devices, and the companies making these products claimed that FDA approval precluded lawsuits in state courts that sought damages for injuries due to the products. The companies argued that approval of the products by an expert agency meant that the government had judged that the products were sufficiently safe, although not without some risks, to be marketed and that additional enforcement of safety through the courts was inappropriate. That is, the FDA had already taken into account in its decision the benefits and costs associated with the product, and the courts should not make decisions pertaining to only one side of that assessment.

Preemption has attracted considerable nonmarket action as firms have sought to obtain explicit language in new legislation to provide preemption, and other interest groups such as trial lawyers and consumer groups have opposed such language. The courts have also addressed the issue in response to cases brought before them, and in a major decision in 2007 the Supreme Court ruled that FDA approval of a medical device shielded the manufacturer from class action lawsuits by people claiming injury from the product. In a related case pertaining to pharmaceuticals, the Supreme Court ruled that a drug approved by the FDA was not shielded from personal injury claims. The court decisions on preemption are considered in more detail in Chapter 14.

A POLITICAL ECONOMY THEORY OF REGULATION

Although the capture and rent-seeking theories are insightful, they give insufficient attention to market imperfections, as is most apparent in the regulation of externalities such as pollution. These theories also give insufficient attention to the role of institutions in structuring the competition among interest groups, and they lack an account of the organization, strategies, and effectiveness of those interest groups. As indicated in Figure 10-2, regulation takes place in a complex institutional and political environment, and the mandates and procedures of those institutions, as well as the policy objectives of the executive branch, can be important. In the case of the regulation of basic cable television prices, members of Congress saw the issue as sufficiently popular with constituents that it was worthwhile for them to enact the Cable Television Act of 1992 and claim credit for it. Price regulation was eliminated during the Clinton administration. By 2008 members of Congress were again calling for restrictions on rate increases for cable television.

Regulation and regulatory change can be more fully understood through the frameworks presented in Parts I and II of this book combined with the characteristics of the regulatory environment and the analysis of market imperfections. This *political economy* theory views regulation as shaped by market imperfections, institutions and their officeholders, and the nonmarket action of private interests. The impact of nonmarket action on regulatory agencies is direct, as well as indirect through Congress and the executive branch. In addition, regulation has procedural requirements imposed by both legislation and due process rights. The economic efficiency objective of addressing market imperfections also influences the policymaking process, particularly if that objective is embraced by the presidential administration. The civil service personnel of the agencies and the nature of bureaucracy also play a role.[26]

EXAMPLE   The Political Economy of Regulation: ATVs

The Consumer Products Safety Commission (CPSC) maintains an information system in which accidents that require hospital emergency room treatment are reported to the CPSC. In 2005, 137,000 people went to the hospital as a result of accidents involving ATVs, and 40,400 children under the age of 16 required treatment in hospital emergency rooms. The commission staff estimated that 90 percent of the children injured were riding adult-size vehicles. The commission identified 467 people who had died from accidents involving ATVs, and the staff believed that when all the data were in, the number would reach 700.

Sales of ATVs had fallen from 912,000 in 2004 to 856,000 in 2006. Moreover, imports from China had increased substantially, putting pressure on the established manufacturers such as Yamaha, Kawasaki, and Polaris. The established manufacturers both supported and opposed regulation of their industry and products. The CPSC had not acted, perhaps because it faced another problem with youth ATVs. Whereas the established manufacturers were required to comply with safety regulations, the products of "new entrant" manufacturers were not required to meet those regulations. The CPSC issued a public statement "that children are at risk of injury or death due to multiple safety defects" from the Kazuma Meerkat 50, a youth ATV imported from China. The commission stated that the ATV had no front wheel brakes, no parking brake, and could be started in gear.[1] The CPSC had not ordered a recall because it lacked a quorum: The Senate had refused to confirm the nominee, who then withdrew from consideration.

The Specialty Vehicle Institute of America (SVIA), which represented the established manufacturers, sought regulation of

all ATVs, including those in the "new entrant" category. The SVIA lobbied Congress to enact legislation making regulation uniform across all manufacturers. The Consumer Product Safety Improvement Act made the prior SVIA voluntary standards mandatory, and the CPSC was preparing to revise those standards in response to updated SVIA standards.

The SVIA also faced regulation of another type. Carolyn Anderson, co-founder of Concerned Families for ATV Safety, had lost her 14-year-old son to an ATV accident and sought a rule by the CPSC banning children under 16 from using ATVs. She said, "Kids under 16 don't have the judgment, they don't have the physical strength a lot of time. They're short on common sense."[2] The American Academy of Pediatrics agreed. Dr. Gary Smith, chair of the Committee on Injury, Violence and Poison Prevention of the Academy, said, "The Academy feels strongly that children aren't developmentally ready until about the age of 16 to operate a complex machine such as an ATV. It has to do with maturity, with judgment, with coordination, with strength."[3]

The SVIA already participated in a voluntary agreement with the CPSC in which retailers were not supposed to sell to people who might let children operate the vehicles. The SVIA opposed going farther. Tim Buche, president of the SVIA, said, "A lot of parents want their kids to ride ATVs. ATVs are loads of fun every day for millions of Americans when used safely and responsibly."[4] The SVIA proposed model state regulation that would require warnings on safety, age restrictions, and certain equipment requirements.

---

[2]Associated Press, June 3, 2007.
[3]Ibid.
[4]Ibid.

---

[1]*Wall Street Journal*, June 6, 2007.

---

[26]See Wilson (1989).

Interest group politics represents a strong force for change in some cases and for preservation of the status quo in others.[27] Regulatory change in the electric power industries considered later in the chapter illustrates the importance of institutions as well as of interests. The example of ATV regulation illustrates that firms can simultaneously seek to obtain certain regulations and avoid others.

Regulation is also shaped by the efficiency consequences of policy alternatives and the policy responses to those consequences. The impetus for deregulation in the transportation industries came from information provided by public policy analysts, the staff of regulatory commissions, and policymakers in the executive branch.[28] Regulatory policy is thus a product of both interest group actions and institutions and their officeholders.[29]

To illustrate this perspective, consider the case of social regulation and small business. One distinctive feature of much of the social regulation enacted over the past 40 years is the regularity of special provisions for small businesses. Many regulations provide small businesses with exemptions, streamlined reporting procedures, reduced compliance burdens, smaller penalties, or less stringent standards. Brock and Evans (1986, Table 4.2) listed 29 federal regulatory programs that provide "tiers" of regulation based on the size of firms. For example, the Family Leave Act of 1993 exempts firms with fewer than 50 employees. Furthermore, the Regulatory Flexibility Act of 1980 encourages regulators not to burden small businesses unduly.

Small business receives these exemptions in part because the compliance costs, and particularly their administrative components, are disproportionately burdensome for small business. Exemptions, however, are also due to the effective political organization of small businesses. As indicated in Chapter 8, small businesses are numerous, have complete coverage of legislative districts, and in the aggregate have substantial resources. Small business is also well organized for nonmarket purposes, with the National Federation of Independent Business, the National Small Business Association, and the Chamber of Commerce having considerable influence in Washington and in state capitols.

Redistribution and Cross-Subsidization

In addition to addressing market imperfections, regulation can be used to redistribute income. Rent control in the housing market is an example, and cable television price regulation is another. In telecommunications the distribution of rents between local and long-distance providers depends importantly on the "access charge" paid for access to the local loops of incumbent telephone companies. These rents have generated nonmarket action at the state level. De Figueiredo and Edwards (2007) showed that the access charges set by state public utilities commissions depended on the campaign contributions made to state legislators by the incumbent companies seeking high access charges and by the entrants to the local telecommunications market seeking low access charges.

Regulation can also be used to redistribute income through cross-subsidization of one customer class by another. Because of distributive concerns, state regulatory agencies have instituted lifeline rates for low-income consumers. In California, at the end of 2001 the number of low-income individuals receiving lifeline rates for basic telephone services reached 3.7 million. Lifeline rates require cross-subsidization by other customers, which in California took the form of a 4 percent surcharge on basic telephone service.

Cross-subsidization occurs when one group of customers pays more and another group pays less than the cost of providing their service. Inefficiency results on both sides of the cross-subsidization. When a price is below costs, some consumers receive service even though the cost of satisfying their demand is greater than their willingness to pay for it. When a price is above costs, some consumers who are willing to pay the cost of the resources required to produce their service are denied the opportunity to do so.

Cross-subsidization is a common feature of the economic regulation of industries. Business telephone services have been used to cross-subsidize basic residential service. When airline fares and routes were regulated, long-distance flights cross-subsidized shorter flights, and high-density airline routes cross-subsidized low-density routes. Cross-subsidization is unsustainable when entry into the industry is possible, since customers who are paying more than the cost of their

---

[27]See Noll and Owen (1983), Wilson (1980), and Francis (1993) for studies of the politics of regulation.
[28]See Derthick and Quirk (1985) for a study of the influence of policy analysts on regulatory policy.
[29]Harris and Milkis (1989) provide an analysis of regulatory change at the FTC and EPA.

service have an incentive to seek alternative suppliers. Much of the deregulation movement in the United States has been the result of forces created by cross-subsidization. The entry of MCI into the long-distance telecommunications market occurred because AT&T's long-distance rates were used to cross-subsidize other services. MCI offered services at prices that did not include the cross-subsidization, and customers switched to it.[30] Similarly, as the airline industry was being deregulated, entry occurred first on high-density, long-distance routes.

Accomplishing Through Regulation What Cannot Be Accomplished Through Legislation

Organized labor is one of the core constituencies of the Democratic Party and was important in the election of President Barack Obama. Unions collect dues from members that can be used to fund political activity, including advertisements, campaign workers, and campaign contribution almost all of which goes to Democrats.

Unions succeeded politically in 2008, but in the marketplace their decline continued. The Bureau of Labor Statistics reported that in 2010 only 6.9 percent of the salaried and hourly private-sector workforce was unionized, down from 25 percent in 1975.[31] In contrast to the private sector, 36.2 percent of the public-sector workforce was unionized, and there were now more union members in the public sector than in the private sector. Public-sector union members were core constituents of Democrats, particularly for state and local governments.

The decline in private-sector unionization was due to a number of forces. The principal force was market competition.[32] The high costs resulting from unionization reduced competitiveness, which had caused companies to move jobs from the North to the union-unfriendly South and Southwest, as well as to other countries. Eight states had private-sector unionization rates below 5 percent, and all were in the South. In addition, the liberalization of international trade exposed high-cost U.S. companies to new competition, as was evident by the decline of the U.S. automobile industry. Another force was the establishment of worker rights through court decisions and legislation, which made union protection of employees less important. Also, companies had become effective in opposing union organizing drives.

With the election of President Obama and with Democrat majorities in both Houses of Congress, labor unions sought to change the forces that had led to their decline, and the president and Democrat majorities were eager to reward their core constituents. Their first objective was to pass legislation that would radically change union organizing campaigns. The instrument was a "card check" bill that would allow certification of a union if a majority of the employees of a plant or company signed a card. Labor laws enacted in the 1920s and 1930s gave workers the right to a secret ballot in union elections, so as to avoid union coercion of workers. Card check would do away with the right to secret ballot elections. It would also make it difficult for employers to campaign against unionization. With card check, unions could quietly obtain signatures with little opportunity for companies to communicate with their employees. Card check failed to gain sufficient support in the Senate to overcome a filibuster, and when Republicans became a majority in the House after the 2010 elections, card check was dead, as was any hope of benefiting unions through legislation.

Blocked in Congress, the Obama administration sought to accomplish through regulation what it could not accomplish through legislation. The principal instruments were the National Labor Relations Board (NLRB), which had jurisdiction over employment practices in most industries, and the National Mediation Board (NMB), which had jurisdiction over the transportation industries. The Obama administration appointed pro-union majorities to both boards, which proceeded to make unprecedented changes in favor of organized labor.

The NLRB began an effort to implement card check by changing the rules governing elections. In August 2011 it reversed an earlier decision that had upheld the rights of workers to demand a secret ballot when an employer voluntarily accepted unionization after a majority of workers had signed a card requesting union representation. With the reversal a union would be recognized as soon as a majority had signed cards, provided the employer agreed. Business groups complained that the reversal was contrary to the will of the Congress.

---

[30]MCI is now part of Sprint.

[31]Bureau of Labor Statistics, Economic News Release, "Union Members Survey," January 21, 2011.

[32]Many public sector jobs were not subject to market forces, which contributed to higher union representation.

In response to the congressional attempt to enact card check, a number of states enacted laws or modified their constitutions to guarantee an employee the right to a secret ballot in union elections. The NLRB filed a lawsuit against two of the states alleging that their actions violated the U.S. Constitution and federal law. The NLRB also sought to change certification from a majority of employees in the proposed bargaining unit to a majority of those voting, which would give an advantage to the better organized pro-union side.

In the never-ending battle over union representation in the transportation industry, the NMB voted under the Railway Labor Act to change the rule on union organizing votes for airline and railroad employees.[33] To obtain representation under the rule that had been in place for 75 years, a majority of all employees in a particular craft (e.g., airline pilots) had to vote in favor of union representation. The NMB changed the rule so that only a majority of those voting was required for the union to win. This change would benefit the well-organized unions in their drives to represent employees at Federal Express and the airlines. After the Republicans obtained a majority of the House, a spokesperson for the new chair of the House Transportation Committee said, "Changes in the way elections are conducted under the Railway Labor Act are the authority of the Congress, not two political appointees of the National Mediation Board."[34] Gina Laughlin, a spokesperson for Delta Air Lines, said, "We don't believe that allowing a minority of employees to elect a union to speak for the majority is in the best interests of Delta employees and is good for labor stability in the airline industry."[35] The Transportation Committee inserted a provision in a Federal Aviation Administration reauthorization bill that would reverse the Board's action. Federal Express lobbied in support of the House provision, and the AFL-CIO and the Teamsters Union lobbied against it. The provision was dropped, but the committee continued to try to overturn the NMB action.

The NLRB sought to slow the movement of union jobs to the south. Boeing had built a $1 billion plant in South Carolina to produce the 787 Dreamliner, which was also produced in Seattle. The workers in Seattle were unionized, whereas those in South Carolina were not nor were they likely to support a union organizing campaign. In an unprecedented action the NLRB general counsel charged Boeing with building the plant in South Carolina in retaliation against the Seattle unions and sought to block the transfer of any production to the new plant. Retaliation against workers for exercising their rights was prohibited under the National Labor Relations Act, but thousands of companies had moved production to lower-cost states. Boeing executives had complained about strikes that disrupted production, but the company said the reason for building the plant in South Carolina was lower costs. Sir Richard Branson, CEO of the Virgin Group of airlines, had complained about the union strikes and disruptions in Seattle which had delayed delivery of aircraft he had ordered. He said, "If union leaders and management can't get their act together to avoid strikes, we're not going to come back here again. We're already thinking 'Would we ever risk putting another order with Boeing.'"[36]

The NLRB action to block Boeing ignited a firestorm of opposition in the business community, and the House voted 238–186 to prevent the NLRB from forcing a business to close or move (e.g., back to Seattle). The NLRB sought a settlement of the Boeing case, but the company refused, and the case went before an administrative law judge, who prepared to hear evidence.

The NLRB went further in its quest to slow the movement of jobs to lower-cost states. It announced that it would review a number of prior cases in which a company had relocated because of high costs. The NLRB also voted to require businesses to provide information to unions when considering relocations because of cost considerations.

The NLRB also sought to make it easier for unions to organize health care workers by reversing a 1991 decision that required unions to organize non-acute health care workers at the company level. To make it easier for unions, the NLRB voted to allow a union to organize "mini-bargaining units" representing a group of employees performing the same kind of job (e.g., nurses). This would give a minority of workers the ability to disrupt operations through strikes, a problem that plagued companies like Boeing where strikes by the machinists union had shut down all production, leading to Sir Richard Branson's comment.

[33]See the Chapter 7 case, *Federal Express and Labor Organization.*
[34]*Wall Street Journal*, March 30, 2011.
[35]Ibid.
[36]*Economist*, May 21, 2011.

The NLRB also sought to reduce to as little as 10 days the time between when a union election was authorized and when the vote took place. This would allow unions to collect signatures for an election on the quiet and leave less time for management to communicate with workers about the election. Small businesses complained that this would put them at a disadvantage because of their limited resources.

The ultimate effect of the changes by the NLRB and the NMB was unclear because the decisions would be contested in the courts. The challengers would argue, among other things, that the actions were arbitrary and capricious and should be overturned under the precedent of *Motor Vehicles Manufacturers Assn. v. State Farm Insurance Co.* The airline industry had already filed a lawsuit against the NMB, and Boeing had challenged the NLRB action and would likely appeal any adverse ruling by the administrative law judge.

COST-OF-SERVICE REGULATION

Regulation in a number of industries has centered on cost-of-service pricing. In industries such as airlines and trucking, entry had been controlled and industry-wide prices were set with cost increases passed on to consumers in the form of higher prices. This allowed inefficiencies to creep into the industries. Because industry-wide wage increases affected all firms similarly and the increased costs could be passed through to consumers, firms had weak incentives to resist wage demands. This moral hazard feature of cost-of-service regulation allowed organized labor, such as the Teamsters, to capture substantially higher wages than would otherwise have been possible.[37] When deregulation occurred in these industries and entry was permitted, wage rates and union membership began to fall. Similarly, in the airline industry pilots and machinists captured high wages, and with deregulation the growth of nonunion carriers put wage pressure on the unionized airlines and their union members.

In the electric power, natural gas transmission, and telecommunications industries prices were set on a firm-by-firm basis to yield the revenue required to cover the firm's actual costs plus an allowed return on equity capital. Price changes occurred only with regulatory approval, and the approval process was similar to formal adjudication. Data and analyses were presented by the firm in support of the price changes, comments were requested from interested parties, hearings were held, witnesses testified and were cross-examined, and the commission issued an order specifying the prices. Much of the contention in this process centered on the rate of return the firm was allowed. In some cases, the emphasis on rate of return caused regulation to focus more on the profits earned by firms than on production efficiency or efficient pricing.

This cost-of-service regulatory system has been blamed for inducing high costs and slowing the introduction of new technology in telecommunications. Firms were said to invest in excess capacity and higher-quality equipment than needed because that increased their asset base. Since profits were determined by applying the allowed rate of return to the asset base, higher profits resulted. This also caused other inefficiencies. AT&T was said to have inhibited the rate at which new technology was introduced because it did not want to write off existing assets and lose the return allowed on those assets. These inefficiencies coupled with cross-subsidization led to deregulation.

DEREGULATION

Electric Power

The electric power industry represents approximately 3 percent of GDP and is nearly the size of the telecommunications and airline industries combined. Electricity prices vary greatly across the states with average 2011 retail prices of 10.58 and 14.39 cents per kilowatt hour in Connecticut and New York, respectively, at the high end, and 6.35 in Wyoming and 6.65 cents per kilowatt hour in Utah, Idaho, and North Dakota. The price differences were in large part due to historical factors including the availability of hydro power and the high costs of nuclear power plants still in the rate base in some states. Renewable Portfolio Standards in some states also required the purchase of high-cost power from renewable power sources as considered in Chapter 13.

---

[37]See Rose (1987).

Technological change in electric power has also had an important effect as improvements in gas turbine generators and the availability of low-cost natural gas have lowered costs and greatly reduced the minimum efficient scale in the industry. In addition, line losses from electricity transmission have been reduced.

These technological changes have made it both feasible and economical to transmit electricity to distant customers. For example, the lower cost of power in adjacent states provided incentives for California's customers to import electricity. In 1992 Congress passed the Energy Policy Act, which required a transmission company to "wheel" electricity from a producer in one state through its lines to a customer in a third state. This, in effect, made wholesale electricity a competitive market. Brokers and trading companies such as Dynegy and Enron made a market in electricity, where industrial customers bought electricity on the spot market in 15-minute blocks. The potential for competition led a majority of states to deregulate their electric power markets.[38] The actions taken by the states varied considerably, and the most extensive deregulation effort was in California.[39]

Strong economic growth in California during the 1990s and the failure to build new generating capacity reduced the peak-load reserve capacity in the state to almost zero. During the summer of 2000 a drought in the Northwest reduced the supply of hydroelectric power and reduced electricity exports to California. California utilities were forced to increase their purchases of electricity on the wholesale market, and the wholesale price skyrocketed. California utilities could not increase prices to their customers and were obliged to meet demand, so they purchased electricity on credit. When the utilities were unable to pay for the electricity, some qualifying facilities, some of which had not been paid for 6 months, refused to generate electricity. Power shortages developed in Northern California leading to occasional rolling blackouts. Pacific Gas & Electric, the utility in Northern California, declared bankruptcy. Southern California Edison also ran out of credit and sought relief from the state government.

The crisis ended in May 2001 as a result of several factors. First, substantial retail price increases were finally allowed, which reduced demand. The higher prices, however, would pay only for future purchases of electricity. Second, cool weather throughout the summer reduced peak demand by approximately 10 percent. Third, the Federal Energy Regulatory Commission instituted a price monitoring system for the western United States and a price mitigation plan for California. Within 2 months wholesale prices in the West had fallen by 80 percent.

The power crisis was over, but the California deregulation effort had been crippled. The failure of the California power market was due to several factors. First, risks, such as the drought in the Northwest, were larger than had been contemplated. Second, nonmarket pressures had prevented construction of new power plants in California. Third, the prohibition against utilities signing long-term contracts forced them to pay spot prices on the wholesale market. Fourth, the fixed retail prices meant that consumers did not curtail their demand when the wholesale price of electricity skyrocketed. Fifth, the refusal of the California Public Utility Commission to raise retail prices caused the utilities to bear all the risk, and they quickly became insolvent. The rules governing the electricity market were revised, and the market began to operate efficiently.

Part of the volatility of wholesale prices was due to the trading strategies of companies such as Enron that exploited flaws in the design of the California electricity market. The chapter case *Enron Power Marketing, Inc. and the California Market* concerns these trading strategies.

An important development in improving the efficiency of the electric power industry is smart grid technology. The technology can improve efficiency on many dimensions of the electric power system. One is to better manage the distribution of power, particularly from intermittent sources such as wind and solar. The Chapter 13 case *Silver Spring Networks and the Smart Grid* considers a company that is a leader in Internet Protocol-based platforms for communications in the management of the electric power system. Another is to allow customers, including residential customers, to better manage their use of electricity and to enable responsive pricing that sets prices based on real-time demand and supply. The Chapter 12 case *Pacific Gas & Electric and the Smart Meter Challenge* considers the challenges faced by an electric utility in rolling out residential smart meters.

---

[38]Wilson (2001) analyzed in detail the market for electricity and the management of that market.

[39]White (1997) analyzed the political economy of electric power deregulation across the states.

Auctions

The FCC has substituted auctions for its comparative license award system for allocating the radio spectrum. The FCC had traditionally allocated broadcast licenses and spectrum, for free, by evaluating applications using a set of noneconomic standards.[40] With the development of cellular technology, the FCC had to allocate portions of the radio spectrum for that service, and it initially turned to the same system it used to allocate broadcast licenses.

It became clear, however, that the traditional allocation system was cumbersome and inefficient and, with a major segment of the radio spectrum to be allocated in 1995 for personal communications services, the FCC needed a better mechanism. For decades economists had urged the use of auctions to allocate scarce public resources such as the radio spectrum. Auctions award resources to the highest bidders—the ones with the highest-valued uses for the resource. In a competitive market the highest-valued uses are determined by how effectively firms can compete to serve customers. Auctions thus yield economically efficient outcomes. Moreover, auctions capture for the government and the public the rents that previously went as gifts to the selected applicants. The 1995 auction for spectrum licenses suitable for personal communications systems attracted 70 bidders and raised $7 billion for the federal Treasury—$7 billion that under the previous system would have been a windfall gain to those receiving the licenses.

The FCC continued to use auctions to allocate the radio spectrum and through 2011 had received $50 billion from its 92 auctions. Other countries began to use auctions to allocate licenses. In Europe spectrum auctions brought in over $100 billion, but overbidding weakened many of the successful bidders. The Part III integrative case *Spectrum for Wireless Broadband: Old Media versus New Media* considers the nonmarket action centering on making spectrums currently held by broadcast television available for high-speed wireless service.

SUMMARY

Government regulation has a long history in the United States, beginning in the populist era, expanding during the New Deal, and taking new directions during the period of social regulation. Although considerable deregulation has occurred, particularly at the federal level, there is still considerable economic regulation in many industries.

The government's right to regulate is unquestioned and broad but is limited by due process and the constitutional protections against the taking of property without compensation. Regulation is conducted by commissions and agencies located at both the federal and the state levels. To implement their guiding statutes, regulatory agencies issue rules through formal and informal procedures.

Regulatory commissions and agencies are embedded in a complex institutional environment. They are influenced by the executive branch, Congress, private interests, and the courts. The president has considerable influence through both the appointment process and the policies advocated by executive branch agencies. In addition to writing the authorizing statutes for a regulatory agency, Congress controls the agency's budget and has oversight responsibility. Private interests affect regulatory agencies directly through testimony and lobbying and through their influence with Congress and the executive branch. The nature and scope of regulation are also shaped by the courts, which review statutes, policies, and individual rules in response to lawsuits filed by private parties.

Regulation is provided in response to both market imperfections and nonmarket forces. Market imperfections include natural monopoly, externalities, public goods, asymmetric information, and moral hazard. One role of regulation is to correct these market imperfections, but regulation itself is imperfect and could be worse than the imperfection it is intended to correct. In some cases regulation is intended to protect incumbent firms and in other cases to redistribute income or provide fairness. The political economy perspective on the locus and form of regulation emphasizes the role of private interests as well as institutions in shaping regulation. Institutions and the regulatory agencies themselves have an important impact, and regulators at the federal level have actively worked for deregulation in the airline, electric power, natural gas transmission, surface transportation, and telecommunications industries.

---

[40]See Breyer (1982, pp. 71–95) for a description and critique of this system.

Merck and Vioxx

On September 30, 2004, Merck voluntarily withdrew its $2.5 billion blockbuster drug Vioxx (rofecoxib) because new clinical research showed a significantly higher probability of cardiovascular events, such as heart attacks, for patients who took the drug for over 18 months. Merck's market capitalization fell by 27 percent on the day of the announcement and subsequently fell another 13 percent. The withdrawal met with instant praise for the quick decision, but soon the praise turned to questions as information became available about whether the company should have recalled the drug years earlier.

Merck defended itself in a series of full-page advertisements in major newspapers. In three full-page ads on November 21, 2004, Merck defended its actions, restated its commitments to patients, and attempted to assure investors about its financial strength and its future. The first ad stated:

> **We extensively studied** VIOXX before seeking regulatory approval to market it.
>
> **We promptly disclosed** the clinical data about VIOXX.
>
> When questions arose, **we took additional steps, including conducting further prospective, controlled studies** to gain more clinical information about the medicine.
>
> When information from these additional prospective, controlled trials became available, **we acted promptly** and made the decision to voluntarily withdraw VIOXX.

Vioxx, along with Pfizer's Celebrex and Bextra, were Cox-2 inhibitors used to treat patients with chronic pain. Traditional painkillers, such as aspirin and ibuprofen, blocked the Cox-1 and Cox-2 enzymes that cause pain. Blocking Cox-1 enzymes had the benefit of reducing cardiovascular risks, such as blood clots and heart attacks, but it could contribute to intestinal and stomach problems including stomach bleeding and ulcers. Cox-2 inhibitors did not block Cox-1 enzymes, so relative to traditional painkillers they provide benefits to patients at risk from intestinal and stomach bleeding. Vioxx had sales of $2.5 billion in 2003, Celebrex had sales of $1.9 billion, and Bextra, a newer version of Celebrex, had sales of $687 million.

THE INITIAL MARKETING DECISION FOR VIOXX

Early Merck memoranda suggested that the company recognized that sales would be limited if Vioxx were restricted to patients with stomach or intestinal bleeding. If the drug were marketed as a general-purpose painkiller for arthritis and other persistent ailments, sales could be much higher. If Merck were to market Vioxx as a general-purpose painkiller, it would use direct-to-consumer (DTC) advertising.

In designing clinical trials for Vioxx in the mid-1990s Merck recognized that to show its effectiveness trial subjects could not take aspirin. Consequently, the trials could show increased blood clots and cardiovascular events.

A Merck scientist proposed that patients with a high risk of cardiovascular problems be kept out of the clinical trials. Information on the final design of the clinical trials was not available.[41]

The Food and Drug Administration approved Vioxx for sale in 1999. The Phase III clinical trials required by the FDA for approval found "there was not an increased risk of cardiovascular events with VIOXX compared with placebo or VIOXX compared with other non-naproxen non-steroidal anti-inflammatory drugs (NSAIDS)."[42]

Preparation Questions

1. Should Merck seek to market Vioxx as a general-purpose painkiller with heavy DTC advertising or limit its marketing to those patients with gastrointestinal problems?
2. Should Merck conduct additional clinical trials to evaluate the risks of blood clots and cardiovascular events?

THE SUCCESS OF VIOXX

Merck aggressively promoted Vioxx as a general-purpose pain reliever for arthritis and other conditions. In 2000 it spent $161 million on DTC advertising for Vioxx. Continued heavy advertising and traditional marketing to doctors resulted in 2003 sales of $2.5 billion worldwide.

THE VIGOR CLINICAL TRIALS

In early 1999 Merck began a clinical study called VIGOR to demonstrate the effectiveness of Vioxx for patients with gastrointestinal problems. The control was naproxen, and participants were prohibited from taking aspirin. Patients with heart problems were not included in the trials. The results were released in March 2000 and showed that patients receiving Vioxx had fewer gastrointestinal problems than those receiving naproxen.[43] The results also showed that of the 4,047 people taking Vioxx, 101 had cardiovascular adverse events, such as blood clotting, whereas 46 of the 4,029 taking naproxen had such events. Because earlier studies had shown no greater cardiovascular problems with Vioxx than with a placebo, Merck suspected that the difference in cardiovascular adverse events was due to the beneficial effects of naproxen rather than to problems with Vioxx.[44] Merck and the FDA began discussions about what information from the VIGOR trial would be included in the new label for Vioxx.

---

[41] *Wall Street Journal,* November 1, 2004.

[42] Merck, "Merck Announces Voluntary Worldwide Withdrawal of VIOXX®," www.vioxx.com/rofecoxib/vioxx/consumer/index.jsp. Naproxen is marketed over-the-counter as Aleve.

[43] The results of the study were published in the *New England Journal of Medicine* in November 2000.

[44] Ted Mayer, an attorney representing Merck, later explained, "The known antiplatelet properties of naproxen strongly suggested that a property of naproxen was responsible for the differential rates in the Vigor trial." *Wall Street Journal,* November 1, 2004.

Preparation Questions

1. In light of the results of the VIGOR trials, should Merck issue a warning to doctors and patients?
2. Should Merck reduce its DTC advertising of Vioxx?
3. Should Merck conduct new clinical trials designed to identify any cardiovascular adverse effects of Vioxx?
4. What information should Merck support for inclusion on the new Vioxx label?

The Approve Study

In August 2001 researchers at the Cleveland Clinic published an article in the *Journal of the American Medical Association* raising concerns about Vioxx's cardiovascular risks. In 2002 a researcher at the Catalan Institute of Pharmacology in Barcelona criticized Merck's handling of Vioxx. The same criticism had been published in the British medical journal *The Lancet.*

The FDA was also concerned about the results of the VIGOR trial and particularly a Merck press release entitled "Merck Confirms Favorable Cardiovascular Safety Profile for Vioxx." In a September 17, 2001, letter to Merck the FDA called the press release "simply incomprehensible" and said that Merck had engaged "in a promotional campaign for Vioxx that minimizes the potentially serious cardiovascular findings that were observed ...." The letter also stated that "patients on Vioxx were observed to have a four- to five-fold increase" in heart attacks.[45] The new label for Vioxx mentioned both the gastrointestinal and cardiovascular results of the VIGOR trial.

As a result of the VIGOR trial, Merck researchers began discussing the possible risks associated with Vioxx and the other Cox-2 inhibitors. In May 2000 Merck considered conducting a cardiovascular study on Vioxx but decided not to do so. Earlier in 2000 Merck had begun enrolling patients for a 156-week study named APPROVe to demonstrate the effect of Vioxx on "the recurrence of neoplastic polyps of the large bowel" in patients with colorectal adenoma. In the study Merck used a placebo as the control and decided to monitor patients carefully for cardiovascular events. Merck established an external safety review board for the study. The board reviewed the interim results periodically. In May 2003 the panel noted a 20 percent higher risk of heart attack and stroke and by February 2004 the risk was 80 percent higher. Two of the five board members had consulting arrangements with Merck.[46]

An article published in *Circulation* in May 2004 found that Vioxx was "associated with an elevated relative risk" compared to Celebrex and to no pain reliever. Vioxx was also criticized at a medical conference in August by an FDA researcher.

In September 2004 the cardiovascular results in the APPROVe study showed 15 heart attacks or strokes per 1,000 patients with Vioxx compared to 7.5 with the placebo. Merck decided to withdraw Vioxx from the market. Merck reported, "In this study, there was an increased relative risk for confirmed cardiovascular (CV) events, such as heart attack and stroke, beginning after 18 months of treatment in the patients taking VIOXX compared to those taking placebo. The results for the first 18 months of the APPROVe study did not show any increased risk of confirmed CV events on VIOXX, and in this respect are similar to the results of two placebo-controlled studies described in the current US labeling for VIOXX."[47] ■

Preparation Questions

1. In light of the criticism of Vioxx and the letter from the FDA, should Merck have withdrawn Vioxx or issued warnings to doctors and patients prior to learning the results of the APPROVe study?
2. Should Merck have conducted a specific cardiovascular study?

CONGRESSIONAL HEARINGS

The Senate Finance Committee held hearings in November on whether the FDA was doing enough to ensure post-approval safety of drugs. The FDA's Dr. David Graham stated, "I would argue that the FDA as currently configured is incapable of protecting America against another Vioxx." He testified that five drugs—Accutane, Meridia, Crestor, Bextra, and Serevent—should be reexamined to determine if they should be withdrawn. Earlier in the year Graham had examined the health records of 1.4 million Kaiser Permanente patients, including 40,405 who took Celebrex and 26,748 who took Vioxx. He found that the risk of heart attacks and sudden cardiac death was three times higher in patients that took high doses of Vioxx. He estimated that Vioxx was responsible for an additional 27,785 deaths from 1999 through 2003. His analysis was posted on the FDA Web site.

Another FDA official, Dr. Sandra Kweder, head of the Office of New Drugs, disagreed with Graham. Dr. Steven Galson, the FDA's director of drug evaluation and research, later said that Graham's numbers "constitute junk science" and were "irresponsible."[48] ■

Preparation Question

1. Should Merck provide testimony on the adequacy of the FDA's post-approval safety monitoring? How should it respond to Dr. Graham's study?

---

[45]*Wall Street Journal,* October 5, 2004.
[46]*Wall Street Journal,* February 7, 2005.

[47]Merck, "Merck Announces Voluntary Worldwide Withdrawal of VIOXX," September 30, 2004.
[48]*New York Times,* November 19, 2004.

Pfizer and Celebrex

On September 30, 2004, Merck withdrew from the market its Cox-2 inhibitor Vioxx because a clinical trial had found an increased risk of cardiac events such as strokes and heart attacks among patients taking the drug for over 18 months. Commentators speculated that there could be problems with the entire class of Cox-2 inhibitors. Pfizer's Celebrex had become the best-selling Cox-2 inhibitor with 21 million prescriptions written in 2003 and 2004, and sales were expected to reach $3.3 billion a year. The chemical formula for Celebrex was different from that of Vioxx, and none of the many studies of Celebrex had shown evidence of increased risk of cardiac events. Pfizer began a brief advertising campaign telling the public and doctors that Celebrex was safe and was not associated with an increased risk of cardiac events. Pfizer considered beginning a clinical study to demonstrate that Celebrex did not cause adverse heart conditions and might even have beneficial effects.

Celebrex was discovered by Monsanto's Searle division, which was subsequently acquired by Pharmacia. In 2003 Pfizer acquired Pharmacia for $60 billion, in part because of Celebrex. Pfizer became the world's largest and most profitable pharmaceutical company. Celebrex's primary indication was for treating pain in patients subject to stomach bleeding, who could not take over-the-counter pain relievers such as aspirin and ibuprofen. Celebrex, however, had been marketed with heavy direct-to-consumer advertising as a more general pain reliever with an emphasis on arthritis pain. Pfizer spent $71 million on Celebrex ads during the first 9 months of 2004. Ads featuring figure skating champion Dorothy Hamill and other middle-aged people were common on television. The purpose of the ads was to have patients ask their doctors for the drug by brand name, and the results confirmed the strategy.

Approximately 40 studies sponsored by the National Institutes of Health (NIH) were under way, exploring other applications for Celebrex. For example, a 5-year study on 2,000 patients was being conducted by the National Cancer Institute (NCI) to determine if high doses of Celebrex could prevent colon polyps and colorectal cancer. Three groups of clinical trial patients were given a placebo, 400 milligrams, and 800 milligrams of Celebrex. An earlier Pfizer study of patients taking 400 milligrams had shown no increase in cardiac events. The European Union had approved Pfizer's Cox-2 inhibitor Onsenal for treating intestinal polyps, and Pfizer planned to begin marketing the drug early in 2005. Onsenal used the same active ingredient celecoxib as Celebrex but was more potent.

Preparation Questions

1. Should Pfizer review the clinical studies in progress to determine if there is any new evidence on cardiac events?
2. Should Pfizer stop its direct-to-consumer advertising of Celebrex?
3. Should Pfizer withdraw Celebrex from the market as a precautionary measure?

THE NATIONAL CANCER INSTITUTE STUDY

As a result of the Vioxx withdrawal, the researchers conducting the cancer study for the NCI began a review of the patient trials in October. After 6 weeks of investigation the researchers had identified six patients with cardiac events in the placebo group, 15 in the 400 milligram group, and 20 in the 800 milligram group. The researchers presented their findings to a safety review panel of cardiologists on December 10, 2004. After reviewing the data, the panel was concerned. The NCI then informed the FDA, NIH, and Pfizer. The NIH notified the researchers conducting the other studies. The panel recommended that the NCI study be halted, and researchers did so. Pfizer learned of the results on Thursday, December 16, in a call from the NCI, and Pfizer CEO Henry McKinnell was called at his home at 7:00 P.M. that evening. McKinnell immediately arranged a conference call with Pfizer's regulatory team for 8:00 P.M.[49] After the Vioxx withdrawal Pfizer had continued to market Celebrex to consumers and doctors. McKinnell had to decide what to do with Celebrex and how to present its decision to the FDA and the public. McKinnell and Pfizer had some experience with such issues. Shortly after Viagra was marketed, patients taking both it and angina medications reported cardiac events, including heart attacks.

Trial lawyers had scheduled a meeting for March 17 and 18, 2005, to plan their strategy for Vioxx, and Celebrex would certainly be added to their agenda. ▪

Preparation Questions

1. Should Pfizer stop its direct-to-consumer advertising of Celebrex?
2. Should Pfizer stop its marketing of Celebrex to doctors?
3. Should Pfizer withdraw Celebrex from the market?
4. What should Pfizer be prepared to do when it informs the FDA of its decision?
5. How should Pfizer present its decision to patients, doctors, and the public?

[49]*Wall Street Journal*, December 20, 2004.

Enron Power Marketing, Inc., and the California Market

Using names such as Death Star, Get Shorty, Fat Boy, and Ricochet, Enron Power Marketing (EPM) deployed an array of electricity trading strategies to take advantage of imperfections in the design of the market for power in California. In a December 2000 memorandum an outside lawyer and an EPM lawyer reminded the company that the California market rules prohibited "gaming" the trading system and warned that penalties could include "fines and suspension" and actions by "the appropriate regulatory or antitrust enforcement agency."[50] In late April 2002 that memorandum and a later memorandum by lawyers engaged by Enron were discovered.[51] The Enron board of directors waived attorney–client privileges and confidentiality rights and turned the memos over to the Federal Energy Regulatory Commission (FERC).[52] An Enron attorney said that it was "the responsible and honest thing" to do. FERC chairman Patrick Wood decided to make the memoranda public, stating, "We have to try to get to the bottom of this and tell the truth. If the capital markets perceive that regulators and customers and elected officials and everybody else are getting comfortable with understanding what went on in California, then you can restore confidence."[53]

Deregulation in the electricity market required establishing a market in which buyers and sellers could trade electricity on a continuous basis.[54] Markets for a nonstorable good such as electricity must be designed and regularized to allow supply and demand to be equilibrated almost minute by minute. One of the largest markets was established in California, where large customers were allowed to purchase electricity from any supplier. The efficiency of such markets can be improved by traders who act as middlemen between electricity producers and customers. EPM, Dynergy, El Paso, Reliant Resources, Duke Power, American Electric Power, Williams, and a number of other companies traded power. In 2000 EPM had an estimated 13.0 percent of the U.S. wholesale electricity market, and the next largest share was 8.9 percent.[55] Enron was believed to have had a significantly larger share of the California market.

No new electricity generation capacity had been built in California during the 1990s, and strong economic growth caused the state to import electricity from other states and Canada, particularly during peak periods. With reserve capacity in California below the minimum needed to ensure that demand could be met, the system was at risk. When a drought in the northwest reduced the power generated by hydroelectric facilities, the California market faced shortages and much higher wholesale prices. Despite the increases in wholesale power prices, the regulated retail prices remained fixed.[56]

The state's energy system and the market for electricity were coordinated by the Independent Service Organization (ISO), which operated the state's power grid. The power grid had a limited capacity, since no new transmission capacity had been built in many years. Moreover, the system had bottlenecks that limited the amount of power that could be moved between the north and south of the state.

The ISO was responsible for ensuring that California's power needs would be met. The ISO attempted to forecast demand and supply and balance the system both in real time and in advance. A trader that contracted to supply large retail customers such as manufacturing plants submitted a daily "schedule" of deliveries for the day-ahead market, and the ISO checked whether there was both a buyer and a seller for each megawatt before scheduling its transmission across the state's power lines.

EPM's "inc-ing" strategy involved overscheduling power deliveries to Enron Energy Services, Enron's retail unit, which contracted with large retail customers. The overscheduling led the ISO to anticipate higher demand and to plan to buy power the next day. Often those purchases were from Enron at high prices. An EPM trader referred to this as the "oldest trick in the books." Enron was in effect speculating based on its forecasts of demand, scheduled power generation, and the ISO's predicted behavior, which was influenced by EPM's scheduling. According to the second memorandum, this strategy offset the practice of independently owned utilities that regularly underestimated their load (demand for their power). In addition to trading on its own account, EPM served as "scheduling coordinator" for other companies. Two power suppliers allegedly involved in the generation side of this practice were Puget Sound Electric and Powerex, a unit of BC Hydro of Canada. Both companies denied having violated either ISO or FERC rules. EPM's strategy was believed to be legal and, according to an ISO official, consistent with the ISO rules at the time. California politicians charged that the companies using this strategy reaped billions of dollars of profits from the California market.

The Get Shorty strategy took advantage of the ISO's policy of maintaining reserve capacity to handle unexpected surges in demand. The ISO referred to this reserve generating capacity as "ancillary services," and power generators were paid to maintain idle capacity that could be switched on at short notice. EPM used a strategy of shorting the ancillary services and then covering them the next morning at a lower price. This speculation was not always successful, since on at least one

---

[50]Memorandum from Christian Yoder of EPM and Stephen Hall, Stoel Rivers LLP, December 8, 2000.

[51]Memorandum from Gary Fergus (Brobeck, Phleger & Harrison, LLP) and Jean Frizzell (Gibbs & Bruns LLP), no date. The two memoranda were available at www.ferc.gov. The lawyers engaged by Enron reviewed the December memorandum and met with traders to discuss the strategies described. They concluded that some of the information in the December memorandum was incorrect. Both memoranda stated that other traders used some of the same strategies.

[52]In 2002 EPM and its trading technology were sold to UBS Warburg, a unit of UBS AG of Switzerland. Six hundred thirty-five employees moved from Enron to UBS.

[53]*New York Times,* May 12, 2002.

[54]The development of the wholesale electricity market was spurred by the Energy Policy Act of 1992.

[55]"Report on EnronOnline," FERC, May 16, 2002.

[56]Pacific Gas & Electric (PG&E) went bankrupt by buying power at spot wholesale prices with its customers paying at the fixed retail rate. When it filed for bankruptcy, PG&E was estimated to owe Enron $500 million.

occasion the ISO asked EPM to deliver ancillary services it had shorted but failed to cover. The December memorandum stated, "This strategy might be characterized as 'paper trading' because the seller does not actually have the services to sell …. As a consequence, in order to short the ancillary services, it is necessary to submit false information that purports to identify the source of the ancillary services."

In the Death Star strategy, EPM profited by relieving congestion in the power grid for deliveries between the north and south of the state. The ISO relieved congestion by paying power suppliers to reduce their deliveries on the congested part of the grid and sell their power elsewhere. EPM would overschedule power to be delivered, knowing that the ISO would not be able to determine whether there were actual users for the power. Since the power grid appeared to be overloaded, the ISO would pay power suppliers, including EPM, to relieve congestion by selling their power elsewhere, such as out of the state.

In its "load shift" strategy EPM overscheduled supply into a congested area and underscheduled power into an uncongested area. EPM then would "reduce" deliveries into the congested area, receiving congestion relief payments, and "increase" deliveries in the uncongested area. In this practice EPM did not have to actually contract for the power, and even if it had contracted for the power, it could sell the power at a loss and still profit. The December memorandum stated, "Because the congestion [relief] charges have been as high as $750 per megawatt-hour, it can often be profitable to sell power at a loss simply to be able to collect the congestion payment."

EPM also took advantage of a price cap imposed by California regulators to prevent price spikes due to shortages. The normal price for electricity was $30 to $40 a megawatt-hour, but price spikes of as high as $1,200 occurred in 2000 and in the spring of 2001 as the ISO desperately sought to obtain power. The price cap of $250, however, covered only California. During a price spike EPM could buy power at $250 in California, export it from the state, and sell it at a higher price. EPM referred to this as arbitrage. The December memorandum stated that this "appears not to present any problems, other than a public relations risk arising from the fact that such exports may have contributed to California's declaration of a Stage 2 Emergency yesterday."

Ricochet trades, or "megawatt laundering," involved completing the arbitrage opportunity by reselling the exported electricity back to the ISO, which was unconstrained in the price it could pay for imported power. In a Ricochet trade EPM would buy power at the $250 price cap during a price spike and sell the power to a party outside the state. That party would charge a small fee, and resell the power to EPM. EPM then would sell the power to the ISO at prices as high as $1,200. Ricochet trading involved other parties often without their knowledge of the nature of the trade. Portland General Electric (PGE), a unit of Enron, Inc., reported that it had participated in a trade in which EPM sold power to a third party, which sold it to PGE, which then sold it to EPM. In June 2001 FERC imposed a price cap of $250 throughout the Western states, ending this arbitrage opportunity.

The December memorandum indicated that some of EPM's trading practices were "potentially criminal," and EPM reportedly halted the practices in December 2000. During the first several months of 2001 electricity prices in California continued to increase and shortages resulted in rolling blackouts and wholesale price spikes. To alleviate the energy crisis, or because he panicked as his critics contended, Governor Gray Davis committed $43 billion of state funds to buy power under long-term contracts at prices substantially above normal market prices. The energy crisis in California abated during the summer of 2001 due to below normal temperatures, lower natural gas prices, and new generating capacity coming on line. The governor subsequently sought to renegotiate the contracts and obtain refunds from energy traders.

After the revelation of the two memoranda Senator Diane Feinstein (D-CA) wrote to U.S. Attorney General John Ashcroft asking for a criminal investigation of Enron's trading practices. She wrote that the memos from the Enron lawyers "indicate that Enron was not only manipulating prices in the West, but also engaged in a number of calculated strategies … to either receive payment for energy not delivered or increase price. In my book, this is outright fraud."[57]

R. Martin Chavez, CEO of Kiodex, an energy risk management company, said, "Energy trading is a football game; it ain't bridge. If you want a nice game because electricity is an important public good, then set up a nice game."[58] Recalling his days as head of energy risk management at Goldman Sachs, he said, "The whole reason for the existence of traders is to make as much money as possible, consistent with what's legal. I lived through this: If you didn't manipulate the market and manipulation was accessible to you, that's when you were yelled at."[59] ■

Preparation Questions

1. Was EPM doing anything wrong in its trading strategies? Was this not just taking advantage of opportunities available in the market?
2. What were the flaws in the California market design?
3. Were EPM's strategies different from the types of strategies used on Wall Street?
4. How should Enron have conducted its trading business?

Source: Copyright © 2000 by David P. Baron. All rights reserved. Reprinted with permission.

---

[57]*Wall Street Journal*, May 8, 2002.
[58]*New York Times*, May 12, 2002.

[59]*New York Times*, May 8, 2002.

11 | FINANCIAL MARKETS AND THEIR REGULATION

INTRODUCTION

The capital markets are an essential component of a capitalist economic system, allowing individuals to save their money in a broad array of financial instruments and transforming those savings into funding for businesses, home-buying, and retirement. Savings and investments carry risks, and financial markets provide diversification that dissipates idiosyncratic risks specific to an individual firm or security. This diversification raises the risk-adjusted return on savings and lowers the cost of funds to borrowers and investors. Systemic risks that affect all securities, however, cannot be diversified away. Financial markets and financial institutions thus can be unstable, and that instability has led to government intervention and regulation. This chapter focuses on the financial markets, the financial crisis of 2007–2009, and the regulation established in the wake of that crisis. The chapter focuses on the United States, which was the principal origin of the financial crisis.

Financial crises are not uncommon. Reinhart and Rogoff (2009) examined and found numerous financial crises over the past eight centuries, many of which followed a similar pattern. The United States has experienced 13 banking crises since 1800, and the United Kingdom and France have experienced 12 and 15, respectively. Since 1945 Argentina has experienced 4 banking crises, Brazil 3, Japan 2, Indonesia 3, and South Africa 2.[1] The recent crises in the United States are:

- Mortgage-related financial crisis, 2007–2009.
- Dot-com bubble, 2000–2001. Speculative investments in Internet and technology companies caused a bubble, which burst resulting in a dramatic drop in share prices and a recession.
- Savings and loan crisis, 1991. Precipitated by a housing boom and risky investments by savings and loan associations, the government was forced to intervene and liquidate nearly 1,000 thrifts. A severe recession followed.

Crises outside the United States have also been severe, as in the Asian financial crisis of 1997, the Russian financial crisis of 1998, and the Mexican crises in the 1980s and 1990s. Spain experienced a severe financial and economic crisis at approximately the same time as the U.S. mortgage-related crisis, and that crisis was preceded by rapidly rising housing prices and a housing construction boom.

THE FORMAL AND INFORMAL (SHADOW) BANKING SYSTEMS

Depository institutions such as banks accept deposits and make loans. These institutions are required to maintain a fractional reserve requirement, which allows the formal banking system to lend a multiple of the deposits held.[2] For example, a 10 percent reserve requirement means that banking system could create $1000 of credit for every $100 of deposits. The bank in which the $100 was first deposited must retain $10 as the reserve requirement and can lend $90. The borrowers then spend the $90 which is deposited in banks. Those banks retain $9 as their reserve requirement and can lend $81. The borrowers then spend the $81, which again is deposited in banks. Those banks retain $8.10, and lend $72.90. The original deposit of $100 thus has resulted in credit of $243.90 and spending of the same amount. But, the $72.90 can provide more credit, just as the original $100 did. This can continue, and in the limit $1000 of credit can be created. The banking system in effect has taken $100 and created economic activity of $1000 (= $100/0.10). Credit is the fuel of the economy.

---

[1] Rinehart and Rogoff, Tables 10.3 and 10.4, pp. 151–153.
[2] Banks are subject to capital requirements under the Basel II agreement and as of 2013 the Basel III agreement discussed later in the chapter.

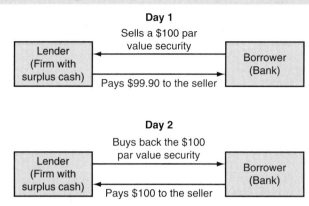

FIGURE 11-1 Repurchase Agreement

If a depositor wants to withdraw her funds, the bank pays the depositor and must replace the funds with other deposits or reduce its loans. Deposits are generally short term but loans such as for the purchase of a house are long term, as are many of the loans to businesses, so banks can have difficulty reducing their outstanding loans when deposits are withdrawn. If many depositors attempt to withdraw their funds at the same time, the bank may not be able to pay them. Bank runs caused by depositors' nervousness about whether they will be able to withdraw their funds can cause a bank to fail, as in the Great Depression. Bank runs by depositors have all but disappeared because of deposit insurance provided by the Federal Deposit Insurance Corporation (FDIC), which covered deposits up to $100,000 and up to $250,000 since the height of the crisis in late 2008.

A principal source of funds for banks is short term borrowing from businesses and investment funds with surplus cash. To accommodate short-term financing, the repurchase, or repo, market developed in which a firm or fund with surplus cash lends, often overnight, to a borrower such as a bank that puts up collateral and makes a payment analogous to interest referred to as a repo rate.[3] This "shadow banking" system operates outside the purview of regulators and provides much of the financing for banks, securities traders, and mortgage lenders.

Figure 11-1 illustrates a basic repurchase agreement. On day 1 a borrower that wants to borrow overnight sells to a lender (e.g., a firm with surplus cash) a security with a value of $100 with an agreement to buy back the security the next day for $100. In exchange for the security, the lender transfers $99.90 to the borrower, where the $0.10 difference represents a "haircut" that covers counterparty risk on the transaction (i.e., that the borrower will not repurchase the security). The borrower thus has $99.90 to use for one day. On day 2 the borrower fulfills the second part of the contract by buying the security back from the lender for $100.[4] The lender thus has earned $0.10, which is analogous to interest. The repo rate is the annualized percentage return and is higher the riskier is the borrower. This shadow banking system functioned efficiently until the financial crisis in 2008, when it froze.

Another component of the shadow banking system is securitization. Securitization involves pooling contractual debt obligations and issuing new securities backed by those obligations. The purpose of securitization is to provide liquidity by mitigating risk through diversification within a class of pooled instruments, yielding a better risk-adjusted return for investors and higher values for the originators of the contractual debt. Credit card borrowings and mortgage loans are the largest securitization categories, but a wide array of financial obligations ranging from automobile loans to student loans to certain insurance contracts are securitized. Well-designed securitizations are an important means of dealing with risk and providing liquidity.

Figure 11-2 illustrates the securitization of mortgage loans. Banks that make mortgage loans and non-depository mortgage loan originators sell most of their mortgage loans, which then provides funds to lend to additional borrowers. A bank such as Goldman Sachs creates a

---

[3]The Federal Reserve has long used repurchase agreements in its open market operations.
[4]One advantage of a repurchase agreement is that it is treated as a single transaction, so the sale of the security and its repurchase are not recorded as an asset sale and the purchase of a new asset.

FIGURE 11-2   Collateralized Debt Obligations

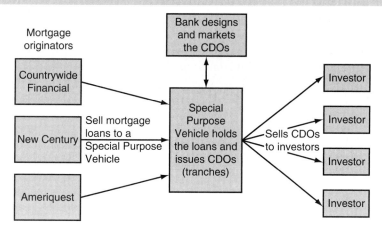

special-purpose vehicle (SPV) that buys the mortgage loans and issues new securities referred to as collateralized debt obligations (CDOs). The bank engineers the new securities so as to diversify risk, which provides a financial gain that is divided between the mortgage loan originators, the purchasers of the CDOs, and the bank.

The diversification comes in two forms. First, the loans used to back the CDOs have idiosyncratic risks that can be diversified by creating a portfolio. To illustrate this diversification, consider a $100 investment in an asset that will pay $160 with probability one-half and $60 with probability one-half. The expected or mean payoff is $110 and the variance is $2,500 = 0.5(60 - 110)^2 + 0.5(160 - 110)^2$. As an alternative, consider investing $50 in each of two assets with the same payoff structure; that is, payoffs of $80 and $30 with equal probabilities, and uncorrelated returns—if one of the $50 investments pays $30, the other is equally likely to pay $30 or $80. The expected payoff is again $110, but the variance is 1,250. Similarly, investing $25 in four such assets has an expected payoff of $110 and a variance of 625. The riskiness on the investment thus decreases as the $100 investment is allocated over more assets, and in the limit the expected return is $110 with the variance approaching 0. This is the Law of Large Numbers. If the returns on the assets are correlated (e.g., if the return on one asset is $30, the return on the other asset is more likely to be $30 than $80), the reduction of variance is smaller than if returns were not correlated. If the returns are perfectly correlated, diversification does not reduce the risk.

In the securitization of mortgages, diversification could be achieved by pooling mortgages for house purchases in different parts of the country. This could include both prime and subprime loans and could include loans with different maturities.

Second, in constructing CDOs, the mortgage loans were sliced into tranches with the cash flows from the mortgages cascading down the tranches as in a waterfall. That is, cash flowed first to the most senior tranche, the remaining cash going to the next (e.g., mezzanine) tranche, and the remainder going to the non-investment grade or equity tranche.[5] The most senior tranches thus were the least risky, whereas the bottom tranches were the riskiest. CDOs corresponding to each tranche were sold to investors who were eager for the higher returns.

As an example of a mortgage-backed CDO, Goldman Sachs Alternative Mortgage Products created the SPV GSAMP Trust 2006-S3, which was one of 83 created in 2006 by Goldman Sachs with a value of $44.5 billion.[6] The principal features of GSAMP Trust 2006-S3 were:

- $494 million of loans representing 8,274 second mortgages
- Average interest rate of 10.51 percent; 2.85 percent was retained to cover defaults.
- Average equity of borrowers in the house was 0.71 percent
- 58 percent were no-documentation or low-documentation loans

---

[5]The equity tranche could be retained by the bank, used in backing other CDOs, or in some cases sold.
[6]Allan Sloan, "Junk Mortgages Under the Microscope," *Fortune*, October 16, 2007. Gorton and Souleles (2006) consider SPVs in detail.

- 13 tranches of CDOs were created
    Top tranches A-1, A-2, A-3
    Mezzanine M-1 through M-7
    3 non-investment grade tranches
- 68 percent of the $494 million of securities were rated AAA
- Another 25 percent were rated investment grade

The payments from the mortgage loans were received by the SPV and used to cover the top tranche CDO A-1 first, the second tranche A-2 next, and so on.[7]

These CDOs were quite risky. First, the borrowers on average had less than 1 percent equity in their homes, so if housing prices fell, the borrowers would owe more than the value of their houses. Second, the CDOs were backed by second mortgages, so if there was a default, the holder of the second mortgage would be paid only after the first mortgage had been paid. Third, the income or job status of 58 percent of the borrowers had not been verified. Yet, 93 percent of the CDOs created were given an investment grade rating by the credit rating agencies. That is, according to the credit rating agencies the CDOs created from the mortgages were of sufficiently high quality that almost all could be purchased by banks, insurance companies, and retirement funds. Moody's Investor Services estimated an ultimate default rate of 10 percent, but within 18 months 18 percent of the loans had defaulted.

As this example indicates, CDOs can be risky, and holders of CDOs often hedge their risks by purchasing credit default swaps (CDSs). Figure 11-3 illustrates a simple CDS. In the top panel a CDO investor such as Goldman Sachs that may have retained an equity tranche enters into a contract with a provider of CDSs such as AIG. The provider promises to pay the $100 face value of the CDO in the case of a "credit event" such as the failure of the assets backing the CDO, and in exchange the investor makes a periodic payment to the provider that is analogous to an insurance premium. If a credit event occurs as in panel two, the provider pays $100 to the investor, which transfers the CDO to the provider of the CDSs. When CDSs are priced efficiently in the market, the periodic payment reflects the risk on the CDO.

A CDS involves another kind of risk because the provider of the CDS might be unable to make the payment in a credit event. To cover this counterparty risk, the purchaser (Goldman Sachs) of a CDS can require the provider to post collateral that the purchaser retains if its counterparty (AIG) defaults. The amount of collateral required depends on the riskiness of the counterparty, and the purchaser can demand more collateral as that risk increases. In 2008 Goldman Sachs became concerned about the financial health of AIG and demanded more

FIGURE 11-3   Credit Default Swap

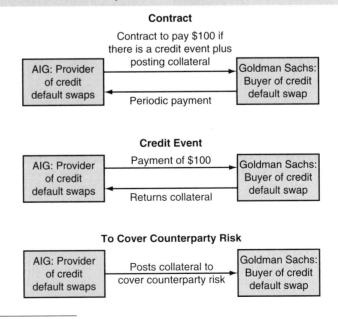

[7]For a description of tranches see John Park, "The Impact of Subprime Residential Mortgage-Backed Securities on Moody's-Rated Structured Finance CDOs: A Preliminary Review," Moody's Investors Service, March 23, 2007.

collateral which contributed to the collapse of AIG. CDOs and CDSs play a central role in the chapter case *Goldman Sachs and Its Reputation*.

The mortgage, securitization, and CDS markets performed efficiently through 2006, and mortgage lenders made increasingly riskier loans as rising housing prices made buying a home attractive. Housing prices began to fall broadly in the United States in 2007, and delinquencies increased. The broad decline in housing prices meant that the risks on subprime mortgages were correlated and had not been diversified, and the prices of mortgage-backed securities began to fall. In 2008 fears that the banks Bear Stearns, Lehman Brothers, and Washington Mutual might fail led to a run on the shadow banking system or a "run on repo" as cash-surplus lenders demanded larger and larger haircuts, effectively cutting off funding to the banks.[8] Bear Stearns and Washington Mutual failed with the government forcing Bear Stearns to be sold to JPMorgan Chase and Washington Mutual being seized by the Office of Thrift Supervision with the banking assets then sold to JPMorgan Chase. In September 2008 Lehman Brothers, which was highly leveraged and dependent on repo financing, failed as repo lenders required greater and greater haircuts. Lehman declared bankruptcy and closed its doors.[9] Fears spread and the financial markets, including the repo, securitization, and CDS markets, froze. This caused a credit crisis and an economic crisis that some have called the Great Recession. As a result of the financial crisis another round of regulation was imposed on financial institutions and on financial markets in the form of the Dodd-Frank Wall Street Reform and Consumer Protection Act of 2010, which is discussed later in this chapter.

THE U.S. REGULATORY STRUCTURE

The Federal Reserve System

The Federal Reserve System was established in 1913 and serves as the central bank of the United States. It has broad responsibilities for managing the money supply and has regulatory authority over national banks and state banks that participate in the Federal Reserve System. The Federal Reserve provides liquidity to the financial system through its credit window and has certain regulatory responsibility pertaining to consumer credit. The Federal Reserve is governed by a seven-member board of governors whose chairman is Ben Bernanke. The Fed is composed of 12 regional Federal Reserve Banks, and the Federal Reserve Bank of New York serves as overseer of banks and managed the bailout of banks during the financial crisis.

The Federal Reserve is independent of the presidential administration, although the members of the board of governors are appointed by the president and confirmed by the Senate. The term of office for a board member is 14 years, and the chairman and vice chairman have 4-year terms. The Federal Reserve is also independent of the congressional budget process, since it earns large profits that finance its operations with its surpluses paid to the Treasury. The Federal Reserve is thus an independent central bank.

The Federal Reserve is subject to the acts of Congress, and Congress has refrained from altering its independence. Congress has, however, assigned the Fed certain responsibilities for consumer credit giving it rule-making authority over the practices of credit card companies, particularly focusing on disclosure. The Federal Reserve also has responsibilities for certain lending practices, such as the subprime lending by consumer finance companies, as considered in the chapter case *Citigroup and Subprime Lending*.

Securities Regulation

Much of the regulatory structure for the financial markets was born in the Great Depression and the New Deal of President Franklin Delano Roosevelt. The stock market crash in 1929 was viewed as a cause of the depression, and Roosevelt sought to reduce the risks in the securities markets. The first New Deal legislation enacted was the Securities Act of 1933 which regulated the issuance of new securities, and the following year Congress enacted the Securities Exchange Act to extend regulation to stock exchanges and the trading of already-issued securities. The

---

[8]Gorton and Metrick (2009).
[9]Lehman's North American assets and operations were subsequently sold to Barclays, and its Asian and certain European businesses were sold to Nomura Holdings.

Securities Exchange Act also established the Securities and Exchange Commission (SEC) to regulate and police the markets and those who trade in them.

The principle embodied in the acts was full disclosure so that the parties to securities transactions could make better-informed decisions. The Securities Act required full disclosure when new securities were issued, and the Securities Exchange Act required full disclosure when securities were traded. This was seen as important to restoring public confidence in the securities markets. Companies with publicly traded securities were also required to make public disclosures of information in conjunction with proxy solicitations and tender offers. The Securities Exchange Act also regulated insider trading and prohibited fraud in securities transactions, with the SEC assigned enforcement powers.

The Glass-Steagall Act of 1933 forced banks to separate their commercial banking and investment banking businesses. As a result, in 1935 the House of Morgan built by J. Pierpont Morgan separated into a commercial bank, JPMorgan & Company, and an investment bank, Morgan Stanley. The Act also established the FDIC to insure deposits in banks.

After two decades of political activity by banks, the Glass-Steagall Act was repealed by the Gramm-Leach-Bliley Act of 1999. After the repeal JPMorgan merged with Chase Manhattan in 2001 to form the present-day JPMorgan Chase & Company. The repeal allowed bank holding companies to engage in broader financial activities, such as insurance, in addition to banking. In anticipation of the repeal Citibank and the Travelers Group insurance company merged to form Citigroup, then the world's largest financial services company. In 2008 Citigroup became insolvent and was rescued with a government infusion of $25 billion.

Credit Card Regulation

Borrowing on credit cards reached nearly $1 trillion in 2008, and Congress has been active in regulating practices in the industry. Consumers complained about large and sudden increases in interest rates on credit card borrowings and about late fees imposed without adequate notice, among other practices. In response Congress passed the Credit CARD (Card Accountability Responsibility and Disclosure) Act of 2009 to increase the regulation of credit card issuers. The Act as well as regulations by the Federal Reserve System provided transparency to credit card users and also significantly restricted the practices of the card issuers.

Regulations intended to eliminate abuses can have effects on markets. The new regulations restricted the ability of card issuers to use risk-based pricing and to re-price risks when a cardholder had a credit event. The reduced pricing flexibility meant that risks could not be priced efficiently. The issuer then had the choice between bearing the risk, imposing the costs on other cardholders, or cancelling the card. Bearing the risk forces other cardholders to cross-subsidize the high-risk cardholder through higher average interest rates, whereas cancelling the card avoids cross-subsidization by letting high-risk cardholders turn elsewhere for credit. Kenneth Clayton of the American Bankers Association said, "Prior to the Card Act, we were able to charge people for the risk they posed and, as a result, also allowed others to pay lower rates."[10] When credit card issuers cancel the cards of high-risk cardholders, fewer people have access to credit.

THE FINANCIAL CRISIS, 2007–2009
Mortgage Lending and Subprime Mortgages

Mortgage lending had been dominated by banks and savings and loans associations, and lenders held some of the mortgages they originated and sold the rest to the government-sponsored enterprises, the Federal National Mortgage Association (Fannie Mae) and the Federal Home Loan Mortgage Corporation (Freddie Mac), which provided guarantees and repackaged loans and sold them to investors. In addition to the loan purchases and guarantees provided by Fannie Mae and Freddie Mac, the Federal Housing Administration (FHA) provided financing for qualified borrowers. Government policy supported expanding home ownership through government support of Fannie Mae, Freddie Mac, and the FHA.

In the 2000s non-bank lenders such as Countrywide Financial, Ameriquest, Long Beach, and New Century Financial innovated with a variety of subprime mortgages that allowed borrowers who previously had been unable to qualify for conventional conforming mortgages to

---

[10]*New York Times*, August 5, 2009.

now obtain mortgages. These companies did not take deposits but instead financed their lending with short-term borrowing in the commercial paper and repo markets and by selling their mortgage loans to banks for securitization. By May 2007 Countrywide had borrowed $18.3 billion in asset-backed commercial paper. As a result of a change in bankruptcy laws in 2005 the repo market began to take CDOs and other derivatives as collateral, greatly expanding repo lending.[11] The short-term financing fueled the rapid growth in subprime lending, and the demand by investors resulted in a huge growth in mortgage-backed CDOs issued by banks. By 2006 privately issued CDOs reached $1.15 trillion, of which 71 percent were subprime or low initial rate loans. "Countrywide's essential business strategy was 'originating what was salable in the secondary market.' The company sold or securitized 87 percent of the $1.5 trillion it originated between 2002 and 2005."[12] Sales contracts typically had provisions that allowed the buyer to demand that the seller take the mortgages back under certain circumstances such as fraud. Bank of America, which bought Countrywide after it failed, was forced to take back over $5 billion in mortgages.

The originators of mortgage loans could be either offices of the lender, as in the case of Countrywide's 1,300 storefront offices and Washington Mutual's retail branches that between 2000 and 2003 grew by 70 percent to 2,200, or independent mortgage brokers.[13] Mortgage brokers accounted for 60–70 percent of the lending during the early part of the decade. Herbert Sanders, head of World Savings, said, "You have to understand how independent brokers work. They are the whores of the world." Yet by 2006 independent brokers were accounting for 60 percent of World Savings' loan business.[14]

Loan originators innovated with a variety of loans including adjustable-rate mortgages (ARMs) with low initial "teaser" interest rates that increased after a stipulated period, Alt-A loans that were interest-only for the first years, and option-ARMs that allowed borrowers to determine how much they paid each month. Payments on these loans were scheduled to increase sharply after the initial period to the point that many borrowers would be unable to meet them. Borrowers whose credit rating had improved were expected to refinance, and those whose credit had not improved were expected to sell their houses. With rising housing prices the latter alternative was not of concern to many borrowers.

In addition to subprime mortgages, lenders began to require less than the standard 20 percent down payment and also provided second mortgages. They also began making no documentation loans, referred to as "no-doc" or "stated-income" loans where the originator did not verify the income of the borrower but instead either accepted the borrower's claim of income or made up an income. These loans were referred to as "liar loans."[15]

In part, the "investor's appetite" drove mortgage lending through the demand for CDOs. Jeff Schaefer, an originator at Lehman Brothers, stated, "How do you blame us? A lot of what we did from an origination standpoint was based on investors' appetite. Do you think we would just go out and say, 'I think we're going to do $100 million in no-doc loans?'"[16] Patricia Lindsay of New Century observed, "Wall Street was very hungry for our product. We had loans sold three months in advance, before they were even made at one point."[17]

The securities sold to investors were rated by the credit rating agencies, but providing a rating was a challenge. Subprime loans were made to a new class of borrowers who previously had not qualified under traditional lending standards, so the models and historical data used by the credit rating agencies were inadequate for rating the new CDOs. In addition, obtaining information to produce better-informed credit ratings was at times difficult. For one CDO, Moody's

---

[11]Financial Crisis Inquiry Commission, Report, Washington, D.C., p. 114.

[12]Financial Crisis Inquiry Commission, p. 105.Originators typically held a portion of their loans to provide assurance to buyers by keeping some "skin in the game."

[13]*New York Times,* December 25, 2008.

[14]Ibid.

[15]Loan origination was subject to many types of fraud by borrowers and brokers, as detailed by the Mortgage Asset Research Institute (2010). The FBI reported that the number of Suspicious Activity Reports from all federally insured financial institutions increased from 3,245 in 2000 to 35,617 in 2006 and 67,190 in 2009. These reports could be associated with loans made in earlier years so the numbers must be assessed with care, but it is clear that the increase was dramatic. Florida, New York, and California had the largest ratios of fraud and misrepresentation cases relative to loan originations, and over a 5-year period more than 60 percent of the cases involved fraud in the application including reported income and employment.

[16]*New York Times*, September 13, 2009.

[17]FCIC, p. 117.

requested the "collateral tapes" from the originating investment bank, and the managing director responded, "Any request for loan level tapes is TOTALLY UNREASONABLE!!! Most investors don't have it and can't provide it. Nevertheless we MUST produce a credit estimate …. It is your responsibility to provide those credit estimates and your responsibility to devise some method for doing so."[18]

Credit rating agencies were also under competitive pressure to give high ratings on CDOs, since issuers of CDOs shopped for the highest ratings. Under competitive pressure the credit rating agencies also showed their ratings models to the investment banks, which then engineered their CDOs to meet the minimum requirements for a rating (e.g., AAA).[19]

Representative Henry Waxman characterized the role of the credit rating agencies, quoting from a Standard & Poor's document, "Ratings agencies continue to create [an] even bigger monster—the CDO market. Let's hope we are all wealthy and retired by the time this house of cards falters."[20] When it began to collapse, the credit rating agencies downgraded the CDOs and by nearly twice the number of notches as the historical average for downgrades. Benmelech and Dlogosz (2010) reported that in 2007 there were 8,000 downgrades, which was eight times the number in 2006, and in the first three quarters of 2008 there were 36,880 downgrades.

With financing readily available and a strong demand for CDOs from investors both within and outside the United States attracted by high returns and AAA ratings, housing prices continued to increase through 2006. "With house prices already up 91% from 1995 to 2003, this flood of money and the securitization apparatus helped boost home prices another 36% from the beginning of 2004 until the peak in April 2006—even as homeownership was falling."[21] Lenders had early signals that mortgages were going bad. "The percentage of Countrywide's option ARMs that were negatively amortizing grew from just 1% in 2004 to 53% in 2005 and then to more than 90% by 2007."[22] This did not stop Countrywide from continuing its subprime lending.

Housing prices began to fall late in 2006, borrowers began defaulting, lenders failed, CDO prices fell, and the financial crisis began. The next section considers explanations for the crisis.

Financial Crisis Inquiry Commission

The Financial Crisis Inquiry Commission (FCIC) was created by Congress to investigate the causes of the financial crisis, and in 2011 it issued a 633-page report with six of its members voting to adopt the report and four members dissenting. The majority concluded that the crisis was avoidable and that stronger regulation and more vigilant enforcement could have prevented the crisis. The majority laid much of the blame on Wall Street and its securitization of high-risk mortgages. The principal conclusions of the majority were:

1. This financial crisis was avoidable
2. Widespread failures in financial regulation and supervision proved devastating to the stability of the nation's financial markets
3. Dramatic failures of corporate governance and risk management at many systemically important financial institutions was a key cause of this crisis
4. A combination of excessive borrowing, risky investments, and lack of transparency put the financial system on a collision course with crisis
5. The government was ill prepared for the crisis, and its inconsistent response added to the uncertainty and panic in the financial markets
6. There was a systematic breakdown in accountability and ethics
7. Collapsing mortgage-lending standards and the mortgage securitization pipeline lit and spread the flame of contagion and crisis
8. Over-the-counter derivatives contributed significantly to this crisis
9. The failures of the credit rating agencies were essential cogs in the wheel of financial destruction

---

[18]Cited by Representative Henry Waxman, "Opening Statement," Hearing on the Credit Rating Agencies and the Financial Crisis, House of Representatives, October 22, 2008.
[19]See Benmelech and Dlugosz (2009).
[20]Representative Henry Waxman, "Opening Statement," Hearing on the Credit Rating Agencies and the Financial Crisis, House of Representatives, October 22, 2008.
[21]Financial Crisis Inquiry Commission, p. 103.
[22]Ibid., p. 108.

The majority gave little blame to the role of Fannie Mae and Freddie Mac or to the Community Reinvestment Act (CRA).[23]

Three of the dissenters characterized the majority report as a compilation of all the bad events that took place rather than as an explanation of the critical factors that caused the crisis. They also criticized the majority for ignoring evidence of a crisis in Europe at the same time as the one in the United States that could not have been caused by regulatory failure in the United States. They wrote, "Not all these factors identified by the majority were irrelevant; they were just not essential."[24] The dissenters identified 10 essential causes of the crisis:

1. Credit bubble
2. Housing bubble
3. Nontraditional mortgages
4. Credit ratings and securitization
5. Financial institutions concentrated correlated risks
6. Leverage and liquidity risk
7. Risk of contagion
8. Common shock (the fall in housing prices)
9. Financial shock and panic
10. Financial crisis causes economic crisis

Causes

The financial crisis was a perfect storm of multiple factors. The United States had run large trade deficits during the 2000s, particularly with China; the federal budget deficits were large; and the savings rate in the United States was low. The budget and trade deficits had to be funded, and with a low domestic savings rate the funds had to come from other countries. The United States continued to be the safest country in which to invest, and foreign investors bought U.S. government bonds and notes. In addition, large amounts of capital flowed into the United States looking for other assets in which to invest.[25] The only market large enough to absorb the inflow was land and housing, and housing prices rose at rates that greatly exceeded their historical average. From 1996 to 2006 housing prices increased 92 percent in real terms.[26] In addition, the inflow of funds reduced interest rates making it cheaper to finance home purchases and new construction. During this period the Federal Reserve kept interest rates low in the aftermath of the bursting of the dot-com bubble. The housing market boomed, particularly in states such as Arizona, California, Florida, and Nevada. The housing market also boomed in Europe, particularly in Spain.

The boom in the United States was fueled by a number of federal policies. The government sought broader home ownership, mortgage interest payments were tax deductible, and the first $500,000 of capital gains on the sale of a house was tax exempt. In the 2000s further steps were taken to broaden house ownership, which meant enabling people who had not been able to qualify for a mortgage in the past to now obtain one. President George W. Bush urged broader home ownership, Fannie Mae and Freddie Mac bought riskier subprime loans, the CRA required broader lending, and activist groups such as ACORN pushed for broader lending to low-income borrowers.[27] In addition, homeowners traded up as the prices of their homes increased, and some people bought houses as speculative investments.[28] Developers rushed in to supply the demand for new housing, and the home construction boom contributed to the growth in the economy.

Lenders innovated with subprime loans, contributing to the increases in housing prices. Lenders were able to make risky subprime loans and sell them quickly for securitization rather than hold them, reducing the risk they faced. Lenders also increasingly relied on mortgage brokers to originate the mortgages they funded, making it harder to monitor lending standards.

---

[23]Under the CRA of 1977 banks were required to lend in the neighborhoods in which they received deposits, which meant making mortgages available in low-income areas where relatively few individuals would qualify under traditional mortgage standards.

[24]Report, p. 416.

[25]See Chinnn and Frieden (2011).

[26]Rinehart and Rogoff, p. 207.

[27]Edward Pinto, "Acorn and the Housing Bubble," *Wall Street Journal*, November 13, 2009.

[28]Sarah Nash, a nurse with a salary of $60,000, purchased three homes for between $120,000 and $200,000 each with no down payments and adjustable-rate loans. She planned to rent the houses, but unable to rent or sell them, she defaulted in 2007. Even with her credit score in ruins, she said, "I consider myself a very smart person and I did some very dumb things. I just have to live with it." *Wall Street Journal,* June 25, 2010.

Mortgage brokers were paid based on the number and not the performance of the loans they originated, so they had strong incentives to originate loans. Low-doc and no-doc loans became prevalent, as did liar loans. The result was that many people bought houses with mortgages they could not afford—unless everything went well. The riskiness of the mortgage loan pool increased substantially.

The increased riskiness of the mortgages being issued was not necessarily a problem because the financial markets can diversify risks by pooling risky assets whose returns are uncorrelated. Price changes in local housing markets had varied considerably over time, but local price movements were largely uncorrelated. This meant that banks could pool mortgages with uncorrelated risks and use them to back CDOs that had lower risk.

As housing prices began to weaken, some homeowners walked away from their homes which were under water, and others became delinquent. The new construction market also began to slump. The changes in housing prices were not uncorrelated as they had been in the past, so much of the diversification claimed in the CDOs was false. The prices of CDOs began to fall. The falling prices of the CDOs began to be felt by banks and investors.

As CDO prices fell, the counterparty risk in the repo market increased, and lenders demanded more collateral or a greater haircut for the repo financing they provided. Bear Stearns, Merrill Lynch, Washington Mutual, and a number of small banks as well as subprime lenders began to fail, and the government intervened, as considered in the next section. The final nail in the coffin was the failure of the highly leveraged Lehman Brothers, which had relied on repo financing and the confidence of repo lenders. When lenders sensed that Lehman might fail, they demanded greater haircuts or more collateral to compensate for the greater counterparty risk. With Lehman unable to meet the collateral demands, the lenders stopped providing funds and Lehman failed. The federal government, which had arranged for the sale of Bear Stearns earlier in the year, did not rescue Lehman Brothers, which then declared bankruptcy. The bankruptcy of Lehman Brothers in September 2008 signaled that the risks were much greater than had been appreciated by many investors. The repo market then froze as nervous lenders stopped providing credit, leading to a severe recession.

TARP, Bailouts, and the Stimulus

As the severity of the crisis became clearer in 2008, a consensus developed that the government had to act to prevent a possible collapse of the banking system. The Bush administration and Congress created the Troubled Asset Relief Program (TARP) administered by the Department of the Treasury. TARP was authorized with funding up to $700 billion to be used to shore up banks and stimulate the provision of credit to borrowers. During the last months of 2008 $294 billion was provided to banks, including the former investment banks, and the insurance giant AIG that had provided huge amounts of credit default swaps that it could not cover.[29] The government received equity warrants or preferred stock in exchange for the funds, and the expectation was that the warrants would be redeemed when the banks' financial health improved. The Obama administration also used $94 billion of TARP funds to bail out General Motors and Chrysler and to provide funds for the "Making Homes Affordable" program to restructure residential mortgages and provide funds to homeowners with under-water mortgages. Although TARP was successful in preventing a collapse of the financial system, it was less successful in stimulating lending by banks.

Most of the TARP funds provided to banks was quickly repaid with interest, and in late 2010 the Treasury estimated that the ultimate cost of TARP would be $29 billion, counting a profit of $22 billion on AIG shares obtained in exchange for warrants. The losses on TARP came from the bailouts of General Motors and Chrysler, or as some commentators said the bailout of the United Automobile Workers union since shareholders in the companies received nothing, and from the residential mortgage restructuring and support program estimated to cost $45.6 billion when completed.

TARP was dwarfed by the Obama administration's $787 billion economic stimulus program. The program provided funding for a variety of projects and included a host of tax credits,

---

[29]The government had intervened in 1998 to prevent Long-Term Capital Management (LTCM) from failing. LTCM, which had obligations of $125 billion, was on the verge of collapse due to the Russian default on bonds in 1998, and the Federal Reserve Bank of New York arranged a $3.625 billion, privately financed bailout with most of the major banks and securities firms providing the funding. The banks and securities firms subsequently liquidated LTCM.

most of which were tied to particular activities. Income tax rates were not reduced, but withholding rates were. Tax credits were given to first-time homebuyers, new car buyers who turned in a clunker, and homeowners who made their homes more energy efficient. A tax credit was also given under the Making Work Pay program designed to help taxpayers avoid the alternative minimum tax.

The effect of the stimulus on the economy was unclear. Proponents argued that it resulted in job creation and that the projects funded would transform the economy, whereas critics pointed to the continuing high unemployment rates, called the projects pork, and viewed the stimulus as a cause of the record federal budget deficit. What was clear was that the United States incurred record budget deficits because of the sharply higher spending and lower tax revenues.

What was also clear was that the stimulus was a political failure. Most Americans did not benefit from the stimulus, unemployment remained high, and the record budget deficit meant sacrifice in the future. These sentiments were reflected in the 2010 elections in which Republicans gained 63 seats and a majority in the House and gained 6 seats in the Senate. The gain in the House was the largest for a mid-term election in over 70 years.[30]

Fannie Mae and Freddie Mac

Fannie Mae and Freddie Mac are government sponsored enterprises (GSE) created to support the issuance of mortgage loans. Their mission was to help make home ownership affordable by providing liquidity for the mortgage market by creating a secondary market in mortgages. Fannie Mae purchased government-supported loans, such as those from the Federal Housing Authority, and private loans from banks and savings and loan associations, and then securitized the mortgages and sold them providing liquidity to the market. Fannie Mae also guaranteed mortgages. Fannie Mae was part of government until it was privatized in 1968. In 1970 Freddie Mac was created as an alternative to Fannie Mae.

In 1992, legislation assigned Fannie Mae and Freddie Mac the responsibility for supporting low-income and moderate-income home ownership and gave them annual affordable housing goals. Those goals increased from 30 percent of the housing units financed to 55 percent in 2007. The companies were also required to expand mortgage loan availability in inner city areas under the CRA. To meet its affordable housing mandates, Fannie Mae loosened its standards and began to purchase subprime mortgages in addition to the prime (or conforming) mortgages that it had traditionally purchased.[31] The pressure for greater low-income housing and the weakening of Fannie Mae standards contributed to the explosion in subprime lending.

Some efforts were made in the 2000s to reduce the riskiness of Fannie Mae and Freddie Mac, but Representative Barney Frank (D-MA) stated his opposition: "These two entities—Fannie Mae and Freddie Mac—are not facing any kind of financial crisis. The more people exaggerate these problems, the more pressure there is on these companies, the less we will see in terms of affordable housing."[32] This assessment proved wrong, and as the financial health of the two companies continued to worsen, the government seized Fannie Mae and Freddie Mac in September 2008 and provided an infusion of funds from the Department of the Treasury.[33] The Obama administration estimated that the bailouts of Fannie Mae and Freddie Mac would cost $224 billion by 2013.

THE DODD-FRANK WALL STREET REFORM AND CONSUMER PROTECTION ACT

Anger with the perceived excesses of Wall Street and a desire to protect consumers from burdensome borrowing led Congress with the support of the Obama administration to enact legislation to increase regulation in an attempt to prevent future crises. In the final stages of work on new legislation, government investigations revealed that Goldman Sachs appeared to have taken advantage of a client to serve another investor's interests by failing to disclose that the securities in a

---

[30]Voters also expressed anger about the recession and the health care reform legislation enacted in 2010.

[31]For 2011 the conforming loan limit for single-family dwellings was $417,000 and for high-cost areas it was $729,750.

[32]*New York Times*, September 11, 2003.

[33]The FHA also failed and was seized by the government.

synthetic CDO had been selected to fail, allowing the investor to profit by shorting the security.[34] The revelation and the subsequent filing of a civil fraud lawsuit against Goldman Sachs by the SEC helped propel the pending legislation to passage in 2010. The chapter case *Goldman Sachs and Its Reputation* considers this and other events that posed a challenge to Goldman Sachs.

The 2,300-page Dodd-Frank Act provided for new regulations, strengthened enforcement, and required new rule making by regulators. It represented the most sweeping regulation of the financial system since the 1930s. Many of the effects of the Act were highly uncertain. Some of the uncertainty was the result of Congress delegating important rule making to government agencies based on studies yet to be conducted. The Act called for 67 studies and the writing of 243 new regulatory rules. As illustrated in Figure 7-1 attention turned to the administrative agencies that would conduct the studies and write the rules.

The Act also created a new regulatory agency, the Consumer Financial Protection Bureau, restricted the pricing of credit card borrowings, increased the exposure of credit rating agencies to lawsuits, restricted securities trading by banks, required derivatives trades to go through clearinghouses, and imposed new capital requirements on banks. The Act did not address the roles of Fannie Mae and Freddie Mac.

Some of the provisions of the Act would be implemented only after a transition period that could last as long as 5 years, as in the case of the regulation of swaps and derivatives. The following sections identify provisions of the Act pertaining to the causes of the financial crisis.

Financial Stability Oversight Council

The Dodd-Frank Act established a Financial Stability Oversight Council composed of the heads of 10 regulatory agencies with responsibility for monitoring the economy and responding to emergencies that threaten the stability of the financial system. To reduce systemic risks, the council by a two-thirds vote can place under regulation by the Federal Reserve a firm that poses a systemic financial risk. The Act imposed a floor on capital requirements for firms and authorized the council to impose a 15-1 leverage ratio on a firm that poses a grave threat to the financial system

Too Big to Fail

The Act authorized the government to seize and break up a firm whose collapse could result in substantial harm to the economy.[35] The Act also required financial companies to develop "living wills" for closing down and provided for the orderly liquidation of failed companies. The public opposition to TARP and the bailout led to provisions in the Act prohibiting taxpayer funds from going to bail out a financial company. The Federal Reserve was also limited in its ability to provide emergency funds to individual companies, but broad-based programs approved by the Secretary of the Treasury could be implemented provided that they did not permit a failing company to benefit.

The Volcker Rule

To reduce speculative investments by banks, former Federal Reserve chairman Paul Volcker advocated prohibiting banks that take deposits from engaging in proprietary trading. A "Volcker Rule" was included in the Dodd-Frank Act after heated debate and was subsequently subject to extensive rule-making activity to refine the restrictions. The rule allowed banks to trade on behalf of clients and to hedge their own risks. Under the rule a bank's ownership in hedge funds and private equity funds was restricted to no more than 3 percent of its Tier 1 capital, composed of common equity, retained earnings, and certain nonredeemable preferred stock. A bank also was restricted from owning more than 3 percent of a hedge fund or private equity fund. These requirements covered non-depository banks such as Goldman Sachs and Morgan Stanley.

Nonbank financial companies including hedge funds were required to register as investment advisors and be subject to restrictions on capital requirements and investments as determined by rules to be determined by regulators. They may also be subject to supervision by the Federal Reserve if so designated by the Financial Stability Oversight Council.

---

[34]A synthetic CDO is not backed by assets such as mortgages, but instead its returns are determined by the performance of other securities such as mortgages or CDOs.

[35]The Federal Reserve had not had this authority and thus could not have seized Lehman Brothers when it failed.

Derivatives and Swaps

To reduce risks and increase regulatory scrutiny, the Act gave the Commodities and Futures Trading Commission (CFTC) regulatory authority over swaps and major swap market participants such as market-makers.[36] The Act also gave the SEC regulatory authority over certain security-based swaps including credit default swaps for a single issuer. Swap dealers and major swap market participants were required to register, and regulators were to set minimum capital requirements for them. The swaps themselves must be traded on exchanges or cleared through a clearinghouse that serves multiple parties, and dealers may be required to post a margin or collateral with the clearinghouse to cover possible losses. Derivatives contracts had traditionally been settled or cleared bilaterally by the parties to the contract, and to reduce counterparty risk, such contracts are required to be cleared multilaterally by a clearinghouse. That is, the seller settles with the clearinghouse, and the buyer also settles with the clearinghouse. Clearinghouses have been used for years for settling futures contracts. At the insistence of Senator Blanche Lincoln (D-AK) no federal assistance could be provided to nonbank entities, swap dealers, and hedge funds.

Securitization and Excessive Risks

Issuers of asset-backed securities such as mortgage-backed CDOs, were required to retain at least 5 percent of the risk unless the assets meet certain loan standards. This requirement meant that issuers of CDOs would have more "skin in the game" with the hope that they will make more prudent lending and securitization decisions. The 5 percent requirement could be shared, for example, by a mortgage lender that made mortgage loans and a bank that issued CDOs backed by the mortgages. Mortgages determined to be "qualified residential mortgages" (QRM) were exempt from the 5 percent requirement, and mortgage lenders worked hard in an attempt to convince the regulators to define a QRM to include most conforming mortgages.

Hedge funds and private equity funds with assets of over $150 million are required to register with the SEC as investment advisors and to provide data on their trades so that their potential impact on systemic risk can be assessed by regulators. As an investment advisor, a fund has a fiduciary duty to its clients. The Act also permits the SEC, after conducting a study, to impose a fiduciary duty on securities brokers, requiring them to provide advice that is in the interest of their clients.

Consumer Protection

Complaints from consumers and consumer advocacy groups about financial products centered on abusive mortgages, high interest rates charged by payday lenders, and the financing practices of automobile dealers and student loan companies. Consumer advocates and the Obama administration pushed for new protections, and despite strong opposition from business, the Dodd-Frank Act created a Consumer Financial Protection Bureau (CFPB). The bureau has authority over banks with assets over $10 billion, mortgage lenders, student loan companies, and payday lenders, but to reduce opposition by business, auto dealers and small businesses were not covered but could face stronger oversight by agencies that already had responsibilities for their practices. The bureau was housed in the Federal Reserve and its budget was paid by the Fed so as to insulate the bureau from political influence by Congress. The following example concerns an interest group that sought exemption from the new regulation.

The Dodd-Frank Act left some ambiguity about which companies would be subject to regulation by the CFPB. Banks had been concerned by the expansion of Wal-Mart in financial services such as check cashing.[37] The Consumer Bankers Association, whose members are retail banks, lobbied for designation of Wal-Mart as a large participant in financial services and hence subject to regulation.[38]

---

[36]The Act used the term *swap* to cover a wide range of derivatives but not futures contracts that involve a physical settlement, as in a commodities futures contract in which a producer agrees to sell a buyer a commodity at some point in the future.

[37]Wal-Mart was not licensed to operate a bank in the United States but did operate banks in Canada and Mexico.

[38]*Bloomberg Businessweek*, August 15–28, 2011.

EXAMPLE   Constituency Power

Some groups were able to avoid regulation by the CFPB. The United States has 18,000 automobile dealers located in every congressional district. Dealers suffered as a result of the financial crisis as auto sales fell sharply, and General Motors and Chrysler eliminated thousands of dealerships when they reorganized under the bankruptcy laws. Consumer-oriented members of Congress took the opportunity of the 2010 financial reform legislation to regulate the lending practices of auto dealers. The Obama administration argued that an automobile was the second largest purchase made by most families and that consumers should be protected as they would be for mortgage loans under the legislation being con-sidered in Congress. The military also supported inclusion under the proposed consumer protection agency to protect military personnel who were said to be subject to abusive auto lending. Automobile lending was already under the purview of the Federal Trade Commission, which was responsible for enforcing laws against deceptive sales and advertising, and subject to truth-in-lending regulations administered by the Federal Reserve.

The automobile dealers sought an exemption from the new regulations. The incentives for dealers to seek an exemption were clear. New regulations could restrict access to financing, which was essential for most buyers. In addition to the availability of financing, dealers received a fee when they arranged the financing. Auto dealers were often prominent members of local communities with access to government representatives. Representative Jeb Hensarling (R-TX) said of the plan to include automobile lending under the proposed CFPB, "This is a way to restrict access to the automobile."[1]

President Obama made a personal statement opposing an exemption for auto dealers, and a spokesperson for the White House said, "The president vowed to fight efforts to weaken the bill and find ways to strengthen it, which is why he opposes carve-outs like this one that would exempt auto-dealer lenders from new consumer protections."[2] Paul Herrnson, director of the Center for American Politics and Citizenship at the University of Maryland, explained, "They've consistently played the lobbying angle, the campaign-finance angle and the grass-roots angle in pressuring members of Congress. And regardless of who runs the administration … members of Congress listen to their constituents."[3]

Auto dealers were well organized through the National Automobile Dealers Association (NADA) which lobbied on behalf of dealers. In 2009 NADA spent $3.5 million on lobbying, and dealers and their employees spent $10 million on contributions during the election cycle. More importantly, NADA conducted numerous fly-ins to Washington by dealers to lobby their members of Congress. Dealers also encouraged their employees to call and write their representatives. The unrelenting pressure from the auto dealers and their complete coverage of congressional districts was overwhelming, and the opponents of an exemption for auto dealers conceded defeat. Representative Luis Gutierrez (D-IL) said, "The political reality is that those of us who have fought against an auto dealer carve-out can't prevail."[4]

---

[1]*New York Times*, June 23, 2010.

[2]*Wall Street Journal*, June 24, 2010.
[3]Ibid.
[4]*New York Times*, June 23, 2010. Financing through GMAC and Carmax was not exempted.

As with the Credit CARD Act some consumer advocates worried about the effects of the new regulations on the availability of credit for low-income individuals. Business associations called the CFPB part of an increasing "nanny state." The following boxed example is an instance of the anticipated consequences of increased regulation.

EXAMPLE   Anticipated Consequences—Credit Availability

Regulation of the financial system had consequences, some of which were anticipated and some of which were not. One anticipated consequence of the credit card regulation resulting from Federal Reserve rule making and congressional action was reduced availability of credit cards because of the restric-tion on pricing based on risk.

The consumer protection provisions of the Dodd-Frank Act and the CFPB were intended to eliminate some of the abuses that had victimized some consumers.

For example, credit card issuers were prohibited from increasing interest rates quickly when the probability that a cardholder would default increased. What was uncertain was less the protection provided and more the effect of the regulation on the availability and cost of credit to consumers.

Scott Talbott of the Financial Services Roundtable said, "There could be some downsides as well. We've seen an increase in the cost of credit and a decrease in the availability of credit."[1] Jamie Dimon, CEO of JPMorgan Chase, wrote to shareholders in the spring of 2010 explaining why it was reducing the number of customers to which it was issuing credit cards: "In the future, we no longer will be offering credit cards to approximately 15% of the customers to whom we currently offer them. This is mostly because we deem them too risky in light of new regulations restricting our ability to make adjustments over time as the client's risk profile changes."[2] The borrowing alternatives for those who lost their cards were payday lenders and other nontraditional credit providers that charge much higher interest rates than on credit cards. "As the chief financial officer of a national payday-lending chain, Advance America, put it, 'We believe that we're starting to see a benefit of a general reduction in consumer credit, particularly … subprime credit cards.'"[3]

---

[1] *Wall Street Journal*, June 15, 2010.

[2] Ibid.

[3] Todd Zywicki, "Dodd-Frank and the Return of the Loan Shark," *Wall Street Journal*, January 4, 2011.

Compensation

The financial crisis harmed millions of people, yet the compensation of Wall Street firms remained high. Whether the Wall Street firms were an essential cause of the crisis will be debated for many years, but the media, politicians, and the public clearly ascribed responsibility to Wall Street. Moreover, TARP funds were used to bail out the Wall Street firms, and although those funds were quickly repaid (except for AIG) with interest, the public viewed the firms as being supported by tax dollars. Politicians seized on the public concern and in the 2009 stimulus legislation established a "pay czar" to oversee the compensation of Wall Street executives and force repayment of any "ill-advised" compensation. In July 2010 the pay czar Kenneth R. Feinberg concluded that there was $1.6 billion of ill-advised compensation in 17 banks, but he declined to order the repayment of any funds.[39]

In addition to the clamor over the level of compensation, the structure of Wall Street compensation was criticized. Compensation for bankers and traders on Wall Street typically consisted of a salary and an annual bonus paid in cash that was several times the base salary. Moreover, when performance was subsequently revealed to have been bad, the bonus was not returned to the company. Critics argued that the current cash bonus system provided strong incentives for short-term performance but weak incentives for long-term performance, creating excessive risk-taking in the financial system.

The concerns over compensation of bankers found their way into the Dodd-Frank Act in the form of directing the FDIC to promulgated rules to regulate any bonus plan that "encourages inappropriate risks."[40] The rules require banks to defer at least half the bonuses for top executives and also for lower level employees whose activities could inflict "material risk" on the bank. Morgan Stanley and Goldman Sachs had already begun to restructure their incentive compensation in this manner for their top executives with deferred incentive compensation and a higher base salary.[41]

The Dodd-Frank Act also directed the SEC to address the compensation issue. The SEC promulgated "say on pay" rules requiring a nonbinding shareholder vote on executive compensation at least every 3 years. The SEC also proposed rules requiring banks and financial services firms to report bonuses paid to individual employees and to block bonuses that posed the risk of "material financial loss" for the firm. In 2012 Citigroup shareholders voted no on the bank's compensation program.

Europe had gone further. The United Kingdom imposed a one-time, 50 percent tax on bank bonuses above £25,000. Banks paid £2.5 billion under the tax with U.S. banks paying the majority. JPMorgan Chase paid $550 million. The European Union also passed a law limiting the cash component of regular bonuses to no more than 30 percent and no more than 20 percent of a large bonus. The United Kingdom had imposed a less restrictive limit of 50 percent.

The banks argued that by limiting compensation they would lose their most talented employees. The fear was less that employees would leave for other banks than that they would leave for private hedge funds. Some hedge funds raised new funds to recruit asset managers from

---

[39] After completing his responsibilities under TARP, Feinberg jumped from the frying pan into the fire, becoming the administrator of BP's $20 billion fund to compensate victims of the Gulf of Mexico oil spill.

[40] The Act also directed the SEC to claw back executive compensation that was improperly awarded, as in the case of earnings that were later restated.

[41] Morgan Stanley also announced that it would reduce overall compensation, after paying out 62 percent of its revenue in compensation. The level of compensation resulted in lawsuits by two institutional investors for overpaying employees.

the banks. The limits imposed on proprietary trading by the Volker rule added to the incentives for traders to leave the banks.

Credit Rating Agencies

Credit ratings provide information to investors about risks associated with securities. Ratings have been provided for over 100 years, and ratings have become an integral component of the financial markets. Credit rating agencies are private companies, and government regulators have delegated to designated Nationally Recognized Statistical Rating Organizations (NRSRO) the assessment of risks associated with securities.

The credit rating agencies were widely criticized for failing to appreciate the risks associated with the collateralized debt instruments and with financial market participants themselves. Moody's gave Lehman Brothers an investment grade rating on its bonds just days before it declared bankruptcy and gave American International Group (AIG) an investment grade rating the week before the company had to be rescued by the government. More importantly, the credit rating agencies failed to recognize the riskiness of the mortgage-backed securities that were at the center of the financial crisis. Approximately 90 percent of the CDOs backed by subprime mortgages issued during 2006 and 2007 have been significantly downgraded, many to junk status. Many critics pointed to a conflict of interest in ratings, since issuers of securities paid the credit rating agencies when they provided a rating.[42] Issuers of debt instruments also "ratings shopped" for the highest rating from the credit rating agencies, since the higher the rating, the higher the price at which they could sell their securities. Critics argued that this gave the credit rating agencies incentives to produce higher than warranted ratings so as not to lose customers.

The credit rating agencies had also missed the Enron and WorldCom collapses in the early part of the decade, and congressional regulation in 2006 gave the SEC regulatory authority over NRSROs. The SEC had also begun to strengthen competition by giving NRSRO designation to new entrants, and DBRS of Toronto gained market share by giving issuers rapid responses about a rating. Jules Kroll, who had sold his investigations company for $1.9 billion, formed Kroll Bond Ratings to provide closer scrutiny of debt offerings.

Despite the actions of the SEC in allowing more competition in the credit ratings industry, critics argued that it did not go far enough. Critics argued for a variety of major reforms ranging from eliminating the NRSRO designation to requiring a user-pays system to relying on the tort system by changing the legal liability of NRSROs. The chapter case *Credit Rating Agencies* considers the alternatives in more detail.

The Dodd-Frank Act added a number of restrictions on the credit rating agencies, including provisions pertaining to the protection of ratings from liability. The Act made suing an agency for fraud easier by allowing investors to bring lawsuits against credit rating agencies that "knowingly or recklessly" failed to "conduct a reasonable investigation of the rated security."[43]

The Dodd-Frank Act reflected the difficulty in addressing the ratings issues. The Act established an Office of Credit Ratings and required stronger internal controls by the credit rating agencies, but it did not restructure the ratings system. One reason was the difficulty in predicting the consequences of seemingly simple measures. The example identifies the unanticipated consequences of a simple designation of credit rating agencies as "experts."

EXAMPLE Unanticipated Consequences—Experts

The credit rating agencies had enjoyed a shield from lawsuits for their ratings based on the free speech rights provided by the First Amendment. The credit rating agencies were careful in labeling their ratings as opinions about the future performance of the securities they rated, and the courts had ruled that such opinions were protected under the First Amendment. In 2010 the credit rating agencies had carefully followed the House and Senate financial reform bills, including the conference committee formed to reconcile the two bills. The language in the House bill caused concern among the

---

[42]Beginning in 2005 one small NRSRO AM Best operated under a users-pay model where investors paid for a subscription service.
[43]*Wall Street Journal*, June 18, 2010.

NRSROs. In April, Moody's CEO Raymond McDaniel told investors, "we remain concerned that the bill's liability provisions would lead to unintended consequences that could negatively impact the credit markets."[1] The agencies were basically satisfied by the language of the Senate bill, which was to be the basis for the final Act.

When the Dodd-Frank Act was signed, the credit rating agencies were shocked to learn that it contained not the language in the Senate bill but that from the House bill that would treat them as "experts" when their ratings were included in offering documents, such as prospectuses filed with SEC registration statements.[2] The law firm Davis Polk wrote, "The bill establishes that the enforcement and penalty provisions of the Exchange Act apply to statements made by credit rating agencies in the same manner and to the same extent as they apply to statements made by registered public accounting firms or security analysts under the securities laws."[3] Dan Curry, president of the bond rating firm DBRS, said, "The inclusion in the final offering documents are an unacceptable risk." He added that the liability standard used for experts was "'really the standard for an auditor' and should not be used for rating agencies, since their opinions are 'an attempt to predict future outcomes.'"[4] The uncertainty created by the Act was compounded because the provision became effective immediately when the Act was signed by President Obama. Moreover, previous law required that ratings be provided for all new securities backed by consumer loans, mortgage loans, credit card borrowings, and automobile loans.

The credit rating agencies responded by refusing to allow their ratings to be used in offering documents. The refusal shut down the bond market on July 22, 2010, as issuers withdrew their planned bond issues. The $1.4 trillion asset-backed bond market was crucial for consumer finance such as auto loans, home mortgages, student loans, and credit card loans. For example, auto dealers offer manufacturer-provided loans to car buyers, and companies such as the Ford Motor Company securitize the loans, allowing the company to offer lower interest rates on the auto loans it financed. Ford's financing unit withdrew its planned bond issue backed by auto loans. The alternative for bond issuers was to turn to the smaller private placement market where ratings could be used without creating expert liability, but issuers would receive less for their bonds in that market.

The credit rating agencies were uncertain about how to proceed. Standard & Poor's stated that it would "explore mechanisms outside of the registration statement to allow ratings to be disseminated to the debt markets."[5] Moody's McDaniel said the company would rethink how to provide ratings "for as many small and perhaps marginal issuers as possible."[6]

With the market effectively shut down and the alternatives unclear, the SEC suspended the rule that required issuers to include ratings in their prospectuses, initially for 6 months and then indefinitely.

---

[1]*Wall Street Journal*, July 21, 2010.

[2]NRSROs that agreed to have their ratings in a securities registration statement submitted to the SEC "would be exposed to liability as experts under Section 11 of the Securities Act for material misstatements or omissions with respect to such included ratings." Davis Polk &Wardell LLP, "Summary of the Dodd-Frank Wall Street Reform and Consumer Protection Act, Passed by the House of Representatives on June 30, 2010," July 9, 2010.

[3]Davis Polk & Wardell LLP, "Summary of the Dodd-Frank Wall Street Reform and Consumer Protection Act, Passed by the House of Representatives on June 30, 2010."

[4]*Wall Street Journal*, July 22, 2010.

[5]*Wall Street Journal*, July 21, 2010.

[6]Ibid.

GLOBAL CAPITAL REQUIREMENTS REGULATION—BASEL III

The Basel Committee on Banking Supervision is an organization of 27 nations that sets capital requirements for banks. The requirements must be approved by the G-20 nations and then enacted into law by each nation. In the late 1990s the Committee had lowered capital requirements in the Basel II agreement, and after the financial crisis the focus in Basel III was on raising capital requirements. The Basel III accord required banks to hold equity capital of at least 4.5 percent of risk-weighted assets plus a 2.5 percent buffer that a bank could draw down during a crisis.[44] Reserves of at least 3 percent of total assets including derivatives and off balance sheet assets were also required. Jean-Claude Trichet of the European Central Bank and chairman of the Basel Committee said, "The agreements reached today are a fundamental strengthening of global capital standards." Mary Frances Monroe of the American Bankers Association commented, "Banks understand the need for heightened prudential standards."[45] The heightened standards in Basel III would reduce the earnings rate on the equity of banks, including the former investment banks, but that effect on the banks' market values could be offset by the lower risk.

---

[44]The requirements were to be phased in from 2013 through 2018.

[45]*New York Times*, September 13, 2010.

SUMMARY

The financial crisis was caused by the conjunction of several factors: large budget and trade deficits caused a massive inflow of funds into the United States at a time when the Federal Reserve was keeping interest rates low in the aftermath of the recession in 2000–2001; housing prices rose at a rate well above their historical rate; pressure to expand affordable housing and home ownership, easy credit, and low interest rates expanded the set of people who could obtain mortgages; mortgage originators lowered standards as did Fannie Mae and Freddie Mac; the securitization of mortgage loans expanded rapidly providing liquidity to the mortgage market and increasing incentives to originate new loans; credit rating agencies had difficulty rating the CDOs and most received investment grade ratings; investors were eager for the seemingly higher returns of mortgage-backed CDOs; banks increased their leverage in part through repo financing; and greed and fraud were present. The crisis was precipitated by falling housing prices over most of the United States, resulting in mortgage delinquencies and defaults, plummeting CDO prices, liquidity problems at banks, and bank failures as a result of excessive leverage and a run on the repo market. The federal government intervened successfully to rescue the banks and financial system, but the government's attempt to stimulate the economy was less successful.

The financial and economic crisis led to the most sweeping legislation affecting the financial markets since the Great Depression. The Dodd-Frank Act contains a number of measures to reduce the likelihood of future financial crises, but the regulation may increase the cost of capital and reduce the availability of credit. Moreover, the financial markets are fluid and innovative, and whether new causes and forms of crises will occur awaits to be seen. As Reinhart and Rogoff remind us, crises are recurrent.

Many government and private lawsuits have been filed against market makers, mortgage originators, banks, and credit rating agencies, so many of the participants in the mortgage and financial markets will be involved in litigation for years to come.

CASES

Goldman Sachs and Its Reputation

Our history of good performance through the crisis became a liability as people wondered how we performed so well and whether we'd received favorable treatment from well-placed alumni. This was not only a poor place to be, it was a dangerous place to be.

Lloyd C. Blankfein, CEO, Goldman Sachs, *Wall Street Journal*, January 11, 2011.

We did a good job of managing risks but we did a less good job of managing our reputation.

Lloyd C. Blankfein, CEO, Goldman Sachs, *Economic Times, India Times*, May 20, 2010.

INTRODUCTION

Goldman Sachs is a bank, but it does not take deposits, issue credit cards, make mortgage loans, or interact with consumers. For most of its history Goldman was organized as a partnership and operated as an investment bank engaging in underwriting new securities to raise funds for corporations and public agencies, advising clients as in mergers and acquisitions, and managing assets for clients. It began to engage in securities trading and risk arbitrage in the 1950s, when it developed its philosophy of being "long-term greedy," which the bank

understood as focusing on long-term profitability rather than short-term performance.

After the repeal of the Glass-Steagall Act in 1999, bank holding companies were allowed to own other financial enterprises. A number of investment banks reorganized as bank holding companies to broaden the financial services they could provide. Goldman did not reorganize but did go public in 1999, forecasting that its investment banking business would continue to provide most of its revenue and profits. Soon, however, its proprietary trading and trading on behalf of clients began to dominate both its revenue and profit streams. The leadership of the firm also shifted from investment bankers to traders, such as Henry Paulson and current CEO Lloyd C. Blankfein. Former Goldman Sachs' executives have served in a variety of government positions. Goldman alumni Robert Rubin and Henry Paulson served as Secretary of the Treasury under Presidents Bill Clinton and George W. Bush, respectively. Goldman alumni populated many of the leading banks, hedge funds, and corporations.

Goldman was the most prestigious and most profitable of the investment banks. In 2010 its revenue was $39.2 billion and profits were $8.35 billion, down from $45.17 billion and $13.39 billion, respectively, in 2009. For 2008 revenue and earnings were $22.22 billion and $2.32 billion, respectively, and for 2007 were $45.99 billion and $11.60 billion, respectively. Despite its profitability it faced heightened financial risks, and on September 21, 2008, Goldman along with Morgan Stanley reorganized as bank holding companies so that they would be under the purview of the Federal Reserve System and could receive capital from it. Goldman accepted $10 billion in Troubled Asset Relief Program funds and also received $5 billion from Warren Buffett's Berkshire Hathaway.

Goldman Sachs had been a major participant in the events leading up to the financial crisis. The Financial Crisis Inquiry Commission wrote:[46]

> From 2004 through 2006, the company provided billions of dollars in loans to mortgage lenders; most went to the subprime lenders Ameriquest, Long Beach, New Century, and Countrywide through warehouse lines of credit, often in the form of repos. During the same period, Goldman acquired $53 billion of loans from these and other subprime loan originators, which it securitized and sold to investors. From 2004 to 2006, Goldman issued 318 mortgage securitizations totaling $184 billion (about a quarter were subprime), and 63 CDOs totaling $32 billion; Goldman also issued 22 synthetic or hybrid CDOs with a face value of $35 billion between 2004 and June 2006.

During the financial crisis Goldman performed much better than other banks; for example, it did not cut its dividend as others did.[47] This led to speculation that it might have taken advantage of clients and counterparties during the crisis. A series of events and revelations also raised questions about its business conduct and challenged its reputation.

THE COLLAPSE AND BAILOUT OF AIG

To hedge its holdings of mortgage-backed collateralized debt obligations, Goldman purchased credit default swaps (CDSs) from AIG, the leading provider. In a CDS contract AIG promised to pay the par value of Goldman-held CDOs, and Goldman paid a regular premium to AIG analogous to the payment of an insurance premium. With such a contract each party faces the risk that its counterparty might fail (e.g., become illiquid or bankrupt) and not be able to fulfill the terms of the contract. To compensate for this counterparty risk, Goldman required AIG to provide it with collateral, for example, a deposit with Goldman of cash, Treasury notes, or securities such as CDOs, that Goldman would keep in the event that AIG could not fulfill the terms of the contracts. Goldman purchased some $20 billion in CDSs from AIG.

In 2007 Goldman became concerned about the financial health of AIG, and began to demand additional collateral to cover the greater counterparty risk. As the prices of mortgage-backed securities began to fall in 2008, Goldman demanded more collateral and other banks followed. AIG became illiquid

and could not meet the demands for collateral. On the verge of collapse and unable to raise funds, AIG turned to the federal government for a bailout in September 2008.[48] The government eventually provided $182.3 billion in TARP funds to AIG. Goldman was criticized for having caused AIG to fail.

A related dispute centered on the basis for the collateral demands Goldman made on AIG. Goldman justified its demands based on its estimates of the market value of the CDOs AIG had provided as collateral, but since CDOs were not actively traded, there was no market price to use in the valuation. The amount of coverage provided by AIG depended on the difference between the face value of the CDOs and their market value, which Goldman estimated using a variety of methods and data sources. Goldman was accused of providing unreasonably low valuations to increase the amount of collateral it could demand from AIG. A November 2008 analysis by the asset management firm BlackRock concluded that Goldman's valuations for the securities covered by AIG were "consistently lower than third-party prices."[49] A Goldman spokesperson said, "We requested the collateral we were entitled to under the terms of our agreements, and the idea that AIG collapsed because of our marks is ridiculous."[50] Goldman CFO David A. Viniar said, "We believed that the value of these positions was lower than they believed … I don't think there is any guilt whatsoever."[51]

Goldman was called to testify before the Financial Crisis Inquiry Commission established to determine the causes of the financial crisis. Goldman explained its valuation methods in a report entitled "Valuation & Pricing Related to Transactions with AIG," but the critics were not satisfied.

When the CDO market collapsed, Goldman sought to collect on the credit default swaps it had purchased from AIG. It was clear that the mortgage-backed securities had lost substantial value, and AIG sought to negotiate a settlement with Goldman Sachs and other holders of the CDSs. AIG hoped to pay less than the face value of the CDSs, asking Goldman to absorb some of the loss. Goldman refused to accept less than the face value, with the implicit threat of filing a lawsuit if AIG refused. The New York Federal Reserve Bank supervised the use of TARP funds by AIG and backed AIG in asking Goldman to absorb some of the losses. Thomas C. Baxter, general counsel of the New York Fed, said, "We asked for concessions, and they said no. I wonder why we even bothered."[52] AIG paid Goldman and the other holders of the CDSs their face value, resulting in $46 billion of TARP funds going to Goldman and other CDS holders.

ABACUS AC1

During the 2000s Goldman Sachs issued a series of CDOs under the Abacus name. Goldman issued both mortgage-backed and synthetic CDOs, a security whose value tracked the

---

[46]Financial Crisis Inquiry Commission, "Report," January 2011, p. 142.

[47]For example, Morgan Stanley's revenue and earnings were $31.6 billion and $3.6 billion, respectively, in 2010; $23.4 billion and –$0.9 billion, respectively, in 2009; $18.2 billion and –$0.7 billion, respectively, in 2008; and $28.0 and $3.1 billion, respectively, in 2007.

[48]As Goldman and AIG began to unwind the CDSs, some of the CDOs rose in value, and Goldman returned some of the collateral to AIG.

[49]*New York Times*, February 7, 2010.

[50]Ibid.

[51]Ibid.

[52]*New York Times*, January 23, 2010.

value of a set of CDOs but did not have the backing of those CDOs. In less than 3 years Goldman issued $73 billion of synthetic CDOs.[53]

In early 2007 Paulson & Company contacted Goldman Sachs asking that a synthetic CDO be created that would track mortgages that John Paulson, a billionaire fund manager, believed would fall in value.[54] Synthetic CDOs can be used to hedge risks or to speculate, and Paulson planned to short the newly created CDO. Goldman assigned a young banker, Fabrice Tourre, to design the synthetic CDO, named Abacus 2007-AC1, and he contacted ACA Management LLC, an asset management company with long experience in CDOs, to participate in constructing Abacus AC1. Paulson recommended mortgage-backed securities to be included in AC1 that he believed would fall in value, but ACA had the final authority to approve the securities. Goldman and ACA contacted the German bank IKB Deutsche IndustrieBank, an experienced investor in CDOs, with the investment opportunity, but IKB was not told of Paulson's role nor that he planned to short Abacus AC1. The underlying securities were chosen, and ACA and IKB were the counterparties, with Goldman receiving a $15 million fee for its services.

John Paulson had done research on the mortgage market and believed that many CDOs were highly risky and could collapse in value. In the spring of 2007 he had written to investors in his fund, "We believe we are in the early stage of a correction in this market and that the market will eventually implode." Paulson reportedly earned a profit of $1 billion by shorting Abacus AC1.

On January 27, 2007, Tourre celebrated the Abacus deal under way with an infamous e-mail in which he wrote, "more and more leverage in the system, the whole building is about to collapse anytime now …. Only potential survivor, the fabulous Fab … standing in the middle of all these complex, exotic trades he created without necessarily understanding all of the limitations." He also sent an e-mail in which he referred to the securities on which Abacus AC1 was based as having been selected by "ACA/Paulson."

THE SECURITIES AND EXCHANGE COMMISSION LAWSUIT

The Abacus AC1 deal closed in April 2007, and the SEC asked Paulson & Company for information about AC1 in early 2008. The SEC began an investigation and served Goldman with a subpoena in August 2008. In July 2009 the SEC served Goldman with a Wells notice that fraud charges could be filed against it, and Goldman met with the SEC to discuss the notice in September. The next several months were quiet, and then on April 16, 2010, the SEC filed a lawsuit charging Goldman Sachs with fraud and also named Fabrice Tourre. Goldman Sachs' share price fell 13 percent that day.

Goldman was caught off guard by the lawsuit and responded calling the allegations "completely unfounded in law and fact." Goldman said it would "contest [the allegations] and defend the firm and its reputation." It quickly recognized,

however, that letting the lawsuit continue would keep the allegations before its clients, the public, and government. Goldman began meeting with the SEC in May seeking a settlement.

The SEC and Goldman reached a settlement of the lawsuit, which was approved by the SEC on a 3–2 vote with the 3 Democrats voting for the settlement and the 2 Republicans voting against it.[55] Without admitting to wrongdoing Goldman agreed to disgorge $15 million in profits on Abacus AC1 and pay a fine of $535 million.[56] Goldman's share price increased by 5 percent on the announcement of the settlement.

In the settlement, "Goldman acknowledges that marketing material for the Abacus 2007-AC1 transaction contained incomplete information. In particular, it was a mistake for the Goldman marketing materials to state that the reference portfolio was 'selected by' ACA Management LLC without disclosing the role of Paulson & Co. Inc. in the portfolio selection process and that Paulson's economic interests were adverse to CDO investors. Goldman regrets that the marketing materials did not contain that disclosure." Goldman was required by the settlement to take remedial action to provide oversight and approval of written marketing materials.[57]

Senator Carl M. Levin (D-MI), chairman of the Senate Permanent Subcommittee on Investigations, commented, "Goldman played fast and loose in the Abacus deal, misled its clients, and got called on it today. A key factor in the settlement is that Goldman acknowledges wrongdoing, in addition to paying a fine and changing its practices."[58]

The lawsuit was filed during congressional debate on financial reform legislation, and Republicans on the House oversight committee accused the SEC of political motivation and asked whether there had been communication between the White House and the SEC regarding the lawsuit and its timing. Other critics accused the SEC of filing the lawsuit to distract attention from a report by SEC Inspector General H. David Kotz concluding that the SEC had repeatedly missed opportunities to detect a $7 billion fraud by R. Allen Stanford. The lawsuit was filed the same day as Kotz's report was released. In congressional testimony Kotz stated, "It would strain credulity to think it was coincidental."

The SEC lawsuit spurred concerns outside the United States as well. United Kingdom Prime Minister Gordon Brown said, "There is a moral bankruptcy reflected in what I am reading about and hearing about," and he ordered the Financial Services Authority (FSA) to investigate the effects of Goldman's actions on UK banks.[59] In September 2010 the FSA fined Goldman Sachs £17.5 million for the failure to disclose

---

[53]Financial Crisis Inquiry Commission, "Report", January 2011, pp. xxiv–xxv.
[54]John Paulson is not related to former Goldman Sachs CEO Henry Paulson.

[55]The fraud allegations in the lawsuit were based on SEC Rule 10b, which was viewed as more serious than Rule 17a1 on which the settlement was based, since the latter allowed for unintentional as well as intentional fraud. Republican Commissioner Kathleen Casey questioned the settlement on the lesser charges and questioned the magnitude of the fine given the lesser charges.
[56]Of the fine and disgorgement, $150 million was paid to IKB, $100 million to the Royal Bank of Scotland which had backstopped IKB, and $300 million to the SEC.
[57]The settlement did not cover the allegations against Fabrice Tourre, who remained under investigation.
[58]*New York Times*, July 15, 2010.
[59]*Wall Street Journal*, April 19, 2010.

that one of its employees in the United Kingdom was under investigation in the United States. The employee was Fabrice Tourre, who had transferred to London in 2008.

GOLDMAN'S RESPONSIBILITIES TO ITS CLIENTS

Goldman viewed its clients as sophisticated investors and hence saw its responsibility as providing them with the risks they wanted to bear. From its point of view there was nothing inappropriate in its construction of the Abacus CDOs, since the parties on both sides of the transaction were sophisticated investors.

Goldman, however, was accused of foisting bad mortgage-backed securities on unsuspecting clients. After deciding in 2007 to reduce its exposure to mortgage-backed securities, Goldman created a $1 billion CDO named Timberwolf I, which was composed of portions of other CDOs and other derivatives. The firm then worked hard to sell securities to investors. A senior Goldman banker wrote in an e-mail, "Boy, that Timberwolf was one shi**y deal." Within 5 months Timberwolf had lost 80 percent of its value and was subsequently liquidated when Goldman made a collateral call.[60] After the e-mail was made public by the Senate Investigations Subcommittee in 2010, Basis Capital, an Australian hedge fund, filed a $1 billion lawsuit against Goldman claiming that one of its funds failed because of Timberwolf and that "Goldman was pressuring investors to take the risk of toxic securities off its books with knowingly false sales pitches."[61] Goldman denied the allegation and responded that the prices Basis Capital paid "were substantially below the face value of the securities and consistent with where other investors were purchasing the same Timberwolf securities during the same time."[62]

In Senate hearings on the Abacus AC1 transaction, Blankfein explained the situation as a perception problem: "We have to do a better job of striking the balance between what an informed client believes is important to his or her investing goals and what the public believes is overly complex and risky."[63] Fabrice Tourre explained, "I was an intermediary between highly sophisticated professional investors—all of which were institutions. The structured products on which I worked … permit sophisticated institutions to customize the exposures they wish to take in order to better manage the credit and market risks of their investment holdings."[64]

Senator Levin introduced hearings on the role of investment banks in the financial crisis, stating, "Goldman Sachs, like all other major Wall Street Firms, got a multibillion-dollar lifeline from the taxpayers in 2008. Goldman Sachs was slicing, dicing, and selling toxic mortgage-related securities on Wall Street like many other investment banks, but its executives

continue to downplay the firm's role in the financial engineering that blew up the financial markets and cost millions of Americans their jobs, homes, and livelihoods, Goldman Sachs made billions of dollars from betting against the housing market, and it placed those bets in some cases at the same time it was selling mortgage related securities to its clients. They have a lot to answer for."[65]

Senator John Tester (D-MT) noted that Goldman witnesses referred to themselves as "market-makers" and asked Blankfein to explain what a market-maker did. He responded, "There are parts of the business where you're a money manager, where you owe a duty to the client. There are parts of the business where you are a principal and you are giving the client what it wants and it's understood—where you have to know that they're suitable, you have to know that the product you do delivers what they expect to have. But the markets couldn't work if you had to make sure it was good for them."

Prior to the hearing focusing on Goldman Sachs, Senator Levin released several Goldman e-mails suggesting that the company profited by going short on mortgage-backed securities. He stated, "In a third email, employees discussed securities underwritten and sold by Goldman relating to a subprime lender, Long Beach Financial. One staffer reported the 'good news' that the wipeout of one security and the imminent collapse of another meant Goldman would make $5 million from a bet against the instruments it had set up and sold."[66] Goldman investigated the episode and concluded there was no wrongdoing. The Senate embarked on an extensive investigation of Goldman Sachs and produced a 650-page report. The investigation continued, and New York State began an investigation.

During the financial crisis Goldman Sachs performed much better than other banks such as Citigroup and Morgan Stanley. Commentators speculated that this was because Goldman had shorted mortgage-backed securities, taking advantage of those who had purchased the securities from the bank. Although Goldman was not net short on mortgage-backed securities, it had aggressively reduced its exposure ahead of the collapse. In his Senate written testimony Blankfein explained, "The fact is we were not consistently or significantly net 'short the market' in residential mortgage-related products in 2007 and 2008. Our performance in our residential mortgage-related business confirms this. During the two years of the financial crisis, while profitable overall, Goldman Sachs lost approximately $1.2 billion from our activities in the residential housing market."[67] CFO David A. Viniar explained that at the end of 2006, "we became collectively concerned about the higher volatility and recent price declines in our sub-prime mortgage-related positions .... We proceeded to sell certain positions outright and hedge our long positions .... As always,

[60]Bear Stearns, which failed and was acquired by JPMorgan Chase in a fire sale, purchased $300 million of Timberwolf securities. Critics accused Goldman of having contributed to the failure of Bear Stearns.

[61]*Bloomberg BusinessWeek*, January 31, 2011.

[62]Ibid.

[63]Lloyd C. Blankfein, Testimony before the Permanent Senate Subcommittee on Investigations, April 27, 2010.

[64]Fabrice Tourre, Testimony before the Permanent Senate Subcommittee on Investigations, April 27, 2010.

[65]"Senate Committee Holds Fourth Hearing on Wall Street and the Financial Crisis: The Role of Investment Banks," U.S. Senate Permanent Committee on Investigations, April 26, 2010.

[66]*The Observer (England)*, April 25, 2010.

[67]Lloyd C. Blankfein, Testimony before the Permanent Senate Subcommittee on Investigations, April 27, 2010.

the clients who bought our long positions or other similar positions had a view that they were attractive positions to purchase at the price they were offered."[68] Goldman continued to reduce its long position during 2007, but in 2008 it still had a long position and incurred losses.[69]

FACEBOOK

SEC rules impose disclosure requirements on corporations with 500 or more shareholders. This requirement imposes a variety of burdensome reporting requirements and invites scrutiny from regulators and the financial markets, and many companies prefer to remain outside the regulatory regime of the SEC as long as they can still raise funds. Facebook was one of those companies, and it needed to raise a large amount of capital to fund its meteoric growth. It sought to remain private until it was ready for an initial public offering (IPO) of its shares, expected in 2012. In conjunction with Goldman Sachs the company embarked on an arrangement in which Goldman would make a $450 million investment in the company and then raise an additional $1.5 billion in a private placement, while keeping the number of shareholders below 500. The arrangement with Facebook was viewed as a coup for Goldman, since it not only was able to take a stake in the company, but it also was in line to manage the IPO and other fund-raising by Facebook. Moreover, many of the private investors who would participate in this funding were said to be clients of Goldman's wealth management division. Orders poured in, and Goldman was quickly forced to close its book on the funding. Goldman trumpeted the deal, and the media covered it extensively because of the parties involved and the magnitudes of the funding.

Facebook already had many private investors through previous rounds of fund-raising, ranging from venture capital firms to corporations such as Microsoft to private investors such as Li Ka-shing and Alisher Usmanov. To accommodate more private investors and facilitate raising the $1.5 billion, Goldman planned to pool the investments of wealthy private investors in a special-purpose vehicle or private equity fund that would count as a single investor.[70] The SEC viewed this with skepticism and announced that it was beginning a review of its rules governing disclosure.

Fearing the outcome of the review, Goldman quickly abandoned its plans for a private placement in the United States and announced that it would raise $1 billion from investors outside the United States. In its announcement, "Goldman Sachs concluded that the level of media attention might not be consistent with the proper completion of a U.S. private placement under U.S. law. The decision not to proceed in the U.S. was based on the sole judgment of Goldman Sachs and was not required or requested by any other party. We regret the consequences of this decision, but Goldman Sachs believes that this is the most prudent path to take." In addition to having egg on its face, Goldman had angered its U.S. clients who had hoped to invest in Facebook.

RECOVERY MEASURES

Shortly after the filing of the lawsuit by the SEC Goldman announced at its May 2010 annual meeting that it was establishing a Business Standards Committee to review its business standards and practices.[71] Blankfein explained that there was "a disconnect between how we view the firm and how the broader public perceives our role and activities."

The Business Standards Committee hired a prominent consulting company to conduct interviews with 200 clients. Goldman was stung by the criticisms that revealed a perception that Goldman put its interests ahead of those of its clients.[72] In January 2011 the Business Standards Committee issued its report with 39 recommendations that Goldman pledged to implement. The report stated, "Clients raised concerns about whether the firm has remained true to its traditional values and business principles given changes to the firm's size, business mix, and perceptions about the role of proprietary trading. Clients said that, in some circumstances, the firm weighs its interests and short-term incentives too heavily."

The report reemphasized the relevance of its Business Principles, the first of which was "Our clients' interests always come first," established over 30 years earlier. The report, however, pointed to reputational concerns, "Goldman Sachs has one reputation. It can be affected by any number of decisions and activities across the firm. Every employee has an equal obligation to raise issues or concerns, no matter how small, to protect the firm's reputation."[73] The report emphasized the importance of communication with clients.

The report identified the roles Goldman assumed as "advisor, fiduciary, market maker and underwriter" and the responsibilities to its clients it had in each of its roles. The report called for making those responsibilities clear to clients. Goldman established a Client and Business Standards Committee to put client interests "at the center of our decision-making processes." To structure its responsibilities to clients it established a "Role-Specific Client Responsibilities" matrix for each of its four roles. For example, as a market maker that provides liquidity to clients, Goldman acts as an agent of its clients "regardless of market conditions and our view of the market." When it considers participating in a market for structured securities, Goldman would now "answer the critical question of whether we 'should' engage in the relevant activity

---

[68]David A. Viniar, Testimony before the Permanent Senate Subcommittee on Investigations, April 27, 2010.

[69]With regard to the AC1 securities Tourre stated, "I recall informing ACA that Paulson's fund was expected to buy credit protection on some of the senior tranches of the AC-1 transaction …. Goldman Sachs also had no economic motive to design the AC-1 transaction to fail. Quite the contrary, we held long exposure in the transaction just like ACA and IKB …. Goldman Sach's overall losses in connection with the transaction exceeded $100 million, including $83 million with respect to the retained long position." He added that both IKB and Goldman Sachs had suggested securities to ACA for inclusion in the transaction, as did Paulson, and that "ACA ultimately analyzed and approved every security in the deal." (Fabrice Tourre, Testimony before the Permanent Senate Subcommittee on Investigations, April 27, 2010.)

[70]Steven Pearlstein, *Washington Post*, January 5, 2011.

[71]Goldman had a governance structure that included several committees that oversaw operations.

[72]*Economist*, January 15, 2011.

[73]Report of the Business Standards Committee, January 2011.

while we consider whether we 'can' engage in the activity operationally." The report also established "Standards of Sophistication: We are committed to knowing our clients and ensuring that they have the ability and background to understand the risks of all transactions they execute with us, including structured products." The report called for consideration of three segments of clients: professional investors, other institutional accounts (e.g., municipalities, pension funds), and high net worth accounts. To provide greater transparency of its activities, the report recommended reorganizing the firm's business segments into four classes: investment banking, institutional client services, investing and lending, and investment management.

In addition to emphasizing client interests, the report focused on reputational risks. It established an Event Review Group composed of rotating senior executives to review "incidents" arising from its activities. It also established a Firmwide Client and Business Standards Committee to replace the Business Standards Committee with the "additional focus on the primacy of client interests and reputational risk." The report also called for additional training of personnel and giving importance to "leadership, culture and values along with commercial productivity" in evaluating performance.

Goldman as well as other banks faced heavy criticism for their compensation systems for their bankers. Criticism focused on the high levels of compensation, as well as the emphasis on short-term profits. Compensation was very high on average. For 2010 Goldman's compensation pool was $15.38 billion, or 39 percent of revenue, which for its 36,500 employees represented an average compensation of $430,000 a person, even though profits were down 37 percent from 2009.[74]

Salaries in Goldman Sachs were relatively low (e.g., Blankfein's salary was $600,000 for 2009) and the bulk of compensation was bonuses based on performance for the year. Blankfein's bonus was $68.5 million in 2007, although it fell to $9 million in 2009. To reduce the short-term emphasis, Goldman increased the base salary for executives and bankers; Blankfein's salary for 2011 was set at $2 million. Goldman also restructured its bonuses for top executives. For 2010 Blankfein received a bonus of 78,111 shares with a current market value of $12.6 million, but the shares vested only after 3 years and could not be sold until 2016.[75]

In December 2010 Goldman became the first Wall Street bank to adopt "say-on-pay," giving shareholders a nonbinding vote on executive compensation. Under the Dodd-Frank financial reform legislation the SEC was directed to consider promulgating rules requiring firms to provide say-on-pay for their shareholders. On a 3–2 vote the SEC approved say-on-pay rules in January 2011.

In addition to restructuring its compensation structure the Business Standards Committee imposed additional controls on structured transactions, such as Abacus, to ensure that client interests were taken into account by traders. Approval was now required by bankers representing client interests. A former Goldman banker quipped, "They recognize that the time has come for adult supervision."[76]

John Whitehead, former chairman of Goldman, summed up the situation, "There's a lot of work ahead for the management to recover its reputation." He added, "They need to maintain some balance in top management of both investment bankers and trading."[77]

CLOSING

Despite the challenges it faced Goldman's average compensation was higher than that of any other bank. It was also considered one of the best banks to work for. Vault.com's survey of 1,300 bankers in 2010 ranked Goldman as the best place to work, and a survey released in January 2011 also had Goldman at the top. Ike Suri of Options Group commented that Goldman's reputation "is still pristine and well-regarded amongst its clients, competitors and its employees. They are cutting-edge and forefront in the marketplace."[78] Goldman reported that in the first quarter of 2011 it lost money on only one trading day and made over $100 million on 32 trading days.[79]

Although Goldman was not selected to lead the IPO of General Motors, its major clients stuck with it. Stephen Schwarzman, CEO of the Blackstone Group, said, "We're a major client of Goldman's and will continue to be a major client of Goldman's. We've never had any circumstance where there's been a question about their ethical behavior." A Ford Motor Company spokesperson said, "We've had a long relationship with Goldman Sachs, and we expect it to continue."[80]

CEO Blankfein observed, "Loss of reputation is—can bring down a firm. It will not bring down Goldman Sachs because we enjoy, I believe, the confidence and trust of our clients. We don't take it for granted, and want to work very, very hard to keep what we have and to gain what we may have lost in some cases, and to even expand it beyond that original point."[81]

As a result of the Senate report and ongoing investigations, Blankfein and other Goldman executives hired criminal defense attorneys, a common practice when companies face possible litigation. Goldman estimated "reasonably possible" costs of legal claims at $2.7 billion. ■

Preparation Questions

1. Were the challenges to Goldman's practices largely due to a failure of the public to understand the complex transactions in which it engaged?
2. Can Goldman Sachs effectively explain its activities to the public? To the media? To members of Congress? To the SEC? To its clients?

---

[74]Average compensation in 2007 during the last year of the financial boom was $661,490. (*The Independent* (London), January 19, 2011.)

[75]In 2008 during the worst of the financial crisis Goldman granted its executives stock options, one-third of which could be exercised in 2010, 2011, and 2012.

[76]*Economist*, January 15, 2011.

[77]*Wall Street Journal*, July 17, 2010.

[78]*Los Angeles Times*, September 10, 2010.

[79]*New York Times*, May 11, 2011.

[80]*Associated Press*, April 27, 2010.

[81]Lloyd C. Blankfein, Interview with Bloomberg Television, May 7, 2010.

3. Did Goldman do anything wrong?

4. What caused the Facebook about-face?

5. Goldman emphasizes the importance of reputation. Reputation with whom? For which of its constituencies should it be concerned?

6. How serious are the events to Goldman's reputation? Will it suffer?

7. Are the measures Goldman is taking to deal with its reputation concerns sufficient? What else, if anything, should it do?

Credit Rating Agencies

INTRODUCTION

Credit rating agencies have played a central role in the U.S. financial markets. Their ratings provide information to investors about the risks on securities, and ratings are required for some investors. Pension funds and financial institutions are required to hold only investment grade securities, and the resulting demand for these securities exceeds their supply.

The credit rating agencies failed to anticipate the financial risks that led to the crisis that began in 2007 and have shared the blame for the crisis. Moody's gave Lehman Brothers an investment grade rating on its bonds just days before it declared bankruptcy and gave American International Group an investment grade rating the week before the company had to be rescued by the government. More importantly, the credit rating agencies failed to recognize the riskiness of the mortgage-backed securities that were a principal source of the financial crisis. Approximately 90 percent of the collateralized debt obligations (CDOs) backed by subprime mortgages issued during 2006 and 2007 were significantly downgraded, many to junk status.

Critics complained that the system in which issuers paid the rating agencies created a conflict of interest and that issuers shopped for the highest rating, putting pressure on the credit rating agencies to give inflated ratings. The calls for reform of the credit rating system were widespread with proposals ranging from tightened regulation to eliminating the rating requirements for investors. The credit rating agencies had to decide which proposals, if any, to support and which to oppose.

THE CREDIT RATING SYSTEM

John Moody began rating railroad bonds at the turn of the twentieth century, and Poor's Publishing began in 1916 and Fitch in 1924. The ratings industry was spurred in the 1930s when the Comptroller of the Currency prohibited banks from buying "speculative investment securities" as determined by "recognized ratings manuals," referring to the thick manuals in which the rating agencies sold their ratings.[82] In the 1970s the Securities and Exchange Commission (SEC) referred to the credit rating agencies in a rule pertaining to brokerages, and in 1975 the SEC established the designation Nationally Recognized Statistical Rating Organizations (NRSROs).

Subsequent legislation and rule-making referred to the NRSROs, and many financial institutions and institutional investors such as pension funds were restricted to buying only "investment grade securities," those receiving a high rating such as AAA. Ironically, Standard & Poor's included the following disclaimer at the bottom of each of its ratings: "[A]ny user of the information contained herein should not rely on any credit rating or other opinion contained herein in making any investment decision."[83]

The Credit Rating Agency Reform Act of 2006 gave the SEC authority to regulate the conduct of the NRSROs.[84] By the end of 2009 the SEC had promulgated rules regarding record keeping, disclosure, reporting, and access to data on rating-related information, and prohibited rating agencies from providing advice on the structuring of asset-based securities.

The credit rating agencies used econometric models to assess the risks on securities, based on data provided by the issuer. Issuers used the ratings in marketing their securities, and a higher rating generally led to a higher price for the securities, particularly for investment grade ratings. How useful the ratings were to investors depended on the investor. Financial institutions and pension funds were restricted to investment grade securities, and other investors could rely on the reputation of the issuer or on their own research or knowledge of the markets. Moreover, if the market for the securities was liquid (i.e., securities could be readily sold without affecting the market price), active investors could easily sell the securities if they became nervous. Investors, however, without expertise in assessing risks often relied on the ratings.

Moody's and Standard & Poor's had approximately 75 percent of the U.S. ratings market with Fitch having a 20 percent share.[85] In 2009 the big three had revenue of $3.6 billion from rating bonds. Smaller firms with NSRSO designation included Egan-Jones, DBRS of Toronto, Lace Financial, and Realpoint.[86] DBRS, which had been formed to rate Canadian bonds, had increased its share of structured finance ratings in the United States by giving an issuer a prompt answer, whereas the large rating agencies were understandably

---

[82]Lawrence White, "Markets: The Credit Rating Agencies," *Journal of Economic Perspectives* 24 (2010): 211–226.

[83]Quoted in White, "Markets," 214.

[84]The Reform Act was enacted in the aftermath of the collapse of Enron and WorldCom.

[85]Moody's Investors Service was owned by Moody's Corporation, Standard & Poor's was owned by McGraw-Hill, and Fitch Ratings was a unit of Fimilac SA of France. Moody's had been spun off from Dun & Bradstreet in 2000.

[86]In 2010 Morningstar purchased Realpoint, paying $52 million for a company with revenue of $12 million. (Crain's New York Business, May 20, 2010)

slow in producing a rating.[87] In 2009 DBRS was involved in rating 41 percent of the CDOs issued, which was an increase from 18 percent in 2008.[88] Standard & Poor's was involved in 42 percent, down from 84 percent in the previous year, and Moody's was down to 6 percent from 40 percent. The latter two firms had tightened their standards for ratings.

The NRSROs had successfully avoided liability for their ratings by arguing that their ratings were opinions about the future and thus protected by the free speech right provided in the First Amendment.[89] That protection continued but was increasingly challenged.

THE FINANCIAL CRISIS

Buoyed by a strong housing market and low interest rates, subprime mortgage lending increased substantially with most lenders operating on an "originate to distribute" business model where mortgage loans were quickly sold. Many loans were "no docs" in which the lender did not verify the borrower's employment or income, and new forms of loans were devised. Adjustable rate mortgages (ARMs) had low initial interest rates which subsequently jumped to a high interest rate, and option ARMs allowed borrowers to determine how much to repay each month, with the deferred interest added to the principal.

The mortgages sold by lenders were used by investment banks to back CDOs. The mortgages were sliced into risk tranches, and the cash flow from the loans cascaded down the tranches. The top (lowest risk) tranche obligations were covered first, the remaining cash flow then covered the second (next lowest risk) tranche, and so on. The investment banks shopped for the highest rating they could obtain for the CDOs in each tranche, and most of the ratings obtained were investment grade. The CDOs were then marketed to investors, who relied on the rating and typically did not investigate the quality of the mortgages backing the CDOs. The credit rating agencies had incentives to give high ratings because of fear that the issuers would turn to a different agency. The credit rating agencies were paid by the issuer rather than the users of the ratings.

As the housing market weakened and the bubble collapsed, most of the ratings given to the CDOs proved to be too high. The credit rating agencies were widely blamed for misleading investors, but most participants in the financial markets had failed to recognize the risks inherent in the securities and the mortgages that backed them. Commenting on Moody's in which Berkshire Hathaway held a 20 percent stake during the bubble, Warren Buffett said, "They made a mistake that virtually everyone in the country made."[90]

Rating agencies made public the models they used to rate securities. This was said to be done to provide transparency so that investors could understand the ratings and issuers would not be surprised by a rating lower than they had expected. This meant, however, that investment banks could engineer the securities they issued to yield the rating they sought. For example, the investment banks could take mortgages and slice the returns from those mortgages into tranches to meet the minimum standards for a rating such as AAA. Goldman Sachs went further and chose cheap bonds to include in the backing for the securities, a practice referred to as "ratings arbitrage."[91] This meant that the quality of a AAA CDO was lower than the average quality of a AAA corporate bond, whose return was determined by the performance of the company. Investment banks had hired former employees of the rating agencies to help design the tranches and other engineered securities. For example, Goldman Sachs hired Shin Yukawa from Fitch to work in its mortgage unit. Yukawa helped design the Abacus 2007-AC1 CDOs that were the focus of the SEC's fraud lawsuit against Goldman Sachs. Within 6 months of issuance 84 percent of the Abacus CDOs had been downgraded.

As a result of the financial crisis the credit rating agencies were subject to many lawsuits, but in 12 of the 15 cases in which the motions had been acted upon the judges had dismissed the lawsuits, and five other lawsuits had been dropped, according to Standard & Poor's.[92] One crack in the First Amendment shield occurred when a federal judge rejected a motion for dismissal on a lawsuit against Cheyne Capital on a private placement. The judge stated that "where a rating agency has disseminated their ratings to a select group of investors rather than to the public at large, the rating agency is not afforded the same protection [by the First Amendment]."[93] On the day of the decision the shares of Moody's declined by 7.1 percent, and the shares of Standard & Poor's fell by 10 percent. In addition the rating agencies were sued in state courts, and a California state judge rejected a motion to dismiss, allowing a lawsuit by CalPERS, a pension fund for state employees, to proceed.

ALTERNATIVES

The principal alternatives under consideration for reforming the credit rating system were:

1. The status quo—issuer pays. (Better the devil you know than the devil you don't know.)
2. A "user pays" or subscriber model where investors paid for ratings.
3. Easy entry and reliance on competition to produce higher quality ratings.
4. End ratings shopping: Establish a commission under the SEC to assign a rating agency to each security issued.
5. Eliminate the requirement that regulated investors invest only in investment grade securities; that is, no longer require investors to have ratings for the securities they purchase.
6. Weaken the liability shield of the credit rating agencies.
7. Tighten regulation by the SEC.

---

[87]DBRS had been able to increase its share of securities rated by getting deals done quickly. Dan Curry, president of DBRS, said that when issuers "can't get an answer from the other guys, we let you know within a week." (*Wall Street Journal*, May 24, 2010.)

[88]DBRS also had the largest share of ratings of resecuritizations or re-remics, where asset-backed securities such as CDOs were used to back new securities.

[89]The shield was subject to an actual malice exception. The credit rating agencies had no shield from fraud.

[90]*Los Angeles Times*, June 3, 2010.

[91]*New York Times*, May 13, 2010.

[92]*New York Times*, May 23, 2010.

[93]*Wall Street Journal*, September 4, 2009.

ISSUER-PAYS SYSTEM

In the early 1970s the ratings industry shifted from a user-pays system to an issuer-pays system.[94] Along with the issuer-pays system came potential conflicts of interest, although there were few complaints prior to the mid-2000s. When the bubble burst, the complaints escalated. Senator Carl Levin (D-MI) said the issuer-pays system was "like having one of the parties in court paying the judge's salary."

Deven Sharma of Standard & Poor's commented, "The market benefits greatly from the issuer-pays model as it increases transparency by allowing us to distribute our ratings to all investors free of charge—that's not the case in a subscriber model that creates haves and have-nots in the marketplace."[95] He added that there were conflicts of interest in any system.

Warren Buffett said, "I'm not arguing that this is a perfect model—I'm just saying that it's very difficult to think of an alternative."[96]

USER-PAYS SYSTEM

Diners pay for restaurant guides, and parents pay for college guides for their college-bound children. William McGurn used the analogy to college guidebooks to argue for competition and a user-pays system. He wrote, "[college guides] competed by persuading students and parents to buy them on the quality and relevance of their findings."[97]

A user-pays system could involve investors paying for ratings on a subscription basis, but the principal issue was whether investors would voluntarily pay for a rating. One concern was how valuable ratings were to investors. Another concern was that information was a public good; that is, it was costly to produce but, once produced, disseminating it electronically was virtually costless. Investors had an incentive to free ride on the information acquired by others, which could mean that few investors would subscribe. Warren Buffett stated in a hearing held by the Financial Crisis Inquiry Commission, "It's very difficult to think of an alternative where the user pays. I'm not going to pay."[98]

EASY ENTRY

The passage of the Credit Rating Agency Reform Act led the SEC to certify additional NRSROs, and by 2010 there were 10.[99] Competition in the credit rating industry could be increased by further easing the standards for designation as a NRSRO. This would require shortening the 3-year period required by the SEC before a firm could offer ratings. Competition could also be increased by entry of firms without an official designation that could sell ratings to investors. McGurn wrote, "the [SEC]

might do well to stop anointing particular credit rating agencies. Forcing these firms to compete for customers the way the college guides do would give us better ratings—and fewer investors lulled into complacency that comes from thinking Uncle Sam has done the due diligence."[100]

Jules Kroll, who had sold his security and investigations firm for $1.9 billion in 2004, planned to launch Kroll Bond Ratings, which he hoped would generate $400 million in revenue within 5 years. Kroll said he planned to conduct real investigations of the assets behind debt instruments, including knocking on doors to see if a house were occupied.[101] He said, "I see this as another version of due diligence. You really need to look at what the facts are, and then you rate them, which is what we've done for years but in a different context."[102] Kroll planned to charge a subscription fee for his firm's ratings.

Public accounting firms potentially had the capability of entering the credit rating industry. John Griffith-Jones, chairman of KPMG UK, commented, "It is something that we talk about as a plausible thing to do. It is effectively something we would be proficient at doing. But it's not on the agenda at the moment."[103]

END RATINGS SHOPPING

The inherent conflict of interest resulting from the opportunity of investors to ratings shop generated pressure for higher ratings.[104] A 2004 internal e-mail by a Standard & Poor's employee stated, "We are meeting with your group this week to discuss adjusting criteria for rating CDOs of real estate assets this week because of the ongoing threat of losing deals. Lose the CDO and lose the base business—a self-reinforcing loop."[105] Another employee complained about having "to massage the sub-prime and ALT-A numbers to preserve market share."[106]

When an issuer decided not to use a rating or not to proceed with a ratings firm that expressed skepticism or required additional data, the issuer often cited a failure to meet its deadline. For example, in 2009 Deutsche Bank AG securitized $1.7 billion of loans made by German banks to U.S. companies and sought a AAA rating. Moody's balked at the deal, but Fitch gave a AAA rating to $1.3 billion of the securities. A Deutsche spokesperson said, "We selected the only ratings firm to meet our deadline."[107]

Senator Al Franken (D-MN) described the current system as follows: "There is a staggering conflict of interest affecting the credit rating issue …. [Issuers] shop around for their ratings, selecting those agencies that tend to offer them the best ratings

---

[94]White, "Markets," discusses alternative explanations for the shift ranging from the introduction of the photocopier, which made copying the manuals cheaper, to the recognition that issuers needed to have their securities rated for regulated investors to buy them so they should be willing to pay for the ratings.
[95]*USA Today*, March 22, 2010.
[96]*Los Angeles Times*, June 3, 2010.
[97]William McGurn, "Let's Grade Wall Street Like Colleges. The more rating agencies the better," *Wall Street Journal*, September 15, 2009.
[98]*Wall Street Journal*, June 3, 2010.
[99]White, "Markets," 222.

[100]William McGurn, op.cit.
[101]*Crain's New York Business*, May 17, 2010.
[102]*Guardian*, May 21, 2010.
[103]*The Banker*, June 1, 2010.
[104]See Vasiliki Skreta and Laura Veldkamp, "Ratings Shopping and Asset Complexity: A Theory of Rating Inflation," *Journal of Monetary Economics* 56 (2009): 678–695.
[105]Documents released by the Senate Permanent Subcommittee on Investigations. *International Herald Tribune*, April 24, 2010.
[106]Documents released by the Senate Permanent Subcommittee on Investigations. Cited in Paul Krugman, "Berating the Raters," *New York Times*, April 26, 2010.
[107]*Wall Street Journal*, May 24, 2010.

and threatening to stay away from rating agencies that are too tough on them." Franken offered an amendment to the pending financial system reform bill to eliminate the conflict of interest. "[A credit rating agency] would be assigned. That means that an issuer will no longer be able to shop around for a rating."[108] Standard & Poor's commented on Franken's amendment, "Credit ratings firms would have less incentive to compete with one another. This could lead to more homogenized rating opinions and, ultimately, deprive investors of valuable, differentiated opinions on credit risk."[109]

ELIMINATE REQUIRED RATINGS

Inside Mortgage Finance estimated that 56 percent of the $2 trillion in CDOs issued during the bubble were private-label securities that did not receive a credit rating.[110] To induce investors to buy the securities, issuers offered high yields (low prices). The private-label market collapsed with the bursting of the bubble but began to revive in 2009–2010. One advantage of going to market without a rating was speed, since obtaining a rating can take considerable time particularly after the bubble had burst. Bob Knuze-Concewitz, CEO of Gruppo Campari of Italy, said of the company's €350 million bond offering, "Our reputation is good … I don't think a rating would have mattered much."[111] With structured finance, however, investors were less likely to rely on reputation and had a stronger incentive to do their own analysis.

Senators George LeMieux (R-FL) and Maria Cantwell (D-WA) offered an amendment to the Senate's financial system reform bill that would remove references to credit rating agencies from the federal laws regulating investments, including the Securities Exchange Act of 1934 and the Federal Deposit Reserve Act. Cantwell said, "It's critical that these agencies like the FDIC and the comptroller of the currency come up with appropriate standards of creditworthiness and not rely on the monopoly of the credit rating agencies."[112] The Senate approved the amendment with all Republicans voting for it along with 37 Democrats. Removing the references would mean that financial institutions and institutional investors would have the responsibility for assessing the riskiness of the securities they bought, subject to oversight by their regulators.

REMOVE THE LIABILITY SHIELD

The financial system reform bill reported by the Senate Banking Committee would weaken the liability shield and encourage lawsuits. Deven Sharma of Standard & Poor's said "the provision would hamper [the CRAs] willingness and ability to [provide updated analysis]. A better answer for consumers and our economy is to turn over to the regulatory agencies enforcement tools of sufficient strength so that mistakes are addressed but

not blown out of proportion for personal gain."[113] Even if the First Amendment shield remained in place, the filing of fraud lawsuits could be encouraged. Congress was considering explicitly allowing investors to bring lawsuits against credit rating agencies that "knowingly or recklessly" failed to "conduct a reasonable investigation of the rated security."[114]

Even in the absence of new legislation the liability shield would continue to be challenged by trial lawyers because the potential awards were so high. As the *New York Times* wrote, "What is happening with the ratings agency lawsuits is what happens every time an industry is attacked through the courts en mass—the plaintiffs lawyers learn from each ruling, including the dismissals, then fine-tune their arguments and refile."[115]

STRENGTHEN REGULATION BY THE SECURITIES AND EXCHANGE COMMISSION

The SEC had rule-making authority over the credit rating agencies and had tightened rules on transparency, disclosure, and reporting. Rule making was complex, however. Mary Schapiro, chairman of the SEC, began a rule-making procedure in 2009, but in early 2010 she said, "It can take more time than one might have thought at the outset. We have to understand the real-life implications of what we're doing, the unintended consequences. We need to digest all the comments and all the economic analysis. And that leads us down a path that sometimes isn't 100 percent predictable at the beginning."[116] Schapiro sought to reform the credit rating industry but some reforms required Congress to expand the SEC's authority. The SEC could be given additional authority over credit ratings, including the authority to mandate disclosure when an issuer had sought a rating and subsequently decided not to use that rating in the marketing of its securities.

The SEC had removed the reference to credit rating agencies for some securities but had added a reference for money market funds.[117] In April 2010 the SEC initiated a rule-making procedure on a 667-page proposed rule that would eliminate the requirement that securities have a rating, relying on issuers to certify the securities and provide information on the underlying assets. ■

Preparation Questions

1. As Moody's which alternatives would you support and what would you do to increase the likelihood that they would be adopted and the other alternatives rejected?
2. As DBRS which alternatives would you support and what would you do to increase the likelihood that they would be adopted and the other alternatives rejected?
3. Which alternative or combination of alternatives would be best from a public policy perspective?

[108]*New York Times*, May 14, 2010.
[109]Ibid.
[110]*Wall Street Journal*, April 2, 2010.
[111]*Wall Street Journal*, October 29, 2009.
[112]*New York Times*, May 14, 2010.

[113]*USA Today*, March 22, 2010.
[114]*Wall Street Journal*, June 18, 2010.
[115]*New York Times*, May 23, 2010.
[116]*Washington Post*, February 16, 2010.
[117]Kathleen Casey and Paul Partnoy, "Downgrade the Ratings Agencies," *New York Times*, June 6, 2010.

Citigroup and Subprime Lending

On September 6, 2000, Citigroup, Inc., announced an agreement to acquire Associates First Capital Corporation in an exchange of shares valued at $31.1 billion. The Associates was the largest publicly traded finance company with managed assets of $100 billion and shareholder equity of $10.4 billion. The Associates had 2,750 offices with approximately 1,000 in the United States and the rest in 13 other countries.[118] The Associates also did business through thousands of independent brokers. Citigroup had managed assets of $791 billion, shareholder equity of $51 billion, and operations in 100 countries. Citigroup chairman and CEO Sanford I. Weill said, "Our consumer finance operations are very well regarded. We are excited about the prospects for the combined operations." Keith W. Hughes, chairman and CEO of the Associates, said, "We are excited to be joining forces in this effort, contributing the energy and drive that has led the Associates to twenty-five consecutive years of record earnings."[119] Citigroup planned to merge the U.S. operations of the Associates into its CitiFinancial unit, which also provided consumer finance. Hughes would be the head of CitiFinancial and join Citigroup's board of directors as vice chairman.

The acquisition of the Associates brought Sandy Weill back to his roots. In 1986 he became CEO of a Baltimore finance company, Commercial Credit Corporation, that lent to working class families. He built the company through internal growth and acquisition and later merged The Travelers Group with Citicorp to form one of the largest financial institutions in the country. As a result of the merger Commercial Credit was succeeded by CitiFinancial, which in 2000 had $18.5 billion in loans and $390 million in profits. The Associates had profits of $409 million in the second quarter of 2000 and had 480,000 home equity loans outstanding. With the acquisition CitiFinancial would become the nation's largest finance company.

A major profit source for CitiFinancial and the Associates was subprime lending—lending to people who did not meet the customary credit requirements of banks. The growth of subprime lending during the 1990s had been spectacular, with lending increasing 13-fold between 1993 and 1999. Outstanding subprime loans were estimated at $150 billion in 1998. This lending had provided access to credit to many people who would not have qualified for prime loans because of their credit history. A study by Freddie Mac, however, estimated that perhaps one-third of subprime borrowers could have qualified for prime loans, and Freddie Mac chairman Franklin Raines believed that as many as half might be able to qualify. One study found that 35 percent of the subprime borrowers were over 55, and African Americans were twice as likely to borrow in the subprime market as in the prime market.

The growth in subprime lending was also driven by aggressive marketing by the subprime lenders. The lenders relied on both mass advertising and direct marketing. One form of subprime lending was home equity loans marketed to borrowers to consolidate their bills. *BusinessWeek* commented on an example of such a loan on the CitiFinancial Web site: "'I now can afford so much more than I thought possible,' says Spencer L. of Worcester, Mass. A sample worksheet shows that Spencer can take out a $20,000 home-equity loan to consolidate his bills, pay off credit cards, and reap $310.57 in 'monthly savings.' The fine print notes that Spencer will pay that back in 120 months at a 13.49 percent interest rate. But nowhere on the Web site does it say that it would cost $36,500 to pay off starting debts of $17,000."[120]

Subprime lending had generated vocal complaints from consumer and activist groups, which referred to it as predatory lending. Many of the people who borrowed in the subprime market were lower income, minority, and elderly, and consumer advocates claimed that they often did not understand the loans and what was bundled with them. Some of these critics referred to the Associates as a "rogue company."

A second aspect of subprime lending was single-premium life insurance sold along with a loan to pay off the principal in the case of the death of the borrower. The insurance premiums for several years were typically charged up front and added to the loan principal. Moreover, the insurance often covered not only the loan principal but the insurance premiums and the interest on the loan. Frequently, the insurance did not cover the entire period of the loan. Because the premiums were packed into the loan principal, the insurance was financed at the high interest rates on the loans. The resulting cost of single-premium life insurance was considerably higher than the cost of term life insurance. This single-premium life insurance was criticized by community activists and government officials because many borrowers did not understand that it was included in the loan principal. The Consumer Federation of America called this "the worst insurance rip-off" in America.

As an example of a complaint involving insurance, Benny and Linda Mackey of Chocowinity, North Carolina, had fallen behind on their $519 monthly mortgage payments, and refinanced their $37,117.76 mortgage with the Associates. The Associates added a $4,231 "loan discount" to their principal and also added $4,910.08 in life insurance premiums to the loan. At a 14.99 percent interest rate the Mackeys' monthly payment rose to $592. When they missed some payments, the Associates harassed them and threatened foreclosure, according to the Mackeys. The Mackeys filed a complaint with the state of North Carolina, and the Associates lowered their payments to $370 at a 9 percent interest rate. Alan Hirsch, a deputy attorney general of North Carolina, said

---

[118]The Associates had been owned for a decade by the Ford Motor Company, which spun off the unit in 1998.

[119]Citigroup press release, September 6, 2000.

[120]*BusinessWeek,* March 19, 2001.

that single-premium credit insurance was the most egregious practice, since "many borrowers don't understand it's been included in the loan." The attorney general of North Carolina had begun an investigation of the Associates in 1999 and subsequently filed a lawsuit against the company. The investigation focused on packing insurance premiums in the loan and financing it at high rates. North Carolina also enacted an anti-predatory lending law.

Both the Associates and CitiFinancial sold single-premium life insurance. The Associates issued insurance through its subsidiary, Associates Corporation of North America, which over the past 5 years had collected $1.8 billion in insurance premiums and recorded earnings of $397.5 million.[121] Fannie Mae and Freddie Mac refused to buy first mortgages with single-premium credit insurance.

One of the principal critics of subprime lenders was ACORN (Association of Community Organizations for Reform Now). ACORN was an organization with 500 neighborhood chapters in 50 cities focusing on supporting low- and moderate-income families. It filed numerous lawsuits on behalf of people whom it viewed as victims. ACORN referred to subprime lending as "legalized robbery" and listed the following among the predatory lending tactics used by subprime lenders:[122]

- Charging excessive interest rates not justified by the risk involved
- Charging and financing excessive points and fees
- Packing loans with additional products like financial credit insurance or club memberships
- Charging extended prepayment penalties that trap people in high-interest-rate loans
- Financing single-premium credit insurance
- Misrepresenting the terms and conditions of loans
- Charging unfair and excessive late fees
- Refinancings, and especially repeated refinancings, that result in no benefit to the borrower
- Balloon payments and negative amortization schedules on high-cost loans
- Targeting high-cost loans to vulnerable borrowers, including the elderly, low-income, and minority families
- Using harassing and intimidating collection techniques

In particular, ACORN had criticized CitiFinancial and the Associates for sales of single-premium life insurance, high up-front fees, and high prepayment fees. ACORN had asked the companies to stop these practices.[123]

AARP (American Association of Retired Persons) also was concerned about predatory mortgage lending because many people over 50 were using subprime borrowing. AARP was studying subprime lending and was considering a campaign

against it. A campaign would involve both public education and support for stringent state legislation to curtail abuses.

Regulation of subprime lending was loose, and the relevant agencies were considering whether tighter supervision was warranted. The relevant regulators were the Comptroller of the Currency, the Federal Reserve Board, the Federal Deposit Insurance Corporation, and the Office of Thrift Supervision.

One lever of the community activists had been taken away in 1999 when Congress passed banking reform legislation. The legislation eliminated a requirement that in approving bank acquisitions the Federal Reserve Board had to solicit and consider consumer opinions on how well the banks met the requirements of the 1977 Community Reinvestment Act. That Act required banks to loan in the communities in which their offices were located. The legislation eliminated this requirement in the case of the acquisition of financial companies that did not take deposits. Since the Associates did not take deposits, Citigroup was only required to provide information to federal regulators about CRA performance. Groups such as ACORN had regularly used the CRA requirement to scrutinize the banks' lending data and extract lending pledges from the banks.

When the acquisition was announced, Representative Stephanie Tubbs Jones (D-OH) said, "Citigroup needs to know there are members of the House banking committee—particularly the Congressional Black Caucus members—who are concerned about the merger and they need to be concerned about our concerns." A North Carolina group had shown the Black Caucus a videotape of a man who had gone to an Associates office for a loan to buy groceries and over the next 10 years had been persuaded to refinance the loan 11 times, resulting in a $50,000 mortgage at an interest rate of 19 percent.[124]

The Associates had been named in approximately 700 lawsuits and had been fined $147,000 by the state of Georgia. The Department of Justice had filed a lawsuit against the Associates alleging that one of its credit card banks had violated fair lending laws in marketing credit cards to Hispanics.[125] The Federal Trade Commission (FTC) had initiated an investigation of the Associates in 1999 for allegations of deceptive marketing practices. Since 1998 the FTC had filed 14 lawsuits involving subprime lending, including complaints against the Associates.

Citigroup was surprised by the intensity of the criticisms of its acquisition of the Associates and more generally of subprime lending. The allegations of predatory lending and deception were serious, and they threatened a highly profitable business. In response to the criticisms, William Street, a Citigroup attorney, said, "Citigroup is committed to improving … the compliance systems and operation systems and anything else they determine needs improving to meet their standards."[126]

---

[121]*New York Times,* October 22, 2000.
[122]ACORN, "Predatory Lending: A Growing Problem," www.acorn.org.
[123]ACORN also launched a campaign against Household Finance for what it called abusive and predatory practices.

[124]*Washington Post,* September 15, 2000.
[125]Ibid.
[126]Ibid.

In a letter to the Comptroller of the Currency, the Superintendent of the New York State Banking Department, and the Chairman of the Federal Deposit Insurance Corporation, the regulators that had to approve the acquisition, Sandy Weill stated, "We prize our long-standing reputation for service to customers and communities and we recognize that CitiFinancial's position as the soon-to-be largest consumer finance company in the U.S. gives it the opportunity to play an even more important and valuable role in communities in which it does business."[127] The motto on Citigroup's 1999 annual report was "Leading by Example." ▪

Preparation Questions

1. Are there ethics concerns associated with subprime lending?
2. What should CitiFinancial do about single-premium life insurance?
3. What should CitiFinancial do about the other allegations of abuse?
4. Should Citigroup support the efforts of ACORN and AARP to weed out unscrupulous practices? Should it support tighter regulatory supervision of the subprime lending market?
5. What policies should Citigroup adopt for subprime lending?

Source: This case was prepared from public sources by David P. Baron. Copyright © 2001 by David P. Baron. All rights reserved. Reprinted with permission.

[127]Citigroup, November 7, 2000.

12

ENVIRONMENTAL MANAGEMENT AND SUSTAINABILITY

INTRODUCTION

The public, government, and business recognize the importance of environmental protection and sustainability. The benefits include improved human health, a more vibrant natural environment, the preservation of ecosystems, and a more sustainable relationship with the natural environment. Achieving these benefits is also expensive. Compliance with existing environmental regulation costs each person in the United States nearly $900 a year in 2004—or a total of $250 billion annually, representing 2.1 percent of GDP. New programs to meet other environmental goals and more stringent regulations have added to that cost. The cost of environmental protection and sustainability require not only that the environment be protected and sustainability be achieved but also that they be accomplished as efficiently as possible. Although there is widespread agreement about general goals, there remains considerable disagreement about how much protection is appropriate and about the distribution of the burden of that protection. These disagreements generate the politics of environmental protection and sustainability.

This chapter focuses on public and private managerial policies for environmental protection and sustainability. The following section considers the global climate change challenge, and the next section introduces a framework for reasoning about externalities. The experiences with the U.S. sulfur dioxide cap-and-trade system and the European Union cap-and-trade system for carbon dioxide are then reviewed. Environmental regulation is then considered with a focus on the policies of the Environmental Protection Agency (EPA). The politics of environmental protection are then addressed. The management of environmental and regulatory issues from a firm's perspective is then considered. Examples include BP's internal emissions trading system, Intel's participation in the EPA's XL program, environmental innovation at Home Depot, Wal-Mart's aggressive environmental programs, an experiment by FedEx, the Responsible Care program in the chemical industry, and McDonald's and Dow Chemicals' cooperative programs with environmental groups. Chapter 13 focuses on renewable energy.

THE ENVIRONMENT AND SUSTAINABILITY

Goals and Actions

Environmental protection and sustainability are widely accepted goals, although disagreement remains about how costly attaining these goals would be. Environmental protection goals pertain to ecosystems, climate change, pollution, habitats, and more, and sustainability pertains to energy, forests, and the environment more generally.

In 1983 the United Nations formed the Brundtland Commission to consider the future of the environment and natural resources. The commission headed by Bro Harlem Brundtland developed a concept to sustainability for society, "Sustainable development is development that meets the needs of the present without compromising the ability of future generations to meet their own needs."[1] From this perspective the present generation is to conduct itself so that future generations will be able to obtain at least the level of well-being of the present generation. The Environmental Protection Agency defines sustainability as, "Sustainability creates and maintains the conditions under which humans and nature can exist in productive harmony, that permit fulfilling the social, economic and other requirements of present and future generations." Although the concept of sustainability is be appealing, it is subject to two principal issues. The first is how to think about population growth. The second is the difficulty of predicting future technological progress and innovation.

---

[1]World Commission on Environment and Development, Our Common Future, Report of the World Commission on Environment and Development, Oxford University Press, 1987.

The challenge for firms is to identify their roles in contributing to sustainability objectives. For example, Unilever stated its goals as, "Through our business and brands, we want to create a better future every day for people all around the world: the people who work for us, those we do business with, the billions of people who use our products, and future generations whose quality of life depends on the way we protect the environment today."

The principal instruments for attaining environmental and sustainability goals come from government, but private initiatives can also play a role, as can the policies of firms and the practices of individuals. Twenty-six companies including General Electric, General Motors, and DuPont joined with six environmental groups including Environmental Defense and the Natural Resources Defense Council to form the U.S. Climate Action Partnership. The partnership has urged the adoption of strong government action to reduce greenhouse gases emissions. Venture capital firms have begun investing in energy start-ups and in companies developing technologies to reduce carbon emissions, including negative carbon technologies. Companies such as Wal-Mart have implemented aggressive corporate environmental programs. Some of these programs are responses to public and private politics pressure, but many are adopted voluntarily in the absence of direct pressure. Individuals have taken measures such as replacing incandescent light bulbs with compact fluorescent bulbs as well as more extensive measures such as installing solar panels and bicycling to work.

Responsibility for environmental protection and sustainability has broadened. Financial institutions, for example, are now held responsible not only for their own carbon footprint but also for the consequences of their lending. JPMorgan Chase, Bank of America, Citigroup, and Goldman Sachs have environmental and sustainability policies. As a consequence of pressure from activist groups and its leadership in establishing the Equator Principles, Citigroup has a greenhouse gases reporting system for the project finance it provides. The bank also has a Sustainable Development Investment Program to fund private equity investments in renewable energy and other environmental improvement prospects.

Global Climate Change

The scientific evidence on global climate change identifies humans as a major contributor to global warming through the release of greenhouse gases. The increase in greenhouse gas emissions is due to a variety of factors, the two most important being population growth and economic growth. The U.S. Census Bureau estimates that the world population increased from 3 billion in 1959 to 7 billion in October 2011. The United Nations, which had projected that the world population would level off at 9 billion in 2050, revised its forecast to 10.1 billion with growth continuing thereafter. Africa and Asia account for approximately three-quarters of the world population and are projected to account for nearly 90 percent of the growth over the next 30–40 years. The most rapid growth is projected for Sub-Saharan Africa, which the UN projects will have three-quarters the population of Asia by 2100. Economic growth has increased more rapidly than population, resulting in an increase in per capita income.

The energy intensity of economic activity has decreased steadily in much of the world by approximately 1.5 percent a year. Denmark has perhaps the lowest energy intensity with slightly more than 3.1 Btu/$1,000 of GDP in 2008, whereas the energy intensity in China was 26.7 Btu/$1,000. The world average was 9.8 Btu/$1,000 of GDP. For the United States the Btus/$1,000 have decreased from 12 in 1990 to 7.6 in 2008. Although energy intensity has decreased steadily in the United States, because of population and economic growth the total emissions of CO_2 have increased by 17.5 percent between 1990 and 2006 and by 38.6 percent since 1974.

Policy

The United States has not and likely will not in the near future adopt a national program for reducing carbon emissions. The northeastern states formed a carbon emission cap-and-trade system, the Regional Greenhouse Gas Initiative (RGGI), with the objective of reducing CO_2 emissions by 10 percent by 2018. The cap, however, was set too high, and RGGI accomplished little. New Jersey withdrew from RGGI citing the burden on the economy during a recession. The remaining states began considering revisions to the cap-and-trade system. California also enacted a carbon emission reduction goal and delegated the implementation plan to the state air resources regulator. The regulator chose a cap-and-trade system, but environmental groups filed a lawsuit to block it, arguing that a carbon tax was preferable. A judge agreed, sending the issue back to the air resources regulator, as considered in the chapter case *Environmentalist versus Environmentalist.*

Global climate change objectives could be achieved using a variety of instruments. One is to increase energy productivity. In two major studies McKinsey & Co. evaluated the opportunities to reduce energy use and found that half of the projected increase in worldwide energy demand could be avoided by investments that had an internal rate of return of at least 10 percent.[2] The capital expenditures required would be $170 billion a year for 13 years, of which half would be in the industrial sector, one-quarter in the residential sector, and the remainder in the commercial and transportation sectors. The greatest opportunity is in the residential sector through better insulation, the use of fluorescent lighting, and more efficient hot water heaters.

If such attractive investment opportunities are available, why are these investments not being made automatically? One explanation is that there are market failures and transactions costs that impede the investments. Individuals may be poorly informed about the opportunities or may be credit constrained, preventing them from retrofitting their homes to reduce energy use. In addition, the transactions costs of making improvements may seem larger to homeowners than the modest annual savings that can be achieved. Because of uncertainty about whether consumers will actually buy a more energy-efficient appliance, manufacturers may be reluctant to produce enough of the appliances to realize the potential economies of scale. One response to these market failures and transactions costs is government subsidies and incentives for reducing energy use and prescriptive regulations mandating energy efficiency. The United States has adopted efficiency standards for appliances and enacted a controversial law to in effect eliminate the use of most incandescent light bulbs.

Tradeoffs

Even if there are attractive investment opportunities, they are unlikely to be sufficient to deal with global climate change. Tradeoffs thus must be made. Most measures to mitigate the harm from externalities require tradeoffs. Tradeoffs are involved in decisions by consumers as well as policies of governments. For example, the use of compact fluorescent bulbs in place of incandescent bulbs causes a mercury pollution problem, since the fluorescent bulbs contain about 4 mg of mercury, a toxic substance. At the government level, Congress has subsidized the production of ethanol as a substitute for oil. Corn has been the principal crop used for ethanol production, and the demand for corn has increased, leading farmers to increase their production at the expense of other crops.[3] The demand for ethanol has resulted in higher prices for corn, palm, and other crops, and crop and food prices escalated rapidly, putting a substantial burden on households as well as developing countries. The Food and Agriculture Organization of the United Nations and the Organization for Economic Cooperation and Development issued a report stating, "The energy, security, environmental, and economic benefits of biofuels production based on agricultural commodity feed stocks are at best modest, and sometimes even negative."

These concerns have refocused biofuel enthusiasts on second-generation feedstock made from nonfood crops such as reeds, jatropha, and wild grasses. Scientists warned, however, that these nonfood crops were often invasive and posed environmental risks. Plans for a giant reed plantation in Florida were opposed by some environmental groups, and jatropha, which is grown in eastern Africa, has been banned in Australia. The International Union for Conservation of Nature warned, "Don't let invasive biofuel crops attack your country."

The U.S. Green Building Council provides standards and certification for sustainable buildings and provides LEED certification for new construction and retrofitting. Certificate levels are Certified, Silver, Gold, and Platinum, representing successively higher levels of sustainability—and costs. San Francisco has adopted stringent building standards requiring the use of clean energy and sustainable building materials. A study by the city's Office of Economic Analysis (OEA) concluded the greenhouse gas emissions would be reduced over time but at a cost of $30 million to $700 million a year through 2027. The OEA indicated that a carbon

---

[2]McKinsey & Co., "The Case for Investing in Energy Productivity," February 2008; "Curbing Global Energy Demand Growth: The Energy Productivity Opportunity," May 2007. The estimates were based on a price of $70 for a barrel of crude oil.

[3]In contrast, Brazil uses the stalks from sugar cane to produce ethanol and has become nearly self-sufficient.

tax would have an immediate effect on emissions and would distort economic activity less. The tax, however, would increase utility rates by 16.5 percent. A framework for the analysis of the tradeoffs in environmental protection is presented in the next section.

SOCIALLY EFFICIENT CONTROL OF EXTERNALITIES

Social efficiency is attained when aggregate well-being is maximal. Aggregate well-being takes into account the harm from an externality and the social costs of reducing that harm. Just as it is not socially efficient to prevent all accidents, it is not socially efficient to prevent all pollution or return carbon concentrations in the atmosphere to pre–industrial revolution levels. Instead, that pollution which is not too costly to prevent should be prevented. The control of externalities, however, has often taken the form of *command-and-control* regulation in which regulators order engineering controls or require the best available technology for pollution abatement. This approach deals with the source of the harm, but it takes into account neither the benefits of the avoided harm nor the cost of abatement. Command-and-control is a blunt instrument that imposes uniform controls and standards on dissimilar sources of pollution, resulting in excessive abatement costs. In contrast, social efficiency requires that the polluter and those affected by the pollution externality take into account both the harm and the costs of abatement. For each source of pollution, social efficiency requires that costs and benefits be considered and that reductions in pollution be attained at the least cost. The lower the cost of reducing pollution, the larger are the reductions that can be made.

Incentive approaches take into account the benefits and costs of attaining environmental objectives and achieve those objectives by aligning the social and private costs of pollution and its abatement. These approaches attain social efficiency by requiring polluters to internalize the social costs of pollution externalities. These approaches also decentralize pollution-control decisions because the generators of pollution rather than regulators have the responsibility for evaluating alternative abatement strategies and technologies. Rather than dictating how environmental goals should be achieved, incentive approaches impose a cost on pollution-causing activities, leaving it to individual polluters to decide how best to respond. Incentives then drive these decisions toward the least-cost means of attaining environmental objectives. The incentives to reduce costs also provide incentives to redesign production processes to reduce pollutants, eliminate harmful components of products, develop better pollution control technologies, and develop alternative production technologies.

The principles underlying incentive approaches to achieving social efficiency in the presence of externalities are provided by the Coase theorem. It addresses the private attainment of social efficiency and the conditions for its attainment.

The Coase Theorem

The *Coase theorem* pertains to market imperfections, including externalities and public goods. It focuses on the standard of social efficiency and provides a conceptual foundation for both regulation and the liability system considered in Chapter 14. The theorem does not address other standards, such as distributive objectives and social justice, that could be used in evaluating alternative social arrangements and public policies. The Coase theorem has gained influence in the economics of externalities and public goods and in the law through applications to issues such as breach of contracts, nuisance law, and torts.[4] Coase's (1960) original exposition focused on externalities.

Coase observed that an externality is reciprocal in the sense that at least two parties are required. In the case of noise pollution, there would be no externality without the polluter or in the absence of anyone to hear the noise. In the case of a toxic risk from an oil refinery, an externality exists because of both the refinery and the presence of homes and businesses near it. When an externality is recognized to be reciprocal, it is clear that there is more than one means of achieving social efficiency. Coase's analysis began with an entitlement protected by a *property rule*. A property rule prohibits other parties from infringing the entitlement without the consent of the party holding it. Homeowners are protected by a property rule that prohibits other persons from taking their home without consent or forcing them to sell it at a price they deem inadequate.

---

[4]See Polinsky (2011) for an exposition of the role of the Coase theorem in the law.

As an example of Coase's analysis, suppose firm A discharges pollutants into a river whose water is used as an input to a production process by a downstream firm B. In principle, the two firms can voluntarily reach an agreement to *internalize the externality* regardless of which firm has the entitlement. That is, social efficiency can be achieved whether A has the entitlement to pollute or B has the entitlement to be free from pollution. If A has the entitlement to pollute, B has an incentive to bargain with A to reduce the pollution. B would be willing to pay A to the point at which the marginal harm done to B's production equals the marginal cost of reducing pollution at A. This minimizes the total cost of abatement and the harm from pollution, resulting in social efficiency.

If B has the entitlement not to have its production harmed by the pollution, A has an incentive to bargain with B to allow A to discharge some amount of pollution into the river. A is willing to pay B up to A's marginal cost of abatement. B would require a payment equal to the marginal harm it would incur from the pollution, so in an agreement the marginal cost of abatement would equal the marginal harm. The assignment of the entitlement to B thus also results in the socially efficient level of pollution. The Coase theorem example illustrates this logic in more detail and extends the analysis to include abatement alternatives.

The Coase theorem states that, in the absence of transactions costs that would impede the bargaining over these private agreements, the socially efficient outcome can be realized if the entitlement is assigned to either party. The role of government thus is to clearly assign entitlements to the parties and allow them to reach private agreements that internalize the externality. Although social efficiency is attained with either assignment of the entitlement, the assignment affects the distribution of the social costs of the externality and its control. The Coase theorem example illustrates this in more detail.

EXAMPLE The Coase Theorem

To illustrate the concept of social efficiency, suppose company A produces apple cider up river from a brewery B. Company A can produce 0, 100, or 200 gallons of apple cider, and its corresponding profit is 0, 40, and 70, respectively. The company's plant also pollutes the river in proportion to its production, and the pollution causes harm to the brewery's product of 0, 20, and 60, respectively. These data are summarized in Table 12-1. Aggregate social well-being or social value is the profit of company A less the harm to company B. As indicated in the table, the social value is maximized at a production level of 100, which yields profit of 40 and harm of 20 for a social value of 20.

Identifying the social optimum is one thing; attaining it is another matter. Company A has an incentive to maximize its profit by producing 200 gallons, which yields a profit of 70. The harm, however, of 60 results in a social value of 10. One means of achieving social efficiency is through bargaining between A and B.

For bargaining to take place, entitlements must be clearly assigned and their protection specified. Suppose that

B has the entitlement not to be harmed by pollution, and the entitlement is protected by a property rule. B thus will not allow A to produce at all unless it is compensated for the harm it incurs. A is willing to pay up to 40 to be able to produce 100 units, and B requires compensation of at least 20 for the harm. Suppose that as a result of their bargaining they split the difference, with A paying 30 to B to be allowed to produce 100 units accompanied by the pollution. Next, consider whether A wants to induce B to allow it to increase its production from 100 to 200. If it does, its profit increases by 30, but B requires at least 40 more to compensate for the additional harm. A thus is not willing to pay enough to induce B to bear the additional harm. Consequently, the bargaining between A and B results in the socially optimal output of 100 and a social value of 20. Through bargaining, the two parties have internalized the externality.

Coase considered such situations and asked whether social efficiency would be obtained regardless of how the entitlement was assigned. That is, suppose that A is assigned the entitlement to produce and pollute as much as it chooses and the entitlement is protected by a property rule. A would then want to produce 200 units. B, however, would incur harm of 60, so it is willing to offer A up to 40 if A will reduce its production from 200 to 100. Since A loses only 30 in profit from cutting back its production to 100, the two parties can strike a bargain (at 35 if they split the difference). It is straightforward to verify that B will not be willing to compensate A enough to induce it to cut its production to zero. The socially efficient outcome has again been obtained.

TABLE 12-1 Production, Harm, and Social Value

A			B	Social
Production	Emissions	Profit	Harm	Value
0	0	0	0	0
100	10	40	−20	20
200	20	70	−60	10

(Continued)

(*Continued*)

The Coase theorem states that social efficiency can be achieved regardless of which party has the entitlement.

Although social efficiency is achieved with either assignment of entitlements, the distributive consequences of the assignments are quite different. If the entitlement is assigned to B, A has profit of 10 (= 40 – 30) and B has 10 (= 30 – 20). If the entitlement is assigned to A, A has a profit of 75 (= 40 + 35) and B has –55 (= –20 – 35). (Note that B's profit is not included here.) These distributive consequences are the source of politics as people seek to have the entitlement assigned to them.

The Coase theorem is more general than indicated by the analysis of a property rule. A property rule is distinguished from a *liability rule*. A liability rule does not prohibit a party from interfering with another party, but if harm is done, compensation must be paid to the injured party. In the example, suppose that the entitlement is assigned to B and is protected by a liability rule. Then A will produce 100 units and compensate B for the actual harm of 20. A will not increase its production to 200 because its profit would increase by only 30, but additional compensation of 40 would be required. Similarly, A would not reduce its output to 0. Social efficiency is again achieved. The same is true if the entitlement is assigned to A and protected by a liability rule. In this case, B would enjoin A from producing 200 and would be required to compensate A for the loss of profits of 30. B is willing to do so since it avoids harm of 40, but B would not want to enjoin A from producing 100, since that would require paying 40 to A, whereas harm of only 20 would be avoided. So, A will produce 100, again achieving social efficiency.

As in the case of a property rule the distributive consequences of the assignment of the entitlement protected

TABLE 12-2 Abatement and Social Value

Reduction in Emissions, %	Cost of Abatement		Social Value*	
	A	B	A Abates	B Abates
0	0	0	10	10
50	15	20	25	20
100	30	40	40	30

*Based on production of 200.

by a liability rule differ. When the entitlement is assigned to B and protected by a liability rule, A has 20 and B has 0. When the entitlement is assigned to A, A has 70 and B has –50.

This analysis can be extended to include an abatement alternative. Suppose that, as indicated in Table 12-2, A and B each have an abatement alternative. Each can reduce the pollution by 50 or 100 percent at different costs. A can reduce the pollution by 50 and 100 percent at costs of 15 and 30 respectively, and the corresponding costs for B are 20 and 40 respectively. The socially efficient outcome is then for A to produce 200 and to expend 30 to reduce its pollution by 100 percent. The social value is 40 (= 70 – 30). This outcome is achieved regardless of to whom the entitlement is assigned and whether it is protected by a property or a liability rule. For example, if the entitlement is assigned to B and protected by a liability rule, A will produce 200, and rather than compensate B by 60 for the harm, it will install the 100 percent abatement technology at a cost of 30. A's profit is then 40, and B incurs no harm.

Since an externality is reciprocal, one approach to dealing with it is to remove one side of the reciprocal relationship between polluter and those harmed by the pollution. Many plants have closed because of the costs they would have to bear to reduce their pollution. Conversely, to reduce the harm to local residents, the American Electric Power Company bought for $20 million the town of Chesire, Ohio, where one of its coal-fired power plants was located. The amount paid was three times the value of the homes, and the residents quickly accepted the offer.[5] Similarly, Exxon paid $4 million to purchase 110 homes and businesses to create a safety zone around its Baton Rouge, Louisiana, refinery. From the perspective of the Coase theorem, the entitlements in these two cases were held by the homeowners and were protected by a property rule. The firms bargained to purchase those entitlements, thereby bearing the cost of reducing the risk of harm.

Although social efficiency can be achieved with any assignment of entitlements, the distributive consequences can differ substantially. Environmental politics often arises from the existing assignment of entitlements and its implications for the distribution of the benefits and costs of environmental protection. As an example, residents of the Old Diamond neighborhood of Norco, Louisiana, conducted a 12-year private and public politics campaign against Shell. The neighborhood was located between a Shell chemical plant and an oil refinery owned by a Shell joint venture. The plants met EPA emissions standards, and Shell had reduced its emissions. The residents, however, wanted further reductions or a higher price for their homes. The entitlement rested with Shell, but the social pressure from the campaign finally forced Shell to buy the residents' homes.

---

[5]*New York Times Magazine*, February 8, 2004.

Transactions Costs and the Limits of the Coase Theorem

The Coase theorem implies that when bargaining between the parties to an externality is possible, social efficiency can be achieved. Consequently, from the Coasean perspective social efficiency is a problem only when there are impediments to bargaining. These impediments are referred to as *transactions costs* because they are associated with the process of arriving at and enforcing a transaction or agreement. When the parties involved are identifiable and their number is small, transactions costs are likely to be low and private agreements can be reached, as in the case of the power plant in Ohio and the oil refinery and chemical plant in Louisiana. When the parties are difficult to identify or are large in number, however, transactions costs can be prohibitively high, preventing private arrangements.

Consider air pollution from automobile emissions. Millions of automobiles generate pollution, and many more people are affected by that pollution. The costs would be exorbitant if all these individuals attempted to reach agreements about measures to reduce emissions or the amount of driving allowed. Because of the very high transactions costs associated with private bargaining, automobile emissions are controlled through government regulation.

In the case of an externality such as automobile emissions with high transactions costs, either a command-and-control approach specifying particular controls can be used or performance standards can be set. Performance standards are preferred because they allow firms to choose the most cost-effective means of achieving those standards based on their superior information about the costs of alternatives. This approach is decentralized with localized information being used to achieve abatement at the lowest cost.

A market is the logical extension of a decentralized system in which entitlements are assigned and can be traded. Markets, or incentive-based systems, have become an effective means of achieving environmental goals at the least cost to society. These systems are considered next.

CAP-AND-TRADE SYSTEMS

Cap-and-trade systems, or *tradable permits systems,* cap the total allowed emissions of a particular pollutant such as sulfur dioxide or carbon dioxide, issue permits (entitlements) for that amount, and allow the permits to be traded. Cap-and-trade systems have been used for sulfur dioxide emissions and nitrogen dioxides, and several systems are in operation regionally, as in Southern California. A tradable permits system has been adopted to reduce greenhouse gases emissions in conjunction with the Kyoto Protocol on global climate change. Although the United States did not ratify the Kyoto Protocol, a voluntary compliance system was established with permits traded on the Chicago Climate Exchange.[6] The European Union has implemented a cap-and-trade system for carbon dioxide, and in the United States 10 northeastern states have formed RGGT to implement a similar system. BP established an internal tradable permits market for greenhouse gases.

The Coase theorem applies to a tradable permits system. That is, given the amount of pollution permitted, the permits can be allocated to polluters for no charge, can be allocated to the public, or can be auctioned to the highest bidder. With any of these allocations, social efficiency can be achieved provided the permits can be traded. The allocation of the permits, however, affects the distribution of the burden of the emissions reduction and hence motivates politics.

The control of an externality in a tradable permits system has three components. The first is providing incentives for abatement by internalizing the cost of the harm done by the pollution. The second is allowing parties to respond to those incentives by choosing the most efficient means of abatement. These means include reducing output, installing pollution-control equipment, redesigning products and production processes to reduce the pollution generated, and reducing the harm from emissions, as when oil refineries create safety zones around their facilities. The third component involves reflecting in the prices of goods and services, the costs of abatement and the social costs of the harm from the remaining pollution. This allows consumers to take into account the full social cost of the goods they consume. These three components operate simultaneously. An equilibrium results when (1) all advantageous trades have been made, (2) emitters have taken the abatement measures they prefer given the market price of permits, and (3) the quantities of products consumers purchase result in total emissions equal to the number of permits issued.

---

[6]The Chicago Climate Exchange ended its trading program in 2011.

A cap-and-trade system is equivalent to a system in which an emissions tax is imposed on each unit of pollution emitted, provided the tax is set so as to reduce the pollution to the level of the cap. A tradable permits system is preferred by some policy analysts to an emissions tax because the amount of abatement is known in advance with a permits system, whereas with an emissions tax the amount is known only after firms have responded to the tax.

An emissions tax is favored by some economists because it is transparent and easy to implement compared to having to develop a market. The Congressional Budget Office in 2008 concluded that a tax could achieve environmental objectives "at a fraction of the cost" of a cap-and-trade system. Moreover, an emissions tax may be less vulnerable to pressure from industry and labor, as suggested by the European Union's experience with its cap-and-trade system in which too many permits were issued and emissions actually increased initially. Industry opposes emissions taxes because companies would have to pay the tax and prefers a cap-and-trade system in which they are given the permits for free.

Emissions taxes or fees are used in Scandinavia for CO_2 emissions, and in Southern California for organic gases, nitrogen oxides, carbon monoxide, sulfur oxides, and particulate matter. Maine uses an emissions fee that increases from $3.28 per ton for emissions up to 1,000 tons to $15.85 per ton for emissions over 4,000 tons. Fees or taxes are used for landfills, grazing on public lands, and hazardous waste disposal. In 2011 Australia adopted a carbon tax of A$23 per tonne to reduce its emissions, which were the highest per person of any rich country. The Chapter 15 case *The European Union Carbon Tax* considers a similar tax.

A cap-and-trade system has an advantage in that it allows people with different preferences to express them in the market for permits. If people have a preference for lower levels of pollution, they can purchase permits and retire them, thereby reducing emissions. Some people have purchased permits and given them as gifts. The Cleaner and Greener Green Energy program facilitates the donation of permits. The Nature Conservancy purchases land and holds it as open spaces.

Cap-and-trade systems and emissions tax approaches to environmental protection provide incentives for dynamic efficiency. Firms have incentives to invest in research and development to find more efficient means of reducing their emissions. If they can do so, they can sell their permits. Similarly, the pollution-control technology industry has an incentive to develop new abatement technologies because firms have a continuing demand for emissions reduction rather than a demand that arises only when more stringent engineering controls are mandated, as in a command-and-control system.

Despite their efficiency advantages, objections arise because under incentive approaches some firms will reduce emissions considerably whereas others will reduce them less. Some people who view pollution as a social wrong rather than as an external cost of production believe that all firms should be forced to reduce their emissions by the same amount so that, for example, neighboring residents all receive the same reduction in pollution. The next section considers a successful tradable permits system that succumbed to these pressures. The chapter case, *Environmental Justice and Pollution Credits Trading Systems,* addresses this issue and the politics it generated.

Cap-and-Trade Systems to Address Acid Rain

The bulk of the sulfur dioxide emissions (SO_2) that cause acid rain come from coal-fired electric power plants in six states: Indiana, Illinois, West Virginia, Pennsylvania, Ohio, and New York. New power plants are subject to New Source Performance Standards (NSPS), but existing power plants had not been subject to emission limits. These six states, and others as well, had lower electricity prices because their plants did not have to meet stringent controls. Adding a scrubber to remove the sulfur dioxide could increase the cost of electricity by 15 percent. Since the damage from acid rain occurred primarily in the northeastern states and Canada, addressing the issue involved benefits for one region and costs to another. Bargaining thus focused on both efficiency and the distributive consequences of policy alternatives. The political competition over acid rain went on for a decade, culminating with the Clean Air Act Amendments of 1990, which provided for an 87 million pounds, or 45 percent, reduction in sulfur dioxide emissions from the 1980 level and a 2 million pounds reduction in nitrogen oxides emissions.

The amendments addressed efficiency through a tradable permits, or cap-and-trade, system and the distributive consequences were addressed through a number of special provisions. Called "allowances" rather than permits, the system reduced the cost of abatement by allowing electric power companies to use the most efficient means of achieving emissions standards. They could choose low-sulfur coal, coal washing to remove sulfur before burning, new technologies such as fluidized bed combustion, or a scrubber. More importantly, the system permitted firms to trade allowances in a market, providing incentives for the efficient distribution of abatement across firms.

In the initial phase of the program, the EPA administrator annually allocated allowances to 110 coal-fired power plants in 21 states in the Midwest, South, and East according to formulas specified in the legislation.[7] The EPA administrator also conducted an annual auction of allowances from a reserve formed by taking a percentage of the allowances allocated to the plants.[8] Unused allowances could be carried forward to the next year and transferred or sold to other companies.

The value of the sulfur dioxide allowances issued in 2004 was estimated at $3.6 billion, and the spot price in 2004 had skyrocketed from $200 per allowance to $650 per allowance. Spot prices in the EPA auction reached $883 in 2006 and declined to $380 in 2008 as a result of reductions in emissions by power plants. The economic harm from a ton of sulfur dioxide emissions was estimated to be $4,000.[9] The tradable allowances system has been estimated to cost less than a uniform command-and-control approach by 50 percent, or $2.5 billion per year.[10] A 2005 study concluded that by 2010 the acid sulfur dioxide reductions attained by the tradable allowances system would yield benefits of $122 billion at an annual cost of $3 billion for a benefit-cost ratio of 40 to 1.[11]

The EPA also established an emissions trading system for nitrogen oxide similar to the one for sulfur dioxide. The program reduces by 28 percent the emissions in 22 states and the District of Columbia and covers coal-fired and oil-fired power plants and industrial boilers. Nitrogen oxides are a major component of smog and can flow to downwind states. In 2006 nitrogen oxide emissions were less than half the 1990 levels.

Tradable Permits for Sulfur Dioxide and Nitrogen Oxides

The sulfur dioxide and nitrogen oxides interstate trading systems were supplemented by the EPA in its Clean Air Interstate Rule (CAIR) issued in 2005. CAIR was intended to reduce SO_2 emissions and NO_x emissions by 60 percent from 2003 levels by 2015. The trading system functioned efficiently, but the achievements in rapidly achieving environmental goals in an efficient manner ended because of distributive considerations. The state of North Carolina challenged the interstate trading of permits on the grounds that upwind power plants could purchase permits rather than reduce their emissions and downwind states would be unable to meet their air quality standards, which were required by the Clean Air Act. The lawsuit focused not on social efficiency but rather on the distribution of the remaining pollution and an implicit claim that all states and their residents had a right to have their air quality standards attained.

In 2008 the DC Court of Appeals ruled in favor of the plaintiff, vacating CAIR and remanding the issue to the EPA to develop a new rule. Distribution had won out over efficiency, as the court in effect established a right of residents of one state not to have their air quality standards impaired. The court left CAIR in place while the EPA developed a replacement rule, but the market for allowances collapsed as a result of the decision with SO_2 allowances trading for $5. The EPA had also developed a tradable permits system for controlling mercury emissions, and the DC Court of Appeals rejected that system as well.

In 2011 the EPA issued a replacement rule that prohibited the interstate trading of allowances but allowed for intrastate trading. EPA administrator Lisa P. Jackson seemed delighted by the elimination of interstate trading. She said, "No community should have to bear the burden of another community's polluters, ... the [new] Cross-State Air Pollution Rule will help ensure that American families aren't suffering the consequences of pollution generated far from home, while allowing states to decide how best to decrease dangerous air

---

[7]See Joskow and Schmalensee (1998) for a study of the political economy of the allocation of allowances.

[8]The proceeds are distributed back to the plants from which the allowances were originally obtained.

[9]The value of the nitrogen dioxide allowances was estimated at $1.4 billion.

[10]Joskow, Schmalensee, and Bailey (1998), Schmalensee et al. (1998), and Stavins (1998).

[11]With a tradable permits system, emissions must be monitored to ensure that they do not exceed the permits held by the firm. The sulfur dioxide cap-and-trade system uses continuous monitoring by sources and is verified by the EPA and posted on the Internet for public inspection. If a source emits more sulfur dioxide than the allowances it has, a fine of $2,900 per ton of excess emissions is imposed (in 2003). (www.epa.gov/airmarkets.)

pollution in the most cost effective way."[12] The court decision and the new EPA rule meant that the cost to power plants of further reductions in emissions would be higher.

The court's ruling and the EPA's embracement of it could mean that a market mechanism for reducing carbon and other greenhouse gases emissions could be rejected by the courts, unless the Clean Air Act were amended to eliminate the implicit right the court saw in the Act. That is, measures to reduce carbon emissions also reduce the emissions of other pollutants, as when a power company replaces a coal-fired generating plant with a plant burning natural gas. The replacement would reduce SO_2, nitrogen oxides, and mercury emissions along with CO_2 emissions. Without a market-like mechanism for valuing the reductions, the costs to some industries and some firms would be higher, which would generate more political opposition to dealing with climate change.

The EPA's new rule was issued during a record heat wave in the south and central parts of the country and record electricity demand. Texas power plants were unable to meet demand and were forced to purchase electricity on the wholesale market at 60 times normal prices.[13] The electric power industry warned about shortages of capacity, since coal-fired power plants would have to be closed and new gas-fired plants could not be built in time to replace the lost capacity. The electric power industry was affected not only by the elimination of interstate cap-and-trade, but also by forthcoming EPA regulations covering coal ash and cooling towers. The cumulative effect of the regulations was difficult to predict.

The EPA had estimated that its forthcoming rules on SO_2, nitrogen oxides, and mercury would lead to the shutdown of 10,000 megawatts of electricity generating capacity, or 1 percent of U.S. capacity. The Southern Company announced that it would close a 4,000 megawatt coal-fired plant, and American Electric Power announced that it would close a 6,000 megawatt coal-fired plant. American Electric Power also listed 25 of its 55 coal-fired plants as possible closures. It stated that it would cost $700 million to upgrade its Big Sandy 2 plant to meet EPA regulations.[14]

The movement to renewable power increased the concerns about the ability of the electric power system to meet peak demand, as in the case of the 2011 heat wave. Renewable power such as solar and wind was unpredictable and its supply was limited during heat waves. The power company PJM "factors in such variability, counting a 100 megawatt wind farm as being worth only 13 megawatts on a peak summer day, for example. While over the course of a year the wind machines can contribute mightily to kilowatt hours produced, they do much of their production on windy winter nights, according to experts at PJM and other grid organizations."[15]

GLOBAL CLIMATE CHANGE AND EMISSIONS TRADING SYSTEMS

In 1998 the Clinton administration signed the Kyoto Protocol on global climate change, which called for country-specific reductions in domestic carbon dioxide emissions averaging 5.2 percent from 1990 levels by 2012. The U.S. target was a 7 percent reduction from 1990 levels. The protocol had strong opposition in the Senate, which in 1997 adopted a resolution opposing the protocol unless developing countries, particularly China and India, made firm commitments to reduce their emissions. President Clinton chose not to submit the protocol to the Senate for ratification. The Clinton administration argued that the Kyoto agreement would have little effect on costs, but the Department of Energy predicted that gasoline prices would increase by nearly 40 percent and electricity prices between 20 and 86 percent in real terms by 2010. President Bush announced that the United States would not ratify the Kyoto Protocol, and instead a voluntary approach was adopted with a 2012 goal of an 18 percent reduction in emission per unit of GDP. Russia approved the protocol in late 2004, enabling it to go into effect. The Kyoto Protocol targets expire in 2012.

The Obama administration sought to establish a national cap-and-trade system, and soon after taking office introduced legislation. Many U.S. businesses participated with environmental

---

[12]EPA News Release—Air, July 7, 2011. Related issues are present in the chapter case, *Environmental Justice and Pollution Credits Trading Systems.*
[13]*New York Times*, August 12, 2011.
[14]Ibid.
[15]Ibid.

groups in the U.S. Climate Action Partnership (USCAP), which had actively sought cap-and-trade regulation of greenhouse gasses. As the climate bill began to work its way through Congress, lawmakers were forced to be specific about provisions of the bill. The House bill included emissions standards for off-road machines, which led Caterpillar, a maker of heavy equipment, to withdraw its support for the bill. The company also opposed a provision to levy tariffs on goods imported from countries that did not curb their emissions of greenhouse gasses. Some provisions were included to "buy" the support of Congress members. One would require automakers to produce vehicles that run on methanol, which obtained the support of Representative Eliot Engel (D-NY) who sought to reduce dependence on foreign oil.[16] General Motors complained about the provision as did the Ford Motor Company. Some oil companies that participated in USCAP withdrew their support of the bill because it allocated 30 percent of the initial emissions permits to electric power companies and only 2 percent to oil refiners. The provision was supported by Exelon, Duke Energy, and DuPont. Several USCAP members opposed the bill because it required contractors on some energy projects to pay locally "prevailing wages," a provision supported by labor unions and their allies in Congress. House Majority Leader Steny Hoyer (D-MA) explained, "when the federal government helps fund new energy projects, it is only right that we ensure that the workers building them get fair wages."[17]

The recession and the sputtering recovery focused attention on the cost of addressing climate change and the impact of higher costs on jobs. The climate bills stalled in Congress, and attention focused on the Obama administration's health care reform initiative, the regulation of financial markets, and its stimulus bill. The 2010 congressional elections sealed the near-term fate of climate change legislation, as Republicans gained control of the House.

Stopped in Congress, the Obama administration began an aggressive program of environmental regulation through the EPA. During the Bush administration the EPA did not act to regulate CO_2 emissions since it had not been declared a pollutant as required for regulation under the Clean Air Act. Twelve states and several cities sued the EPA to force it to regulate CO_2 emissions. In *Massachusetts v. Environmental Protection Agency* 549 U.S. 497 (2007) the Supreme Court ruled that under the Clean Air Act the EPA had to formally decide whether CO_2 was a pollutant. The Court did not draw a conclusion about whether CO_2 was a pollutant and instead deferred to the EPA. The matter was remanded to the EPA, and when the Obama administration took office, its EPA declared that CO_2 and other greenhouse gases were pollutants and subject to regulation. This gave the EPA broad authority to regulate sources such as vehicle emissions.

Kyoto Protocol

The accomplishments under the Kyoto Protocol are a subject of disagreement. Developed countries have reduced their domestic emissions, but research shows that this is due to increased imports displacing local production. Since imports from China and other developing countries have high CO_2 emissions in their manufacturing industries, emissions caused by developed countries have increased. A 2011 study published in the Proceedings of the National Academies of Sciences found that domestic CO_2 emissions in developed countries that had quantified reduction targets had stabilized from 1990 to 2008, whereas emissions from developing countries doubled.[18] The achievements for the developed countries resulted from replacing domestic emissions-generating activities such as manufacturing with imports. If CO_2 emissions are counted based on which country caused them (i.e., counting CO_2 emissions as the basis of consumption), the developed countries increased their emissions by 0.3 percent per year or 7.0 percent over the 1990–2008 period. From the perspective of the Kyoto objectives, the accomplishments have been disappointing at best.

China accounted for 55 percent of the growth in global CO_2 emissions from 1990 to 2008 and 75 percent of the growth in imported emissions in the developing countries. Without participation by China in quantifiable CO_2 limits beyond 2012, a renewal of meaningful Kyoto targets seemed unlikely.

---

[16]*Wall Street Journal*, July 13, 2009.
[17]Ibid.
[18]Peters, Minx, Weber, and Edenhofer (2011).

Emissions Trading in the European Union

The signatories to the Kyoto Protocol agreed to use an emissions permits trading system to reduce the cost of achieving their commitments. Countries earned credits, referred to as Kyoto mechanisms, toward their Kyoto goals by investing in emissions reduction programs in developing countries. The European Union took the lead on multination emission trading with the European Trading System (ETS) commencing in 2005. The ETS is a cap-and-trade system that covers 12,000 facilities in 15 EU member states. The EU goal was an 8 percent reduction by 2012 from a 1990 base.

To implement the European Trading Scheme (ETS) the EU issued the permits to the companies in their countries. Pressure from the companies that feared a loss of competitiveness and unions that feared the loss of jobs resulted in the issuance of more permits than the emissions companies had made in the previous year. The market value of the permits was around €20 per tonne of CO_2, but when the EU released a report that there was an extra supply of credits, the market collapsed with the price reaching €1. Not facing any cost of emissions, the firms increased their emissions. For example, Point Carbon, a carbon market research and consulting firm in Oslo, Norway, reported that the firms in the EU increased their carbon emissions by 1.1 percent in 2007. Emissions had also increased in the previous 2 years by about 1 percent.[19] The EU announced that it would reduce permits allocated for 2008–2012 by 6.3 percent below projected levels, and the price of a permit rose to the €15–25 range. For the first half of 2009 the price averaged €13. The ETS has expanded to cover 11,000 plants in 30 countries, and allowance for 2013 and beyond will be auctioned. The 2020 ETS target was a 21 percent reduction from 2005 levels.

The European Environment Agency (EEA) estimated that 2009 emissions would be 6.9 percent below 2008 levels, but much of the decrease was due to the severe recession in many of the countries and in their export markets. The EU also established a 2020 target for domestic greenhouse gases emissions for the 27 member states of a 20 percent reduction from 1990 levels. The EEA estimated that 2009 emissions would be 17.3 percent lower than 1990 levels, and the ETS was a principal contributor to the accomplishments.[20] The ETS has been a major success and played a major role in accomplishing the EU's greenhouse gases goals. The EU extended its cap-and-trade system to cover airlines serving the EU market. A number of the EU member states had used Kyoto mechanisms to meet their targets.

Kyoto mechanisms referred to credits bought by countries to help finance projects in developing countries that would reduce greenhouse gases. Qualifying projects had to be such that they would not have been undertaken absent the funds provided by the sale of the credits. Projects were qualified by the United Nations under its Clean Development Mechanism (CDM) program, and approval was given by the CDM board. In its first year the board approved almost all the proposed projects, but concerns began to mount that some of the projects would have been funded independently of the credits. In addition some of the projects were found not to have generated the reductions projected. The board then applied additional scrutiny to the proposed projects and began to reject a higher percentage.

The Regional Greenhouse Gas Initiative (RGGI)

RGGI was formed in 2005 by 10 northeastern U.S. states to operate a cap-and-trade system for reducing greenhouse gases emissions. RGGI began operating in 2008, and auctioned 86 percent of the allowances generating $790 million through 2010. Most of the funds generated in the auctions were used by the states to fund energy efficiency programs and renewable power, as well as providing subsidies for low-income ratepayers. RGGI was supported by companies that benefited from the funds generated by the auctions, but other companies argued that it drove up costs and drove jobs away.

The price of allowances had been set very low, and the recession reduced emissions below the RGGI cap, resulting in a price of allowances at the minimum allowed of $1.89 a ton of emissions. In addition the price of natural gas fell, and power companies burned gas instead of oil or coal, reducing emissions. RGGI had accomplished little in the way of emissions reductions.

---

[19]The U.S. Energy Information Administration reported that carbon emissions in the United States increased by 0.6 percent in 2005, decreased by 1.3 percent in 2006, and increased by 1.6 percent in 2007.

[20]European Environment Agency, "Tracking progress towards Kyoto and 2020 targets," November 7, 2010.

Environmentalists argued that the cap should be reduced so that it would have bite, and RGGI officials were considering measures to strengthen the program. Kenneth Kimmell, commissioner of the Massachusetts environmental protection agency, said, "Everyone who looks at RGGI understands we need to address the fact that the cap currently greatly exceeds emissions. We've got to tread carefully here, in terms of making sure whatever we adopt does have a short-term impact on the economic recovery."[21]

The failure of RGGI to affect environmental goals led states to consider withdrawing from the initiative. The governor of New Jersey announced that the state would withdraw at the end of 2011 and vetoed a bill passed by the state legislature that would have continued participation. Governor Chris Christie stated, "RGGI has not changed behavior and it does not reduce emissions …. RGGI does nothing more than tax electricity, tax our citizens, tax our businesses, with no discernible or measurable impact on our environment. Because states such as Pennsylvania are not RGGI members it's just possible by making the cap too stringent, clean New Jersey plants would be forced to close only to be replaced by power from dirty Pennsylvania coal plants. It doesn't make any sense environmentally or economically."[22] The New Hampshire state legislature passed a bill to withdraw from RGGI, but the governor vetoed it. Governor John Lynch referred to the $16 million the state had received from the auctions through 2010 in stating, "These are funds that have been invested directly in helping New Hampshire families, businesses and local governments become more energy efficient, reduce costs and create jobs."[23] The future of RGGI was uncertain.

Emissions Trading Within BP plc (British Petroleum)

Emissions trading can occur not only among firms and nations but also within firms. To address the global climate change issue, in 1998 BP plc committed by 2010 to reduce its emissions of greenhouse gases (GHGs) by 10 percent from 1990 levels. BP's greenhouse gases policy was guided by a target for the earth of 500 to 550 parts per million (ppm) of GHGs compared to the present level of 370 ppm and 280 ppm before the industrial revolution.

To achieve its goal, BP worked with Environmental Defense to develop an internal GHGs trading system for the company. Each BP business unit was given an annual cap that it had to meet either through emissions reduction projects or by purchasing allowances (permits) on the internal company market. No additional allowances were given for growth, although the baseline was adjusted in the case of an acquisition. A central broker within the company administered the market. In the first year of the market 2.7 million tons of allowances were traded, and an average price was $7.60 per ton. Trading operated as it does in the basic theory of tradable permits systems. A chemicals unit that installed a new furnace that improved combustion freed allowances that it could sell to a business unit whose cost of CO_2 reduction was greater than the price of an allowance.

BP's internal trading system was instrumental in enabling the company to achieve its 2010 goal by 2001. Having achieved its goal, BP ended its emissions trading system and set a new goal of no increase in GHG emissions through 2012. BP also participated in the UK emissions trading scheme and the sulfur dioxide and nitrogen oxides trading systems in the United States.

GOVERNMENT POLICY

The EPA

The EPA, an independent agency located in the executive branch, is headed by an administrator appointed by the president and confirmed by the Senate.[24] The EPA was created by an executive order of President Nixon in 1970 to bring together in a single agency a number of environmental regulation programs then housed in different federal agencies. Congress quickly passed several measures expanding the new agency's responsibilities. The EPA is now responsible

---

[21]*Financial Times*, August 21, 2011.

[22]www.environemtnalleader.com, May 27, 2011.

[23]*Concord Monitor*, July 7, 2011.

[24]See *Congressional Quarterly* (1994) for a description of the EPA and its powers.

FIGURE 12-1 Principal Environmental Acts

Federal Insecticide, Fungicide and Rodenticide Act of 1947 (amended in 1972, 1988)
Clean Air Act of 1963 (amended in 1970, 1977, 1990)
Solid Waste Disposal Act of 1965
Air Quality Act of 1967
National Environmental Policy Act of 1969
Water Quality Improvement Act of 1970
Federal Environmental Pesticide Control Act of 1972
Federal Water Pollution Control Act (Clean Water Act) of 1972 (amended in 1987)
Marine Protection, Research and Sanctuaries Act of 1972
Noise Control Act of 1972
Endangered Species Act of 1973
Safe Drinking Water Act of 1974 (amended in 1997)
Toxic Substances Control Act of 1976 (amended in 1988)
Resource Conservation and Recovery Act of 1976
Clean Water Act of 1977
Comprehensive Environmental Response, Compensation, and Liability Act of 1980 (amended in 1986)
  [Superfund]
Emergency Planning and Community Right-to-Know Act (1986)
Water Quality Act of 1987
Ocean Pollution Dumping Act of 1990
Pollution Prevention Act of 1990
Oil Pollution Act of 1990
Reclamation Projects Act of 1992
Food Quality Protection Act of 1996

for administering the major acts listed in Figure 12-1. As was characteristic of the new social regulation, the acts were written in the fear that they would not be enforced because the agencies would be captured by industry. The acts thus are often highly detailed and frequently include timetables intended to force the agency to act.[25] Many of these measures established specific goals for environmental protection without reference to costs. The goals in some cases were unrealistic and served more as symbols than as commitments.[26] The Federal Water Pollution Control Act of 1972, for example, established the goal of eliminating all discharges of pollutants into navigable waters by 1985.

Federal environmental regulation is a major undertaking. The EPA had a budget of $8.7 billion in 2011 and over 17,000 employees. The EPA has responsibility for air and water quality, drinking water safety, waste treatment and disposal, toxic substances, and pesticides. The Department of the Interior has responsibilities for some conservation programs, and the Department of Agriculture has responsibilities for some pesticide control programs.

A number of the statutes assign to the states the responsibility for formulating implementation plans for attaining federal environmental standards. Under the Clean Air Act, states are responsible for developing State Implementation Plans to meet air quality standards. This gives the states a considerable role in environmental protection. States have their own environmental laws and regulatory agencies as well, and some enforcement is delegated to those agencies.

Enforcement

The EPA enforcement process requires the filing of a notice of a complaint and a hearing before an administrative law judge (ALJ). The ALJ's decision can be appealed to the agency's administrator and to the courts. Under some statutes the EPA has the authority to forward cases to the Department of Justice, which can file a civil proceeding in federal district court. Typically, however, the EPA seeks voluntary compliance. Some environmental laws also allow lawsuits by private citizens against polluters who violate regulations.

---

[25]Vogel (1986) provides a comparison of U.S. and UK environmental policy.
[26]See Kneese and Schultze (1975) for an early critique of environmental legislation.

The federal government can seek both civil and criminal convictions of polluters, both of firms and individual managers. In 2010 the EPA referred for prosecution 346 criminal cases and obtained conviction of 198 criminals. The EPA imposed fines of $151 million. In the wake of the Alaskan oil spill by the *Exxon Valdez,* felony and misdemeanor criminal charges were brought against Exxon and the captain of the tanker. The captain was acquitted of three of the four charges, including the felony charges, and convicted on one charge of misdemeanor negligence. In 1991 Exxon agreed to a settlement with the federal and Alaska governments in which it pleaded guilty to three misdemeanor charges and agreed to pay $1.15 billion in civil and criminal fines and restitution, of which $287 million was for actual damages. In addition, Exxon spent over $2 billion on the cleanup. In 1994 a federal court jury found that Exxon had acted in a negligent and reckless manner and ordered it to pay $5 billion in punitive damages to Alaskans. After a series of appeals, punitive damages were reduced to $507 million, which equaled the compensatory damages. (See Chapter 14 for a discussion of compensatory and punitive damages.)

Standards Setting and Engineering Controls

EPA regulation has largely been command and control, in which uniform rules or standards are ordered and then enforced. This type of regulation is often a blunt instrument, imposing uniform rules in dissimilar circumstances. Under this approach the EPA, for example, sets emissions limits for each pollution source, where a source may be as specific as an individual piece of equipment in a chemical plant. Uniform stationary-source pollution standards that ignore differences in abatement costs and achievable benefits across emissions sources have created both economic inefficiency and administrative nightmares. This experience contributed to the decision to use a cap-and-trade system for the reduction of sulfur dioxide and nitrogen oxides emissions.

The EPA sets emissions standards and air quality standards. In 2008 the agency set stringent standards for soot emissions by trains and ship diesel emissions. The agency also tightened the standard for ozone from 84 parts per billion to 75 parts per billion. The soot regulations drew praise and the ozone regulations drew criticism from environmental groups.

In addition to establishing overall standards, such as for ambient air quality, the EPA specifies engineering controls to reduce emissions. The engineering controls, in order of increasing stringency, are the "best practicable technology," "best conventional technology," "best available technology," and "maximum achievable control technology." The use of engineering controls has been criticized on efficiency grounds, but its advocates believe it is necessary to force polluters to comply.

In a standard setting case involving water intake systems for power plants, the EPA decided to use cost–benefit analysis to determine the best-available technology. The activist group Riverkeeper sued arguing that the EPA was not allowed to use cost–benefit analysis. The Court of Appeal held for Riverkeeper, and for the majority judge Sonia Sotomayor wrote, "The Agency is therefore precluded from undertaking such cost-benefit analysis because the [best technology available] standard represents Congress' conclusion that the costs imposed on industry in adopting the best cooling water intake structure technology available (i.e., the best performing technology that can be reasonably borne by the industry) are worth the benefits in reducing adverse environmental impacts." The decision was appealed to the Supreme Court which overturned the Court of Appeals decision stating that the Clean Water Act was ambiguous and that using cost–benefit analysis to determine the best available technology was reasonable.

The command-and-control approach is a blunt instrument and often imposes high administrative costs on firms and limits their flexibility in responding quickly to market changes and product developments. For example, an Intel semiconductor plant may have 35–40 chemical process changes a year, and each change can require EPA approval. For a company like Intel that introduces a new generation of microprocessors every year or two, the delay caused by the required process approvals can be more costly than the administrative and compliance costs. To deal with such problems Intel and the EPA reached an agreement on simplifying the permit and compliance process in the context of the EPA's Project XL. The example describes the project.

EXAMPLE   Intel and Project XL

The objective of the EPA's Project XL was to "provide a forum for companies to test new technologies and alternative regulatory approaches that eventually might be used by more companies to boost efficiency and achieve better environmental protection." In 1996 Intel and the EPA reached an agreement on the first XL project at its Chandler, Arizona, semiconductor plant.[1] The plant was subject to regulations under four principal statutes administered by five different EPA offices:

- Clean Air Act administered by the Office of Air Quality Planning and Standards
- Clean Water Act administered by the Office of Wastewater Management and the Office of Wetlands, Oceans, and Watersheds
- Resource Conservation and Recovery Act administered by the Office of Solid Waste
- Pollution Prevention Act administered by the Office of Prevention, Pesticides, and Toxic Substances

In addition, the Intel plant was subject to regulation by the Arizona Department of Environmental Quality, the Maricopa County Bureau of Air Pollution Control, and the city of Chandler.

The Intel project had two principal features: (1) elimination of case-by-case process change reviews by the EPA, provided that Intel emissions remained below a capped amount, and (2) preapproval of major plant expansions, provided that emissions remain below a cap for the entire site. Environmental groups initially criticized the agreement. The National Resources Defense Council said, "We are disappointed with the environmental performance required by this agreement."[2] Local environmental and labor groups also criticized the agreement, charging that it "allows Intel to expose its employees and the communities of Chandler and Phoenix to increased toxic chemical hazards."[3] Intel has remained well below the emissions caps.

According to the EPA, "Intel also has avoided millions of dollars in production delays by eliminating 30 to 50 new source permit reviews a year. The company has found the emissions caps so successful that it will invest $2 billion to build a new wafer fabrication facility (Fab 22) at the site. Under the existing cap, Intel can proceed with expansion without first going through regulatory review." The Project XL was one of the factors that led Intel to build its Fab 22 at the Chandler site.

The project also included an informational component. The project allowed Intel to use a consolidated reporting system for all the regulatory statutes, with the exception of the Toxic Release Inventory. Intel invited local stakeholders to participate in designing environmental reports, and those reports were made available on Intel's Web site. Intel also participated in an emergency preparedness program with the city of Chandler.

[1]EPA, "Project XL Progress Report: Intel Corporation," 100-R-00-031, January 2001.

[2]*New York Times*, November 20, 1996.
[3]Ibid.

Incentive Approaches

In addition to imposing engineering controls and establishing standards, the EPA has increasingly used incentive approaches.[27] One approach used in local air quality regulation under the Clean Air Act is the "bubble" program. Under the command-and-control approach, engineering controls are specified for each individual processing unit in an oil refinery, chemical plant, or steel mill. Under the bubble policy, the EPA sets permitted emissions levels for the entire plant—imagine a bubble around the plant—and allows the producer to achieve those levels in the most efficient manner. The plant, for example, may achieve the required reduction on a single processing unit or through controls on several units.

Another program to improve the efficiency of air quality regulation in nonattainment areas—those that do not meet federal air quality standards—uses *credits* and *offsets*. For example, under the Clean Air Act Amendments of 1990, the EPA allocates credits to states for implementing enhanced auto emissions testing and maintenance programs. Under the offset program, to construct a new plant in a nonattainment area a firm must reduce pollutants elsewhere in the area by the amount to be released by the new plant. The firm can reduce emissions at another of its facilities or may purchase credits from another firm. In 1995 the California Institute of Technology and the Pacific Stock Exchange created an electronic market for trading credits in four Southern California counties. The Regional Clean Air Incentives

[27]Ellerman, Joskow, and Harrison (2003) provide an introduction to incentive approaches in the United States. Fiorino (2006) discusses and evaluates environmental program innovations at the EPA.

Market (RECLAIM) hosts trades of credits in sulfur dioxide and nitrogen oxides. Trading has been active, and a state review concluded that the program was efficient and effective.[28]

The EPA does not have the authority to tax pollution, but Congress has taken an interest in pollution taxes. In 1989 a federal law imposed a tax on chlorofluorocarbons (CFCs) as a means of reducing the use of the ozone-depleting chemicals while production was being phased out. To address the global climate change issue, some firms, members of Congress, and environmentalists have urged the use of a broadscale carbon tax on fuels. In 1993 the Clinton administration attempted to have a closely related Btu tax enacted by Congress, but the political pressure from those who would bear the distributive consequences of the tax caused the plan to fail. The Chapter 15 case *The European Union Carbon Tax* concerns a similar measure.

Superfund

The EPA administers the Superfund for the cleanup of existing toxic waste disposal sites. Estimates placed the number of sites requiring Superfund cleanups as high as 20,000, and cost estimates were as high as $600 billion. Under the Superfund program the EPA attempts to identify the source of the dumping and force it to clean the site. If the EPA does the cleanup, it can go to court to recover the costs. In 2010 the EPA secured nearly $1.6 billion from private parties. As of 2010 the EPA had completed work on 1,098 of the over 1,627 sites on the National Priorities List and another 475 were "sitewide ready for anticipated use." The Superfund program has been criticized both for moving too slowly and for spending funds where there was little hope of a successful cleanup. In recent years the pace of cleanup of toxic waste sites has increased. Of the $30 billion spent by business and government on the Superfund program, however, a third is estimated to have gone to lawyers in litigation over who is liable for the cleanup costs. Another criticism of the program is that it requires the same cleanup level of all sites, regardless of their future use or the costs of cleanup.

In addition to the litigation costs the Superfund has been criticized for its "retrospective liability" feature that requires companies to pay for the cleanup of wastes that had been disposed of legally. The Clinton administration responded to this criticism by proposing to exempt small firms. The criticisms and disagreements over the Superfund caused its congressional reauthorization to be mired in politics for most of the 1990s, and the taxes imposed on firms to fund the program expired in 1995. The Superfund is now financed by the federal budget and by fees imposed on identified polluters. Approximately 70 percent of the cleanup costs are paid by the party held responsible for the pollution with the rest paid by the government.

State Policy Initiatives

Electric utilities have incentives to build new capacity to meet projected demand, and to reduce the incentives to build new capacity, regulators in California have begun a program in which utilities are rewarded for their energy savings. The California Public Utilities Commission (CPUC) establishes energy-savings goals for each utility, and for any savings beyond the target, it receives 12 percent, which is higher that the rate of return allowed by the CPUC on new investments. If the savings are within 85–100 percent of the target, the utility receives 9 percent; within 65–85 percent there is no return; and below 65 percent a penalty is imposed. The state estimates that the total bonuses and penalties could be in the $324 million to $450 million a year, and the CPUC has estimated spending $2 billion over 3 years on conservation programs. One program is to subsidize compact fluorescent light bulbs. Consumers pay for these programs in their utility bills, including an approximate $8 per pack of two light bulbs. California regulators expect that the program will eliminate half the new capacity that otherwise would be built, although lighting savings are primarily at night and capacity is determined by daytime peak demand.

States can also act to countermand federal regulations. The Energy Independence and Security Act of 2007 effectively banned 40–100 watt incandescent lamps by requiring that they become 25–30 percent more efficient. The House majority sought to rescind the law arguing that the government was micromanaging people's lives. Texas went further and passed a law declaring that light bulbs manufactured and sold in Texas do not involve interstate commerce and hence are not subject to federal regulation. The matter would ultimately be settled by the courts.

---

[28]Each trade is listed at www.aqmd.gas/reclaim/reclaim/html.

THE POLITICAL ECONOMY OF ENVIRONMENTAL PROTECTION

The Nature of Environmental Politics

Environmental issues are of concern to everyone, and hence to interest groups and the news media, and they often advance rapidly in their life cycles. Since most of the costs of environmental protection are borne by private parties, government budget considerations have imposed few limits on the advance of environmental issues.[29] The costs of environmental protection are borne by firms, their employees, and consumers, and those costs generate opposition to more stringent regulation. Similarly, the benefits of environmental protection are both widespread and concentrated on those with strong concerns about particular issues such as health impairment from pollution, air quality at the Grand Canyon, wetlands, logging in national forests, or cattle grazing on Bureau of Land Management lands. Environmental issues thus are the subject of intense public politics.[30] Environmental issues are also the subject of private politics led by environmental and activist groups, as considered in Chapter 4 and in the Chapter 4 case *Anatomy of a Corporate Campaign: Rainforest Action Network and Citigroup (A)(B)*.

Environmental issues are complex, in part because of scientific uncertainty about the consequences of pollution, incomplete information about the costs and benefits of environmental protection, and disagreements about alternative approaches, such as incentive-based systems versus command-and-control, to protection. Environmental issues are also complex because of differing perspectives about the protection of entitlements. From the social efficiency perspective, the entitlement to be free from the hazards of pollution should be protected by a liability rule because the transactions costs associated with a property rule would be prohibitive. Yet many individuals treat the environment and their health as if they were protected by a property rule. They seek to prohibit activities that may pose a risk to their health or to the environment. The Court of Appeals decision ending the interstate cap-and-trade systems for SO_2, nitrogen oxides, and mercury is an example. In one instance, Congress responded to these sentiments by enacting the Delaney amendment, which prohibited the use of any food additive found to be a carcinogen in laboratory animals. Environmental politics—including the NIMBY movement—thus is motivated both by distributive consequences and normative perspectives about the protection of the environment and health.

Judicial Politics

The politics of environmental protection often moves into judicial arenas. The National Resources Defense Council (NRDC) sued the EPA, seeking enforcement of the Delaney amendment for pesticides used in the production of foods. As a practical means of dealing with potential risks, the EPA had followed a practice of allowing pesticide use if the risk to human health was "negligible." The courts held for the NRDC, requiring the EPA to enforce the Delaney amendment. This decision required the banning of dozens of widely used pesticides. The court decision added to the pressure for congressional action to repeal the Delaney amendment, which occurred in 1996.

Environmental groups have succeeded in inserting citizen provisions in environmental statutes. Under the citizen provision of the Clean Water Act the environmental group Water Keeper Alliance sued Smithfield Foods, the nation's largest hog producer, alleging that runoff from its hog farm in North Carolina polluted the state's rivers. Such lawsuits are not uncommon, but this one was potentially important because it was financed by the trial lawyers who had successfully filed class action lawsuits against the tobacco companies. Such litigation can also be backed by interests seeking to preserve their rents. Some populist farm groups backed the lawsuit because the efficiency of Southfield's operations threatened family-owned hog farms.

Advocacy Science

Much remains unknown about environmental hazards and their control, and this scientific uncertainty is a source of contention in environmental politics. For example, the EPA estimated that 8 million homes were contaminated by dangerous levels of radon, a naturally occurring

---

[29]Some regulation does have budget effects. For example, municipalities are one of the largest water polluters, and the federal government provides subsidies to municipalities for the construction of waste treatment plants.

[30]See Greve and Smith (1992), Rosenbaum (2007), and Vaughn (2007) for treatments of environmental politics.

radioactive gas formed as radium decays in the ground. The EPA projected that the exposure to radon over a lifetime could cause 20,000 lung cancer deaths a year. The EPA issued an Indoor Radon Health Advisory that said, "Radon causes thousands of deaths each year." Other scientists placed the number of households with radon concentrations at the EPA's action level as low as 100,000. In one study, the lung cancer rate of people exposed to radon was found to be no different from that of people who were not exposed.[31] The EPA backtracked and issued voluntary guidelines for new homes and an information pamphlet for homeowners.

The scientific uncertainty about the harm to the environment caused by pollution and about the risks to people's health, as in the case of radon, provides an opportunity to use advocacy science—proclaiming dangers to health and the environment—as a component of a private politics strategy. The Alar episode considered in Chapter 3 provides an example of the effectiveness of such a strategy. Because the media sees health and environmental risks as having societal significance and considerable audience interest, environmental issues quickly find their way to the public's attention and are frequently contested in full view of the public. These issues often arise from data provided in epidemiological studies. Feinstein (1988) characterized the pattern: "The episodes have now developed a familiar pattern. A report appears in a prominent medical journal; the conclusions receive wide publicity by newspapers, television, and other media; and another common entity of daily life becomes indicted as a menace to health— possibly causing strokes, heart attacks, birth defects, cancer .... The reported evidence is almost always a statistical analysis of epidemiological data, and the scientific tactics that produced the evidence are almost always difficult to understand and evaluate." He criticized the studies because "the research methods seldom have the precautions, calibrations, and relative simplicity that are taken for granted in other branches of science."

Another source of contention in environmental politics results from laboratory studies. Studies of health risks are often conducted on laboratory animals, which are exposed to pollutants at concentrations higher than human beings would ever encounter.[32] The laboratory results then must be extrapolated to the size, weight, and physiology of people. Whether such results bear a reasonable relationship to the health risks to human beings can be a matter of disagreement.

Distributive Politics

In addition to concerns about hazards, environmental politics is motivated by the distributive consequences of environmental policy, the costs of environmental protection, and the benefits from the reduction in pollution and hazards. Much of the battle over the Clean Air Act Amendments requiring reduction of sulfur dioxide emissions from power plants was between "clean" and "dirty" states. The clean states wanted credit for their accomplishments and wanted to avoid having to pay the dirty states' cleanup costs. The dirty states were primarily in the Midwest, and many of them also mined high-sulfur coal. Their representatives in Congress sought both to hold down electricity prices and preserve jobs for coal miners. The dirty states also sought cost sharing through federal tax subsidies for scrubbers and compensation for jobs lost.

At the federal level, attention had focused primarily on major sources of pollution, often exempting small business. The 1990 amendments to the Clean Air Act, however, addressed emissions not only by automobiles and electric power plants but also by dry cleaners, furniture manufacturers, and printers, which were required to install costly pollution-control systems. Joe Gerard, vice president of the American Furniture Manufacturers, stated, "What's unnerving for our industry is that the law would affect the application of [wood] finishing materials, and that's what gives us our competitive edge over imports." Linda Greed of the NRDC responded: "Everything that comes down the pike, we're told it'll put them out of business .... When they come up with the data to show it costs too much, they usually do get some relief. But when it's just arm waving, they don't. We hear it too often to be credible."[33]

---

[31]*New York Times*, January 8, 1991.

[32]This is often because of the short life span of some laboratory animals and the desire to reduce the cost of experiments and speed completion of the research.

[33]*Wall Street Journal*, November 13, 1990.

Private and Public Politics

There are many environmental NGOs active in public politics at the federal, state, and local levels. Environmental groups testify regularly in legislative and regulatory hearings, and some demonstrate to attract media coverage to their side of the issue. Environmental groups are also active in private politics, as considered in Chapter 4 and in the Chapter 4 cases *Shell, Greenpeace, and Brent Spar* and *Anatomy of a Corporate Campaign: Rainforest Action Network and Citigroup (A)(B)*. Some environmental groups have been active participants in the antiglobalization protests against the World Trade Organization and other international economic organizations such as the World Bank and the International Monetary Fund. Environmental groups also monitor the activities of government officials. The League of Conservation Voters annually rates members of Congress based on their votes on a set of environmental bills. The Sierra Club and some other environmental groups endorse candidates in federal and state elections. The example on the Equator Principles illustrates the role of environmental groups and private politics at the global level.

EXAMPLE   The Equator Principles

Project finance provides the funding for dams, pipelines, telecommunications systems, transportation systems, mines, power plants, and other infrastructure projects. The financing was typically secured by the anticipated revenue from the project. Many of these projects were in developing countries, and environmentalists complained that some of the projects caused environmental damage and disrupted the lives of indigenous peoples. For example, the Three Gorges dam in China displaced many thousands of people and resulted in considerable environmental damage. The Export-Import Bank (Eximbank) of the United States refused to provide financing for the dam because of concerns about potential environmental damage. Within the Organization for Economic Cooperation and Development (OECD), the Eximbank began to promote better environmental standards, but as chairman James Harmon observed, "To my amazement, opposition to our proposal was not only intense, but came from virtually every OECD member."[1]

The campaign for higher standards was subsequently led by NGOs. Environmental groups advocated stronger guidelines for projects and targeted individual lenders as well as the construction companies. WestLB of Germany had been targeted because of a pipeline project in Ecuador. The Rainforest Action Network (RAN) targeted Citigroup because of its major role in project financing. RAN blamed Citigroup for contributing to "rainforest destruction, climate change and the disruption of the lives of indigenous peoples." RAN's tactics included hanging a large banner across Citigroup's headquarters "accusing it of 'banking on' global warming and deforestation." RAN also urged college students not to accept Citigroup credit cards and for those with cards to cut them and mail the pieces to the bank. In addition to targeting by individual environmental activist groups, a group of 100 advocacy groups signed the Collevecchio Declaration calling for financial institutions to adopt more responsible lending practices.[2]

Under pressure from the NGOs, four banks, ABN Amro, Barclays, Citigroup, and WestLB, began discussions under the auspices of the International Finance Corporation (IFC), the private-sector financing unit of the World Bank. The IFC hosted negotiations involving the four banks and environmental groups, and the result was the Equator Principles, a set of voluntary principles for project financing. In addition to the initial four banks, Credit Lyonnais, Credit Suisse, HVB Group, Rabobank, Royal Bank of Scotland, and Westpac joined in the initial signing of the Principles. By 2011, 72 banks in 27 countries had subscribed to the principles. In 2007, 71 percent of the $74.6 billion of project finance debt in emerging market economics was subject to the Equator Principles.

The Equator Principles applied to all projects of $10 million or more and categorized projects as A, B, or C (high, medium, and low) for their environmental or social impact. For A and B projects an environmental assessment was required, and the loan contracts from subscribing banks included a covenant stipulating that the borrower must comply with the environmental assessment. If a borrower did not fulfill its commitments, the bank could declare the loan in default. The principles are available at www.equator-principles.com.

Citigroup proclaimed, "We are extremely proud to be part of this voluntary, private-sector initiative and we are confident that we will see more and more banks active in project finance adopt these principles in the coming months." Peter Woicke of the IFC said, "The adoption of these principles by the private sector marks a profound victory for sustainable development ... some of the banks came under pressure from NGOs. They also realized without the best graduates they cannot compete, and the best people want to work for companies which pay attention to environmental and social issues."[3]

Fred Krupp of Environmental Defense praised the actions of the banks: "This is a major step forward in trying to achieve environmental standards for the global economy."[4] He added, "It is remarkable to have a private bank committing

---

[1]*Financial Times*, April 9, 2003.
[2]*Wall Street Journal*, June 4, 2003.

[3]*Financial Times*, June 4, 2003.
[4]*Financial Times*, April 7, 2003.

to this even ahead of supposedly green governmental institutions like the European public export credit agencies."[5]

Those sentiments were not uniformly shared within the environmental activist community. Ilyse Hogue of RAN said, "We're glad to see banks responding to pressure that's been brought on them. But I think that you'll find broad consensus around the NGO (nongovernmental organization) community that the Equator Principles don't go far enough. The loopholes are wide enough for bulldozers to move through."[6] Michelle Chan-Fishel of Friends of the Earth

commented, "We are pleased that banks are responding to public pressure and are trying to address the environmental and social impact of their transactions. But one of the key weaknesses of most corporate-led voluntary initiatives is the lack of accountability in implementation mechanisms. This may be the fatal flaw of the Equator Principles."[7] The participating banks met with the NGOs, including Environmental Defense, Friends of the Earth, and RAN, to discuss progress in implementation of the Equator Principles. The environmental groups were generally satisfied with Citigroup's implementation.

[5]*Financial Times*, April 9, 2003.
[6]*Wall Street Journal*, June 4, 2003.

[7]*Financial Times*, June 4, 2003.

Company policies can also generate public and private politics. Tesco, the largest retailer in the United Kingdom, announced a carbon label program to inform customers of the carbon emissions associated with the products they buy. The program covered all products it sold ranging from food to appliances. The program required suppliers to determine the carbon associated with their products, which was a complicated matter since a product could be produced in several plants and countries. In the first phase of implementing its carbon label program, Tesco placed an airline sticker on products shipped by airfreight. The stickers generated protests from companies and governments of developing countries that complained that their fresh food products were being discriminated against. Abraham Barns, an agricultural attaché in Kenya's embassy in the UK, said, "The moment consumers looked at this sticker, they would stigmatize those products."[34]

The Bush administration applied a more consistent and refined cost–benefit analysis on new regulations issued by agencies including the EPA. One controversial aspect of the cost–benefit analysis was the use of life-expectancy analysis, which estimates benefits based not on the number of deaths prevented by a regulation but the number of years that life expectancy would be increased. This meant that the benefits from preventing a death of an elderly person were lower than from preventing a death of a younger person. This approach was used in medical research and had been used for years by the Food and Drug Administration. When environmentalists learned in a footnote in a report that the EPA used it as a secondary method in estimating benefits, they labeled it a "senior citizen death discount" and ran an advertisement showing an elderly person with a price tag hanging from her glasses. On the tag was written "37% off." Fearing that the method would lead to less stringent regulation, environmentalists and health care advocates created a firestorm of criticism that led the EPA to end use of the method. (The life-expectancy approach is considered in more detail in Chapter 21.)

NIMBY and Private Politics

William Ruckelshaus, former EPA administrator and then CEO of Browning-Ferris industries, a worldwide waste disposal company, wrote of the coming solid waste disposal crisis, "More than a third of the nation's landfills will be full within the next decade. New York will exhaust its capacity in 9 years, Los Angeles in 6, and Philadelphia is out of capacity now and must engage in continuous negotiations to dispose of its 800,000 tons per year. Why? Nobody wants garbage put down anywhere near where he lives, the 'not-in-my-backyard' syndrome—the dreaded NIMBY."[35] The NIMBY movement focuses on local environmental concerns, particularly as they involve possible risks to person or property. The movement is often directed toward refuse disposal sites, toxic waste sites, chemical and oil plants, and other facilities that may emit toxins. Hamilton (1993) studied the location decisions and expansion plans of hazardous waste disposal and incineration facilities and found that companies take into account the anticipated opposition by local groups in making their site decisions for capacity expansion.

---

[34]*BusinessWeek*, March 17, 2008.
[35]*Wall Street Journal*, September 5, 1989.

The NIMBY movement has been energized by information provided by the federal government's Toxics Release Inventory (TRI), which provides detailed information on the emissions by 22,000 plants of over 300 chemicals believed to have health consequences.[36] The TRI is a result of the "right-to-know" amendment to a 1985 Superfund reauthorization bill. The amendment was passed by the House on a 212 to 211 vote.[37] The TRI has become the focus of considerable nonmarket activity with some industries seeking to have chemicals they emit dropped from the TRI and industries such as agriculture, forestry, and mining working to preserve their exemptions. Environmentalists have sought to eliminate exemptions and expand the list of chemicals. The release of the TRI has become a strategic event for environmentalists. The NRDC uses the data in the TRI to release the names of the largest emitters of those chemicals listed by the EPA as "probable human carcinogens."

In addition to allowing national organizations to take action, the TRI facilitates private politics in the form of local NIMBY action. The data in the TRI are provided for each plant, so emissions can be identified for individual communities. This allows local citizens to take nonmarket action against the plants. As an example, in 1989 the NRDC released an analysis of the TRI data listing Shendahl of Northfield, Minnesota, as the 45th largest emitter of the 11 chemicals analyzed by the NRDC. Shendahl had been legally emitting 400 tons a year of methylene chloride, a chemical whose emission was unregulated at both the federal and state level. The firm had no visible chemical emissions and had routinely been issued a permit for the discharges.[38]

When residents of Northfield learned of the emissions, their reaction was immediate. Within a week of the revelation, Shendahl announced that it would reduce emissions by 90 percent by 1993 and eliminate them entirely by 2000, switching to flammable solvents. Residents and activists formed Clean Air Northfield to continue the pressure. The activists charged that the company had withheld information on its emissions from the public, knowing that the EPA had listed methylene chloride as a probable carcinogen. One activist group sought closure of the plant, but employees, arguing that the plant was the largest employer in town, sought an orderly reduction in emissions to save their jobs. The Amalgamated Clothing and Textile Workers Union, which represented the employees, was concerned that reducing emissions by the planned 90 percent might cause a hazardous accumulation of methylene chloride inside the plant, threatening employees. The union sought and won contract rights to monitor the emissions reduction program. The activists and the union also took action at the state level, persuading the state to include in Shendahl's emissions permit a required 93 percent reduction by 1995. Clean Air Northfield then lobbied the state government for the elimination of all methylene chloride emissions.

Empirical studies by Hamilton (1995) and Konar and Cohen (1997) found that the market value of companies included in the TRI fell upon release of the TRI, and those with the greatest decreases subsequently had the largest reduction in their toxic releases. Maxwell, Lyon, and Hackett (2000) studied voluntary reductions in TRI releases and concluded that reductions were larger the higher the membership in the Sierra Club and the NRDC in the locales where the reductions were made. Since the toxic chemicals released were within the levels permitted by environmental regulations, the identified effects were likely due to local environmental pressures and private politics.

MANAGEMENT OF ENVIRONMENTAL PROTECTION ISSUES

The management of environmental and sustainability issues involves both external and internal activities. Externally, firms and their managers must address a set of issues that arise in their market and nonmarket environments. These issues may be addressed in government institutional arenas such as Congress, state legislatures, courts, and regulatory agencies; or outside those institutions, as with NIMBY activities and direct interactions with environmentalists and local communities.

Environmental issues have become so important, pervasive, and costly that high-level attention must be given to them. Some firms have established committees of their boards of directors to assume oversight responsibility for sustainability and environmental issues. Some

---

[36]Firms are required to notify the federal, state, and local governments of any emission of the chemicals.
[37]See Hamilton (1997) for a study of the voting on the amendment.
[38]This account is based on an article in the *New York Times*, January 2, 1991.

CEOs have personally declared a commitment to environmental protection. When DuPont Chairman Edgar S. Woolard Jr. assumed the role of the company's chief environmentalist, the level of awareness rose. DuPont's vice president for safety, health, and environmental affairs commented on the difference: "I used to have to do a real selling job to line up people .... Then suddenly it wasn't just me trying to get the organization to do things, it was Ed. Now they call all the time."[39] Some firms established corporate environmental groups and audit units. IBM created the position of vice president for environmental health and safety in its corporate office and gave that office responsibility for ensuring compliance with environmental regulations and company policies. Home Depot has been aggressive in its environmental policies, particularly in its wood procurement, as considered in the example later in the chapter.

To implement its new environmental lending policy for project finance, Citigroup placed the group responsible for its Environmental and Social Risk Management policy in a position in which it interacted directly with senior lenders. Ilyse Hogue of RAN commented, "Having only five full-time staff dedicated to what the majority of the world is concerned with still falls short. But they have made smart choices by not locating [Environmental and Social Risk Management] staff in a marginalized environmental affairs office, instead placing them in positions of power with real access to senior decision-makers. That has really been key."[40]

A commitment from top management may be necessary for successful management of environmental matters, but it is not sufficient, since compliance takes place at the level of the individual facility. Sensitivity to environmental issues and compliance responsibility must be distributed throughout the firm. Furthermore, ideas for waste reduction and pollution control often are generated at the plant level. The Carrier Corporation, for example, was able to eliminate through engineering redesign its degreasing operation in the manufacture of air conditioners.

Wal-Mart was the subject of an unrelenting private politics campaign as considered in the Part I integrative case *Wal-Mart: Nonmarket Pressure and Reputation Risk (A)*. Wal-Mart began to work with Conservation International and the Natural Resources Defense Council (NRDC) on environmental initiatives.[41] The company evaluated the packaging of products it sold and found that reducing packaging also reduced shipping costs. Wal-Mart also opened an Environmental Demonstration Store and planned to open another. The store used solar panels, wind turbines, burned the used oil from oil changes, and burned fat used to fry chickens.[42] It also had a computerized heating and cooling system and used low-mercury fluorescent lamps and electronic ballasts.

In 2005 Wal-Mart announced a $35 million, 10-year Acres for America program to offset the nearly 140,000 acres that its current stores occupied plus its planned expansion over the next 10 years. The company formed a partnership with the Fish and Wildlife Foundation for the purchase of the acreage. The land would be available for hunting, fishing, and other outdoor activities and for sustainable logging.

Wal-Mart also announced a major environmental initiative focused on reducing energy use. The initiative included improving the efficiency of energy use in its supercenters and other stores. It also pledged to improve the fuel efficiency of its huge truck fleet by 25 percent over 3 years and by 100 percent over 10 years. The company announced that it would invest $500 million annually to reduce its emissions of greenhouse gases by 20 percent over 7 years. Wal-Mart also pledged to use its power to encourage its suppliers to be more energy efficient and to reduce their packaging. The initiative drew praise from Environmental Defense and the Sierra Club. A spokesperson for WakeUpWal-Mart.com, however, said, "It is a diversionary tactic. Wal-Mart understands that they have a growing public relations disaster on their hands."[43]

In 2009 Wal-Mart CEO Mike Duke announced that the company would lead an effort to create a "sustainability index" that would cover all the products it sold. The company created the Sustainability Consortium with participation by two universities and companies including Pepsi and Procter & Gamble.[44] The task of creating a meaningful sustainability index was herculean, progress was slow, and Wal-Mart became more cautious in creating expectations about what could

---

[39]*New York Times,* March 3, 1991.

[40]www.equator-principles.com/inc/printversion.php.

[41]For further information on Wal-Mart's sustainability strategy, see the case *Wal-Mart's Sustainability Strategy,* OIT-71, Graduate School of Business, Stanford University.

[42]"Lee Scott on Why Wal-Mart Is Playing Nicer," *BusinessWeek,* October 3, 2005.

[43]Michael Barbaro and Felicity Barringer, "Wal-Mart to Seek Savings in Energy," *New York Times,* October 25, 2005.

[44]*Fortune,* July 25, 2011.

be accomplished. Len Sauers, Procter & Gamble vice president of global sustainability commented, "So much has to go into a sustainability score and there are so many variables, the question is whether you can come up with a number that's accurate enough to drive meaningful decisions."[45]

Many companies attempt to instill the attitude that environmental matters are the responsibility of all employees. Many have established Environment, Health, and Safety (EHS) programs with explicit goals and public reporting on the progress made on those goals. BP reports publicly on its EHS performance, which is independently reviewed as part of its sustainability reporting.

Managers must interact with a host of regulatory officials, ranging from those who grant permits and inspect facilities to those who write implementation regulations. Managers should deal with regulators on the basis of trust and mutual respect but must also be prepared to suggest new means for achieving environmental goals and to oppose rules that may be overly burdensome. Managers should recognize that just as they face competing pressures for profits and environmental goals, regulators face competing pressures from environmental groups, oversight by political principals in Congress, and monitoring by those who bear the cost of regulation. Recognizing the pressures regulators face can be important in developing workable relationships.

Many firms have extended their internal environmental management programs to include external advice and consultations with local communities. Dow Chemical formed a Corporate Environmental Advisory Council to advise the company on its environmental stewardship policies and programs. Dow also encouraged its plant managers to form community advisory councils to address local issues and assure the community that its activities met environmental standards. Dow's emphasis was on pollution prevention through the four Rs: reduce, reuse, recycle, and recover. Source reduction was the preferred method followed by recycling and recovery.[46] The example illustrates the importance of source reduction in pollution. King and Lennx (2002) found that source reduction reduces total production and pollution control costs as argued by Porter and van der Linde (1995).

With increasing frequency companies are joining with environmental groups to discuss issues and solve particular environmental problems. As indicated in Chapter 4, most companies prefer moderate, science-based groups such as Conservation International and Environmental Defense (ED). ED has embraced the objective of efficiency in pollution control and advocates

---

EXAMPLE   Dow Chemical and Local Environmentalists

Dow Chemical, in conjunction with the NRDC, invited five local activists to join in a project at its Midland, Michigan, plant complex to make environmental improvements that would also save the company money.[1] Despite concerns about the possible release of proprietary information, Dow agreed to reduce toxic chemicals by 35 percent and to reduce emissions into the air and water by the same amount. These reductions were beyond any required by government regulations and were to be achieved only through pollution prevention approaches. More strikingly, Dow allowed the environmentalists to choose which toxic chemicals to be included, and it accepted without challenge the 26 selected.

Dow and the environmentalists agreed to use an outside environmental engineering expert to provide recommendations for how to achieve the reductions. Often the reductions were for small changes in processes or equipment settings that reduced the production and release of the toxic chemicals. Many of these changes had been overlooked by Dow

engineers, whose focus had been on satisfying regulations rather than going beyond those requirements. Dow reported that it spent $3.1 million on process changes yielding cost savings of $5.4 million a year. A major part of the savings occurred in its waste treatment facilities, which no longer had to treat certain toxics. Moreover, the company exceeded the targeted 35 percent reductions.[2]

The project also had less tangible benefits. Samuel Smolnik, vice president for global EHS, commented on a practical benefit of the project, "When you reduce waste and emissions, a community is a lot more willing to issue permits for other operations down the road."[3]

The NRDC offered to cooperate with other companies and expressed disappointment that it had no takers. Part of the explanation may be due to its other stances, such as its criticism of Intel's Project XL program with the EPA, discussed earlier in the chapter.

---

[1]This example is based on an article in *New York Times*, July 18, 1999.

[2]The final project report is available from the NRDC.
[3]*New York Times*, September 9, 2001.

---

[45]Ibid.
[46]See Popoff (1992).

the use of incentive approaches to achieve that end. This earned ED a role in the development of the provisions of the Clean Air Act Amendments of 1990 and in the design of the emissions permits trading system for the Kyoto Protocol. As indicated previously, ED also joined with BP to develop an internal tradable permits system for CO_2 emissions. ED has also developed a working relationship with McDonald's, resulting in over 20 joint projects. Their first project, a waste reduction program, is discussed in the example.

Not all cooperative arrangements between environmental NGOs and companies produce positive results. Federal Express and Environmental Defense joined in a project to explore the feasibility of a hybrid-electric truck that would be more environmentally friendly than its standard pickup and delivery trucks. William Logue, executive vice president of FedEx, reported on the experience with the 93 trucks in its Opti-Fleet E700 fleet. Compared to its standard trucks, the hybrids were "shown to increase fuel economy by 40 percent while decreasing particulate emissions by 90 percent and greenhouse gases by more than 25 percent." He also said, "The Opti-Fleet E700 costs almost twice as much as a standard pickup and delivery truck and, while we embarked on this program with a rallying call for others in the transportation sector to get on board, very few companies have committed to the technology, and the main reason is cost."[47]

EXAMPLE McDonald's and Waste Reduction

McDonald's is the largest restaurant system in the world and also one of the world's largest generators of solid waste. For a number of years McDonald's had been reducing its use of packaging materials. The packaging weight for a Big Mac, fries, and a shake had been reduced from 46 grams in the early 1970s to 25 grams by the 1990s. McDonald's had also conducted a number of waste reduction experiments, including a test program in 800 restaurants to recycle polystyrene containers. Environmental groups, however, pressured the company to make further reductions in its solid waste.[1] The Citizens' Clearinghouse for Hazardous Waste worked for 3 years, pressuring McDonald's to replace its polystyrene clamshell sandwich container. McDonald's replaced it with paper in 1990.

In the same year McDonald's decided to work with ED on the solid waste reduction issue. ED had a staff of over 110, including scientists, engineers, economists, and attorneys. It also had both a moderate stance on environmental protection and considerable experience in dealing with solid waste issues. The relationship began when Ed Rensi, president of McDonald's U.S.A., accepted ED president Fred Krupp's invitation to discuss the waste issue. After a number of joint staff meetings, McDonald's and ED established a joint task force project to study options for reducing solid wastes. The task force studied McDonald's operations and its 39 regional distribution centers and visited suppliers and disposal and recycling facilities. Each ED member also worked for a day in a McDonald's restaurant to gain an appreciation for its operations.

In 1991 the task force released its final report, identifying 40 steps that could reduce McDonald's solid wastes by 80 percent.[2] An important part of the task force study was a detailed investigation of McDonald's solid waste generation.

The study revealed, for example, that 79 percent by weight of on-premise waste was generated behind the counter. "'The results of the task force far exceed all of our expectations and original goals,' said Keith Magnuson, McDonald's director of operations development and a task force member. 'We started out to study waste reduction options. Instead, we developed a comprehensive waste reduction plan that is already being implemented....' 'The task force has set forth a long-term vision bolstered by concrete actions to be taken in the short term,' said Dr. Richard Denison, a senior scientist with ED and a task force member."[3]

The task force study also resulted in changes in McDonald's decision-making criteria. In its purchasing decisions on disposable packaging, McDonald's had considered three factors: availability, functionality, and cost. As a result of the task force study, it added a fourth: waste reduction.

In addition to the specific measures, the task force emphasized instilling a commitment to waste reduction throughout the McDonald's system. Three-quarters of McDonald's 8,500 U.S. restaurants were owned by independent franchisees. In addition, McDonald's had over 100 packaging suppliers. McDonald's had a tradition of standardization and strict enforcement of policies, so institutionalizing the waste reduction commitment was not difficult. Overall compliance assurance rested with the Environmental Affairs Department, but the commitment was lodged in all areas of its operations, including with suppliers and franchisees. McDonald's senior environmental officer reported directly to the board of directors on progress in implementing the task force recommendations.

[1]See the Chapter 1 case *The Nonmarket Environment of McDonald's*.
[2]The McDonald's Corporation–Environmental Defense Fund Waste Reduction Task Force report is available at www.environmentaldefense.org.

[3]McDonald's Corporation press release, April 16, 1991. In contrast to these statements, the original agreement between McDonald's and ED sought options rather than an action plan and contained language allowing for separate opinions to be issued and for either side to withdraw from the project.

[47]William J. Logue, "Testimony," Committee on Energy and Natural Resources, U.S. Senate, January 30, 2007.

EXAMPLE   Environmental Activism at Home Depot

Home Depot was founded in 1978 and became the world's largest home improvement specialty retailer with 1,707 stores in all 50 states. Its sales reached $64.8 billion in 2003 and earnings were $4.3 billion. Home Depot was the world's second largest retailer and had 300,000 associates. It had frequently been ranked as one of the nation's most-admired companies.

After Earth Day in 1990 Home Depot established its Environmental Principles and initially focused on recycling and offering some green products. In 1992 the company faced its first challenge from environmental groups. The Rainforest Action Network (RAN) challenged the company to eliminate its use of old growth tropical timber. Home Depot phased out its line of teak furniture and pledged to buy wood from sustainable sources. Environmental activists, including RAN, again targeted Home Depot and other companies in 1997 to stop their use of old growth redwood, and Home Depot and the other companies did so. RAN then launched its old growth market campaign in 1998, again targeting Home Depot. RAN hung a banner on Home Depot's headquarters and held protests at hundreds of stores.[1] Concerned about the public criticism of its timber sourcing, Home Depot agreed to stop buying old growth products. It also agreed to give preference to Forest Stewardship Council (FSC) certified wood.[2]

Home Depot's environmental practices were recharged when in 2000 Ron Jarvis was appointed as merchandising vice president with authority to terminate timber supply contracts. When Jarvis learned that an Indonesian supplier was using slash-and-burn harvesting, he cancelled the contract. Subsequently, Home Depot reduced by 90 percent its sourcing from Indonesia, where illegal logging was commonplace. The remaining purchases from Indonesia were from sources with sustainable practices. Rewarding those sources for their practices, however, did not cause other loggers in Indonesia to change their practices.[3] Jarvis also cancelled all purchases from Gabon when suppliers refused to change their practices.

When it was targeted by the activists, Home Depot realized that it had no means of identifying the sources of the wood products it sold nor how much wood it purchased from those sources. It began a major tracking effort that bore fruit in 2002. Home Depot now knows the source of every wood product it sells. In 1999 it issued its first Wood Purchasing Policy, and in 2002 it issued its current Policy. Ninety-four percent of its wood products now comes from North American timber, where forestland had increased by 1.5 percent during the past decade.[4] Home Depot pledged to purchase wood only from "forests managed in a responsible way and to eliminate wood purchases from endangered regions of the world …"

Home Depot went beyond its own practices and began corporate environmental activism. Along with Lowe's and other companies, it joined with environmentalists to convince the Canadian government to stop logging in the Great Bear Rainforest in British Columbia. Home Depot joined with The Nature Conservancy and a British agency to put bar codes on timber from Borneo. Home Depot had reduced its purchases of Indonesian lauan by 70 percent and worked with The Nature Conservancy, Tropical Forest Foundation, Tropical Forest Trust, and the World Wildlife Fund to improve practices in Indonesia. RAN executive director Michael Brune, however, criticized any purchasing from Indonesia: "This is not a time to establish small toeholds of good production."[5] RAN wanted all purchases from Indonesia halted.

Home Depot recognized only FSC certification, but the supply was too small to satisfy its demand, let alone other retailers and home builders. Home Depot decided to increase the supply. It worked with Tembec, a large Canadian lumber producer, to increase FSC certified lumber. Tembec agreed to obtain FSC certification for all its lumber by 2005, compared with 25 percent in 2003.[6]

After a call from the environmental activist group Forest Ethics claiming that tree farms were wiping out the natural forests in Chile, where Home Depot purchased 10 percent of the country's timber production, Jarvis called the heads of the two timber suppliers in Chile that had been targeted by a boycott by U.S. and Chilean activists. The timber executives disputed the activists' claim, stating that in the past they had cleared less than a million acres of forests and had discontinued the practice. The companies now planted their tree farms on agricultural and ranch land. Jarvis invited the activists and the Chilean timber producers to Home Depot's headquarters in Atlanta to discuss the matter. The next meeting was in Chile, where the timber companies gave the activists a tour of their farms. Jarvis said, "I basically told both sides, 'If you want to win on this, you have to give.'"[7] The timber companies agreed not to buy recently cleared land for their tree farms and made some changes in their practices. The activists agreed to call off the boycott and praised the companies. Randy Hayes, president of RAN, observed, "If you've got Home Depot carrying your water, you're going to get a lot farther than as just an environmental group."[8] The environmentalists stopped targeting Home Depot.

Ron Jarvis commented, "I think that maybe this is a template we can use in other countries."[9]

---

[1] See the case *Strategic Activism: The Rainforest Action Network*, Case No. P-44, Graduate School of Business, Stanford University.

[2] FSC was backed by environmental groups including RAN and Greenpeace.

[3] *Wall Street Journal*, August 6, 2004.

[4] www.homedepot.com.

[5] *BusinessWeek*, November 24, 2003.

[6] Canada News Wire, December 3, 2003.

[7] *Wall Street Journal*, August 6, 2004.

[8] Ibid.

[9] Ibid.

Source: This case was prepared from public sources by Professor David P. Baron. Copyright © 2004 by David P. Baron. All rights reserved. Reprinted with permission.

VOLUNTARY COLLECTIVE ENVIRONMENTAL PROGRAMS

A number of voluntary self-regulation programs have been established. These programs are relatively new, and their effectiveness has only begun to be evaluated. The International Organization for Standards has established ISO 14001, a worldwide voluntary environmental program for improved environmental management systems. In contrast to government regulation, ISO 14001 does not establish environmental standards or specify pollution-control practices. Instead, it emphasizes managerial processes to improve environmental performance. Over 36,000 companies have obtained ISO 14001 certification, with over 1,500 in the United States. Delmas (2000, 2001) studied the participation of firms in ISO 14001. Potoski and Prakash (2005) studied participation of U.S. facilities in ISO 14001 and concluded that, although it is costly, participation provided reputational benefits for participants. They, however, were not able to determine how effective it was in achieving improved environmental performance beyond that required by government and induced by private politics.

The Responsible Care program is a worldwide EHS voluntary regulation program operated by the chemical industry. Initiated in Canada in 1985, Responsible Care was established in the United States in 1989 following the accident at the Bhopal chemical facility that killed thousands. Responsible Care programs are now conducted by chemical industry associations in 47 countries that account for over 90 percent of worldwide chemicals production. Responsible Care focuses on improved practices for human and environmental protection. In addition to the direct benefits from improved practices, the program provides reputational benefits to the industry. Participation is voluntary, and not all chemical companies participate. Among the participants, companies with public faces and brand names are overrepresented, suggesting that the reputational benefits are important to those firms.

King and Lennox (2002) evaluated the Responsible Care program in the United States and found that companies with poor performance were disproportionately represented in the program. They also found that participants did not improve their performance at a faster rate than companies not participating in the program. The former is consistent with the hypothesis that companies with the worst performance have the most to gain from an improvement in the collective reputation of the industry, and the latter is consistent with the hypothesis that some participants shirk on their commitments to improve performance. Responsible Care subsequently strengthened their standards and provided for voluntary inspections of facilities.

A number of programs such as Responsible Care have been called "greenwash" by environmental groups. The allegations are that the programs sound good to the public, but they fail to live up to their promises. That is, the walk does not match the talk. The same criticisms have been levied against some of the voluntary programs run by the EPA and other government agencies. For example, Lyon and Kim (2007) found that participation in the Department of Energy's voluntary greenhouse gas registry had no effect on the carbon emissions per unit of electricity generated by electric utilities.

SUMMARY

Environmental protection and sustainability have broad support among the public, government, and the business community. Environmental protection is costly, however, and the more efficient the approach taken to reducing pollution, the greater reduction can be attained for any given expenditure. Conversely, for a given level of pollution reduction, the approach used to achieve that reduction affects the costs that society must bear. The social efficiency approach to environmental protection seeks to minimize the sum of the harm from pollution and the cost of reducing that harm.

An emissions tax system imposes a charge on pollutants emitted, which increases the costs of emissions and provides incentives to reduce them. A cap-and-trade system caps emissions, issues permits equal to the emissions cap, and allows the permits to be traded. A polluter with relatively low costs of reducing emissions has an incentive to reduce emissions by more than its permits require and sell the unused permits to another firm that has higher costs of reducing emissions. Both systems provide incentives to achieve social efficiency. The EPA has also used other incentive approaches in its bubble, offset, and credits programs, but the most successful system in operation is the transferable permits program for controlling greenhouse gases in the European Union.

Environmental policies such as a cap-and-trade system are the product of a political competition in which distributive consequences and efficiency considerations weigh large. The Clean Air Act Amendments of 1990 involved bargaining on several specific measures affecting those distributive consequences. On the acid rain provisions, bargaining occurred on both the stringency of the cap and the distribution of permits. The same incentives for nonmarket action are present in the broader effort to establish a cap-and-trade system for greenhouse gases emissions.

Environmental issues spark a wide range of private politics in addition to public politics. At the local level, environmental groups have been increasingly active in addressing environmental issues. The NIMBY movement and private politics have grown in importance. NGOs have been successful in pressuring firms to strengthen their environmental and sustainability programs.

Environmental protection and compliance are important components of management responsibility. Firms and their managers must address a variety of nonmarket issues that involve local communities, environmental groups, legislators, and regulators. A number of firms and environmental groups have developed relationships that allow them to address issues in a nonconfrontational manner. Some firms have worked directly with environmentalists, as in the case of the McDonald's–Environmental Defense project on reducing the company's solid wastes. Firms have developed a variety of innovative voluntary programs that go beyond the requirements of regulation.

CASES

Pacific Gas & Electric and the Smart Meter Challenge

We know the science has come out and said there is no harmful effect [from SmartMeters]. But there is a group of our customers that believe it does affect them, and that's fair. The question is then how do you design something that makes sense that is an alternative that can still allow you to go forward with what is good for society.[48]

Chris Jones, President, Pacific Gas & Electric

Most CEOs struggle over this issue more than anything else. You could have a real rebellion.[49]

Ted Carver, CEO of Edison International

INTRODUCTION

A wireless smart meter relays fine-grained information on electricity usage to utilities and allows utilities to send customers information such as hourly prices that depend on the level of demand and on the prices utilities pay for power on the wholesale market. One objective of public policymakers and environmentalists has been to reduce peak demand, so as to avoid

the highest cost power sources and to avoid building new power plants. Ahmed Faruqui of the Brattle Group estimated that responsive pricing could account for $45 billion of the estimated $227 billion of cost savings from a smart grid.[50] In addition, to the extent that customers reduced their overall electricity usage, responsive pricing provided environmental benefits.

Smart meters also allowed utilities to avoid a number of other costs. For example, meter-reading costs, which amounted to between 50 cents and $1 per meter per month, could be eliminated, and power could be turned on or off remotely without sending a truck and crew to do it. These savings would lower electricity rates for customers, but they had to pay for the meters, which cost Pacific Gas & Electric (PG&E) $220 apiece including installation. PG&E was the leader in installing smart meters and planned to spend $2.2 billion on the installation of 9.3 million smart meters by 2012.

The social benefits from responsive pricing enabled by smart meters were evident, but even taking the first step of installing the smart meters proved to be a challenge. Responsive pricing could be even more difficult.

---

[48]*San Jose Mercury News*, March 11, 2011.
[49]*Wall Street Journal*, February 22, 2010.

[50]*The Economist*, October 8, 2009.

PEAK DEMAND PRICING AND DEMAND RESPONSE

Peak demand times can be predicted in advance, and time-of-use pricing sets higher prices for peak hours and lower prices for off-peak hours. Power costs also depend on a utility's purchases of power on the wholesale market, and dynamic pricing adjusts prices in response to those wholesale market prices. A number of electric utilities used dynamic pricing for industrial and commercial customers. For example, Georgia Power had a voluntary program in which customers were given day-ahead and hour-ahead prices and decided how much power to use, paying a premium for usage above a baseline and receiving a rebate for usage below the baseline. Customer satisfaction with the program was high, and their peak usage decreased substantially and by more the greater the price premium.[51]

Would households respond to pricing differentials by shifting their demand to off-peak times? Faruqui and Sergici (2008) surveyed 17 real experiments with time-of-use pricing and dynamic peak pricing and found that demand was shifted and the magnitude depended on the price increase and whether customers had "enabling technologies" such as two-way programmable thermostats and gateway systems. With time-of-use pricing, peak demand was reduced 3–6 percent, and with dynamic peak pricing demand was reduced 13–20 percent. They found that enabling technologies resulted in reductions in peak demands from 27 to 44 percent.

PEPCO Inc., in conjunction with the Public Utility Commission of the District of Columbia, conducted a dynamic pricing experiment titled PowerCents DC in which 1000 randomly selected households in Washington DC were given smart meters. The households were randomly stratified across three pricing plans with half given enabling technologies, principally an automated control thermostat.[52] The Critical Peak Pricing (CPP) plan set peak prices at least 5 times higher during 4 hours a day for 15 days a year with lower rates at other times. The Critical Peak Rebate (CPR) plan offered a rebate for reductions in peak usage, and the Hourly Pricing (HP) plan adjusted prices based on the wholesale market price for electricity. All three pricing plans were designed to be revenue neutral. The households were given online information about rates. The changes in peak demand are given in Table 12-3.

The HP plan yielded little improvement, and the rebate plan only modest improvement. The critical peak pricing plan with substantial price penalties for peak usage, however, yielded a large reduction in peak usage, particularly during the summer air-conditioning months. With smart thermostats the reductions in peak usage averaged 50 percent, and the

TABLE 12-3 Washington, DC Program Tests

Price Plan	Summer Peak Reduction (%)	Winter Peak Reduction (%)
CPP	34	13
CPR	13	5
HP	4	2

Source: PowerCents DC, "Smart Grid Washington DC," A Case Study in Empowering Consumers," Briefing to White House Officials, July 1, 2010.

reductions were greater the higher the outside temperature. Over 91 percent of the participating households had a reduction in their electricity bills with an annual average savings of $43.83, and the other 9 percent had an increase that averaged $17.43 a year. Satisfaction of the participating households with PowerCents DC was very high, and 93 percent preferred their PowerCents DC pricing plan to the former pricing plan.

The price penalties in the CPP plan yielded the greatest reductions in peak demand and the greatest savings, but Pepco was reluctant to use it. Steven Sunderhauf of Pepco explained, "Our general sense is that consumers would prefer a rate structure with no downside. From a purist's standpoint, I may prefer critical peak pricing because it gets the boldest response … but using rebates will help people get comfortable with smart meters."[53]

The Attorney General of Connecticut was concerned that customers would pay for the smart meters but not receive benefits because they would not respond to the price differentials. Connecticut Light & Power conducted an experiment to determine the extent of the savings that could be realized by responsive pricing. The company "gave new meters to 3,000 residential and business customers, testing three types of rates. Like other utilities, it found that homes facing the highest peak hour pricing—$1.60 per kwh at certain times—responded the most, cutting peak use 16–23 percent, depending on whether they had other aids like smart thermostats. Commercial customers, in a similar test, cut their demand far less, only 7 percent."[54] The Connecticut utility planned to develop a smart meter deployment program and initially to offer consumers a rebate for conservation.

Southern California Edison also planned to offer a rebate program. "The utility chose rebates over penalties partly because a law passed during the California energy crisis a decade ago limits its ability to involuntarily switch people to higher peak-hour pricing plans right now. A new law may allow it in 2013."[55] Using rebates provided weaker incentives to shift usage.

[51]Demand Responses and Advanced Metering Coalition, "Real-Time Pricing Case Study: Georgia Power Company," No date. www.drsgcoalition.org.
[52]Also participating were the International Brotherhood of Electrical Workers, The Office of the People's Counsel, and the DC Consumer Utility Board.

[53]*Wall Street Journal*, February 22, 2010.
[54]Ibid.
[55]Ibid.

CONSUMER BENEFITS?

Would consumers see lower electricity bills from peak-demand pricing? In the short run average electricity bills should be somewhat lower to the extent that utilities can avoid using high cost power sources at peak demand periods. The more important efficiency gains from smart meters came in two forms. First, capacity costs would be lower in the future than they would otherwise be to the extent that reductions in peak demand allowed utilities to avoid building new power plants. Second, smart meters would aid utilities in accommodating intermittent sources of power such as from solar modules, solar farms, and wind turbines, particularly in states with renewable power standards. These are longer-run savings that customers would not realize for years. With higher energy costs and continued inflation even at moderate rates, consumers would likely never have lower electricity bills and might associate smart meters and other smart grid technologies with the higher bills. Instead, electricity rates would be lower than they would be in the absence of smart grid applications.

The question was how to achieve the social benefits from shifting demand from peak to off peak times. Two things were essential. First, electricity usage had to be metered by time of day and customers given time-specific prices. Second, a significant price differential had to be set so that consumers would actually shift usage from peak to off-peak times. Both posed problems.

Joshua Hart, of the activist group Stop Smart Meters, said, "The meters don't benefit the consumer; they cost a lot of money, and we can't opt out."[56] Customers did not have the right to reject a smart meter. Under California Public Utility Commission (PUC) regulations PG&E had the right to enter a premise to provide service, including installing meters, and if a customer tried to block an installation, the company had the right to terminate electric or gas service.[57]

COMPLAINTS

Accuracy of Smart Meters

Soon after their introduction in California customers began to complain about skyrocketing electricity bills, and many attributed the cost to inaccurate smart meters. Many of those complaints came from the Bakersfield area. PG&E found that there had been a few billing errors, but maintained that the meters were accurate. The company explained that the higher bills were due to unusually hot temperatures resulting in heavy air-conditioning use and higher tier rates as usage increased. In July 2010 Bakersfield had 17 days with high temperatures above 100 degrees, compared to 6 the previous year.[58] In addition to the extreme heat California electricity rates had five tiers with sharply increasing rates for Tiers 3, 4, and 5. The extreme heat and high air-conditioning use moved consumers into higher tiers.

Customers continued to complain, and PG&E responded with an advertising campaign to explain the consumer benefits from Smart Grid applications. The ads referred to hourly billing with prices based on the wholesale rates at which the utility purchased power and demand shifting in response to peak and nonpeak prices. Customers continued to complain.

The complaints led PG&E to check the accuracy of its smart meters. In April 2010 it reported that it had found 43,376 cases of problems out of 5 million installed smart meters. It found that 23,000 meters had been improperly installed, 11,376 had failed to retain customer information, and 9,000 had problems connecting to the wireless network.[59] Some of the problems might have resulted in billing errors.

The complaints attracted the attention of state politicians, who asked the PUC to investigate. Consumer advocates also urged investigation of the complaints. Mindy Spatt of The Utility Reform Network (TURN), a longtime opponent of PG&E, said, "Given the large number of consumer complaints, we hope that every consumer's complaint is taken seriously."[60] The PUC took the complaints seriously, although its members were skeptical about there being an accuracy problem. The PUC hired The Structure Group of Houston, a consulting firm specializing in the energy and utilities industries, under a $1.4 million contract to conduct tests on the smart meters and PG&E's downstream billing and to investigate customer complaints.[61] The consultants found that the smart meters were more accurate than the electromechanical meters they had replaced. Texas regulators had hired Navigant Consulting to evaluate 5,600 existing meters against 600 smart meters and also concluded that the smart meters were more accurate than the old meters.[62] The Structure Group faulted PG&E for not doing a better job educating the public about the smart meters.

Health Claims and Tin Foil Hats

More important than the accuracy issue, consumers complained that the electromechanical field (EMF) of the smart meters caused a variety of illnesses. Some consumers believed they had "electromagnetic hypersensitivity," or EHS, which with the EMF of wireless smart meters caused illnesses.

The World Health Organization (WHO) had reviewed the science on EHS and concluded:[63]

> EHS is characterized by a variety of non-specific symptoms that differ from individual to individual. The symptoms are certainly real and can vary widely in their severity. Whatever its cause, EHS can be a disabling problem for the affected individual. EHS has no clear diagnostic criteria and there is no scientific basis to link EHS symptoms to EMF exposure. Further, EHS is not a medical diagnosis, nor is it clear that it represents a single medical problem.

---

[56]*Bloomberg Businessweek*, September 20–26, 2010.
[57]*CBS 5*, March 11, 2010.
[58]Michael Kanellos, "PG&E and Its Discontents," www.greentechmedia, August 12, 2010.
[59]*San Jose Mercury News*, April 28, 2010.
[60]*San Jose Mercury News*, March 31, 2010.
[61]Structure Consulting Group, "PG&E Advanced Metering Assessment Report," September 2, 2010.
[62]*Wall Street Journal*, July 7, 2010.
[63]World Health Organization, "Electromagnetic Fields and Public Health: Electromagnetic Hypersensitivity," Fact sheet N 296, December 2005.

TABLE 12-4 Comparison of RF Power Density in the Everyday Environment

Power Density in Microwatts per square centimeter (µW/cm^2)	
Adjacent to a gas SmartMeter™ (1 foot)	0.00166
Adjacent to an electric SmartMeter™ (10 feet)	0.1
Adjacent to an electric SmartMeter™ (1 foot)	8.8
Microwave oven nearby (1 meter)	10
Wi-Fi wireless routers, laptop computers, cyber cafes, etc., maximum (~1 meter for laptops, 2–5 meters for access points)	10–20
Cell phones (at head)	30–10,000
Walkie-Talkies (at head)	500–42,000

Source: Richard Tell Associates, Inc.

The WHO also reviewed the controlled studies of EHS and stated:[64]

A number of studies have been conducted where EHS individuals were exposed to EMF similar to those that they attributed to the cause of their symptoms. The aim was to elicit symptoms under controlled laboratory conditions.

The majority of studies indicate that EHS individuals cannot detect EMF exposure any more accurately than non-EHS individuals. Well controlled and conducted double-blind studies have shown that symptoms were not correlated with EMF exposure.

A review by Kings College, London, of 46 studies of electromagnetic fields and health effects concluded, "despite the conviction of … sufferers that their symptoms are triggered by exposure to [electromagnetic] fields, repeated experiments have been unable to replicate the phenomenon under controlled conditions."[65]

After receiving complaints, the Maine Public Utilities Commission reviewed the science on EHS and concluded, "The majority of studies indicated that people who described themselves as suffering from such sensitivity could not detect whether they were being exposed to electromechanical field in experiments any more accurately than non-EHS individuals."[66] Elisa Baker-Cook, who had been leading the protests against the smart meters installed by Central Maine Power, responded, "When someone is sensitive to wireless, they don't need a causal link. Our bodies' reaction is the causal link, and we learn to trust that."[67]

PG&E spokesperson Jeff Smith said, "'We do understand that some of our customers have concerns' even though 'the evidence shows overwhelmingly' that no link to health effects have been established."[68] PG&E took the complaints seriously as did the PUC. Bloggers were less charitable, referring to the

complainers as "tin foil hats."[69] The density of the radio frequency waves from the meters was far lower than from common devices such as laptop computers, cell phones, and wireless baby monitoring systems. Table 12-4 presents radio frequency power density for a variety of common electronic devices.[70] Joshua Hart said, "People with electrosensitivity are always accused of being tinfoil-hat crazies. But this is not like cell phones, where you can choose not to buy them."[71]

The California Council on Science and Technology examined the health claims lodged against smart meters and concluded that the meters "result in much smaller levels of radio frequency (RF) exposure than many existing common household electronic devices, particularly cell phones and microwave ovens."[72] The report stated that the emissions were well within Federal Communications Commission standards and that those standards were sufficient to protect human health even under "worst-case" scenarios.[73] The Council also reported that it could find no study that had confirmed negative health effects of RF emissions like those from smart meters. The worriers were not assuaged. Sandi Maurer of the EMF Safety Network said, "People are really getting sick—we're getting all kinds of anecdotal reports about sleep problems, nausea, headaches and ringing in the ears. This report simply says that there's no proof. That's not reassuring."[74]

The Council report also pointed out that there was an alternative to wireless meters. A hard-wired equivalent was possible with meter reading transmitted over wires. Assemblyman Jared Huff stated, "Whether or not you believe there are health issues, utilities should give consumers complete

---

[64]Ibid.
[65]*Wall Street Journal*, September 9, 2010.
[66]*New York Times*, January 31, 2011.
[67]Ibid.
[68]Ibid.

[69]"One may wear the hat in the belief that it acts to shield the brain from such influences as electromagnetic fields, or against mind control and/or mind reading; or attempt to limit the transmission of voices directly into the brain.

The concept of wearing a tin foil hat for protection from such threats has become a popular stereotype and term of derision; the phrase serves as a byword for paranoia and persecutory delusions, and is associated with conspiracy theorists." Wikipedia, "Tin Foil Hat," accessed March 19, 2011.
[70]www.pge.com/myhome/edusafety/systemworks/rf.
[71]*San Jose Mercury News*, November 9, 2010.
[72]*San Jose Mercury News*, January 12, 2011.
[73]Ibid.
[74]Ibid.

and accurate information regarding RF emission from smart meters, and customers should be allowed the alternative of having a hard-wired smart meter."[75]

To better understand the complaints and to monitor the activities of those leading the protests, PG&E's director of the SmartMeter program William Devereaux joined the activist California EMF Coalition online under the name "Ralph" to obtain access to the group's private Web site. Devereaux used a Gmail address, but activists discovered his true identify. The activists also alleged that he had joined the forum SmartWarriorMarin without identifying himself. Joshua Hart said, "The fact that this guy who is responsible for the entire SmartMeter program is spending his time trying to infiltrate groups that are worried about health issues shows that PG&E has something to hide. These are symptoms of a deeper malaise, and a corporate culture of dishonesty and recklessness."[76] PG&E suspended Devereaux and after an investigation fired him.

PRIVACY CONCERNS

Some consumers claimed that the smart meters were threats to their personal privacy. The North Bay Patriots affiliated with the Tea Party held a meeting to voice their complaints. Jed Gladstein complained that the smart meters were "the sharp end of a very long spear pointed at your freedoms."[77] The privacy NGOs the Center for Democracy and Technology and the Electronics Frontier Foundation expressed their privacy concerns to the PUC. David K. Owens, executive vice president of the Edison Electric Institute, said, "We've always gotten information about customers' usage and always keep it confidential. We're going to honor their privacy."[78]

Two women from the West Marin Citizens Against Wireless Smart Meters tried to block PG&E contractors' trucks from delivering smart meters. One of the arrested, Katherina Sandizell, said, "I'd love to work out a peaceful solution where people's concerns are honored."[79] A blogger wrote that not only were the Tea Party members against the smart meters, but "the hippies in West Marin as well ...."

Customers also complained that the smart meters were causing interference with other electronic devices, such as baby monitors. PG&E explained that the meters satisfied Federal Communications Commission standards and that the baby monitor was not built to a standard that would avoid interference with FCC standard devices.[80]

The complaints about smart meters were not confined to California. A woman in Michigan complained in a township meeting, "This plan was invented as another means of control of the masses. Smart meters will allow your power to be shut off instantly, whether by a consumer service agent or automatic computer control. All of your appliances will eventually be under observation and under control, including your climate control in your refrigerator. Your food consumption and diet will be monitored, and video and audio alarms, and surveillance can be incorporated into this. They will be able to tell who is in your home, where they are and what they are doing. They will even be able to tell which members of the house is eating what and even when they flush the commode."[81]

FAIRNESS CONCERNS

Concerns were expressed about the impact of responsive pricing on vulnerable consumers. Low-income consumers could face higher electrical bills if they were unable to shift their demand. Some states such as California had low lifeline rates for low-income consumers and higher prices for higher income consumers. PG&E provided a California Alternate Rates for Energy (CARE) program and a Family Electric Rate Assistance (FERA) program. For 2010 a family of 4 with an income no more than $43,200 was eligible for CARE and between $43,201 and $54,000 for the FERA program. Responsive pricing could require greater cross-subsidization.

The elderly and others could have difficulty responding to real-time pricing, and their inability to cope with the real-time displays and controls could leave them with higher electricity bills. Utility executives worried that responsive pricing could harm such vulnerable customers. Kevin DelGobbo, Connecticut utilities commissioner, said, "I'm mindful that an elderly person with medical equipment can't say, 'I'm not going to run the equipment at the 'peak' time.' We have to be careful with these rate structures."[82]

Utilities were also concerned about higher bills for customers who failed to shift their demand or found it inconvenient to do so. For example, consumers might not want to reduce their use of air-conditioning during the late afternoon and early evening on scorching hot days.

DEVELOPMENTS

The strategy of the opponents of smart meters in California was to use the media to pressure government officials and speak to the broader public. City councils and county commissions passed resolutions calling for a moratorium on new installations, and the anti-smart meter activists lobbied newly installed governor Jerry Brown to appoint pro-moratorium commissioners to the PUC. A bill was introduced in the state assembly to impose a moratorium. By January 2011 PG&E had installed 7.5 million meters and was continuing its installations at the rate of 15,000 a week.

In March 2011 the PUC ordered PG&E to present within 2 weeks opt-out alternatives for it to evaluate. PUC President

[75]Ibid.

[76]*San Jose Mercury News*, November 9, 2010.

[77]Andrew Dalton, SFist, January 7, 2011.

[78]*New York Times*, January 31, 2011.

[79]*San Jose Mercury News*, December 29, 2011.

[80]*San Jose Mercury News*, September 10, 2010.

[81]*Advisor & Source Newspapers*, March 8, 2011.

[82]*Wall Street Journal*, February 22, 2010.

Michael Peevey asked that the alternative be "at a reasonable cost, to be paid by the customers who choose to opt out." PG&E responded that it had been studying opt-out alternatives and would be able to meet the 2-week time period. PG&E president Chris Johns commented, "Some of these alternatives are pretty expensive, and who pays for that? Does the whole community pay for that? Or do you try to make the person who wants the alternative pay for that?"[83]

The strident critics were not satisfied. Joshua Hart said the PUC action was "too little, too late. We will not rest until we have a moratorium on installation and public hearings on the health concerns."[84] ▨

Preparation Questions

1. Could the smart meter crisis in California have been avoided? What steps would you have taken in hindsight?
2. Could the crisis have been avoided by anything other than giving an opt-out alternative?
3. What opt-out alternatives would you propose to the PUC?
4. What steps would you take in introducing responsive pricing? Should an opt-out alternative be part of the responsive pricing program?
5. Are regulators likely to be willing to implement sufficiently large difference between peak and off-peak prices to cause households to shift demand significantly?

Environmental Justice and Pollution Credits Trading Systems

As executive vice president for West Coast operations of Westco Oil Company, Jeremy Bentley was proud of the environmental accomplishments of his company in California. Emissions at the company's Long Beach refinery had been reduced, and oil spills at its marine terminal in El Segundo had been reduced dramatically.

Jeremy was aware of the Environmental Protection Agency's environmental justice campaign and supported its concern about the siting of facilities, such as hazardous waste disposal sites, in areas in which minorities and the poor were overrepresented. He was shocked, however, when Westco was confronted by the environmental justice movement. Not only were the arguments made by the activists novel, but they also struck at the heart of the evolving system of air pollution control being implemented in the Los Angeles area and elsewhere in the United States. That system emphasized attaining environmental goals using the least costly means of abatement. Attaining the goals at least cost to society required greater reductions in emissions at facilities with low costs of abatement and smaller reductions at facilities with high costs of abatement.

To implement this system the South Coast Air Quality Management District (AQMD) had established a pollution credits trading program that allowed abaters to earn credits for emissions reductions and sell those credits to emitters of pollution that had high costs of abatement. The trading of credits reduced the aggregate costs of attaining environmental goals, and the AQMD had supported the development of markets in credits. Under one program approved by the AQMD, automobile scrap yards bought old, high-pollution automobiles for $600 to $700 and received a credit that they could sell either to the AQMD, a company such as Westco, or an environmental group. If a company purchased a credit, it would not have to reduce its emissions by as much as it would otherwise have to reduce them. Under Jeremy's leadership Westco had participated in the AQMD program and purchased credits that it used at its marine terminal. Jeremy had also purchased credits through other programs and used those credits at its Long Beach refinery.

Environmental justice and pollution credits trading systems collided in July 1997 in Southern California as environmental groups and advocates for low-income groups, led by the interest group Communities for a Better Environment, filed lawsuits seeking to force the EPA to rescind the authority granted to the AQMD and the California Air Resources Board to operate a pollution credits trading system. One focus of the lawsuits was the pollution credits trading system and the purchase and scrapping of old, high-pollution automobiles. One lawsuit filed by Communities for a Better Environment against five oil companies including Westco alleged that residents in San Pedro and El Segundo had been exposed to harmful hydrocarbon emissions because the companies violated the federal Clean Air Act by failing to reduce emissions at their marine terminals. Instead, the companies had earned pollution credits by purchasing and scrapping 7,400 old cars as allowed under the AQMD program. Westco had been one of the leading purchasers of the credits.

Unocal, which had initiated the program to purchase and scrap high-pollution cars, operated a subsidiary, Eco-Scrap, that purchased old cars for companies that wanted to earn pollution credits. Spokesman Barry Lane said, "We still believe that the emission control program is of great value, it makes good sense."[85]

In another lawsuit, the Center on Race, Poverty and the Environment and the National Association for the Advancement of Colored People joined Communities for a Better Environment in alleging that the pollution credits trading system violated the civil rights of minorities by subjecting communities in which they were disproportionately represented to high levels of health-threatening pollutants. The lawsuit cited Title VI of the Civil Rights Act of 1964, which prohibits discrimination, such as against minorities and women, in programs and activities receiving federal funds.

In conjunction with the filing of the lawsuits, the activist and advocacy groups held a press conference at which local residents told of the harmful effects of the pollutants. Fifth-grader Laurie Johnson, who was on medical leave from

[83]*San Jose Mercury News*, March 11, 2011.

[84]Ibid.

[85]*Los Angeles Times*, July 23, 1997.

Wilmington Park Elementary School, reported that she and other children at the school had health problems attributable to the emissions. She said, "It's time for our corporate neighbors to be responsible and give us a hand."[86] Sixty-nine-year-old Lily Camarillo, who lived near a Texaco refinery, said, "I've raised several kids there, lost three others and you wouldn't believe the problems we've had. Headaches, sick stomachs; my daughter has leukemia."[87]

Richard Drury, attorney for Communities for a Better Environment, turned the pollution credits trading system principle on its head by arguing that it exposed residents to the equivalent of "thousands of cars idling at each marine terminal." He also said, "It's a good thing to get old cars off the road; they cause a lot of pollution. But you don't trade the health of workers and the residents who live near those facilities in exchange for that."[88] Later on CNN he said, "If you have enough money, you can buy enough pollution credits and pump out as much pollution as you want to. That's going to create toxic hot spots."[89]

AQMD spokesman Tom Eichorn stated, "These people think they're being affected by air pollution problems ... our job is to respond to their complaints." But he added that the agency did not believe that emissions were higher than before the pollution credits trading system was instituted.[90] Barry Wallerstein of the AQMD said, "The preliminary analysis by our legal department indicates that we're in full compliance with federal law."[91] "James Lents, the AQMD's outgoing executive officer, said he believes that the agency is not violating civil rights because toxic hot spots around industries are reduced under a separate rule, which prohibits fumes that pose a risk exceeding 100 cases of cancer among every million people exposed. However, that standard is less stringent than environmentalists and some health officials have wanted. AQMD board members, skeptical of the cancer danger posed by the [hydrocarbon] fumes, set the scaled-back standard in 1994."[92]

Faced with moral accusations, lawsuits, and community pressure, Jeremy had to decide what to do. First he wanted to evaluate the moral claims being made by the activists and residents. Then, he would have to assess whether their claims, if morally supported, warranted a change in Westco's environmental protection programs. Jeremy also wondered whether he should meet with the residents or the activists to see if there was common ground from which they could work to resolve the issues.

ENVIRONMENTAL JUSTICE

The environmental justice movement began with concerns raised by activists that the poor and minorities were disproportionately affected by pollution. Since housing prices were naturally lower near industrial areas, low-income individuals tended to disproportionately locate in those areas. Concern for their well-being centered not only on issues of poverty and opportunity but also on the effects of pollution on their health. In 1992 the EPA issued a report raising the environmental justice issue. When President Clinton appointed Carol Browner, an environmentalist who had worked for Vice President Al Gore, to head the EPA, she initiated an environmental justice program. In 1994 President Clinton issued an executive order directing federal agencies to ensure that public health and environmental programs were nondiscriminatory and provided environmental justice. The president referred to Title VI of the Civil Rights Act in his order.

Many environmental interest groups and activists opposed the use of pollution credits trading systems. Some were suspicious of using incentive systems to control a social bad such as pollution. Some preferred uniform command-and-control regulations that forced a direct abatement requirement on all pollution sources and hence would result in a similar reduction in pollution in every locale rather than different levels of abatement across locales, depending on where the pollution credits were used. More fundamentally, however, most of the activists preferred lower emissions than allowed by legislation and EPA regulations.

As some commentators observed, with the mainstream environmental groups "under the thumb of Vice President Al Gore, their political patron," the cause of environmental justice has been led by some of the smaller and newer environmental interest groups.[93] In the 1990s those groups emphasized the twin themes of health, particularly for those at risk, and of environmental justice. These groups argued that pollution control policies should take into account the special interests of low-income people who disproportionately live and work in areas of high pollution. President Clinton and Vice President Gore embraced both the concept of environmental justice and the use of pollution credits trading systems.

In 1997 the U.S. Court of Appeals gave individuals the right to challenge state environmental permits on the grounds of a disparate effect on low-income and minority groups. The Supreme Court, however, chose to review the decision.

As the EPA began its implementation planning, the environmental justice movement met with increasing opposition as business groups and members of Congress became concerned about the objectives of the movement and the consequences of such a policy. The U.S. Chamber of Commerce and the National Black Chamber of Commerce led a campaign to revoke the EPA's environmental justice program.[94] "We fully support the U.S. Chamber's efforts to repeal the EPA's misguided policy," Black Chamber president Harry Alford said. "This represents the beginning of a close working relationship between the U.S. Chamber and our organization to support black businesses around the country."[95] "It's an economics problem; it isn't race," Alford said. "If you're going to dump trash, you're going to dump it on land that's cheap. We feel the EPA is exploiting the Civil Rights Act and exploiting

---

[86]Copley News Service, July 23, 1997.

[87]Ibid.

[88]*All Things Considered*, National Public Radio, July 24, 1997.

[89]*CNN Today*, August 1, 1997.

[90]Copley News Service, July 23, 1997.

[91]*CNN Today*, August 1, 1997.

[92]*Los Angeles Times*, July 23, 1997.

[93]*In These Times*, July 28, 1997.

[94]The National Black Chamber of Commerce had 180 chapters representing 62,000 black-owned businesses.

[95]*Washington Times*, July 20, 1998.

the black communities in an attempt to gather a vocal constituency in its ever-growing fight against big business."[96]

Alford was particularly concerned that the policy would drive jobs away from the areas in which minorities live. He pointed to the case of a permit sought by Shintech, a Japanese-owned company, to build a $700 million polyvinyl chloride plant in Louisiana's St. James Parish. Local activists had protested the plant, even though it would bring badly needed jobs to the parish.

Alford and others also argued that the EPA's environmental justice program would hinder attempts by cities to attract businesses to so-called "brownfields," some half million abandoned industrial sites, most of which were located in inner city areas. The U.S. Conference of Mayors spoke out against the EPA's environmental justice program, urging the EPA to develop a new policy that would encourage rather than hinder brownfield developments.

Congress also took an interest in the EPA program. The House Appropriations Committee inserted language in the EPA's fiscal 1999 appropriation barring it from taking any new civil rights actions under the program. The House Commerce Committee launched an investigation of the EPA's environmental justice program.

In a challenge to President Clinton, Carlos Porras, director of Communities for a Better Environment for Southern California, said, "[Environmental justice] is a defining issue for the president's administration. This has national significance and we're very interested to see where the Clinton administration draws the line."[97]

POLLUTION CREDITS TRADING SYSTEMS

For decades economists and business leaders had advocated the use of pollution credits trading systems to achieve environmental objectives at the least cost to society. Pollution credits trading systems had been implemented in the Midwest and Northeast for sulfur dioxide and nitrogen oxides, and several systems were in place in Southern California to control a number of pollutants. Many other states were considering using similar systems, and with the recent promulgation of costly new federal regulations regarding microscopic airborne particulates, additional states and regions were expected to consider these systems.

To illustrate the difference between pollution credits trading systems and the traditional command-and-control approach, consider an environmental objective of reducing emissions of hydrocarbons by 50 percent in the oil industry in the Los Angeles basin. Under a command-and-control system all pollution sources would be required to reduce their emissions by 50 percent. In a pollution credits trading system the 50 percent reduction would be achieved by requiring a source to hold a permit for each pound of hydrocarbons emitted. Permits would be issued equal to 50 percent of the pre-reduction emissions. For example, one permit could be issued for each pound of hydrocarbon emissions allowed with

TABLE 12-5

	Costs of Abatement by Source ($)		
Pounds Abated	a	b	c
100	10	15	20
200	20	30	35

the permits allocated among the emitters according to some baseline such as their prereduction emissions. Then, an emitter with low costs of abatement that reduced its emissions below the number of permits it was allocated could sell its excess permits, or credits, to an emitter with high costs of abatement, which would reduce its emissions by less than 50 percent. Thus, low-cost abaters would reduce their emissions by more than high-cost abaters, allowing the environmental objective to be achieved at the lowest total cost. In characterizing pollution credits trading systems, David Roe, a senior attorney for Environmental Defense, said, "What this allows for the first time is that companies that have the technical ability to go beyond the law in reducing their emissions have a reason to do it."[98]

As an example, consider a region with three pollution sources a, b, and c in locations A, B, and C, respectively. Suppose the sources each have been emitting 200 pounds of hydrocarbons and that the new environmental objective is to cut emissions by 50 percent to 300 pounds in total. Also assume that each source is allocated 100 permits. Suppose that the costs of abatement for each source are as given in Table 12-5.

For example, if source a were to abate 100 pounds, its cost would be $10, and if it were to abate 200 pounds, the cost would be $20. The corresponding costs for source c are $20 and $35, respectively. If under a command-and-control system each source were to reduce its emissions by 100 pounds, the total cost of the 300 pounds of abatement would be 10 + 15 + 20 = $45.

The environmental objective of a 300-pound reduction can, however, be attained for $35 if a reduced its emissions by 200 pounds (at a cost of $20) and b reduced its emissions by 100 pounds (at a cost of $15). Source a would then have zero emissions, b would have emissions of 100, and c would have emissions of 200.

For this outcome to be realized, source c must purchase 100 credits. By purchasing the 100 credits, c would avoid the abatement cost of $20 that it would incur if it were to abate 100 pounds. By reducing its emissions by 200 rather than 100 pounds, a incurs a cost of only $10. Since c is willing to pay up to $20 for 100 credits and a requires only $10 of compensation to reduce its emissions from 100 to 0 pounds, the two sources can reach an agreement. Thus, source a reduces its emissions by 200 pounds, source b reduces its emissions by 100 pounds, and source c purchases 100 credits from a rather than reducing its emissions. The equilibrium price for a credit is $15, since

[96]*National Journal*, July 11, 1998.
[97]*Los Angeles Times*, July 23, 1997.

[98]*Wall Street Journal*, July 24, 1997.

if *a* were to attempt to sell credits for more than $15, *b* would offer to sell credits for slightly less. Then the competition between *a* and *b* would drive the price down to $15. Similarly, if the price were less than $15, *b* would offer to buy credits from *a*. Then *b* and *c* would compete for the credits, driving the price up to $15. The distribution of the cost of achieving the environmental objective with a price of $15 is then $5, $15, and $15, respectively, for sources *a, b,* and *c.*

In designing a pollution credits trading system, an important factor is the geographic region the system covers. The basic principle is that the region include those affected by the emissions, as in the Los Angeles basin. Then the focus is on the aggregate reduction in emissions in that region rather than in specific locations. In the example, a reduction of 200 pounds was achieved by source *a* and 100 pounds at *b.* This result can also be stated in terms of the remaining emissions, which are 0, 100, and 200 pounds in locations *A, B,* and *C,* respectively. ▨

Preparation Questions

1. Evaluate a pollution credits trading system from the perspective of a system that maximizes aggregate utility.
2. Compare command-and-control and pollution credits trading approaches in terms of economic efficiency.
3. Evaluate the claims of the activist and advocacy groups based on conceptions of justice. Is the AQMD's "separate rule" for hot spots an appropriate response to justice concerns?
4. Do oil companies have a duty to reduce their emissions at their marine terminals and refineries rather than purchasing credits, even though doing so would reduce the efficiency of the pollution credits trading system?
5. What should Jeremy Bentley do and why? Should he voluntarily stop purchasing credits? Should he meet with the residents and activists?

Source: This case was written by Professor David P. Baron. Copyright © 1998 by the Board of Trustees of the Leland Stanford Junior University. All rights reserved. Reprinted with permission.

Environmentalist versus Environmentalist

In 2006 with the support of environmental groups and opposition by business groups California enacted AB 32, a landmark Global Warming Solutions Act that directed the California Air Resources Board (ARB) to establish rules to reduce greenhouse gas emissions to 1990 levels by 2020. ARB could choose how to achieve the objective either through direct regulation, a market mechanism such as an emissions credits trading system, or other means such as a carbon tax. In its scoping plan ARB chose a cap-and-trade system in which major emitters would be issued permits and allowed to buy or sell permits or purchase offsets such as planting trees or funding emissions reductions in developing countries. In the process of making its choice, ARB was directed to convene an Environmental Justice Advisory Committee to advise it regarding the impact of its choice on vulnerable community members, and the committee met many times during the decision-making process.

Most of the business community opposed the Act, although the clean tech industry and the venture capital firms funding the industry saw the Act as a means to drive the demand for renewable energy. Politicians touted the creation of clean tech jobs in the state, and the opposing businesses warned that the Act would increase the already-high cost of doing business in California. With unemployment soaring to over 12 percent in the state as a result of the recession, taxpayer groups and business groups collected signatures for a ballot initiative for the November 2010 election. The initiative would suspend the Global Warming Solutions Act until unemployment was below 5.5 percent for four consecutive quarters, something that had not been achieved since 1980. The groups collected sufficient signatures to qualify it as Proposition 23. Environmental groups campaigned vigorously against Proposition 23, and voters rejected it with 61.6 percent voting against it.

While Proposition 23 was attracting all the attention, a group of environmental justice advocates filed a lawsuit against ARB claiming that it had failed to meet procedural due process requirements in not considering sufficiently the impact of its choice on vulnerable communities and the poor. Plaintiff Jane Williams of California Communities Against Toxics said, "During passage of AB 32, the legislature instructed ARB to both maximize reductions in greenhouse gas emissions and protect vulnerable communities and the poor. ARB's scoping plan does neither of these things."[99] Adrienne Bloch of Communities for a Better Environment added, "The effect of this will be higher energy costs for Californians with little to no environmental benefit, and exporting jobs and public health co-benefits out of state in the midst of soaring unemployment and a statewide budget crisis."[100] The plaintiffs argued that reducing greenhouse gas emissions had a co-benefit in that emissions of pollutants and toxics were also reduced. Emissions of pollutants and toxics were already regulated, but the plaintiffs wanted further reductions, and they wanted those reductions in California rather than exporting them as would result when offsets were bought out of state. The plaintiffs complained that ARB failed to consider alternatives to a trading system such as direct regulation that would specify "maximum technologically feasible and cost-effective reductions." The plaintiffs also argued that ARB should have considered a carbon tax.

On March 17, 2011, San Francisco County Judge Ernest Goldsmith blocked further implementation of the Act, ruling that the ARB had failed to adequately justify its choice of a

---

[99]Press Release, "Environmental Justice Advocates File Suit to Force California to Follow the Law in Implementing the AB32 Global Warming Solutions Act," June 10, 2009.
[100]Ibid.

cap-and-trade system relative to alternative means of reducing greenhouse gas emissions.[101] He dismissed the direct regulation approach but held that a carbon tax should have been given greater consideration, noting that only two paragraphs in ARB's environmental study were devoted to justifying its choice. The plaintiffs were delighted. Bill Gallegos of Communities for a Better Environment said, "Allowing the most entrenched polluters to increase pollution violates our environmental rights and is not the way to stop poisoning our air and slow catastrophic climate change. Now the ARB has a chance to do it right and consider real alternatives to pollution trading."[102]

The author of AB 32, Fabian Nunez, responded, "It's a false assertion. There won't be more pollution."[103] In their press release the plaintiffs wrote, "Cap and trade is pollution trading that allows the worst polluters to continue or increase their pollution by buying 'reductions.' These polluters are disproportionately located in low income communities of color."[104] Tom Frantz of the Association of Irritated Residents commented, "This ruling will compel ARB to fully consider

those of us most affected by its decisions, and not just move forward in its haste to make major polluters happy."[105] Caroline Farrell, executive director for the Center on Race, Poverty & the Environment, said, "ARB refused to do its job so we were left with no other choice but to sue to protect public health."[106]

Preparation Questions

1. Is there merit in the claims by the environmental justice advocates that pollution by "major polluters" will increase under cap-and-trade?
2. Is a carbon tax any different from a cap-and-trade system if the tax is set to achieve 1990 emissions levels?
3. In addition to environmental justice considerations, were there other considerations that motivated the lawsuit? That is, is their objection to cap-and-trade or to offsets?
4. Will a carbon tax satisfy the plaintiffs?
5. How should ARB take environmental justice considerations into account?

---

[101]*Association of Irritated Residents v. California Air Resources Board (CARB)*. Case No. CPF-09-509562.
[102]*San Jose Mercury News*, March 22, 2011.
[103]Ibid.

[104]Press release, "Environmental Justice Groups Win: California Air Resources Board Forced to Revisit Alternatives to Unjust Pollution trading System," March 17, 2011.
[105]Ibid.
[106]Ibid.

THE INVESTOR'S PERSPECTIVE: RENEWABLE ENERGY

INTRODUCTION

Managing effectively in the nonmarket environment is essential for firms, particularly for a company at a major strategic crossroads or when there are market or nonmarket challenges. Strategy implementation is also essential on an ongoing basis at an operational level to achieve performance goals, address challenges, and seize opportunities. The competence of management in market and nonmarket strategy formulation and implementation is also important to investors in a company. Competence assures investors that the company will be able to address important market and nonmarket challenges effectively and lead the company successfully in its environment. From the investor's perspective the opportunities available to companies and the risks facing them in both their market and nonmarket environments must be assessed as well as the ability of the companies' leaders to chart a successful course through those environments. Managers must understand the concerns of those investors and hence understand their perspective.

This chapter adopts the investor's perspective and focuses on the analysis of risks and opportunities in the nonmarket environment of a company viewed as an investment opportunity. The perspective is that of a large investor such as a private equity fund or hedge fund that invests in post-start-up firms. To provide a specific context in which to apply the framework developed, the focus is on renewable energy and particularly solar power. In most countries solar power depends heavily on government subsidies, and those subsidies not only provide opportunities but also pose risks. The framework presented is applied to the case of a solar panel producer that was the first to receive a large loan guarantee from the U.S. government. The loan guarantee allowed it to build a state-of-the-art manufacturing plant to grow its solar panel business and attempt to become competitive, particularly relative to Chinese producers.

Investment Decisions

In making their decisions, investors assess both the opportunities and risks associated with firms and the quality of their management. The assessment of managerial quality depends not just on a firm's leadership and market strategy but also its nonmarket strategy and the ability of management to anticipate and deal effectively with the emergence and development of nonmarket issues.

For example, in 2011 renewable energy companies had attractive market opportunities in the United States but faced market risks including competition from domestic and foreign rivals, innovation and technological change, and changes in prices, exchange rates, and factor input prices. The opportunities depended importantly on government subsidies, and those subsidies required government appropriations, and their authorizations often had expiration dates that required renewal. In the absence of the subsidies many renewable energy companies would fail.

For example, wind power benefitted from a federal loan guarantee program that covered up to 80 percent of the cost of constructing wind projects. The loan guarantee allowed wind power producers to borrow on favorable terms and to borrow more than they would otherwise be able to borrow, but the loan guarantee program was scheduled to expire in September 2011. In addition, wind power producers were eligible for a 30 percent investment tax credit on construction costs, and producers could receive the credit up front in cash under the Department of the Treasury's 1603 program. The option to receive it in cash rather than as a credit against income taxes was scheduled to expire at the end of 2010. The loan guarantee and the cash option were in jeopardy for several reasons. First, the huge federal budget deficit required measures to reduce expenditures. Second, the 2010 congressional elections brought 63 new Republican representatives to the House and 6 new Republican senators, and many of them had pledged to reduce the budget deficit. Third, wind energy prices were determined by state public utility regulatory agencies, and many of them gave a large premium for wind power through high "feed-in tariffs." The cost of wind energy was then averaged into the prices residential and business customers paid. The high feed-in tariffs, however, were regulatory decisions that could be changed. One concern was that the higher electricity prices could drive some businesses out of the state or into bankruptcy, creating political pressure for lower prices. In addition, the growing market shares of Chinese wind tower and turbine producers generated complaints that the subsidies provided to U.S. wind power companies were being used to purchase equipment from abroad rather than to create jobs in the United States.

Nonmarket risks arise from public politics through legislation and regulatory decisions, as well as administrative rule making and court decisions. Nonmarket risks can also arise from private politics, including consumer reactions, activist and NGO challenges, and changes in public sentiment. Private politics generally was supportive of renewable power unless there were adverse environmental consequences.

THE ENVIRONMENT OF WIND AND SOLAR POWER

The long-term opportunities for wind and solar power were enormous. Supply costs were falling as efficiencies were achieved and new technologies were introduced and refined. Demand for renewable power was expected to continue to grow as fossil fuel prices increased and environmental concerns were attended to, particularly global climate change. Demand growth had been led by Europe as a result of generous subsidies, but as those subsidies were reduced, growth slowed. At the same time demand grew in China and the United States, and more countries began to support wind and solar power. Demand was expected to grow substantially in China and developing nations, but growth hinged on government support and the cost of other energy sources.

A 2011 study by the Solar Energy Industries Association and GTM Research found that the solar market in the United States grew from $3.6 billion in 2009 to $6.0 billion in 2010 with California the leader in installations with 259 megawatts (MW) of projects in 2010. The market included both the familiar rooftop installations of solar panels to solar farms and solar thermal plants that concentrated sunlight to heat water to drive turbines.[1]

Demand growth in the United States depended on government subsidies provided by both the federal and state governments, as well as on the costs of alternative power sources, primarily coal, natural gas, and nuclear. The 2011 study explained that part of the growth in the market in 2010 was due to the rush to begin projects before a subsidy program was expected to expire. "The U.S. PV [photovoltaic] market made the most significant strides in 2010, more than doubling installation totals from 2009 according to the latest U.S. Solar Market Insight[TM] report. This expansion was driven by the federal section 1603 Treasury program, completion of significant utility-scale projects, expansion of new state markets, and declining technology costs. The section 1603 Treasury program helped fourth-quarter installations surge to a record 359 MW and was critical in allowing the solar industry to employ more than 93,000 Americans in 2010. Originally set to expire at the end of 2010, the 1603 Treasury program was ultimately extended through 2011."[2]

Markets and Government Involvement

Retail electricity prices varied greatly across the states. The lowest average price was ¢6.21/kwh for Wyoming, and the highest on the continent was ¢17.41/kwh for Connecticut, with Illinois at ¢8.89, California at ¢13.16/kwh, and Texas at ¢8.7/kwh. The average for the United States was ¢9.62/kwh.[3] The attractiveness of solar power thus depended on the state as well as the subsidies provided. Solar and wind power were high cost, particularly because coal and natural gas prices were low. Natural gas prices decreased by 30 percent during 2010 before increasing slightly at the end of the year.

Both solar and wind power were quite variable. Wind generated 4 percent of the United Kingdom's electricity on a windy day and 0.04 percent on a calm day.[4] Solar power output also depended on the weather. Solar power could supply 10 percent of Germany's electricity demand—on sunny days. Wind power was most attractive in locations where the wind blows

---

[1] Solar Energy Industries Association and GTM Research, "U.S. Solar Market Insight 2010," March 11, 2011.
[2] Ibid.
[3] U.S. Energy Information Administration, Washington, D.C. Prices are for the year ending November 2010.
[4] *The Times* (London), February 15, 2011.

hard and steadily, as in the Great Plains region of the United States. Solar power was most efficient in the Southwest.

Wind power differed from solar power in that blades and tower sections were more costly to ship than were solar panels. This provided incentives to locate production of tower sections near the installation locations, whereas solar panel production could be located where manufacturing costs were low. Denmark's Vestes Wind Systems, the world's largest wind system producer, thus located tower production in the U.S. Midwest, whereas the largest solar panel manufacturers were in China. Turbines were high value relative to shipping costs, and their manufacture could be located anywhere.

China had the objective of being the world leader in renewable power and provided considerable support for its industry. One form of support was low-cost loans from government supported banks. The Obama administration countered with loan guarantees for renewable power included in its stimulus program the American Recovery and Reinvestment Act. The Department of Energy administered the loan guaranties and awarded the guarantees based on applications by companies. Critics of the program said the government was trying to pick winners rather than allowing the market to determine the winners.

Europe and particularly Spain and Germany had used high feed-in tariffs to spur renewable power, making those countries attractive markets for renewable power producers and their suppliers. Spain signed 25-year contracts with solar power producers paying €0.45 per kilowatt hour, which was nearly 10 times the rate paid for power from coal and gas power sources.[5] In 2009 Spain provided €2.6 billion in solar power subsidies.[6] The subsidies collided with the financial crisis that hit Spain, and the country lowered the tariffs for new solar power plants. It also sought to reduce its payments on existing contracts. Germany also began to reduce its feed-in tariffs in response to complaints by customers about the price of electricity. Germany cut its subsidies by 25 percent, and France halted high feed-in tariffs for household electricity. The chapter case *T-Solar and the Solar Power Market* concerns a Spanish solar panel producer that faced a changing environment for renewable power.

Suppliers began to feel the effects of the high cost of renewable power. General Electric reported that orders for wind turbines in the third quarter of 2010 decreased by 30 percent, and Vestes Wind Systems announced the layoff of 3,000 workers in Denmark and Sweden, although not at its 4 factories in the United States. Subsidies became more crucial.

Solar power faced nonmarket opposition not only because of the cost of subsidization but also because of environmental NIMBY. The federal government had opened public lands to renewable energy development but required reviews of environmental impacts and also granted individuals the right to sue. California had set an ambitious renewable power goal, and developers proposed large-scale solar power generation projects. After lengthy reviews and strong protests from environmentalists and others, California approved 11 plants. After approval, the environmental opponents turned to the courts to stop five of the plants in the Mojave Desert with planned output sufficient to power 2 million homes.[7] In 2011 Solar Millennium abandoned its planned project because of concerns about the impact on the Mojave ground squirrel. The Sierra Club and a labor union filed a lawsuit to block a project because of a threat to the desert tortoise and other desert wildlife. The Quechan American Indian Tribe obtained a preliminary injunction stopping a solar plant on its ancestral lands, and an American Indian group sought an injunction to stop five other plants.[8] The boxed example illustrates the challenges, and the chapter case *BrightSource Energy* considers a company dealing with those challenges.

Market Signals

The market for solar panels in Europe and the United States slowed to a crawl in 2010, whereas the market in China grew at a rapid pace. Although the short-term prospects in the Unites States were modest, the longer-term prospects were substantial. Analysts anticipated a fivefold increase in the market for solar panels and related technologies over the next 5 years. General Electric, which was a major supplier of wind turbines generating $6 billion in revenues in 2010, decided to become a major supplier of solar panels as part of its renewable energy strategy. In April 2011

---

[5]*Wall Street Journal*, December 23, 2010.
[6]Ibid.
[7]*New York Times*, February 26, 2011.
[8]Ibid.

EXAMPLE   Environmentalist Opposition

Solargen Energy of Cupertino, CA, designed a $1.8 billion project to build a solar power facility with 1.2 million solar panels on 4,717 acres of an 18,000 acre ranch to be purchased in the Panoche Valley in California. CEO Mike Peterson explained, "This is renewable energy. It doesn't cause pollution, it doesn't use coal or foreign oil, and it emits no greenhouse gasses."[1] The location had 90 percent of the solar intensity of the Mojave Desert, was 20 miles from the nearest town, and a major transmission line ran through the ranch. When operational the facility would supply 420 megawatts of electricity, enough to power 315,000 homes. The solar panels would be 3 feet off the ground to allow wildlife and animals such as sheep to pass under them.

Opposition to the facility began to mount. Local chapters of the Audubon Society opposed the project. Shani Kleinhaus said, "There is really very little information on how these sorts of projects impact the environment. We really

don't know....Put solar panels over parking lots. Put them along the freeways, in airports, landfills. There's plenty of space. In 5 years, with new technology, they may not even need this much space." The Audubon Society chapter noted that the Panoche Valley was home to several endangered species, including the San Joaquin kit fox, the blunt-nosed leopard lizard, and the giant kangaroo rat.[2] NIMBY opposition also arose from residents who expressed concern about the effects of the facility on the character of the area.

Peterson commented, "It was like everyone was in favor of renewable energy. But the solar industry is finding the politics are complicated. There's a lot of 'we love renewable, but not here, and not in my backyard.'"[3] The fate of the project rested with the San Benito County Board of Supervisors. Approval was finally given by the Board after 4 years, but lawsuits against the project remained. In addition, the company faced the challenge of obtaining funding of the project.

---

[1]*San Jose Mercury News*, December 23, 2009.

[2]Ibid.
[3]Ibid.

GE announced that it would build a solar panel plant with a capacity of 400 megawatts, making it the largest plant in the United States, exceeding the capacity of the Hillsboro, Oregon, plant of SolarWorld AG of Germany. GE's announcement followed its acquisition of PrimeStar Solar, which according to the Department of Energy produced the highest efficiency thin-film solar panels. The long-run prospects for solar panels anticipated by GE were soon after confirmed as Total SA of France, the world's sixth largest oil company, bought 60 percent of SunPower for $1.37 billion, representing a 40 percent premium above the company's share price. SunPower CEO Tom Werner said, "This is old energy betting on new energy. This is a bet for the future."[9]

The actions by GE and Total represented good and bad news for other solar panel producers. The good news was that two huge companies were optimistic about the growth of the solar panel market in the United States and worldwide. The bad news was that solar power start-ups now faced two more large competitors with deep pockets and access to alternative technologies.

ECONOMIC AND POLITICAL RATIONALES FOR SUBSIDIZATION

The economic rationales for the subsidization of renewable power are three fold. First, subsidization provides environmental improvements by displacing carbon-based power generated from coal or natural gas. Second, subsidization provides security benefits to the extent that it reduced the dependence on imported fuels.[10] Third, the subsidies could enable producers to realize economies of scale that would reduce costs and allow output to expand. The first and second rationales are based on positive externalities, whereas the third is intended to achieve cost efficiencies and increased output.

Subsidies are provided on both the demand and supply sides of the market for renewable power. Demand-side subsidies are provided to consumers, and supply-side subsidies are provided to power producers and their suppliers. Demand-side subsidies include grants or tax credits for households and businesses to install solar panels on rooftops or to purchase electric cars. Supply-side subsidies include high feed-in tariffs for power producers and grants and loan guarantees to solar panel producers, solar power producers, and electric utilities for smart grid infrastructure. The feed-in tariffs act like a tax on electricity used to finance the benefits from the

---

[9]*San Jose Mercury News*, April 29, 2011.
[10]Wind and solar power provided only modest reductions in oil imports.

first and second economic rationales for subsidization. In addition, 29 states had a Renewable Portfolio Standard (RPS) for power generated by wind, solar, geothermal, and biomass. This forced electric utilities to invest in alternative energy production or to contract with private producers. In some states the RPS led electric utilities to subsidize the installation of solar power panels by homeowners.

Subsidies were also either direct or indirect. Direct subsidies were provided to consumers and producers and required government expenditures, whereas indirect subsidies such as high feed-in tariffs were funded by higher prices to consumers of electricity. Direct subsidies were at risk at the federal level and in states with large budget deficits. High feed-in tariffs and RPS did not contribute to government budget deficits (other than through government as a consumer of electricity) and hence were less likely to be victims of the budget process.

There were also political rationales for the subsidization of renewable power. First, the positive externalities for the environment and security benefitted constituents, although those benefits were often difficult to observe. Second, subsidization generated pork, since the recipients of the subsidies and their suppliers earned rents from the economic activity stimulated by the subsidization. Demand-side rents were earned by installation companies and their employees, power producers and their employees, and suppliers. Rents from supply-side subsidization were earned by power producers and the producers of power generation inputs, such as solar panels. The U.S. government regularly cited the number of jobs created in the solar panel production and installation industries. An associated political rationale was that subsidies built interest group support for continued subsidization in a manner that the dispersed environmental and security benefits typically could not build.

Demand-side subsidies differed from supply-side subsidies in a way important for nonmarket risk analysis. The additional demand generated by demand-side subsidization could be satisfied by production located in the United States or overseas. The first political rationale thus was satisfied because the higher demand generated positive environmental externalities. The second political rationale of creating jobs, however, could only be realized by production located in the United States. Supply-side subsidization more directly served the second political rationale.

The Costs of Subsidization

The direct costs of subsidies such as grants and loan guaranties are the corresponding government budget expenditures and liabilities. Those expenditures ultimately require higher taxes, which distort economic activity, resulting in inefficiencies. Subsidization in the form of high feed-in tariffs raises electricity prices, which also distorts economic activity. Higher costs to businesses reduce their competitiveness, which reduces employment. Higher electricity prices also were regressive, harming low-income households more than high-income ones. U.S. consumers had benefited from the cost-efficient location of production in China and other low-cost countries, even though it meant the loss of high-paying jobs in the United States.

Subsidies are supplied through a political process. The renewable power lobby was well organized and active, and its interests were aligned with those of the Obama administration. Client politics prevailed, and subsidies were obtained on both the demand and supply sides of the market. The demand-side subsidies increased the supply of renewable power and decreased the negative externalities from emissions. The political question was whether the jobs created were in the United States or in other countries and whether jobs created in the United States would remain there. Supply-side subsidies were more likely to create U.S. jobs, since they were restricted to companies producing in the United States. At the dedication of a solar power plant in Arcadia, Florida, President Barack Obama, speaking about the effects of a grant funded by the American Recovery and Reinvestment Act, said, "It will provide smart meters to 2.6 million more customers. And most importantly, it will create thousands of jobs—good jobs, by the way, that can't be outsourced; jobs that will last and jobs that will pay a decent wage."[11] The economic and political rationales for the subsidization of renewable energy were well understood, and the more difficult question was the appropriate level of the subsidies.

The nonmarket dimensions of subsidization differed in another way. Direct grants required annual appropriations by a legislature whose members faced elections. High feed-in tariffs

---

[11]Barack Obama, "Remarks by the President on Recovery Act Funding for Smart Grid Technology," Arcadia, Florida, October 27, 2009.

were authorized by legislatures but once authorized remained in place. The tariffs required no appropriations and were set by regulators who in most states were appointed rather than elected. The cost of the high feed-in tariffs was paid by electricity customers through higher prices, and households were poorly organized to deliver political action to reduce the cost. Moreover, many consumers were happy to pay higher prices to support renewable power. Commercial and business customers, however, were better organized and motivated by competitiveness considerations. These customers posed a threat to high feed-in tariffs.

Although renewable energy production such as solar and wind power was not cost competitive and hence was dependent on subsidies, many smart grid applications were driven more by opportunities for efficiency than by government support. Companies involved in smart grid applications thus faced one fewer risk than did renewable energy producers and their suppliers. The chapter case *Silver Spring Networks and the Smart Grid* considers one such company.

Examples

California had a 20 percent RPS target for 2017, and the governor mandated that utilities generate or obtain 33 percent from renewable sources by 2020. California also provided state tax credits for home solar generation systems with a cap of $10,000 per home. The state budgeted $2.167 billion for 2007–2016 with the objective of generating 1,940 megawatt of new solar power. California had huge budget deficits, however, which threatened the subsidies.

As an example of the subsidies, the estimated cost of home solar panel installation cost for a 4 megawatt system in California was $26,000. The Federal/State Tax credit was $6,072, and the State/Utility Rebate was $5,760 for a net cost of $14,168.[12] The state's electric utilities opposed the tax rebates. Jennifer Briscoe of San Diego Gas & Electric said, "We want to make sure there isn't an unfair level of cost shifting."[13] "Cost shifting" referred to the higher rates borne by ratepayers who were unable to afford a solar power installation or were not located in areas where solar power was an attractive alternative.

Supply-side subsidies took one of three basic forms. The first was a grant for research and development. For example, the Department of Energy's ARPA-E grant program supported research at start-up firms. The second was a direct grant to a solar power producer to reduce the capital needed to build a solar farm. The third was the subsidization of a factor input such as capital. The federal government provided loan guarantees for renewable energy companies allowing them to borrow at lower interest rates than they would otherwise be able to obtain and allowing them to raise more funds that they otherwise could. For example, Abengoa Solar Inc., a unit of Spanish utility Abengoa S.A., received a $1.45 billion loan guarantee for the construction of a 250-megawatt solar power plant in Arizona that would use molten salt tanks to store heat to use in generating power when the sun was not shining.[14]

Subsidies were also provided by states to attract jobs. Stion, a manufacturer of thin-film solar panels located in San Jose, California, raised $70 million in Series D financing in June 2010, with $50 million from Taiwan Semiconductor Manufacturing Company (TSMC), the world's largest contract semiconductor manufacturer, which took a 21 percent ownership share in Stion. In September 2010 Stion received a $5 million loan with an interest rate of 2.75 percent from the California Energy Commission toward the $22.5 million expansion of its 10 megawatt pilot production factory in San Jose. The Commission trumpeted the 73 full-time jobs that would be created by the expansion and the 140 megawatts of annual capacity. Four months later Stion announced that it would build a $100 million factory in Hattiesburg, Mississippi, with an initial capacity of 100 megawatts and an anticipated $400 million of additional investment over the next 6 years to reach a production capacity of 500 megawatts. The factory was financed by a $75 million loan from the state of Mississippi along with other tax incentives. The company stated, "Our expansion in Hattiesburg is an integral part of our capital-efficient scale-up plan. The cost and time-to-market advantages of building here will provide a significant competitive advantage."[15] Stion cancelled its planned expansion of its San Jose facility and entered into negotiations with the California Energy Commission over the

---

[12]www.dasolar.com/energytaxcredit-rebates-grants/california, accessed November 27, 2010.
[13]*Los Angeles Times*, July 6, 2009.
[14]*Wall Street Journal*, December 31, 2010.
[15]Stion, Press release, January 4, 2011.

$5 million loan. In conjunction with its investment, TSMC licensed Stion's technology and contracted to produce panels for Stion to sell.

Companies must survive in the short run to succeed in the long run. Survival and success depend on the demand for renewable power, which is largely outside the control of firms operating on the supply side of the market. Survival and success also depend on the cost side, and firms competing in the solar power market developed a variety of technologies. Which would survive would be decided through competition and innovation. The location of production also would be determined by cost considerations. Competition in solar power had intensified as producers in China had achieved economies of scale, driving down costs. The example illustrates both a location choice and the market risks.

One hope for U.S. producers was new technology that would lower costs below those that could be achieved with silicon-based photovoltaic panels. As the Evergreen Solar example indicates, however, production using a new technology could always be moved to a low-cost location. One company with a new technology was Solyndra.

EXAMPLE   The Market Threat from China

In 2010 Evergreen Solar was the third largest producer of solar panels in the United States, and its innovative String Ribbon® products were widely used in Europe and the United States. Its principal manufacturing plant was in Devens, Massachusetts, and the company had received $43 million in assistance from the state government for the plant, which opened in 2008. The company had been able to lower its manufacturing costs more rapidly than it had anticipated, but the prices of photovoltaic (PV) solar panels had been dropping more rapidly as Chinese manufacturers increased their scale. Eleven Chinese producers had greater output in 2010 than the largest U.S. producer, and three of them—Suntech Power, Yingli Green Energy, and Trina Solar—were five times larger.[1]

The cost advantage of photovoltaic panel producers in China was due to scale economies, labor and supply chain costs, and government support. The average factory wage in China was $300 a month compared to $5,400 in Massachusetts. In addition, an efficient supply chain had developed to support producers in China. Photovoltaic solar panel production was capital intensive, so the labor cost advantage provided only part of the explanation for the cost differential. SunTech Power CEO and founder Zhengrong Shi noted that when his company began in 2001 the cost of solar panels was $6 per watt, and by 2011 it had fallen to $1.60, "This is all because of manufacturing innovation, innovation along the supply chain. And it is not revolutionary. It looks more incremental, but it is very effective."[2]

In January 2011 Evergreen Solar's CEO Michael El-Hillow stunned the state of Massachusetts by announcing that the company was closing its Devens plant and transferring output to its joint-venture plant in Wuhan, China, which had been ramping up production.[3] He explained, "Although production costs at our Devens facility have steadily decreased, and are now below originally planned levels and lower than most western manufacturers, they are still much higher than those of our low cost competitors in China." He added, "While overall demand for solar may increase, we expect that significant capacity expansions in low cost manufacturing regions combined with potential adverse changes in government subsidies in several markets in Europe will likely result in continuing pressure on selling prices throughout 2011. Solar manufacturers in China have received considerable government and financial support and, together with their low manufacturing costs, have become price leaders in the industry. While the United States and other western industrial economies are beneficiaries of rapidly declining installation costs of solar energy, we expect the United States will continue to be at a disadvantage from a manufacturing standpoint."[4] El-Hillow explained that low-cost financing in China was provided by state-owned banks and by local governments.[5] Evergreen Solar had a loss of $27 million in the third quarter of 2010 on sales of $86.5 million. Its share price had fallen from over $100 in 2008 to $3 in January 2011. Evergreen finally gave up in August 2011, declaring bankruptcy and hoping to reorganize and operate from China.

Innovalight, a start-up thin-film module producer, began producing solar panels in 2008 in a 10-megawatt capacity factory using silicon ink that improved efficiency. By 2010 the company had abandoned production and begun licensing its technology to Chinese producers. Innovalight's CEO Conrad Burke commented, "How do you fight against enormous subsidies, low-interest loans, cheap labor and scale and a government strategy to make you No. 1 in solar?"[6]

[1]*New York Times*, January 15, 2011.
[2]*San Jose Mercury News*, July 19, 2011.
[3]SunPower had moved its production to the Philippines, and FirstSolar had moved production to Malaysia.
[4]Evergreen Solar, Press Release, January 11, 2011.
[5]*New York Times*, January 15, 2011.
[6]*New York Times*, October 15, 2010.

EXAMPLE: SOLYNDRA, INC.

The principal technology for solar power was photovoltaic, which used materials similar to silicon-based semiconductors. Two layers of silicon were covered by metal and glass to form a flat panel, with one layer positively (p) charged and the other negatively (n) charged. Sunlight striking the p-layer caused an electron to jump to the n-layer. An opening in the p-layer was then filled by an electron from an adjacent atom, causing electricity to flow when wires were attached to the p- and n-layers. The cost of solar panels had been high in part because of the scarcity and high price of pure silicon in 2006 and because the low volume of most producers was insufficient to generate substantial economies of scale.

In response to the high price of pure silicon, thin-film technology was developed using copper indium gallium selenide (CIGS) or other less costly materials. CIGS cells could be deposited on materials such as glass or metal in a manner similar to printing with ink on paper. Solyndra, Inc., founded by a veteran of Applied Materials and funded by venture capital, had developed a new thin-film technology applied to cylinders. The cylinders were less efficient in capturing solar energy and converting it to electricity than flat panels but were expected to cost less to produce and install. Solyndra's technology used CIGS.

In 2008 Solyndra and Solar Power, Inc., a leading installer of solar panels, agreed to a supply arrangement for $325 million of solar panels over the 2008–2012 period. Solar Power CEO Steve Kircher stated, "Solyndra's panels are highly innovative and offer unique design features that differentiate them from conventional panels. Their panels and simple mounting systems are quick to install and have outstanding energy production."[16] The supply agreement called for increasing volumes over time and decreasing prices per watt of electricity generated. Solyndra panels were ideal for white-coated roofs, since they produced electricity from reflective as well as direct sunlight. They also had the advantage of being lightweight in addition to their low installation cost.

As 2010 began, optimism was widespread for renewable energy. The research firm Clean Edge forecast that the global market would increase from $30 billion in 2008 to $81 billion in 2018. Silicon Valley expected to be the leader, since the technology of solar power generation was closely related to the technology for semiconductor manufacturing. T. J. Rodgers, the founder of Cypress Semiconductor and chairman of SunPower, a San Jose-based solar panel producer, said, "Energy is the biggest opportunity Silicon Valley has ever seen."[17] John Doerr, a leading venture capitalist, said that Silicon Valley could someday be known as Solar Valley.

In 2009 California received over $2 billion in venture capital for clean tech with Khosla Ventures raising $1.1 billion. Vinod Khosla commented on the clean tech opportunities: "This is one of the largest new opportunities that Silicon Valley has seen, but competition from other areas will be extensive. We (in Silicon Valley) don't have a natural advantage in talent—like chemical engineers, fermentation experts, engine designers and physicists. But we do have a support culture for entrepreneurship and a culture of risk-taking. This gives us a head start."[18] Congress and President Barack Obama backed the industry with moral and financial support, arguing that the support would spur economic growth.

In 2010 the *Wall Street Journal* ranked the clean tech venture capital-funded companies, and Solyndra headed the list. Solyndra applied for a federal loan guarantee and after a 6-month review received a guarantee for a $535 million loan provided by the Treasury's Federal Financing Bank. The loan guarantee was the first granted under the Department of Energy (DOE) program established by the Energy Policy Act of 2005 and expanded in 2008 and then greatly expanded in the American Recovery and Reinvestment Act of 2009. The stimulus also extended the 30 percent Residential Solar Investment Tax Credit for 8 years through 2016 and removed the $2,000 cap on the credit for residential solar generation.

The DOE had moved slowly in reviewing loan guarantee applications under the Energy Policy Act in part because of the failed 1980s loan guarantee program for alternative fuels production. Every company that had borrowed under that program had defaulted on the loans, costing taxpayers $15 billion. In part the defaults were due to the withdrawal of price supports for alternative fuels by the Reagan administration as oil prices dropped. DOE said it would be different this time and approved the loan guarantee for Solyndra in record time. DOE press secretary

---

[16]*New York Times*, October 15, 2010.
[17]*San Jose Mercury News*, January 30, 2010.
[18]Ibid.

Stephanie Mueller stated, "The market for photovoltaics has been growing by 40 percent a year, so we expect that Solyndra will have a very bright future."[19]

To qualify for the loan guarantee Solyndra raised nearly $198 million in equity financing led by Argonaut Private Equity and broke ground for a $733 million, 300,000 square foot factory called Fab 2 in Fremont, California. California governor Arnold Schwarzenegger and Secretary of Energy Steven Chu attended a groundbreaking celebration at Solyndra's existing Fab 1 facility, and Vice President Joe Biden spoke via close-circuit television to the attendees. Chu said, "At the Energy Department we've moved aggressively to move these dollars out the door to help with American recovery. It's about laying a foundation for our future prosperity …. We're helping turn groundbreaking ideas like Solyndra's into groundbreaking ceremonies like this."[20] Solyndra CEO and founder Dr. Chris Gronet said the plant would help "save our planet from the threat of global warming."[21]

The Obama administration made Solyndra the poster child for its clean energy program. In May 2010 President Obama visited the factory site while still under construction and said, "The true engine of economic growth will always be companies like Solyndra." The company expected to begin production in November 2010 in Fab 2. Sales reached $70 million in 2009. Solyndra reported that 2,000 temporary jobs were created in the construction of the factory, and it expected to have 1,000 full-time employees.

In December 2009 Solyndra filed for an initial public offering (IPO), anticipating raising $300 million. It expected to have a production capacity of 610 megawatts by 2013. Stephen O'Rourke, an analyst with Deutsche Bank, observed, "The first CIGS company to deliver will be an enormous hit. A lot of people bought tickets, and now it's time to deliver."[22]

The market opportunities for thin-film solar panels received a boost from Wal-Mart's corporate sustainability program. Wal-Mart signed a contract with SolarCity to install solar panels on its retail outlets and reserved a significant proportion of them for thin-film panels.[23]

Risks and Opportunities Assessment

This section focuses on the risks and opportunities in the market and nonmarket environments of Solyndra. Solar power was not cost competitive with power generated by burning coal or natural gas, so the opportunities hinged on government support, making nonmarket forces crucial for the company. As considered below in more detail, public politics at the federal level took the form of client politics with solar panel customers, solar power producers, and suppliers supporting the subsidies. Support was also provided by states that had renewable power standards, folded high costs into the prices paid by consumers, and provided direct subsidies. The other side of the government-support coin was the risk that the subsidies would be scaled back. Reductions in the subsidies would require a political entrepreneur to lead the public politics competition between the pro-subsidy interests and the opposing interests. Opportunities could also be restricted through regulation, which in the case of solar power was largely at the state level.

NGOs, social activists, and green consumers were supportive of renewable energy, but there was little they could do in the absence of government. They could play a role in public politics, although their views were already well known. They generally supported the subsidization of renewable power, and many of their renewable power goals could be met by demand-side support such as subsidies for installed systems and high feed-in tariffs. The demand side could be satisfied by producers located overseas or in the United States. The NGOs were less focused on the second political rationale of providing jobs, which was crucial for Solyndra's success, at least in the short run.

One institutional arena in which NGOs might have an impact was with state public utility commissions (PUCs) that set the feed-in tariffs for renewable power. The high feed-in tariffs were key to the economics of large-scale solar generation plants and also allowed customers with rooftop installations to reduce their electricity bills and to sell excess power into the grid. Some states also allowed customers to buy green power at a price premium, although these programs had experienced only limited success.

---

[19]Platt's *Global Power Report*, September 10, 2009.
[20]Ibid.
[21]Ibid.
[22]*San Jose Mercury News*, January 31, 2010.
[23]*New York Times*, October 13, 2010.

TABLE 13-1 Solar Power Opportunities and Risks—Market and Nonmarket Factors

Opportunities

Market Factors	Nonmarket Factors
Growth in electricity demand	Subsidies
Costs of alternative power sources	High feed-in tariffs
Green preferences of customers	Loan guarantees
	Direct grants (e.g., installation)
	Research and development
	Protections
	Renewable power standards

Risks

Market Factors	Nonmarket Factors
Competition	Reductions in subsidies
Technology	Electricity customer opposition
Innovation	Subsidization of producers by other countries
Factor price changes	Environmental NIMBY

Table 13-1 identifies the market and nonmarket factors that affect the performance of Solyndra, organized by opportunities and risks. The opportunities have been identified above and in earlier sections, and the risks are considered in more detail next.

Market Risks: Prices and Costs

In the factor input market the price of pure silicon fell substantially in 2009 reducing the cost cushion relative to photovoltaic solar panels that Solyndra and other CIGS producers had anticipated. This spurred sales of photovoltaic panels, and producers began to achieve economies of scale that also lowered prices substantially. In addition, Chinese producers received subsidies in the form of low-cost loans, and received free land provided by provincial and local governments for plants. SuntechPower, JA Solar, and Yingli became low-cost producers of photovoltaic modules. JA Solar reported that by the end of 2010 it would have 1.8 gigawatts of capacity and 11,000 employees.[24] The prices of solar panels plummeted by 40 percent in 2010 and by 30 percent in 2011. The anticipated price advantage for thin-film solar modules had shrunk or disappeared, putting pressure on producers to reduce their costs. Ben Bierman of Solyndra commented on the effect of low-cost suppliers, "It definitely puts more pressure on us to bring our costs down as quickly as possible by ramping up volume."[25]

In addition to low prices, Chinese photovoltaic panel producers offered attractive financing and captured 40 percent of the California market. Arno Harris, CEO of solar developer Recurrent Energy of San Francisco, explained why his company had signed a supply contract with Yingli, "We realized that would enable us to bid competitive power prices from projects that could also be efficiently financed."[26]

Low-cost production and solar efficiency were keys to success in the solar panel industry, and a measure of competitiveness was the cost per watt of electricity generated. By the end of 2010 First Solar had reduced its cost to $0.75/watt, and Chinese producers had lower costs. Solyndra's initial costs were high, and it worked hard to reduce them.

Nonmarket Risks

The public politics risks centered on Congress, which had to approve the subsidies and other federal support for renewable power. The severe recession, the slow and uneven recovery, the huge federal budget deficit resulting from the recession and the stimulus expenditures, and the Obama administration's seeming focus on issues other than the economy resulted in voter

---

[24]*New York Times*, October 15, 2010.
[25]*New York Times*, October 13, 2010. The growth in demand for solar panels in 2010 caused the price of pure silicon to rise. DigiTimes forecasted that prices would increase by 15–30 percent in late 2010.
[26]*New York Times*, October 15, 2010.

anger with incumbents in Congress. The predictions for the 2010 election were borne out with Republicans gaining a majority in the House, substantial gains in the Senate, and large gains in state governments. Voter sentiment supported reducing the federal deficit without raising taxes. Although public sentiment continued to support the environment, renewable power was not immune to deficit reduction pressures or from opposition to the subsidies provided on both the demand and supply sides of the renewable power market. Solar power also competed with other renewable power sources, such as wind, geothermal, and biomass, all of which sought subsidies. The nonmarket risks for Solyndra were substantial.

The recipients of the subsidies were consumers who purchased solar systems, solar power producers, and suppliers. Consumers were poorly organized for political action, although installation companies could represent their interests. Solar power producers and their suppliers were well organized.

The cost of the subsidies was borne by taxpayers, and electricity customers bore the cost of high feed-in tariffs. Taxpayers would eventually be required to cover the cost of the subsidies, and in the short run the subsidies increased the budget deficit. The analysis of the support for and opposition to the subsidization of solar power is considered in more detail in the next section.

The challenge to the subsidies for renewable power and solar power in particular came from entrepreneurial politics, and there were many entrepreneurs in the newly elected Congress and state governments. At the federal level support for solar power was protected to some extent by the presidential veto, but subsidies had to be reauthorized and appropriations made, which required positive action by Congress. Political entrepreneurs could build a blocking majority or could muster a filibuster in the Senate to force lower subsidies. This could lead to bargaining between the administration and those opposed to large subsidies.

Distributive Politics Analysis

The market opportunities and the government subsidization provided distributive benefits that motivated public politics in support of and opposition to continued government subsidization. The beneficiaries include the supply-side participants in wind, solar, geothermal, and biomass segments of the renewable power industry. The beneficiaries also include citizens with green preferences or security concerns. To simplify the exposition, the focus here is on solar. The beneficiaries are solar panel producers such as Solyndra, companies that install solar panel systems, suppliers, the public (from reduced carbon dioxide emissions), and green consumers and NGOs. Those who bear the costs are taxpayers, electricity customers, local residents (those located near wind and solar farms), and some environmentalists. Electric utilities are conflicted, with interests on both sides. They bear costs to the extent that they purchase power from solar installations at high feed-in tariffs, since the resulting higher prices add to the pressure on state-level rate setting. They benefit to the extent that they are under RPS mandates, since the additional power generated counts toward their mandate. This benefit results whether the suppliers of solar panels are located in the United States or in other countries. The utilities operate in a relatively transparent regulatory environment and under scrutiny by the media, NGOs, and large customers, so their efforts are likely to be muted at the federal level. The state level is their focus.

The costs of federal subsidization are widely distributed among taxpayers and electricity customers, who are large in numbers but the per capita costs they bear are small. The exceptions are large industrial and commercial electricity customers that are forced to pay higher rates for electricity, affecting their competitiveness. Some have the alternative of moving their facilities to states with lower power costs or to other countries. Local residents frequently oppose (NIMBY) large installations such as solar farms, but those residents are few in number. Moreover, their protests often center on licensing, which is a state prerogative.[27] Their incentives for political action may be stronger at the state level than at the federal level.[28] Environmentalists, such as those that opposed renewable power projects as in the Solargen Energy example, also had incentives to oppose certain individual projects.

---

[27]The federal government is involved in licensing and approvals for solar power production on public lands. See the chapter case *BrightSource Energy: The Challenges.*

[28]Protests by residents slowed the development of onshore wind power in the United Kingdom, and the wind power industry announced that it would pay local communities £2,000 for each turbine installed in the community. The anti-wind campaigners said they would not be dissuaded from their protests, calling the payment a bribe. (*The Times* (London), February 15, 2011.)

The benefits from continued subsidization were widely dispersed among the public as well as concentrated on a relatively small number of producers, suppliers, and those electricity customers who sought installation subsidies. The costs were widely distributed, so client politics led by those with concentrated benefits characterized the political competition. That is, the beneficiaries sought to have government view them as clients who warranted continued subsidization. The other side of the client politics coin is entrepreneurial politics, where an entrepreneur seeks to eliminate the subsidization by representing those who bear its cost. The entrepreneurs were members of Congress who represent the interests of taxpayers and electricity customers and could claim credit for acting in their interests.

Among the beneficiaries, the producers of solar panels and the installers for residential and commercial customers are direct beneficiaries. Solar panel producers are relatively few in number, and the direct employment they provide is modest. Moreover, the producers have limited resources and limited coverage of congressional districts. Installers, however, are more numerous, and they are labor intensive. They provide much greater coverage than do producers, but coverage is better in regions that are more conducive to solar power production. Solar power producers such as companies that operate solar farms are small in numbers, and they are relatively concentrated in areas where the sun is most intense. Suppliers include not only those that supply components but also those that provide financing and professional services to producers and customers. The following section on implementation describes the suppliers and their activities.

The public is a beneficiary from reduced emissions of pollutants and greenhouse gasses, but their incentives to take political action are weak, although their interests are represented by green NGOs. The public also consumes electricity, and as taxpayers they pay the cost of the subsidization. The interests of taxpayers and customers are represented by a different set of NGOs. In many states residential customers are represented by NGOs in rate setting proceedings of the public utility regulators, but those NGOs are often aligned with green NGOs and are not likely to oppose high feed-in tariffs. The influence of NGOs is likely to be limited and in support of continued subsidies.

In client politics the clients face weak opposition and frequently win. The Obama administration proposed large increases in spending for renewable energy projects, particularly for solar, biomass, and geothermal. The huge budget deficits at the federal and state levels provided an opportunity for entrepreneurs in Congress and state legislatures to represent taxpayers and future generations that would bear the cost of the deficits. Moreover, many new members of Congress were elected because of their opposition to high government spending.

Implementation

The incentives of suppliers were strong, and 18 suppliers had formed an association, the U.S. Partnership for Renewable Energy Finance (US PREF), to advocate their interests. Members included the banks Citigroup, Deutsche Bank, Credit Suisse, Morgan Stanley, Bank of America, and GE Capital; Google; professional services firms; and the renewable energy companies Solar City, First Solar, and Starwood Energy Group. Their influence activities focused on the jobs created by renewable energy subsidization and in particular the 1603 Treasury grant program, a demand-side subsidy program.

The 1603 program was created to provide tax credits for renewable energy projects, but much of the credits could not be used by qualified participants, since their profits were too low to use the credits. This problem was solved by the participants selling their credits to "tax equity" investors, usually financial institutions that used the credits to offset their taxes. The financial crisis, however, caused some of these investors to fail, and others had losses or much lower profits and could not use the tax credits. Congress responded by allowing qualified participants to take the tax credits in the form of an immediate cash grant.[29] The cash grants were crucial for solar and wind producers, including residential and business customers that installed solar panels.

The clients had two objectives in 2010. The immediate objective was renewal of the 1603 program, which would expire at the end of the year. The broader objective was the renewal of the subsidization programs for renewable power at both the federal and state levels. The strategy was to emphasize the direct benefits to constituents, and the clearest direct benefit was jobs—the

---

[29]Tax equity investors were still needed to purchase the depreciation deductions, which participants also sold.

political rationale for subsidization. The strategy was implemented through informational lobbying. In addition, members of Congress were reminded of the more difficult to quantify environmental and security benefits. Producers of solar panels and wind turbines emphasized the need to achieve scale economies to be competitive.

To preserve the 1603 program, US PREF reminded Congress members of earlier studies of the jobs created by the subsidization, and in addition it developed its own projections for 2011.[30] The Lawrence Berkeley National Laboratory and the National Renewable Energy Laboratory had estimated that the Treasury grant program would create 143,199 jobs in wind power, and the Solar Industries Energy Association and International Solar estimated that 58,180 jobs would be created in solar power through 2016. US PREF also reported that the share of imports per dollar spent on wind power had declined from 85 percent in 2006 to 39 percent in 2009, so domestic suppliers had gained market share. US PREF estimated that if the Treasury grant program were not renewed for 2011 104,068 jobs would be lost and $24.6 billion of scheduled projects would not proceed.[31] The presidents of the Solar Energy Industry Association and the American Wind Energy Association also argued that 20,000 presently employed workers would lose their jobs if the 1603 grant program were eliminated. US PREF broke out its estimates of projects by state, identifying 17 states affected. Coverage of congressional districts was relatively good for client politics.

This jobs information was the basis for informational lobbying in Congress. Large wind power producers such as wind farm companies were active lobbyists as were companies such as General Electric with a 40 percent share of installed wind turbines. Members of both the House and Senate circulated letters seeking signatures supporting the grant program. By early December 2010 between 15 and 20 percent of the members had signed.[32] The 1603 Program was renewed for 1 year in December 2010 during the last days of Democrat majorities in Congress, but would it survive congressional budget cutting in 2011 and beyond?

Nonmarket Risks: China

The market for solar panels is global, and firms in many countries are capable of producing the panels. Photovoltaic solar cells are based on a technology similar to that used to produce semiconductors, and most semiconductors are produced in East Asia with some production in Europe and the United States. Although Solyndra had an innovative CIGS technology, its panels competed with the more conventional photovoltaic panels. A firm installing a solar system or building a solar generation plant could use panels with either technology, and price was an important factor in the choice. Chinese manufacturers with conventional photovoltaic technology set the cost standard for the industry. Moreover, China maintained a lower dollar–yuan exchange rate than if the market were allowed to set the rate, although China had allowed the exchange rate to rise somewhat in 2010.

Chapter 16 addresses the political economy of China, and a principal message in that chapter is that the Chinese government is authoritarian and can act quickly and decisively. Moreover, the size of the Chinese economy means that resources can be readily mobilized by government in the domestic capital and factor input markets. The Chinese government views renewable energy as an attractive industry for growth and also for dealing with China's substantial pollution problems and its high-energy usage. That the Chinese government would provide incentives for renewable energy companies, and even generous subsidies, was not surprising.

To address the subsidy and exchange rate policies of China, the United States first attempted to pressure the Chinese government to reduce its subsidization but with little effect. The United States could file a trade complaint with the World Trade Organization (WTO) on Chinese subsidization, but such complaints can take years to resolve (see Chapter 19). Moreover, it is not clear that the WTO would decide in favor of the United States. In addition, a trade complaint would likely lead China to file a trade complaint focusing on U.S. subsidization. Action by the WTO could be outside the time frame of Solyndra and its investors.

The United Steel Workers Union filed a Section 301 petition complaining that China subsidized wind turbine production and provided other subsidies for renewable power that were in violation of WTO rules. No U.S. company joined the union in the complaint. The United States

---

[30]US PREF, "Impact of Jobs through the Extension of the ARRA 1603 Cash Grant," September 2010.

[31]The job estimates did not include jobs at U.S. solar panel producers, where the numbers would be smaller.

[32]Cleanenergyauthority.com, December 9, 2010.

Trade Representative conducted an investigation of the complaints and in December 2010 initiated the consultation phase of the WTO dispute settlement procedure. (This procedure is considered in more detail in Chapter 19.) China reacted angrily to the complaint. Zhang Guobao, head of China's National Energy Administration, said, "The United States will not win this trade war against China's new energy sector. The probe will backfire by exposing more of the huge subsidies to America's own clean energy sector."[33]

Developments

In the audit report included in the April 2010 prospectus for Solyndra's IPO, Pricewaterhouse Coopers criticized the company's performance: "[Solyndra] has suffered recurring losses from operations, negative cash flows since inception and has a net stockholders' deficit that, among other factors, raise substantial doubt about its ability to continue as a going concern."[34] In June 2010 Solyndra withdrew its IPO because of an anticipated weak demand for its shares, and instead raised $175 million in a private placement of secured convertible promissory notes. Christopher Gronet resigned as CEO, but remained chairman of the board. The company recruited Brian Harrison from Intel as CEO.

Solyndra opened its $733 million Fab 2, state-of-the-art robotic factory 2 months early on September 13, 2010. Seven weeks later it announced that it was closing its Fab 1 factory and consolidating production in its more efficient plant. CEO Harrison commented on the decision, "Fab 2 is much more efficient and cost-effective than our existing facility. We're adjusting our plans to be more in line with where the market is and where our business is at the moment."[35] The closure of Fab 1 resulted in the layoff of 135 contract workers and 20 to 40 employees; Solyndra capped its workforce at 1,000. The company also scaled back its estimates of its projected capacity. Spokesperson David Miller explained, "Solar has become incredibly competitive …. Our customers tell us we have to keep our prices competitive. Our greatest challenge is to lower that cost."[36] Solyndra also postponed the planned expansion of Fab 2.

Solyndra lost $119.8 million for the first 9 months of 2010 and did not expect to be cash-flow positive until 2011. Shyam Mehta, an analyst for GTM Research, commented, "Solyndra has a new technology, a new product design. It has potential. The question is whether the potential reward justifies the risk."[37]

Things turned for the worse in January 2011 as the politics of renewable power subsidization focused on Solyndra. The House Energy and Commerce Committee launched an investigation of Solyndra's $535 loan guarantee and asked the Department of Energy for all documents related to the guarantee. Chairman Fred Upton (R-MI) and Oversight Subcommittee Chairman Cliff Stearns (R-FL) wrote to Secretary Steven Chu explaining that "subsequent events raise questions about whether Solyndra was the right candidate to receive a loan guarantee in excess of half a billion dollars."[38] They pointed to the auditor's report, the closing of Fab 1, and the postponement of plans to expand Fab 2.[39] Commentators speculated that the investigation might have been motivated by suspicion that the loan guarantee was a political decision, since the majority investor in Solyndra was Argonaut Private Equity, controlled by the George Kaiser Family Foundation of Oklahoma billionaire George Kaiser, who was a fund-raising bundler for the Obama–Biden campaign in 2008. The subcommittee issued subpoenas for documents pertaining to the loans.

In February 2011 Solyndra restructured, obtaining a $75 million loan from current investors, and the Department of Energy restructured its loan agreeing to an extension of the amortization period and giving priority to the loan from the current investors. The company also stated that it expected to have the installed cost of its solar cells down to $2 per watt by 2013. Sales for 2010 exceeded $140 million.[40]

---

[33]*The Times* (London), December 12, 2010.
[34]Platt's *Electric Utility Week*, April 26, 2010.
[35]*New York Times*, November 3, 2010.
[36]*San Jose Mercury News*, November 13, 2010.
[37]Ibid.
[38]Fred Upton and Cliff Stearns, Letter to Steven Chu, February 17, 2011.
[39]Andrew Malcolm, "Top of the Ticket," *Los Angeles Times*, February 23, 2011. John Rossomando, "Green jobs company endorsed by Obama and Biden squandered $535 million in stimulus money," *The Daily Caller*, February 22, 2011.
[40]Solyndra, Inc., "New Investment Funds Rapid Manufacturing and Sales Growth," February 28, 2011.

In August 2011 Solyndra abruptly closed its plant, let go all its 1,100 employees without severance payments, and filed for bankruptcy. The company had drawn $527 million on its loan guarantee, and whether the government would recover any of the funds was unclear. Private investors had invested over $1 billion in the company. Solyndra's failure was the third by solar panel producers in the month. In addition to Solyndra and Evergreen, SpectraWatt, a spin-off of Intel, declared bankruptcy. In 2011 seven U.S. solar panel producers led by SolarWorld Industries America filed a trade complaint against China charging subsidization and dumping of panels, but it was too late for the failed companies. China vigorously opposed the complaints.

After Solyndra failed, Chairman Upton stepped up the investigation of the loan guarantee, issuing a subpoena for White House correspondence with the Department of Energy on the guarantee. The FBI raided Solyndra's offices to collect documents. Critics renewed their objections to the government trying to pick winners.

SUMMARY

Investors assess the opportunities and risks associated with their investment alternatives, and this chapter has focused on the risks associated with renewable power companies. Market risks come from both domestic and overseas companies, and those companies differ because of their home country market and nonmarket environments. Chinese solar panel producers benefitted from a number of government policies that lowered their costs, but their primary advantage came from the markets. Labor costs were very low relative to the costs in Europe and the United States, and domestic demand for solar panels grew rapidly. Moreover, countries subsidized the demand side, allowing Chinese producers to achieve economies of scale. In addition, the price of pure silicon fell dramatically as supply caught up with demand, giving an additional advantage to photovoltaic panels, the primary product of the leading Chinese producers. Solar panel producers in the United States faced price pressure with panel prices falling sharply.

The U.S. government provided subsidization on both the demand and supply sides of the market for renewable power. The subsidies were motivated in part by the objectives of reducing greenhouse gases emissions and reliance on oil imports. The subsidies were also motivated by political concerns as the Obama administration sought to create jobs during the faltering economic recovery. The political objectives posed nonmarket risks, since subsidies were costly and their benefits were difficult to identify. Supply-side subsidization such as the loan guarantees faced both nonmarket and market risks, whereas subsidization through high feed-in tariffs was largely independent of budget pressures. The principal risk to subsidization through high feed-in tariffs was from business customers forced to pay higher prices for electricity, as was developing in Europe.[41] The nonmarket risk to demand-side subsidization stemmed both from government budget concerns and imported solar panels that hindered achieving the political objective of creating jobs. Client politics had prevailed but was threatened by opposition entrepreneurial politics motivated by the objective of reducing government expenditures.

CASES

BrightSource Energy: The Challenges

INTRODUCTION

In the 1980s Arnold Goldman's company Luz International built nine solar thermal plants in the California desert using parabolic troughs to concentrate sunlight to boil oil that drove turbines to generate electricity. Falling crude oil prices put an end to solar thermal projects until a revival near the end of the first decade of the 2000s. Solar thermal plants were built in Spain supported by high feed-in tariffs. A solar thermal plant in Seville used tracking mirrors called heliostats to concentrate the sun's rays to boil water to drive turbines. The Spanish company Acciona built a solar thermal plant in Nevada in 2007. With support for solar thermal growing in the United States, Goldman formed BrightSource Energy with the objective of building large-scale solar thermal plants. BrightSource's first U.S. project was the Ivanpah plant.

---

[41]See the chapter case *T-Solar and the Solar Panel Market*.

THE IVANPAH SOLAR ELECTRIC GENERATION SYSTEM

The Ivanpah solar thermal plant would be the largest in the world when completed in 2013.[42] The technology used heliostats to concentrate sunlight on a boiler to produce superheated steam to drive a conventional turbine to generate electricity. The boiler and turbine were to be mounted on a 459-foot-high tower, and three towers were planned for Ivanpah. The first tower was expected to be completed by mid-2012 and the other two by 2013. Construction began on the first plant and tower in October 2010, and the governor of California and the Secretary of the Interior were present at the groundbreaking.

The $2.1 billion plant was located on public land in the Mojave Desert northeast of Los Angeles near the Nevada border. The plant received a $1.37 billion loan guarantee, one of the first approved under the federal program established by the 2009 American Recovery and Reinvestment Act. The plant also qualified for the Department of Treasury's Section 1603 cash grant program that would reimburse the developer for 30 percent of the construction costs when the plant came online.[43]

The generation costs for the Ivanpah plant were necessarily uncertain. Nathaniel Bullard, a solar analyst for Bloomberg New Energy Finance, estimated that solar thermal plants could generate electricity at approximately 13–17 cents per kwh after including the federal subsidies, compared to about 10 cents for natural gas fueled plants.[44] Bullard estimated that solar thermal plants like Ivanpah would generate electricity at a cost of 17.5 cents per kwh without subsidies.[45]

When completed the Ivanpah plant capacity of 394 gross-megawatts would power 140,000 homes annually and reduce CO_2 emissions by 2.5 million tons annually. The reduction in CO_2 emissions was equivalent to taking 70,000 cars off the road.

BrightSource signed 20- and 25-year supply contracts with Pacific Gas & Electricity and Southern California Edison for the power. The contracts had been approved by the California Public Utilities Commission (PUC) with tariffs established under a "cost reasonableness" standard, which required comparison to other Renewables Portfolio Standard (RPS) projects.[46]

Southern California Edison planned to spend $314 million to construct transmission lines to connect the Ivanpah solar power plants to the California electricity market. The company sought incentive rates that required approvals from the Federal Energy Regulatory Commission and the California Independent System Operator, which owned and operated the transmission system in the state.

APPROVALS

The Ivanpah plant required approval from five government agencies, and the public was allowed to intervene. Environmentalists were divided on the project with some supporting approval because of the renewable energy and others opposing it because of the harm to the desert habitat.[47] Gloria Smith, a senior attorney with the Sierra Club, stated, "Looking at the new proposal, it will not do anything to protect the desert tortoise …. We will support this project but just want it to have a more beneficial footprint."[48] San Bernardino County, where the plant was to be located, objected to the plant because the county would not receive much tax revenue because of required state tax breaks and because the construction jobs would largely go to workers in Nevada, since the closest town was Primm, Nevada.

As the approval process ground along, time became an increasing concern. To qualify for the 1603 cash grant program, construction on the Ivanpah plant had to commence before the end of 2010. A fast-track approval process was instituted in which five agencies simultaneously reviewed the proposal. The final approvals from the U.S. Bureau of Land Management (BLM) and the California Energy Commission were obtained in the fall of 2010, allowing construction to begin.

The approval process took 3 years, and the company made a number of changes in the Ivanpah project to mitigate environmental impacts and to address objections by the BLM and the California Energy Commission. The company reduced the plant size by 12 percent to 3,500 acres of federal land. The technology used water rather than oil to drive the turbine, avoiding the possibility of environmental damage from oil. To conserve water the plant would use air cooling to condense the spent steam, reducing water usage by 95 percent compared to water-cooled solar thermal plants. The heliostats were to be mounted on pylons above the ground to allow vegetation and wildlife to coexist with the plant. This also allowed the natural contours of the land to be followed, avoiding grading.

The focal point for environmental objections to the Ivanpah project was the desert tortoise. BrightSource went to extraordinary steps to protect the tortoise. Mercy Vaughn, chief biologist for BrightSource, said, "Nobody is allowed on site without a biologist to escort them …. We have someone tracking all the tortoises continuously, so whenever we determine one's at risk, someone gets put on it."[49] Each desert tortoise on the site was fitted with a radio transmitter. The company placed signs in parking areas on the work site stating, "Look under your car for desert tortoise before you drive away!"[50]

BrightSource also agreed to acquire 7,200 acres of desert land to mitigate the impact of the project. The company also agreed to test for any disease in all desert tortoises on the site, relocate them to comparable habitat, and continue to monitor them. To overcome the objections by San Bernardino County and union complaints, BrightSource and Bechtel, the

---

[42]German developer Solar Millennium planned to build a $6 billion solar thermal plant on 11 square miles of desert near Blyth, California. Also, Tessara Solar planned a 709 megawatt plant in the Imperial Valley of California.

[43]The cash-grant program was scheduled to expire at the end of 2010, although the underlying tax credit program was authorized until 2016.

[44]*New York Times*, October 29, 2010.

[45]*San Jose Mercury News*, April 26, 2011.

[46]The tariffs were deemed confidential by the PUC.

---

[47]The Ivanpah area was open to off-road vehicles.

[48]*New York Times*, February 11, 2010.

[49]*International Herald Tribune*, November 29, 2010.

[50]Ibid.

construction company for the project, reached an agreement on hiring with the State Building and Construction Trades Council of California and the Building and Construction Trades Council of San Bernardino and Riverside counties.

FINANCING

In addition to the loan guarantees by the Department of Energy, NRG Solar LLC, a subsidiary of NRG, a large power producer headquartered in Princeton, New Jersey, invested $300 million in the plant and Google invested $168 million. Bechtel also was an equity investor in the plant.

During the approval process BrightSource raised equity capital, including $55 million from Alstom SA of France in May 2010 and $122.5 million from private investors in March 2011. BrightSource completed its equity financing with $75 million from Alstom in April 2011. BrightSource had earlier received equity financing from Vantage Point Capital Partners, Black River, DBL Investors, and google.com. MorganStanley, Draper Fisher Jurvetson, BPalternativenergy, and StatoiHydro Ventures also provided funds. With construction on the Ivanpah plant underway, in April 2011 BrightSource announced an initial public offering to raise $250 million.

RISKS

With the approvals by California and the U.S. government in hand and construction underway, environmentalists and Native American groups again sought to stop the plant. In January 2011 the Idaho-based Western Watersheds Project environmental group filed a lawsuit alleging violation of the Endangered Species Act because of the threat to the desert tortoise. BrightSource had estimated that 38 tortoises were on the Ivanpah site, but the BLM estimated that 3,000 tortoises would be disturbed by the construction and 700 juvenile tortoises would be killed during construction. In April 2011 federal officials ordered construction to halt on two-thirds of the project site. Kelly Wachs, spokesperson for BrightSource, said the government numbers "are not consistent with the actual number of tortoises found on the project site. It appears that the largest concentrations of tortoise are outside the project and in areas that we designed the project to avoid."[51]

Cory J. Briggs, an attorney for La Cuna de Aztlan Sacred Sites Protection Circle Advisory Committee, which filed a lawsuit against the Ivanpah and four other solar power projects, said, "There's no good reason to go into these pristine wilderness areas and build huge solar farms, and less reason for the taxpayers to be subsidizing it. The impacts to Native American culture and the environment are extraordinary."[52] Alfredo Acosta Figueroa, who had founded La Cuna, "explained how the giant image of the creator etched into the earth guides the souls of mothers and children toward Old Woman Mountain."[53] He said, "There's no way these people can circumvent all the sacred sites out here, and

no way to fix it when the damage is done."[54] Threats to cultural heritage represented a new challenge to desert projects.

Arnold Goldman and the CEOs of 33 other renewable-energy companies went to Washington in April 2011 to lobby against a continuing resolution that would reduce the Department of Energy's loan guarantee program by $25 billion. The reduction had been approved by the Republican-controlled House of Representatives as part of the effort to reduce the enormous federal budget deficit. The reduction would include rescinding loan guarantees already approved. The CEOs argued that their projects involved $24 billion in private investment and would employ 35,000 workers when completed. Goldman and seven other CEOs wrote to House and Senate members stating, "We are deeply concerned that eliminating funding for this critical program will not only destroy thousands of pending jobs and hinder the growth of critically needed U.S. domestic energy production, but also defeat America's effort to compete with China, Germany, and others in the clean technology marketplace .... Eliminating funding at this late stage would literally pull the rug from under our projects, just as we are about to break ground."[55] Senator Diane Feinstein (D-CA) said, "American industry has asked Congress to provide a predictable business environment. Yet the House [Continuing Resolution] would eliminate the DOE's loan-guarantee program without warning and without provision for loan applicants who have negotiated with DOE in good faith for multiple years."[56] The $25 billion reduction was in part in response to a House inquiry into the federal loan guarantee to Solyndra Inc. for the construction of a plant to produce solar panels.

BrightSource had signed long-term contracts with Southern California Edison and Pacific Gas and Electric, and normally such contracts would be upheld by the courts if there were a breach and compensation would then be awarded to the injured party. The tariffs for renewable energy, however, were set by the California PUC and hence were subject to regulatory approval and hence to regulatory risk. Regulatory commitments could be reviewed as to the reasonableness of tariffs, and the state legislature could also intervene. Altering contracts would, however, send a signal to other renewable power producers and affect future projects.

The marketplace also posed risks. One longer-term risk for BrightSource was competition from photovoltaic solar power plants. Solar panel prices had fallen sharply because of expanded production in China, making photovoltaic plants that convert sunlight directly to electricity potentially more competitive than solar thermal. Moreover, photovoltaic plants could have smaller footprints and be constructed on private land. Ted Sullivan, an analyst with Lux Research, said, "The real concern is that if these solar thermal projects don't get done in a timely fashion in 2011 and 2012, prices will come down and it will make more sense to go photovoltaic."[57]

[51] *San Jose Mercury News*, April 28, 2011.
[52] *New York Times*, February 24, 2011.
[53] *Los Angeles Times*, February 24, 2011.

[54] Ibid. The environmental group Californians for Renewable Resources also joined in the lawsuit.
[55] Inside Energy with Federal Lands, *Platt's Inside Energy*, April 4, 2011.
[56] Inside Energy with Federal Lands, *Platt's Inside Energy*, February 21, 2011.
[57] *New York Times*, February 24, 2011.

Another risk for BrightSource beyond Ivanpah was the scale of the footprint required for its generation technology. The opposition to large-scale solar thermal plants was substantial, and finding the required land was problematic. Some analysts believed that solar generation plants that used photovoltaic solar panels would ultimately prevail because they could be built on smaller sites, such as urban brownfields.[58] ■

Preparation Questions

1. Assess the opportunities for BrightSource.
2. Assess the market and nonmarket risks BrightSource faces.
3. What should BrightSource do about the challenges from environmentalists and Native Americans?
4. Identify the regulatory and legislature risks BrightSource faces. How should the company deal with those risks?

Silver Spring Networks and the Smart Grid

Smart meters will allow you to actually monitor how much energy your family is using by the month, by the week, by the day, or even by the hour. So coupled with other technologies, this is going to help you manage your electricity use and your budget at the same time, allowing you to conserve electricity during those times when prices are higher, like hot summer days.[59]

Barack Obama

Technology is expensive, but not using it will be even more expensive.[60]

Ahmad Faruqui, The Brattle Group

INTRODUCTION

Silver Spring Networks (SSN) provided platforms for enabling communication within a smart grid. A smart grid in the United States was projected to reduce electricity costs in the United States by over $200 billion by 2020 through improved efficiency. In addition, using smart technology in the home to provide customers with information on their electricity usage and on prices that reflected real costs would allow them to manage their usage and shift demand from peak to off-peak times, reducing costs by $45 billion. These efficiency savings required communication between customers and the grid and among components of the grid structure, and those components had to be managed and integrated. For example, growth in the use of rooftop solar panels produced an intermittent supply of electricity that had to be meshed with other generation capacity, taking into account transmission capacity.

SSN provided Internet Protocol-based platforms for the communication needed to manage the components of electricity generation, distribution, and use. SSN provided the software platforms for advanced or smart meters that provide customers with real-time usage information; distribution automation; demand response that provided real-time price information to customers; smart home software to allow heating, cooling, and appliances to respond automatically to price information; and electric vehicles to accommodate the demand resulting from the use of plug-in electric vehicles. SSN's customers were primarily electric utilities and companies that operated components of the electricity grid, such as public distribution grid companies. SSN's customers were regulated, and their regulatory environments differed across the states. The principal nonmarket challenge for SSN was to facilitate the rapid deployment of smart grid applications, and that had to be accomplished through its customers and their regulators. The market challenge for SSN was to sustain its technological advantage and its market leadership in the face of numerous start-ups and the presence of giants such as Cisco Systems and IBM.[61]

THE COMPANY

Founded in 2002 in Milwaukee, Wisconsin, the company moved to California in 2004 for better access to venture capital funding and engineering talent. The company had remained private, receiving funding from venture capital firms. In 2009 the company raised $100 million from Foundation Capital, Kleiner Perkins Caufield & Byers, Northgate Capital, and Google Ventures.[62] The company had been expected to announce an initial public offering of its shares in 2010 but decided not to go public. The company had received numerous awards. In November 2010 it was ranked first in the 2010 Global Cleantech 100 out of 3,138 nominated companies from 50 countries.

The opportunities for SSN were exciting with the expectation that the smart grid investments would continue at a rapid pace. In 2009 President Obama had announced a goal of 40 million smart meters installed over the next 5 years with 25 million projected by 2012. The administration's stimulus bill, the American Recovery and Reinvestment Act, included $3.4 billion in Smart Grid Investment Grants to utilities for smart grid projects, including smart meter installation.[63] Whether those expenditures would continue was uncertain because of the pressures for reducing the enormous federal budget deficit.

SSN had become the leading provider of software for smart meters, which was an essential component of the smart grid. The strategy followed by SSN was to partner with smart meter manufacturers such as General Electric and Swiss meter giant Landis+Gyr so that its software platform would work with

---

[58]*Economist*, April 16, 2011.

[59]Barack Obama, Speech at Arcadia, Florida, October 27, 2009, www.white-house.gov

[60]*The Economist*, June 6, 2009.

[61]In later 2010 Cisco acquired smart-grid software firm Arch Rock and joined with Itron in an effort to develop smart-grid communication technology.

[62]Generation Investment Management had also provided capital.

[63]The Act also provided $630 million in Smart Grid Demonstration Grants.

any meter. A utility, however, could not replace a smart meter with SSN's communication software with a smart meter with another company's communication software. A number of companies participated in an interoperability committee to establish a standard to allow one company's communication software to work with another company's communication software.

In 2011 SSN entered into a strategic reselling agreement with Control4, allowing Control4's automatic thermostat and software to be integrated with SSN's advanced metering platform for use by utilities in getting customers to adopt intelligent thermostats. The agreement moved SSN deeper into the demand response component of home area networks. SSN also introduced a prototype of a plug-in charging system for the 2012 Prius plug-in model. SSN viewed the opportunities for smart grid platforms overseas as particularly attractive. SSN partnered with Landis+Gyr to provide smart grid applications in Brazil, which had mandated the installation of 61 million smart meters. Landis+Gyr was the first company to have its smart meter certified by Brazilian regulators. The European Union had also mandated the installation of smart meters, and the United Kingdom planned to install 50 million electric and gas smart meters by 2018.

A SMART METER REBELLION?[64]

The foundation for many smart grid applications was advanced metering using smart meters at the customer's premises that transmitted usage information to the utility and could receive information such as time-sensitive prices customers could manage their electricity. At the forefront of the installation of smart meters was Pacific Gas & Electric (PG&E) which by the end of 2010 had installed about 7 million meters on the path to having over 9 million installed by 2012. PG&E's rollout of the smart meters had not gone smoothly as customers complained that the new meters resulted in higher electricity bills, caused illnesses, and threatened privacy. PG&E was SSN's largest customer.

Shortly after PG&E began installing smart meters, residential customers started to complain that their electricity bills were higher and that inaccurate smart meters were the cause. Many of the complaints came from Bakersfield, and PG&E investigated and found that the higher bills were due to unusually hot weather that led to greater air-conditioning use and sharply higher prices as usage increased. The company checked all its meters and found problems with fewer than 1 percent. A majority of the problems were due to improper installation and others due to communication and data retention problems. The California Public Utilities Commission (PUC) hired an independent consultant to study the accuracy of the smart meters, and the consultant concluded that the smart meters were more accurate than the electromechanical meters they had replaced.

Some customers complained that the wireless communication technology used in smart meters would allow hackers to enter through the meters into the electronic control and communication systems within a house. Others complained that hacking into one smart meter could provide access to other smart meters. SSN's platform had protections that isolated each meter so that entering other meters was not possible nor could a virus propagate through the network. Customers anxious about privacy were not persuaded.

The most common complaint was by consumers who claimed to be sensitive to the electromagnetic field (EMF) generated by smart meters resulting in a variety of illnesses. The possible relation between EMF and illness had been studied by many researchers over the previous decades, and no study had found a relation. Moreover, in controlled experimental conditions individuals claiming EMF sensitivity could not detect whether an EMF was present or not. The California Council on Science and Technology examined the health claims lodged against smart meters and concluded that there was no evidence of a causal relation and that there was much less radio frequency exposure from a smart meter than common devices such as cell phones, baby monitors, and wireless Internet connections.[65] Sandi Maurer of the EMF Safety Network said, "People are really getting sick—we're getting all kinds of anecdotal reports about sleep problems, nausea, headaches and ringing in the ears. This report simply says that there's no proof. That's not reassuring."[66]

Consumers asked the PUC for a moratorium on the installation of smart meters and for the option of opting out from having a smart meter. Asked about the health concerns and the request for an opt-out option, Eric Dresselhuys, executive vice president and chief marketing officer of SSN, said, "It's a Northern California phenomenon, and it's a highly emotional issue because people feel they have very legitimate health concerns. But it would be hugely inefficient, and expensive, if a small amount of customers were allowed to opt-out."[67] In March 2011 the PUC asked PG&E to submit within 2 weeks alternatives to allow customers to opt out "at a reasonable cost, to be paid by the customers who choose to opt out." Opting out not only would limit the demand for SSN's smart meter platform, but would also jeopardize demand generated by home automation and responsive pricing.

A principal concern was that responsive pricing might not reduce customers' electricity bills, and consumers might associate smart meters and responsive pricing with higher costs. Some states such as Connecticut and Texas had been concerned that consumers' electricity bills would not be lowered, and ordered pilot studies with responsive pricing to be conducted before smart meters were deployed. Several states had conducted responsive pricing experiments and found that consumers reduced their peak-time usage significantly only if peak-time prices were very high. Some states that had conducted successful responsive pricing experiments that were very well received by customers were worried about consumer reactions to high rates for critical peak periods and low rates for off-peak periods. Pepco, a utility serving Washington DC and two counties in Maryland, decided not to increase peak-use prices, choosing instead to

---

[64] For additional information see the Chapter 12 case *Pacific Gas & Electric and the Smart Meter Challenge*.

[65] *San Jose Mercury News*, January 12, 2011.
[66] Ibid.
[67] *San Jose Mercury News*, January 8, 2011.

offer rebates for consumption. Steven Sunderhauf of Pepco explained, "Our general sense is that consumers would prefer a rate structure with no downside. From a purist's standpoint, I may prefer critical peak pricing because it gets the boldest response … but using rebates will help people get comfortable with smart meters."[68]

THE CHALLENGE

SSN faced the possibility that the rollout of smart meters could be slowed in California, and complaints in Maine threatened installation there. The reluctance of regulators to use higher peak-use prices threatened the largest home application–demand response. SSN had worked through its customers, the utilities, to gain public acceptance of smart grid technology. The utilities were largely on board but were cautious because of possible customer complaints that might lead regulators to slow the transition to the smart grid.

The challenge for SSN was whether it should do more than work with and through its customers. ▪

Preparation Questions

1. Are the consumer complaints likely to be only a California phenomenon? Could the complaints spread to other states?
2. If utilities are unwilling to use high prices at peak periods and instead use rebates, the demand response would likely be small, calling into question the benefit from smart meters. Should SSN support a cautious approach (e.g., rebates) to responsive pricing or an approach that would yield greater benefits to society?
3. Should SSN lobby the PUCs to shore up support for smart meter deployment?
4. Should SSN work for greater public support for the smart grid?
5. Should SSN work for the continued subsidization of smart grid installation?

T-Solar and the Solar Power Market

Grupo T-Solar Global, S.A. (T-Solar) was the largest producer in the solar photovoltaic (PV) power market in Spain with an installed capacity of over 155 MWp in 28 plants with additional plants under construction in Italy and Spain. T-Solar also produced large-area (5.7 m²) thin-film amorphous silicon solar panels in its state-of-the-art plant in Orense. T-Solar, based in Madrid, was privately held and had invested over €1 billion in its operations since its founding in 2007. Raising capital had been easy in the booming European solar power markets in Germany and Spain. For 2009 the company had revenue of €128.7 million, EBITDA of €84.8 million, and 224 employees. T-Solar had borrowed extensively on the euro market, and its debt was said to be 10 times its EBITDA.[69]

T-Solar had a 5 MWp solar power plant under construction in Italy with plans for an additional 122 MWp. T-Solar and Global EcoPower of France formed a 50–50 joint venture to build 120 MWp of solar photovoltaic power plants in France between 2010 and 2013. The companies were attracted by high feed-in tariff of €0.314 per KWh plus indexation established in January 2010 by the French government. In addition to projects in Europe, T-Solar looked to India, South America, and the United States for growth. T-Solar and Solarpark Espana won an auction to construct and operate 20 megawatt solar PV power plants in Peru with the output sold to Sistema Electrico Nacional under a 20-year purchase contract.

To reduce its debt and raise capital for its global expansion, T-Solar announced on March 29, 2010, that it would raise nearly €250 million in an initial public offering. CEO Juan Laso explained, "The company wants to fund its international expansion, leveraging its project pipeline, which currently consists of 664 MWp in different stages of development, and on its sound network of partners in countries where it already operates. T-Solar's objective is to quadruple its installed capacity over the next three years and consolidate its position as one of the largest independent producers of solar photovoltaic power in the world."[70]

THE ECONOMIC AND POLITICAL ENVIRONMENT OF T-SOLAR

T-Solar's profitability depended on 25-year power supply contracts with the Spanish government at high feed-in tariffs intended to spur clean energy production. The tariff for solar plants in service before September 2008 was €0.45 per megawatt hour, which was 10 times greater than the price paid for coal or natural gas generated power. The high feed-in tariffs attracted an investment of €18 billion in solar power generation with a capacity of 3,200 MWp, which was six times the capacity anticipated by the Spanish government. Spain reduced its feed-in tariff for new plants by 29 percent in 2009 and limited the subsidization of new installations.

The European Photovoltaic Industry Association (EPIA), representing 240 firms, joined with Greenpeace and issued a report on the development of the solar power industry: "Global investments in solar PV technology could double from €35–40 billion today to over €70 billion in 2015, … The estimated investments in the European Union alone would rise from

---

[68]*Wall Street Journal*, February 22, 2010.
[69]The company had hedged the interest rate risk on it project finance. Bloomberg.net, April 9, 2010.

[70]T-Solar, Press release, March 29, 2010.

today's €25–30 billion to over €35 billion in 2015. This report on the global market outlook for solar photovoltaic, named 'Solar Generation 6' foresees that PV could account for 12% of the European power demand by 2020, and up to 9% of the global power demand by 2030."[71]

Germany had been the early leader in building solar PV power capacity, and in 2008 Spain surpassed Germany in new capacity installed. New installation slumped in 2009 as a result of the lower feed-in tariffs, and France reduced its feed-in tariffs by 29 percent for rooftop installations. The United Kingdom countered the trend by instituting in April 2010 a $0.62 per KWh feed-in tariff, which was 10 times the market price.[72] Japan continued its subsidies for rooftop installations, and established a feed-in tariff in November 2010.[73] The PV industry was helped by a large increase in capacity for crystalline silicon solar cells which led to a 40 percent decrease in wholesale solar panel prices in Europe. In addition, scale economies, particularly for PV panel producers in China, had driven prices down. The Chinese government had the goal of being the global leader in solar power.

A severe financial crisis struck Spain in 2007 as a result of a housing bubble, and most other European countries experienced an economic slowdown or recession. Many of the countries incurred large budget deficits that jeopardized their ability to borrow. The capital markets reacted by driving up interest rates of government borrowings in Greece, which forced the European Union to establish a lending facility to provide emergency funding for the country. Similar problems developed in Ireland, which also received funds from the European Union. Standard & Poor's downgraded Portugal's debt rating, and commentators opined that Spain and Italy could be next. Share prices of European companies declined broadly.

Spain had a large budget deficit, and the socialist government of Prime Minister Jose Luis Rodriguez Zapatero pledged to reduce the deficit, as the financial markets watched. The budget deficit in 2009 was 11.0 percent of GDP, and although the government met its deficit goal of 9.3 percent in 2010, achieving the European Union target of 3 percent by 2013 would be a challenge. The unemployment rate was 20 percent, and the projection for 2011 was 19.3 percent. The opposition had made gains in the 2010 regional elections in Catalonia, with national elections looming in 2012.

Solar power attracted attention in the budget discussions because subsidies amounted to €2.6 billion. In addition to government subsidies, the high feed-in tariffs had increased the price of electricity, and the government became concerned about the competitiveness of Spanish companies, which had complained about the high price of electricity. The Ministry of Industry had already cut feed-in tariffs for new solar power plants in 2009, and it had the authority to cut tariffs on contracts already in effect. Minister of Industry Miguel Sebastian told Parliament, "In dialogue with the sector and political forces, we'll make a reasonable adjustment to avoid damaging the competitiveness of industry."[74] The Ministry announced that it was considering retroactive cuts on existing contracts. Speaking for the industry, Juan Laso, who headed Spain's Photovoltaic Business Association, said, "This implies bankruptcy."[75]

The day after the minister's statement, T-Solar announced that it was postponing its IPO. Laso stated, "The lack of clarity from the Ministry of Industry regarding the generation model it wants to foster in Spain and the legal uncertainty created by the fact that its department has publicly questioned the sustainability of the remuneration system...has generated an atmosphere of mistrust amongst investors looking at industrial plans in Spain."[76]

"Mark David, an analyst at Panmure Gordon, said: 'A retroactive cut would be catastrophic for the Spanish solar market. Aside from the obvious damage to the profitability of projects and the issues for lending banks, it would stop investments in new projects in Spain. If the government cuts once, it could clearly do it again.'"[77] Jamie Richards of the Foresight European Fund noted, "If the government reneges on projects in solar then why not in other sectors during these difficult times?"[78]

Italy planned to reduce its feed-in tariff for new solar projects by 18 percent, Germany was considering a 15 percent cut for new solar power plants, and within a year of introducing its feed-in tariff the United Kingdom announced that it would review its tariff a year earlier than planned. The Czech Republic chose a different approach to deal with solar power subsidization. The government authorized a 26 percent tax on the revenue of solar plants with capacity above 30 KWp that had begun production in 2009 or 2010. The EPIA condemned the decision, stating

—the retroactivity changes the conditions guaranteed to the operators of solar power plants already on the grid in 2009 and 2010. Current law guarantees them a [feed-in tariff] FIT already set for these years. A special tax of 26% retroactively reduces that guaranteed FIT

—it substantially interferes with the legitimate expectations of operators of solar power plants. One may therefore expect a number of litigations and arbitrations against the Czech Republic government[79]

Commenting on Germany cutting its feed-in tariff, James Britland, an analyst for Allianz RCM, said, "Things were too liberal in Germany. The government realized it was costing them too much money. The volume rise was too big as installations were way higher than expected. Spain had a gold rush in solar, and Germany saw a similar thing was happening to them last year."[80] The German feed-in tariff was €0.39 per KWh under a 20-year contract, which was eight times the market

[71]EPIA, Press Release, February 2, 2011.
[72]*New York Times*, March 31, 2010.
[73]PRWeb, February 22, 2011.

[74]Bloomberg, April 28, 2009.
[75]*Financial Times*, February 23, 2010.
[76]T-Solar, Press Prelease, April 27, 2010.
[77]*The Sunday Times*, July 4, 2010.
[78]Ibid.
[79]EPIA, Press Release, December 9, 2010.
[80]*New York Times*, March 31, 2010.

price. "The difference is passed on to consumers, who pay an average $5 extra each month in electricity fees per household."[81]

By December 2010 the Spanish government was expected to cut retroactively by up to 30 percent the tariffs on contracts already in effect. Tom Murley of HgCapital in the UK, representing 20 funds that had invested in the Spanish photovoltaic industry, said, "If they proceed on this path, they'll endanger not only our investment, but the whole sector."[82]

In response to a call by the European Commission for more harmonized policies for supporting solar power, the EPIA issued a statement: "EPIA fully supports this general objective, in particular the importance to adapt instruments in order to avoid excessive returns on capital." "PV investment profitability should be assessed on a regular basis and support schemes adapted accordingly in a predictable manner," said Eleni Despotou, Ad-Interim Secretary General of EPIA. "Well-designed and evolutionary support schemes are the key market drivers for a sustainable photovoltaic (PV) deployment. We think that Feed-in-Tariffs should evolve within a predefined 'corridor' that could help avoiding stop-and-go policies or retroactive measures," she added.[83]

Preparation Questions

1. From the investor's perspective evaluate for T-Solar
   a. The market risks
   b. The nonmarket risks
2. What should T-Solar do about the anticipated retroactive change in the contracts?
3. Should T-Solar support the "corridor" proposal?

[81]Ibid.
[82]*Wall Street Journal*, December 28, 2010.
[83]EPIA, Press Release, January 31, 2011.

14 | LAW AND MARKETS

INTRODUCTION

Markets are the cornerstone of a free enterprise system. For markets to function efficiently, individuals must be confident that the terms of their exchanges will be fulfilled. An exchange may be supported by a contract that establishes mutual expectations about terms such as the quality and quantity of an item, delivery, and payment. An exchange may also carry with it some residual obligations not explicitly included in the contract. For example, a party may be responsible for harm to the other party or to third parties caused by the item exchanged. That harm could involve environmental damage, personal injury during use, or adverse health consequences. An exchange may also involve other risks for the parties. For example, does a party actually have a property right to the item to be exchanged? Can the attributes of the item be easily appropriated by a third party without payment? Does the contract cover the possible events that could affect its execution? What if there is an extenuating circumstance, such as an act of nature or human intervention, that leads one party to be unable to fulfill the contract? Is compensation due? What if there is an accident or injury associated with the item exchanged? These uncertainties can impair the functioning of markets and the realization of the gains from trade. The law plays a principal role in reducing such uncertainties and in supporting exchange in markets.

Law is established by constitutions, statutes enacted by legislatures, rules promulgated by regulators, and decisions made by judges. Statutory law, for example, specifies the length of a patent and the statute of limitations on filing lawsuits. The common law, or judge-made law, is a body of law that has evolved through cases brought before the courts by private parties. The decisions made by judges serve as precedents for future cases, and the set of precedents establishes a body of law. Judges also interpret statutes, and their interpretations can become part of the law. This chapter addresses aspects of the law that support the functioning of markets and private agreements.

Despite its importance the law is not the principal means of reducing uncertainty and improving reliance in exchanges. The alternative to public order provided by the law is private order based on private assurances among trading partners. Private means of assurance include trust, honesty, reputations for fulfilling promises, and bargaining to resolve disputes. Anyone who has purchased an online item relies more on the reputation of Amazon or L.L. Bean than on law. Similarly, buyers on eBay pay in advance for items, relying on the descriptions and pictures of items offered and on the reputations of sellers established through feedback from other buyers. Disputes are also resolved between a company and a customer through return and refund policies. On eBay the parties to a dispute can use an online dispute resolution mechanism, and if that does not work, an online mediator can be engaged for a modest fee.

In some instances the law plays even less of a role in resolving disputes. A private ordering could be established through face-to-face and repeated interactions that allow norms to develop and be sustained. Ellickson (1991) studied the norms of ranchers and homeowners in Shasta County, California, and found that they settled disputes based on norms largely without reliance on the law and often in a manner contrary to the law. The ranchers and homeowners were able to rely on norms and punishments, primarily through gossip, because they had repeated interactions and were proximate. Repetition and proximity allowed norms to be respected.

Private orderings, however, function in the shadow of the law, which provides a final recourse for disputes. The homeowners at times resorted to lawsuits when the norms failed to resolve recurring problems. Similarly, cases of suspected fraud on eBay are turned over to law enforcement authorities. In areas where the stakes are high, the law remains the principal basis for supporting expectations about future performance. The cost of developing a new drug is over $1 billion, and a pharmaceutical company wants assurance that other companies will not simply copy its discovery. Patent law and its enforcement provide the assurance, and the decisions of judges have refined the law of patents to address new issues that arise.

This chapter first considers the common law and contrasts it with civil law. The concept of property is then introduced, and the establishment of incentives to develop property is analyzed. The focus is on intellectual property and its protection through patents and copyrights. Contracts are then considered along with principles governing their enforceability and breach. Torts and the liability system are considered next with a focus on establishing incentives to guide the actions of buyers and sellers to reduce accidents associated with a product. Products liability is considered both because of its importance and because it illustrates the evolution of the common law. The chapter cases deal with product safety, possible liability for a health problem, and patent protection.

THE COMMON LAW

One perspective on the law is that it is imposed from above by a legislature or, in earlier times, by a ruler. In issuing decrees, even a ruler may look for guidance to how the people have organized their activities. For example, people privately developed practices for the control and management of land, and in England the king often looked to those practices as the basis for the king's law.[1] That law then evolved both as the practices of people evolved and through the precedents set by the king's court and subsequently by public courts. The resulting body of law is referred to as the *common law*. It is used in the United Kingdom, the United States, and most of the other former English colonies. Common law countries typically have an adversarial system of litigation in which each party advocates its side of the dispute and judges and juries render decisions based on the evidence, the arguments provided, and precedents.[2]

The role of the common law is to help people accomplish what they want to accomplish. The advantage of the common law is that it can adjust to changing circumstances without having to wait for new statutes to be enacted by legislation. The common law evolves through lawsuits filed by people in response to the problems they need addressed. As considered in a later section, the evolution from a law of warranty to the law of products liability occurred as a result of the changing nature of products.

In contrast, on the European continent, in Latin America, and elsewhere, *civil law* is used rather than common law. Civil law was developed by the Romans and served as the basis for the Napoleonic Code written after the French revolution by legal scholars commissioned by Napoleon. The Napoleonic code spread through the European continent and to the colonies of those countries. Civil law is also used in Louisiana and Puerto Rico in the United States, Quebec in Canada, and Scotland in the United Kingdom. Japan has a civil law system developed from German civil law. Civil law is written in codes based on legal principles, and judges decide cases based on those codes and the principles expressed in them. Civil law thus does not evolve in as flexible a manner as does the common law. Civil law countries typically do not use an adversarial system, and in many cases a judge is as much a fact finder as an adjudicator. Civil law countries also generally do not use juries as widely as in the United States, where the Constitution grants people the right to a jury trial in both criminal and civil cases.

The origins of commercial law are similar to those of common law. The origins were in the medieval Merchants Law and in institutions such as the law merchant that developed to facilitate long-distance trade. Trade centered around fairs, such as the Champagne fair, to which merchants would travel great distances to arrange the exchange of goods. The trades often involved future delivery, with merchants agreeing to deliver goods of a particular quality in the future. The traders themselves were often from different regions and relied on their reputations for fulfilling promises. Disputes naturally arose even when merchants sought to fulfill their promises. The law merchant was an office established by the merchants to resolve disputes. Moreover, over time merchants developed understandings about how particular uncertainties were to be handled. These understandings formed the basis for the development and evolution of commercial law.

In the United States, the common law governs a number of important domains, including property, contracts, torts, products liability, and some aspects of labor contracting. The decisions of judges and the precedents established have been codified in a number of areas. On some matters statutes have been enacted to address specific issues in the domain of the common law.

---

[1]See Cooter and Ulen (1997, Ch. 3).
[2]See Carp and Stidham (2001) for information on the courts.

PROPERTY

Property is a set of rights to control a tangible or intangible thing. In the terminology of the Coase theorem introduced in Chapter 12, a property rule protects an entitlement by allowing the holder to use the entitlement, transfer it to another person, or prevent unwanted infringement of that entitlement. That is, a property right is the right to do whatever one chooses with the entitlement. Some property is well defined, whereas others are more difficult to define. Real property in the form of land, buildings, and physical assets is well defined. Ideas, inventions, and expressions are more difficult to define. The former are easier to protect than the latter, and their protections may differ. Real property is generally protected indefinitely, whereas intellectual property is generally protected for a limited time.

The economic efficiency rationale for property is twofold. First, property rules facilitate bargaining, allowing economic transactions to be made and gains from trade to be realized. Second, property rules provide incentives to create assets, as in the case of intellectual property.

Bargaining

Property allows persons to reach mutually beneficial agreements. To illustrate this, consider a manufacturer that wants to buy components from two suppliers and assemble them to produce a final product. Component *a* is supplied by firm A, and component *b* is supplied by a number of firms in a competitive market. The manufacturer can produce its final product by buying *a* and *b* and assembling them at a cost of $100. Because of complementarities in its technology, firm A could assemble the two components at a cost of $80 and supply the assembled components to the manufacturer. The manufacturer and firm A thus have an incentive of $20 to reach an agreement under which firm A assembles the two components. Because the manufacturer and firm A have property rights, they can bargain with confidence to reach an agreement. How the gain of $20 is divided between the manufacturer and firm A depends on their bargaining power and by their reservation values, but any division is efficient. The courts are not concerned with how the gain is divided, provided that the manufacturer and firm A have bargained over the division.

Incentives and Appropriability

The second efficiency role of property is to provide incentives to create assets. The incentives are clear in the case of physical assets such as a house. The incentive to build a house arises from a property rule that allows the holder to exclude others from the use of the house, with enforcement provided by public authorities. In the case of intellectual property, exclusion can be considerably more difficult. A music recording company that releases a recording can have it pirated and distributed instantaneously over the Internet. Similarly, a pharmaceutical company can develop a new drug, but once developed it can be easy to copy. The same is true for any invention whose technology can be copied at low cost. Many intellectual creations have low costs of replication, making exclusion difficult. It thus can be hard for the creator to appropriate the returns from the creation. When those returns are not appropriable, the incentives to create are weakened. Since innovation and discovery are engines of economic growth, means are needed to strengthen those incentives. The law of property is intended to provide for appropriability by the creator.

Some means of establishing appropriability are private.[3] Firms may keep their intellectual assets proprietary. Microsoft keeps its operating system code proprietary. The formula for Coca-Cola is kept secret. Similarly, some production technologies are kept within the company. The private protection of intellectual assets is often incomplete or expensive, however. Recording companies may be able to encrypt their products, but codes can be cracked.

INTELLECTUAL PROPERTY

The characteristics of intellectual assets and the difficulty in excluding others from their use implies that those assets can be undersupplied in markets. To address this undersupply, protection is publicly provided. Article I of the Constitution states, "Congress shall have the Power ... to

---

[3]Some incentives to develop information can be provided by the opportunity to take financial positions in the information. For example, some private equity investment firms appropriate returns from their investment in information by acquiring stakes in companies.

Chapter 14 • Law and Markets

FIGURE 14-1 Information and Incentives

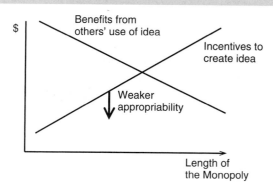

promote the Progress of Science and useful Arts, by securing for limited times to … Inventors the exclusive Right to their respective writing and Discoveries." The issues for Congress and the courts are then what can be protected, what type of protection should be provided, and how long that protection should last.

The basic trade-off in the protection of intellectual property is between the benefits to society from the use of ideas and inventions and the incentives for their creation. Consider the issue of the duration of a patent. A patent grants a monopoly on use of the invention, and the longer the duration, the greater are the returns that may be appropriated, and hence the greater are the incentives to invent. The longer the duration of the monopoly, however, the lower are the benefits to society, since the holder of the patent restricts use so as to appropriate the monopoly returns. This is illustrated in Figure 14-1. The optimal duration of a patent maximizes the sum of the benefits to society and to the inventor. The same principle applies to the breadth of protection for an invention or idea.

The appropriability of the returns from a discovery thus depends on two principal factors. The first is how easy it is for others to replicate the discovery. The second is the strength of the public protection for the discovery. Figure 14-2 is adapted from Teece (2000, p. 19) and relates these factors to appropriability. The cost of replicating a movie is very low, whereas the cost of replicating an oil refining process may be high. The protection given to pharmaceutical patents in the United States is generally tight, whereas the protection in India was loose because Indian patent law granted a patent if the method of production of a product was original or different. Hence, one company's patented drug could be produced in India by another company that used a different manufacturing process. Returns to pharmaceuticals in India were weakly appropriable, whereas in the United States they are more strongly appropriable. In 2005 India changed its patent law to allow patents on products and discoveries, including drugs. The change was required by

FIGURE 14-2 Appropriability of Returns

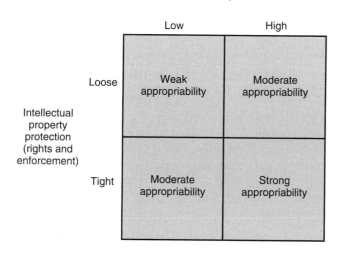

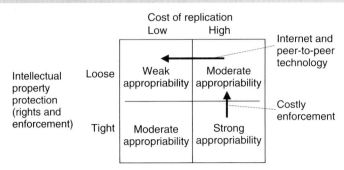

FIGURE 14-3 Appropriability of Returns and Peer-to-Peer Systems

the World Trade Organization, but it was also supported by Indian pharmaceutical companies that sought to develop their own proprietary drugs and needed assurance of appropriability.

Changing technology can dramatically alter the costs of replication of intellectual creations. The Internet and MP3 technology made it possible to exchange digital music and video files with little degradation in quality. Napster seized the opportunity provided by the technological developments to launch a peer-to-peer file sharing service. This lowered the costs of replicating music to close to zero, reducing the appropriability of returns to recording companies, music publishers, and film studios. Appropriability also depends on intellectual property protection accorded to recordings and films and whether peer-to-peer services infringe copyrights. Moreover, enforcing intellectual property rights is costly because legal proceedings are expensive and it is difficult to identify the persons copying files. As illustrated in Figure 14-3, the high cost of enforcement means that protection is loose rather than tight, and technological change reduces the cost of replication. The appropriability of returns in the music and film industries was weakened.

Intellectual Property Protection

The principal forms of protection for intellectual assets are *patents, copyright, trade secrets,* and *trademarks.*

PATENTS A patent may be granted for an invention of "any new and useful process, machine, manufacture, or composition of matter, or any new and useful improvement thereof." A patent establishes a property right that allows the holder to exclude others from using the invention; that is, a patent grants a monopoly to the inventor. As a result of a 1981 Supreme Court decision, computer software may be patented, but software patents are not easily obtained. Patents are also granted for designs and for plants as well as for business methods such as eBay's "buy-it-now" feature. The principal type of patent is a utility patent, which has a duration of 20 years beginning with the filing of the patent application with the Patent and Trademark Office. The number of utility patent applications filed in 2010 was 490,226, nearly double the number from 10 years earlier, out of which 219,614 patents were granted. Patents are enforced by the courts, which may enjoin others from infringing the patent or may order compensatory damages.[4] Beginning in 2005 the Supreme Court in a series of cases has made it more difficult for a patent holder to enforce its patent against infringement, including ordering royalties rather than imposing an injunction for infringement. In 2008 the Court ruled that a patent holder could not require royalties from downstream users of a product produced under a license from the patent holder.

In addition to the duration of a patent, the breadth of the patent is important. Breadth pertains to issues such as whether a patent for a discovery also covers closely related applications and improvements thereon. Inventors seek as broad a patent as possible, whereas competitors and potential users of the invention want a narrow patent. The appropriate breadth of patents is a source of contention both within the courts and among legal scholars.

In 2011 Congress passed the America Invents Act, the principal feature of which was to change the U.S. patent system from a "first-to-invent" to a "first-to-file" system, which was the

---

[4]Treble damages can be awarded but seldom are, unless there is intentional and continuing infringement. See Bouchoux (2001).

system used by European and Asian countries. Secretary of Commerce Gary Locke said, "The first-inventor-to-file provision is consistent with the practices of our economic competitors, and would benefit U.S. businesses by providing a more transparent and cost-effective process that puts them on a level playing field with the rest of the world."[5] The Act was expected to reduce the Patent Office's backlog, which had grown to 700,000 applications awaiting review and shorten the time for a decision to be reached. The Act also provides a grace period for filing if the inventor publicly discloses the innovation. The first-to-file provision created incentives to file patent applications quickly even if the innovation was not fully developed, but the provision would eliminate much of the litigation under the previous system as inventors fought in the courts over who actually first discovered the innovation. Small businesses complained that the first-to-file system put them at a disadvantage, since patent applications are expensive and time consuming. To address their concerns, the Act provided discounts on filing fees for small businesses and an ombudsman system to help start-ups.

Patents are the driving force in the pharmaceutical industry, providing strong incentives for research, development, and testing of new chemical entities. A patent on a new drug and approval for marketing by the Food and Drug Administration gives the innovating company a monopoly on the sale of the drug. Reflecting this monopoly, the company appropriates returns by charging a high price. When a patent expires, generic versions of the drug can be marketed. This typically drives the price down significantly and broadens the use of the drug. This increases the benefits to society from the drug. Not only do pharmaceutical companies have strong incentives to innovate, but they also have strong incentives to enforce their patent rights and to obtain extensions of their patents through congressional and other actions. The Chapter 1 case *The Nonmarket Environment of the Pharmaceutical Industry* and the chapter case *Patent Games: Plavix* address these issues. The latter case considers the lengths a company may go to protect a patent.

Licensing makes an invention available to others and hence increases its benefits to society. Licensing also allows the discoverer to appropriate returns. Licensing is attractive when there are complementary goods whose value is enhanced by the intellectual asset.[6] A biotechnology company that develops a gene may license it to another company that can use it to develop a non-competing pharmaceutical. Similarly, to appropriate returns an engineering company may license a refining technology to oil companies rather than go into the oil refining business. In some cases an intellectual asset may be given to the producers of complementary products. Microsoft provided its application programming interfaces (APIs) to software developers because the more software written for Windows, the greater the demand for its operating system and other proprietary software.

Software patents are the underpinnings of the mobile communications business, but software development typically involves incremental progress that can lead to patent races and wars as the example indicates.

Patent Wars

The mobile communications explosion was accelerated by the introduction of the iPhone and tablets. Google had obtained the open source Android system and developed it as a platform for mobile communications, but the company was a latecomer with Apple, Microsoft, and others having more experience. Since technological progress in mobile communications was incremental, the early entrants had amassed a substantial holding of patents that Google did not have. Moreover, Google had focused on generating revenue—and profits—and had not been very aggressive in obtaining patents. By 2011 Google held 307 mobile-related patents, whereas Research in Motion held 3,134, Nokia 2,655, and Microsoft 2,594.[1] Google CEO Larry Page said, "Computing is moving onto mobile. Even if I have a computer next to me, I'll still be on my mobile device."[2] Google's Android system was used in 43.4 percent of smart phones, more than any other system, but the smartphones were produced by 39 companies that used different versions of Android.

Companies began filing lawsuits against other firms alleging patent infringement. Apple sued HTC, Samsung, and

---

[1]*Bloomberg Businessweek*, August 8–14, 2011.
[2]*New York Times*, August 18, 2011.

(*Continued*)

---

[5]*San Jose Mercury News*, August 17, 2011.
[6]See Teece (2000, Ch. 8) for strategic considerations in licensing.

(Continued)

Motorola Mobility, and Microsoft also sued Motorola Mobility regarding Android. Motorola Mobility had filed lawsuits against Microsoft and other companies alleging patent infringement. Oracle sued Google for up to $6 billion alleging improper use of its Java programming language. Apple argued that Android devices were using its intellectual property and that some Android-based mobile devices were essentially copies of Apple's iPhone and iPad. In conjunction with an Apple patent infringement case against Taiwan's HTC, CEO Steve Jobs said, "We can sit by and watch competitors steal our patented inventions, or we can do something about it. We think competition is healthy, but competitors should create their own original technology, not steal ours."[3] A judge found in favor of Apple in the case against HTC, and Samsung reached a settlement in which it agreed not to import its pad into Australia. In another lawsuit Microsoft had reached a settlement with HTC, in which the company agreed to pay Microsoft $5 for each handset it sells.[4] Additional fees could result from the Apple case that was decided in favor of Apple in 2011.

The best protection against patent infringement lawsuits was to hold a portfolio of patents that could be presented as defense against the lawsuits. This provided incentives to acquire patents. In December 2010 Apple and Microsoft acquired 880 patents from Novell for $450 million, and in July 2011 a consortium led by Apple, Microsoft, and Research in Motion outbid Google for 6,000 patents of bankrupt Nortel, paying $4.5 billion. David Drummond, chief legal officer of Google, criticized the consortium stating that it was a "hostile, organized campaign against Android by Microsoft, Oracle, Apple and other companies, waged through bogus patents."[5] Google had purchased 1,000 patents from IBM.

In a bold move Google acquired Motorola Mobility for $12.5 billion, representing a 63 percent premium above its market price. Google obtained a handset pioneer and major producer, which would allow it to better integrate software and hardware. More importantly, it obtained Motorola's 17,000 patents and 7,500 patent applications. Herbert Hovenkamp, a University of Iowa law professor said, "The best way to fight a big portfolio of patents is to have your own big portfolio of patents. This appears to be what Google is doing here, arming itself with patents to be able to defend itself in this fast-growing market."[6] Drummond said in a blog post, "We're determined to preserve Android as a competitive choice for consumers, by stopping those who are trying to strangle it. Unless we act, consumers could face rising costs for Android devices—and fewer choices for their next phone."[7]

[3]*San Jose Mercury News*, August 4, 2011.
[4]*Bloomberg Businessweek*, August 8–14, 2011.

[5]*New York Times*, August 16, 2011.
[6]Ibid.
[7]*San Jose Mercury News*, August 4, 2011.

COPYRIGHT Works of original expression may receive a copyright allowing the recipient to restrict use, reproduction, and distribution of the work. A copyright can be claimed even without a filing with the government. The first copyright law in 1790 established a maximum duration of 28 years. Since then Congress has extended the duration 11 times. The most recent extension in 1998 was stimulated by the imminent expiration of the copyright on early Mickey Mouse cartoons, as considered in the example. The duration of a copyright is now the life of the author plus 70 years, or in the case of a disguised authorship it is a minimum of 75 years or 100 years after creation. The breadth of a copyright pertains to the uses one is allowed without authorization by the author. The fair use doctrine allows limited unauthorized use for research, scholarship, and literary criticism.

EXAMPLE   Mickey Mouse Politics and Law

The copyrights on the early Mickey Mouse cartoons (e.g., *Steamboat Willy*) were due to expire in 2003, and Pluto, Goofy, and Donald Duck would lose their protection in 2009. Disney and other entertainment and media companies saw this as an opportunity to extend the duration of copyright. The European Union had issued a directive in 1993 to extend the copyright duration to 70 years, and the U.S. interests, arguing for harmonization, sought a 20-year extension to 70 years. The issue was characterized by relatively quiet client politics, and in 1998 Congress provided the extension by passing the Sonny Bono Copyright Term Extension Act.

The opponents of the extension soon challenged the Act in the courts. The opponents included individuals and companies that relied on public access to materials. They made two arguments. First, they argued that the extension violated Article I of the Constitution by essentially giving nearly unlimited rights to creations. Second, they argued that the law stifled free speech in violation of the First Amendment. The district court, the Court of Appeals, and in 2003 the Supreme Court upheld the Act. In the majority opinion Justice Ruth Bader Ginsburg wrote that Congress had acted within its authority as granted by the Constitution and that copyright was intended to "promote the creation and publication of free expression." With respect to the wisdom and the public policy effects of the extension, Ginsburg wrote "that it is generally for Congress, not the courts, to decide how best to pursue the copyright clause's objectives …"[7]

[7]*Eldred v. Ashcroft.* 537 US 186 (2003).

An important issue in information technology and information services industries is whether the "look and feel" of software or a Web site can be protected by copyright. This is an unsettled matter. In an important case Apple Computer filed a copyright lawsuit against Microsoft arguing that the user interface of Microsoft Windows operating system copied the look and feel of Apple's system. The court held in favor of Microsoft.

The issue of what may be copyrighted has required both legislation and court interpretation. Consider the issue of whether compilations of facts can be protected by copyright. A 1991 Supreme Court decision (*Feist Publications, Inc. v. Rural Telephone Service Co.*, 499 U.S., 340) held that "facts," even if collected through "sweat and effort," remained in the public domain. Earlier court decisions had held that databases were protected by copyright under the "sweat of the brow" doctrine. This doctrine prevailed despite 1976 amendments to the Copyright Act that required a degree of creativity or originality for compilations of data to be protected. In *Feist* the court affirmed the originality and creativity requirement and stated that "all facts—scientific, historical, biographical and news of the day … are part of the public domain available to every person." For example, the telephone white pages cannot be copyrighted because they are simply an alphabetical list of names and numbers, whereas the Yellow Pages can be copyrighted because the information is arranged by category, which has a degree of originality.

Trademarks and Trade Secrets

A trademark provides social and private value. The social value results from reducing search costs for consumers by allowing branding of products. Branding can also support a reputation for quality, uniformity, or service. The word Coke is a trademark, as are eBay and Intel. Trademarks can be registered at the federal or state levels and if maintained can be perpetual. Remedies for infringement can take the form of injunctions and compensatory damages. The requirement for a trademark is distinctiveness. Generic terms such as "online auction" cannot be protected by a trademark, but the name eBay can be protected. As mentioned in Chapter 2, a new entrant into the online auction market used a front page that closely resembled eBay's homepage. The most defensible trademarks are those that are "arbitrary and fanciful," and an eBay attorney explained, "eBay is a completely coined name. It means nothing."[8] eBay filed a successful trademark infringement lawsuit against the entrant.

As an example of a trademark dispute, Johnson & Johnson, the health care company that makes Tylenol, Band-Aids, and Johnson's Baby products along with pharmaceuticals, sued the American Red Cross for infringing its red cross trademark. Johnson & Johnson had begun using the red cross symbol in 1887 before the American Red Cross was established. In 1895 the two parties entered into an agreement under which the American Red Cross acknowledged Johnson & Johnson's "trademark for chemical, surgical and pharmaceutical goods of every description."[9] Johnson & Johnson did not oppose the occasional sale of products by the American Red Cross as a fund-making device, rather it was a supporter, having contributed $5 million over the past 3 years. In 2004, however, the American Red Cross began licensing the red cross symbol to companies for use on a variety of products that competed with Johnson & Johnson products, such as first-aid kits. The company filed the lawsuit after the failure of several months of negotiations, about which a company spokesperson said, "We deeply regret that it has become necessary to file this complaint. The company has the highest regard for the American Red Cross and its mission." The American Red Cross's president characterized the company's action as "obscene" and said it was done "simply so that J & J can make more money."[10] A judge ruled in favor of the American Red Cross.

A trade secret is almost anything that is unique and of value or potential value to a company. This includes process information, operating methods, programs, and business plans. To receive protection the information must be adequately protected by the company on a continual basis. Trade secret protection can be perpetual, and the secrets do not have to be registered. Remedies for violations of trade secrets include injunctions and compensatory damages. Trade secret law has been used to prohibit employees who move from one company to another to take along information from their former employer. Google protects its search engine as a trade secret rather than through patents, since patents require the disclosure of information.

---

[8]*San Jose Mercury News*, July 31, 2001.
[9]*New York Times*, August 9, 2009.
[10]*New York Times*, August 9, 2007.

CONTRACTS

Contracts are governed both by the common law and by statutes pertaining to particular types of contracts and transactions. This section focuses on the principles of contract law derived from the common law, which developed over time to resolve economic problems associated with noncontemporaneous trades. People benefit from the exchange of goods and services, and because of their knowledge of the specific circumstances, people know best how to realize the gains from trade. The objective of the law is to support people in what they want to do by addressing impediments to those trades. In this sense the common law looks to what people do and want to do to arrange and complete exchanges. Contracts are one means by which people arrange mutually advantageous trades.[11]

In a contract both parties seek assurances. A mortgage lender wants assurance that the borrower will repay the loan with interest. To make it costly for the borrower to fail to repay the loan, the house is pledged as collateral. The borrower wants to induce the lender to provide funds and does so by pledging the house as collateral. Contracts thus are mutually advantageous to the participating parties. Without a contract no lender would extend funds with a repayment period that extends for 15 or 30 years. Contracts make the mortgage lending market possible.

Contracts are also entered into to induce *reliance.* Reliance refers to a change in behavior by a party. For example, an electric power plant wants a steady source of coal, and rather than develop a mine itself, it prefers to have a coal company with the required expertise develop the mine. Opening a mine requires major expenditures that the coal company is unwilling to make without assurances that the coal will have a buyer. To induce the coal company to make the reliance expenditures, the power company must provide assurances to the coal company. The power company may agree to build a generating plant at the mine mouth and to purchase at market prices specific quantities of coal for an extended period such as 50 years. With such an assurance, the coal company is willing to make the reliance expenditures. In the event of default on the contract by the power company, the reliance expenditures provide a basis for damages.

A contract is an agreement over which parties are to have bargained. The contract then is mutually advantageous, making each party better off than it would be in its absence. As in the case of mortgage lending, some markets would not exist if it were not for contracts. Contracts cover promises to take particular actions in the future, such as making mortgage payments, and the promises are credible because the failure to follow them is costly. For example, a lender may foreclose on the house provided as collateral.

Contracts, however, are seldom complete in the sense of providing for all the possible contingencies that could arise. The transactions costs associated with completely specifying the responsibilities of the parties in every conceivable circumstance are typically too high, so contracts have a degree of incompleteness. When one of those contingencies arises, the courts may be called on to resolve the ambiguity or resulting conflict. The Genentech and City of Hope example illustrates this in the case in which a long-term licensing contract contained sections that appeared to have conflicting implications.

Contracts can be either written or oral and generally involve an offer, acceptance, and consideration. Consideration is what a promisee gives to a promisor to induce the latter to make the promise, and mutual consideration is usually given. In the purchase of an automobile, the seller gives the automobile as consideration to the buyer to elicit a promise to pay for the car. To induce the seller to provide the car, the buyer gives the seller a down payment and a promise to pay as well as recourse to the car in the event of breach of the contract. In the case of financing the purchase of a house, the buyer provides as consideration a lien or deed of trust on the house to induce the lender to provide the funds. The lender provides the funds to induce the borrower to agree to the lien or deed of trust.

Enforceability

The central issues in contracts are which contracts are enforceable, when can they be breached, and what damages are due in the event of a breach. A contract may be voided if an individual, such as a minor, does not have the authority to enter into it. Similarly, a contract to sell one's vote

---

[11]Other means include contemporaneous exchange (at the grocery store), relational contracts built on long-term relationships (as in supply chains), and reputation (as in online auctions).

EXAMPLE   Genentech and City of Hope

In 1976 as a fledgling company, Genentech entered into a contract with the City of Hope Medical Center (COH) under which two COH researchers agreed to splice a human gene into bacteria to synthesize the DNA for human insulin.[1] In 1978 the scientists were successful, resulting in the first genetically engineered pharmaceutical and the birth of the biotechnology industry. The contract provided that all research findings and resulting patents were the property of Genentech, and Genentech obtained 127 patents related to the COH research. Upon the discovery Genentech licensed the DNA patent for human insulin to Eli Lilly & Co. Under the license Lilly agreed to pay a 6 percent royalty to Genentech and a 2 percent royalty to COH. COH had received $285 million in royalties from human insulin and also from the human growth hormone.

In the mid-1990s COH began inquiring into Genentech's licensing of the DNA patents to pharmaceutical companies other than Lilly. Genentech had licensed the patents to 22 companies, and COH filed a breach of contract lawsuit, claiming that Genentech owed it $445 million in additional royalties. COH also claimed that Genentech intentionally concealed the licensing, which opened the possibility of punitive damages. COH based its lawsuit on a paragraph of the

16-page contract that stated, "Should Genentech license any third party under any patent acquired by it hereunder, then Genentech shall secure from that party and pay to City of Hope the same royalty City of Hope would have received had Genentech itself carried out the licensed activity."

Genentech rejected COH's claim and argued that the governing section of the contract was the section that stated, "Genentech shall pay to City of Hope a royalty of 2 percent of the net sales of all polypeptides (proteins) sold by it or its affiliates, provided only that manufacture of the polypeptide employs DNA synthesized by City of Hope under this agreement."[2] Genentech stated that the term "provided only" meant that royalties were due only on products that used the DNA developed by the COH scientists. Genentech not only argued that it had not violated the contract but that the case was actually about patent law and hence should be tried in federal, not state, court.

The case was tried in state court in 2001 and the jury split seven in favor of Genentech and five in favor of COH. Since nine votes were required to decide the case, the judge was forced to declare a mistrial. The case was retried and the jury voted 9–3 that Genentech had breached the contract and 10–2 that it had done so with fraud or malice. The jury awarded COH $300 million in compensatory damages and $200 million in punitive damages.

---

[1] COH is a world-renowned nonprofit cancer research center that in addition to giving birth to the first genetically engineered pharmaceutical also pioneered bone marrow transplants and opened a facility to produce experimental drugs for untreatable diseases.

[2] *San Francisco Chronicle*, September 10, 2001.

---

in an election is voidable because the right to vote is inalienable; that is, it is not transferable. A contract is generally not enforceable if it is illegal or unconscionable and is voidable under certain conditions such as fraud or a mistake. These conditions may be augmented by statutes. In California, individuals have 3 days during which they can cancel certain contracts. Unconscionability may be either procedural or substantive. The former pertains to contracts entered into under duress or unfair circumstances such as when one party has no bargaining power. The latter pertains to contracts that, for example, may obligate a person to pay a penalty that has no relation to the value of the item under contract.

Duress and unconscionability are ex ante concepts in the sense that the conditions are present when the parties agree to the contract. Circumstances may develop after signing a contract that make it unenforceable. One such circumstance is impossibility, where a party is unable to fulfill a contractual promise. For example, an act of nature such as a fire may destroy a company's plant, making it impossible to fulfill a supply contract. The responsibility in such a case should be assigned to the party that is able to cope with the situation at the least cost. For example, if the buyer can obtain the contracted supplies from another producer, the factory owner may have no remaining obligation. If the buyer had made reliance expenditures, however, for a unique product produced by the destroyed plant, the factory owner may be responsible for damages. In the case in which reliance expenditures are made by the buyer, the factory can take out insurance against the risk of both the fire and the inability to fulfill the contract.

Another situation that can make a contract unenforceable is frustration of purpose. If an event occurs that causes the purpose of the contract to disappear, the courts have held that the contract is unenforceable, since there is no point to its fulfillment. As with impossibility, damages may be awarded. From the perspective of economic efficiency, responsibility for the risk that the purpose of the contract could vanish should be assigned to the party that can best avoid the risk or, if that is not possible, deal with it ex post at the least cost. This principle of the least-cost avoider is considered in more detail in the section on Torts.

Breach

Contracts and their enforcement provide credible commitments about the actions of parties. These contracts, however, cannot be complete, so circumstances can arise under which one or both parties prefer not to fulfill its terms. In such circumstances the parties could mutually agree, perhaps with the payment of compensation, to terminate a contract.

A party may also unilaterally *breach* a contract. Breaches are allowed because under some circumstances it is economically efficient not to fulfill the conditions of the contract. For example, if a change in the market makes a necessary input to the production process prohibitively expensive, it may be better to breach a purchase contract and allow the buyer to contract for a product made with different inputs.

If the circumstances can be anticipated under which it may be economically inefficient to fulfill the commitments, the contract can be written to specify the obligation each party has to the other in those circumstances. There may be disagreement, however, about whether the circumstances are as claimed by the breaching party. One purpose of contracts is to reduce transactions costs associated with circumstances that develop during fulfillment of the agreement. When contract terms do not specify the obligations of the parties, the contracting parties can anticipate the consequences of a broken promise by referring to the rules used by courts for ordering remedies.

Remedies

Courts use two basic types of remedies in the event of breach: damages and specific performance. Damages can be compensatory for the harm caused or punitive, as in the Genentech and City of Hope example. Compensation for foreseeable damages depends on the baseline used by the courts.[12] One baseline is to leave the plaintiff as well off as she expected to be if the contract terms had been fulfilled. These *expectations damages* can differ from the amount required to allow the plaintiff to contract with someone else for the provision of the product or service. For example, in the case of an antique, a promisee may have expected to pay a certain amount for the item, but finding another identical item may be considerably more expensive because of search costs, transportation costs, and special handling. In such a case the court could order *consequential damages* based on the opportunity cost of the next best alternative. Another rule for awarding damages is to put the promisee in the same position she had been in prior to signing the contract. This rule corresponds to *reliance damages,* since it compensates the promisee only for reliance expenditures made as a result of the contract. In some cases the courts may simply require the defendant to return the item provided by the promisee. For example, an auto dealer may repossess an automobile when a purchaser defaults on payments.

Court awards of damages take place ex post, and anticipation of those awards provides ex ante incentives to fulfill promises, while leaving the flexibility to breach contracts when it is efficient to do so. The parties to a contract may also write into the contract contingencies in the event of breach. This *liquidated damages* approach is ex ante and is based on the principle that more complete contracts can be more efficient. Liquidated damages are limited to compensation for harm and are not intended as penalties for particular actions.

In cases in which it is difficult to determine the actual damages incurred as a consequence of a breach, the courts may provide relief in the form of *specific performance*. This generally involves an order directing the promisor to take the action called for in the contract. The court could, for example, order the antiques dealer to deliver the item to the buyer.

---

[12]In *Hadley v. Baxendale, Restatement (Second) of Contracts*, § 351(1) 1979, the court held that the defendant was not responsible for damages in circumstances that could not be reasonably foreseen. This decision is consistent with the notion that the common law provides incentives for actions to increase economic efficiency, and if something cannot be foreseen, no action can be based on it. Hence, there is no efficiency rationale for awarding damages.

Many contracts contain mandatory arbitration clauses that require disputes to be resolved outside the courts. The purpose of these clauses, which have been used for credit card and brokerage accounts for years, are intended to avoid the legal and administrative costs associated with a court case. Arbitration clauses are being used more broadly by a wider set of industries. Arbitration itself can be costly, so some companies have turned to jury waivers. In signing a contract such as a residential lease or an automobile loan agreement, an individual may waive the right to trial by jury. The purpose of the waiver is to avoid what some companies view as unreasonable awards by juries. In some states, however, including California, such waivers have been held to be in violation of the state constitution.

TORTS

Torts are civil wrongs—wrongs done by one person to another.[13] The law of torts is common law that evolves through decisions made by judges in cases brought by private plaintiffs. The common law of torts evolves as innovative cases are brought before the courts. Obesity has become a health concern, and trial lawyers have brought lawsuits against restaurants for their alleged contribution to obesity and the associated health risks. The chapter case, *Obesity and McLawsuits,* concerns the litigation against McDonald's. Tort claims also are laid to rest. In 2002 the claims of 1,900 plaintiffs who said their health was damaged by radiation from the 1979 Three Mile Island nuclear plant accident were finally resolved when the Court of Appeals upheld the district court's summary dismissal of the claims. The court concluded that not enough radiation leaked to cause adverse health effects. The plaintiffs decided not to appeal the decision to the Supreme Court.

The law of torts is applied in situations in which, because of transactions cost, for example, people are unable to bargain over the compensation that would be due in the event of a wrong such as an injury. Accidents that involve damage to real property or injury to a person are one subject of torts. The purpose of the tort system is to provide incentives to people and firms to take care to avoid harm. A study by Towers Perrin Tillinghast estimated that the cost of the tort system in the United States was $255 billion in 2008, or $838 per person, which represented 3.3 percent of GDP. In 1950 the cost per person was $12 (not adjusted for inflation).[14]

The basic elements of a tort case are an injury, an action that caused the injury, and the breach of a duty owed to the injured party. In the case of an automobile accident, the injury may have been caused by a brake failure, and if the brake failure was due to a faulty design or a failure of a part, the injured party may be able to recover damages from the automaker. If, however, the injured party was at fault as a result of negligence, the court may find for the defendant and not award damages. For example, if the owner of an older car had a safety inspection that revealed that the brake pads and rotors needed replacement but the owner did not have repairs made, the court could find that the owner had acted negligently. This could relieve the automaker of liability or reduce the damages awarded.

Some tort lawsuits that involve similar wrongs may be consolidated by the courts into a class action lawsuit. Class action lawsuits increased substantially in numbers during the 1970s and 1980s but in recent years have declined as a result of legislation and court decisions. Particularly in securities litigation the number of class action cases has plummeted since the peak in 1998.[15]

To identify the role of the law of torts in markets, the issue of product safety is used. The next section introduces the product safety problem and the concept of social efficiency. The following sections introduce the role of the liability system in achieving social efficiency, the development of the law of products liability, and the performance of the products liability system.

---

[13]See Franklin and Rabin (1996) and Cooter and Ulen (2007) for treatments of the law of torts.

[14]Towers Perrin Tillinghast, "2009 Update on U.S. Tort Cost Trends," 2009.

[15]The leading law firm, Milberg Weiss, in filing class action securities lawsuits made illegal kickbacks to plaintiffs in 225 lawsuits extending over several decades. The law firm's most feared securities class action attorney, William Lorach, was fired and sentenced to 2 years in prison for his participation, and Melvin Weiss, cofounder of the firm, pleaded guilty to criminal conspiracy charges and was sentenced to 30 months in prison. The law firm, renamed Milberg, paid a $75 million criminal fine.

THE PRODUCT SAFETY PROBLEM AND SOCIAL EFFICIENCY

Safety is a primary concern for responsible management and occupies a prominent place on the nonmarket agendas of most firms. No firm wants injuries in its workplace or associated with one of its products, yet preventing all injuries could be prohibitively costly if not impossible. The issue thus is the extent of care to take in reducing the number and severity of injuries. The principal and most comprehensive source of institutional guidance on safety is the law of torts. Lawsuits filed by injured persons bring both a specific case and broader issues of responsibility into the institutional arena of the courts. The law of products liability has developed from these cases, and the awards courts make and the costs of litigation and liability insurance provide firms with incentives to take care in manufacturing and in the incorporation of safety features, instructions, and warnings.[16]

The product safety problem can be conceptualized as shown in Figure 14-4. The producer makes a number of ex ante decisions, including product conception, research and development, design, manufacturing, and marketing. Once the product is put on the market, it becomes the property of the consumer. Ex post some consumers may be injured or incur property damage through their use of the product. From the perspective of social efficiency, decisions by both the producer and the consumers should take into account the social cost of possible injuries to persons and property as well as the costs of preventing those injuries.

Both producers and consumers take into account the social costs of the care they take to reduce injuries. The producer can make design changes, improve manufacturing quality, add safety features, and provide instructions and warnings. The consumer can develop skill in using the product and take precautions against accidents. In the case of a chain saw the producer can add safety features such as a safety tip, provide warnings about the hazard of kickback, and provide instructions on proper use, including a videotape. The consumer can purchase goggles, a hard hat, and steel-tipped boots. The costs of these measures constitute the cost of care by the producer and the consumer. The cost of care also includes any loss of benefits, for example, from the product because of safety features or additional costs from use. In the case of a chain saw a safety tip reduces the cutting length of the blade and increases the weight of the saw, contributing to fatigue of the user. Similarly, using a chain saw safely can lengthen the time required to complete a job.

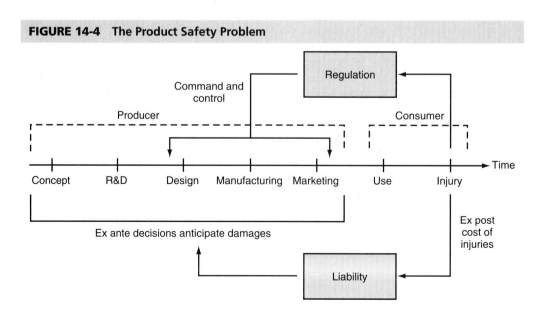

FIGURE 14-4 The Product Safety Problem

---

[16]The law of torts served as the principal source of institutional guidance on a broad range of safety issues until the 1970s, when the wave of social regulation led to the creation of regulatory agencies, such as the National Highway Traffic Safety Administration (NHTSA), the Consumer Product Safety Commission (CPSC), and the Occupational Safety and Health Administration (OSHA), to address particular safety issues. These agencies focused on specific hazards and mandated controls and safety standards.

FIGURE 14-5   Social Cost of Injuries Prevented

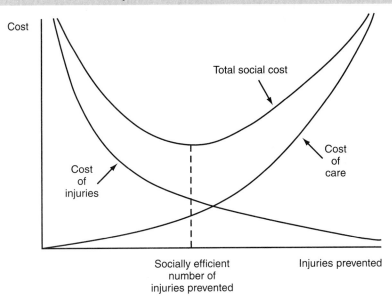

Social efficiency requires balancing the costs of injuries and the costs of care. This perspective is illustrated in Figure 14-5, which graphs costs as a function of injuries prevented. The social cost of injuries decreases as more injuries are prevented. If all injuries were prevented, however, the cost of care—the cost of injury avoidance—would be very high. In the case of a chain saw, this would require not producing the product. Total social costs are the sum of the costs of care and the costs of injuries, as illustrated in the figure. The socially efficient number of injuries prevented, or equivalently the optimal amount of care, minimizes total social costs and is determined by a trade-off between the cost of injuries and the cost of preventing them.[17] As shown in the figure, society tolerates some injuries because preventing them is too costly. That is, society prevents those injuries that are not too costly to prevent. Society allows chain saws to be produced and used despite many thousands of injuries annually.

The cost of care curve in Figure 14-5 reflects the most efficient, or least cost, combination of care taken by producers and consumers. Thus, for any given level of injuries prevented, the socially efficient allocation of care between the producer and consumers is that which minimizes the total costs of care. This is referred to as the principle of the *least-cost avoider;* that is, efficiency requires care by the producer or the consumer or both, depending on which has the lower cost of preventing injuries.

The social costs of injuries and the cost of care taken by producers are reflected in the prices consumers pay for products. The higher price required to cover these costs reduces the demand for a product and thus the injuries resulting from it. Consumers will not purchase a product whose price and the associated cost of taking care during use exceed the benefits anticipated from its use. Those who value the product more highly than those costs will purchase it. Over 1.5 million chain saws are sold each year.

As illustrated in the lower part of Figure 14-4, the institution of liability is intended to assign the ex post social costs of injuries to producers and consumers so that each takes the efficient level of care. The prices of products demanded and supplied then fully reflect those costs. This then results in the socially efficient number of injuries prevented, as illustrated in Figure 14-5.

In the United States and in other countries, the institution of liability is the principal institution that guides producers and consumers in most product safety decisions. Liability operates through the courts, which assign the social costs of injuries to consumers and producers through the damages assessed in cases brought by injured consumers. These assignments of costs are intended to induce consumers and producers to take the socially efficient level of care.

---

[17]The socially efficient number of injuries prevented is identified by the point at which the marginal social cost of injuries equals the marginal cost of care.

By aligning private and social costs, the liability system not only provides incentives for the socially efficient level of care but also allows decentralized decision making on the part of producers and consumers rather than relying on government regulation through command and control.

The actual institution of liability, however, differs from this ideal. Distributive considerations influence courts, which can focus on compensating the injured as well as on aligning private and social costs. These distributive consequences also motivate nonmarket action to alter liability standards. The product liability system is also costly to operate. Products liability law and measures to reform it are considered in more detail after the distinction between liability and property rules is developed.

ENTITLEMENTS, LIABILITY, AND SOCIAL EFFICIENCY

Entitlements and Their Protection

Starting from the perspective of the Coase theorem, Calabresi and Melamed (1972) defined an entitlement, or right, as the ability of an individual to control a particular resource or to take an action, with the state protecting that control or action from infringement. The type of protection given to entitlements is important. Calabresi and Melamed distinguished between two types of rules for protecting entitlements—property rules and liability rules.[18]

A *property rule* prohibits other parties from infringing the entitlement without the consent of the party holding it. Home owners are protected by a property rule that prohibits a person from either taking their home without consent or forcing them to sell it at a price they deem inadequate.

A *liability rule* protects an entitlement in quite a different manner. When an entitlement is protected by a liability rule, a person may infringe the entitlement but must compensate its holder for the objectively assessed harm resulting from that infringement. Although a home is protected by a property rule against infringement by a person, it is protected only by a liability rule against infringement by the state. Eminent domain is a liability rule that permits the state to take a home for a public purpose and requires the state to compensate the owner for its objectively assessed value. Even if owners would prefer to hold out for greater compensation, as would be their right under a property rule, eminent domain does not allow them to do so. An injury in an accident associated with a product is governed by a liability rule.

The remarkable feature of the Coase theorem is that in the absence of transactions costs social efficiency is achieved when entitlements are protected with either a property rule or a liability rule (also considered in Chapter 12 in the context of the control of externalities). An entitlement protected by a property rule allows parties to a possible accident to bargain over the allocation of care to reduce the likelihood of an accident. This bargaining was illustrated in the section on Property. To illustrate the role of a liability rule in protecting an entitlement, consider the case of chain saws and the risk of kickback, where the chain saw bucks sharply back toward the user as a result of hitting a knot in a tree, from the chain binding in the cut, or from boring with the tip. If the entitlement to compensation for an accident is assigned to the chain saw user and is protected by a liability rule, the manufacturer will add a safety feature, such as a safety tip to prevent boring, if the cost of the feature is less than the expected cost of the additional harm from not adding the feature. If the cost is greater, the feature will not be added. This is consistent with social efficiency, which requires that the accidents to be avoided are those that are not too costly to avoid. The chapter case *California Space Heaters, Inc.* provides an opportunity to consider such decisions.

As another example of the role of a liability rule in inducing social efficiency, consider the case of a swimming pool in a person's backyard. An externality is present because of the swimming pool and the presence of neighbors. Because the greatest likelihood of injury centers on neighborhood children, they are be the focus here. If the swimming pool owner posts a clear and obvious warning not to trespass, anyone who trespasses and is injured in the pool is in some sense "at fault." From the perspective of fault, the swimming pool owner should be protected so

---

[18]Calabresi and Melamed also consider inalienability rules. When an entitlement is protected by an inalienability rule, an individual is not allowed to give up or transfer the entitlement, even voluntarily. An individual's entitlement to vote in a public election is governed by an inalienability rule, since a person is not permitted to transfer that entitlement to another person.

that people neither trespass nor use the pool without the owner's consent. The costs of avoiding harm then would be assigned to the neighborhood children and their parents. Parents then would take care in supervising their children when they are outside and take measures such as building a fence around their own yards to prevent their children from going to the pool. Is this assignment likely to result in social efficiency; that is, is it likely to result in actions that minimize the sum of the costs of harm and the costs of the care by the pool owner and the neighbors? No, it would be more efficient for the pool owner to build a fence around the pool than for all the neighbors to build fences to keep their children away from the pool. This suggests that the swimming pool owner should be assigned the costs of injuries—that is, be liable for injuries associated with the pool. That assignment then creates incentives to build a fence around the pool.

Protecting certain entitlements with a liability rule is believed to involve fewer transactions costs than protecting them with a property rule. For example, it would be prohibitively expensive to negotiate agreements between each motorist and every other motorist and all pedestrians regarding compensation for injuries. Consequently, accidental injuries are governed by liability rules rather than by property rules. The next section addresses the issue of transactions costs and their implications for the use of property and liability rules.

The Assignment of Social Costs and the Choice Between Liability and Regulation

The Coase theorem pertains to situations in which entitlements can be clearly assigned and private agreements can be reached without substantial transactions costs. When entitlements are not well defined or there are substantial transactions costs, the assignment of responsibility for the social costs of injuries is a task for government.

Calabresi and Melamed provide five principles for the assignment of costs and the choice between the institutions of liability and regulation.

1. The assignment of entitlements should favor knowledgeable choices between social benefits (e.g., preventing injuries) and the social costs of obtaining them.
2. When it is unclear whether the social benefits exceed the social costs, "the cost should be put on the party that is best located to make such a cost-benefit analysis."
3. When there are alternative means of achieving social benefits (or of avoiding social costs), the costs of achieving them (or avoiding social costs from accidents) should be assigned to the party that can do so at the lowest cost.
4. When it is not clear who that party is, "the costs should be put on the party or activity which can with the lowest transactions costs act in the market to correct an error in entitlements by inducing the party who can avoid social costs most cheaply to do so."
5. Given principles one through four, protect the assignment with a liability rule or government regulation, depending on which is more likely to lead to social efficiency.

Breyer (1982) gives examples of the application of the *Calabresi and Melamed principles* to safety and pollution:

> When it is uncertain whether a benefit (such as a lawnmower with a certain risk) is worth the potential costs (such as the harm of related accidents), one should construct liability rules such that the costs (of the harm) are placed on the party best able to weigh the costs against the benefits. This principle is likely to place costs upon the party best able to avoid them, or, where this is unknown, on the party best able to induce others to act more safely. This principle seems to argue for making the lawnmower manufacturer strictly liable if he is best able to weigh the benefits, risks, and avoidance costs involved. Similarly, in the case of pollution, the rule would place liability on the factory owner, for he is in the best position to determine whether it is more efficient to curtail pollution or to compensate the victims of his noisome emissions.

In the case of lawnmower safety, the fifth principle pertains to the choice among government regulation, voluntary standards, and reliance on the liability system.

Principles three and four call for placing social costs on those who can most efficiently reduce them or induce others to take care to reduce them. In many cases, this means that the producer should be liable, as in the case of the risk of fire or explosion from a lithium-ion battery. In other cases, the producer and the consumer should each bear some portion of the social costs of injuries, so as to induce each to take the efficient level of care.[19]

In the case of a chain saw, the producer is better placed than is the consumer to determine whether, for example, the social benefits of a safety feature exceed its costs. If accidents can be reduced either by a safety feature or by care taken by the consumer, the producer is likely better placed to determine which can do so at lower cost. For example, the producer is better placed to determine if a safety tip is more effective in reducing the risk from kickback than are warnings to the consumer not to bore with the tip. If the hazard is from a branch falling on a chain saw user, the consumer is best placed to reduce the risk by, for example, wearing a hard hat. The producer then may be liable only if it failed to inform consumers about the hazard. If it were not clear whether a safety feature would reduce the hazard at lower cost than a precaution taken by the consumer, the costs should be put on the party best able to correct an error in the assignment of the cost. The producer typically is better placed to induce the consumer to change his behavior through warnings and instructions than is the consumer able to induce the firm to change its product. In the case of a chain saw, liability rather than regulation is used to govern the provision of safety, although the industry has adopted some voluntary standards to lessen the risk that a producer would free ride on the safety reputation generated by other producers.

PRODUCTS LIABILITY

The Development of Products Liability Law

Products liability is a branch of the common law of torts. Products liability cases that are litigated—particularly those that reach a state or the U.S. Supreme Court—establish legal precedents under which future cases are decided. Those precedents also provide the basis for plaintiffs' and defendants' expectations about likely court decisions in their own cases and so provide the basis for settlements.

The issues brought before the courts change over time, and the common law evolves to address those changes. Technological progress changed the nature of many consumer products, particularly as electronics replaced mechanical functions, making it more difficult to determine a product's likely hazards through casual inspection. In this situation, the Calabresi and Melamed principles suggest shifting the cost of injury prevention toward the producer because the producer is likely to have a lower cost of preventing injuries through design and manufacture than the consumer has in inspecting the products and taking precautions. The producer is also better placed to take actions in the market, such as providing warnings and instructions that can induce consumers to take care. Court decisions have followed a similar logic, resulting in evolving legal standards on which courts decide cases.[20]

The common law of products liability has evolved considerably since the 1950s, with legal standards originating in the law of contracts evolving into a standard of *strict liability* under which a producer may be held fully responsible even if it was not at fault and could not have prevented the injury. Some activists and legal scholars have advocated going further to a system of absolute, or total, liability. Under such a system a producer would be held liable for any injury associated with a product. Such a system would be equivalent to a producer attaching to each product it sells an insurance policy with no deductible or copayment.

This section provides an introduction to the principal changes in and central principles of products liability. One reason for the complexity is that products liability is largely state law, and not all states have adopted the same legal standards. Nearly all states have adopted the standard of strict liability, but some allow certain defenses that others do not allow. For example, a number of states allow state-of-the-art design defenses. Firms thus have the challenge of dealing with dissimilar laws across the states. This has led some business groups and some lawyers to advocate a uniform federal code for products liability.

---

[19]These principles also provide the basis for the choice among remedies for breach of contract, as discussed earlier in the chapter.

[20]Some legal scholars, such as Posner (1981), argue that social efficiency is the cornerstone of legal justice and that court decisions will in the long run produce a common law that supports efficiency. Rubin (1983) and Priest (1977) have argued that the natural incentives for parties to bring lawsuits when social efficiency gains can be realized will lead to new legal precedents that promote social efficiency.

The law pertaining to product safety developed from the laws of contracts and *warranties,* which focus on economic well-being. The law of warranties is codified in the Uniform Commercial Code, which has been adopted for commercial transactions by all the states. In addition, the Magnuson–Moss Warranty Act of 1975 regulates the content and clarity of written warranties. Warranties include those expressly made by the producer and those implied by, for example, the fact that the product was put on the market for sale. *Express* warranties are made in writing by the producer and, as part of the sales agreement, represent obligations binding on the producer. If the manufacturer states that a chain saw will cut at a particular speed and it does not, the consumer may sue for damages under the law of warranty.

Implied warranties are not made by producers but are held by the courts to be associated with a product put on the market. Products are held to have an implied *warranty of merchantability.* A chain saw is supposed to cut wood—if it does not, the consumer may sue. However, a chain saw is not supposed to cut cement blocks or metal pipe. A product also has an implied warranty for fitness for a particular purpose. A food or drink carries an implied warranty of *fitness for human consumption.*

The legal foundations provided by the law of contracts and warranties were transformed through two steps into the current law of products liability. The first step was a movement away from the rules of contract law by expanding the concept of who has standing to sue whom. In addition, certain principles of tort law were applied to injuries associated with products. The second was the replacement of the standard of negligence by strict liability. A negligence standard is still used in many parts of tort law, but the standard of strict liability is used in most jurisdictions in cases of products liability.

At the turn of the twentieth century, state laws generally required *privity of contract* in which a party incurring a loss of property associated with the use of a product could sue only the party from whom the product had been purchased. A producer who sold a product through a retailer could not be sued by a consumer because the consumer had privity of contract only with the retailer. This standard changed when the State Appeals Court of New York in *MacPherson v. Buick Motor Company,* NY Court of Appeals, 111 N.E. 1050 (1916), held that an injured consumer could sue the manufacturer when the manufacturer had been negligent in failing to detect a defect in a product. The court stated, "If the nature of a thing is such that it is reasonably certain to place life and limb in danger when negligently made, it is then a thing of danger …. If he is negligent, where danger is foreseen, a liability will follow." This decision not only eliminated the privity requirement but also led to injuries associated with products being treated as torts. This began the development of products liability.

The limits of privity of contract were further eroded by a court decision that extended the implied warranty of merchantability to cover an automobile driver, in this case the spouse of the purchaser, who was not in privity with the seller.[21] These two cases extended the reach of tort law to users other than the purchaser and back through the channel of distribution to the manufacturer. In most jurisdictions, a consumer is now able to sue the producer as well as virtually all those in the channel of distribution through which the product passed. In addition, other people, including injured bystanders, can sue for damages.

The *MacPherson* decision applied to cases in which negligence was shown. *Negligence* is defined as "the omission to do something which a reasonable man, guided by those ordinary considerations which ordinarily regulate human affairs, would do, or the doing of something which a reasonable and prudent man would not do."[22] The second phase of the evolution of products liability was the abandonment of the negligence standard and its replacement by the standard of strict liability in tort. Under a negligence standard, the burden of proof was on the plaintiff to show that the producer was at fault. Fault was determined by whether the producer had taken *due care* in the manufacture of the product and whether adequate warnings had been given. Cases often focused on showing that the product had a defect that caused an injury that would not have occurred had the manufacturer exercised due care.

Under strict liability the concept of fault is irrelevant and negligence is not required.[23] The courts do not inquire into who was at fault but instead are concerned only with whether the

---

[21]*Henningsen v. Bloomfield Motors,* 32 N.J. 358, 161 A.2d 69 (1960).

[22]*Black's Law Dictionary* (Black, 1983, p. 538).

[23]Negligence, for example, due to careless manufacturing may expose a company to punitive damages.

product in question was associated with the injury.[24] The courts also may not allow a due care defense, so a producer may be held liable even if everything possible had been done to prevent the defect that caused the injury.

The transformation to strict liability was the result of a set of cases decided in state courts. In *Escola v. Coca-Cola Bottling Co.*, 24 Cal. 2d 453, 150 P.2d 436 (1944), a case involving a person injured by an exploding Coca-Cola bottle, California Supreme Court Judge Traynor stated in a dissenting opinion: "I believe the manufacturer's negligence should no longer be singled out as the basis of a plaintiff's right to recover in cases like the present one. In my opinion it should now be recognized that a manufacturer incurs an absolute liability when an article that he has placed on the market, knowing that it is to be used without inspection, proves to have a defect that causes injury to human beings." Judge Traynor provided two rationales for his conclusion: one based on ex ante social efficiency and one based on which party can best bear the distributive consequences of the injuries. "Even if there is no negligence, however, public policy demands that responsibility be fixed wherever it will most effectively reduce the hazards to life and health inherent in defective products that reach the market. It is evident that the manufacturer can anticipate some hazards and guard against the recurrence of others, as the public cannot. Those who suffer injury from defective products are unprepared to meet its consequences. The cost of an injury and the loss of time or health may be an overwhelming misfortune to the person injured and a needless one, for the risk of injury can be insured by the manufacturer and distributed among the public as a cost of doing business."

Judge Traynor's call for a system of absolute liability has not prevailed, but his opinion influenced later court decisions that established the somewhat narrower standard of strict liability. In *Greenman v. Yuba Power Products*, 59 Cal. 2d 57 (1963), a person injured by a piece of wood when using a shop tool was awarded damages under the principle that "a manufacturer is strictly liable in tort when an article he places on the market, knowing that it is to be used without inspection for defects, proves to have a defect that causes injury to a human being." The explanation given for strict liability was "to insure that the costs of injuries resulting from defective products are borne by the manufacturers that put such products on the market rather than by the injured persons who are powerless to protect themselves." The definition of strict liability given in the *Restatement (Second) of Torts (1965)* is presented in Figure 14-6.[25]

The courts have adopted a broad interpretation of what constitutes a defect in a product. Defects include those that come from manufacturing, as, for example, a defective Coca-Cola bottle. It is often difficult to prove whether a product had a manufacturing defect, so many courts assume that if a person was injured by a product, the product was defective. Defects can also result from the design of the product. If a shop tool were designed in such a manner that a piece of wood could fly out of it during use, the product may be said to have a defect. Defects can also be associated with the instructions provided with a product or with the warnings given. Producers thus have a *duty to warn*. A defect in a warning is complicated because it involves both the warning given by the producer and the consumer's understanding of it. Many firms tailor their warnings to the lowest common denominator, and some use

---

FIGURE 14-6 Strict Liability Section 402A of the *Second Restatement of Torts* (1965)

(1) One who sells any product in a defective condition unreasonably dangerous to the user or consumer or to his property is subject to liability for physical harm thereby caused to ultimate user or consumer, or to his property, if (a) the seller is engaged in the business of selling such a product, and (b) it is expected to and does reach the user or consumer without substantial change in the condition in which it was sold.

(2) The rule in Subsection (1) applies though (a) the seller has exercised all possible care in the preparation and sale of his product, and (b) the user or consumer has not bought the product from or entered into any contractual relation with the seller.

---

[24]Even proof of direct causation need not be given, as indicated by the DES decision considered later in the chapter.

[25]A restatement is a collection of the rules established through court decisions, prepared by the American Law Institute, an association of legal scholars. A restatement is intended to reflect the case law in a majority of the states. A restatement is not itself the law but instead provides guidance to plaintiffs, defendants, and the court in reasoning about particular cases.

pictographs because some consumers are illiterate. The adequacy of warnings and instructions is evaluated by the courts.

Design defects include both those that are knowable and in some cases those that are unknowable—for example, because of the limitations of science at the time the product was manufactured. Manville was held liable for some asbestos-related injuries because of a failure to warn even though the court concluded that the danger was unknown to science at the time and thus the company could not have warned against it.[26] A defense that a firm used *state-of-the-art design* may not prevail when a standard of strict liability is applicable. Producers have thus been held liable for injuries from "defects" that were neither knowable nor preventable. Some states allow state-of-the-art defenses.

Warnings about the product's proper and intended use may not protect producers from liability. Proper and intended use is an imprecise concept. Is the proper and intended use of a screwdriver only to turn screws, or does it include opening paint cans and serving as a chisel? Because a product such as a screwdriver can be anticipated to be used for a variety of purposes, courts have assigned to producers the duty to *anticipate misuse.* A manufacturer of a pickup truck, for example, was held liable for an injury caused by a rollover when a user attached a camper that exceeded the truck's stated carrying capacity. In recent years companies have substantially increased their warnings. After an award to a woman scalded when she spilled a cup of its coffee, McDonald's added the warning on its cup, "Caution: Contents Hot." A manufacturer of a Batman costume warned, "Parents: Please exercise caution … cape does not enable user to fly."

Since the *Restatement (Second),* products liability has become both more important and increasingly controversial as courts have addressed a variety of difficult issues. In 1998 the American Law Institute issued the *Restatement (Third) of Torts: Products Liability* to reflect changes in the law as developed in the states. The *Restatement (Third)* is itself controversial; for example, it does not reflect the law in California and Oregon, and the Supreme Court in Connecticut has rejected the restatement as it pertains to design defects. How influential it will eventually be is unclear.

The *Restatement (Third)* distinguishes between manufacturing defects, design defects, and inadequate instructions and warnings defects. Strict liability applies only to manufacturing defects and applies "even though all possible care was exercised." A design is defective if a "reasonable alternative design" is available to reduce or avoid a foreseeable risk. The burden is assigned to the plaintiff to show that there is a reasonable alternative design. This assignment represents a departure from the law in many states and makes establishing liability considerably more difficult for the plaintiff. The *Restatement (Third)* also requires that an improved design be used rather than a warning to reduce or avoid a foreseeable risk. It also states that a manufacturer has a duty to warn if a risk is identified after the sale.

Allowable Defenses Under Strict Liability

Some defenses are allowed under strict liability, but they vary among the states. In all of these defenses, the burden of proof is on the defendant. The only absolute defense is that the product was not associated with the injury or was not the *proximate cause* of the injury. The concept of proximate cause was broadened considerably in the DES case to that of probabilistic causation. A woman whose mother had taken the drug DES during her pregnancy developed cancer over 20 years later.[27] The woman did not know which of several manufacturers had produced the DES her mother had taken, but the court held for her and apportioned damages among the producers according to their market shares.[28] Third-generation DES lawsuits have been filed as granddaughters of women who had taken DES sought compensation.

The other defenses are not absolute. One is based on the *assumption of risk* by the consumer. If a consumer voluntarily and knowingly assumes a risk, a producer may be protected. Such assumptions are routine for surgery and certain medications, but they may provide little protection if the patient did not understand the risk. The burden of proof is on the defendant

---

[26]*Beshada v. Johns-Manville Prods. Corp.,* 90 N.J. 191, 447 A.2d 539 (1982).

[27]The FDA banned DES in 1971 as a result of an abnormal cancer rate in the daughters of women who had used the drug.

[28]*Sindell v. Abbott Laboratories,* 26 Cal. 3d 588, 607 P.2d 924 (1980). In 1989 the Supreme Court let stand a New York court verdict holding DES manufacturers liable.

to prove that the assumption was both voluntary and understood. A producer may also have a defense if the consumer accepted a known and avoidable danger.

As indicated in the statement of strict liability in Figure 14-6, a producer may have a defense if a product had been altered by someone other than the producer in a manner that caused injury to the plaintiff. The *correction of a defect* may also provide a degree of protection in some instances.

In some jurisdictions a defense of *contributory negligence* on the part of the plaintiff is allowed. The burden of proof is on the defendant to show that the plaintiff was negligent in the use of the product; if proven, the defendant may avoid damages or have the damages reduced by the plaintiff's share of responsibility.[29] Producers are generally held responsible for anticipating misuse, however.

A producer may be able to use *disclaimers* to limit liability, but the courts have held some disclaimers to be invalid. The Magnuson–Moss Act prohibits producers from disclaiming express warranties and any implied warranties that go with it. Disclaiming is a concept from contract law and as such is intended to be a factor over which the parties bargain. Otherwise the courts may hold that it is invalid. One type of disclaimer that is upheld by courts is that associated with an assumption of risk in which a consumer voluntarily and knowledgeably agrees to bear the risk. Courts, however, typically examine closely whether the consumer actually understood the disclaimer. Disclaimers that limit the remedies available to parties, such as the right to sue, may not be upheld.

In most jurisdictions, products liability cases are covered by a *statute of limitations,* which is often 4 years. For capital equipment, a *statute of repose* serves the same function as a statute of limitations, but the time allowed is much longer. Compliance with government safety standards can in some cases be used as a defense, although such standards may be viewed by the courts as providing only the minimum level of safety.

Preemption

Some federal legislation preempts states from adding requirements beyond those stated in the federal law. This preemption could be explicit or implicit in the law. A 1976 law dealing with the FDA premarket approval of medical devices contained a preemption clause that prohibited states from imposing "any requirement … different from, or in addition to" the federal law. In 2008 in an 8–1 decision, *Riegel* v. *Medhome*, 552 U.S. 312 (2008), the Supreme Court held that this explicit preemption precluded the imposition of damages by state courts in a liability lawsuit pertaining to a large class of medical devices.[30] The case pertained to injuries due to the risks from a medical device that the FDA had already taken into account in its premarket approval of the devices. An award of damages was judged to be precluded by the statute. Justice Antonin Scalia provided an efficiency argument in the majority opinion that what state courts do is consider the danger of the device but not its benefits. He wrote, "The patients who reaped those benefits are not represented in court." Compensation for those injured would then be provided by insurance or by funds provided by state or federal government.

In contrast to the explicit preemption in the medical devices statute, pharmaceutical companies claimed that a similar preemption was implicit in the premarket approval for drugs. In 2008 the first case to reach the Supreme Court resulted in a 4–4 tie with Chief Justice John Roberts not participating. The tie allowed the Court of Appeals decision allowing a liability lawsuit involving a diabetes drug to go to trial. The following year the Supreme Court in *Wyeth* v. *Levine*, 555 U.S. 555 (2009) held that the FDA's approval of labels does not preempt lawsuits alleging a failure to disclose information or adequately warn. In 2011 the Supreme Court in *Williamson* v. *Magdo* (no. 08-1314) ruled unanimously that regulation does not preempt lawsuits regarding automobile seat belts.

Damages

The principal form of damages awarded in liability cases is *compensatory*—compensation for the loss incurred. The determination of compensation is straightforward in the case of property

---

[29]See Cooter and Ulen (1988, pp. 354–360) for an analysis of the efficiency consequences of a contributory negligence defense. Negligence is not the same as misuse but is better understood as gross misuse.

[30]Cases alleging manufacturing defects would be unaffected by the decision.

that has a readily established value. In other cases measurement is more difficult. It is possible to determine the cost of medical care for an injury, but measuring pain and suffering or the loss of a limb or a life is more difficult. Juries do make such decisions, however. Moreover, trial lawyers have available detailed data on the damages awarded in personal injury lawsuits. For example, Jury Verdict Research (2001) annually publishes its *Personal Injury Valuation Handbook*, which provides data on awards in a variety of categories such as vehicular liabilities and products liability with breakdowns by type of injury. In 1999 the median jury award in products liability cases was $1.8 million compared to $500,000 6 years earlier. Awards ranged from $11,000 to $285 million.[31] Part of the explanation for the higher median award is that trial lawyers have shied away from cases they expect will yield only modest awards. Jury Verdict Research conducts statistical analysis of cases and awards and provides probabilities of a plaintiff victory and predictions of awards for particular types of cases. For example, the median jury awards for burns and leg fractures were $891,000 and $500,000, respectively. Most cases do not reach trial, and out-of-court settlements are substantially lower than awards in litigated cases, perhaps because stronger cases are more likely to be litigated than weaker ones.

In cases in which both the producer and the consumer are responsible for the injury, some courts assess *comparative damages.* If the consumer is found to be 30 percent responsible for an accident and the producer 70 percent responsible, the producer is assessed damages equal to 70 percent of the consumer's loss. *The Restatement (Third) of Torts: Products Liability* requires comparative liability, which is used in all but six states and the District of Columbia.

Defendants often complain about the magnitude of some awards. The awards may reflect the sympathy jurors feel for accident victims and the deep pockets they see in firms. The awards in many of these cases are reduced by the trial judges or on appeal. Most cases are settled out of court with the settlement amounts not made public. The largest settlement was in 1998 when a class action suit against Dow Corning involving silicone breast implants was settled for $3.2 billion.

The number of personal injury lawsuits of all types has declined in recent years, although class action lawsuits and "mass torts," such as those involving tobacco and asbestos, increased until the mid-2000s. The overall decline in the number of cases in California, for example, has been attributed to several factors, including declines in accident rates, trial lawyers pursuing fewer but larger award cases, the use of alternative dispute resolution mechanisms such as arbitration, court decisions making certain types of cases more difficult to win, and tort reform. The size of awards and settlements has continued to increase. Settlements, awards, and court costs in asbestos cases have totaled nearly $54 billion, and projections are that the total will be over $200 billion. Eighty-five corporations have gone bankrupt as a result of the litigation.[32]

In most jurisdictions *punitive* damages can be assessed. The legal standard for imposing punitive damages is higher than that for compensatory damages and generally requires a finding of negligence and fault. This allows defendants to use defenses, such as state-of-the-art design, that may not be allowable under strict liability. Jury Verdict Research reported that in 1995 and 1996 punitive damages were awarded in 12 percent and 6 percent, respectively, of the products liability cases litigated. The median awards were $1.25 million and $2.5 million, respectively. The magnitude of some of the punitive damages awards has attracted considerable attention. In a case in which a Pinto's gas tank caught fire and caused injury, a jury awarded $3.5 million in compensatory damages and $125 million in punitive damages. The judge reduced the punitive damages to $3.5 million.[33] In 1994 the Georgia Court of Appeals struck down an award of $105 million in punitive damages mentioned in the Chapter 3 case *General Motors: Like a Rock? (A)*, involving an accidental death in a GM pickup truck with gas tanks mounted outside the frame rails.

The Politics of Products Liability

The costs and consequences of liability cases, and the proportion of awards that go to trial lawyers, provide strong incentives to take liability issues into the legislative arena. Liability costs not only affect safety decisions, but they also affect the prices of products and in some cases

---

[31]Current data are available only to subscribers.
[32]See White (2004).
[33]See Cooter and Ulen (1988, pp. 403–407) for an analysis of Pinto cases.

whether products are produced. In part because of soaring liability costs, production in the small aircraft industry fell from 17,811 aircraft in 1978 to 964 in 1993. Cessna Aircraft stopped producing single-engine, piston-powered aircraft in 1986 because of liability costs. The plight of the industry led to enactment of the General Aviation Revitalization Act, which prevents lawsuits against manufacturers for accidents associated with aircraft more than 18 years old. When the law went into effect in 1994, Cessna announced that it would resume producing single-engine, piston-powered aircraft.

Producers of medical implants such as heart valves have been subject to numerous liability lawsuits. Fearing that they would be included as defendants under joint and several liability (discussed later in this chapter), the suppliers of biomaterials began to stop supplying implant makers. The amount of biomaterials used in an implant is small and represented little loss of revenue to the suppliers. Implant makers and patient advocacy groups feared that a shortage would develop and worked for federal legislation shielding suppliers from liability. The Biomaterials Access Assurance Act was enacted in 1998.

Business has worked for decades for federal products liability legislation.[34] With Republican majorities in both houses of Congress as a result of the 1994 elections, business hopes for reform were buoyed. The American Tort Reform Association—which included 300 nonprofit organizations, professional societies, trade associations, and businesses—had actively worked for tort reform. The 60,000-member Association of Trial Lawyers and its consumer advocate allies, such as Public Citizen, renewed their opposition to reforms and geared for another battle.[35]

The foci of the federal efforts were (1) caps on punitive damages for small companies, (2) limits on the liability of wholesalers and retailers in products liability lawsuits unless they altered a product, (3) heightened standards for punitive damages by requiring evidence of "conscious, flagrant disregard" for safety, (4) restrictions on damage awards if the plaintiff misused a product or was under the influence of alcohol or drugs, and (5) a cap on noneconomic (pain and suffering) damages. Federal tort reform, however, succumbed to filibusters in the Senate and a presidential veto during the Clinton administration. In 2004 the House passed bills to cap pain and suffering awards at $250,000 and penalize lawyers who file frivolous lawsuits and engage in venue shopping. The Senate, however, did not act on the measures. A filibuster in the Senate by Democrats stopped a bipartisan compromise to move class action lawsuits from state to federal courts.

After the 2004 elections President Bush pledged to try again on tort reform. At an economic conference attended by the president, economists, and business executives, Home Depot CEO Robert Nardelli described the concerns of business: "What you have today is business on one side, and you've got the trial lawyers on the other side … You've got deep pockets colliding with shallow principles." Todd Smith, president of the Association of Trial Lawyers of America, responded, referring to the president and his tort reform objectives, "He [unashamedly] advocates legislation that would protect insurance industry profits and prohibit any punishment for the makers of dangerous drugs like Vioxx, while penalizing your mother for being abused in a nursing home or your daughter for having her baby killed by medical malpractice."[36] In 2005 the Bush administration prevailed and Congress passed a law requiring most class action lawsuits to be tried in federal rather than state courts. The law was intended to stop venue shopping, where plaintiffs attempt to have cases tried in jurisdictions friendly to plaintiffs.

Tort reform at the state level has been more successful than federal efforts. Many states have acted to cap and otherwise limit damage awards. In addition to the limits imposed by recent Supreme Court decisions, 36 states have adopted some limits on punitive damages. In addition, many states have capped awards in medical malpractice cases in an attempt to slow the increases in the cost of insurance for doctors. Several states have also abolished or otherwise restricted joint and several liability. The American Tort Reform Association (www.atra.org) tracks changes in tort law in each state. One proposal for reform is to have punitive damage awards paid to the government rather than the plaintiffs. This would preserve the deterrence effects of punitive damages without providing additional incentives for trial lawyers to file lawsuits. In 2003 Texas

---

[34]See Cohen (1990) for a review of the early legislative efforts.
[35]The trial lawyers renamed their association the American Association for Justice.
[36]*San Jose Mercury News*, December 16, 2004.

limited noneconomic damages in medical lawsuits, and in 2011 passed a law requiring plaintiffs to pay defendants' legal costs in meritless lawsuits.[37]

In a study of the effects of changes in state liability laws over the 1970–1990 period, Campbell, Kessler, and Shepherd (1998) found that states that had decreased their levels of liability awards experienced statistically significant higher gains in productivity of approximately 1–2 percent.[38] Other studies have indicated that high levels of awards in liability cases reduce innovations.[39] As indicated in the next section, businesses shied away from the state of Mississippi because of its litigation record.

IMPERFECTIONS IN THE LIABILITY SYSTEM

The products liability system has been criticized on equity, distributive, and efficiency grounds.[40] The equity arguments often express a belief that cases should be decided on the basis of fault and negligence. In particular, firms consider it inequitable to be assessed damages when there was nothing they could have done to prevent the injury. Objections have been made to the inability to use state-of-the-art design as a defense in cases governed by strict liability. In the absence of a statute of repose for capital equipment, this means that an injured party may be able to sue successfully for an injury caused by a product manufactured many years earlier when technological capabilities were more limited. The *Restatement (Third) of Torts* addressed this issue.

The distributive objection is that the awards in many cases are too large and seem to provide a prize, as in a lottery, rather than providing compensation for actual losses. The deep pockets of producers are seen by some jurors as a means of helping those who were unfortunate enough to have been injured. Criticism has centered on damages awarded for pain and suffering, which some argue are often unreasonable and unguided by legal standards. Whether awards are too large is unclear, however, and limits on awards remain the subject of considerable disagreement.

Most products liability cases are filed in state courts, and trial lawyers shop for the state venue most likely to favor their cases. The state of Mississippi earned a national reputation for large jury awards to plaintiffs, and many trial lawyers attempted to have their cases tried in that venue.[41] Venue shopping focused on Mississippi's 22nd Judicial Circuit, which the American Tort Reform Association designated a "Judicial Hellhole."[42] The governor of Mississippi pushed for state tort reform, citing not only the bad reputation the state had earned but also the business opportunities the state had lost. In explaining why Toyota had decided not to build a plant in the state, the company stated that "the litigation climate in Mississippi is unfavorable ...." Similarly, the CEO of Caterpillar explained why the company was not expanding operations in the state: "Unfortunately, Mississippi's current lawsuit environment makes us very reluctant to consider expanding our activities in the state."[43] Mississippi took the first steps toward reform by eliminating joint and several liability, reducing the liability of retailers, and capping awards for noneconomic damages at $1 million except for medical liability, which was capped at $500,000.

As the Coase theorem indicates, the distributive consequences of a legal standard can be independent of their efficiency consequences. However, liability awards can force firms into bankruptcy or dissuade them from producing certain desirable products. Because a number of pharmaceutical companies had stopped producing certain vaccines as a result of liability costs, Congress passed the Childhood Vaccine Act of 1986, which established a no-fault compensation system and capped pain and suffering awards. Similarly, there might be no nuclear power plants in the United States were it not for the Price–Anderson Act, which limits liability in the case of an accident.

Some critics argue that the development of drugs to treat conditions associated with pregnancy has been chilled by lawsuits such as those involving Bendectin, a drug used to treat

---

[37]*Economist*, August 20, 2011.

[38]Kimmel (2008) reached a similar conclusion finding that an additional tort reform increased productivity by 1 percent.

[39]See Viscusi and Moore (1993) and Huber and Litan (1991).

[40]See Viscusi (1991) for an analysis of products liability and recommendations for reform.

[41]In a dispute over legal fees in a case involving Hurricane Katrina, Mississippi lawyer Richard F. Scruggs, who had received millions of dollars in fees in asbestos and cigarette litigation, pleaded guilty in 2008 for conspiring to bribe a federal judge in Mississippi and was sentenced to 5 years in prison.

[42]The American Tort Reform Association issues an annual Judicial Hellholes® Report.

[43]*Associated Press State & Local Wire*, April 28, 2004.

EXAMPLE Silicone Breast Implants

In the 1970s and 1980s, 600,000 women received silicone breast implants in the United States. In 1982 a woman claimed that she became seriously ill when her breast implants leaked into her body. She sued and received an award of over $1 million. The Dow Corning Company subsequently was sued by 170,000 women, filing bankruptcy in 1995 as a result of a proposed settlement that collapsed shortly thereafter. Three other manufacturers settled the claims against them later in 1995. In 1998 Dow Corning reached an agreement with the plaintiffs in which it agreed to pay $3.2 billion over 15 years.

The litigation was coordinated by trial lawyers and was well orchestrated. The trial lawyers hired Fenton Communications to conduct a public relations campaign to highlight the claims of serious illness resulting from the implants.[1] The settlements reached were in spite of consistent scientific evidence that there was no link between the leaks and serious illness. The American College of Rheumatology stated that the scientific evidence was "compelling" that there was no link between implants and systemic disease. The Council on Scientific Affairs of the American Medical Association stated, "To date, there is no conclusive or compelling evidence that relates silicon breast implants to human auto-immune disease." The American Academy of Neurology stated that "existing research shows no link between silicon breast implants and neurological disease." Dr. Marcia Angell, executive editor of the *New England Journal of Medicine* and author of a book on breast implants, said that 15 scientifically valid epidemiological studies had been conducted and none showed any higher rate of illnesses among women with breast implants than women without them. She referred to the systemic diseases reported by women as "coincidental." Dr. David Kessler, who in 1992 as head of the Food and Drug Administration banned the sale of silicone-gel implants and later became dean of the Yale University School of Medicine, said, "There's no evidence that they cause systemic disease."[2]

Citing a Supreme Court decision calling on judges to act as "gatekeepers" to rule out unscientific testimony and speculation in favor of "pertinent evidence based on scientifically valid principles," a federal district court judge hearing implant cases barred plaintiffs' expert witnesses from testifying that the implants cause systemic diseases.[3] A special panel of independent experts appointed by the judge studied the issue for 2 years and in December 1998 issued its report concluding that there was no evidence that implants induce systemic diseases. The plaintiffs vowed to continue to press their cases.

The evidence continued to accumulate. A 1999 Institute of Medicine study found no increase in risk of cancer, autoimmune diseases, or neurological problems. A National Cancer Institute (NCI) study published in 2001 concluded there was no increased risk of cancer. Louise Brinton, an NCI researcher said, "[The study] helps lay to rest much of the concern."[4] Dr. Stuart Bondurant, chair of the Institute of Medicine committee, said, "We could find no evidence to support a causal relationship between the breast implants and any systemic disease. As far as I know there has been no information since the report was written that would naturally change that conclusion."[5] In 2000 the FDA approved for marketing saline-filled breast implants produced by two companies, and in 2006 it approved two silicone-gel breast implants produced by the same two companies.

At the end of August 2011, the FDA convened a 2-day meeting on the safety and monitoring of silicone breast implants. Dr. William Maisel, chief scientist of the FDA, said the implants were safe, "We felt that way before the meeting, and we continue to feel that way after the presentations and discussions over the past two days."[6] He added, "women should feel assured that the FDA continues to believe that currently marketed silicone breast implants are safe."[7] The FDA and the outside scientific panel recommended that monitoring using MRIs should not be required.

---

[1]Fenton Communications was the firm that orchestrated the nonmarket campaign against the apple-ripening chemical Alar discussed in Chapter 3.
[2]*New York Times*, July 11, 1998. The European Union never banned the implants, but in 2001 it required that recipients be at least 18 years of age.

[3]Some women suffered some scarring and hardening of tissue from leaks.
[4]*Milwaukee Journal Sentinel*, April 27, 2001.
[5]*New York Times*, October 11, 2003.
[6]*New York Times*, September 1, 2011.
[7]Ibid.

---

morning sickness. Congenital abnormalities occur naturally in about 3 percent of newborns, and pharmaceutical companies can face lawsuits if a mother used one of their products. As the silicone breast implants example indicates, liability cases can result in large settlements even when there is little scientific evidence linking a product to a disease.

In addition to concerns about the standards on which cases are decided and awards based, the liability system is costly to operate. Court costs and legal expenses for defendants are high, and under the contingent fee system, attorneys for plaintiffs typically receive one-third of any award or settlement. Of the $54 billion cost of asbestos litigation, approximately $34 billion has gone to lawyers (White, 2004). Investigating the facts in a case can also be expensive. Products liability cases are frequently consolidated into class action lawsuits, which generally reduces the costs of litigation. The high cost of taking a case to trial encourages settlements, but it can also encourage frivolous lawsuits that seek to extract a settlement from defendants who prefer to avoid the legal fees and court costs.

The high costs of litigation associated with the products liability system led Polinsky and Shavell (2010) to conclude that the system may not be worth the cost. They argue that market forces lead firms to provide safety in their products. But when they fail to do so, their reputation and brand equity will be harmed, resulting in lower sales. They also argue that NHTSA and the CPSC require safety in important classes of products. Moreover, consumers with insurance have the direct costs of injuries covered, although pain and suffering, which are difficult to evaluate, are not covered. They report that studies have shown that for every dollar received by plaintiffs another dollar is spent on the costs of operating the products liability system. Given the difficulty in demonstrating the benefits and the evident costs of operating the systems, Polinsky and Shavell concluded that the case for products liability is tenuous and that elimination of the system should be considered.

A particular concern of business is *joint and several liability.* In a case in which several parties have a role in an injury, such as a manufacturer and a distributor or a manufacturer and a government, all may be held liable. A motorist who hits a pothole, loses control of the car, hits a telephone pole, and is injured may sue both the city government and the telephone company under the principle that the harm to the victim is indivisible.[44] In such a case, the damages awarded are allocated among the defendants in proportion to their responsibility for the injury. But if one of the defendants is unable to pay its share of the damages, the defendant with "deeper pockets" can be required to pay the entire award. This standard focuses on compensating the injured party rather than providing appropriate incentives for care.

Another criticism is that punitive damages awards are governed neither by statute nor clear constitutional guidelines. Instead, juries have been largely free to assess punitive damages as they see fit. The imposition of punitive damages without standards to guide their award has been a source of concern to both firms and jurists. In a concurring opinion Supreme Court Justices Sandra Day O'Connor and Antonin Scalia, discussing punitive damages, wrote, "The impact of these windfall recoveries is unpredictable and potentially substantial … this grant of wholly standardless discretion to determine the severity of punishment appears inconsistent with due process."[45]

Although there are no explicit constitutional limits on punitive damages, in 1996 the Supreme Court threw out as constitutionally excessive a decision against BMW of North America in a case in which a jury awarded $4,000 in compensatory damages and $4 million in punitive damages because the paint on a new car had been retouched.[46] In an important decision in 2003 the Supreme Court overturned a punitive damages award that exceeded the compensatory damages award by a ratio of 145 to 1.[47] The court stated that the award was an "irrational and arbitrary deprivation of the property of the defendant." The court also stated that an award with a double-digit ratio was unlikely to be constitutional and that when compensatory damages are substantial, an award "at or near the amount of compensatory damages" would likely be justified. The decision quickly had effects as the Court of Appeals ruled that punitive damages of $5 billion against ExxonMobil for the *Exxon Valdez* oil spill were excessive and reduced the award to $2.5 billion. Exxon appealed the decision, arguing that the $3.4 billion it had already paid for compensation, criminal fines, and cleanup was sufficient punishment. In 2008 the Supreme Court reduced the award to $507 million, which was the amount of compensatory damages.

From the perspective of producers, damage awards are difficult to predict, complicating the estimation of the ex post consequences of their ex ante decisions. The insurance system allows firms to insure against that risk, but the insurance system itself is imperfect and costly to operate. Also, many firms are unable to purchase liability insurance. In response, Congress passed the Risk Retention Act of 1981, which allows firms in the same industry to form their own insurance pool.

The standard of strict liability is said by some to assign too much of the cost of injuries to firms and too little to consumers, distorting the incentives for care. This can cause firms to take

---

[44]See Cooter and Ulen (2004, pp. 362–64, 429–431).

[45]*Bankers Life & Casualty v. Crenshaw*, 486 U.S. 71 (1988). Quoted in Mahoney and Littlejohn (1989).

[46]*BMW of North America v. Gore*, U.S. Supreme Court, 116 S.Ct. 1589 (1996).

[47]*State Farm Mutual Automobile Insurance Co. v. Campbell*, No. 01-1284, 2003 WL 1791206 (2003).

more care and consumers to take less care than is efficient. The *Restatement (Third) of Torts* reflects this concern by allowing defenses in design defect cases. Efficiency is improved by allowing a defense of contributory negligence and assigning damages on a comparative basis. In an imperfect world, however, the Calabresi and Melamed principles indicate that liability should be assigned to the party that is best placed to evaluate costs and benefits and to induce the other party to take appropriate care. Producers are generally better placed than consumers for these purposes, so efficiency may be served by assigning liability to producers rather than to consumers.[48]

Tort law evolves as cases with new issues are brought before the courts. This means that tort innovation is ongoing. As an example, shortly after Mattel's second toy recall because of lead in the paint on toys, a lawsuit was filed in Los Angeles on behalf of a California family claiming that Mattel was negligent and should establish a fund to pay for medical monitoring of children who might have been harmed by the toys (discussed in the Chapter 5 case *Mattel: Crisis Management or Management Crisis*). The lawsuit filed by attorney Jeffrey Killino of Philadelphia sought class action status. The lawsuit was based on the medical monitoring theory that a fund could be ordered by the courts even though there was no evidence of actual injury. A 1993 California Supreme Court decision had supported a fund for monitoring if there was "a reasonably certain consequence" of exposure to a toxic substance.[49] In 1997 the U.S. Supreme Court rejected the establishment of such a fund, but the decision did not apply to state courts. Justice Stephen Breyer cautioned against medical-monitoring funds because they could harm plaintiffs "who depend on a tort system that can distinguish between reliable and serious claims on the one hand, and unreliable and relatively trivial claims on the other."[50]

SUMMARY

The law is an important institution for improving the efficiency of markets and private agreements. The United States has three basic types of laws. The first are those enacted by Congress, state legislatures, and local government bodies. The second includes rule making and decisions of administrative agencies, at times involving an administrative law judge, as considered in Chapter 10. The third is the common law, which is law developed from the rulings of judges on cases brought by plaintiffs. Common law consists of the precedents established by those decisions and forms the basis for important branches of the law, including the law of property, torts, and contracts. The common law evolves as courts address new issues brought before them by plaintiffs.

The fundamental efficiency perspective on the law is provided by the Coase theorem, which identifies two basic principles. The first is that when transactions costs are low, efficiency can be attained by assigning the entitlement to either party to a transaction, agreement, or hazard. The second is that efficiency can be attained with either a property rule or a liability rule. When transactions costs are high, as in the case of accidents, a liability rule is more efficient. In some cases regulation may be used, particularly if there is a market imperfection.

In the case of real property a property rule is natural, since the parties can reasonably be expected to bargain to an efficient outcome. In the case of an idea or invention, an intellectual property rule is required to allow the creator to appropriate returns from the creation. Appropriability is stronger, the tighter is intellectual property protection and the higher the cost of replicating the creation. Intellectual property is protected by patents, copyright, trademarks, and trade secrets.

The law of contracts allows parties to make credible commitments to future actions. This can provide the needed assurances for noncontemporaneous trades and for reliance expenditures. Contracts may be unenforceable if they are made under duress, violate statutes, or are unconscionable. Breach of a contract can be efficient, and courts award damages for both efficient and inefficient breach and may order specific performance such as fulfillment of the contract. Damages may be awarded based on expectations, reliance, or opportunity costs, and the parties to a contract may stipulate liquidated damages. Contracts may be judged unenforceable ex post or damages may be reduced because of impossibility or a frustration of purpose.

---

[48]See Epstein (1980) for an argument supporting strict liability.
[49]*Wall Street Journal*, August 20, 2007.
[50]Ibid.

Torts are civil wrongs, and strict liability in torts applies to manufacturing defects and in most states to many other types of product defects. Under strict liability a producer may be held liable even if it has exercised all possible care. The social efficiency role of products liability is to provide incentives to producers and consumers to take appropriate care to avoid those injuries that are not too costly to avoid. The assignment of the entitlement to consumers is generally supported by the Calabresi and Melamed principles. In practice, courts have also assigned the entitlement to consumers to compensate them for the losses they incur. Under strict liability that compensation can be independent of fault. The defenses allowed under strict liability vary among the states and include the absence of proximate cause, the assumption of risk, product alteration, and contributory negligence.

Products liability law continues to evolve as courts consider cases involving new issues. This has led to a broadening of the definition of products liability and at the same time a narrowing of the grounds for lawsuits as reflected in the *Restatement (Third) of Torts: Products Liability*. The Supreme Court has also limited punitive damages. Tort reform has occurred in many states, and to a limited extent at the federal level. Business has sought federal legislation to limit liability awards and expand the allowable defenses, but intense political competition over this legislation has limited reform.

CASES

California Space Heaters, Inc.

California Space Heaters had developed a line of unvented, convection kerosene space heaters using a new technology and was making preparations to sell them. For a modest purchase price the heaters could heat a room economically, without requiring a central heating system. A particular advantage of the heaters was that they allowed the consumer to focus the heat where and when it was needed. Because of high energy prices in the early 1980s, the demand for the heaters was expected to be brisk. Demand was anticipated to be particularly strong among low-income consumers and homeowners who had electric heating systems, especially in the East where electricity prices were very high. The heaters would also inevitably be used by people whose electricity had been cut off.

Although the heaters were very economical, there were safety hazards associated with their use, ranging from the risk of fire to adverse health effects from their emissions. The hazards were functions of the heater's design, its maintenance, and the conditions of use, including the fuel used. The company could incorporate a variety of safety features in the heaters, but safer heaters had a significantly higher cost and somewhat lower efficiency, requiring more fuel for the "effective warmth" produced.

In terms of hazards, a heater could cause a fire if it were placed too near curtains or furniture. The heaters could be designed so that the temperature could be as low as 320 degrees or as high as 500 degrees. The higher the temperature, the more efficient the heating but the greater the fire hazard, and the greater the risk that small children and others could be burned by touching the heater. The temperature in the heater depended in part on the wick adjustment, which could be controlled manually or by a thermostat. Fires could also occur from "flare up." Should that happen, closing the shutoff valve would extinguish the flame.

Ignition also posed a fire hazard. Electric spark ignition of the wick was safer than match ignition. Fires were a risk each time the fuel tank was refilled, particularly if the unit was already hot. This risk could be reduced by incorporating a removable fuel tank that could be filled outside the house. A siphon could also be incorporated into the tank to lessen the risk of spills when using a funnel. Because kerosene expands when warmed, the tank should never be completely filled; instead, some air space should be maintained to allow for expansion. Kerosene itself was difficult to burn without a wick, but if spilled, a carpet or curtains could act as a wick. The units with electric spark ignition—a battery-operated ignition device—could be equipped with an automatic cutoff system that instantly stopped combustion if the heater were tipped over or jarred. These units could also be equipped with a power-loss shutoff system that stopped combustion if the batteries lost power.

In addition to the risk of fire, toxic emissions from the heaters posed a potential hazard because the heaters were not vented to the outside as were central heating systems and fireplaces. Inhaling noxious fumes could be harmful, particularly if substandard kerosene were burned or combustion were incomplete. Kerosene came in two grades: 1K, which had a low sulfur content and was appropriate for the heaters, and 2K, which had a higher sulfur content and was inappropriate. Grade 2K kerosene was used in diesel automobiles and trucks and was available at many gasoline stations, whereas 1K kerosene usually had to be purchased at a hardware or specialty store. Since the two grades of kerosene could not be distinguished without conducting a chemical test, consumers could not easily verify which grade they had purchased and had to rely on the supplier. Gasoline should never be used in the heater, nor should fuel oil, which has a significantly higher sulfur content than kerosene.

Proper ignition involved raising the wick, igniting it, and lowering it until the flame burned cleanly. Some consumers might attempt to regulate the heat by adjusting the height of the wick. If the wick were set too low, combustion was less complete and emissions were increased. A wick stop could be incorporated into the heater to prevent the wick from being lowered too far. Because the heater rested on the floor, it could be difficult to adjust the wick properly, requiring the consumer to bend low to see the flame.

The hazard from improper combustion and the burning of the wrong kerosene centered on carbon monoxide and nitrogen dioxide emissions, which posed particular problems for asthmatics, children, the elderly, and pregnant women. EPA standards for outside air were nine parts per million (ppm) for carbon monoxide and 0.05 ppm for nitrogen dioxide.[51] U.S. Navy standards for submarines were 15 and 0.5 ppm respectively, and NASA's standards for the space shuttle were 25 and 0.5 ppm. The company's studies indicated that its heaters would not meet the EPA standards but would meet the Navy and NASA standards by a comfortable margin. The EPA had not issued standards for indoor air nor was it expected to do so within the next few years.

The risk associated with emissions could be reduced by using a kerosene additive that improved clean burning. The wick should be replaced each year, since the cleanliness of the burn depended on wick quality. Even if combustion were complete and the proper grade of kerosene were used, however, injury or asphyxiation could occur if the room were inadequately ventilated and the heater consumed too much of the oxygen in the room. A window should be left open to prevent oxygen depletion.

Kerosene heaters using old technologies had been banned by several states and municipalities, but most state legislatures had decided to allow the new-technology heaters because of the savings in fuel costs they provided. No federal safety standards

for kerosene heaters had been promulgated, but such standards could be forthcoming if injuries resulted from the heaters. The cognizant regulatory agency was the Consumer Products Safety Commission (CPSC), but the CPSC had been immobilized recently and was unlikely to mandate standards, at least for several years.

The design alternatives available to California Space Heaters centered on the safety features that could be incorporated into the heaters. Table 14-1 lists the potential hazards and the design steps, beyond the least expensive model, the company could take to respond to the hazards. Each safety feature was expected to be effective in reducing the specific hazard. The production process for the heaters involved standard technologies and methods, so the chance of a manufacturing defect was slight.

Consumers could also take care to reduce the likelihood of accidents and injury, such as making sure the room was properly ventilated. They could purchase the proper grade of kerosene and could use the "clean burn" additive that sold for $3.99 per 12-ounce bottle. The heater should be cleaned and the wick changed at least at the beginning of each heating season. The consumer should, of course, purchase the appropriate wick.

The least expensive model of kerosene space heater with match ignition could be manufactured for $44, and the standard markup was 100 percent for a discount store and slightly higher in an appliance store. With proper use, the least expensive model was safe. The demand for the low-end heaters was expected to be strong and price elastic. At a price of $88 sales could reach 2 million units per year. The safest and most expensive model the company could make would include all the safety features listed in Table 14-1. It could be manufactured for $189. The

TABLE 14-1 Heater Hazards and Remedies

Potential Hazard	Design Remedy	Cost ($)
Temperature adjustment	Thermostat	7.50
Overheating due to flare-up	Automatic temperature shutoff	22.00
Tank overflow	Tank level gauge	3.00
Tip-over fire	Automatic cutoff	8.00
Contact fire	Low burn temperature*	—
Spill during filling	Siphon filling system	12.00
Ignition fire	Electric spark ignition	19.50
	Large tank	12.00
Fire during refilling	Removable tank**	6.00
Noxious emissions		—
Substandard kerosene	None	—
Incomplete combustion	(a) wick stop	6.50
	(b) electric wick adjustment	32.00
Oxygen depletion	None	—

Note: * Estimated loss in efficiency of $40 per year.

** Only effective if tank is removed and taken outside.

---

[51]The EPA standard was set to protect individuals with angina while they exercised.

demand for the safest heater was expected to be limited. The venture capitalist backing the company commented, only partly in jest, that at a price of $378 the only sales would be to the wealthy for use in their ski cabins.

To indicate the savings attainable from use of the heaters, a marketing analyst compared the cost of heating a house to 68 degrees with heating it to 55 degrees and using a kerosene space heater to bring the living room up to 68 degrees. The estimated savings was $470 a year for a house in New England that used fuel oil; if the house had electric heat, the savings would be $685 per year. Smaller savings could be attained with a portable electric heater, which cost less than a kerosene heater.

The heaters could be marketed through various channels of distribution, ranging from discount stores to appliance stores to heating and air-conditioning shops. Appliance stores might be interested in carrying a full line of heaters, but discount stores were expected to be interested in only the least expensive model. Heating and air-conditioning stores were not expected to stock the heaters but would order them for customers. Their customers were likely to be interested in the more expensive models. The channels of distribution differed significantly in their ability to provide consumers with information on safety features and proper use.

The company consulted a lawyer who indicated that products liability lawsuits were probable should there be injuries or adverse health consequences associated with the use of the heaters. Strict liability in tort would in all likelihood be the applicable liability standard, so the company could be held liable even if an injury were due to foreseeable misuse by a consumer. The costs to the company included the cost of liability insurance, legal and court costs, and the management time required by the cases. These costs could be reduced by adding

more safety features to the model. The lawyer had investigated the cost of insurance and roughly estimated that insurance costs plus legal fees might be as much as $55 per unit for the lowest priced model and $10 per unit for the safest model given the estimated sales. The lawyer also estimated that the purchasers of the lowest-cost heaters were less likely to file lawsuits in the event of an injury because they were less familiar with the legal process.

The likelihood of an injury associated with a heater was difficult to estimate, but the company's engineers gave a ballpark estimate of one in a million of a manufacturing defect resulting in a death or a permanent disability from a fire. They estimated that the likelihood of a fire death from misuse was approximately 5 in 100,000 with the least expensive model over the life of the heater and 4 in a million with the most expensive model. The lawyer asked the engineers for estimates associated with each safety feature, but so far they had provided only two estimates. They estimated that adding electric spark ignition to the least expensive model would reduce the probability of a death by 50 percent, whereas electric wick adjustment would reduce the probability of a death by less than 2.5 percent. ■

Preparation Questions

1. How should California Space Heaters reason about its responsibility for the safety of its heaters and their use?
2. What safety features should be incorporated into the heaters? Should electric spark ignition be incorporated? Electric wick adjustment? What criteria should be used for those decisions?
3. What other actions should be taken in the design or marketing of the heaters?
4. How should prices be set; that is, on what cost basis?

Patent Games: Plavix

In 2001 Apotex, a Canadian manufacturer of generic drugs, filed an application with the U.S. Food and Drug Administration (FDA) to market clopidogrel bisulfate as a generic version of the world's second–best-selling drug, Plavix, an anticlotting drug. Sanofi-Aventis, the French pharmaceutical giant, held a composition of matter patent on Plavix, but Apotex claimed that the 1989 Sanofi patent was invalid because the ingredient clopidogrel bisulfate could be inferred from an earlier 1985 patent that had expired. Sanofi-Aventis argued that the later patent was valid and would not expire until 2012.[52] In 2002 Sanofi-Aventis filed a patent infringement lawsuit in federal court, claiming that the patent provided it with exclusive rights to produce and market Plavix. Plavix was marketed in the United States by Bristol-Myers Squibb, and U.S. sales were $3.5 billion in 2005 with worldwide sales of over $6 billion. Plavix was the best-selling of Bristol-Myers Squibb's drugs and was crucial to the success of the company.

Apotex was a privately held generics producer located in Toronto, Canada, and its CEO, Richard Sherman, was known as an aggressive risk taker. Sherman said, "They say I stalk my prey. I say I don't ever shy away from a fight."[53] He added, "The system is being screwed up by greedy people who see this big pot to be split, and they have no interest in consumers, who get screwed by paying more than they should for medications they need." He referred to the payments that drug makers made to keep generic drugs off the market as "poison pills." Sherman had a net worth of $3.7 billion, according to *Forbes* magazine.

The FDA approved Apotex's version of Plavix in January 2006. The approval allowed Apotex to market the drug at its own risk. That is, if it marketed the drug and lost the patent infringement case, it could be liable for damages. Apotex had invested millions of dollars to construct production facilities and began to produce clopidogrel bisulfate in late 2005.

---

[52]*Wall Street Journal*, September 2, 2006.

[53]*Ottawa Citizen*, August 19, 2006.

Bristol-Myers Squibb and Sanofi-Aventis learned that Apotex had built an inventory of clopidogrel bisulfate, and with a trial on the merits of the patent infringement lawsuit scheduled for June 2006, they initiated settlement negotiations with Apotex. On March 21 the three companies reached an agreement granting Apotex the right to market its generic drug in September 2011, 8 months before the patent on Plavix would expire. The agreement gave Apotex a 6-month period before the companies could offer their own generic. Bristol-Myers Squibb and Sanofi-Aventis also agreed to pay Apotex at least $40 million if the agreement were approved and a $60 million break-up fee if the agreement were rejected on antitrust grounds. In a required disclosure, Sanofi-Aventis and Bristol-Myers Squibb stated that there was a significant risk that the agreement would not receive antitrust approval. The trial on the patent infringement lawsuit was postponed pending approval of the agreement.

Bristol-Myers Squibb was operating under a 2003 consent decree with the Federal Trade Commission (FTC) and state attorneys general pertaining to attempts to delay the entry of generic versions of two of its drugs—Taxol and BuSpar. Under the consent decree the FTC and the state attorneys general had to approve any Bristol-Myers Squibb arrangements that could be anticompetitive. The agreement with Apotex was submitted to the regulators for review. The FTC had expressed opposition to agreements that restricted the introduction of generic drugs. On May 5 the state attorneys general told the three companies that they would not approve the agreement, and the FTC also was said to be opposed. The FTC was reportedly concerned about the break-up fee and the 6-month period before Bristol-Myers Squibb and Sanofi-Aventis could begin marketing their own generic drug.

After the agreement was rejected, Bristol-Myers Squibb CEO Peter R. Dolan sent executive vice president Dr. Andrew G. Bodnar to Toronto to negotiate a modified agreement that would satisfy the regulators. The modified agreement was submitted on May 26 to the FTC and state attorneys general. It did not include the 6-month period and allowed Apotex to license and manufacture a generic version of Plavix in June 2011.

Apotex said that in addition to the modified agreement submitted to the FTC and the state attorneys general, Bodnar had made two oral agreements with Sherman that had been in the original agreement but were not in the modified agreement. One was that Bristol-Myers Squibb and Sanofi-Aventis would not market its own generic version of Plavix until Apotex's generic had been on the market for 6 months. The other was that Bristol-Myers Squibb and Sanofi-Aventis would pay Apotex the $60 million break-up if the modified agreement were rejected by the government.

One provision retained in the modified agreement was that Bristol-Myers Squibb and Sanofi-Aventis could not file for an injunction to stop generic sales of clopidogrel until 5 days after a sales launch. The modified agreement also limited damages to 50 percent of Apotex's sales of the generic if it launched the drug and the modified agreement were rejected and Apotex lost the patent infringement case.[54] These provisions were to

remain valid even if the agreement were rejected by the government.

Robert S. Silver, an attorney for Apotex, demanded payment of the $60 million break-up fee after regulators rejected the initial agreement. On May 27, one day after the modified agreement had been concluded, Dr. Bodnar sent an e-mail message to Sherman stating, "You explicitly assured me that you would not initiate such action at this point and would wait until matters had resolved themselves. Unless Silver immediately withdraws his demand, I will consider myself not bound by any restriction as to this issue to which I am bound by agreement with you."[55]

On July 26 Federal Bureau of Investigation agents raided Bristol-Myers Squibb's headquarters, including the office of CEO Dolan, as the Antitrust Division of the U.S. Department of Justice began a criminal investigation of the agreement. The investigation was initiated at the request of the FTC. Bristol-Myers Squibb commented that it "believes that all of its conduct relating to the proposed Plavix settlement has been entirely appropriate and coordinated throughout with senior outside counsel."

The state attorneys general indicated that they would not accept the modified agreement, and the FTC indicated that it was not satisfied with the modifications. This rejection and the provisions of the agreement that remained valid gave Apotex an opportunity to market clopidogrel with only limited risk.

Apotex launched its generic drug on August 8. Sherman said, "There should be no mistaking that our decision to launch a generic version of this blockbuster product at risk is a testament to our commitment to patients, consumers, and taxpayers." The drug had an expiration date of nearly 2 years, so drug distributors could buy large quantities and sell it out of inventory. Apotex had talked with the major drug distributors prior to launching its sales, and they had expressed eagerness to purchase the drug, since they had mandates to obtain drugs at the lowest possible cost. Medco Health Solutions and other pharmacy benefits companies purchased the generic, and Rite Aid said it would have the generic on its shelves in a day. Apotex charged $124 for a 30-day supply, compared to a price of $148 for Plavix. Bristol-Myers Squibb was reported to be offering rebates. Verispan LLC, which provided information on prescription sales, reported that Apotex's generic drug had 60.2 percent of total prescriptions written and 74 percent of new prescriptions for the week ending August 18.[56]

Surprised by Apotex's flooding the market, Sanofi-Aventis responded by filing a lawsuit in federal court seeking an injunction to halt the sales. Prior to the first hearing on the lawsuit, Apotex's lawyers advised Sherman to disclose the oral agreements, and on August 17, 2006 Apotex filed a statement in federal court revealing the oral agreements. Bristol-Myers Squibb said that the side agreements had been suggested by Sherman and that they had refused. Bristol-Myers Squibb held that there were no oral agreements.

After Apotex began shipping its generic, Sherman said in an interview, "I thought the FTC would turn [the modified agreement] down, but I didn't let on that I did. But they seemed

---

[54]*Wall Street Journal*, September 2, 2006.

[55]*New York Times*, August 18, 2006.
[56]AFX.COM, September 1, 2006.

blind to it."[57] He also commented, "They couldn't see that maybe certain things were going to end them up in prison."[58] Sherman's belief that the modified agreement would be rejected was supported by a July 7 letter to three U.S. senators in which Sherman wrote, "I must comment on the well-publicized perception that Apotex has entered into an anticompetitive settlement with Sanofi/Bristol-Myers Squibb concerning clopidogrel (Plavix). That perception is incorrect. Apotex has negotiated only to remove barriers to immediate launch. To achieve that objective, we entered into a somewhat bizarre arrangement that will enable immediate launch, if and when the FTC refuses to approve a settlement."[59]

At the hearing on the lawsuit seeking an injunction, attorneys for Bristol-Myers Squibb claimed that failure to issue an injunction would "kill future clinical efforts." Federal judge Sidney Stein granted a preliminary injunction, halting sales on August 31. Judge Stein wrote that Sanofi-Aventis "clearly established a likelihood of success on the merits." The judge, however, refused to order Apotex to recall the product it had already shipped, and Bristol-Myers Squibb was required to post a $400 million bond to compensate Apotex if it won the lawsuit. Apotex had asked for a $4 billion bond and said that the amount of the bond was "grossly inadequate." Apotex filed with the U.S. Court of Appeals for an emergency stay of the injunction,[60] and the U.S. Court of Appeals rejected the appeal, ending Apotex's foray. Analysts estimated that Apotex had shipped several hundred million dollars worth of clopidogrel.

In 2005 Bristol-Myers Squibb and the U.S. Attorney in New Jersey had reached a deferred-prosecution agreement in a case involving charges of conspiracy to commit securities fraud relating to an accounting scandal. Under the agreement Bristol-Myers Squibb agreed to exemplary conduct for 2 years and supervision by an independent federal monitor, retired judge Frederick B. Lacey, appointed by the court. The U.S. attorney asked Lacey to examine the Apotex affair, and Lacey conducted a review. In September 2006 Lacey told the Bristol-Myers Squibb board of directors that CEO Dolan should be fired. The board promptly did so. Bristol-Myers Squibb's share price had fallen 60 percent since Dolan was appointed CEO in 2001. ∎

Preparation Questions

1. Why did Bristol-Myers Squibb and Sanofi-Aventis seek a settlement rather than let the patent infringement case go to trial?
2. Should Bristol-Myers Squibb and Sanofi-Aventis have attempted to pay Apotex to prevent it from launching a generic version of Plavix?
3. Was Sherman's strategy that of a shrewd business executive? Did Sherman act ethically in his strategy?
4. Should the FTC and the state attorneys general have rejected the agreements?
5. Did Bristol-Myers Squibb likely violate the deferred prosecution agreement?

Obesity and McLawsuits

In 2001 New York trial lawyer Samuel Hirsch filed a liability lawsuit against McDonald's alleging that his 5-feet 10-inch, 272-pound client had become obese from eating at McDonald's and other fast-food restaurants. The man had continued to eat at fast-food restaurants despite two heart attacks. After dropping that lawsuit, Hirsch represented two obese teenagers who claimed to have eaten at McDonald's regularly for several years and to have developed obesity-related illnesses.

Hirsch was advised by Professor John Banzhaf of the George Washington University Law School, whose students had earlier filed a lawsuit against McDonald's for claiming that its french fries were fried in vegetable oil when they were also par-fried in beef fat at the potato processing plant.[61] The case was settled in 2002 for $12.5 million. Banzhaf "teaches unique world-famous courses—'Legal Activism' [Law 637], which has been dubbed 'suing for credit' and 'Sue the Bastards'—where his law students, which the press dubbed 'Banzhaf's Bandits,' learn to become public interest lawyers by bringing their own legal actions …. He and his students are widely known for bringing hundreds of innovative public interest legal actions …"[62]

After their success in litigation against tobacco companies, trial lawyers sought a new mass tort, and obesity was their next campaign. Banzhaf said, "A fast-food company like McDonald's may not be responsible for the entire obesity epidemic, but let's say they're 5 percent responsible. Five percent of $117 billion is still an enormous amount of money."[63] The Public Health Advocacy Institute of Boston held a seminar at Northeastern University on "Legal Approaches to the Obesity Epidemic." Brian Murphy, an attendee and a recent graduate of the Rutgers Law School, said, "It's a very important and pressing issue, and its outcome will be with us for years to come. I'm hoping to be able to build a career out of this."[64]

Lisa A. Rickard, president of the U.S. Chamber Institute for Legal Reform, stated, "Lawyers hungry for more money should resist the temptation to take a bite out of the fast-food industry. Overweight Americans will not find the solution to obesity in the courtroom but in making wise choices to eat smaller portions and healthier foods wherever they go."[65] Brendan Flanagan of the National Restaurant Association commented that "people who are filing these suits are trying to legislate via the court system."[66]

[57]*Wall Street Journal*, September 2, 2006.
[58]*New York Times*, August 15, 2006.
[59]Ibid.
[60]The judge stated that the claims of an oral side agreement were not affecting his decision "as of now."
[61]The Daily Buzz, www.foodservice.com, March 12, 2004.
[62]http://banzhaf.net.

[63]*Time,* August 3, 2003.
[64]Ibid.
[65]Press release, U.S. Chamber of Commerce, July 2, 2003.
[66]Associated Press Online, March 10, 2004.

OBESITY

Interest in the obesity issue intensified after a government study revealed that Americans had become heavier and that obesity had become a serious health problem. A study released in February 2004 by the Centers for Disease Control and Prevention (CDC) stated that in 2000, 400,000 deaths were caused by obesity-released illnesses compared to 435,000 deaths caused by tobacco.[67] The Surgeon General estimated that health care costs resulting from obesity were $117 billion annually, and the Department of Health and Human Services began an advertising campaign promoting personal responsibility and urging more exercise and less eating. The U.S. government and the World Health Organization urged food manufacturers and restaurants to offer healthier foods.

The body mass index (BMI), defined as a person's weight in kilograms divided by height in meters squared, was used to measure obesity. A BMI in the 19–25 range was considered healthy, 26–30 was overweight, and over 31 was obese. The BMI had increased by 0.9 from 1971–1975 to 1988–1994, and the proportion of people considered obese increased from 15 percent to 31 percent from 1980 to 2000.[68] Sixty-four percent of American adults were overweight or obese. The average weight of an adult male had increased from 168 pounds in the early 1960s to 180 pounds at the beginning of the twenty-first century. The average weight for an adult female increased from 143 to 155.

Substantial increases in weight occurred throughout the twentieth century with the BMI for people in their 40s increasing by 4 units.[69] This increase was accompanied by only a modest increase in calorie intake. During the last century, however, technological change reduced the strenuousness of work both in the home and in the marketplace. Another long-term factor was a substantial decline in the relative price of food as a result of technological progress in agriculture. Lakdawalla and Philipson estimated that in the post–WWII period approximately 40 percent of the increase in BMI was due to the expansion in the supply of food, and 60 percent was due to demand-side factors such as a decrease in physical activity.[70]

From 1977–78 to 1994–96 the average intake of calories increased from 1826 to 2002. Surveys based on food diaries indicated that the increase did not come from meals but instead from snacks between meals. Cutler, Glaeser, and Shapiro concluded, "Fast food has certainly increased, from about 60 calories per day to over 200 calories per day. But this increase is largely at formal meals, where it has been offset by reduced home consumption."[71] They concluded that "the evidence also rules out the view that fattening meals at fast-food restaurants have made America obese." Their explanation for the increase in obesity was that technological change had led Americans to switch from home-prepared food to mass-produced food. For example, the total potato consumption in the United States increased by 30 percent from 1977 to 1995 as a result of improved technologies for producing potato chips and french fries. The lower cost of mass-produced food also led to greater consumption.

In a report prepared for the U.S. Chamber of Commerce, Todd Buchholz argued that the increase in obesity was caused by a variety of factors, including the lower real price of food, changes in the nature of work, and the failure to exercise more as the calorie intake increased.[72] Buchholz reported that in 1961 consumers spent 17 percent of their income on food and in 2001 spent 10 percent. He also cited U.S. Department of Agriculture (USDA) data indicating that the ratio of the prices of restaurant meals to supermarket prices had declined from 1.82 in 1986 to 1.73 in 2001. Moreover, a smaller percent of people were employed in jobs requiring physical work than in the past. Buchholz also argued that fast food meals derived fewer of their calories from fat than "a typical home meal from 1977–78."

Buchholz argued that the greatest increase in BMI from 1971–75 to 1988–94 was accounted for by college-educated people rather than those who had a high school education or less. On average Americans were consuming 200 more calories a day and not compensating for it with exercise. The USDA's "Continuing Survey of Food Intakes by Individuals" indicated that Americans were not eating larger meals but instead were eating more between meals.

MCDONALD'S MARKET RESPONSE TO THE OBESITY ISSUE

For nearly 20 years McDonald's had provided nutrition information in each of its restaurants, but it did not provide information for individual menu items. After the government reports on obesity, McDonald's announced that it was discontinuing its supersize meals to simplify its menus. It also introduced the "Go Active" meal with a salad, water, a pedometer, and an activity log; an all-white-meat chicken McNugget; and other healthier items. McDonald's, the International Olympic Committee, and the American College of Sports Medicine opened a Web site, www.goactive.com. McDonald's also introduced an educational campaign, Real Life Choices, about how to track diets and put menu items into three categories: Watching Calories, Watching Fat, and Watching Carbohydrates.[73] McDonald's also provided nutritional information on its Web site. Chuck Horton of Virginia commented, "If I want to eat healthy, I'll eat at home. I come to McDonald's for one reason: the fries ... I think this healthy eating thing has gone too far."[74]

---

[67]Obesity is associated with greater risk of developing type 2 diabetes, chronic lower back pain and joint disorientation, cardiovascular diseases, certain cancers, respiratory problems, and depression.

[68]Cutler, Glaeser, and Shapiro (2003) concluded that demographic changes did not explain the increase in obesity.

[69]Dora Costa and R. Steckel, "Long-Term Trends in Health, Welfare, and Economic Growth in the United States." NBER Historical Working Paper No. 76. National Bureau of Economic Research, Cambridge, MA, 1995.

[70]Darius Lakdawalla and Tomas Philipson (2009).

[71]Cutler, Glaeser, and Shapiro, op. cit.

[72]Todd G. Buchholz, "Burger, Fries and Lawyers: The Beef Behind Obesity Lawsuits," U.S. Chamber of Commerce and the U.S. Chamber Institute for Legal Reform, July 2, 2003.

[73]PRNewswire, January 6, 2004.

[74]Associated Press Online, April 16, 2004.

OBESITY LAWSUITS

In dismissing the case brought by Hirsch on behalf of the two teenagers, U.S. District Court Judge Robert W. Sweet wrote "that the dangers of over-consumption of … high-in-fat foods, such as butter, are well-known. Thus any liability based on over-consumption is doomed if the consequences of such over-consumption are common knowledge …. Thus, in order to state a claim, the Complaint must allege either that the attributes of McDonald's products are so extraordinarily unhealthy that they are outside the reasonable contemplation of the consuming public or that the products are so extraordinarily unhealthy as to be dangerous in their intended use. The Complaint—which merely alleges that the foods contain high levels of cholesterol, fat, salt and sugar, and that the foods are therefore unhealthy—fails to reach this bar."[75] He also wrote that under New York law, "The standard for whether an act or practice is misleading is objective, requiring a showing that a reasonable consumer would have been misled by the defendant's conduct."[76]

Judge Sweet, however, left the door open for a lawsuit based on showing that fast food was addictive or that it was deceptive because it contained more harmful content than consumers anticipated. He wrote that "Chicken McNuggets, rather than being merely chicken fried in a pan, are a McFrankenstein creation of various elements not utilized by the home cook." Judge Sweet also stated that this lawsuit could "spawn thousands of similar 'McLawsuits' against restaurants."

STRATEGY ALTERNATIVES

To deal with the McLawsuits, McDonald's and other restaurants could continue to defend themselves in court on a case-by-case basis. Cases could be brought in both state and federal courts, and the incentive for trial lawyers was to attempt to qualify for a class action lawsuit.

Some state courts were believed to be friendlier than federal courts to plaintiffs. Mississippi in particular had been a favorite venue for trial lawyers, who would shop in the state for plaintiffs whom they could represent. A study by Harris Interactive for the U.S. Chamber of Commerce and the U.S. Chamber Institute for Legal Reform concluded that Mississippi had the worst, most unfair liability system among the 50 states.[77] The new governor of Mississippi had campaigned on the theme that the state had earned a reputation as hostile to business, which discouraged companies from locating in the state. The governor sought legislation to limit and cap tort awards. Many states had placed caps on medical malpractice awards, and in tort cases states had imposed limits on punitive awards. A number of states also adopted liability standards based on comparative liability and had narrowed and limited joint and several liability.

McDonald's could also seek legislation to shield restaurants and food processors from liability. Legislation could be pursued in federal or state legislatures. The House of Representatives, whose members faced reelection every 2 years, were often responsive to issues that appeared to be popular with voters. The House quickly passed the Personal Responsibility in Food Consumption Act, dubbed the cheeseburger bill, on a 276–139 vote. The bill provided protection from obesity and weight-based lawsuits unless the weight gain had been due to the violation of a state or federal law. Author of the bill Ric Keller (R-FL) said, "We need to get back to the old-fashioned principles of common sense and personal responsibility and get away from this new culture where everybody plays the victim and blames other people for their problems."[78] James Sensenbrenner (R-WI) was more direct, stating that "fat people should 'look in the mirror' and that parents need to monitor children's eating habits to make sure that 'little Johnny' doesn't become 'big Johnny.'"[79] House Speaker Dennis Hastert (R-IL) commented, "We as Americans need to realize that suing your way to better health is not the answer. Trial lawyers need to stop encouraging consumers to blame others for the consequences of their actions just so they can profit from frivolous lawsuits against restaurants."[80] The White House added, "Food manufacturers and sellers should not be held liable for injury because of a person's consumption of legal, unadulterated food and a person's weight gain or obesity."[81] During floor debate on the bill representatives cited a Gallup poll indicating that 89 percent of those surveyed "oppose the idea of holding fast-food companies legally responsible for the diet-related health problems of fast-food junkies." The bill had also been introduced in the Senate, but the Senate was often less willing to go along with such measures than was the House.

Commenting on the cheeseburger bill, Representative James McGovern (D-MA) said, "It protects an industry that doesn't need to be protected at this particular point and we're dealing with a problem that doesn't exist. The problem that does exist is that we have an obesity problem in this country."[82] Neil Barnard, president of the Physicians Committee for Responsible Medicine, commented, "[The bill] is an unsavory attempt to protect corporate profits at the expense of American health. The bill strips the public of its right to seek any redress against food manufacturers for their contribution to the obesity crisis, and the related epidemics of heart disease and diabetes. Given that we are just now beginning to discover the industry's involvement, granting them sweeping immunity is, at best, dangerously short-sighted."[83] Ben Cohen of the Center for Science in the Public Interest (CSPI) argued, "If Congress really believed in personal responsibility, it would help them make responsible choices by passing legislation that would require fast-food chains to post signs showing the calorie count for each item on their menu."[84]

[75]*Pelman v. McDonald's Corporation*, 2003 U.S. Dist. Lexis 707, 13.

[76]*Second Opinion in Pelman v. McDonald's*, September 3, 2003.

[77]Harris Interactive, Inc. "State Liability Ranking Study." U.S. Chamber of Commerce and the U.S. Chamber Institute for Legal Reform. March 8, 2004.

[78]The Daily Buzz, www.foodservice.com, March 11, 2004.

[79]Ibid.

[80]Associated Press Online, March 10, 2004.

[81]Ibid.

[82]Ibid.

[83]The Daily Buzz, www.foodservice.com, March 9, 2004.

[84]The Daily Buzz, www.foodservice.com, March 11, 2004.

The restaurant industry backed the Commonsense Consumption Act, the state version of the cheeseburger bill, which would shield restaurants and food processors from liability. As of mid-2004 the cheeseburger bill had been introduced in 23 state legislatures, and 12 had enacted it.

The public attention to the obesity issue led to the introduction of the Menu Education and Labeling Act (MEAL) in the House and the Senate in November 2003.[85] The so-called McMenu bills applied to chains with 20 or more locations operating under one trade name. The Senate bill required disclosure "in a statement adjacent to the name of the food on any menu listing the food for sale, or by any other means approved by the Secretary [of Health and Human Services], the number of calories, grams of saturated fat plus trans fat, and milligrams of sodium contained in a serving of the food, offered for sale, in a clear and conspicuous manner" and "information, specified by the Secretary by regulation, designed to enable the public to understand, in the context of a total daily diet, the significance of the nutrition information that is provided."

In April 2004 Ruby Tuesday, Inc. began providing nutritional information on its menus for every item served. The nutrition analysis cost the 750-restaurant chain $650 per menu item, and whenever the chain changed a portion size for an item, it would have to determine the nutritional information and reprint the menus. The company found that customers' ordering was unaffected by the information, and after 4 months the company stopped providing nutritional information on its menus and substituted cards at every table with the information. For years McDonald's had provided nutritional information on a placard in each restaurant and in 2004 began to provide that information on tray liners.[86]

The fast-food industry also faced the possibility that state attorneys general would use the same strategy they used against the tobacco industry by filing lawsuits seeking reimbursement for Medicare costs of obese people.

Later in the year the CDC concluded that its estimate of the number of deaths from obesity contained errors and stated that it would substantially revise downward its estimate. Other researchers were also concerned about the CDC's estimates and criticized the assumptions on which the estimates were prepared, suggesting that the actual number of deaths was far lower. For example, the death rates used by the CDC were based on people who became obese early in their life, whereas many people became obese later in life. Their death rates from obesity were believed to be considerably lower. ■

Preparation Questions

1. Given the *Restatement (Second) of Torts,* assess the likelihood of a plaintiff prevailing against McDonald's on an obesity lawsuit.
2. How would the doctrine of comparative liability address the obesity issue?
3. Is McDonald's likely to prevail in the courts?
4. Should McDonald's portray the lawsuits as being led by trial lawyers eager for large fees?
5. What market and nonmarket strategies should McDonald's use to address the obesity issue?
6. Should McDonald's fund research on a possible obesity–fast-food link, such as addiction? If so, should it pledge in advance to release the results of the research regardless of the results? Should it instead require the researchers to sign a nondisclosure agreement so that it could keep the results secret in the event that they supported a possible link?
7. Will the cheeseburger bill be broadly adopted? How active should McDonald's be in supporting the bills?
8. In which institutional arenas is McDonald's most likely to be successful?

---

[85]The CSPI supported the MEAL bill.
[86]*Wall Street Journal*, August 31, 2004.

PART III

Spectrum for Wireless Broadband: Old Media versus New Media

Mobile communication was revolutionized by the introduction of the iPhone and by tablets such as the iPad. The growth in use of these devices to connect to the Internet and the downloading of videos, movies, and games greatly accelerated the demand for wireless broadband capacity. Streaming video, for example, took 100 times the bandwidth as a telephone call. Forecasts estimating demand were quickly obsolete, and companies in the industry became concerned about dropped calls and pages that would not load. Mobile communications companies were reluctant to price based on usage, so there was little to limit the use of wireless capacity. Capacity could be increased by providing more spectrum for wireless broadband, and in 2009 the Federal Communications Commission (FCC) had allocated 108 MHz to mobile communications from the "white spaces" between channels when television broadcasting switched from analog to digital transmission. This had allowed wireless carriers such as AT&T and Verizon to rollout 4G networks.

The government was also concerned about spectrum capacity for wireless broadband, and in 2009 Congress passed a law directing the FCC to develop a plan to make broadband accessible nationwide. In March 2010 the FCC released a National Broadband Plan that sought a 500 MHz increase in spectrum for wireless broadband with 120 MHz coming from spectrum currently held by television broadcasters.[87] The 120 MHz would represent a 22 percent increase in the capacity for wireless broadband. The FCC determined that the spectrum to be made available for wireless broadband would be most valuable if the spectrum were contiguous, but this would require moving some TV stations to different channels. The spectrum held by TV broadcasters was ideal for wireless broadband because signals could penetrate buildings and travel long distances.

FCC chairman Julius Genachowski explained the goal of the National Broadcast Plan, "Broadband will be the indispensible platform to assure American competitiveness, ongoing job creation and innovation, and will affect nearly every aspect of American's lives at home, at work, and in their communities."[88] He added, "History teaches us that nations that lead technological revolutions reap enormous rewards. We can lead the revolution in wired and wireless broadband. But the moment to act is now."[89] President Barack Obama directed the National Telecommunications and Information Administration to identify spectrum controlled by the government that could be redeployed within 5 years for wireless broadband.

In his 2011 budget President Obama called upon Congress to pass legislation authorizing "voluntary incentive auctions" in which holders of spectrum licenses could

voluntarily sell their spectrum in an auction conducted by the FCC.[90] This request was made to induce broadcasters and other licensees to sell voluntarily their underutilized spectrum at a price to be determined in an auction. Under current law the proceeds of any FCC auction must go to the U.S. Treasury and hence cannot be paid to the licensee.

President Obama had also pledged to make broadband available nationwide. An estimated one-third of Americans either did not have access to or chose not to have high-speed Internet service. The FCC planned to expand service in rural America and could use the Universal Service Fund that is funded by surcharges on telephone service and provides subsidies of $8 billion for rural telephone service and Internet connections to schools and libraries. Funds from the auction could also be used to expand wireless broadband services. The FCC was also considering a "digital literacy corps" to help unwired Americans learn online skills.[91]

In addition, government policymakers sought to create a nationwide, interoperable broadband network for public safety and personal security. Wireless carriers provided some capacity for first responders, but multimedia communication was generally limited. Funding from the network could come from the auction.

"We're in full battle mode to protect broadcasters from being forced to give up spectrum," said Gordon H. Smith the president of the National Association of Broadcasters.[92] He also said lack of spectrum was only a problem in New York and Los Angeles. Smith said, "Why should people in Kentucky have their local stations' signal potentially downgraded so urbanites in Manhattan can have a faster download of the app telling them where the nearest spa is located?"[93] Steve Largent, president of the Cellular Telephone Industries Association which renamed itself The Wireless Association, responded by accusing the NAB of "desperate and inaccurate tactics."[94]

Former NAB president Edward Fritts warned about "an entire telecommunications industry out to minimize or dismiss the invaluable contributions that local broadcasters provide every day, across America for the public good. Theirs is a campaign characterized by sharp elbows, enormous war chests and a public notion that if it computes, it must be good."[95] Dennis Wharton, vice president of the NAB said, "You can't take that much spectrum from broadcasters and not have devastating

---

[87]The European Union was considering setting aside 800 MHz for mobile broadband, some of which would come from television broadcasters.

[88]*New York Times*, March 13, 2010.

[89]TECHWEB, March 17, 2010.

[90]A voluntary incentive auction could be implemented as a "double auction" in which buyers decide how much spectrum to bid for and what price to bid and simultaneously sellers determine how much spectrum to offer and what price to accept.

[91]*New York Times*, March 13, 2010.

[92]*New York Times*, April 22, 2011.

[93]*Los Angeles Times*, April 13, 2011.

[94]*New York Times*, April 22, 2011.

[95]*Daily Variety*, April 12, 2011.

consequences for delivery of mobile digital television, HDTV and other innovative services."[96]

Genachowski pledged, "No broadcaster will be forced to offer up spectrum for auction." The FCC, however, was believed to be planning to repack the broadcast spectrum to provide a contiguous band for wireless broadband. Genachowski explained that "voluntary can't mean undermining the potential effectiveness of an auction by giving every broadcaster a new and unprecedented right to keep their exact channel location."[97] Alan Frank, CEO of Post-Newsweek Stations, commented, "I had the honor of serving in the Army, and I understand 'voluntary.'"[98] The FCC was believed to be willing to cover the cost of moving channels and had given assurances that no station would be moved from VHF to UHF. The NAB said in a statement, "Going forward, we believe policymakers have an obligation to maintain digital TV services currently provided by broadcasters and to allow free TV viewers to benefit from DTV video innovations. NAB will oppose government-mandated signal strength degradations or limitations, and new spectrum taxes that threaten the future of free and local broadcasting."[99]

Gary Shapiro, vice president of the Consumer Electronics Association (CEA), said, "Broadcasters are gearing up for a huge political battle, but the reality is that fewer people are watching over-the-air television, and we're fighting for our future of innovation."[100] In April 2011 the CEA released a nationwide survey that found, "By a six-to-one margin, Americans believe that underutilized spectrum—the nation's airwaves used for everything from local broadcast television to wireless devices—should be auctioned off to raise money to lower the federal deficit, ..."[101] The survey also indicated that fewer than 10 percent of Americans got breaking news from over-the-air broadcasts.

Television stations were currently allocated 300 MHz of spectrum, but most of it was unused. In markets with populations less than 1 million only 36 MHz was used on average, and in the largest markets 150 MHz was used. For example, channels 31–51 were lightly used.[102] The broadcasters said that the unused spectrum was needed to reduce interference. Approximately 10–15 percent of the population used over-the-air broadcasts, and the number had been declining steadily. In addition, the NAB warned that cities like Detroit that border Canada or Mexico could lose over-the-air television if the reallocated spectrum conflicted with the spectrum used in those countries.

Broadcast licenses had fixed durations, and the FCC could simply not renew the licenses when they expired and then reallocate the spectrum. The broadcasters would then in all likelihood sue the FCC on the grounds that they had not violated any of the conditions of their licenses and that the licenses should be renewed as they had been in the past. The process of reclaiming the licenses would at a minimum be lengthy and uncertain.

Broadcasters argued that the wireless carriers were not efficiently using the spectrum they already had and that they had alternatives to increase the capacity of their spectrum. Smith said the issue is "more investment in towers and infrastructure and receiving standards that maximize the use of the huge swaths of spectrum that wireless carriers have already been allocated."[103] In May 2011 the NAB released a study that concluded that the FCC had not taken full account of measures that wireless carriers could take to increase the capacity of the spectrum they already held. The study pointed to increased use of femtocells, better receiver standards, and spectrum sharing.[104]

The House Committee on Energy and Commerce began the process of drafting legislation as did the Senate Commerce Committee. ■

Preparation Questions

1. As an Apple or Verizon executive, what legislation would you propose to the House and Senate committees to advance the reallocation of spectrum to wireless broadband? Make sure you both deal with the concerns raised by opponents of the reallocation and build broad support for the reallocation.

2. If you propose authorizing a voluntary incentive auction, would you impose any restrictions, such as minimum or maximum prices or a specified sharing rule for broadcasters that offer spectrum?

3. What contingency, if any, would you provide if broadcasters do not make sufficient amounts of spectrum available?

4. As a broadcaster what strategy would you use to address possible congressional legislation and FCC rule making?

---

[96]*Washington Post*, January 20, 2011.
[97]*New York Times*, April 22, 2011.
[98]*Daily Variety*, April 12, 2011.
[99]www.adweek.com, November 30, 2010.
[100]*Washington Post*, January 20, 2011.
[101]CEA Press Release, April 11, 2011.
[102]*Washington Post*, January 20, 2011.

[103]*Los Angeles Times*, April 13, 2011.
[104]http://spectrum.ieee.com, May 6, 2011.

15

THE POLITICAL ECONOMY OF THE EUROPEAN UNION

INTRODUCTION

The European Union (EU) has taken landmark steps toward economic and political integration. It has established a single market with half a billion consumers in 27 nations to provide for the free movement of people, goods, services, and capital. The EU has strengthened political integration establishing the office of president and has moved toward greater commonality in defense and foreign policy. Seventeen member states have adopted a common currency, and the EU has an independent central bank. The eventual breadth of the union remains an open question with other nations seeking to join, and the eventual depth of integration, particularly with respect to political union, remains unclear.

The European Union admitted Bulgaria and Romania in 2007, and official candidates for future entry are Croatia, Republic of Macedonia, and Turkey. Five other countries are potential candidates for entry. Norway was approved to join the EU, but in 1994 Norwegian voters rejected membership as they had done in 1972. The member states differ considerably with populations ranging from 418,000 to 82 million, a ratio of more than 4 to 1 in per capita income, and unemployment rates ranging from 3.7 to 21.2 percent in 2011. The EU has 23 languages. The 12 new countries that became members in 2004 and 2007 increased the differences among the member states. For example, the highest statutory corporate tax rate in the European Union was 33.4 percent in France, but the rate in Bulgaria was 10 percent. The average price-level index in the 10 new members that entered in 2006 was 52 percent of that in the other 15 member states. The average labor cost in Belgium was €38 an hour, whereas the average in Bulgaria was only €3. Yet, remarkable progress toward economic integration has been made, and the commitment to deeper integration remains strong in most of the member states.

This chapter considers the nonmarket environment in the European Union using the structured pluralism framework introduced in Chapter 6. The next section traces the history of the EU and considers the two principal instruments for economic integration. The principal institutions are then considered along with the legislative procedures used by the EU. The monetary union, fiscal harmonization, competition policy, state aid, market opening, and social democracy are then discussed. Issues and interests are considered, and these foundations are used to identify effective nonmarket strategies in the European Union.

THE EUROPEAN UNION

In the aftermath of World War II, Europeans recognized the need to increase trade and encourage political cooperation. In 1951 six nations—Belgium, France, Italy, Luxembourg, the Netherlands, and West Germany—signed the Treaty of Paris, which established the European Coal and Steel Community (ECSC). The ECSC's goal was to improve the efficiency of its member states' coal and steel industries through the reduction of trade barriers.

In 1957 those same nations signed the Treaty of Rome, which provided the basic framework for the European Union of today. The Treaty of Rome established the European Economic Community (EEC), or the common market, with the objectives of opening domestic markets to the members and rationalizing their industries.[1] The 1965 Treaty of Brussels represented an important step toward European integration by unifying the administration of the EEC, ECSC, and European Atomic Energy Community (EURATOM). This provided an administrative structure upon which further steps toward economic and political integration could be built. The European Monetary System was established in 1979 to provide fixed, but adjustable, exchange rate bands for the currencies of the member states. In 1973 Denmark, Ireland, and the United Kingdom joined

---

[1]The six nations also formed the European Atomic Energy Community (EURATOM).

the EEC. Greece joined in 1981, Portugal and Spain in 1986, and Austria, Finland, and Sweden joined in 1995. The 2000 Treaty of Nice provided a road map for enlargement of the Union, and in 2004 the European Union admitted 10 new members: Cyprus, Latvia, Lithuania, the Czech Republic, Estonia, Hungary, Malta, Slovakia, Poland, and Slovenia, with Bulgaria and Romania joining in 2007.[2]

In addition to the broadening of the EU through the admission of new member states, the member states and their citizens faced the issue of the depth of political integration. Some supported a deeper union in which more authority would be transferred from the member states to the EU government. This could involve substantial changes in the institutions and the representation in those institutions. One possibility was a federal system such as the one in Germany or the United States. In contrast to those who sought a deeper union, a number of EU citizens began asking whether political union had already gone too far. This Euroskepticism stemmed from the view that once economic integration had been achieved, a deeper political union would provide little in the way of benefits.[3]

The three most recent major steps toward economic and political union have been the Single European Act, the Maastricht Treaty on European Union, and the Treaty of Lisbon, which are considered next.[4]

The Single European Act

Economic growth in the common market was strong during the 1960s, but beginning in the 1970s and particularly in the early 1980s growth slowed markedly, unemployment rolls swelled to over 10 percent, and job creation came to a crawl. The slow growth, the high cost of labor, and the difficulties and costs involved in workforce reductions made many firms reluctant to hire. Europeans called their economic disease "Eurosclerosis" and worried about worsening competitiveness relative to Japan and the United States.

Many business leaders recognized that competitiveness was inhibited by a set of barriers that limited trade and increased costs. Progress in reducing many of the barriers had been slow because each state reserved the right to veto changes it believed were contrary to its interests. To document the potential gains from further market integration, the European Commission sponsored the Cecchini study, which concluded that the formation of a single market could increase GDP by 4.3–6.4 percent.[5]

The Single European Act (SEA), which took effect in 1987, addressed several impediments to trade and provided measures to facilitate access to national markets.[6] The SEA also increased the power of the EU government relative to the governments of the member states, particularly by limiting the use of the unanimity rule for decision making. The SEA mandated the realization of a single market by the beginning of 1993. The program to realize market integration involved the removal of three types of barriers: physical, technical, and fiscal. The removal of physical barriers pertained to the movement of both goods and people, eliminating customs and other goods inspections, removing restrictions on the entry of people, and allowing individuals to work in any member state.

The European Union took two approaches—harmonization and mutual recognition—to the removal of internal barriers to trade. *Harmonization* refers to the development of a common set of policies for all member states. Because of the complexity of the bargaining, progress on technical issues such as product standards, product certification, and the licensing of professional services had become tediously slow as nationalistic considerations complicated negotiations. To avoid the roadblocks of the past, the principle of *mutual recognition,* first articulated by the European Court of Justice in the Cassis de Dijon case, was adopted.[7] The EU member states

---

[2]Cyprus is partitioned, and only the Greek portion of the island has become a member.

[3]See, for example, Alesina and Wacziarg (1999).

[4]The 1997 Treaty of Amsterdam strengthened the human rights provisions of the EU, committed the EU to take steps to increase employment, adopted the objective of sustainable development, strengthened the Common Foreign and Security Policy, elevated the formal powers of the European Parliament, and prepared for institutional change when new members were admitted.

[5]See Cecchini et al. (1988) and Emerson et al. (1988).

[6]See Overturf (1986) for an analysis of the benefits from economic integration.

[7]In 1979 the court ruled that a German regulation on the alcohol content of liqueurs could not be used to block the sale of the French liqueur Cassis de Dijon.

were able to agree on mutual recognition, whereas they had been unable to agree on a common set of standards. The principle of mutual recognition represented a major change in EU policy and increased the speed with which internal barriers were removed.

Fiscal harmonization pertains to tax policy, particularly value-added taxes (VAT), excise and corporate profits taxes, government fiscal policy, and subsidization or "state aids." The member states differed substantially in their tax and other fiscal policies, and those differences distorted trade, the location of facilities, and the movement of people. For example, VAT rates were as high as 38 percent on some goods and as low as zero on others. Furthermore, some countries had multiple tiers of VAT rates, whereas others had a single rate. Progress on fiscal harmonization has been slow.

With the entry of 12 new member states since 2004 the disparity in tax rates increased. The countries of Eastern Europe generally had low corporate tax rates, and several of them had reduced their tax rates prior to joining the EU. The average corporate tax rate of the 10 new entrants in 2004 was 21.3 percent, whereas the average for the 15 prior members was 31.3 percent. Tax harmonization was even farther in the future, although many of the member states have reduced their corporate tax rates.

Harmonization is also the approach taken to the sensitive and important issues of public health, safety, and the environment. The approach was to reach agreement on a set of basic standards and then allow the individual member states to go beyond those standards as they chose.

The Maastricht Treaty

In 1992 the member states agreed to the Maastricht Treaty on European Union. The Treaty ran into immediate problems as the United Kingdom opted out of part of it, Denmark first rejected and then narrowly accepted it, and French voters only narrowly approved it.

The treaty established a timetable for a common European currency and an independent European Central Bank.[8] Twelve member states that had met targets on inflation rates, government budget deficits, and interest rates formed a monetary union with a common currency—the euro—and a European Central Bank. Denmark, Sweden, and the United Kingdom met the targets but chose not to join.

Political integration was considerably more difficult than monetary union, but some steps toward political union were taken. The member states entered into a protocol to establish a joint social policy. Nine of the member states agreed to establish a joint defense policy. Additional proposals included strengthening the European Parliament, establishing a European citizenship, and changing the unanimity rule still in effect for certain decisions.

The Treaty of Lisbon

To advance the cause of political union, a constitutional convention was convened and developed a constitutional proposal that was subsequently rejected by France and the Netherlands. The EU then repackaged most of the proposed constitution as the Treaty of Lisbon, which was ratified by all member states and took effect in December 2009. The treaty amended the Treaty of Rome [renamed the Treaty on the Functioning of the EU (TFEU)] and the Maastricht Treaty.

The Treaty of Lisbon formally recognized the Charter for Fundamental Rights, making human and civil rights enforceable by the European Union. The Treaty extended the legislative procedure requiring approval of both the Council of Ministers and the European Parliament (EP) to cover 95 percent of EU lawmaking and changed the voting rule of the Council. Matters of taxation, social policy, and foreign and defense policy would continue to require unanimity. The Treaty established the positions of High Representative for Foreign Affairs and Security Policy and established the European Council, composed of the heads of states of the member states, as a separate institution with a president with a 2 1/2-year term.

The Treaty of Lisbon made the institutions more transparent and democratic, although the EP remained the only popularly elected body. To strengthen the role of national governments, the Commission was required to review a legislative proposal if one-third of the national parliaments believed the proposal was not in accord with the principle of subsidiarity.

---

[8]See Committee for the Study of Economic and Monetary Union (1989) and Goodman (1992).

FIGURE 15-1   EU Legislative and Administrative Institutions

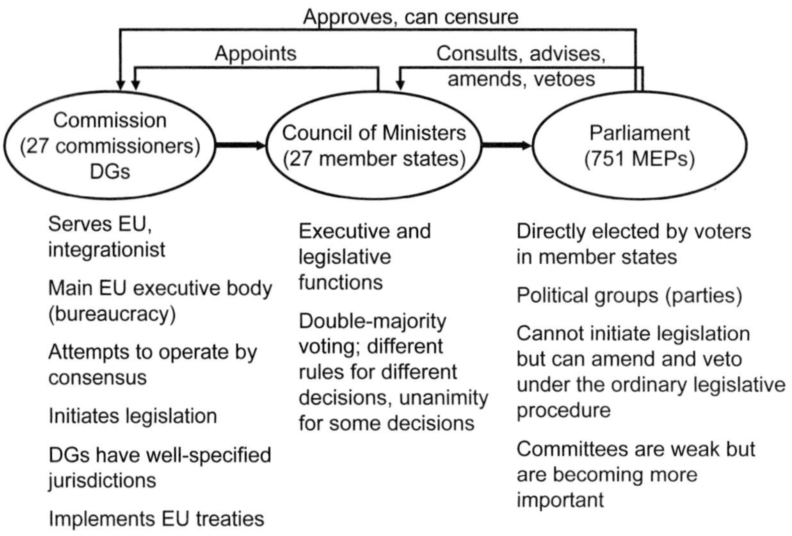

THE INSTITUTIONS OF THE EUROPEAN UNION

The four principal institutions of the European Union are the European Commission, the Council of Ministers, the European Parliament, and the Court of Justice. The following sections consider the institutions in more detail and the changes that resulted from the ratification of the Treaty of Lisbon. Figure 15-1 highlights the principal roles of the three institutions involved in legislation and administration.

The European Commission

The European Commission, located in Brussels, is the executive and administrative body of the European Union. The Commission administers EU policies and enforces the various treaties. It is responsible for monitoring the implementation of EU legislation and ensuring that the member states comply with EU law. The Commission is responsible for trade negotiations and manages the EU budget. The Commission is the only body with the power to initiate legislation. The European Parliament and the Council of Ministers, however, can ask the Commission to review proposals and consider issues. The European Commission's role in initiating legislation and administering policies makes it a target for lobbying. Moreover, the Commission is obligated to consult with interest groups and to notify the Council of Ministers and the parliament that it has done so. The Commission has a relatively small staff (25,000), so it needs information and expertise, and its consultations with interest groups are a means of obtaining information.

Each member state has one commissioner, who is obliged to serve the interests of the European Union and not those of their own countries.[9] Commission terms are 5 years, and commissioners are nominated by the individual member states. The commissioners must be approved as a whole by the European Parliament, and the Parliament can dismiss the Commission on a vote of no confidence. In an unprecedented event in 1999 all the commissioners resigned under a threat from the European Parliament stemming from allegations of corruption and mismanagement. In 2004 the incoming president of the Commission withdrew his nominees for commissioners because of certain rejection by the parliament.

One commissioner serves as president and five as vice presidents, and the others have responsibility for one or more of the 33 Directorates-General (DGs). A DG is a department, with a particular policy or administrative jurisdiction. For example, one DG has responsibilities for economic and financial affairs, and the competition DG has responsibility for antitrust, mergers, and state aid. The Commission also has several services.

---

[9]The Treaty of Lisbon capped the number of commissioners at two-thirds of the number of member states but allowed the European Council to drop the cap, which it did to obtain Ireland's ratification of the treaty.

The conflict between national and EU laws creates a tension within the community. EU law takes precedence over national law when a conflict arises, but not all national laws have been harmonized with EU law. In a number of cases member states have not complied with EU law, and the Commission attempts to obtain compliance. In 2003 the Commission initiated 1,552 infringement proceedings against member states for violating treaties or failing to implement directives. For example, the Commission filed complaints against a number of member states for delays in implementing the Directive on Data Protection.

The Commission formally makes decisions by majority rule, but in practice it operates on a collegial basis, and no public reports of its deliberations or votes are issued. Conflict within the Commission, however, can develop over policies, particularly those that have impacts across more than one DG. For example, the commissioner for industry proposed the elimination of price controls on pharmaceuticals as a means of encouraging firms to invest more in the development of innovative drugs. The Commission, however, rejected the proposal in favor of asking the member states to bring their divergent pharmaceutical pricing policies into alignment.

The Council of Ministers and the European Council

The Council of Ministers, based in Brussels, is the principal legislative body of the European Union.[10] In contrast to the Commission, whose members are obliged to serve the European Union, Council members are the individual member states. The Council consists of one minister from each state, but the nations have different voting weights based on population, with Germany having 16.5 percent of the population and the vote and Luxembourg and Malta having 0.1 percent.

The presidency of the Council rotates among the member states every 6 months, and which ministers belong to the Council depends on the issue under consideration. On an issue involving economics and finance, the cognizant ministers of the member states meet as the Economic and Financial Affairs Council (ECOFIN). The Council operates in private, but since 1995 its votes have been reported publicly.

Twice a year, the heads of state or government of the member states meet as the European Council, which sets the general direction for the European Union. The President of the European Council serves for 2 1/2 years and has largely administrative responsibilities and represents the EU externally.

Associated with the Council is the Committee of Permanent Representatives (COREPER), composed of ambassadors, or "permanent representatives," of the member states. COREPER represents the member states before the Commission and serves as the secretariat of the Council of Ministers. It prepares the agenda, forms working parties, and negotiates informal agreements prior to council deliberations. Before the Council considers proposals, COREPER appoints an ad hoc working party composed of government officials from the member states. Members of the Commission may also participate. The working party gives its opinion on a legislative proposal to COREPER. If COREPER agrees with the opinion, it forwards the proposal to the Council. COREPER is said to resolve 90 percent of the issues before they come to the Council, leaving only the most politically sensitive issues for Council deliberations.

Council decisions had been governed by a unanimity rule, which gave a veto to the member states. Because this created long delays on some issues, the SEA provided for decisions by majority rule. On most procedural matters the council acts under simple majority rule. Most of its substantive actions, however, require a "qualified" majority. The Treaty of Lisbon changed the qualified majority rule to a "double majority" of countries constituting 55 percent of the member states and at least 65 percent of the EU population. To avoid a situation in which three large countries could stop an action, four countries representing at least 35 percent of the population are required for a blocking minority. The voting rule will be phased in beginning in 2014.

The Treaty of Nice and the Treaty of Lisbon replaced unanimity with qualified majority on most substantive issues, including negotiated agreements on trade in services and intellectual property protection. Decisions involving foreign and security policy, justice and home affairs, some aspects of fiscal policy, and enlargement of the community, however, require unanimity.

---

[10]See Hoscheit and Wessels (1988) and Nugent (2003) for an analysis of the Council of Ministers.

The European Union can take four types of actions, which differ in the extent to which they are binding on the member states.[11]

1. Regulations are legally binding on the member states and are enforced by the Commission.
2. Directives are legally binding with respect to the result sought, but national governments are responsible for how the result is achieved.
3. Decisions are legally binding but pertain only to the parties identified in the decision.
4. Recommendations and opinions are not legally binding but may provide guidance and foretell future action on issues.

EU law becomes effective in a member state when that state accepts it as its law.

The Union operates under the principle of subsidiarity, meaning the intention to accomplish as much as possible at the level of the member states.[12] Article 35 of the Consolidated Treaty states that the Union can act "only if and in so far as the objectives of the proposed action cannot be sufficiently achieved by the Member States and can therefore, by reason of the scale or effects of the proposed action, be better achieved by the Community." This statement has been clarified by guidelines developed by the Council. Any conflict over the application of the principle can be taken to the Court of Justice.

The European Parliament

The European Parliament (EP) has 750 members plus the president of the Parliament and are directly elected for 5-year terms under proportional representation by voters in the member states. Although the European Parliament's power has increased over time, the turnout in the elections has decreased over time. Parliament members organize by parties or political groupings. After the 2009 elections the European People's Party held 265 seats, the Liberals and Democrats held 84, and the Conservatives and Reformists had 56, giving the loose coalition a majority. The Socialists Group held 185 seats. The EP meets in Brussels and Strasbourg.

As the only popularly elected institution in the European Union, the EP has powers of "democratic supervision."[13] The EP approves of and can dismiss the Commission and can ask questions of commissioners in writing or during "Question Time" when the EP is in session. The EP and the Council share legislative authority, but Parliament cannot initiate or enact laws, as described later in the chapter. Parliament also has budgetary authority, but the EU budget is relatively small.

The EP elects a president, who serves a 2 1/2-year term, and vice presidents from the other member states. It has 22 standing committees to which proposals are referred for consideration, and they are a focus of lobbying. Neither the committees nor the EP has the ability to delay a proposal, since action must be taken within a specified time period. The EP operates under simple majority rule.

Individual citizens and firms may petition the EP on issues arising from either EU actions or conflicts between EU law and national laws. Petitions are reviewed by a Petition Committee; if accepted for consideration, the Petition Committee evaluates the petition and may hold a hearing. Interest groups often work through their national representatives in the petition process.

The Court of Justice

The Court of Justice, located in Luxembourg, is the supreme judicial body of the Union and has the authority to overturn decisions that conflict with the EU treaties.[14] The court has one judge from each member state, with one judge elected as president for a 3-year term.[15] The court makes decisions by majority vote in 13-judge chambers, and some cases are decided in three- and five-judge chambers. Dissenting opinions are not issued. The judges serve 6-year terms

---

[11]See Nugent (2003).

[12]The pledge to abide by the principle of subsidiarity was important in obtaining Denmark's support for the Maastricht Treaty.

[13]The term "democratic supervision" refers to the fact that the council is not popularly elected.

[14]See Nugent (2003).

[15]Europe also has a Council of Europe that has a European Court of Human Rights, which hears cases under the European Convention on Human Rights.

and are assisted by eight advocates general who provide independent and impartial opinions. The court hears cases pertaining to the various treaties of the European Union and other cases involving disputes between the community's institutions. Some of the cases brought to the court involve complaints by the European Commission against the member states. Some cases can be brought directly to the court by individuals and legal entities of the member states. Although the court has the final word on EU law, treaties give the courts of the member states some responsibilities for implementing EU law. The court also hears cases from member states when the states' own courts are uncertain about EU law.[16] Because of the court's workload, the Council of Ministers established the Court of First Instance, which was renamed the General Court by the Treaty of Lisbon. The General Court applies the law established by the Court of Justice, and its decisions may be appealed to the higher court.

The Court of Justice also hears appeals of Commission decisions. For example, cases involving the competitive practices of firms are usually decided by the commission's DG for competition. Firms can appeal its decisions and the penalties assessed. As indicated later in the chapter, European airlines appealed the commission's decision to allow France to subsidize Air France, and Microsoft appealed a decision in a competition case.

The European Economic and Social Committee

The European Economic and Social Committee (EESC), based in Brussels, is an advisory body whose 344 members represent employees, employers, farmers, trades, and other interests. The EESC has six sections, or committees, that provide forums to express opinions on Commission proposals and suggest changes in them. Interest groups interact with the EESC through the representatives of their home countries in the relevant sections. The final opinions of the EESC can have influence because they reflect the concerns of interest groups. On some policy matters the Council and the Commission are required to consult the EESC.

The EU Legislative Process

The European Union has three basic procedures—consultation, co-decision, and assent—for developing directives and regulations.[17] The SEA established the assent procedure, which gives the EP a veto over council action. The assent procedure is used for decisions about admission of new member states, international agreements, and the structure of the European Central Bank. The consultation procedure was used for nearly all important issues prior to the SEA, and subsequent treaties replaced it with the co-decision procedure.

The Maastricht Treaty established the co-decision procedure, and the scope of its use was expanded in the Treaty of Amsterdam and the Treaty of Nice, and further expanded in the Treaty of Lisbon, which renamed it the ordinary legislative procedure. This procedure, as illustrated in Figure 15-2, gives the EP a greater role and more power relative to the Commission and the Council. This procedure begins as in the consultation procedure, but once the opinions of the EP and the EESC have been obtained, the Council develops by qualified majority a "common position" on the proposal. It is then sent to the EP for a second reading. If the EP approves the proposal, it is enacted. If an absolute majority of the EP votes against the common position, it is defeated and the process ends. If the EP amends the common position, the Council can accept the amendments, thereby enacting the proposal. If the Council rejects the amendments, a conciliation committee composed of members of the Council and the EP is formed. If they reach agreement, the amended proposal is enacted by qualified majority of the Council and a simple majority of the Parliament at the third reading. If no agreement is reached, or if either the Council or the Parliament fails to approve the amended proposal, the proposal fails.[18]

---

[16]A major difference between the United States and European countries results from the due process requirements of the U.S. Constitution. As discussed in Chapter 10, due process imposes a complex set of requirements on government processes intended to ensure individuals the right to participate in governmental decision-making processes. Unless provided for by specific legislation, the European Union and most European countries do not have the same requirements.

[17]See Nugent (2003) and Hix (2005).

[18]The stages of the process each have timetables; for example, the conciliation committee has 6 weeks to reach an agreement.

FIGURE 15-2 Ordinary Legislative Procedure

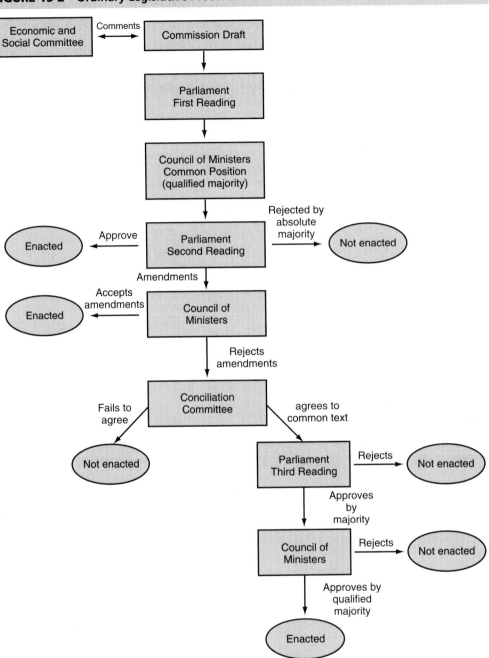

The ordinary legislative procedure is said to be bicameral, since approval by both the Council and Parliament is required. The procedure is not fully "democratic," however, because the popularly elected Parliament cannot enact laws itself. The ordinary legislative procedure is thus best viewed as a legislative process in which both the Parliament and the Council have a veto.

The European Central Bank and Monetary Union

The European Union's interest in a monetary union officially began in 1989 when the Council of Ministers endorsed a series of steps to realize an Economic and Monetary Union (EMU). The EMU commenced in 1998 with the formation of the European System of Central Banks and the European Central Bank (ECB) to conduct a single monetary policy for its members. The ECB is an independent central bank patterned after Germany's central bank (the Bundesbank). The primary objective of the ECB is "to maintain price stability." The Treaty establishing the ECB stated that "without prejudice to the objective of price stability, the ECSB shall support the general economic policies in the Community...." The ECB is independent of the governments of the member states, but some governments have sought to influence the policies of the ECB to stimulate economic growth and create jobs.

In 1999 the euro became the common currency of the member states that chose to participate, and euro notes and coins replaced national currencies in 2002.[19] Seventeen member states have adopted the euro. The European Union estimated that the savings on transactions costs associated with currency exchange would be 0.4 percent of GDP. The euro has become an important global currency and an emerging reserve currency. Some countries such as Italy saw another advantage in the EMU. It would serve as a commitment device that would provide price stability to which its governments had had difficulty committing.

The flaw in the euro system was that the ECSB could control monetary policy, but the member states controlled their own fiscal policies. The participants were required to have a budget deficit no greater than 3 percent of GDP and government debt no greater than 60 percent of GDP, but some countries such as Greece failed to comply.[20] With the financial crisis of 2008 and the subsequent recession, the budget deficits of several member states increased and the recession slowed economic growth. Fearing default, the financial markets put pressure on Greece and then Ireland and Portugal and then Spain and Italy. The EU was forced to provide funding to Greece, Ireland, and Portugal in exchange for austerity measures. The euro crisis is considered in more detail in the chapter case *The Euro Crisis.*

Competition Policy

Competition policy includes EU policies involving the structure, conduct, and support of industries, including state aid. Antitrust policy is the centerpiece of competition policy, and this section addresses EU antitrust law and its administration. The member states also have their own competition laws. In 1998 France rejected Coca-Cola's planned acquisition of Orangina, after objections by PepsiCo and Orangina employees who feared layoffs.

The basic antitrust law of the European Union is found in Articles 101 and 102 of the TFEU, the principal components of which are presented in Figure 15-3. The articles have two antecedents. The first is the Treaty of Rome goal of market integration. The second is U.S. antitrust law. Articles 101 and 102 correspond to Sections 1 and 2 of the Sherman Act, but EU antitrust law differs somewhat from U.S. law. Both aim at promoting competition, but EU law allows defenses, such as economic consequences, not explicitly provided for under U.S. law. Hence, EU law does not have per se offenses.

As with Section 1 of the Sherman Act, Article 101 refers to group activities that may limit competition or constitute a barrier to trade among member states. Much of the text addresses vertical restraints, which were a concern at the time of establishment of the economic community because of the possibility that firms would use such arrangements in their channels of distribution to preserve national markets for themselves. Parts a, b, and c of Article 101, paragraph 1, pertain to vertical arrangements that might foreclose markets, and part d deals with price discrimination. Part e pertains to tying arrangements or reciprocal deals that might foreclose markets. The feature of Article 101 that distinguishes it most from Section 1 of the Sherman Act is the allowable defenses provided in paragraph 3. A firm may make the affirmative defense that an arrangement improves efficiency. The firm is obligated to use the least restrictive means to achieve that efficiency, and some of the efficiency gains must be passed on to consumers. The United States has adopted a similar perspective by considering whether a practice benefits consumers. Paragraph 3 virtually grants block exemptions for a variety of agreements—exclusive distributorships, exclusive purchase arrangements, patent licensing, motor vehicle distribution, specialization, research and development, franchises, and know-how licensing.

Article 102 deals with unilateral actions and differs from Section 2 of the Sherman Act. The article is not concerned with how a dominant position was obtained but rather with whether that position is abused. Its specific provisions apply to unfair practices, monopoly restriction of output, price discrimination, and tying.

---

[19]The European Union had a long history of coordinating exchange rate policies. In the 1970s European countries maintained the "snake" with fixed exchange rates, and subsequently a stable Deutschmark zone developed. The European Monetary System (EMS) was established to band exchange rates together. The EMS also used a weighted average of exchange rates, the ECU, that was a forerunner of the euro.

[20]In 2012 Eurozone countries ratified a Fiscal Compact that required countries to write the deficit and debt limits into their national laws with fines to be imposed by the Court of Justice if they failed to meet the limits. The Compact was intended to reassure the capital markets, but whether it would work was unclear.

FIGURE 15-3 European Union Antitrust Law: Articles 101 and 102 of the Treaty on the Functioning of the European Union

Article 101:

(1) The following practices shall be prohibited as incompatible with the internal market: all agreements between undertakings and all concerted practices which may affect trade between Member States and which have as their object or effect the prevention, restriction or distortion of competition within the internal market, and in particular those which:

  (a) directly or indirectly fix purchase or selling prices or any other trading conditions;

  (b) limit or control production, markets, technical development, or investment;

  (c) share markets or sources of supply;

  (d) apply dissimilar conditions to equivalent transactions with other trading parties, thereby placing them at a competitive disadvantage;

  (e) make the conclusion of contracts subject to acceptance by the other parties of supplementary obligations which, by their nature or according to commercial usage, have no connection with the subject of such contracts.

(2) Any agreement or decisions prohibited pursuant to this Article shall automatically be void.

(3) The provisions of paragraph 1 may, however, be declared inapplicable in the case of:

   –any agreement or category of agreement between undertakings

   –any decision or category of decisions by associations of undertakings,

   –any concerted practice or category of concerted practice

which contributes to improving the production or distribution of goods or to promoting technical or economic progress, whilst allowing consumers a fair share of the resulting benefit, and which does not: (a) impose on the undertakings concerned restrictions which are not indispensable to the attainment of these objectives; (b) afford such undertaking the possibility of eliminating competition in respect of a substantial part of the products in question.

Article 102:

Any abuse by one or more undertakings of a dominant position within the internal market or in a substantial part of it shall be prohibited as incompatible with the internal market in so far as it may affect trade between Member States. Such abuse may, in particular, consist in:

(a) directly or indirectly imposing unfair purchase or selling prices or other unfair trading conditions;

(b) limiting production, markets or technical development to the prejudice of consumers;

(c) applying dissimilar conditions to equivalent transactions with other trading parties, thereby placing them at a competitive disadvantage;

(d) making the conclusion of contracts subject to the acceptance by the other parties of supplementary obligations which, by their nature or according to commercial usage, have no connection with the subject of such contracts.

ENFORCEMENT Antitrust enforcement is by the DG for Competition, which investigates practices, initiates proceedings, serves as prosecutor, decides cases, and imposes fines. In contrast to the United States where antitrust cases are decided by judges or by an independent commission in the case of the Federal Trade Commission, the DG serves as both prosecutor and judge. The courts play no role unless there is an appeal of an action. Appeals are heard by the General Court and then by the Court of Justice if necessary. Private parties may file complaints with the European Commission, but private lawsuits are not permitted by Articles 101 and 102 of the TFEU.[21] The DG is also required to consult with national competition officials before

---

[21]Private lawsuits may be filed under the antitrust laws of the member states.

initiating proceedings. Those officials participate in the Advisory Committee on Restrictive Practices and Monopolies. In terms of remedies, the Commission is limited to imposing fines and supervising conduct. Criminal penalties are not allowed. In 2004 the DG for Competition was given additional investigatory authority, and responsibility for certain merger approvals was devolved to the member states to allow the DG to concentrate on breaking up cartels. The commission has proposed that it be allowed to use structural remedies, such as ordering the divestiture of business units. The Microsoft example includes a range of remedies.

Fines of up to 10 percent of a company's sales are the principal enforcement instrument of the DG for Competition. In 2000 the Commission imposed fines of €110 million on Archer Daniels Midland, two Japanese companies and one Korean company, for cartel price fixing of lysine used in animal foodstuffs. In 2001 the Commission fined eight companies €855 million for cartel price fixing of vitamins. Roche Holding AG was fined €462 million as the ringleader of the price-fixing cartel. (U.S. actions against the cartel members are discussed in Chapter 9.) The French company Saint Gobain was fined €896 million in 2004 for fixing prices on auto glass. In 2009 the Commission fined Intel €1.06 billion for abusing its dominant position in the market for microprocessors by offering rebates and conditioning some rebates on not using AMD chips.[22] Intel rejected the Commission's conclusion, and appealed the decision, and sought a settlement.

EXAMPLE   Microsoft and EU Competition Policy

Microsoft's competitive practices and dominance of the operating system and desktop software markets have been a concern of the DG for Competition for nearly 20 years. In 1991 the U.S. Department of Justice (DOJ) and the European Commission signed an agreement to cooperate on antitrust investigations. The DOJ and the Commission, acting under a complaint from Novell, Inc., cooperated in an antitrust case against Microsoft with both agencies pressuring the company to enter into a consent decree to change its software licensing practices. At the end of the 1990s, the DG for Competition prevented Microsoft from exercising joint control over the United Kingdom's Telewest Communications, in which Microsoft had invested $3 billion.

Sun Microsystems filed a complaint with the DG for Competition (and not with U.S. antitrust authorities) alleging that Microsoft withheld interface (API) information for connecting servers to PCs in a network. Sun hoped to benefit from a precedent in which the Commission had ordered IBM to share certain interface information with Amdahl. A similar complaint was filed pertaining to interface information for Windows 2000. The Commission combined the two complaints and added new allegations about the bundling of Microsoft's music and video-streaming software with Windows XP. In 2003 a group of global telecommunications, electronics, and software companies joined the case as intervenors, alleging that Windows XP incorporated broader bundling, exclusionary practices, and screen bias favoring Microsoft software.

After 5 years of investigation and several attempts to reach a settlement, in 2004 the DG for Competition found Microsoft guilty of abusing its dominant position in computer operating systems in violation of Articles 101 and 102. As remedies, the DG fined Microsoft €497 million and ordered it to offer a version of Windows without Media Player. The court also ordered Microsoft to disclose substantive portions of its Windows code to allow server manufacturers to develop software that worked with Windows. The DG and Microsoft again attempted but failed to reach a settlement, and Microsoft appealed the decision to the General Court and sought a suspension of the remedies order. The president of the Computer and Communications Industry Association (CCIA), which was among the intervenors, said, "Their history is to appeal everything so as to delay."[1]

Microsoft subsequently settled with Novell for $536 million and with the CCIA for an undisclosed amount. Microsoft had earlier settled with AOLTimeWarner and Sun Microsystems, leaving Real Networks as the only remaining intervenor. The General Court rejected Microsoft's appeal.

Microsoft took a number of steps to comply with the judgment, but the Commission concluded that the company had not adequately disclosed information on its server protocols. The Commission announced that it would fine Microsoft €2 million a day until it complied, and in 2006 it fined the company €280.5 million. Microsoft lost its last appeal in 2007 and complied. In early 2008 the Commission fined Microsoft an additional €899 million for its past failure to comply. Microsoft appealed the fine to the General Court.

---

[1]*New York Times*, October 2, 2004.

---

[22]After the EU decision the U.S Federal Trade Commission (FTC) filed an antitrust complaint against Intel alleging that it abused its monopoly in microprocessors through anticompetitive processes. Intel and the FTC reached a settlement in 2010 in which Intel agreed to change its rebate and other practices.

In 2004 the DG for Competition reached a settlement with Coca-Cola after a 5-year investigation. In member states in which its market share exceeded 40 percent and its sales were double those of the next largest company, Coca-Cola agreed to end restrictive practices, including offering large discounts on its popular brands in exchange for stocking its less popular brands. Coca-Cola also agreed to stop offering rebates for reserving shelf space as well as "target" and "growth" rebates. In addition, Coca-Cola agreed to make up to 20 percent of the space in its branded refrigerators available to competitors, including Pepsi, which had complained to the European Union about Coca-Cola's practices. The settlement avoided fines and years of appeals.

MERGERS The Treaty of Rome did not address mergers because they were viewed as a desirable means of enabling small-scale European firms to attain the scale needed to compete globally. In 1989 the Council of Ministers adopted a Merger Control Regulation, assigning the Commission responsibility for reviewing large mergers, those in which the combined unit has sales of over €2.5 billion and the individual firms have sales of over €250 million.[23] Companies registered outside the European Union must submit a merger notification if they have sales in the European Union of €100 million. Merger review by the Commission is based solely on the effect on competition. The member states have authority to review smaller mergers and can seek permission from the Commission to conduct their own review of large mergers. If two-thirds of the revenues of each of two merging firms are from a single member state, that state rather than the Commission has authority over the review. A country thus can allow the merger of two of its major companies.

The EU has been active in the review of mergers, and its decisions have generally been consistent with those of the United States. In 2000 both the European Union and the United States blocked the merger of MCI (then WorldCom) and Sprint Communications. Also, in 2000 the United States approved the merger of AOL and TimeWarner after requiring the companies to provide rival Internet access through TimeWarner's cable systems. The EU also approved the $118 billion merger with the requirements that AOL TimeWarner scrap joint ventures with Bertelsmann AG, Vivendi SA, and EMI Group that threatened competition in the music business.

In 2001, however, the EU blocked the merger of General Electric and Honeywell International after the United States and 15 other countries had approved it. The DG for Competition was concerned about General Electric's dominant position in aircraft leasing and the portfolio effect if combined with Honeywell's avionics business. Critics charged that the decision was intended to protect Airbus Industrie from stronger competition. General Electric and Honeywell dropped the merger, but the companies decided to appeal the decision to the European Court of Justice so that the case would not set a precedent for future acquisitions. The General Court rejected the General Electric appeal.

In 2003 the General Court overturned a DG for Competition decision to block the merger of two UK travel agencies. The court used unusually harsh language in its decision, stating that the DG had been guilty of "manifest error" and "exceeded the bounds of its discretion." The court added that the DG's analysis was "vitiated by errors" and that it was necessary to show a "direct and immediate effect" on creating or maintaining a dominant position. The DG subsequently announced that greater oversight and additional reviews, including a peer review panel, would be applied before making merger decisions.

State Aids and the Common Agriculture Policy

State aids are subsidies paid by member state governments to their industries or government-owned companies.[24] Compared with the United States and Japan, EU member states provide considerably more subsidization for their firms. In 2009 the EU member states provided €107 billion in state aids. Much of the subsidization has gone to declining industries in an attempt to protect labor and capital, but more recently has been used for relief in the economic crisis.

The Commission monitors state aids and, for example, directed Italy to obtain a refund for a subsidy given to Fiat and ordered France to stop the large-scale subsidization of Renault.

---

[23]See Fishwick (1993) and Cini and McGowan (1998) for analyses of EU competition policy.
[24]State aids are governed by Articles 107–109 of the TFEU.

Private parties can file complaints with the DG for Competition to stop state aid. For example, the European Banking Federation complained about German loan guarantees to state-owned savings banks and regional banks. The DG for Competition made 510 decisions in state aid cases in 2000—more than the number of antitrust and merger cases combined.

EU member states also provide subsidies to failing companies. In 2004 France provided a €2.2 billion bailout of Alstom, an engineering conglomerate, to avoid having the company broken up and the parts purchased by foreign companies. Such bailouts must be approved by the DG for Competition, which gave its approval to stem the declining prospects for a number of companies. France and Germany sought to create globally competitive industrial champions by consolidating firms in some industries. Germany began with the consolidation of its shipbuilding industry.

In addition to state aid to agriculture and fisheries, the EU's Common Agriculture Policy (CAP) provided subsidies to farmers totaling €41 billion in 2009. The European Union sought to rein in CAP and made some progress, although opposition from farmers and some member states remained intense. The CAP, along with agricultural subsidization in the United States and Japan, has been a source of considerable international trade tension, as considered in Chapter 19. CAP also complicated enlargement negotiations with applicant countries. France, for example, sought to avoid any diversion of payments from its farmers to the new EU members.

The Social Charter, Social Democracy, and Labor Markets

The European Union adopted a Social Charter as part of the Treaty Establishing the European Community. The charter provides a vision for the free circulation of labor and the rights to fair wages, improvement of living and working conditions; social security; free association and collective bargaining; vocational training and education; equal treatment for men and women; information; consultation and participation for workers; health protection and safety in the workplace; protection for children, adolescents, and the elderly; and protection of the disabled.[25] Translating the vision of the Social Charter into law has been marked by several disagreements between business and labor and by the reality of national policy differences.[26] This led to the practice of an open method of coordination for implementation. Many of the actions under the Social Charter have been directed at increasing employment.

The SEA and other EU laws reflect the objectives of empowering labor and protecting individuals from risk and hardship through extensive social programs.[27] The European Union requires works councils or a consultative process between management and workers, or "social partners" in the terminology of European Union. At the plant level in Germany, workers have both representation and participation rights.[28] Those rights are in the areas of personnel policy, working conditions, and information, such as required notification of business plans that affect workers. Works councils can effectively prohibit weekend and overtime work and have powers over dismissals and reassignments.[29] Works councils use their rights to influence management, and management thus has an interest in accommodating council interests. Management, however, controls most decision making.

Much of the European labor force is well educated and highly skilled, and labor costs in many EU member states are high. Workweeks are shorter and vacations longer in Europe than they are in the United States and Asia. The OECD reported that on average Americans worked 1,777 hours in 2003, whereas the French and Germans worked less than 1,400 hours and the Dutch 1,309 hours.[30] Edward Prescott, the 2004 Nobel laureate in economics, attributed the difference in hours worked between the United States and Europe to differences in the tax rates on income. During the 1970–1974 period, the hours worked in France exceeded those in the United States, and tax increases in France and tax decreases in the United States led to the divergence, he argued.[31]

---

[25] See Nugent (2003, pp. 313–315) and Pierson (1999).
[26] See Wise and Gibb (1993).
[27] See European Commission (1988).
[28] See Streeck (1984, Ch. 3).
[29] See Streeck (1984, Ch. 7).
[30] The hours worked in South Korea were 2,390, followed by Poland (1,984), Mexico (1,980), Czech Republic (1,882), Japan (1,825), and Greece (1,811). Source: OECD.
[31] *Wall Street Journal*, October 21, 2004.

The short work hours led one German industrial relations manager to observe that "the German worker doesn't work very often, but when he does work, he works very, very hard."[32] Hard work was not enough, however, and the high labor costs led some German companies to move jobs to the new, low-wage members of the EU. Some German unions began to accept longer work hours to keep jobs in Germany. In contrast, France reduced its workweek to 35 hours in 2000 in an effort to reduce its unemployment rate.

With labor costs in the new EU member states far lower than those in the other member states, two threats faced the high-wage countries. One was that jobs could flow east to take advantage of both low wages and low taxes. This would increase unemployment and force wage concessions in the west. The other was that workers would flow west seeking higher wages. Anticipating this, the 15 existing EU member states reserved the right to restrict for up to 7 years the right of workers from the new member states to work in the west. Restrictions were imposed by several of the 15, including Austria, Denmark, Germany, the Netherlands, and the United Kingdom.

In 1995 most EU member states signed the Schengen Agreement, which eliminated border checks so as to allow the free flow of people within the signatory states. The Agreement caused friction, and by 2011 some member states adopted restrictions. Denmark reinstated border checks for people coming from Germany and Sweden, and Spain with an unemployment rate over 20 percent imposed restrictions on the inflow of people from Romania, whose numbers in Spain had quadrupled in the previous 5 years.[33] The presidents of France and Italy called for a revision of the Shengen Agreement after an influx of refugees from North Africa. Both countries had set up border checks in response to the influx. The Commission, however, proposed centralizing control of the EU's internal borders and requiring approval by a weighted majority vote of the council before temporary checks could be used. France, Germany, and Spain opposed the proposal.

Economic growth in the Netherlands far outstripped that in other European countries during the 1990s, and by 2003 unemployment was less than 3 percent in contrast to over 9 percent in Germany and France. The economic performance of the Netherlands was credited to moderate wage growth and labor market flexibility, including temporary and part-time work, and increased authority of companies to hire and fire. In addition, the country cut unemployment and disability benefits, which increased the incentives to find work. Disability claims fell by 80 percent. The country also shifted the burden of sick pay from the government to employers, which reduced significantly the number of employees calling in sick. Many of these reforms came under the leadership of a prime minister who was a former labor leader.

In the aftermath of the financial crisis and the subsequent recession, the Netherlands government implemented a short-work program under which companies could reduce workers' hours by as much as 50 percent and the government subsidized the lost wages. The program was credited with holding unemployment down to 3.7 percent in 2011, when the EU average was 9 percent. Some 1,500 companies participated in the program with the benefits to continue for 9–15 months.

NONMARKET ISSUES

Nonmarket issues in the European Union may be categorized by the level at which they are addressed, the EU level versus that of a member state, and whether they are specific to an industry or to an individual firm. At the EU level, important issues include the euro crisis, deeper political integration, the administration of competition policy, persistent high unemployment, further reforms of the common agriculture policy, trade policy, defense, harmonization of fiscal policies, the continued opening to competition of industries such as energy and financial services, and takeover policy. As an example, the governments of several member states held golden shares in companies, which in effect gave the governments a veto over any takeover attempt. This impeded the free flow of capital with the European Union. Some member states had voting rights caps that were intended to protect companies such as Volkswagen and the

---

[32]*New York Times*, January 25, 1985.
[33]*New York Times*, July 22, 2011.

United Kingdom's BAA. The DG for Competition ordered Germany to revise the governance laws for Volkswagen, including the majority of shareholders that had to approve major decisions such as closing a factory. Volkswagen had an 80 percent required majority, compared to 75 percent for other German companies, because the state of Lower Saxony held more than 20 percent of the shares of Volkswagen. The Commission directed Germany to lower the majority to 75 percent, but Germany refused to do so. The Commission sent a formal notice to Germany, which could take the issue to the Court of Justice.

At the national level the overall tax burden remains an issue. Countries including Denmark, France, and Sweden have a taxes-to-GDP ratio over 50 percent, compared to 31 percent in the United States and 33 percent in Japan. Citizens receive important services, such as health care, for the taxes, but many firms are concerned about the effect of taxes on their global competitiveness. Moreover, the tax rates of the member states differ considerably, making some relatively attractive as locations for new plants and enterprises.

An important difference between the European Union and the United States is the nature of regulation. The European Union more readily uses what may be called "precautionary regulation" than does the United States. One example is the policy restricting the use of genetically modified organisms (GMOs) in food on the grounds that they might pose health risks. This approach generated a major trade conflict between the European Union and the United States, as considered in Chapter 19. The United States tends to regulate known, as opposed to unknown, hazards, and GMO foods are widely available in the United States and other countries.

Another difference is that the United States more frequently relies on voluntary approaches to regulation, as in the case of Internet privacy. The policies of the European Union and the United States diverge substantially on the protection of personally identifiable information. For example, Americans were amused by the woman who complained that Google's Street View showed her cat sitting in her apartment window (discussed in the Chapter 1 case *The Nonmarket Environment of Google*). In response Google voluntarily agreed to blur the faces of people visible in Street View. The EU's top data protection officer, however, warned that Street View would have to comply with the data protection directive. Google and Street View continue to be embroiled in controversy in Europe.

Many Europeans are quite concerned about privacy, and these concerns have led to strong EU measures to protect personal information. At the EU level the Directive on Data Protection (95/46/EC) took effect in 1998 and required that a person grant explicit permission to a company before it could obtain personal information. In preparing its in-house telephone directory, General Motors had to obtain permission from each of its employees in the European Union to include their work telephone numbers, which were considered personal information. Individuals also have the right to inspect any files maintained and to correct any errors. Furthermore, an individual must be notified in advance if any personal information is to be sold. According to a spokesperson for Oracle, "Your business is essentially tubed until you get this resolved. It can be a life-or-death situation for some businesses."[34]

A number of the issues addressed by the European Union have major impacts on other countries. The Directive on Data Protection has caused some countries to issue new data protection rules that satisfy the EU requirements for data transfers. In this sense the EU has been driving regulation not just among its member states but also around the world. This has generated concerns in other countries about regulations driven by extreme caution. The United States refused to change its policies in response to the Directive on Data Protection and entered into negotiations with the EU, resulting in a safe harbor agreement.

The EU Directive on Data Protection was scheduled for revision in 2012, and one point of contention was whether the law should require Internet users to opt in before cookies could be deposited on computers and other online devices. The cookies were used to develop a profile of a user for placing online advertisements based on the user's behavior. The industry had self-regulated by creating a Web site where users could opt out of having cookies deposited. Commissioner Viviane Reding stated, "Companies must obtain prior consent before individuals' data is used."[35] Kimon Zorbas of IAB Europe said, "I am afraid it would kill a significant part of

[34]*San Jose Mercury News*, October 26, 1998.
[35]*New York Times*, September 19, 2011.

the industry."[36] The chapter case *The European Union Data Protection Directive (B)* considers the issue in more detail.[37]

As another example, because of the health fears underlying the precautionary principle, the European Union faced the issue of what to do about existing materials and products that might pose health or safety risks. The Commission embarked on a campaign to force the testing of 30,000 industrial chemicals either manufactured in or imported into the EU. The testing would be required even if there were no indication that there was any risk associated with the chemical. The chemical industry complained of the burden, and companies in the United States and other countries accused the EU of using regulation as a trade barrier. After intense lobbying, the Commission scaled back its proposed regulation, known as REACH (Registration, Evaluation, Authorization, and Restriction of Chemicals), and the Parliament approved it after considering a record 6,000 amendments. REACH created a new regulatory body, the European Chemicals Agency, to administer the regulation. Testing requirements would be phased in over 11 years, beginning with chemicals considered "risky." Testing was to focus on safety, and for more heavily used chemicals on health as well. Some 1,500 chemicals viewed as "hazardous" were required to go through a new authorization process to stay on the market. Firms are responsible for assessing the safety of chemicals they use, including manufacturers and importers, producers or importers of articles containing the chemicals, distributors, and downstream users, so the responsibility falls broadly on the business community. Since the EU represents a large market for foreign firms, REACH in effect requires firms in other countries to know the chemicals used in their products and ultimately to comply with the testing and possible ban of the chemicals.

The European Union has been a leading advocate of reducing greenhouse gas emissions, and the chapter case *The European Union Carbon Tax* considers an early attempt to regulate carbon emissions. The EU agreed to an aggressive Kyoto Protocol goal of reducing CO_2 emissions by 6 percent compared to 1990 levels.

The EU had made considerable early progress toward its Kyoto goals because electric utilities had switched from coal to natural gas and the high price of energy had led to investments in efficiency. To meet its goal, the EU implemented a cap-and-trade system for controlling emissions from factories as discussed in Chapter 12, but in the first 3 years of operation emissions actually increased because member state governments, worried about the possible loss of jobs, issued too many permits. The EU then reduced the number of permits and broadened the coverage, but whether the Kyoto goal would be realized was unclear.

The EU expanded the scope of its emissions permits trading system to cover the emissions of airlines that use EU airports. U.S. airlines backed by the U.S. government objected strongly to the EU action. The U.S. government lobbied the EU government arguing that the control of airline emissions required a global accord, which was being led by the United Nations' International Civil Aviation Organization. The EU rejected the argument stating that the UN effort was insufficiently ambitious and moving too slowly. The U.S. airlines argued that they were being unfairly taxed for activity outside the EU. Joe LePochet of American Airlines said, "It is not right that foreign carriers are charged by Europe for operating on their own airspace. Essentially, I'm charged for burning fuel on the ground in New York or Chicago."[38] They took their arguments to the Court of Justice. U.S. environmental groups joined the lawsuit on the EU side. An Environmental Defense Fund spokesperson said, "We think that the EU law is fully consistent with international law."[39]

At the level of the member states, issues affecting business include pharmaceutical approvals and price controls, tax policies to attract business, harmonization of financial services regulation, the convergence of products liability laws, Internet taxation, and the opening of government procurement to competition among the member states. Issues also pertain to individual firms, including the privatization of government-owned firms and the subsidization of firms through state aids. Many of the issues at the level of the member states involve the implementation of EU regulations and directives.

Many nonmarket issues are company-specific. Responsibility for advertisements of fake goods on online marketplaces has been a contentious issue with producers of the authentic goods

---

[36]Ibid.

[37]See the sixth edition of this book for the case *The European Data Protection Directive (A)*.

[38]*Wall Street Journal*, June 30, 2011.

[39]Ibid.

working to force eBay and others to remove the advertisements. In the United States the online marketplaces are not responsible provided they remove the ads when asked to do so by a producer.[40] In the EU, the Court of Justice ruled in a case brought by L'Oréal against eBay that the online marketplace provider was responsible for removing advertisements for fake goods if it played an "active role" in helping sellers in the promoting or advertising of fake goods or if it failed to remove items that infringed trademarks. In a related case U.S. movie studios had filed a lawsuit against a UK Internet service provider alleging that the Web site Newzbin allowed users to unlawfully download movies.[41]

Many nonmarket issues result from actions taken by activists, as considered in the Chapter 4 case *Shell, Greenpeace, and the Brent Spar.* Activist groups, for example, protested a Benetton advertisement showing a bloody uniform of a fallen Croat soldier in the Yugoslav civil war. The ad was intended as a plea for peace, but Benetton was accused of exploiting the war. A German court banned Benetton ads, and the French minister for humanitarian affairs called for a boycott of Benetton and urged people to "pull [Benetton sweaters] off the people who are going to wear them."[42]

INTERESTS AND THEIR ORGANIZATION

Interests are pluralistic in the European Union as they are in the United States and other countries, but their organization is different, in part because the governments of the member states are parliamentary.[43] Some firms are directly involved in issues at the EU level, and more are involved in the issues at the level of the member states. At the EU level, Philips Electronics worked for the creation of a center to conduct research on semiconductors. Much of the nonmarket activity at the EU level, however, is conducted by peak associations that represent businesses within the member states.

Several European countries, such as Germany and Sweden and others to a lesser extent, have a strong corporatist system in which interests are represented by national associations that interact directly, and often with formal sanction, with government. In a corporatist structure, unions and businesses have peak organizations that advise government and negotiate on policy. In Germany, for example, manufacturing enterprises, agricultural interests, service companies, and professionals are organized by law into "chambers," which exercise self-regulation authority over members and represent their members' interests before the government. The Federation of German Employers' Associations (BDA) is composed of 56 employer associations and represents business on social and labor issues. The Federation of German Industry (BDI), whose members are 39 national federations that include 40,000 businesses and 85 percent of German industry, is more active in nonmarket arenas.[44] It provides expert testimony on legislation, lobbies government institutions, and consults with government leaders. The peak business organizations cooperate both formally and informally. Informally, their leaders consult on issues, and formally the BDA and the BDI interact through organizations such as the Joint Committee of German Trade and Industry.

In many industries the national associations join to form EU-wide associations that implement nonmarket strategies directed at the EU institutions. The largest of these associations is the Union of Industrial and Employers Confederations of Europe (UNICE). The European Roundtable of Industrialists represents large companies in Brussels and in the member states. These peak associations take much of the nonmarket action that individual firms and ad hoc coalitions take in the United States. For example, the European Confederation of Retail Trade represents retail interests in the European Union, and the European Chemical Industry Council (CEFIC) includes as members the national associations of chemical companies. A peak organization such as CEFIC represents relatively homogeneous interests, whereas the Confederation of Food and Drink Industries represents relatively heterogeneous interests including soft drinks, beer, beef, and cheese. CEFIC was active in the chapter case *The European Union Carbon Tax.*

---

[40]See Chapter 2 for more details.

[41]*Financial Times,* July 13, 2011.

[42]See the Chapter 14 case *Benetton, Advertising Protests, and Franchising* in Baron (2000).

[43]In a parliamentary system the government is formed by a majority party in parliament or by a coalition of parties that constitute a majority. The government and the parliament are thus aligned allowing them an opportunity to act without direct restraint but with consideration for their fate in the next election.

[44]A third, less active, peak organization is the Diet of German Industry and Commerce.

Foreign firms are organized in a similar manner. The EU Committee of the American Chamber of Commerce (Amcham) represents over 100 U.S. companies in Brussels and is highly regarded.[45] In addition, several U.S. associations formed the U.S. Industry Coordinating Group.[46] Some industry associations, such as the Pharmaceutical Research and Manufacturers Association, maintain offices in Brussels.

Much of the nonmarket action at the industry level has been conducted by EU-wide associations representing the industry associations in the member states. For example, the pharmaceutical industry had sought the decontrol of pharmaceutical prices, which have been kept low in countries such as France to relieve the government's health care budget. Issues involving the pharmaceutical industry are addressed by the European Federation of Pharmaceutical Industries' Associations. In some cases ad hoc groups of firms from various member states join together to seek support, as when Philips, Siemens, Thomson, and General Electric (UK) sought support for the European computer and semiconductor industries.

Unionization in the European Union is more extensive than in the United States, and unions are also organized in national federations and in EU-wide umbrella associations. For example, German unions typically are organized by industry and bargain with associations of employers in those industries. Seventeen German unions are members of the federation Deutscher Gewerkschaftsbund (DGB). The unions have considerable power because of the high rate of unionization and also because of their links to political parties, particularly socialist parties. In Germany the DGB exercises political power both through the political parties and through its interactions with the executive branch and the legislature. Many Social Democrat members of the Bundestag (parliament) are union members.

Activists and NGOs are active in the European Union, particularly in northern Europe. Consumer groups such as Consumentenbond in the Netherlands are linked to consumer groups in other countries. Some interest groups, such as the Greens, have formed political parties. Green activists have vigorously opposed biotechnology and have had considerable success in slowing the growth of the industry. The Chapter 4 case *Shell, Greenpeace, and Brent Spar* concerns an activist protest in Europe against a company's actions.

NONMARKET STRATEGIES IN THE EUROPEAN UNION

Many nonmarket strategies are implemented at the levels of both the member states and the institutions of the European Union. To illustrate the multiple levels of nonmarket strategies, the European Union committed to achieving the goals established in the Kyoto Protocol on global climate change and worked for a cap-and-trade system among the signatories. Within the EU, opposition occurred at both the EU and member state levels. A spokesperson for the Federation of German Industries said, "What we are against is the exaggerated ecological leadership which...the European Union wants to administer."[47] The Commission was forced to delay the proposal because of complaints by pan-European associations and industry associations, such as those for autos and chemicals, concerned about the effect on their international competitiveness. The European Trading System (ETS) finally began in 2005. The opposition by business led the member states to issue more permits than needed. The United Kingdom had started a cap-and-trade system, and Blue Circle, a UK cement company owned by Lafarge Coppée of France, successfully lobbied to have its emissions goal stated in terms of CO_2 emissions per ton of cement produced, as opposed to an absolute cap. This allowed the company to expand its output.

The member states have parliamentary systems of government, but they differ considerably in terms of their institutions, their party organization, and the strength and organization of various interests. Van Schendelen (1993) presents an analysis of interests and lobbying in EU countries, and the Part IV integrative case *Toys 'Я' Us and Globalization* considers strategies for individual countries. The focus here is on nonmarket activities and strategies at the EU level.[48]

---

[45]See, for example, Coen (1999).
[46]See Calingaert (1993).
[47]*Wall Street Journal*, July 13, 2001.
[48]Calingaert (1993) provides a description of the organization for nonmarket action at the EU level.

FIGURE 15-4 EU Institutions, Constituencies, and Access

Institution	Constituency	Access
European Commission	EU-wide constituency— member states, citizens, interests	DGs, commissioners, staff
Council of Ministers	Member states	Member states, political parties, COREPER, working groups
European Parliament	Voters	Committees, political parties, members of Parliament
Economic and Social Committee	Interests	Representatives, associations

In the terminology of Chapter 7, both representation and informational strategies are important in the European Union. Representation strategies are based on the constituency for each of the principal EU institutions, as indicated in Figure 15-4. For example, the constituency of the Council of Ministers is the member states, and hence representation strategies targeting the council are implemented primarily through the member state governments. Because those governments are parliamentary and often controlled by coalitions, political parties are an important focus of these strategies. The national ministries are a locus of expertise and play important roles in how a member state votes in the Council of Ministers. The primary points of access to the council are COREPER and the working groups it forms to address issues. For example, in the chapter case the *European Union Data Protection Directive (B)*, the Article 29 Working Party composed of data protection regulators in each of the member states met with industry groups and companies about the revision of the directive.

Much of the nonmarket action in the European Union takes place behind the scenes, and most businesses avoid taking public action that might be subjected to criticism. In addition, because of the pervasive influence of government in many EU countries, companies seldom engage in open confrontation with government, as is more often the case in the United States.

Lobbying is the principal political activity for implementing both representation and informational strategies in the European Union. A lobbyist's strategy is to demonstrate that the interests of a company or industry are aligned with those of the person or office being lobbied. In the case of the European Union, those interests are a mixture of economic efficiency and social objectives at the EU level; sectoral interests in the case of agriculture, steel, or computers; and local interests in the case of some members of the EP and the Council of Ministers. EU officials face pressures from their home country constituents and from their mandate for economic and political integration.

Lobbyists are not required to register with the EU, but estimates put their number at around 15,000. In 2008 the EU adopted a code of conduct for lobbyists and established a voluntary registry. The European Parliament provides a 1-year pass to its premises in exchange for a lobbyist signing a code of ethical behavior. The EU does not require disclosure of lobbying activity, the funds spent on hired lobbyists, or the policy issue on which the lobbyists work.

Former EU and national government officials have formed lobbying firms to represent interests. EU lobbyists have backgrounds similar to their counterparts in the United States. Companies hire former EU officials, trade negotiators, ambassadors, and former officials of national governments as lobbyists. Lobbying services are also provided by law firms and consultants. Companies have opened offices in Brussels to be close to the EU and to track its activities. Managers frequently participate in lobbying along with heads of industry associations and peak organizations. In addition, in a number of countries business leaders have close personal relationships with government officials. In some countries, such as France, these relationships may have been formed through attendance at the same *grandes écoles.* In Germany top government officials consult with business leaders because of the status and strength of business in the country.[49]

---
[49]See Calingaert (1993).

Peak associations play a number of roles, including the monitoring of government activities, the funneling of information and expertise from their members to the government, and lobbying. Lobbying, for example, is pervasive in German politics, but because of the omnipresence of associations it tends to be collective in its nature. Much of the political influence takes place through the executive branch and the interactions of high-ranking government officials, particularly bureaucrats, with the leaders of the peak associations. Seventy percent of the BDI's contacts were with the bureaucracy and only 5 percent with the Bundestag. As a result of the SEA and the increasing importance of the EU government, German associations increased their presence and lobbying in Brussels.

Informational strategies center on the strategic provision of information to EU officeholders, and the nature and content of these strategies is the same as characterized in Chapter 7. The key to successful lobbying is the provision of information useful to the institutional officeholders. Successful lobbying requires an understanding of their interests, the relationship between policy alternatives and consequences, and the procedures and practices of EU institutions. Lobbying also takes place within each member state in attempts to convince government officeholders of the importance of the interests affected. Figure 15-4 identifies the points of access.

The form that lobbying takes depends on the institution in question. The European Commission is perhaps the most important body because it is the agenda setter for much of the legislation and also administers policies. Because the Commission has a relatively small staff, it needs information and expertise for its legislative and regulatory actions. The Commission stated, "The Commission has always been open to ideas from the outside world. It believes that openness is crucial for developing its polices. This dialogue has proved valuable to both the commission and interested outside parties.... The Commission will remain very accessible to the interest groups."[50] The Commission has established a set of informal and formal consultation procedures, including the formation of advisory committees and policy forums. To provide voice to groups that would otherwise be underrepresented, the EU provides funding for NGOs to participate in political and policy-making processes.

The EU uses several thousand working groups and committees in writing and implementing legislation as part of its "comitology" procedures. These include advisory, management, regulation, and oversight committees. Some committees are composed solely of members of government, whereas others include representatives of business for their expertise. Interests direct their lobbying at these committees, particularly those that are involved in advising the commission on the implementation of policies.

The respect garnered by the American Chamber of Commerce (Amcham) in Brussels is due in part to the detailed information it provides on issues and its accurate representation of American concerns. As Coen (1999, p. 35) characterized the situation in the mid-1990s, "U.S. firms demonstrated to their European rivals the importance of direct, regular, and reliable representation at the European Commission.... Amcham and its EU committee demonstrated the importance of both direct firm membership (at the collective European level) and the participation of senior executives with expertise in the policy debate. By adapting the organizational structure around 12 specialized technical committees on issues such as competition, trade, social affairs, and the environment, Amcham was able to complement the new European Commission's issue-based forums..."

Interests interact with the Commission directly through its DGs, but interests can also be represented by members of either the European Parliament or the Economic and Social Committee. Also, member governments intervene on behalf of interest groups in their own countries. The targets of lobbying are the commissioners and their cabinets. Because the DGs are the repositories of expertise and deal with the specifics of issues, access to members of the relevant DGs is important. Participation in working parties and advisory committees can be an important means of access as well as a source of information. The Commission initiates legislation in the form of drafts that are circulated for comments before the legislative process begins (see Figure 15-2). Lobbying thus begins early in the process and is directed at the formulation of the initial draft as well as the subsequent legislative process. Affecting the agenda can be an effective means of laying a path to be followed with subsequent lobbying. Lobbyists are also active at the implementation stage, as the Commission makes decisions and issues directives to implement legislation.

---

[50]europa.eu.int/secretariat/general/sgc/lobbies/approche/apercu_en.htm.

The Council of Ministers is the principal legislative institution, but it is difficult to influence directly because it operates in private. The principal route to influencing the Council is through member state governments and their relevant ministries. National interests also are represented by a country's permanent representatives (COREPER) to the EU. COREPER is required by law to consult directly with interests, and industry and labor organizations maintain close contacts with it. COREPER is expected to resolve political issues on behalf of the Council.

As a result of the Maastricht Treaty and the Treaty of Lisbon that mandated the increased use of the ordinary legislative procedure, the EP has become more important due to its powers to amend and veto Commission proposals. The EP's constituencies are voters and the political parties that represent them, and the principal points of access are the party organizations, individual members, and committees. The EP members are both issue oriented and concerned about the effects of issues on constituents. Members represent a variety of interests and may be willing to act as allies in advancing the interests of firms and industries. Although the EP has committees that formulate amendments, most of the lobbying takes place outside the formal committee structure. In addition, the organization of the EP by political party means that a path to influence is through the party system in the firm's home country. The attention given to lobbying the EP is growing, but still less than that given the Commission, COREPER, and member state governments.

The custom in Europe has been to use peak organizations, such as UNICE and the Roundtable of European Industrialists, for political and other nonmarket actions. Issues involving the internal market and international trade, however, are industry-specific and have differing impacts on individual firms. Industry associations play a major role on such issues.[51] Also, coalitions are formed that cut across the lines of peak associations. These coalitions may include companies domiciled in different member states acting together on a trade issue or a company and a union joining together to advance their joint interests.

As an example of an ad hoc coalition formed to address a specific issue, in 1996 the EP proposed amendments to a Commission policy on the media industry. France, backed by socialist members of the EP, pushed for tighter quotas on the foreign content on television and multimedia outlets. According to one report, American companies produced 80 percent of the programming shown on European television. Opposition to the proposed amendments included not only American interests and private broadcasters but also a broad set of other interests. Advertisers opposed the amendments because they would restrict advertising on home shopping channels. Retailers opposed the amendments because they would restrict the number of hours regular TV channels could devote to teleshopping. The prospect of quotas on Internet content led one Bertelsmann lobbyist to comment, "It's very silly what they want to do. It won't work in an Internet, online environment."[52] The chapter case *The European Union Carbon Tax* concerns another issue involving a broad set of interests.

Some firms undertake independent political action or form ad hoc coalitions to advance their agenda. Philips Electronics has been one of the most active. It was an early advocate of the creation of a single market and also worked to limit competition from outside the European Union. For example, it lobbied successfully for protection against Japanese compact disc systems. In addition to its extensive lobbying, Van Schendelen (1993) reports that Philips was successful in "parachuting" one of its technology experts into the DG responsible for subsidies for technology programs. Philips obtained R&D subsidies for 150 projects. Philips was also one of the principal forces behind the EU subsidies for the development of a European HDTV system. Working with the European Information Technology Roundtable, Philips also led the effort to obtain $4 billion for semiconductor research.

Philips Chairman Cornelis van der Klugt was personally active, lobbying in Brussels to obtain import protection for Philips. He argued that free trade with the European Union required "real reciprocity." To protect its VCR business, Philips pushed through the European Union a 30 percent levy on Japanese and South Korean VCRs. He worked to have the European Union investigate dumping charges against Asian producers of small televisions and compact disc players and to have semiconductors assembled by Japanese firms in Europe classified as imports so

---

[51]John and Schwarzer (2006) studied the lobbying of the European automobile industry.
[52]*Wall Street Journal*, February 12, 1996.

they would be subject to tariffs. An antidumping complaint against six Japanese semiconductor manufacturers led to an agreement between the European Union and Japan that set a price floor on imported semiconductors. Van der Klugt defended his efforts: "It's not necessary for the Japanese to export unemployment to Europe. We have enough unemployment."[53] At the same time that he worked for protection, van der Klugt pushed the European Union to scrap its internal trade barriers as quickly as possible.

Nonmarket issues and strategies are often complicated by national concerns. Pharmaceuticals is far from a single market. Under the principle of subsidiarity, the member states are responsible for health care and can institute their own price controls. The Commission has expressed concern that very stringent price controls were driving pharmaceutical innovation out of the EU.[54] France, for example, required pharmaceutical companies to sign broad conventions that covered not only prices but also commitments to create jobs in France and to support state-owned research institutes. To hold down the cost of its national health care system, pharmaceutical prices were set at very low levels. This in part led the three largest French pharmaceutical companies to either merge or spin off their pharmaceutical operations into a jointly owned affiliate. The French Parliament also enacted a law that made pharmaceutical companies responsible for any costs above ceilings set by parliament for the national health service. Industry members challenged the new law in France and before the Commission and the Court of Justice.[55]

Specific nonmarket issues can also arise in the normal course of EU activities. An example of such an issue, a German court decision about wedding dresses that had important implications for franchising, is considered in the example.

Firms also employ judicial strategies in the European Union. A German environmental law favored reusable materials such as glass bottles over recyclable materials such as plastic

EXAMPLE   Pronuptia and Franchising

A German court had invalidated a franchise agreement that required a German retailer, Pronuptia, to sell only the wedding dresses of its French franchiser and only in specific territories. The French franchiser appealed the decision to the Court of Justice. U.S. franchisers saw the decision as crucial to their use of U.S.-style franchise arrangements in the European Union. They launched a lobbying campaign directed at the Commission, which planned to file an opinion on the case with the court. The lobbyist engaged by the U.S. franchisers conducted a "teach in" about U.S. franchising practices for officials of the DG for Competition. The commission subsequently argued before the court that the franchise restrictions were necessary to maintain product quality, among other things. In 1986 the court overruled the German court and upheld the rights of franchisers to restrict the actions of their franchisees on several dimensions.[1]

U.S. franchisers were still concerned that the franchising arrangements allowed by the court might be challenged under the antitrust provisions in Article 101. Some franchisers, including Pronuptia, sought and received exemptions from the Commission. They also encouraged the commission to grant a broader exemption from antitrust rules for franchise arrangements. The U.S. interests, including McDonald's, Pizza Hut, Kentucky Fried Chicken, Midas Muffler, Coca-Cola, Holiday Inns, and others, were represented by the International Franchising Association (IFA), which was active in Brussels. The IFA met with a variety of officials, including the competition commissioner, who was also lobbied when he visited the United States.

The lobbyist for the U.S. franchisers said, "The most important lessons we've learned so far are for American interests to get in early; in a European, not American, way; and demonstrate from the start that American interests are compatible with European interests." An official with the DG for Competition said the IFA "made their points forcefully, but also gave us a lot of useful information about how the U.S. system works."[2]

U.S. franchisers obtained "96.5 percent" of what they sought, but they were prohibited from requiring franchisees to purchase one brand exclusively. A fast-food chain thus cannot force its franchisees to carry only one soft drink brand.

---

[1]*Pronuptia de Paris GmbH v. Pronuptia de Paris Irmgard Schillgalis* (case 161/84), January 28, 1986, Common Market Report (CCH) para. 14,245 (1986). See Rosenthal (1990) for a discussion of this case. Also see Hawk (1988).

[2]*Wall Street Journal*, May 17, 1989.

---

[53]*New York Times*, June 4, 1989.
[54]European Commission press release, November 25, 1998.
[55]*Wall Street Journal*, December 7, 1998.

and cans. Since glass bottles were much more costly to transport than other containers, beverage firms were effectively excluded from the German market. French mineral-water companies complained that it was prohibitively costly to collect and truck the empty bottles back to their springs for refilling. The 50-member packaging association Europen, whose members included Coca-Cola and Nestlé, successfully lobbied the Commission to file a lawsuit against Germany. In 2004 the Court of Justice ruled that the German law discriminated against foreign companies.

SUMMARY

The Single European Act represented a major step toward economic integration within the Union. It also increased the political power of the EU institutions relative to the governments of the member states. The Maastricht Treaty provided for a monetary union and for steps toward a political union. The European Union has also broadened with 10 additional countries joining the Union in 2004 and two others joining in 2007. The Maastricht Treaty and the Treaty of Lisbon increased the power of the European Parliament, which exercises democratic supervision.

The principal institutions of the European Union are the European Commission, the Council of Ministers, the European Parliament, and the Court of Justice. The Economic and Monetary Union established both an independent European Central Bank and a common currency among the 17 participating states. Considerable progress has been made in eliminating internal barriers to trade, but several difficult issues, including fiscal harmonization, remain. Rigid labor markets, high wages and taxes, and the high costs of laying off workers have resulted in a high unemployment in many member states.

Interests take nonmarket action both individually and through associations and peak organizations, which play an important role at the EU level. The pattern of interest group activity and the nature of nonmarket action have evolved as companies, unions, and other organizations have adapted their strategies to institutional changes. The growth in lobbying is a sign of both the increased importance of the EU government and the stakes involved in its actions. Lobbying is the principal nonmarket strategy for influencing the EU institutions. Since much of the legislative and regulatory activity takes place outside the view of the public and prior to the formal procedures beginning, it is important to participate both early and continuously in the EU governmental processes.

Although the powers of the EU institutions have increased, the governments of the member states continue to be the focus of considerable nonmarket activity. Those governments are parliamentary but differ in their institutional structures and their politics. The organization of interests in a number of member states is corporatist with peak associations active in nonmarket and governmental matters. Individual companies, however, also undertake their own nonmarket activities and form alliances with companies in other EU member states.

CASES

The European Union Carbon Tax

Whether and to what extent global warming was occurring remained the subject of considerable scientific uncertainty, disagreement, and debate during the early 1990s, but the scientific evidence increasingly supported the global warming hypothesis. The principal contributor to global warming was believed to be the burning of carbon-based fuels, principally coal, petroleum, and natural gas.

A European Union (EU) Joint Council of Energy and Environment Ministers declared in 1990 that the member states would by the year 2000 stabilize CO_2 emissions at the 1990 level. Because of projected economic growth, stabilization would require a reduction in emissions of approximately 10 percent from the unstabilized level. Some of the reductions required to stabilize emissions were anticipated to come from improved energy efficiency induced by the current prices of fossil fuels. These "no regrets" conservation measures were estimated to reduce emissions by 5.5 percent by 2000, leaving a reduction of 5 percent to be accomplished by other measures. In October 1991 the European Commission issued a draft directive informing the member states of its plans to propose a variety of measures to reduce CO_2 emissions. These measures included R&D programs and a carbon/energy tax to achieve the remaining reduction of 5 percent. The proposed carbon/energy tax was intended to reduce carbon emissions by making fuels, particularly carbon-based fuels, more costly, thereby inducing conservation and the substitution of less carbon-intensive fuels.

The European Commission operated under collective responsibility but frequently deferred to the commissioner with policy jurisdiction if the issue was not controversial. This was not an uncontroversial issue. The lead commissions for this issue were DG XI (environment) and DG XVII (energy). Mr. Carlo Ripa di Meana, EU commissioner for the environment, pushed for a formal proposal on the tax by June 1992 in time for the Rio Earth Summit. Mr. Jacques Delors, president of the commission, also supported the tax and the leadership position it would give the European Union in Rio. Mr. Antonio Cardoso e Cunha, EU commissioner for energy, supported the tax because it would promote energy efficiency.

The European Commission proposal involved specific (per unit) taxes that would impose half the burden on carbon-based fuels and the other half on energy. The commission estimated that the full tax would increase the price of natural gas for industry by 33 percent, hard coal by 60 percent, and gasoline by 6 percent.[56] Because emissions of CO_2 were difficult to measure by source, the taxes would be applied to inputs rather than emissions. The proposed carbon tax would begin at $3 per barrel of oil and increase by $1 per year for the next 7 years, reaching $10 per barrel. (The $10 per barrel tax was equivalent to a tax of $75 per ton of carbon.) An equivalent tax would be applied to coal and natural gas. The energy tax would apply to all energy sources except renewable sources. The energy tax was included to satisfy environmentalists who opposed a pure carbon tax because it would provide incentives for the expansion of nuclear power. Countries such as Germany, Greece, and the United Kingdom, with carbon-intensive energy supplies, also favored an energy tax. Denmark and the Netherlands and two European Free Trade Association (EFTA) countries, Finland and Sweden, already had imposed a carbon tax.[57] Denmark's carbon tax averaged $16 per ton of carbon for individual consumption and $8 per ton for industry. Energy-intensive industries, however, could be granted an exemption of up to 100 percent of the tax. The Netherlands' carbon tax was $12.50 per ton. The tax in Sweden was $62 per ton of carbon, and in Finland the tax was $6.50 per ton.[58]

Neither Japan nor the United States had a carbon tax in 1992. The Japanese government argued that its regulations already set standards that were at least as strong as those the EU tax would achieve. Presidential candidate Bill Clinton had pledged during his campaign to address the global warming issue using efficient means, including taxes on carbon and/or energy. The Congressional Budget Office estimated that to stabilize CO_2 emissions a tax of $100 per ton of carbon would

be required.[59] Representative Pete Stark (D-CA) introduced a bill to impose a tax of $15 per ton on coal, $3.25 per barrel of oil, and $0.40 per MCF of natural gas. The European Commission urged the member states to make every effort to ensure that other OECD countries, in particular Japan and the United States, adopted measures similar to its proposed carbon/energy tax.

The carbon/energy tax would affect production and consumption decisions throughout the European Union. It would also affect the competitiveness of EU businesses, particularly those that used energy-intensive technologies. Mr. Ripa di Meana, however, argued, "This is a chance to update European industry and make it a leader in a green-oriented market." To lessen the impact on the international competitiveness of European companies, the commission proposed to at least partially exempt from the tax those industries that had energy-intensive production processes.

The tax would ultimately be borne in large part by individuals and would have the greatest impact on those who intensively used energy, and particularly carbon-based fuels. Because lower-income individuals spent a higher portion of their income on energy, the tax would be regressive.

A carbon/energy tax also would generate substantial revenue for governments. For example, a tax of $100 per ton of carbon was estimated to generate revenue equal to 1.99 percent of GDP based on consumption in 1988. For France the revenue would be 1.28 percent of GDP, and for Germany and the United Kingdom it would be approximately 2.3 percent. The commission suggested that the carbon tax should be "fiscally neutral" for each country, although Mr. Ripa di Meana argued that a portion of the tax revenue should go to developing countries to prevent deforestation. Fiscal neutrality would require that any additional revenue generated by the tax be offset by fiscal incentives or reductions in other taxes. Because the individual member states rather than the European Union would receive the revenue from the tax, each member state would determine its own use of the revenue. Under EU law the member states would be responsible for the implementation of the tax.

The EU legislative process required that the imposition of a carbon/energy tax be decided under a unanimity rule. Some bargaining among the member states would likely be involved with compensation given to certain countries that otherwise would be substantially impacted by the tax. As part of its annual budget, the European Union provided grants of structural funds for economic development to countries and to regions within countries. In 1992 these funds were approximately 19 million ECUs ($25 billion). The budget and thus the amount and allocation of structural funds were decided by a qualified majority of the Council of Finance Ministers. In 1992 a qualified majority required 54 of the 76 votes. The number of votes for each member state is presented in Table 15-1.

---

[56]The percentage increase for gasoline was low because gasoline was already heavily taxed.

[57]In 1995 Austria, Finland, and Sweden joined the European Union.

[58]See Poterba (1991, pp. 71–98).

[59]The United States had imposed a tax on CFCs as a means of speeding the elimination of their production. In addition to contributing to ozone depletion, CFCs were greenhouse gases and contributed to global warming.

TABLE 15-1 Votes of Member States in the Council of Ministers, 1992	
Member States	Votes
Belgium	5
Denmark	3
France	10
Germany	10
Greece	5
Ireland	3
Italy	10
Luxembourg	2
Netherlands	5
Portugal	5
Spain	8
United Kingdom	10
Total	76

TABLE 15-2 CO_2 Emissions (million tons) with No Further Abatement: 10 EU Countries		
	1988	Projected, 2010
Belgium	109	110
Denmark	61	60
France	374	370
Germany	718	677
Greece	84	127
Italy	399	489
The Netherlands	146	165
Portugal	28	51
Spain	196	265
United Kingdom	561	505
Total	2,676	2.819

Source: Coherence (1991). "Cost-effectiveness analysis of CO_2 reduction options." Synthesis report and country reports for the Commission of the European Communities, DG XII. May 1991.

In December 1991 the EU Joint Council of Environment and Energy Ministers unanimously endorsed the European Commission's draft directive. Denmark, Germany, Italy, Belgium, and the Netherlands came out clearly in favor of the proposal, whereas the lower-income southern countries led by Spain, along with Luxembourg, were concerned about how the abatement burden would be divided among the countries. The United Kingdom agreed in principle but was hesitant about the additional taxes. France, which generated much of its electricity from nuclear power, supported the proposed taxes but wanted to tilt the taxes more toward fossil fuels. Both endorsed the report. A few days later the EU finance ministers took note of the proposal and asked for a detailed study on the practical details of the tax.

THE ECONOMICS OF EMISSIONS CONTROL IN THE EUROPEAN UNION

Before the European Commission presented its proposal for meeting the EU-wide stabilization target, it commissioned a study of the costs and benefits of CO_2 emissions reduction. Although emissions were to be stabilized by the year 2000, the Council of Ministers requested that the study analyze the effects in the year 2010, since the stabilization target was to hold indefinitely and some investments in energy conservation would take several years before they were fully implemented. Table 15-2 outlines the "base-case" scenario that was predicted to occur in 2010 if no EU-wide emissions control took place. Column 1 of Table 15-2 presents 1988 CO_2 emissions for 10 EU countries for comparison purposes (Ireland and Luxembourg are omitted from the analysis because they had the lowest CO_2 emissions in the European Union and because important data were not available). Not surprisingly, the largest and wealthiest countries—France, Germany, Italy, and the United Kingdom—had the highest levels of CO_2 emissions in 1988. However, the projected growth in emissions for 1988 to

2010 exhibited a very different pattern. The lower-income countries—Greece, Portugal, and Spain—were predicted, respectively, to emit 52, 82, and 35 percent more CO_2 by 2010 if no additional measures were taken, compared with decreases in emissions in France, Germany, and the United Kingdom. The declines were projected to result from increased energy efficiency.[60]

If emissions were to be stabilized in 2000 and beyond, the European Commission had to make a proposal that achieved a 143 million ton reduction in CO_2 by the year 2010. A uniform tax would induce efficient emissions control across countries by giving polluters in each country the incentive to abate up to the point at which the marginal cost of abatement equaled the emissions tax. As a result, the marginal cost of reducing pollution in any one country would equal the marginal cost of reducing pollution in every other country. The tax required to achieve the target reduction of 143 million tons of CO_2 was calculated by researchers to be approximately $75 per ton of carbon at an exchange rate of $1.30/ECU.[61]

COSTS AND BENEFITS OF A CARBON/ENERGY TAX

The relative impact of a carbon tax would be greatest on the lower-income countries. The tax would reduce their growth rate in addition to imposing high costs of abatement. The countries that would be most severely affected were Greece, Italy, Portugal, and Spain. A reduction in CO_2 emissions by the European Union would constitute a public good, since all

---

[60]For example, CO_2 emissions in the United Kingdom in 1992 were below the emissions levels in 1972.

[61]See "Reaching a CO_2-Emission Limitation Agreement for the Community: Implications for Equity and Cost Effectiveness," *European Economy*, Special Edition No. 1, *The Economics of Limiting CO_2 Emissions*, Directorate-General for Economics and Financial Affairs, Commission of the European Communities, 1992.

countries would benefit from the reductions. The benefits for individual EU member states would be roughly proportional to their populations.

The reactions to the proposed tax by industry were predictable. The trade association Euroelectric, representing the EU electricity industry, opposed the tax and argued for voluntary conservation measures. Electric power generators—Electrabel (Belgium), Endesa (Spain), PowerGen (United Kingdom), RWE (Germany), Scottish Power (United Kingdom), Union Fenosa (Spain), and VEAG (Germany)—pointed to the uncertain effects of the imposition of a tax and proposed a series of conservation measures as well as the export of energy-efficient technologies to Eastern Europe. In addition to the efforts of the coalition and the trade association, individual power generation companies lobbied to prevent the adoption of the tax.

The European Coal and Steel Council Consultative Committee also opposed the tax and argued for voluntary programs and payments to developing countries to stop deforestation. Opposition also developed within countries. For example, in France 14 major companies, including Electricité de France, Renault, Rhone Poulenc, Total, Elf Aquitaine, Pécincy, and Unisor Sacilor, organized "Business for the Environment" to oppose the tax. In exchange, the coalition offered help in cleaning up toxic waste sites.

Chemicals was one of the premier industries in Europe. The industry was energy intensive, and the petrochemical component of the industry used petroleum feedstocks. The global competitiveness of the industry thus would be significantly impacted by the proposed taxes. The industry estimated that the impact of the taxes when fully implemented would be $4.45 billion per year. The chemical industry pointed to the success of voluntary measures undertaken by individual companies. The managing director of Montedison Primary Chemicals stated that since 1974 the European chemicals industry had reduced by 35 percent the energy usage per unit of output and that another 15 percent reduction would be achieved by the year 2000.[62]

As was the case in many European industries, the chemical industry in each country was represented by an association that included most of the companies operating in that country. These national associations acted on behalf of their members within their countries. The associations in the individual countries were organized into the European Chemical Industry Council (CEFIC) that acted at the level of the European Union. As the importance of the EU governmental institutions had grown, individual companies had begun to take actions in addition to those of their national and pan-European associations. ▪

Preparation Questions
Economics

1. Identify the efficiency and distributive consequences of a carbon/energy tax.
2. What are the effects of a carbon tax for the global competitiveness of EU companies?

Government

1. What types of politics should be anticipated in the consideration of a carbon/energy tax in the European Union? Which EU institutions will be involved in the decision?
2. If structural funds could be provided to countries through the EU budget, what outcome would you expect? Assume for the purposes of this question that the European Union makes its decision on structural funds by a qualified majority of ECOFIN.

Nonmarket Strategy

1. As a European chemicals company dependent on petroleum feedstocks, what effects do you anticipate from the proposed carbon/energy tax?
2. What objectives and strategy should the company adopt to address the carbon/energy tax? How should that strategy be implemented? Which institutions should be targeted?

The European Union Data Protection Directive (B)

In 1995 the European Union enacted a Directive on Data Protection (95/46/EC) to protect the privacy of EU residents when using the Internet, telecommunications, and various commercial transactions (PII). The Directive protected personally identifiable information, defined as any information that pertains to an "identified or identifiable natural person." The Directive covered persons for data transferred within the EU and between the EU and outside countries. Those countries entered into agreements with the EU or adopted the Directive as their own law. The United States had very limited government

regulation of online privacy relying on self-regulation and had negotiated a voluntary US–EU Safe Harbor agreement with the EU. The Directive was generally viewed as successful in protecting the privacy of EU residents, and the safe harbor agreement was also viewed as generally successful.

By 2009 changes in technology and innovations had exposed shortcomings in the Directive. The growth of e-commerce, the widespread use of GPS devices, the spread of mobile communications and wireless broadband, and cloud computing raised new issues some of which were in

---

[62]*The Economist*, May 9, 1992.

gray areas of the Directive. GPS devices, for example, gave location information which represented PII. Innovations such as social media, Internet search and advertising, and instant messaging also raised new issues. Moreover, identity theft, hacking, and terrorism raised security concerns that extended beyond personal information.

Under the Directive the EU had been dealing with issues as they arose. For example, in 2011 Google was said to have violated EU law by maintaining a registry of residential Wi-Fi routers that could identify the location of cellphones and owners within range of the routers. Google conceded stating, "At the request of several European data protection authorities, we are building an opt-out service that will allow an access point owner to opt out from Google's location service. Once opted out, our services will not use that access point to determine users' locations."[63] Google planned to offer the opt-out service worldwide.

Similarly, the EU did not have an explicit rule about personal information processed through cloud computing, and since the processing could take place anywhere in the world, concerns were raised. In response Amazon established a data center in Dublin to host cloud computing.[64] Microsoft had also established a data center in the EU for cloud computing.

The EU embarked on the process of modernizing the Directive led by commissioner Viviane Reding of the DG for Justice, Fundamental Rights and Citizenship (JUST). A new Directive would have to be approved by both the Council of Ministers and the European Parliament. The Treaty of Lisbon had officially incorporated the Charter of Fundamental Rights as part of the EU treaties. The Charter established a right of privacy that was implemented by the Directive and could require broader protections. Reding pledged to "strengthen individuals' rights and enhance the Internal Market dimension of data protection" and to "ensure consumers of surfing and shopping online without worrying about the safety of their personal information." She also said, "Data should be collected and processed only under informed consent of a person to whom they relate."[65] The implementation of the 1995 Directive differed across the member states, and JUST sought better harmonization of procedures.

The modernization of the Directive could have broad ramifications for e-commerce, social media, and mobile communications companies. For example, the implementation of the present directive required storage of data for no longer than required for the purpose of the communication or transaction, and the EU had reached agreements with companies such as Microsoft and Google about data retention.[66] JUST was considering a new "right to be forgotten" that would allow a person to remove the data that was stored by a company and a "right of portability" that would allow persons to move all of their personal content from one website to another. The latter would

reduce switching costs and make lock-in harder to achieve, whereas the former could limit the ability of websites to develop and maintain information to use for advertising placement. The United States did not have a right to be forgotten. Marc Rotenberg, executive director of the Electronic Privacy Information Center, said, "As a general matter, companies in the United States don't have to recognize your right to be deleted. They may choose to accommodate you, but they are not required to."[67]

JUST also was considering measures to clarify the EU's criteria for adequacy of data protection in third countries and to improve standards. A Working Party formed by the Commission and composed of the data commissioners of all the member states called for the EU "to ensure a strict and far reaching general privacy agreement with the United States."[68] The Trans Atlantic Consumer Dialogue, composed of 80 consumer groups in Europe and the United States, sent letters to the European Commission and to Congress stating, "There is much the United States could learn from other countries about how to address such challenges and the EU Data Directive provides a very good starting point."[69] A US House of Representatives subcommittee held a hearing in September 2011 on "The impact and burden of EU regulation," and witnesses were critical of the EU Directive. Professor Catherine Tucker of the Massachusetts Institute of Technology testified that the effectiveness of advertising fell by 65 percent as a result of the EU's privacy policies.[70]

The 1995 Directive articulated a number of specific rights: "the right to know who the data controller is, the recipient of the data and the purpose of the processing; the right to have inaccurate data rectified; a right of recourse in the event of unlawful processing; and the right to withhold permission to use data in some circumstances."[71] The latter right had been implemented by the provision of "opt out" opportunities. For example, in 2011 the industry association Interactive Advertising Bureau Europe (IAB Europe) had set up an opt out website that allowed individuals not to receive advertisements based on profiling. European consumer and privacy advocacy groups were pushing for an "opt in" requirement before any data could be processed. Kostas Rossoglu of the European Consumers' Organization explained, "We believe that by having consumers opt in, rather than opt out, they will be better protected and informed about what happens with their information."[72] Stephan Noller, CEO of nugg.ad of Berlin and head of the policy committee of IAB Europe, disagreed stating that opt out "fits with the needs of today's Internet users. Information is provided contextually where relevant and is instantly available. We use the dynamism and interactivity of the Internet to provide pragmatic privacy control."[73] The

---

[63]*New York Times*, September 14, 2011.

[64]*International Herald Tribune*, July 25, 2011.

[65]Viviane Reding, Press Release, September 22, 2010.

[66]The 2006 EU Data Retention Directive limited the length of time a company could retain personal information obtained, for example, in an economic transaction.

[67]*International Herald Tribune*, September 6, 2011.

[68]Electronic Privacy Information Center. www.epic.org/privacy/int/eu_data_protection_directive.html.

[69]*New York Times*, September 19, 2011.

[70]*Europolitics*, September 19, 2011.

[71]Electronic Privacy Information Center. www.epic.org/privacy/int/eu_data_protection_directive.html.

[72]*New York Times*, September 19, 2011.

[73]Ibid.

Working Party of member state data commissioners stated that opt out was inadequate and "Only statements or actions, not mere silence or inaction, constitute valid consent." Reding stated, "Companies must obtain prior consent before individuals' data is used."[74] Kimon Zorbas, vice president of IAB Europe observed, "Consumer profiling is basic to any business, not just online business. I am afraid [banning profiling] would kill a significant part of the industry."[75]

France had introduced a voluntary charter for data protection and urged companies to sign it. Google and Facebook refused to sign. The companies argued that self-regulation was sufficient and that restrictions interfered with their right to freedom of expression. Referring to a right to be forgotten, Kevin Townsend, a UK writer and founding editor of ITsecurity.com, said, "If Google, Facebook, Microsoft and Apple, et al., simply say 'no', what is the EU going to do? Some of these companies are financially as big or bigger than some EU nations. They could and should be responsible for removing personal data, but they won't do it."[76]

In November 2011 Commissioner Reding announced that she planned to add to the revised directive proposal an extension of the jurisdiction of EU data protection regulation. She said, "We both believe that companies who direct their services to European consumers should be subject to EU data protection laws. Otherwise they should not be able to do business on our internal market. This also applies to social networks with users in the EU. We have to make sure that they comply with EU law and that EU law is enforced, even if it is based in a third country and even if its data are stored in a 'cloud'."[77] This would have implications for the safe harbor agreement and more importantly for how foreign companies with users and customers in the EU conduct their businesses. The extended jurisdiction would also pose enforcement challenges. ▪

Preparation Questions

1. What in electronic commerce is included in the EU's "personal information"?
2. Is opt in an appropriate granted right? What are its implications for electronic commerce? Should Google and Facebook support a right to be forgotten?
3. As Google would you use opt in worldwide for location services if the new Data Protection Directive required its use in the EU?
4. As Facebook would you support or oppose a US–EU agreement requiring the use of opt in for any processing of personal data of EU residents? Is there another alternative?
5. What are the implications of Commissioner Reding's proposed extension of EU jurisdiction?
6. Should companies oppose the establishment of a right to be forgotten?
7. Should the leading Internet companies join together to addresses the EU's modernization of the Data Protection Directive?

The Euro Crisis

THE CRISIS

The Maastricht Treaty required all member states of the European Union (EU) to adopt the euro as their currency, but Denmark and the United Kingdom were granted exemptions and remained outside the euro zone. Sweden decided not to adopt the euro and did so by intentionally failing to meet the criteria for participation. The new members of the EU pledged to join but had not yet met the qualifying criteria. The other 17 member states had adopted the euro beginning in 1999. The European Central Bank (ECB) was responsible for monetary policy.

The basic flaw in the euro structure was that while the ECB could set monetary policy the member states controlled their own fiscal policy. To address this potential problem, euro zone countries were required to have a budget deficit no greater than 3 percent of GDP and to limit their sovereign debt to no more than 60 percent of GDP. The countries were also to meet limits on their inflation rate and the long-term interest rate on their sovereign borrowing.

The common currency produced a convergence in the interest rates at which euro zone members could borrow, and countries with otherwise weak credit were able to borrow at lower interest rates than they would otherwise have been able to borrow. In part this was due to the belief that the euro zone members would rescue a country in financial trouble. This also made it easier for some countries to borrow more than they otherwise could. In addition to sovereign borrowing, banks and companies in those countries were able to borrow at lower interest rates to finance consumption and investment. The result was that southern European countries, banks, and companies borrowed heavily from northern European banks. In Ireland, Portugal, and particularly Spain the borrowing flowed into the housing market.[78] The economy in Spain grew rapidly driven by the home construction industry, but the bubble burst in 2008 creating a financial crisis that coincided with the broader financial crises that originated in the United States.

The bankruptcy of Lehman Brothers sent a shock through the world financial system, causing an economic slowdown and recession in many developed countries. Initially, the financial markets were concerned about banks and companies failing,

---

[74]Ibid.
[75]Ibid.
[76]*Prague Post*, August 17, 2011.

[77]*New York Times*, November 11, 2011.
[78]Jeffrey A. Frieden, "Europe's Lehman moment," Reuters, September 16, 2011.

but by 2010 the concerns turned to sovereign debt. Greece had the weakest financial situation.

Greece joined the euro zone in 2002 but never met the qualification criteria. In 2002 its budget deficit was 4.5 percent of GDP, and by 2007 it was 6.4 percent as the country continued to borrow and spend. When the financial crisis struck, Greece continued its spending while its economy slumped. The budget deficit soared to 15.4 percent of GDP in 2009 before falling to 10.5 percent in 2010 as the country began austerity measures. The sovereign debt of Greece reached 143 percent of GDP in 2010 and long-term borrowing became increasingly difficult to arrange. Fearing the possibility of default, lenders demanded higher interest rates on loans to the country, and soaring interest rates put even greater pressure on the Greek budget. With earlier borrowings coming due, Greece faced very high borrowing costs and concerns that it would be unable to turnover its debt, which would represent a default. Economic growth had stalled in much of the euro zone, and in Greece growth was negative in 2009, 2010, and 2011 in part because of the austerity measures taken by the government. By mid-2011 the unemployment rate in Greece was over 16 percent, up from 8 percent 2 years earlier.

Greece had structural problems that made it difficult to reduce its budget deficit. First, tax evasion was widespread in the country making it difficult to generate additional tax revenue. Second, the Greek government provided generous social services and pensions on which citizens had come to depend. Third, the payroll of the Greek government was bloated with excess employees many of whom were paid above market wages. Fourth, the government owned a number of companies some of which were used to benefit party stalwarts and supporters. These companies represented an asset that could be sold to raise funds, but the powerful labor unions opposed any sales for fear of losing jobs. The government was formed by the Socialist Party, which held 155 of the 300 seats in parliament.

THE MAGNITUDE OF THE RISK

The risk of default was borne by the holders of Greek sovereign debt and lenders to Greek banks and companies. Investors demanded a premium, or spread, above the risk-free rate of interest, and the greater the perceived risk the higher the spread demanded. The spread was determined in a financial market equilibrium with investors on one side of the market and debt issuers on the other side. The equilibrium relationship between the spread and the probability of default provided a means of estimating the default probability on a debt security. Consider a sovereign bond with a maturity of 1-year that sells in the financial markets at a spread s above the risk-free interest rate, traditionally measured by the interest rate on U.S. treasury bills. Suppose that if there were a default the holder of the bond would recover a fraction r of the face value of the bond. Then, in the financial market equilibrium the spread would exactly compensate for the risk $1 - r$, so $s = \rho(1 - r)$, where ρ is the probability of default on the bond. Hence, $\rho = s/(1 - r)$. As an example, if $s = 0.03$ (300 basis points) and $r = 0.6$, the default probability as assessed by the financial markets is $\rho = 0.075$ or 7.5 percent.

The default probabilities are easily estimated from market data. Many investors in sovereign debt purchase credit default swaps, analogous to insurance, to protect themselves in the event of default. The "price" of the insurance is the spread, so if the recovery rate can be estimated, the probability of default can be calculated. Using this method, Deutsche Bank Research provided the following 1-year probabilities of default on September 16, 2011.

Country	Default Probability (%)
Germany	1.3
Greece	19.0
Ireland	9.7
Portugal	11.7
Spain	5.3
Italy	6.2
United Kingdom	1.3

These data indicate that the financial market's implicit estimate of the probability of default on Greek sovereign debt within a year was 0.19 or approximately one chance in five, whereas the corresponding probability for Germany was 13 in 1,000. As the table indicates, the financial markets were not only concerned with Greece but also with Ireland and Portugal and to a lesser extent Italy and Spain. These default probabilities take into account the rescue packages already in place for Greece, Portugal, and Ireland.

RESCUE ATTEMPTS

The initial response to the crisis in Greece was to rescue the country to prevent a collapse. The EU, the International Monetary Fund (IMF), and the ECB joined together to provide a rescue package. The euro zone countries were led by Germany, which had the strongest economy and the greatest capacity, and by France. Those two countries were also at risk in the event of a default by Greece, since they held large amounts of Greek sovereign debt. In addition, banks, particularly in France and Germany, held Greek sovereign debt as well as private debt of Greek banks and companies. Government officials feared that a default by Greece could trigger the failure of the Northern banks, which would contract the availability of credit. Worse, a default could trigger a run on the banks similar to that which occurred after the collapse of Lehman Brothers, resulting in a credit freeze and further weakening of the economies of the euro zone countries and beyond.

With the situation dire the so-called troika, EU, IMF, and ECB, provided €100 billion to Greece in May 2010. The funds were provided in tranches conditional on austerity measures put into place by Greece. Soon after the rescue package was approved, Ireland and Portugal experienced sharply higher interest rates as the financial markets became nervous about their ability to finance their sovereign debt. Concerns were also raised about Italy and Spain.

The troika provided €78 billion to Portugal, and Ireland received a total of €70 billion primarily to shore up its banks, quelling the immediate concerns but perhaps not the longer term concerns. The ECB also announced that it would accept as collateral government bonds with any credit rating. Portugal could have further problems, since its budget deficit for 2010 was 8.6 percent of GDP.

The EU recognized the need to establish a larger fund to deal with the potentially broader financial crisis. The 17 countries in the euro zone created the European Financial Stability Facility (EFSF) with the capacity to purchase €440 billion in bonds of countries in financial difficulty. Germany provided nearly half of the funds. In addition, the EU provided €60 billion from its budget, and the IMF provided €250 billion, for a total of €700 billion. The funds were administered by the EU, ECB, and IMF.

In July 2011 the troika arranged a second rescue package of €109 billion for Greece, but approval required unanimous consent by the 17 euro zone members. The Treaty of Lisbon contained a "no bailout" provision that no member state would be liable for the debts of another member state, so any rescue required a new treaty that had to be ratified unanimously by all member states. Finland demanded that any further assistance to Greece be backed by collateral. Since unanimity was required, negotiations were extended. The second rescue package included a structured default in which some investors would exchange their Greek bonds for new bonds and take a haircut of 21 percent. Greek bond prices had fallen sharply in value after the July decision, leading the German minister of finance to observe that the July agreement might have to be revised.

The austerity measures taken by Greece had reduced government expenditures, but they also contributed to an economic contraction with growth at –5.3 percent in 2011. This reduced tax receipts and increased the budget deficit. The ECB had bought between €40 and €50 billion of Greek bonds in an attempt to hold down the country's borrowing costs, but the financial markets were too powerful. The credit ratings agencies rated Greece as in selective default.

By September 2011 Greece was running out of cash, and the final €8 billion tranche of funds from the first rescue package required cutting the budget deficit by €6 billion. The IMF estimated that Greece was €4.6 billion short of its target for deficit reduction, or 2 percent of GDP. The troika demanded that Greece take further austerity measures. With few available options the Greek government said it would impose a new property tax, cut pensions, sell government-owned companies,[79] impose a tax on low income workers who were not currently taxed,[80] and put 30,000 government workers into a reserve workers program at reduced salaries after which their jobs could be eliminated.[81] The measures were very unpopular particularly with public sector unions, which were part of the base of the governing Socialist party. Violent protests resulted, and the public sector labor unions scheduled nationwide strikes.

Critics complained that the rescue plan simply kicked the can down the road, and that default was inevitable. The troika was reluctant to allow a default because of fears of contagion and disagreement about how the losses should be distributed. The troika initially decided to have losses absorbed solely by governments and not private parties such as the banks that held Greek debt. The fear was that forcing banks to write down the value of Greek bonds they held would weaken their capital structure forcing them to restrict credit. Several major French banks were believed to be in precarious financial condition, as the market had concluded in driving the share price of Société Générale down by 50 percent.

Many European banks were undercapitalized and hence were at risk in the event of a Greek default. The availability of short-term funding was contracting, and the use of Greek, Irish, and Portuguese government bonds as collateral for repo borrowing had fallen by half in the second half of 2010 according to economists at the Bank of International Settlements.[82] U.S. mutual and investment funds reduced their short-term lending to European banks, and European banks cut back on their loans to other EU banks, depositing their excess cash with the ECB. This forced EU banks to reduce their lending in U.S. dollars and to turn increasingly to the ECB for their short-term funding. A banker in Frankfurt said, "Nobody really wants to lend to anybody where there is the slightest doubt. Any counterparty where the market suspects underlying problems will have trouble finding liquidity from sources other than the ECB."[83] This forced the weaker banks that in the absence of a debt crisis would have borrowed from other banks to borrow from the ECB. Dexia SA, one of the 20 largest banks in Europe, was on the verge of collapse. Concerns about contagion grew.

Dorthea Schäfer, a banking expert at the German Institute for Economic Research, said, "Banks certainly do not have enough capital in relation to their government bonds."[84] She estimated "that the 10 largest German banks would need to raise €127 billion to bring their capital reserves to 5 percent of gross assets—a level she considered barely adequate."[85] In September 2011 the IMF estimated that European banks were at risk of losing €300 billion in the euro zone debt crisis of which €200 billion was in sovereign debt and the rest in private debt. The IMF urged the banks to raise additional capital.

Some European governments hoped that China and Brazil would provide funds that could be used to deal with the financial crisis, but the head of the World Bank warned that Europe should not count on aid from them. Brazil rejected the idea of providing assistance and called on Europe to put its house in order.

THE END GAME

The ultimate resolution of the euro zone financial crisis could take one of three forms, each of which was unattractive. One was the preservation of the current euro zone through the continued rescue of countries with weak finances. To prevent

---

[79]The value of some of the companies was problematic, since they would continue to be regulated by the Greek government.

[80]The tax was to be collected through electricity bills to avoid tax evasion.

[81]Under the Greek constitution public sector workers cannot be fired, and the public sector unions claimed that the reserve worker program was equivalent to firing. (*New York Times*, September 22, 2011)

[82]*New York Times*, September 23, 2011.

[83]Ibid.

[84]Ibid.

[85]Ibid.

the financial crisis from recurring, the euro zone countries would have to control their fiscal policies to prevent countries from living beyond their means. This could require the creation of a new fiscal authority, which would require new treaties that would have to be approved by unanimous consent. It would also mean that the cost of the rescue would ultimately be borne by the financially strong northern countries, whose citizens would surely oppose such an alternative. A majority of German citizens was strongly opposed to using their country's resources to rescue what they considered an irresponsible country that knowingly continued to live beyond its means. Citizens of other northern European countries also opposed using their funds to rescue Greece. Voters in Finland gave surprising support to a right-wing party, and the government took a tougher stance on the bailout of Greece. To counter the popular opposition, the German Confederation of Trade Unions took out advertisements supporting the second rescue package. The unions said, "Our mothers and fathers built a peaceful Europe from the rubble of the second world war. It is our responsibility that we maintain a united Europe for our children and our grandchildren."[86]

The second alternative was an orderly default by Greece while remaining in the euro zone. An orderly default would involve propping up the country while sovereign, and possibly private, debt was restructured. This could force bondholders to absorb part of the cost of default; i.e., to write down the amount that Greek borrowers owed them. This would weaken banks that had heavy exposure to Greek sovereign and private debt. Some of those banks would then need an infusion of capital, which would have to come from the EU or their home country. Unless the banks were assured of being propped up, a credit crisis could result. An orderly default by Greece could trigger fears within the financial markets that Portugal and Ireland would also require an orderly default, and that Italy and Spain could follow.

An orderly default could be accompanied by Greece remaining in or exiting from the euro zone. If it remained in, the issue of fiscal discipline would remain. If it abandoned the euro, it would have to fend for itself as it had before the euro. The interest rate it would have to pay on its borrowings would be high, since lenders would be nervous about its fiscal policy.

The third alternative was for Greece to leave or be expelled from the euro zone and to fend for itself. The country would default and restructure its sovereign debt, and the new Greek drachma would plummet in value relative to the euro. In addition to the challenge of reintroducing the drachma, capital would flee the country, so bank deposits would likely have to be frozen, and foreign borrowing would come to a standstill. In the short-run, many Greek companies would fall into bankruptcy, since it would be harder for them to repay their debts denominated in other currencies. The low value of the drachma relative to the euro would represent a loss of wealth for Greek citizens, and the economy would contract severely causing further suffering. Vassilis Korkdis, president of the National Confederation of Hellenic Commerce, said, "Greece is going to go decades back. This is going to be a disaster."[87]

The advantage of this alternative was that the insolvency would be dealt with rather than continuing to linger over the country and the euro zone. Market forces and the Greek people then could determine the fate of the country. Hans-Werner Sinn of the Institute for Economic Research in Munich said, "If Greece were to exit the euro, it would be able to devalue its currency and thus become competitive once again."[88] Supporters of this alternative pointed to the case of Argentina, which defaulted on its sovereign debt in 2002. The economy collapsed causing widespread hardship, but soon it began to grow rapidly fueled by exports and was able to borrow on international markets. Critics of this alternative pointed out that Argentina had benefited from a high demand for agricultural commodities, which Greece would not have.

Critics also feared that the financial markets would drive other countries out of the euro and that panic could result, affecting the other euro zone countries, the rest of the EU, and the world economy. If the euro were to unravel, the financially healthy countries could link their exchange rates to the German deutschemark as they had done before the default, and if one of them experienced financial difficulty, it could simply devalue relative to the deutschemark. The countries could go further and form a fiscal union within the EU, giving the EU a two-track system. ■

Preparation Questions

1. As the head of Société Générale what advice would you give to the French government about what should be done in the Greek crisis?
2. As the head of the ECB what should be done in the Greek situation? Will your decision make it more or less likely that other countries in the euro zone will have to be rescued?
3. Should Germany continue to fund the rescue of euro zone countries?
4. Should the EU move toward fiscal integration? Would this prevent future crises?

---

[86]*Wall Street Journal*, September 28, 2011.

[87]*Bloomberg Businessweek*, September 19–25, 2011.
[88]www.dw-world.de, May 8, 2011.

16 | CHINA: HISTORY, CULTURE, AND POLITICAL ECONOMY

INTRODUCTION

China is an ancient country that since 1978 has embarked on a remarkable economic path in which markets and foreign direct investment have been encouraged and economic reforms have been frequent and often successful. Yet China remains a country under the domination of the Chinese Communist Party (CCP) with little popular participation in political activity and continuing restrictions on civil and human rights. The importance of a country with over 1.3 billion people cannot be underestimated for both foreign businesses and governments, but the absence of democratic institutions and weak legal protections present challenges. Economic reforms have led thousands of companies to set up operations in China and, combined with the liberalization of business opportunities for Chinese citizens, have resulted in spectacular economic growth. Real growth in GDP has averaged 9 percent annually since the open-door policy began in 1978. The remnants of the planned economy era, however, posed a particular challenge for China as it attempted to make its state-owned enterprises (SOEs) more efficient while replacing the social services they had provided for workers and retirees. Economic growth was not led by the SOEs but by private enterprises and enterprises supported by provincial and municipal governments. Continued economic liberalization had to be accomplished while preserving the supremacy of the CCP.

In 2001 China joined the World Trade Organization, which brought both opportunity and new challenges. Membership provided additional access to foreign markets, but it also required China to open major industries to imports and foreign direct investment. This put additional pressure on SOEs and on the country to strengthen legal protections.

This chapter provides background on the history and culture of China and characterizes the four I's with an emphasis on government institutions and business issues. The next section provides a historical background on China beginning with the pre-republican era and concluding with the current era. The following section considers Confucianism and its implications for business, society, and politics. The nonmarket environment is then discussed with an emphasis on the institutions of government. Business in China is considered with a focus on SOEs, foreign direct investment, and international trade. Several current issues, including human rights, piracy, corruption, product safety, energy and the environment, and workers' rights, are then considered. The chapter cases provide an opportunity to address particular managerial challenges in the context of China's political economy.

HISTORICAL BACKGROUND[1]

Pre-Republican

Ethnic Chinese, also known as Han people, originated in the Yellow River Valley in North-Central China. Organized rural society has existed in this region for over 10,000 years, and political control was typically divided by rival dynastic kingdoms. Invasion by barbarians resulted in centuries (c. 771–221 B.C.) of political fragmentation, during which much of China's most impressive philosophy was developed. Three important schools of Chinese philosophical thought emerged in this period: Daoism, Confucianism, and Legalism.[2] These laid the basis for much of China's future political thought and made the unification of China a paramount ideal. Confucianism, considered later in the chapter, had a profound impact on the organization of Chinese government, as it advocated the concept of government by meritocracy. This provided the intellectual foundation for the imperial bureaucracy.

---

[1]This section is based on a note prepared by Michael M. Ting under the supervision of Professor David P. Baron. Copyright © 1998 by the Board of Trustees of the Leland Stanford Junior University. All rights reserved. Reprinted with permission.
[2]See Pye (1978, pp. 32–59; 1985) for an introduction to the early Chinese schools of thought.

Many historians regard the victory of the Qin kingdom after a period of prolonged conflicts known as the Warring States Period (403–221 B.C.) as the beginning of China's existence as a unified nation. The resulting state controlled an area roughly half the size of today's People's Republic of China. Technology played a central role in the Qin's success, as it had mastered iron-working in advance of most of its rivals. The Qin Dynasty played an important role in shaping the institutions and practices of imperial China. It eliminated the remnants of China's ancient feudal society and established the beginnings of a central bureaucracy based on Confucian principles. It also standardized the currency, weights, and measures; built some of China's first extensive irrigation projects; introduced a uniform system of writing; and consolidated many of the nation's defensive walls.

BUREAUCRACY IN IMPERIAL CHINA Despite the immense political changes made by the Qin, China's society and politics were dominated by regional aristocracies for almost another millennium. Each succeeding dynasty, however, expanded and strengthened the bureaucratic system, and by the Tang Dynasty (A.D. 618–907) the imperial bureaucracy was considered the preeminent political authority.[3]

Since the Early Han Dynasty (206 B.C.–A.D. 8), membership in the bureaucracy was attained through highly competitive national examinations that in theory were open to all. The wealth, power, and prestige afforded by passing the examinations were so great that families often invested handsomely in educating their young men. Successful examinees spent their entire youth studying the Confucian classics in preparation for the examinations and often were in their mid-30s when they passed. The bureaucracy played an important role in ensuring social stability by preventing the rise of rival sources of political power while still permitting the accumulation of family wealth.[4]

FOREIGN RELATIONS Imperial China faced external military threats for much of its history. The Ming Dynasty (1368–1644) constructed the Great Wall of China to ward off northern barbarians, but it proved to be a military failure, as it could not stop a Manchurian invasion that resulted in the last dynasty, the Qing (1644–1911). In general, the pre-Ming Chinese welcomed foreign commerce. Trade with the Middle East and European nations flourished, and in the early 1400s a fleet of Chinese vessels successfully completed a trade and diplomatic mission to Africa. During the fifteenth century, however, Chinese leaders began to view foreign interactions with a peculiar contempt. Costly border wars and fiscal crises caused the Ming to pull back on their efforts to establish foreign relations and build a navy. Convinced that foreigners could offer little of value to China, conservative Confucian scholars of the period increasingly advocated xenophobic foreign policies.[5]

Notwithstanding the Qing's hostility, the British, led by the British East India Company, vigorously attempted to maintain trade ties in southern China. With the end of the Napoleonic Wars in 1815, England gradually increased its commercial interest in China. China's defeat in the Opium War at the hands of Britain's vastly superior military technology resulted in the 1842 Treaty of Nanjing. The terms of the treaty were widely regarded as humiliating to the Chinese, as they required massive reparations to Britain, the turnover of Hong Kong, and the opening of five coastal cities to British residents and commerce. Many of the Western powers also insisted on reciprocal "most favored nation" agreements that automatically granted to every foreign country the concessions made to any one country, thus hastening the pace and extent of economic concessions.

COLLAPSE OF IMPERIAL CHINA The latter half of the nineteenth century was marked by numerous large-scale revolts that reflected the inability of the Qing to maintain domestic peace and contain foreign influence. The imperial bureaucracy was increasingly perceived as an incompetent and backward institution, incapable of performing even its traditional duties of maintaining China's important waterways. As the nineteenth century drew to a close, internal calls for reforms became increasingly prevalent, and the Qing initiated many ambitious reforms. They attempted to copy several Western-style government institutions and abolished

---

[3]See Shue (1988, pp. 84–85) and Moore (1966, p. 164).
[4]Fairbank (1992, pp. 179–182).
[5]Ibid., pp. 138–140.

the centuries-old examination system in 1905. Their drive toward modernization resulted in the outfitting of a Western-style military and plans for a new national rail network.

THE REPUBLICAN ERA By the first decade of the twentieth century, local warlords had ascended to political prominence in China. Many raised their own armies, collected their own taxes, and showed questionable loyalty to the Qing. In addition, revolutionary societies and fraternities, many loosely organized into a group called the Revolutionary Alliance, were increasingly active in China's major urban centers. The Revolutionary Alliance, led by Dr. Sun Yat-sen, had relatively strong popular backing, but lacked an army. By early 1912, a large military faction led by former Qing general Yuan Shikai gained the upper hand, and the last Qing abdicated his throne in 1912.

While many credit Sun Yat-sen with the founding of the Republic of China in 1911, China at the time was hardly a coherent political entity. Yuan proved incapable of ruling China, as he insisted on central control over proposed modernizations but lacked substantial authority over local governments. He also actively attempted to undermine his Revolutionary Alliance allies, many of which had organized themselves into the Guomindang (GMD), or Nationalist Party, under Sun.

Sun's death in 1925 cleared the way for the ascendancy of Chiang Kai-shek as the new GMD leader. Capitalizing on both the strength of his National Revolutionary Army and a wave of nationalist sentiment in the mid-1920s, Chiang launched military offensives in 1926 and 1928 that established a new capital in Nanjing and brought most of China under GMD rule. His sudden success convinced many that the GMD was China's best hope for modernizing its economy and political system. This hope proved to be illusory, however, as the Nanjing leaders lacked sufficient control over many regions to execute their policies. The GMD's support base was primarily urban, but since China's urban-industrial sector was still very small, its base and resources were limited.

The main unifying force for the GMD was the threat from the Chinese Communist Party formed in 1921. Chiang continually harassed the CCP and, in response, several communist uprisings took place, only to be crushed by GMD armies. The CCP did not recover until 1933, by which time it had transformed itself into a rural party largely independent of the international communist party. Headed by Mao Zedong, an early revolutionary leader who had carefully studied the rural economy, the CCP was once again strong enough to be of concern to the GMD. Chiang's continuous attacks drove the CCP to seek a new base, and in late 1934, 100,000 soldiers and party members began their famous Long March.

WAR AND CIVIL WAR In 1937 Japan invaded and Chinese armies were quickly routed by superior Japanese tactics and technology. Chinese resistance to Japan was highly fragmented in spite of the initial promise of a united front between the GMD and CCP. During the war and occupation, Mao was able to consolidate his leadership and develop his own distinctive brand of Marxism. As part of his program the CCP began to institute land reform in friendly areas, thus enlisting peasant support and swelling the ranks of CCP troops.

As World War II drew to a close, both sides prepared for a civil war. In 1945 the CCP was stronger than at any point in its history, but its army had little foreign support and was only half the size of Chiang's American-equipped army. American support, however, could not forestall the subsequent rout of the GMD in the 1946–1949 civil war. By mid-1949 the communist victory was nearly complete, and on October 1, 1949, Mao proclaimed the founding of the People's Republic of China.

As Chiang's losses mounted in 1948, he transferred the remains of the Republic of China to Taiwan, which as part of the Yalta agreements in World War II had been formally returned to the Republic of China after 50 years of Japanese colonization. The GMD instituted comprehensive land reforms and compensated landlords with government bonds. With American economic aid, it embarked on vigorous industrialization by attracting foreign investment and targeting export markets.[6]

The Communist Era

Although the communist victory had been complete, Mao and his followers still faced a daunting task that had eluded Chinese rulers for centuries: establishing a state with unquestioned

---

[6]See Deyo (1987) and Haggard (1990) for a comparative perspective on Taiwanese industrial policy.

control over the entire nation. The CCP's assumption of power took two distinct tracks. First, in the countryside, it sought to complete the process of land reform that had begun in Northern China earlier in the decade. Because peasants benefiting from land redistribution overwhelmingly outnumbered landlords, the process was quickly and enthusiastically embraced.[7] Second, in keeping with Marxist philosophy, the party sought to control all commerce, but again the magnitude of the task demanded considerable flexibility. Only the largest companies came under state control in the early years, and most urban professionals were allowed to continue working regardless of their political background. Meanwhile, governments at all levels gradually asserted control over prices, the banking system, and the allocation of various important goods.[8]

The end of the Korean War allowed policymakers to concentrate on their next task: the transformation of the Chinese economy into a socialist system. Following the early Soviet model, planners in Beijing hoped to stimulate the development of heavy industry by taxing the agricultural sector. They also believed that greater productivity could be best achieved by wiping out the remnants of capitalism and developing huge, self-contained production units in agriculture and industry.

A central feature of the First Five Year Plan was the collectivization of agriculture. Shortly after land reform was completed, the CCP began to organize peasant households into ever-larger cooperative associations. A similar process was under way in the industrial sector. State takeovers of large enterprises accelerated throughout the 1950s, until only the smallest street merchants were allowed to remain independent. With the aid of Soviet loans, CCP industrial policy emphasized sectors such as steel, petroleum, and chemicals at the expense of consumer goods. In addition to their economic importance, these enterprises also served a vital social role. Labor was furnished through the *danwei* ("work unit") system, under which workers were permanently assigned to enterprises upon completing their education. The *danwei* provided its members with housing, child care, schooling, health care, shops, post offices, and other social services. It was also an instrument of social control. Because there was no welfare system, urban residents had no access to even the most basic social services outside of their *danwei*, and opportunities for changing enterprises were rare.

Convinced that China's lagging production could be blamed not on poor economic reasoning but on a lack of mobilization, the CCP unleashed a flurry of production efforts to spur the economy. Many of these projects launched in the Great Leap Forward in 1958 were at best ill conceived, and at worst destructive.[9] Agricultural cooperatives were rapidly combined into even larger county-size communes, but in 1959 poor weather highlighted the inefficiency of the communes. Production plummeted and China suffered a famine that claimed over 20 million lives through 1962.

The clear failure of the large communes prompted authority to devolve back to smaller production units, so that individual households were once again held responsible for meeting production quotas. More importantly, the government legalized private plots on which peasants were allowed to raise and market their own vegetables and animals while their communes produced grain. On a larger scale, leaders also began to question the Soviet-inspired strategy of developing heavy industry first.

Mao's allies—notably his wife Jiang Qing and army chief Lin Biao—insisted that China's problems were the result of insufficient dedication to the CCP's revolutionary principles. Mao's gambit to reassert power combined this message with his still considerable populist appeal in launching the Great Proletarian Cultural Revolution in 1966. Mao and Lin organized thousands of Red Guard units, consisting largely of fanatical students who were directed to purge their jurisdictions of the four "olds"—old ideas, old customs, old cultures, and old habits. Their campaigns destroyed many of China's most valuable cultural artifacts and degenerated into destructive excess and mob rule in the name of Mao. Finally, in 1967, the army stepped in to control the chaos, often by imposing martial law. The Cultural Revolution had decimated much of the party's organization, especially at the provincial and lower levels. It had also elevated the army's status within the party hierarchy.

---

[7]Vogel (1980, pp. 91–124) discusses policy debates during the early years of land reform.

[8]See Naughton (2007, Ch. 3) for an analysis of economic policies in this period.

[9]See the Chapter 16 case *Wugang and the Reform of State-Owned Enterprises* in the sixth edition of this book for a description of one of these projects.

As a result of the split of the Sino-Soviet alliance in 1958, successive American administrations expressed interest in renewing relations with China, and these efforts culminated in President Nixon's historic visit to China in 1972. As a result of improved relations, both nations gained a powerful ally against the Soviet Union.

The Reform Era

The deaths of Mao and foreign minister Zhou Enlai in 1976 led to Deng Xiaoping assuming the leadership of China. Deng's rise occurred during a period of tremendous foreign and domestic ferment. The United States formally switched its recognition of China from Taiwan to the People's Republic on January 1, 1979, after which Deng made historic visits to America and Japan. Inspired by the beginnings of political liberalization, many Chinese began to express their bitterness toward the communist party with large posters on various city walls, the most famous of which became known as the Democracy Wall in Beijing. The party, which was ready to commit itself to many reforms, had little intention of sharing its authority, and to emphasize its control, Deng consolidated power.

Deng's economic reforms were headlined by the "Four Modernizations"—agriculture, industry, defense, and science and technology.[10] Recognizing that China needed more exposure to Western products, ideas, and capital, Beijing lifted import restrictions in 1978 under its open-door policy. Four Special Economic Zones were opened in southern China, where foreign investors could take advantage of low-wage labor and preferential tax rates. Small, household-run enterprises were once again legalized. Finally, larger enterprises such as agricultural production teams and many SOEs were subjected to a new fiscal regime under which some profits from above-quota production could be retained for the enterprise's use. This exposure to market forces resulted in a dramatic increase in nationwide investment in 1979 and 1980.[11]

A second, more intensive wave of reforms occurred between 1983 and 1985. In the agricultural sector, the government replaced mandatory grain purchases with a contracting system known as the Household Responsibility System, and prices for many goods were allowed to "float" to market levels. In the cities, SOEs were given increased discretion over their profits, and individual managers were made more accountable for their performance. Beijing also granted 14 additional coastal cities and Hainan Island Special Economic Zone status. The sudden changes and influx of wealth, however, created economic and social backlashes. Economic crime and corruption were rampant, and leaders often voiced concerns about excessive Western cultural influence.

Another period of retrenchment occurred in 1986, as restrictions were placed on investments and imports in an attempt to cool the economy. More ominously, however, large-scale social unrest had become evident throughout the country, and students and intellectuals grew increasingly disappointed that the nation's rapid economic change was not accompanied by changes in the authoritarian political system. For many students, Hu Yaobang personified many of the disappointments they faced. An outspoken progressive, Hu was forced to resign as party general secretary in January 1987 after other party leaders blamed him for not stopping student protests. His sudden death in 1989 set off a wave of nationwide student demonstrations, the most prominent of which attracted as many as a million demonstrators to Beijing's Tiananmen Square. For weeks the demonstrators and sympathetic civilians successfully resisted attempts to impose martial law, but in a move that was condemned worldwide, crack army units crushed the protests.

The repercussions of the Tiananmen massacre showed that China's efforts to join the world community were imposing constraints on the CCP and the government. China's desire for an international role commensurate with its growing economic strength had generated numerous frictions. Foremost among these were China's foreign economic relations. Both the United States, one of China's largest trading partners, and the GATT/World Trade Organization, which China hoped to join, insisted that China adhere more closely to international norms in its economy.

---

[10]Naughton (2007, Ch. 4) provides some detail on the economic policies of the reform era and the transition toward a market economy.

[11]Harding (1987, p. 4).

One foreign policy success was the 1984 agreement with the United Kingdom, returning Hong Kong to China in 1997. Under China's "One Country, Two Systems" policy, Hong Kong was to retain its autonomy, including a separate currency, for 50 years. Shortly before the return, the British government attempted to bolster the colony's legislative body as a popular institution, but Beijing ensured that only its own hand-picked representatives were permitted to sit. In 1999 Macao was returned to China by Portugal.

A potentially more serious sovereignty issue was the status of Taiwan. In their claims to sovereignty over both the mainland and Taiwan, both the CCP and GMD agreed that there was only a single Chinese nation. Because of their disparate political systems, however, movement toward reunification has been virtually nonexistent. Beijing originally proposed the One Country, Two Systems policy for Taiwan, but it was quickly rejected by the GMD government, which refused to unite with a communist regime. Beijing made clear that it would not tolerate a declaration of Taiwanese independence.

DOMESTIC REFORM IN AN AUTHORITARIAN FRAMEWORK   Domestically, China resumed its economic reforms shortly after the furor over Tiananmen subsided. The 1990s saw the increasing autonomy of SOEs, reforms of the nation's financial system, as well as a fully convertible currency. The government also handled the political transition of Deng's death in 1997 with few problems. The country, however, faced challenges that were as formidable as ever. One of the most urgent was the reform of over 300,000 obsolete SOEs. Few of these enterprises were profitable because they had functioned too long in the absence of competitive pressures. Many were hopelessly inefficient, saddled with old technology and employing up to 15 million excess workers nationwide. Moreover, these enterprises had accumulated combined debts approaching $120 billion (almost 20 percent of GDP), while absorbing most of China's domestic credit.[12] The problem was tightly linked with a crisis in the national banking system, whose long-standing practice of granting loans on the basis of political connections rather than commercial merit had resulted in high levels of bad debt. Transforming these enterprises into profitable entities would inevitably require the dismantling of the *danwei* system, but there was no social welfare system to replace it.

The economy continued to grow rapidly as a result of export growth and the growth of domestic demand. Beijing, however, also faced a host of long-term economic and political issues. The country's labor and housing markets required revamping. Corruption and cronyism were prevalent at all levels of government. The growing demand by an increasingly affluent population for energy and consumer goods was exacerbating China's already dire environmental problems. As SOEs were restructured, millions of workers lost their jobs, and they and millions of rural workers moved to the cities in search of work. The rapid adoption of information technology, wireless communication, and social media provided challenges to the government, which feared collective protests that could challenge its control. The CCP faced the daunting task of addressing these issues without once again raising demands for political liberalization.

CONFUCIANISM AND SOCIAL EXPLANATIONS

An important factor in understanding Chinese social and economic organization is its rich cultural heritage. This section considers Confucianism, which has had a significant influence not only in China but also in several other Asian nations.[13] With its emphasis on hierarchy, deference, moral rectitude, and behavioral norms, Confucianism was well suited to the needs of social stability. Indeed, many historians have credited China's long existence as a unified nation to its Confucian heritage. Yet the attribution of highly complex social phenomena to a single body of philosophical work would be unwarranted. Over more than 2,000 years of development, a wide variety of theories have worked their way under the Confucian umbrella. Thus, the general framework of Confucian thought displays considerable flexibility. On the one hand, as Confucius

---

[12]See Tomlinson (1997) for an example of the privatization of a state-owned enterprise.
[13]This section is adapted from a note prepared by Michael M. Ting under the supervision of Professor David P. Baron. Copyright © 1998 by the Board of Trustees of the Leland Stanford Junior University. All rights reserved. Reprinted with permission.

might suggest, a degree of modesty is warranted in drawing conclusions about social and economic organization from this highly complex ethics system.[14] On the other hand, attempting to understand Chinese groups, organizations, and behavior without sensitivity to the Confucian heritage would be incomplete at best.

During the political turmoil following the fall of the Zhou Dynasty, Confucius (551–479 B.C.) recorded and organized the extant body of ethical thought and extended it by de-emphasizing religious aspects and instead giving priority to the human condition (De Bary, 1991). Under this humanistic reorientation, virtue figured prominently in personal and political affairs, and individuals were to possess virtue and follow rules of behavior just as emperors did. Thus, Confucius was responsible for initiating the central preoccupation of Chinese philosophical thought: moral self-cultivation (Ivanhoe, 1993).

Perhaps the fundamental distinction between Confucianism and many Western systems of thought lies in its orientation toward the fundamental problem of social organization. As Yang (1959, p. 172) explained:

> Self-cultivation, the basic theme of Confucian ethics … did not seek a solution to social conflict in defining, limiting, and guaranteeing the rights and interests of the individual or in the balance of power and interests between individuals. It sought the solution from the self-sacrifice of the individual for the preservation of the group.

Confucianism links self-cultivation and social harmony through the development of group relations because it views the family as the ideal setting for moral self-cultivation. According to the Zhongyong, "Five Relationships" (*wu lun*) must be perfected before social harmony is achieved: father and son, husband and wife, sibling and sibling, friend and friend, and ruler and subject. Taking a pragmatic view of human nature, Confucius felt that most people could achieve perfection only in their intrafamily relationships. By extension, if virtue and harmony could be found most readily in family relationships, the process by which virtue is acquired must be present there as well (Schwartz, 1985, p. 99). As the individuals most responsible for this process, the leaders of such groups—family elders or bureaucrats—were accorded a high degree of deference and respect. Groups were therefore a vital part of the Confucian ethical system, as the individual goal of moral self-cultivation was in some sense an achievement of a larger group, be it a family or a nation.

The objectives of self-cultivation are two interrelated concepts: *ren*, or humanity, and *li*, or propriety. Loosely speaking, the former refers to one's internal discipline, whereas the latter concerns one's social relations. Confucius regarded *ren* as the more fundamental of the two concepts and considered it the ultimate object of moral self-cultivation. In its most abstract sense, the concept refers to the love of all human beings, and all people were thought to have an innate capacity for it.

Li is the external, or social, manifestation of *ren*. Although *li* is most commonly interpreted as "propriety," the term is also synonymous with "ceremony," "ritual," "decorum," and "good form," since it addresses all aspects of human behavior, including personal, familial, social, religious, and political conduct (Tu, 1979, pp. 20–21, 29). The Confucian tradition places a strong emphasis on behavioral minutiae because of its belief that self-cultivation is not a solitary endeavor, but rather occurs in a social context.

Confucian behavioral norms display a strongly particularistic, as opposed to universal, inclination. In contrast with ethics systems that require equal treatment of all individuals, Confucianism explicitly condoned behavior differentiated on the basis of social relationships. That is, differing standards could be applied to different social relationships, such as within a group to which a person belonged versus with regard to strangers. Appropriate behavior in a group could also differ depending on the person's position. For example, within a family

---

[14]Although the best exposition of Confucian thought is the *Analects*, over the centuries *Rujia* philosophers added dozens of major variations and extensions to this work. Zhu Xi grouped its existing strands into a two-tiered program of study that is regarded as the Confucian canon. First came the "Four Books": the *Analects, Mencius, Daxue (The Great Learning)*, and *Zhongyong (Doctrine of Man)*. Next were the "Five Classics": *Shujing (Book of History), Liji (Book of Rites), Shijing (Book of Odes), Spring and Autumn Annals*, and *Yijing (Book of Changes)*. Thus, while Confucianism lacks a single, comprehensive statement, a commonly accepted body of tenets emerges from these works.

a parent follows a particular form of proper behavior with regard to a child, whereas within a work group the same parent may be in the position of the "child" in relation to his or her employer.

The notion that appropriate behavior is specific to particular social relationships is largely attributable to the group foundations of moral self-cultivation, which forces numerous concessions out of necessity. Self-cultivation ideally encompasses relations with all people, but in practice most individuals can achieve only a limited degree of success in perfecting relationships. A family bond, for instance, creates opportunities for developing *ren* and *li* that may elude those outside the family. Thus, self-cultivation is seen as a process of gradual inclusion, beginning with the individual, then progressing to relations with family, nation, and the world. In this framework, universalism exists as an ideal, but discrimination and favoritism within groups should be expected because Confucians would find the notion of universalistic humanity incoherent without the prior achievement of harmony within smaller groups (Tu, 1979, p. 28).

Another feature of *li* in Confucian ethics is its distinctive conception of reciprocity. Many cultures have some variation of the Golden Rule: "Do unto others as you would have them do unto you." Beginning with the *Analects*, Confucians have devoted a great deal of attention to the idea of *shu*, or consideration. Confucius's classic statement of the rule is:

> Tzu-kung asked saying, Is there any single saying that one can act upon all day and every day? The Master said, Perhaps the saying about consideration: "Never do to others what you would not like them to do to you." (Analects 15.23)

Numerous variations and extensions on the Golden Rule exist in the Confucian canon. Taken together, they share the characteristic of emphasizing hierarchy. Nivison (1996, p. 73) constructs the following synthesis of the idealized version of *shu:*

> What I do to you, if I am in a superior position, should be what I would find it acceptable for you to do to me, if our positions were reversed. I should be kind, lenient, considerate .... What I do for you, if I am in an inferior position, should be what I would expect you to do for me, if our positions were reversed. I should be "loyal," and so should be strict with myself even when what I am doing might hurt me …

Western variants of the Golden Rule typically make no allusions to the social position of the actors.

Confucianism does not include an independent notion of individual rights. As considered in Chapter 22, Western concepts of rights involve liberty, choice, and autonomy. These rights impose duties on others not to interfere with those rights. Chang (1998, p. 133) argues that "although the Confucians did not talk about 'human rights,' they maintained that people should treat each other as fellow human beings and help one another to live a good, human way of life. This idea is clearly comparable with the concept of 'human rights.'" Cheng (1998) explains the nature of rights in terms of the relationship between a person and a ruler and their duties within that relationship. A ruler, or government, has a duty to help develop virtue in subjects, and the "rights" of those subjects are to consideration by the ruler. Cheng (1998, p. 145) writes, "we can see how a Chinese might see his rights as his duties and define his own self in terms of his consciousness." That is, instead of independently identified rights, Confucianism focuses more on duties required by a relationship, and those duties give expectations of certain types of treatment for the others in the relationship.

Applications in Society, Politics, and Business

POLITICAL INSTITUTIONS   The Confucian ideal of hierarchical relations within the family also extends to the political realm. Whereas family heads could exercise near-absolute authority over other family members, households were expected to defer to the state on nonhousehold matters. The promotion of one's self-interest in society was considered just as inappropriate as a child's selfishness before her or his parents (Pye, 1985). The analogy helped to justify the Confucians' advocacy of authoritarian rule by a meritocratic elite. It also identified some of the highest political priorities of the state: security, cohesion, loyalty, and stability. Confucius wrote extensively on the behavior expected of a ruler. The following passage touches on some important aspects of a ruler's behavior:

> The Master said, Govern the people by regulations, keep order among them by chastisements, and they will flee from you, and lose all self-respect. Govern them by moral force, keep order among them by ritual and they will keep their self-respect and come to you of their own accord. (Analects 2.3)

Confucius saw the ruler as a moral exemplar, but the primary purpose of governing by moral force was not divine reward but the moral development of the people. To achieve this, the ruler could use formal rules or coercion, but setting a virtuous example was both necessary and sufficient for improving society's moral character and inducing social harmony.

One of the most striking differences between Confucian and Western political thought is that the former does not conceive of a role for "civil society," or the collection of intermediate organizations between the family and state (Shils, 1996).[15] Because households were to show the same loyalty to the state that children showed to their parents, allegiance to other organizations had the potential for destabilizing society. Remarkably, imperial Chinese society mirrored these priorities for over two millennia, as merchants never achieved any substantial social status and social advancement was secured exclusively through advancement in the state bureaucracy (Pye, 1985, p. 57). The lack of recognition of legitimate interests outside the state and the deference expected of citizens also rendered Confucianism inconsistent with modern conceptions of democracy.

FIRMS AND BUREAUCRACIES   In more modern settings, Confucian paternalism may be seen in the context of other organizations, such as firms and bureaucracies (Abegglen and Stalk, 1985; Dollinger, 1988; Durlabhji, 1990; Taka, 1994). Because of the imperative of maintaining group harmony, decision making is typically achieved through consensus building. This process requires the cooperation of leaders and subordinates. Leaders must demonstrate decision-making ability commensurate with their position, treat subordinates fairly, and set a good example for all. Personal negotiation may be used to resolve disputes among peers. In return, subordinates are to recognize a leader's authoritarian prerogatives and subsume personal desires to the attainment of group goals. Little emphasis is placed on formal rules, and quiet suasion and deference are often sufficient for making decisions and maintaining organizational unity.

This familistic orientation can exert a powerful influence outside the boundaries of formal organizations. Informal personal ties in Chinese society are often referred to as *guanxi*. These relationships may be either vertical (e.g., between teacher and student) or horizontal (e.g., between residents of the same village). *Guanxi* ties create a form of diffuse reciprocity, allowing individuals to exchange favors even years after a formal relationship has been dissolved. Their importance in Chinese society should not be underestimated. Throughout history, decisions ranging from hiring to the sale of scarce goods have gone in favor of those possessing good *guanxi*. Such practices have persisted despite the increased bureaucratization of Chinese society during the communist era. Because these relationships are usually not reflected in formal laws, *guanxi* often makes Chinese organizational behavior appear nontransparent and at times resemble cronyism to outsiders. The strength of such ties in China frequently has frustrated Westerners, who are more accustomed to legally circumscribed contracts or quid pro quo arrangements (Pye, 1988).

The importance of *guanxi* is such that individuals must concern themselves with acquiring it. Some ties arise in the course of normal social interaction, for instance through school or family. Others require investment and must be cultivated directly through the giving of gifts and favors, for which an elaborate set of norms has evolved. Gift giving in China frequently serves the instrumental goal of initiating a relationship. Whereas gifts may sometimes be used to secure specific favors, the diffuse nature of *guanxi* requires that exchanges occur in private some time before the desired favor to avoid the public appearance of a quid pro quo (Yang, 1994, p. 144).

Confucianism's strong focus on group cohesion and solidarity has implications for other relationships. Because intragroup relations are so important, relationships of subordinates within

---

[15]Gold (1996) argues that large family networks serve as the functional equivalent of civil society.

a group with individuals outside the group are often frowned upon. Such relationships are the responsibility of the group leader, who may require the outsiders to acknowledge his or her moral authority (Pye, 1985, p. 63). As a result, outsiders hoping to influence a group must simultaneously respect the group leader's appearance of control while also exerting effort toward establishing trustworthiness and becoming more of an insider. The latter may entail a significant investment in the establishment of *guanxi* relationships prior to the execution of any significant interaction.

BUSINESS RELATIONSHIPS   Confucianism has often been linked with the development and operation of capitalism in China and other Asian countries.[16] In particular, the Chinese tendency toward small, family-owned businesses that operate within tight networks shows many traces of the Confucian heritage (Hamilton, 1996). The high status associated with public office, which required tremendous investment in education, and the traditional practice of dividing inheritances equally among children, mitigated the concentration of wealth in large firms.[17] Instead, wealthy merchant families would establish multiple small businesses that could be distributed evenly to the next generation. These multiple businesses relied on often vast *guanxi* networks to conduct their affairs. The success of such businesses depended critically on the level of trust, and *guanxi*-based ties proved to be extremely successful in this regard.[18] Over the past century during which Chinese have migrated throughout the Pacific Rim, these ties have proven to be invaluable to the success of Chinese business communities throughout the region. In China's reform era, these ties have also been credited with aiding overseas Chinese who sought to do business in China.

Commercial and political success were closely linked in imperial China, as successful businessmen could more easily afford to invest in education, and bureaucrats used their political influence to favor family businesses. Thus, relationships between businesses and government traditionally have been close, often to the point of inappropriateness by Western standards. *Guanxi*-based influence networks remain pervasive throughout Asia, and while they can play an important role in facilitating business, today they are increasingly criticized for inducing favoritism, poor economic decisions by political institutions, and corruption. The state banking system in China, for instance, faced a bad debt crisis as a result of loans given on the basis of cronyism instead of merit.

Li (2004) described another purpose of *guanxi*:

> In China's relation-based system, personal connections are used to circumvent the legal and regulatory system to obtain public goods and to protect one's property rights when the legal system fails. The formal legal system in China tends to be opaque, unfair, and particularistic. This is the fundamental reason why circumventing laws and regulations by using personal connections is widely practiced in China and thus viewed as ethical by some investors as well as scholars. Furthermore, investors should realize that when they use *guanxi* to protect their interest, their local partners or competitors may use their *guanxi* to take advantage of the foreign investors—and very often the local partners and competitors tend to have stronger *guanxi*.

THE NONMARKET ENVIRONMENT AND THE FOUR I'S

The framework of structured pluralism relevant to China is illustrated in Figure 16-1, but the importance of the components differs from that in other countries. With regard to culture and history, China has a long history as a relatively unified nation, but it has no democratic tradition. Instead, institutions have been dominated by the bureaucracy and in the postwar period by the CCP. Culturally, China has a rich tradition, and only one aspect of that culture, Confucianism, has been considered here. This section briefly considers the other components of the structured pluralism perspective, the four I's—issues, interests, institutions, and information—and pertains only to the current period.

A host of market and nonmarket issues faced business and government in China. Externally, the European Union and the United States criticized China's policy of pegging the yuan to the

---

[16]See Weidenbaum (1996).

[17]By contrast, "primogeniture," or the granting of the entire inheritance to the first son, was practiced in Japan, which encouraged the concentration of capital.

[18]See Redding (1996) for a discussion and comparison of trust networks in other cultures.

FIGURE 16-1   Structured Pluralism and Culture and History

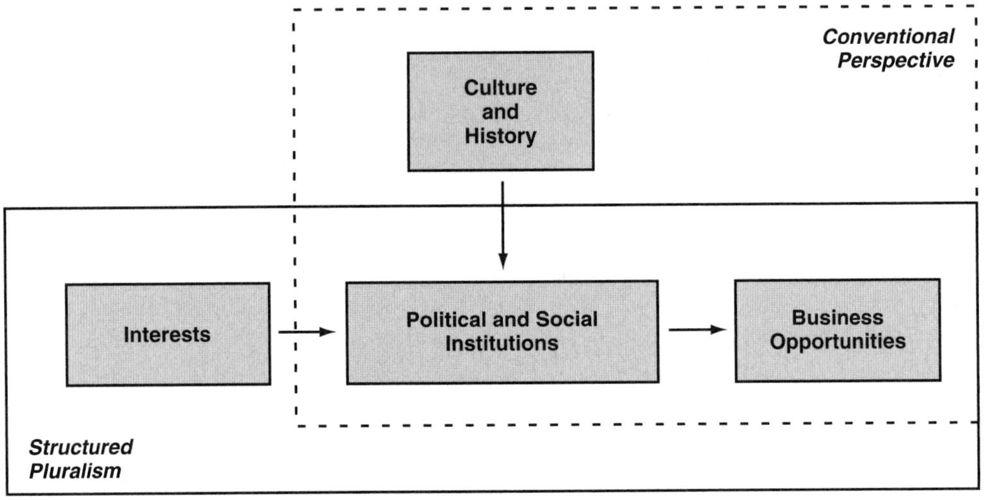

Structured Pluralism

• Interests change more rapidly than culture and history
• Interests motivate the action that shapes business opportunities
• Institutions intermediate between interests and opportunities

dollar at a low exchange rate. This kept its export prices low, and the prices of imports high, resulting in a huge trade surplus with the United States. The International Monetary Fund and the Group of Seven (G-7) nations urged China to float the yuan. China pledged to act, but some observers believed that inclusion in the G-7 was China's price for floating or revaluing the yuan. In late 2004 China's central bank raised its lending rate for the first time in 9 years to slow inflation, and by the end of the decade it began slowly increasing the value of the yuan.

Internally, China had the problem of reforming or closing a large number of inefficient SOEs. Many of the SOEs had close ties to the CCP and the ministries that controlled them. China's inclusion in the World Trade Organization (WTO) resolved one issue, but compliance with WTO requirements was difficult. China had to address commercial piracy, quotas on imports, and restrictions on entry in many markets. A variety of human rights complaints had been lodged against China, ranging from the absence of civil rights to the enforcement of the one-child-per-family policy to the working conditions in factories. Nonmarket issues stemmed from the weak protection of intellectual and other property rights in China and the widespread corruption stemming in part from the government's extensive involvement in business and in the regulation of business.

Interests in China are pluralistic, but because of the domination of the CCP there is little interest group activity and collective nonmarket action is rare. Moreover, independent labor unions are not permitted. Instead, interests manifest themselves through client politics narrowly tailored to specific issues. This means that interests do not drive outcomes in the same manner as in a democracy such as Japan, the European Union, or the United States.[19]

The government is sensitive to the possibility of popular unrest and attempts to anticipate problems. Riots and demonstrations break out in China as a result of local issues. For example, as inflation increased, retirees protested that their pensions were not indexed to inflation. Farmers rioted against some local governments that had taken their land for development purposes without adequate compensation. The large population of migrant workers who had left the countryside to find work constituted a potential for unrest. The Chinese Academy of Social Sciences estimated that there were 80,000 "mass protests" in 2007, and commentators speculated that by 2011 it was nearly 100,000.

Ethnic conflicts have also occurred. In Urumqin in Xinjiang province, Muslim Uigurs and Han Chinese battled, leaving over 150 people dead. Protests also developed in Inner Mongolia in response to the death of a Mongolian herdsman caused by a coal truck driven by a Han Chinese.

---

[19]Kennedy (2005) provides an analysis of lobbying in China.

The Chinese government was very sensitive to the development of ethnic conflicts. Protests also occurred in Lhasa, Tibet, which the Chinese government suppressed.

Information is important in China in part because of the presence of a dominant political party and a hierarchical government. It is also important because government rules and regulations are not transparent and can be changed without due process or electoral sanction. This situation is exacerbated by the dominance by the CCP of both business and the administration of laws. *Guanxi* relationships between business and government facilitate obtaining information, but this also makes it difficult for those who do not have *guanxi*. The chapter case *Direct Selling in China* illustrates some of these features.

The institutions in China are dominated by the CCP and include a strong and encompassing bureaucracy and a relatively weak legislature and judiciary. Despite the tight political control exercised by the CCP, China has devolved considerable authority to the provinces and local governments.

Institutions and Government

China's government is characterized by close ties between the CCP and state institutions. In practice, a government body wields power to the extent that its leadership is influential within the CCP. The constitution of the PRC places the party in the highest position of authority and requires that government policies and civil liberties conform to its direction. As a result, the informal configuration of power within the party leadership is usually more informative than the government's organization charts for determining where policies are made.

Since the ascendance of Deng Xiaoping, three general trends have developed. First, political power has steadily devolved to local governments, thus shifting the locus of a considerable body of policymaking away from Beijing. Second, the relationship between party and state has been weakened by new restrictions on joint appointments in the leaderships of both bodies. This has been coupled with significant advances in administrative law and an increasing professionalization of the bureaucracy. Third, although their influence remains small, democratic procedures, such as elections to local People's Congresses that were once considered mere formalities, have become more important.

PARTY ORGANIZATION   The CCP claims to represent the Chinese working people and is the highest source of political power in China. Moreover, the People's Liberation Army, which historically has been closely linked with the CCP, is sworn to defend the party rather than the state. In 2010 CCP membership stood at 78 million, or about 6 percent of the population. At the local level, the party is represented in virtually all significant societal organizations, including townships, factories, and rural collectives. At higher levels, party organizations mirror the hierarchy of the national government. Decisions at all levels are made by a process known as democratic centralism, whereby party units may set their own policies in a democratic manner but may not contradict the directives of a higher level. This system of representation and centralization of authority guarantees significant party influence over potentially all aspects of political and economic activity.

NATIONAL PARTY CONGRESS   Nominally the highest authority of the CCP, Party Congresses meet every 5 years. The 17th Party Congress in 2007 had 2,217 delegates, elected from local party organizations, the central party, and the military. Because meetings are brief (usually a few days) and the number of delegates is large, the Congress usually does little more than rubber-stamp the decisions of its delegated bodies.

CENTRAL COMMITTEE   When the Party Congress is not in session, authority passes to the 198-member Central Committee, which convenes at least twice annually. The Central Committee is elected by the National Party Congress, but until 1987 ballots were not secret and the number of candidates did not exceed the number of seats. Members represent the central party, local party organizations, the government, and the military. The committee makes decisions by majority rule and has veto authority over many party decisions. Many of Deng's reforms catered to local governments to avoid a Central Committee veto.[20] The Central Committee also supervises many of the party's internal functions, such as propaganda and party organization.

---

[20]Shirk (1993, Ch. 4).

POLITBURO The Politburo is responsible for the ongoing administration of the party. This 25-person body meets regularly and makes decisions by majority rule. It holds a veto over many of the decisions of the Standing Committee and supervises the policy branches of the party organization (e.g., military, foreign affairs, and finance). Much of the Politburo's authority comes from its personnel powers.

STANDING COMMITTEE OF THE POLITBURO In 2010 the Standing Committee consisted of nine members. This group handles the day-to-day affairs of the party and, like other CCP bodies, makes decisions by majority rule. Much of its leverage comes from its ability to convene Politburo meetings and set their agendas.[21]

THE CCP AND POLICYMAKING The prevalence of majority rule in CCP decision making may seem surprising, but in accordance with the principles of democratic centralism, the procedure is taken seriously. However, CCP decision making has an authoritarian character because delegated groups such as the Standing Committee of the Politburo exercise tremendous agenda control over their parent groups. The CCP's appointments process also contributes to intraparty unity. Because career advancement within the party is typically achieved through patronage, intraparty factions tend to be highly cohesive.

As a given policy's importance increases, the number of veto bodies it must pass through also increases. For example, Five-Year Plans must be approved all the way down through the National Party Congress. Because the Congress and the Central Committee are composed of very diverse groups (including geographically based representatives), major policies must satisfy some particularistic interests.

Virtually all high-ranking party officials belong to an "entrance" (*kou*) that covers a major policy area. The most important *kou*s, such as Party Affairs and Military Affairs, are led by members of the Standing Committee of the Politburo, while other Politburo members lead less important or subordinate *kou*s. *Kou*s often form the basis of intraparty factions, and their members typically hold positions both within the party leadership as well as in the state institutions that carry out the policies associated with the *kou*.[22]

State Institutions

THE LEGISLATIVE BRANCH The National People's Congress (NPC) is both the highest legislative body and formally the highest institution of the central state. One of its duties is the election of a premier, who serves as the PRC's head of state. The PRC constitution grants the NPC authority to pass legislation and to appoint and remove most executive branch officials. Membership selection has a reciprocal character similar to that of the upper echelons of the CCP: the plenum elects a Standing Committee which in turn selects representatives to the plenum. The NPC's 3,000 delegates are elected to 5-year terms, but the plenum meets for only 2 weeks annually, leaving most day-to-day activities to the 150-member Standing Committee. Representation is both geographical and functional (or corporatist). Large social interests such as the People's Liberation Army, ethnic minority groups, and peasants, among others, are granted fixed proportions of representatives. Non-CCP members account for 20–30 percent of NPC delegates.

Historically, the divergence between the NPC's formal and actual powers has been large due to the domination by the CCP elite of all aspects of statecraft. Since the early 1980s, however, the NPC has with increasing frequency defeated or forced the rewriting of bills submitted by the State Council. In addition, the NPC has established specialized committees, such as an environmental committee founded in 1990, that have given it some leverage in policy debates.[23] Public appreciation for this trend is evidenced by the increased volume of constituent letters written to NPC delegates.[24]

THE EXECUTIVE BRANCH The four principal positions in the Chinese government are the general secretary of the CCP, the president of the country, the head of the Chinese Army, and the premier of the State Council. The first three positions are frequently held by the same

---

[21]Christiansen and Rai (1996, pp. 110–111).
[22]See Lieberthal (1995).
[23]Christiansen and Rai (1996, pp. 106–107).
[24]See Pei (1997).

person. Jiang Zemin held the positions into the early 2000s. In 2002 Hu Jintao replaced Jiang as head of the CCP and in 2003 replaced him as president. Jiang remained as chairman of the Central Military Commission, that is, head of the Chinese Army, a position he had held since the Tiananmen Square massacre. Hu replaced him as chairman of the Central Military Commission in 2004. The premier, or prime minister, is Wen Jiabao, whose term extends until 2013.

China's paramount executive body is the State Council, which is headed by the premier and serves as China's cabinet. The State Council is composed of about 50 people, including the premier, several vice premiers, and ministers and vice ministers of all major ministries and commissions. Like most deliberative groups in Chinese government, much of the State Council's day-to-day responsibilities are delegated to a Standing Committee. This committee consists of about 15 of the council's highest-ranking members and meets roughly every 2 weeks.

The State Council presides over dozens of commissions, which coordinate policies functionally across specific ministries. Commissions correspond roughly to departments in the U.S. executive branch; the National Defense Commission, for example, is analogous to the Department of Defense. Sometimes referred to as the "little State Council," the State Planning Commission (SPC) had been one of the most powerful commissions in the PRC. As its name suggests, the SPC was charged with overseeing China's vast planned economy. The magnitude of that task has resulted in SPC alumni being well represented in the Politburo. The decline of the planned sector relative to the private sector has reduced the SPC's authority, and the State Council's current formal delineation of its responsibilities reflects this. The SPC was merged with other economic agencies to form the National Development and Reform Commission (NDRC) in 2003. The NDRC has responsibility for economic performance, macroeconomic policies, finance, credit, and approves major capital construction projects, energy planning, industrial restructuring, and regional development.

Below the commissions stand the provinces and ministries. Each of the 22 provinces holds ministerial rank, as do some of China's largest cities (Beijing, Tianjin, Shanghai, and Chongqing). Ministries have more specific jurisdictions than commissions and often find themselves subject to oversight from many commissions. An important exception is the Ministry of Finance, which is the most powerful ministry and informally holds commission rank in the State Council hierarchy. Ministers are typically high-ranking party officials, and departments within ministries are staffed by contingents of party cadres to ensure compliance with CCP directives.

Each national-level commission or ministry is the head of a hierarchy, or *xitong*, of local offices that perform the same role for the corresponding local government. A *xitong* generally is under the informal control of a *kou*. A provincial government's Education Commission is therefore a branch of the State Education Commission. *Xitongs* are known for protecting institutional turf. Very little information is shared across hierarchies, and the incentives for vertical integration are strong. Many *xitongs* owned companies and operated colleges to satisfy funding and personnel needs. In response, the reform-era CCP leadership has become increasingly active in reorganizing and abolishing ministries, as well as strengthening interdepartmental professional organizations. For example, the Ministry of Power and Water Conservancy was broken up to fragment opposition to the Three Gorges Dam project.[25]

In 2008 China began the process of establishing five "super-ministries" to improve coordination and reduce interagency turf battles. For example, the National Energy Commission (NEC) was established to centralize authority for energy policy while allowing the implementation of that policy to remain with the NDRC. The NEC includes the minister of the NDRC and the minister of finance, reflecting the economical political power of those two ministries. Premier Wen heads the NEC. Other superministries include industry and information, transportation, and environmental protection. The last elevates the importance of environmental protection in the bureaucratic hierarchy.

THE JUDICIAL BRANCH   China has no tradition of an independent judiciary, and its highest court, the Supreme People's Court, has long been little more than a reflection of the CCP. There is no judicial review process in China. Likewise, the Supreme People's Procurator has little ability to pursue cases on its own initiative. Nevertheless, the emphasis of Deng's reforms on a stable and predictable legal environment has resulted in a growing role for the national judiciary. Citizens have increasingly turned to the courts to resolve disputes.

---

[25]Christiansen and Rai (1996, pp. 111–114).

Provincial and Local Governments

The governments and party organizations at the provincial, county, and city levels essentially mirror those at the national level. The highest state institution at each level is the People's Congress, a legislative body that has formal, but often weak, authority over the executive branch, the People's Government. Many representatives to People's Congresses are elected by popular vote at the county and township levels. The general devolution of fiscal authority to the provinces (as well as lower levels of the state hierarchy) has made local governments the locus of interest group activity.

Most provinces share their revenues with the central government according to a fixed formula that is renegotiated periodically. These formulas typically allow the provinces to keep a certain proportion of the earnings of provincial enterprises. Across China, lower levels of government also work under similar financial arrangements. As a result, local governments exercise a large amount of budget and taxation discretion and frequently are the locus of bargaining with private interests. Local governments, for example, can offer a prospective enterprise favorable tax treatment in exchange for taking on extra workers to alleviate local unemployment.[26]

BUSINESS: STATE-OWNED ENTERPRISES, FOREIGN DIRECT INVESTMENT, AND INTERNATIONAL TRADE

State-Owned Enterprises

The SOE is a unique entity that has represented the single most important type of company in China in terms of employment, as well as in problems for the country. The SOEs are not the future of the Chinese economy, however, nor have they been responsible for China's growth in the reform era. Economic growth has been fueled on the demand side by both domestic and export demand and on the supply side by foreign direct investment and local companies formed by entrepreneurs and local governments. Strong economic growth has been essential for China, since growth absorbed the unemployed as SOEs were forced to improve their efficiency. China has privatized many of the SOEs, but in 2008 there were still 154,000 SOEs. The SOEs held 44 percent of the assets in the industrial sector. With the consolidation of SOEs their average size has increased dramatically, in part because of continued government support and funding.[27]

The labor policies of the SOEs were the heart of the socialist economic system and gave SOEs a distinctive dual purpose. In addition to production, SOEs provided virtually all the major social services required by employees, their families, and retirees, including education, health care, and housing. Moreover, because many goods such as housing and food staples were rationed, workers could only receive necessities through enterprise-issued coupons. This set of services essentially served as China's social welfare system and became known as the "iron rice bowl." A major constraint on the Chinese government's willingness to take strong measures to reform SOEs has been the lack of social security and welfare systems for its citizens.

Since the late 1970s, SOE reform has been a constant priority for Chinese leaders. Managers have been given more authority to evaluate employees, and the growth of the private sector has allowed many SOEs to shed some excess labor.[28] Enterprises were permitted to retain profits, which were taxed by the state. The deregulation of prices and increasing competition from private, foreign, and rural industries increasingly exposed SOEs to market discipline. Subsidies provided to SOEs accounted for 21 percent of China's budget in 1989, but by 1996 subsidies accounted for only 4 percent of the budget as the state reduced its support.

Despite these changes, much of the system, and its dual role and chronic inefficiencies, remained intact at the beginning of the new century. SOEs were still losing money, underutilizing capacity, and consuming much of the country's available capital. The Chinese government ceased using its budget to subsidize SOEs, but in its place the state-run banks made "policy loans" to many of the SOEs. These, however, were more in the form of subsidies than loans, and expectations were that the loans would never be repaid. These loans were in large part the cause of the financial

---

[26]Ibid., pp. 232–233.
[27]See Lardy (1998) for an analysis of SOEs.
[28]See Groves et al. (1994, 1995) for studies of incentives and the managerial labor market in SOEs.

difficulties experienced by state banks. The government planned to retain many of the larger and more competitive SOEs, but the remainder were to be sold, merged, privatized, or closed.

Foreign Direct Investment

JOINT VENTURE POLICY   One cornerstone of Deng's liberalizations was the Central Committee's July 1979 decision to establish four Special Economic Zones (SEZs).[29] As a result of this liberalization, foreign direct investment (FDI) and joint ventures in the PRC skyrocketed, with over 100,000 in operation in the mid-1990s.[30] For example, in the chapter case *Direct Selling in China*, Amway's plant in Guangzhou was a joint venture with a government development agency.

Among the several forms of joint ventures, a prominent one is the equity joint venture (EJV). EJVs are limited liability companies in which the Chinese and foreign partners both manage day-to-day operations and divide the risk in direct proportion to their capital contributions to the project. Contractual (or cooperative) joint ventures (CJVs) divide risks by contract rather than by capital contribution. These arrangements permit greater flexibility for parties in allocating responsibilities. Such ventures are often riskier, however, because China's legal system is not well equipped to deal with contractual disputes between partners. CJVs were once quite popular but have declined in importance.

The third type is the wholly foreign-owned enterprise (WFOE). These give the foreign firm the greatest control and the greatest risk. The 1990 Law on Wholly Foreign-Owned Enterprises prohibited them from operating in markets such as media, insurance, and communications and restricted their activities in public utilities and real estate. Article 3 of the law permits WFOEs if they are technologically advanced and export most of their production. Large Western firms such as Motorola, 3M, and Shell entered China as WFOEs because they provided the best protection from being forced to share sensitive technology.[31] Beijing realized that the autonomy offered to such enterprises was necessary for attracting export-oriented, high-technology firms that could help develop the Chinese economy, and as a result WFOEs have been the fastest-growing segment of FDI.

FDI as a percent of GDP increased dramatically from 1 percent in 1991 to 6 percent in 1994, after which it declined to 3 percent in 2005.[32] This reflected the growth of the domestic economy. As China joined the WTO, FDI was over $60 billion in 2005. WTO membership required China to open its markets to foreign firms, although the opening was gradual. Major industries, including banking, insurance, telecommunication, and agriculture were not yet fully opened.

International Trade Policy and WTO Membership

In the pre-reform era trade increased substantially, but trade policies remained essentially the same. All trade had to be approved by the Ministry of Foreign Economic Relations and Trade (MOFERT), and imported items were marketed directly by the cognizant state-owned firm. Deng's reforms and the open-door policy allowed China a wide range of international finance arrangements, including direct loans, export credits, and development assistance from foreign governments. In 1980 China joined the International Monetary Fund and World Bank, which gave it access to loans and other development aid.

Trade policy became one of the primary concerns of China's international relations in the 1990s. The PRC's application for membership in the WTO was a protracted and contentious issue. Many advanced industrialized nations, particularly the European Union and the United States, insisted that China open its markets further to foreign businesses as a condition for membership. Beijing resisted many market-opening initiatives because of worries about social instability caused by workers laid off by uncompetitive SOEs.

The large U.S. trade deficit with China aroused animosity from some American policymakers and drew attention to PRC trade practices, including inadequate protection of intellectual property rights. Concerns over Chinese domestic policies and human rights abuses blocked

---

[29]Grub and Lin (1991, p. 65).
[30]See Urata (2001) for a study of European FDI in China.
[31]Grub and Lin (1991, Chs. 4–5, Appendix 3).
[32]Naughton (2007, p. 404).

WTO membership. After nearly 15 years of negotiations China was admitted to the WTO at the end of 2001.[33] During that period China made many domestic reforms to qualify for membership, and it was forced to make important changes in its foreign trade policies. It pledged to lower tariffs, reduce import quotas, open markets to imports, and open industries such as telecommunications and banking to FDI. In addition, companies, such as the express companies, were no longer required to operate through joint ventures with a Chinese company. China also agreed to reduce by 40 percent its tariffs, which averaged 15 percent. Foreign banks would be allowed to have wholly owned subsidiaries and branches and to accept deposits. China was also required to improve its legal system, which in the late 1990s had become independent of the other parts of the government.

Market opening resulted in continuing nonmarket issues at the level of industries as well as a set of societal-level problems. Domestic firms resisted the opening of their markets to imports and FDI. Retailers had been restricted to selling only products made in China, but as a result of WTO membership they were, after a transition period, allowed to sell imported goods. At the societal level reductions in tariffs on agricultural imports threatened farmers, and those imports were expected to increase the already high unemployment in rural provinces. More than 100 million migrant workers had moved to cities seeking employment, and millions more would follow. Coupled with the competitive pressures on SOEs, China faced the challenge of developing social welfare programs to meet the needs of the unemployed and those harmed by the reforms.

China began to train judges to handle trade cases and established a WTO Department to develop policies for implementing WTO requirements. The *Direct Selling in China* chapter case involves an opportunity to use WTO membership to challenge a directive barring the principal component of the direct sellers' business model.

Regulation

Regulation in China is established through the ministries and commissions and through agencies associated with the State Council. Many of the regulations pertain to the same issues as in more developed countries. An example is fuel economy standards. China's automobile market boomed in the 2000s, and as incomes grew, Chinese consumers bought larger vehicles, and SUVs became popular. Economic growth and increased driving made China more dependent on imported oil and also pushed up the price of oil. To address the dependence on foreign oil, China issued fuel economy standards.

The standards were developed over more than 2 years and did not involve public inputs, although Volkswagen, which had a quarter of the market in China, was consulted. The standards, which had been developed by the Automotive Technology and Research Center, were issued by the State Council. A fuel tax, which would be the most effective means of reducing fuel use, was considered but rejected because of concerns about public anger and increased inflation. Three basic types of fuel economy standards were used in other countries. The European Union had a voluntary program, Japan had standards for each model, and the United States had a corporate average system. China chose a weight-based system for automobiles, vans, and SUVs. The standards did not apply to pickup trucks, which were primarily used by business in China. The standards took effect in 2005 and were strengthened in 2008.

CONTINUING ISSUES

Human Rights

The issue of human rights in China became internationalized in the 1990s. Foreign governments as well as human rights groups targeted China as a major abuser of human rights. International concern focused on four areas.[34] First, China's criminal justice system was said to allow arbitrary imposition of the death penalty, the torture of prisoners, detention without trial, and the use of prison labor in industrial production. Second, China was accused of persecution of ethnic (primarily Tibetan) and religious (primarily Christian) minorities. Third, Beijing had little tolerance for political dissidents and held many political prisoners. Finally, critics argued that the

---

[33]Two days later Taiwan was admitted to the WTO.
[34]See Levine (1997) for a summary of human rights concerns in China.

condition of Chinese women had deteriorated despite the advances in gender equality made during the communist era. Beijing often dismissed these complaints as interference in domestic affairs. The U.S. State Department's "Annual Country Reports on Human Rights Practices" identified specific abuses and discussed trends in their occurrence. The 2007 report dropped China from the list of 10 worst violators of human rights, but the report concluded that China's "overall human rights remained poor." The 2010 report stated, "A negative trend in key areas of the country's human rights record continued, as the government took additional steps to rein in civil society, particularly organizations and individuals involved in rights advocacy and public interest issues, and increased attempts to limit freedom of speech and to control the press, the Internet, and Internet access." The Chapter 23 case *Fresenius Medical Care in China* concerns a human rights issue.

China censored the content on the Internet and as well as blocked responses to searches on topics such as Tibet and the spiritual Falun Gong movement. In 2011 the government established the State Internet Information Office to consolidate regulation of the Internet including "online content management."[35] Internet companies were not only subject to censorship, but they also could be required to turn over e-mails to the Chinese government. Yahoo! provided information to the government that led to the arrest and imprisonment of the journalist Shi Tao. Yahoo! was sharply criticized by human rights groups as well as members of the U.S. Congress. The chapter case *Google in China* concerns Google's entry into China and the associated censorship and human rights issues. The Chapter 24 case *Google Out of China* considers Google's subsequent decision to move its search business out of China.

Several long-standing practices continued to provoke complaints and posed problems for companies. To control its population growth, China unofficially adopted a one-child-per-family policy with birth targets for each province.[36] The average number of children per woman decreased from nearly six in 1970 to 1.8 by the 2000s. Women who had more than one child without permission were fined, or otherwise punished. These measures were a continuing source of conflict between citizens and the government. Moreover, a survey by the National Population and Family Planning Commission found that prominent and wealthy Chinese generally had two children and 10 percent had three. The wealthy simply paid the fine. In a rural province the government revoked the membership in the CCP of 500 people, most of them government officials, who had violated the one-child-per-family policy.

Beijing began studying population issues to determine if it would have enough workers to support an aging population. The 2010 census found that the percent of the population under 14 had decreased from 23 percent in 2000 to 16.6 percent and the percent over 60 had increased from 10.3 to 13.3 percent. The National Population and Family Planning Commission maintained the one-child policy but began to consider pilot programs where two children would be allowed for some families.

Some Chinese preferred male to female children. The national ratio of male to female births was 120–100 and was believed to be due to selective abortions made possible by advances in ultrasound technology. The one-child-per-family policy along with the preference for boys was blamed for both selective abortions and for female infanticide. The Chapter 18 case *Advanced Technology Laboratories, Inc.* addresses this issue in India.

In 1998 China signed the International Covenant on Civil and Political Rights and released the imprisoned leader of the Tiananmen Square democracy demonstrations. Although some elections have been held at the local level, the CCP has maintained itself as the sole political party in China. When a group of democracy supporters formed the China Democratic Party in November 1998, the government arrested party leaders, including three prominent dissidents sentenced to between 11 and 13 years in prison. In 2007 China arrested Hu Jia, one of its most prominent human rights activists. In 2009 China sentenced Liu Xiaobo, a prominent human rights and democracy campaigner, to 11 years in prison for subversion. In 2010 Liu was awarded the Nobel Peace Prize.

Despite the human rights abuses and political restrictions, Chinese citizens enjoyed greater freedoms than at any time since the communists gained control of the country. Much of the improvement resulted from growing economic prosperity that had given people the means to

---

[35]*New York Times*, May 5, 2011.

[36]Exceptions to the one-child policy were provided in the case where both parents were single children, when the first child was a girl, or for minorities.

exercise more control over their lives. In addition, the accumulation of personal property led people to attempt to protect it, resulting in greater use of the courts. Moreover, with the widespread use of the Internet, computers, and mobile communication devices, information was more readily available and actions could be coordinated. This inevitably led to pressure for greater freedoms and a more responsive government, but democracy was not in the foreseeable future. In 2007 Premier Wen wrote that democracy was consistent with "socialism with Chinese characteristics," but he added, "We are still far away from advancing out of the primary stages of socialism. We must stick with the basic development guidelines of that stage for 100 years."[37]

PIRACY OF INTELLECTUAL PROPERTY   A major concern of firms has been the piracy of intellectual property ranging from pharmaceuticals to software to consumer goods. Copies of movies and books often appeared on Chinese street corners before they were available in stores in the United States. Even the CCP had been a victim of piracy. The party sponsored production of an anticorruption movie, and prior to its release pirated copies were being shown in Chinese stateowned cinemas.[38] The Chinese automaker Jonway UFO exported to Europe a copy of the RAV4, which Toyota had failed to patent in China. The U.S.-based Business Software Alliance estimated that in 2000, 91 percent of the software in China was pirated. One reason it was difficult to stop the pirating of intellectual property was that local officials were said to support it. The pirating companies paid local taxes and more importantly provided badly needed jobs.

Chinese joint venture partners have set up competing companies with technology taken from their foreign partners.[39] Many foreign joint venture partners complained to their home countries and began to take their cases to China's courts. The earlier excerpt from Li about *guanxi* provides one perspective on the role of the courts in such matters. The example illustrates a case of piracy taken to the U.S. courts.

Demonstrating that almost anything can be pirated, enterprising Chinese opened fake Apple stores in Kumming, Chongqing, and other cities. With the popularity of Apple's iPhone and the slow pace of its opening of full-service retail outlets, pirates capitalized on the gap and began opening fake stores that were nearly identical to the real stores. When found, the police closed the stores.

In some cases the piracy appeared to be legal. For example, patents on proprietary pharmaceutical formulas can receive administrative protection in China, but first an open and lengthy public comment period was required in which drug patents were available for inspection. Chinese pharmaceutical companies could inspect the patent filings and immediately file for permission to

---

EXAMPLE   An Intellectual Property Challenge

Huawei Technologies, located in Shenzhen, was founded in 1988 and by 2004 had 22,000 employees and sales of over $4 billion. Huawei manufactured telecommunications equipment and had begun producing routers and servers. Huawei told customers that the commands for its router were similar to those for routers made by Cisco Systems, and Cisco believed that Huawei had copied its software. Cisco engineers found many lines of Huawei code identical to its code, including spelling errors and other Cisco glitches. Huawei's manual also included paragraphs copied from Cisco's manual.[1]

Cisco wrote to Huawei, which immediately withdrew its router from the U.S. market, but continued to sell it outside the United States. Cisco followed with a lawsuit alleging

copyright violation. This was the first intellectual property lawsuit ever filed by Cisco, which commented, "We don't go around suing people."[2] Huawei stated in court filings that it had copied the code but stated that it was unintentional and had not believed it was copyrighted. A federal court issued a preliminary injunction against Huawei, ordering it to stop immediately "using, importing, exporting or selling" any software system using the Cisco code. A Huawei spokesperson stated, "Before Cisco initiated its legal action against Huawei, the company had already taken good-faith, voluntary action to proactively remove from the U.S. market the obsolete products outlined in the injunction." Huawei commented that the court order was immaterial because it was unenforceable outside the United States.

---

[1]Cisco also believed that Huawei had copied source code from its network operating system.

[2]*San Jose Mercury News*, January 24, 2003.

---

[37]*Washington Post*, February 28, 2007.
[38]*New York Times*, October 5, 2000.
[39]See *BusinessWeek*, October 6, 1997, for examples.

produce and market the drug. If the application was approved before the patent received administrative protection, the local company could sell its knockoff drug. For example, a Chinese pharmaceutical company received approval to produce Eli Lilly's Prozac before the patent had been protected. The company beat Eli Lilly to market with its drug. Eli Lilly sued in court, but lost at the lower court level. The deputy director of the Chinese company said, "Eli Lilly's effort against us can't possibly lead to any positive result, as any resolution must have a legal basis. And everything we have done is in perfect conformity with the law."[40]

Pressure from other countries resulted in some progress on intellectual property protection, particularly as China prepared for entry into the WTO. Additional progress has occurred as a result of domestic rather than foreign pressure. As Chinese companies have grown and matured, many have developed their own brands and intellectual property. Between 2003 and 2007 the number of patents granted doubled, and trademark registrations increased by 60 percent. Chinese firms holding property rights faced the same piracy risks as did foreign firms, and the number of patent infringement lawsuits filed in Chinese courts has doubled over this period. The Chinese government has encouraged the press to champion the lawsuits.[41]

The Chinese government sought to acquire technologies used in electric vehicles, and used incentives to induce auto companies to transfer their technology. China provided a subsidy of up to $19,300 for the purchase of an electric vehicle, but to qualify for the subsidy, a foreign automaker had to transfer at least one of three technologies to a Chinese automaker with whom it could have a joint venture: "electric motors, complex electronic controls, and power storage devices."[42] China also required that the foreign automaker form a joint venture with a Chinese automaker to receive the technology. European and Asian automakers planned not to sell their electric vehicles there because of the required transfer. General Motors sought to sell the Volt in China and to qualify for the subsidy without a technology transfer, but it subsequently formed a joint venture with S.A.I.C. Motor and transferred some technology for batteries and inverters. GM vice-chairman said, "This is not a political decision today. It's a business decision."[43]

PRODUCT SAFETY   Several widely publicized incidents in 2007 and 2008 involving the safety of products such as children's toys, food, and pharmaceuticals drew widespread news coverage and criticism. Some consumers avoided Chinese products, and politicians called for bans on imports. The Chapter 5 case *Mattel: Crisis Management or Management Crisis* considers incidents in which lead was found in the paint on children's toys. China initially was reactive but quickly shifted to trying to correct the problems.

CORRUPTION   Transparency International ranked China tied for the 78th among 178 countries in its 2010 corruption perception index. Citizens protested the corruption, and the evident corruption reached the point at which the CCP became concerned that it could undermine confidence in the government and the party.

Corruption was present at all levels of the government. For example, farmers protested that local governments took their land for industrial development. The farmers complained that the government paid too little, promised jobs that never materialized, and sold the land at a large profit. Local governments also took independently owned oil wells and paid only a fifth the value, according to the former owners. The Chinese central government sought to stop corruption, but uprooting it proved difficult.

The government launched an anticorruption drive that resulted in the bribery conviction of the head of the State Food and Drug Administration. He was executed in 2007. Over 20 people in and connected to the Shanghai government were convicted of corruption charges, including the head of the CCP in Shanghai. China established a National Bureau of Corruption to strengthen investigation and prosecution. The Bureau decided to establish a Web site where citizens could report corruption and identify corrupt officials. The site was deluged by citizens complaining about corruption, primarily of local government officials, and praising the Bureau for its apparent willingness to combat corruption.

---

[40]*Wall Street Journal*, March 25, 1998.
[41]*Economist*, April 12, 2008.
[42]*New York Times*, September 6, 2011.
[43]*New York Times*, September 21, 2011.

The CCP's anticorruption watchdog, the Central Commission for Discipline Inspection, reported that 106,000 government officials were found guilty of corruption in 2009. The anticorruption unit planned greater scrutiny of the executives of SOEs.[44] A *China Daily* survey found that citizens viewed corruption as the country's biggest problem.

WORKERS' RIGHTS Labor unions and human rights groups have been critical of working conditions in China and other countries that produced for the developed world. Labor unions complained because China denied "freedom of association," referring to the right to form a union that is independent of the government. NGOs and rights activists pressured firms in the United States and Europe to ensure that the factories that supply their brands meet certain minimal labor standards.[45] These foreign firms have generally responded, having established codes and subjected factories to inspections. The apparel and footwear industries established the Fair Labor Association, considered in Chapter 24. Most factories in China, however, supplied the domestic market or were in industries not covered by the monitoring.

Workers in China complained of harsh working conditions, unfair dismissals, failure to make severance payments, and failure to pay overtime. In 2007, parents of 400 missing children posted a letter on an Internet site describing how they had rescued 40 children who had been kidnapped and sold as slaves to work in brick kilns in Shanxi province. Local government officials, however, prevented the families from locating more of the children. Outrage broke out in China, and the government sent 35,000 police to the area to search 7,500 workplaces. The police rescued and released nearly 1,000 workers, many of whom were dazed, bleeding, and exhausted. Pictures of the released men and boys added to the popular anger. This incident provided the final impetus for legislation to establish certain rights for workers.

The Labor Contract Law took effect in 2008 and provided for basic rights, although those rights are not as extensive as those found in Europe and the United States. The law was vigorously opposed by foreign corporations that argued that costs would rise substantially, making Chinese factories less competitive. The law went through three drafts and received 190,000 comments before being enacted.

The Labor Contract Law requires an employer to give a contract to a worker within 1 month of employment. The employer must also specify the nature of the job, working conditions, and compensation. Employees are also required to give 30 days notice if they intend to terminate employment, and the circumstances under which a worker can be let go are limited to factors such as poor performance or theft, or changing circumstances, such as the loss of a supply contract or financial distress. Severance pay is due upon termination. Employers are required to consult with the worker or a worker's representative before terminating employment. Wages must be at least the minimum wage for the municipality where the place of employment is located. One effect of the law was to give individual workers the opportunity to stand up to their employers and take unresolved disputes to the courts.

Energy and the Environment

In 2007 China surpassed the United States to become the largest emitter of CO_2. Nearly 70 percent of its energy demand was met by coal, and it has the third largest coal deposits in the world. For security purposes China has embarked on an energy conservation campaign to reduce its dependence on imported oil. In 2006 it introduced a "Save energy, cut emissions" campaign to reduce its energy use per unit of GDP by 20 percent over 5 years. The Beijing Olympics were the first to be carbon neutral.

By 2011 environmental conditions had become sufficiently bad that the government spoke openly of the problem. Premier Wen said, "We must not any longer sacrifice the environment for the sake of rapid growth and reckless rollouts, as that would result in unsustainable growth featuring industrial overcapacity and intensive resource consumption."[46] Environmental minister Zhou Shengxian warned, "In China's thousands of years of civilization, the conflict between humankind and nature has never been as serious as it is today. The depletion, deterioration, and exhaustion of resources and the worsening ecological environment have become bottlenecks and

---

[44]BBC News, January 8, 2010.

[45]See the Chapter 4 case *Nike in Southeast Asia*.

[46]*New York Times*, March 1, 2011.

grave impediments to the nation's economic and social development."[47] The government reported closing 2,000 plants because of their energy inefficiency. The government objective was to reduce its CO_2 emissions per unit of GDP, so as not to limit economic growth. The government established a goal of reducing CO_2 emissions per unit of GDP by 40–45 percent by 2020. Renewable energy was supported by the government and accounted for 9.9 percent of energy consumption in 2009.[48]

China is not covered by the Kyoto Protocol, which expired at the end of 2012, but it will be expected to participate in any post-Kyoto agreement. China has been a major beneficiary of the Kyoto Protocol because of the Clean Development Mechanism, or Kyoto mechanism, under which countries can invest in carbon reduction projects in developing countries in lieu of making reductions at home. As of 2008, China had received $5.4 billion, or nearly three-quarters of the total, mostly from European countries.[49]

China's principal environmental concerns have not been global warming but rather domestic pollution, including acid rain from burning coal to generate electricity. In advance of the Olympics China announced some progress in reducing pollutants. Scrubbers installed at coal-fired power plants helped reduce sulfur dioxide emissions by over 4 percent, and industries reduced their solid waste discharges by 8 percent. Emissions of organic pollutants into waterways were reduced by over 3 percent. Despite the progress on these dimensions SEPA reported that overall pollution in the country increased. After detecting unhealthy levels of lead in several children, the Shanghai government suspended operation of 14 plants using lead. Earlier lead was found in the paint on toys exported from China, as considered in the Chapter 5 case *Mattel: Crisis Management or Management Crisis.*

An emerging phenomenon in China was citizen protests against planned construction projects. Using the Internet and cell phones for coordination, middle-class citizens protested the construction of a $5.5 billion ethanol plant in Sichuan province. Thousands of protesters had shut down the construction of a chemical plant in Fujian province, and protesters in Shanghai had stopped the extension of a rail line. The protesters complained that the projects were too close to population centers and the environmental reviews of the projects were inadequate. The protests were covered by the news media. In 2011, nearly 12,000 protesters in Dailan marched on the city government offices demanding that a 2-year-old petrochemical plant be closed after a tropical storm had damaged a dyke around the plant. Rather than suppressing the protests, the government responded by ordering the plant to close.

Although the Chinese government was wary of collective action and protests that could develop widespread support, NGOs have been established and private politics was emerging. NGOs from outside China added to the private politics. In July 2011, the U.S.-based China Labor Watch charged that the largest electronics technology companies, including Apple, had created "electronic sweatshops" in China and shared responsibilities for a series of worker suicides, including 12 at Foxconn, the world's largest supplier of electronics. Apple had revealed in its annual responsibility report that child labor had increased at its suppliers' factories.[50] In September 2011, Greenpeace alleged that millions of tons of hazardous waste threatened Chinese citizens. Greenpeace pointed to the dumping of chromium waste in Qujing in Yunnan province and warned that the pollution could spread to rivers.[51] The chapter case *Apple and Private Politics in China* concerns a challenge to Apple posed by environmental NGOs.

SUMMARY

China provides tremendous business opportunities yet poses a host of challenges, particularly in the nonmarket environment. China has no democratic tradition, and its Confucian heritage provides a degree of deference for hierarchical authority. It also has a long history as a unified nation and a willingness to assert and defend its independence. China has been building a modern economy with less dependence on foreign direct investment, yet with 1.3 billion people it faces a considerable challenge

---

[47]Ibid.
[48]*China Daily,* January 28, 2010.
[49]*Economist,* June 7, 2008.
[50]*Daily Telegraph,* July 22, 2011.
[51]*Straits Times,* September 2, 2011.

to create jobs and provide social services. Economic progress enabled people to have better control over their lives and generated pressure for political and economic liberalization. The Chinese Communist Party, however, continued to dominate government at every level. Political competition was not tolerated, and human rights were restricted. The government was concerned about problems such as the environment that were of increasing concern to citizens. The government was also sensitive to the possibility of popular dissent arising from economic dislocations and dissatisfaction with government performance, as in the case of corruption. Despite the limitations on rights, Chinese citizens enjoyed greater liberty than at any time in the postwar period.

The nonmarket environment was important not only because of the government and party involvement in business but also because of issues pertaining to human rights, intellectual property, and the natural environment. The nonmarket environment was structured by the hierarchical nature of government that persisted despite the devolution of authority to provincial and local governments. Since the government was not checked by opposition parties, elections, or organized interest or activist groups, some policies could be changed quickly, as in the case of environmental policy and the Labor Contract Law. The judicial system in China did not provide the protection available in other countries, but citizens were increasingly turning to the courts to resolve disputes and enforce rights. The capabilities of the judicial system had improved.

The importance of *guanxi* networks, not only between companies but also between business and government, complicated strategies of those companies new to China. Joint ventures with domestic companies, most of which were enterprises owned by national, provincial, or local government units, could also provide the *guanxi* networks and access needed to address nonmarket issues. Joint ventures, however, posed their own set of problems, which led most foreign entrants to China to establish wholly owned subsidiaries.

CASES

Apple and Private Politics in China

Apple had revolutionized mobile communications with its iPhone, iPod, and iPad, and its product introductions were closely-guarded secrets. The company also held information on its operations close to its vest. Apple provided on its website an "Apple and the Environment" section with information on products and its environmental footprint. The section also included a report on supplier compliance with Apple's policies and workplace standards, including summaries of steps taken as a result of its supplier audits. In contrast to Nike, however, Apple did not release the audit reports or identify its suppliers. This made it a target for environmental activists in China.

The Beijing-based Institute of Public & Environmental Affairs issued a 46-page report entitled "The Other Side of Apple II" that focused on Apple's Chinese suppliers that it cited for discharging hazardous materials into the environment. The report said that Apple was "'stubbornly evasive' and its refusal to discuss suppliers 'can only be seen as a deliberate refusal of responsibility' for environmental issues."[52] The Institute had released a report earlier in the year to which Apple had not responded, which resulted in the Institute focusing on Apple. Ma Jun, director and founder of the Institute, said, "Apple has made this commitment that it's a green company. So how do you fulfill your commitment if you don't consider you have responsibility in your suppliers' pollution."[53] "Mr. Ma said the IPE focused its latest report on Apple because other technology companies have been willing to discuss their

suppliers with the IPE, while Apple hasn't."[54] He said, "The company refuses to make the identities of suppliers public and to fulfill its responsibility to disclose information about the environmental effects of suppliers' actions."[55]

The report was based on inspections of 22 factories believed to be Apple suppliers. Some information was also obtained from people living near the factories. Li Chunhua of the environmental group Green Stone, who had inspected the Kaedar Electronics (Kunshan) Co. Ltd. factory and had interviewed local residents, said, "Only about 50 people live in the village [Tongxin], and nine of them have had cancer."[56] The report named seven factories supplying Apple and identified specific problems primarily concerning the disposal of hazardous materials including copper, cyanide, and nickel. The Institute also released videos posted on a video sharing website of pollution at "suspected" Apple suppliers. The report contained maps of suspected and confirmed suppliers and photos of environmental damage. Ma said, "We believe Apple customers cannot accept the fact that these faddish gadgets are made at the cost of poisoning the environment, harming communities, and sacrificing employees' rights."[57]

Apple spokesperson Carolyn Wu responded to the report stating that the company "is committed to driving the highest standards of social responsibility throughout our supply

---

[52]*Wall Street Journal*, September 1, 2011.
[53]*New York Times*, September 2, 2011.

[54]*Wall Street Journal*, September 1, 2011.
[55]Chinadaily.com.cn, September 1, 2011.
[56]Ibid.
[57]Ibid.

base."[58] Apple's Steve Dowling said, "We require that our suppliers provide safe working conditions, treat workers with dignity and respect, and use environmentally responsible manufacturing processes wherever Apple products are made."[59] Apple responded to the Institute by letter and said that it took the report seriously but that there were inaccuracies in it. The company asked for a "private conference call" with the Institute and the other sponsors of the report.

One of the plants identified as an Apple supplier was Unimicron (Kunshan) near Shanghai, where the report said the residents faced toxic wastes and noxious odors. Mr. Wang of the Kunshan local government said, "It's true that it smells here, but the level of pollution is actually better than national standards. But when the wind blows, the smell is just unavoidable."[60]

Pollution and the disposal of toxic wastes were regulated by the government, but Mr. Ma said, "The costs of flouting a regulation are lower than following it."[61] ■

Preparation Questions

1. What should Apple do about the Institute report? Does this have the potential to turn into a crisis?
2. How much responsibility should Apple assume regarding its suppliers?
3. Should Apple disclose the names and locations of its suppliers? Why or why not?
4. What effect might the report have on Apple's market in China? In the United States?
5. Formulate a strategy for dealing with this issue.

Direct Selling in China

With over 1.2 billion people China represented an extremely attractive market for direct sellers such as Amway, Avon Products, Mary Kay Cosmetics, Sara Lee, and Tupperware. Also, in the 1990s the restructuring of state-owned enterprises had reduced workforces, providing an ample supply of people interested in becoming direct sellers, many of whom made door-to-door sales calls. With the Asian and Russian financial crises beginning in 1997 the supply of potential direct sales personnel increased further. In 1995 Amway opened a factory in Guangzhou and began sales in China. By 1997 it had 70,000 independent sales agents in China producing revenue of $178 million.[62] Avon's revenue in China was $75 million.

Companies such as Amway and Avon operated by enlisting independent sales agents who bought product from the company and sold it door-to-door. Amway used its standard business model in China with the exception that all other markets were supplied from U.S. plants. Its sales agents were compensated by their own sales and also were paid for the number of new sales agents they recruited. They also received a commission on the sales of those they recruited as well as those their recruits recruited. The companies operated distribution centers and provided training for their sales agents in both sales techniques and in the company's culture, which emphasized empowerment. Amway had a policy of buying back all unsold product, providing a full refund.

The success of U.S. direct sales companies led to a boom in home-grown direct sales companies selling everything from foot massagers to water beds to elixirs. By 1998 some 20 million Chinese were estimated to be working in direct selling.[63] It was said that 50,000 people had come to Wuhan seeking jobs selling Xingtian Company's foot massaging machine. Some of these companies operated pyramid and Ponzi schemes in which they profited by recruiting sellers and selling them products rather than making sure that products were being purchased by consumers. Other companies duped unsuspecting consumers. In a front-page article the *China Daily* said that these companies "have been behaving badly, getting involved in underworld crimes and preying on innocent people through their superstitions."

On April 21, 1998, the State Council published a directive banning all direct sales in the country. The directive stated, "Criminals have used direct selling to set up sects and cults, spread superstition and carry out illegal activities, affecting the country's social stability." The directive expressed concern about the massive sales meetings of direct sellers in which they clapped and chanted to build enthusiasm. The directive also stated that direct selling had attracted people, including teachers, members of the military, and officials of the Chinese Communist Party, who were legally prohibited from such sales activity. The *People's Daily*, the official newspaper of the Chinese Communist Party, justified the State Council's decision: "Due to immature market conditions, inadequate legislation and immature consumer psychology, direct sales have proved unsuitable for China and thus must be resolutely banned." The newspaper also referred to "excessive hugging" at the mass sales meetings held by the direct selling companies.

The State Administration for Industry and Commerce, which was responsible for the distribution industry, asked local officials to enforce the ban and avoid civil disorder. Its director Wang Zhongfu said, "It's necessary to stop the operation of pyramid sales since it has begun to hurt social stability and economic development."[64] Government officials said that if the

---

[58]*Wall Street Journal*, September 1, 2011.
[59]*New York Times*, September 2, 2011.
[60]*San Jose Mercury News*, September 2, 2011.
[61]*Straits Times*, September 2, 2011.
[62]Amway had 667,000 independent sales representatives worldwide.

[63]In the United States 8.5 million people were engaged in direct selling.
[64]China Business Information Network, May 12, 1998.

U.S. direct selling companies established normal retail shops they could stay.

This was not the first time China had addressed direct selling. In 1995 it had suspended all direct sales activity for several months over concerns about the "revival meeting atmosphere" used by some of the companies. Avon was forced to change its credo from "God first" to "Faith first."

Once the State Council had banned direct selling, many independent sales representatives were left with goods they could not sell. Protests occurred when they were unable to obtain refunds from companies. According to press reports, 10,000 disgruntled door-to-door salesmen came to the town of Zhangjiajie seeking refunds from a company that made foot massagers, but it had closed its doors. "'It has left me worse than bankrupt,' says Chen, an unemployed steelworker, who has been left with 60 mechanized foot massagers and, now barred from selling them, losses of roughly $4,830."[65] Riots broke out leaving four people dead and 100 injured.

The directive issued by the State Council came as U.S. Trade Representative Charlene Barshefsky was in Beijing making preparations for President Bill Clinton's upcoming state visit. In a news conference in Beijing she stated, "The ban has effectively shut down the legitimate operations of these and other U.S. companies in China. These companies have invested over $120 million in China and provide income to more than 2 million Chinese." She added, "It is a serious matter when the [Chinese] government simply bans the legitimate business of foreign-invested companies ... [the ban] goes well beyond China's legitimate need to pursue consumer protection." Wu Yi, China's minister for trade and foreign investment, told her that in addition to consumer protection concerns the direct selling companies were breaking the rule requiring them to sell only goods manufactured in China.

Steve Van Andel, chairman of Amway Asia Pacific, said, "We understand and respect the Chinese government's decision to take additional steps to protect consumers from illegal scams, which have become a more serious social problem in recent months .... We have invested over $100 million in China over the past 5 years and we continue to believe in the long-term business opportunities of this enormous market .... While management of Amway China has established strong government relations and is hopeful that discussions with government officials will be successful, it is too early to project the short-term and long-term impact of the directive on our business."[66] Amway and other direct sellers began to evaluate alternatives for restructuring the way they conducted their sales activities.

Richard Holwill, Amway's director of international relations, said, "We're frustrated that this sledgehammer approach gets rid of ours as well as the ones they're really trying to get rid of. 'Shut it down and sort it out later' seems to be the attitude."[67] Holwill also stated, "We don't want to be part of the problem, we want to be part of the solution."

Holwill served as co-chairman of the Asia Task Force of the U.S. Chamber of Commerce and discussed the ban in testimony before the House Ways and Means Committee in June during hearings on renewal of most favored nation status for China. China was also in the process of negotiating entry into the World Trade Organization (WTO). This involved negotiations with the European Union and the United States regarding specific reforms and market openings in China. ■

Preparation Questions

1. Why did China ban direct selling?
2. How might the U.S. direct sales companies restructure their sales activities to satisfy the concerns of the Chinese government? Should they establish retail stores?
3. Should U.S. direct marketers form a coalition or act independently to address this challenge?
4. Should the U.S. companies attempt to enlist the aid of the U.S. government?
5. What nonmarket strategy should the U.S. direct sellers in China adopt?

Source: This case was written by Professor David P. Baron. Copyright © 1998 by the Board of Trustees of the Leland Stanford Junior University. All rights reserved. Reproduced with permission.

Google in China

It's an imperfect world, we had to make an imperfect choice.

—Elliot Schrage, Google vice president
for global communications and public affairs

INTRODUCTION

Using servers located in the United States, Google began offering a Chinese-language version of Google.com in 2000. The site, however, was frequently unavailable or slow because of censoring by the Chinese government. Google obtained a significant share of searches in China but lagged behind market leader Baidu.com. To achieve commercial success, Google concluded that it was imperative to host a Web site from within China. Given its motto, "Don't Be Evil," Google had to decide whether to operate from within China or to continue to rely on Google.com. If it decided to establish operations in China, the company had to decide how to deal with the censorship imposed by the Chinese government.

As a result of an extensive debate within the company, cofounder Serge Brin explained their decision: "We gradually came to the realization that we were hurting not just ourselves but the Chinese people."[68] Google decided to establish the site Google.cn, but without features that allowed users to provide content. To avoid putting individuals in jeopardy of being

---

[65] *Financial Times*, May 5, 1998.

[66] Amway press release, April 21, 1998.
[67] *Los Angeles Times*, April 24, 1998.
[68] *San Jose Mercury News*, March 3, 2006.

arrested, Google offered neither e-mail nor the ability to create blogs, since user-generated material could be seized by the Chinese government. This allowed Google to avoid putting individuals in jeopardy of being arrested. Because Google would be required by Chinese law to censor search results associated with sensitive issues, it decided to place a brief notice at the bottom of a search page when material had been censored, as it did in other countries such as France and Germany which banned the sale of Nazi items. Google planned to exercise self-censorship and developed a list of sensitive items by consulting with third parties and by studying the results of the Chinese government's Internet filtering. Senior policy counsel Andrew McLaughlin stated, "Google is mindful that governments around the world impose restriction on access to information. In order to operate from China, we have removed some content from the search results available on Google.cn, in response to local law, regulation or policy. While removing search results is inconsistent with Google's mission, providing no information (or a heavily degraded user experience that amounts to no information) is more inconsistent with our mission."[69]

Google's approach to entering China irritated the Chinese government. Within a month of offering Google.cn, Google was criticized by two government-run newspapers in China. The *Beijing News* criticized the company for not doing enough to block "harmful information." Referring to Google's practice of informing users when search results had been censored, the *China Business Times* wrote in an editorial, "Is it necessary for an enterprise that is operating within the borders of China to constantly tell your customers you are following domestic law?" Both publications claimed that Google was operating as an Internet content provider without a proper license.[70]

Reporters Without Borders, a Paris-based organization campaigning for freedom of expression, called the establishment of Google.cn "a black day for freedom of expression in China." It stated:

> The firm defends the rights of U.S. Internet users before the U.S. government, but fails to defend its Chinese users against theirs. United States companies are now bending to the same censorship rules as their Chinese competitors, but they continue to justify themselves by saying their presence has a long-term benefit. Yet the Internet in China is becoming more and more isolated from the outside world.[71]

Other activists demanded that Google publish its censorship blacklist in the United States.

Internet Censorship in China

According to the U.S. State Department, companies offering Internet services were "pressured to sign the Chinese government's 'Public Pledge on Self-Discipline for the Chinese Internet Industry.'" Under the agreement, they promised not to disseminate information that "breaks laws or spreads superstition or obscenity" or that "may jeopardize state security and disrupt social stability."[72] Providing Internet services required a license, which in turn required not circulating information that "damages the honor or interests of the state" or "disturbs the public order or destroys public stability …"[73]

Censorship in China involved self-regulation by Internet companies as well as government actions. The government did not provide a list of objectionable subjects—instead companies inferred which topics were out of bounds by observing what the government censors removed. The State Council Information Office also convened weekly meetings with Internet service providers. An American executive explained, "It's known informally as the 'wind-blowing meeting'—in other words, which way is the wind blowing. They say: 'There's this party conference going on this week. There are some foreign dignitaries here on this trip.'"[74] Xin Ye, a founder of Sohu.com, a Chinese value-added Internet services firm, was asked how hard it was to navigate the censorship system. He said, "I'll tell you this, it's not more hard than dealing with Sarbanes and Oxley."[75]

Zhao Jing, a political blogger in China, "explained that he knew where the government drew the line. 'If you talk every day online and criticize the government, they don't care. Because it's just talk. But if you organize—even if it's just three or four people—that's what they crack down on. It's not speech; it's organizing.'"[76] In December 2005 Zhao called for a boycott of a newspaper because it had fired an editor. In response, the Chinese government asked Microsoft's MSN to close Zhao's blog and Microsoft complied.[77] Brooke Richardson of MSN said, "We only remove content if the order comes from the appropriate regulatory authority."[78]

Yahoo! and MSN, as well as other sites, complied with Chinese law as well as exercising self-censorship.[79] Robin Li, chairman of the Chinese search company Baidu.com, said, "We are trying to provide as much information as possible. But we need to obey Chinese law."[80] Baidu had reached an agreement that allowed the Chinese government to oversee its Web site and in exchange it avoided the disruptions of service and strict operating rules that plagued foreign Internet companies.[81]

In 2004 Yahoo! provided information to the Chinese government that led to the arrest of the journalist Shi Tao. Shi

---

[69]*New York Times*, January 25, 2006.

[70]*Washington Post*, February 22, 2006. Google shared a license with a Chinese company, Ganji.com. This practice was common among foreign Internet firms.

[71]*New York Times*, January 25, 2006, op. cit.

[72]*Business Week*, January 23, 2006.

[73]Clive Thompson, "Google's China Problem (and China's Google Problem)," *New York Times Magazine*, April 23, 2006.

[74]Ibid.

[75]Ibid.

[76]Ibid.

[77]Microsoft's blogging servers were located in the United States. Clive Thompson, "Google's China Problem (and China's Google Problem)," *New York Times Magazine*, April 23, 2006.

[78]*BusinessWeek*, January 23, 2006, op. cit.

[79]Yahoo! lagged behind other Internet companies in China and in 2005 invested $1 billion for a 40 percent interest in the Chinese company Alibaba.com. Yahoo! then turned operating control of Yahoo! China over to Alibaba.com.

[80]*BusinessWeek*, January 23, 2006, op. cit. Baidu had a 46.5 percent share of Internet searches in China; Google was second with 26.9 percent. Google had a small stake in Baidu but sold it in June 2006.

[81]*New York Times*, September 17, 2006.

was subsequently sentenced to 10 years in prison for releasing state secrets on a foreign Web site. Shi had provided information by e-mail about a Communist party decision. Yahoo! general counsel Michael Callahan said the company regretted that action but had no alternative, since its Chinese employees could have been arrested on criminal charges for not providing the information to the government. Callahan also said that Chinese law prohibited disclosing how many times the company had provided information on users to the government.[82]

The agencies that regulated the Internet employed 30,000 people who monitored e-mail, Web sites, blogs, and chat rooms. Internet cafes were required to use software that stored data on all users. Anyone establishing a blog was required to register with the government. Telephone companies were required to incorporate software that censored text messaging.

A key part of the censorship system was the control by the government of all gateways into China. This allowed the censors to block undesired content on Web sites and restrict Internet search results. Referred to as the Great Firewall of China, routers at China's nine Internet gateways examined messages and search requests and were programmed to block or censor information. It was this firewall that made accessing Google.com slow or at times unavailable from China.

China also blocked certain news sites including the BBC News, Voice of America, Amnesty International, Human Rights in China, and Wikipedia, in addition to any information on the spiritual movement Falun Gong, which was banned in China. Search results on terms such as "Tiananmen Massacre," "Tibet," and "Dalai Lama" were also suppressed.

Censorship was also practiced elsewhere, including at universities. University computer systems and bulletin boards banned certain subjects such as politics, and student monitors directed chatroom conversations away from sensitive subjects to those that helped build a "harmonious society." Student monitor Hu Yingying said, "We don't control things, but we don't want bad or wrong things to appear on the Web sites. According to our social and educational systems, we should judge what is right and wrong. And as I'm a student cadre, I need to play a pioneering role among other students, to express my opinion, to make stronger my belief in Communism." Another student, Tang Guochao, said, "A bulletin board is like a family, and in a family, I want my room to be clean and well lighted, without dirty or dangerous things in it."[83]

The censorship system was in a technology race with those attempting to evade it. Bill Xia, who arrived in the United States as a student in the 1990s and subsequently founded Dynamic Internet Technology (DIT), developed software called FreeGate that masked the Web sites that users visit.[84] Companies such as DIT and UltraReach also used software to create new Web sites to elude the Chinese censors.[85] For Voice of America, for example, DIT established uncensored proxy sites that directed users to the real site. DIT and UltraReach sent millions of e-mails a day alerting users to the uncensored sites. The Chinese censors worked to shut down the proxy sites and were often able to close the sites within a few days. The companies then would develop new software to evade the censors.

The Chinese government sought to justify its practices. Liu Zhengrong, deputy director of the State Council Information Office's Internet Affairs Bureau, argued that China's efforts to keep out "harmful" and "illegal" information were similar to those in Western countries. He said, "If you study the main international practices in this regard you will find that China is basically in compliance. The main purposes and methods of implementing our laws are basically the same."[86] He observed that the *New York Times* and *Washington Post* Web sites deleted content that was illegal or in bad taste. He added, "Our practices are completely consistent with international practices." He continued, "Many of our practices we got from studying the U.S. experience."[87] He noted, "It is clear that any country's legal authorities closely monitor the spread of illegal information. We have noted that the U.S. is doing a good job on this front."[88]

Liu commented, "No one in China has been arrested simply because he or she said something on the Internet."[89] Reporters Without Borders claimed that 62 Chinese were in prison for "Posting on the Internet articles and criticism of the authorities."[90]

Despite the international criticism of Internet censorship in China, it was not clear that the Chinese people were concerned. Kai-Fu Lee, who headed operations for Google in China said, "People are actually quite free to talk about [democracy and human rights in China]. I don't think they care that much. I think people would say: 'Hey, U.S. democracy, *that's* a good form of government. Chinese government, good and stable, *that's* a good form of government. Whatever, as long as I get to go to my favorite Web site, see my friends, live happily.'"[91]

Ji Xiaoyin, a junior at Shanghai Normal University, commented, "I don't think anybody can possibly control any information in the Internet. If you're not allowed to talk here you just go to another place to talk, and there are countless places for your opinions. It's easy to bypass the firewalls, and anybody who spends a little time researching it can figure it out."[92]

Google's Perspective

In response to criticism that Google should lobby the Chinese government to change its censorship system, CEO Eric E. Schmidt said during a visit to China, "I think it's arrogant for us to walk into a country where we are just beginning operations and tell that country how to run itself." He also explained, "We had a choice to enter the country and follow the law. Or we had

---

[82]*San Jose Mercury News*, February 20, 2006.

[83]*New York Times*, May 9, 2006.

[84]Human Rights in China and Radio Free Asia were also DIT clients.

[85]Both DIT and UltraReach were said to be connected to the Falun Gong movement. *San Jose Mercury News*, July 2, 2006.

[86]*New York Times*, February, 15, 2006.

[87]*Wall Street Journal*, February 15, 2006.

[88]*New York Times*, February 15, 2006, op. cit.

[89]*San Jose Mercury News*, February 20, 2006, op. cit.

[90]*San Jose Mercury News*, July 2, 2006.

[91]Clive Thompson, op. cit.

[92]*New York Times*, May 9, 2006, op. cit.

a choice not to enter the country." Earlier he had said, "We believe the decision that we made to follow the law in China was absolutely the right one."[93]

Speaking at an ethics conference on Internet search at Santa Clara University, Peter Norvig, director of research at Google, commented on the decision not to offer services such as e-mail and blogging in China. "We didn't want to be in a position to hand over users' information .... We thought that was just too dangerous .... We thought it was very important to keep our users out of jail."[94]

Norvig justified Google's policies in China. "Yes, it's important to get information about democracy and Falun Gong. They also want to know about outbreaks of bird flu. We thought it was more important to give them this information that they can use even if we have to compromise."[95]

Google continued to debate internally whether and how it should operate in China. It also hoped for guidance from the U.S. government and the industry. Norvig said, "We feel that the U.S. government can stand up and make stronger laws, and we feel that corporate America can get together and have stronger principles. We're supporting efforts on both those fronts. We feel we can't do it alone."[96]

Norvig disclosed that Google was not keeping search logs in China. "They don't have personally identifiable information but they do have IP addresses that are potentially identifiable with an individual."[97] That information was kept in the United States, and China could request that information through the U.S. State Department.

Political Pressure in the United States

In advance of congressional hearings on China and censorship, the State Department announced the creation of a Global Internet Task Force to decrease censorship and encourage change in other countries. Paula Dobriansky, undersecretary of state for democracy, human rights, and labor, said, "The Internet, especially, can be a liberating force. Topics once politically taboo can become freely discussed, and people can communicate anonymously. We must ensure it does not become a tool of repression."[98]

Representative Chris Smith (R-NJ), chairman of the House Subcommittee on Africa, Global Human Rights, and International Operations, introduced the Global Internet Freedom Act that would impose restrictions on U.S. companies operating in China. It included a code of conduct, requiring that e-mail servers be located outside the country and licensing requirements for the export of technologies that could be used for censorship. Smith held a hearing in which Cisco Systems, Google, Microsoft, and Yahoo! testified and were grilled by subcommittee members. Commenting on China's sophisticated censorship system, Smith said, "It's an active partnership with both the disinformation campaign and ..., and the secret police

in China are among the most brutal on the planet. I don't know if these companies understand that or they're naïve about it, whether they're witting or unwitting. But it's been a tragic collaboration. There are people in China being tortured courtesy of these corporations."[99] The bill was passed by the subcommittee and sent to full committee for consideration.

Representative Tom Lantos (D-CA), leader of the Congressional Human Rights Caucus and a survivor of the Holocaust, said, "These captains of industry should have been developing new technologies to bypass the sickening censorship of government and repugnant barriers to the Internet. Instead, they enthusiastically volunteered for the censorship brigade."[100]

In congressional testimony Elliot Schrage, vice president of global communications and public affairs at Google, explained that China was an important market for the company. He said, "It would be disingenuous to say that we don't care about that because, of course, we do. We are a business with stockholders, and we want to prosper and grow in a highly competitive world. At the same time, acting ethically is a core value for our company, and an integral part of our business culture."[101]

Earlier in 2006 Google had refused to comply with a request from the U.S. government to provide information on Internet search requests.[102] The government had asked Google for a random sample of 1 million Web addresses and a week's search requests with any information that could identify the user removed. The information was to be used for a study to show that Internet filters were not sufficient to prevent children from accessing pornographic Web sites. The Department of Justice sought the information to help revive the 1998 Child Online Protection Act, which had been blocked by the Supreme Court and sent to the Court of Appeals for reconsideration. Google strongly objected to the request on privacy grounds and refused to provide the information. The Department of Justice then took Google to court to force it to provide the information. In the court hearing the government substantially scaled back its request, and the judge ordered Google to provide 50,000 random Web addresses. The judge also stated that providing the requested 50,000 random search queries could harm Google through a loss of goodwill among its users.[103]

In June Brin commented on the criticism Google had received. He said, "We felt that perhaps we could compromise our principles but provide ultimately more information for the Chinese and be a more effective service and perhaps make more of a difference .... Perhaps now the principled approach makes more sense."[104]

In July Amnesty International launched a campaign against Internet oppression, mentioning Sun Microsystems, Nortel, Cisco, Yahoo!, Google, and Microsoft. Amnesty

[93]*New York Times*, April 13, 2006.

[94]*San Jose Mercury News*, March 1, 2006, and March 3, 2006, op. cit.

[95]*San Jose Mercury News*, March 1, 2006, op. cit.

[96]Ibid.

[97]*San Jose Mercury News*, March 3, 2006, op. cit.

[98]*San Jose Mercury News*, February 15, 2006, op. cit.

[99]Ibid.

[100]*San Jose Mercury News*, February 19, 2006.

[101]*Wall Street Journal*, March 10, 2006.

[102]The government also sought similar data from AOL, Microsoft's MSN, and Yahoo!, all of which complied with the request.

[103]The judge also stated that the search queries could be within the scope of a subpoena. *San Francisco Chronicle*, March 18, 2006.

[104]*San Jose Mercury News*, June 7, 2006.

International stated, "Internet companies often claim to be ethically responsible—these pledges will highlight how their cooperation in repression risks making them complicit in human rights abuses and damages their credibility."[105] ▥

Preparation Questions

1. What principles are relevant for Google's decision to enter China? Is censorship consistent with Google's core values? Should compromises be made?

2. Why does the Chinese government censor information so aggressively?

3. Should Google have entered China?

4. Given that Google decided to enter China, should it have offered e-mail and hosted blogs? Should it have restricted its offerings more than it actually did?

5. Are Google's practices sufficient? What else should it do?

6. Should Google lobby the Chinese government to change its censorship policies?

7. Should Google lobby the U.S. government to develop a policy to guide U.S. Internet companies in China?

Source: This case was prepared from public sources by Professor David P. Baron. Copyright © 2006 by the Board of Trustees of the Leland Stanford Junior University. All rights reserved. Reprinted with permission.

---

[105]Amnesty International, press release, July 20, 2006, www.amnesty.org.

17 EMERGING MARKETS

INTRODUCTION

Eighty percent of the world's population lives in emerging markets countries, and 90 percent of the world's population growth will be in these countries over the next 30 years. Per capita income is growing rapidly in the BRIC countries (Brazil, Russia, India, and China) and in other countries with relatively open economies. Opportunities in many emerging market countries are very attractive to firms, and foreign direct investment has flowed to the relatively stable and lower-risk countries.

Yet more than half the people in the world still live on less than $2 a day. The informal sector plays an important role in many of these countries with estimates of over 40 percent of GDP accounted for by the informal sectors in Africa and Latin America. More than half the people live in nondemocratic countries, and some democratic countries are at risk of a military coup. Four coups occurred in Africa during 2008–2010. Corruption plagues many emerging markets countries, and the rule of law is unevenly enforced. Refugees flow across borders in Africa, and civil wars rage in a number of countries. Cultural, ethnic, and religious conflict is present in many of these countries. Risk often accompanies opportunity. Changes can occur rapidly in emerging markets countries, and at times the change can be abrupt, as in the "Arab Spring" in 2011.

Countries are distinctive, so making generalizations is difficult. Moreover, the principles of nonmarket strategy for operating in democracies cannot simply be transported to emerging markets, particularly for countries that are not democratic and where the rule of law is weak. This chapter focuses on opportunities in emerging market countries and on the risks present in those countries that are not present in the established democracies of the developed world. The next section identifies sources of information available for evaluating a country, and the following sections address opportunities and risks. Nonmarket strategies for emerging markets are then considered. The political economy of China is considered in Chapter 16, and the political economy of India is the subject of Chapter 18.

COUNTRY ASSESSMENT

Opportunities for successful participation in an emerging markets economy depend not only on the characteristics of the particular markets in which a firm participates but also on the characteristics of the country. The market environment may be different from that of the company's home country, and the nonmarket environment can be even more different. Just as a company entering an emerging markets economy will study in detail the demand and supply relations in the market, investigate the competitiveness of incumbent companies, and assess the labor market, the company also needs to study the nonmarket environment. This includes understanding the government and its role in the market and nonmarket environments, the impact of corruption, divisions within the populace, freedoms, and risks associated with both the government and its policies.

Ian Brenner (2005), president of the Eurasia Group, defined an emerging markets country as "a country where politics matters at least as much as economics to the market." The importance of market and nonmarket forces is indicated by the variety of assessment measures developed for countries and the growth of political risk consultancies. This section identifies several indexes relevant to assessing conditions in a country. These indexes should not be viewed as conclusions about a country but instead should be viewed as identifying possible concerns that warrant further investigation.

Individual Freedoms

Freedom House, an independent, nonpartisan organization founded in 1941, supports the expansion of freedom in the world. The organization annually publishes an evaluation of the following freedoms for countries around the world: Political Rights with components Electoral Process, Political Pluralism and Participation, and the Functioning of Government and Civil Liberties with components Freedom of Expression and Belief, Associational and Organizational Rights, Rule of Law, and Personal Autonomy and Individual Rights. Freedom House also provides a Freedom of the Press index.

Economic Freedom

Recognizing the relationship between economic prosperity and economic freedoms, the Heritage Foundation and the *Wall Street Journal* annually publish an Index of Economic Freedom based on 10 freedoms: business freedom, trade freedom, fiscal freedom, government size, monetary freedom, investment freedom, financial freedom, property rights, freedom from corruption, and labor freedom. The creators of the Index stated, "A systematic analysis of the 10 freedoms has demonstrated again this year that economic freedom is the key to creating an environment that allows a virtuous cycle of entrepreneurship, innovation, and sustained economic growth and development to flourish."[1] The 2011 Index covered 179 countries, with Hong Kong and Singapore having the highest scores and Cuba, Zimbabwe, and North Korea having the lowest.

Corruption

Corruption has a corrosive effect on a country and its people. It favors those in positions of influence and with resources to pay bribes and extend favors. It distorts economic activity and can substantially reduce GDP. A number of countries have hired private companies to run their ports so as to reduce corruption. Corruption is typically hard to observe, difficult to measure, and hard to eradicate. Several measures of the extent of corruption in a country are available, perhaps the best known of which is Transparency International's Corruption Perceptions Index (CPI).

Concerned by what he had observed from his position in the World Bank, Peter Eiger founded Transparency International (TI) in Berlin in 1993 as an NGO to lead in the curtailment of corruption.[2] In his introduction to TI's "Global Corruption Report 2001" he wrote:

> Corruption respects no national boundaries. It deepens poverty around the globe by distorting political, economic, and social life. Transparency International (TI) was born from the experience of people who witnessed first hand the real threat to human lives posed by corruption—and from its founders' frustration that nobody wanted to talk about it.

The instrument for TI's attack on corruption was the construction of a corruption index as a way of calling attention to the issue and putting pressure on countries. The CPI pertains to the corruption in a country or the demand side of corruption and is based on surveys asking people about their perceptions of corruption in a country.[3] For 2010 Denmark, New Zealand, Singapore, and Finland headed the list, and Afghanistan, Myanmar, and Somalia were at the bottom of 180 countries.

Ease of Doing Business

The World Bank provides an evaluation of the Ease of Doing Business in a country, which reflects the bureaucratic, regulatory, and administrative barriers a company can face. The evaluation is based on nine factors, including starting a business, dealing with construction permits, registering property, and enforcing contracts. The 2010 survey ranked Singapore and Hong Kong at the top and Burundi, Central African Republic, and Chad at the bottom of 183 countries.

Competitiveness

IMD Switzerland conducts an assessment of the competitiveness of 59 countries covering economic performance, government efficiency, business efficiency, and infrastructure. For 2011 the leaders in overall competitiveness were Hong Kong and the United States followed

---

[1]2008 Index of Economic Freedom, "Executive Summary," p. 2.

[2]Transparency International has chapters in 85 countries.

[3]According to its chairman, "Transparency International is not saying in this index that one country is more corrupt than another. We are reporting how business people, political analysts, and the general public around the globe perceive levels of corruption in different countries."

by Singapore, and Venezuela was last. The United States was first in economic performance and infrastructure, whereas Hong Kong and Singapore were first in government and business efficiency.

Political Risk

A number of consultancies, such as Country Watch, Euromoney Country Risk, Eurasia Group, PRS Group, and Continuity Central, provide detailed assessments of the political risks in a country. Country Watch provides an index of political risk "based on criteria including stability, democratic accountability, and economic risk," where the last includes the transparency of regulation and the nonservicing of payments by the country, among other factors. The highest scores for 2007 were for Austria, Canada, Denmark, Finland, Luxembourg, Netherlands, Norway, Sweden, and Switzerland. The lowest score was for Iraq, followed by Lebanon, North Korea, Somalia, Sudan, and Zimbabwe.

Sovereign Default Risk

The 2011 euro crisis highlighted the risks associated with the sovereign borrowings of countries. Investment houses provide assessments of these risks, and the financial markets also yield a measure of the default risks based on investors' trades of credit default swaps, which provide a form of insurance or hedge against sovereign default risk. (The methodology is discussed in the Chapter 15 case *The Euro Crisis*.) In 2011 Deutsche Bank Research provided estimates of the probability of default on sovereign debt for countries for which credit default swaps were traded. For example, the probability of default within 1 year of U.S. sovereign debt was 0.8 percent, whereas the probability for Greece was 19.9 percent. For emerging markets countries the probability of default was 2.0 percent for China and 12.6 percent for Venezuela.

Use of the Measures

The measures and rankings discussed here should not be used to judge a country, but instead should be used to identify areas to investigate further. Corruption, for example, can vary by industry as well as region of a country. The World Bank's Ease of Doing Business provides an indication of the types of hassle that may be found in a country. For example, Malaysia is ranked first in the ease in "getting credit" but 113th in starting a business and 108th in "dealing with construction permits." With these countries in mind Table 17-1 presents indices and rankings for the BRIC countries.

TABLE 17-1 Rankings of BRIC Countries

Index	Brazil	Russia	India	China	No. of countries
Freedom—Political Rights (1–7 scale)[1]	2	6	2	7	183
Freedom—Civil Liberties (1–7 scale)[1]	2	5	3	6	183
Economic Freedom[2]	113	143	124	135	179
Freedom of the Press[1]	90	173	77	184	196
Corruption[3]	69	154	87	78	179
Ease of Doing Business[4]	127	123	134	79	183
Competitiveness[5]	44	49	32	19	58
Probability of Default (%)[6]	2.6	3.3	NA	2.0	

[1] Freedom House

[2] Heritage Foundation

[3] Transparency International

[4] World Bank

[5] IMD

[6] Deutsche Bank Research

Culture

Culture can also be important, not only shaping the opportunities and risks in a country but also whether a company can implement its market strategy. Lincoln Electric was renowned for its high productivity resulting from its piece-rate compensation system that provided strong individualized incentives to increase output. The company decided to expand overseas and selected a number of countries in which to make acquisitions and build plants. In some countries Lincoln Electric's system of individualized incentives clashed with local culture that was more collectivist in nature and hostile to individualized incentives. After a series of costly trial and error attempts to establish high-productivity plants, the company concluded that there were only two countries where its incentive approach worked—China and Poland.[4]

OPPORTUNITIES

Opportunities in emerging markets are of two basic types. The first is to use a country to export goods to better developed countries and markets. The extractive industries are the prime example, as are the factories in Asia that supply the apparel and footwear markets. This requires foreign markets to be open, which is generally the case in developed countries. The European Union, however, has placed a moratorium on products containing genetically modified organisms, which has restricted the opportunities for African farmers who seek the higher yields available with genetically modified seeds.

The second type of opportunity stems from the domestic economy. Emerging market economies have been growing rapidly and the middle class was emerging in many countries. India and China had large middle classes, and the middle class in Africa was as large as that in India. McKinsey & Company projected continued strong economic growth in Africa. In part the rapid growth in Africa was due to large price increases for oil and minerals, which contributed to export growth and attracted foreign direct investment. Much of FDI was from China, which sought to secure supply sources for its economy. Two-thirds of the growth during the decade of the 2000s was due to the domestic consumption economy, including wholesale and retail sales and transportation and telecommunications. McKinsey estimated that consumer-facing industries, agriculture, resources, and infrastructure could grow by $1 trillion by 2020.[5]

A study by *The Economist* reported that emerging markets accounted for 38 percent of world GDP in 2010, up from 19 percent in 1990, and were projected to surpass the GDP of developed countries before the end of the present decade.[6] Emerging market economies account for nearly half of the world's retail sales, more than half of automobile sales, 80 percent of mobile telephone subscriptions, and 80 percent of foreign exchange reserves. The investment rate in countries like China is much higher than that in most developed countries.

The World Bank estimated that the growth rate in emerging economies would average 4.7 percent between 2011 and 2025, whereas the growth rate of developed countries would average 2.3 percent. Six countries, Brazil, China, India, Indonesia, South Korea, and Russia are projected to account for more than half of GDP growth by 2025. The World Bank pointed to the projected growth in South-South trade and foreign direct investment.

Kose and Prasad (2010, p. 170) studied the performance of emerging markets economies (EMEs) and concluded: "the growing size of EMEs and their rapidly rising per capita incomes are expanding the size of their domestic markets, making them less reliant on demand in advanced economies. Since the emerging markets have high savings rates, they are also becoming less dependent on foreign finance, especially from advanced economies. This gradual process of structural divergence of EME business cycles from advanced economy business cycles, along with the strong growth potential of the former group, suggests that advanced economies should be looking to expand trade relationships with the EMEs in order to diversify their export base and benefit from the growth potential of EMEs."

---

[4]See Siegel and Larson (2007).

[5]*McKinsey Quarterly*, June 2010.

[6]*Economist*, August 6, 2011. On a purchasing power parity basis emerging market countries have greater GDP than developed countries.

At the level of an individual firm, successful participation in a domestic market requires specific knowledge of that market so as to apply the firm's expertise. A firm with superior know-how could also acquire a local firm supplying the domestic market and operate it more efficiently or better serve the market. Cemex began as a regional cement producer in Mexico and through internal growth and acquisitions became the third largest producer in the world. One component of its globalization strategy was to acquire inefficient producers in emerging markets where cement was sold as a branded product directly to consumers rather than in bulk to construction companies. In South America Cemex bought cement plants in Argentina, Columbia, and Venezuela. It improved the efficiency of the plants to lower their costs. In Venezuela it became the largest producer of cement and ready-mix concrete.

Hewlett-Packard's decision to source in Vietnam was in part motivated by the rapid income growth in a country with 100 million people, an increasing proportion of whom were potential customers. In addition, the government represents an important potential customer.

Underdeveloped Markets and Business Groups

Often the set of markets on which a new firm depends for inputs is incomplete. In particular, domestic capital markets may be inadequate for the financing needed in emerging market economies. Over time this has led to the formation of business groups in a number of countries as a means of providing financing and diversifying risks. The companies in these business groups are independent legal entities, but they are tied together by cross shareholdings or familial ties. These groups have been important to the development of the economy in many countries but also some have been blamed for a failure of a country to reform and liberalize. Khanna and Yafeh (2007) surveyed the research on the performance of business groups in emerging markets, studying the data on business groups in Argentina, Brazil, Chile, India, Indonesia, Israel, South Korea, Mexico, Philippines, Taiwan, Thailand, and Turkey. In many cases the business groups were family controlled.[7] Khanna and Yafeh concluded that differences in structure, the industries covered by the groups, and the countries in which they operate meant that some groups were paragons and others parasites. An example of a paragon is the Tata Group of India, considered in Chapter 18.

Business groups as well as individual companies have strong incentives to interact with government when it controls markets, lets contracts, and regulates business activity. Leuz and Oberholzer-Gee (2006) examined the performance of firms with and without relationships to the Suharto regime in Indonesia. Firms with strong political relationships relied less on global financial markets than did firms that had no political relationship. These political relationships increased the returns on those firms, but access to global financial market also increased returns. The higher returns for firms with political relationships were due to preferential financing, and those firms sought to avoid the global financial markets because greater transparency was required and because it was more difficult for management to extract benefits from control of the firms when they were monitored by global lenders.

Relying on political relationships can also increase risk. The firms that relied on political connections underperformed during the Asian financial crisis and significantly underperformed once Suharto was gone and replaced by a new government hostile to the Suharto regime. Political relationships can become a liability when there is a regime change, and those relationships may be hard to reestablish with a new regime.

Opportunity at the Bottom of the Pyramid?

C. K. Prahalad (2004) argued that companies had overlooked as customers the 4 billion people in the world who lived on less than $2 a day. Moreover, he argued that private companies could make a "fortune" serving these consumers, helping to bring them out of poverty. He further argued that multinational companies could play a leading role in selling to the poor, in particular because the poor wanted quality products. Prahalad presented a series of examples to illustrate his thesis. One of his most cited examples was a start-up company in India that made single-serve packages of shampoo that were said to be more affordable than conventional-size packages.

Karnani (2007) criticized all aspects of Prahalad's thesis, arguing that it was "logically flawed and inconsistent with the evidence." He examined the examples and concluded that most

---

[7]Family-related business groups have been important to the success of the overseas Chinese in Southeast Asia.

did not show profitability. Moreover, he estimated that the market at the bottom of the pyramid was not that large and was costly to serve. He argued that the single-serve packages were not affordable, and moreover, no multinational company produced the packages. Hindustan Lever Limited did sell salt in small packages, but the salt sold for the same price per kilogram as in the larger packages. Moreover, the salt sold at nearly three times the price of unbranded salt. Whether there is a fortune in selling to the bottom of the pyramid remains an open question.

One example of serving the poor that has been successful is microfinance. Banco Compartamos has been highly profitable serving the poor in Mexico, but it charged interest rates of 90 percent.[8] It, however, has helped hundreds of thousands of people to improve their lives.

Another company that has been highly successful in serving consumers in emerging markets is MTN Group, a provider of mobile telephone service and enhancements in Africa and the Middle East. Its customer base, however, pays on average $20 a month, which means that many customers are not at the bottom of the pyramid. The chapter case *MTN Group Limited* provides an opportunity to assess its business model and the opportunities and risks it faces.

Microfinance

Microfinance has a long history, but the modern version is due to Muhammad Yunus, a Bangladesh economist, who in 1974 became concerned about the devastating poverty from which people were seemingly unable to escape. As he interviewed people, he learned that many women made by hand small objects that they sold in local markets. Many borrowed in the morning from local moneylenders, purchased materials, made and sold the objects, and repaid the lender at the end of the day. The interest rates were usurious, leaving the women at best with a subsistence income and unable to improve their situation. He quickly identified 42 people in a similar situation and found that in total they needed only $27 a day in lending. Yunus began borrowing from a bank on his own account and lending to the people. The loan funds were used for agriculture, home business, and a variety of other purposes and made a large difference in the lives of the people. The borrowers repaid the loans, and Yunus established the Grameen Bank to expand the number of people served. By 2004 Grameen Bank had loaned over $4 billion and had 3.5 million current borrowers, 95 percent of whom were women. Grameen loaned to groups or circles of women, who were responsible for allocating the borrowings among themselves and for ensuring that the borrowings were repaid. Grameen reported a 99 percent repayment rate. Yunus received the Nobel Peace Prize in 2006 for his work.

By 2010 Grameen Bank had $10 billion in loans outstanding to 8.3 million people in Bangladesh, and it established Grameen America to make loans to Americans who could not otherwise obtain them. In 2011, however, the government of Bangladesh ousted Yunus as managing director of Grameen Bank. Commentators speculated that the government was still angry at Yunus for his aborted 2007 attempt to form a political party in Bangladesh to challenge the incumbent government.[9]

Yunus also developed an innovative approach to helping the poorest people—beggars. They could obtain a Grameen identity card that enabled them to borrow merchandise from stores and sell it door-to-door, with their borrowing financed by a loan from the bank. Yunus then turned to stationary beggars, many of whom were blind or missing a limb. Since they typically positioned themselves in strategic places, Grameen enabled them to sell drinks, food, and other objects from their places.

Inspired by the work of Yunus, thousands of other nonprofit microfinance institutions (MFIs) were formed. Most of these MFIs were subsidized by donors and provided low interest rates relative to the rates of local moneylenders. By 2010 microfinance customers of lenders participating in Microcredit Summit Campaign (MSC) were estimated at 190 million, of which 128 million were among the very poorest. Including family members the MSC estimated that 640 million people were affected.[10]

---

[8]See the chapter case, *Social Entrepreneurship: Banco Compartamos.*

[9]Grameen Bank had been accused by the Norwegian government of improperly transferring its $100 million donation to an affiliate of the bank. After a complaint by the Norwegian government the funds were retransferred, and a later investigation cleared the bank and Mr. Yunus. (*New York Times*, April 6, 2011.)

[10]Microcredit Summit Campaign, "State of the Microcredit Summit Campaign Report 2011," www.microcredit summit.org

One means of reaching more of the poor was for-profit microfinance. Some entrepreneurs had started for-profit institutions, but the potential became clear in 2007 when Carlos Danel and Carlos Labarthe took Banco Compartamos public in an IPO valued at $1.53 billion. The bank had been started as a nonprofit in Mexico and received funding from NGOs and international development institutions such as the International Finance Corporation. The bank was converted to for-profit status in 2001 and expanded its customers from 60,000 to 839,000 in 2007. Banco Compartamos had profits of $81.5 million and a loan portfolio of $400 million with only 1.36 percent of its loans nonperforming.

The interest rates charged by the bank were in the 90 percent range, which was substantially less than the interest rates of local moneylenders. (Interest rates were generally much higher in Latin America than in Africa and Asia.) Yunus strongly criticized Banco Compartamos for its interest rates and argued that microfinance should be provided by nonprofit institutions. He said, "They're absolutely on the wrong track. Their priorities are screwed up.... Microcredit was created to fight the money lender, not to become the money lender."[11] Supporters of Banco Compartamos argued that for-profit status allowed the bank to raise capital and expand its services far more rapidly than it could as a nonprofit. Some participants in microfinance estimated that access to the capital markets could expand microfinance funding from $4 billion a year to $30 billion and serve 1 billion low-income customers.[12] The chapter case *Social Entrepreneurship: Banco Compartamos* provides an opportunity to consider these issues in more detail. The for-profit approach to microfinance can be contrasted with a nonprofit online microfinance approach pioneered by Kiva, as considered in the chapter case *Social Entrepreneurship: Kiva*.

For-profit microfinance companies have been formed in many countries, and their ability to raise capital has allowed them to expand rapidly. SKS Microfinance of India raised $350 million through stock sales in 2011 but was subsequently criticized by local politicians and subjected to an interest rate cap as considered in Chapter 18.

Microfinance is itself subject to nonmarket risks. In the state of Andhra Pradesh in India microfinance had grown rapidly in part because of the presence of for-profit lenders that were able to raise capital. One-third of the microfinance in India was accounted for by Andhra Pradesh, but that lending was halted by opportunism by local politicians. Opposition party politicians highlighted abuses of some microlenders, the burden imposed on some of the poor who struggled to repay their loans, and the threat it provided to traditional means of finance such as "self-help groups."[13] The local politicians began urging borrowers not to repay the loans, and the state assembly passed a law capping interest rates and restricting collection practices. This led banks to halt their lending to the microfinance companies, threatening the microfinance market. Suresh K. Krishna, managing director of Grameen Financial Services in Bangalore, which had laid off 600 employees, said, "This is frustrating. This is not what we set out for. The whole idea was to support entrepreneurs and support people in the rural areas and people below the poverty line."[14]

Activists and politicians in Bangladesh, Bolivia, Nicaragua, and Pakistan also turned on microfinance. The prime minister of Bangladesh accused microlenders of "sucking the blood from the poor in the name of poverty reduction."[15] President Daniel Ortega of Nicaragua had supported a no-pay movement, which led to the closing of the Banco del Exito. Elisabeth Rhyme, an official at Accion International, which funds microlenders, said, "These crises happen when the microfinance sector gets saturated, when it grows too fast, and the mechanisms for controlling overindebtedness are not well developed. On the political side, politicians or political actors take advantage of an opportunity. When they see grievances, they go, 'Wow, we can make some hay with this.'"[16]

Microfinance came under attack not only from politicians for the burden imposed on some borrowers but also for the unsubstantiated claims of success by its proponents. Critics noted that comparison of borrowers and non-borrowers was subject to selection bias, since those who sought microcredit loans to start businesses were people who were more likely to be entrepreneurs than those who did not seek loans. Any comparison of the proportions of the two groups that successfully started new businesses thus would be biased. The best way to control for selection and

---

[11]*BusinessWeek*. December 13, 2007.
[12]See Cull, Demirgüç-Kunt, and Morduch (2008).
[13]*New York Times*, January 6, 2011.
[14]Ibid.
[15]Ibid.
[16]Ibid.

other factors that could compromise evaluations of microlending was to use randomized controlled experiments. Two such experiments were conducted, and the results showed very heterogeneous effects of microlending and little evidence that it had much effect on households.

Banerjee, Duflo, Glennerster, and Kinnan (2009) conducted an experiment in the slums of Hyderabad in the Indian state of Andhra Pradesh. Microlender Spandana, which had 1.2 million borrowers in India, identified 104 neighborhoods in the slums of Hyderabad that it had an interest in entering to provide microloans. The researchers then randomly selected 52 neighborhoods, and Spandana opened offices in those neighborhoods but did not open offices in the other 52 neighborhoods. Loans were made to women's circles. Prior to this random selection, the researchers had conducted surveys of households in the Hyderabad slums to establish a baseline for the comparison. They then conducted an endline survey after Spandana had been making loans for 15–18 months. At the baseline there were no microlenders in the neighborhoods, but 69 percent of the households had outstanding loans from local moneylenders, family members, and others, and the average interest rate was 3.85 percent a month. The research study found that the loans to households with existing businesses or that started businesses reduced their household nondurable spending presumably to help make a larger investment in their businesses. Those who borrowed for non-business purposes increased their household consumption, suggesting that they were borrowing from the future for the present. The researchers also found that the microlending "appears to have no discernible effect on education, health, or women's empowerment."

Karlin and Zinman (2009) conducted a randomized controlled experiment in the outskirts of Manila, the Philippines, in which the for-profit microlender First Macro Bank randomly approved and rejected microenterprise loan applications from marginal borrowers. The loans made were to individuals, and they had higher incomes than the average for the Philippines and most were male, so the study was of so-called second-generation microcredit. The researchers found that the scope of the businesses funded actually shrank as the businesses shed unproductive employees. The loans reduced the outside work of household members and increased their likelihood of attending school, reduced the use of formal and informal insurance, and may have somewhat increased the profits of the enterprises. There was no self-reported sense of greater well-being among the borrowers and instead was "some evidence of a small *decline* in self-reported well-being." The researchers also found that the effects of the lending were greater for male than female borrowers and greater for higher-income borrowers.

As the researchers caution, the studies do not report long-run effects of microlending, which could be more beneficial. The randomized controlled experiments call into question some of the claims of the advocates of microcredit. In part the response of the advocates is provided in the "State of the Microcredit Summit Campaign Report 2011" prepared by the Microcredit Summit Campaign.[17]

An alternative or perhaps a complement to microfinance is to facilitate safe saving by the poor. Most of the very poor are "unbanked." That is, they do not have bank accounts or opportunities to make low cost financial transactions. The rapid rollout of mobile telecommunications in many emerging markets countries has transformed their economies and spurred growth. It has also allowed people to make payments by cellphone, and for many the payments systems allow them to "store" their cash electronically. This form of savings allows them to use their savings in emergencies rather than to turn to local moneylenders. Savings can also be used to start businesses or expand existing businesses. The use of cellphones for financial transactions spread rapidly in Africa and India.

Savings can also be facilitated by innovations in banking. In India and other countries, banks have begun using mobile tellers who visit villages educating people about banking, establishing accounts, and helping with financial transactions such as paying electricity bills. These banks and mobile tellers allow people to accumulate savings to help smooth consumption and invest in businesses. An example is the Equity Bank of Kenya, which has innovated in extending banking to the previously unbanked through branchless banking.

Equity Bank of Kenya began in 1984 as a mortgage lender, but was unable to become profitable. In 2004, under the leadership of CEO James Mwangi, the bank transformed itself into a savings and loan bank with an emphasis on microfinance.[18] The focus was on the 58 percent of

---

[17]www.microcreditsummit.org

[18]See the case "Equity Bank (A)," Case No. E260, Graduate School of Business, Stanford University, 2007.

Kenyans who lived on less than $2 a day, many of whom were women, who represented 70 percent of the illiterate in Kenya. By 2006 Equity Bank had 1 million customers with savings accounts, which after 6 months qualified the account holder for borrowing. Loans were from KSh500 to KSh50 million, and interest rates averaged 17.5 percent. To expand its coverage, it had opened 42 branches by 2006 and planned to have 70 by 2008. Equity Bank sought to serve its customers with low fees and services tailored to their needs. In return, it earned record revenues and profits and became the seventh largest for-profit bank in Kenya. The chapter case *Equity Bank of Kenya* considers the growth strategy of the bank in 2011.

Fair Trade

The fair trade movement was begun to improve the lives of poor farmers and workers trapped by market conditions. The movement can be understood as an approach to improving the well-being of poor farmers in developing countries by circumventing markets and coordinating market behavior. The fair trade system attempts to intervene directly on both the demand and the supply sides of the market by coordinating the flow of consumer revenue to participating producers. Coffee producers participating in the fair trade system are primarily cooperatives of small farmers that agree to meet certain production and environmental standards. Participating coffee brokers agree to pay a fixed, fair trade price, which exceeds the market price, so the income of coffee farmers is increased. The brokers charge a higher price for fair trade coffee, and retailers generally sell the coffee at a higher price. Fair Trade certification allows consumers to pay high prices on the expectation that their payments benefit the farmers, and the fair trade movement monitors the system to ensure that the higher prices actually benefit farmers. The FAIRTRADE mark is now available on over 3,000 products, including coffee, tea, rice, bananas, mangoes, cocoa, sugar, honey, fruit juices, flowers, gold, handicrafts, and soccer balls.[19]

Coffee production had been governed by the International Coffee Agreement (ICA), a cartel that established export quotas for the producing countries to maintain prices within a range called the corset. The quotas were waived in times of shortage when prices could rise substantially. Growing opposition to cartels led to criticism of the ICA, which collapsed in 1989 when the United States withdrew from the agreement. The ICA was succeeded by the International Coffee Organization (ICO), but it was unable to limit production. Prices began to fall, and with the exception of two periods of high prices due to frost in Brazil, prices remained below the corset levels. After a small price increase in 1999 coffee prices fell by 50 percent over the following 3 years.

The price drop was due to increased supply and slow growth in demand. In particular, Vietnam had provided incentives for farmers to grow coffee, and the country quickly became the second-largest exporter after Brazil. Brazil also had increased production as a result of increased mechanization and a shift away from frost-prone regions. Demand growth was slowed by increased competition from soft drinks and the movement to natural fruit drinks, particularly in the United States. From 1970 to 2000 coffee consumption per capita fell from 36 to 17 gallons annually in the United States, while soft drink consumption increased from 23 to 53 gallons per capita.[20] Coffee retailers attempted to increase sales by introducing specialty and flavored coffees. The latter increased the demand for low-quality coffee.

OxfamAmerica reported that 70 percent of coffee production was accounted for by small farmers, who were devastated by the price drop. Oxfam reported that in 1980 a coffee grower could purchase a Swiss Army knife with 4.171 kilograms of coffee, but by 2001, 10.464 kilograms were required. Oxfam estimated that 25 million coffee farmers were affected.

THE FAIR TRADE SYSTEM The fair trade movement began in the Netherlands in 1988 with the introduction of Max Havelaar brand coffee, named after a nineteenth-century Dutch novel depicting the exploitation of plantation workers in Dutch colonies. The objective of the movement was to protect small growers from fluctuating and falling prices. The movement grew in Europe and spread to the United States and other countries.

The fair trade coffee system paid farmers $1.26 a pound for their coffee or $1.41 for organic coffee. The market price for coffee in early 2004 was $0.65 a pound. To qualify for the

---

[19]Fair Labeling Organizations International, www.fairtrade.net/sites/aboutflo/faq.html.
[20]Oxfam International, "Mugged: Poverty in Your Coffee Cup," 2002, p. 19.

fair trade system farmers had to form a producer organization such as a democratically operated cooperative or association. The production practices of the producer organization were then monitored to ensure compliance with the fair trade standards.

The fair trade system had two wings. One focused on the certification of coffee producers, the monitoring of coffee brokers, and enforcement to ensure that funds reached the producers. The other focused on building a demand for fair trade products, primarily in the consuming countries. The fair trade system was led by the Fairtrade Labeling Organizations (FLO), headquartered in Bonn, Germany. The FLO established FLO-Cert Ltd., which verified that the farmers benefitted from the program.

The fair trade program in the United States was administered by TransFair USA, which tracked fair trade products from fair trade producers.[21] TransFair was a member of the FLO. TransFair worked on the demand side of the market to increase the retail availability of fair trade coffee and other fair trade products. TransFair reported that 110 million pounds of fair trade coffee was certified in the United States in 2009. TransFair certified coffee provided $11 million in premiums to farmers in 2010.

In addition to TransFair and the FLO, NGOs worked to increase the availability of Fairtrade coffee. OxfamAmerica, Global Exchange, Co-Op America, and the Interfaith Fair Trade Initiative targeted coffee companies and retailers and sought to educate the public as well as coffee retailers. OxfamAmerica headed a private politics campaign to convince Procter & Gamble and Dunkin' Donuts to sell fair trade coffee. Adding to the direct pressure on the companies, the Center for Reflection, Education and Action (CREA) and Domini Social Investments registered shareholder resolutions for the P&G annual meeting, the first-ever shareholder resolution on fair trade. The U.S. Senate and House approved resolutions calling for support of coffee farmers in developing countries.

Dunkin' Donuts agreed to sell fair trade espresso in the spring of 2003. After 2 years of efforts by the NGOs, Procter & Gamble agreed to sell Fair Trade Certified coffee through its Millstone specialty division and over the Internet. Sister Ruth Rosenbaum of CREA praised P&G: "P&G's action is an excellent example of what can be accomplished through collaboration of shareholder activists and nonprofit organizations. It's a win-win for the world's small-scale coffee farmers, for the environment, and for P&G itself."[22]

Oxfam established a ratings system for the four largest coffee companies, assessing for the previous 12 months their actions to address the global coffee crisis. Procter & Gamble received a rating of 49 out of 100, Nestlé 43, Kraft 38, and Sara Lee 27. Phil Bloomer, the Make Trade Fair campaign director for Oxfam, said, "These companies continue to make massive profits while coffee farmers get poorer and poorer."[23]

CHALLENGES One concern with the fair trade concept was whether retailers would charge such a large price premium that demand would be suppressed. "'Supermarkets are taking advantage of the label to make more profit because they know that consumers are willing to pay a bit more because it is fair trade,' said Emily Daradaine, fruit-product manager" at the FLO.

At its 435 outlets Café Borders sold fair trade coffee for $16 a pound, whereas non–fair trade coffee was sold at $12 a pound. After an inquiry by a reporter for the *Wall Street Journal,* Café Borders said it would lower the price for a bag of fair trade coffee by 20 percent. At the online site of the United Kingdom's largest supermarket chain Tesco, fair trade coffee sold at 46 percent more than non–fair trade coffee. Luuk Laurens Zonneveld, managing director of the FLO, said he was concerned about high retail margins because they reduce the market share for fair trade products. He said some of the FLO's affiliates might "approach" the companies about their practices.[24]

Whole Foods Markets had declined to participate in the fair trade program because it believed that the system was unfair to family farms that did not qualify as a producer organization. Instead, Whole Foods started its own program, High Five for Farmers, through Allegro Coffee

---

[21]TransFair USA became Fair Trade USA in 2010.

[22]OxfamAmerica, "Advocacy Groups and Shareholders Persuade Procter & Gamble to Offer Fair Trade Coffee," press release, September 15, 2003.

[23]OxfamAmerica, press release, December 9, 2003.

[24]*Wall Street Journal,* June 8, 2004.

and initiated FairTrade practices for farmers. Royal Ahold NV of the Netherlands also set up an alternative certification program. " 'If you are a large supermarket brand or a large roaster, to buy all your products under the fair-trade conditions is just not economically possible,' said David Rosenberg, director of Utz Kapeh," the foundation Royal Ahold helped establish to certify coffee.[25]

The fair trade movement claimed that fair trade coffee was higher quality. Tadesse Meskala, who managed a farmers' coffee cooperative in Ethiopia, commented, "Better payments leads us to make sure the coffee is a better quality." Farmers "care for the coffee because people care for us. They pay us a fair price."[26] Starbucks, however, had delayed selling Fair Trade coffee because of concerns about its quality. Once quality was assured, Starbucks began selling fair trade coffee.

Ultimately, as the FLO stated, "The impact of Fair Trade in the end always depends on the goodwill and loyalty of the consumer."[27] Paul Rice, founder and chief executive of TransFair USA, said, "It is guilt-free coffee, but I would not call it that. I would call it feel-good coffee."[28] Bill Conerly of the National Center for Policy Analysis commented, "It's a feel-good program. I don't expect it to be a broad trend because people don't like to spend more money. I expect the impact to be trivial."[29] By the end of 2009 worldwide sales of fair trade products had reached £3.4 billion, and 827 producer organizations in 58 countries had been certified.

In 2010 TransFair USA changed its name to Fair Trade USA, and in 2011 it quit the FLO to pursue its own Fair Trade for All Initiative. Fair Trade USA sought to increase awareness of fair trade products among U.S. consumers and to provide higher benefits to producers. The principal objective of the separation was to extend eligibility of producers beyond cooperatives to include coffee estates and small individual farmers. This would allow an increased supply of products such as coffee to meet the unsatisfied demand of corporate coffee buyers.

RISK ASSESSMENT

Risks in emerging markets can differ in magnitude and nature from those in developed countries.

- Risks are greater in magnitude in emerging markets. In 2007 Venezuelan president Hugo Chávez began to nationalize foreign businesses as a way of consolidating his power and realizing his vision of "21st century socialism." Nationalization is no longer an immediate risk in most developed countries.
- Foreign risks arise from a broader range of factors than do domestic risks. These include ethnic and religious differences, ideology, and class and income differences.
- Risks can depend on the country of origin for foreign direct investment and trade.

In 2008 demonstrators in France disrupted the carrying of the Olympic torch to China as a protest against suppression in Tibet. France had also granted honorary citizenship to the Dalai Lama and to Hu Jia, a human rights activist in China. Some Chinese citizens were offended by the criticism and the honorary citizenship and launched protests against France. Many chose to demonstrate at the stores of Carrefour, the giant French retailer. Whether the protests affected sales is unclear, but it was clear that demonstrations against the company were because of its country of origin.

Sources and Types of Risks

The immediate source of many risks is the weak rule of law in a country. This means that agreements and contracts may not be enforced, even if their terms are unambiguous. It can also mean that the law is not enforced impartially and that regulations can be applied in a discriminatory manner. Moreover, politics and political ties can override the rule of law. This section identifies a set of risks in emerging markets that differ from those in most developed countries.

---

[25]Ibid.
[26]*San Jose Mercury News,* April 28, 2004.
[27]www.fairtrade.net.
[28]*San Jose Mercury News,* April 28, 2004.
[29]Ibid.

COUPS Sudden changes can occur because of a military coup, as in Thailand. In 2006 the Thai military overthrew the elected regime of Prime Minister Thaksin Shinawatra, disbanded his political party, and reversed many of his policies. The military government forced Google to censor its searches because of YouTube postings objectionable to the government. The military pledged to allow elections in 2007, and Thaksin's supporters formed a new party backing him and his policies. The party was successful in the election and formed a new government that pledged it would reinstate Thaksin's policies.

DEMOCRATIC REVOLUTION Venezuelans first elected President Hugo Chávez in 1998 and reelected him twice. In 2007 he embarked on a campaign to establish twenty-first-century socialism and to consolidate and extend his power. He seized many companies owned by foreigners, including operators of oil fields and firms in the electricity and telecommunications industries. He nationalized a milk producer, sugar plantations, and a cold storage and distribution company. He closed a television station that was critical of him. Despite skyrocketing oil prices, his policies worsened the economy, and he responded by nationalizing more companies. Because of a housing shortage he seized all the cement companies in the country, including the company owned by Cemex. In May 2008 he seized the Luxembourg-owned steel company Sidor and pledged to make it a "socialist company." The economy continued to weaken. To extend his influence in other countries, he financed rebels in neighboring Colombia and sent an envoy to Argentina with $800,000 in cash intended for the Argentine presidential campaign. Customs officials found the cash in a suitcase. Venezuela consistently ranks near the bottom on the measures of freedoms and economic opportunities used in Table 17-1. The country is last in the world competitiveness scoreboard by a wide margin, 175th in economic freedom, 172nd in ease of starting a business, 164th in corruption, and 166th in freedom of the press. Chavez planned to stand for reelection in 2012.

Festering Anger and Revolution

In December 2010 a young Tunisian fruit vendor, Mohamed Bouazizi, set himself on fire to protest the desperation in which he and many of his countrymen lived. More demonstrations forced President Zine al-Abidine Ben Ali, who had controlled the country for 24 years, to flee the country. The revolution swept to Egypt forcing the end of Hosni Mubarak's regime of 30 years. In both countries the military refused to fire on the demonstrators, and the regimes quickly fell. In Libya the army fired on the protestors, resulting in an armed revolution ending in the death of Muammar Qadafi and his 42-year rule. Mass protests in Syria and Yemen were checked by the government, but the protesters persisted and the eventual outcome was uncertain. In the richer oil-producing countries of the Middle East the status quo persisted, despite increased sectarian tensions in Bahrain. In other countries such as Morocco and Jordan the kings instituted reforms.

The sources of the revolutions were varied and differed across the countries. Some protesters sought to rid the country of an autocratic ruler. Some sought democracy. Some sought an Islamic state. Some women sought liberation and greater freedom or to protect the liberties they had. Some sought greater freedoms. Many of the young sought change. Most sought a better life.

The Arab Spring was an unexpected event at least with respect to its timing, and the underlying anger and forces were varied, making predictions of the outcomes uncertain. In Egypt, Libya, and Tunisia elections and new constitutions were the initial steps of the revolution, but where that would lead was uncertain.

What might result? There seems to be a wide range of possibilities. One is a flourishing democracy, perhaps leading to a system like that in Turkey where the secular and religious coexist peacefully if not always harmoniously. Another is illustrated by Lebanon, whose Cedar revolution in 2005 continued the festering problems of "sectarianism, corruption, the insecurity brought about by a weak central state, foreign meddling and armed party militias."[30] Another possibility is an Islamic state as in Iran, where religious leaders control the state and God's law rather than man's law is used. Or, the pre-revolution system could evolve but remain much the same, as would be the case if the military retained control in Egypt. A moderate Islamic party won the Tunisian election for the council to write a new constitution, and the head of the revolutionary council in Libya declared that the country would be Islamic with sharia law.

---

[30]*Economist*, July 16, 2011.

POLICY RISK   When the military took over in Thailand, it looked for policies that would be popular with citizens. One was to take on the global pharmaceutical companies. As discussed in Chapter 19, the TRIPS agreement as amended in the Doha Round WTO negotiations allowed countries in a national emergency to issue a compulsory license for the importation or production of a patented drug. Thailand issued compulsory licenses for Merck's AIDS drug Efavirenz, Abbott Laboratories' AIDS drug Kaletra, and the Sanofi-Aventis' heart drug Plavix. Brazil followed by issuing a compulsory license for Efavirenz. The Chapter 19 case *Compulsory Licensing, Thailand, and Abbott Laboratories* considers the issue in more detail.

REGULATORY RISK   Islamic finance has grown quickly since the Malaysian government issued the first Islamic bond in 2002. The most popular *sukuk,* or sharia-compliant bonds, structures were *musaraka,* a type of Islamic joint venture, and *mudaraba,* a form of trust financing.[31] In November 2007, the Islamic scholar Sheikh Muhammad Taqi Usmani stated that 85 percent of the *sukuk* being issued violated two principles of Islamic law. Usmani was the head of the religious board of the Accounting and Auditing Organization for Islamic Financial Institutions, based in Bahrain. No sizable international *sukuk* was issued during the next 3 months. The concerns were that the structures in effect had a guaranteed return, which is not in accord with Islamic law, which calls for the sharing of risk and profit. Financial institutions participating in Islamic finance relied on Islamic scholars as advisors, but those scholars were frequently in disagreement. Islam does not have a hierarchical structure with a head who can make proclamations to resolve differing views and establish a uniform religious policy.

PRICE CONTROLS   In 2008 Mexico approved a price freeze on 150 food products. The freeze was accepted by business and was intended to control inflation of food prices, which has traditionally been a powder keg for political protests in Latin America. At the same time Vietnam, the world's second largest exporter of rice, imposed a minimum export price of $800 a tonne. The price had risen from slightly over $300 a tonne in 2007 to a peak of $1,100 a tonne in 2008, before decreasing to $800. Given the action by Vietnam, $800 was likely to be the minimum price of rice until the next harvest was available.

India also felt the increase in food and energy prices. It initially banned the export of rice and some edible oils. Because of rising prices the government threatened to list steel as an "essential commodity," which would give it the authority to control output and distribution. This led the steel companies to enter into a voluntary agreement under which they cut the prices of steel used in the construction of homes.

FINANCIAL RESTRICTIONS   Emerging markets countries have imposed a variety of restrictions on foreign direct investment, foreign exchange transactions, and the repatriation of earnings. Some of these restrictions are temporary, but many are long lasting. India restricts foreign investment in telecommunications companies to 74 percent. Restrictions can also be imposed by developed countries. The European Union and the United States have imposed restrictions on financing of companies in the Sudan, and the United States has restrictions on doing business with Iran.

NATIONALIZATION AND SEIZURES   During the 1960s and 1970s a number of countries expropriated the assets of firms, primarily foreign-owned firms. This discouraged investment in the countries and often led to mismanagement of the expropriated companies. By the late 1980s nationalizations and expropriations had largely ended—until Hugo Chávez began his campaign.

POLITICAL MEGALOMANIA   Zimbabwe was the breadbasket of Africa. In 2000 voters rejected a constitutional amendment that would allow the government to seize farmland, and President Mugabe then turned his supporters loose to seize the farmlands.[32] They took over the farms, most of which were owned by whites. Some of the whites resisted, but most fled the country. Agricultural output plummeted, and soon the country had been turned into an importer, rather

---

[31]*Financial Times,* June 19, 2008.
[32]Robert Mugabe was a national hero, having led the revolt that ended colonial rule in Rhodesia. He was elected president in 1980.

than an exporter, of food. Mugabe continued with his disastrous economic policies, including price controls, and conditions continued to worsen. Between 2000 and 2007, the economy contracted by 40 percent. Zimbabwe fell in the Heritage Foundation's index of economic freedoms to 155th of 157 countries, ahead only of Cuba and North Korea.

POLITICAL CORRUPTION Hunger gripped Zimbabwe, and the opposition went to the polls in 2008 in an attempt to defeat Mugabe in his reelection bid. Although the facts are not completely clear, many observers believed that Mugabe and his supporters engaged in voter fraud. Voters gave his opponent more votes but not a majority, forcing a runoff. Mugabe then began a campaign of intimidation in an attempt to secure the election. He then pledged to stay in power even if he lost the runoff. His opponent withdrew because the election would not be fair. The violence continued, and world leaders pleaded with Mugabe to postpone the election, but he refused.[33] A boatload of weapons from China destined for the Mugabe government was turned away by dock workers when it tried to unload in South Africa. Mozambique and other countries also refused to let the boat dock and eventually it returned to China with its cargo.

Zimbabwe is also one of the worst in competitiveness as measured by the World Bank, ranking 157th of 183 countries. The World Bank reported that to start a business nine procedures are required, taking on average 90 days and costing 182.8 percent of per capita income in the country. Dealing with construction permits required 17 permits and took 1,012 days on average and cost 8,020.6 percent of per capita income. Starting a business was thus both costly and time consuming, sufficient to discourage much private entrepreneurship. This contributed to the size of the informal sector and provided incentives for corruption to speed the process of launching a business.

Under pressure from other African countries, Mugabe entered into a power sharing agreement with the opposition leader Morgan Tsvangirai of the Movement for Democratic Change party, but Mugabe retained most of the power including control of the police. After a period of hyperinflation the country abandoned its currency and removed price controls which spurred economic growth, aided by the rapid expansion of the Marange diamond fields. By 2011 political violence had returned in advance of what commentators speculated would be an early election called by the 87-year old Mugabe, who had been in power for 31 years. African nations again urged fair elections, and the heads of state of South Africa, Zambia, and Mozambique called for a halt to political violence and assigned a team to help set up free and fair elections.[34] Mugabe had regularly rebuffed pressure from his neighbors in the past.

The economy in Zimbabwe remained weak, and the country ranked very low on international comparisons: 157 on ease of starting a business, 134 in corruption, 178 in economic freedom, and 173 in freedom of the press. In 2011 the Minister of Indigenization ordered several multinational companies to submit plans within 2 weeks to turn over at least 51 percent ownership to local ownership or to the government. The minister said, "Those foreign firms will have to comply or else we will ask them to leave."[35] The chapter cases *MTN Group Limited* and *Equity Bank of Kenya* concern possible expansion by the companies into Zimbabwe.

ETHNIC AND RELIGIOUS CONFLICT Kenya had a long record of stability since its independence in 1963. The country was led initially by Jomo Kenyatta, followed in 1978 by Daniel arap Moi after Kenyatta's death. Moi established a single-party state, and the economy deteriorated under his reign. International pressure including the holding up of international aid finally forced Moi to return the country to a multiparty system. In 2002, in the country's first democratic election, voters elected Mwai Kibaki, who embarked on economic reform that resulted in strong economic growth. Corruption scandals, however, tarnished the government and led the World Bank to suspend aid. In the election at the end of 2007, Kibaki was widely believed to have engaged in election fraud to obtain the highest vote share. The opposition protested, and Kibaki suppressed the protests, resulting in many deaths. The alleged election fraud gave rise to the first major ethnic conflict in Kenya. Kibaki was a Kikuyu, whereas his opponent was a Luo.

---

[33]Queen Elizabeth II revoked Mugabe's honorary knighthood as a "mark of revulsion" against his human rights abuses and his "abject disregard" for democracy.

[34]*New York Times,* June 13, 2011.

[35]*Wall Street Journal,* August 20, 2011.

With relatively open markets, Kenya's economy grew rapidly, but growth dropped in 2008 as a result of the global financial crisis. Growth quickly resumed, and Kenya had East Africa's premier economy. The turmoil in Kenya calmed, and in 2010 voters approved a new constitution to take effect after the next election. The calm allowed the country to recover from the slump caused by the global financial crisis, with growth reaching 5 percent in 2010 and being projected at more than 6 percent for 2011–2012. Kenya expected to benefit from the growth in the east African Community (Kenya, Uganda, Tanzania, Rwanda, and Burundi), and from its position as the gateway to East Africa. The government, however, had a large and persistent budget deficit. The high growth rate, however, was accompanied by inflation that rose to 16 percent in 2011, causing the Kenyan shilling to drop sharply in value. This aided exports, but caused food prices to increase, imposing hardship on the poor and threatening unrest in advance of the 2012 elections.

The Equity Bank of Kenya had flourished, becoming the fourth largest in the country. It had expanded into Uganda and opened branches in South Sudan and Tanzania. The chapter case *Equity Bank of Kenya* considers its expansion plans and the accompanying risks.

MEDIA RESTRICTIONS   As an example of religious risks, YouTube was shut down in most of the world by a routing error by Pakistan. When a posting contained a trailer for an as-yet unreleased film by a Dutch lawmaker that was critical of Islam, Pakistan directed all YouTube traffic to a "black hole" where all content was discarded. A routing error, however, resulted in most of the world's access to YouTube to disappear for several hours. The Internet in many countries is censored on religious or other grounds. Freedom House assessed the "level of Internet and new media freedom for 37 countries based on three criteria: obstacles to access, limits on content, and violations of user rights." The countries were classified as free, partly free, and not free. Brazil and Saudi Arabia were ranked as in the free category, India, Russia, and Pakistan as partly free, and China as not free.

ENVIRONMENTAL RISKS   Environmental risks center on both harm to the environment in an emerging markets country and the harm from cross-border externalities such as global climate change. Many countries were encouraging major extractive projects, some of which involved the construction of mines or the exploration for oil. The financing for major projects was largely governed by the Equator Principles, a voluntary set of principles observed by major banks that have subscribed to the Principles. The Equator Principles applied to all projects of $50 million or more and categorized projects as A, B, or C (high, medium, and low) for their environmental or social impact. For A and B projects, an Environmental Assessment was required, and the loan contracts from subscribing banks included a covenant stipulating that the borrower must comply with the Environmental Assessment. If a borrower did not fulfill its commitments, the bank could declare the loan in default.[36]

Another environmental risk centered on the successor to the Kyoto Protocol for controlling greenhouse gas emissions. Neither China nor India was subject to Kyoto goals, but both countries would be under pressure to participate in goals for beyond 2012. India had done little with respect to greenhouse gas emissions. To meet its economic growth objective of 8 percent annually, it would need to increase its power generation by a factor of six.[37] India had said in the past that increased emissions were justified to increase the standard of living of its people. That is, economic growth was an "overriding priority" as recognized by the Framework that gave rise to the Kyoto Protocol.

MARKET RISK HEDGING   Most emerging markets countries are not well integrated into global markets, and this can increase the cost of capital yet provide a measure of insulation from risks in global markets. For example, the 2008 financial crisis originated in the United States and spread to Europe and other developed countries through the tightly integrated global financial markets. Most of the emerging market countries escaped the crisis since their financial systems were not integrated with the global market. Moreover, the economies of most emerging markets countries, with the exception of some countries that relied on exports, were not as affected by the subsequent recession in the United States and Europe. Nor were the countries as adversely

---

[36]The Principles are available at www.equator-principles.com.
[37]*Economist*, June 7, 2008.

affected by the euro crisis in 2011 as were the countries in the European Union and the United States (also discussed in the Chapter 15 case *The Euro Crisis*). The insulation of many emerging markets countries was buttressed by strong domestic economies.

Kose and Prasad (2010) identify seven factors that explain the resilience of emerging market economies (EMEs) during the recent global financial and economic crises.

1. Less dependence on foreign finance and a shift away from external debt denominated in foreign currencies
2. Large buffers of foreign exchange reserves
3. Greater trade linkages among EMEs
4. More diversification in EME production and exports
5. Separation of EMEs' business cycles from advanced economies' business cycles
6. Better macroeconomic policies, including flexible exchange rates, in emerging markets
7. Rising per capita incomes and a burgeoning middle class

MANAGEMENT IN THE NONMARKET ENVIRONMENT

Operating in an emerging markets country requires an integrated strategy with a strong nonmarket component to shape opportunities and deal with risks. Management and strategy formulation in the nonmarket environment are based on the same conceptual frameworks developed earlier in the book with some exceptions. Some of the frameworks, such as legislative and electoral strategies, however, are not appropriate for countries with authoritarian governments as found in many emerging markets countries. Frameworks such as identifying the issues, interests, institutions, and information in the nonmarket environment are broadly applicable.

A second qualification is that in nondemocratic countries developing relations with influential members of government becomes more important because government is not bound by due process requirements and strong courts may not be present to discipline government officials and resolve disputes. In both democracies and nondemocracies, however, obtaining access to government officeholders, whether for the purpose of lobbying or using personal ties or political relationships, can be important for success. Similarly, obtaining information about the agenda of regulators and administrators can be crucial to developing a successful strategy. One concern about personal relationships in emerging markets, however, is that they can become a locus for corruption. Foreign firms may be at a disadvantage relative to domestic firms if there is mistrust of foreigners. In that case, the rationale for having local management and a domestic face are stronger. More generally, the stronger the rent chain in an emerging markets country, the more effective a nonmarket strategy is likely to be.

Another difference in nonmarket strategy between developed and emerging market countries results from the nature and magnitude of risks. For some risks such as those associated with currency fluctuations it may be sufficient simply to hedge the risk in the currency futures market. Similarly, insurance can be purchased for some risks, including the risk of seizure of a business. A firm can also borrow locally as a means of reducing its exposure. For other risks, strategies such as those developed in Parts I and II of this book can be useful. In some cases new strategies may be available. When Venezuela seized oil fields from ExxonMobil, the company filed lawsuits in Europe and the United States to freeze the financial assets of the country.

For some risks it may be possible to draw on an international institution or a home country government. For an issue involving international trade, the WTO is available, but it can only be accessed by governments. This then requires working with the home country government. For other risks the home country may be able to intervene directly, although there is often a risk of backlash against foreign intervention. The Part IV integrative case *Toys 'Я' Us and Globalization* provides an opportunity to decide if the company should attempt to enlist the U.S. government to intervene on its behalf.

Henisz and Zellner (2008) propose a three-component approach to managing policy risk. The first is to understand the preferences of the actors in the market and nonmarket environments. The second is to have a structure analogous to that of the intelligence community that can provide information and assessments. The four I's provide a framework for identifying preferences and collecting information. The third is to influence the risk through collective action and coalitions. The strategy frameworks developed in earlier chapters provide guidance for doing so.

A useful perspective on risk management is risk reduction, which is applicable to private politics as well as public politics. This can involve working with NGOs and local stakeholders to reduce the likelihood that private politics against the firm will arise. This may involve formal interactions with stakeholders as is frequently done in developed countries. A firm may also participate in industry associations to mitigate risk and may work on preparedness in the event that a risk materializes. In the event that a private politics campaign arises against a company, the crisis management approaches presented in Chapter 5 can be helpful.

SUMMARY

Much of the world's future rests with emerging markets countries, which have over 80 percent of the world's population and an even larger market share of expected population growth. Nearly half the people in these countries live in poverty. A number of countries have had very high growth rates that have helped lift more of their people out of poverty and create a middle class. Accompanying that growth are further demands on energy and the environment.

Emerging markets present enormous opportunities not only to source products and extract raw materials but also to market to consumers with rising incomes. Most of these market opportunities are analogous to those in developed countries at present or in their past. Some, however, such as microfinance and serving the consumption needs of the poor, involve more creative business models. Some opportunities are blocked by government restrictions, and others are accompanied by risks that can differ from those in developed countries in terms of their nature, breadth, and magnitude.

Managing in the nonmarket environment of emerging market economies is at least as great a challenge as in developed countries. Many of the same strategies are applicable, but some of the emerging market countries are not democracies and others apply the rule of law inconsistently. This means that the strategies must be tailored to the specifics of the countries, their markets, and their nonmarket environments. For nondemocratic countries strategies for influencing outcomes on issues often involve the development of relationships with government officials. This provides a setting for corruption, and vigilance is required to make certain that managers and advisors do not succumb to temptation.

Some of the issues encountered in emerging markets are moral in nature and require additional frameworks to address them responsibly. Those frameworks are developed in Part V of the book, and Chapter 24 deals specifically with moral issues in international business with an emphasis on emerging markets. The Chapter 18 case *Advanced Technology Laboratories, Inc.* and the Chapter 23 case *Fresenius Medical Care in China* are set in emerging markets countries. The Chapter 21 case *Gilead Sciences (A): The Gilead Access Program for HIV Drugs* concerns the company's attempts to make its HIV/AIDS drugs accessible in low-income countries.

CASES

Social Entrepreneurship: Banco Compartamos

In April 2007 Carlos Danel and Carlos Labarthe took Banco Compartamos public in an IPO that valued the bank at $1.53 billion. Compartamos had been formed in 1990 as a nongovernmental organization by Gente Nueva, a Catholic service organization, to aid the poor in rural areas of Chiapas and Oaxaca, Mexico. In 2001 the two Carloses took the organization private as an SOFOL, a non-deposit-taking financial services company. At that time Compartamos received capital from international development organizations, including ACCION International which provided $1 million for an 18 percent share, and the IFC, the private sector arm of the World Bank. The IFC also provided an initial loan and later provided a partial credit guarantee for a $47 million bond offering.[38]

In the IPO the executives of the bank received $150 million of the $450 million proceeds, and ACCION sold half its share for $135 million, which it invested in new initiatives to help the poor. In 2007 Compartamos had profits of $81.5 million and a loan portfolio of $400 million with only 1.36 percent of its loans nonperforming. Compartamos had become one of Mexico's most successful banks, with an average return on equity of

---

[38]The IFC subsequently provided a $50 million financing package.

40 percent since becoming for-profit. Danel was named a Young Global Leader by the World Economic Forum.

Compartamos' business was microfinance. After taking the bank private, it increased its customers from 60,000 to 839,000 in 2007, and its goal for 2008 was 1 million customers.[39] The bank made loans without collateral to groups composed of friends and neighbors, 99 percent of whom were women.[40] The group then served to monitor the repayments by its members. For example, a group in Villa de Vázques met weekly to plan borrowings and repayments. Micaela Rivera and her mother Alejandra Abúndez had borrowed $3,550 for animal feed and supplies for their homemade cheese business, and another woman had borrowed to start and expand a small restaurant in her home.

Compartamos had 252 service centers in 27 Mexican states and hired over 1,000 new employees in 2006. Its mission statement read,

> Compartamos is a social company committed to the people. We generate development opportunities within the lowest economic segment, based on innovative and efficient models on a wide scale as well as transcending values that create external and internal culture, fulfilling permanent trusting relationships and contributing to a better world.

The interest rates charged by Compartamos were nearly 90 percent, 15 percent of which was a tax. The Mexican nonprofit social service organization Pro Mujer had interest rates only a little lower than those of Compartamos, but the interest rates were far higher than the average of 25–40 percent for microfinance in other countries. Compartamos reported that its interest rates had been reduced by 30 percentage points over the past 5 years as a result of efficiencies that were passed along to borrowers. Costs of operating in Mexico were high. For example, Compartamos agents collected payments on loans weekly, riding busses in rural areas to reach the borrowers. Compartamos employees also met with individual borrowing groups.

Labarthe explained the importance of being able to raise capital rather than relying on donations to fund lending, "It's marvelous to have one creditor, but it's marvelous to have one million creditors, and that's where we really start to change the face of opportunity."[41] Maria Otero of ACCION noted, "This is one strategy that doesn't remain small and beautiful."[42] The two Carloses argued that in a middle-income country like Mexico it was better to resort to the capital markets to raise funds than compete for donations. Compartamos' target customer base was the 14 million Mexican households without access to banking services.

The critics of Compartamos were vicious and vociferous.[43] Muhammad Yunus, the pioneer who started microfinance and received the 2006 Nobel Peace Prize, said, "They're absolutely on the wrong track. Their priorities are screwed up. When you discuss microcredit, don't bring Compartamos into it. Microcredit was created to fight the money lender, not to become the money lender."[44] Yunus also said, "A true microcredit organization must keep its interest rate as close to the cost of funds as possible. There is no justification for interest rates in the range of 100 percent. My own experience has convinced me that microcredit interest rates can be comfortably under the cost of funds plus 10 percent, or plus 15 percent at most."[45] Alex Counts, president of the Grameen Foundation, held that Compartamos' borrowers "were generating the profits but were excluded from them."[46]

Sam Daley-Harris, head of the Microcredit Summit Campaign, said, "Microfinance started in the 1970s with a focus on using this breakthrough to help end poverty. Now it is in great danger of being about how well the investors and the microfinance institutions are doing and not about ending poverty."[47] The microfinance industry group, Consultative Group to Assist the Poor, housed at the World Bank, estimated that 23.6 percent of Compartamos' interest went to profits and that the bank's return on assets was 45 percent compared to an average of 15 percent for Mexican banks. Charles Westerfield, a consultant and critic of Compartamos, said, "Not only are they making obscene profits off poor people, they are in danger of tarnishing the rest of the industry. Compartamos is the first but they won't be the last."[48]

Danel noted, "We don't only see ourselves as a specialist in microfinance but also as the builder of an industry."[49] Bob Patillo of the fund Gray Ghost observed, "This has got Wall Street's eye, London's eye, Geneva's eye—to have one out there to say that if all the dots got connected this can be quite profitable."[50]

Compartamos means "let's share" in Spanish. ◾

Preparation Questions

1. Why do the banks in Mexico not serve more of the poor?
2. What, if anything, are the advantages of Compartamos relative to traditional microfinance organizations that operate as described by Muhammad Yunus?
3. Are the critics of Compartamos right? Should the company lower its interest rates substantially?
4. Should more for-profit microfinance companies be formed? If you were to form such a company, what would you do differently?

Source: This case was prepared by David P. Baron from public sources, including the article "Microloans, Big Profits," by Elizabeth Malkin, *New York Times*, April 5, 2008. Copyright © 2008 by the Board of Trustees of the Leland Stanford Junior University. All rights reserved. Reprinted with permission.

---

[39]Seguros Banamex began offering low-cost life insurance to Compartamos customers in 2006.

[40]The bank also began to make loans to individuals.

[41]*New York Times*, April 5, 2008.

[42]Ibid.

[43]MicroCredit.org hosted an online debate on Compartamos.

[44]*BusinessWeek*, December 13, 2007.

[45]PRNewswire, December 18, 2007.

[46]*New York Times*, April 5, 2008.

[47]Ibid.

[48]Ibid.

[49]Ibid.

[50]Ibid.

Social Entrepreneurship: Kiva

Jessica Jackley moved to California in 2001 and began working for the Stanford Business School. In 2003 Muhammad Yunus, the Bangladesh economist who in 2006 would receive the Nobel Peace Prize, spoke at the school about an innovative program to provide loans to beggars who had been certified with a Grameen identity card. Jessica thought microfinance "was the coolest thing in the world."[51] Shortly thereafter she went to Kenya, Uganda, and Tanzania to interview recipients of microfinance loans. In 2004 her husband of a year, Mark Flannery, also went to Africa. He commented, "I liked the independent spirit of an informal economy. It's much more fun than formal economies. You could buy an entire business there for $500—*that* was exciting."[52]

The Flannerys began to discuss how they could contribute to microfinance, and an Internet approach seemed natural. In October 2005 they ran a pilot trial with eight Ugandan entrepreneurs, as borrowers were called. The Flannerys sent e-mail to their wedding guest list announcing the opportunity to lend, and over the weekend all eight were funded. They also sent out a press release that was posted on Daily Kos, and $10,000 was raised in one day. The first person-to-person micro-lending organization had been born.

At the time Jessica was enrolled in the Stanford MBA program, and Mark quit his job at Tivo to work full-time on Kiva. Mark explained, "We had no idea what we were getting into. Legally, it's a minefield."[53] For example, if they took funding over the Internet, would the financing arrangements be considered securities subject to regulation by the Securities and Exchange Commission? Jennifer was able to find legal assistance, and Kiva was established as a 501(c)(3) nonprofit organization.

A year later Kiva was featured in a 15-minute segment on PBS, and it was deluged with funds. The Flannerys also appeared on *Oprah* and other television programs, and Kiva was featured in Bill Clinton's book *Giving: How Each of Us Can Change the World*. Most loans were funded in less than a day. Kiva also introduced gift certificates, and sold $2.2 million of them over the 2007 Christmas holiday season.

Kiva recruited as president Premil Shah from PayPal, who obtained a commitment from the company to handle Kiva's transactions without charge. Shah had become interested in microfinance as an undergraduate at Stanford University and had worked in India for a microfinance organization. Shah commented on the organization of Kiva, "We have all the complexity of being a Silicon Valley start-up that is growing real fast, coupled with the complexity of international financial transactions. It's a complicated model, with a lot of due diligence and screening required."[54]

Lenders received no interest on their loans, but their principal was repaid and lenders could take their funds or relend them to other borrowers. Most of the lenders reloaned their funds. Although lenders received no interest, Kiva hoped to be able to provide a small return to lenders in the near future. Interest payments would also help with the problem that "…some causes are more popular than others. Widows in Africa are almost always funded immediately, but men in Central America often have to wait longer. The Kiva team plans to experiment with higher interest rates on less popular causes to help attract funders."[55]

Kiva, which means "unity," "agreement," or "concord" in Swahili, matched lenders with entrepreneurs over the Internet. Fiona Ramsey of Kiva explained the role the organization played, "People are by nature generous and want to help others, but they want to do it in a way…where they can really see how they're making an impact on somebody's life. We all see [the philanthropic work that] Bill Gates and Oprah do, and we'd love to do that ourselves. But few of us can afford it." She added, "Right now, we can't offer a financial return on your investment. But we can offer you an emotional return."[56]

The matching of lenders and entrepreneurs took place on www.kiva.org, which not only provided the match but also established a personal link. Shah explained that people do not give to beggars on the street or charities over the telephone because of a lack of transparency. He said, "I don't know where that money's going to go. I don't know if it will be well used. So we back off on giving."[57] Through Kiva, lenders could see the persons to whom they were lending as well as descriptions of the use of the loans and learn about the differences the loans could make in their lives. Approximately 100 entrepreneurs were listed at any one time. Lenders chose how much and to whom to lend. Lenders received e-mail progress reports on the use of the loans, and entrepreneurs made monthly payments on the loans. Kiva later decided to limit to $25 the amount any one lender could lend to a single entrepreneur, so that more people had a chance to lend to the person.

Kiva did not select the entrepreneurs but instead relied on field partners—microfinance organizations with people on the ground in various countries. Field partners identified and screened entrepreneurs, and funds were sent by Kiva to the field partner, who passed them on to the entrepreneur. The field partner administered the loans, collected the monthly payments, and remitted them to Kiva. In some cases the field partners visited borrowers on a daily basis by bicycle. Field partners set the interest rates on loans, which overall averaged 22 percent. The rates varied considerably—from 4 to 50 percent. Rates in Latin America were the highest but were less than those charged by money lenders, which were as high as 100 percent. The interest payments were retained by the field partner to cover costs. As of the spring of 2008 Kiva had 96 field partners in 45 countries, although not all partners were active.

Loans were short term with most maturities between 6 and 12 months. Entrepreneurs could borrow again, and their

---

[51]*Stanford Business,* November/December, 2007.
[52]Ibid.
[53]Ibid.
[54]Ibid.

[55]*BusinessWeek,* July 31, 2006.
[56]*Los Angeles Times,* October 18, 2007.
[57]*Toronto Star,* June 14, 2007.

credit histories were displayed on the Internet page next to their biography and planned use of the loan. In addition to a picture and information about the entrepreneur, the Internet page displayed information about the field partner, including its risk rating, total loans, time with Kiva, delinquency rate, and default rate.

On its Risk and Due Diligence page Kiva warned lenders about the potential risks associated with their lending. Risks were associated with the borrower, the field partner, and the country. Loans were made in countries such as Afghanistan and Iraq, which posed risks. Kiva's relations with field partners could also be subject to risk such as fraud or embezzlement, and each field partner was either active, paused, or closed. Entrepreneurs also posed risks ranging from uncontrolled events like a bad crop to diversion of the funds. Fiona Ramsey of Kiva observed, however, "We have a perception of the poor as a [poor] credit risk, but actually they're a very good credit risk. The poor are motivated to be successful. Usually, this is their only chance for a loan."[58]

As of the spring of 2008 Kiva had 27 employees and 250 volunteers, had funded loans of $27.2 million, and reported a repayment rate of 99.67 percent. Kiva's operating expenses were covered by donations by individuals and foundations. Lenders could donate 10 percent of their funds to Kiva for operating expenses, and those donations provided the bulk of its funding. Silicon Valley firms also assisted with operations.

The limits on Kiva's growth were not in obtaining funds but rather in identifying borrowers and maintaining integrity in the lending process. Field partners had difficulty expanding because their work required people on the ground to visit entrepreneurs and verify the needs of prospective borrowers, distribute funds, and collect payments. Kiva monitored its field partners and gave them a rating of one to five stars. The maximum amount Kiva provided was $100,000 a month for a five-star partner and $10,000 a month for a one-star partner. Finding field partners was time consuming, requiring considerable due diligence and financial and reference checks. The objective was to find reputable and reliable partners, so as to maintain the integrity of the Kiva system. ■

Preparation Questions

1. What role does the Internet play in the success of Kiva?
2. Identify the management challenges Kiva faces.
3. What are the limits to the growth of Kiva?
4. Are there additional roles or services that Kiva could provide to help the poor?
5. What potential threats does Kiva face?

Source: This case was prepared by David P. Baron from public sources, including the article "Small Change, Big Payoff," by Cynthia Haven, *Stanford Business*, November–December 2007. Copyright © 2008 by the Board of Trustees of the Leland Stanford Junior University. All rights reserved. Reprinted with permission.

Equity Bank of Kenya

Beginning in 1984 as a microfinance lender, Equity Bank of Kenya had focused on providing banking services to the unbanked and to small account holders. It recorded impressive growth, maintaining its focus on expanding retail banking services for the Kenyan people. After ethnic conflict surrounding the 2008 elections the situation in Kenya stabilized, and with the signing of the East African Community Common Market protocol among Burundi, Kenya, Rwanda, Uganda, and Tanzania in 2009 and the approval in a public referendum of a new Constitution, optimism and rapid economic progress returned to Kenya. By 2010 Equity Bank had become Kenya's fourth largest bank in assets and the largest in number of customers. Its next stage of growth was to extend its business model of mobile and agency banking to other East African countries.

CEO Dr. James Mwangi said, "we want to focus on a high volume, low margin business model." Consistent with its business model, the bank had the lowest average deposits per account, KSh19,000, of all major banks in Kenya but had the largest customer base that grew to 5.4 million in 2010, representing 57 percent of the banked population in Kenya. Its large customer base reduced its cost of funds. Mwangi said, "Our borrowing is funded disproportionately from our current and savings accounts that come at a low cost."[59] Equity Bank also had a lower wage bill than did other leading Kenyan banks. At the end of 2010 Equity Bank had 5,007 employees and a wage bill of KSh4.3 billion, whereas Barclay's Bank had 5,325 employees with a wage bill of Ksh7.2 billion.[60] Equity Bank had profit of KSh7.1 billion in 2010 for a return on equity of 28.5 percent, and in the first half of 2011 the bank earned KSh4.74 billion.

Equity Bank's vision was "To be the champion of the socio-economic prosperity of the people of Africa," and its mission statement said: "We offer inclusive, customer focused financial services that socially and economically empower our clients and other stakeholders." Equity Bank had received numerous awards from banking associations, and Dr. Mwangi was named African Banker of the Year in both 2010 and 2011.

The bank had begun to expand the scope of its banking activities beyond those of its individual and household base. It had bought a 24 percent interest in Housing Finance, and it had begun making corporate loans, including participating in a syndicate to provide funding for the Kenya-Uganda railroad. Equity Bank also worked with the China Development Bank in providing financing for small and medium sized enterprises. Equity Bank was the agent for China Union allowing its customers to use the bank's ATMs and point of purchase terminals.[61] The Bank was also considering a venture with Chinese real estate developers that would put it in the mortgage business. Mwangi said, "What we will do is, for example, put

[58]*Wall Street Journal*, March 20, 2008.
[59]*Africa News*, July 26, 2011.
[60]*Nation* (Nairobi), January 19, 2011.
[61]*Nation* (Nairobi), November 1, 2011.

up a 20 floor flat to maximize on the land that is available. Land is currently a major issue within Nairobi and we will effectively utilize this."[62]

Despite the broadening of the scope of its banking activities, the primary focus of the bank's growth strategy was to take its successful retail banking business to other countries, emphasizing mobile and agency banking.

MOBILE PHONE BANKING

Mobile phone usage had exploded in East Africa, and users began to use their phones for money transfers by purchasing minutes in one location, transferring them by text, and then cashing them in another location.[63] This informal system gave developers at Safaricom, a unit of Vodafone and the largest mobile phone carrier, the idea of building a commercial system. The result was M-Pesa, which by 2011 had 14 million subscribers in Kenya, about 70 percent of adults. A study revealed that many unbanked subscribers used their M-Pesa accounts like a savings account for small amounts of money. Jan Chipchase of Frog Design described it, "Don't think of [M-Pesa] as mobile money transfer. Think of it as taking money out of circulation."[64] Equity Bank joined with Safaricom to develop a mobile savings account system called M-Kesho. Njuguna Ndung'u, governor of the Central Bank of Kenya, said, "Mobile phone technology has in a few years of its existence demonstrated how financial inclusion can be leapfrogged on a major scale and in a short-time span using appropriate technological platforms."[65] Wireless penetration was projected to reach 50 percent in Africa by 2012.

In addition to M-Kesho, Equity Bank had partnered with Tekom Kenya's Orange to develop Iko-Pesa for agency account users to transfer funds, which gave Equity Bank access to Orange's national service network.[66] Equity Bank's software was embedded in Tekom Kenya's SIM cards. The Bank had an exclusive arrangement for Iko-Pesa for a year, so other banks would be unable to copy its service as they had with E-Kesho. Mwangi said, "This is going to be the biggest mobile banking solution and e-commerce platform that should position Equity as the biggest provider of financial services in Eastern Africa."[67]

AGENCY BANKING

Agency banking had the potential to revolutionize commercial banking. Under the agency banking model a shopkeeper, for example, would act as the front office with the bank managing and guaranteeing deposits. The agent would receive training and be provided with the necessary technology to handle a variety of banking transactions such as deposits, withdrawals, and small loans. Agency banking would make banking available to the poor and to the participants in the informal

sector, which was estimated to represent 30–40 percent of the economy.[68] Mwangi observed, "It will also increase efficiency of the mobile money transfer business, because it allows withdrawals and deposits from M-Pesa, M-Kesho, Iko Pesa, and Yu-cash, the cellphone bank accounts networked with Equity Bank."[69]

By mid-2011 the bank had 2,000 agents that accounted for 20 percent of its transactions. Mwangi said, "About 2,000 agents are working and we envision a situation where agency banking will handle deposits and withdrawals as the staff focus on high business such as loan processing."[70] Equity Bank had innovated in mobile and agency banking by allowing people to open accounts without making a deposit. Other banks had copied the successful innovation. In 2011 the bank allowed customers to reactive their accounts without a charge.

Mwangi explained, "We are able to link about 3,000 accounts a day, suggesting that the demand for these products is high in this market. We may leapfrog on this new innovation to skip some of the steps that Western countries went through such as debit and credit cards."[71] By 2011 agency banking generated transactions with a daily value of KSh200 million.[72]

According to the Central Bank of Kenya, the number of Kenyans with bank accounts increased by 1.1 million in the third quarter of 2010, and agency banking played a large role in that expansion.

INTERNATIONAL EXPANSION

Equity Bank initially decided to take its successful business model to neighboring countries through acquisitions. It began in Uganda with the acquisition in 2008 of Microfinance Ltd., and by 2011 it had 40 branches in the country. Equity Bank was the fastest growing bank in Uganda, becoming the 10th largest in 2011. It entered South Sudan more cautiously with three branches. Integrating the branches into its culture was challenging and costly, and for further entry into foreign markets it planned to bring future employees to work in its headquarters in Nairobi before working at new branches.

Equity Bank's overall strategy was to expand in COMESA (Common Market of East and Southern Africa) countries. The bank planned to open 10 branches in each of Rwanda and Tanzania in 2011. Other foreign banks had entered the markets in those two countries, and Equity Bank planned to focus on the young, women, and the agricultural sector with its agency banking model. "Winning in banking will require us to take our services closest to the people. Mobile and agency banking are the next frontier for growth in the sector."[73] In its Financial Report filed for approval for entry into Rwanda, the bank said, "Agency and mobile banking will decongest the branch banking halls and will also enhance overall customer

---

[62]*Nation* (Nairobi), November 1, 2010.

[63]*Bloomberg Businessweek*, September 12–19, 2011.

[64]Ibid.

[65]*Business Daily* (Nairobi), October 26, 2011.

[66]Equity Bank also had an agreement with Essar Telecom to use its Yu system.

[67]*Africa News*, October 12, 2011.

[68]*East African* (Nairobi), January 2011.

[69]Ibid.

[70]*Nation* (Nairobi), July 25, 2011.

[71]*Nation* (Nairobi), February 8, 2011.

[72]*Africa News*, July 26, 2011.

[73]*East African*, January 2011.

experience including convenience and ease of access."[74] Eric Musau, an analyst at African Alliance, said, "Mobile banking is convenient and cheap, making it attractive to customers in areas where it would not make sense for banks to set up brick and mortar branches."[75]

In July 2011 Mwangi announced, "We have received regulatory approval from the Central Bank of Rwanda to rollout mobile and agency banking there."[76] "The Governor of Central Bank of Rwanda, Clever Gatele, told *Business Times* in a phone interview that Equity Bank's entry will add more value to the market as it is a respected brand in the region, adding that the bank is known to attract every segment in the market, starting from ordinary people to big businesses."[77] The Governor of the National Bank of Rwanda Francois Kanimba said, "It will increase competition in the retail market because currently we have banks which focus on corporates with little activity in the retail market; we believe this will also increase access to finance for SMEs."[78] Kanimba added, "Knowing that Equity is an innovative bank, very dynamic we have already given consent and they can start preparing themselves for the operations."[79] Only 20 percent of Rwandans had access to banking services.

Despite the promising market opportunities in East Africa, shares in Equity Bank fell to a 20-month low in October 2011 as the Kenyan shilling plummeted in international trading due to inflation fears and government budget concerns. With elections scheduled for 2012 some investors were concerned about the possibility of renewed ethnic conflicts between Kalenjin and Kikuyu people as had occurred in conjunction with the 2008 elections. ▪

Preparation Questions

1. Why has mobile and agency banking been so successful in Kenya?
2. What are the competitive advantages of Equity Bank?
3. Is its expansion into Rwanda and Tanzania subject to nonmarket risks?
4. Should Equity Bank expand further south to Zimbabwe? What risks are associated with operating in Zimbabwe?

MTN Group Limited

INTRODUCTION

In May 2008 MTN Group, a very successful South African wireless telephone company, began exclusive discussions with Reliance Communications Ltd., the second largest wireless company in India, regarding possible business combinations including a merger. The previous month discussions between MTN and Bharti Airtel Ltd., India's largest wireless company, had collapsed, reportedly because MTN balked at becoming a subsidiary of Bharti. MTN served 68 million customers in Africa and the Middle East and had a market capitalization of $32 billion.[80] Reliance Communications served 48 million customers and had a market capitalization of $26 billion. Reliance Chairman Anil Ambani said a combination "would provide investors, customers, and the people of both companies a unique and global platform for exponential growth."[81] The day of the announcement of the discussions the share prices of both companies fell by over 5 percent.

The two companies operated in different markets, with Reliance Communications operating in India and MTN operating in 21 countries in Africa and the Middle East. The two companies had somewhat different strengths according to observers. MTN was experienced in entering new national markets and in efficiently building infrastructure. Reliance Communications was experienced in serving very poor customers in rural areas, and its average monthly revenue per subscriber was $8.80 a month. MTN's average customer spent less than $20 a month on wireless service, compared to $40–50 a month in Europe and the United States.

Regardless of whether MTN entered a combination with Reliance Communications, it had to deal with challenges in its ongoing operations and evaluate opportunities in emerging markets in which it was not yet present.

MTN GROUP LIMITED

MTN began in 1994 with the founding of the cellular telephone company M-Cell, which was 25 percent owned by MTN Holdings. Through internal growth and acquisitions the company grew rapidly from 800 employees in 1997 to 20,000 in 2008. In 2001 MTN acquired licenses in Nigeria and built a nationwide microwave transmission system. It continued its expansion in Africa with operations in Rwanda, Swaziland, Uganda, and Ghana. Cellular telephones were popular in Africa because of the lack of access to land-line telecommunications in many countries. In 2005 MTN paid $5.5 billion for Investcom LLC of Lebanon, which provided 21 million subscribers and entrance to the Middle East and North Africa.

In 2008 MTN had operations in the following countries: South Africa, Botswana, Ghana, Nigeria, Zambia, Cameroon, Ghana, Sudan, Uganda, Côte d'Ivoire, Benin, Syria, Afghanistan, Iran, Swaziland, Rwanda, Cyprus, Guinea-Bissau, Guinea-Conakry, Republic of Congo, and Yemen. The company was organized in three geographic regions: South and East Africa

---

[74]*New Times* (Kigali), July 27, 2011.
[75]*Business Daily* (Nairobi), November 10, 2010.
[76]*Africa News*, July 26, 2011.
[77]*New Times* (Kigali), July 27, 2011.
[78]*East African* (Nairobi), April 2011.
[79]Ibid.
[80]For comparison, the largest U.S. wireless company, AT&T Wireless, served 71.4 million customers.
[81]*Wall Street Journal*, May 27, 2008.

(SEA), West and Central Africa (WECA), and the Middle East and North Africa (MENA). In 2007 19 million of its subscribers and 43 percent of its revenues were in SEA, 28 million and 43 percent in WECA, and 14 million and 14 percent in MENA. MTN's EBITDA increased by 43 percent in 2007 resulting in an after tax profit of R11.9 ($1.6) billion on revenue of R73.1 ($9.7) billion. MTN's strongest growth was in South Africa and Nigeria. In its marketing MTN went to the people, using vans in rural areas and selling its prepaid phones at traffic lights.

MTN provided mobile telephone service along with the following enhanced applications: Data Solutions, BlackBerry, International Roaming, Banking, EVD, Mobile TV, Me2U, and CallerTunes. MTN also had begun to invest in broadband in Nigeria and had acquired an Internet service provider in Cameroon.

One component of MTN's strategy was to build and rely on local talent in its operations in each country. Another component was to have local shareholder participation in its national operations, but MTN always maintained a controlling interest. In Uganda it had increased local shareholder participation to 5 percent and in Côte d'Ivoire to 40 percent.

MTN also embraced social responsibility. Mrs. Amina Oyagbola of the MTN Foundation explained, "Corporate Social Responsibility is an integral part of MTN's business strategy. As you know we set up the MTN Foundation to focus on implementing our CSR programmes. To date, MTN is the only organization in the telecom industry that sets aside a percentage of its earnings, annually to CSI (corporate social investment) initiatives in which the MTN executes."[82]

In 2007 MTN introduced "21 Days of Y'ello Care" in Nigeria and the other countries in which it operated. Its staff performed a wide variety of community services in addition to their work obligations. MTN Nigeria CEO Ahamad Farroukh had apologized for quality of service problems, "My firm assurance to you is that despite the infrastructural constraints we face, we remain firmly committed to ensuring that the quality of service on the network continues to improve. In the past nine months, we have embarked on one of the most aggressive network expansion programmes anywhere in the world. We are building dozens more of base station controllers, and several mobile switching centres."[83]

MTN also contributed R5 million for the relief efforts for refugees who had fled to South Africa from countries such as Zimbabwe. Some South Africans had attacked the refugees in the camps they had set up.

MTN was committed to sustainability, which for MTN meant:[84]

- Promoting ethical responsibility and sound corporate governance practices
- Providing a safe working environment in which the health of employees is protected and their opportunities for self-development are enhanced
- Promoting cultural diversity and equity in the workplace
- Minimising adverse environmental impacts
- Providing opportunities for social and economic development within the communities we operate

MTN was proud to have been chosen as the global sponsor of the 2010 FIFA World Cup to be held in South Africa.

OPPORTUNITIES AND RISKS

Although the risks of operating in emerging markets were substantial, those markets provided tremendous opportunities. Market penetration of mobile telephones in Africa was 29 percent, 34 percent in India, 70 percent in the United States, and more than 90 percent in Europe. Because of poor transportation infrastructures and the low penetration rate of Internet service, banking transactions were now beginning to be conducted by cell phones in emerging markets countries. In South Africa many wireless customers use their handsets for even small transactions such as services and retail purchases. In much of Africa many people did not have bank accounts, but the opportunity to make transactions remotely by cell phone could lead them to open a bank account. Moreover, cell phones could be used to make payments on microfinance loans rather than requiring the lender or the borrower to make a physical trip.

One limit to growth in emerging markets was the price of a handset. The cheapest handset was made by Motorola and sold for $30, but with half the people in the world living on less than $2 a day even that price could be prohibitive. To reach rural customers some wireless companies had set up "telephone ladies" who rented their handsets, one customer at a time.

Entry into new markets required a license, and MTN both bid for licenses and acquired licenses from other parties. MTN faced competition from other wireless companies in Africa as well as companies from outside Africa. The largest wireless company in Africa was Orascom of Egypt with 71 million customers. Vodafone had a subsidiary in Egypt and operated in eight countries in Africa, and Orange had investments in 13 African countries. Vodafone also owned Vodacom, a wireless company in South Africa.[85] U.S. firms had shown little recent interest in Africa. Robert Chaphe, who was CEO of MTN from 1995 to 2002, explained, "Many big U.S. telcos eventually lost interest in these markets: they were too small. Now U.S. telcos see more opportunity closer to home. After all, risk ratios are lower in Kansas than in Africa."[86]

In some countries a government-owned or regulated company provided fixed-line service and wireless service as well. Countries belonging to the World Trade Organization (WTO) were required to open their telecommunications industries and issuing a second license for wireless service was a straightforward way of meeting this obligation. For example, Saudi Arabia joined the WTO in 2005, and auctioned a second wireless license. In 2007 it auctioned a third license for wireless service, as well as a license for fixed-line service.

---

[82]*Africa News,* June 9, 2008.

[83]Ibid.

[84]www.mtn.com.

[85]*New York Times,* May 27, 2008.

[86]Ibid.

MTN outbid Altech for Internet service provider Verizon Business in South Africa. MTN's competitors immediately complained about antitrust violations. Angus MacRobert, CEO of Internet Solutions, said, "We have seen how MTN operates around interconnection and mobile data and it is anticompetitive. This is going to intensify it."[87]

Wireless companies in South Africa were subject to reselling of airtime. The Competition Tribunal had scolded Vodacom for trying to eliminate resellers. MTN faced a decision on whether to block an acquisition bid by the Huge Group for reseller iTalk Cellular, which was 41 percent owned by MTN. MTN could do so by buying a majority share. CEO Anton Potgieter of Huge said, "It's been such a game of poker that it's hard to know how hard MTN will try to push it, but I believe we have the moral and legal high ground."[88]

The regulatory systems in each of the countries in which it operated posed a variety of challenges. For example, MTN had experienced problems in repatriating funds from Ghana and Syria, and Benin had suspended the MTN network for 3 months in 2007. MTN described the regulatory environment:[89]

Telecommunications is a regulated industry and MTN engages actively with governments and regulators in all the countries in which it operates. MTN respects the fact that the frequency spectrum is a natural and national resource, and that the management thereof is subject to much public scrutiny.

MTN strives to participate fully in dialogue with governments and regulators on policy and legislative issues and frameworks. While we will lobby for fair treatment in the business interest, we respect the laws of countries in which we operate and the terms of our licence conditions. We endeavour to fulfill the terms of our license obligations, and to go the extra mile in facilitating universal access to communications services. We will not in any way compromise the national interest of countries where we do business. We also participate actively in industry forums that promote improved health and safety issues relating to mobile telephony.

A major problem for wireless companies operating in emerging markets was taxation. The billings systems of wireless companies provided an opportunity for countries to raise funds at little cost to the government by simply taxing wireless phone service and requiring the operator to remit the taxes to the government. Particularly in Africa where most countries were strapped for revenue, taxing wireless service was an opportunity too good to pass up. In addition to a value-added tax countries imposed special levies on wireless service. According to the GSM Association, an industry association, the tax on wireless service represented 47 percent of mobile phone service charges in the Congo, 35 percent in Ghana, 27 percent in South Africa, and 22 percent in Nigeria. Countries faced a tradeoff, however.[90] Wireless phones increased productivity and business activity, so a tax increase could reduce economic growth.[91]

Another challenge was to keep infrastructure costs low to be able to price to attract customers lower on the pyramid. Serving customers in a new country or expanding into new areas in a county required building infrastructure. In Nigeria MTN had not only to build base stations and transmission facilities but also its own power supplies. Some carriers had begun to experiment with new business models, such as franchising parts of the system. For example, Nokia Siemens Networks has been exploring a model in which a local entrepreneur or a village would own a base station and handle service and billings.

THE BUSINESS COMBINATION

One complication to a business combination with Reliance Communications was that billions of dollars of cash might have to be raised to complete the deal. U.S. banks were unlikely to be able to participate in the funding because of U.S. restrictions on facilitating business in Iran. MTN and its local partner Irancell had 6 million customers. Moreover, MTN had 2.1 million customers in the Sudan, and the European Union and the United States had imposed restrictions on companies doing business in that country. The United States also had financial restrictions on companies doing business in Syria, where MTN had 3.1 million customers.[92]

South Africa had regulations governing mergers. Any offer to purchase more than 35 percent of a company required the purchaser to make an open offer for the rest of the shares. India capped foreign direct investment in a telecommunications company at 74 percent, and a purchase of 15 percent of a company required an open offer for the remainder of the shares.[93] Ambani thus could obtain 34.9 percent of MTN, while retaining a share of Reliance Communications. The two companies were bargaining over the exchange of shares. During MTN's negotiations with Bharti, the Indian consumer group Telecom Watchdog had threatened to file a lawsuit to block the merger if a share swap was used in the transaction and violated the FDI restrictions.

After discussions were underway between MTN and Reliance Communications, Reliance Industries LTD., whose chairman was Mukesh Ambani, the older brother of Anil, wrote to MTN stating that it had first rights of refusal on acquiring Reliance Communications. A spokesperson for MTN said, "We are aware that something is going on between the two brothers."[94] ∎

[87]*Africa News,* June 6, 2008.
[88]*Africa News,* May 28, 2008.
[89]www.mtn.com.

[90]The GSM Association represented 750 wireless companies operating in 218 countries and territories and serving 82 percent of the world's users.
[91]*Economist,* May 29, 2008.
[92]*International Herald Tribune,* May 27, 2008.
[93]*Times* (London), June 10, 2008.
[94]*New York Times,* June 14, 2008.

Preparation Questions

1. Why has MTN been so successful?
2. Identify the risks MTN faces.
3. Why does MTN want local shareholders in the countries in which it operates? Why does it want to staff its operations with locals? Why is corporate social responsibility important to the company?
4. How should MTN deal with the risk of higher taxes on wireless service?
5. Suppose that a license were to be auctioned in Zimbabwe. Assess the opportunities and risks in that country.

18 | THE POLITICAL ECONOMY OF INDIA

INTRODUCTION

India is the world's largest democracy and the second largest country in the world with a population over 1.2 billion. With a growth rate of 1.3 percent, it is projected to overtake China by 2030 as the largest country. Its economy has been growing at over 7 percent annually since 1997, and it weathered the financial crisis and economic recession of 2008 better than most developed countries. Yet, its GDP per capita ranked 162 of 227 countries and was less than half that of China and 10 percent that of the European Union.[1] Poverty has diminished as a result of economic growth, but poverty remains one of the greatest challenges for the country. Government data show that the proportion of the population below the poverty level decreased from 45.6 percent in 1983 to 27.5 percent in 2004–2005, but over 300 million people remained below the international poverty level of $1.25 a day.[2] Education, health services, and the development of infrastructure remained major challenges for the country.

Despite its challenges, India provided great opportunities and huge potential. It has developed world-class companies, has a rapidly growing technology sector, and provides broad entrepreneurial opportunities. The country has a vibrant democracy with diverse political parties, but has religious and ethnic divisions and faces a number of domestic insurgencies in addition to tensions with neighbors. The country has several principal religions, a lingering caste system, and a variety of languages spoken. The 2001 census indicated that 30 different languages were spoken by over a million people and 122 by at least 10,000 people. There were a reported 1,500 dialects spoken in India. Although discrimination based on caste was banned by the Constitution, the caste system remained a part of Indian culture. Considerable change has occurred in the implications of caste for individuals, however. An "untouchable" was elected chief minister of the state of Uttar Pradesh, and another headed the Supreme Court.

This chapter focuses on the political economy of India, with an emphasis on nonmarket issues and on the challenges facing the country.

INSTITUTIONS

Government

India is a union of states with a parliamentary system of government and a federal structure. The country has a president, but the government is led by the prime minister who heads the council of ministers (cabinet). The principal government institution is the Parliament, which is bicameral. Members of the House of the People (*Lok Sabha*) are elected for 5-year terms using a proportional representation system, and the prime minister and council of ministers are responsible to the House of the People. The House of States (*Rajya Sabha*) is composed of 250 representatives elected by state assemblies for 6-year terms, with one-third of the members retiring every 2 years.[3] Each of the 28 states has an elected assembly, and a state government is led by a chief minister who heads the state council of ministers. The governor of a state corresponds to the position of president of the country.

Consent of both houses is required to pass legislation, but money bills are the responsibility of the House of the People. A motion of no confidence can be introduced in the House of the People, and if passed on majority vote, the prime minister and the council of ministers must resign.

The federal system in India is composed of the states and 7 union territories. Although the national government has greater powers, the states are important components of the government with some

---

[1]Central Intelligence Agency, The World Book, GDP per Capita (Purchasing Power Parity), 2010 estimates.
[2]World Bank, "Perspectives on Poverty in India," 2011.
[3]Twelve members are nominated by the president.

independent authority and responsibilities for implementing policies. The country has an extensive bureaucracy and regulatory system, and some industries such as railways and electric power are dominated by government-owned firms.

India has an independent judiciary with a Supreme Court of 26 justices and a chief justice. The Supreme Court hears cases in smaller benches. The judiciary is patterned after the British system, with 19 High Courts below the Supreme Court with authority over the judiciaries in the states. The Supreme Court in India has taken a more activist role than has the Supreme Court in the United States in part because India has a system of public-interest litigation in which third parties can file lawsuits on a policy issue and the cases can go directly to the Supreme Court.

History and Economic Development

British colonial India included what is today Bangladesh, India, and Pakistan. India and Pakistan became independent from Britain in 1947, and Bangladesh was formed from East Pakistan as a result of the 1971 war supported by India against West Pakistan (the current Pakistan). West Pakistan countered by attacking India, which was supported by the Soviet Union, while the United States supported Pakistan.

The independence movement had been led by Mohandas Gandhi, who used nonviolent methods in seeking independence from the British. The Constitution established parliamentary political institutions based on the Westminster model from Britain. At independence India was led by Jawaharlal Nehru, its first prime minister, and the successor to Gandhi as political leader. Nehru and the Congress Party embarked on a socialist path and implemented a socialist economic policy for several decades. The policy involved a Soviet-style 5-year planning process under which the country emphasized the development of heavy industry at the expense of consumer goods. The policy included import substitution and restrictions on foreign direct investment and little emphasis on international trade. Domestically, economic policy involved extensive regulation and increasingly tight controls over the economy. Beginning in the 1970s the government led by Indira Gandhi began the process of nationalization of companies, and by 1973 all banks, insurance companies, coal mines, and oil companies had been nationalized. The government also sought to force foreign companies to hold only minority stake in their ventures. Gandhi also controlled international trade and foreign exchange. During her government, the Constitution was amended in 1977, inserting "socialist secular" into the preamble's identification of the country."[4] Gandhi's socialist policies were a failure, resulting in economic stagnation, inefficiency, and little progress in reducing poverty.

A change of government brought the beginning of economic liberalization using a piecemeal approach, and slow liberalization continued on and off until 1991. In that year, the Congress Party prime minister appointed economist Dr. Manmohan Singh as minister of finance. The opportunity for liberalization of the economy was a balance-of-payments crisis in 1991 and intervention by the World Bank. Dr. Singh took the occasion to address Parliament on July 24, 1991, stating, "the room for maneuver, to live on borrowed money or time, does not exist any more."[5] He abandoned central planning and began a comprehensive process of economic liberalization that has continued, although more slowly in recent years. The liberalization has resulted in sustained high levels of growth in the economy and helped make India an important world player.

Economic liberalization accelerated in the early 2000s under the government formed by the National Democratic Alliance (NDA). The government lowered tariffs, reformed the tax system, privatized a number of companies, opened the insurance industry to competition, allowed competition in banking, and restructured the telecommunications industry. The liberalization had a positive effect on the economy, but the NDA lost the 2004 elections and

---

[4]The preamble of the Constitution states, "WE, THE PEOPLE OF INDIA, having solemnly resolved to constitute India into a SOVEREIGN SOCIALIST SECULAR DEMOCRATIC REPUBLIC and to secure to all its citizens:

    JUSTICE, social, economic and political;

    LIBERTY of thought, expression, belief, faith and worship;

    EQUALITY of status and of opportunity; and to promote among them all

    FRATERNITY assuring the dignity of the individual and the unity and integrity of the Nation."

[5]*Economist*, July 23, 2011.

the Congress Party led a coalition government with Dr. Singh as prime minister.[6] The most powerful politician in India was Sonia Gandhi, widow of former prime minister Rajiv Gandhi, who was assassinated in 1991. She was president of the Congress Party and leader of the United Progressive Alliance (UPA) in the Lok Sabha, which formed the government headed by Dr. Singh.

The country has been politically stable but faces lingering tensions between its Hindu and Muslim populations, a Maoist insurgency in the eastern states, conflict with Pakistan over Kashmir, and foreign-based terrorism. The CountryWatch Political Risk Index is 8, compared to 7 for China and 9 for the United States. The Freedom House scores for political rights and civil liberties are 2 and 3, respectively, compared to 1 and 1 for the United States and 7 and 6 for China.

Economic Restrictions

Despite the economic liberalization, restrictions remained in some sectors. The government had relaxed many of the restrictions on foreign direct investment (FDI), and FDI had increased from $8.28 billion in 2003 to $29.4 billion in 2011, but that was down from its peak of $41 billion in 2009. Unrestricted FDI was allowed in most industries, but was restricted to minority ownership in several industries, including insurance, print media, and air transportation. FDI was allowed up to 74 percent in banking, telecommunications, coal and lignite, mining, and airports. The limits were often binding. In 2011 UK-based Vodafone bought Essar Group's one-third interest in a joint venture for $5 billion, but because Vodafone already has a 42 percent share of the joint venture, it was forced to sell 1.3 percent of the company. Other regulations restricted the growth of foreign companies. For example, foreign banks were required to obtain approval from the government for each branch they sought to open. FDI was still banned in four industries: retail trading (with the exception of single-brand retailing), atomic energy, lottery business, and gambling and betting.

India's impressive economic growth rate stood in contrast to the effect of regulations, permits, and licenses on new business. The World Bank *Doing Business 2011* report ranked India 134th of 183 countries in the ease of doing business. India was near the bottom in the categories of Starting a Business, Dealing with Construction Permits, Paying Taxes, and Enforcing Contracts. The rankings were based on both costs and the time required, for example, to obtain a permit.

The restrictions on retailing reflected the potential threat to small shops and stall retailers. An estimated 30 million Indians were employed in retailing, and the government feared that lifting the restrictions could drive many of them out of business. Foreign retailers were banned from using FDI for direct sales to individuals, and multi-brand retailers were barred from owning and operating their own stores. Foreign retailers could make franchise arrangements, however, with local retailers, but India had few large retailers. Foreign retailers could also establish joint ventures. In 2007 Wal-Mart and Bharti formed a joint venture in which Wal-Mart would operate the back-end of Bharti's retail operations. Protests erupted from activists and others who feared that Wal-Mart's presence would harm small retailers.

The chapter case *Tesco PLC in India?* considers the issue of whether the largest retailer in the United Kingdom should enter the Indian market and if so, how it should do it, given the restrictions on FDI. Tesco PLC was attracted to the Indian retail market by the size and structure of the market. The retail market in India had sales of $200 billion in 2005 and was growing rapidly with a projected market potential of $300 billion in 2010. The organized sector, consisting of establishments with 10 or more employees, accounted for only 3 percent of sales but was projected to account for 10 percent of sales by 2010. The unorganized sector consisted of nearly 11 million outlets, including kirana shops and other small stores, with only 4 percent having over 500 sq ft. of floor space.[7] The restrictions on FDI in retailing meant that Tesco either had to stay out of India or find a way to enter that would prepare the company for when the restrictions were relaxed.[8]

---

[6]Panagariya (2008) provides a detailed account of the economic policies and performance in India. Mukherji (2007) presents a collection of papers on Indian economic development and policy.

[7]www.thehindubusinessline.com, June 1, 2006.

[8]In 2011 India began considering initial steps to liberalize foreign direct investment in retailing.

OPPORTUNITIES

Market Opportunities

The principal market opportunities in India stemmed from domestic demand. McKinsey & Co. studied the marketplace in India and concluded that at the projected growth rates the middle class would increase from 50 million to 583 million people by 2025 and 291 million people would move from "desperate poverty to a more sustainable life...."[9] Exports also represented an opportunity, with Indian companies being leaders in the outsourcing movement. Manufacturing exports had increased to the point where they exceeded services exports by a factor of two. The inflation rate was approaching 10 percent in 2011, however.

The economy was the 10th largest in the world, and it was projected to be the third largest by 2030. Michigan State University developed a Market Potential Index for 26 emerging markets taking into account factors such as market size, growth rate, market intensity, market consumption capacity, commercial infrastructure, economic freedom, market receptivity, and country risk. The 2010 index ranged from Hong Kong at 100 and Venezuela at 1, with India at 48 and China at 92. India lagged on the commercial infrastructure index and market receptivity, a measure of international trade. In terms of competitiveness, India was 32nd of 59 countries in the 2011 IMD Overall Competitiveness rankings, whereas China was 19th and the United States tied for first with Hong Kong. India was not a major exporter as was China, but an export oriented economy was developing in Gujarat state. The western state had 5 percent of the population, 16 percent of India's industrial output, and 22 percent of the country's exports.[10]

GDP per capita in India for 2010 was $1,477, compared to $4,393 for China and $47,184 for the United States, as determined by the World Bank. Correcting for purchasing power parity, GDP per capita was $3,560 for India, $7,570 for China, and $47,020 for the United States.

The industry composition of GDP has changed significantly over the past 20 years with the services sector increasing from 45 percent of GDP to over 55 percent. The increase has been at the expense of agriculture, which declined from over 30 percent to under 17 percent, whereas manufacturing has remained constant at 16 percent. The so-called "black economy" was estimated to have increased dramatically in India even as the economy grew. Arun Kumar, chairman of a research center at Jawaharlal Nehru University explained, "The reason it has grown is that illegality in society has become more and more tolerable."[11] Another explanation is that the black economy grew when the economy was hampered by excessive regulations. Prime Minister Singh stated, "I affirm our commitment to a new wave of reform. I am aware of the fact that much more needs to be done to make our economy competitive."[12]

The rapid economic growth had produced a large and growing middle class in India. The middle class generated demand for products similar to those in developed countries, providing opportunities for foreign companies. For example, the market for mobile telecommunications had exploded, resulting in some 700 million cellphone users. The growth was stimulated by low prices for handsets and for service, but the available networks were only 2G. Corruption was involved in the 2008 allocation of operating licenses, and the ensuing crisis had made regulators cautious. The potential for 3G and 4G networks was enormous, but intense competition had left the mobile communications companies without the resources to build faster networks. The mobile communications companies complained that merger rules prohibited any company from having more than 40 percent of the subscribers in any market. This resulted in inefficiencies, including an excessive number of carriers in many markets. Some markets were served by a dozen or more carriers, and competition for subscribers had driven prices and profits down, leading the companies to reduce their rate of investment in infrastructure. The Indian government sought to have fewer but stronger companies.

Additional spectrum was also needed, and stung by the corruption scandal, the telecommunications ministry auctioned some spectrum for 3G service in 2010. Companies bid aggressively and prices were high. The telecommunications minister Kapil Sibal said referring to future spectrum allocations, "The big companies who have deep pockets only want an auction

---

[9]McKinsey Global Institute, "The 'Bird of Gold': The Rise of India's Consumer Market." May 2007.
[10]*Economist*, July 9, 2011.
[11]*Wall Street Journal*, March 30, 2011.
[12]Ibid.

because they can snuff out everybody else."[13] The ministry pledged to use a market-based mechanism for future spectrum allocations but one that would yield a fair price.

Carriers complained that the ministry continued to impose additional regulations on them. Srinivasa Addepalli, senior vice president of Tata Communications, said, "You can't launch a service and then be told after the fact that you need some new permissions. It leads to uncertainty in the market and a waste of resources."[14] Carriers were also nervous about the possibility that the licenses allocated in the 2008 corruption scandal could be reallocated as a result of a pending court decision.

The explosion in demand for mobile communications had not carried over to the Internet. Data from 2009 indicated that Internet users represented only 5.5% of the population, whereas the comparable figure for Brazil was 39.2% and 29% for both China and Russia. With a growing middle class, the Internet opportunities in India were enormous. In addition, Indians were underbanked and few had credit cards. Mobile communications devices could be used for making banking and payment transactions as well as online purchases as they were in Africa. The opportunities led local entrepreneurs to establish their own dot.coms often along the model of those in developed countries.

E-commerce was relatively underdeveloped, and business models faced the risk of liability for information provided or posted on a Web site. India's constitution established the right to free speech, but that right was subject to "reasonable restrictions" to protect "public order, decency, or morality."[15] Web sites were required to take down objectionable material, and a company that hosted Web sites could be required to take down a Web site. Objectionable material is that which "threatens the unity, integrity, defense, security or sovereignty of India, friendly relations with foreign states or public order."[16] The chapter case *Google in India* considers the issues from the perspective of Google.

India embarked on an ambitious solar power program to produce 22,000 megawatts of power by 2022, and it planned to fund the first few years of the program with $20 billion in subsidies. To keep the benefits from the subsidization in India, the Ministry of New and Renewable Energy issued rules that banned the importation of solar panels. Foreign companies were allowed to operate in India but only through joint ventures with Indian companies. The rules favored Indian companies, the largest of which were Moser Baer India and Tata BP Solar. Critics of the imports ban argued that the protection would both cut Indian companies off from technological innovations in solar power and lead domestic companies to increase their prices. Bryan Ashley of the U.S. solar panel producer Suniva, who represented U.S. producers in discussions over the rules, stated that "This has been pushed by some in the Indian industry to give themselves a monopoly."[17] K. Subramanya, CEO of Tata BP Solar, explained that the goal of the new rules was "to create a whole new solar ecosystem generating employment, entrepreneurship, and technical innovations."[18]

Opportunities were substantial in the food and household products markets. The food market was complex because of ethnic differences and religious traditions across the country. Household products such as refrigerators and cleaning supplies had more homogeneous demand. Both Nestlé and Unilever had operated in India for many years, and both had developed the local market knowledge necessary for success in the country. Local knowledge was more important for Nestlé because some religious and ethnic groups had their own food restrictions. To better understand the market, Nestlé conducted "Project Epicure" in 2006 making "1,500 visits to Indian homes, rich and poor, to see how people cook and eat."[19] Hindustan Unilever focused less on the religious and ethnic characteristics of the market and more on determining the size of packages and prices. Other foreign companies sought to obtain market knowledge through joint ventures or acquisitions.

In 2011 Starbucks decided to enter the market in India and entered into an alliance with Tata Coffee, which had coffee plantations in India. Corey duBrown of Starbucks said, "We are

---

[13]*Wall Street Journal*, May 31, 2011.
[14]Ibid.
[15]*Wall Street Journal*, January 2–3, 2010.
[16]*New York Times*, April 28, 2011.
[17]*Wall Street Journal*, December 15, 2010.
[18]Ibid.
[19]*Economist*, August 6, 2011.

excited about the great opportunities that India presents to Starbucks."[20] Earlier in the year the two companies signed an agreement under which Starbucks would source and roast coffee. The venture was expected to take advantage of other companies in the Tata Group such as its hotels and retail operations. Dunkin' Brands also entered into an agreement with Jubilant FoodWorks Ltd. under which the company would open between 25 and 30 Dunkin' Donuts stores in the next 3 years. Coffee drinking had been increasing in popularity, with demand increasing by 80 percent over the past decade.

Business Groups

Many emerging markets countries have domestic business groups, which are frequently family controlled. In emerging market economies with underdeveloped capital and resources markets and uncertain government regulation and policies, business groups can provide efficiencies similar to those that can be achieved through contracting in developed economies. A number of the business group conglomerates have expanded overseas primarily through acquisitions. Many of India's business groups are family controlled, including Reliance Industries led by Mukesh Ambani and the telecommunications, electric power, and finance conglomerate led by his brother Anil. Other business groups include Bharti and Sterlite Industries (Vedarta). The largest of the business groups is led by Ratan Tata, whose family founded the group in 1868.

The Tata Group includes 98 operating companies that employ 395,000 people. The companies include Tata Motors, Taj Hotels Resorts and Palaces, Tata Steel, Tata Chemicals, Tata Power, Tata Sky, and Tata Consultancy Services among other companies. Tata Global Brands is the world's largest producer of branded tea.

Tata has expanded overseas both through extension of its product lines and acquisitions and joint ventures. Tata Consultancy Services is among the world's largest consultancies and Asia's largest software company. Through acquisitions Tata became the largest manufacturer in Britain. In 2000 Tata Tea bought the UK's Tetley Tea; in 2007 Tata Steel bought steel producer Corus for $12 billion, the successor to British Steel; in 2006 Tata Chemicals acquired Brunner Mond chemicals; and in 2008 Tata Motors bought Jaguar Land Rover for $2.3 billion. In 2011 Tata employed 40,000 people in the United Kingdom, including 4,900 employed by Tata Consultancy Services, and nearly 15,000 employees in India supported British services providers.[21] The group also had a number of joint ventures in emerging markets, although its British operations accounted for over half of its revenues.

One of the most ambitious efforts of Ratan Tata was the development of an affordable automobile, the Nano, to replace the bicycles and motor scooters used by many lower income Indians for both personal and business purposes. Farmers in West Bengal demonstrated against the construction of the Nano production plant in their state, and Tata moved the plant to Gujarat in the west of the country. The four-door car was sold at a price of $2,900 beginning in 2009, and sales were modest in part because of limited dealerships and limited credit for buyers. Tata Motors hoped to export the Nano to other emerging markets countries.

Some businesses have emerged and prospered because of the inefficiency of the Indian economy and particularly its infrastructure. A number of large companies built their own power companies because of the unreliable power supply in some parts of the country. Gautam Adani built a successful business group by working around the Indian infrastructure and political system. His Adani Group owned an electric power company in the state of Gujarat that was supplied by coal from the Group's company in Indonesia because it was too costly to transport Indian coal to the power plant. He also owned the ships that hauled the coal and the port where it was unloaded. The success of his venture led to plans to build eight additional power plants. Needing a connection to the government-owned Indian Railroads system, he built his own 40-mile railroad spur rather than wait for Indian Railroads to build the line.[22]

Patent law

Some of India's economic liberalization was required by membership in the World Trade Organization. For example, Indian patent law allowed patents on methods of production but

---

[20]*Wall Street Journal*, October 11, 2011.
[21]*Economist*, September 10, 2011.
[22]*New York Times*, July 27, 2011.

not on products themselves. This allowed an Indian pharmaceutical company to produce a drug patented in Europe and the United States if it used a different production process. This spurred the development of a vigorous pharmaceutical industry in India, with many companies producing generic versions of patented drugs. With the adoption of the TRIPS agreement for the protection of intellectual property, India was forced to change its patent system to conform with the type of intellectual property protection found in Europe and the United States (TRIPS and the WTO are discussed in Chapter 19). This changed the incentives for Indian pharmaceutical companies, and some began to develop their own proprietary drugs.

Pharmaceuticals

As a result of its patent law, India's pharmaceuticals industry had some 5,000 pharmaceutical companies producing 20 percent of the world's generic drugs. One advantage of the pharmaceutical companies was that doctors tended to prescribe drugs using brand names, and pharmacists were prohibited from substituting another generic equivalent drug. In addition, pharmaceutical advertising was prohibited. These factors had three effects. First, they reduced competition among generics. Second, they provided incentives for pharmaceutical companies to market their drugs directly to doctors. India had an estimated 100,000 sales representatives, and McKinsey estimated that by 2020 the country would have 3 sales representatives for every 10 doctors. Third, companies had an incentive to introduce generic drugs with brand names. India had 92,000 registered brand name drugs, and 43 brands of the blood pressure drug olmesartan.[23] Chandra M. Gulhati, editor of the Indian edition of *Monthly Index of Medical Specialties*, said, "The number of medicine brands sold in India is at least 30 times that in the U.S. and Europe."[24]

Pharmaceutical sales had increased by 14 percent a year since 2005, and projections were for continued rapid growth as incomes grow and the country improves its health care system. Domestic sales reached $12 billion in 2010, and industry revenue, including exports, reached $19 billion with projected sales of $50 billion by 2020.[25] The size and growth of the Indian pharmaceutical market and the new patent protection provided under TRIPS attracted foreign pharmaceutical companies. Pfizer and GlaxoSmithKline had units in India, and other major global pharmaceutical companies began to acquire Indian firms. Mylan Laboratories of the United States acquired a majority interest in Marix Laboratories, Daiichi Sankyo of Japan acquired a majority interest in Ranbaxy Laboratories, Sanofi-Aventis of France acquired a majority interest in Shanta Niotechnics, Reckitt Benckiser of the United Kingdom acquired Para Pharmaceuticals, and Abbott Laboratories of the United States acquired Piramal Healthcare. The acquisitions raised concerns about the future development of the Indian health care market and about the prices of drugs.

One policy alternative considered by the government was to restrict acquisitions, but that could signal to a resurgence of protectionism and spur a reaction from global financial markets that could reduce foreign direct investment. A more attractive alternative was to have all pharmaceutical acquisitions reviewed by the Competition Commission, the antitrust regulator. Arun Maira, an official of the Planning Commission, explained, "Please come inside and enjoy yourself, but we want to make sure you don't cause any harm."[26] The Indian Pharmaceutical Alliance (IPA), an industry association, advocated stricter controls on acquisitions. Secretary General D.G. Shah said, "If one were not to take note of it and initiate appropriate action, the damage to the domestic industry and the public health will be irreversible."[27] Shah argued for required approval of any acquisition by the Foreign Investment Promotion Board. The U.S.–India Business Council (USIBC) wrote to the Indian government seeking "to prevent the enactment of protectionist measures in the industry."[28]

---

[23]*Bloomberg Businessweek*, September 12–18, 2011.
[24]Ibid.
[25]*Wall Street Journal*, September 27, 2011.
[26]*Wall Street Journal*, September 27, 2011.
[27]Ibid.
[28]Ibid.

NONMARKET ISSUES

Corruption

Corruption is widespread in India ranging from small payments demanded by low level bureaucrats to corruption involving major businesses. In its Corruption Perceptions Index, Transparency International ranked India tied with Albania, Jamaica, and Liberia for 87th of the 178 countries included in its survey. China was tied for 78th. Corruption was a major concern of citizens, but many individuals were complicit. Tax evasion was widespread, and many Indians were involved in the theft of electricity. Author Amir Kumar estimated that tax evasion cost the country $314 billion a year.[29]

Electricity theft was widespread in some areas. According to Power Secretary P. Uma Shankar, approximately one-third of the electric power generated in India was lost to theft and dissipated in transmission, whereas in China the losses were 8 percent.[30] Much of the power theft was due to individual households hooking wires to power lines or bypassing meters. Power Secretary Shankar commented, "In a government-owned company there can be corruption, which interferes with the task of reducing theft. Private companies tend to have much better governance and have very clear targets."[31] One approach taken by the government was to turn over administration of the power system to private companies. In New Delhi, administration had been turned over to Reliance Power and Tata Power, which had been able to reduce theft by two-thirds. The government sought investment of $400 billion in the power sector, but theft reduced the incentives to invest.

In a major corruption episode in 2008, a state government allocated 2G mobile telecommunications licenses based on favoritism, costing the government an estimated $36 billion in lost revenue. The minister of Telecommunications and Information Technology at the time and several other government officials were imprisoned, and the previous minister was charged with rigging the allocations. The case was taken to the Supreme Court, and the companies involved could be subject to penalties. Corruption was also present in India's hosting of the Commonwealth Games 2010, and widespread corruption was found in the iron ore industry.

Part of the difficulty in exposing corruption was the Indian law that imposed penalties on both the government official demanding a payment and the person making the payment, discouraging citizens from filing complaints. One response by citizens was to set up a Web site ipaidabribe.com, which attracted 14,516 reports of corruption as of October 2011.

Corruption also manifested itself in electoral competition. In 2006 in the state of Tamil Nadu, the DMK party promised every voter a free color TV if it won the election. The DMK won the election and delivered 16 million color TVs, paid for by the government. The DMK was also at the center of the telecommunications scandal, and as a result it was vulnerable in the 2011 elections. In Tamil Nadu the party promised free laptop computers for engineering students, and the opposition AIADMK party promised free laptops to all college and 11th and 12th grade students. The DMK countered by pledging to give all voters a "mixie" (blender) or a grinder used in preparing meals in south India. The party also promised an insurance program for fishermen, and washing machines and refrigerators to some voters.[32] Not to be outdone, the AIADMK promised "a blender, a grinder, and a fan for all women; four free sheep for poor families; four grams of gold for poor brides (for the necklaces brides wear on their wedding day); 60,000 cows for 6,000 villages and free cable-TV connections for all."[33] Giving or promising gifts to voters in exchange for their votes was illegal in India, and a lawsuit on the practice was before the Supreme Court. The political parties explained that they were not buying votes or bribing voters but were providing welfare programs. A DMK spokesperson explained, "There are people in rural areas who still use the hand-grinding method. It's a lifestyle improvement."[34] The voters tossed the DMK out of power in Tamil Nadu largely because of its involvement in the telecommunications scandal.

---

[29]Amir Kumar, *The Black Economy in India*, Penguin Books, New Delhi, 2002. Cited in *Bloomberg Businessweek*, August 1–7, 2011.

[30]*Bloomberg Businessweeek*, June 20–26, 2011.

[31]Ibid.

[32]*Wall Street Journal*, April 11, 2011.

[33]Ibid.

[34]Ibid.

In the Gandhian tradition, activist Anna Hazare led a populist campaign against corruption in 2011. Hazare went on a hunger strike to mobilize support for the creation of an anticorruption Lokpal, an ombudsman that would be largely independent of government. It would have broad powers to investigate and bring cases against government corruption at all levels, including the judiciary and the prime minister. Opponents of an independent Lokpal warned that such an organization would be outside the usual democratic checks in India. The Singh government agreed to establish a Lokpal, but the government's draft bill exempted the prime minister and the judiciary. The fate of the bill was uncertain.

Poverty and Welfare

The growth in the economy had lifted many Indians out of poverty, but there were many who were left behind. Ravi Venkatesan, former chairman of Microsoft in India, commented, "we could end up with a rather unstable society, as aspirations are increasing and those left behind are no longer content to live out their lives. You already see anger and expressions of it. I strongly have a sense we're at a tipping point: There is incredible opportunity but also dark forces. What we do as an elite and as a country in the next couple of years will be very decisive…. What has globalization and industrialization done for India? About 400 million have seen benefits, and 800 million haven't."[35]

Life expectancy in India increased from 58 years in 1991 to 64 years in 2008, and mortality for children under six years had decreased substantially. Despite the improvements, its health statistics lagged far behind those of China. Infant mortality in 2010 was 48.2 per 1,000 in India compared to 15.8 in China, and maternal mortality in 2008 was 230 per 100,000 in India and 38 in China.[36] To improve maternal and infant care, India began offering $30 to a woman who had her baby in a hospital rather than at home.[37]

A detailed study of poverty in India by the World Bank 2011 was published in *Perspectives on Poverty in India.* Poverty was present in the cities, but it was widespread in rural areas. In her 2009 election campaign, Sonia Gandhi campaigned on the platform of lifting the common man out of poverty. Succeeding in the election, the government established a $9 billion jobs program in rural areas to build irrigation projects and other public facilities. The program raised incomes but may not have enabled workers to emerge from poverty. Government statistics revealed that 41.6 percent of the population lived on $1.25 a day or less.[38]

Microfinance had grown in India, providing loans to people who were too poor to borrow from a bank or were far from a bank (microfinance is discussed in Chapter 17). Many of these borrowers had traditionally borrowed from local loan sharks at very high interest rates. Microlending had flourished in the state of Andhra Pradesh and large private lenders operated in the market. SKS Microfinance was one of the largest and had raised $350 million in the Indian stock market. The interest rates on loans were high in part because of the costs of administering and collecting payments. The microlenders preferred lending to women's circles but also made loans to individuals. Local politicians in Andhra Pradesh became concerned about high interest rates and about high-pressure collection tactics used by some agents. Politicians also blamed microlending for 70 suicides in the state, although local residents disputed that microlending, rather than loan sharks for example, was to blame.[39] One woman committed suicide because of pressure from microcredit lenders and from the women's circles she had joined to borrow money. She had borrowed a total of $3,400 on eight loans and used most of it for her daughter's wedding.[40]

Local politician A. Subramanyam said, "I told them [a women's circle] if they don't have the money, they don't have to pay. I have seen them sell their wedding jewelry to pay the installments, why should they do that? No one here has prospered with these loans"[41] In December 2010 the Andhra Pradesh state assembly enacted a law to cap the interest rate on

---

[35]*Wall Street Journal*, March 30, 2011.
[36]World Bank, "World Development Indicators," July 28, 2011.
[37]*Wall Street Journal*, July 30–31, 2011.
[38]*Wall Street Journal*, April 30–May 1, 2011.
[39]*Wall Street Journal*, October 29, 2010.
[40]Microcredit Summit Campaign, "State of the Microcredit Summit Campaign Report 2011: Introduction." www.microcreditsummit.org.
[41]*Wall Street Journal*, October 29, 2010.

microlending and to regulate collections. This and political activity in other parts of the country led banks to curtail their lending to microlending companies and organizations. The festering revolt by politicians threatened the lenders and put in jeopardy the availability of this form of credit for the poor. Vikram Akula, founder and chairman of SKS Microfinance said, "This is potentially going to devastate lending to rural areas for a long time. We are confident that we will survive, but certainly this is going to change how things could and should be done."[42]

An alternative to microfinance was to bring banking to the poor, particularly in rural areas, so as to lower their transaction costs and make saving easier. Two-thirds of Indians lived in 600,000 villages, and there were only 35,000 branch banks in the country, so most villages had no ready access to banking. Banks developed a business model in which they sent "business correspondents" to visit a circuit of villages and serve as mobile tellers, explaining about banking, helping people establish an account, and making small transactions for them. When people needed funds for a family emergency, for example, they could withdraw funds from their account rather than borrow from the local loan shark.[43] Deposits in the accounts earned 4 percent interest. The Reserve Bank of India had pushed the idea, and by 2011 there were 60,000 business correspondents taking banking to the people. Abhijit V. Banerjee, a professor of economics at the Massachusetts Institute of Technology, commented, "This is something that could be powerful. It's true that this will not make them rich, but it will make them less likely to face starvation someday."[44]

In China a huge number of people had moved from rural areas to cities and industrial areas, but a similar mass movement has not yet occurred in India. Approximately two-thirds of India's population lived in rural areas. McKinsey predicted that by 2030 urban populations in India would increase by 250 million and that cities might not have the means to provide the services demanded by the greater numbers.[45]

Education continued to be a challenge for the country, even though the literacy rate had increased from 65 percent to 74 percent over the past decade. India had elite schools and universities, but the poor were often left with subpar schools and education. The low quality of public schools led to higher-income families sending their children to private schools. The District Information System for Education reported that for the first through the eighth grades 130 million students were enrolled in public schools and 57 million in private schools.[46] In response, India enacted the Right to Education Act in 2009 that required all private schools to allocate 25 percent of their seats to low-income and underprivileged children.

The Missing Girls

The 2011 census revealed that the gender ratio of children five and under decreased to 914 girls for 1,000 boys compared to 927 in 2001. In Haryana state the ratio was 830. The natural relation was slightly more boys than girls, so approximately 600,000 girls were missing each year. The explanation was a preference for boys that resulted in sex selection through the abortion of female fetuses and much less commonly female infanticide. Sex selection was a phenomenon as well in China and a number of other countries, but in India it appeared to be worsening. Demographer Alaka Basu commented that it "seems to spread son preference to places that were once more neutral about the sex composition of their children."[47] Some states where sex selection was the worst were some of the highest income states, including Punjab, Haryana, and Gujarat. In addition to sex selection, some families neglected their young girls.

One explanation for the preference for boys over girls was the tradition of providing a dowry. A family with a daughter may incur expenses in arranging a marriage and must provide an expensive dowry that can leave some families in debt. In contrast, a boy will obtain a wife and a dowry. The practice of providing a dowry had spread to states that had not previously had the tradition and had become more prevalent in wealthier states. The *Economist* wrote, "as Indians

[42]Ibid.

[43]Banerjee and Duflo (2011) provide an insightful analysis of the causes of poverty.

[44]Ibid.

[45]McKinsey Global Institute, "India's urban awakening: Building inclusive cities, sustaining economic growth." April 2010.

[46]*Wall Street Journal*, June 4–5, 2011.

[47]*Economist*, April 9, 2011.

grow wealthier, dowries are getting more lavish and are spreading to places where they were once rare, such as Tamil Nadu and Kerala, in the south."[48]

Technology played a role in sex selection. In particular, ultrasound devices were routinely used during pregnancies, and they could early on identify the sex of a fetus. It was illegal in India for a medical professional to reveal the sex of a fetus, but it was easy to find someone who would do so. Portable ultrasound machines made possible an illegal mobile sex selection business. The chapter case *Advanced Technology Laboratories, Inc.*, concerns a producer of portable ultrasound devices that must decide how to operate in India where its devices could be used for illegal sex selection.

Some hope for reducing sex selection was provided by a change in attitude of the people. South Korea had a distorted sex ratio in the 1990s, but the country had had success in reducing sex selection. The 2011 census in India stated, "female literacy, improving female health care, improving female employment rates [are] slowly redefining motherhood from childbearing to child rearing. Census 2011 is perhaps an indication that the country has reached a point of inflection;…"[49]

SUMMARY

India is a vibrant democracy with 1.2 billion people and an increasing presence in the world economy. Since the economic reforms that began in 1991, the growth in its economy has been rapid, lifting many millions of people out of poverty and creating an attractive domestic market for companies. Yet, 300 million people remain in poverty, many of whom have been untouched by the growth of the domestic economy. Per capita income has increased rapidly but remains less than half of that of China. The economy of India is not intertwined with those of the developed countries, which has allowed it to avoid the financial crises and recessions stemming from the United States and Europe.

Economic reforms have been successful in spurring growth, but additional reforms were needed. Foreign direct investment was allowed in most industries, although ownership in some industries such as banking is capped. India has become the leader in the outsourcing industry, but foreign companies have not used India as a source of low-cost supplies for the developed economies. In part this is due to infrastructure problems, including the transportation system and unreliable power in parts of the country. Much of the growth in the Indian economy has been driven by domestic entrepreneurs and by large business groups, often family controlled. Export industries have developed, and some have focused on supplying the emerging markets countries rather than developed countries.

Despite its economic success, India faced an array of challenges. The gravest was poverty, which remained a massive problem in both rural and urban areas. The public education system remained inadequate. Corruption was widespread producing both inefficiency and inequity. Government restrictions on businesses increased costs and limited market competition.

In spite of its remaining challenges India presents enormous opportunities as it rises to prominence in the world.

CASES

Tesco PLC in India?

INTRODUCTION

India represented an attractive opportunity for retailers. With 1.2 billion people, more than half of whom are under 25 years of age, and a dearth of major retail chains, the market in India presented tremendous opportunities for global retailers. The retail market had sales of $200 billion in 2005 and was growing rapidly with a projected market potential of $300 billion in 2010. The organized sector, consisting of establishments with 10 or more employees, accounted for only 3 percent of sales, but was projected to account for 10 percent of sales by 2010. The unorganized sector consisted of nearly 11 million outlets, including kirana shops and other small stores, with only 4 percent having over 500 sq ft. of retail space.[50] Some 21 million people were employed in retailing.

---

[48]Ibid.
[49]Ibid.
[50]www.thehindubusinessline.com, June 1, 2006.

The booming economy and the absence of major retail chains provided opportunity to both domestic and foreign firms. The entry of foreign retailers, however, was limited by restrictions on foreign direct investment (FDI) in retailing. India had gradually been removing its restriction on FDI in other sectors but had not done so in retailing because of concerns about the fate of small retailers. Some restrictions had recently been relaxed as in the case of single-brand retailers, and removal of restrictions on FDI in retailing was inevitable. But when that would occur was unclear.

Most of the large industrial groups in India were scrambling to enter the retailing sector before the FDI restrictions were lifted. In 2006 Reliance Industries, the largest business group in India, announced that it would invest $6 billion over 5 years to open 1,500 convenience stores and 1,000 hypermarkets. Chairman Mukesh Ambani said the strategy was to establish "a pan-India footprint of multi-format retail outlets" with large rural hubs to purchase produce and dairy products directly from farmers as part of its "field-to-fork" control of the supply chain.[51] This posed a substantial problem for the global retailers. They could enter the market now with constraints on their investments and hence on their organizational forms, or they could wait for further relaxations of the FDI regulations.

Tesco PLC was the largest retailer in the United Kingdom and accounted for £1 in every £7 spent on food. Tesco had begun selling nonfood items and had a successful Internet sales operation. In 1992 Tesco began diversifying internationally to take advantage of market opportunities. By 2005 over 50 percent of Tesco's floor space and over 20 percent of its sales were outside the UK. Chairman Sir Terry Leahy said, "Our international business is our biggest opportunity, both for growth and delivering returns."[52] In the year ending 2006 Tesco's revenue was £39.5 billion, and after-tax profit was £1.576 billion. Tesco's core purpose was "to create value for customers to earn their lifetime loyalty," and its strategy was based on six elements: be flexible, act local, keep focus, be multi-format, develop capability, and build brands.

FDI IN INDIA

As the Indian government relaxed restrictions, FDI had increased from $8.28 billion in 2003 to $25.66 billion in 2006. FDI up to 51 percent was allowed in 35 high-priority industries, and most recently, FDI had been allowed in real estate. FDI was still banned in four industries: retail trading (with the exception of single-brand retailing), atomic energy, lottery business, and gambling and betting. The restrictions on retailing reflected the potential threat to small shops and stall retailers. In contrast to India, Thailand, for example, had allowed global retailers to enter, and 7 of the top 10 global retailers operated there. China also allowed global retailers, including Carrefour, Wal-Mart, and 7-Eleven, to invest in the country.

FDI also was capped at "24 percent in the equity capital for units manufacturing items reserved for small scale industries." The small-scale industries restriction reflected the sensitivity of

competition for small businesses in India and the priority given to growth in those businesses.[53]

Foreign retailers were banned from using FDI for direct sales to individuals, and multi-brand retailers were barred from owning and operating their own stores until at least 2009, and then only if the FDI restrictions were changed. In lieu of FDI, foreign retailers could use franchise arrangements. International retailers, including Marks and Spencer, Shoprite Checkers, Reebok, Nike, Cartier, Woolworths (Australia), Debenhams, and McDonald's used franchising to operate in India.

FDI was unrestricted in wholesale operations that supplied registered retailers, but Metro Group, operator of Metro Cash-and-Carry GmbH wholesale stores for business customers, was the only firm to have entered the Indian market. Metro had begun operations in Bangalore, and in 2006 announced it would invest €300 million to expand to 33 cities.

Beginning in 2006 single-brand retailers were allowed to use FDI up to 51 percent. For example, Lladro of Spain announced a joint venture with SPA Agencies to open Lladro India stores to sell its porcelain products. The French boutique retailer Fendi, owned by the Louis Vuitton and Moet Hennessey (LVMH) Group, announced a 51 percent joint venture with Fun Fashion India to establish a single-brand retail chain. The government approved the FDI, but even for a single-brand retailing venture added restrictions. The LVMH venture had proposed selling ballpoint pens, umbrellas, and cuff links, which were items reserved for small-scale industries and hence under the jurisdiction of the Ministry of Small-Scale Industries. The Ministry attached a rider to the approval of the FDI requiring LVMH to export at least 50 percent of any product manufactured in India. The government also imposed a requirement that if the joint venture sought to add another brand for sale it would have to obtain a new approval from the Foreign Investment Promotion Board (FIPB).[54]

Approval for FDI ventures was the responsibility of the FIPB. Approval for investments up to 51 percent in high priority industries was automatic upon application to the Reserve Bank of India.

In addition to restrictions on FDI, the organized retail sector faced a variety of regulations. The organized sector was prohibited from using hourly or part-time employees. The organized sector typically had lifetime employment, pension benefits, and union representation.

Retailers also faced differing regulations across the states, since the Shops and Establishments Acts, which regulated retailing, were implemented at the state level. For example, some states restricted certain types of promotions including prize offerings used to attract customers. Some states required retailers to close one day a week. Minimum wages also differed across the states.

[51]*Sunday Telegraph*, August 13, 2006.

[52]*The Independent,* October 4, 2006.

[53]"The present policy of encouraging growth of small scale industries is based on several promotional measures—one of these is reservation of products for exclusive manufacture in the small scale sector in areas where there is techno-economic jurisdiction for such an approach. Large/medium units can, however, manufacture such reserved items provided they undertake to export 50% or more of their production." www.smallindustryindia.com.

[54]*India Business Insight*, September 2, 2006.

Carrefour, the world's second largest retailer, had explored entering the Indian market but in 2004 announced, "We have postponed our plans for India. It is an important market and we hope to revisit it at a later date. We don't want to comment further." Carrefour had explored a franchise arrangement, but had rejected that route. The company was thought to want to retain direct control over operations.

NONMARKET FORCES

Local merchants feared being driven out of business by major retailers, and they put nonmarket pressure on the governing Congress Party. Over 41 million people were unemployed in India, and the small retailers argued that many of those in retailing would lose their jobs if FDI restrictions were relaxed and foreign retailers entered. For example, "The West Bengal Minister in charge of Commerce and Industry, Mr. Nirupam Sen, has lauded the city-based [Kolkata] Merchants' Chamber of Commerce (MCC) for 'categorically' expressing its reservations against free flow of foreign direct investment in the retail sector."[55] The MCC president argued that the state should not allow FDI where it had the potential to displace employment. Arvind Singhal, chairman of Tecknopak, a retail consultancy, said, "Shopkeepers are asking, 'is Reliance going to kill us?'" Jageshwar Prasad, who operated a vegetable shop and pavement stall, said, "It will affect us very much because [Reliance] will take both the rich and the poor customers with lower prices."[56] Montek Singh Ahluwalia, the deputy chairman of the government's Planning Commission, stated, "I do believe (that) the introduction of modern retailing is very crucial and overdue … (However) I want to emphasize one thing. FDI in retail is not in my view critical in the next few years to achieve 8.5 percent growth."[57]

Mohan Guruswamy, the head of the Center for Policy Alternatives, in Delhi said, "You can't stop the Chinese forever and you can't stop Wal-Mart forever, but you can take it in phases." Referring to the $28 billion in goods Wal-Mart bought in China, he said, "that pipeline is directly set up to come into India, and could be set to wipe out small industry."[58]

The Ministry of Commerce and Industry was responsible for initiating proposals for changes in FDI regulations. Referring to the FDI policy in the retail sector, the Minister of Commerce and Industry, Kamal Nath, stated, "We need a model that doesn't replace existing retailers."[59] Assocham, the Associated Chambers of Commerce and Industry of India, opposed the elimination of the regulations, but supported allowing 51 percent FDI.

Local retailers also used nonmarket strategies against foreign retailers. Retailers complained that Metro Cash & Carry was selling to retail customers in violation of its licensing conditions. The retailers were led by the Federation of Associations of Maharashtra (FAM), which was "supported by the Karnataka and Tamil chambers of commerce at the state level and by the Confederation of India Industry at the national industry chamber level."[60] FAM renewed its criticism in 2003 when Metro launched a membership drive with loyalty cards. FAM claimed that the cards had been issued to groups not covered by its license. The communist newspaper, the People's Democracy, claimed that loyalty cards were being issued to employees of the groups and that Metro was "indulging in nothing but retail trade."[61] The Karnataka government, backed by the central government, filed a writ petition against Metro in a Bangalore court. Muralidhara Rao, national convener of the Swadeshi Jagaran Manch, the nationalist wing of the Bharatiya Janata Party, criticized Metro in a speech to the Karnataka Chambers of Commerce and Industry. He said, "Our market is an asset [that should not be] sold to multinationals."[62]

Local merchants had also taken direct action. The Supreme Court of India had ordered the city of New Delhi to enforce its long-ignored zoning laws which required closing 40,000 illegal shops that lined roadways. An estimated 5,000 shopkeepers broke through police lines to protest at the city's assembly building.[63]

THE OPPORTUNITY

A study by McKinsey & Co. and the Confederation of Indian Industry reported that a number of major international retailers, including Tesco, Kingfisher, Carrefour, and Ahold, were contemplating entering the Indian market. The report projected that the retail sector would reach $300 billion by 2010 if restrictions on FDI were relaxed. A study by AT Kearney concluded that India was the most attractive market for international retailers. It projected that sales in the organized sector would increase from $7 billion in 2006 to $21 billion in 2010. Technopak, a retail consultancy, estimated that the share of the organized sector would expand to 16–18 percent by 2010. This estimate depended on the strategies of the large global retailers.[64]

Modern retailing had begun to boom in India with the growth of shopping malls in metropolitan areas. Large domestic companies, such as Tata, RPG group, ITC, and HLL, had seized the opportunity in retailing and developed chains, primarily supermarkets. For example, the Tata group had the West Side chain, and Foodworld was owned by RPG.[65] Infiniti Retail of the Tata group announced an alliance with Woolworths to establish a retail chain, Croma, for consumer durables.[66] Woolworths owned the wholesale company in India that would supply the Croma stores. Pantaloon Retail and

[55]*Business Wire,* August 31, 2006.

[56]*Economist,* November 4, 2006.

[57]*Statesman (India),* August 30, 2006.

[58]*San Francisco Chronicle,* November 25, 2006.

[59]*Economist,* November 4, 2006.

[60]Jayanthi Iyengar, "China, India Confront the Wal-Marts," Asia Times Online, www.atimes.com, 2004.

[61]Ibid.

[62]Ibid. The Communist Party of India (Marxist) had the third largest number of seats in Parliament.

[63]*San Francisco Chronicle,* November 25, 2006.

[64]*Economist,* November 4, 2006.

[65]S. Majumder, "FDI in Retailing: India as a Supermarket," Business Line, September 17, 2002.

[66]*Business Times Singapore,* October 5, 2006.

Spencer's were accelerating the expansion of their operations. In 2006 Carrefour resumed exploring alternatives to enter the Indian market and was in discussions with the Landmark Group of Dubai.

Wal-Mart received approval from the government to set up an office in India to conduct market research. Spokesperson Amy Wyatt of Wal-Mart stated, "India is an emerging retail market in which we have a high interest. We continue to monitor the Indian government's policy on FDI and continue our market research."[67] Wal-Mart was rumored to be in discussions with DLF Universal, India's largest real estate developer. Wal-Mart said that its recent sale of its 85 German stores to Metro AG provided capital to invest in emerging markets. Wal-Mart had also sold its 16 stores in South Korea for $882 million.

Some Indian firms were actively seeking to partner with a foreign firm entering the retail sector. Bharti Enterprises had initiated discussions with Tesco and Wal-Mart about forming a venture. Sunil Mittal, chairman of the Bharti Group, said, "Government policy allows foreign equity in back-end wholesale and logistics and in real estate, so we'll do a joint venture with a foreign partner in those areas, and we will own the retail business 100 percent till the government allows FDI there, and then we'll do a joint venture there with our partner."[68] In late November 2006 Bharti and Wal-Mart announced that they would form a joint venture that would be responsible for logistics, supply-chain management, distribution, and wholesale operations, and Bharti would own the retail stores that sold directly to consumers.

In 2003 Tesco entered the markets in Japan and Turkey, and in 2004 it entered China and had 39 stores there by 2006. In 2006 it decided to enter the U.S. market with a chain of convenience stores patterned after its successful Express format. India was the last remaining major market opportunity, and Tesco had to decide whether to enter the market, how to enter it, and when to do it. ■

Preparation Questions

1. How attractive are the opportunities given the FDI regulations in retailing?
2. Would it be better to delay entry until the FDI restrictions are eliminated?
3. What strategy should Tesco adopt for entering the Indian market?
4. Should Tesco adopt a nonmarket strategy to influence the pace of relaxation of FDI regulations in India? Should it implement the policy in India or through the European Union and the World Trade Organization?

Source: This case was prepared by David P. Baron based on public sources. Copyright © 2006 by the Board of Trustees of the Leland Stanford Junior University. All rights reserved. Reprinted with permission.

Google in India

An estimated 110 million Indians were on the Internet, and the market was expected to reach 300 million by 2014 according to Rajan Anandan, Google head in India. Although the number of Internet users was nowhere near its potential, there were already 700 million cellphone users in 2011, spurred in part by low-cost phones. Almost half of India's 1.2 billion people were younger than 25. Gautam Gandhi, head of new business development for Google India, said, "We are very excited about the Indian market. The number of people online is very small and new users are going online through the mobile phone."[69] In 2011 Google unveiled "Indic web," which allowed users to translate among several Indian languages: Hindi, Bengali, Gujarati, Kannada, Tamil, and Telugu.[70] This allowed Indians who otherwise could not communicate with those speaking a different language to expand their reach on the Internet. This innovation had increased the scope of blogging in India.

Google was the leading Internet site in India, and its social-networking site Orkut was the sixth largest site, according to ViziSense.[71] Google was estimated to obtain only a very small portion of its 2010 revenue of $29.3 billion from India, since the market for online advertising had not yet blossomed as it had elsewhere. Anandan was trying to get major advertisers in India to change their advertising strategy. He said, "You should actually have a digital first strategy. That's not to say you shouldn't do significant TV advertising, but for many industries digital today can not only reach the audience that's most valuable to them but also target them in a very interesting way."[72] In addition to the challenge of developing the digital advertising business in India, Google faced the problem of complying with a new law pertaining to the responsibilities of Internet service providers. The law had been clarified by new rules promulgated in 2011, but those rules posed additional challenges to the company.

In 2008 terrorists based in Pakistan launched an attack in Mumbai that killed 163 people. Shortly afterward Parliament enacted a law that gave the government expanded powers over electronic communications and also established certain privacy rights of individuals. India's constitution established the right to free speech, but that right was subject to "reasonable restrictions" to protect "public order, decency, or morality."[73] The Indian government made 1,400 requests for data from Google in the first half of 2010, whereas the United States

---

[67]*Press Trust of India,* August 1, 2006.
[68]*Economist,* November 4, 2006.
[69]*Straits Times,* October 20, 2010.
[70]*International Herald Tribune,* August 10, 2011.
[71]*Wall Street Journal,* May 11, 2011.

[72]*Wall Street Journal,* September 16, 2011.
[73]*Wall Street Journal,* January 2–3, 2010.

made 4,200 requests, many of them presumably related to security matters and terrorism. Google reported that many of the requests from India pertained to postings on Orkut.[74]

The Indian law required Web sites to take down objectionable material or the Web sites themselves, and the maximum penalty for failing to do so was a fine and a jail sentence of up to 7 years.[75] Internet companies viewed the law as better than the previous law because it removed liability for companies as long as they did not create content that was objectionable. Subho Ray, president of the Internet and Mobile Association of India, commented, "The new IT Act (2008) is, in fact, a large improvement on the old one."[76]

In 2011 when the government was in the process of issuing rules to implement the law, Google submitted comments on a draft version of the rules, but it took no other nonmarket action. In its comments Google had said it was "troubled" by a provision that could make it liable for material posted on an Internet site and possibly subject to imprisonment and fines.[77] The proposed rule stated that an Internet company "shall not itself host or publish or edit or store" material that was banned.[78] Google also objected to a provision that required an Internet company to remove banned material after notification or "obtaining actual knowledge by itself."[79] Both provisions remained in the final rules, the Information Technology (Intermediaries guidelines) Rules, 2011.

The Indian rules banned material that was "grossly harmful, harassing, blasphemous" or "ethnically objectionable," "disparaging," or "impersonates another person." The rules explained that the banned material "threatens the unity, integrity, defense, security or sovereignty of India, friendly relations with foreign states or public order."[80] As an example of the sensitivity, Google was alerted to offensive comments posted on Orkut about the chief minister of the state of Andhra Pradesh, who had recently died in an airplane crash. Google responded by taking down the offensive comments and the user group as well.[81] As another example, the most important politician in India is Congress Party President Sonia Gandhi, the widow of former prime minister Rajiv Gandhi, who was assassinated in 1991. In 2008 a person posted on Orkut a site entitled "I hate Sonia Gandhi." Google removed the site and turned over the person's IP address. He was arrested under India's obscenity law.

Sunil Abraham, executive director for the NGO Center for Internet and Society in Bangalore, commented on the 2011 rules, "These rules overly favor those who want to clamp down on freedom of expression. Whenever there are limits of freedom of expression, in order for those limits to be considered constitutionally valid, those limits have to be clear and not be very vague. Many of these rules that seek to place limits are

very, very vague."[82] Abraham also said, "With this kind of blanket surveillance regime, we are on a very slippery slope. The language is so vague that it is open to arbitrary interpretations.... In comparison with other democracies in North America and Europe, the Indian rules appear to be on the China end of the spectrum."[83] Pushkar Raj, general secretary of the People's Union for Civil Liberties in New Delhi, exclaimed, "What are we, Saudi Arabia? We don't expect this from India. This is something very serious."[84]

Commenting on the criticism of the new rules, Sachin Pilot, deputy minister for communications and information technology, said, "We believe in freedom of speech through all media, including the Internet, although there are some codes of conduct that are expected to be followed by all. We have sought to balance the rights of consumers with those of service providers and other stakeholders in this space. We must draw a distinction between freedom of expression and freedom of expression with intent to harm or defame someone."[85]

Google spokesperson Nicole Wong said, "India does value free speech and political speech, but they are weighing the harm of free speech against violence in their streets."[86] She added, "In those gray areas, it is really hard. On the one hand, we believe very strongly in political speech and, on the other hand, in India they do riot and they blow up buses."[87]

In 1992 riots involving Hindus and Muslims resulted in over 1,000 deaths. Gulshan Rai of the Ministry of Communications and Information Technology said, "If you are doing business here, you should follow the local law, the sentiments of the people, the culture of the country. If somebody starts abusing Lord Rama on a Web site, that could start riots."[88]

In 2007 Shiv Sena supporters attacked Internet cafes near Mumbai after postings criticized the group's founder and a seventeenth-century king revered by ethnic Marathis.[89] Google took down several groups at the request of local government officials. Shailest Patel, a spokesperson for Shiv Sena, said, "This is a country with a lot of religions and sentimental values. If that censorship is not there, some people may utilize these mediums to disturb the harmony of the country, and it may lead to chaos."[90] ▪

Preparation Questions

1. Why is India so concerned about speech on the Internet?
2. Compare the restrictions on speech on the Internet in India with those in China. (See the Chapter 16 case *Google in China,* and the Chapter 24 case *Google Out of China.*)

---

[74]*International Herald Tribune*, January 10, 2011.
[75]*Wall Street Journal*, January 2–3, 2010.
[76]*New York Times*, April 28, 2011.
[77]*Wall Street Journal*, May 11, 2011.
[78]Ibid.
[79]Ibid.
[80]*New York Times*, April 28, 2011.
[81]*Wall Street Journal*, January 2–3, 2010.

[82]*New York Times*, April 28, 2011.
[83]*Washington Post*, August 2, 2011.
[84]*New York Times*, April 28, 2011.
[85]*Washington Post*, August 2, 2011.
[86]*Wall Street Journal*, January 2–3, 2010.
[87]Ibid.
[88]Ibid.
[89]Shiv Sena is a Hindu nationalist political party.
[90]*Wall Street Journal*, January 2–3, 2010.

3. Google has moved its search business to Hong Kong, services such as YouTube are blocked in China, and Orkut is not offered there. Should Google restrict its services in India?

4. Formulate a policy for Google for compliance with the new rules?

5. Should Google try to convince the Indian government to change the 2008 law or the 2011 rules?

Advanced Technology Laboratories, Inc.

Advanced Technology Laboratories, Inc. (ATL), with worldwide headquarters in Bothell, Washington, and European headquarters in Munich, Germany, was a leader in digital diagnostic ultrasound technology and equipment. "Ultrasound is a noninvasive technology that uses high frequency sound waves to image the body's soft tissues, organs and fetal anatomy and to display blood flow in real time."[91] ATL's ultrasound systems were used by cardiologists, radiologists, vascular surgeons, obstetricians, and gynecologists. Applications of ultrasound technology in gynecology included diagnosis of ovarian cysts, endometrial hyperplasia, the endometrium, and ovarian flow.

ATL ultrasound systems were sold in 100 countries to village clinics and world-renowned medical research centers. The worldwide ultrasound market was estimated at $2.5 billion. In 1996 ATL earned $21.8 million on sales of $419 million. Its competitors included such companies as General Electric and Siemens.

ATL's principal subsidiaries were located in OECD countries as well as in Argentina and India. In other countries ATL sold its systems through agents. Demand in the United States was sluggish, and ATL's worldwide competitors had introduced new products during the past 2 years. ATL looked to developing countries for growth.

The most attractive growth opportunities were in large countries with high growth rates of spending for medical care and health services. India, with a population of 800 million and a forecasted growth rate of 15–20 percent a year for medical devices, represented a particularly attractive market. ATL India, a joint venture with an Indian company that made low-end ultrasound instruments, was responsible for sales in India and Nepal. China, with a population of 1.2 billion, also represented an attractive market, and the installed base of ultrasound equipment was lower in China than in India. In 1997 ATL formed ATL China, where it had sold ultrasound systems since 1978. ATL also had a technology transfer agreement with the Shantou Institute of Ultrasonic Instruments.

In 1997 ATL introduced its HDI 1000 system, which replaced 50 percent of the hardware components with multitasking software, making digital ultrasound technology available at a substantially lower cost. ATL's Handheld Systems Business Division had also developed its FirstSight high-resolution digital imaging technology that would bring "highly portable, handheld ultrasound devices … to the examining table, the bedside and the field." ATL Chairman and CEO Dennis C. Fill said, "We believe that in the next few years these handheld ultrasound devices could have the same impact on patient care as the stethoscope and have the potential to create entirely new markets across many medical disciplines."[92]

In certain cultures some parents valued sons more than daughters. In the 1990s ultrasound devices became an effective means of allowing parents to engage in sex selection. Ultrasound was capable of identifying the sex of a fetus as early as 16 weeks, and local ultrasound clinics began to spring up throughout a number of Asian countries. A study by the Indian government revealed that for every 1,000 baby boys born, only 929 baby girls were born. A study reported that of the 8,000 abortions performed at one Bombay hospital, all but one were female fetuses.

One explanation for the preference for boys was given in a *CNN World News* story. "Sons are favored in India because it is they who are expected to carry on the family name and take care of the parents in their old age. Daughters are seen as a liability, and an expensive one at that. Families pay small fortunes in dowries to get their daughters married…. For those Indians too poor to afford tests, there is a grimmer option. Skakuntala admits to killing her newborn daughter several years ago. She already had two girls and didn't want another. 'We were poor,' she says. 'I put my sari over her face and she stopped breathing. It was the only thing to do.'"[93] CNN also reported that 25 percent of the girls born in India did not reach the age of 25, and in some families boys are given disproportionate shares of food, medical care, and education.

In 1994 India responded to the practice of using ultrasound to identify the sex and abort female fetuses by enacting the Pre-Natal Diagnostic Techniques (Regulation and Prevention of Misuses) Act. The law limited the use of ultrasound to women who were at high risk due to age or other factors and banned abortions of female fetuses identified by either amniocentesis or ultrasound. However, the use of ultrasound combined with abortion for purposes of sex selection continued unabated. According to the *New York Times*, "[f]or an investment amounting to a few thousand dollars, a mobile clinic operator can reap a small fortune from rural women, many of whom have never used a telephone or watched a television. Charges for the test can run as low as 150 rupees in poorer regions, about $5…."[94] The same report noted that the law did not require registration of ultrasound machines, so it was virtually impossible to control their use in mobile clinics.

[91]ATL Web site: www.atl.com.

[92]Ibid.
[93]*CNN World News*, September 17, 1995.
[94]John F. Burns, *New York Times*, August 27, 1994, Section 1, p. 5.

Gender selection was also practiced in several other Asian countries, including China. The natural ratio of boys to girls at birth worldwide was 105 to 100, but the actual birth rates in China it was 114 to 100 and was considerably higher in some rural districts.[95] Chinese law prohibited gender selection through abortion, infanticide, and child abandonment.

Sex selection was widely criticized. The United Nations International Conference on Population and Development opposed sex selection. In the United States the President's Commission for the Study of Ethical Problems in Medicine and Biomedical and Behavioral Research strongly opposed the practice, as did the American College of Obstetricians and Gynecologists' Committee on Ethics. The Ethics Committee of the American Society for Reproductive Medicine argued that doctors should use "moral suasion" to convince couples to avoid sex selection.

In 1995 the Canadian minister of health ordered Canadian doctors to cease providing sex selection services for nonmedical purposes, and the British Columbia College of Physicians and Surgeons issued guidelines urging doctors and sonographers not to reveal the sex of fetuses. Vancouver, which had a substantial population of Asian-Canadians, was concerned about people going to the United States for fetal sex identification and returning to Canada for an abortion paid for by the government. Dr. Dalip Sandhu said, "I tell them it's a sin. But they're not here to ask for my opinion. They want the information. They don't get it from me. It doesn't mean it stops them."[96]

Shashi Assanand, director of the Lower Mainland Multicultural Family Support Services Centre in Vancouver, blamed the dowry system. "Besides paying for a lavish wedding, the bride's family is expected to buy her a complete wardrobe and jewelry, as well as clothes and jewelry for the new son-in-law's family, with whom their daughter will be living. 'That's the minimum,' says Assanand. Those who can afford more are expected to give their new in-laws 'cash, furniture, appliances, a car and even property.'"[97]

Another group concerned with sex selection and women's issues was the Women's Environment and Development Organization (WEDO). WEDO and other women's groups were concerned about what was becoming known as the "missing women" of Asia.[98] ■

Preparation Questions

1. Identify the moral concerns in using ultrasound for sex selection.
2. What possible reactions might ATL encounter on this issue?
3. Does ATL have any responsibility regarding the use of its products in sex selection?
4. Should ATL introduce its FirstSight handheld product in India?
5. Develop a strategy for ATL with respect to the issues discussed in the case. Be sure to include specific steps you would take to implement your strategy.

---

[95]The ratio in South Korea was 114 to 100 and in Taiwan it was 110 to 100.
[96]*Chicago Tribune*, August 3, 1997.

[97]Ibid.
[98]See also *The Endangered Sex: Neglect of Female Children in Rural North India*, by Barbara Miller, 1981. Ithaca, NY: Cornell University Press.

19

THE POLITICAL ECONOMY OF INTERNATIONAL TRADE POLICY

INTRODUCTION

International trade policy is the result of economic and political forces. The principal economic force is the gains from trade, which provides the economic rationale for free trade. The principal political force is the benefits that firms, consumers, employees, and suppliers can obtain through favorable trade policies. The beneficiaries of those policies have incentives to adopt nonmarket strategies to protect and increase those benefits. Not all interests benefit, however, often resulting in contentious political competition.

Since the Smoot–Hawley Act of 1930, which raised tariffs dramatically and contributed to the depth and duration of the Great Depression, the United States and other developed countries have supported reductions in tariffs and other barriers to international trade. In the aftermath of World War II, the reductions in trade barriers were largely the result of U.S. hegemony. As other countries recovered from the war and the U.S. share of international trade declined, the principal mechanism for reductions in trade barriers has been multilateral negotiations, most of which have been conducted in the context of the General Agreement on Tariffs and Trade (GATT). In 1995 the World Trade Organization (WTO) was established to encompass GATT and other multilateral agreements. The WTO also provided a continuing forum for addressing trade issues and resolving disputes among nations. In addition, a number of regional trade agreements, such as the North American Free Trade Agreement (NAFTA) and the treaties that established the single market in the European Union, have reduced barriers and increased trade. The United States and other countries have also concluded bilateral agreements to spur trade in services such as air transportation. The result has been a steady, if not uniform, reduction in trade barriers, and the resulting increase in international trade has been dramatic. The most recent Doha Round of multilateral trade negotiations, however, failed as a result of disagreement between developing and developed countries.

Trade policy consists of agreements among countries, domestic laws pertaining to international trade, and procedures for administering those laws and resolving disputes. International trade agreements are the result of bargaining among countries, but the positions from which countries bargain depend on domestic economic considerations and hence on domestic politics. The interactions between international trade policy and domestic politics are illustrated in Figure 19-1. The international negotiations, shown at the top of the figure, and the agreements reached, shown at the bottom, determine the rules of the game for the export and import practices of firms. The competition between imports and domestic production and the opportunities to trade in world markets provide incentives for interests—firms, employees, suppliers, and consumers—to seek support for exports and/or protection from imports. The opportunities to engage in domestic politics and the rights granted under domestic trade laws allow interests to affect trade policy directly by filing trade petitions as well as indirectly through the bargaining positions of their governments in bilateral and multilateral negotiations. Trade policy thus depends not only on government actions but also on the market and nonmarket strategies of private interests. Conversely, international trade policy has important consequences for the market and nonmarket environments of business.

This chapter addresses the political economy of international trade policy, its connection to domestic politics, and the role of business and other interests in those politics. The perspective taken is that the system depicted in Figure 19-1 is animated by the incentives generated in domestic and international markets. Those incentives give rise to nonmarket strategies, implemented in both domestic and international institutional arenas, that shape trade policy. The next section considers the economics of international trade with an emphasis on competitive theory and strategic trade theory. Economic theory does not explain well many of the trade practices of countries, so the following section considers the political economy of international trade policy using the perspective developed in Chapter 6. The chapter also discusses the WTO and the agreements under its purview. The international trade policy of the United States is considered, including an analysis of the political economy of market opening and protectionism, including U.S. efforts to protect the steel industry. Current trade issues are considered, including the recent Doha Round of WTO multilateral trade negotiations.

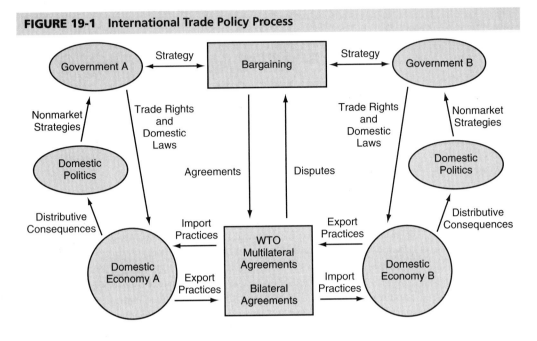

FIGURE 19-1 International Trade Policy Process

THE ECONOMICS OF INTERNATIONAL TRADE

Competitive Theory

The competitive theory of international trade is based on the *gains from trade*. Those gains are evident in the case of a country that cannot produce a product that its citizens wish to consume. Gains from trade are also evident when one country can produce a good more efficiently than another country, and the latter country can produce a different good more efficiently than can the former country. There are also gains from trade when one country is absolutely more efficient than the other in the production of both goods. That is, even though a country has an absolute disadvantage, gains from trade can be achieved if it produces the good for which it is relatively more efficient and the other country produces the good for which it is relatively more efficient. This result, known as the law of *comparative advantage*, provides the basic rationale for free trade—all countries, even those with an absolute disadvantage, can gain from trade.

The gains from trade can be demonstrated when two countries either determine the terms of their trade through bargaining or trade goods in a competitive market. Consider two countries, each of which can produce two goods, A and B. The production possibilities of each country are characterized by its resources and the technology it uses to produce the goods. To simplify the analysis, suppose that each country has one resource: 12 units of labor. Country I has a technology that requires 2 units of labor to produce 1 unit of A and 1 unit of labor to produce 1 unit of B. Country II can produce 1 unit of A with 1 unit of labor and 1 unit of B with 2 units of labor. These production possibilities are illustrated in Figure 19-2. As the figure illustrates, Country I is more efficient in the production of good B, and Country II is more efficient in the production of good A.

In the absence of trade, the consumption possibilities of each country are its own production possibilities. That is, Country I can produce and consume 12 units of B and none of A, 6 units of A and none of B, or any linear combination of those two outputs. Each country will produce and consume at the point on its production possibility frontier that yields the greatest aggregate well-being of its citizens. To be precise, suppose that the preferences of citizens in each country are identical and that their well-being is measured by the product of the quantities consumed of the two goods. For example, the goods could be bread and butter, and well-being is greatest when there is butter for each loaf of bread. The best combination of consumption is thus an equal amount of each good.

In the absence of trade, referred to as *autarky*, Country I can do no better than to produce and consume 3 units of A and 6 units of B. Analogously, under autarky Country II will produce and consume 6 units of A and 3 units of B. These autarky points are indicated in Figure 19-2 and correspond to levels of well-being of 18 for each country.

FIGURE 19-2   Production and Consumption Possibilities—Autarky

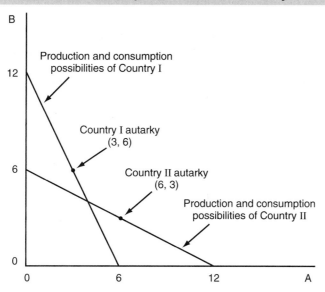

Trade benefits a country by allowing consumption to diverge from production. To illustrate this, Figure 19-3 presents the production and consumption possibilities of Countries I and II when they are able to trade. Gains from trade are possible because trade expands the consumption possibilities of each country beyond those of its own production. That is, both countries can benefit if Country I produces more of good B, for which it has an absolute advantage, and Country II produces more of good A, for which it has an absolute advantage. In this example, Country I will specialize in producing 12 units of good B and none of good A, whereas Country II will produce 12 units of A and none of B. Country I then will export 6 units of B and import 6 units of A. Country II's imports and exports will be the opposite of those of Country I. With the trades indicated in the figures, the resulting consumption in each country is 6 units of A and 6 units of B. The well-being of each country is 36, so both are better off with trade.[1] Both countries gain from trade.

FIGURE 19-3   Production and Consumption Possibilities with Trade

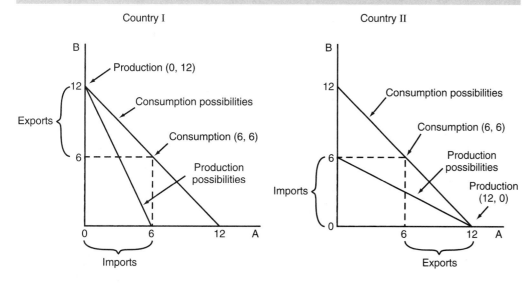

---

[1]This outcome is a competitive market equilibrium in the sense that each country, taking prices as given, produces the quantities of the two goods that maximize its well-being, and each country consumes the quantities it prefers given the prices for the goods. In this example, the price, or rate of exchange, is one unit of A for one unit of B. The value of imports thus equals the value of exports for each country.

This example illustrates the gains from trade for the case in which Country I is more efficient (has an absolute advantage) in the production of good B and Country II is more efficient (has an absolute advantage) in the production of good A. Even if Country I is absolutely more efficient in the production of both goods, there are gains from trade. To illustrate this, suppose that Country I's technology is the same as above, but Country II's technology requires 3 units of labor to produce 1 unit of A and 4 units of labor to produce 1 unit of B. In the absence of trade, Country II would produce 2 units of A and 1.5 units of B for a level of well-being of 3. Both countries can gain, however, if, for example, Country II produces 4 units of A and no units of B and Country I produces 2 units of A and 8 units of B. Country II then can trade 2 units of A to Country I for 3 units of B.[2] The well-beings of the two countries are then 20 and 6, respectively, compared with 18 and 3 in the absence of trade. This gain is possible because Country II is relatively more efficient in the production of good A than is Country I. That is, the ratio of the number of units of labor required to produce a unit of A and a unit of B is $3 \div 4 = 0.75$ for Country II, whereas the corresponding ratio for Country I is $2 \div 1 = 2$. Country II thus has a comparative advantage in the production of A even though it has an absolute disadvantage in the production of both goods. Gains from trade thus result from comparative advantage.

Gains from trade are also present if there are differences in the relative prices of untraded factor inputs such as labor. That is, if one country has lower wage rates than another, gains can be achieved from trade. The high-wage country can gain by importing labor-intensive goods from the low-wage country and allocating its high-wage labor to the production of goods for which it has a comparative advantage. Consequently, a country such as the United States, with high labor costs, and a country such as India, with low labor costs, can gain by China producing labor-intensive textiles and apparel for export to the United States and the United States producing capital-intensive machinery for export to India. The United States, however, has for decades restricted textile and apparel imports to protect employment in its domestic industries. The gains from trade thus are not sufficient to explain the trade policies of countries. That is, politics can intervene in international trade, as indicated in Figure 19-1. The political dimensions of international trade and trade policy are examined in more detail after a consideration of strategic trade theory.

Strategic Trade Theory

The theory of comparative advantage is based on the assumption of perfectly competitive markets. Information is assumed to be complete, consumers and producers act as price takers, goods are undifferentiated, and production is characterized by constant returns to scale or by decreasing returns to scale with costless entry and exit. From these assumptions, theories such as the law of comparative advantage demonstrate the gains from trade among open economies. The theory also implies that intervention by governments in perfectly competitive domestic or international markets will reduce aggregate well-being. Competitive theory thus provides a compelling rationale for free trade, and the role of government is then to join in international efforts to reduce tariff and nontariff barriers to trade.

Economists have also considered whether a nation can gain from a strategic trade policy—that is, intervention to protect domestic industries, subsidize exports, or stimulate demand for domestic goods.[3] These interventions can be beneficial for a country only if one or more of the conditions for perfect competition is not satisfied. Theories of strategic trade policy thus are set in the context of imperfect competition.

As an example, consider the case of an undifferentiated good that is produced by only two firms, one domestic and the other foreign. Suppose they engage in Cournot competition where each firm chooses the quantity it will produce and both sell their quantities in the world market. Because there are only two firms, they each restrict output. Suppose one government subsidizes the production of its domestic firm, thus lowering that firm's marginal cost. This has two effects. First, the lower marginal cost induces the firm to expand its output. Second, as it expands its output, the foreign firm will react by reducing its output. This then allows the subsidized domestic firm to increase its output even more. This second effect is said to be strategic because the subsidization has altered the strategic relationship between the two firms by lowering the cost of

---

[2]Other mutually beneficial trades are also possible. For example, Country II could trade 2 units of A for 2 units of B.
[3]For a nontechnical exposition of these theories, see Krugman (1986, 1990).

one firm. In the new equilibrium, the subsidized firm makes greater profits than it did in the absence of the subsidy. Moreover, even taking into account the cost of the subsidy, subsidization can increase the aggregate well-being of the subsidizing country by expanding output.[4] The European subsidization of Airbus Industrie may be an example of this strategy. Although the subsidization of domestic firms in certain industries could increase well-being, it often does not. For example, the subsidization by the European Union of agricultural exports resulted in large reductions in well-being because agricultural markets generally satisfy the conditions for perfect competition.

The gains from strategic trade practices can turn to losses if other governments retaliate. If one country adopts a strategic trade policy, other countries can retaliate either by adopting the same policy or by taking measures to offset the effect of the other country's strategy. For example, the United States retaliated against the European Union's subsidization of agricultural exports with its own export subsidies, resulting in large losses to both.[5] Once both are subsidizing exports, they are in a dilemma, since neither has a unilateral incentive to stop the subsidization. To resolve the dilemma, countries negotiate agreements prohibiting such policies and establish institutions to enforce the agreements. This approach, represented by the WTO, is favored by most countries. Before considering international trade agreements, the nature of the politics of international trade is considered.

THE POLITICAL ECONOMY OF INTERNATIONAL TRADE POLICY

The Dual Nature of the Politics of International Trade

As illustrated in Figure 19-1, the politics of international trade policy is driven by domestic politics, which arises from the interactions between international trade policy and the domestic economy. Trade policy has differentiated distributive consequences with some interests benefiting from trade liberalization and others harmed by it. Trade politics thus has two components—measures to liberalize trade and measures to support domestic interests harmed by liberalization.

According to the typology of political competition presented in Figure 6-2, the politics of international trade policy is at one level majoritarian. That is, everyone is affected by international trade. Because liberalized trade policy is beneficial in the aggregate, countries generally gain from multilateral reductions in tariff and nontariff barriers. The benefits, however, are often widely distributed, so preferences for trade liberalization may not be transformed into policy. In the United States, as in most countries, the politics of trade liberalization are basically entrepreneurial. In the United States, Congress has delegated the role of entrepreneur to the president. Congress is willing to delegate because the aggregate benefits of trade liberalization exceed the aggregate costs, and the benefits are sufficiently widely distributed that leadership must be exercised. Since the constituency of the president is the nation as a whole, as opposed to a congressional district or a state, presidents generally support trade liberalization.

The distributive consequences of a liberalized trade policy, however, are not uniform. Instead, liberalization has concentrated effects on particular interests, and those interests have an incentive to take nonmarket action to increase the benefits they receive or reduce the costs they bear.[6] In the case of trade policies that reduce domestic barriers to trade and thereby increase imports, the benefits typically are distributed broadly among consumers, whereas the costs are concentrated on import-competing industries. For example, in the United States steel companies and the United Steel Workers (USW) were hurt by imports and had strong incentives to seek protection. Protectionism is thus characterized by client politics. In most countries, interests, including companies and unions, can seek protection and relief from injury due to imports. For example, countries have antidumping laws that allow domestic firms to petition to have duties placed on imports sold at "less than fair value."

---

[4]Indeed, worldwide aggregate surplus is increased because the total quantity produced is greater than it would be without the subsidy. This results because the subsidization leads to a price that is closer to marginal cost. These conclusions, however, are not completely robust and may be reversed if firms compete in a manner different from that assumed in Cournot competition.

[5]The depressed commodity prices also harmed developing countries that produced the same crops.

[6]Magee, Brock, and Young (1989) provide a theory of rent-seeking to explain aspects of international trade policy.

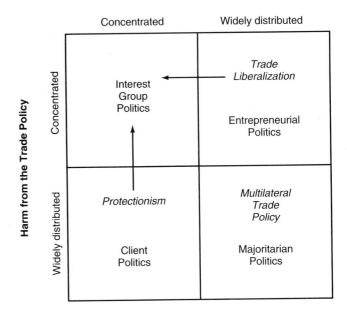

FIGURE 19-4 The Politics of International Trade Policy

The benefits from protection are concentrated on those interests that compete against imports, whereas the costs of protection are widely distributed among consumers and other users of the protected goods. Although consumers are harmed by these policies, the harm is typically small on a per capita basis, and hence consumers seldom take nonmarket action to oppose protection. Importers, however, are often harmed and have incentives to oppose protectionism. The steel companies and the USW sought protection from imports, but General Motors and Caterpillar opposed it because it would raise the price of the steel they use. Interest group politics can thus develop. Interest group politics can also result in political competition between import-competing industries and exporters as in the case of the ratification of broad trade liberalizations, such as NAFTA, that require reciprocity.

The politics of international trade policy is summarized in Figure 19-4. In the aggregate, trade policy is characterized by majoritarian politics. At a disaggregated level, the nature of the politics depends on the specific policy alternative in question. Export oriented trade liberalization and market opening are basically characterized by entrepreneurial politics. Client politics characterizes protectionism, since the benefits from supporting protectionism are concentrated and the costs are typically widely distributed. Protectionist policies may generate a response by importers, and reciprocity in market opening policies may generate a response by import-competing industries, so the number of interest groups involved can expand. The politics of protectionism and the politics of market opening thus can lead to interest group politics.

Asymmetries in the Politics

Although trade policy liberalization creates opportunities for exporters and threats for import-competing industries, the domestic politics of international trade are asymmetric. The asymmetry is due to sunk resources and the rents on those resources. Consider the case of a firm that would construct a new plant dedicated to exports, provided that foreign barriers to trade were lowered. Its incentive to undertake nonmarket action to open the foreign market depends on the profit it can earn, which is given by the export revenue less the full cost of the resources required to produce the exports. In contrast, domestic firms faced with import competition typically have sunk resources. Because of sunk resources, the domestic firms earn rents. When there are sunk resources, the import-competing industry can have more to lose than the exporting industry has to gain, so in the short run the incentives for protection can be stronger than the incentives for market opening.

To illustrate this, consider the case of labor. Trade liberalization creates new jobs in exporting industries, but at the time at which the trade policy is chosen those new jobs are not yet identified, let alone occupied. Those jobs might be filled by many people, and hence the probability that any one person would obtain one of the jobs is small. The incentive for an individual to take nonmarket action thus is weak. As the managing director of one of the largest U.S. investment banks commented on organized labor's opposition to NAFTA, "The jobs that will be lost are identifiable; the jobs that will be created are as yet unidentified." Cisco Systems projected that its increased exports to Mexico would create 200 additional U.S. jobs at its suppliers, but who would hold those jobs was as yet unidentified. Thus, Cisco had clear incentives to support NAFTA, but those unidentified individuals who would hold the new jobs could not support it.

In contrast, workers in import-competing industries are often earning rents in their jobs; that is, their wages are higher than the wages they could obtain elsewhere. Rents are thus concentrated on identified individuals, and their incentives to oppose trade liberalization and seek protection from imports can be strong. This is the case for organized labor, where, for example, the wages of USW members are higher than the wages most members would earn in other employment. Not surprisingly, the USW and similarly the United Automobile Workers have sought protection for the U.S. steel and auto industries, respectively, and have opposed liberalized trade. Organized labor vigorously, but unsuccessfully, opposed NAFTA and the Uruguay Round accord that established the WTO.

Global firms often have mixed incentives. As with any import-competing firm earning rents, a global firm would benefit from protection of its domestic market. A global firm would also benefit from opening foreign markets for its products. The simultaneous protection of domestic markets and the opening of foreign markets is not sustainable, however, since protectionism can result in retaliation by other countries and market opening may require reciprocity. Most global firms support liberalized trade because of the aggregate gains from trade and because liberalized trade creates opportunities to pursue their competitive advantages.

INTERNATIONAL TRADE AGREEMENTS

The World Trade Organization

At the conclusion of World War II, a group of countries led by the United States established the International Trade Organization (ITO). They hoped the ITO would allow them to avoid the disastrous trade policies that had contributed to the depression and the pressures for war. When the U.S. Senate failed to provide the two-thirds majority to ratify the organization's treaty, the ITO disbanded. However, a set of principles for international trade in goods had been drafted in conjunction with the ITO, and in 1948 those principles were formalized as the GATT by 23 countries. Seven subsequent rounds of multilateral trade negotiations among the signatories have resulted in major reductions in tariffs and nontariff barriers to trade.

The focus of international trade policy through the 1960s was on tariffs. Because tariffs limit the gains from trade, the United States and other countries sought in the Kennedy Round (1964–1967) of GATT negotiations to reduce tariffs on a more or less uniform basis among all signatories. The result was an average reduction of 36 percent in tariffs, and the volume of international trade increased substantially as a result.

After reducing tariffs to the point at which they no longer constituted a major barrier to trade, the focus of GATT turned in the Tokyo Round (1974–1979) to nontariff barriers to trade. Nontariff barriers were more complex and difficult to address and were often deeply rooted in both domestic politics and business practices that protected rents.[7] Trade in agricultural products, for example, had been distorted by a variety of policies such as import quotas, domestic subsidies, and export subsidies. Although the Tokyo Round focused on nontariff barriers, it also resulted in an average reduction of 34 percent in tariffs. As a result of the Tokyo Round agreements, the average tariff in developed countries was 6.3 percent. Thirty-two percent of U.S. imports were duty free, and the average duty on the rest was 5.5 percent.[8]

The Tokyo Round left several sectors, such as agriculture, unaddressed, and several others, such as services, became more salient. The Uruguay Round (1986–1993) was intended to improve GATT provisions on trade in goods and expand the multilateral trade agreements to

---

[7]Grieco (1990) provides an analysis of the compliance with Tokyo Round nontariff barrier agreements.
[8]See Lande and VanGrasstek (1986, p. 4).

include trade in services, agriculture, intellectual property protection, government procurement, and other issues. After nearly 8 years of negotiations an agreement was concluded that made major improvements in international trade policies and, in addition, reduced tariffs by 38 percent to an average of 3.9 percent in developed countries. To encompass this broader set of agreements, the WTO was established. The WTO agreements include GATT, GATS, TRIPS, dispute settlement, and trade policy reviews. The WTO also encompasses the Agricultural Agreement and an agreement on government procurement.

The WTO has 154 member countries, including Russia which joined in 2011, and 30 others are observers with the intent to become members. The WTO has three principal roles. First, it provides a system of agreements that helps trade move more freely. Second, it provides a forum for trade negotiations such as the telecommunications agreement concluded in 1997. Third, it provides a dispute settlement mechanism to resolve trade disputes in a timely manner.

The central principle of the WTO agreements is embodied in the most favored nation (MFN) requirement that each signatory accord all other signatories the most favorable terms for trade provided to any country; that is, trade policies are to be nondiscriminatory.[9] A second principle is national treatment; that is, domestic and foreign goods are to be treated the same. For example, Canada imposed higher postage rates on U.S. magazines than for Canadian magazines, and a WTO dispute resolution panel held that the Canadian practice violated the national treatment principle.

GATT covers a variety of practices and policies governing trade in goods.[10] Article VI covers antidumping and countervailing duties and requires a finding of less than fair value sales or subsidization, respectively, and a finding of material injury. Article XI sets a framework for the elimination of quantitative restrictions on trade, but Article XVIII allows exceptions for balance of payments problems of developing countries. Article XIX allows for temporary safeguard relief from imports. Article XVI is the subsidies code, and Articles XX and XXI provide exceptions to the free trade provisions of the other articles. For example, a country may impose trade restrictions if they are required by national security considerations.[11]

General Agreement on Trade in Services (GATS)

U.S. service industries had complained that their international expansion was hindered by the protection many countries provided for their domestic industries. The effort to reduce barriers to trade in services was led by a number of CEOs, including James Robinson of American Express, who for years personally campaigned to open foreign markets. In 1982 the Coalition of Service Industries was formed and was successful in including trade in services in the Uruguay Round agenda.

The result was the General Agreement on Trade in Services (GATS), which covers all services and provides for MFN and national treatment. The agreement also requires countries to make transparent all regulations and conditions of service. Since the services markets of many countries were largely closed to foreign firms, GATS temporarily allowed countries not to apply MFN treatment.

Two services, telecommunications and finance, posed particular problems because of heavy regulation and the government ownership of firms. The Uruguay Round and GATS agreements were signed while negotiations on telecommunications and financial services continued. In 1997 over 68 countries agreed to open their telecommunications market in various degrees. The telecommunications agreement provided opportunities for telecommunications companies by requiring that countries grant licenses through a mechanism open to foreign firms, as in the Chapter 17 case *MTN Group Limited.*

Later in 1997, 102 countries reached agreement to open banking, insurance, investments, and other financial services to international competition. Some countries, however, limited foreign ownership stakes in their financial services companies. GATS now covers all international trade in services.

---

[9]Exceptions to the equal treatment principle include colonial preference arrangements in effect when GATT was established, preferences for developing countries, and certain multilateral agreements such as the Multi-Fiber Arrangement. The quotas established in the Multi-Fiber Arrangement were phased out, ending in 2005.

[10]Prior to 1995 GATT was not a single agreement but instead a set of agreements, each of which countries could choose to sign. For example, GATT included a subsidies code intended to limit the domestic subsidization of export industries, but the signatories were largely the members of the Organization for Economic Cooperation and Development (OECD), an association of industrial democracies.

[11]With the exception of Article II, the GATT articles have counterparts in U.S. trade law.

Trade-Related Aspects of Intellectual Property Rights (TRIPS)

Intellectual property rights include copyrights, patents, trademarks, brand names and logos, industrial designs, semiconductor circuit designs, and trade secrets. Such rights allow individuals and firms to capture the benefits from their efforts to create new concepts and products; infringement of these rights reduces the incentives to create (see Chapter 14). TRIPS provides broad protection and is included in the WTO dispute settlement system, allowing trade sanctions to be imposed in the event of violations. Because many countries had weak domestic laws for protecting intellectual property rights, developing countries were given 5 years to comply and the least developed countries were given 11 years.

Intellectual property is a contentious issue between developed and developing countries. Many developing countries believe that intellectual property rights allow companies to unfairly preclude their countries from obtaining important products such as pharmaceuticals that are priced beyond their means. TRIPS includes sections that allow a country to invoke compulsory licensing and to import generic versions of drugs in the event of a public health emergency. The chapter case *Compulsory Licensing, Thailand, and Abbott Laboratories* concerns the imposition of compulsory licenses by Thailand and the response by Abbott Laboratories. Drug pricing, compulsory licensing, and parallel imports are also considered in the Part V integrative case *GlaxoSmithKline and AIDS Drugs Policy.*

As an example of the contentious nature of intellectual property rights, under the auspices of the World Intellectual Property Organization, a unit of the United Nations, a treaty providing protection for intellectual property was negotiated. Developing nations, however, initially refused to sign it, but a negotiated 2004 accord led to 183 signatories.

Agriculture

Agriculture has been the sector with the greatest distortions in trade. An OECD report concluded that farm subsidies and import controls cost consumers and taxpayers $361 billion in 1999. The European Union accounted for the largest distortions, followed by the United States and Japan. The principal roadblock to an agreement on agricultural trade was the European Union's Common Agriculture Policy (CAP). CAP was intended to maintain farmers' incomes and did so by establishing prices high enough to yield a reasonable income for high-cost farms. The high prices, however, induced efficient farms to expand their output, resulting in huge crop surpluses, some of which were exported at subsidized prices. The European Union's export subsidization resulted in retaliatory subsidization of agricultural exports by the United States.

The Uruguay Round produced the Agricultural Agreement to reduce tariffs, domestic support, and export subsidies in agriculture. By 2000 developed countries were to reduce their tariffs by an average of 36 percent with a minimum reduction of 15 percent. Domestic support was to be reduced by 20 percent and export subsidies by 36 percent. The reductions required for developing countries were lower, and they were given until 2004 to comply. Because many countries used quotas to restrict imports, the agreement adopted a "tariffs only" policy in which quotas were replaced by equivalent tariffs, which were then subjected to the required reductions. The agreement on agriculture also addressed health and safety issues. It required that regulations be based on science and that they "be applied only to the extent necessary to protect human, animal, or plant life or health."

The Agricultural Agreement, however, left unresolved many issues. The European Union reformed CAP by decoupling the subsidies received by farmers from the amount they produced. A WTO trade policy review, however, concluded that "the reform of the Common Agricultural Policy (CAP) falls short of liberalizing EU's agriculture."[12] The United States has continued to subsidize its farmers.

Developing countries complained that the agricultural subsidies and protection provided by the European Union, Japan, United States, and other countries impeded their economic development in two ways. Domestic subsidies and import barriers reduced export opportunities for the developing countries, and export subsidies unfairly competed with their exports. NGOs such as Oxfam America called attention to the subsidies and lobbied for their elimination. Agriculture was the main stumbling block to progress in the Doha Round of multilateral negotiations.

---

[12]WTO press release, October 27, 2004.

Government Procurement

The Uruguay Round negotiators reached a new Government Procurement Agreement (GPA) that extended the existing agreement to include construction and services and some procurement by sub-central governments and government-owned firms. The GPA is a "pluralateral" agreement among 39 WTO members. Developing countries were given special conditions. In a bilateral agreement with the European Union, the procurement of 15 U.S. states and seven major cities was opened to EU firms in exchange for opening the European Union's $28 billion heavy electric equipment market.

Antidumping, Countervailing Duties, and Safeguards

The Kennedy Round of GATT negotiations incorporated provisions in Article VI allowing domestic laws to include antidumping measures. From the perspective of economic theory, dumping occurs when a company sells a good at a price below the cost of producing it. As applied in international trade, however, antidumping pertains to sales at "less than fair value" that materially injure domestic industries. In response, a duty on imports can be imposed to bring their price up to fair value. Antidumping provisions are thus intended to provide for "fair trade" rather than free or socially efficient trade. Antidumping provisions have been criticized as being protectionist because they can result in the imposition of duties on imports even when prices are above costs. Antidumping basically compares the domestic price of a product in the exporting country with the price in the importing country, so antidumping actually pertains to price discrimination rather than to dumping. In addition to a price less than fair value, the imports must cause material injury to domestic interests. The chapter case *Cemex and Antidumping* centers on this issue.

The Uruguay Round agreement standardized the procedures for calculating the dumping duty and for conducting investigations. It also imposed a 5-year sunset limit on any antidumping duty, unless ending the duty would result in imminent material injury.

Antidumping had been used almost exclusively by developed countries with the number of actions initiated averaging about 200 per year in the early 1990s.[13] The number of actions initiated by developed nations has decreased sharply and developing countries have become active in using antidumping and by now initiate more actions than developed countries. India became one of the largest users of antidumping, and China was the most frequent target. In 2008 India initiated 54 antidumping cases, Brazil 23, and Turkey 22, with the EU initiating 19 and the United States initiating 16. China was the target in 73 cases, and Thailand was second with 13. Most antidumping cases do not result in disputes filed with the WTO. Despite the protectionist nature of antidumping, most countries prefer to retain the provisions as a safety valve to relieve pressure for broader protectionist measures.

Countervailing duties are allowed by the WTO agreements to offset the effects of subsidies provided by another country. These duties are subject to the same standards as antidumping duties. Special provisions are provided for developing countries.

Temporary safeguards against a surge in imports can be taken to avoid "serious injury" to a country. The United States invoked the safeguards provision to protect its steel industry, as indicated in the example presented later in the chapter.

Dispute Settlement

Under GATT, disputes between countries could be brought before a panel that investigated the matter and issued a recommendation. The recommendation became binding, however, only if all countries agreed to it, and countries including the United States frequently withheld their agreement. A major achievement of the Uruguay Round was to establish the WTO Dispute Settlement Body (DSB) to hear disputes and issue binding orders to resolve them.[14] The DSB encourages the parties to resolve disputes through negotiation and compromise; if that is unsuccessful, a country may request that a special panel be established to hear the dispute. The entire process, from the filing of the initial complaint to the issuance of a final report by

---

[13]Bellis (1989) and Schuknecht (1992) provide analyses of the European Union's antidumping policies and procedures.
[14]The DSB is not an organization, but instead is the General Council of the WTO. It is better thought of as a procedure for resolving disputes.

the panel, is to be completed within 1 year, and any appeal is to be resolved in 3 months. Correction of a violation, however, can take considerable time.

If the DSB finds against a practice, the country is supposed to correct the fault.[15] Failure to comply can be brought to the attention of the DSB, which can authorize the petitioner to impose trade sanctions against the violator. Thus, countries need not change their laws or practices to comply with the decision of the DSB, but if they fail to do so, sanctions can be authorized by the WTO. The sanctions typically take the form of a suspension of trade concessions previously granted to the violator. The violator is to accept the sanctions. The United States and other countries have generally complied with the decisions of the DSB.

The United States has been involved in more disputes than any other country. The United States has been the complainant in 90 and the respondent in 99 disputes filed with the WTO, followed by the European Union with 78 and 62, respectively. Thirty-one of the complaints by the United States were against the EU, and 31 of the EU complaints were against the United States. Brazil has been the complainant in 23 disputes and the respondent in 14.

TRADE DISPUTES The first case decided by the DSB involved a complaint by Venezuela, later joined by Brazil, that rules issued by the U.S. Environmental Protection Agency (EPA) for reformulated gasoline violated the WTO national treatment principle. The EPA had written its rules based on data that were readily available for U.S. refiners. Because foreign refiners had not kept the same data, the EPA required them to meet a more stringent standard. The DSB decided in favor of Venezuela, and the United States complied by rewriting the EPA rules to provide for national treatment.

Disputes typically center on specific protectionist practices. The European Union maintains a set of preferences for the overseas territories and former colonies of its member states. In 1993 the United States and five Latin American countries filed a complaint against EU rules for preferential treatment for bananas from the overseas territories and former colonies, particularly in Africa.[16] Banana exports from Honduras to the European Union fell by 90 percent as a result of the rules. The DSB decided against the European Union and rejected an appeal. The European Union then revised its rule under contentious internal bargaining, pitting Germany and other countries that opposed the preferences against France and other countries that favored them. The United States and Latin American countries, however, contended that the revised rule did little to remove the barriers to Latin American banana imports. The United States proposed that the new rule be taken to the WTO for an expedited DSB process, but the European Union refused. When the DSB failed to authorize sanctions by the required deadline, the United States announced 100 percent punitive tariffs on $500 million of imports of wine, cheese, and other products. The DSB subsequently found for the United States and authorized it to impose punitive tariffs on $191 million of imports. Finally, a settlement was reached in which the United States lifted the punitive tariffs in 2001 and the EU agreed to phase out its preferences over 5 years. The EU announced reductions in its tariffs on bananas, but the reductions were insufficient to satisfy the Latin American countries and they filed new complaints. Finally in 2009 the EU, the United States, and Latin American, African, and Caribbean countries negotiated a settlement to the 16-year dispute.

The trade conflicts continued as the United States filed a trade complaint claiming that the European Union provided billions of dollars of subsidies in the form of low-interest rate loans to Airbus Industrie. The European Union countered with a trade complaint claiming that the United States subsidized Boeing through military research and development grants. Negotiations to resolve the dispute collapsed. The chapter case *The Airbus and Boeing Trade Disputes* considers the two cases.

A controversial case was brought by the United States against the European Union on its ban of beef from cattle treated with growth-enhancing hormones. The EU ban did not violate the national treatment principle, because it applied to any hormone-treated beef, nor was it intended to protect European beef producers. Instead, the ban was enacted because of consumer health concerns. The DSB concluded that the EU had no scientific basis for concluding that the

---

[15] A DSB finding can be overcome by a majority of the WTO members.

[16] The United States was a petitioner because Chiquita Brands and Dole Food Company export Latin American bananas to the European Union.

hormone-treated beef might be a health hazard. The EU, however, was given a period of time to conduct its own safety tests on the hormone-treated beef. After 2 years of inaction by the European Union, the WTO authorized the United States to impose 100 percent punitive tariffs on $117 million of imports of European goods. The EU subsequently reviewed the scientific literature and concluded that the hormone-treated beef constituted a health risk because some hormone residue could cause cancer. The EU then enacted new legislation banning six beef hormones. The United States replied that the review provided no new scientific evidence. A spokesperson for the office of the U.S. trade representative said, "The hormone levels they are concerned about—represent a tiny fraction of what occurs naturally in an egg or one glass of milk."[17]

The beef dispute was part of a broader U.S. complaint against the EU ban on imports of foods with genetically modified organisms (GMOs). In 1998 the European Union and the United States had agreed to an EU moratorium on new approvals of imports of GMO foods and animal feed. The EU lifted the ban in 2003, replacing it with regulations requiring documentation of the genetic history with a comprehensive paper trail for all food imports. U.S. exporters of agricultural products claimed that it would be impossible to provide such documentation. The European Union had substituted a regulatory ban for its explicit ban, and agricultural exporters turned to the WTO. Since the EU ban on GMO foods was seen as a violation of the WTO agreements, Argentina, Canada, and the United States filed a trade complaint. The WTO ruled against the EU, and the EU did not appeal because it claimed that the approval process it had implemented after 2003 was compliant with the WTO ruling. The approval process was painstakingly slow from the perspective of the genetically modified foods industry.

The ban and documentation requirement were based on the EU's "precautionary principle" under which temporary bans could be imposed on products that might pose risks. A member of the EU trade delegation explained that "in a democracy you have to take into account fears of the people, and the people in many European countries are concerned about genetically modified food."[18] In a case in which Monsanto claimed that Italy had illegally banned imports of GMO corn, the European Court of Justice upheld temporary bans under the precautionary principle "without having to wait until the reality and seriousness of risks become fully apparent, even if a full risk assessment becomes impossible because of the inadequate nature of scientific data available." The court, however, also said that the risks "must not be purely hypothetical or founded on mere suppositions which are not yet verified."[19] In 2008 only two GM crops were grown in the EU, and France filed a petition with the EU Commission to ban one, a corn that had been grown in Spain for over a decade. More trade complaints were likely.

The beef and GMO foods cases are important because they pertain to the question of whether countries can respond to citizen preferences whatever might be the basis for those preferences. Another example involves environmental protection. A U.S. law banned the sale of shrimp caught with nets from which sea turtles were unable to escape. The DSB upheld a complaint by India, Malaysia, Pakistan, and Thailand against the U.S. law on the grounds that the WTO agreements did not permit discrimination against products on the basis of how they were produced. The dispute continued with Vietnam filing a WTO complaint against the United States regarding shrimp. Prior to the establishment of the WTO, a GATT panel had on the same grounds ruled against the U.S. Marine Mammal Protection Act ban on yellow-fin tuna caught in purse seine nets in which dolphins could get caught and drown. In the case of the tuna decision, the United States withheld its consent and the panel decision did not take effect. Mexico subsequently took the issue to the WTO, and in 2011 the WTO ruled in favor of Mexico, allowing Mexican yellow-fin tuna to carry the "dolphin-safe" label. Greenpeace opposed the decision, and U.S. tuna companies were expected to continue their refusal to buy tuna caught in association with dolphins. Environmental issues such as these and health issues such as the EU ban on hormone-treated beef and GMO foods spurred calls for a new round of WTO negotiations.

[17]*Wall Street Journal*, November 9, 2004. The European Union took its evidence to the WTO in an attempt to have the sanctions lifted.

[18]*New York Times*, January 10, 2003.

[19]*Wall Street Journal*, September 9, 2003.

The Doha Round of WTO Negotiations

The Uruguay Round and follow-up agreements were generally successful, and the WTO dispute settlement process had been effective. Nevertheless, many trade issues remained unresolved. The members of the WTO had planned to adopt an agenda for a new round of multilateral trade negotiation at the 1999 Seattle ministerial meeting, but demonstrations by activist groups disrupted the meeting.[20] Finally, in 2001 after tense negotiations, particularly between developing and developed countries, the members agreed to a broad agenda for the Doha Round.[21]

Despite intense political pressure from the pharmaceutical industry, developing countries, led by India, received a pledge that TRIPS "does not and should not prevent Members from taking measures to protect public health." This would allow developing countries to violate pharmaceutical patents and produce or import generic drugs to protect public health without being subject to trade penalties.

Other issues added to the Doha agenda reflected bargaining among the members. Despite the opposition of France, the European Union agreed to negotiations on agricultural subsidies and market access. The European Union pledged to support sustainable development and for discussions on the relationship between trade and multilateral environmental agreements, but more specific environmental objectives were not specified. The United States agreed to negotiations on the clarification of antidumping procedures, much to the anger of U.S. industries that had used antidumping for protection from imports. The WTO members also agreed to reduce or eliminate tariffs on industrial goods. Activist groups failed to obtain commitments to labor protection due to objections by developing nations. The negotiations in the Doha Round were to pay special attention to the situations of developing countries. For example, developing countries were given until 2016 to bring their patent laws into accord with TRIPS.

Negotiations were also scheduled for the trade effects of competition (antitrust) policy, intellectual property protection under TRIPS, and services under GATS. The members also committed to a review of DSB procedures, discussions on rules pertaining to investments, and negotiations on transparency in government procurement.

Reaching agreement on the Doha Round agenda was hard, but making progress on substantive issues was far more difficult. The disagreements between the developing and developed countries were at the heart of the problem. Developing countries wanted the developed countries to bear the brunt of the costs of further trade liberalization. They sought reductions in U.S. agricultural subsidies, reductions in EU tariffs on agricultural products, and greater access to EU markets. For example, Brazil was the leader of the G22 block that had successfully filed trade complaints against EU sugar subsidiaries and U.S. cotton subsidies. In exchange for reducing agriculture supports, the developed countries sought reductions in industrial tariffs in developing countries and the opening of services markets (see the Chapter 17 case *Tesco PLC in India?*). The developing countries rejected those demands. In 2008 the negotiators gave up, and negotiations were suspended.

In 2011 WTO Director General Pascal Lamy revived discussions hoping to reach a narrow agreement before the expiration of the Doha Round at the end of the year. Negotiators abandoned discussions on the issues of importance to developed nations and focus on several narrow issues of importance to developing countries. Whether agreement would be reached on those issues was unclear. The lack of progress on the Doha Round led countries to pursue bilateral trade agreements outside the multilateral negotiating framework of the WTO.

Other Trade Agreements

A number of regional free trade agreements have been concluded. The largest of these free trade areas are NAFTA and the Common Market of the European Union. In 1994 the 16 countries participating in the Asia-Pacific Economic Cooperation (APEC) forum agreed to work toward removing all barriers to trade by the year 2020. In Latin America there are four regional trading areas: the Central American Common Market, the Andean Community, Caricom, and Mercosur. Mercosur members are Argentina, Brazil, Paraguay, and Uruguay, with Bolivia, Chile, Colombia,

---

[20]See Prakash (2001) for an analysis of the Seattle meeting. The principal effect of the demonstrations in Seattle was to delay the next round of negotiations 2 years rather than to affect the agenda significantly.

[21]Esty (2001) analyzes the trade and environment issues.

Ecuador, and Peru as associates. Venezuela was accepted into Mercosur, but full membership was blocked by Paraguay. Despite Mescosur, Argentina and Brazil enacted a number of measures to restrict imports, tax exports, restrict the ownership of land, and favor domestic companies. Global Trade Alert reported that Argentina had more trade distorting restrictions than any country other than Russia.[22]

In addition to WTO trade agreements, a large number of bilateral and multilateral agreements are in force. For example, in 2004 the United States concluded a free trade agreement with Chile, which already had such an agreement with Canada and the European Union. Also, the United States has worked to deregulate international air transportation, which had been governed by a cartel supported by countries with state-owned airlines. The U.S. strategy had been to negotiate bilateral agreements deregulating air fares and schedules with other countries. This increased competition and brought prices down, although restrictions remained in some markets because landing slots were limited.

U.S. TRADE POLICY

The Structure of U.S. Trade Policy

Article 1, Section 8 of the Constitution gives Congress the power "to regulate commerce with foreign nations" and to "lay and collect duties." In 1934 in the aftermath of the disastrous Smoot–Hawley tariff, Congress passed the Reciprocal Trade Agreement Act, which delegated to the president the authority to negotiate trade agreements. The authority for U.S. trade negotiations has remained largely with the president. The Office of the U.S. Trade Representative (USTR), located in the Executive Office of the President, serves as the president's representative in trade negotiations. The United States has supported trade liberalization through the multilateral policies embodied in the WTO agreements, regional free trade agreements including NAFTA and APEC, and bilateral arrangements such as those promoting competition in international air transport.

In the late 1980s, Congress began to assert its constitutional authority. The USTR is now required to consult with Congress on both trade policy and specific actions that implement that policy.[23] Being closer to constituents than the president, members of Congress have been concerned with protecting their constituents' interests. The result has been a series of amendments to the trade laws that make it easier for industries both to obtain protection and to initiate action to open foreign markets to their products. U.S. trade laws establish rights of private parties to initiate trade actions to further their own interests, so U.S. trade actions have both public and private initiation.

The politics of international trade takes place in four institutional arenas—cabinet departments, regulatory agencies, Congress, and the Office of the President. The administration of trade policy has been placed with executive branch agencies, primarily the Departments of the Treasury, State, and Commerce. The International Trade Administration (ITA) in the Department of Commerce and the International Trade Commission (ITC), an independent regulatory commission, have administrative responsibilities for certain sections of U.S. trade law. Cabinet departments participate in international trade policy, both administratively and politically, and regularly conduct policy research, provide congressional testimony, and lobby for their policy objectives and the interests they represent.

U.S. Trade Law and Its Administration

The major components of U.S. trade law are embodied in the Trade Act of 1974 and the Tariff Act of 1930. The principal sections and their purposes are as follows:[24]

- Section 201 (temporary safeguards) provides for temporary relief for domestic industries seriously injured by increased imports; no unfair trade practice is required.
- Section 301 (presidential retaliation) provides for action against countries that restrict imports of U.S. goods or subsidize exports to the United States.
- Section 731 (antidumping) provides authority for the imposition of duties on goods imported to the United States at a price that is less than fair value (LTFV).

---

[22]*Economist*, September 24, 2011.

[23]See O'Halloran (1994) for a study of the development of U.S. policy and the choice of trade institutions.

[24]See Trebilcock and York (1990) for studies of the administration of trade laws in a number of countries.

- Section 303 (countervailing duties) provides authority for the imposition of duties against countries that subsidize their domestic industries.
- Section 337 (intellectual property) allows retaliation against countries that violate U.S. patents, copyrights, or protected trade secrets.
- Trade Adjustment Assistance provides assistance for those injured by imports.

These laws establish rights that private interests may exercise either directly or indirectly through administrative channels. For example, firms, unions, and other interests may file antidumping petitions to initiate a complex administrative process that can result in duties assessed on imports. Antidumping and countervailing duty petitions are considered by the ITA and the ITC. In Section 201 and 301 cases, the president has final authority, as illustrated in the steel imports example in this chapter. Decisions by the ITC can be appealed to the U.S. Court of International Trade and the Court of Appeals (Federal Circuit), and many of the decisions are appealed. The chapter case *Cemex and Antidumping* provides details on the ITC and ITA administration of an antidumping case and considers a firm's market and nonmarket strategies for addressing a dumping complaint.

THE POLITICAL ECONOMY OF PROTECTIONISM

Formal Policies

Although official U.S. trade policy has promoted free and fair trade, the client politics arising from import competition has been important since the eighteenth century. Protection may extend indefinitely, have a specified duration, or be extendable. Protection for coastal shipping has continued since 1789, but most of the recent protectionist measures are intended to be temporary to give an industry time to improve its competitiveness.

Protection applies to two kinds of conditions. The first involves a predatory trade practice, such as export subsidization or predatory dumping, where a foreign firm sells in the United States at a price below its cost. The second involves relative efficiency—when foreign firms have lower costs than U.S. firms and sell in the United States at prices above their costs yet below the prices of domestic goods. Economic efficiency requires allowing nonpredatory imports and calls for blocking predatory practices if they will lead to long-run inefficiency. The political process, however, has not drawn the same line as economists and instead focuses on fair trade and protection from injury.

Predatory and discriminatory trade practices are addressed by the antidumping provisions of Section 731 and countervailing duties under Section 303. From 1980 through 2007, 1,606 cases were filed, 70 percent of which were antidumping cases. The number of cases filed peaked in 2001 at 116 and declined thereafter, but increased again in 2007. Thirty-eight percent of the cases were decided for the complainant, 39 percent for the respondent, and 22 percent were terminated or suspended. Few of these cases involved predatory practices.

The duties in antidumping cases had been paid to the U.S. government, but in 2000 Congress enacted a provision, the Byrd Amendment, under which the duties were paid to the companies that were injured by the trade practice. The European Union and eight other countries filed a complaint with the WTO against the practice. The WTO ruled against the United States and authorized $150 million in duties on U.S. goods. The United States repealed the Byrd Amendment in 2005.

The relative inefficiency of domestic industries is addressed in four ways. First, those injured may be compensated under the Trade Adjustment Assistance Act, which is intended to help a domestic industry adjust by improving its efficiency. Trade adjustment assistance compensates those, such as workers, who are injured, thereby reducing their political opposition to liberalized trade. The assistance is generally restricted to workers and has primarily focused on retraining programs. Trade adjustment assistance has been provided sparingly because of concerns that it might become an entitlement for workers or be used as a pork barrel program.

Second, safeguards relief can be granted under Section 201 in the form of temporary tariffs, import quotas, the suspension of previously granted trade concessions, or trade adjustment assistance. Relief under Section 201 is infrequently requested and seldom granted. Relief for the steel industry, considered in the example later in the chapter, was the first Section 201 case in 17 years. Relief can also be sought under Section 301 in the case of subsidized exports. As discussed in Chapter 13, in 2010 the United Steel Workers filed a Section 301 complaint against China claiming that the country's subsidies for wind turbine production violated WTO rules. The United States agreed and took the complaint to the WTO.

Third, relief is granted under Section 731 when a petitioner's dumping complaint is affirmed by the ITC and the ITA. A finding of dumping requires only that the imported good is sold at LTFV and that the petitioner has been materially injured by the imports. Antidumping thus is not restricted to predatory practices but instead can be used to protect domestic firms from imports. The example considers Section 301 and Section 731 complaints by the renewable power industries against China.

Fourth, protection is provided by measures ranging from tariffs to voluntary agreements to limit imports. The United States imposes a 2.5 percent duty on passenger cars but imposes a 25 percent duty on light trucks. Textile and apparel exports to developed countries had been restricted by quotas specified in the Multi-Fiber Arrangement (MFA). The Uruguay Round accord eliminated the MFA and its quotas beginning in 2005. In anticipation of the end of the quotas, the U.S. textile and apparel industries sought protection from what was expected to be a huge increase in imports from China and India. U.S. manufacturers and textile unions petitioned the Bush administration for temporary safeguards protection under Section 201, and 1 week before the 2004 elections the president agreed to consider the petition.[25] Using a provision in the agreement allowing China to join the WTO, the United States imposed quotas on some clothing imports. Under pressure from both developed and developing countries, China announced that it would impose a tariff on its textile exports.

EXAMPLE Renewable Power and Trade Complaints

U.S. renewable power companies were under considerable price pressure from producers in China that were supported by the Chinese government (discussed in Chapter 13). In September 2010 the United Steel Workers Union filed a 5,800 page Section 301 complaint against alleged subsidization by China of wind turbine manufacturing and other support for renewable power. After an initial investigation by the USTR, the United States initiated the WTO dispute settlement process by requesting consultation with China over the allegations. During the investigation China had agreed to lift two support policies, and possible WTO action pertained only to the subsidization of wind turbines.

The U.S. investigation focused on China's subsidy program for wind turbines that provided manufacturers with grants ranging from $6.7 million to $22.5 million with firms eligible for multiple grants for producing larger turbines. The grants appeared to be contingent on using domestic components, and Chinese wind power developers were seen to favor domestic producers. The United States viewed this as an import substitution program that subsidizes domestic producers with their output intended to replace imports. USTR Ron Kirk said, "Import substitution subsidies are particularly harmful and inherently trade distorting, which is why they are expressly prohibited under WTO rules. These subsidies effectively operate as a barrier to U.S. exports to China. Opening markets by removing barriers to our exports is a core element of the president's trade strategy."[1] USW president Leo W. Gerard commented, "The goal is not litigation. It's to end their practices."[2] Kirk explained the next steps, "We will continue to work closely with the USW and other stakeholders in the months ahead on the remaining allegations. If we are able to develop sufficient evidence to support those allegations and they can be effectively addressed through WTO litigation, we will pursue the enforcement of our rights at the WTO independently of Section 301."[3]

The striking thing about the Section 301 petition was that no U.S. producer joined in the complaint. General Electric, which was a major global producer of wind turbines, had no comment on the complaint. The only company supporting, but not signing, the petition was SolarWorld Industries America, the U.S. subsidiary of SolarWorld AG of Germany, which had plants in the United States but none in China. U.S. companies were said to be fearful of retaliation by China if they supported the petition. China was the largest and fastest growing market for wind power.

---

[1]*New York Times*, December 23, 2010.
[2]Ibid.
[3]Ibid.

---

[25]At the same time a group of the least-developed countries sought protection from the WTO for their domestic industries, which were expected to lose export markets to China.

Solar panel producers were under severe price pressure from producers in China, and three U.S. companies had recently gone bankrupt, as discussed in Chapter 13. In October 2011, seven U.S. solar panel producers filed Section 301 and Section 731 complaints against China. The lead company was SolarWorld Industries America, and the other six companies chose to remain anonymous. Senator Ron Wyden (D-OR) said, "American solar operations should be rapidly expanding to keep pace with the skyrocketing demand for these products. But that is not what is happening. There seems to be one primary explanation for this; that is, that China is cheating."[4] Senator Jeff Merkley (D-OR) said China used "rogue practices." SolarWorld Industries America was headquartered in Oregon and had a large plant there.

Antidumping cases were easier to win against China than against developed economy countries because the United States had designated China as a "nonmarket economy." In considering the antidumping complaint, the U.S. International Trade Administration then compared prices at which solar panels were sold in the United States with prices at which they were sold in third countries.

Chinese solar panel producers such as Suntech Power had subsidiaries in the United States, so the Solar Energy Industries Association, of which the subsidiaries were members, was split and decided to take no position on the petitions. The seven complainants then formed their own association, the Coalition for American Solar Manufacturers, to support the petitions.

---

[4]New York Times, October 20, 2011.

THE COST OF PROTECTIONISM   Ultimately, the cost of protectionism is borne by consumers. Hufbauer and Elliott (1994) estimated that in 1990 special trade protection cost consumers over $70 billion, or approximately $280 per capita. U.S. producers were estimated to have captured approximately 45 percent of that amount as additional profits. Of the 21 cases of protection they studied, the annual cost per job saved ranged from $3,000 to $256,000, with an average of $54,000 for the 192,000 jobs saved by the protection. Over 152,000 of those jobs were in the apparel industry, and the cost to consumers per job was over $50,000 per year.

Although they bear the cost of protectionism, consumers are costly to organize, and individual consumers are unlikely to act politically on trade protection issues. Furthermore, organized consumer groups have largely been inactive in cases involving protection of domestic industries. This leaves the political arena open to domestic industries, with political opposition coming primarily from importers, U.S. exporters, and those in government who support free trade and economic efficiency. For example, in the Section 201 petition, the U.S. textile manufacturers and unions were opposed by the United States Association of Importers of Textiles and Apparel.

Channels of Protection

Firms, labor unions, and industries can seek protection from imports through political and/or administrative channels. The political channel is through Congress and is directed either at specific legislation, such as a quota on sugar imports, or at the criteria used in the administrative channel. In addition to enacting new legislation, the political channel represents a threat that may strengthen the U.S. bargaining position with other countries. The protection obtained by an industry through the political channel depends on its ability to generate nonmarket pressure, as considered in Chapter 6, and on the pressure from opposing groups. Industries such as automobiles, steel, dairy farming, sugar, and textiles with large numbers of employees have been able to generate considerable nonmarket pressure.

The administrative channel involves regulatory and executive branch agencies and is accessed by a petition filed pursuant to the U.S. trade laws. Much of the administration of trade policy is delegated to the ITC, the ITA, and the president. In the chapter case *Cemex and Antidumping* labor unions and U.S. cement producers filed an antidumping petition against Mexican cement imports. The administrative process imposes a series of gates through which a case must pass before relief is granted, and a petition may fail at any of several points in the process. In some cases, the threat of action is used to negotiate a voluntary settlement or suspension of the complaint. The steel imports example illustrates the use of both political and administrative channels.

EXAMPLE   Steel Imports and the Nonmarket Campaign

Overcapacity in the steel industry worldwide caused employment in the U.S. steel industry to drop by 325,000 during the 1980s, much of it at the hands of imported steel. Employment at Bethlehem Steel fell from 130,000 in the 1960s to 16,400 in 1998. To improve its competitiveness, the industry invested $50 billion in modernization and new technology. Despite the investment a number of inefficient plants were still in production, and the United States remained a high-cost producer. By the second half of the 1990s strong demand returned the U.S. industry to health, and prices and profits were up. The situation changed quickly, however, in 1997 as a result of the financial and economic crises in Asia and Russia and to a lesser extent in Latin America. Steel imports increased dramatically as foreign producers looked for markets for their excess capacity, and the robust U.S. economy with open markets was by far the most attractive opportunity. The imports drove prices down sharply and resulted in layoffs and the bankruptcy of one small steel company. The price of hot rolled steel fell by 18 percent in 1998 to the lowest level during the 1990s.

In response, the USW and 12 leading steel producers joined in a broad client politics campaign to limit what they viewed as unfairly dumped steel. Curtis Barnette, CEO of Bethlehem Steel, said, "We're sometimes viewed as protectionist and rust belt in our thinking when we are a high-tech, low-cost, world-class industry. We believe in open markets. But when the rules are breached, they should be enforced."[1] Barnette was referring to U.S. laws against unfair competition resulting from dumping and the subsidization of foreign producers. To implement its nonmarket strategy the industry began the "Stand Up for Steel" campaign to bring the issue to the attention of the public, Congress, and the president.

Four producers of stainless steel and the USW filed antidumping petitions against eight countries and countervailing duty petitions against Belgium, France, Italy, and South Korea for subsidizing their steel makers. Stainless sheet steel prices had fallen from $2,700 a metric ton in 1996 to $1,800 in 1998. Industry profits on stainless sheet steel fell from $466 million in 1995 to $141 million in 1997. The industry also filed antidumping and countervailing duty petitions against Brazil, Japan, and Russia for dumping hot rolled steel and against Brazil for subsidizing its steel producers. With the downturn in the U.S. industry reflected in layoffs and lower prices and profits, the material injury standard was expected to be met.

In addition to pursuing its case in administrative channels, the industry pursued relief through political channels, deploying a nonmarket strategy intended to pressure the U.S. government to act. The industry lobbied Congress, and the House passed a nonbinding resolution calling for a ban on steel imports for a year. The industry also succeeded in inserting a provision in an appropriations bill requiring

the Clinton administration to produce a plan for aiding the industry by January 5, 1999. Barnette and others lobbied in the Senate and convinced the Senate Steel Caucus to call on the administration to restrict imports.

The Stand Up for Steel campaign spent $3 million on a public advocacy campaign, including full-page newspaper advertisements presenting a letter calling on President Clinton to act.[2] George Becker, president of the USW, said, "We're fighting for the heartland of America. All the blood is gone from our industry; we can't bleed anymore."[3]

On the trade petitions, the ITA found in favor of the steel industry and announced duties ranging from 3.44 percent to 67.68 percent. Overall, however, only about half the petitions were ultimately approved. The industry also sent a message to the president and the Democratic Party. In the 1997–1998 election cycle, the USW and the steel companies provided $1.2 million in campaign contributions, most of which came from the USW, with over 80 percent going to Democrats. More importantly, the USW had been very effective in "get out the vote" efforts on behalf of Democrats. The president and vice president were not only concerned with rewarding their important political backers but also feared having unemployed steel workers when the 2000 elections arrived.

The campaign by the steel industry did not go unopposed. Steel purchasers formed the Consuming Trade Action Coalition, which argued that any restraints on steel imports would result in higher prices for consumers. Both General Motors and Caterpillar criticized the antidumping and countervailing duty petitions. Caterpillar stated, "We strongly object to suggestions that steel trade should be subject to 'special' protection. The quotas used to protect the steel industry in each of the last four decades hurt American industries that use steel and rewarded foreign steel traders with a guaranteed share of a restricted market."[4]

Under the threat of action, Brazil and Russia agreed to quotas on imports of their steel products. The Clinton administration's report on the steel industry recommended that the administrative processes of U.S. trade law be accelerated, but the administration took no formal action under U.S. trade law. Some commentators believed that the failure to take action cost Vice President Gore the state of West Virginia and the election.

In 2001 President Bush ordered a review of the state of the steel industry. Employment in the industry had dropped from 800,000 in 1980 to 160,000 in 2001. Imports accounted for 27 percent of U.S. steel consumption, down from 30 percent during the Asian crisis, but prices for some steel products had fallen to their lowest levels in 20 years. In addition, 18 steel companies including LTV—one of the largest—had filed for bankruptcy.[5] The situation in the industry was due in

---

[1]*New York Times*, December 10, 1998.

[2]*New York Times*, September 10, 1998.
[3]*New York Times*, December 10, 1998.
[4]Ibid.
[5]Bethlehem filed for bankruptcy later in the year.

part to the inefficiency of U.S. integrated steel producers, which had lost market share not only to imports but also to domestic mini mills. The market value of all U.S. steel producers was $10 billion, approximately 3 percent of the value of Microsoft.

As a result of its review, the Bush administration took the rare action of filing a Section 201 petition for relief for the industry, the first such petition since 1985. The Emergency Committee for American Trade, a business organization that supported free trade, criticized the action.

Later in the year the ITC concluded that the industry had been "seriously injured" by imports in 12 product categories representing 74 percent of the imports under investigation.[6] The ITC recommended duties from 5 percent to 40 percent on products representing 80 percent of imported steel. Economist Gary Hufbauer estimated that the cost to consumers for each steelworker job saved by the duties would be $326,000.[7]

The European Union and South Korea announced that they would file a complaint with the WTO if any new restrictions were imposed as a result of the Section 201 case. Pascal Lamy, the EU trade commissioner, said, "The cost of restructuring in the U.S. steel sector should not be shifted to the rest of the world."[8]

The steel industry and the USW mounted an intense political campaign along with their allies in Congress. Under pressure the Bush administration imposed temporary 3-year tariffs on certain steel imports under Section 201. The ostensible purpose of the tariffs was to allow the steel companies to consolidate and improve their efficiency. The tariffs began at 30 percent and decreased to 24 percent the next year and to 18 percent in the third year. Developing countries were exempted, and the tariffs were primarily

applied to industrialized countries and advanced developing countries. The Bush administration stated that the temporary tariffs were permitted under the WTO's safeguard provision, which allowed temporary relief in the event of a surge of imports.

Part of the assistance sought by the steel industry and USW was to cover the cost of health and pension benefits for 600,000 retired workers. The estimate of the cost over the next 10 years was more than $10 billion. The Bush administration refused to assume the pension obligations.

In response to the Section 201 action, the European Union took immediate action by filing two petitions with the WTO. First, it filed a complaint under the WTO dispute resolution process and identified U.S. imports to be targeted if the WTO ruled in its favor. Second, it filed a complaint that the United States had improperly imposed tariffs selectively under the "safeguards" procedures.

The direct effect of the tariffs on EU steel producers was small, since only 2.5 percent of EU production was affected. The principal concern was that low-cost steel that had been exported to the United States would now be diverted to the European Union, forcing prices down. The European Union announced that it would impose temporary tariffs on steel imports from any country that exceeded 2001 import levels. Canada also considered imposing temporary tariffs.

In late 2003 the WTO ruled that the U.S. tariffs were illegal and authorized punitive tariffs on $2.1 billion of U.S. exports to the European Union. In 2004 President Bush withdrew the safeguards tariffs. During the 2 years the tariffs were in effect, the U.S. steel industry consolidated and efficiency improved. As the tariffs were being withdrawn, U.S. demand for steel increased, raw material and energy costs increased, and the U.S. dollar fell, making steel imports more expensive. Steel prices in the United States rose sharply, and the industry returned to profitability.

---

[6]The ITC found no serious injury in 17 product categories.
[7]*New York Times*, December 8, 2001.
[8]*New York Times*, June 7, 2001

THE POLITICAL ECONOMY OF MARKET OPENING

Market opening occurs through majoritarian policies such as those embodied in the WTO and NAFTA and through entrepreneurial politics, with the president attempting through multilateral and bilateral negotiations to reduce foreign tariff and nontariff barriers to trade. In some cases, market opening is characterized by client politics as interest groups pressure the government to take action to open specific foreign markets. This section considers the political economy of NAFTA, market opening under the threat of retaliation, and bilateral market opening.

The North American Free Trade Agreement

The North American Free Trade Agreement established, subject to certain exceptions, free trade among Canada, Mexico, and the United States. NAFTA was an expansion of the United States–Canada Free Trade Agreement that had been in effect since 1988, and it adopted many of the features of that agreement. NAFTA is a free trade agreement and not a market integration agreement as is the Single Market Act in the European Union. The agreement thus does not cover the movement of people or the harmonization of domestic laws.

NAFTA provided for the elimination of tariff and nontariff barriers over a 10-year period, although some barriers were to be phased out over 15 years. To the extent that external trade barriers remained in effect, the elimination of trade barriers within North America gave foreign firms an incentive to locate operations in the NAFTA countries. Because of both market and nonmarket considerations, Japanese automobile manufacturers had incentives to shift light-truck production to North America. The principal market factor was the lower wages in Mexico. The principal nonmarket factor was to avoid the 25 percent U.S. tariff on imports from outside the NAFTA countries.

Despite the expected economic gains, political opposition to the agreement was strong in Canada and the United States. In the United States, opposition was led by organized labor, which feared the loss of jobs to Mexico, and by environmentalists. To overcome the opposition, the George H.W. Bush administration, which negotiated the agreement, and the Clinton administration, which obtained congressional passage, made a number of deals and provided safeguards to obtain the needed votes. Nevertheless, 60 percent of the House Democrats voted against the agreement, and it passed as a result of strong Republican support.

The politics of NAFTA were similar to those of other trade liberalization measures. The weight of majoritarian interests was in favor of liberalized trade, and the opposition came from concentrated interests that were likely to be injured. Without concessions those interests and the client politics they generated might have defeated the agreement. Three types of measures were taken to reduce opposition. First, NAFTA included transition provisions for a gradual phaseout of trade barriers to give industries time to adjust. Moreover, to reduce opposition from agricultural interests that feared a flood of low-priced Mexican produce, NAFTA included safeguards that would take effect if there were large surges of imports that depressed agricultural prices.[26] Second, to obtain congressional votes, the Clinton administration made a number of side deals outside the trade area, including approval of public works projects in members' districts. Third, side agreements were concluded to reduce the opposition of environmental groups concerned about higher pollution as production expanded in Mexico and of organized labor that feared that high-paying jobs would be lost to Mexico.

The elimination of tariff and nontariff barriers did not mean that trade disputes disappeared. NAFTA left domestic trade laws in place, so antidumping and countervailing duty cases continued. The Canada–U.S. bilateral free trade agreement had established a dispute settlement mechanism to avoid use of the courts. NAFTA incorporated this feature by establishing a trilateral Trade Commission, composed of cabinet level officials, to hear complaints and resolve disputes on issues such as the application of antidumping laws. When the United States refused to allow Mexican trucks unrestricted access to U.S. roads, Mexico filed a complaint. A dispute settlement panel ruled in favor of Mexico, and fines could be imposed if the United States failed to grant access. The opposition in the United States was led by the Teamsters Union and by activists concerned that the United States did not have the safety inspection capacity to ensure that the trucks met U.S. safety standards. President Clinton refused to allow Mexican trucks into the United States, but President George W. Bush announced that the United States would comply with the panel decision. Mexican trucks were finally allowed into the United States in 2007. As soon as he took office, President Obama banned Mexican trucks to benefit the Teamsters Union, and Mexico retaliated by imposing punitive tariffs on $2.3 billion U.S. agricultural and industrial imports. Finally, in 2011 the United States and Mexico ended the 17-year saga by negotiating an agreement under which some Mexican trucks were allowed into the United States, U.S. trucks were allowed into Mexico, and the Mexican punitive tariffs were eliminated.

Market Opening Under the Threat of Retaliation

The most effective means of addressing foreign barriers to trade is through negotiations, but countries, and particularly the United States, have used retaliation and its threat to provide leverage. In the 1980s the Semiconductor Industry Association filed a Section 301 petition to pry open the Japanese market to foreign-made semiconductors. Pressure from the United States and the threat of success in the administrative channel resulted in an agreement in which Japanese semiconductor manufacturers pledged not to sell in the United States at less than fair value, to open the Japanese market, and to increase the market share of foreign semiconductors to 20 percent.

More often, however, bilateral negotiations have been lengthy and only moderately successful. Increasingly frustrated by what it viewed as inadequate action and by a process that

---

[26]In 2008 the last Mexican tariffs on corn, beans, milk, and sugar were eliminated under NAFTA. Mexican farmers took to the streets to protest the elimination and called for renegotiating NAFTA.

placed much of the power in the hands of the president, Congress sought to increase its influence over both the relief and the retaliation processes. In 1988 Congress enacted the Omnibus Trade and Competitiveness Act, which established a mechanism for retaliation under a strengthened Section 301, referred to as Super 301.

Super 301 provided for mandatory sanctions against countries that engaged in unfair trade practices that injured U.S. industries. The USTR prepared the National Trade Estimate Report (NTER) listing the countries with which the United States had a large trade deficit and the policies and practices that inhibited U.S. exports. The threat of mandatory retaliation under Super 301 contributed to an agreement under which Japan pledged to open its markets for wood products, communications satellites, and supercomputers.

Super 301 was sharply criticized by other countries, and both the European Union and Japan retaliated by issuing reports identifying U.S. tariff and nontariff barriers. Authorization for Super 301 expired at the end of 1990, but President Clinton issued an executive order reinstating a revised version of Super 301 under which sanctions were not mandatory. The rancor caused by Super 301 and the responses to it convinced most countries to pursue market opening through multilateral negotiations under the WTO.

The United States continues to issue the NTER and in 2008 put Thailand on the priority watchlist because of the compulsory licenses it had authorized. Fearing possible trade sanctions, Thailand prepared a plan for improving intellectual property protection and sought to convince the United States to take it off the priority watchlist. The chapter case *Compulsory Licensing, Thailand, and Abbott Laboratories* considers this issue from the perspective of a company whose patent has been violated by the compulsory license.

Bilateral Free Trade Agreements

The United States had 17 bilateral free trade agreements in effect, and free trade agreements were negotiated with South Korea, Panama, and Columbia in 2006 by the Bush administration. Congressional Democrats backed by labor unions blocked ratification of the three agreements fearing the loss of jobs. President Obama had opposed the agreements during his presidential campaign but as the recession lingered, the president saw the pacts as a way to stimulate the economy. The administration renegotiated the agreement with South Korea obtaining a more gradual phaseout of U.S. tariffs on automobile imports, and the United Auto Workers agreed to support the free trade pact. The administration feared that the United States would be at a competitive disadvantage, since a trade agreement between South Korea and the European Union and Canada and Columbia would take effect in the summer of 2011. The administration's stimulus bill had expanded the Trade Adjustment Assistance (TAA) program, but the expansion ended in 2011. Republicans supported the three free trade agreements, and to buy support in the Senate, they agreed to a modest expansion of TAA in exchange for putting the agreements to a vote. Organized labor led by the AFL-CIO opposed all these agreements, but with support from Republicans and some Democrats, the administration submitted the three trade pacts and the TAA compromise to Congress 5 years after they had been approved. All were passed.

SUMMARY

The gains from trade and the law of comparative advantage provide a compelling rationale for free trade. Under certain conditions, however, a nation can benefit from a strategic trade policy that restricts imports or subsidizes exports. In such situations countries may be in a prisoners' dilemma in which each has an incentive to adopt a strategic trade policy, but all are worse off when they do so. International trade agreements are intended to avoid these dilemmas and allow gains from trade to be realized.

International trade policy is driven by economic incentives but governed by the politics that stem from those incentives. The politics of international trade are basically majoritarian, but because of rents associated with sunk resources, the support for protectionism is often strong. Protectionism is characterized by client politics, whereas the politics of trade liberalization is entrepreneurial. Opposition to protectionism can develop from importers and their customers and from exporters concerned about retaliation by other countries. Interest group politics can be the result.

Multilateral trade liberalization policies are incorporated in the agreements that govern trade and dispute resolution. The WTO agreements cover trade in goods, services, and agricultural products and provide for intellectual property protection. Several regional free trade agreements, including NAFTA, the single market of the European Union, and Mercosur, have been established to eliminate internal barriers to trade.

The political economy of international trade is best understood by focusing on domestic politics and the negotiations among countries on trade policy. Trade negotiations reflect the desire to open foreign markets while avoiding injury to domestic interests. The political forces supporting protectionism are naturally strong because of the rents that accrue to sunk resources, but the long-run gains from trade liberalization are greater than the rents that would be dissipated by trade liberalization. In the United States the president usually advocates trade liberalization, and protectionism manifests itself primarily in Congress and administrative agencies.

Whereas the United States has generally supported free trade, it provides both administrative and political channels for relief of industries injured by imports. Because protectionism is costly to an economy, the administrative channel has been designed to provide easy access but to make relief relatively hard to obtain. Success for an industry seeking relief in the political channel requires an ability to generate nonmarket pressure, and this requires numbers, resources, and coverage of political districts.

The Part IV integrative case *Toys "Я" Us and Globalization* considers a firm that took its domestic market strategy to other countries and encountered a variety of trade and other barriers.

CASES

Cemex and Antidumping

Lorenzo Zambrano was accustomed to making tough decisions. During his 6-year tenure as chief executive officer of Cementos Mexicanos, S.A. (Cemex), he had transformed Cemex from a small Mexican cement manufacturer to an industry superpower. In the fall of 1990, however, Zambrano faced perhaps his most difficult challenge. In August the U.S. International Trade Commission ruled that Cemex had unfairly depressed cement prices in the southern and southwestern United States by dumping cement and cement clinker. As a result, a duty of 58 percent was levied on all subsequent Cemex exports from Mexico into the region. The ruling threatened Cemex's expansion and its access to the lucrative U.S. market. Cemex needed a strategy to address the threat.

In early 1989 cement producers in the southern portion of the United States were concerned about the erosion of their domestic market share due to increased imports from Mexico. Imports of gray portland cement and cement clinker, two principal cement products, had been increasing steadily over the previous 5 years. At the same time the lackluster performance of the economy in the region, and in particular the depressed level of new construction, was reducing the demand for cement.

Historically, the cement industry was a very regionalized business with high overland transportation costs preventing the commodity from freely flowing between regional markets. This insulation helped cement producers ride out hard times in the highly cyclical industry. Throughout the 1980s, however, Mexican producers were able to transport their cement across the border and still remain competitive on price, sometimes undercutting domestic producers. The majority of Mexican cement imported into the United States came from one producer, Cemex.

U.S. cement companies in the South and Southwest realized that imports from Cemex and other Mexican companies presented a threat to their profitability and perhaps to their survival. They believed that with high transportation costs, Mexican producers must be selling their cement at less than fair value, which would constitute dumping under Section 731 of U.S. trade law. Cement producers in Arizona, New Mexico, Texas, and Florida filed an antidumping petition claiming that Cemex and the Mexican cement industry were dumping cement and clinker in their markets.

THE MEXICAN CEMENT INDUSTRY

Portland cement was used predominantly in the production of concrete, and cement clinker was the primary component in the production of portland cement. Demand for cement was cyclical and followed the general economic climate, demographic trends, and construction expenditures. In Mexico approximately 60 percent of cement expenditures were in residential construction, 20 percent in public works, and 20 percent in commercial construction.

A principal input to cement production was oil, with energy costs accounting for 40–50 percent of cement production expenses. Mexican cement firms had benefited from governmental policies. Mexico's vast oil resources allowed it to implement targeted domestic industrial policies, and in 1986 the government provided its domestic producers with oil for as little as $4 a barrel, compared with a weighted-average world price ranging from $14 to $16 a barrel.[27] In 1990, however, Mexican oil prices were raised to world levels.

---

[27]"Cement Makers Fight, Yet Buy from, Importers," *Business Marketing,* August 1986, and *Energy Statistics Sourcebook,* 1987.

The Mexican cement industry was dominated by Cemex, which by the early 1990s was the largest cement company in North America and the fourth largest in the world. By the end of 1991 its capacity had grown to 24 million tons, which was 63 percent of Mexican capacity. Cemex's primary Mexican competitor was Grupo Cementos Apasco, S.A. de C.V. (Apasco), which was 60 percent owned by Holderbank Financière Glarus Ltd. (Holderbank), a Swiss company that was the largest cement company in the world.[28] Apasco had 17 percent of the Mexican market in 1991. The next largest competitor was Cruz Azul, which had 13 percent of the market.

Part of Cemex's rapid growth had come through acquisitions. Cemex had spent nearly $1 billion on acquisitions acquiring Cementos Anahuac, then Mexico's third-largest cement producer, in 1987 and in 1989 acquiring Empresas Tolteca, Mexico's second-largest producer and Cemex's chief competitor. Geographic diversification in addition to locating plants close to major markets rationalized production. Cemex also spent $950 million on new plant and environmental control equipment. This made the plants more energy efficient, raised labor productivity, and added 4.8 million tons of new capacity. Another $330 million was spent to develop international operations, including U.S. distribution facilities in Arizona, Texas, and California. Cemex subsequently acquired for $1.8 billion the two largest Spanish cement producers, giving it a presence in the European Union.

In 1991 Cemex's sales were approximately $1.7 billion with exports accounting for 15 percent of the total. The combination of its plant modernization and capital expenditure programs and its management and engineering know-how had given Cemex very low costs. Cemex had outstanding plant management practices and had been able to reduce plant downtime substantially, which increased its effective capacity and reduced costs.

Cemex had high brand loyalty in Mexico. In most countries, cement was a commodity purchased primarily by industrial and commercial buyers. In Mexico, however, about 78 percent of cement sold was through retailers in bags under brand names. In 1991 Cemex's bagged cement was sold through 4,500 exclusive retail distributors. Cemex provided technical and marketing assistance to its dealers and maintained long-term relationships with them.

Cemex had several plants located close to the U.S. border. Cemex's headquarters in Monterrey was only 130 miles from Texas, and the rapid economic growth in Mexico along the U.S. border provided an attractive location for new cement plants. Since cement production involved economies of scale, large plants were desirable, leaving some capacity for exports to the United States.

THE U.S. CEMENT INDUSTRY

As in Mexico, the U.S. industry was highly cyclical, depending on the general state of the economy and the construction industry in particular. Because of high overland transportation costs 95 percent of all gray portland cement shipments were made to customers located within 300 miles of the production site.

The U.S. industry was not nearly as concentrated as the Mexican industry. The leading U.S. cement producer in 1990 was Holnam, which was owned by Holderbank and had 11.8 percent of the domestic market.[29] Holnam was followed by Lafarge (6.7 percent), Southdown (6.1 percent), Lone Star Industries (5.5 percent), Ash Grove Cement (4.9 percent), and numerous other companies, at least five of which each had a domestic market share of over 3 percent. During the 1980s European companies began buying U.S. cement companies, and by 1989, 60 percent of the U.S. industry was owned by foreign companies. For example, Lafarge was owned by Lafarge Coppée of France, which was the world's second largest cement producer.

Cement imports accounted for 22 percent of the approximately 90 million tons of annual U.S. cement consumption, and imports had somewhat higher shares in the southern tier states. The Portland Cement Association estimated that in 1986 U.S. producers bought and resold approximately two-thirds of the cement imported into the country. The rationale provided by U.S. producers was that import prices were attractive, and since cement was a commodity, they were forced to serve their customers from the lowest-cost source.

The U.S. construction industry was weak at the end of the 1980s. The growth of the U.S. cement market was 1.3 percent in 1989 and 2.9 percent in 1990, whereas the growth rates of the Mexican cement market for the same years were 3.7 percent and 7.3 percent, respectively. In the southern and southwestern United States in particular, the success of Mexican cement importers contrasted sharply with the decline of local cement firms. In 1988, Mexican imports accounted for 14 percent of the Arizona–New Mexico–Texas market and 22 percent of the Florida market. In addition, since 1983 seven domestic cement plants had closed in the Arizona–New Mexico–Texas region and two had closed in Florida.

Domestic firms believed that Mexican firms were dumping cement in the United States by selling their exports at less than fair value (LTFV). The antidumping petitioners included two unions and eight companies, which formed the Ad Hoc Committee of AZ-NM-TX-FL Producers of Gray Portland Cement. The committee was led by Southdown, the largest U.S.-owned cement manufacturer. "Our investigation to date convinces us that the Mexicans' success in U.S. markets is due to dumping and not to any other factor," stated Clarence Comer, chief executive of Houston-based Southdown and chairman of the committee.[30]

The petitioners claimed that they had been materially injured by Mexican cement producers. The petition alleged that the dumping of cement depressed prices in the United States, caused investors to abandon the industry, and threatened their markets, production, and jobs. Comer summarized the allegation: "U.S. cement producers should not have to accept declining returns, declining employment, and declining capital investment. We should not have to cede U.S. markets and U.S. jobs to unfairly

---

[28]Holderbank subsequently changed its name to Holcim.

[29]Holnam was formed by the merger of Dundee Cement and Ideal Basic, and in 2001 was renamed Holcim.

[30]"U.S. Cement Companies Charge Mexican Producers with Dumping Cement in U.S. Markets," *Business Wire*, September 27, 1989.

priced imports from Mexico. If we lose out to fair competition from Mexico, so be it."[31] Comer surmised that additional injury to the cement industry in the southern and southwestern United States was imminent. "Mexican producers continue to build export oriented capacity aimed at American markets."[32]

The petitioners identified two principal reasons the U.S. cement producers were vulnerable to imports from Mexico. First, because cement was a commodity, a small price change could result in large shifts in market shares. Thus, even a small price difference would cause a large loss of volume for domestic producers if they did not meet the lower import price. Second, cement imports displaced domestic production ton for ton because aggregate demand for cement was derived from the demand for construction, and cement represented a small share of construction costs. Consequently, the aggregate demand for cement did not vary appreciably with price, so lower prices did not create additional demand.[33]

A similar but unsuccessful antidumping petition had been filed in 1986 by all U.S. cement producers against Mexico, Colombia, Venezuela, France, Greece, Japan, South Korea, and Spain.[34] In that case, the International Trade Commission (ITC) determined that there was no material injury to the U.S. cement industry because it had begun its recovery from the recession. The 1989 case, however, was different in three key respects: the petition was more narrowly focused; demand for cement in Arizona, New Mexico, and Texas was depressed; and Mexican imports were rising while U.S. cement prices were falling.

U.S. ANTIDUMPING LAW

The antidumping laws codified in Section 731 allowed either a private party or the International Trade Administration (ITA), an arm of the Department of Commerce (DOC), to file a petition for redress. The executive branch agencies charged with the administration of trade law in dumping cases were the ITC and the ITA. The ITC conducted a preliminary investigation to determine if there was a "reasonable indication" of material injury, or the threat of such injury, to the industry. Typically, the investigation covered the previous 3 years of activity. If no indication of injury were found, the petition was dismissed.

With a positive preliminary determination from the ITC, the ITA investigated whether there was a "reasonable likelihood" that imports were being sold at LTFV and calculated a preliminary estimate of the dumping margin. With an affirmative finding that a reasonable likelihood existed, the importer was required to make a cash deposit or post a bond or other security to guarantee the potential dumping liability. Upon concluding its investigation, the ITA announced its final determination of whether dumping was found. A positive finding included the final estimate of the dumping margin. A negative finding resulted in the petition being dismissed. Following an affirmative finding by the ITA, the ITC began the industry analysis stage. Here, the ITC investigated whether the imports

in question caused or threatened to cause injury to the domestic industry. Unless the ITC found material injury, the case was dismissed. If the ITC found material injury, the case returned to the ITA for the negotiation of settlements and/or the imposition of duties.

THE ITC AND ITA DETERMINATIONS

To find material injury or the threat of material injury, the ITC had to first determine the "like product" and the "domestic industry." The petitioners and respondents agreed that gray portland cement and cement clinker comprised a single like product. On November 8, 1989, the ITC issued a unanimous affirmative preliminary determination in favor of the petitioners. The DOC then formally notified the Mexican cement producers that they had to submit to and fully cooperate with an administrative review if they wished to continue exporting to the United States. Questionnaires sent to Cemex requested general information on Cemex's strategy, production capacity, and number of plants. They also requested specific information on the Mexican and U.S. markets, including Cemex's costs, prices, pricing policies, market share, and customer information for the different markets.

The ITA concluded that Type II gray portland cement was the "like product" and that the bulk cement market was the relevant market for the basis of comparison. To test for dumping or the selling of a product at LTFV, the ITA considered the weighted-average price (for all the different plants from which U.S. sales were made) of the product as sold by the foreign firm to the first unrelated party in the importing country. This price was then compared with the price at which the same or a similar product was sold in the home country. Since data for the price comparisons were limited, the ITA "constructed" prices at the mill gate using an administrative provision in its procedures that subtracted transportation and other costs. The price comparison thus was of mill net prices, determined by taking the sale price and deducting all costs other than those incurred in the mill. Dumping would be found if the price at which a ton of cement left the mill to a U.S. customer was lower than the price at which a ton of cement left the mill to a Mexican customer. The dumping margin was then the average of all the margins for those comparison sales for which dumping was found. Table 19-1 presents a sample calculation.

TABLE 19-1 Example of the Antidumping Margin

	Matched Pair of Sales in	
	Mexico	**United States**
Price ($)	85	80
Transportation to terminal	10	30
Customs	0	2
Terminal and distribution	11	7
Other expenses	12	10
Mill net price ($)	52	31
Dumping margin = 100 (52 − 31)/31 = 68 percent		

---

[31]Ibid.
[32]Ibid.
[33]Ibid.
[34]In contrast to shipping by land, shipping by sea is low cost.

The ITA set the dumping margin for Cemex at 58.38 percent and for Apasco, Cementos Hidalgo, and all others at 53.26 percent, 3.69 percent, and 58.05 percent, respectively. Thus, if the ITC were to find injury, Cemex would be assessed a duty of 58 percent of the dollar value of each ton of cement leaving the mill for the U.S. market.

To determine whether there was "material injury" or the "threat of material injury" from imports of Mexican cement, the ITC assessed the effects of Mexican cement imports on U.S. prices, production, capacity, capacity utilization, shipments, inventories, employment, wages, financial performance, capital investments, and research and development expenditures. The data showed that from 1986 to 1989 the total quantity of cement shipped by U.S. producers had increased by 4.7 percent, but declining prices caused the total value to decrease by 3.7 percent. Capacity for cement and clinker production changed little, and capacity utilization decreased slightly. Additionally, the employment, wages, and hours worked of production workers fell by 19 percent, 13.8 percent, and 14 percent, respectively. Productivity rose by 23 percent. The financial performance of southern tier producers deteriorated, as gross profit fell by 18.1 percent and operating income dropped by 36.7 percent. Some firms had curtailed planned investment. The data also indicated that the volume of Mexican imports had increased 24 percent.

In August 1990 the ITC issued an affirmative final determination in favor of the petitioners. To continue importing cement and clinker, Mexican importers were required to tender cash deposits to the U.S. Customs Service equal to the estimated dumping margins. For Cemex and Apasco, those margins were 58 percent and 53 percent of their mill net prices, respectively. The antidumping order had an unlimited duration, so the duties would remain in effect until the dumping ceased. The duties, however, were to be recalculated every year based on updated data. As a result of the duties, all the Mexican producers except Cemex left the U.S. market.

CEMEX'S STRATEGY

From the beginning of the process, Cemex complied fully with the requests for data. Cemex also opened its operations to the DOC as much as possible to expedite the administrative process and to demonstrate that the company was confident that it would prevail.

Cemex assigned the dumping issue top priority and created a new department to oversee the implementation of a multipronged strategy to address the issue. First, a U.S. law firm specializing in dumping cases was hired to provide advice. Second, Cemex sought to use the media in Mexico to build support and call the attention of the Mexican people to the alleged "unfair" treatment. Cemex also sought coverage from the U.S. media, including the *Wall Street Journal,* to educate the American people about Cemex and its overall strategy and performance both in Mexico and in the United States. Third, a presentation was made to the Mexican Commerce Department to demonstrate the importance of the petition and the effect it would have on Cemex and Mexico. The goal was to obtain the Mexican government's support against the U.S. action.

The Mexican government, however, was concerned about possibly jeopardizing the ongoing North American Free Trade Agreement (NAFTA) negotiations and decided not to pressure the U.S. DOC.

The opportunity for lobbying in Washington was limited because the issue was in the jurisdiction of regulatory rather than legislative institutions. As a result, little lobbying was done, although certain government leaders (including senators and governors in states where Cemex had operations) were contacted to explain the antidumping petition and Cemex's position.

Cemex believed that in reaching their conclusion that dumping had occurred the U.S. agencies had ignored Cemex's actual price and shipping costs. For example, Cemex sold its cement in the United States at market prices, but nearly a third of that went to the cost of transporting the cement from its plants south of the border. Zambrano noted that the ITC deducted the transportation costs and thus concluded there was dumping.[35]

Cemex argued that the antidumping petition was nothing more than an attempt by its competitors to halt its expansion in the United States. "Some of our competitors thought we were a rather weak neighbor," stated Zambrano. "And it just so happens that we grew, and they didn't like it."[36]

The ITC ruling had potentially devastating ramifications for Cemex's expansion drive into the U.S. market, and Zambrano implemented an integrated strategy, combining both market and nonmarket components. The market component consisted of a revamped short-term business strategy in response to the duty assessed. The nonmarket component focused on lowering the duty and reversing the ruling. It was designed to seek redress through three institutional arenas: administrative, judicial, and international.

CEMEX'S MARKET STRATEGY[37]

First, Zambrano decided to reduce substantially Cemex's exports to the United States. This was offset to some extent by growth in Cemex's home market, which had become much more attractive because Mexico initiated a number of public works projects that caused demand for cement to grow by about 10 percent.

Second, the 58 percent duty made shipments unprofitable in states where cement prices were low, so Zambrano withdrew completely from some U.S. states and focused only on those with higher prices. Cemex abandoned Florida outright after the ITC ruling and was content with breaking even in the higher-priced markets. Selling only in regions with high prices had the advantage of reducing the difference between U.S. and Mexican mill net prices, which would result in a lower dumping margin at the next annual review.

Third, Cemex maintained a substantial Type II (bulk) cement market in Mexico so that the ITA would compare the product sold in the U.S. market with the Mexican

---

[35]"Cement Wars," *Forbes,* October 1, 1990.
[36]Ibid.
[37]Ibid.

Type II (bulk) cement market. Cemex wanted to avoid the ITA concluding that the like product was its branded bagged cement in Mexico, which would substantially increase the dumping margin.

CEMEX'S NONMARKET STRATEGY

As part of its nonmarket strategy Cemex requested administrative reviews of the duty, and in the first review the petitioners alleged that Cemex had created a fictitious bulk market in its home country to reduce the duties. The ITA found that no fictitious market had been created, and as a result of Cemex's new market strategy of limiting exports to regions with high prices, the duty was reduced to 30.74 percent.

Zambrano also attempted to have the ITC's ruling reversed in judicial arenas. Cemex appealed the ITC determination of material injury to the U.S. Court of International Trade (CIT), arguing that the ITC had not followed proper procedures. The CIT rejected Cemex's argument, and Cemex appealed, using the same argument, to the U.S. Court of Appeals, but was also unsuccessful. Cemex also appealed to the CIT the duties imposed by the ITA, arguing that the ITA had followed neither statutory requirements nor precedents in determining the dumping margin. The CIT, however, ruled that the overall weight of precedent was in favor of the approach used in the Cemex case. The CIT upheld the dumping duty.

After failing in the U.S. judicial arenas, the Mexican government petitioned the General Agreement on Tariffs and Trade (GATT) requesting that a panel be established to review the antidumping dispute. In July 1992 the GATT panel found that the United States had improperly imposed duties on the Mexican cement industry and recommended that $30 million in duties already collected be returned. The order to refund duties was rarely made by GATT, so the decision was considered severe. The panel did not address whether the Mexican companies had sold at less than fair value. Rather, the panel concluded that the U.S. Department of Commerce had not verified that the ad hoc committee of petitioners that brought the action was sufficiently representative of the industry. The committee represented only 61.7 percent of all U.S. cement producers in the region, but under GATT antidumping rules, the petitioner in a regional dispute must represent all or almost all of the production in the region.

Since all GATT member nations had to adopt the panel's recommendation for it to take effect, any single member could effectively block action. Concluding that the basis for the GATT panel's determination was contrary to U.S. law, the United States withheld its approval and the duties and findings imposed under U.S. trade law remained in effect.

Frustrated by the U.S. rejection of the GATT panel's decision, Cemex faced four immediate problems. First, the antidumping duty remained in effect on Cemex's remaining exports to the United States, and the U.S. producers were sure to argue at each annual administrative review that the bulk cement market in Mexico was fictitious and that bagged rather than bulk cement was the relevant like product. This posed the threat of an even higher duty. Second, Cemex had some stranded assets in terminal and distribution facilities in the United States. Third, the reduction in exports to the United States left Cemex with excess capacity in Mexico. Fortunately, domestic demand for cement had grown somewhat. Fourth, Cemex had to decide what to do about the U.S. market.

U.S. demand continued to exceed domestic capacity, creating a demand for imports. Cemex could import cement from Spain, but this left the risk of another antidumping petition. Cemex could also directly invest in the United States by building new plants. This would meet some of the shortfall in domestic supply but would reduce the need for imports, and Cemex continued to want to export to the United States. Cemex could also attempt to purchase existing capacity from a U.S. producer. This would be advantageous if Cemex were confident that it could operate the plants more efficiently than the seller. Purchasing capacity would not reduce the demand for imports, leaving export opportunities if the antidumping problem could somehow be resolved. ▪

Preparation Questions

1. Why might the price of cement be higher in Mexico than in the United States?
2. Is the dumping of cement likely to be harmful to the U.S. economy?
3. What was the motivation of the U.S. producers in filing the antidumping petition? Is this protectionism?
4. Evaluate Cemex's strategy for addressing the antidumping ruling. How well were its market and nonmarket components integrated?
5. After the United States withheld its approval of the GATT decision, what should Cemex do about the four problems?

Source: This case was written by Justin Adams under the supervision of Professor David P. Baron. It draws upon two previous case studies, "Cemex and Mexican Cement Imports," by Darryl E. Walsh, and "Cemex vs. U.S. Sunbelt Competitors," by Juan Prestarno, as well as "Gray Portland Cement and Cement Clinker from Mexico," Determination of the ITC in Investigation No. 731–TA–461 (Preliminary) and (Final). Copyright © 1998 by the Board of Trustees of the Leland Stanford Junior University. All rights reserved. Reprinted with permission.

Compulsory Licensing, Thailand, and Abbott Laboratories

TRIPS AND COMPULSORY LICENSING

The Trade Related Intellectual Property Rights (TRIPS) agreement negotiated in the Uruguay Round of multilateral trade negotiations was a major victory for the brand name pharmaceutical companies. Patent life was extended to 20 years in the United States, and countries participating in the World Trade Organization (WTO) agreed to bring their national patent law into conformity with the laws in the developed countries. This forced India, for example, to change its patent laws, preventing the Indian generic pharmaceutical companies from copying patented pharmaceuticals by using a different production process.

Article 31 of TRIPS, however, allowed for violation of a patent (compulsory licensing) without being specific about the reasons for the violation but also imposed certain requirements on governments. Under Article 31(f), entitled "Other Use Without Authorization of Right Holder," the country must first attempt to obtain a voluntary license under reasonable commercial terms. Pharmaceutical companies, however, typically do not license their patents, so Article 31 allowed countries to proceed in the cases of "national emergencies," "other circumstances of extreme urgency," or for "public noncommercial use" such as in research. If a compulsory license was issued, it normally was only for the domestic market, and a royalty (e.g., 5 percent) had to be paid to the patent holder.

Developing countries were unhappy with TRIPS, and when the Doha Round of WTO multilateral negotiations began, those countries insisted on more flexibility in interpreting Article 31. In 2001 the WTO ministers issued a Declaration on TRIPS and Public Health that supported actions by members to protect public health. In 2003 the General Council of the WTO allowed member countries to waive Article 31(f) under certain conditions to allow countries with no manufacturing capacity to import drugs made under a compulsory license. The Declaration stated that TRIPS should not prevent members from protecting public health and underscored "flexibilities" associated with compulsory licensing and parallel imports.[38] The General Council also extended to 2016 the deadline for least-developed countries to bring their laws regarding patent protection into compliance with TRIPS. Twenty-three developed countries pledged not to use the Declaration provisions, and 11 other countries said they would use the provisions only in the case of national emergencies or extremely urgent situations. Thailand was not one of those countries.

In 2005 the WTO added Article 31bis to TRIPS, which allows least developed countries to import a drug from another country for the treatment of HIV/AIDS, tuberculosis, and malaria epidemics. The article would go into effect if two-thirds of the WTO members ratified it. The European Union ratified the provision, bringing the number of members having approved it to 12. Rwanda was the first country to invoke the provision by arranging for the importation of an AIDS drug from Canada.

The pharmaceutical industry interpreted the language of Article 31 as applying to a health crisis such as virulent infectious flu or SARS. The industry knew, however, that the language was subject to interpretation. Compulsory licensing had been threatened but never invoked.

Brazil had threatened to invoke compulsory licensing in 2000 on three AIDS drugs, including one produced by Abbott Laboratories. The companies entered into negotiations with the Health Ministry, resulting in substantial price reductions, but compulsory licensing was not invoked. Brazil had a very successful national AIDS treatment program and had sought to reduce its cost by forcing down the prices of the drugs. The confrontation with the pharmaceutical companies was popular in Brazil, and its initiator, Health Minister Luiz Inacio Lula da Silva, subsequently was elected president of the country.

Pharmaceutical companies typically used a tiered-pricing system for their AIDS drugs. For developed countries prices were market based, whereas for the lowest income countries prices were at a major discount. Some companies priced at cost. Prices of AIDS drugs for the lowest-income countries had been reduced in response to pressure from governments and private politics initiated by activist organizations. For middle-income countries, such as Brazil, Mexico, and Thailand, the pharmaceutical companies priced at an intermediate level. Abbott Laboratories priced its AIDS drug Kaletra, a second-line AIDS drug used when first-line medications lost their effectiveness, at $7,000 a year in developed countries, $500 a year for the least developed countries, and $2,200 a year for low-income and low-middle income countries, which included Thailand. The World Bank categorized countries such as Thailand and Brazil as Upper Middle Income countries. The per capita gross national income of Thailand was $2,190 and Brazil was $2,760, whereas the per capita gross national income of the Least Developed Countries was $300 or less a year.[39]

THAILAND AND ABBOTT LABORATORIES

In 2004 Thailand introduced a national health care plan. In August 2006 a study funded by the World Bank and the health ministry estimated that compulsory licensing would save the government 100 billion baht through 2025.[40] In October 2006 a military coup in Thailand replaced the elected government. The military junta appointed Dr. Mongkol na Songkhla as Health Minister. He had been critical of pharmaceutical companies, and shortly after being appointed he launched a campaign to relieve the pharmaceutical burden on the national health care plan. On November 29, 2006 Dr. Mongkol sent a letter to Merck announcing that Thailand

---

[38]The WTO allowed parallel imports, which were imports from a third country of a drug manufactured by a patent holder. A country that was paying a high price for a patented drug thus could import that drug from another country where it was sold at a discount.

[39]Source: World Bank, http://www.finfacts.com/biz10/globalworldincomepercapita.htm (October 26, 2006).

[40]*Straits Times*, January 31, 2007.

had invoked Article 51 of its 1992 Patent Law that allowed the government to produce or import a generic version of Merck's patented AIDS drug Efavirenz, sold in Thailand under the name Stocrin. The government declared a public health emergency to justify importing the drug under TRIPS. Merck offered to reduce the price to avoid compulsory licensing, but Thailand went ahead and arranged for the supply of the drug from India.

In January 2007 Thailand notified Abbott and Sanofi-Aventis that compulsory licenses would be issued for Kaletra and Palvix, respectively. Thailand claimed that because of the price only about 40,000 of the 200,000 people who needed Plavix, a heart medicine, were receiving it. The government estimated that compulsory licensing would reduce the cost from $2 a pill to as low as 20 cents.[41]

In justifying its action, the Thai government issued a 96-page white paper in which Dr. Mongkol wrote, "The Thai ministry of public health views these decisions on the government use of patents as a form of social movement that aims at improving access to essential medicines and the health of the people. The public health interest is thus the main and final goal of this social movement …. We are convinced and committed to the view that Public Health interest and the life of the people must come before commercial interest."[42] Approximately 1 percent of the Thai population was estimated to have HIV/AIDS and less than 1 percent had chronic coronary disease.[43]

Dr. Mongkol also said, "We ask for the understanding of pharmaceutical companies. Much of our affected population cannot afford your drugs and we want people to have access to the medicines that they need. We are willing to negotiate with the companies if they are willing to give some discounts for the import of their originals."[44] "If they voluntarily reduce prices to let the poor people access to essential drugs, there is no need to do compulsory licensing. We are doing everything to help the poor people."[45] The decision by the Thai government was endorsed by the Clinton Foundation, 22 U.S. senators, the World Health Organization, and UNAIDS, the United Nations agency responsible for coordinating AIDS care and prevention.

Compulsory licensing allowed a country to manufacture a patented drug, authorize a domestic company to produce it, or ask a pharmaceutical company in another country to supply the drug. Thailand planned to import a version of Efavirenz from India and pay for it with funds from the Global Fund to Fight AIDS, Tuberculosis, and Malaria.[46] The Thai government decided to produce domestically its copy of Kaletra through its Government Procurement Organization (GPO), a state-owned company.

About 20 percent of the 500,000 people in Thailand living with HIV/AIDS were receiving treatment with a first-line antiretroviral drug produced by GPO, but an estimated 20,000 people had developed resistance to the drug. Those people would benefit from Kaletra. Another 60,000 patients could also benefit from Kaletra. Mongkol estimated that the cost of treating those patients could be reduced by two-thirds with compulsory licensing. The health ministry estimated that the country would save $24 million as a result of the three compulsory licenses.

ABBOTT'S DECISION

Abbott reacted angrily to Thailand's action. It publicly objected and announced that it was withdrawing all pending applications for marketing new drugs in Thailand. Abbott withdrew applications for seven drugs: Aluvia, a version of Kaletra that required no refrigeration; a painkiller, Brufen; Abbotic, an antibiotic; a blood-clotting drug, Clivarine; Humira, an arthritis drug; Tarka, a high-blood-pressure medication; and a kidney disease drug, Zemplar.[47] Aluvia was particularly important because unlike Kaletra it did not require refrigeration, which was often not available to patients. "Without Aluvia in the arsenal of drugs to fight HIV/AIDS, Thailand will now have to maintain expensive cold storage for the drug, and poorer infected populations, who often cannot afford refrigeration, will continue to go without access to any form of Kaletra," said Dr. Homayoon Khanlou, AIDS Healthcare Foundation's director of global advocacy.[48]

Dirk Van Eeden, public affairs director of Abbott International, said, "Thailand has revoked the patent on our medicine, ignoring the patent system. Under these circumstances, we have elected not to introduce new medicines there."[49] He added, "Actions that don't respect patents make it difficult to justify bringing forward new medicines in Thailand."[50] Melissa Brotz, an Abbott spokeswoman, explained, "The Thai government has chosen to limit access to medicines by breaking patents and discouraging companies like Abbott from bringing new medicines forward there. This matter is about intellectual property and the integrity of the patent system."[51]

Bayer of Germany expressed support for Abbott. Arthur Higgins, head of Bayer's healthcare unit, said, "I fully support Abbott and I fully support the very strong stance the industry is taking. This is not the way forward. I do not believe it is in the long-term interest of the Thai people because Abbott has already said they will not bring any new products to the Thai market. This is what will happen."[52]

The Pharmaceutical Research & Manufacturers Association of Thailand, composed of 38 pharmaceutical companies mostly from Europe and the United States, warned that the government's

[41]Thailand entered into discussions with India for the supply of a copy of Plavix. Thailand asked for bids and M-cure was the lowest of the four bidders. The price was 1.01 baht per pill compared to 70 baht for the French-made Plavix.

[42]Inter Press Service/Global Information Network, March 21, 2007.

[43]The HIV/AIDS rate for the United States and Brazil was approximately 0.3 percent.

[44]Associated Press Worldstream, January 29, 2007.

[45]Agence France Presse, March 18, 2007.

[46]The Global Fund was an independent organization formed as a result of an initiative by United Nations Secretary General Kofi Annan. The Global Fund was funded by developed nations.

[47]Associated Press Worldstream, March 21, 2007.

[48]PR Newswire US, March 14, 2007.

[49]Associated Press Financial Wire, March 14, 2007.

[50]*Financial Times*, March 14, 2007.

[51]Associated Press State and Local Wire, March 22, 2007.

[52]Reuters, March 15, 2007. Quoted in the *Nation* (Thailand), March 20, 2007.

move could discourage foreign investments. President Teera Chakajnarodom said, "Leading members of the association ... have confirmed to me that their plans for further investment in Thailand will be put on hold pending a review of the foreign investment climate. They are concerned about continuing to invest in a country where the government cannot provide a basic guarantee for the safety of their assets. We fully appreciate the health challenges and financial constraints that the Ministry of Public Health faces. However, the best response to this situation is to engage constructively with industry to find a mutually agreeable solution."[53] Teera added, "We realize the problem of budget constraints of the Ministry of Public Health and we appreciate their efforts to provide better healthcare to patients. But compulsory licensing won't solve the problem. The best way is to negotiate."[54] Teera also said, "We don't want to see compulsory licenses used as a bargaining chip."[55] The Association said that Thailand was considering similar actions on 11 more AIDS, heart, and cancer drugs.

The International Federation of Pharmaceutical Manufacturers Associations said countries should initiate "direct discussions with the companies that invest, develop and market medicines to directly address key health challenges." President Harvey Bale added, "Compulsory licensing can be a route to commercial abuse and can put patients at risk."[56] The American Chamber of Commerce in Thailand said that compulsory licensing sends "a negative signal to foreign investors in Thailand regarding the government's commitment to transparency and support for intellectual property rights."[57]

Peter Mandelson, the trade commissioner of the European Union, wrote to the Thai government to protest the compulsory licensing of the Sanofi-Aventis drug. The European Parliament, however, disagreed and supported making HIV/AIDS and malaria drugs available in poor countries through breaking patents. The EU, however, did not define "poor," although the Commission of the European Union stated that it did not consider Thailand to be poor.

REACTIONS

Paul Cawthorne, head of Doctors Without Borders in Thailand, reacted to Abbott's decision to withdraw its new drug application, "I'm actually lost for words, if they really are going to do this. For me, it's just evil. It's appalling. If they really are going to do this, it reflects so badly on the multinational companies."[58] Cawthorne added, "It was the first time I have seen such a reaction from a drug company. If they think Thailand has broken a law, they should have challenged it in court instead of acting like a spoiled child."[59]

In May the Clinton Foundation announced that it had negotiated a major price reduction for generic second-line

AIDS treatments. Making the announcement in Thailand accompanied by Dr. Mongkol, Bill Clinton commented, "Abbott has been almost alone in its hard-line position here over what I consider to be a life and death matter."[60]

Michael Weinstein, president of the AIDS Healthcare Foundation, the largest U.S. AIDS health care and education organization, said, "This is a new low, and I am horrified that Abbott would deprive poor people in need of lifesaving medications, particularly for those living with HIV/AIDS, in a country as hard-hit by the epidemic as Thailand .... Abbott has the hubris to blacklist a courageous country like Thailand simply trying to do the right thing for its people. Astounding."[61] "What they did is synonymous with holding our patients hostage," said Kriengsak Vacharanukulki-eti, head of the Rural Doctors' Society. "It's not just a threat to Thai patients, it's a threat to patients in poor countries everywhere."[62]

"Abbott's move goes to show that they take no social responsibility and only care about maximum profit, especially since Thailand has not broken any laws or trade agreements," said Kamol Upakaew, an AIDS activist and former president of the Thai Network of People living with AIDS/HIV.[63]

Abbott was criticized in the United States by Christian Brothers Investment Services and 13 other religious investors. "We believe the company is overlooking risks that have a serious effect on brand, its relationships with patients, and ultimately, shareholder value."[64] The Interfaith Center on Corporate Responsibility (ICCR), which advised institutional investors such as universities, issued a report "Benchmarking AIDS: Evaluating Pharmaceutical Company Responses to the Public Health Crisis in Emerging Markets" in which it wrote, "there is an urgent clinical need for a number of products Abbott could provide including pediatric drugs, fixed dose combinations and low-cost generic versions of Kaletra. ICCR called on Abbott to ensure that its new, heat-stable version of Kaletra be registered, available and affordable in adult and pediatric formulations. ICCR continues to urge Abbott to bring its policies in line with these recommendations."[65]

Kannikar Kitjiwatchakul of Médecins Sans Frontières (MSF) Bangkok called for a local boycott of Abbott. Saree Aongsomwang of the Foundation for Consumers called for a global boycott. She said, "Since Abbott has challenged Thailand and shown it doesn't care about Thai consumers, please stop using any of its products. This act by Abbott is totally unacceptable. Please don't ignore this pressure against the government over stopping what really benefits the consumer."[66]

At the Eighth International Conference on AIDS in Asia and the Pacific attended by representatives of 70 countries, Prasada Rao, director of the UNAIDS regional support team, said, "Thailand has made a strong statement by invoking a compulsory license for the production of second-line

---

[53]*Associated Press Worldstream*, January 25, 2007.
[54]*Christian Science Monitor*, January 31, 2007.
[55]*International Herald Tribune*, February 16, 2007.
[56]*Financial Times*, January 30, 2007.
[57]*Associated Press Worldstream*, January 31, 2007.
[58]*Wall Street Journal*, May 14, 2007.
[59]*Associated Press Worldstream*, March 21, 2007.

[60]*New York Times*, May 9, 2007.
[61]*Associated Press Financial Wire*, March 14, 2007.
[62]*Associated Press Worldstream*, March 21, 2007.
[63]*Associated Press Financial Wire*, March 14, 2007.
[64]*Associated Press State and Local Wire*, March 22, 2007.
[65]*PR Newswire US*, March 22, 2007.
[66]*Nation* (Thailand), March 20, 2007.

antiretroviral drugs. It's the right thing to do because we just can't provide those who need with only the first-line drugs because of the high cost. I urge countries in Asia and the Pacific region to use the WTO flexibilities to do more and show more commitment to AIDS responses."[67]

Relative to the importance of compulsory licensing, Thailand's savings of $24 million from compulsory licenses seemed small for a middle income country with 65 million people and a high growth rate of the economy. With no acute national health emergency the savings seemed a small reward for being the first country to invoke compulsory licensing of a pharmaceutical. Referring to Brazil's threat to use compulsory licensing, Tadataka Yamada, president of the Global Health Program of the Gates Foundation, observed, "Brazil is not Rwanda, which cannot afford to pay."[68] "Bruce Lehman, a lawyer who worked on the TRIPS accord in the Clinton administration, thinks it is cynical for middle-income countries 'to avoid paying their fair share of drug-discovery costs.' In doing so, he fears, they risk provoking a backlash from Americans who will, in effect, have to pay more as a result."[69] "Richard Epstein of the University of Chicago law school has observed that there is nothing to stop AIDS organizations or foreign governments from buying these products at a negotiated price and giving them away free. 'Charity can come from anywhere, not just drug companies,' he notes."[70]

A CHANGE OF STRATEGY

After discussions with the World Health Organization, Abbott agreed in April 2007 to reduce the price of Kaletra to $1,000 a year for several developing countries, including Thailand. The price in developed countries remained at $7,000.

The same month Abbott decided to change its strategy and negotiate with the Thai government. The company offered to resubmit its application for Aluvia and when approved sell it at $1,000 a year if Thailand would drop its plan to invoke compulsory licensing. Melissa Brotz of Abbott explained, "We are willing to have discussions to come to a solution, but we have not backed down on protecting intellectual property."[71] Abbott did not offer to reinstate the applications for the other six drugs. Miles D. White, Abbott CEO, explained the decision: "In this particular case, in the name of access for patients, we offered to resubmit Aluvia at our new price, which is lower than any generic, provided they wouldn't issue a compulsory license." He explained that the decision was the result of a "concern that compulsory licensing would be abused ever more widely, using HIV as an excuse."[72] The Thai government refused the offer, and Abbott did not resubmit the Aluvia application.[73] Yusuf Hamied, chairman of Cipla in India, which already produced a

copy of Kaletra and was working on a copy of Aluvia, stated, "Let the multinationals go. We will supply whatever drugs the Thai or other governments may want."[74]

Michael Weinstein of the AIDS Healthcare Foundation supported Thailand's rejection of Abbott's offer, stating "Abbott took a huge hit from AIDS activists and advocates the world over when it first announced its drug blacklist against the people of Thailand last month, and the company bowed to pressure from activists by quickly announcing price cuts on its AIDS drugs in Thailand and 40 other low and lower middle-income countries. We fully support Thailand's right to exercise flexibility in promoting public health by issuing these compulsory licenses. We ask Abbott to immediately back off the 'quid pro quo' offer which holds Thai people in need of this lifesaving AIDS medicine hostage. We also question Abbott's real commitment to 'turning science into caring'—Abbott's hollow corporate slogan—when the company continues its blacklist on six other drugs in Thailand."[75]

ABBOTT'S RESPONSE TO ACTIVISTS

The French AIDS activist group Act Up–Paris launched a cyber attack on Abbott's Web site which disrupted services, including its online sales. An Act Up–Paris member explained, "We use symbolic violence to call attention to real violence …," such as against AIDS victims. Act Up–Paris responded to a call from a Thai patient advocacy group by setting up a link on its Web site that between 500 and 1,000 activists in 12 countries used in an International Day of Action to overload Abbott's Web site during a 4-hour period. The attack was launched on the evening before Abbott's annual meeting. Abbott wrote to the advocacy group and then filed a lawsuit in a French criminal court alleging that the group had violated two articles of French criminal law prohibiting disruption of a Web site and providing the means for others to do so.

Abbott characterized its lawsuit as "a principled action." A spokesperson explained, "We respect the right to protest and, while our organizations can disagree on various matters, it is important to convey those disagreements in a respectful, appropriate and lawful manner."[76] Michael Harrington, executive director of the Treatment Action Group in New York said, "It's the latest in a long line of miserable actions by Abbott."[77] Michael Weinstein said, "I've spoken to pharmaceutical industry executives who think that Abbott's position is a PR disaster for the industry."[78] Jerome Martin of Act Up–Paris said that the group would use the media attention and the trial to criticize Abbott's policy. He said, "We're going to use the forum they're offering us to talk about Thailand again and the horrible consequences their decision has had there."[79]

[67]*BBC Worldwide Monitoring*, August 23, 2007.

[68]*Economist*, June 9, 2007.

[69]Ibid.

[70]Ibid.

[71]*Wall Street Journal*, April 24, 2007.

[72]*Wall Street Journal*, April 23, 2007.

[73]Sanofi-Aventis also offered a lower price for Plavix but also attached conditions. The Thai government rejected its offer.

[74]*Wall Street Journal*, April 24, 2007.

[75]*Biotech Business Week*, August 13, 2007.

[76]*Wall Street Journal*, June 18, 2007.

[77]Ibid.. Abbott had infuriated AIDS activist groups in 2003 by increasing the price of Norvir by 400 percent to get patients to switch to Kaletra. (Datamonitor, June 20, 2007.) Both a Bristol-Myers Squibb and a GlaxoSmithKline drug needed a Norvir boost to be effective.

[78]*Wall Street Journal*, June 18, 2007.

[79]Ibid.

In July Abbott dropped its lawsuit after a discussion with Act Up–Paris at a conference in Australia. An Abbott spokesperson said she did not anticipate any further attacks, but Martin stated, "If we have to organize another net strike we will, because access to treatment is more important than information they have on their Web site."[80]

BRAZIL

Brazil decided to use compulsory licensing as a bargaining tactic. Brazil had a highly successful and acclaimed AIDS program that had brought the adult infection rate to the level of that in the United States. The program emphasized prevention and provided free drugs for those infected, but the cost of providing the drugs had doubled in the past 4 years. In May President Lula da Silva authorized Health Minister José Temporão to invoke compulsory licensing for Merck's drug Efavirenz, after negotiations over a price reduction broke down.[81] Brazil then began importing a substitute drug from India. Brazil was also attempting to negotiate lower prices for a number of other drugs. One was Abbott's Kaletra. ■

Preparation Questions

1. Evaluate Abbott's strategy regarding Thailand's compulsory licensing. Will it be successful?
2. What should Abbott have done once Thailand rejected its offer?
3. What should Abbott do in Brazil?
4. What does Thailand's compulsory licensing do for pharmaceutical companies' opportunities in rapidly growing lower- and middle-income countries?
5. How should the pharmaceutical industry deal with compulsory licensing?

The Airbus and Boeing Trade Disputes

THE MARKET FOR LARGE CIVIL AIRCRAFT

The market for Large Civil Aircraft (LCA), aircraft that can carry more than 100 passengers and weigh over 30,000 pounds, is dominated by two producers: Boeing and Airbus. These include large wide-body aircraft with two passenger aisles: the Airbus A330, A340, A350 and A380; and the Boeing 747, 767, 777 and 787. Both companies also produce large narrow-body aircraft: the Airbus A318, A319, A320 and A321 (the A320 family); and the Boeing 737 and 757. These aircraft can typically carry no more than 200 passengers, and tend to have a maximum flight range of less than 4,000 miles, whereas large wide-body aircraft can usually carry more passengers and fly farther. The market for large narrow-body aircraft is more competitive than the market for large wide-body aircraft and is not be the main focus of the trade disputes.[82]

Over the years, competition between Airbus and Boeing has become more intense. For decades Boeing was the dominant firm in the LCA market. Airbus first equaled Boeing, as far as the numbers of orders are concerned, in 1994. Since 1999 their numbers have been similar. As far as aircraft deliveries are concerned, Airbus took the lead in 2003 and has retained it ever since.

Both companies have similar product offerings but have pursued somewhat different strategies in other respects. During the 1990s Boeing increasingly diversified into the defense, space and security markets. Today its commercial aircraft division accounts for little more than half of its revenues. Airbus, by contrast, remains focused on the production of LCA. The LCA market was projected to continue to grow rapidly.

The characteristics of the LCA market explain the emergence and persistence of the current duopoly. First, the *launch costs* of an aircraft program are very high, usually up to 50 percent of the total costs (Knorr et al., 2010). There are thus strong economies of scale. An aircraft program is the complete sequence of actions from the design to the last sale of a particular airplane model. Launch costs include the costs of development, construction and overhead related to the start-up of a new aircraft program. Launch costs may in some cases exceed the value of the company, as was the case for Boeing in the 1970s when it developed the 757 and 767. The uncertainty about the success of a new model makes the launch of an aircraft a risky business. The high-risk nature of the LCA industry is at the heart of the disputes between the European Union and the United States.

Second, the LCA market is characterized by a steep *learning curve* due to the technological complexity of the production processes (Pavcnik, 2002). Labor costs related to the production of an airplane decline by 30–40 percent as the accumulated output doubles (Benkard, 2000).

Third, there are important *economies of scope*. Research achievements and innovative technologies can be transferred easily from one model of aircraft to another (Heymann, 2007). To reap the benefits of the economies of scope, aircraft manufacturers often develop and produce variations of existing airplane models, and establish product families rather than design new models. Both Boeing, with its many variations of the Boeing 737, and Airbus, with the A320 family, have pursued this route. Moreover, airlines prefer to buy products from the same family, since doing so lowers their maintenance and training costs.

---

[80]*Wall Street Journal*, July 24, 2007.
[81]*Wall Street Journal*, July 5, 2007.
[82]The market for large narrow-body aircraft includes such other producers as Aviastar (manufacturers of the Tupolev aircraft), Bombardier and Embraer. The Chinese company Comac is scheduled to deliver its first large narrow-body aircraft in 2012.

Fourth, due to the launch costs, learning curve, and economies of scope, the LCA industry has enormous *barriers to entry*. Moreover, the huge development and production costs were largely sunk and thus constitute important barriers to exit.

THE 1992 BILATERAL AGREEMENT BETWEEN THE EU AND THE US

The rise of Airbus and the resulting duopoly led to tensions between the EU and the US. These were temporarily relieved with the conclusion of a Bilateral Agreement in 1992. The agreement did not seek to eliminate subsidies in the LCA industry, but instead allowed the EU and the US to continue to provide a limited level of support to their respective aircraft industries (Pritchard and MacPherson, 2004). The agreement was not concluded under the auspices of the World Trade Organization (WTO) and thus could not be the basis for a WTO dispute.

The Bilateral Agreement limited direct subsidies to 33 percent of total launch costs. Moreover the support had to be in the form of loans. The interest rate for these loans was not to be lower than the government's cost of borrowing, and the loans had to be repaid within 17 years. Furthermore, the Bilateral Agreement limited indirect government support to 3 percent of the country's LCA industry sales. Indirect support did not need to be repaid. The rules on direct support were mainly targeted at Airbus, which benefited from such support. The rules on indirect support, in turn, limited the US practice of providing support to Boeing through the National Aeronautics and Space Administration (NASA) and the Department of Defense (DOD).

In the 1990s the US was considered to benefit more from the agreement than the EU (Hayward, 2005). Whereas the EU had to abandon production subsidies and became severely limited in the launch support it could grant, the US only had to accept limits on indirect subsidies, which were difficult to verify.

THE DISPUTES

On October 6, 2004, a few weeks after Airbus announced the launch of its A350 program and a month before the US presidential elections, the US withdrew from the Bilateral Agreement. In conjunction with the withdrawal the US filed a complaint against the EU and four of its member states (Germany, France, the United Kingdom and Spain) under the WTO's dispute settlement system.[83] At the time Harry Stonecipher, President and CEO of Boeing, declared: "It is clear that the 1992 agreement does not reflect current market realities and has outlived its usefulness." US Trade Representative Robert Zoellick justified the US move as follows, "Since its creation 35 years ago, some have justified subsidies to Airbus as necessary to support an 'infant' industry. If that rationalization were ever valid, its time has long passed. Airbus now sells more LCA than Boeing …. Terminating this agreement reinforces our belief that now is the time to end subsidies, ideally through a new agreement." EU Commissioner for External Trade Pascal Lamy responded, "If this is the path

the US has chosen, we accept the challenge, not least because it is high time to put an end to massive illegal US subsidies to Boeing which damage Airbus, particularly those for Boeing's new 7E7."

The US claimed that Airbus had received subsidies inconsistent with the 1947 General Agreement on Tariffs and Trade (GATT) and the 1995 WTO Agreement on Subsidies and Countervailing Measures (SCM). The EU responded by filing a counterclaim (DS317 United States–Measures Affecting Trade in Large Civil Aircraft) on the same day, alleging that Boeing had received illegal indirect subsidies. It filed an updated complaint in June 2005 (DS353 United States–Measures Affecting Trade in Large Civil Aircraft—Second Complaint).

THE US COMPLAINT

The US complained about several forms of aid allegedly granted by the EU and its member states for a total of more than $100 billion, including: (1) launch aid; (2) research funding; (3) infrastructure-related grants; (4) corporate restructuring aid; and (5) equity infusions and European Investment Bank (EIB) and other loans. The US argued that these measures constituted specific subsidies under Articles 1 and 2 of the SCM Agreement and that it suffered adverse effects from the subsidies, in violation of Articles 5 and 6 of the SCM Agreement. The US further claimed that certain launch aid provided for the A340 and A380 constituted illegal export subsidies, in breach of Article 3 of the SCM Agreement.

Specifically, the US argued that Airbus had benefited from generous government support since its founding in 1970. The main focus of the US complaint was the launch aid for the A380 and A350. Another major channel of support was the EU's series of framework programs for research. In addition national, regional and local authorities in France, Germany, Spain and the United Kingdom allegedly granted support to Airbus. The EIB provided additional support. It partially funded airlines' investment projects, thus accelerating the renewal of passenger fleets and spurring aircraft demand.

The WTO panel issued a ruling on the US complaint in June 2010. It found that Airbus received subsidies of $18 billion, according to Boeing's calculations. Specifically, it ruled that all launch aid given constituted specific subsidies, but that the US had failed to show that the planned launch aid for the A350 was a specific subsidy. It further found that some of the aid constituted prohibited export subsidies. Only some of the research funding, infrastructure-related grants, restructuring aid, loans, and equity infusions, however, were found to constitute specific subsidies. The panel further concluded that the specific subsidies had displaced imports and exports, but it did not find evidence that they depressed prices. The EU and its member states were ordered to withdraw the subsidies or remove the adverse effects on the US. WTO rulings are concerned with future actions and are thus not retroactive.

The US and the EU both appealed the ruling in August 2010. In May 2011 the WTO's Appellate Body issued its ruling, which was somewhat more favorable to the EU, reversing the earlier ruling on close to $4 billion. The EU agreed to implement the ruling.

---

[83]This case is known as: Dispute Settlement (DS) 316 European Communities - Measures Affecting Trade in Large Civil Aircraft.

THE EU COMPLAINT

The EU and its member states filed a counterclaim accusing the US of providing subsidies to Boeing that were inconsistent with the SCM Agreement and the GATT. In particular it claimed that the following measures constituted subsidies inconsistent with the SCM Agreement: various tax and non-tax incentives provided by the state governments of Kansas, Illinois and Washington, and local authorities in these states; financial and other support provided by NASA, the DOD, and the Departments of Commerce and Labor; and tax exemptions under legislation on Foreign Sales Corporations (FSC) and the Extra-Territorial Income (ETI) Exclusion Act and its successor acts. The EU put the total amount of the alleged subsidies at $19.1 billion between 1989 and 2006. More than half, $10.4 billion, was in the form of NASA research subsidies. The DOD was alleged to have provided dual use technology worth more than $2.4 billion to Boeing at no cost. Furthermore, NASA and the DOD allegedly waived intellectual property rights worth more than $700 million and granted more than $3 billion in technology subsidies.

The WTO panel issued a ruling on the EU complaint in March 2011. It found some of the US support for Boeing to be specific subsidies, in the amount of $5.3 billion for the 1989–2006 period. The panel also found that the FSC and ETI benefits constituted prohibited export subsidies. Some of the subsidies were ruled to have had adverse effects on EU interests, such as trade displacement, price suppression and lost sales. The US was ordered to remove the adverse effects or withdraw the subsidies.

The EU and the US both appealed the ruling in April 2011. ■

Preparation Questions

1. What is the nature of nonmarket relationships between Boeing and Airbus and their home nations?
2. Why did the United States withdraw from the Bilateral Agreement?
3. What is likely to happen after the Appellate Body ruling on the EU complaint is made? Are the United States and EU likely to stop supporting Boeing and Airbus, respectively?

PART IV

Toys 'Я' Us and Globalization

Charles Lazarus began his career working in his father's used bicycle shop. He subsequently started selling children's furniture out of the shop, and when customers kept asking if he carried toys, he added some toys in addition to the children's furniture. He soon recognized, however, that he was not getting any repeat business. "Furniture lasts forever," Lazarus pointed out. "But toys," he continued with a laugh, "toys are great because they have built-in obsolescence. Kids break them."[84]

Lazarus was intrigued by the success of self-service supermarkets and conceived the idea of selling toys in a similar manner. He opened his first Toys 'Я' Us store in 1957 using shopping carts, a large selection, and low prices. Because toy sales were highly seasonal, he advertised to build a year-round demand. To raise funds for expansion, in 1966 he sold the company to Interstate Stores, a retailing conglomerate, for $7.5 million. Lazarus retained operating control, and when Interstate went bankrupt, the court made him president. After selling off the Interstate assets, in 1978 he renamed the company Toys 'Я' Us and launched a rapid expansion program. Toy industry analysts had estimated that over the next 10 years industry-wide sales of toys by specialty retailers would increase to $2.4 billion. Over that period, the sales of Toys 'Я' Us alone increased by over tenfold, reaching $4 billion in 1989, including clothing sales at Kids 'Я' Us stores. Profits were $268 million. Because of his vision and the company's tremendous success, Lazarus was widely viewed as a retailing genius.

The Toys 'Я' Us market strategy was built on three principles: price, selection, and stock. The original idea was to sell at discount prices in stores with supermarket-style service and limited sales staff. It soon became clear that consumers wanted one-stop shopping, leading to larger stores, more varieties of items, and a broad range of goods including items such as disposable diapers. Toys 'Я' Us then began to stock an average of 18,000 items in its stores. The key, of course, as Lazarus explained, was "to pick the right toy at the right time—the toys that sell. We're very much like the fashion industry. Customer tastes are very fickle, and you have to move quickly when they change. Otherwise, you'll be out of business. It's that simple."[85] The third principle was to have the goods on hand, so Toys 'Я' Us operated a sophisticated inventory tracking and supply system designed to avoid stock-outs. The company used electronic point-of-purchase sales terminals in each store, which were linked to its central computers in its headquarters.

To supplement these principles, Toys 'Я' Us relied on advertising to get consumers to purchase toys year round, which both increased demand and reduced seasonality. It also provided a money-back guarantee policy under which a customer could return any item for any reason. In the United States, the location of stores was crucial. Toys 'Я' Us preferred locations with ample and adjacent parking so that customers could go out the door of the store and directly to their cars. Toys 'Я' Us also sought to keep its stores open 7 days a week, 365 days a year, where local ordinances permitted it. Toys 'Я' Us owned all its stores so as to maintain standardization and control.

GLOBALIZATION

By 1984 Toys 'Я' Us operated 169 stores in over 40 states and had revenue of $1.3 billion and profits of $92 million. Although it operated only within the United States, it had developed a worldwide supply system, purchasing toys from around the world. East Asia represented the largest source of supply.

The company's initial international steps were cautious. It opened its first store outside the United States in Canada and then opened a store in England. Lazarus explained that "the Canadians seemed to be much like ourselves, and [our approach] seemed to work pretty well. And we went to England." Toys 'Я' Us continued to expand in Canada and the United Kingdom. Its other early international steps were serendipitous. Toys 'Я' Us had been approached by Jopie Ong, director of Singapore's Metro retail group, which wanted a franchise to open a store in Singapore. The Toys 'Я' Us policy was not to use franchisees, and hence it rejected the request. Ong persisted, however, and was eventually able to persuade the company to form a joint venture. Toys 'Я' Us–Metro opened its first Singapore store in 1984.

Its entry into Hong Kong was also serendipitous. Joseph Baczko, president of the Toys "Я" Us international division, had met Victor Fung when they were both at Harvard. When Fung became chairman of Li & Fung Ltd., a Hong Kong trading company, the two companies were natural partners. The Toys 'Я' Us–Li & Fung joint venture was formed and opened a store in Hong Kong in 1985. The success of its stores in Singapore and Hong Kong led Toys 'Я' Us to develop a globalization strategy. Lazarus explained that the company was "interglobal." "Our registers in Hong Kong take eight currencies. They just punch in what kind of currency you're giving them. It's a really international kind of thing. You have to see it to believe it." The company also preferred to hire locals as store and country managers.

Toys 'Я' Us viewed opportunity in a country as stemming from a large population and high income. Those factors "combined with the lack of any dominant toy retail competition in Europe and Asia, afford Toys 'Я' Us with an ideal climate for aggressive international expansion."[86] As Lazarus put it, "We can go anywhere there are supermarkets and kids because we are, after all, a supermarket for kids."[87]

---

[84]*Solutions*, March/April, 1988.
[85]*Solutions*, March/April, 1988.

[86]Toys 'Я' Us, Annual Report, 1991, p. 7.
[87]*Solutions*, March/April, 1988.

Each country posed different hurdles, however. Some were market based and others were nonmarket. Germany, Japan, and Sweden posed particular challenges.

GERMANY[88]

With one of the highest standards of living in the world, Germany offered considerable potential. Although Germany had a relatively open economy, a number of rules, regulations, and traditional relationships presented difficulties for foreign entrants. Entry into retailing, in particular, was more difficult than might have been expected.

Toys '月' Us G.m.b.H. was formed in 1986, but as it attempted to enter the German market it encountered several hurdles. In contrast to the United States, a number of European countries had laws favoring employees over consumers. Germany protected employees in the retail trade by imposing strict rules on store-opening hours, except for gasoline stations and stores in railroad stations and airports. A federal law enacted in 1956 was intended to protect employees from having to work long hours, and it had continuing strong support from the 500,000-member union representing retail, banking, and insurance workers. Union members worked a 37.5-hour week. Many small retailers also supported the law, believing that extended hours would not increase sales enough to warrant the additional cost. Stores were required to close by 6:30 P.M. except on Thursday when they could remain open until 8:30 P.M. The 6:30 P.M. closing time gave employees little time to shop after work. Moreover, stores had to close by 2 P.M. on Saturday and were not allowed to open on Sunday.[89] In addition, in smaller towns many retailers closed at lunchtime.

Other federal laws also imposed hurdles. Not only were profits taxes the highest in Europe at 50 percent, but Germany also had regulations that were as strict as any in Europe, particularly in the retail sector. For example, German law prohibited discounts of more than 3 percent from previous prices except during certain restricted periods. German antitrust law also restricted the use of loss leader pricing, and the Cartel Office could order price increases. German law also prohibited lifetime guarantees.

German labor laws made it difficult to dismiss an employee and gave rights to employees on some policy issues. For example, employees had a say in any legislative effort to revise the store opening laws. In addition, the worker participation requirements in Germany were foreign to an American company and reduced a company's flexibility. Wages and benefits were very high—German workers typically had 6 weeks of vacation a year and received a thirteenth month of salary as a bonus. German employees were well educated and highly productive, however.

Most German toy retail stores were small, family-owned shops, and many were located in city centers. These retailers were often active members of local organizations. As managing director Arnt Klöser of Toys '月' Us G.m.b.H., who had been hired from a leading German department store chain, said, "When you ask a city for a construction permit, the first thing they do is ask the local chamber of commerce and retailers' association what they think of your idea. They always say the same thing: A toy store belongs in the city center, not the meadow on the edge of town."[90] To obtain store approval, Klöser's strategy was to try to convince the local toy retailers that the entry of Toys '月' Us would actually benefit them by expanding the market.

German toy manufacturers opposed the entry of Toys '月' Us because of concerns about the consequences for their current retail customers. To support local retailers, some manufacturers argued that a self-service retailer such as Toys '月' Us could place children in danger. They said that customers needed the assistance of a Fachmann to provide expert advice. The German Toy Manufacturers Association complained about the Toys '月' Us practice of selling such items as diapers, baby food, clothes, and sporting goods in addition to toys. Some manufacturers went further. The leading manufacturer of model trains, Gebruder Märklin, announced that it would not sell to Toys '月' Us because doing so would damage its image.

Toys '月' Us was willing to commit whatever resources were necessary to enter the German market, but it needed a strategy for dealing with the hurdles it faced.

JAPAN

By 1989 Toys '月' Us's sales had reached $4 billion and net income was $238 million. The company operated nearly 500 Toys '月' Us and over 100 Kids '月' Us stores. Toys '月' Us operated over 70 stores in countries other than the United States. However, the company had not yet entered the Japanese market.

The opportunities in Japan were substantial. The Japanese toy market was over $5.5 billion, and personal income was growing rapidly. Less than 5 percent of the $5 billion toy market was accounted for by imported toys, however. Domestic toy manufacturers had a lock on the distribution system that supplied the thousands of small toy stores that accounted for virtually all the toy sales in the country.

One estimate was that over 50 percent of all retail sales in Japan was accounted for by shops with one or two employees. Many of these "mom and pop" shops were owned by retirees. The aging of shop owners and their children's reluctance to take over the businesses resulted in a decline of 9.3 percent in the number of shops from 1982 to 1985 and a 7 percent decline from 1985 to 1988. In spite of the decline, over 1.4 million small shops remained in Japan. These shops represented an important component of the clientistic and reciprocal exchange relationships with the Liberal Democratic Party (LDP) and the bureaucracy. Local merchants also often played an important role in the *koenkai*, a local support group, of many Diet members.

These small shops were an important part of the fabric of Japanese society, but they were also the cap of a very inefficient distribution system. Japan had several more layers

---

[88]This section is based in part on an article in the *New York Times*, August 18, 1991, and on additional public sources.

[89]Stores could remain open until 4 P.M. on the first Saturday of every month and the four Saturdays before Christmas.

[90]*New York Times*, August 18, 1991.

to its distribution system than most other countries and two to three times the number of small shops per capita. This increased costs and prices. The high prices provided an important profit opportunity for an efficient, large-scale retailer such as Toys 'Я' Us.

Charles Lazarus saw a potential for 100 stores in Japan and hoped to open the first Toys 'Я' Us store in Niigata, 160 miles north of Tokyo. Toys 'Я' Us planned to supply the stores directly, bypassing the Japanese distribution system. Approximately 80 percent of the merchandise sold in its Japanese stores would be the same as that sold in the other Toys 'Я' Us stores.

Toys 'Я' Us' market opportunities were controlled by government regulations. As Vice President Michael Goldstein explained, "A lot will depend on whether the Japanese government will relax [its] rules. We think we're going to expand the market there for toys. It'll be good for us, good for our suppliers and will be good for Japan in that we're going to bring a diversity of consumer products for Japanese children."

Entry into the Japanese market was complicated by a variety of factors. The structure of Japanese retailing persisted in part because of the Large-Scale Retail Store Law (LSRSL), which made it difficult to open a large store. Notice had to be given to the Small and Medium-Size Enterprises Agency (SMEA) of MITI to open a store larger than 1,500 square meters.[91] SMEA typically recommended postponing the opening as it sought the advice of a local large-scale retail council. Notice of any store larger than 500 square meters also had to be given to the governor of the prefecture, which had authority similar to MITI's. Two laws enacted in 1977, the Coordinating Sphere of Activities Law and the Small and Medium-Size Business and Cooperative Law, strengthened the position of small enterprises by giving them a stronger voice in the local large-scale retail councils. Those councils sought the advice of the "commercial business arrangement committee," established by the local chamber of commerce. The committee's advice was often reflected in the decision of the governor or minister. Local councils played a role in setting not only store size but also store hours.[92] These laws and the local consultation process provided an opportunity for local merchants to oppose entry. As Tatsuki Kubo of McDonald's (Japan) explained, "It's a Japanese custom. If a big company wants to move into a local area, the people oppose it."[93]

These laws and the complex approval process did not preclude the opening of large stores, but they could result in long and often prohibitive delays. The laws placed no limit on the length of the consultation period, and there had been delays as long as 10 years. When faced with strong opposition some large-scale retailers had given up, whereas others had chosen to "negotiate" with the local store owners to overcome their opposition.

In spite of these restrictions, some supermarket and department store chains had expanded in Japan. Isao Nakauchi founded the Daiei chain in 1957; by 1988 Daiei had 181 outlets that sold clothing and other merchandise as well as groceries. Nakauchi complained that opening a new store took from 5 to 7 years and that 73 applications had to be filed for 26 permits under 12 laws.

Because of the size of their outlets, companies such as McDonald's and 7-Eleven were often unaffected by the LSRSL.[94] Indeed, McDonald's, led by President Den Fujita, had expanded rapidly and by 1989 had 675 restaurants in Japan. McDonald's Japan was skilled at dealing with the relevant bureaucracy and the local government units whose approval was needed to open a restaurant. McDonald's (Japan) also employed *amakudari* bureaucrats for their relationships with and knowledge of the ministries from which they had descended.[95]

In recent years, the approval process had been somewhat streamlined, and in some cases the delays had been reduced to as little as 2 years. Restrictions on store hours and expansion had also been eased. Rumors of the possible entry of Toys 'Я' Us, however, stirred concern in the retail industry. A toy wholesaler in Niigata commented, "This is not just a local problem; Toys 'Я' Us will have a big impact on the entire toy industry. We are opposed to their plan."[96] He said he would be meeting with other members of the industry to formulate a strategy against Toys 'Я' Us. Masao Sakurai, a toy retailer with eight shops in Niigata, predicted, "If Toys 'Я' Us comes in, Japanese shops will be wiped out."[97]

In 1989 MITI issued a report, "Vision of the Japanese Distribution Industry in the 1990s," which criticized the inefficiency in the distribution system and explored possible improvements. One possibility would be to limit the ability of local governments to impose restrictions that favored local retailers. As was frequently the case in Japan, MITI could make some changes through "administrative guidance," although it would have to obtain the consent of the Ministry of Local Autonomy.

The Toys 'Я' Us market strategy was to attempt to bypass the Japanese distribution system by opening large stores and supplying them directly. To implement this strategy, the company faced not only the problem of the LSRSL but also a host of local regulations on retailing. One strategy Toys 'Я' Us could adopt was to attempt to place the issue of retailing restrictions on the agenda of the ongoing U.S.–Japan trade negotiations. U.S. Trade Representative Carla Hills was believed to be sympathetic to this issue and might make Toys 'Я' Us a cause célèbre. Toys 'Я' Us also faced the difficult problem of finding store locations because the price of land in Japan had reached astronomical levels.

SWEDEN

Operating from its base in the United Kingdom, Toys 'Я' Us entered Sweden in September 1994, opening stores in Gothenberg, Malmo, and Skarholmen, a suburb of Stockholm.[98]

---

[91]Toys 'я' Us stores were up to four times this size.

[92]Store hours and the number of employees permitted were regulated in the same manner.

[93]*Wall Street Journal*, February 7, 1990.

[94]McDonald's Company (Japan) Ltd. was a 50–50 joint venture of the U.S. McDonald's Corporation and Fujita & Company. 7-Eleven stores were owned by Ito Yokuda, a supermarket and department store chain, which licensed the 7-Eleven name.

[95]*Japan Economic Journal*, May 26, 1990.

[96]*Wall Street Journal*, February 7, 1990.

[97]Ibid.

[98]Toys 'я' Us became one of the few foreign retail chains operating in Sweden.

In accord with its policies in other countries, the company required its 110 employees to sign the company handbook, which specified the work rules under which the company operated.

Unions were particularly strong in Sweden with over 90 percent of Swedish employees represented by a union. The Swedish model of labor relations had been an important factor in the country's long record of industrial peace. The Handelsanstalldas Forbund, the Retail Workers Union, had signed up a number of workers in Toys '*Я*' Us stores and demanded that the company sign the standard nationwide collective labor agreement. The objective of the collective agreement was to allow organized labor to bring broad pressure on employers as a means of balancing corporate power. "'In all shops where we have members we want a collective agreement,' said Mr. Bjorn Sjoblom of Handelsanstalldas Forbund. 'This is quite normal in Sweden. We have not had any problems before with other companies.'"[99]

Toys '*Я*' Us refused to accept the collective agreement but remained willing to negotiate an agreement with the union. "'Toys '*Я*' Us does not have any difficulty in accepting an agreement with the union, but considers itself to have the right to participate in negotiations to formulate a firm-adapted agreement,' Sten Yetraeus, attorney with the business law firm Lagerlof & Leman, explained. '[Accepting the collective agreement] would mean that we would be bound to a detailed book of regulations that is the product of many years of negotiations between the Retail Workers and the Retail Employers without us,'" Yetraeus added.[100] Frank Heskjer, the company's head for Scandinavia, said, "We get by without such agreements in other countries and we'll do the same in Sweden." Retail Workers Union chairman Kenth Pettersson said, "We haven't had a conflict like this for years. Signing collective agreements is a virtual formality these days."[101] The Retail Workers Union and its chairman were at the more militant end of the labor spectrum in Sweden.

A government commission failed in its efforts to mediate a settlement, and the first strike by the union in 20 years began. Toys '*Я*' Us stated, "[Unions] have forced our employees to strike solely because we will not unconditionally sign a collective agreement." David Rurka, managing director of the company for the United Kingdom and Scandinavia, said, "The problem is the culture here. Many of our people don't want to strike. But they say they have fathers or other family members in unions who say they must support the union. The union has motivated the staff with fear and fear alone."[102]

The union provided the strikers with 100 percent pay and took out national advertisements asking the public to support the strike and boycott Toys '*Я*' Us stores. The union not only picketed each of the stores but attempted to blockade the stores from supplies. It enlisted the aid of the Transport Workers, and truckers refused to cross the picket lines. The Seamen's Union forced the Swedish flagged carrier Tor Lines to refuse to carry goods from the distribution facility in the United Kingdom to Sweden. The Seamen's Union also announced that it would take actions against Stena Line, Lion Ferry, and SweFerry AB. A Seamen's Union spokesperson said, "A struggle like this is well known within our own union." The expanded actions by the union were in part the result of shoppers who crossed the picket lines to buy low-priced diapers that the union learned were being imported from Denmark. Other unions also announced sympathy measures of support for the Retail Workers Union. For example, the financial sector union refused to handle the Toys '*Я*' Us daily receipts.

Toys '*Я*' Us paid a wage slightly higher than union members earned elsewhere and provided the same insurance. The principal concern, however, was job security. The employee handbook specified performance conditions that could lead to a firing, and one of the strikers explained, "You never felt really secure there, that you can stay." Therese Karlsson, who was let go by the company in Skarholmen during the provisional period, said, "Just prior to [being fired], management said that they were finished making cutbacks in personnel. Those of us who remained could feel secure, and a few were even promised permanent employment. Then they called me at home on a Saturday evening and told me 'you may leave.'"[103] Therese was one of the strikers on the picket line.

The conflict between Toys '*Я*' Us and the union also involved other work rule issues. For example, the company handbook stated that employees were forbidden to "speak to or be interviewed by the mass media without special permission in advance from the managing director."[104] Gunnar Jonsson, manager of the Gothenberg store, explained, "Our rules about uniforms, searches at the end of the shift, about not talking to the media and so on do look hard on paper. But all stores demand a neat appearance from their staff, check purses and bags, and so on. Of course our employees may speak with the media—except when it has to do with the internal affairs of the company"[105] Fredrik Larsson, an employee since the store opened, commented, "In my personal opinion, the company's rules don't bother me. I don't see anything against a uniform, and the check that I have to undergo is not insulting, as I see it. After all, it's my own boss who does it. We know each other, and they do it mostly because they have to report to their manager that they have done it."[106]

In response to the strike Toys '*Я*' Us halted its planned expansion in Sweden and speculated to the media that it might close its stores and leave the country. The company had planned 15 stores in Sweden employing 500 permanent and 1,000 seasonal workers.

As the strike continued, commentators viewed the conflict between Toys '*Я*' Us and the union as a test for the Swedish model of collective bargaining in its new role as a member of the European Union. Peter Skogh, who managed the store in Malmo, said, "We are an international company coming into a new market. Of course we are trying to adapt to the conditions here. But Sweden, in order to survive, must also

[99]*Financial Times*, May 11, 1995.
[100]*Dagens Nyheter*, May 10, 1995.
[101]*Reuter Business Report*, May 8, 1995.
[102]*Financial Times*, May 11, 1995.

[103]*Dagens Nyheter*, May 24, 1995.
[104]*Dagens Industri*, May 10, 1995.
[105]Ibid.
[106]Ibid.

adapt to the European and international business climate."[107] "One self-employed mother who drove her four children past the pickets said, 'Swedish trade unions are inflexible and only interested in sticking to old principles. Sweden is sick to the back teeth of them.'"[108] Toys 'Я' Us began to receive expressions of support from other companies. ■

Preparation Questions

1. What is the Toys 'Я' Us market strategy?
2. In what kinds of national markets are its opportunities the most attractive? Which companies are its natural competitors? Are any of them global?
3. What nonmarket forces potentially impede the success of its market strategy?
4. What overall market and nonmarket strategies should Toys 'Я' Us develop, and how should those components be integrated?
5. What specific strategy should it adopt to gain entry to the Japanese market?
6. What specific strategy should it adopt to enter the German market successfully?
7. What should it do about the situation in Sweden?

---

[107]*Guardian*, May 13, 1995.
[108]Ibid.

20

CORPORATE SOCIAL RESPONSIBILITY

INTRODUCTION

Corporate social responsibility has received increased attention from business, the public, and researchers. A survey by the Economist Intelligence Unit found that 47 percent of the firms responding agreed that corporate social responsibility (CSR) "is a necessary cost of doing business" and 47 percent agreed that it "gives us a distinctive position in the market." Only 4 percent of the respondents believed that corporate social responsibility was a "waste of time and money." The *Economist* observed, "It is almost unthinkable today for a big global corporation to be without [a CSR policy]."[1]

Many firms go beyond what is required by their market and nonmarket environments, and some explicitly attempt to serve directly the needs of their stakeholders or, more broadly, of society. For these firms, successful performance not only requires compliance with laws and regulations but also requires fulfilling broader responsibilities. Firms make charitable contributions, provide pharmaceuticals to those in need, respect and support human rights, exercise self-regulation, and take measures beyond those required by law to protect the environment and the safety of employees and customers. Firms vary considerably in the extent of these activities, however. The extent depends on their conceptions of corporate social responsibility and the role of business in society.

The previous chapters provide a basis for addressing issues in the market and nonmarket environments of business under the objective of maximizing shareholder value. The focus in those chapters was primarily on the nonmarket challenges directed at firms. In contrast, social responsibility focuses less on pressures and more on normative principles that identify duties based on conceptions of well-being, rights, and justice. These principles can require an objective broader than shareholder value maximization.

This part of the book thus adds another consideration—moral concepts—for management in the environment of business. As illustrated in Figure 20-1, formulating integrated strategies requires consideration of the market and nonmarket environments as well as attention to moral concerns and social responsibilities. This does not mean that the objective of shareholder value maximization is inappropriate; instead, it means that strategies and actions should be evaluated in terms of moral principles in addition to their effects on shareholder value.

This chapter examines the social responsibilities of business and provides a framework for reasoning about corporate social performance. The normative content of social responsibility is developed in the following chapters in terms of ethics systems and their application in management. Chapters 23 and 24 address the implementation of ethics systems and conceptions of corporate social responsibility.

THE TRUST GAP

In interacting with the public or with stakeholders, it is useful to begin with caution. The public trust in large firms is low, and criticisms of business are often viewed with a degree of credibility that is not accorded to the communication by firms. This may be due to the self-interested objectives of firms and a lack of confidence that competition in markets will serve society's interests. It may also be due to greater trust among parts of the public in the critics of firms, such as social activist organizations and NGOs. Their objectives are frequently viewed as better aligned with society's interests than are the objectives of firms.

In 2005 GlobeScan Inc. organized interviews with over 20,000 people in 20 countries to assess their degree of trust in society's institutions.[2] The question asked respondents was how much trust they had in the

---

[1]*Economist*, January 17, 2008.
[2]www.globescan.com/news_archives/WEF_trust2005.html. The survey was conducted for the World Economic Forum.

FIGURE 20-1   Integrated Strategy Framework

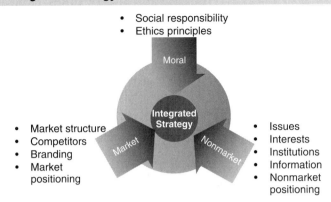

- Social responsibility
- Ethics principles

Moral

Integrated Strategy

Market

Nonmarket

- Market structure
- Competitors
- Branding
- Market positioning

- Issues
- Interests
- Institutions
- Information
- Nonmarket positioning

institutions to "operate in the best interests of our society." For 14 countries also surveyed in previous years, the surveys indicated an overall decrease in trust in all institutions.[3] More interesting is the ranking and ordinal scores (the percent responding "Trust" minus the percent responding "Don't Trust") of the five institutions covered:[4]

Institution	Scores
• NGOs	29
• United Nations	13
• Large local companies	2
• National governments	−9
• Global companies	−15

The apparent lack of trust in global companies stands in stark contrast to the trust in NGOs. To the extent that NGOs are critical of the conduct of business, as many are, firms are at a considerable disadvantage in communicating with the public. That is, the trust gap between NGOs and global firms gives the advantage to NGOs in most contexts involving communication with the public. Closing this trust gap through corporate social responsibility is a considerable challenge.

An individual firm may have earned a reputation for operating in a manner consistent with society's interests, but reputations can be fragile. Most of the public knows little about the conduct of the firm, and a reputation can be tarnished and trust dissipated by the conduct of not only the firm itself but also other firms, particularly those in the same industry. Moreover, because of the trust gap, criticism by an NGO or a media story about high executive compensation or an environmental accident can negate several positive accomplishments by a firm. This means that management should have realistic and perhaps modest expectations about building and sustaining a reputation and public trust.

WHAT IS CORPORATE SOCIAL RESPONSIBILITY?

Many conceptions of corporate social responsibility have been offered. This section considers one provided by Milton Friedman and another by the Business Roundtable. Friedman argues, based on economic theory and a conception of morality based on liberty, that the social responsibility of business is to maximize profits. The Business Roundtable, based on a conception of

---

[3]The countries were Argentina, Brazil, Canada, China, Germany, Great Britain, India, Indonesia, Italy, Nigeria, Russia, Spain, Turkey, and the USA. The only country with an increase in trust in institutions was Russia. The only countries with a positive trust in global companies were China, Indonesia, and India, whereas the only countries with a trust in government were Indonesia, Turkey, India, the United States, and Argentina.

[4]These surveys have been continued as the Edelman Trust Barometer, although the institutions are now NGOs, businesses, government, and media. NGOs continue to have the highest levels of trust with business next followed by government. Trust in business in 2011 was highest in Brazil and India and fell sharply among U.S. respondents from 2010 levels. Trust in government was highest in Brazil and China, and trust in NGOs was highest in Brazil.

obligation to stakeholders, provides a broader conception of the responsibilities of a firm, while leaving the specifics to management.

Milton Friedman's Profit Maximization

MARKETS AND RESOURCE ALLOCATION   Adam Smith (1776) wrote that the surest way to achieve societal well-being was to place resources in the hands of individuals and allow them to transact in markets. Not only are markets the best means of allocating scarce resources to society's needs, but they are also a source of protection for consumers who can turn to other suppliers if they become dissatisfied with a product or service. Markets also allow decentralized decision making and, coupled with the protection of private property, encourage innovation. Smith concluded that it was better to rely on the profit incentives that private ownership provides than to rely on goodwill:

> It is not from the benevolence of the butcher, the brewer, or the baker, that we expect our dinner, but from their regard to their own self-interest. We address ourselves, not to their humanity but to their self-love, and never talk to them of their own necessities but of their advantages.

The corporate form is important in implementing this perspective because share ownership and the limited liability of owners allow ownership and management to be separated. This allows a person working in one field to invest capital in enterprises in other fields with the capital markets coordinating the allocation of capital between investors and business opportunities. Managers of an enterprise are then the agents of the owners—the investors of capital—and are to serve their interests by maximizing the value of the capital they provide. When markets are competitive, value maximization by firms results in economic efficiency and maximizes aggregate societal well-being.

From this perspective, the role of business in society is to generate well-being through economic efficiency. Private property, the corporate form, and markets are the principal institutions for organizing economic activity. Economic theory identifies the maximization of shareholder value—or long-term profit maximization—as the objective that provides the strongest incentives, and competition directs those incentives toward efficiency. Profit maximization and the efficient use of resources then make society in the aggregate as well off as possible.

CORPORATE SOCIAL RESPONSIBILITY   With this foundation Friedman's (1970) conception of corporate social responsibility is "to conduct the business in accordance with [owners'] desires, which generally will be to make as much money as possible while conforming to the basic rules of society, both those embodied in law and those embodied in ethical custom." The objective of a corporation thus is the maximization of its profits, or shareholder value, subject to the constraints imposed by the rules of society. Friedman concludes that those who argue that a "corporate executive has a 'social responsibility' … must mean that he is to act in some way that is not in the interest of his employers"; that is, the shareholders. In maximizing its profits the firm is to respect both the law and ethical custom, as considered in Chapters 21 and 22.

He argues further that corporate executives who serve some social purpose are acting as civil servants by making expenditures and imposing taxes on shareholders that shareholders would not approve. They act as if "political mechanisms, not market mechanisms, are the appropriate way to determine the allocation of scarce resources to alternative uses." According to Friedman, that amounts to socialism rather than capitalism. Furthermore, calls for a broader social responsibility may, in Friedman's view, actually promote that which corporations should seek to avoid. That is, by calling for the adoption of objectives other than profit maximization, managers are advocating the use of a political process to direct the allocation of corporate resources. Friedman believes that these calls for social responsibility will weaken the free enterprise system and the well-being of society that flows from it.

From Friedman's perspective, a corporation is a voluntary association of individuals who have joined together for a mutual purpose. That purpose may be the generation of profits in which they will share or the achievement of some social or nonprofit objective. In the case of a for-profit corporation, shareholders have a property right to its assets and hence to the return on those assets. As indicated in Figure 20-2, shareholders are principals and the corporation is

FIGURE 20-2   Friedman's Conception of a Corporation

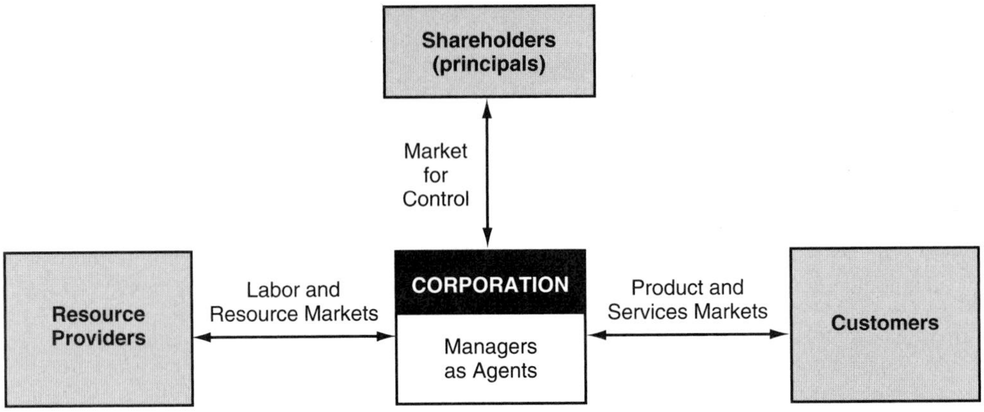

managed by agents—the managers—who are to operate it in the best interests of the principals. In an efficient capital market, shareholders will unanimously prefer that the firm be operated to maximize its market value. If one shareholder prefers to donate all his returns to charity and another prefers to spend all her returns on consumption, both will prefer that the firm be operated to make those returns as great as possible. If management does not maximize the value of the firm, the market for control of firms will replace management through a takeover or proxy contest.

From this perspective, the corporation engages in voluntary transactions with both resource providers and customers. As Figure 20-2 illustrates, labor and resource markets intermediate between resource providers and the corporation, and product and services markets intermediate between customers and the corporation. If markets are competitive, maximizing shareholder value is consistent with economic efficiency and yields the greatest aggregate well-being for society.

According to Friedman, then, the responsibility of managers, serving as agents of the owners of the firm, the principals, is to maximize profits (shareholder value) by engaging in free and open competition. In that competition, firms engage in voluntary exchanges with others, while abiding by the law and ethical custom.

THE ROLE OF GOVERNMENT   It is impossible to have a conception of the responsibilities of business without also having a conception of the responsibilities of government. In Friedman's view, government is to impose taxes and determine expenditures, and the judiciary is to mediate disputes and interpret the law. When there are market imperfections and private costs diverge from social costs, the role of governments is to assign clear entitlements and protect them with a property or liability rule, as called for by the Coase theorem considered in Chapters 12 and 14. Individuals then will internalize the social costs of their actions and reach socially efficient decisions through private bargaining. When transactions costs are high, the government may equate private and social costs through market-like mechanisms such as cap-and-trade systems for pollution control, as considered in Chapter 12. These functions are reserved for government, with its coercive powers limited by a system of checks and balances, individual rights, and the popular election of representatives. According to Friedman, a call for corporate social responsibility "amounts to an assertion that those who favor the taxes and expenditures in question have failed to persuade a majority of their fellow citizens to be of like mind and that they are seeking to attain by undemocratic procedures what they cannot attain by democratic procedures."

Friedman does not indicate whether and to what extent firms should take political action to influence government policies. The natural extension of his perspective, however, is that political competition moves government toward social efficiency just as competition in markets drives firms toward social efficiency.[5]

---

[5]See Becker (1983).

PHILOSOPHICAL UNDERPINNINGS   Friedman views a corporation as a voluntary association of individuals that maximizes the value of their property not only because of economic efficiency considerations but also because it is consistent with a philosophy of individualism, liberty, and personal responsibility. From this perspective, society is a collection of individuals with differing interests who can be free only if they can act voluntarily. The role of government then is to protect private property and other rights. Since individual liberty and voluntary actions take priority over government direction, resource allocation is to take place through markets rather than through a political process.[6] In this philosophy, competition not only promotes efficiency but also allows people to protect themselves by providing alternatives in the marketplace. Friedman also identifies "the great virtue of private competitive enterprise— it forces people to be responsible for their own actions and makes it difficult for them to 'exploit' other people for either selfish or unselfish purposes. They can do good—but only at their own expense."

THE SOCIAL RESPONSIBILITY LABEL   A firm that maximizes shareholder value may directly benefit others. A value-maximizing firm may make philanthropic contributions because doing so strengthens the communities in which it operates, thereby helping it to attract and retain employees. A firm may institute worker participation programs to improve productivity by enhancing worker satisfaction. A firm may design high-quality products and inform consumers of their safety and performance features because doing so reduces liability costs and increases demand. According to Friedman, when such actions increase shareholder value, they should not be given the label of social responsibility. Those actions are simply another component of a strategy of profit maximization.

From Friedman's perspective, a conception of CSR that differs from shareholder value maximization must be costly and can have only two interpretations—either a political process is to be used to make decisions or managers are to act as principals rather than as agents. In the former case he argues that political processes are to be reserved for government and not business. If managers are acting as principals, they are determining who should bear the cost of social responsibility. When the markets in which the firm operates are competitive, however, the costs of social responsibility must ultimately be borne by shareholders. The firm could then become the target of a takeover attempt by investors who would operate it to maximize its value. In principle, unless restricted, the market for control should drive a firm in which managers act as principals toward value maximization.

UNDERSTANDING FRIEDMAN'S PERSPECTIVE[7]   The economic justification for Friedman's position is based on an environment in which citizens can both invest their funds in the capital markets and make personal gifts to social causes. Social causes can also be served by firms, and citizens can obtain satisfaction from corporate giving as well as from their personal giving. If shareholders as principals wish to support social goals, however, they can do so with the returns from their shareholdings rather than through the firm. If an entrepreneur starts a firm and makes it clear to investors that the firm will engage in social activities that may decrease profits, then investors will take this into account when determining how much they will pay for the shares of the firm. Any cost of the social activities will then be borne by the entrepreneur rather than subsequent investors. Since shareholders do not bear the cost when they anticipate the social activities, Friedman would have no objection to those activities. The entrepreneur as the principal can operate the firm under any combination of financial and social objectives, provided that investors are informed in advance of those objectives. That is, Friedman's objection is not to CSR that is anticipated, since then shareholders do not bear the cost. Instead, Friedman's objection is to CSR that cannot be anticipated by investors.

---

[6]See Friedman (1962, Chapter 8). The moral underpinnings of Friedman's conception of corporate responsibility as profit maximization are individual liberties similar to those of individualism. Lukes (1973) characterizes individualism as consisting of four elements: (1) accepting the intrinsic *moral worth* of individual human beings, (2) advocating the *autonomy* of individual thought and action, (3) acknowledging the existence and importance of individual *privacy,* and (4) expressing *self-development* or self-regulation as a desirable goal.

[7]This section is based in part on Baron (2007).

The perspective that entrepreneurs rather than current shareholders choose the objectives of the firm and bear the cost of CSR was articulated by John Mackey (2005), CEO of Whole Foods, who wrote,

> I believe the entrepreneurs, not the current investors in a company's stock, have the right and responsibility to define the purpose of the company. It is the entrepreneurs who create a company, ... and who negotiate the terms of trade with all of the voluntarily cooperating stakeholders—including the investors. At Whole Foods we "hired" our original investors. They didn't hire us.
>
> We first announced that we would donate 5 percent of the company's net profit to philanthropy when we drafted our mission statement .... Our policy ... predates our IPO by seven years. All seven of the private investors at the time we created the policy voted for it when they served on our board of directors .... How can Whole Foods' philanthropy be "theft" from the current investors if the original owners of the company unanimously approved the policy and all subsequent investors made their investments after the policy was in effect and well publicized?

When costly social activities cannot be anticipated, Friedman views managers as imposing taxes on shareholders and spending the proceeds as they choose. In doing so, he argues that managers become "in effect a public employee, a civil servant," and argues that if they are to play that role they should be chosen through a "political process." As indicated in the framework presented later in the chapter, a social entrepreneur can be willing to form a CSR firm at a financial loss because of either the good it does for others (altruism) or the personal satisfaction from providing that good (a warm glow). As an example of warm glow preferences, Paul Rice, founder and chief executive of TransFair USA, the U.S. fair trade coffee organization, said, "It is guilt-free coffee, but I would not call it that. I would call it feel-good coffee."[8]

The perspective of Friedman and Mackey that social policies of firms should be announced in advance so that investors can make informed choices about whether to invest in the firm may not be sufficient to sustain those policies. Friedman (1970) points to the discipline of the market for control, "Will not the stockholders fire [the manager]? (Either the present ones or those who take over when his actions in the name of social responsibility have reduced the corporation's profit and the price of its stock.") Even if the original shareholders supported CSR, the market for control could result in new shareholders taking over the firm, eliminating the costly CSR, and capturing the gain in market value. T. J. Rodgers (2005), CEO of Cypress Semiconductors, wrote, "Mackey spouts nonsense about how his company hired his original investors, not vice versa. If Whole Foods ever falls on persistent hard times—perhaps when the Luddites are no longer able to hold back the genetic food revolution using junk science and fear—he will quickly find out who has hired whom, as his investors fire him." To persist, CSR firms thus need insulation from the market for control. Social entrepreneurs may protect the firms they found with antitakeover provisions, or socially responsible mutual funds can be formed to hold the shares of CSR firms. Socially responsible mutual funds can raise the share price of firms that engage in social activities, making a takeover less likely.

The Timberland example concerns a successful family-controlled company known for its social responsibility and sustainability policy but which had experienced cost and profit pressures. It was acquired by a larger company with a record of cost reduction and margin improvements that saw an opportunity to increase profits.

Corporate social activities may not be costly. Some are undertaken for strategic reasons because they will be rewarded by consumers, investors, or employees or other suppliers of inputs to the firm. This is discussed in more detail later in the chapter and is only illustrated here. As an example of activities carried out under the banner of CSR that can be motivated by strategic considerations, referring to days on which each store donates 5 percent of its sales to local charities, Mackey wrote, "While our stores select worthwhile organizations to support, they also tend to focus on groups that have large membership lists, which are contacted and encouraged to shop our store that day to support the organization. This usually brings hundreds of new or lapsed customers into our stores, many of whom then become regular shoppers. So a 5 percent Day not only allows us to support worthwhile causes, but is an excellent marketing strategy that

---

[8]*San Jose Mercury News*, April 28, 2004.

EXAMPLE   Timberland Company

The Timberland Company was founded in 1952 in New England and promoted a reputation for social responsibility and sustainability. The producer of boots, apparel, and outdoor gear had a guiding environmental perspective: "We live by a simple challenge and common commitment—to be environmentally responsible. We call it Earthkeeping." The company had planted more than a million trees and had developed a recycled rubber compound used in its boots. The company assumed responsibility for climate, products, factories, and services. President and CEO Jeff Schwartz referred to the company's approach as "strategic sustainability." He wrote, "Timberland's social and environmental initiatives help our company to save money, operate more sustainably, make better products and create a positive social impact … all of which add real value." The company had developed a clientele that resonated with the company's commitment.

In 2011 Timberland was acquired by VF Corporation, a large apparel maker with brands North Face, Nautica, and Wrangler jeans, for $2 billion, representing a 43 percent premium above its share price. Timberland's sales in 2010 were $1.43 billion, but its profits had fallen by 30 percent and its share price by 25 percent. Leather prices were sharply higher and wages in China had increased by 20 percent forcing the company to look for suppliers in lower wage countries. Timberland had refused to raise prices significantly in spite of higher costs. It reportedly tried to sell itself in 2006 during a strong stock market, but found no takers. Facing cost and profit pressure, the company, of which the Schwartz family controlled 73.5 percent of the voting shares, agreed to the takeover.[1]

VF planned to cut overhead, expand distribution, and improve Timberland's operating margin, which was 9 percent in 2010, compared to 20 percent for VF. In addition to cutting costs, VF planned to improve profitability at Timberland's 230 stores in North America. VF CEO Eric Wiseman explained the premium it paid, "Our confidence is based on the fact that we've accomplished that over and over before."[2] VF also saw advantages in combining an "above the tree line" brand with a "below the tree line" brand.

---

[1]*Wall Street Journal,* June 14, 2011.
[2]Ibid.

---

has benefited Whole Foods investors immensely." Friedman would support such policies if they increase profits, but he would see no reason to label the policies as CSR—unless that was an effective advertising term.

An entrepreneur seeking to pursue social objectives may be able to form a nonprofit firm to pursue those objectives. The Chapter 17 case *Social Entrepreneurship: Kiva* concerns an innovative microfinance enterprise organized as a nonprofit. In contrast, the Chapter 17 case *Social Entrepreneurship: Banco Compartamos* considers a microfinance enterprise organized as a for-profit firm.

COMPLIANCE WITH THE LAW

Any conception of the social responsibility of business must include compliance with just laws. Both civil and criminal laws apply to firms and their managers. Criminal prosecution can occur under the antitrust laws, securities and exchange laws (as with insider trading considered in the Chapter 23 case *Insider Trading*), certain environmental laws, and many others. Individual managers and corporations are also subject to fines and can be liable for damages under both statutory and common law. These laws proscribe actions that legislatures or the courts have held to be socially unacceptable.

Compliance with the law is a fundamental component of responsible management, yet in recent years the number and size of corporate scandals and incidents of wrongdoing have been alarming. A partial list from the past decade includes Adelphia Communications, AIG, Arthur Andersen, Citigroup, Computer Associates, Crédit Lyonnais, Enron, Global Crossing, HealthSouth, ImClone, Marsh and McLennan, Merrill Lynch, Metallgesellschaft, The New York Stock Exchange, Parmalat, Qwest Communications, Rite Aid, Shell Oil, Siemens, Sumitomo, Tyco, Vivendi, WorldCom, and Xerox. In addition, prominent executives including Jack Welch, former CEO of General Electric, were found to have received special treatment, and some such as Martha Stewart went to prison. *Fortune* (June 9, 2008) provided a rogue's gallery of corporate criminals: Conrad Black of Hollinger International, Bernard Ebbers of WorldCom, Andrew Fastow and Jeff Skilling of Enron, Dennis Kozlowski of Tyco, Sanjay Kumar of Computer Associates, John Rigas of Adelphia, Richard Scrushy of HealthSouth, and Sam Waksal of ImClone. The financial crisis has resulted in numerous fines by regulators and court decisions against banks and other lenders (see Chapter 11 and the case *Goldman Sachs and Its Reputation*).

Some individual companies have been involved in a series of wrongdoings. Citigroup agreed to the following settlements:

- 2002: paid $215 million to settle Federal Trade Commission charges on subprime lending
- 2003: paid $400 million on Securities and Exchange Commission (SEC) charges of biased research
- 2003: paid $145 million on SEC and New York State charges involving Enron
- 2003: paid $325 million to settle New York State charges of biased research
- 2004: paid $70 million on Federal Reserve charges on subprime lending
- 2004: paid $2.58 billion to settle a class action lawsuit on its involvement in the WorldCom scandal

In mid-2004 Citigroup increased its reserve for "Enron and pending litigation" to $6.7 billion, while Chairman Sandy Weill received a $29 million cash bonus for 2003. In addition, Japan ordered Citigroup's private banking group to close because of violations of banking rules, and shortly thereafter Citigroup fired three of its highest ranking officers. In 2007–2008 Citigroup was deeply involved in the subprime mortgage crisis and was subject to numerous lawsuits. The CEO brought in after the scandals in the early part of the decade was fired, and his replacement came under fire as the subprime mortgage crisis worsened. In 2010 Citigroup settled SEC charges regarding disclosure for $75 million and two executives were fired. In 2011 it paid $255 million to settle SEC charges that it defrauded investors. In 2011 Bank of America paid $8.5 billion to settle a lawsuit by private investors regarding bad mortgage lending, and Citigroup was expected to settle for approximately $3 billion. Many other lawsuits were pending.

Whether there have been more such incidents in recent years than in the past is unclear, but what is clear is that a substantial number of major companies have violated the law or entered into settlements to end legal complaints. Responsible management requires compliance with laws, yet a company's policing of the actions of its managers cannot be perfect. Some managers violate the law because of greed, some because they think they "can get away with it," some because they believe others are doing the same thing without reprimand, and others because they are pushing into gray areas where there is ambiguity in the law. Regardless of the source of the problem, a foundation of responsible management is compliance with the law and caution in areas where the law is ambiguous. Moreover, violations of the law by business can lead to more stringent regulation, such as the Dodd–Frank financial reform act considered in Chapter 11 and the Sarbanes–Oxley corporate governance requirements considered later in the chapter.

In addition to proscribing actions, the law assigns certain duties to firms and managers. For example, the Americans with Disabilities Act assigns an extensive set of duties to firms to provide for the disabled in the workplace. Duties assigned by law are not always the limits of social responsibility, however. Duties also arise from moral considerations. The law thus is an essential guide for responsible management, but reliance solely on the law is rarely sufficient. The next section raises the issue of whether responsible management requires more than compliance with the law and serving the interests of shareholders.

MARKET AND GOVERNMENT FAILURES AND STAKEHOLDERS

The market perspective of Friedman leaves unresolved a number of issues about the role of business in society. First, market imperfections as considered in Chapter 9 can cause a divergence between private and social costs and can warrant a role for government regulation and antitrust policy. In some cases the divergence can be addressed through incentive-based regulation and the liability system that align—albeit imperfectly—private and social costs and direct economic activity toward efficiency even in the presence of market imperfections. Nevertheless, market imperfections can remain, which may require self-regulation by companies.

Second, the reliance on private ownership and markets to generate well-being is justified by the moral philosophy of utilitarianism, considered in Chapter 21. Other conceptions of morality, such as those based on rights and justice considerations, however, are also important. They may call for restrictions on the use of private property, the restructuring of incentives, and government intervention for purposes other than the correction of market imperfections. For example, principles of distributive justice may warrant the redistribution of wealth and income to those who are less advantaged, and basic rights may require that the fair equality of opportunity be assured in society.

Third, just as markets can be imperfect, so too can government. Because government may be ineffective in correcting market imperfections, providing social justice, and assuring rights, some critics of Friedman argue that business has an affirmative duty to address societal needs unfulfilled by government.

A fourth concern results from agency problems. The corporate form involves a separation of ownership and management. This separation is essential for the efficient allocation of capital, but it also gives managers a degree of discretion to pursue interests other than those of owners.[9] The separation of ownership from management and the resulting managerial discretion means that Adam Smith's *market capitalism*—the reliance on markets to direct the allocation of resources—coexists with *managerial capitalism*—the reliance on managers for the allocation of resources.[10]

In principle, managerial capitalism could be more efficient than market capitalism. It allows the accumulation of resources through retained earnings and their allocation within the firm without having to incur the transactions costs of raising funds in the capital markets. It may also have advantages if management has information whose value would be dissipated if disclosed when raising capital. Managerial capitalism, however, can result in inefficiency when the incentives of management are not structured properly. For example, some firms cross-subsidize losses in one line of business with profits from another line of business. The more open are domestic and international markets, the stronger is competition, and the more active is the market for control, the greater are the pressures for efficiency, leaving less discretion to managers.

A firm interacts with a number of constituencies, including employees, suppliers, customers, the communities in which it operates, and the public in general.[11] To the extent that these constituents have an interest, or "stake," in their relationship with the firm, they are referred to as stakeholders.[12] Some stakes are protected by the law, as in the case of an employment contract or shareholder voting rights for approval of a merger. Most stakes, however, are protected by a relationship of mutual advantage with the firm. That is, a firm is attentive to the interests of stakeholders because it is advantageous to do so, and the stakeholders are attentive to the interests of the firm because they benefit from the relationship with it.

A stakeholder relationship centers on an exchange, as when an employee provides labor services to a firm in exchange for wages. Both parties presumably benefit from the continuation of the exchange relationship or else they would terminate it. Employees who have developed firm-specific human capital may earn a higher wage with their current employer than if they reentered the labor market. Similarly, the firm may have a stake in the relationship with employees to the extent that wages are less than the value of employees' contributions plus the costs of finding and training replacements. Both the firm and the employees then have incentives to take into account the interests of the other party in the relationship. Their stakes are voluntarily maintained through mutual advantage.

Does a firm have a responsibility to stakeholders other than to maintain mutual advantage? Using an analogy to contract law (Chapter 14), an employee may have made reliance expenditures in the form of investing in firm-specific human capital that has little value to other prospective employers. Similarly, a supplier may change its workplace practices to satisfy the requirements of its customers. Responsibility in such cases is to create realistic expectations about the continuation of mutual advantage. It is those expectations that induce the firm-specific reliance investments by stakeholders. Those expectations may include how the firm will deal with the termination of the relationship. For example, the firm may compensate employees in the event of a plant closing and provide support to the community in which the plant was located. A firm thus has a responsibility to create and fulfill realistic expectations, and if it does not do so, it may have a further obligation to compensate stakeholders.[13]

[9]Berle and Means (1932) first called attention to the issue of the separation of ownership and control and to its implication. Fama and Jensen (1983) provide a contractual perspective on the issue.

[10]See Chandler (1977) and Chandler and Tedlow (1985).

[11]See Freeman (1984) for an examination of stakeholder concepts and business strategy and Pfeffer and Salancik (1978) and Thompson (1967) for organizational perspectives.

[12]Those with a direct economic stake in the relationship with the firm are sometimes referred to as primary stakeholders, whereas others such as the public without a direct economic stake are referred to as secondary stakeholders.

[13]Post, Preston, and Sachs (2002) and Jensen (2001) provide opposing views of the stakeholder perspective.

Levi Strauss & Company had a strong commitment to its stakeholders and successfully sustained that commitment for decades. It had also continued to manufacture jeans in the United States, despite the high costs. When in 1997 it was forced by declining sales to lay off over 6,000 employees in the United States, the company was obligated by its principles to provide generous severance packages for the employees who lost their jobs and for the communities in which plants were closed. The cost to Levi Strauss was over $200 million. In 2002 it closed another eight plants at a cost of $113 million, and in 2003 it was forced to close its last plants in Canada and the United States, eliminating 21 percent of its workforce. Again, the company provided a generous severance package for those affected.

BROADER CONCEPTIONS OF SOCIAL RESPONSIBILITY

The Business Roundtable was founded to "examine public issues that affect the economy and develop positions which seek to reflect sound economic and social principles."[14] The Roundtable is composed of the CEOs of 150 major corporations, with combined employment of 10 million in the United States. In 1981 one of its task forces issued a "Statement on Corporate Responsibility." This statement reflects a constituency or stakeholder perspective and states that business is to "serve the public interest as well as private profit." The Roundtable stated that "some leading managers … believe that by giving enlightened consideration to balancing the legitimate claims of all its constituents, a corporation will best serve the interest of its shareholders."

The Roundtable's basic view of the firm is illustrated in Figure 20-3. The Roundtable identified seven constituencies: customers, employees, financiers, suppliers, communities, society at large, and shareholders. "Responsibility to all these constituencies in total constitutes responsibility to society, making the corporation both an economically and socially viable entity." The corporation thus is an entity whose existence depends on society's approval. That is, a corporation is a legal entity granted certain privileges, including limited liability, indefinite life, and special tax treatment such as depreciation allowances. In exchange for these privileges, the corporation has a responsibility to the society that granted them.

According to the Roundtable, customers have "a primary claim for corporate attention," so in Figure 20-3 they are represented separately as the providers of revenue for the firm. Shareholders also "have a special relationship to the corporation" but are viewed as "providers of risk capital" rather than as principals, as Friedman views them. The Roundtable goes further and criticizes institutional investors because "a high proportion of [shareholders] is made up of institutionally grouped and often unidentified short-term buyers most interested in near-term gain. This has affected their role among business constituencies." Ownership of the firm is never mentioned in the Roundtable statement, which suggests that the corporation exists as a legal entity. In contrast to Friedman's perspective, the principals in the Roundtable's view are managers.

FIGURE 20-3   The Business Roundtable View of a Corporation

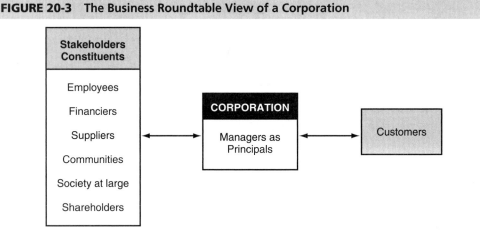

---

[14]See Business Roundtable (1981).

The objective of a corporation is not as clearly identified in the Roundtable statement as it is in Friedman's theory. Instead, managerial decision making involves "weighing the impacts of decisions and balancing different constituent interests …." The statement adds, "The shareholder must receive a good return but the legitimate concerns of other constituencies also must have the appropriate attention." Although the term "good return" is not defined, this balancing is presumably different from shareholder value maximization. Management is to ensure that the corporation remains viable, but beyond a reasonable return on investment all constituents can have a claim to the resources and returns of the firm. The Roundtable statement intentionally provides little guidance about how a corporation makes trade-offs between the interests of various constituencies, since that is the responsibility of managers as principals.[15] As Vogel (1991, p. 114) noted, part of the "universal appeal of the concept of corporate social responsibility rests on the concept's ambiguity," allowing management to formulate its own vision of social responsibility.

The Roundtable argues that the legitimate concerns of constituents are to be taken into account, but it does not want those constituents to participate in managerial decision making. Although "[i]t is important that all sides be heard … ," managers as principals are to give attention to constituents' interests and decide whether and how much to respond to those interests.

According to MacAvoy (1981), the Roundtable's concern for constituents "implies that the large corporation is a political entity subject to the votes of interest groups, rather than an economic organization subject to the market test for the efficient use of resources." He continued, "Political interests should not be served from corporate investment returns. If the stockholder wishes to support the local schools, or solutions to international problems, then he or she should do so with his or her own dividends." If managers operate their firms otherwise, they are acting as "politicians of the Roundtable," according to MacAvoy.

In a later statement "Corporate Governance and American Competitiveness," the Business Roundtable (1990, p. 5) stated, "It is important that all stakeholder interests be considered, but impossible to assure that all will be satisfied because competing claims may be mutually conflicting." In this statement, the Roundtable argued that corporate governance differs from political governance on several dimensions, including the speed and boldness with which businesses must act and the means through which shareholders can influence the course of management.

Perspectives

Business leaders advocate CSR for a variety of reasons. Some argue that there are societal objectives that can be achieved only through corporate action. Business, for example, may be more efficient than government or educational institutions at training workers for certain jobs. Other business leaders call for restraint on the pursuit of profits and for self-regulation in the hope that it will forestall additional government regulation. These calls are viewed by some as a necessary response to pressures from the nonmarket environment, which if ignored could lead to more serious threats to the free enterprise system. Some calls for CSR are directed to the public with the intent of increasing public support for business. Some who call for CSR believe that unless business uses at least the rhetoric of social responsibility, more onerous intervention by government will result.

Businesses thus advocate CSR for a variety of reasons, many of which are strategic. This has led skeptics to view as very limited what CSR can be expected to accomplish in meeting society's needs. Christian Aid, an agency of churches in the United Kingdom and Ireland, called "on the politicians to take responsibility for the ethical operation of companies rather than surrendering it to those from business peddling fine words and lofty sentiments."[16] In his evaluation of CSR, Vogel also sees its impact as limited. He states that "while the CSR movement has measurably improved the performance of some firms in some areas, its overall impact has been and will remain more modest than many of its advocates claim, or hope—or some of their critics fear." If business is to do more, he concludes, government will have to prescribe conduct.

---

[15]The absence of specifics increased the support for the statement among members of the task force.
[16]Christian Aid, press release, January 21, 2004.

Self-Regulation

Many businesses support a notion of CSR as voluntary self-regulation. At the Earth Summit in Rio de Janeiro in 1992 this perspective was challenged by a United Nations recommendation for international regulation of corporate behavior. The World Council for Sustainable Development, a coalition of businesses, opposed this recommendation and succeeded in obtaining endorsement for a manifesto of voluntary self-regulation. Similarly, in its definition of CSR the European Commission stated that businesses are to take into account the social and environmental consequences of their operations but on a voluntary basis.

The initial conception of CSR within the Commission of the EU was as a voluntary framework but with a set of obligations spelled out in a 2001 Green Paper. As Ungericht and Hirt (2010) discussed, however, the published communiqué of the Commission had a different orientation focusing on the economic contribution of business and the asserted benefits "from the inclusion of social and environmental issues into their daily operations." In 2006 the Commission in conjunction with the Council issued a revised conception of CSR emphasizing the role of business in sustainable economic growth, competitiveness, job creation, and innovation. The Commission and Council rejected the need for additional regulations or obligations for business and viewed voluntary CSR as contributing to that role.

Another voluntary approach to CSR is that taken by the International Organization for Standards (ISO), which in 2010 issued ISO 26000, "Guidance in social responsibility," intended for public sector organizations in addition to businesses.[17] ISO 26000 addresses seven components of social responsibility; human rights, labor practices, the environment, fair operating practices, consumer issues, community involvement, and development. It argues that these components should be integrated throughout a company's decisions and activities. "Guidance is provided for implementation recognizing that 'what social responsibility' means may vary from one program to another."

CORPORATE SOCIAL RESPONSIBILITY AND CORPORATE SOCIAL PERFORMANCE

Corporate social responsibility focuses on the responsibility of a firm for social performance, but where does that responsibility and duty come from? The perspective presented here is that responsibility comes from a moral obligation; that is, the content of corporate social responsibility is found in moral principles. Corporate social responsibility thus arises from the combination of (1) an ethical failure that establishes a moral duty and (2) the assignment of that duty to the firm. The concept of a moral duty is developed in Chapters 21 and 22 from the perspectives of three foundational ethics systems—utilitarianism, moral rights, and justice—that correspond to basic moral intuitions. Some moral standards such as freedom of speech impose a duty on everyone to respect. In other cases the set of parties that can address an ethical failure may be small, and assigning of duty requires identifying the party, such as a firm, government, or an individual, that is best positioned to address the ethical failure.

As an example, some people view obesity as a social problem if not a moral problem. Is there a duty on a fast-food company such as McDonald's to address the obesity problem?[18] The party best positioned to deal with the obesity problem is clearly the individual, and government may be best positioned to provide information about obesity and its consequences. McDonald's, however, is well positioned to respond by broadening its menu items and providing more information about those items. The assignment of duty in such situations is considered more generally in Chapters 21 and 22 to identify corporate social responsibilities.

Another aspect of the concept of responsibility is motivation. If a self-interested, profit-maximizing company produces a green product because consumers are willing to pay a sufficiently high price that profits increase, is it the company or consumers that are being environmentally responsible? If a self-interested, profit-maximizing company accepts government subsidies in exchange for building a solar power plant, is the company being socially responsible or simply opportunistic? If a self-interested, profit-maximizing company self-regulates because it faces social pressure and the threat of government regulation, is the company being

---

[17]www.iso.org/isa.social_responsibility.
[18]See also the Chapter 14 case *Obesity and McLawsuits.*

socially responsible or simply responsive? Rather than answer these questions here, the broader concept of *corporate social performance* will be used.

In contrast to corporate social responsibility, corporate social performance need not be motivated by moral considerations but instead could be strategic or a response to the social pressure a firm faces. For example, McDonald's could broaden its menu items to include salads because an increasing number of consumers prefer salads. Similarly, McDonald's could offer salads because of criticism of its menu offerings, as depicted in the movie *Supersize Me*. Or it could offer salads because of pressure from lawsuits claiming it was liable for the obesity of its customers. Corporate social performance thus could be motivated by a number of considerations.

The tuna and dolphins example illustrates the difference between social performance that is in response to social pressure and social performance that is morally motivated. Heinz's decision not to purchase tuna caught in purse seine nets was consistent with ethical consensus in the United States, but the decision was a response to the social pressure it faced. Heinz's motive appears to have been to reduce the actual and potential damage from a boycott and the effect on its brand. Heinz was well aware of the fishing practices in the Eastern Pacific and the number of dolphins being killed. The company also understood the widespread concern about the issue once the videotape was broadcast in March 1988. That Heinz took 2 years to change its policy

---

EXAMPLE   Tuna and Dolphins

Environmental and animal rights groups protested the use of purse seine nets to catch yellow fin tuna in the Eastern Pacific fishery. In the Eastern Pacific, yellow fin tuna swim underneath dolphins, and fishing boats cast their nets around the dolphins knowing that the tuna will be caught. Environmental groups estimated that more than 100,000 dolphins a year were being caught in the nets and drowned. However, August Felando, president of the American Tuna Boat Association in San Diego, argued that the 30-vessel U.S. fleet accounted for the deaths of only 12,643 dolphins in 1989, compared with the U.S. limit of 20,500 established by the Marine Mammal Protection Act of 1972. He added that the number had been decreasing because U.S. fishers had become skilled in freeing the dolphins from the nets. All U.S. tuna boats carried U.S. observers to monitor fishing practices. The United States also attempted to enforce its regulations on foreign boats, with 30 percent of foreign tuna boats, mostly from Latin America, also carrying U.S. observers.

H. J. Heinz, which owned StarKist Seafood Company, and other tuna companies had been under pressure for some time. The "save the dolphins" project had been working to convince tuna companies to change their practices and had led a national boycott of yellow fin tuna products. The Humane Society, Greenpeace, the Earth Island Institute, and the Dolphin Coalition were also pressuring the tuna companies. The key event in the campaign was a 1988 videotape taken by a biologist who had signed on as a crew member on a tuna boat. The videotape showed dolphins drowning in purse seine nets. The videotape was broadcast by the national television networks, and suddenly the public became involved. The Earth Island Institute, which had helped organize a boycott of StarKist, took out newspaper advertisements calling on Heinz to stop the "dolphin massacre." Consumers responded, school children boycotted tuna, and the boycott found its way into movies such as *Lethal Weapon 2*. Politicians also became

interested in the issue, introducing legislation to require "dolphin-unsafe" labels on cans containing tuna caught with purse seine nets.

Over 2 years later on April 12, 1990, Heinz President Arthur O'Reilly announced that StarKist would purchase only "dolphin-safe" tuna and would no longer use tuna caught in purse seine nets.[1] StarKist planned to market its tuna under a "dolphin-safe" label. In an interview in the film *Where Have All the Dolphins Gone?*, O'Reilly said, "I think it would be a poor chief executive officer that was not attentive to his customers … because of the affection children have for Flipper … there was a growing barrage of criticism, well-orchestrated, which I think served to convey a growing sentiment among schoolchildren that the previous fishing methods were no longer acceptable." O'Reilly said that his children had asked him to stop killing dolphins.

In 1988 Hobee's restaurants, a popular and growing chain, switched from yellow fin to Tongol tuna, which is not caught in a manner that contributes to dolphin deaths. In early 1990 the 10 Hobee's restaurants in the San Francisco Bay area began a boycott of all tuna products. Hobee's replaced many of its tuna items with chicken, placed pamphlets on each table explaining its policy, and provided training to its servers so that they could provide more information on the subject if asked. Hobee's also began a boycott of all Heinz products, substituting other brands for such staples as Heinz ketchup. The boycott sent a signal to Heinz.[2]

---

[1]Shortly thereafter, Bumble Bee Seafoods and Van Camp Seafood Company, producer of Chicken of the Sea brand tuna, announced that they would likewise. Bumble Bee was owned by Unicord of Thailand, and Van Camp was owned by the Mam Trust of Indonesia.

[2]Hobee's lifted its ban on other Heinz products after the company's April 12 announcement, but it continued its boycott of StarKist tuna, awaiting implementation of Heinz's program.

and not until it had become a boycott target suggests that its action was in response to the social pressure it faced. In contrast, Hobee's restaurants did not act in response to pressure. Its motive was to protect dolphins, even if doing so reduced its profits. Hobee's actions reflected its conception of corporate social responsibility.

A FRAMEWORK FOR UNDERSTANDING CORPORATE SOCIAL PERFORMANCE

Terminology

The term corporate social performance (CSP) will be used to refer to social activities that satisfy two conditions. First, the social activities extend beyond the requirements of the law and regulations.[19] Second, the social activities involve the private provision of public goods or private redistribution. For example, the McDonald's project with Environmental Defense discussed in Chapter 12 reduced solid waste in the company's restaurants, which benefited the public by relieving a negative externality. Wal-Mart's corporate philanthropy also benefits the public and represents private redistribution from the company to local communities. Having a "dolphin safe" policy benefits dolphins and those who value their well-being. CSR implies CSP, but CSP need not be morally motivated. Most of the popular discussion as well as the empirical analysis pertains to CSP, since identifying moral duties is difficult. That task is the subject of Chapters 21 and 22.

From one perspective what matters is social performance and not the motivation for it. That is, if the objective is to serve society's needs, then actions and not motives matter. It should not matter whether a firm takes an action to maximize profits, avoid a challenge from an activist group, or fulfill a moral duty. If the objective is to predict the future behavior of firms, however, then motive matters. A firm that undertakes social activities only for strategic reasons or because of social pressure will act only when there is an opportunity for profits or when forced to act by its nonmarket environment. A firm motivated by moral principles can act in the absence of a profit opportunity or social pressure. From the perspective of anticipating when a firm will act, it is important to understand motive as well as market opportunities and social pressure.

The Setting

The framework for CSP begins with individuals who can allocate their resources among consumption goods, investments in the shares of firms that do and do not conduct social activities, and direct contributions to social causes.[20] Individuals have preferences for consumption and the financial return on their investments, and many also have preferences for social causes. For example, in the United States contributions to charities in 2010 topped $300 billion, or approximately $1,000 a person.[21] Those contributions may be motivated by altruism for those whose lives are improved by the contributions or because the individual as a donor feels better about herself or himself because of the contribution. As an illustration of the latter type of preferences, in 2004, 34 percent of the Prius purchasers stated that their primary reason for buying a Prius was that it "makes a statement about me." By 2007 that number had increased to 57 percent.[22] Prius purchaser Mary Gatch stated, "I felt like the Camry Hybrid was too subtle for the message I wanted to put out there. I wanted to have the biggest impact that I could, and the Prius puts out a clearer message."[23] Such preferences are referred to as "warm glow" preferences and pertain to the act of contributing to a social cause in addition to the benefit to the social cause. Many actions by individuals are motivated by both altruism and warm glow preferences.

---

[19]The *Economist* survey found that 23 percent of the firms agreed that corporate social responsibility "is meaningless if it includes things that companies would do anyway" (*Economist,* January 17, 2008).

[20]The theory underlying the framework presented here is developed in Baron (2007, 2008, 2009).

[21]Press Release, GivingUSA Foundation and Center on Philanthropy at Indiana University, June 26, 2011.

[22]The surveys were conducted by CNW Marketing Research.

[23]*New York Times*, July 4, 2007. Sexton and Sexton (2011) tested for the Prime effect, or "conspicuous conservation" in their terminology, by statistically relating auto sales to the characteristics of the communities in which the buyers resided using data from Colorado and Washington. They found that 32.9 percent of its market share in Colorado and 10.1 percent in Washington was due to conspicuous conservation and that the willingness to pay for the "Prius halo effect" was between $1,400 and $4,200 in Colorado and between $420 and $1,290 in Washington.

To satisfy their desire to support social causes, individuals can make direct contributions to those causes but they can also buy shares in firms that conduct social activities. Corporate social activities, however, may be only an imperfect substitute for personal contributions since, for example, the individual may be opposed to some of the social activities conducted by the firm.[24] Those individuals who view the corporate social activities as a good substitute for personal contributions would then hold shares of such firms, whereas other individuals who view those activities as a poor substitute for personal contributions to social causes would instead purchase shares of firms without those activists and contribute personally to their preferred social causes. Firms thus attract an investor clientele corresponding to their social performance. Those clienteles could operate through socially responsible investment funds.

Motivations for CSP

Corporate social performance can be costly. As the opening quotation from the *Economist* survey indicates, many companies view CSP as a "necessary cost of business." Social activities can be rewarded, however, and the strength of those rewards can depend on the motivation of the firm. Punishment can also result. Consumers may stop buying a product such as canned tuna, activist groups could target a company, or employee recruiting and retention may suffer. Four motivations for CSP are considered here. The first is moral motivation, the second is managerial perquisites, the third is to relieve social pressure, and the fourth is strategic, that is, to exploit available rewards for CSP.

MORAL MOTIVATION Social activities can be undertaken because of a moral concern for which the duty is assigned to the firm. The moral concern could be associated with the stakeholders of the firm, the environment, or the general public. The firm may voluntarily take actions to relieve global warming, support community activities, oppose corruption, aid victims of natural disasters, or protect dolphins as in the case of Hobee's. Examples of such activities are presented in Chapters 23 and 24, and the moral foundations for the activities are considered in Chapters 21 and 22.

MANAGERIAL PERQUISITES CSP could be a perquisite for management in the sense that managers themselves have a preference for the social activities or receive a warm glow from the accolades of the advocates of broadened social performance. Managers could have a personal preference for those activities, altruistic preferences for those whose lives are better as a result of the activities, or a warm glow from having conducted the activities. For example, managers could receive a warm glow from their company being included in a socially responsible investing index such as the Dow Jones Sustainability Group Index. As a former employee of an investment bank commented, "the CEO liked birds, so we [the company] liked birds."

Firms could also undertake CSP because of social norms or audience effects. For example, if most firms discuss their CSP more than their profits, a firm may follow suit so as not to be conspicuous.

SOCIAL PRESSURE A firm could conduct social activities in response to social pressure from government or NGOs and social activists. Citigroup was under pressure from environmental NGOs, as considered in the Chapter 4 case *Anatomy of a Corporate Campaign: Rainforest Action Network and Citigroup (A)(B)* and took the lead along with three other banks in establishing the Equator Principles with environmental and human rights standards for project finance, as considered in Chapter 12. This *responsive CSP* can be undertaken in the absence of any moral concerns and may or may not be rewarded by consumers, investors, or employees. Responsive CSP could relieve social pressure that affects financial performance.

---

[24]One rationale for a preference for CSP over personal giving is that firms may have opportunities to make social improvements that are not available to individuals. Individuals, however, may be able to contribute to NGOs that conduct social activities at the scale of those undertaken by a firm. Moreover, with the Internet the range of social activities in which an individual can participate has expanded enormously. Another rationale is that firms can provide social improvements more efficiently than can individuals or the nonprofit organizations to which they give. Firms and most managers, however, typically have little experience or training in conducting social activities. One illustration of this is the eagerness of firms to partner with NGOs such as Environmental Defense and Conservation International on environmental practices and projects.

Punishments could also result. Social pressure could have a direct effect on the financial performance of a firm if it causes consumers, investors, or employees to shun the firm. Social pressure could also damage the reputation of the firm or a brand, and it could also portend future problems arising from private or public politics, using the terminology of Chapter 4, as in the Chapter 11 case *Goldman Sachs and Its Reputation.*

Social pressure can be applied to all firms as in the case of criticism of business for excessive executive compensation, but it is often targeted to individual firms or industries. Social activists select targets for their campaigns, and government often focuses enforcement activities on particular firms or industries. Similarly, the threat of new legislation often focuses on particular industries, such as electric power, or on particular practices such as backdating stock options granted to executives. Social pressure stemming from private politics and public politics thus can be targeted to particular firms and industries.

Targeting could focus on *worst offenders,* those firms with poor social performance, or it could focus on firms that are *soft targets* and more likely to bow to the social pressure. A firm could be a soft target because it has in the past conducted social activities or been responsive to social pressure or because it is financially weak or vulnerable to brand or reputation damage. Argenti (2004, pp. 110–111) explained the decision by the activist group Global Exchange to target Starbucks to sell Fair Trade Coffee: "Truly socially responsible companies are actually more likely to be attacked by activist NGOs than those that are not …. Our interviews with Global Exchange suggested that Starbucks was a better target for the fair trade issue because of its emphasis on social responsibility, as opposed to a larger company without a socially responsible bent."

STRATEGIC (CSR) MOTIVATION Corporate social activities could be undertaken for strategic reasons; that is, they increase profits. The activities could strengthen local community relations or improve employee morale and productivity. Wal-Mart is the largest corporate philanthropist, and most of its contributions are made at the local store level with employees participating in the allocation of the contributions. The contributions strengthen the communities in which the stores are located, and participation by employees improves morale. Whole Foods' 5 percent Days are a similar example. Corporate social performance could also strengthen a brand as in the case of Starbucks and Whole Foods. Corporate social performance could make hiring of talented people easier. It could also attract a clientele of shareholders who value the social activities of the firm.

CSP may also provide better access to government institutions and their officeholders. This may increase the effectiveness of lobbying and other nonmarket strategies, which can result in more favorable government policies or decisions. CSP may also result in activists having greater trust in a firm. This may provide an opportunity to communicate with them on an emerging nonmarket issue in a less hostile context than might otherwise exist.

If strategic CSP is rewarded, a firm could maximize profits by undertaking social activities such as producing a green product, sourcing only from suppliers that respect worker rights, or meeting more stringent environmental standards than called for by regulations. If consumers will pay a premium for green products or for organic foods, a firm motivated by self-interest will supply those products regardless of its position on CSP. Similarly, if consumers prefer products produced from recycled materials or produced by a company with a reputation for environmentally friendly policies, a firm may find it profitable to develop such a policy. These policies can have nothing to do with social responsibility and everything to do with profit maximization. Strategic corporate social performance thus could be undertaken to maximize the profits of the firm and may have no moral motivation. Indeed, many companies state that they engage in social activities when they make "business sense." One interpretation of business sense is that the activities increase profits.

To illustrate the notion of CSP that makes business sense, Figure 20-4 presents a hypothetical relation between CSP and profit for a firm, where associated with the CSP are social benefits to others in addition to shareholders. For the upper curve a profit-maximizing firm would conduct strategically motivated CSP to the point A, which maximizes profits. A firm that values CSP in addition to profits would conduct CSP to some point between A and B, since those levels increase profits and social benefits. Extending CSP beyond B would not make business sense, however, although it may make social or moral sense. The low curve in the figure is a reminder that social performance may not be rewarded.

FIGURE 20-4   Corporate Social Performance and Business Sense

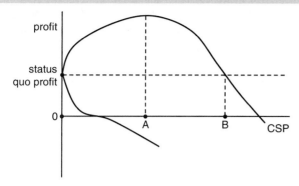

Rewards

CSP can be rewarded, although costs can accompany the rewards. Rewards could come directly from investors, consumers, or employees or other inputs to production. Rewards could also be indirect through relieving social pressure that could arise from either private politics or public politics. CSP that responds to the interests of stakeholders or the demands of NGOs can also build support for the firm in the market and the nonmarket environments. Firms may develop loyal customers, suppliers, and local communities whose support they may need for permits and approvals. Rewards can also come from government in the form of regulatory forbearance, as an example.

CONSUMER REWARDS   Individuals could reward a firm in their roles as consumers. Consumers could prefer to buy a product from a firm with CSP rather than from a firm without CSP. That is, social activities could provide a form of product differentiation. Some consumers prefer Timberland boots because of the company's commitment to social performance, and some consumers shun gasoline from ExxonMobil because of the *Exxon Valdez* oil spill.

Elfenbien and McManus (2010) compared the prices of identical items auctioned on eBay's non-charity and charity auction formats, where the charity format involves designating all or a share of the proceeds to go to a charity. They found an average 6 percent premium for items sold on the charity auction. Casadesus-Masanell, Crooke, Reinhardt, and Vasishth (2009) found that consumers were willing to pay a premium for Patagonia's organic cotton sportswear. Hiscox and Smyth (2006) conducted an experiment in which two identical versions of products, towels and candles, were sold with and without a "Fair & Square" label that identified the products as being produced under good working conditions. Consumers were willing to pay a substantial premium for the labeled goods, but the authors caution that the retailer was known for selling cause-related goods to high-income people. The authors state, "it is safe to say that we were looking for a market for labor standards in a place where one might expect to find it." How the willingness to pay compares to the cost of providing CSP is not clear.

EMPLOYEE REWARDS   Individuals as employees could also reward a firm through higher productivity motivated by the social activities of their employees. Alternatively, a firm that conducts social activities could attract higher-ability employees or find it easier to retain them. Policies such as allowing employees to volunteer in community organizations on company time can improve employee morale and may be rewarded through higher productivity and lower turnover. Similarly, charitable contributions to local organizations can strengthen a community and improve employee satisfaction and morale as well as attract better employees. A firm that conducts social activities could also be included in the supply chain of a firm with a commitment to CSP. Even if the CSP does not improve productivity, hiring, or retention, CSP could be rewarded by employees who value the CSP and are willing to accept lower wages. Nyborg and Zhang (2011) found that firms in Norway with a reputation for CSP paid lower wages than firms without such a reputation.

INVESTOR REWARDS   Purchasing shares of a firm with CSP provides both a financial return and a social return, and the market value of the firm is composed of the value of its financial return and the value of its social return. Costly social activities may not be fully valued in the capital market, however, since investors may prefer to make personal contributions to social causes than to hold shares in firms with CSP. The market value of the firm thus could be less than if it eliminated the social activities. If the reward for those activities exceeds the cost, the market value could be higher. Investors thus may reward the firm in part for its social activities by holding its shares or may penalize a firm that engages in a business the investor dislikes. For example, Hong and Kacperczyk (2007) found that the market prices of sin stocks were depressed and concluded that investors shunned those stocks.

GOVERNMENT REWARDS CSP could be rewarded by government. Politicians may be more willing to listen to a firm with good CSP, which can facilitate lobbying and other nonmarket strategies. Richter (2011) assembled data on CSR activities and lobbying intensities of firms and found that the two were strategic complements in the sense that neither individually affected the market value of firms, but firms that engaged in both CSR and lobbying had significantly better financial performance. CSP in the form of self-regulation could also deter government from regulation. The movie industry has self-regulated and escaped regulation. Similarly, Internet firms have practiced self-regulation both individually and collectively, and privacy regulation has not been imposed in the United States.

Summary

The framework identifies relations among the financial and social performance of firms and social pressure from their nonmarket environment. A firm could be rewarded for its social performance by consumers, investors, or employees, but whether those rewards exceed the cost of social performance depends on the specifics of the market and nonmarket environments in which the firm operates. Social performance could be morally motivated, but it also could be a response to social pressure, which itself could depress share prices. Social activities could also be undertaken as a perquisite for management, and if so, social performance should be greater the greater are the slack resources available to managers; for example, when financial performance is better. Social pressure results from private and public politics and is directed to selected firms and industries. The selection may be based on worst offenders or soft targets. Researchers have attempted to assess these complex relationships among CSP, social pressure, and financial performance.

Empirical Research

Vogel (2005) assessed the research literature and concluded that CSP has a small impact both on social issues and on corporate financial performance (CFP). Margolis and Walsh (2003) identified 127 empirical studies and 13 surveys focusing on the relation between CSP and CFP. Although a number of studies found no relation, they concluded that the overall weight of the studies showed a positive but weak correlation between the two components of corporate performance. Griffin and Mahon (1997), Mahon and Griffin (1999), Roman, Hayibor, and Agle (1999), and Orlitsky, Schmidt, and Rynes (2003) also examined and interpreted many of these studies. The overall conclusion from this literature is that although there are considerable differences among the studies in terms of methods, measurement, and findings, the weight of evidence supports a weak, positive correlation between CSP and CFP.

Research, however, has not established the direction of causation. That is, good CSP could cause good CFP, or good CFP could provide slack resources to spend on CSP. As the *Economist* put it, "whether profitable companies feel rich enough to splash out on CSR, or CSR brings profits."[25] Waddock and Graves (1997) evaluated the relationship between CSP and CFP and the direction of causation and concluded that good financial performance leads to good CSP. McGuire, Sundgren, and Schneeweis (1988) also suggest that "It may be more fruitful to consider financial performance as a variable causing social responsibility than the reverse." They and McGuire, Schneeweis, and Branch (1990) reach the same conclusion regarding causation as Waddock and Graves. Orlitsky, Schmidt, and Rynes conclude that causation runs in both directions: "Financially successful companies spend more [on CSR] because they can afford it, but CSP also helps them become a bit more successful [in CFP]."

---

[25]*Economist*, January 17, 2008.

Baron, Harjoto, and Jo (2011) conducted an empirical study of the relations among CFP, CSP, and social pressure and also examined the direction of causation between CSP and CFP. The study is based on financial and operational data, indices of CSP and social pressure from Kinder, Lydenberg, Domini Research & Analytics (KLD)'s Socrates database, as well as data on corporate governance. KLD, an independent research firm, compiled data on the social performance of firms.[26] Its Socrates database is the most comprehensive and widely used data on social performance and includes social ratings data for more than 3,000 companies. KLD's "inclusive" social criteria contain "strength" ratings and "concern" ratings for community, diversity, employee relations, environment, governance, human rights, and product. The KLD strength ratings are an indicator of CSP, and the KLD concerns ratings can be interpreted as an indicator of social pressure. The KLD concerns include government actions such as regulatory enforcement actions, investigations, and fines, as well as private actions such as community protests and poor relations with indigenous peoples.

In the study, financial performance is measured by Tobin's Q, a standard measure used in economics and finance. Tobin's Q is the ratio of the market value of the firm divided by the capital invested in the firm, measured as total assets, and the market value is the value of all securities issued by the firm. Higher values of Tobin's Q represent better CFP.

The empirical estimation involved three simultaneous equations. One had Tobin's Q as the dependent variable representing the financial performance of the firm with independent variables CSP and social pressure as well as measures of operations (e.g., R&D ratio), financial structure, and capital market factors such as the percentage of shares held by institutional investors and the number of analysts covering the firm. The second equation had CSP as the dependent variable and as independent variables had financial performance and social pressure, as well as the operational and market measures. The third equation had social pressure as the dependent variable and CFP and CSP as independent variables, as well as the operational and market measures. The equations were estimated for a balanced panel of 484 firms, most of which were in the S&P 500, for the 1996–2004 period, as well as for a broader sample with fewer years of data for some firms.[27]

The estimations indicate the following. CFP is uncorrected with CSP and is decreasing in social pressure. Thus, social pressure worsens the financial performance of the firm, whereas CSP has no significant relation to financial performance. That is, in comparing two firms, one with low CSP and one with high CSP, the one with high CSP is no more likely to have better financial performance. This does not necessarily mean that there is no causal relationship between CSP and CFP for an individual firm; that is, consumers, investors, or employees could sufficiently reward firms for their CSP and the rewards could offset the cost of those social activities.[28] Moreover, firms could be choosing their CSP to maximize their market values, but looking across the population of firms in the study could reveal no statistically significant relation between CSP and CFP. That is, there is a "social Modigliani–Miller" property analogous to that in finance theory where in a financial market equilibrium there is no relation between CFP and CSP because investors respond optimally to the CSP of the firms.

The results for the CSP equation provide no support for the perquisites hypothesis and strong support for the responsive CSP hypothesis. That is, better CFP results in lower CSP. CSP is also increasing in the social pressure, implying that firms respond to pressure by increasing their CSP. The data do not allow a test of whether social performance is morally motivated or strategically motivated, although if social performance were morally motivated, it should be nonincreasing in financial performance, as is the case in the estimates.

The results for the social pressure equation support the soft target hypothesis over the worst offenders hypothesis. That is, social pressure is increasing in the CSP and decreasing in CFP, suggesting as in the comment about Starbucks that social pressure may be directed at those firms that are vulnerable and more likely to respond than firms, such as ExxonMobil, that are tough targets and not likely to respond. Social pressure is decreasing in CFP indicating that firms that are financially weaker face greater social pressure, which is also consistent with the soft-target hypothesis.

---

[26]KLD was acquired by Risk Metrics which merged with MSCI in 2010.

[27]The three equations have endogenous variables on the right side, so they were estimated using instrumental variables formed through two-stage least squares. The equations were identified through exclusion restrictions.

[28]No data are available on the actual cost of the activities included as KLD strengths.

Firms differ in terms of the industries in which they operate, and the firms in the database are classified as operating in either consumer-facing ("consumer") or business-facing ("industrial") industries. For consumer industries, CFP is positively correlated with CSP, whereas for industrial industries it is negatively correlated with CSP. The results for the full dataset are thus due to the positive correlation for consumer industries offsetting the negative correlation for industrial industries. Again, these are correlations and not causal relations. For consumer industries, CSP is increasing in CFP, which is consistent with the managerial perquisites hypothesis, whereas for industrial industries CSP is decreasing in CFP, which is consistent with a moral management hypothesis that CSP is undertaken because it is required. These results suggest that the relations among CFP, CSP, and social pressure vary across industries.

Empirical studies such as the one reported here provide a picture of the landscape in which firms operate, but it does not provide a roadmap for individuals firm. From the perspective of an individual firm the challenge is to determine the relation between its CFP, its CSP, and the social pressure it encounters. This requires specific information on the possible rewards that it might receive for its CSP and how the social pressure it faces depends on its CSP and financial performance. The chapter case *Wal-Mart: Nonmarket Pressure and Reputation Risk (B): A New Nonmarket Strategy* provides an opportunity to consider a company under intense social pressure that must decide whether it should embark on a CSP program and if so, how extensive it should be. In addition, it must assess the extent of any moral obligations it might have. These issues are also the subject of Chapters 21–24. The chapter case *Facebook and Online Privacy* considers a company that must address the social pressure that accompanied its rapid growth.

CORPORATE GOVERNANCE

Social Accountability

Accountability continues to be an issue for firms that adopt social responsibilities. Some firms experimented with independent "social audits" of their efforts, and some published those audits. The call for social audits faded in the 1980s as the impact of such reports was questioned, but in the mid-1990s they began to receive increased attention. Many firms now conduct their own assessments of social performance and publish reports. Some of these assessments are comprehensive, and some focus on a specific issue such as the environment or employee safety. BP provided an extensive and detailed report on its greenhouse gas emissions, including a report of an independent audit of its individual facilities. Dow Chemical provides a detailed report on its environment, health, and safety performance.

In 2004 the Gap Inc. issued its first social responsibility report.[29] Along with reporting on the company's charitable and volunteer activity and its corporate governance policies, the report provided a detailed summary of the findings by its 90-person compliance team that conducted 8,500 inspections of over 3,000 garment factories that supplied the company. As a result of the compliance inspections, 136 suppliers were terminated. Many more suppliers were found to have deficiencies, and the Gap worked with them to correct the deficiencies. For example, between 10 and 25 percent of the factories in China, Saipan, and Taiwan were found to have used psychological coercion or verbal abuse. Half the factories in sub-Saharan Africa did not provide adequate safety equipment. The Gap also inspected 653 other garment factories that sought to supply the company and rejected 16 percent of them. The Reverend David Schilling of the Interfaith Center on Corporate Responsibility (ICCR) praised the report as a "major step forward."[30]

Social performance is not only self-assessed by firms but is also assessed through external monitoring and evaluation by activist and other groups. "Socially responsible" investment funds have grown considerably but represent less than 10 percent of the market. Several independent organizations provide investment funds and institutions, such as universities and pension funds, with evaluations of the social performance of firms. In preparing its social responsibility report, the Gap formed a public reporting working group with members from Domini Social Investments, the Calvert Group, the As You Sow Foundation, the Center for Reflection, Education and Action, and the ICCR. Organizations such as the ICCR provide evaluations of

---

[29]Gap Inc., Social Responsibility Report, 2004, www.gapinc.com.
[30]*Wall Street Journal,* May 12, 2000.

corporate policies on particular issues that are the subject of shareholder resolutions voted at annual shareholder meetings.

Proponents of the stakeholder responsibility perspective, as articulated by the Business Roundtable, have argued for stakeholder representation on boards of directors to improve corporate social performance. Hillman, Keim, and Luce (2001) studied the relation between stakeholder directors and CSP.[31] Their statistical analysis revealed no aggregate relation between CSP and board representation, and when they disaggregated the components of CSP and types of board representatives, they found little evidence of a relation. Even if an empirical relation had been found of a link between stakeholder representation and CSP, the direction of causality still would be unclear. As the authors noted, firms with poor CSP could be the ones that added stakeholder directors.

The Duties of Boards of Directors

Corporations are "managed under the direction" of a board of directors, and board members have legal obligations that generally fall into categories referred to as the *duty of loyalty* and the *duty of care*. The duty of loyalty pertains to conflicts of interest and requires that directors serve the interests of the corporation and its shareholders. According to Clark (1985, p. 73), "Case law on manager's fiduciary duty of care can fairly be read to say that the manager has an affirmative, open-ended duty to maximize the beneficiaries' wealth ...." The duty of care requires directors to take care in their direction of the corporation under the "prudent person" standard and to make informed decisions. (Officers of the corporation have the same duty.) Directors are not expected to participate in the day-to-day management of the corporation.

The courts judge the discharge of the obligations of directors according to a common law standard referred to as the *business judgment rule*. Under this standard, actions taken by the board generally are not subject to judicial review if they are taken in accord with the duty of loyalty and the duty of care. The business judgment rule is based on the view that courts have no special expertise in second-guessing business decisions and that business decision making would be unduly hampered if it were subject to judicial review. Furthermore, the courts are likely to be less effective in monitoring managerial decisions than is the market for control.[32]

If directors do not exercise due care, they may be held liable. In *Smith v. Van Gorkom* (1985), 488 A.2d 858 (Del.), the Delaware Supreme Court held that the directors of Trans-Union Corporation were grossly negligent, and hence not protected by the business judgment rule, since they failed to independently value the firm in a leveraged buyout.[33] A subsequent case, *Hanson Trust PLC v. ML SCM Acquisition* (1986), 781 F.2d 264 (2nd Cir. 1986), established that being adequately informed is not sufficient to be protected by the business judgment rule. Directors must be well informed when they make decisions. Consequently, boards now seek the advice of independent experts in any valuation decision and in many other decisions as well. Reliance on experts is not sufficient, however, and directors are required to inquire into the content and quality of the reports given by management. The *Van Gorkom* and *Hanson* decisions caused the cost of directors and officers insurance to increase sharply. Most states responded by enacting statutes that allowed shareholders to limit the liability of directors and officers.

In addition to legal requirements, boards have a number of specific roles and functions. The Business Roundtable (1997, pp. 4–5) identified five principal functions of the board:

i. Select, regularly evaluate and, if necessary, replace the chief executive officer, determine management compensation, and review succession planning.

ii. Review and, where appropriate, approve the major strategies and financial and other objectives, and plans of the corporation.

iii. Advise management on significant issues facing the corporation.

iv. Oversee processes for evaluating the adequacy of internal controls, risk management, financial reporting and compliance, and satisfy itself as to the adequacy of such processes.

v. Nominate directors and ensure that the structure and practices of the board provide for sound corporate governance.

---

[31]Performance was measured using the same data used by Waddock and Graves.
[32]See Easterbrook and Fischel (1981).
[33]Corporations are incorporated under state law, and Delaware is the most popular state for incorporation. The decisions by its Supreme Court are influential in the courts in other states.

The Roundtable also argued that board attention should focus on strategic decisions and the social impacts of corporate decisions, although it drew considerably narrower boundaries on social responsibility than did the task force statement on corporate social responsibility.

The Roundtable recommended a board composed of "a substantial majority of ... outside (nonmanagement directors)" and recommended inclusion of more women and minorities on boards. The Roundtable also stated that "it is highly desirable for a board to have a central core of experienced business executives." Many corporations assign only nonmanagement directors to the audit, compensation, and nominating committees of their boards to ensure that the shareholders' interests are being served by management.

The duty of loyalty supports both Friedman's position and the strategic use of CSR. The business judgment rule, however, means that management and the board have a substantial range of discretion in deciding the extent of that responsibility. Concerns about managerial capitalism and the objectives that management pursues have resulted in direct pressure from institutional investors for a more independent and vigilant board of directors. The nation's largest fund, the California Public Employees' Retirement System (CalPERS), for example, pressures firms to have more independent boards and improve their financial performance. TIAA-CREF, a pension fund for teachers and professors, joined with CalPERS in seeking changes in boards of directors of companies such as Heinz, arguing that the board was not sufficiently independent.

Sarbanes-Oxley

In the wake of the Enron and WorldCom bankruptcies Congress enacted the Public Company Accounting Reform and Investor Protection Act, known as Sarbanes–Oxley after its congressional authors. The law requires a company to identify an independent "financial expert" on its board audit committee and requires the CEO and CFO to certify the firm's financial statements. If those statements are found not to meet the standards in Sarbanes–Oxley, prison terms of up to 10 years and a fine of up to $1 million can be imposed. The law also prohibits audit firms from providing consulting services while conducting an audit. It also established the independent Public Company Accounting Oversight Board as a watchdog over accounting firms. Penalties for destroying, falsifying, or altering records include prison terms of up to 20 years.[34]

Critics of Sarbanes–Oxley argued that it went too far. They worried that it would make it harder to recruit new board members, spur a rash of lawsuits, impose heavy costs for meeting documentation requirements for financial controls, and make firms risk averse. The first two concerns have not materialized, but firms, particularly small firms, have complained about the costs of documentation of their internal controls as required by Section 404.[35] The SEC has sought to lighten the administrative burden on small firms. Whether firms have become more risk averse remains unclear.

Say-On-Pay

A provision in the Dodd–Frank financial reform act of 2010 required corporations to conduct a nonbinding shareholder vote on executive compensation at least once every 3 years. The provision was spurred by criticism of high executive compensation that often did not appear to be the result of good corporate performance. Median CEO compensation for S&P 500 companies was $8.4 million in 2010. The first shareholder votes took place in 2011. Seventy percent of the shares were held by institutional investors, and many of those investors were advised by International Shareholder Services (ISS), founded by corporate governance activist Robert A. G. Monks. ISS advised "no" votes on 293 companies, but shareholders rejected only 39 of 2,532 companies holding votes.[36] Among the 39 were Hewlett-Packard and Stanley Black & Decker. Monks complained, "Say-on-pay is at best a diversion and at worst a deception. You only have

---

[34]The law also separated stock analysis from deal-making of financial services firms. Sarbanes–Oxley increased the maximum prison sentence for mail and wire fraud from 5 to 10 years.

[35]Both management and the external auditors are required to report on the firm's Internal Controls over Financial Reporting.

[36]ISS was criticized by the Center for Executive Compensation for "bias and errors," and the Center director called for stricter regulation of proxy advisory services including ISS. (*Bloomberg Businessweek*, June 20–26, 2011).

the appearance of reform, and it's a cruel hoax." Some of the companies that were given "no" recommendations made changes in their compensation so as to remove the negative recommendation. General Electric received a no recommendation because of an options grant of 2 million shares to CEO Jeffery Immelt, and the options were revised to make the options conditional on meeting performance standards.[37]

The Market for Control

The market for control disciplines management and directors to serve shareholder interests through mergers, acquisitions, hostile takeovers, proxy contests, and depressed market valuations.[38] However, many managers want to be insulated from the market for control, arguing that they are best able to chart the firm's course.[39] Investors often disagree and favor the discipline of the market to the discretion of management; that is, they prefer market capitalism to managerial capitalism. For example, through a series of acquisitions, United Airlines, which had renamed itself Allegis, had included in its system Hertz Rent-A-Car, Westin Hotels, and Hilton International. Pressure on the company for better financial performance caused its board of directors to replace the CEO. Under new management Allegis was broken up, with UAL, Inc., the surviving entity. In his letter to shareholders, the new chairman and CEO wrote, "My objective ... has been ... enhancing near-term stockholder values and the goal of permitting United Airlines to operate successfully and gain in value in the future in a very competitive environment .... We have determined to proceed immediately with the sale of all of our non-airline businesses—Hertz, Westin, and Hilton International—and to distribute the net proceeds from those sales to stockholders."[40]

Institutional investors are an increasingly important force in the market for control. During the 1970s and most of the 1980s, institutional investors were relatively passive and seldom attempted to influence the management of firms. Most institutions voted with management on proxy issues. With institutions now holding 70 percent of the shares of U.S. corporations, compared with slightly over 20 percent in 1970, institutional investors have been crucial in forcing management changes in companies such as General Motors and Eastman Kodak. Pension funds, such as CalPERS, have been concerned about the return on their investments and have increasingly opposed management on proxy challenges, antitakeover charter amendments, and shareholder resolutions directed at forcing management to improve profitability. In addition, the Department of Labor has instructed pension fund managers to vote on proxy issues in the best interests of their beneficiaries.[41] In 1992 the Securities and Exchange Commission issued rules giving shareholders new powers, such as calling special meetings and maintaining confidentiality on proxy measures, which make it easier to take action against management. Although the market for control is active and limits the exercise of managerial capitalism, the imperfections in the market for control leave considerable discretion to management.

Under pressure from corporations and organized labor, Pennsylvania enacted an antitakeover law intended to protect its firms and the jobs they provided in the state. This action provided evidence on both the market for control and managerial responses to the protection of firms and their management. A unique feature of the law was that it gave corporations a window during which they could opt out of one or more of the law's protective provisions. The capital market reaction occurred soon after the bill was introduced in the state legislature. The price of a market basket of 60 companies incorporated in Pennsylvania fell over 5 percent relative to the Standard & Poor's 500 index. As the likelihood increased that the bill would pass, the gap increased. When the state senate passed the bill, the gap was 6.9 percent.[42] Since some firms were expected to opt out of the law, the decrease in market value for those firms that were expected to choose the protection of the law was considerably greater than the average. The capital markets penalized those companies that protected management from the market for control.

---

[37]*Bloomberg Businessweek*, June 20–26, 2011.

[38]See Weston, Chung, and Hoag (1990) for a comprehensive treatment of the market for control, Jensen (1988) for an analysis of the role of takeovers, and Tirole (2005) for insight into the market for control.

[39]See Coffee, Lowenstein, and Rose-Ackerman (1988).

[40]April 25, 1987, letter to Allegis Corporation stockholders from Frank A. Olson.

[41]The Department of Labor has regulatory authority under the Employee Retirement Income Security Act of 1974.

[42]See Karpoff and Malatesta (1989).

SUMMARY

The role of business in society and the extent of its social responsibilities remain subjects of debate. The duties of care and loyalty and the business judgment rule leave considerable discretion to directors and management, but management is not free to rely on its personal preferences for charting the paths of the firms they control. Management and directors face continuing pressure for improved financial performance, which limits management's discretion to pursue social objectives. The chapter case *The Collapse of Enron: Governance and Responsibility* addresses the responsibilities of directors when management pushes the envelope of acceptable practices.

Corporate social responsibility is distinguished from corporate social performance by the presence of a moral duty assigned to the firm. CSP can be conducted for strategic as opposed to moral considerations, and can be rewarded by consumers, investors, or employees. CSP can also be a perquisite for management or can be undertaken in response to social pressure. Social pressure is directed at firms, as in the Wal-Mart chapter case, and can be directed at worst offenders as well as soft targets.

Many companies argue that corporate social performance and corporate financial performance can, and do, go hand in hand. Surveys of the empirical literature indicate that there is a positive but weak correlation between CSP and CFP, and the direction of causation remains an open question. The empirical study, discussed earlier, of the relations among social performance, financial performance, and social pressure found no relation between CSP and CFP, but CFP is decreasing in social pressure. CSP is responsive to social pressure and is decreasing in CFP. Social pressure is decreasing in CFP and increasing in CSP suggesting that soft targets are selected to receive social pressure. For consumer industries, CFP is positively correlated with CSP, and CSP is increasing in CFP. For industrial industries CFP is negatively correlated with CSP, and CSP is decreasing in CFP.

Even Friedman's dictum to maximize profits is subject to the limits of the law and ethical custom, both of which leave a gray area between what is clearly responsible and what is clearly irresponsible. On such issues managers obtain guidance from two primary sources. The first is government, which proscribes as well as prescribes certain actions and provides incentives to adopt certain types of policies. The tax deductibility of philanthropic contributions and the tax advantages provided for hiring disadvantaged youths are examples of such incentives.[43] The second source of guidance is ethics. Ethics provides a basis for reasoning about and evaluating actions and policies. The content of social responsibility ultimately is found in these principles and their moral foundations. Moral foundations, however, do not always provide unambiguous prescriptions nor are the prescriptions provided by different ethics frameworks necessarily the same. The following chapters develop these frameworks and consider applications within the scope of the corporate social responsibility debate.

CASES

The Collapse of Enron: Governance and Responsibility

In an interview with PBS in March 2001 when doubts were being raised about Enron, President and CEO Jeffrey Skilling said, "We are the good guys. We are on the side of the angels."

Addressing Jeffrey Skilling in a House hearing, Representative Edward J. Markey (D-MA), said, "You are employing the Sergeant Shultz defense of 'I see nothing. I hear nothing.'" (Sergeant Shultz was a character in the television series Hogan's Heroes.*)*

Representative James Greenwood (R-PA) referred to Enron CFO Andrew Fastow as the "Betty Crocker of cooked books."

Enron was a great business success soaring to a market capitalization in excess of $60 billion and ranking seventh on the Fortune 500 list. It was frequently voted one of the most admired companies and one of the best companies to work for. Enron also had a cutthroat corporate culture in which pushing the envelope was routine and failure led to departure.

Enron was creative in its financial arrangements, entering into numerous partnerships with a variety of entities. The purpose of some of the partnerships and their related-party transactions was to transfer certain assets, their associated borrowings, and their profits, or more often losses, to the

---

[43]Corporations can deduct charitable contributions up to 15 percent of their net income.

partnership. This allowed Enron, with the approval of its auditor Arthur Andersen, to keep losses off its income statement and debt off its balance sheet. Many of the partnerships were organized by Enron executives, some of whom invested in them with guaranteed returns. Negotiations with the partnerships were thus not at arm's length, with Chief Financial Officer Andrew Fastow both representing Enron and participating through limited partnerships in deals with Enron. Fastow and several lower-level employees "were enriched, in the aggregate, by tens of millions of dollars they should never have received."[44] The participation of the employees other than Fastow had not been approved by the chairman and CEO.

The partnerships allowed Enron to keep substantial losses off its financial statements. From the third quarter of 2000 through the third quarter of 2001 Enron reported a before-tax profit of $1.5 billion, but if certain partnerships referred to as Raptors had been consolidated into its financial statement, its earnings would have been $429 million. Although Enron stated that the partnerships protected the company from risk, the risk was actually borne by Enron through guarantees to the Raptors. As Enron's share price declined in 2001 the Raptors' ability to protect Enron's earnings disappeared. CEO Jeffrey Skilling resigned abruptly in August 2001, while proclaiming that Enron was in good health.

Under increasing pressure from its own failed investments, facing difficulty in obtaining financing, and under scrutiny from Wall Street, on October 16 Enron reported a third-quarter pre-tax loss of $710 million and subtracted $1.2 billion from shareholders' equity. One billion dollars of the write-down was due to the correction of "accounting errors," and $200 million was due to the termination of the Raptors. In November Enron restated its earnings back through 1997. The restatements of earnings included the consolidation of a number of partnerships that had been used to keep debt and earnings fluctuations off Enron's financial statements. Fastow was asked to leave the company on October 23, and the Securities and Exchange Commission began an investigation. Revelation of the hidden losses destroyed any remaining confidence in the company, and its share price continued its decline from its peak of $81.39 on January 25, 2001, to less than a dollar in December 2001. Enron filed for chapter 11 bankruptcy on December 2.[45] A flurry of class action and other lawsuits were filed against Enron and Arthur Andersen for securities fraud and other violations.

HISTORY OF THE COMPANY

After stints as a corporate economist, assistant professor, Federal Power Commission staff member, and undersecretary of the Department of Interior, Kenneth Lay became vice president of Florida Gas and then of the Continental Group. He then became president and CEO of Transco, a Houston-based gas company, and then of Houston Natural Gas. In 1985 he arranged the merger of Houston Natural Gas and InterNorth, and the merged companies subsequently became Enron.[46] Enron operated fixed assets in power generation and natural gas transmission and organized an energy trading market in which it traded electricity and natural gas. Enron also had a large merchant investment business in structured transactions in fixed assets and trading. Enron was an aggressive advocate of deregulating energy markets.

In 2000 Enron had sales of $101 billion and assets of $47.3 billion. Enron operated 30,000 miles of pipelines and 15,000 miles of fiber optic cable and had 19,000 employees in 2002.

SPECIAL PURPOSE ENTERPRISES AND ACCOUNTING STATEMENTS

A central component of Enron's strategy was to utilize subsidiaries and special purpose entities including partnerships for the funding and structuring of projects. Enron was estimated to have 3,000 partnerships and subsidiaries. It had over 140 subsidiaries in the Netherlands, where tax laws gave favorable treatment to holding companies with subsidiaries in other countries. The holding companies could loan funds to subsidiaries such as Enron Columbia Energy BV, and the interest on the loan was not taxable.

In partnerships named Marlin and Osprey, Enron formed an investment trust, lending its stock to the partnerships for use as collateral.[47] The partnership raised small amounts of outside equity and raised most of its funds by issuing debt with the Enron stock as collateral. The partnership then formed a joint venture with Enron in which Enron provided real assets to the joint venture in exchange for funds used to pay off debt on the assets. The debt in the joint venture did not appear on Enron's books, but if the joint venture were to fail or be unable to repay its debt obligations, Enron would have to provide shares to cover the debt payments. These partnerships were disclosed only in the fine print of Enron's annual report. In marketing such structured transactions Citigroup described one of the benefits as removing "certain items from 'plain view,' thus enhancing the appearance of the balance sheet."[48]

Enron used a variety of other means to keep debt off its books, one of which was a prepaid swap. For example, in December 2000 Enron signed a contract to deliver natural gas to Mahonia Ltd. over a 5-year period and simultaneously signed a contract with Stonehill Aegean Ltd. to purchase the gas to be delivered to Mahonia. In the deals Mahonia prepaid the fair value of the contract, while Enron's payment to Stonehill was to be spread over 5 years. This in effect gave Enron a loan of $330 million at a 7 percent interest rate, but the loan did not appear on Enron's balance sheet. Mahonia and Stonehill were affiliated companies linked to JPMorgan Chase, which structured the swap.[49] Citigroup reportedly loaned $2.4 billion to Enron through a series of prepaid swaps.[50]

[44]The Report of Investigation by the Special Investigative Committee of the Board of Directors of Enron Corp., February 1, 2002 [Special Report], p. 3.
[45]Subsequent to filing for bankruptcy Enron agreed to a merger with Dynergy, but Dynergy backed out of the agreement shortly thereafter.

[46]*New York Times,* February 3, 2002.
[47]*New York Times,* February 14, 2002.
[48]Ibid.
[49]*New York Times,* February 19, 2002.
[50]*New York Times,* February 17, 2002.

Enron also established special purpose enterprises that participated in related-party transactions to keep certain assets and debt off its balance sheet and shield its earnings. Accounting for the enterprises was subject to generally accepted accounting principles. Enron could avoid having to consolidate these special purpose enterprises in its financial statements if they satisfied two conditions. One was that the enterprises were independently controlled, and the other was an SEC requirement that 3 percent of its assets be at risk; that is, outside equity of at least 3 percent was required.

CHEWCO

In 1993 Enron established a partnership named JEDI (Joint Energy Development Investments) with the California Public Employees' Retirement System (CalPERS) as the limited partner. JEDI initially invested in natural gas pipelines and was not consolidated in Enron's financial statements because Enron and CalPERS exercised joint control.

In 1997 CalPERS wanted out of JEDI, and Fastow established Chewco Investments LP to buy CalPERS's interest for $383 million.[51] Accounting rules would have required disclosure of the partnership if an Enron senior executive, such as Fastow, were to manage Chewco, so Fastow assigned Michael J. Kopper, who reported to Fastow, to manage Chewco. Disclosure was not required because of Kopper's rank.

Chewco was financed by a $240 million loan from Barclays Bank PLC, guaranteed by Enron, and by an advance of $132 million from JEDI. To keep Chewco off Enron's books, a minimum 3 percent equity investment, or $11.5 million, had to be invested. To provide the outside equity, Fastow and Kopper established Big River Funding as Chewco's limited partner, and Little River Funding was established to own Big River Funding. Kopper invested $125,000 of his own funds in the two entities and arranged to borrow the remaining $11.4 million "equity" from Barclays.[52] The credit document was written so that Barclays could treat it as a loan and Enron could treat it as equity for accounting purposes. For example, instead of referring to interest, the credit document referred to "yield." Barclays ultimately loaned only $6.8 million, so Chewco did not meet the SEC outside equity requirement.[53] Chewco thus was incorrectly kept off Enron's books with neither its debt nor its losses consolidated. Enron repurchased Chewco in March 2001, and Kopper and his partner Dodson received $10.5 million for their investment. In November 2001 Enron disclosed Chewco when it revised its financial statements.

Enron also engaged in a variety of questionable accounting practices regarding revenue and income from JEDI and Chewco. For example, Chewco held 12 million shares of Enron stock, which were carried at fair value. As its stock appreciated, Enron recorded a share of the appreciation as its own income, which is contrary to generally accepted accounting principles. Moreover, as its stock price began to fall, Enron's $90 million share of the loss on the shares held by Chewco was not recorded as a decrease in income. Arthur Andersen approved both the recognition of appreciation as income and not recognizing the decrease in value as a reduction in income.

LJM PARTNERSHIPS

In 1999 Fastow proposed establishing a partnership LJM Cayman LP (LJM1) for the ostensible purpose of hedging Enron's investment in Rhythms NetConnections by obtaining investments from outside investors.[54] Fastow would be the general partner, since, he explained, that would help attract outside investors. He said he would personally invest $1 million in LJM1. The proposal was approved by Lay, Skilling, and the board, which determined that Fastow serving as managing partner of LJM1 would not "adversely affect the interests of Enron." Such a determination was required by Enron's code of conduct.

Enron also sought to take advantage of the "embedded" value resulting from a forward contract with an investment bank to purchase Enron shares at a fixed price. Enron restructured the contract, releasing 3.4 million shares of its stock to be used as collateral. To "hedge" Enron's investment in Rhythms, LJM1 received these Enron shares in exchange for a note to pay $64 million to Enron. LJM1 then transferred the shares to a newly created limited partnership, Swap Sub, that gave Enron a put option on Enron's entire investment in Rhythms.[55] The put option entitled Enron to sell its Rhythms shares to Swap Sub at $54 per share in June 2004.[56] Enron had purchased its 5.4 million shares in Rhythms at $1.85 per share in March 1998, and when Rhythms went public in 1999 Enron's holding was valued at $300 million. This arrangement, however, did not provide a true hedge because if Enron's shares declined in value, Swap Sub would be unable to cover the put. In addition, Swap Sub did not have the required 3 percent equity investment. Arthur Andersen, which had not objected to the arrangement, concluded in October 2001 that it had made an error.

Enron began to unwind the hedging arrangement in the first quarter of 2000 in a series of complicated transactions. Five lower-level Enron employees plus Fastow formed a limited partnership, Southampton Place LP, to participate with LJM1 in the unwind. Within 2 months a $25,000 investment returned $4.5 million funneled into a "family foundation," whose limited partners were Fastow and the other five employees. Two of the five also invested $5,800 and received a return of $1 million in 2 months. These employees did not seek a determination from Lay and Skilling that their participation would not adversely affect the interests of Enron. The Report of the Special Committee established by the board in the wake

---

[51]Following a *Star Wars* theme, there were partnerships named JEDI, Obi 1, and Chewco, after Chewbacca.

[52]Shortly thereafter, Kopper transferred his financial interests to his domestic partner, William Dodson.

[53]The remaining $6.6 million was funded from a distribution by JEDI from the sale of an energy company.

---

[54]Fastow named the LJM partnerships using the first letters of his wife's and children's names.

[55]Enron could not sell its shares in Rhythms before the end of 1999.

[56]PricewaterhouseCoopers reviewed the transactions and concurred that the arrangement was fair to the parties.

of the collapse stated, "Enron employees involved in the partnerships were enriched, in the aggregate, by tens of millions of dollars they should never have received—Fastow by at least $30 million, Kopper by at least $10 million, two others by $1 million each ...." The Special Committee report concluded, "We have not seen any evidence that any of the employees, including Fastow, obtained approval from the chairman and CEO under the code of conduct to participate financially in the profits of an entity doing business with Enron. While every code violation is a matter to be taken seriously, these violations are particularly troubling."

LJM1 was also used to take certain assets off Enron's balance sheet and increase its current income. Enron had a 65 percent interest in a Brazilian company building a power plant that was "experiencing significant construction problems." Enron sold a portion of its interest to LJM1, leaving it no longer technically in control of the company and allowing Enron to take its investment in the company off its balance sheet. This also allowed Enron to mark-to-market the value of a gas supply contract an Enron unit had with the Brazilian company. This increased Enron's income for the second half of 1999 by $65 million.[57]

On Fastow's recommendation the board approved the establishment of a second (LJM2) partnership with Fastow as the general partner.[58] LJM2 raised $394 million primarily from 50 limited partners, including Merrill Lynch, JPMorgan Chase, and Citigroup. In addition, Fastow and other Enron employees invested in LJM2 through two limited partnerships, one of which, Big Doe, was managed by Kopper, and the other by Fastow himself. The LJM partnerships were in a gray area of accounting standards and were not consolidated with Enron's financial statements.

RAPTORS

Raptor was Enron's name for a partnership used to hedge its merchant investments portfolio in projects and companies. The Raptors were a result of the initial success of the Rhythms "hedge." Because its merchant investments were marked-to-market, changes in their value affected Enron's earnings on a quarterly basis. The first Raptor, named Talon, was established in April 2000. To provide the 3 percent equity required to keep Talon off Enron's balance sheet, LJM2 provided $30 million. LJM2 was guaranteed a payment of $41 million before Talon could engage in hedging. For accounting purposes the $41 million was treated as a return on LJM2's investment, leaving its $30 million to satisfy the 3 percent requirement. However, Enron, which contributed its shares to Talon, would keep 100 percent of its earnings. Talon's only assets thus were Enron's shares.

To pay LJM2 Enron signed a contract with Talon under which Enron paid $41 million in exchange for a put option, the right to sell Enron shares to Talon at a fixed price. Talon then paid the $41 million to LJM2, allowing Talon to begin operations. Enron and Talon then signed a contract under which

Talon agreed to cover Enron's losses on certain investments in exchange for sharing in any appreciation of the investments. This protected Enron's income statement from losses on the merchant investments. The Raptor's ability to cover losses depended on the price of Enron shares, however. If Enron's share price were to decline to a $47 trigger, Talon would be unable to cover Enron's losses.

Four Raptors were used to keep $504 million of losses off Enron's books, but as its stock price fell, triggers were tripped that threatened their ability to protect Enron's reported earnings. Early in 2001 Enron restructured the Raptors to reestablish the facade that they were covering risks, but after the restructuring they were even more vulnerable. Within weeks of the restructuring Enron reported a profit of $425 million for the first quarter of 2001.

In referring to Talon the Board secretary wrote, "Does not transfer economic risk, but transfers P&L volatility."[59] The Board Special Committee stated, "Enron still bore virtually all of the economic risk. In effect, Enron was hedging risk with itself." The Special Committee concluded, "Especially after the restructuring, the Raptors were little more than a highly complex accounting construct that was destined to collapse."

As the Raptors were collapsing, Enron and Andersen accountants discovered that Enron's accounting for three of the Raptors was wrong. The shares Enron contributed to the Raptors had been treated as an increase in notes payable and a corresponding increase in shareholders' equity. This increased shareholders' equity by $1 billion during the first half of 2001. In October and November Enron restated its income and balance statements and consolidated the LJM partnerships.

In August Skilling abruptly resigned. After the resignation Sherron Watkins, an Enron vice president, wrote to CEO Kenneth Lay warning of the "inappropriateness" of some transactions. She wrote, "To the layman on the street it will look like we recognized funds flow of $800 million from merchant asset sales in 1999 by selling to a vehicle (Condor) that we capitalized with a promise of Enron stock in later years."[60] She also wrote, "I am incredibly nervous that we will implode in a wave of accounting scandals."[61]

As a result of Watkins's letter Enron asked its outside law firm Vinson & Elkins to prepare a report on its transactions. The report presented on October 15 concluded that nothing wrong had been done, although it noted that both Enron and Andersen agreed that the accounting had been "creative and aggressive." Although the law firm found nothing wrong, the report stated, "Within Enron, there appeared to be an air of secrecy regarding the LJM partnerships and suspicion that those Enron employees acting for LJM were receiving special or additional compensation."

---

[57]Special Report, pp. 136–137.
[58]The LJM partnerships participated in 20 transactions with Enron.

[59]The reference to "P&L volatility" meant that the profit and loss effects would not appear on Enron's books.
[60]Later in congressional testimony she referred to the culture at Enron as "arrogant."
[61]See Watkins (2003) for her analysis of moral responsibility in the Enron episode.

Not everyone was fooled by Enron. A few analysts issued warnings, but most analysts followed the herd. In a conference call with analysts, Enron released its first quarter 2001 earnings and proclaimed the quarter a great success. One skeptical analyst asked why the company was issuing an income statement without the accompanying balance sheet and cash flow statement. Skilling brushed aside the question, mocking the analyst.

Citigroup, a major lender to Enron, decided to hedge some of its risk. Fifteen months before Enron's collapse and again in May 2001 Citigroup sold 5-year notes to investors who were guaranteed a return plus their principal unless Enron went bankrupt or failed to repay a loan. In those events the investors would be paid in Enron debt. This was the largest hedge Citigroup had ever taken against a company.

401(k) PLANS AND DEFERRED COMPENSATION

Enron employees participated in 401(k) retirement plans, and most of them held Enron shares. The company matched employee contributions with equal contributions of Enron shares, and employees were prohibited from selling their shares until age 55.[62] Enron shares represented approximately 65 percent of the assets of the plans. During 2001 the company continued to tout its stock to employees as a good investment. Enron's collapse caused many employees to lose most of their retirement funds.

In addition to its 401(k) plans Enron had a deferred compensation plan under which managers could defer portions of their compensation. During 2001 before Enron filed for bankruptcy a number of executives withdrew funds from their deferred compensation plans, but others, including executives who had already retired, did not do so. As a result of the bankruptcy filing, those participating in the plan became unsecured creditors of the firm with their compensation to be determined by the bankruptcy court. Allegations were made that current executives were able to withdraw funds from their deferred compensation plans and were paid their bonuses in November prior to the bankruptcy filing, while others were not allowed to do so.

During Enron's slide in 2001 Kenneth Lay sold $100 million in Enron shares, including $70.1 million sold back to the company. Sales in public markets had to be disclosed in the month following the sale, whereas sales back to a company did not have to be disclosed until the following year.

Days before filing for bankruptcy, Enron paid $100 million in retention bonuses to 600 key employees deemed essential to the continued operation of the company. Enron also laid off 4,500 employees, giving them severance pay of $4,500.

POLITICAL CONTRIBUTIONS

Enron and its executives made substantial political contributions to members of Congress and state legislatures. Since 1989 it had given $5.7 million to members of Congress, with $2.0 million contributed in the 2000 election cycle. Approximately two-thirds went to Republicans. Approximately half the House and two-thirds of the Senate had received contributions from Enron executives. Enron also contributed substantially to state officeholders and parties. The company also lobbied intensely for the deregulation of energy markets and had participated in Vice President Richard Cheney's energy task force. Enron had also implemented a plan to cultivate a relationship with Vice President Al Gore during his presidential campaign.[63]

The contributions provided access in both Washington and state capitols for Enron's lobbying campaign. When it was collapsing, Enron executives sought relief from the Bush administration. Although he and President George W. Bush were well acquainted, Kenneth Lay went to the Secretaries of Commerce and Treasury, neither of whom contacted the president.[64] Secretary of Commerce Donald Evans rejected Lay's request for assistance. Evans commented on *Meet the Press,* "If I had stepped in, I think it would have been an egregious abuse of the office of Secretary of Commerce." Lay also called Secretary of Treasury Paul O'Neill and enlisted Robert Rubin, former Secretary of Treasury in the Clinton administration and currently a top executive at Citigroup, to call the Secretary urging assistance for Enron.[65] Secretary O'Neill rejected Enron's request.

Enron also attempted to lobby for deregulation with the Federal Energy Regulatory Commission headed by Pat Wood III, who had previously headed the Texas Public Utility Commission. Wood, however, was unresponsive to Enron and angered the company by imposing caps on wholesale prices of electricity in the West.

THE BOARD OF DIRECTORS

The Board of Directors was responsible for the performance of the company and had a fiduciary duty to shareholders. As Enron increased its use of related-party transactions, the board increased the control over those transactions and ordered annual reviews of all LJM transactions. The Special Committee (p. 12) concluded, however, "These controls as designed were not rigorous enough, and their implementation and oversight was inadequate at both the management and board levels." In addition, Enron's outside counsel "Vinson & Elkins should have brought a stronger, more objective and more critical voice to the disclosure process" (p. 26). Referring to Enron management and Arthur Andersen, outside director Robert K. Jaedicke, chairman of the Board Audit Committee, said in congressional testimony, "It now appears that none of them fulfilled their duty to [the board]. We do not manage the company. We do not do the auditing. We are not detectives …. I am not confident as I sit here today that we would have gotten to the truth with any amount of questioning and discussion."[66]

---

[62]Contributions in stock and restrictions on when the shares could be sold were common features of corporate retirement plans.

[63]*New York Times,* February 18, 2002.

[64]Lay had been chair of then-Governor Bush's business council.

[65]In 1999 Enron invited Rubin to join its board of directors, but he declined the offer.

[66]Six board members including Jaedicke resigned in March 2002.

Throughout the rise and fall of Enron the board apparently did not block the questionable transactions and financial arrangements that led to the collapse. The board maintained that it was unaware of some of the deals and that data were withheld from it. For example, Chewco was approved by the board during a telephone conference call without disclosure of the "equity" loan by Barclays to Chewco's limited partner. Kopper's management of Chewco was approved by Skilling, but Enron's code of conduct required it to be brought to the board.

After the announcement of its third-quarter 2001 loss, Enron named William Powers, dean of the University of Texas School of Law, to its Board of Directors. The board then appointed a Special Committee headed by Powers to produce a report on the collapse. The Special Committee concluded that the board had failed in "its oversight duties."

The Special Committee assigned much of the responsibility to Kenneth Lay in his role as a director. The report stated, "Lay approved the arrangements under which Enron permitted Fastow to engage in related-party transactions with Enron and authorized the Rhythms transaction and three of the Raptor vehicles. He bears significant responsibility for those flawed decisions, as well as for Enron's failure to implement sufficiently rigorous procedural controls to prevent the abuses that flowed from this inherent conflict of interest. In connection with the LJM transactions, the evidence we have examined suggests that Lay functioned almost entirely as a director, and less as a member of management. It appears that both he and Skilling agreed, and the board understood, that Skilling was the senior member of management responsible for the LJM relationship." In the initial congressional hearings on the collapse, five Enron executives, Lay, Fastow, Kopper, chief accounting officer Richard Causey, and chief risk officer Richard Buy, exercised their constitutional right under the Fifth Amendment to protection against self-incrimination.[67] Jeffrey Skilling testified but had difficulty recalling what had happened.

ARTHUR ANDERSEN

Enron's auditor was Arthur Andersen, one of the big five accounting firms. Andersen also provided consulting services to the company. In 2000 Enron paid a total of $52 million to Andersen with approximately half for audit services. Enron paid $5.7 million to Andersen for nonaudit services provided to Chewco and the LJM partnerships.

Andersen issued no qualifications in its audit reports and apparently approved all transactions brought to it. Andersen claimed to be ignorant of most of the questionable partnership arrangements, however. Andersen indicated that it was not given access to data on Chewco, and if it had been it would have required a restatement of earnings.

Andersen CEO Joseph Berardino subsequently testified before Congress that it had questioned $51 million in earnings in 1997 and considered requiring adjustments in reported earnings. Andersen, however, decided that the adjustments were not "material" and did not require them. Berardino stated that the adjustments were "less than 8 percent" of normalized earnings. In November when Enron corrected its financial statements back to 1997, the $51 million adjustment was made. Berardino also stated that the Chewco/JEDI arrangements involved "possible illegal acts."

In October after the announcement of Enron's third-quarter loss and the write-down in its shareholders equity, Andersen's Houston office, which had the principal responsibility for the audits, began shredding documents associated with its audits.[68] The managing director said that he had consulted with a lawyer in Andersen's headquarters and had been advised to shred the documents. After the telephone conversation the lawyer had sent an e-mail reminding the Houston office that Andersen policy required the retention of certain audit documents and allowed the shredding of other documents. The managing director was subsequently fired. ▮

Preparation Questions

1. What factors led to the collapse of Enron?
2. Should Enron have used partnerships in the manner it did? What, if anything, is wrong with using partnerships such as the Raptors, Chewco, and the LJMs?
3. What responsibilities does the board of directors have in such situations? What responsibilities did and should Enron and its directors have for its employees' 401(k) plans?
4. Why did Arthur Andersen and Vinson & Elkins not conclude that there were problems with Enron's structuring of transactions?
5. Is there an inherent conflict of interest for an outside auditor that also provides other services to its client?
6. What, if anything, was wrong with Enron's political contributions and lobbying? What assistance did the contributions buy Enron when it was collapsing?
7. How much of its financial arrangements should Enron have disclosed?
8. What responsibilities does an audit firm have?

Source: This case was prepared by Professor David P. Baron from public sources including the Report of Investigation by the Special Investigative Committee of the Board of Directors of Enron Corp., February 1, 2002 [Special Report]. Copyright © 2002 by David P. Baron. All rights reserved. Reprinted with permission. This case was written in February 2002 when facts were still being revealed.

---

[67]Causey and Buy were fired in February 2002.

[68]The managing director of the Houston office asked the staff to work overtime so that the shredding would not delay service to other clients.

Wal-Mart: Nonmarket Pressure and Reputation Risk (B): A New Nonmarket Strategy[69]

In 2004 Wal-Mart decided to reduce the nonmarket pressure it faced by establishing a "gentler" image with respect to its competition. It decided not to threaten its competitors aggressively with low price promotions during the holiday period, as it had done the previous year with toys. Instead of lowering its prices, Wal-Mart raised its prices slightly. Its competitors responded by cutting their prices and taking business away from Wal-Mart. Wal-Mart was forced to cut its prices in response. Wal-Mart reversed its strategy in 2005, announcing it would match its rivals' price discounts and offering door-busters on Black Friday, the Friday after Thanksgiving. "I would rather be accused of driving people out of business than getting fired because we don't have any sales," said CEO H. Lee Scott.[70]

To deal with the nonmarket pressures it faced, Wal-Mart established a war room at its Bentonville headquarters and staffed it with people with political experience, since many of the criticisms of the company were orchestrated by former political operatives. The company also established an Action Alley in Bentonville and one in Washington, D.C. to deal with breaking issues. Wal-Mart hired advisors including Michael Deaver, former advisor to President Reagan, and Leslie Dach, a former media consultant to Bill Clinton.[71] The company also hired Edelman, a public relations firm that had worked with activist groups.

To deal with grassroots critics, Wal-Mart opened eight community relations offices in various locations, including Chicago, Los Angeles, and New York where local opposition had blocked new store openings.

Wal-Mart began to respond to its critics. Scott began meeting with a number of critics including the Investor Responsibility Research Center (IRRC) and environmental and anti-sweatshop groups. To address the sweatshop criticism, Wal-Mart worked with Business for Social Responsibility and met with IRRC leaders. In addition, Scott met with members of Congress and the Congressional Black Caucus.

On January 13, 2005, Wal-Mart took out full-page advertisements in 100 newspapers nationwide explaining its wage and benefit policies and its employment practices. In the ad Scott wrote, "When special-interest groups and critics spread misinformation about Wal-Mart, the public deserves the truth. Everyone is entitled to their own opinions about our company, but they are not entitled to make up their own facts."[72] The ad stated that Wal-Mart's average wage was nearly twice the minimum wage and reported that more than half its employees viewed benefits as important to their employment

decisions. The company also stated, "Seventy-four percent of Wal-Mart's hourly associates work full-time. That's well above the 20–40 percent typically found in the retail industry." More than half its associates owned Wal-Mart stock through a profit-sharing/401(k) plan.

Earlier Wal-Mart had test marketed an ad explaining the company's policies. The company reported an average hourly wage of $10.37 an hour and stated that medical coverage was available to both full- and part-time employees. The ad also explained, "Many of our jobs are held by working 'retirees,' working spouses supplementing a family income and students working through school." A unique feature of the ad was pointing out the benefits consumers received. The ad cited a study by the Los Angeles Economic Development Corporation that concluded, "with the entry of Wal-Mart into Southern California, area consumers will save $3.7 billion annually, or $589 per household per year, once Wal-Mart reaches 20 percent market share in the region."[73]

In April 2005, Wal-Mart held its first-ever media conference. In response to criticism by Wal-Mart Watch, Scott reported that an internal company audit revealed that 7 percent of workers were on government health benefits prior to being hired, but 2 years later only 3 percent were still on government assistance.[74] Referring to the large number of people who applied for jobs at new Wal-Mart stores, Scott said, "It doesn't make sense that people would line up for jobs that are worse than they could get elsewhere, with fewer benefits and less opportunity."[75] Scott urged Congress to raise the minimum wage, and critics noted that that would harm Wal-Mart's competitors more than Wal-Mart itself.

Wal-Mart also ran ads in Asian languages on Chinese, Vietnamese, and Filipino television stations. It also ran a series of television ads in which minority and women associates told of their satisfaction working for Wal-Mart. Earlier Wal-Mart had agreed to sponsor PBS and NPR programs and began a $500,000 fellowship program for minority journalism students at nine universities. The company also sponsored *The Scholar*, a reality series in which students competed for a full-ride college scholarship worth $300,000. Wal-Mart was woven into the plots of the shows.[76]

Wal-Mart began to work with Conservation International and the Natural Resources Defense Council on environmental initiatives. The company evaluated the packaging of products it sold and discovered that reducing packaging also reduced shipping costs. Wal-Mart also opened an Environmental Demonstration Store and planned to open another. The store used solar panels, wind turbines, burned the used oil from oil

---

[69]See the Part I integrative case *Wal-Mart: Nonmarket Pressure and Reputation Risk (A).*

[70]Michael Barbaro, "Back to Basics at Wal-Mart: Spare No Rivals," *New York Times,* November 23, 2005.

[71]Michael Barbaro, "A New Weapon for Wal-Mart: A War Room," *New York Times,* November 1, 2005.

[72]"Wal-Mart Launches Nationwide Campaign to Set the Record Straight," press release, Wal-Mart, January 13, 2005, http://walmartstores.com/GlobalWMStoresWeb/navigate.do?catg=26&contId=4901 (May 23, 2006).

[73]*San Jose Mercury News,* September 23, 2005.

[74]Ann Zimmeran, "Wal-Mart Stores Defends Its Image, Wages and Benefits," *Wall Street Journal,* April 6, 2005.

[75]Steven Greenhouse, "Wal-Mart's Chief Calls Its Critics Unrealistic," *New York Times,* April 6, 2005.

[76]Stuart Elliott, "Wal-Mart's New Realm: Reality TV," *New York Times,* June 3, 2005.

changes, and burned fat used to fry chickens.[77] It also had a computerized heating and cooling system and used low-mercury fluorescent lamps and electronic ballasts.

In 2005 Wal-Mart announced a $35 million, 10-year Acres for America program to offset the nearly 140,000 acres that its current stores occupied plus its planned expansion over the next 10 years. The company formed a partnership with the Fish and Wildlife Foundation for the purchase of the acreage. The land would be available for hunting, fishing, and other outdoor activities and for sustainable logging.

In October 2005 Wal-Mart announced a major environmental initiative focused on reducing energy use. The initiative included improving the efficiency of energy use in its supercenters and other stores. It also pledged to improve the fuel efficiency of its huge truck fleet by 25 percent over 3 years and by 100 percent over 10 years. The company announced that it would invest $500 million annually to reduce its emissions of greenhouse gasses by 20 percent over 7 years. Wal-Mart also pledged to use its power to encourage its suppliers to be more energy efficient and to reduce their packaging. The initiative drew praise from Environmental Defense and the Sierra Club. A spokesperson for WakeUpWalMart.com, however, said, "It is a diversionary tactic. Wal-Mart understands that they have a growing public relations disaster on their hands."[78]

In 2005 Wal-Mart established a $25 million private equity fund to support businesses owned by women and minorities that could supply the company—approximately 8.5 percent of Wal-Mart's U.S. suppliers were women or minority owned. Spokeswoman Linda Blakely reported that women and minority-owned suppliers sold $3 billion of goods to the company compared to $2 million in the mid-1990s.[79] Blakely denied that the establishment of the fund was in response to the class-action lawsuit on behalf of 1.6 million current and past women employees or the lawsuit filed by two black truck drivers who claimed they had been denied jobs because of their race.

In November 2005, Wal-Mart went further and held a conference in which economists presented analyses of its economic impact. Wal-Mart presented its own study conducted by Global Insight.[80] The study concluded that between 1985 and 2004 Wal-Mart had lowered the Consumer Price Index by 3.1 percent, representing an annual savings of $2,329 for an average household. Wages were depressed by 2.2 percent, which was less than the decrease in the CPI. Benefits were not taken into account, however. The study concluded that Wal-Mart did not pay less than market wages, was more capital intensive than its competitors, and had efficient distribution and inventory control systems. The study reported that on net Wal-Mart had created 210,000 jobs. The other studies presented mixed findings, with one finding a similar impact on wages as in the Global Insight study. One study showed that Wal-Mart's entry into the grocery business reduced prices by 5 percent more than supermarkets would have reduced their prices in the absence of competition by Wal-Mart.

Wal-Mart also announced expanded health care benefits including reduced co-payments for generic drugs and extended its $11 a month health care coverage to at least half its employees. It also planned to open 50 clinics in its U.S. stores that would provide treatment for both customers and employees.

Wal-Mart decided to review its employment practices pertaining to diversity. It formed Business Resources Groups composed of women, African-Americans, Latinos, Asian-Americans, American Indians, gays, and disabled employees that met at Wal-Mart headquarters to provide advice.[81] The groups also provided advice on marketing.

In December 2005, "Working Families for Wal-Mart" was formed to counter the company's critics. Its Web site, www.forwalmart.com, stated that the organization was "standing up for Wal-Mart and helping it keep doing great things for families and communities." The site stated the organization was "committed to fostering open and honest dialogue with elected officials, opinion makers and community leaders that conveys the positive contributions of Wal-Mart to working families." The steering committee for the organization included religious leaders, community leaders, a former woman marine, and Pat Boone. Working Families for Wal-Mart was partly funded by Wal-Mart as well as supported by Taylor Gross, media operations coordinator for the Republicans in the 2000 elections.[82]

Working Families for Wal-Mart commissioned a survey by RT Strategies, a bipartisan firm. The survey found that:

- 71 percent of Americans believe Wal-Mart is good for consumers while 63 percent of union households hold the same belief.
- 58 percent of Americans and 54 percent of union households believe union leaders should make protecting union jobs a higher priority than attacking Wal-Mart.
- 60 percent of Americans say the campaign against Wal-Mart is not a good use of dues and 44 percent of union households agree.
- 54 percent of Americans and 42 percent of union households believe the campaign against Wal-Mart makes labor union leaders less relevant to solving the economic challenges facing working families today.

Critics of the survey noted that the "preface to some questions contrasted nonunion Wal-Mart's job growth with unionized General Motors' job losses."[83]

To reduce opposition to its store openings in urban areas, Wal-Mart announced a policy to reduce the impact on small businesses. Scott said, "We see we can be better for communities than we have been in the past if we are willing to stretch

[77]"Lee Scott on Why Wal-Mart Is Playing Nicer," *BusinessWeek,* October 3, 2005.

[78]Michael Barbaro and Felicity Barringer, "Wal-Mart to Seek Savings in Energy," *New York Times,* October 25, 2005.

[79]Michael Barbaro, "Wal-Mart to Start Equity Fund to Help Diversify Its Suppliers," *New York Times,* October 19, 2005.

[80]Global Insight was formed by the merger of DRI and Wharton Econometric Forecasting Associates.

[81]*San Jose Mercury News,* January 8, 2006.

[82]*Arkansas Democrat-Gazette,* December 22, 2005.

[83]Associated Press State & Local Wire, January 4, 2006.

ourselves and our resources."[84] Wal-Mart established jobs and opportunities zones in 50 cities in which it hoped to open stores and vowed to locate in areas that traditionally had been shunned by other retailers. Wal-Mart planned to help local businesses directly by placing advertisements for them in newspapers and on its in-store radio network. It also planned to provide coaching for local retailers and financial support for local chambers of commerce.

To reduce opposition from local banks to its industrial bank application in Utah, Wal-Mart pledged not to open any branch banks. The application was opposed by the Independent Community Bankers of America, the North Dakota Bankers Association, the American Bankers Association, and individual banks. Wal-Mart received support from the Salvation Army and the National Center for Missing and Exploited Children, both of which had traditionally been supported by the company.

Wal-Mart had refused to sell the Plan B contraceptive, also known as RU-486 or the morning-after pill, in its 3,700 pharmacies. When the state of Massachusetts ordered Wal-Mart to sell the pills, the company announced that it would do so in all states with the same requirement. Wal-Mart also announced a so-called conscientious objector policy in which a pharmacist could direct a customer to another pharmacist or pharmacy.

Wal-Mart announced a new position of senior director of stakeholder engagement and sought "an innovative, out-of-the box thinker" to "help pioneer a new model of how Wal-Mart works with outside stakeholders, resulting in fundamental changes in how the company does business."[85] Wal-Mart also announced a search for a person to conduct "opposition research" and oversee its "crisis communications program" and another for a person to "mobilize resources" during a "crisis situation."[86] ▪

Preparation Questions

1. Evaluate the steps Wal-Mart has taken in developing a nonmarket strategy in response to the social pressure it faces.
2. What is Wal-Mart's motivation for its nonmarket strategy?
3. What else should Wal-Mart do, if anything?

Source: This case was prepared from public sources by David P. Baron. Copyright © 2006 by the Trustees of the Leland Stanford Junior University. All rights reserved. Reprinted with permission.

Facebook and Online Privacy

INTRODUCTION

In 2011 Facebook users exceeded 800 million people, and on one day 500 million people logged into Facebook. User's spent more time on Facebook than the total on the next four most popular sites. In the first quarter of 2011 Facebook had 346 billion ad impressions (views of advertisements). Revenues were expected to reach nearly $2 billion in 2011. Growth on Facebook had continued at a torrid pace as more and more users used it as their interface with the Internet. Research firm eMarketer estimated that online advertising revenue would increase to $132 billion by 2015, a two-thirds increase from 2011.

Facebook had remained privately held and had limited the number of shareholders to fewer than 500 to avoid Securities and Exchange Commission (SEC) reporting and disclosure requirements. The company had raised capital through private placements, including $1.5 billion raised in 2011 through a private placement led by Goldman Sachs (see also the Chapter 11 case *Goldman Sachs and Its Reputation*). Facebook was widely expected to go public in 2012 and could have a valuation of $50 billion to $100 billion.

The strategy challenge for Facebook was described by Professor Eric Brynjolfsson of the Massachusetts Institute of Technology, "As Facebook becomes more and more synonymous with the Internet experience, that is going to benefit Facebook shareholders. Facebook has been very successful in getting the lion's share of people's time and attention. Their challenge in the coming years is to convert that dominance in time and attention into a bigger share of consumer wallets—a bigger share of money they spend either directly or indirectly through advertising."[87] One continuing threat to that task was online privacy, which threatened usage as well as government regulation in the United States, Europe, and other countries.

ONLINE PRIVACY

Online privacy was not directly regulated in the United States, which had relied on self-regulation by individual companies and the industry. Most major Web sites posted a privacy policy, and some allowed users to opt out of data collection. Tracking of Internet browsing was widespread, with Google leading the way. Incidents raised concerns among users, attracted the media, and led to government efforts to protect privacy. Some regulatory proposals if enacted could severely limit data collection and reduce online advertising revenue directly. In addition, existing laws in the United States posed challenges to online companies, and pending privacy regulation in the European Union could affect online businesses worldwide. Legislation had been introduced in Congress to regulate online privacy, and President Obama had called for a "consumer privacy bill of rights."

[84]Michael Barbaro, "Wal-Mart Offers Aid to Rivals," *New York Times,* April 5, 2006.

[85]Aaron Bernstein, edited by Dan Beucke, "A Social Strategist for Wal-Mart," *BusinessWeek,* February 6, 2006.
[86]Michael Barbaro, "Wal-Mart Begins Quest for Generals in P.R. War," *New York Times,* March 30, 2006.
[87]*New York Times,* September 22, 2011.

The United States had little regulation of the Internet or online commerce, but the practices of online companies were subject to other laws, including antitrust laws. The Federal Trade Commission (FTC) had authority to regulate "deceptive trade practices," and this authority covered privacy policies. The FTC had the authority to initiate civil proceedings against companies, and citizens could file complaints with the FTC.[88]

The European Union had more strict data protection regulation than had the United States, and the United States and the EU had reached a safe harbor agreement that allowed U.S. firms to process data outside the EU. Companies that operated in the EU as did Facebook, Google, and Twitter abided by its data protection laws. Those companies stored data on clouds and operated their clouds from Ireland. A number of other countries had been forced to adopt the EU rules. The EU commissioner for justice Viviane Reding had been developing an updated regulation to present to the Parliament and Council of Ministers in January 2012. The revision would strengthen privacy protections on a number of dimensions. One was to require opt-in for permission for Web sites to use personally identifiable information. Another was to establish a right to be forgotten, which would require a Web site to delete all information about a person upon request (see also the Chapter 16 case *The European Union Data Protection Directive (B)*). In November 2011 Reding announced in a speech that she intended to go much further than the changes in the proposed revision. She said, "We both believe that companies who direct their services to European consumers should be subject to EU data protections laws. Otherwise, they should not be able to do business on our internal market. This also applies to social networks with users in the EU. We have to make sure that they comply with EU law and even if its data are stored in a 'cloud.'"[89] Reding had criticized Facebook for its data retention policies.

The bold proposal to regulate outside the European Union was opposed by U.S. businesses. The American Chamber of Commerce to the European Union had filed a 42-page brief, with the commission warning against revisions to the directive that would inhibit the free flow of information.[90]

A USA Today/Gallup Poll in 2011 found that 26 percent of respondents who used Facebook daily were "very concerned" about privacy compared to 35 percent who used Facebook less regularly. Surveys of Internet users regularly found that when asked about privacy, respondents express concerns, but when respondents were asked to list things that concern them, online privacy was not high on their lists. A study by three Google researchers found that survey responses depended significantly on how the questions were asked.

FACEBOOK AND DATA

Facebook did not sell personal information to anyone or share it with advertisers. In 2010 it was revealed that some apps including FarmVille had transferred data including users' ID numbers off Facebook's Web site. Moreover, some apps developers sold data to data brokers. Privacy concerns also arose in connection with the introduction of its Places feature in 2010. Facebook tightened its practices.

Facebook also had a "hate and harassment" team that policed its Web site, taking down objectionable material. Nevertheless postings by users continued to be a problem. Moreover, the company faced issues pertaining to free speech. In one case Facebook allowed postings that led Pakistan to block Facebook. Team member Nick Sullivan said, "In the same way that efforts to combat bullying offline are not 100 percent effective, the efforts to stop people from saying something offensive about another person online are not complete either."[91]

In December 2009 Facebook had trumpeted a new privacy platform that it said was "setting a new standard in user control." The new privacy features "include added control for each piece of content users share, simplified privacy settings, help in choosing settings and expanded privacy education materials." What Facebook did not disclose was that the default had been reset to make publicly available a variety of personal information, including name, picture, location, gender, and friends list. This led to a firestorm of complaints and protests. A number of privacy NGOs leaped on the issue, and the Electronic Privacy Information Center (EPIC) and other NGOs filed a complaint with the FTC.

Facebook introduced its Sponsored Stories, which allowed advertisers to use the online equivalent of word-of-mouth advertising. Advertisers could pay to send an advertisement to the friends list of a user that clicked the Like button on an advertisement or brand. Privacy setting were maintained, so the advertisement would go only to those in the user's selected group.[92]

New Facebook features also posed challenges. In June Facebook introduced its face-recognition technology that allowed users to tag and identify friends in photos. Then, when a user posted a photo, the face-recognition technology identified and suggested the name of the person tagged from the user's set of friends. The photo then provided a link to the page of the person linked. Facebook explained, "If for some reason someone doesn't want their name to be suggested, they can disable the feature in their Privacy Settings." It was easy for users to hide a photo on their home pages, but the tag remained on the page of the person who tagged it. Eliminating the tag was more cumbersome. When it rolled out the technology, Facebook made it the default and a user had to opt-out if it wanted to avoid the tagging. Marc Rotenberg, executive director of EPIC, complained, "Facebook users thought they were simply tagging their friends. Turns out Facebook was building an image profile database to automate online identification."[93] Representative Edward J. Markey (D-MA), who had sponsored privacy legislation in the House of Representatives and was an advocate of opt-in, said, "If this new feature is as useful as Facebook claims, it should be able to stand on its own, without

---

[88]The enforcement powers of the FTC are discussed in Chapter 9.
[89]*New York Times*, November 10, 2011.
[90]Ibid.

[91]*New York Times*, December 13, 2010.
[92]*San Jose Mercury News*, January 27, 2011.
[93]*Wall Street Journal*, June 7, 2011.

an automatic sign-up that changes users' privacy settings without their permission."[94]

Data protection regulators in the European Union reacted quickly to the introduction of the face-recognition technology. Data protection regulators in Hamburg, Germany and the Netherlands asked Facebook to disable the technology and the Commission's data protection advisory panel took up the issue of whether the feature violated a user's privacy. A Facebook spokesperson in Berlin said, "We will consider the points the Hamburg Data Protection Authority have made about the photo tag suggest feature but firmly reject any claim that we are not meeting our obligations under European Union data protection law."[95] Facebook said it had received few complaints about the face-recognition feature.

In July 2011 the privacy commissioner of Canada, Jennifer Stoddart, raised concerns about data gleaned by third-party apps such as games and quizzes on Facebook. In August Facebook responded by announcing new privacy features that required apps to notify user of and obtain permission for specific information at the time it is needed, rather the current blanket approval. The new features would be implemented worldwide. Stoddart commented, "application developers have had virtually unrestricted access to Facebook users' personal information. The changes Facebook plans to introduce will allow users to control the types of personal information that applications can access."[96]

The August announcement included other features to give users better control over the content they posted. The changes allowed users to edit and remove content and improved "Who can see this?" by changing the label "Everyone" to "Public." Some privacy controls were also moved to a user's home page. Privacy advocates generally praised Facebook for the changes. Facebook vice-president Chris Cox, said, "We want to make this stuff unmistakably clear. It has to clear that Facebook is a leader in how people control who sees what."[97] Skeptics observed that the changes came 6 weeks after Google introduced its new social network Google+. Justin Brookman, director of the privacy program at the Center for Democracy and Technology, who had consulted with Facebook on the changes observed, "This is Facebook competing on privacy."[98] Simon Davies, director of Privacy International, said, "Google has shamed the company into reform but even now most Facebook executives don't understand why privacy is a critically important design component."[99]

In September 2011 Facebook introduced its new Timeline format for storing and sharing. Mark Zuckerberg said, "We wanted to make Timeline a place you were proud to call your home. Timeline is a completely new aesthetic for Facebook. It's the story of your life. You have all your stories, all your apps, and a new way to express who you are."[100] When he introduced Timeline, Zuckerberg said Facebook users would be given 7 days to review and edit their entries before the Timeline was shared.

In response to the announcement of Timeline, Rotenberg commented, "It's getting really difficult to evaluate the changes that Facebook makes, and I say that as a privacy professional. I can't imagine what the typical user goes through."[101] Rotenberg planned to write the FTC about his concerns. Ben Barr of the technology blog Mashable, wrote, "We're at the point of no return. Facebook's passive sharing will change how we live our lives. More and more, the things we do in real life will end up as Facebook posts. And while we may be consoled by the fact that most of this stuff is being posted just to your friends, it only takes one friend to share that information with his or her friends to start a viral chain."[102]

SETTLEMENT WITH THE FTC

Facebook and the FTC reached a settlement on the EPIC complaint that Facebook had engaged in "deceptive trade practices." The settlement required Facebook to undergo independent privacy audits for 10 years and prohibited the company from making public information that a user had previously shared with a limited group. The settlement did not require Facebook to obtain permission from users to be included in new features nor did it require the company to agree to changes in features.

Referring to earlier privacy features introduced by Facebook, Amber Yoo of the Privacy Rights Clearinghouse, said, "Companies know that making a user go through an extra step to secure greater privacy over their account is something a majority of users aren't going to do."[103]

Jeff Chester, executive director of the Center for Digital Democracy, commented on the settlement, "We have not read the fine print, but the fact is that business realities are going to shape Facebook's data collection practices—not regulation. In the absence of a major consumer revolt, Facebook is going to continue to push the envelope."[104] He continued, "I have my doubts about the impact of the settlement. Does the consent decree provide new rights for users on Facebook to control their data, or it is a digital bump in the road that will do nothing to deter the social network's voracious appetite for consumer information?"[105]

The settlement between the FTC and Facebook was patterned after a similar settlement with Google over privacy controls on its now-defunct Buzz social media site. Twitter had also reached a settlement with the FTC. Both settlements required an annual independent audit of the companies' privacy policies.

PRIVACY ENFORCEMENT IN THE EUROPEAN UNION

In Germany people who were not Facebook users complained that they were receiving Facebook solicitations because their email addresses were culled from Facebook users' email lists.

[94]Ibid.
[95]*New York Times*, August 4, 2011.
[96]*San Jose Mercury News*, August 28, 2011.
[97]*Wall Street Journal*, August 24, 2011.
[98]Ibid.
[99]*Financial Times*, August 23, 2011.
[100]*San Jose Mercury News*, September 23, 2011.

[101]*San Jose Mercury News*, September 27, 2011.
[102]Ibid.
[103]*San Jose Mercury News*, November 11, 2011.
[104]Ibid.
[105]Ibid.

Facebook was publicly criticized by the German data protection commissioner and the consumer protection minister.[106] The Hamburg state data protection supervisor Johannes Caspar reviewed Facebook's privacy practices, and prosecutors were considering taking formal action against the company. Faced with possible fines and additional damage to its reputation, Facebook agreed to make changes in its Friend Finder service to make it easier to block users from accessing address books.[107]

An Austrian law school student Max Schrems requested the information Facebook had on him, as the EU Data Protection Directive provided. Facebook provided him with a CD with 1,222 pages of information. He said that there was information that was not included in the files. He and friends then established the online campaign Europe-v-Facebook that issued 22 complaints that the group sent to the Irish Data Protection Commissioner, who had jurisdiction over Facebook. The campaign inundated Facebook with requests by users for their data.[108]

The German state of Schleswig-Holstein had ordered government agencies to take Facebook's Like button off their computers. The European Commission also stopped using Facebook's public relations service.

APPLICATIONS AND DEVELOPERS

Many marketing companies had developed detailed information on consumers and sought to link their data with the information on Facebook's users so they could offer better targeted advertisements, offers, and promotions. Intermediaries such as Merkle and Lithium Technologies worked with companies to develop applications to place on Facebook. For example, Disney Destinations, which operated Disneyland and Walt Disney World, had detailed information on visitors to its parks, and nearly 18 million of its visitors were on Facebook.[109] Tom Boyles, senior vice president of Disney Destinations, said, "Understanding our guests' past stays, favorite experiences and attractions, entertainment preferences and desires allows us to create the most magical vacations possible. Social media is adding to our core 'Know me' strategy."[110]

Facebook did not share information with advertisers about individual users, but it did aggregate information about users who, for example, clicked the like button on a brand or advertisement. Facebook could provide that information to apps developers and advertisers.

Facebook's popularity led some entrepreneurs to abandon their plans to develop their own user base and to work off Facebook's user base. This "platformatizing" has "enabled us to grab the things we need to generate commerce and allows us to do what we do best," said Danny Leffel, CEO of Yardsellr Inc.[111] Developers had been allowed on Facebook since 2007, but as apps proliferated, two types of problems resulted. One

was an increase in spam that led Facebook to crack down beginning in 2010. The other was that the apps would take user information off the platform or misuse that information. In 2010 applications on Facebook's site were found to have transmitted personal information on users to outside parties.

To make platformatizing work, companies needed access to Facebook users and data. In September 2011 Zuckerberg announced that the company would update its "open graph" to allow developers enhanced access to users. The system "allows outside applications—which users must sign up for—to tap into Facebook users' data. The open graph will now allow a variety of media companies and start-ups to create applications for consuming and sharing content inside of Facebook."[112] Facebook had partnered with Sweden's Spotify to allow Facebook users to allow their friends to see in real time the music they were listening to. Daniel Ek, CEO of Spotify, said a person was twice as likely to purchase music if they have a recommendation from a friend on Facebook.[113] Ek said, "We are bringing people back to paying for music again."[114] Zuckerberg said, "It's amazing how much music you can discover from your friends. Knowing that you helped a friend discover something new, and that they like your taste in music, is awesome."[115]

Netflix similarly sought to increase demand by having Facebook users share information on the movies they rented. This, however, was thwarted in the United States by the Video Privacy Protection Act that prohibited the release of information on video rentals.[116] The law would have to be revised or repealed for rental information to be shared. The video rental sharing feature could still be made available outside the United States.

POST-LOGOFF TRACKING

In September 2011 Nik Cubrilovic, an Australian blogger, detected that Facebook placed cookies on users' browsers, and that those cookies tracked browsing after the user had logged out. Andrew Noyes, a Facebook spokesperson, said, "There was no security or privacy breach. Facebook did not store or use any information it should not have."[117] The cookies had unique identifiers, but Facebook did not keep the identifiers so it could not use any data after a user logged out. Facebook fixed the problem.

Privacy activists were not satisfied, however. Ten NGOs wrote to the Federal Trade Commission calling for an investigation of Facebook's tracking. The group wrote, "These changes in business practices give the company far greater ability to disclose the personal information of its users to its business partners than in the past. Options for users to preserve the privacy standards they have established have become

---

[106]*New York Times*, January 25, 2011.
[107]Ibid.
[108]*Irish Times*, October 15, 2011.
[109]*Wall Street Journal*, October 3, 2011.
[110]Ibid.
[111]*Wall Street Journal*, September 22, 2011.

[112]*Wall Street Journal*, September 23, 2011.
[113]Ibid.
[114]*San Jose Mercury News*, September 23, 2011.
[115]Ibid.
[116]This law was passed in 1998 after opponents of Supreme Court nominee Robert Bork obtained his video rental records from Blockbuster and used the information against him in a media campaign.
[117]*San Jose Mercury News*, September 30, 2011.

confusing, impractical, and unfair."[118] David Jacobs of EPIC, one of the authors of the letter, said, "We would like the FTC to investigate the extent to which Facebook's recent changes and its secret tracking of users after they have logged out constitute unfair and deceptive business practices." Greg Stefancik, a Facebook engineer, said, "We do not share or sell the information we see when you visit a Web site with a Facebook social plugin to third parties and we do not use it to deliver ads to you."[119] A user from Illinois quickly filed a lawsuit seeking redress for wrongs committed by Facebook. Representative Markey and Representative Joe Barton (R-TX) wrote to the FTC urging that the residual cookie should be investigated as an "unfair and deceptive act."

Jodee Rich of People Browser, which analyzed social network data, warned, "Facebook wants to be omnipresent in the Web by adding commerce, video and mail to their early success with news feeds and picture tagging. Trying to be all things to all people was the undoing of Microsoft and AOL. If Facebook continues to overreach, they will stumble."[120]

FACEBOOK AND CHILDREN

In 2011 Consumer Reports released a survey that showed that 7.5 million children under 13 years of age were on Facebook, and 5 million were under 5. Federal law and Facebook policy prohibit children under 13 to have online accounts. Consumer Reports said that the children's accounts "were largely unsupervised by their parents, exposing them to malware or serious threats such as predators and bullies." The magazine stated, "Clearly, Facebook presents children and their friends and families with safety, security, and privacy risks."[121] Technology editor Jeff Fox said, "Despite Facebook's age requirements, many kids are using the site who shouldn't be. What's more troubling was the finding from our survey that indicated that a majority of parents of kids 10 and under seemed largely unconcerned by their children's use of the site."[122] Facebook had a Family Safety Center on its Web site and had introduced new security tools making it easier to report bullying and abuse content. Bret Taylor, chief technology officer for Facebook, said, "Whenever we find out that someone's misrepresented their age on Facebook, we shut down their account. We don't allow people to misrepresent their age."[123]

The National Center on Addiction and Substance Abuse at Columbia University conducts an annual back-to-school survey of 12–17 year olds. The 16th annual survey asked about the use of social media and found:[124] Compared to teens that spend no time on social networking sites in a typical day, teens that do are:

- Five times likelier to use tobacco;
- Three times likelier to use alcohol; and
- Twice as likely to use marijuana.

The Children's Online Privacy Protection Act (Coppa) prohibited online companies from registering children under 13 as users. Zuckerberg opposed Coppa and said, "[Coppa] will be a fight we take on at some point."[125] Facebook had a "safety advisory board" that included heads of two children's safety NGOs. Both advocated allowing children under 13 on Facebook and allowing Facebook to protect them. Both NGOs received financial support from online firms including Facebook.[126]

PROPOSED REGULATION

In December 2010 the FTC issued a report on online privacy.[127] The report criticized companies for their practices, particularly for the ability of third-party tracking of online users. The FTC report called for "privacy by design," greater transparency of company policies, better consumer education about data practices, and streamlined privacy policies including "do not track" mechanism that a user could use to prevent tracking. The report stopped short of recommending detailed regulation of online activity, but called on Web sites to make it easier for users to control their data. FTC Chairman Jon Leibowitz explained, "Despite some good actors, self-regulation of privacy has not worked adequately and is not working adequately for American consumers. We'd like to see companies work a lot faster to make consumer choice easier."[128] Mark Zaneis of the Interactive Advertising Bureau (IAB) said that if a "do not track" mechanism were established and participation was high as it was for the "do not call" mechanism for telephone calls, the online advertising industry would suffer "significant economic harm."[129]

The FTC did not have the authority to establish a do-not-track mechanism, so Congress would have to act. In March the Obama administration called on Congress to give the FTC authority to enforce privacy protections. "The administration urges Congress to enact a 'consumer privacy bill of rights' to provide baseline consumer data privacy protections," wrote Lawrence Strickling of the Department of Commerce.

Senators John Kerry (D-MA) and John McCain (R-AZ) sponsored The Commercial Privacy Bill of Rights Act of 2011 to "establish a right to protect every American when it comes to the collection, use, and dissemination of their personally identifiable information (PII)." Kerry said "Every single day each of us produces a staggering amount of personal information on the Internet. This journey can be tracked, it can be stored and it can be shared on an almost unimaginable scale."[130] The three principal rights that would be established by the bill were:

- The right to security and accountability
- The right to notice, consent, access, and correction of information
- The right to data minimization, distribution constraints, and date integrity

[118]*Washington Post*, September 30, 2011.

[119]*San Jose Mercury News*, September 30, 2011.

[120]*New York Times*, September 22, 2011.

[121]*New York Times*, October 16, 2011.

[122]*San Jose Mercury News*, May 11, 2011.

[123]*San Jose Mercury News*, May 20, 2011.

[124]National Center on Addiction and Substance Abuse, Press Release, August 24, 2011.

[125]*New York Times*, October 16, 2011.

[126]Ibid.

[127]Federal Trade Commission, "Protecting Consumer Privacy in an Era of Rapid Change," December 2010.

[128]*New York Times*, December 2, 2010.

[129]Ibid.

[130]*New York Times*, April 13, 2011.

The second right provided for opt-out and not opt-in. The bill also did not contain a do-not-track provision. Kerry explained that do-not-track "didn't seem to fit into our ability to get the balance between consumer support and industry support that we were able to get," but he added that it would likely be an amendment that would be considered.

In March 2011 Microsoft announced that forthcoming Internet Explorer 9 would include Mozilla's do-not-track privacy feature that displayed a header when a user connected to a Web site that asked users if they wanted their activity tracked on that site. Microsoft also planned to retain its current Tracking Protection Lists. Google planned a "Keep My Opt-Outs" feature for Chrome.

The threat of legislation and FTC regulation spurred industry self-regulation. The IAB, whose members include the major online companies including Facebook, adopted a code of conduct that included a version of a do-not-track mechanism. The IAB members agreed to display a turquoise triangle with an "i" in the center that allowed a user to click through to a Web site where it could opt out of tracking by participating companies. Carmen Balber of Consumer Watchdog caustically characterized the IAB mechanism, "The IAB's program does not give consumers the ability to opt out of tracking—either in theory or practice. Companies who participate agree to stop targeted advertisements for consumers that opt out. However, they may continue to track (others) at will."[131]

Although Facebook did not track users outside its Web site, any regulation of online activity would have ramifications for the company. Perhaps the greatest regulatory uncertainty came from the proposed revision in the EU Data Protection Directive.

In light of the pressure Facebook faced, it increased the size of its Washington office and established a political action committee FB PAC to "give our employees a way to make their voice heard in the political process by supporting candidates who share our goals of promoting the value of innovation to our economy while giving people the power to share and make the world more open and connected."[132] Facebook hired Tim Sparapani, a former privacy expert at the American Civil Liberties Union, for its Washington office. Sparapani said, "We need to be here to define ourselves before someone else does it for us. It's clear we need to be part of the new thinking of Washington—and early in the company's maturation process."[133] ▪

Preparation Questions

1. Are users really concerned about these privacy issues? Is it mainly a small set of privacy activists who are raising concerns?
2. Is competition in privacy sufficient to protect users?
3. How big a threat is the proposed revision to the EU's Data Protection Directive?
4. Should Facebook establish a right to be forgotten for its community of users?
5. How should Facebook handle the default setting on the introduction of its next new feature?
6. Should Facebook ask users for permission before targeting advertising to users?
7. What data protection policy should Facebook adopt?

---

[131]*USA Today*, August 30, 2011.
[132]*New York Times*, September 27, 2011.
[133]*USA Today*, January 13, 2011.

ETHICS SYSTEMS: UTILITARIANISM

INTRODUCTION

The content of corporate social responsibility is provided by ethics. This and the following chapter address the role of ethics in management and provide an introduction to three principal ethics systems. The objective is to increase moral sensitivity and provide frameworks for reasoning about issues based on ethics principles and moral standards. No single ethics framework encompasses all the moral intuitions of people, so it is important to consider issues from the perspectives of several systems. The ethics systems considered are utilitarianism, rights, and justice. (Confucianism is considered in Chapter 16.) These systems correspond to basic intuitions about the good and the right and are important guides to firms and managers in the evaluation of alternative courses of action.

Ethics and its application in management constitute a broad and deep subject. The approach taken here is to address the subject in a series of steps. This and the following chapter introduce the three ethics systems and evaluate nonmarket issues with moral concerns based on those systems. Chapter 23 considers behavioral ethics, that is, how people behave in situations in which moral concerns are present, and the implementation of ethics systems in domestic contexts. Chapter 24 focuses on the implementation of ethics systems in international contexts. The chapter cases provide opportunities to reason from the perspectives of ethics systems and apply ethics principles and methods to managerial problems.

This chapter focuses on the nature of ethics in managerial contexts and on utilitarianism, a consequentialist ethics system that evaluates actions in terms of the human well-being they yield. The next two sections consider the role of ethics in management and the distinction between ethics and other forms of managerial decision making. The following sections address the relationship between ethics and self-interest, politics, and casuistry. The methodology of ethics and the relationship between ethics and moral and political philosophy are then considered. Utilitarianism, the principal consequentialist ethics system, is then introduced, including the distinction between act and rule utilitarianism. A framework for applying utilitarianism in competitive situations is presented, and the difficulties in its application are considered. Examples of utilitarian reasoning are presented, and those examples are then reconsidered in Chapter 22 from the perspectives of rights and justice.

THE MANAGERIAL ROLE OF ETHICS

Ethics has several managerial roles. As a normative approach, ethics provides principles for evaluating alternatives and formulating policies to take into account the interests, rights, and liberties of those affected. In the context of the framework for nonmarket analysis presented in Chapter 2 and Figure 2-5, ethics in its normative role is used in both the screening and choice stages. In the screening stage, ethics provides the underpinnings for policies that guide managers in determining which alternatives should be screened out and which should be considered further. In the choice stage, ethics provides a basis for evaluating whether claims have moral standing and thus whether they are to be respected in the firm's decision making. Ethics also provides a basis both for assessing whether moral consensus is present and for justifying a firm's actions to stakeholders, government, and the public.

Ethics is also an important foundation for the positive analysis of nonmarket issues. Individuals, activists, interest groups, and government officeholders can be motivated by moral concerns about a firm's conduct. In the analysis stage of the framework in Figure 2-5, ethics contributes to the prediction of morally motivated nonmarket action. Managers must be sensitive to how the moral determinants of nonmarket action can affect the firm and shape its nonmarket environment. Because individuals have a range of ethical intuitions, it is important to view issues from the perspectives of several ethics systems. In its normative and positive roles, ethics thus provides a basis for analysis, decision making, and the formulation of strategies for addressing nonmarket issues and the nonmarket actions associated with them.

WHAT ETHICS IS AND IS NOT

Ethics is a systematic approach to moral judgments based on reason, analysis, synthesis, and reflection. It addresses matters of importance to human well-being, autonomy, and liberty. Ethics is based on moral standards that are independent of the declarations of governments or other authoritative bodies. Moral standards are impartial, take precedence over self-interest, and are to apply to everyone; that is, they are to be universal.[1] Ethics thus is the discipline concerned with judgments based on moral standards and the reasoning therefrom.

Moral philosophers have proposed an array of ethics systems without arriving at consensus on a single system. On some issues, a decision alternative may be consistent with one ethics system and inconsistent with others. Random drug testing of employees may reduce social costs, and hence satisfy a utilitarian standard, yet it may violate an individual's right to privacy. Similarly, an absolute right to privacy could be unjust if it prevented drug testing of employees whose responsibilities include public safety.

The issues considered in this and subsequent chapters involve significant moral concerns not easily resolved through approaches that are independent of moral standards. The focus thus is not on simple temptation. There are many managerial situations in which an action is contrary to the law, a well-established company policy, or widely shared ethics principles, yet managers may be tempted to take the action because they, or the firm, may benefit from it. Since what is good or right is clearly evident, these situations have only limited interest from the perspective of ethics. Addressing the issue of temptation remains important, however. One responsibility of management is to develop procedures to reduce the temptation that often arises, for example, from how performance is compensated. Approaches to reducing temptation and guiding managers through situations in which temptation may arise are considered in Chapters 23 and 24. The Chapter 10 case *Enron Power Marketing, Inc., and the California Market* considers a company that succumbs to the temptation to manipulate a market for electricity, and insider trading considered in Chapter 23 concerns temptation.

The focus of ethics is not on issues involving direct mutual advantage. Such issues generally do not require ethics analysis. Every sale a firm makes benefits the firm and its customer. In the absence of external consequences, the transaction is generally free from moral objection. Mutual advantage may also control temptation. A consulting or investment services firm often has an opportunity to serve its own rather than its clients' interests. To attract future clients, however, the firm must maintain a reputation for effectively serving client interests. Honoring expectations in such cases can be explained by self-interest independently of moral standards. Serving client interests, however, is not sufficient. Firms must assess whether client interests are consistent with ethics principles and the law, as in the Chapter 11 case *Goldman Sachs and Its Reputation* in which the company's design of securities and its marketing may have violated ethics principles, the law, and the interests of some clients.

PERSONAL AND BUSINESS ETHICS

Business ethics is the application of ethics principles to issues that arise in business. There is no separate discipline of business ethics. As opposed to personal ethics, where an individual is the principal in the sense of Chapter 20, business ethics pertains to situations in which individuals are in an organizational position and act as agents of the company and its owners.

Business ethics also differs from personal ethics because a manager has accepted the responsibilities associated with the position occupied. The set of issues faced also differs from those one encounters in one's personal life. In an organizational setting an individual may have duties, such as preventing sexual harassment by others or meeting fiduciary responsibilities, that may not be encountered in one's personal life. Moreover, in one's personal life an individual may focus on the virtuous life in an Aristotelian sense or a life of propriety in a Confucian sense. In an organization role, however, a manager must reason about situations in which virtue is not always present, conceptions of what is good or right differ among individuals, and interests are in conflict. The focus here is on ethics systems as applied to moral issues that arise in an organizational context.

---

[1]Moral claims are distinguished from prudential claims, which are based on considerations of self-interest.

ETHICS AND INDIVIDUAL INTERESTS

Ethical behavior enables society to realize the benefits from social interactions and allows individuals to rely on the word and conduct of others. Ethical behavior does not always make an individual or a firm better off, however. In some countries a policy of refusing to pay bribes to government officials can result in costly delays or the loss of sales. Furthermore, ethical behavior may not be self-evident to others and, even if it is, it may not be rewarded. Ethical behavior thus can conflict with profit objectives or with an individual's self-interest. That is, ethics principles prescribe behavior based on considerations that take precedence over self-interest. This is perhaps clearest in a utilitarian framework in which a person's own interests are given no greater consideration than the interests of any other person. Good ethics is thus not necessarily beneficial to an individual or profitable for a firm; however, good ethics is good for society and is a requirement of good management.

Although good ethics may not always be profitable, unethical behavior can result in substantial losses, as evidenced by the series of business scandals and violations of the law discussed in Chapter 20. Unethical actions by a firm can worsen the environment for all firms by causing the public to become suspicious of business and its motives and increasing the trust gap. In the long run, harmony between business and society requires conduct consistent with the principles embodied in the social contract under which business operates. Business and its management thus are evaluated not only in terms of financial performance but also in terms of moral performance.

ETHICS, POLITICS, AND CHANGE

Ethics involves an inquiry into whether a proposition has moral status. Propositions may be classified as claimed or granted. A granted proposition is one that has been established either by ethical consensus or by an authoritative body such as government. Claims often are made that a proposition has moral status. Frequently, these claims are intended to increase the likelihood that the proposition will be granted by government. For example, in some areas delivery services are plagued by robberies and threats to the safety of delivery personnel. As a result of reports from drivers concerned about their safety, a Federal Express district manager suspended after-dark pickups in Gary, Indiana. Similarly, a Domino's Pizza franchisee refused to deliver in certain high-risk areas in Miami. Consider the proposition that delivery services may not refuse to serve parts of their normal service area, even if the motive is to avoid possible harm to delivery personnel. One use of ethics is to determine whether such a proposition results in an injustice or a violation of rights. The use of ethics to establish the moral status of a proposition is illustrated by the horizontal arrows in Figure 21-1, which classifies propositions as claimed and granted and according to their moral status.[2]

Politics pertains to the vertical status of propositions in Figure 21-1. Most politics centers on private interests and is advanced in the absence of arguments about moral status, as illustrated

FIGURE 21-1   Ethics, Politics, and Change

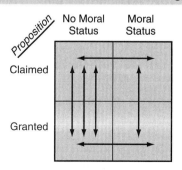

Proposition: A delivery service may not refuse to deliver in its regular service area.

❶ *Politics* can be interpreted as attempts to change the vertical status of claims; e.g., to delivery service. Most politics is about private interests rather than about propositions with moral status.

❷ *Ethics* can be interpreted as disciplinary arguments about the horizontal status of claims and grants. In principle, ethics is independent of politics and of whether the proposition is presently granted or claimed.

---

[2]This figure was prepared by Keith Krehbiel.

by the three arrows in the left column of the figure. Some politics focuses on propositions with established moral status, as indicated by the arrow in the right column. The policies restricting deliveries were prohibited by the mayor of Gary and by a court order in Miami. San Francisco passed an ordinance making it illegal to refuse to deliver in parts of the regular service area of a restaurant.

Change can come from both ethics and politics. The Chapter 12 case *Environmental Justice and Pollution Credits Trading Systems* focuses on the ethics and politics of the proposition that less-advantaged persons, including minorities and women, are disproportionately and adversely affected by certain environmental protection policies, in this case a cap-and-trade system.

CASUISTRY

Ethics is principled reasoning and is distinguished from casuistry, which is an approach to moral practice that seeks to balance competing considerations by making exceptions to ethics principles in particular cases. Casuistry is an ancient approach that reemerged during the Reformation in the sixteenth century as the argument that different principles were applicable to different situations and in different roles. For example, a ruler might violate principles in an attempt to benefit his subjects. Casuistry was attacked by Pascal, who argued that although they may have been well intentioned, casuist methods were flawed and the results therefore questionable. Casuistry has been characterized as a false art of making exceptions in particular situations, resulting in the violation of underlying principles.[3] This approach is contrary to the ethics systems considered here, which are intended to apply universally. Thus, the familiar saying that "a diplomat is a person who lies abroad for the benefit of his country" may characterize politics but not ethics.

The example illustrates casuist reasoning.

EXAMPLE   Saving the Division

Leyden Corporation was a small manufacturer of household appliances, including blenders, food processors, mixers, and coffee makers. Competition had intensified in all its lines of business, particularly as companies in China had entered its markets. In 2006 Leyden incurred a loss of $6.4 million, and the first half of 2007 was worse. Leyden saw little opportunity to turn the situation around.

The most serious problem was with its line of blenders, which because of low-priced imports had experienced decreasing sales and was losing nearly $12 million a year. The blender division had done all it could to reduce costs, including freezing wage rates for the past year. If the profitability of the division could not be improved, Leyden's only alternative would be to close its plant. The general manager of the blender division formulated a plan that he believed would save the plant for a few years to buy time in the hope that something favorable, such as a change in exchange rates, might occur.

The general manager's plan involved cutting the quality of the blenders but marketing them as if they were the previous models. The plan was to use a lower-quality motor and cheaper internal materials, which together would reduce costs by nearly 14 percent. This would enable the plant to remain open, as long as volume could be maintained. Although the blenders would not be as durable, a consumer would have no way of knowing that at the time of purchase. To conceal the lower quality, the general manager proposed keeping the same model numbers, charging the same price, advertising and marketing the blenders as before, and making certain that the new blenders had the same external appearance as the current ones. The general manager was confident that neither retailers nor customers would soon detect the changes.

The general manager reasoned that the plan would benefit employees and shareholders, and Leyden could be said to have a social responsibility to both groups of stakeholders. Consumers would be worse off compared to their expectations, but employees were a more immediate constituency, and consumers would still be getting a serviceable blender. From the point of view of responsibility to stakeholders, the general manager decided to implement the plan.

The general manager's reasoning is an example of casuistry. That is, the reasoning proceeds from a concept of responsibility to the specifics of a case without reliance on principles. From a utilitarianism perspective, selling a lower-quality product as if it were a higher-quality product reduces aggregate well-being because some customers would be better off buying other blenders if they knew of the change. The plan also involves deception, which is difficult to support in any ethics system. Furthermore, it treats consumers as a means of saving the division. From a rights perspective, the company is not respecting consumers' autonomy as considered in Chapter 22.

---

[3]See Jonsen and Toulmin (1988) for a history of casuistry and for its defense as practical ethics.

The casuist approach is dangerous precisely because it shortcuts the application of principles in favor of conceptions of responsibility that may be inconsistent with moral standards. Furthermore, those conceptions can be a disguise for the self-interest of the decision maker. Several factors indicate when casuistry is being practiced. It is often present in situations in which the action the manager wants to take is identified by self-interest, the firm's interest, or stakeholders' interests. Casuistry may be present when managers find themselves searching for a justification for the actions they wish to take based on self-interest. It may also be present when a manager tries to rationalize around principles using the justification that stakeholders benefit. The chapter case *Consumer Awareness or Disease Mongering? GlaxoSmithKline and the Restless Legs Syndrome* provides an opportunity to assess the attraction of casuistry.

THE METHODOLOGY OF ETHICS

The methodology of ethics is illustrated in the left panel of Figure 21-2. It involves the identification of decision alternatives, evaluation of those alternatives in terms of ethics principles and moral standards, and choice based on those evaluations. Ethics analysis is to be applied early rather than late in the process. As illustrated in the right panel of Figure 21-2, ethics that serves only to explain decisions made on other bases is inappropriate. It encourages managers to choose actions that serve their and their firms' interests and then to search among the various ethics systems to find one that comes closest to justifying the already-chosen action. This does not mean that when correctly applied, ethics cannot be used to justify the action taken. That justification, however, should be consistent with the basis for the decision.

Figure 21-3 provides more detail on the methodology of ethics. The methodology begins with the identification of the facts about the issue, since if the facts are incorrectly understood, even a correct analysis can result in an inappropriate decision. Along with the facts, the moral concerns associated with the issue must be identified. They may involve concerns about well-being, rights and liberties, and fairness for those involved. Management also must identify alternatives for addressing the issue, and creativity should be used in generating alternatives.

Once the facts have been discerned, moral concerns identified, and alternatives generated, ethics principles and moral standards are used to analyze the alternatives. Analysis involves reasoning that is logical, systematic, consistent, and reflective. The results of the analysis are judgments about whether the alternatives are consistent with ethics principles and moral standards. When ethics is directed at decision making, the final stage involves choice and

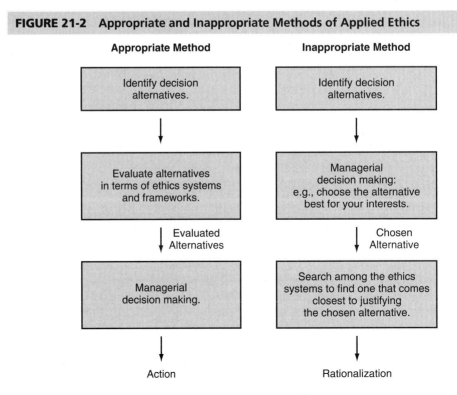

FIGURE 21-2   Appropriate and Inappropriate Methods of Applied Ethics

Appropriate Method	Inappropriate Method
Identify decision alternatives.	Identify decision alternatives.
Evaluate alternatives in terms of ethics systems and frameworks. *(Evaluated Alternatives)*	Managerial decision making: e.g., choose the alternative best for your interests. *(Chosen Alternative)*
Managerial decision making.	Search among the ethics systems to find one that comes closest to justifying the chosen alternative.
Action	Rationalization

FIGURE 21-3   **Process of Ethics Analysis**

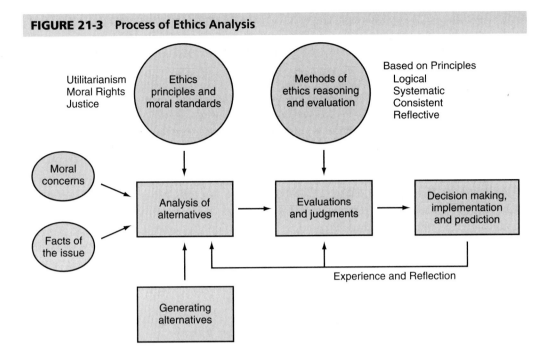

implementation. When ethics is used to understand whether there will be a reaction to a decision, the final stage involves predicting whether objections to a decision are likely and whether nonmarket action can be expected. Finally, experience and reflection provide lessons for refining the methods of analysis and evaluation.

THE RELATIONSHIPS AMONG MORAL PHILOSOPHY, ETHICS, AND POLITICAL PHILOSOPHY

Figure 21-4 illustrates the relationship between moral philosophy and ethics. Moral philosophy is concerned with deducing moral principles and standards from axioms or self-evident principles. The self-evident principle that what matters is human well-being is the basis for utilitarianism. From that principle, the standard of maximizing aggregate well-being is deduced. The action that maximizes aggregate well-being then has moral standing because it yields the greatest good in

FIGURE 21-4   **Relationship between Moral Philosophy and Ethics**

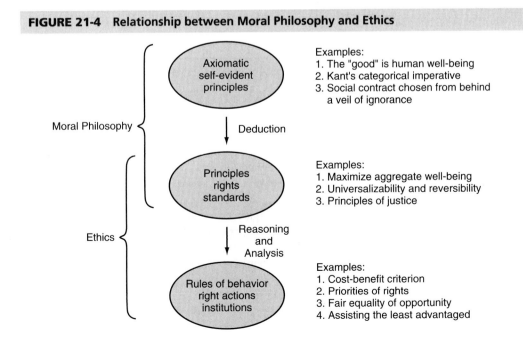

terms of well-being. As considered in Chapter 22, Kant's categorical imperative provides a basis for deducing maxims to guide behavior, which in turn provide a basis for identifying individual rights. Choosing a social contract from an impartial position provides the basis for principles of justice as considered in Chapter 22.

As indicated in Figure 21-4, ethics is concerned with analysis and reasoning based on principles and standards. That reasoning may be directed at the design of society's institutions, such as the public education and justice systems, the identification of rights, and provisions for social justice. Analysis and reasoning may also be directed at determining which actions provide the greatest aggregate well-being or whether a right, such as a right to privacy, takes precedence over other considerations.

Political philosophy is related to ethics and moral philosophy but focuses on institutions to govern the interactions among individuals. Political philosophy naturally focuses on conceptions of the state, how the state should grant and limit liberties and ensure justice, and the extent to which markets or other institutions are used to organize economic activity.

Moral and political philosophies come together when they provide principles to govern the interactions among individuals. Utilitarianism provides a basis for a political philosophy in which the choice between private institutions, such as markets, and public institutions, such as government, is made according to which maximizes aggregate well-being.

UTILITARIANISM: A CONSEQUENTIALIST SYSTEM

Utilitarianism has a rich history with its origins in the work of Jeremy Bentham (1789), who argued for a calculus of pain and pleasure, and then of John Stuart Mill (1859). The moral standing of utilitarianism, however, is better understood in more recent expressions to which the criticisms applied to hedonism are less applicable. Utilitarianism is better understood as a particular form of a consequentialist moral philosophy.

In a consequentialist system, an action is moral if it produces better consequences than any other alternative. Utilitarianism is a consequentialist system with two particular features. First, consequences are to be evaluated in terms of the preferences of all individuals affected, and second, those preferences are to be aggregated. Aggregation is required because an action may make some individuals better off and others worse off. The standard of human well-being and the need to consider the consequences for all persons correspond to fundamental ethical intuitions.

As an example, because of the oil crisis of 1973 the United States adopted a national speed limit of 55 miles per hour. As oil prices dropped and Americans increased their driving, the pressure for higher speed limits mounted. In 1995 Congress abolished the federal speed limit, and by 1998 all but one state had increased their speed limits. Many increased their speed limit to 70 or 75 on rural stretches of interstate highways. Data subsequently indicated that the higher speed limits increased fatalities and injuries. The higher speed limits also saved motorists and their passengers many hours of travel time. The overwhelming revealed preference among the states for higher speed limits suggests that the benefits from the time saved outweighed the safety costs. As one motorist said referring to the greater risks, "I'll take that trade-off."

Utilitarianism does not focus on the numbers of people who are better or worse off because of an action, nor is it equivalent to a vote among alternatives. If an action makes 100 people worse off by one unit each and makes one person better off by 101 units, the action should be taken. Utilitarianism also is not equivalent to "the greatest good for the greatest number." That statement is ambiguous because, as the example indicates, one alternative could produce the greatest good yet another alternative could produce benefits for the greatest number. Utilitarianism chooses the action that yields the greatest good.

Table 21-1 illustrates the basic utilitarian approach. A decision maker is to choose between two alternatives, A and B. The well-being for each of the four members of society, measured in terms of their preferences or utilities for the consequences, is presented in the body of the table. The aggregate well-being is the sum of those utilities; that is, utilitarianism aggregates the utilities of all the individuals. Alternative A yields an aggregate utility of 11, whereas action B yields a greater aggregate utility of 14. Utilitarianism identifies action B as the moral action, since it yields the greater good.

Pure transfers among individuals have no effect on the utilitarianism calculus. If one firm signs a supply contract with another firm to provide a product, both firms presumably are better off as a result of the transaction. From a utilitarian perspective the transaction is morally right provided

TABLE 21-1 Utilitarianism Example

Individual	Utility from Alternative	
	A	**B**
1	3	3
2	3	5
3 (the decision maker)	3	2
4	2	4
aggregate utility	11	14

there are no associated externalities. Moreover, as long as both parties agree to the contract, the price at which the product is exchanged is irrelevant. That is, if the value of the product to the buyer is 20 and the cost to the supplier is 15, the transaction results in a net benefit of 5 regardless of whether the price is 19 or 16. The price paid is a pure transfer between the buyer and the seller, and the transfer nets to zero in the utilitarian calculus. In Table 21-1 if alternative B provided utility of 4 to individual 3 and 3 to individual 2, the conclusion that B is the moral action would remain.

Utilitarianism and Self-Interest

Utilitarianism is nearly the antithesis of self-interest because one's own interests are to be given no more consideration than those of any other person. That is, decisions are to be impartial. The interests considered thus are not just those of the decision maker but those of everyone affected by the action. In the Leyden Corporation example, marketing the blenders as proposed would likely make customers worse off by more than the gain to the company and employees. In Table 21-1 individual 3 is worse off with action B than with A, but as a utilitarian decision maker, individual 3 has a moral duty to choose B over A. Note also that as utilitarians each of the four individuals would choose alternative B. That is, with utilitarianism there is unanimity about the moral action. Utilitarianism is also universalizable in the sense that as moral persons each would be willing to have everyone act in accord with the principle of maximizing aggregate well-being.

In the chapter case *Consumer Awareness or Disease Mongering? GlaxoSmithKline and the Restless Legs Syndrome*, the company recognized an opportunity to develop a new indication for its existing drug Requip. People experiencing "restless legs" were the new market. Few people who had restless legs recognized that they had a disorder, and GlaxoSmithKline used heavy direct-to-consumers television and print advertising to stimulate demand for treatment. The company said it was simply raising awareness of "a disorder that was generally overlooked by most physicians and individuals." Critics argued that the company was disease-mongering by "turning normal people into patients." The case focuses on whether the company should have created a market for Requip, how aggressive it should have been, and what to do as the controversy swirled around it.

Aligning Self-Interest with Societal Well-Being

Utilitarianism coincides with self-interest only when societal consequences are aligned with private consequences. One role of government is to establish institutions that provide this alignment. When alignment has been achieved, individuals can evaluate actions in terms of the consequences for themselves rather than having to take into account the consequences for all others affected by an action.

Many of society's institutions are based on aligning the interests of firms and individuals with the aggregate interests of society. The institutions of private property and markets provide one means of alignment, since a voluntary transaction, such as a supply contract between two firms, makes both the buyer and seller better off. In the case of environmental protection, cap-and-trade systems align the interests of polluters and society, as considered in Chapter 12. The law of torts considered in Chapter 14 is an institution that assigns the social costs of accidents to individuals and firms, providing incentives to minimize the social costs of accidents and the cost of avoidance.

When markets are competitive and institutions are in place that align self-interest with societal well-being, the maximization of profit by a firm results in the greatest aggregate societal well-being; that is, the greatest difference between societal benefits and societal costs. This alignment of private interests and societal interests provides a justification for Milton Friedman's view that the social responsibility of business is to maximize profits, as considered in Chapter 20.

Utilitarianism, Distribution, and Altruism

Utilitarianism aggregates individuals' well-being as evaluated in terms of their preferences, and every person's utility is given equal weight. In the example in Table 21-1 the distribution of utility is more equal with alternative A than with alternative B, but since utilitarianism is concerned with aggregate well-being, it does not matter how that utility is distributed across individuals. Alternative B yields the greater aggregate utility and hence is the moral choice.

Although utilitarianism gives equal weight to the utilities of all persons, this does not mean that redistribution is irrelevant. The transfer of a dollar from a rich person to a poor person can increase aggregate well-being if the poor person is made better off by more than the rich person is made worse off; that is, if the gain in the utility of the poor person is greater than the loss in the utility of the rich person. Utilitarianism thus evaluates redistribution as it does any other alternative—in terms of the aggregate utility of all persons. In the illustration of one firm supplying a product to another firm, the "marginal utilities" of the two firms are the same, so the price paid for the product does not affect the utilitarian conclusion that the transaction increases aggregate well-being.

Utilitarianism also takes into account altruism. If some individuals have altruistic preferences for the well-being of others, the well-being of those others receives consideration in the utility function of the altruist. For example, if a rich person has altruistic preferences for the well-being of the poor, the rich person has greater utility for alternatives that benefit the poor than for alternatives that do not, other things being equal. The rich person's preferences for the well-being of the poor cannot be hypothetical, however. Instead, the rich person must be willing to act on those preferences by redistributing some of her wealth or contributing time to improving the well-being of the poor.

In evaluating two alternative government programs designed to benefit the poor, the preferences on which the rich person is willing to act are what is counted. Thus, a person concerned for the well-being of the poor is not able to assign a hypothetical or an arbitrary weight to their well-being. Similarly, a person cannot ascribe one's own altruism to others, that is, cannot assume that others are also altruistic. A person, however, may attempt to persuade others also to be altruistic or may engage in nonmarket action to have the government establish programs to provide benefits to the poor. If the resulting taxes reduce economic efficiency, the cost of that inefficiency must be taken into account in evaluating the programs to benefit the poor. Cost-benefit analysis incorporates these considerations.

Summary of the Components of Utilitarianism

Utilitarianism is a moral philosophy that holds that

- Moral good is judged in terms of consequences.
- Consequences are evaluated in terms of human well-being.
- Human well-being is evaluated in terms of individuals' preferences.
- The rightness of an action is judged by the aggregate well-being, or good, it yields.
- The morally justified action maximizes aggregate well-being.

Moreover, utilitarianism is the antithesis of self-interest, and the two are equivalent only if private well-being and societal well-being are aligned.

UTILITARIAN DUTY AND THE CALABRESI AND MELAMED PRINCIPLES

One of the most difficult aspects of applying utilitarianism, or any other ethics system, is determining who has the duty to take a moral action. For example, if aggregate utility would be increased by transferring a dollar to a poor person, from whom should that dollar come? The answer is that it should come from the person or persons with the smallest decrease in utility from giving up the dollar. If there are many such people, each could give up some portion of their dollar if that would result in a smaller decrease in their aggregate utility. Most managerial situations are more complex.

The Calabresi and Melamed principles introduced in Chapter 14 provide a framework for reasoning about the assignment of duty. The principles are intended to identify which party is in the best position to determine whether the benefits of an action outweigh its costs and which party is in the best position to either act or induce others to take actions that yield benefits that exceed the costs. The party identified by those principles then has the duty to act.

For example, the appropriate level of safety to incorporate into a product depends on the safety features the manufacturer could incorporate and on the care the user of the product could take. To determine if the manufacturer or the user has the duty to add safety features or take care, respectively, the Calabresi and Melamed principles provide the following tests:

1. Assign the duty to the party—the manufacturer or the user—that can best achieve improvements in the difference between aggregate benefits and costs.
2. If it is not clear which party that is, the duty should be assigned to the party that is in the best position to assess the aggregate benefits and costs and then act on that assessment.
3. If that is unclear (and hence a mistake in the assignment of duty could be made), assign the duty to the party that can at the lowest cost induce the other party to take actions to improve the difference between aggregate benefits and aggregate costs in the event of a misassignment.

In the case of product safety the duty is usually assigned to the manufacturer who is better positioned than a consumer to assess aggregate costs and benefits and to reduce accidents through the incorporation of safety features. Moreover, the manufacturer is usually better positioned to induce the consumer through instructions and warnings to take care when the cost of that care is lower than the cost of adding additional safety features. Furthermore, a manufacturer may have a duty to anticipate carelessness and, in some situations, misuse of a product by a consumer. This assignment of duty is warranted when the manufacturer is better positioned to avoid the harm from carelessness and misuse through product design, the addition of safety features, and warnings to consumers. This does not mean that all potential harm from the use of the product should be eliminated, as in the case of a chain saw, since costs and possible reduced benefits must be taken into account.

In identifying the locus of duty in situations not involving government institutions, the Calabresi and Melamed principles can be simplified to answer the question, "Which party is best positioned to act, or to induce others to act, to yield benefits that exceed the costs?" For example, in the Chapter 11 case *Citigroup and Subprime Lending,* Citigroup acquired the Associates First Capital Corporation, a large subprime lender that had been accused of predatory lending. Citigroup could continue to market subprime loans aggressively and rely on customers to determine whether they wanted to borrow or it could attempt to restrict its lending to customers who would actually benefit from the loans. The Calabresi and Melamed principles ask whether Citigroup or a borrower is better positioned to assess whether the loans were beneficial or predatory. Many of the borrowers were poor or elderly and could easily succumb to aggressive marketing, and many of them would be worse off with a loan. The Calabresi and Melamed principles indicate that in many cases Citigroup is better positioned than are the borrowers to assess whether a subprime loan would be beneficial. Hence, the duty is on Citigroup to ensure that its subprime lending makes borrowers better off where there is a doubt.

ACT AND RULE UTILITARIANISM

Utilitarianism may be applied in two forms, *act utilitarianism* and *rule utilitarianism.* The classical distinction between these two forms is considered in this section, and the following section considers an alternative form of rule utilitarianism applicable to settings in which consequences are jointly determined by more than one party.[4]

Act utilitarianism focuses on the consequences of a particular action in a particular situation and prescribes the action that yields the greatest aggregate well-being for everyone affected by that action. Rule utilitarianism focuses on a general rule of behavior to be followed by all individuals in all similar situations. A moral rule is then the one that does best in terms of its consequences for everyone affected in those similar situations. An action is then moral if it is consistent with the

---

[4]See Brandt (1959, 1979) for the classical distinction.

moral rule appropriate for that type of situation. As an example, in the Chapter 19 case *Compulsory Licensing, Thailand, and Abbott Laboratories* and the Part V integrative case *GlaxoSmithKline and AIDS Drugs Policy,* a candidate for a rule could be

> ***In the event of a public health emergency, a developing country may violate a patent and produce a life-preserving pharmaceutical under a compulsory license.***

The evaluation of this rule requires the specific information in the cases and only a brief analysis is presented here. The benefits resulting from the rule are measured in terms of lives saved. The costs are the production costs and the future loss in well-being from the diminished incentives for pharmaceutical companies to conduct research and development to develop new life-saving drugs when patents are not respected. In addition to aggregating the consequences, the rule must be compared with alternative rules such as having the pharmaceutical company provide the drug at preferential prices or developed countries purchase the drug and give it to the developing country. Further analysis is reserved for the cases.

Rule utilitarianism is viewed by its advocates as providing a set of rules for guiding the behavior of all individuals in society in a mutually advantageous manner. Act utilitarianism focuses on individual actions and does not explain what the overall consequences would be for society if everyone were to act in that manner.

To illustrate the substantive and methodological distinctions between act and rule utilitarianism, suppose that in a particular situation deception rather than dealing with a person honestly would yield benefits that exceed the costs. Under act utilitarianism, deception would be a morally justified action in this situation. If a general rule of behavior, however, were "People may deceive others in a particular situation whenever the benefits exceed the costs," relying on the word of others could become problematic, since others might not know the benefits and costs or in which particular situations the benefits would exceed the costs. Aggregate well-being then would be lower because people would not be able to trust others, and mutually advantageous reliance on the word of others would require costly enforcement mechanisms, such as explicit contracts. A rule such as "Always deal with people in an honest and forthright manner" would yield greater aggregate well-being if everyone followed the rule. This rule thus would have moral standing under rule utilitarianism.

Act utilitarianism also risks slipping into self-interest. Since act utilitarianism focuses on an individual's action in a specific situation rather than on general rules of behavior, individuals may be tempted to follow their self-interest. That is, the focus of act utilitarianism can place decision makers on a slippery slope leading to evaluating actions based on their self-interest rather than the consequences for all affected.

The weakness of rule utilitarianism, however, is precisely the strength of act utilitarianism. If deception in a particular situation X yields benefits that exceed the costs, the following modification of the rule would yield greater aggregate well-being: "Always deal with people in an honest and forthright manner except in situation X in which deception is permitted." Amending the rule to allow an exception in situation X improves the utilitarian calculus and hence yields a morally superior rule. Then, any exception that yields benefits in excess of its costs would also yield a morally superior rule. Rule utilitarianism then degenerates into act utilitarianism.[5]

The response of a rule utilitarian is that utilitarian methods are necessarily applied in an imperfect world in which some facts about the particular situation are missing, information is incomplete, and not all consequences can be foreseen, let alone evaluated. In such a world, it is better to evaluate general rules of behavior to guide individuals than to apply utilitarian methods separately to each action in each situation.[6] Rule utilitarianism encourages individuals to think about whether they would want everyone to follow the same rule of behavior in all similar situations. That is, rule utilitarianism encourages universalism. Rule utilitarianism thus is the preferred form of utilitarianism.

As an example, in the late 1980s American Airlines and United Airlines became concerned about the changes in medical standards adopted by the new federal air surgeon, an officer of the Federal Aviation Administration (FAA). The federal air surgeon had responsibility for granting medical waivers, referred to as "special issuances," that allowed reinstatement of pilots who had had their certification suspended. Under the new standards one pilot who had blacked out in the

---

[5]See Lyons (1965).
[6]See Hardin (1988).

cockpit had been granted a special issuance, as had a pilot who had had bypass surgery. An airline was not required to put a pilot with a special issuance back in the cockpit, and both American and United had kept their pilots grounded until receiving clearance from their own chief medical officers. The moral question was whether the airlines should take any action with regard to the new standards being followed by the federal air surgeon. Since the airlines could ground any of their pilots with special issuances that were questioned by their own medical officers, the airlines were not concerned about their own pilots. The broader concern was with general aviation pilots and other airlines that might not be aware of or concerned by the changes made by the federal air surgeon. American and United extrapolated from their own situations to the broader population of pilots and airlines; that is, they considered a general rule. They concluded based on reasoning analogous to the Calabresi and Melamed principles that they had a duty to make their concerns public. The airlines went to the FAA and to the congressional committee with oversight responsibility for the FAA, which held hearings leading to a review of the medical standards.

Jointly Determined Consequences

In many situations consequences are jointly determined by the actions of more than one person. In such a situation, a second form of rule utilitarianism is applicable.[7] As an example of such a situation, consider a firm seeking to sell telecommunication equipment to a government agency in a country in which corruption is known to be widespread. Suppose the firm believes that a competitor with inferior equipment is likely to be offering a bribe to the head of the agency. How should the firm reason about whether it should offer a matching bribe?

In act utilitarianism an individual chooses the action that maximizes aggregate well-being, taking the behavior of others as given. A matching bribe in this situation would increase aggregate well-being because the firm has superior equipment. In rule utilitarianism an individual chooses not only a rule for one's own action but also simultaneously for the actions of all individuals. In so doing the individual is choosing a rule of behavior to be followed by everyone, so the rule is universal. In addition, as utilitarians all persons would choose the same rule, since each person maximizes aggregate well-being. Each individual thus is choosing not only in an impartial manner but also chooses the same rule, so there is unanimity.[8] Bribery and the resulting corruption reduce aggregate well-being, so the moral rule is that neither firm is to offer a bribe. This leaves the issue of the appropriate moral action when another party is recognized to violate the moral duty. Bribery is considered in more detail in Chapter 24, and decision making in the face of a moral transgression is considered here after presenting a quantitative example.

Consider two individuals who each must decide whether to act honestly or dishonestly. Table 21-2 presents their utilities as a function of the actions each takes, where the first entry in each cell is the utility of individual 1 and the second is the utility of individual 2. Acting honestly is better for individual 1 if and only if individual 2 acts honestly, but acting dishonestly is better for 2 regardless of whether 1 acts honestly or dishonestly. With rule utilitarianism consider two alternative rules: (H) All act honestly and (D) All act dishonestly.[9] Rule H yields aggregate

TABLE 21-2 Rule Utilitarianism and Joint Determination

		Individual 2	
		Honest	Dishonest
Individual 1	Honest	10,7	2,8
	Dishonest	7,2	4,7

---

[7]See Harsanyi (1982, p. 57) for this characterization and also Harsanyi (1977).

[8]As developed further in the next chapter, such a rule meets the two higher order moral standards—universalizability and unanimous impartial choice—that give it moral standing.

[9]Note that there are other possible rules, such as, "Individual 1 is to act honestly and individual 2 dishonestly." The two rules H and D are considered because they are symmetric.

utility of 17, whereas rule D yields aggregate utility of 11. As rule utilitarians both individuals would choose rule H, so they are unanimous in their choice.

Act utilitarianism takes the other individual's action as given, so it is necessary to form expectations about which action the other individual is likely to take. In the example in Table 21-2 if individual 2 were to act dishonestly, as an act utilitarian individual 1 would act dishonestly, since that yields aggregate utility of 11 instead of 10. If 2 were to act honestly, 1 would act honestly. As an act utilitarian individual 2 would reason in an identical manner, acting honestly if 1 were to act honestly, and acting dishonestly if 1 were to act dishonestly. Which actions would be taken thus depends on what the other individual can be expected to do. Suppose that 1 suspects that individual 2 might not be a utilitarian but instead might be self-interested. If 1 harbors such suspicions, the better action would be to act dishonestly. That is, if 2 were indeed self-interested, 2 would act dishonestly, since that is a dominant strategy for a self-interested person; that is, acting dishonestly is better for 2 regardless of how 1 acts. If instead 2 were an act utilitarian but believed that 1 was suspicious and might believe that 2 was self-interested and act dishonestly, then 2 would act dishonestly. In this case incomplete information about what the other individual will do could easily cause act utilitarianism to degenerate into both being dishonest.[10]

Decision Making in the Face of a Moral Transgression

Next consider the case in which individual 1 is a rule utilitarian and 2 is known to be self-interested and hence will act dishonestly. Is 1 morally justified in acting dishonestly? The answer at one level is no because the moral rule is for both to act honestly. It is 2 who is acting immorally. Under act utilitarianism 1 is morally right to act dishonestly, however, since doing so is justified by avoiding an even worse outcome. Rule utilitarianism, however, correctly indicates that the moral rule is for both to act honestly, so it is right for 1 to be honest. The moral obligation in such a case is to convince individual 2 to act honestly or more generally to initiate collective action to achieve a binding agreement for all to act honestly. In the case of bribery, the duty is on the firm, and all firms, to eliminate bribery and to reject extortion by government officials. This approach is considered in more detail in Chapter 24 in the case of bribery in international business, where the collective action among firms and nations occurred through the OECD.

UTILITARIANISM AND RIGHTS

Rights may be classified as intrinsic or instrumental. Intrinsic rights are to be respected because they have moral standing independent of the consequences they yield. Instrumental rights are to be respected because they lead to desirable consequences. Instrumental rights are justified in a consequentialist system, such as utilitarianism, when in a wide variety of settings such rights improve well-being. Property rights are an example of instrumental rights in utilitarianism, since they facilitate beneficial economic transactions. Utilitarianism provides a means of evaluating instrumental rights but does not provide a basis for evaluating intrinsic rights, which must be justified by other considerations as identified in Chapter 22. The Chapter 22 case *Genetic Testing in the Workplace* includes issues of instrumental and intrinsic rights.

CRITICISMS OF UTILITARIANISM

Philosophical Criticisms

One criticism of consequentialist systems is that they do not give adequate attention to intrinsic rights and liberties, which are said to be fundamentally important. A related criticism is that consequentialist systems treat all things alike in their calculus. Thus, aspirations, wants, needs, liberties, and opportunities are relevant only with regard to their consequences. As Sen (1987, pp. 74–76) argues, however, consequences must remain an essential focus even of an ethics system that considers intrinsically important concepts.

Another concern with utilitarianism pertains to how duty is assigned when consequences are jointly determined or transgressions are possible. If there is only one person who can take the moral action, the assignment of duty is clear. In some cases, however, there may be several

---

[10]Note that the situation in Table 21-2 is not a prisoners' dilemma.

parties who could take the action, or the consequences could be jointly determined as in the example in Table 21-2.[11] One resolution is that the duty should be assigned to everyone who could take the action, but that leaves a collective choice problem that could be difficult to resolve. If there are costs associated with taking the action, the utilitarian resolution of the collective choice problem is that the person with the lowest cost of acting should be assigned the duty, as indicated previously. More generally, the assignment of duty can be based on the Calabresi and Melamed principles. In some cases the assignment may be either to a firm or to the government. For example, in the case of permanent layoffs, the duty to retrain laid-off employees could rest with the employer, the government, or the employees. The duty to retrain workers has been assigned primarily to government and the employees themselves, whereas many companies have assumed the responsibility for upgrading the education and skills of their current employees.

Assigning duty is also difficult when circumstances change. Most large companies provide health, life, and disability insurance for their employees, but if an employee becomes permanently disabled and unable to work, which party has the responsibility for the worker? An increasing number of employers fire permanently disabled workers, frequently after a specified time period such as 6 months. A Mercer Human Resource Consulting study found that 51 percent of the companies surveyed fired employees on long-term disability.[12] Disability insurance payments continue after firing, but health care and life insurance benefits are no longer provided by the employers, which could impose a financial burden on the former employees. The employers argued that the fired workers were no longer employees, since they could not work. Moreover, the purpose of the disability insurance was to provide for the employee in the event of a disability, including providing funds to pay for health and life insurance. Who has the duty in such cases—the employer, the employee, or government?

Utilitarianism is also criticized for its focus solely on human well-being. Some critics claim that it should be expanded to include the well-being of other living creatures such as animals and trees and inanimate objects such as rocks and soil as well. For example, in the protection of nature what matters is not the pleasure that individuals obtain from an undisturbed mountain lake. Instead, the claim is that the well-being of the lake itself is to be taken into account. This is the subject of much disagreement, but if the claim were accepted, the approach to taking these broader considerations into effect would be similar to how altruism is taken into account, as considered above.

Interpersonal Comparisons of Utility

A fundamental problem with utilitarianism is the difficulty, if not the impossibility, of making interpersonal comparisons of utility. The preferences considered in the discipline of economics are ordinal in the sense that they indicate only how an individual orders one consequence relative to another. Those preferences do not reflect intensity. The Pareto criterion avoids interpersonal comparisons, since it requires only that an action make at least one person better off and no one worse off, evaluated in terms of the preferences of each person. A rule that produces a Pareto improvement thus has a strong claim to moral standing in a consequentialist ethics system. When actions make some individuals better off and others worse off, however, interpersonal comparisons are necessary in applying utilitarianism. Interpersonal comparisons are problematic, though, unless some common measure of preference intensity can be devised.

In spite of the difficulties in making interpersonal comparisons of preferences, utilitarianism is regularly used to evaluate public policies by measuring benefits and costs in monetary units. Measurement may involve a direct estimate of how much individuals are willing to pay, or accept, for one consequence rather than another. Indirect estimates—using wage premiums to evaluate the cost of hazardous jobs such as high steel work or housing price differentials as a function of the distance from an airport to estimate the cost of noise pollution—are also possible. Because of the difficulties in making interpersonal comparisons, cost-benefit calculations are often only one of several considerations used in public policy analysis. These issues are also present in business decisions, as in the chapter case *Pricing the Norplant System.*

---

[11]See Hardin (1988).
[12]*Wall Street Journal,* July 14, 2003.

Identifying Costs and Benefits

A difficulty in the application of utilitarianism centers on whether well-being can be identified from observed actions; that is, from revealed preferences. If people choose to smoke or be obese or hang glide, actions that can reduce their life expectancy, is that a benefit or a cost? If preferences are revealed by actions, these choices presumably have benefits to the person that outweigh the costs. In the case of smoking, however, addiction can mean that actions are not voluntary and hence do not reveal preferences.

Since utilitarianism considers the consequences for everyone, certain consequences net out. In the cap-and-trade systems for controlling sulfur dioxide emissions from power plants considered in Chapter 12, it did not matter from a social efficiency perspective whether the allowances were given free to power plants or were auctioned, or whether the benefits from reduced emissions where in Ohio or North Carolina. Yet, because it was not receiving sufficient benefits, North Carolina challenged the cap-and-trade system and was successful, ending the interstate trading of allowances. Similarly, in Chapter 14 the focus of the analysis of the liability system was on efficiency—that is, which party could reduce accidents at lowest cost—rather than on the distributive consequences. It does matter, however, whether the FCC auctions licenses to use the radio spectrum rather than awarding them based on noneconomic criteria. An auction allocates the licenses to their highest valued use, which is consistent with utilitarianism. Auctions also redistribute wealth from telecommunications and broadcast companies to the government and hence to the public, but that redistribution may net to zero in the utilitarian calculus.

The Measurement Problem

Most applications of utilitarianism involve difficult measurement and estimation problems. Social costs and benefits typically are measured in monetary units based on the amount a person would accept in exchange for a beneficial consequence or would forego to avoid a harmful consequence. Consequences are thus measured in terms of their monetary equivalents. The methods of measuring monetary equivalents in cost-benefit analysis in the public sector serve as guides for utilitarian analysis. These methods are presented in Boardman et al. (2006).

Economists look at what individuals reveal through their actions rather than what they say. That is, rather than asking people how costly is noise pollution, economists estimate the price differentials of homes on airline flight paths.[13] Wage differentials are used to measure certain social costs. Are the wage premiums paid for dangerous construction work an appropriate measure of the social costs of the accidents and deaths associated with that work? One answer is that workers have chosen those jobs in exchange for higher wages, and those choices reveal their trade-off of wages for risk.

The Food and Drug Administration routinely uses an age-adjusted value of a life saved because the elderly have a shorter remaining life expectancy than do younger persons. When the Environmental Protection Agency (EPA) conducted a secondary analysis in which it reduced by 27 percent the estimated health benefits for a person over 70, activists labeled it "the senior citizen death discount." Private politics pressure led the EPA to stop using the measure.[14]

After an airline crash in 1989 safety activists led a movement to require the use of infant safety seats in aircraft. Children under the age of 2 years had been permitted to travel on airlines without tickets if they were held by a parent. Safety activists argued that parents should be required to purchase a ticket for the child and use an infant safety seat. The FAA conducted a cost-benefit analysis of the safety seat issue and concluded that requiring the use of safety seats would actually increase injuries and deaths. The FAA estimated that requiring infant safety seats would save one infant's life over a decade. Requiring infant safety seats, however, would increase the cost of air travel for families, which would cause some families to drive rather than fly. Since driving is considerably more dangerous than flying, deaths and injuries would increase. The FAA's estimate was nine additional highway fatalities, 52 serious injuries, and 2,300 minor injuries. The methods and conclusions of the FAA study were criticized on several dimensions, including the estimated cost increase for air travel for families. Others attacked the conclusion itself. Representative Jim Lightfoot (R-IA) stated, "What's your child worth? Is it worth the

---

[13]This approach takes into account the location decisions of people who have various tolerances for noise.
[14]In 2010 the EPA set a value of $9.1 million for the value of a life, and the FDA set a value of $7.9 million. The Department of Transportation has used $6 million for the value of a life.

price of an airline ticket?"[15] The FAA began a rule-making procedure in 1998 but decided not to require safety seats despite pressure from the National Transportation Safety Board.

An alternative to a cost-benefit analysis in cases involving hazards is a cost-risk analysis or comparative risk analysis. Cost-risk analysis focuses on the costs required to reduce risks (e.g., to avoid the loss of a life) and compares the alternative in question with other alternatives. In evaluating the use of infant safety seats, the FAA estimated the lives that would be saved by the seats and the lives that would be lost because more families would drive rather than fly. The decision was then clear without attempting to value a child's life. In the chapter case *Pricing the Norplant System,* instead of attempting to measure social benefits, Wyeth-Ayerst Laboratories examined the relative effectiveness of its product compared with others on the market. The Chapter 22 case *Genetic Testing in the Workplace* provides an opportunity to use cost-risk analysis.

The Information Problem

Another problem in the use of utilitarianism is obtaining the information required to evaluate the consequences for all those affected, either directly or indirectly. In the case of an action that affects only the firm and its immediate stakeholders, the required information may be available. If the action affects others or if the effects are indirect, as when intermediated by markets or other institutions, or when consequences depend also on the actions of other parties, the information problem can be more serious. The information problem also is more serious in the application of rule utilitarianism because the rule is intended to be applicable to many decision makers and many similar situations. Obtaining information about those other situations can be difficult.

One response to this information problem is extrapolation. If other firms are facing the same issue and if the situation of one firm is reasonably representative of the others, a firm may extrapolate to the broader set of firms based on its own information. If the issue is a chronic health problem, such as carpal tunnel syndrome resulting from repetitive tasks, the experiences of most firms and their employees may be similar. On such issues, extrapolation may be straightforward. The case of American Airlines and United Airlines and the special issuances is one such example.

UTILITARIANISM IN APPLICATION

Categories of Situations

In applying utilitarianism it is useful to distinguish between two categories of situations. The first includes those in which institutions are in place to align the interests of the decision maker with societal well-being. The second includes those in which institutions are either not in place or only imperfectly align private and social interests.

In the first category, the interests of the firm and society are aligned, so the firm can act based on its own interests. If a firm makes a product that is hazardous when misused, and if misuse can be anticipated, the firm can make decisions about safety features under a utilitarian standard as considered in Chapter 14. The firm can maximize its profits and choose safety features based on their cost and the anticipated reductions in liability awards and legal costs. Even though these costs are not perfect measures of social costs, they represent the guidance of an institution, the law of torts, that has evolved over time in response to the social cost of wrongs. The law of torts is an institution consistent with utilitarianism.

Similarly, if markets are competitive, a decision regarding closing a plant can be made on the basis of profitability. If the plant's costs are too high for it to be competitive, utilitarianism concludes that the resources used in that plant be reallocated to higher-valued uses. Furthermore, the government has established a set of institutions, such as unemployment insurance and job training programs, to deal with unemployment and reemployment. Decisions based on profitability then serve society's long-term interest in the efficient use of resources—although in some cases they do so only imperfectly. This does not mean, however, that the firm should not take measures to ease the transition for its former employees if it is best positioned to do so on some dimensions. It also does not mean that other ethics considerations such as rights and justice are not relevant.

The second category of situations includes those in which institutions are not in place to align the interests of the firm and society. In these situations, utilitarian analysis must be applied directly, as considered in the following section. Government agencies use cost-benefit analysis to provide

---

[15]*Washington Post,* July 13, 1990.

information to policymakers. Firms may also use a cost-benefit analysis, as the chapter case *Pricing the Norplant System* indicates. These analyses may not be without controversy, however.

Methodology

The framework for the application of utilitarianism is illustrated in Figure 21-3. It begins with the identification of the facts of the situation and the moral concerns. As applied in the form of cost-benefit analysis, the analysis then involves the following steps:

1. Identify the alternatives—rules of behavior and actions.
2. For each alternative, identify the set of consequences for all persons and organizations affected.
3. Determine which of the consequences are social costs and which are social benefits.
4. Evaluate and estimate the social costs and social benefits.
5. Choose the action or rule that yields the greatest difference between social benefits and social costs.

The objective of a complete utilitarian analysis is to arrive at a decision in step 5. A more modest objective is to encourage managers to think broadly, rather than narrowly, about the consequences of actions. Even if a complete analysis cannot be conducted because, for example, of measurement and information problems, completing the first three steps can deepen the understanding of an issue and provide a sounder foundation for the application of ethical intuition and judgment. In particular, those steps encourage managers to consider the consequences of alternatives for all those affected.

The chapter case *Gilead Sciences (A): The Gilead Access Program for HIV Drugs* concerns a company committed to making its market-leading HIV drugs accessible to those who needed them throughout the world. The step from a commitment to actually having the drugs reach HIV/AIDS victims in Africa and Asia, however, posed a considerable challenge. The company needed an implementation mechanism to fulfill the objectives for its access program, as considered in the case.

To illustrate the analysis at this level, several examples are presented. These examples will also be considered in Chapter 22 from rights and justice perspectives.

EXAMPLE   Integrity Tests

In 1988 a federal law took effect prohibiting the use of prehiring polygraph tests, which had been given to approximately 2 million current and prospective employees annually.[1] The law also placed certain restrictions on the use of polygraph tests for employees suspected of violating laws or company policies. In response to the ban on prehiring polygraph tests, employers began to use more extensive background checks and written "integrity tests."

Integrity tests are paper-and-pencil tests intended to identify individuals with desirable or undesirable traits.[2] Examples of questions on the tests include, "Do you think a person should be fired by a company if it is found that he helped the employees cheat the company out of overtime once in a while?" and "If you found $100 that was lost by a bank truck on the street yesterday, would you turn the money over to the bank, even though you knew for sure that there was no reward?"[3] Firms use these tests, along with information about an applicant's ability, education, and experience, to screen for integrity and potential loyalty to the firm. Some firms have found the tests useful in identifying individuals who might be a problem on the job.

From the perspective of costs and benefits, integrity tests can produce benefits to the extent that they help better match prospective employees to the jobs in which they can be most productive. The tests may yield substantial benefits for some jobs and few for others.

From the perspective of rule utilitarianism, the use of integrity tests is warranted if it better matches prospective employees to jobs. Integrity can be particularly important for jobs that involve security, as in defense industries; jobs that involve access to confidential information, such as that pertaining to clients; or jobs in which an employee is entrusted with resources, as with accountants, couriers, and bank tellers. Integrity tests may also be beneficial if they enable employers to select employees who are more likely to fit with the firm's culture. For these purposes, an integrity test may be one of several sources of information used in hiring decisions, alongside personal interviews and reference checks. Such tests can also be advantageous competitively. W. Thomas Van Etten,

---

[1]Exemptions from the law were provided for security guards and jobs that involved health and safety. Pharmaceutical companies were also exempt, as was government.
[2]See Sackett and Harris (1984).

[3]The questions are from the Integrity Attitude Scale published by Reid Psychological Systems (*New York Times,* November 28, 1997).

senior vice president of Sun Bank in Miami, commented on his bank's use of an integrity test, a background check, and urinalysis for prospective employees, "People with a substance-abuse or integrity problem are more likely to look for work with our competitors who don't take as close a look as we do."[4]

If integrity tests are used to better match potential employees to jobs, they pass the cost-benefit test and are morally justified from the perspective of utilitarianism. Integrity tests, however, raise concerns about rights. They may invade

privacy if the questions are personal. The tests also raise concerns about arbitrary treatment to the extent to which the tests are imperfect measures and hence may misclassify individuals. Employers, however, have a right to hire whomever they prefer as long as they do not engage in illegal discrimination, and they may use relevant means in making hiring decisions. The tests also raise justice considerations because they may deny opportunity to those who, for whatever reason, do not perform well on such tests. Justice considerations may also be involved if the tests put at a disadvantage individuals with past experiences that cause them to perform poorly on the tests. In Chapter 22, integrity tests are reconsidered from rights and justice perspectives.

---

[4]*New York Times,* October 1, 1989.

EXAMPLE   Life Insurance Screening for Preexisting Conditions

To determine eligibility for individual life insurance policies, the insurance industry uses medical examinations to screen for preexisting health problems such as a heart condition or a stroke.[1] Once people have a life-threatening condition, they have an incentive to purchase life insurance to provide for dependents and others. Screening is intended to prevent someone from purchasing a large policy once his or her health is impaired. This provides incentives for people to purchase life insurance ex ante, that is, before they have a life-threatening condition, rather than ex post, after they have such a condition.

The ethics issue is whether people with preexisting conditions should be screened and hence not included in an insurance pool with those with no preexisting conditions. The rule to be evaluated is:

> ***Screening is permitted for preexisting conditions as a requirement for eligibility to purchase an individual life insurance policy.***

If this rule were not followed, insurance companies would have to increase the price of insurance to cover the higher

expected payments to the beneficiaries of those with preexisting conditions. The higher price would cause some individuals without preexisting conditions not to purchase insurance. This is an instance of adverse selection in which those with higher risks choose to buy life insurance, which increases the price of insurance and causes others who would have purchased insurance at the lower price not to do so at the higher price.[2] If enough people with preexisting conditions were to buy life insurance, the price could ratchet up to the point at which those without preexisting conditions would drop out of the market. Those with preexisting conditions would then be alone in the pool, and the price would reflect solely the risks of their conditions. Many persons with pre-existing conditions would then find the price of life insurance to be so high that they would choose not to buy the insurance. The entire market could then fail.

Screening for preexisting conditions results in higher aggregate well-being because insurance would be available to those without preexisting conditions, which would lead more people to buy insurance before their health is impaired. Utilitarian analysis thus supports a rule permitting screening for preexisting conditions. This analysis may be questioned from the perspective of ethics systems that take into account other considerations, as addressed in Chapter 22.

---

[1]Group life insurance plans, such as those provided by an employer, do not require screening for preexisting conditions, but group policies are experience-related and premiums are adjusted annually. The cost of coverage for individuals with preexisting conditions is thus borne by the group members. In contrast, premiums for an individual life insurance policy are fixed at the time of purchase.

[2]Adverse selection is considered in Chapter 10.

EXAMPLE   Redlining

A significant problem in the insurance and banking industries arises from imperfect information about risks. The costs of investigating and assessing risks are often high, and risk assessment is itself imperfect. The collateral for a mortgage on a home or a commercial establishment serves as a means of reducing the risk to the lender, but the value of the collateral

depends not only on the property itself but also on property values in the area in which it is located.

Insurance companies have similar difficulties assessing property and casualty risks on homes or automobiles when the risks depend on location as well as on the precautions taken by owners. Even if an applicant takes every measure of

(Continued)

(Continued)

care, the likelihood that an automobile will be stolen or vandalized is higher in some neighborhoods than in others. When prices are required to be uniform over broad geographic areas, policies written on high-risk areas can result in losses for insurance companies.

To deal with the costs of risk assessment and evaluation, some financial institutions and insurance companies identified high-risk regions of cities and refused to lend or write policies in those regions. This practice, referred to as redlining, might have been efficient, and hence ethical from a utilitarianism perspective, if the costs of risk and credit evaluation were high and the likelihood was low that a loan or policy application would be approved. That is, if the average cost of credit evaluation were high and demographic data indicated that most residents in an area would not purchase insurance or qualify for a policy or a mortgage, it could be efficient for the insurance company or financial institution not to solicit or consider applications from the area.[1]

Although redlining could be ethical from the perspective of utilitarianism, it is said to be unethical from other perspectives. Redlining is said to violate a fundamental right, since it denies opportunity to those who would qualify for loans or insurance but who do not have the opportunity to do so because they happen to reside in a redlined area. Redlining is also said to result in unjust de facto discrimination against minorities and the poor to the extent that they are overrepresented in high-risk areas. Rights and justice frameworks thus bring important considerations to bear on issues such as redlining and have resulted in laws prohibiting the practice. The redlining issue illustrates that a practice could be acceptable from the perspective of one ethics system but unacceptable from the perspective of another.

---

[1]Similar practices exist in a number of other industries, as indicated by the previous discussion of delivery services.

SUMMARY

Ethics is intended to provide mutually beneficial rules of behavior without requiring government regulation and enforcement. Some of those rules are incorporated into constitutions and statutes, but ethics extends beyond the law to provide guidance to people in their behavior and to firms in their formulation of policies.

Ethics standards are impartial and are to be applied universally, in contrast to casuistry, which holds that leaders may violate ethics standards to fulfill responsibilities to constituents. Ethics generally differs from self-interest, and utilitarianism holds that every individual's well-being is given equal weight.

Utilitarianism is a consequentialist system of ethics that defines the good in terms of human well-being and evaluates that well-being in terms of individuals' preferences. Utilitarianism then aggregates those preferences to obtain a measure of societal well-being. The right action is the one that yields the greatest societal well-being. Utilitarianism's practical usefulness is in providing a system for evaluating actions that make some individuals better off and others worse off.

Act utilitarianism focuses on an individual action taking the actions of others as given. Rule utilitarianism focuses on rules that all individuals are to follow in similar situations. Act utilitarianism is criticized for allowing exceptions to general rules of behavior, which can then degenerate into self-interest. Rule utilitarianism seeks rules of behavior that apply universally to all individuals. When consequences are a function of the actions of more than one individual, rule utilitarianism considers the actions of all individuals simultaneously. The moral rule is the one that yields the greatest aggregate well-being when everyone follows that rule.

An applied form of utilitarianism is cost-benefit analysis that evaluates actions and rules in terms of the costs and benefits they generate. The application of utilitarianism, however, involves three basic problems: (1) determining what counts as a benefit or a cost, (2) making interpersonal comparisons, and (3) conducting analysis with imperfect information about consequences and preferences. Utilitarian principles are applied in the form of cost-benefit analysis, but often, critics say, that approach fails to account for other important considerations. For example, utilitarianism considers rights only in their instrumental role of producing well-being.

Despite the challenges in applying utilitarianism, it is perhaps the most widely used ethics framework in business and economics. Utilitarianism is supported by a number of government institutions intended to align the interests of individuals and firms with the well-being of society.

Pricing the Norplant System

Toward the end of the summer of 1993, Wyeth-Ayerst Laboratories, a unit of the American Home Products Corporation, was enjoying the continuing success of its contraceptive, the Norplant System. Introduced in 1991 in the United States, 1992 revenues from the Norplant System were $105 million, which exceeded initial projections by nearly 100 percent. Executives at Wyeth-Ayerst expected annual sales of the Norplant System to stabilize just below $165 million for the near term. Given the current hostile political and regulatory environment faced by the pharmaceutical industry, this success was indeed welcomed.

The Norplant System is a progestin (levonorgestrel) encased in six permeable polymer capsules (Silastic). The capsules, which are inserted in a woman's upper arm, continuously release the progestin into the bloodstream for 5 years. The progestin alters the chemical balance of a woman's own progesterone levels. This alteration prevents ovulation, decreases circulating sperm concentrations, and creates within the uterus an environment hostile for pregnancy.

The popularity of the Norplant System was not surprising. It exhibited several advantages over alternative forms of contraception. Clinical studies indicated that the Norplant System was a highly effective contraceptive method.[16] The average pregnancy rate for women using the system over the entire 5-year period was less than 1 percent, and the first-year pregnancy rate was less than 0.2 percent. In contrast, the first-year pregnancy rate was 3 percent for oral contraceptives and intrauterine devices (IUDs), 18 percent for diaphragms, and 0.4 percent for tubal ligation. The Norplant System also required no effort to use and was easily reversible. The Norplant System did, however, require surgical implantation and removal and provided no protection from sexually transmitted diseases. Clinical tests of the Norplant System were conducted on over 55,000 women in 46 countries prior to introduction in the United States.[17] The Norplant System had a strong record of safe use, having been used by 500,000 women worldwide for the past 20 years.

PRICING THE NORPLANT SYSTEM

The Norplant System was developed jointly by Wyeth-Ayerst and the Population Council, a nonprofit organization. In the development of the Norplant System, the Population Council received $10 million in grants from the federal government and private philanthropic organizations. The system used Wyeth-Ayerst's hormone levonorgestrel, which was licensed by Wyeth-Ayerst from its developer. Wyeth-Ayerst held the exclusive right to produce and distribute the Norplant System and could set its price. It paid the Population Council a royalty of no more than 5 percent of the sales price.

In its process of establishing a price for the Norplant System, Wyeth-Ayerst first conducted a study of the relative costs and benefits of alternative contraceptive methods. The direct costs to consumers included the financial costs of the contraceptive (i.e., average retail price), any additional costs related to the use of the contraceptive (i.e., fitting a diaphragm and spermicidal cream; inserting an IUD, insertion and removal of the Norplant System), additional physician follow-up visits (i.e., checkup and monitoring, recuperation, or development of side effects and complications), and the convenience and ease of use (i.e., the need to take oral contraceptives daily). The indirect costs included the need for medical treatment of the side effects resulting from contraceptive use (i.e., medical treatment of hypertension caused by oral contraceptives), the possibility of hospitalization due to side effects (i.e., cost of hospitalization for treatment of pelvic inflammatory disease), supplies used to treat side effects (i.e., the costs of the prescription and nonprescription drugs and supplies needed post vasectomy), the loss of productivity due to side effects (i.e., absenteeism during recuperation), and the costs of contraceptive failure (i.e., the medical costs of abortion or delivery). Certain indirect benefits (i.e., the fact that oral contraceptives reduced the risk of ovarian and endometrial cancers) were also considered. Based on these studies and using the actual average retail price of other contraceptive methods, Wyeth-Ayerst concluded that even at an initial price of $600, the annual expected costs of the Norplant System would be 5 percent less than the IUD, 31 percent less than oral contraceptives, and 50 percent less than diaphragms. The annual expected costs of the Norplant System at an initial price of $600 were, however, 8 percent higher than tubal ligation and 375 percent higher than vasectomy.

Apart from scientific studies on the relative benefits of the Norplant System, Wyeth-Ayerst also had to consider the market for contraceptive devices in the United States. Marketing studies indicated that women perceived a benefit from the Norplant System that justified high initial retail prices in the $400 to $600 range. The scientific and practical advantages of the Norplant System were evident to potential consumers.

Two important features of the market complicated Wyeth-Ayerst's pricing decision, however. First, a significant percentage of all contraceptives were distributed through not-for-profit family planning clinics. These clinics financed their purchases of contraceptives and compensated their health professionals through grants from governments and philanthropic organizations. These clinics, which were usually strapped for funds, often enjoyed discounts from pharmaceutical manufacturers. For instance, Wyeth-Ayerst deeply discounted the price it charged these clinics for oral contraceptives. Such clinics would expect similar discounts on the Norplant System. Second, most contraceptives distributed in the United States were financed by third-party payers such as insurance companies, state, county, and city governments, and health maintenance organizations. In a world of rapidly escalating health care costs, these third-party payers were not simply

[16]Population Council, *Norplant: A Summary of Scientific Data.* New York, January 1989.
[17]I. Sivin, "International Experience with Norplant® and Norplant®-2 Contraceptives." *Studies in Family Planning,* 1988: pp. 1981–1994.

price takers but, instead, engaged in tough negotiations with pharmaceutical companies to obtain as low as possible price on drugs. The discounted prices that some pharmaceutical companies offered family planning clinics were often used as targets in negotiations by third-party payers. Any discounts to family planning clinics would almost certainly be sought by medical insurers and government agencies.

The other consideration in the pricing of the Norplant System was cost. The actual costs of producing the Norplant System were quite small, less than $50 per unit including the insertion kit. An additional cost was the training of doctors and other health professionals in the insertion and use of the Norplant System. Wyeth-Ayerst estimated that these costs would be approximately $15 million annually. The other relevant cost was that of liability, since lawsuits followed from the use of virtually all contraceptive systems.

Under these circumstances Wyeth-Ayerst adopted a uniform price of $350 for the introduction of Norplant. This price included the six progestin capsules and the disposable kit required for insertion. The patient also had to pay a doctor for the insertion and removal of Norplant. No discounts were given to family planning clinics or third-party payers. Wyeth-Ayerst, however, helped establish and fund the Norplant Foundation to distribute the Norplant System free of charge to indigent patients.

PUBLIC REACTION TO THE PRICING OF THE NORPLANT SYSTEM

Although commercial success of the Norplant System heartened Wyeth-Ayerst executives, public reaction to its pricing decision was not positive. Health professionals in family planning establishments criticized the pricing of the Norplant System on several grounds. Critics pointed to the $23 price per unit in bulk shipments of the Norplant System to developing countries (without the insertion kit) to highlight the glaring difference between the costs of production and average retail price of the Norplant System in the United States.[18] Critics charged that Wyeth-Ayerst was price-gouging American consumers. Whereas executives said that the success of the system indicated that it was priced fairly, critics countered that the pricing reflected the monopoly Wyeth-Ayerst enjoyed on the supply of the Norplant System.[19] This monopoly position was particularly troublesome for critics, who charged that the bulk of the development cost of the Norplant System had been provided by public funds through the activities of the Population Council.

Critics also charged Wyeth-Ayerst with betrayal and creating a "financial nightmare" for family planning clinics.

Many family planning officials believed that they were instrumental in gaining approval for the Norplant System in the United States. However, as a result of Wyeth-Ayerst's pricing decision, they claimed, their budgets had been ruptured. For example, the director of a family planning unit in a major hospital said that shortly after the introduction of the Norplant System, 500 women applied for it. The costs of supplying the system to all these women would have been $175,000, but the clinic's yearly budget for all contraceptives was $20,000. "All of the income for Norplant goes right to the drug company," said Mr. Salo of Planned Parenthood in San Diego. "We don't charge a margin on it. We lose money on each patient that we serve because Medicaid doesn't reimburse the full cost. Staff members have had to forgo raises, and plans for outreach have been shelved as a result."

Critics were also concerned about the implications of Wyeth-Ayerst's pricing of the Norplant System for the pricing of other advances in women's health care products scheduled for introduction in the coming years. For example, Upjohn introduced a new contraceptive, Depo-Provera, which was priced much higher in the United States than it was overseas; and some were concerned about the pricing of RU-486, the so-called abortion pill, scheduled to begin clinical tests in the United States the following year. "Are we going to see RU-486 come into this country at a price that makes it no cheaper than getting a first trimester abortion?" asked Mr. Kring, vice chairman and treasurer of the Norplant Foundation. "It's a trend that scares me to death—that people are making huge profits in women's health care."

The pricing of the Norplant System also attracted the attention of lawmakers. Representative Ron Wyden (D-OR), a senior member of the Subcommittee on Health and the Environment of the House Energy and Commerce Committee, vowed to hold hearings on Wyeth-Ayerst's pricing decision. "You have a situation where clearly Americans are being charged more," said Representative Wyden. "We have a chance to expose these kinds of pricing practices and create a more competitive price."

THE ASSIGNMENT

The Executive Committee on Pricing for Wyeth-Ayerst hastily gathered for a meeting. The members were concerned with the public criticisms directed at the pricing of the Norplant System and about the unfolding nonmarket threats. The committee, composed of the top executives of Wyeth-Ayerst, knew that a good deal of their time over the coming months would be spent on this issue.

They were also concerned with a more general issue that had become increasingly important as the health industry came under closer public scrutiny. The issue revolved around the pricing of proprietary medicines. What factors or principles should guide the Pricing Committee's decisions? Up to this point, the Pricing Committee's primary consideration was the relative quality and costs of available substitutes. In the view of the committee, if Wyeth-Ayerst could provide a better product at or below the costs of existing medicines, everyone would be better off. This focus had led to the comparison of

---

[18]Wyeth-Ayerst pointed out that these units were produced by a Danish manufacturer that held the exclusive right to distribute the Norplant System in certain African countries.

[19]Pharmaceutical prices generally involved a large markup above costs, since the prices of successful pharmaceuticals had to cover the research and development costs of both successful and unsuccessful attempts to discover new drugs. This also explained in part why prices of pharmaceuticals were higher in the United States and in other countries that have a pharmaceutical industry engaged in research and development than prices in countries that had no research and development-intensive pharmaceutical industry.

the Norplant System with oral contraceptives in determining the $350 price. But were other factors important as well? For instance, would the pricing of the Norplant System continue to be a nonmarket issue, or would the issue dissipate with time? Did Wyeth-Ayerst's responsibilities extend beyond providing a more effective contraceptive at a price below those of available substitutes? Should the fact that contraceptives were primarily a women's health care product have a bearing on the price it charged?

Should the fact that family planning clinics play an important role in the distribution of contraceptives to poor women be a factor? Should the fact that the Norplant System was deeply discounted in developing countries play a role in determining the prices charged in the United States? Should the fact that Wyeth-Ayerst discounts oral contraceptives to family planning clinics impact the decision of whether to discount the Norplant System to the poor? What should Wyeth-Ayerst do with respect to the family planning clinics?

The Pricing Committee has asked you to provide specific criteria for pricing proprietary medicines and to apply them to the pricing of the Norplant System. That is, you are to come up with a number that you would have adopted for the price of the Norplant System if it had been your decision to make. The Pricing Committee has asked you for an oral and written presentation of clarity sufficient to implement your proposed

criteria. To help your analysis, the committee has set the following set of parameters:

1. The variable costs of the Norplant System (including insertion kit) were $50 per unit. This figure included all production and delivery costs as well as the expected costs of liability claims. This cost also included the royalties Wyeth-Ayerst paid the developer of levonorgestrel and the Population Council.

2. Wyeth-Ayerst employed 2,700 staff, executives, health care professionals, and salespeople, who educated health professionals on the insertion and use of the Norplant System. To this point, Wyeth-Ayerst had trained over 28,000 doctors on the use of the Norplant System. With benefits, the average annual cost per employee was roughly $65,000. The Norplant System was expected to generate nearly 6 percent of Wyeth-Ayerst's total revenues of $2.8 billion. If the total labor costs were amortized to each of Wyeth-Ayerst's products based on their contribution to revenues, nearly $11 million in annual labor costs would be assigned to the sale of the Norplant System.

3. Wyeth-Ayerst allocated approximately $5 million annually for the advertising and promotion of the Norplant System. ▪

Source: This case was prepared by Thomas Gilligan from materials and information contained in the *Wall Street Journal,* August 30, 1993; the article "Contraceptive Pharmaco-Economics: A Cost Effectiveness Analysis of the Norplant System (levonorgestrel implants)," *Medical Interface,* a publication of the Medicom International, pp. 4–8; and other public sources. Copyright © 1994 by Thomas Gilligan. All rights reserved. Reprinted with permission.

Gilead Sciences (A): The Gilead Access Program for HIV Drugs

In October 2001, Gilead Sciences received approval from the U.S. Food and Drug Administration for the commercial sale of Viread (chemical name: tenofovir disoproxil fumarate), a significant new drug for the treatment of HIV/AIDS. Viread proved to be an immediate success, increasing rapidly in sales and market share in the United States within its first year on the market. As Gilead made plans to take the drug global in early 2003, a high priority was to make the drug readily available to millions of people in the least developed nations, where the HIV virus was having its most devastating effects. Pricing and distribution were key considerations. Gilead did not have a distribution system in place in any of these countries, and the price charged in the United States would be prohibitive in the developing world. If it could solve these problems, Gilead was confident that Viread would make a major contribution to the treatment of AIDS throughout the world.

AIDS

Nearly 20 million people had died from AIDS by 2001, and about 40 million worldwide were infected with the HIV virus.[20] The daily death toll from AIDS was a staggering 8,500. Sub-Saharan Africa had been the hardest hit of all by AIDS with

over 28 million people infected, which constituted more than 8 percent of the adult population. The incidence rate was as high as 30–40 percent in some countries. Primarily spread through unprotected heterosexual contact, the rapid spread of HIV had been exacerbated by the high prevalence of other sexually transmitted diseases, which weakened the body's immune system. The inferior status of women, workforce intermigration and mobility, poverty, unemployment, and lack of care exacerbated the situation. Lack of knowledge about how HIV was spread, combined with an inadequate health infrastructure for testing and treatment, added to the crisis.

Education and precautions had limited the spread of HIV in North America and Western Europe, and the introduction of antiretroviral drugs in 1996 had made HIV/AIDS a treatable chronic disease. In poor countries neither individuals nor their governments could afford the drugs, leaving few of the victims able to access treatment.

GILEAD SCIENCES: EARLY DAYS

Gilead Sciences was founded in 1987 with a mission of discovering new drugs that addressed significant unmet medical needs. The company's name was derived from a region of the ancient Middle East known for a balm with medicinal qualities, referred to in the Bible as "the balm of Gilead," and subsequently cited in Poe's "The Raven," Negro spirituals, and

---

[20]The material in this section was originally published in "Note on AIDS and the Pharmaceutical Industry," GSB No. P-41, p. 3.

a Roald Dahl short story. Gilead Sciences was initially funded by prominent venture capital firms in the San Francisco Bay Area and had an initial public offering in 1992, which raised $86 million.

John Martin joined Gilead in 1990 as vice president for research and development, and shortly after joining the company he negotiated licensing of rights to a portfolio of nucleotides, several of which Gilead later developed into antiviral medicines for HIV, hepatitis and cytomegalovirus. Martin became president and CEO of the company in 1996. That same year, the company gained approval from the Food and Drug Administration (FDA) for its first commercial drug, Vistide (cidofovir injection), used in the treatment of cytomegalovirus retinitis in patients with AIDS. The product, however, did not gain widespread use, generating only $11.7 million in sales in its first full year and $6.1 million the following year.

Gilead's research and development pipeline proved increasingly fruitful, and the company successfully launched a string of new products. Tamiflu, approved in 1999, was a neuraminidase inhibitor for the treatment of influenza. Gilead co-developed the product with Hoffmann-La Roche, which held exclusive marketing rights and paid Gilead a royalty on sales.

The most successful of Gilead's early products was AmBisome, an antifungal agent that combated serious fungal infections and showed activity against visceral leishmaniasis, a parasitic infection. AmBisome achieved sales of $165 million in 2001, representing 86 percent of Gilead's total product sales that year. Despite the success of AmBisome and other products, Gilead had still not posted an operating profit since its founding.

GILEAD'S AIDS DRUGS

Because the HIV virus is prone to mutation and eventual resistance to drugs, HIV/AIDS treatment typically consisted of three drugs used in combination, in what was called a drug cocktail. Drug cocktails included at least three agents that targeted the virus at two or more steps in its replication cycle. Nucleoside/nucleotide reverse transcriptase inhibitors (NRTIs) and non-nucleoside reverse transcriptase inhibitors (NNRTIs) both combat the HIV virus when it first enters the human cell. Protease inhibitors prevent the HIV virus from being successfully assembled and released from an infected cell.[21]

A major milestone in AIDS treatment therapy was reached in October 2001 when the FDA approved Gilead's breakthrough drug Viread as a first-line treatment for AIDS patients. This meant that the drug's use was not restricted to patients who had developed resistance to an initial treatment.

Viread was a significant improvement over existing drugs because it was the first NRTI based on a nucleotide analogue and not a nucleoside analogue. The body naturally converted nucleosides into nucleotides, and drugs based on nucleotide analogues allowed this conversion process to be skipped, resulting in less toxic build-up in the body. For AIDS patients, this meant that treatment with Viread would have a dramatically

better side-effect profile and half-life in the body. Because of its once-a-day dosage and fewer side effects, patients were more likely to adhere to their treatment schedules, which improved their long-term health. Adherence to treatment schedules freed clinical space and resources for the treatment of new patients.

The director of research at the Community Research Initiative of New England and Harvard Vanguard Medical Associates praised the new drug, stating:

> Viread addresses many of the needs of people living with HIV today. The drug has demonstrated a significant antiviral response, even in patients who may no longer respond well to available therapies due to the development of viral resistance …. Viread is an important new option because it is powerful and convenient—it has a strong track record of safety in clinical studies, is well tolerated and is dosed as one tablet once a day. These are all important attributes for patients taking these types of drugs.[22]

In the pharmaceutical trade press, one pharmacist stated that he expected Viread "to be on all the formularies. There's no real secondary choice, there's no other option, and there's no generic."[23]

Viread was launched in the United States at a price of $4,135 for a treatment for a year.[24] A 1-year supply cost approximately $475 to manufacture. After only 1 year on the market, Viread had become Gilead's largest product by revenue in 2002, achieving sales of $226 million. Largely because of Viread, Gilead reported its first operating profit.

Gilead also had several clinical studies under way for promising new drugs. One of these drugs, Emtriva, was a nucleoside reverse transcriptase inhibitor. Although not expected to be a significant therapeutic advancement like Viread, Emtriva (emtricitabine) was important as an extension of Gilead's AIDS drug franchise. If successful, Emtriva was to be included as one ingredient in a new combination pill, Truvada (emtricitabine and tenofovir disoproxil fumarate), also under development. Truvada was a once-a-day pill that included both Viread and Emtriva, helping to simplify the therapy regimen for AIDS patients by combining two of the three drugs in an AIDS drug cocktail into one pill. When approved by the FDA, Truvada was expected to result in greater regimen compliance by AIDS patients, a major concern of doctors who worried about patients skipping doses.

THE GILEAD ACCESS PROGRAM

Gilead was motivated by the suffering of patients with HIV/AIDS and wanted its drugs to be available to those who needed them in the least developed countries. The challenge was to design an access program to accomplish this objective. Gilead would have to be sensitive to the diverse institutional

---

[21]"AIDS & HIV Antiretroviral Drug Treatment in Resource Poor Communities," AVERT, 2006.

[22]"FDA Approves Gilead's Anti-HIV Drug Viread," *Biotech Business,* vol. 14, issue 12, December 1, 2001.

[23]Kathy Hitchens, "HIV Treatment Advances with First Drug in a New Class," *Drug Topics,* November 19, 2001.

[24]Gilead spokesperson cited in Tom Abate, "Gilead HIV Drug OK'd for Wide Use; Viread Allowed for Initial Therapy," *San Francisco Chronicle,* October 27, 2001, p. E1.

environments of these countries. Gilead had a proven track record of success in the U.S., but the international situation, especially in developing nations, was more complicated.

International Institutions

No single governing body provided regulatory standards and oversight for pharmaceuticals. The World Health Organization (WHO), an agency of the United Nations, acted in a coordinating capacity by collecting and disseminating information on diseases and therapies to health ministries around the world. The WHO deliberated on global policies with regard to human health but did not have regulatory authority over countries. The WHO provided technical support for countries implementing treatment programs, including treatment guidelines, prequalification of medicines, and an essential medicines list. Since Gilead had not yet marketed Viread outside the United States and Europe, it was not included on the essential medicines list as either a first-line or second-line therapy.

Through its published treatment guidelines, the WHO recommended to health ministries best-practices in administering all aspects of a treatment program, including patient testing and monitoring, drug use, and education and prevention. Through its prequalification process, the WHO inspected and certified manufacturers for compliance with WHO Good Manufacturing Practices (GMP) which assured clinics that they were procuring medicines from suppliers that met WHO quality standards. In its essential medicines list, updated every 2 years, the WHO listed the medicines and vaccines that a clinic would need to serve its local patients.

National Institutions

A drug had to be registered in each country before it could be used. A company was not required to conduct additional trials to register the drug, but it was required to submit an application to the local ministry of health. In Africa, the registration process tended to be modeled after those of European countries, but the regulatory agencies were typically under-resourced. Approval could be quick in some countries but take 2 or 3 years in others. A drug could also be brought into a country while the registration application was pending through an import waiver. The import waiver could be requested either by local wholesalers or by the clinic prescribing the drug.

Funding

International organizations played an important role in funding drug purchases for clinical programs. The main source of funding in 2003 was the Global Fund to Fight AIDS, Tuberculosis, and Malaria. The Global Fund, a UN-related nonprofit organization, provided grant money directly to the health ministries of developing nations. Grants by the Global Fund averaged $1 billion per year and were collected from the pledges of 50 countries around the world, with the United States as the largest donor providing approximately 33 percent of total funds.[25]

In his 2003 State of the Union address, President George W. Bush asked Congress to allocate $15 billion over 5 years to fight AIDS in Africa and the Caribbean. The President's Emergency Plan for AIDS Relief (PEPFAR), when approved, would be the largest source of funding for AIDS treatment in the developing world. Unlike the Global Fund, whose grants were distributed to governments and health ministries through application, PEPFAR funds could be given directly to local clinics or health care organizations. The administrator of PEPFAR could actively seek recipients for funding. Governments and regional organizations that received funds directly from the U.S. government agencies were referred to as "prime" partners. Many prime partners redistributed funds to local clinics and organizations, referred to as "subpartners," to conduct AIDS treatment programs. Although drugs purchased with PEPFAR funds could be generics, clinics were required to purchase from manufacturers whose plants were FDA approved, which was a stricter quality standard than the WHO GMP.[26]

Intellectual Property

Patent protection allowed pharmaceutical companies to control drug pricing and distribution. Historically, the standards of patent and intellectual property protection varied widely around the world. The 1986–1994 Uruguay Round of multilateral trade negotiations resulted in the Agreement on Trade-Related Aspects of Intellectual Property Rights (TRIPS) which harmonized how these rights were protected by the members of the World Trade Organization. Under TRIPS, governments had to ensure that intellectual property rights were enforceable under their laws and that infringement penalties were sufficiently stringent to dissuade violations. TRIPS, however, provided for exceptions under Article 31, which allowed a government to supersede patent protection and force compulsory licensing of a product in the case of "national emergency or other circumstances of extreme urgency." In issuing a compulsory license, governments could grant to a third party the right to produce the patent-protected product domestically and, in some cases, to export it to a third country.[27] With a critical drug in the treatment of the AIDS epidemic, Gilead faced the threat of compulsory licensing for Viread if the product was not appropriately available or the price was too high.

In addition to the risk of compulsory licensing, Gilead faced the risk that its intellectual property rights would be violated by low-cost generic manufacturers, particularly those in India. Encouraged by India's lenient patent law regime, an extensive drug manufacturing industry had developed that was capable of reengineering advanced therapies for sale in India and other developing markets. With their advanced manufacturing techniques, these firms could copy Gilead's drugs and compete at very low prices. These firms also sold in the United States generic drugs produced in FDA-approved manufacturing facilities in India.

[25]"The Global Fund to Fight AIDS, Tuberculosis, and Malaria," AVERT, 2006, http://www.avert.org/global-fund.htm (October 19, 2006).

[26]"President's Emergency Plan for AIDS Relief (PEPFAR)," AVERT, 2006, http://www.avert.org/pepfar.htm (October 19, 2006).
[27]"Note on AIDS and the Pharmaceutical Industry," p. 7.

Another closely related risk was that drugs made available to poor countries at very low prices could be reimported into the U.S. market or sold in Europe, cannibalizing sales. Gilead decided to produce a white pill for developing nations that was easily differentiated from the blue version sold in the United States, Europe and other high-income regions of the world.[28]

Distribution

Distribution also posed a problem. In most developing countries, the company had no physical presence, local contacts, nor in-house expertise about potentially critical social and cultural forces. Furthermore, each country posed different regulatory challenges. The relevant political institutions varied widely across countries, so strategies that could work in Country A might not work in Country B. Similarly, the identities of key actors within a given regulatory body were usually unknown in advance and, once identified, were often uninformed about Viread (and medicines more generally), skeptical of drug companies, or corrupt. In some countries, government officials in the agencies that reviewed registration applications could demand payments. Failure to make such payments could result in significant delays in approval times. Also, drugs delivered to government agencies could be held up in customs or diverted from their intended recipients. Gilead risked similar problems from private distributors.

Public Perception

Gilead was developing its access program in a charged environment. AIDS activist groups, health care providers, and some governments were strong critics of pharmaceutical companies and their pricing and protection of intellectual property. Most pharmaceutical companies with HIV/AIDS drugs had been targeted by activists and criticized in the press for not doing more to make their drugs accessible. Although Gilead was trying to do the right thing, it had to consider how its efforts would be portrayed by the international organizations and AIDS activist groups that were watching carefully and critically.

The Outlook (2003)

In early 2003, CEO John Martin called 2002 "a remarkable year of transformation and achievements for Gilead." He was equally confident about the impact that Viread would have in treating AIDS patients around the world, stating: "With its efficacy, strong safety profile, and simple, one-tablet, once-daily dosing, Viread has an attractive profile to help address the HIV epidemic in developing parts of the world."[29] After only 1 year on the market, Viread was already the leading product for the treatment of HIV/AIDS in the United States. By offering the drug to the developing world at affordable prices, Gilead was certain that the demand would be very high from governments, health ministries, international organizations, and local clinics that were eager to help the victims of AIDS.

Optimism notwithstanding, Gilead had to decide how best to resolve distribution and pricing issues. It could rely on third parties to implement the Access Program. Some pharmaceutical companies that were part of the Accelerated Access Initiative had used the Ireland-based advisory company Axios to design and manage their access programs.[30] Axios served as a strategic advisor in designing and implementing health care systems in developing nations. Axios consulted on market entry strategies, program design, identification of local partners, implementation, and monitoring. Gilead believed Axios could greatly help its efforts to distribute to the developing world, since Gilead itself did not have any employees or partners in those countries. Reliance on Axios would represent a very significant outsourcing of the Access Program and require much less direct staffing and resource dedication on Gilead's part.

As part of its effort to make Viread available broadly, Gilead would have to develop a pricing strategy that was appropriate for each local market. Gilead had grouped the nations of the world into four tiers by per capita gross national income. The top tier included developed nations, and the second tier included upper-middle income nations with per capita gross national income at least that of Brazil ($3,000 per year). The third tier included lower-middle income nations (per capita GNI less than $3,000). The lowest tier included developing nations with GNI less than $825. ◾

Preparation Questions

1. Does Gilead have responsibility to make its drug available to people who cannot afford it? How far does this responsibility extend? Does Gilead's responsibility extend to developing distribution networks and supervising the proper use of its drugs?
2. Is it wise to rely on Axios for distribution of Viread in Africa?
3. Should Gilead register Viread in each country or attempt to expedite the process by relying on import waivers?
4. Are the government agencies in the developing countries likely to expedite approval of the sale of Viread?
5. Are the media and AIDS activist groups likely to monitor and critique the success of the Gilead Access Program?
6. What, if anything, should Gilead attempt to accomplish with the WHO, and how successful is it likely to be?
7. In designing its Access Program with whom should Gilead work or consult?

---

[28]Gilead believed that the risk of reimportation was lower for AIDS drugs than for other medicines because most AIDS drugs were paid for by state health services programs called AIDS Drug Assistance Programs (ADAP), which received funding from the U.S. government.

[29]"Q4 2002 Gilead Sciences Earnings Conference Call," Voxant FD (Fair Disclosure) Wire, January 20, 2003.

[30]The Accelerated Access Initiative (AAI) was a cooperative effort between organizations such as UNAIDS, WHO, UNICEF, UNFPA, and the World Bank and pharmaceutical companies to broaden access to AIDS drugs. AAI was launched in May 2000 and the founding pharmaceutical companies included Boehringer Ingelheim, Bristol-Myers Squibb, F. Hoffman-La Roche, Glaxo Wellcome, and Merck & Co. See "Fostering Access to Treatment," Merck & Co., http://www.merck.com/cr/enabling_access/developing_world/hiv/hiv_access.html (November 30, 2006).

8. How significant are the risks to Gilead's intellectual property rights for Viread, specifically those posed by compulsory licensing and Indian generic manufacturers?

9. How significant are the risks of drug reimportation and counterfeits? What strategy should Gilead develop to deal with these risks?

10. What other problems or obstacles not mentioned above should Gilead be worried about? How should Gilead mitigate them?

11. How should Gilead price Viread in each of the income tiers? Defend your pricing scheme based on strategic and/or moral principles.

Source: Brian Tayan, Professor David Baron and Professor Keith Krehbiel prepared this case as the basis for class discussion rather than to illustrate either effective or ineffective handling of an administrative situation. Copyright © 2007 by the Board of Trustees of the Leland Stanford Junior University. All rights reserved. Reprinted with permission.

Consumer Awareness or Disease Mongering? GlaxoSmithKline and the Restless Legs Syndrome

"The words 'It's frustrating,' shaped to look like a pair of legs, float across the screen. A voice intones: 'It's frustrating. Just when you're ready to relax, you feel the compelling urge to move.' Eventually, the legs morph into those of a woman draped lazily across a recliner."[31] "When I saw the ad, it pretty much described me to a tee. If that doesn't do it, then I'll talk to my doctor about trying something else," said Frank Stevens of Gillette, Wyoming.[32]

The advertisement was promoting GlaxoSmithKline's (GSK) drug Requip for the treatment of restless legs syndrome (RLS), a neurological condition causing an itchy, restless sensation in the legs. Requip (ropinirole) had earlier been approved for the treatment of Parkinson's disease, and in 2005 it was approved for RLS with 2–4 milligrams doses versus 15 milligrams for Parkinson's disease.

In 2005 GSK spent $36 million to advertise Requip according to Nielsen Monitor-Plus. Sales increased by $50 million, or over 50 percent, in the United States. Worldwide, Requip was projected to have sales of over $500 million in 2006 with more than half accounted for by RLS.

GSK had begun an intensive promotional campaign for Requip prior to approval by the Food and Drug Administration. It began issuing press releases in 2003 referring to research presentations at an American Academy of Neurology conference. It then began advertising to doctors in medical journals and then turned to direct-to-consumer advertising. In 2003 it began developing consumer awareness of RLS with an advertising campaign stating a "new survey reveals a common yet underrecognized disorder—restless legs syndrome—is keeping Americans awake at night."[33] The initial ads did not mention the drug but instead urged people to consult their physician. In preparation for the direct-to-consumers advertising campaign GSK had recruited sleep-disorder specialists to speak to doctors at hosted dinners at restaurants.[34]

GSK argued that its campaign was simply raising awareness of RLS. A GSK spokesperson said that it was "sharing medical information on a wide variety of conditions, including RLS, which is what we see as our mission."[35] John Winkelman of Harvard Medical School who treats sleep disorders said, "This was a disorder that was generally overlooked by most physicians and individuals."[36]

Others disagreed. "The argument the pharmaceutical industry is always making is that this is patient education—that this is an under-diagnosed condition and 'we're just trying to raise awareness,'" said Michael Wilkes of the University of California at Davis. "If you're talking about something like hepatitis C or measles, that might be true. But if you're talking about toenail fungus or baldness or restless legs syndrome, I just don't buy it."[37]

Some accused drug companies of disease mongering.[38] Lisa M. Schwartz of the Veteran Affairs Outcomes Group and the Center for the Evaluative Clinical Sciences of the Dartmouth Medical School said, "We're increasingly turning normal people into patients. The ordinary experiences of life become a diagnosis, which makes healthy people feel like they're sick."[39]

"Researchers say it is surprisingly easy for patients to persuade doctors to prescribe medications, especially for unfamiliar conditions. Richard Kravitz of the University of California at Davis said of RLS, 'physicians don't know much about it and may be wanting to follow the path of least resistance and prescribe a medication for a condition that a patient might not have."[40]

RESTLESS LEGS SYNDROME

Restless legs syndrome "is a neurological disorder characterized by an uncontrollable urge to move the legs, usually accompanied by unpleasant and sometimes painful sensations in the legs. RLS affects up to 10 percent of the population worldwide aged between 30 and 79 years and around one-third of sufferers experience symptoms more than twice weekly causing

---

[31] *Washington Post,* May 30, 2006.
[32] Ibid.
[33] *BusinessWeek,* May 8, 2006.
[34] *Wall Street Journal,* October 26, 2006.
[35] Ibid.
[36] Ibid.
[37] *Washington Post,* May 30, 2006.
[38] Disease mongering was a term coined by Lynn Payer in a 1992 book *Disease-Mongers: How Doctors, Drug Companies, and Insurers Are Making You Feel Sick.* New York: John Wiley. See also R. Moynihan and A. Cassels. (2005). *Selling Sickness. How the World's Biggest Pharmaceutical Companies Are Turning Us All into Patients.* New York: Nation Books.
[39] *Washington Post,* May 30, 2006.
[40] Ibid.

moderate to severe distress. The motor-restlessness worsens during the evening and night causing difficulty initiating and maintaining sleep. The sleep disruption can lead to excessive daytime sleepiness and compromise work performance. RLS also has considerable impact on social activities that require immobility."[41]

GSK recognized the potential of Requip to treat RLS after doctors had begun to prescribe it for the disorder. Some doctors stated that RLS afflicted approximately 3 percent of people with symptoms at least twice a week, but GSK claimed that it affected up to 10 percent.[42] Steven Woloshin and Lisa Schwartz indicated that the 10 percent estimate was based on study responses to a single question rather than "the four standard criteria."[43] In a large-scale study only 7 percent reported all four criteria, and only 2.7 percent reported symptoms occurring sufficiently frequently that treatment might be appropriate.[44] Woloshin and Schwartz also argued that the 2.7 percent figure was likely too high because of selection bias.

Pharmaceutical companies regularly sought applications of their drugs beyond their primary indication. Use for new indications required approval by the Food and Drug Administration, and GSK had conducted the required clinical tests to establish the safety and efficacy of Requip for the treatment of RLS.[45] Similarly, Boehringer Ingelheim's pramipexole had been approved in 1997 for treatment of idiopathic Parkinson's disease, and the company sought approval for treatment of RLS. "Pramipexole was approved in April 2006 throughout the European Union for the symptomatic treatment of moderate to severe idiopathic restless legs syndrome and is also approved in Australia, Brazil, Mexico and others."[46] The lead investigators on an RLS research study concluded, "These studies provide evidence that supports the efficacy and safety of pramipexole for RLS across a range of symptoms which were sustained over time."[47] UCB SA of Belgium was also seeking approval for its Parkinson's drug for treating RLS.

THE RESTLESS LEGS SYNDROME FOUNDATION

The Restless Legs Syndrome (RLS) Foundation, of Rochester, Minnesota, conducted research on and provided education about RLS. The foundation organized support groups with over 2,500 people attending and also provided information at health fairs. Georgianna Bell, executive director of the RLS

Foundation, said, "There's still people out there who have the condition and don't know they have it. It's a serious condition. Raising awareness is important. It can help a lot of people." The number of visits to the foundation's Web site nearly doubled to 4,500 a day after GSK's advertising campaign for Requip.

Robert H. Waterman, Jr., chair of the foundation, wrote in the 2005 annual report, "With our newfound visibility comes the realization that people living with RLS are a big audience. From relative obscurity, we have now become a market. We are a market for medications, a market for publications, a market for untested therapies, and a market for information, the bulk of which will be reliable and some of which will not …. Of all the major sources of information on RLS, our foundation aims to be the most consistently reliable, objective, unbiased, and science-based."

In 2005 the RLS Foundation received $578,000 in contributions, which represented over 40 percent of its total income. GSK was the only Gold Corporate Partner contributing over $250,000.[48] In addition GlaxoSmithKline—USA was a Leader, contributing at least $10,000. The foundation also reported grants receivable of $300,000 in 2005. The grants "represent promises to give from pharmaceutical companies." Boehringer Ingelheim was also a Leader.

DISEASE MONGERING?

Referring to the promotion of drugs for an underappreciated malady, "to a growing chorus of physicians and health-care specialists, the very idea of treating the risk of a risk is wrong. They have labeled the phenomenon 'disease-mongering,' defined as the corporate-sponsored creation or exaggeration of maladies for the purpose of selling more drugs."[49] Dr. Robert L. Klitzman of Columbia University said, "The problem is that mild cases are being made to seem more serious than they are." Dr. David Henry of the University of Newcastle in Australia stated, "Drug companies are playing off the desire we all have to get rid of things that bother us."[50]

Woloshin and Schwartz identified some of the costs of such promotions: "Helping sick people get treatment is a good thing. Convincing healthy people that they are sick is not. Sick people stand to benefit from treatment, but healthy people may only get hurt: They get labeled 'sick,' may become anxious about their condition, and, if they are treated, may experience side effects that overwhelm any potential benefit."[51] They noted that "The market for treatment gets enlarged in two ways: by narrowing the definition of health so normal experiences get labeled as pathologic, and by expanding the definition of disease to include earlier, milder, and presymptomatic forms …"[52]

[41]"Boehringer Ingelheim's Pramipexole Can Provide Benefit of Improved Mood Disturbance for People with Restless Legs Syndrome," *PR Newswire Europe*, September 5, 2006.

[42]Phillips B., Young T., Finn L., Asher K., Hening W. A., et al. (2000). "Epidemiology of Restless Legs Symptoms in Adults." *Arch. Intern. Med.* 160:2137–2141.

[43]Woloshin, Steven and Lisa M. Schwartz. "Giving Legs to Restless Legs: A Case Study of How the Media Helps Make People Sick." *PLoS Medicine*, 3(4): e170 DOI, April 11, 2006.

[44]Allen R., Walters A., Montplaisir J., Hening W., Myers A., et al. (2005). "Restless Legs Syndrome Prevalence and Impact: REST General Population Study." *Arch. Intern. Med.* 165:1286–1292.

[45]There was no evidence to connect RLS and Parkinson's disease.

[46]"Boehringer Ingelheim's Pramipexole Can Provide Benefit of Improved Mood Disturbance for People with Restless Legs Syndrome," *PR Newswire Europe*, September 5, 2006.

[47]*Pain & Central Nervous System Week*, May 1, 2006.

[48]GSK was the only corporate partner in 2005.

[49]*BusinessWeek*, May 8, 2006.

[50]Ibid.

[51]The label on Requip noted nausea and dizziness as side effects. Woloshin and Schwartz report: "Nausea (40% in ropinirole group versus 8% in placebo group) and dizziness (11% versus 5%, respectively). Somnolence and fatigue (ostensibly, the real target of the drug) were also higher in the ropinirole versus the placebo group (12% versus 6%, 8% versus 4%, respectively)." Woloshin and Schwartz, op cit.

[52]Woloshin and Schwartz, op cit.

The promotional campaigns of the pharmaceutical companies were often amplified by coverage in the media. Woloshin and Schwartz studied media coverage of RLS and found 33 articles on the syndrome, most of which exaggerated the prevalence and seriousness of the disease. *The Daily Telegraph* proclaimed, "… The condition sounds like a joke, but its consequences can be devastating. Driven to despair by years of sleepless nights, patients have become suicidal."[53] Many of the articles suggested that the symptoms should be treated, and half mentioned ropinirole, often with testimonials from patients who had used the drug. None of the articles suggested the possibility of overdiagnosis.

For a year in advance of approval of ropinirole in the United Kingdom GSK had advertised in doctors' magazines to promote awareness of RLS, which is also known as Ekbom's syndrome. The ads stated that the syndrome was serious and that sufferers should consult the Web site of the Ekbom Support Group. The Web site mentioned ropinirole as effective for the syndrome. GSK supported the Web site financially.

As a result of the advertising campaign a physician in the United Kingdom complained that GSK was advertising an unapproved drug.[54] "The Prescriptions Medicines Code of Practice Authority, set up by the Association of the British Pharmaceutical Industry, ruled that GSK broke the authority's rules by promoting an unlicensed drug. 'GSK was, in effect, directing patients to a Web site that contained misleading messages about the safety of ropinirole, which might indirectly encourage patients to ask their doctors to prescribe it,' the authority said."[55] The physician said, "The Ekbom Support Group was hijacked by GSK to promote restless legs syndrome and the GSK drug ropinirole. I am not saying some people do not experience pain and restless legs but claims on the Web site that it is a widespread and serious condition are disproportionate."[56] The head of the support group said that she had taken ropinirole for 7 years and it was legitimate to tell others about it.

A spokesperson for GSK stated, "We realize that not every medicine is for every person. The labels contain important information about whether it's appropriate, and we're confident that doctors consulting with patients will assess their health-care issues and the risks and rewards and make an appropriate decision."[57]

GSK made drugs not only for RLS but also for social anxiety disorder and other criticized applications. ▪

Preparation Questions

1. Did GSK act responsibly in seeking approval for Requip for the treatment of RLS?
2. Has GSK acted responsibly in promoting Requip? Should it have restricted its marketing to doctors? Should it have conducted a direct-to-consumers campaign? Has GSK violated any patient rights? Has it been fair to patients? Was it disease mongering?
3. Should GSK continue to support the RLS Foundation to the extent it has been?
4. How should GSK deal with the criticism of its conduct?
5. Did the introduction and marketing of Requip likely increase or decrease societal well-being?

[53]*Daily Telegraph,* December 1, 2004.
[54]Ropinirole was not approved until April 2006.
[55]*Sunday Times,* August 6, 2006. The Prescription Medicines Code of Practice Authority was established by the Association of the British Pharmaceutical Industry.

[56]*Sunday Times,* August 6, 2006.
[57]*BusinessWeek,* May 8, 2006.

ETHICS SYSTEMS: RIGHTS AND JUSTICE

INTRODUCTION

Consequentialist ethics systems such as utilitarianism focus on the good and evaluate the good in terms of individuals' preferences for consequences. Rights established under a consequentialist system are instrumental, since their justification is in terms of the consequences they yield. Some moral philosophies hold instead that there are certain rights and liberties justified by considerations independent of their consequences. Basic liberties such as freedom of speech and rights such as equal opportunity are fundamental concepts that express considerations of autonomy and basic equality. Other moral philosophies emphasize justice, which requires comparisons of the situations of individuals. For example, in the redlining example in Chapter 21, concerns were raised about the violation of a right to opportunity and an injustice to individuals who happened to live in a redlined area. This chapter considers ethics systems that emphasize considerations of rights and justice.

The following two sections consider classes of ethics systems and classes of rights, respectively. The next section introduces and critiques Kant's system of moral rules, which establishes intrinsic rights. An approach to rights analysis and to resolving conflicts among claimed rights is then presented. An alternative—neoclassical liberalism—to Kant's system is then considered. Categories of justice theories are introduced with a focus on compensatory and distributive justice. Rawls's system of justice as fairness is presented, and his principles of justice are evaluated. The role of incentives in his system is identified and contrasted with utilitarianism and egalitarianism. The assignment of duty and the application of the justice principles are then considered. The chapter concludes with higher order principles used to evaluate ethics systems.

CLASSIFICATION OF ETHICS SYSTEMS

Ethics systems are classified as *teleological* or *deontological*. Teleological, or consequentialist, systems define the rightness of an action in terms of the good its consequences yield. Deontological ethics systems hold that moral right takes precedence over the good and can be evaluated by considerations independent of, or in addition to, consequences.[1] From a deontological perspective, the objective is to deduce from fundamental axioms a set of principles that have moral standing and then to identify rights and rules of behavior that correspond to those principles. Those rights and rules of behavior are intrinsic; that is, they are important in and of themselves. The principal deontological system considered here is Kant's theory of moral rules. Rawls's theory of justice brings together elements of deontological and consequentialist theories and prioritizes them.

As illustrated in Figure 22-1, both teleological and deontological systems are ultimately concerned with the evaluation of actions. Teleological systems approach this task by examining the relationship between actions and consequences. Deontological systems approach this task by examining the relationship between actions and the reasons or motives for taking those actions. In a teleological system, consequences are evaluated in terms of a value theory that is a part of the particular system. Utilitarianism, for example, uses a value theory based on individual preferences and their aggregation.

In deontological systems, the motive or reason for taking an action, or abiding by a principle, is required to have moral standing. A principle, for example, could be "respect each person's liberty by treating each person as he or she has freely consented to be treated." The reason to abide by the principle then is that individuals are willing to have everyone abide by it and are willing to have the principle applied to themselves.

Teleological and deontological systems are sufficiently different in their nature and structure that they do not necessarily yield the same evaluations of actions. Because no ethics system is immune to criticism, the objective here is not to decide which system is the more appropriate but instead to understand the guidance that each provides.

---

[1]The root of deontology is *deon,* which means obligatory, to bind.

FIGURE 22-1   Teleological and Deontological Ethics Systems

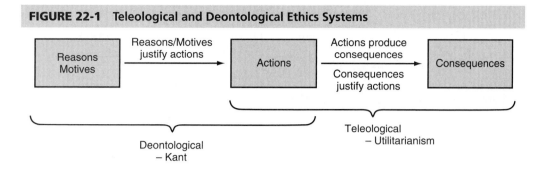

CLASSES OF RIGHTS

Rights may be derived from moral principles or may be established through political choice. Rights established by political choice often reflect moral principles. The U.S. Constitution identifies individual liberties, such as the freedom of speech, and rights of political participation. Rights are also established through legislation, such as the Civil Rights Act of 1964, which prohibits discrimination on the basis of race, color, religion, sex, or national origin. Legislation has also established entitlements, such as a right to education. Rights are also established by private agreements, such as contracts, that specify mutual obligations and expectations that are enforceable by the courts. Rights may also be established by implicit contracts such as those associated with the employment policies and practices of a company.

Rights are often categorized as negative or positive. Reflecting the intellectual tradition at the time it was written, the U.S. Constitution primarily establishes negative rights that impose duties on people and the state not to interfere with the actions of a person. Freedom of speech and assembly are negative rights because they prohibit others from interfering with those activities. A property right is a negative right because others are prohibited from compelling the holder to take an action with respect to that property. In contrast, positive rights impose affirmative duties on others to take particular actions. For example, a person has a positive right to some level of public education, and that right imposes duties on others to pay the corresponding taxes. Some individuals argue that people should have positive "economic rights" to food, housing, and medical care. Others believe that positive rights such as economic rights have lower standing than negative rights because positive rights impose duties that necessarily limit the liberty and autonomy of others.

An important difference between rights established by the state and those based on moral principles is that the former can be publicly enforced, whereas for moral rights there is no enforcement mechanism other than individual sanction. Rights granted by the state or by private agreements are generally specific; if ambiguity exists, an authoritative body such as a court clarifies the right. As considered in Chapter 14, for example, the common law has established precedents for determining remedies for the breach of contract rights.

Rights and entitlements evolve over time as a consequence of demographic change, changes in preferences, and technological developments. Rights may also evolve because of changing perceptions about the appropriate extent of liberties, the scope of justice, or the relative importance of various rights. Rights also evolve as a consequence of interest group pressures acting through the institutions of government and public sentiment.

The evolution of the rights of university students provides an example. In the 1960s many universities followed the principle of in loco parentis, under which the distribution of rights between the university and the student was analogous to that between a parent and a child. The distribution of rights has evolved to the point at which enrollment now carries with it a well-defined set of rights and access to quasi-judicial mechanisms intended to ensure fair treatment.

Rent control is an example of a right resulting from the collective action of interest groups. Rent control, such as on apartments, is a means of redistributing wealth from landlords to renters. If apartment renters have sufficient political power, they may be able to institute rent control as a means of benefiting themselves at the expense of landlords. Rent control on apartments also affects those people who would like to rent, since rent control decreases the incentives to build apartments and spurs the conversion of apartments to condominiums.

KANTIAN MAXIMS OR MORAL RULES

For Kant (1785, 1797) freedom and rationality are the foundations of a theory of morality. The expression of freedom is found in the concept of individual autonomy, and the requirement of rationality is found in the relationship between free will and maxims that govern actions. These maxims, or rules, are derived independently of their consequences by reasoning about the implications of freedom of the will. That is, maxims are evaluated based on the reasons or motives for them. The resulting maxims are thus impartial and universal—a person is to will universal rules. The purpose of the maxims is to allow individuals to judge their actions, and the actions of others, from the point of view of those maxims. As indicated in Figure 22-1, Kant's system is based on the motive, or mental disposition, and the reason for the action. Kant thus emphasizes the "right" over the "good."

Kant argued that because individuals are rational and each individual deduces maxims from a conception of freedom and autonomy that resides in everyone, all individuals will deduce the same maxims; that is, there will be unanimity. Reasoning in Kant's system is to be based on a fundamental axiom known as the *categorical imperative*.[2] The categorical imperative serves two basic functions. First, it provides a basis for determining maxims and moral rules. Second, it prescribes that individuals are to act in accord with those rules. Kant provides several formulations of the categorical imperative, but they basically hold that individuals are to be treated as autonomous beings, as ends rather than solely as means, and are to act based on a reason that each would will to be universal. Kant's basic formulation of the categorical imperative is:[3]

Act according to the maxim that you would will to be a universal rule.

According to Kant (1785, p. 39), "All rational beings stand under the law that each of them should treat himself and all others never merely as means but always at the same time as an end in himself." Morality for Kant then is the condition in which each individual can be an end, and ethics "is conceived as the law of one's own will …" (1797, p. 47). This yields a second formulation of the categorical imperative:

Treat individuals always as autonomous ends, and so never solely as means.

This does not mean that a person cannot be treated as a means, for example, a means of production, but that person is also to be treated as an end with autonomy. An employee can thus be required to meet the standards for a particular job but has the right to quit or attempt to qualify for a different job.

The strength of Kant's conception of morality is that it focuses on motives or reasons for acting that are universal—apply to everyone—and thus are reversible—apply to oneself. The categorical imperative thus embodies two standards for the evaluation of maxims—*universalizability* and *reversibility*. Universalizability may be thought of as "Would I want everyone to behave according to that rule?" Reversibility may be thought of as "Would I want that rule applied to me?"[4] For example, if the rule under evaluation is "Discrimination based on height is not allowed," reversibility requires that I do not discriminate based on height. Universalizability requires that I would will a society in which no one discriminates on the basis of height. The third and equivalent standard for evaluating a proposed maxim or moral rule is, "Does it treat people always as ends and never solely as means, respecting their autonomy?"

The Relationship between Maxims and Rights

Kant's system is expressed in terms of maxims, which individuals have a moral duty to respect. That duty establishes moral rights. Those moral rights are intrinsic, since they are derived from the categorical imperative and not from other considerations such as consequences. To illustrate the relationship between maxims, rights, and duties, consider the maxim, "A firm must sell its

---

[2]The term *categorical* means that the imperative is not conditioned on any purpose other than the imperative itself. Kant (1785, p. 26) wrote, "It is not concerned with the matter of the action and its intended result, but rather with the form of the action and the principle from which it follows: what is essentially good in the action consists in the mental disposition, let the consequences be what they may."

[3]This formulation applies to a broad class of maxims including some that could be contemplated but never acted on, so the categorical imperative is sharpened to pertain to rules that could be acted on. That is, the maxims must have meaning.

[4]Reversibility is implied by universalizability, but it is useful to state it separately as a reminder.

product to anyone who wants it, regardless of the price they are willing to pay."[5] This maxim violates the categorical imperative of treating individuals as autonomous ends, since the owners of the firm would be treated as means when forced to sell the product regardless of whether they wanted to do so.

Consider next the maxim, "A firm must sell its product to anyone who is willing to pay the price set by the firm." This maxim satisfies the categorical imperative because it treats everyone as autonomous and as ends. Hence, it is a moral rule. This rule then has implications for rights and duties. First, it establishes property rights as moral rights. Second, it establishes the right of the firm to set the price for its product. Third, it does not allow the firm to distinguish, or discriminate, among buyers based on any considerations other than their willingness to pay the price set by the firm. This establishes a right not to be discriminated against and a corresponding duty not to discriminate on irrelevant considerations in making sales.

Consider another maxim, "A firm must sell its product to anyone who is willing to pay the cost of producing it." This rule violates the categorical imperative by not treating the owners of the firm as autonomous ends, since they are compelled to sell at a particular price. The regulation of a natural monopoly by setting price equal to average cost thus would not be permitted in a Kantian system unless the owners of the firm were compensated sufficiently so that they would freely choose to sell at that price.

Rights consistent with Kant's system include the freedoms of speech and conscience, since otherwise a person would not be autonomous. Rights also include political equality and the right to vote. Kantian rights require the opportunity to exercise individual autonomy, which includes the right not to be discriminated against on dimensions irrelevant to those opportunities. The categorical imperative draws a line between a right to opportunity without discrimination and the claim that individuals should be provided with the means to pursue opportunity and hence that others have a duty to provide those means. That claim may treat the recipients as ends and respect their autonomy and freedom, but it does not so treat those who have the duty, since it uses them solely as means for serving others. Consequently, economic rights, such as rights to food or housing, are not consistent with Kant's ethics system. From this perspective, claims about economic rights are statements about political goals rather than moral rights.

There are thus few rather than many rights that follow from Kant's system. For example, Kant's system allows the voluntary provision of economic goods to individuals but does not compel anyone to provide those goods. In contrast, Rawls's system of justice, as considered later in the chapter, requires the fair equality of opportunity, which requires that individuals have the means to pursue opportunities.

As an example of Kant's framework, consider the nature of the relationship between an employer and an employee. In the nineteenth century, the employment relationship was governed by the "at-will" legal doctrine derived from the theory of free contract under which either party was free to terminate the relationship whenever it chose. The Kantian right to be treated as an end rather than solely as a means suggests that even though both human beings and machines are factors of production, human beings differ from machines in that they are also to be treated as ends. The employer's right to free contract and to dismiss an employee at will thus may be limited by an employee's right to be discharged only for cause. The maxim thus is, "An employer may dismiss an employee based only on considerations relevant to his or her performance on the job." A corresponding duty is associated with any right, and in this case the duty is assigned to the employer. An employer thus cannot dismiss an employee for her political views but can dismiss a disabled employee who can no longer work.[6] What constitutes "relevant to his or her performance," however, remains a matter of disagreement; particularly as it pertains to issues such as the testing of employees, as in the chapter case, *Genetic Testing in the Workplace.*[7]

Intrinsic and Instrumental Rights

Rights can be instrumental or intrinsic. Instrumental rights are to be respected because they contribute to achieving better consequences, by, for example, enabling individuals to pursue their interests. The right of free contract, that is, to enter into contracts, is intrinsic, but specific

---

[5]This example was suggested by Daniel Diermeier.

[6]See the discussion in Chapter 20.

[7]Kupfer (1993) provides an ethics analysis of genetic testing.

contract provisions are instrumental because they exist to facilitate mutually beneficial economic consequences by ensuring payment and the delivery of goods and services. Claims that individuals have economic rights to housing or food are claims about instrumental rights intended to improve their well-being.

Intrinsic rights are to be respected in and of themselves and do not require any justification in terms of consequences. Intrinsic rights are derived from fundamental moral concepts such as autonomy and liberty, as in Kant's system. Examples of intrinsic rights are freedom of speech, equal protection including equal opportunity, and certain aspects of privacy. Some rights, such as the right to contract, are intrinsic when viewed from the perspective of autonomy and liberty and instrumental when viewed in terms of the consequences they yield. These rights may be stated in constitutions and laws, but intrinsic rights are to be respected independently of formal institutions. Intrinsic rights are frequently negative rights in the sense that respecting autonomy precludes others from infringing that autonomy. Many claims are made about the extent and scope of intrinsic rights, and formal institutions are often relied on to resolve conflicting claims. The extent of a right to privacy in the employment relationship, for example, remains a subject of competing claims as indicated in the privacy example below.

To illustrate the distinction between instrumental and intrinsic rights, consider a consequentialist example presented in Figures 22-2 and 22-3. These figures depict the possible

FIGURE 22-2   Instrumental Rights and Consequences

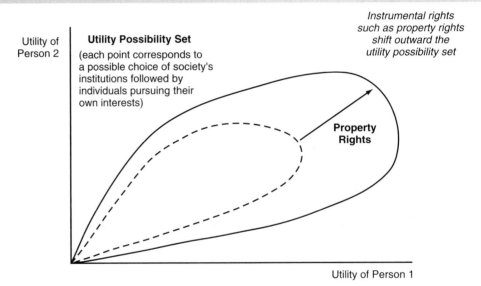

FIGURE 22-3   Intrinsic Rights and Consequences

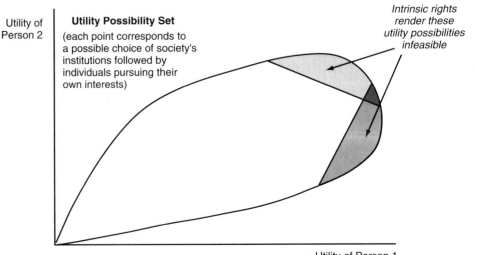

combinations of utility, or well-being, for two individuals, 1 and 2, as a function of the activities in which they may engage, given society's institutions. That is, each point in the oblong shapes—the utility possibility sets—corresponds to the utilities the two individuals could attain if they acted to pursue their own interests, given the opportunities and incentives provided by a particular configuration of society's institutions. The institutions might correspond to various assignments of rights, the tax and transfer payment systems, the laws of torts and contracts, and public education. A point in the figure reflects the incentives provided by those particular institutions, so if the tax system dampens incentives for capital formation, aggregate output and the utility of both individuals could be lower than if stronger incentives were provided.

Instrumental rights affect the shape and size of the utility possibility set. For example, the dotted line might correspond to the set of institutions in communist countries such as the former Soviet Union and the nations of Eastern Europe under its control. The economies of those countries failed because the institutions of centralized state planning resulted in both insufficient capital formation and weak incentives for effort. As an instrumental right, a property right in which individuals keep the fruits of their labor provides stronger incentives for effort and capital formation and expands the utility possibility set, as illustrated in Figure 22-2. The privatization of companies in the former communist nations and in many other countries is one manifestation of this.

Intrinsic rights impose duties on individuals to respect those rights. Viewed from a Kantian perspective, property rights allow individuals to act as autonomous ends, and hence they have moral standing as intrinsic rights. In the context of Figure 22-2, the duty to respect those rights prevents moving from the larger to the smaller utility possibility set. Similarly, an intrinsic right to equal opportunity can expand the utility possibility set. An intrinsic right to equal opportunity, however, is not established in the Kantian system with reference to its effect on consequences but instead is established from the categorical imperative and the requirement of treating each person as autonomous with the opportunity to choose.

Other intrinsic rights may restrict the utility possibility set as illustrated in Figure 22-3. The claimed intrinsic right to privacy may limit the possible levels of utility attainable in a society. That is, intrinsic rights can constrain the set of available alternatives, and from a consequentialist perspective this can make at least some, and perhaps all, individuals worse off in terms of consequences. A right to privacy, for example, could be argued to prohibit genetic testing in the workplace, making it more difficult to move genetically susceptible individuals away from possible exposure to harmful chemicals.

The set of intrinsic rights established by Kant's ethics system is small and generally corresponds to negative rights that allow individuals to act as autonomous ends. The set of instrumental rights that enable people to pursue their interests is larger, and those rights may treat people solely as means if required to realize those rights. The right to some basic level of public education is one such right, and taxpayers are treated as a means. The set of rights established through political processes is larger still. That set includes measures such as rent control and the right to file an antidumping petition against imported goods. A right to file an international trade complaint is instrumental and is established by political authority.

EXAMPLE Privacy

Privacy is important, but it remains controversial. In the employment relationship, for example, privacy pertains to issues such as whether employers can inspect the contents of an employee's locker, whether workplace surveillance of employees is permitted, whether supervisors can listen in on telephone order takers to determine how they handle customer calls, and whether employees can be tested for substance abuse.

A right to privacy is said to arise both from moral standards and from legal guarantees. In the Kantian framework an intrinsic right to privacy can be viewed as arising from the notion of freedom and autonomy. Freedom of conscience is restricted when privacy is violated. In this sense people are said to have a sphere in which their thoughts can remain private. The question is the extent to which this personal sphere extends beyond thoughts to behavior.

The notion of autonomy pertains to the size of the sphere, since a person can choose to allow others access to information about himself or herself. For example, in an employment relationship management generally has the right to supervise and monitor an employee's performance. This right can extend beyond actual performance to factors that

(*Continued*)

(*Continued*)

could affect that performance. For example, many employers require drug tests of their employees, even though such tests primarily provide information about conduct outside the employment relationship. By accepting a job for which drug testing is required, individuals voluntarily sacrifice some of their personal sphere. Individuals thus can contract away some of their personal sphere. In that sense a right to privacy cannot be as important as inalienable rights such as speech and assembly. The intrinsic right in this example is a right not to be forced to accept or work in a job against one's will.

With regard to legal rights the U.S. Constitution does not mention privacy. The Fourth Amendment establishes a right "to be secure in their persons, houses, papers, and efforts, against searches and seizures …" but that right is generally held to apply to searches and seizures by government. Thus, in the private sector there is no constitutional prohibition against drug testing of employees, but in the public sector in which government is an employer, employees have a right not to submit to drug tests unless they are in sensitive positions or are involved with public safety. The Supreme Court has concluded that other rights explicitly established by the Constitution imply that there is a right of privacy in a personal sphere.[1]

The extent of a right to privacy, or the size of the personal sphere, is difficult to identify. One has a right to the privacy of one's body and mind, but as the cases of drug tests and integrity tests indicate, that right can be limited in an employment relationship. One has a right to the privacy of certain behavior, but surveillance is not generally prohibited. One also has privacy rights with respect to information about one's self, but many parties, such as doctors, employers, governments, and others, have records of that personal information. Surveys of the Internet users find that they would exchange their personal data, such as name, address, and contact information, for a $100 gift certificate. The Chapter 15 case *The European Union Data Protection Directive (B)* concerns the issue of data generated through Internet transactions and browsing, and the Chapter 20 case *Facebook and Online Privacy* addresses the multiple dimensions of online privacy. The chapter case *Genetic Testing in the Workplace* concerns another privacy issue.

---

[1]See *Griswold v. Connecticut,* 381 U.S. 479 (1965).

Criticisms of Kantian Rights

The criticisms of Kant's ethics system include both those that pertain to deontological systems in general and those specific to his system. The fundamental criticism of deontological systems is that they fail to explain why a principle or right should be respected. When one attempts to do so, one is often led to justifying it in terms of the extent to which it protects or promotes human interests. For example, why is treating individuals as ends important if it is not to give them the opportunity to pursue their interests? Thus, critics contend that consequences rather than motives actually underlie the moral standing of these principles.

More specific criticisms of rights-based ethics systems are that they may not (1) identify sufficiently precisely where the corresponding duty lies, (2) indicate priority when one right conflicts with another, and (3) indicate when—if ever—it would be acceptable to violate a right. With respect to the first criticism, every right is accompanied by an associated duty, but who is to bear the burden of that duty is not always clear. Some negative rights, such as the right of free speech, impose a duty on everyone not to interfere with that speech. In the case of a claimed positive right, such as a right to medical care, however, the duty may fall on the individual, family, employer, or government. In such situations, legislation is often required to clarify where the duty lies. Legislation, however, reflects interests, and hence preferences and consequences.

A second criticism is that Kant's system does not clearly indicate whether or when one right has priority over another. The categorical imperative requires that individuals be treated as autonomous and so always as an end and never solely as a means. Kant's view was that there would be no conflict among the rights consistent with the categorical imperative. When a person, however, attempts to articulate the set of intrinsic rights, conflicts frequently appear. In such a case, Kant would argue that the person should reexamine those rights from the perspective of the categorical imperative, eliminating those inconsistent with it. In practice, this is difficult, and an approach to prioritizing rights, as presented in the later section "Conflicts Among Rights," is needed.

A third criticism centers on whether there are any circumstances in which it would be acceptable to violate a maxim or right. For example, if rights are in conflict, it may be necessary to violate one to respect another. A violation of a right for whatever reason is a moral wrong, but the seriousness of the violation must be considered. In the language of justice theory, the issue is when it is acceptable to violate one right to avoid a violation of a more important right. For example, paternalism is a wrong, but there may be circumstances, as considered later in the chapter, in which it may be acceptable to take an action to benefit a person even though that action violates the person's autonomy.

In spite of these criticisms, individual rights are a fundamental component of our ethical intuition. Rights are embedded in constitutions, statutes, and moral understandings. The duties corresponding to legal and moral rights provide fundamental constraints on the actions of managers and on the policies and practices of firms.

The practical difficulties with the application of rights-based ethics systems pertain to the evaluation of claims about rights, the priority of various rights, and the relationship between rights and other concerns such as well-being and justice. The next section addresses these issues in the context of applied rights analysis.

APPLIED RIGHTS ANALYSIS

In managerial decision making, rights have two effects. First, as illustrated in Figure 22-3, they rule out certain alternatives, such as those that would violate moral principles or legally protected rights. Second, a right may impose an affirmative duty that requires a firm to take particular actions. The equal employment opportunity laws prohibit discrimination, whereas affirmative action regulations impose affirmative duties on employers to address the effects of past discrimination. The second effect is addressed later in the chapter in the context of equal employment opportunity and affirmative action. The focus here is on rights that rule out alternatives.

Claimed and Granted Rights

A granted right is established by moral consensus or by government and is accompanied by a clear assignment of the corresponding duty. If the duty has not been clearly assigned, moral consensus is absent, or government has not spoken, the right in question is said to be claimed. Individuals claim rights and make demands on others by asserting moral justifications, but others may view those claims as morally unjustified.

To illustrate the distinction between claims and grants and their moral standing, consider the issue of foods containing genetically modified organisms (GMO). A claim that a person has a right to ban imports of GMO foods neither has moral status nor is granted by government. A claim that a person has a right to have GMO food labeled as such may have moral standing because it enables persons to exercise their autonomy in their choice of foods. This right is not granted in the United States but is in the European Union. Even if there were moral consensus that GMO foods should be labeled, government need not play a role. Some grocers have policies of selling GMO-free foods, and some food manufacturers supply such products. A person then exercises autonomy by choosing where to shop and what to buy.

Although it has no moral standing, people have a granted right through government to ban imports of GMO foods and to bear the sanctions authorized by the World Trade Organization (WTO), as in the case of the European Union as considered in Chapter 19. People have a granted right (in the United States a constitutional right to petition government) to lobby government to change WTO rules to require labeling or even the separation of GMO foods. The right to petition has moral standing as a form of free speech and as people acting as autonomous ends.

Private and public policy regarding GMO foods involves both ethics and politics, as illustrated in Figure 22-4. Ethics pertains to the moral standing of claims. Politics involves efforts to turn claimed rights into granted rights or vise versa.

To address nonmarket issues where rights are claimed, managers must evaluate contesting arguments. To illustrate the evaluation of a claimed right, consider the claim that the poor have, or should have, entitlements different from those of other people. In *Kadrmas v. Dickinson Public Schools,* 487 U.S. 450 (1988), the Supreme Court affirmed its 1973 ruling that the equal protection clause of the Constitution does not give special protection due to income. Plaintiff Kadrmas challenged a North Dakota law that allowed school districts to charge a fee for school bus service. The Dickinson School provided bus service for rural students, picking them up at their doors, but charged them $97 per year for the service. The Kadrmases' income was close to the "officially defined poverty level," and Kadrmas refused to pay the fee. The school bus then no longer stopped for Sarita Kadrmas. Since the Kadrmases lived 16 miles from the school, they had to incur an additional expense for Sarita's

FIGURE 22-4 Rights and Moral Standing

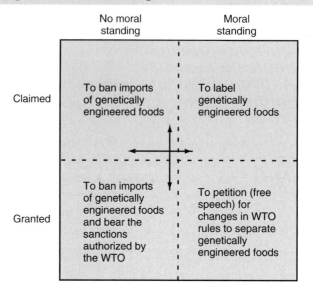

Politics may be construed as attempts to change the "vertical status" of rights in this framework.

Ethics may be construed as disciplinary disputes about the "horizontal status" of rights.

transportation. They sued, and the case reached the Supreme Court. For the majority in a 5-to-4 decision, Justice Sandra Day O'Connor wrote,

> The Constitution does not require that such [school bus] service be provided at all, and it is difficult to imagine why choosing to offer the service should entail a constitutional obligation to offer it for free .... We have previously rejected the suggestion that statutes having different effects on the wealthy and the poor should on that account alone be subjected to strict equal protection .... Nor have we accepted the proposition that education is a "fundamental right," like equality of the franchise, which should trigger strict government scrutiny when government interferes with an individual's access to it.[8]

The majority's opinion thus distinguishes the constitutional grant of equal protection under the law from the claim that because of income individuals should be relieved of certain economic burdens. Equal protection is a right consistent with the Kantian system, whereas the economic right to free bus service is not. Managers must make similar judgments about claimed rights, and a method for the analysis of claims about rights is presented next.

A Methodology for Rights Analysis

Rights analysis has two principal components. The first is determining whether a claimed right has moral standing. The second is determining how conflicts among rights are to be resolved. The methodology of rights analysis is as follows:

1. Identify the rights claimed and their claimed moral bases.
2. Determine which claimed rights satisfy moral standards; for example, Kantian standards or a utilitarian standard that establishes instrumental rights.
3. If a claim is not morally justified, check whether it is established by government. If it is, it is granted and is to be respected. If not, the claim need not be respected.[9]
4. Identify the actions consistent with the protection or promotion of any morally justified rights.
5. Identify conflicts among rights. If there are none, those claimed rights with moral standing are to be respected.

---

[8]*United States Law Week* (56), 6-21-88, 4777–4783, p. 4780.
[9]Claims should not be ignored, however, since they may motivate nonmarket action.

EXAMPLE   **Life Insurance Screening for Preexisting Conditions**

The reasoning in the *Kadrmas* decision suggests that individuals have no granted right to life insurance nor to purchase insurance at a particular price. That is, requiring the provision of life insurance to anyone who demands it violates the autonomy of insurers and treats them as a means. Insurance companies thus need not provide insurance to everyone or anyone. When individual life insurance is offered, however, screening for preexisting conditions is claimed to be discriminatory and an invasion of privacy. A person can act as an autonomous end, however, by not applying for insurance, so no intrinsic right is violated by screening. In addition, in most jurisdictions an insurance company has a granted right to screen for preexisting conditions and to deny or at least limit coverage.[1] That right can be withdrawn or limited through

politics and government action, but in the absence of restrictions most insurance companies screen for preexisting conditions based on utilitarian considerations, as considered in Chapter 21. More generally, claims about privacy violation and discrimination warrant further examination because if they have moral standing, legal and moral rights would be in conflict. Conflicts among rights are considered in the following section.

---

[1]The grant may extend considerably beyond screening. In 1990 a federal district court judge dismissed a lawsuit filed by an employee with AIDS who had charged that it was illegal for a firm that self-insured to limit medical coverage for AIDS. The judge held that the firm had complied with the requirements of the Employee Retirement Income Security Act (ERISA) by notifying employees that its medical plan could be revised on an annual basis. The Court of Appeals rejected the plaintiff's appeal, and in 1992 the Supreme Court let that decision stand.

---

6. If there are conflicts among rights with moral standing, investigate the importance of the interests those rights are intended to protect or promote.
7. Prioritize the rights based on the importance of those interests and determine the extent to which each is constrained by the others.
8. Choose the action that does best in terms of the priorities established.

The life insurance screening example introduced in Chapter 21 illustrates the first four steps in the methodology, and the last four steps are considered in the following section.

CONFLICTS AMONG RIGHTS

Kant argued that the intrinsic rights established in accord with the categorical imperative do not conflict. When the set of rights is expanded to include instrumental rights and granted rights established by government through politics, however, rights can be in conflict. Those conflicts may mean that there is no action that respects all rights. This section presents an approach to steps 5, 6, and 7 of the applied rights methodology. The approach addresses conflicts by prioritizing rights based on the importance of the interests they support. This approach thus adds considerations of consequences to the evaluation of rights.

Rights and Interests

In the case of moral rights, or rights more generally, one approach to reasoning about, if not resolving, conflicts is to assess the importance of the rights by considering the interests they are intended to promote or protect. Rights established by deontological systems are intrinsic, however, and are justified independently of the interests to which they contribute, so they have high standing. Nevertheless, the approach of inquiring into interests is a practical method for addressing conflicts in managerial applications and is consistent with ethical intuition.

To illustrate the inquiry into the interests a claimed right is intended to promote, in his dissent in *Kadrmas* Justice Thurgood Marshall stated his view of the constitutional basis for a right:

> The statute at issue here burdens a poor person's interest in an education. The extraordinary nature of this interest cannot be denied. By denying equal opportunity to exactly those who need it most, the law not only militates against the ability of each poor child to advance herself, but also increases the likelihood of the creation of a discrete and permanent underclass. Such a statute is difficult to reconcile with the framework of equality embodied in the Equal Protection Clause.
>
> As I have stated on prior occasions, proper analysis of equal protection claims depends...upon identifying and carefully analyzing the real interests at stake.[10]

---

[10]*California Reporter,* 829 (1987), p. 4782.

Justice Marshall thus turned to the interests of the individual in attempting to determine the priority of the claimed right to free school bus service. Justice O'Connor, in contrast, focused on whether a right has been granted by the Constitution rather than on the interests affected.

Prioritization

The framework for analyzing conflicts among rights begins with an identification of a right, an assessment of whether it is claimed or granted, and its bases. The possible bases for a right are moral and legal, where the latter includes the Constitution, statutes, court precedents, and contracts. A granted right is established by the state, by another individual or entity as in a contract, or by moral consensus and has a clearly assigned duty. A claimed right either does not have a clearly assigned corresponding duty or has not been established by either a grant or moral consensus.

The first four steps in the methodology presented earlier in the chapter identify rights and their status. Because moral and granted rights can be in conflict in managerial settings, they must be prioritized. Priorities are established by the institutions of society and by moral principles. The Constitution establishes certain priorities. For example, one has a right in one's home to prohibit others from trespassing for commercial purposes. However, one does not have the same right when its exercise denies others the opportunity to exercise their rights of free speech or religion. Consequently, home owners do not have the right to call on the state to prevent people from distributing religious materials on the sidewalk in front of their homes. Constitutional rights also take precedence over legislatively granted rights, particularly because many constitutional rights also have a moral justification. Rights that both are granted and have a moral basis have priority over claims that have a disputed moral basis. Intrinsic rights have priority over instrumental rights. More difficult are cases in which a granted right is in conflict with a claimed right.

To assess priorities in such a case, the interests those rights protect and promote are examined. Those interests may range from the opportunity to pursue one's own well-being to personal privacy, which has a moral basis in the right of conscience in a Kantian framework. The interests identified are intended to be fundamental, as in Justice Marshall's statement about the importance of education to opportunity. Once the interests have been identified, the rights that further those interests are to be assigned priority. At this point individuals may have differing assessments of priorities, but the assignment of priorities is intended to be impartial and based on the importance of the interest and not on the personal preferences of the person conducting the analysis. The final step identifies actions that are consistent with a right.

The result of the analysis may be that there is no action that does not violate some right with legal or moral standing. Prioritization is then based on the seriousness of a violation. Given the assessment of priorities, the managerial task is to determine the extent to which a right should be limited to protect other rights and then to identify the actions that come closest to meeting the priorities. This framework for prioritizing conflicting rights is presented in Figure 22-5 and illustrated with the integrity tests issue.

FIGURE 22-5   Applied Rights Analysis: Integrity Tests

Right	Claimed/ Granted	Bases*	Interests the Right Protects	Priority	Actions Consistent with the Right
Privacy	Claimed	Moral	Liberty Human dignity	$2^\dagger$, $3^\ddagger$	Limited use of tests
Free from arbitrary treatment	Claimed	Moral	Opportunity to qualify for jobs	1	Test verified; professional interpretation of results
To use test in hiring; (firm)	Granted	Moral/ Legal	Autonomy of employer Economic efficiency	$3^\dagger$, $2^\ddagger$	Test where integrity is important to job performance

*moral, legal (constitutional, statutory, and common law)
†for jobs where the efficiency interest is not compelling
‡for jobs where the efficiency interest is compelling

EXAMPLE   Integrity Tests

Integrity tests are currently legal under federal law and under the laws of at least 49 states, so the focus is on moral claims. The rights claimed are the prospective employees' right to privacy, their right not to be subject to arbitrary treatment as a consequence of an inaccurate test, and the employer's right to choose standards for hiring, as long as those standards do not discriminate on an illegal basis. Since these rights are in conflict, it is necessary to evaluate and prioritize them.

The right to privacy is granted by statute as it pertains to certain types of tests, such as polygraphs, but it is claimed as it pertains to integrity tests. Congress might in the future extend the right of privacy to integrity tests, but it has not yet done so. The right to be free from arbitrary treatment is based on the claim that the tests may misclassify individuals because of inherent inaccuracies. The firm's right to use the tests in selecting among prospective employees, as long as it does not illegally discriminate, is granted and has both a moral and a legal basis. The moral basis derives from the autonomy of the employer (and employee) and the liberty to enter into contracts. The legal basis follows from property rights. The bases for the rights are indicated in Figure 22-5.

To investigate priorities, the interests the rights are intended to promote or protect must be identified. The claimed right to privacy is intended to promote liberty and protect human dignity. The claimed right to be free from arbitrary treatment protects the opportunity to qualify for jobs and positions. The employer's right to choose standards for hiring is, as an instrumental right, intended to promote economic efficiency by allowing employers to match prospective employees to jobs.

In addressing the conflicts among these rights, intrinsic rights have priority, because in a deontological system the right takes precedence over the good. The right not to be subjected to arbitrary treatment seems important in this case. In the last column in Figure 22-5, the actions consistent with this right center on ensuring accuracy in testing. The American Psychological Association issued a report concluding that "the preponderance of the evidence" indicates that integrity tests can be useful, but it expressed concerns about some of the tests, the claims made for them, and their use in the absence of supervision by a qualified psychologist. Given these concerns, the tests should be carefully evaluated and supervised by trained personnel. Furthermore, because of possible inaccuracies, passing an integrity test should not be a necessary condition for employment but could be one of several factors considered.

With respect to privacy, the fundamental issue is whether it is morally acceptable to base employment and job assignments on psychological considerations. Integrity and other forms of psychological tests are said to invade privacy by asking questions that are too personal and not closely linked to job requirements. Such questions might pertain to lifestyle and off-the-job activities. Privacy can be limited, however, when there is a compelling reason, and individuals can choose whether to accept a position that requires the sacrifice of a degree of privacy. Consequently, the claimed right to privacy can be limited when the employer has an important interest served by the integrity test.

The employer's right to use tests to select employees on nondiscriminatory grounds is intended to respect autonomy and promote the interest of economic efficiency. In a deontological framework, the former right may be limited if otherwise the liberties or rights of individuals would be restricted. Economic efficiency is clearly an important interest, but the right that promotes it is instrumental. Furthermore, deontological systems can require restrictions on that right to avoid infringing intrinsic rights. The actions consistent with this right to test thus might be to use the test depending on how important integrity and loyalty are for a particular position. A position such as security guard, bank teller, or purchasing agent might warrant an integrity test, whereas a custodial position might not.

Although there is ambiguity in the application of rights-based analysis in this case, the freedom from arbitrary treatment seems to have priority. The liberty and human dignity protected by a claimed right to privacy can be protected by not applying for a position for which an integrity test is required. This, however, would mean that opportunities are reduced by the tests. The interest that justifies the employer's use of an integrity test thus must be important to justify compromising the claimed right to privacy. For jobs in which integrity and loyalty are important to job performance, the employer's right to use the tests seems to have priority. For jobs in which integrity and loyalty are not important to job performance, the claimed right to privacy seems to have priority. Consequently, necessary conditions for the use of the tests is that they be reasonably accurate and administered by qualified individuals, that they be limited to jobs for which the tested traits are important to the interests of economic efficiency, and that they be only one of several factors considered in employment decisions.[1] The chapter case *Genetic Testing in the Workplace* raises similar considerations about rights and their priorities.

---

[1]Dalton and Metzger (1993) reach a different conclusion based on concerns about the accuracy of the tests.

EQUAL EMPLOYMENT OPPORTUNITY

Equal employment opportunity is a principle supported by virtually all ethics systems. Its importance is supported by legal grants that provide for its public enforcement. Its legal manifestation is Title VII of the Civil Rights Act of 1964, which prohibits discrimination on the basis of "race, color, sex, religion, or national origin." Most states have similar laws applicable to businesses operating within their state.

Concerns about illegal discrimination in the employment relationship now focus less on intentional discrimination and more on employment practices and policies that, while appearing neutral with respect to an identifiable group, have a disparate impact on the members of that group. An employment policy that is neutral with respect to race, for example, has a disparate impact if the proportion of minorities hired is lower than the proportion of whites hired. Employers then must establish that the policy is required by business necessity—a bona fide occupational qualification (BFOQ). The concept of a disparate impact is broad and applies to hiring, promotion, and compensation. More subtly, it may also apply to grooming rules, physical requirements, language requirements, and information about an individual's past, such as an illness, criminal conviction, or past substance abuse. Other laws have applied the same principles to other attributes, including age, disability, and pregnancy.

Title VII is administered by the Equal Employment Opportunity Commission (EEOC), an independent administrative commission with five members appointed by the president. The EEOC can act on its own or in response to a complaint filed by an individual. In addition, the EEOC has rule-making authority over compliance with Title VII and may file suit in federal court if conciliation fails. An individual may also file suit in federal court once the EEOC has attempted to resolve the issue. Because most states have laws similar to Title VII, the EEOC allows state agencies to handle many of the cases.

The remedies available to the EEOC or a court under Title VII include injunctions and mandated changes in practices. A complainant may be awarded reinstatement, promotion, payment of back wages, attorney fees, or other awards. As an example, in 1996 Texaco settled a racial discrimination lawsuit for $176.1 million and agreed to establish an "equality and tolerance task force." Texaco also settled a complaint by the EEOC, allowing it to scrutinize the company's hiring and promotion policies for 5 years.

In 1993 Shoney's, Inc., agreed to a $105 million settlement in a case alleging discrimination against African Americans. Shoney's also agreed to institute an aggressive affirmative action program with a 10-year goal of 20–23 percent African American managers and assistant managers in its 754 company-owned restaurants. The Chapter 23 case *Denny's and Customer Service* addresses a discrimination case outside the employment relationship.

An employer has several defenses in a Title VII case. One is that of "business necessity," such as testing individuals for job-relevant skills. A second defense against a disparate impact charge is that of a BFOQ, but the EEOC and courts have interpreted this quite narrowly. A BFOQ defense pertains only to discrimination based on sex, religion, and national origin under Title VII and age under the Age Discrimination in Employment Act of 1967. Racial discrimination is never justified by a BFOQ. Third, seniority systems are not covered by Title VII, so a plaintiff must show intent of discrimination rather than a disparate impact. Seniority systems have been held to be protected under Title VII against complaints that they perpetuate the effects of discrimination.[11]

In addition to Title VII, the Civil Rights Act of 1866, codified as Section 1981 of Title 42 of the United States Code, provides protection against discrimination based on race. Section 1981 states that "all persons ... have the same right to make and enforce contracts ... as enjoyed by white persons." Since employment is viewed as a contract, Section 1981 covers the employment relationship. Protection from discrimination applies not only to minorities but to majorities as well. In *McDonald v. Santa Fe Trail Transportation Co.,* 427 U.S. 274 (1976), the Supreme Court held that Section 1981 protects whites from discrimination.

In 1968 the Supreme Court held that Congress enacted the Civil Rights Act of 1866 pursuant to the Thirteenth Amendment, which abolished slavery, rather than pursuant to the equal protection clause of the Fourteenth Amendment. This meant that the act applies not only to government actions but also to private actions. This considerably expanded the scope of application of Section 1981 and had a number of significant implications beyond those of Title VII. First, unlike Title VII, the act has no statute of limitations. Second, the act imposes no limit on the awards the courts may make, allowing both compensatory and punitive damages. Third, the act

---

[11]See *International Brotherhood of Teamsters v. United States,* 431 U.S. 324 (1977); *American Tobacco Company v. Patterson,* 452 U.S. 937 (1982); and *Firefighters Local Union No. 1784 and Memphis Fire Department v. Carl W. Stotts et al.,* 467 U.S. 561 (1984).

applies more broadly than Title VII, since it covers all employers whereas Title VII covers only those with at least 15 employees. Fourth, an individual can file a lawsuit directly without having first to go to the EEOC.[12]

Title VII bars discrimination in employment but is silent about how a finding of discrimination is to be made. In *Griggs v. Duke Power,* 401 U.S. 424 (1971), the Supreme Court held that an employment policy that is "fair in form, but discriminatory in operation" is in violation of Title VII. Duke Power had required a high school diploma for employment, but its policy had a disparate impact on African Americans, who were less likely than white applicants to have graduated from high school. Griggs also established that the burden of proof rests on the employee or the EEOC to show that the policy in question has a disparate impact on a protected class.[13]

The George H.W. Bush administration and Congress negotiated a compromise resulting in the Civil Rights Act of 1991, which amended several civil rights laws and overturned several Supreme Court decisions. It reversed one Supreme Court decision by placing the burden on the employer to show that a practice was a business necessity. The act also allowed punitive damages for intentional discrimination on the basis of sex, religion, national origin, or disability.[14] The act also overturned a 1989 Supreme Court decision that had restricted Section 1981 to hiring decisions. Section 1981 as amended now covers hiring, working conditions, promotion, and termination.[15]

Complex issues involving equal opportunity and discrimination continue to arise in the employment relationship, as the following example indicates.

EXAMPLE   Disparate Impact versus Disparate Treatment

Fire departments in the United States were often the locus of nepotism where jobs went to relatives of firefighters or members of the same ethnic group. Efforts to diversify the ethnic composition over the next several decades were often successful. By 2003 the New Haven, Connecticut fire department was composed of 30 percent African Americans, 16 percent Hispanics, and the rest white. This diversity, however, was not reflected in the ranks of the officers with only 1 of 25 captains an African American.

Promotions to the ranks of lieutenant and captain were governed by the city's contract with the firefighters union. The contract required two examinations, a written examination counting for nearly 60 percent and an oral examination counting for 40 percent. The city's contract with the firefighters required a rule of three where the top three candidates were considered for promotion when there was a vacancy. To fill the vacancies in 2003, the city hired at a cost of $100,000 an experienced firm to prepare the examinations. The firm conducted a job analysis that was reviewed by the fire chief, who was white, and the assistant fire chief, who was black. "At every stage of the job analyses, [the firm], by deliberate choice, oversampled minority firefighters to ensure that the results—which [the firm] would use to develop

the examinations—would not unintentionally favor white candidates."[1] The firm was careful to prepare examinations that were not discriminatory and pre-tested them on panels of firefighters, 66 percent of whom were minorities, from several cities outside Connecticut. The examinations were written for a 10th grade reading level. The city accepted the examinations prepared by the firm and gave preparation instructions for those firefighters seeking promotion to lieutenant and captain along with a 3-month study period.

The results shocked the mayor and many in the city. On the lieutenant examination, 25 of the 43 whites, 6 of the 19 blacks, and 3 of the 15 Hispanics who took the examinations passed, and on the captain examinations, 16 of the 25 whites, 3 of the 8 blacks, and 3 of the 8 Hispanics passed.[2] Eight lieutenant positions were open at the time, and the test results and the rule of three meant that only whites were eligible for the positions. Similarly, seven captain positions were open, and under the rules seven whites and two Hispanics were eligible for promotion. The highest scoring African American on the

---

[1]*Ricci ET AL. v. DeStefano ET AL.*, No. 07-1428, Opinion of the Court, p. 4–5.
[2]Passing the examinations qualified the candidate for promotion during a 2-year period.

(Continued)

---

[12]In 2008 the Supreme Court broadened the applicability of the Civil Rights Act of 1866 by ruling that it protected a worker who was fired because he had complained that another worker had been fired because of her race (*CBOCS West, Inc. v. Humphries,* No. 06-1431).
[13]See also *McDonnell Douglas Corp. v. Green,* 411 U.S. 792 (1973) and *Texas Department of Community Affairs v. Burdine,* 447 U.S. 920 (1981).
[14]The Civil Rights Act of 1866 allowed punitive damages only for racial discrimination.
[15]The Supreme Court has clarified the requirements and procedures for filing complaints. The Court ruled against "stale claims," requiring that claims be filed within 180 days of the alleged act of discrimination. The Court also ruled that a claim could not be rejected because an employee had filled out the wrong form for the complaint.

(*Continued*)

lieutenant test was 13th and the top Hispanic candidate was 26th. The mayor and other officials of New Haven, whose population is 60 percent black and Hispanic, held hearings on the results. Minority firefighters threatened the city with a lawsuit if the test results were certified alleging disparate impact discrimination under Title VII of the Civil Rights Act of 1964, and white firefighters threatened a lawsuit alleging disparate treatment discrimination under Title VII if the examination results were not certified. The city decided not to certify the results because they believed that certification would have a disparate impact on minorities, which would constitute illegal discrimination. Seventeen white and one Hispanic firefighters who were denied the opportunity for promotion filed a lawsuit alleging that the decision by the city constituted disparate treatment based on their race.

Title VII prohibits "intentional discrimination (known as 'disparate treatment') as well as, in some cases, practices that are not intended to discriminate but in fact have a disproportionately adverse effect on minorities (known as 'disparate impact')."[3] Disparate impact discrimination was defined in *Griggs v. Duke Power Co.* as practices that were facially neutral but were "discriminatory in operation." The Civil Rights Act of 1991 codified the prohibition on disparate impact discrimination, but provided for defenses based on qualifications that were "job related for the proposition in question and consistent with business necessity."

The District Court issued a summary judgment rejecting the lawsuit without a trial, and on appeal the Court of Appeals provided a one paragraph concurring decision. The case was appealed to the Supreme Court, which on June 30, 2009 overturned the lower court decisions, ruling that the action of the city constituted illegal disparate treatment discrimination against the plaintiffs. Writing for the majority in the 5–4 decision, Justice Anthony Kennedy wrote that "the District Court rejected the test results because 'too many whites and not enough minorities would be promoted were the lists to be certified.'"[4] Justice Kennedy continued, "the City made its employment decision because of race. The City rejected the test results solely because the higher scoring candidates were white. The question is not whether that conduct was discriminatory but whether the City had a lawful justification for its race-based action." The Court concluded that the defendants had to have a "strong basis in evidence" to justify disparate treatment and that the City did not meet that standard. Kennedy wrote, invalidating the test "amounts to the sort of racial preference that Congress has disclaimed, … and is antithetical to the notion of a workplace where individuals are guaranteed equal opportunity regardless of race."[5] The lawsuit filed by the firefighters also argued that the action of the City of New Haven violated the Equal Protection

Clause of the Fourteenth Amendment, but the Court chose not to rule on the Constitutional issue, since the plaintiffs had won their case.[6]

Writing for the minority Justice Ruth Bader Ginsburg stated that the "conclusion [the defendants'] had reached and the action thereupon taken were race-neutral in this sense: '[A]ll the test results were discarded, no one was promoted, and firefighters of every race will have to participate in another selection process to be considered for promotion,'" quoting the District Court. She also wrote, "I would therefore hold that an employer who jettisons a selection device when its disproportionate racial impact becomes apparent does not violate Title VII's disparate treatment bar automatically or at all, subject to this key condition: The employer must have good cause to believe the device would not withstand examination for business necessity."[7] Justice Ginsburg thus used intent or motivation as the justification for discarding the results, whereas the majority required a strong basis in the evidence and concluded that the city had no such basis. Justice Ginsburg argued that the examinations were discriminatory and that the city should not have abided by the union contract but instead should have relied more on oral examinations using "real-life scenarios," as was the practice in some other cities. Citing the history of discrimination in fire departments, she argued that it is "against this backdrop of entrenched inequality that the promotion process at issue in this litigation should be assessed." Speaking from the bench Justice Ginsburg said, "Congress endeavored to promote equal opportunity in fact, and not simply in form. The damage today's decision does to that objective is untold."

Many companies wanted to use tests for hiring and promotion. Maria Konev of Liquid Transport Corporation said that safety was their principal concern and any "testing that brings us closer to that goal is certainly something that we will consider."[8] A spokesperson for Southern Company, a utility based in Atlanta, said, "In our, view, the court's ruling validates the testing process we have in place."[9] Southern had been using tests since the 1970s. Karen Harned, executive director of the National Federation of Independent Business, stated, "Now employers have some assurance that they're not going to be sued if it turns out that despite their best effort, the process impacts one of the protected categories. The Supreme Court was sending a message to all employers. You shouldn't engage in a form of intentional discrimination to avoid unintentional discrimination."[10]

---

[3]*Ricci ET AL. v. DeStefano ET AL.*, No. 07-1428, p. 17.
[4]Ibid., p. 19.
[5]Ibid., p. 25.

[6]On July 2, 2009 President Barack Obama commented on the Supreme Court decision stating, "I do think that there are still circumstances in which on a college admissions or on a hiring decision, taking into account issues of past discrimination or taking into account issues of diversity of a workforce or a student body can still be appropriate."
[7]*Ricci ET AL. v. DeStefano ET AL.*, No. 07-1428. Dissent, p. 19.
[8]*Wall Street Journal*, July 1, 2009.
[9]Ibid.
[10]*New York Times*, June 30, 2009.

PATERNALISM

A basic issue for management is when, if ever, a firm is justified in acting paternalistically by taking an action intended to benefit others but in so doing violating a moral standard. For example, should firms require obese employees to lose weight so as to reduce health care costs or encourage employees to vote for a particular candidate?

Paternalism refers to actions taken to benefit a person without that person's consent. In any ethics system emphasizing individual autonomy and liberty, consent is essential for an action or a rule to have moral standing. Paternalism is thus a moral wrong. Paternalism is also objectionable from a consequentialist perspective because it denies individuals the opportunity to make choices that would further their interests. Gert (1988, pp. 286–287) provides a definition of paternalism:

One is acting paternalistically toward a person if and only if …:

1. one's action benefits that person,
2. one's action involves violating a moral rule with regard to that person,
3. one's action does not have that person's past, present, or immediately forthcoming consent, and
4. that person is competent to give consent (simple or valid) to the violation.

Actions taken on behalf of others are often justified by claims that if those others had the information that the action taker has, consent would have been granted. According to Gert's definition, an action taken to benefit a person who has incomplete information about a situation is not paternalistic if the person would grant consent once the action has been explained and the information presented.

In some cases, it is easy to know whether consent would be granted. Firms take a variety of actions to benefit their stakeholders. A firm may bargain with HMOs over the price for health care services, and the firm's bargaining power can lower the cost to both employees and the firm. In such a case, it is in the interests of both employees and shareholders to have the firm represent them. Consent would surely be given.

In contrast, few companies endorse candidates for public office or try to influence how employees vote. Voting is an exercise of individual autonomy, and individuals have the fundamental right not to be coerced into associating with ideas, positions, or candidates with which they disagree. Consent by individuals for the endorsement of candidates by their employer likely would not be granted. Labor unions, however, regularly endorse candidates for office without the consent of their members. Labor unions differ from firms in an important dimension, however, since union members have the right to elect their leaders.

NEOCLASSICAL LIBERALISM

Liberalism emphasizes the liberty of individuals and is concerned with the relationships between liberty and morality and between liberty and the state.[16] The former pertains to which rules or rights have moral standing, whereas the latter pertains to how individual liberty should be limited by the liberty of others and by the institutions individuals establish to govern their interactions. Liberal theory has a rich intellectual tradition, including Hobbes (1651) and Locke (1690), but only a relatively recent version of that theory, that of Nozick (1974), is considered here. Nozick's theory is considered because it stakes out a position for a minimal state and because it provides a conception of rights and justice that is quite different from that of Kant and Rawls.

As with Kant, Nozick attempts to deduce principles that define the scope of autonomy and liberty and then from those principles derive a concept of justice. His starting point is the self-evident principle of requiring the free consent of individuals to any restrictions that might be imposed on their personal liberty. Nozick derives his system based on the side constraint that "no moral balancing act can take place among us; there is no moral outweighing of one of our lives

---

[16]The term *liberal* is generally used in the United States to refer to positions that are to the left on an ideological dimension in which individual responsibilities and limited government are on the right and collectivist responsibilities and larger government are on the left. In many countries, liberalism refers to positions on the right of this dimension, and that is its use here.

by others so as to lead to greater overall social good. There is no justified sacrifice of some of us for others" (p. 33). In Nozick's view, this side constraint ensures that individuals will be treated as ends—as the categorical imperative requires—and not as means. This is a stronger version of the categorical imperative than Kant employs, because Kant argues that individuals may be treated as means as long as they are also treated as ends.

Nozick recognizes that in the exercise of their own rights individuals could coerce or infringe the liberty of others. Individuals thus will form voluntary associations to protect their liberties. Such an association is one to which individuals freely consent, and it is the only entity allowed to use force to prevent violations of rights and liberties. That association may be viewed as a state, and the activities it is empowered to undertake have moral standing because they are the result of individuals exercising their autonomy. It thus satisfies the categorical imperative. Nozick concludes that the state would have minimal powers, limited to "protecting its citizens against violence, theft, and fraud, and to the enforcement of contracts ..." (p. 26). Individuals thus have the negative right not to be coerced by others, and the state has the duty to enforce that right.

In Nozick's system the purpose of justice is to protect liberties. The fundamental principle of free consent provides his conception of distributive justice, which pertains to an individual's entitlements to goods and to the corresponding duties of others to satisfy those entitlements. Because any concept of distributive justice must be based on free consent, Nozick's conclusion is that what is just is whatever is the result of the voluntary actions of individuals. His maxim (p. 160) is expressed as, "From each as they choose, to each as they are chosen."

Nozick's theory has been criticized for its sole reliance on free consent. One line of criticism is based on the utilitarian perspective that actions should be evaluated in terms of their consequences. Another line of criticism is that his theory ignores, other than through what others choose to give them, the situation of those who are poorly off because of their initial endowments of abilities and resources. More importantly for applied purposes, Nozick's conception of a minimal state seems quite removed from modern society. It does, however, provide a basis for the justification and extension of liberties.

CATEGORIES OF JUSTICE THEORIES

Theories of justice add a comparative dimension to moral standards. Justice theories are concerned with how different individuals stand relative to each other on dimensions including, but not limited to, rights, liberties, and consequences. Rawls's theory of justice as fairness, for example, concludes that equality of moral and political rights is required but that economic rewards and burdens can be distributed unequally.

The three principal categories of justice theories are (1) distributive, (2) compensatory, and (3) retributive. Distributive justice is concerned with providing incentives to contribute to well-being in society and with providing a fair and just distribution of the rewards of those contributions. Compensatory justice is concerned with determining how individuals should be compensated for the harm done by others. Retributive justice is concerned with punishment for actions that are contrary to a moral rule or societal well-being. Retributive justice may be used to justify deterring harmful actions. Only distributive and compensatory justice are considered here.

Distributive Justice

Distributive justice is concerned with the distribution of the rewards and burdens of social interactions. A distributive standard is necessarily comparative, since it identifies how those rewards and burdens are assigned to individuals with particular attributes or in particular situations. Tax policy, for example, assigns the tax burden based on income, asset holdings, and spending. Distributive justice is concerned with the question of which attributes are relevant for particular matters. Just as rights can rule out certain decision alternatives, as illustrated in Figure 22-3, justice principles can also rule out alternatives. Those principles can also impose duties to ensure that the distribution of rewards and burdens is just.

The basic comparative principle of distributive justice is that "Equals should be treated equally and unequals, unequally." Velasquez (1998, p. 105) elaborates by stating the principle,

Individuals who are similar in all respects relevant to the kind of treatment in question should be given similar benefits and burdens, even if they are dissimilar in other irrelevant respects; and individuals who are dissimilar in a relevant respect ought to be treated dissimilarly, in proportion to their dissimilarity.

This principle implies that individuals should receive different pay if their productivity is different and should receive the same pay if their productivity is the same even though they differ in terms of irrelevant factors such as race or gender.

Distributive justice has a variety of conceptions. Egalitarianism requires the equal distribution of the rewards and burdens of society. This concept is typically rejected because an equal distribution of rewards would distort the incentives to produce those rewards. That is, at some point the more equally a society attempts to divide its pie, the smaller the pie will be. Rawls's theory of justice concerns distributing the rewards and burdens of society in a manner that is fair, yet gives attention to incentives to increase the size of the pie.

To illustrate the differences, consider the example in Table 22-1 of a three-person society in which individual 1 is more productive than individual 2, who is more productive than individual 3. The society has three possible systems of organizing the interactions of its members. A utilitarian system has the strongest incentives for individuals to use their abilities to pursue their interests, resulting in greater aggregate utility than the other systems. The distribution across individuals, however, is unequal due to the differences in productivity, as indicated in the utilitarianism column of the table. Compared with the utilitarian system, an egalitarian system redistributes aggregate utility equally among the three individuals. To accomplish this, incentives have to be distorted by, for example, taxing the more productive individuals and redistributing the proceeds to the less productive individuals. In the example in Table 22-1, the diminished incentives to produce reduce aggregate utility from 18 to 9. In contrast, Rawls's theory of justice requires making the least advantaged individual, who in this society is individual 3, as well off as possible. In doing so Rawls also seeks to preserve incentives to the extent possible so that individuals can use their abilities to pursue their interests. This can also benefit the least advantaged individual through, for example, increased economic production. Aggregate utility is lower than that under utilitarianism, since incentives are distorted and there is redistribution in favor of individual 3. Aggregate utility is greater than under egalitarianism, however, since individuals have stronger incentives to pursue their interests and utilize their abilities.

Compensatory Justice

Compensatory justice is concerned with whether and how a person should be compensated for an injustice. Compensatory justice has fairness and restitution as its goals. If a person is injured, the institutions of society may be designed to compensate the person. The principal institutions through which compensation for accidents is provided are the liability, workers' compensation, and insurance systems. Compensation serves two objectives. First, it provides restitution for the injury. Second, it provides incentives to reduce injuries and their social costs by imposing the burden on the parties best placed to avoid accidents. If compensation is not well designed, however, it can result in a moral hazard problem that generates social costs by distorting the incentives to avoid accidents. In such a case, the benefits of compensation must be weighed against the distortions of economic incentives the compensation causes. For example, the provision of government-backed flood insurance results in more home building in flood-prone areas than would be warranted by economic efficiency considerations.

Because of past injustices from discrimination in hiring and promotion practices, the courts ruled that compensation was owed to minority group members as a class, rather than solely to the

TABLE 22-1 Distributive Justice: Utilitarianism, Egalitarianism, and Rawlsian Justice

Individual	Utilitarianism	Egalitarianism	Rawlsian Justice
1	10	3	6
2	6	3	5
3	2	3	4
Aggregate utility	18	9	15

identifiable victims of discrimination. Rawls's principle of fair equality of opportunity provides a different justification for this ruling by focusing not on the nature of past injustices but on ensuring that all individuals have fair equality of opportunity. This requires not only the absence of discrimination, but also the fair opportunity for all to qualify for positions and pursue their interests. From this perspective, measures to ensure opportunities are warranted even if they extend beyond the set of actual victims of past discrimination.

Injustice

A general principle advanced in conceptions of justice is that an injustice is morally tolerated only if it is necessary to avoid a greater injustice. Such a principle requires an ordering of injustices. Gert (1988, pp. 110–111) offers a standard for when a violation of a moral rule is justified:

> A violation can be justified by providing reasons which would result in either some impartial rational persons advocating that that kind of violation be publicly allowed or less frequently, all impartial rational persons advocating that such a violation be publicly allowed.

Gert thus requires that the violators have reasons for the violation and that an impartial observer, or all observers, would understand those reasons and be willing to have that form of violation publicly allowed.

An applied version of Gert's principle is the public disclosure test: "If I disclosed publicly that I had taken an action that violated a moral standard and explained my reasons for doing so, would the public understand and approve of my action?" One such explanation would be that a greater injustice was avoided. Since the public disclosure test is intended to be a hypothetical and reflective test for the person contemplating the action, it is important that the test not turn into a rationalization of a violation of a moral standard in the absence of a greater injustice. For this reason the public disclosure feature of the test is crucial. That is, others must agree that the injustice was warranted.

This principle is applied in Chapter 24 to the issue of whether avoiding a greater injustice justifies paying a bribe demanded as a condition for a sale. In the chapter case *Genetic Testing in the Workplace,* a central issue is whether the injustice of the invasion of privacy through genetic testing is warranted to avoid the greater injustice of a genetically susceptible person incurring serious physical harm from exposure to chemicals in the workplace.

RAWLS'S THEORY OF JUSTICE

The Framework for Justice as Fairness

Rawls (1971) provides a theory of distributive justice set in the tradition of the social contract theory of Locke (1690), Rousseau (1762), and Kant. Rawls argues for the priority of the right over the good, but he is less concerned with developing maxims for judging the reasons or motives that individuals have for their actions than with developing principles to guide the design of society's institutions. According to Rawls (1971, p. 7), "the primary subject of justice is ... the way in which the major social institutions distribute fundamental rights and duties and determine the division of advantages from social cooperation ... the legal protection of freedom of thought and liberty of conscience, competitive markets, private property in the means of production, and the monogamous family are examples of major social institutions."

Because any contemporaneous choice of principles by individuals would be based at least in part on who those individuals are and what roles they have in society, Rawls concludes that just principles are those that would be "chosen behind a veil of ignorance" from an "original position" in which one does not know one's personal characteristics or the place one will subsequently have in society. In this original position each individual is equal to every other individual, so the principles chosen will have moral standing, it is argued, because they will be deduced impartially where no one has an advantage.[17]

---

[17]One concern with deducing maxims in Kant's framework is that individuals, knowing their present positions in society, might not reason in an impartial manner. Kant argues that the sense of freedom and autonomy in everyone leads everyone to reason impartially and to will the same maxims, resulting in unanimity. Rawls seeks to ensure impartiality and unanimity through the device of the original position.

FIGURE 22-6 Rawls's Contractarian Framework

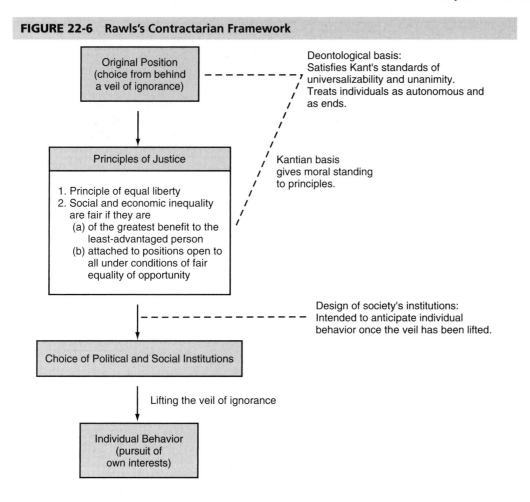

Rawls's contractarian method is illustrated in Figure 22-6. In the original position, individuals do not know which abilities they will have, which positions in society they will occupy, or what their tastes will be. What they do know is that there is a set of possible abilities, tastes, and positions they might be fortunate or unfortunate enough to have once the veil of ignorance has been lifted. They also know the laws of the natural sciences and the understandings gained from the social sciences, so they can anticipate the behavior that will result once society's institutions are in place and the veil has been lifted.

In the original position all individuals are equal, and the principles they choose will apply to everyone and thus to themselves, so the original position satisfies the Kantian standards of universalizability and unanimity. From the original position, individuals will also treat people always as ends and never solely as means. Since Kant's categorical imperative is satisfied, the principles chosen in the original position will have moral standing, according to Rawls.[18] Those principles constitute the social contract.

Once the principles have been chosen, society's political and social institutions are to be chosen based on those principles. Once those institutions are in place, the veil of ignorance is to be lifted, and individuals learn their abilities and tastes and may pursue whatever interests they have. An important feature of Rawls's theory is that it does not suppose that once the veil has been lifted people will necessarily behave according to a set of rules that take precedence over self-interest. Understanding that individuals may pursue their own interests, Rawls focuses on the role of institutions in guiding the pursuit of those interests in a mutually advantageous manner. The central task of Rawls's method then is to determine which principles and which institutions would be chosen in the original position.

The relevance of Rawls's system for management is found both in the principles of justice he identifies and in the concept of the design of institutions consistent with those principles.

---

[18]See Rawls (1980) for a further analysis of the Kantian construction.

The principles provide a basis for reasoning about issues with moral dimensions. The choice of institutions corresponds to the formulation of policies to guide managers in dealing with nonmarket issues with moral dimensions. These policies are used in the screening stage of the framework for nonmarket analysis and strategy formulation introduced in Chapter 2 and summarized in Figure 2-5. In the case of integrity tests, for example, the principles provide a basis for reasoning about whether such tests involve an unjustified intrusion on the liberties of prospective employees, whether they distort opportunities, and whether they have desirable distributive consequences. The Levi Strauss example presented later in the chapter illustrates this approach.

The Principles of Justice

Rawls argues that individuals would adopt two principles as a basis for justice as fairness.[19]

> First: each person is to have an equal right to the most extensive basic liberty compatible with similar liberty for others.
> Second: social and economic inequalities are to be arranged so that they are both (a) to the greatest benefit of the least advantaged and (b) attached to positions and offices open to all under conditions of fair equality of opportunity.[20]

The first principle is referred to as the *equal liberty* principle; part (a) of the second principle is the *difference principle*; and part (b) is the *fair equality of opportunity* principle. Rawls's principles can be thought of as incorporating both deontological considerations (in the form of liberty and opportunity) and consequentialist considerations of well-being (in terms of the benefit to the least advantaged).

Rawls argues that the principle of equal liberty has precedence over the fair equality of opportunity, which has precedence over the difference principle. By the first precedence, Rawls means "that liberty can be restricted only for the sake of liberty itself." The second precedence means that the difference principle is to be applied only after conditions ensuring the fair equality of opportunity are in place. In Rawls's system, no trade-off is permitted between basic liberties and social and economic conditions. Rawls thus concludes that society's institutions should be characterized by political equality but that social and economic inequalities are acceptable as long as they are arranged in accord with the fair equality of opportunity and difference principles.

The equal liberty principle pertains to liberties such as the freedom of conscience and speech, the right to vote, the right to be eligible for office, freedom of assembly, freedom from arbitrary arrest, and the right to hold property. Such liberties can be limited only as necessary to maintain conditions of reasoned discourse and public order. For example, rules of recognition and procedure may be instituted to allow everyone to speak in a manner that allows that speech to be heard. With respect to political liberties, Rawls argues that there must be limits on "the scope of majority rule," such as limits like those in the Constitution and in the Bill of Rights.

Fair equality of opportunity is necessary to allow individuals to realize the worth of their liberty, and it requires that positions in society be open to all and that all individuals have a fair opportunity to qualify for those positions. When fair equality of opportunity has been assured, the difference principle requires that the least advantaged individuals be able to realize the worth of their liberty through the pursuit of their interests. The second principle thus is comparative and may require, for example, provisions for the disabled that provide them access to public facilities and to reasonable accommodations in the workplace. Rawls further argues that policies that improve the well-being of the least-advantaged individual would also improve the well-being of most, if not all, of the disadvantaged because their positions are "closely knit." Thus, a policy that benefits the least advantaged person also benefits other less advantaged persons.

To apply the difference principle, Rawls faces the task of determining who are the least-advantaged persons. This involves making comparisons among individuals, but as indicated in the discussion of utilitarianism in Chapter 21, such interpersonal comparisons are problematic.

---

[19]Rawls (2001) subsequently provided a restatement of his theory of justice as fairness.
[20]Rawls (1971, pp. 60, 83). He gives a more extensive statement of the principles on pages 302–303.

Rawls attempts to avoid this problem by identifying a set of "primary goods" that all individuals require to be able to pursue their interests, whatever those interests might be. The primary goods are divided into broad categories—rights and liberties, opportunities and powers, and income and wealth. Rawls argues that an index of these primary goods be used to assess the well-being of individuals. This allows for interpersonal comparisons. The difference principle thus takes well-being into account.

The Role of Incentives

From Rawls's perspective, once the equal liberty and fair equality of opportunity principles are satisfied, the institutions of society allow one individual to be better off than another if that is necessary to make the least-advantaged person better off. This is illustrated in Table 22-1 where the Rawlsian choice results in lower aggregate utility than utilitarianism, but makes the least-advantaged person better off than under the other two systems. The Rawlsian choice allows more-advantaged persons to pursue their interests resulting in greater aggregate well-being than with egalitarianism. Rawls, however, is concerned with the well-being of the least advantaged rather than aggregate well-being.

The role of incentives and the comparison between the utilitarian, egalitarian, and Rawlsian systems are illustrated in Figure 22-7, where the utility possibility set corresponds to societal institutions that satisfy the equal liberty and fair equality of opportunity principles. In the figure individual 1 is more advantaged than individual 2, since more of the alternatives result in a higher utility for 1 than for 2. Egalitarianism requires that the institutions be chosen to attain point A, which yields the greatest utility for each individual subject to the restriction that both are equally well-off. The difference principle states that it is just to move from A to B, even though individual 1 does relatively better than 2. It is just because the less advantaged person 2 is as well-off as possible at B. Rawls thus would choose institutions that provide incentives to allow society to achieve B rather than A. Institutions that would allow C to be attained, however, would be unjust, since moving from B to C reduces the well-being of the less-advantaged person even though the well-being of 1 increases by more than the well-being of 2 decreases. A utilitarian system that weights the well-being of each individual equally would choose institutions that result in point C.[21]

FIGURE 22-7   Difference Principle, Utilitarianism, Egalitarianism

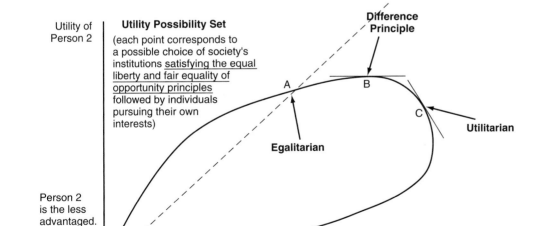

---

[21]Rawls's difference principle requires that the choice of institutions be Pareto optimal. That is, any choice of institutions that yields a point in the interior of the utility possibility set in Figure 22-7 can be improved to make both individuals better off.

Rawls thus recognizes the role of incentives and markets in attaining economic efficiency but supports incentives and markets only in so far as they benefit the least advantaged person. Economic efficiency and aggregate well-being thus can be sacrificed, through distortionary taxes and redistribution, for example, if doing so improves the situation of the least advantaged.

Duty in Rawls's Theory

The assignment of duty in Rawls's theory of justice is part of the choice of political and social institutions based on the principles of justice. Duty may be assigned to government, individuals, firms, or other organizations. All have a duty to respect and promote the basic liberties identified by the principle of equal liberty. The duty to ensure fair equality of opportunity is generally assigned to government and employers. Offices and positions are to be open to all, and employers may be assigned the duty to ensure that their employment practices provide all individuals with the opportunity to qualify for positions. The duty can extend further by requiring employers to take positive measures to ensure that employees have the means to qualify for better positions.

The duty to attend to the interests of the least advantaged under the difference principle should be assigned so that incentives are not distorted to the point that they jeopardize capital formation, investment, and the creation of jobs. That is, in the terminology of economics, incentives should be preserved so that society remains on the frontier of the utility possibility set in Figure 22-7. Thus, the party that is best positioned to attend to the interests of the least advantaged, and to do so efficiently, should be assigned the duty under the difference principles. That duty is often assigned to government when the means is a transfer of income to the least advantaged. Assigning the duty directly to individuals would violate the equal liberty principle, but individuals may through their voluntary choice contribute time and money to charitable and related activities to benefit the least advantaged. Firms as the property of owners may also contribute to such activities on the same grounds. Some duties to attend to the interests of the least advantaged are assigned to firms. For example, injured workers are compensated through the workers' compensation system funded by taxes on employers. The example on clinical trials provides another case.

On some matters, such as equal opportunity in employment, the duty naturally falls on the employer. Similarly, the duty to assure fair equality of opportunity and nondiscrimination in housing rests with landlords. But the duty to provide Rawls's primary goods, such as a minimum standard of living, so that individuals have a fair opportunity to realize the worth of their liberty, is a collective responsibility. As such, the assignment rests primarily with government.

EXAMPLE   Clinical Trial Obligations

CV Therapeutics, a small biotechnology company, developed a new drug, ranolazine, for treating angina.[1] Because it had become increasingly difficult to recruit participants for clinical trials in the United States, pharmaceutical companies began conducting trials in Eastern Europe and Russia where people were eager for Western medicines. CV Technologies was completing its successful clinic trials in Russia, and CEO Dr. Louis G. Lange was concerned about whether the company had a continuing duty to those participants in the trials who had benefited from its drug.[2] In the United States companies typically continued to provide a drug for clinical trial participants until it was approved by the FDA for marketing. Also, many pharmaceutical companies had compassionate-use programs that made life-prolonging drugs available in poor countries. Ranolazine did not prolong life but improved the quality of life. Making it available for sale in Russia did not make economic sense, since few patients could afford it and obtaining approval and setting up a sales force would be prohibitively expensive for a company that did not yet have a product on the market. Providing the drug for free in a compassionate-use program would also be very expensive. CV Therapeutics would have to train doctors in the use of the drug, set up a distribution system, and monitor use for any adverse side effects.

From the perspective of Kantian rights and Nozick's system, CV Therapeutics seems to have no duty to the clinical trial participants, as long as they were not promised that

---

[1]This example is based on an article in the *New York Times,* March 5, 2004, and other public sources.

[2]Ranolazine was approved for sale in the United States in 2006 under the brand name Remexa.

the drug would be provided after the trial was completed. The participants voluntarily entered into the trials and thus had acted as ends and exercised their autonomy. Given the infrastructure cost, providing the drug would likely not be warranted under utilitarianism. From the perspective of Rawls's system basic liberties and the fair equality of opportunity principles seem not to be violated by not providing the drug, so is there a duty to provide it stemming from the difference principle? The Russian participants suffering from angina are certainly less advantaged, but providing the drug could result in an outcome in the interior of the utility possibility set in Figure 22-7. If providing drugs to trial participants were a general rule, the cost of conducting clinical trials overseas would be increased substantially, thus reducing the incentives for pharmaceutical R&D, particularly for start-ups and small companies. In that case any duty to provide the drug seems to rest with the Russian government or with private aid organizations.

Criticisms of Rawls's Theory

One form of criticism centers on whether all individuals in the original position would choose the same principles and, if so, whether they would choose Rawls's principles rather than some other principles.[22] For example, if the first principle is to take precedence over the second, then the "most extensive basic liberty compatible with similar liberty for others" could be viewed as implying the neoclassical liberalism principle of a minimal role for government. Rawls, however, concludes that the role of government is extensive.

Another criticism centers on Rawls's conclusion that in the original position, once liberties and equal opportunity have been assured, society would choose institutions that provide the maximum benefit to the least advantaged. Some critics have argued that this principle would not be chosen in the original position because the chance of any one person being the least disadvantaged is minuscule. Harsanyi (1982) argues that in the original position people would choose a principle corresponding to average rule utilitarianism, since that maximizes the expected well-being of each person when in the original position. Rawls's use of primary goods as a means of assessing the advantages of individuals is also subject to the same criticisms as is interpersonal comparisons of utility.

As with utilitarianism and rights theories, a conceptual and applied difficulty in justice theories pertains to how duty is to be assigned. The issues pertaining to basic liberties are similar to those previously addressed in the analysis of Kant's system. The assignment of the burden of ensuring fair equality of opportunity and improving the position of the least advantaged is similar to the assignment of duty considered in Chapter 21 in the context of utilitarianism. Affirmative action, considered in the example, is an institution that corresponds to these principles.

Nozick (1974) argues that any response to the least advantaged should rest with the free choice of individuals who may, if they so choose, contribute to the well-being of others. Private charity is one reflection of this principle.

Nozick also observes that Rawls's theory pertains to a "time slice" in which the allocation of rewards and burdens of society must necessarily be judged by "end results" and independently of history. That is, to apply the difference principle, the positions of people must be evaluated at a point in time, and Rawls does not inquire into how people came to be in those positions. Nozick argues that how individuals arrived at their current positions is important from a moral perspective. For example, if an injustice were done to a person in the past, it would be necessary to examine the subsequent chain of events to determine what compensation, if any, was warranted. If people had made voluntary choices that worked to their disadvantage, however, is there any duty to compensate them? The chapter case *Environmental Injustice* concerns this issue.

Nozick also argues that Rawls's system of justice is necessarily patterned according to characteristics of individuals or their situations, as required in the application of the difference principle. Whatever form of patterning is used, Nozick argues, must interfere with basic liberties.[23] This, he argues, means that no action can satisfy both Rawls's equal liberty principle and the difference principle.

Although Rawls's theory has been criticized on a variety of dimensions, it remains an important philosophical work and provides a useful framework for reasoning about managerial

---

[22]The same criticisms may be made about Kant's system. Brandt (1979) argues that individuals could choose a variety of different principles. Gauthier (1986) provides a moral theory that addresses the issue of compliance with the initial choice. Binmore (1994) provides a strategic theory with a framework similar to Rawls's.

[23]See Nozick (1974, pp. 160–164).

problems. His theory brings together several considerations, including liberties, opportunities, and well-being, that ethical intuitions recognize as important. It also provides a degree of prioritization that can be used in resolving conflicts. The Chapter 12 case *Environmental Justice and Pollution Credits Trading Systems* provides an opportunity to reason from Rawls's perspective about both managerial policies and one of society's institutions. The Chapter 11 case *Citigroup and Subprime Lending* raises justice concerns.

EXAMPLE   Affirmative Action

Affirmative action is a conscious attempt to realize equal opportunity. It includes steps to remedy the effects of past discrimination and may involve preferential treatment for individuals in protected classes. The EEOC oversees affirmative action plans and issues guidelines for their design. Affirmative action requires that employers adopt recruiting policies that ensure that minorities and women are included in the pool of candidates and that all those who meet the qualifications, or are qualifiable, are given fair consideration. Compliance may require changes in recruitment, hiring, or promotion policies, additional training programs, and the establishment of explicit goals. Affirmative action plans have been adopted more broadly than required by law and have become part of the social fabric of many companies.

Compensatory justice and fair equality of opportunity provide foundations for affirmative action. Compensatory justice is intended to compensate individuals for injustices and, in the context of affirmative action, applies to both individuals and protected classes. From this perspective, compensation for the actual victims of illegal discrimination is justified. Compensation may also be justified for classes, even though the individuals receiving the compensation have not themselves been the subjects of discrimination. The rationale for compensation for a class is that its members' "starting positions" have been adversely affected by past discrimination.[1] This is consistent with the principle of fair equality of opportunity, which holds that individuals are to have a fair chance to qualify for positions. If individuals are at a disadvantage because of their education, training, or other conditions important for qualification, justice considerations may call for providing them additional education or other means to enable them to pursue opportunities.

Affirmative action is not immune to criticism on ethics grounds. Criticism centers on who is to bear the burden of the compensation and how the opportunities of others are to be altered to provide opportunity to those who have been disadvantaged. One means of compensation that generates little opposition is providing additional education and training. Other means have resulted in reverse discrimination resulting from the preferential treatment given to others. Section 703(j) of Title VII of the Civil Rights Act of 1964 states: "Nothing contained in this title shall be interpreted to require any employer...to grant preferential treatment to any individual or to any group because of race, color, religion, sex, or national origin..."

An important attribute of many of the affirmative action programs that have withstood court scrutiny is that they are voluntary. The court, however, may block a program that constitutes a permanent obstacle or barrier to those bearing the burden of an affirmative action program. In *Regents of University of California v. Bakke,* 438 U.S. 265, the Supreme Court struck down a voluntary policy that established a quota for minority admissions to a medical school because it precluded the admission of a qualified white male. In contrast, in *United Steelworkers of America v. Weber,* 443 U.S. 193 (1979), the court upheld a voluntary agreement between an employer and a union that established numerical goals for minority inclusion in a company training program. The court ruled that the agreement did not constitute discrimination against a white male with more seniority who was denied inclusion, since the goals were temporary and did not constitute an absolute barrier to his future inclusion in the program or to promotion.

In contrast to the language of Title VII, the federal government has had a variety of programs that explicitly took race or sex into account. These include minority preference programs for broadcasting licenses, small business loans, college scholarships, and highway construction and defense contracts. For example, federal law specified that 10 percent of the contract dollars on federally aided road projects be set aside for minorities. In 1988 Congress included women under the same program. On federal highway contracts a company qualified as "disadvantaged" was given up to a 10 percent price advantage over other firms.[2] When Adarand Construction lost a contract to a minority-owned firm even though it had the lowest bid, it sued the federal government, arguing that its right to equal protection under the Fifth Amendment had been violated. The Supreme Court in *Adarand Constructors v. Peña.* 515 U.S. 200 (1995) held in favor of Adarand, thereby forcing changes in federal set-aside programs.

The courts have upheld minority preference programs when they served a compelling interest. As an example of a compelling interest, the Supreme Court in *Metro Broadcasting v. F.C.C.,* 110 SCt 2997 (1990), upheld a Federal Communications Commission (FCC) policy that gave preference to minorities seeking to acquire a broadcasting license. The Court held that the FCC policy was important to the

---

[1]Groarke (1990) offers a moral justification for compensation and restitution.

[2]That is, in a procurement context if a disadvantaged firm bids $109 on a supply contract and a nondisadvantaged firm bids $100 the contract is awarded to the disadvantaged firm at the bid of $109.

interest of providing a diversity of viewpoints and programming on the airways.[3] A federal appeals court, however, subsequently held that the *Adarand* decision implied a higher standard of scrutiny and concluded that the FCC policy was important but not compelling. Although the FCC policy was invalidated, many broadcasters vowed to continue following the FCC guidelines.[4]

Colleges and universities have affirmative action programs for student admissions, and in two 2003 decisions involving the University of Michigan, the Supreme Court clarified the legality of those programs. Relying on the *Bakke* decision, the court upheld a program of the Michigan Law School that considered minority applicants on an "individualized" basis.[5] The court, however, declared

unconstitutional the university's affirmative action program for undergraduate admissions. That program automatically awarded 20 points on a 150-point admissions scale to African American, Hispanic, and Native American applicants. In a 6-to-3 decision the court held that the program was quota-like.[6]

Although court scrutiny of government affirmative action and preference programs continues, the affirmative action programs of most companies are likely to remain intact since they are by now a part of the fabric of those companies. The objectives of many of those programs are as yet unrealized, however.

In addition to issues pertaining to employees, affirmative action may be extended to other constituencies. Many firms have a considerable underrepresentation of minorities and women among their distributors, franchisees, and agents, and civil rights advocates have worked to extend affirmative action goals to those positions.

---

[3]See Spitzer (1991) for an analysis of the justifications for minority preference in broadcasting. In 1992 the U.S. Court of Appeals ruled that the FCC policy giving preference to women constituted illegal discrimination against men.
[4]In 1995 Congress repealed a law that gave a tax break to broadcasters that sold a station to a minority-owned firm.
[5]*Grutter v. Bollinger,* 539 U.S. 982, 124 S.Ct. 35.

[6]*Gratz v. Bollinger,* 539 U.S. 244, 123 S.Ct. 2411.

Applying the Principles of Justice

Although Rawls's system of justice is as much a political as a moral philosophy and is thus directed at the design of institutions more than at the evaluation of actions, it provides a set of considerations helpful to managers who must establish policies. Company policies are the managerial analogues of Rawls's institutions.

Because of its close relationship to Kantian rights, the application of Rawls's principle of equal liberty involves the same considerations found in rights analysis, as indicated in the integrity tests example. This section thus focuses on fair equality of opportunity and the difference principle.

For firms, the principle of fair equality of opportunity is most directly applicable to policies associated with the employment relationship. As considered earlier in the chapter, Title VII of the Civil Rights Act of 1964 provides for equal opportunity by prohibiting discrimination in employment. Rawls's principle, however, goes beyond the prohibition of discrimination and requires the "fair equality" of opportunity. Fair equality requires not only that positions be open to all, but that individuals have the means to attempt to qualify for them. Justice Marshall's argument in the *Kadrmas* case is consistent with this principle. Affirmative action programs may be viewed as one application of this principle.

EXAMPLE   Integrity Tests

Much of the rights analysis of integrity tests presented earlier in the chapter is also relevant from the perspective of justice, so the focus here is on the difference principle and fair equality of opportunity. One concern with an integrity test is whether it puts those who are already disadvantaged at a further disadvantage. If they are already disadvantaged for a reason that would be revealed by the integrity test and would result in a "failure" on the test, an objection on justice grounds could be raised, provided the reason were not relevant to the job. Similarly, if the test systematically affected the opportunities of individuals

with particular attributes that were irrelevant to job performance, the test would be unjust. Such concerns are reflected in laws in a number of states that prohibit employers from inquiring about criminal records of job applicants or about their lifestyles. Justice principles require that the tests not adversely affect individuals on irrelevant grounds, but otherwise the tests may be used if they enable the firm to improve its performance; that is, to stay on the frontier in Figure 22-7. The more compelling the firm's interests and the more important the tested traits for a particular job, the more likely the tests are to be justified.

The difference principle is applicable once liberties and fair equality of opportunity have been assured. That principle calls for affirmative consideration of those who are the least advantaged or who would be put in such a position by policies or actions of a firm. As Rawls argues, the position of the least-advantaged person is closely linked to the positions of other less-advantaged persons. Consequently, responding to the situation of the least-advantaged person affects many less-advantaged persons. The difference principle provides a justification, for example, for special programs that make facilities accessible to the disabled and provide opportunities for the disadvantaged. It also provides a justification for policies that respond to the needs of laid-off employees and the communities in which they live. The chapter case *Chipotle Mexican Grill and Undocumented Workers* concerns a company with some workers who may be undocumented and hence illegally employed.

The methodology for applying Rawls's framework involves the elimination of policy alternatives by using first the equal liberty principle and then the fair equality of opportunity principle. The remaining alternatives are then evaluated for fairness, and the choice among those remaining alternatives is based on the difference principle. The methodology may be summarized as follows:

1. Identify the liberties and rights involved.
2. The principle of equal liberty: Evaluate alternative policies in terms of how extensive are the corresponding liberties and rights of individuals consistent with equal liberties and rights for all. Prioritize rights and liberties when conflicts arise. Eliminate alternatives that limit liberties for reasons other than assuring the liberties themselves.
3. The principle of fair equality of opportunity: Identify the opportunities associated with each remaining alternative, and evaluate those alternatives in terms of how extensive the opportunities are. Eliminate alternatives that unnecessarily limit opportunities.
4. For the remaining alternatives, evaluate their fairness implications for the pursuit of opportunities by those affected.
5. Choose among the remaining policies based on the difference principle by favoring policies that benefit the least advantaged even if those policies sacrifice aggregate well-being, but avoid inefficiencies unless they benefit the least advantaged.
6. Identify which parties have which duties.

In this methodology a departure from equal liberty cannot be justified by an advantage in social or economic matters for any individual, including the least advantaged. The following two examples illustrate the analysis.

EXAMPLE   Redlining

Redlining, the practice of refusing to lend or write insurance policies in a designated geographic area, may be economically efficient if few of the people in the area are likely to qualify for a loan or insurance policy. That is, redlining could correspond to point C in Figure 22-7. Redlining, however, is inconsistent with Rawls's principles of justice. Redlining does not seem to violate the principle of equal liberty, but it may violate both the fair equality of opportunity principle and the difference principle. Redlining denies opportunity to people in a redlined area, and while it may not directly affect their ability to qualify for employment positions, it does restrict their opportunity to become a homeowner or to have an automobile insured. Redlining may also violate the difference principle, since redlined areas frequently are low-income areas that are often populated by disadvantaged people. Banning redlining then can result in point B in Figure 22-7.

EXAMPLE   Life Insurance Screening for Preexisting Conditions

If screening for preexisting conditions for life insurance is not a violation of the principle of equal liberty or the principle of fair equality of opportunity, does it conflict with the difference principle? Treatment of diseases such as AIDS can be very expensive, and to the extent that the cost is borne by the victim and the victim's family it can represent a heavy and in many cases insurmountable burden. To the extent that the cost of treatment substantially disadvantages some persons, the difference principle requires that institutions be designed to relieve at least some of that burden. Rawls then asks to which institution the duty should be assigned. The institution of life insurance seems less appropriate than the use of medical insurance or public funds, since adverse selection by those with preexisting conditions could substantially reduce the efficiency of the life insurance system, resulting in a point in the interior of the utility possibility set in Figure 22-7.[1] Screening for preexisting conditions thus seems consistent with Rawls's system.

---

[1]Medical insurance without restrictions on preexisting conditions is also subject to adverse selection. For example, the Obama administration abandoned its plan for a market for long-term insurance because the market could not be self-sustaining, since young, healthy people would not purchase the insurance because of the cost.

Implementing Ethics Principles: Levi Strauss & Company and Global Sourcing

Levi Strauss & Company is a privately owned firm that has integrated core values into its internal policies and earned a reputation for adherence to ethics principles and concern for the interests of its stakeholders.[24] In the 1980s the company made two important market decisions: to broaden its product lines, particularly into casual wear, and to expand internationally in both the markets in which it sells and in its sourcing of products.[25] The expansion of its markets and product lines, sales growth in the United States, and pressure for low-cost sources of supply resulted in a rapid expansion in the number of suppliers. Levi Strauss soon found that a high percentage of its garments was no longer being produced in its own facilities but instead was being produced by over 700 foreign suppliers.

The company became concerned about whether its suppliers met the safety and other standards it maintained in its own production facilities. In addition, it was concerned about possible damage to its brand name resulting from the conditions in its suppliers' facilities. The company had concerns pertaining to child labor, prison labor, plant safety, and environmental protection. The company also had concerns about the human rights conditions in several countries in which its suppliers were located. Its market strategy of expanding its markets and sourcing globally had generated a set of complex issues. Its challenge was how to bring its supplier relationships into congruence with its ethics principles and core values.[26]

Levi Strauss formed a task force to develop two policies to guide its managers: one for suppliers and the other for determining in which countries it would do business. The former focused on working conditions in suppliers' factories and covered dimensions such as safety, working hours, discrimination, child labor, dormitories for workers, and environmental protection. The latter focused on human rights concerns, political stability, the safety of company employees, and legal protection for trademarks and commercial interests.

These policies affected its market strategy in two ways. First, the company terminated its arrangements with suppliers in Burma because of widespread human rights violations in the country. Also due to human rights concerns, it decided to withdraw from China over several years. Not only did the China decision eliminate a low-cost, high-quality source of supply, it also precluded Levi Strauss from investing in its own facilities in China.[27] Second, the Terms of Engagement policy required inspections of suppliers' factories and possibly the termination of supply arrangements. The inspections were conducted by audit teams that regularly visited each supplier and provided a detailed assessment of the conditions at the supplier's facilities.

The process used by Levi Strauss to develop the guidelines can be interpreted through the framework of Figure 2-5. The top panel of Figure 22-8 represents the development of policies to guide its managers, and the bottom panel represents the application to two issues: (1) whether to source in Burma and (2) how to address a safety issue in suppliers' factories. Referring to the top panel, Levi Strauss developed policies pertaining to suppliers and countries and considered alternatives ranging from complete withdrawal from countries to requiring suppliers to meet U.S. building codes. Screening involved the application of fundamental ethics principles in

---

[24]The company had backed its principles with action. It was a leader in integrating its factories in the South in the 1950s, and during the Depression it kept employees on its payroll rather than laying them off. See Schoenberger (2000).

[25]This example is based on Baron (1995b).

[26]Levi Strauss developed its policies for supplier engagements before the sweatshop issue had emerged. See the Chapter 4 case *Nike in Southeast Asia*.

[27]Levi Strauss returned to China in 1998.

FIGURE 22-8 Levi Strauss & Company Global Sourcing Guidelines

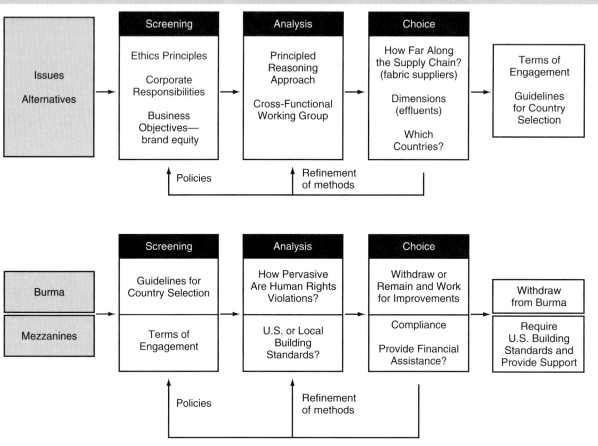

addition to its business objectives. Analysis involved the application of its "principled reasoning approach," in which stakeholder interests were explicitly taken into account.

The third stage involved developing recommendations and choosing among them. Choice included decisions about how broad the policies should be—should they cover effluents from washing operations—and how far down the supply chain they should go. Should the policies extend only to cutting and sewing operations or also to fabric producers? The results of this process were a Country Selection policy and a Terms of Engagement policy to guide managers in their decision making about contractor practices and involvement in countries, respectively.

The bottom panel illustrates the application of the process to specific decisions about doing business in Burma and concerns about the safety of makeshift interior mezzanines used for storage in suppliers' factories in the Caribbean. The screening stage involved the application of the two policies, and analysis centered on the impact of alternatives on stakeholders as well as on specific concerns, such as how pervasive the human rights violations in Burma were and whether U.S. safety standards should be applied in the case of the mezzanines. Choices then were made between withdrawal and constructive engagement in the case of Burma and about who should pay for the safety improvements in the case of the mezzanines.

HIGHER ORDER STANDARDS FOR EVALUATING ETHICS SYSTEMS

The ethics systems based on utilitarian, rights, and justice considerations use two general standards for determining which principles or rules have moral standing. The first is universalizability (which implies reversibility). A principle or rule has moral standing if one would be willing to have everyone, including oneself, behave in accord with it. This standard, however, does not necessarily imply that everyone would choose the same set of principles or rules. The second standard is unanimous impartial choice as in Rawls's original position. The notion of reasoning about principles from the original position is important because ethics principles are to be impartial and not based on the actual position a person occupies in society.

Rule utilitarianism and the rules derived from it have moral standing because each individual chooses a rule to be followed by everyone and, since each individual is maximizing aggregate well-being, everyone would choose the same rule. That is, the principle of maximizing aggregate well-being is universalizable, since each individual would will that everyone abide by it. The principle also would be chosen unanimously from the original position, since everyone would choose the rule that yields the greatest well-being.

Rawls's principles of equal liberty and fair equality of opportunity meet both the standards of universalizability and unanimous choice from the original position. With respect to Rawls's difference principle, individuals might be willing to have everyone abide by it, but it is not at all clear that in the original position everyone would choose the difference principle and not some other principle such as maximizing average aggregate well-being.

Kantian maxims meet both standards. The categorical imperative implies that maxims will be universal. The view that every individual is rational and deduces maxims from a conception of freedom and autonomy that resides in everyone means, according to Kant, that each will choose the same rule, so unanimity results. Kant's view of rationality and a common conception of freedom and autonomy serve as the original position, so reasoning and choice are impartial.

SUMMARY

Rights and justice are important concepts and correspond to fundamental ethical intuitions. Rights may be classified as intrinsic or instrumental. Intrinsic rights are justified independent of consequences by their consistency with conceptions of liberty and autonomy. Instrumental rights have moral standing because they lead to higher levels of well-being. Instrumental rights are an important component of teleological systems, which judge the good in terms of consequences. Intrinsic rights are a central component of deontological systems, which are based on considerations other than, or in addition to, consequences.

Kant's theory of moral rules is based on the categorical imperative, which holds that individuals are to be treated always as autonomous ends and never solely as means, and that rules of behavior are to be universal. Moral rules identify intrinsic rights of individuals and the corresponding duties to respect those rights. Intrinsic rights take precedence over considerations of well-being, but the ethical intuition that well-being is important remains strong.

Justice theories add an explicit comparative dimension to deontological systems. The three principal categories of justice theories are distributive, compensatory, and retributive. Distributive theories focus on the distribution of the rewards and burdens of social interactions. Compensatory theories are concerned with compensating for injustice. Retributive theories focus on punishment for moral wrongs. An injustice is a moral violation and is to be tolerated only if it is necessary to avoid a greater injustice.

Rawls provides a theory of justice as fairness that incorporates the Kantian framework and focuses on liberties, rights, and the comparative treatment of individuals. Rawls's theory prescribes that individuals are to be treated equally with respect to basic liberties but that individuals may be treated unequally in terms of rewards and burdens as long as the inequality satisfies conditions of fairness as embodied in the principle of fair equality of opportunity and the difference principle. Rawls argues that liberties have first priority, and when they are assured, the provision of fair equality of opportunity is required. The difference principle, which requires that institutions and policies be designed to benefit the least-advantaged person, is then applied.

Higher order standards are used to evaluate ethics systems and principles. One such standard is universalizability, which requires that an individual would will that everyone follow the rule or abide by the principle. The second standard is unanimity, which requires that everyone would impartially choose the same rule or principle. Reasoning about which rules and principles would be unanimously supported is intended to be based on Kant's conceptions of autonomy, freedom, and rationality and is to take place impartially as if from the original position. In business applications these two higher order standards provide a basis for evaluating alternative policies and provide guidance for managers in nonmarket analysis and strategy formulation.

Managers must make decisions in situations in which there are competing moral claims that require judgments about the effects of decisions on individuals, their rights, and their well-being.

An understanding of ethics systems and sensitivity to the moral dimensions of issues are important for managers for several reasons. First, sensitivity to the ethics dimensions of issues and the use of ethics frameworks can help managers avoid wrongs that may otherwise result from a narrow focus on the firm's interests. Second, sensitivity to the moral concerns of others about the policies and practices of a firm can help management anticipate nonmarket actions and pressures. Third, managers will be more likely to make decisions that serve the long-run interests of society and ultimately of business itself. Fourth, the content of corporate social responsibility is found in ethics principles, which guide the identification of those responsibilities.

CASES

Genetic Testing in the Workplace

Companies and their employees have an important interest in reducing health risks in the workplace. One approach to doing so is to alter production processes and the workplace to reduce hazards. For some companies, this is quite costly, and in some work situations it is impossible to eliminate all health risks. Another approach is to choose the workforce to minimize the risk. This may be done through evaluating workers' qualifications and experience and through subsequent training. It may also be done by determining workers' susceptibility to certain diseases that could result from exposure in the workplace. That susceptibility could be genetic.

Perhaps the first person to suggest the use of genetic information to improve workers' health was J. B. S. Haldane who in 1938 wrote,[28]

> The majority of potters do not die of bronchitis. It is quite possible that if we really understood the causation of this disease we should find out that only a fraction of potters are of a constitution which renders them liable to it. If so, we could eliminate potters' bronchitis by regulating entrants into the potters' industry who are congenitally disposed to it.

After the U.S. military found a susceptibility of soldiers with G-6-PD (glucose-6-phosphate dehydrogenase) deficiency to develop anemia, Stokinger and Mountain argued for the use of genetic testing for G-6-PD deficiency in workers who might be exposed to oxidants in the workplace:[29]

> Most important, the determination affords, for the first time, an opportunity to make a susceptibility evaluation during a job placement examination, and, thus, avoids placing a worker in exposures to which he is inordinately susceptible. This is preventive toxicology in the highest form; no previous single development in toxicology has opened such prospects for the medical supervision of workers.

In 1982 Representative Al Gore, chair of the House Subcommittee on Investigations and Oversight, warned that genetic testing had "the potential to serve as a marvelous tool to protect the health of workers or a terrible vehicle for invidious discrimination."[30]

Genetic testing to determine susceptibility to certain hazards can be done from a sample of blood or other bodily fluid. Such tests are generally quite accurate. Although they can be expensive, they offer a basis on which to select and assign workers to minimize the risks from exposure to certain health hazards and the possible tragedy of chronic or terminal diseases.

G-6-PD is an enzyme required for the stability of red blood cells. "Those with the deficiency are highly susceptible to having their red-blood-cell membranes destroyed by certain drugs or other oxidizing agents. It is especially a problem for blacks and some Mediterranean people."[31] The G-6-PD deficiency is carried by a sex-linked recessive gene, and approximately 100 million males worldwide are estimated to have the deficiency.

Another genetic test is for alpha-1-antitrypsin (AAT) deficiency, which results in susceptibility to respiratory irritants such as those found in many workplaces. Exposure to "dust and/or fumes" is one of the environmental risk factors and can result in lung and liver disease.[32] Approximately 100,000 Americans have severe AAT deficiency. AAT deficiency is a hereditary condition, and its most common abnormal gene originated in Scandinavia.[33] Treatment of the deficiency involves intravenous injections of AAT on a frequent basis.

Genetic testing can be used for either screening or monitoring purposes. In screening, genetic testing is used to select among job applicants for positions that may involve a potential health hazard. Screening can also be used in assigning current employees and new hires to jobs so as to minimize risks. Screening can also identify susceptible individuals who can take precautions to protect themselves or be moved to other jobs with less exposure to possible irritants such as oxidizing agents.

---

[28]Haldane, J. B. S. 1938. *Heredity and Politics*. New York, NY: Norton.
[29]Sokinger, H. E. and J. T. Mountain. 1963. "Test for Hypersusceptibility to Hemolytic Chemicals." *Archives of Environmental Health* 6: 57–64.

[30]Quoted in Brandt-Raul, Paul W. and Sherry I. Brandt-Rouf, 2004. "Genetic Testing in the Workplace: Ethical, Legal, and Social Implications." *Annual Review of Public Health* 25: 139–153.
[31]*Wall Street Journal*, February 24, 1986.
[32]The other environmental risk factors are personal smoking history, parental smoking history, and frequent lung infections. Robert A. Sandhaus, www.razziniusa.org/jan01/geneticprofiles.htm.
[33]The link between AAT and lung disease was made in Sweden. Robert A. Sandhaus, www.razziniusa.org/jan01/geneticprofiles.htm.

Genetic testing can also be used to monitor groups of employees over time to determine if they experience chromosome damage due to exposure in the workplace. This could be important for employees who work with oxidants, lead, beryllium, and other potentially toxic metals and chemicals. In addition to providing information that could be used to reduce risks, some companies believe that genetic testing could give them a degree of protection from liability if a worker chose to stay in a job after being notified that he or she was genetically susceptible to a disease that could be triggered by exposure in the workplace.

Many companies were hesitant to use genetic testing because of uncertainty about the relevant law. In 2002 the Burlington Northern Santa Fe Railway Company reached a settlement for $2.2 million with the Equal Employment Opportunity Commission (EEOC) of a lawsuit filed under the Americans with Disabilities Act. The company had tested without their knowledge 36 employees who complained of carpal tunnel syndrome to determine if they were genetically susceptible to the syndrome. The company did not acknowledge violating the law nor did the EEOC find that the company had violated the law. The case, however, served as a warning to companies.

Finally, in 2008 Congress enacted and the president signed the Genetic Information Nondiscrimination Act which defined as an unlawful employment practice:

1. to fail or refuse to hire, or to discharge, any employee, or otherwise to discriminate against any employee with respect to the compensation, terms, conditions, or privileges of employment of the employee, because of genetic information with respect to the employee; or

2. to limit, segregate, or classify the employees of the employer in any way that would deprive or tend to deprive any employee of employment opportunities or otherwise adversely affect the status of the employee as an employee, because of genetic information with respect to the employee.

The act also made it illegal "to request, require, or purchase genetic information with respect to an employee or a family member of the employee except—

where (A) health or genetic services are offered by the employer, including such services offered as part of a wellness program; ... (5) where the information involved is used for genetic monitoring of the biological effects of toxic substances in the workplace, but only if (A) the employer provides written notice of the genetic monitoring to the employee; (B)(i) the employee provides prior, knowing, voluntary, and written authorization; or ..."

the information was required by federal or state law.

With the completion of the Human Genome Project the possibilities for more accurate and extensive genetic testing in the workplace were seemingly unlimited. ▪

Preparation Questions

1. Is genetic testing in the workplace warranted from a utilitarian perspective; that is, by the potential benefits it can yield? What ethics concerns does it involve?

2. Consider the use of genetic testing for screening job applicants, for assigning current employees to jobs, and for monitoring employees for genetic damage from exposure in the workplace. Which rights might be said to be violated by either the use or the prohibition of the use of genetic testing for these purposes? How would you prioritize those rights? Does the law accord with your assessment?

3. Who should be informed of the results of a genetic test? Is the use of genetic testing for monitoring more or less appropriate than its use for screening purposes?

4. Prepare a rights table as in Figure 22-5.

5. Design a wellness program for employees that includes an opportunity for an employee to have a genetic test and also provides the employer with an opportunity to use genetic information in screening and/or monitoring.

6. Organized labor and some activists oppose genetic testing on the grounds that the employer should ensure a safe workplace. Does an employer have a moral duty to reduce risks in the workplace to the point at which any qualified person regardless of his or her susceptibility can safely occupy the position?

7. If an employee with full understanding of his or her genetic susceptibility chooses (because, for example, of higher pay) to work in an area in which exposure is possible, should the employer assign the employee to that job?

8. Consider the case of a company with a production process that requires the processing of a metal, such as beryllium, that can be toxic to workers with a particular genetic deficiency. The company has installed dust collection and ventilation equipment, and the workplace meets all government safety requirements by a substantial margin. Nevertheless, an individual with a particular genetic deficiency can develop chronic and serious long-term illnesses from exposure to the metal. At an annualized cost of $1 million the company could install additional equipment that would reduce by half the risk to an employee with the genetic deficiency, but illness could still occur. For jobs in the metals processing unit, the company could also screen job applicants for the genetic deficiency and not hire those who have the deficiency. The cost of the screening would be approximately 10 percent of the cost of the additional equipment and would reduce the risk of disease by 90 percent. The company also has the alternative of replacing 80 percent of the workers in the metals processing unit with sophisticated and expensive robotic equipment at a net annualized cost of $3 million (net of the savings in labor costs). This would result in the layoff of 48 employees. What should the company do?

Chipotle Mexican Grill and Undocumented Workers

INTRODUCTION

Founder, Chairman, and Co-CEO Steve Ells was proud of the growth and success of Chipotle Mexican Grill. By the end of the first quarter 2011 the company had nearly 1,100 company-owned restaurants in the United States, profits in the first quarter showed a 24 percent increase over the same quarter in 2010, the share price had soared as the country emerged from the recession, and the company had just entered the Standard & Poor's 500 Index. The restaurant sold gourmet burritos and tacos and emphasized "food with integrity," made with natural ingredients and range-raised meats. The company planned to open 135–145 more restaurants in 2011 and also was preparing to introduce restaurants serving South East Asian food.

Despite the success of the company in the marketplace, Ells and the management team faced a difficult challenge in its nonmarket environment. Immigration and Customs Enforcement (ICE), a unit of the Department of Homeland Security (DHS), had stepped up enforcement of the immigration laws by reviewing the employment documentation of workers at companies suspected of employing illegal immigrants. An initial ICE investigation in Minnesota had identified a large number of Chipotle workers who had presented false information upon hiring and lacked the documentation to work in the United States. Chipotle fired over 400 workers in Minnesota; most of whom were illegal immigrants. ICE had also begun investigating Chipotle restaurants in other states. Chipotle could voluntarily use the government's E-Verify system to verify that its workers were eligible to work, but it had not done so other than in states such as Arizona, where it was required by state law. More of its employees could lack documentation and be in the country illegally. Chipotle had to decide what to do as the ICE investigation continued.

BACKGROUND

Steve Ells opened the first Chipotle restaurant in 1993 in Boulder, Colorado, and its success led to the opening of more restaurants in the state. In 1998 McDonald's made a minority investment in the company, providing capital to expand outside of Colorado. In 2001 McDonald's obtained a majority interest in Chipotle as it expanded its restaurant formats by investing in specialized restaurant chains. McDonald's invested $350 million in Chipotle, fueling its rapid growth. In 2006 McDonald's decided to focus on its core McDonald's restaurants, and spun off Chipotle along with Donato's Pizza and Boston Market. Chipotle went public in 2006, and by 2011 its share price had increase by more than a factor of five. The company was one of the fastest growing restaurant chains, and its growth was forecast to continue in the United States as well as in Canada, the United Kingdom, and France, where it had recently opened restaurants. Later in 2011 Chipotle planned to launch its new ShopHouse Southeast Asian Kitchen restaurants. Ells commented, "I have always believed that the Chipotle model would work well with a variety of different cuisines. Chipotle's success is not necessarily about burritos and tacos, but rather about serving great, sustainably raised food that is delicious, affordable, and convenient."[34]

ENFORCEMENT OF EMPLOYMENT LAWS

The United States was estimated to have over 11 million illegal immigrants, many of whom were employed in relatively low paying jobs in agriculture, construction, cleaning services, restaurants, and other service industries. Although the inflow of illegal immigrants had slowed during the recession, illegal immigration and undocumented workers remained contentious issues in the country. Voters wanted immigration reform, but the reforms they sought differed greatly, and the Democratic and Republican parties had been cautious in advocating specific reforms for fear of alienating voters. Some voters wanted stronger border controls to prevent illegal immigrants from entering the county, reduced incentives to enter by making it more difficult to obtain work, and deportation of illegal immigrants. Other voters wanted illegal immigrants to be granted amnesty, protected from deportation, and have a pathway to citizenship. Several states including Arizona, Florida, and Georgia had enacted laws to reduce illegal immigration and crack down on illegal immigrants already in the state. Several other states were expected to enact similar laws. Maryland acted to make it easier for illegal immigrants to obtain education benefits.

The Obama administration had steered a cautious course on the politics of undocumented workers and illegal immigrants and had chosen to focus on undocumented workers. Unlike the previous administration that had emphasized raids on factories and the arrest of undocumented workers, the Obama administration decided to focus on employers. The administration began to review the employment records of companies in what commentators called "silent raids." Over 2,740 employment audits were conducted in 2010 and over 1,000 were underway in 2011.[35] Chipotle with 26,000 employees was one of the companies under review.

In its Strategic Plan for 2010–2014 ICE stated that it "will pursue an effective enforcement program to reduce the incentive for aliens to come to, and enter and remain unlawfully." It continued, "The opportunity to work in the United States motivates many to seek illegal entry. Therefore, enforcing the immigration-related employment laws is a critical component of border security. To create a culture of compliance among employers, ICE will use the following two-pronged strategy: (1) aggressive criminal and civil enforcement against those employers who knowingly violate the law; and (2) continued implementation of programs, such as E-Verify and ICE's IMAGE program, to help employers comply."[36]

The IMAGE program provided education and training to companies for use of the E-Verify system and adherence to best hiring practices. The participating companies agreed to undergo

---

[34]Chipotle Mexican Grill, Press Release, April 12, 2011.
[35]In a silent raid in 2009 American Apparel was forced to let go 2,500 workers in its garment factories in California.
[36]U.S. Immigration and Customs Enforcement, "ICE Strategic Plan FY 2010-2014," no date.

an I-9 audit by ICE and to sign a partnership agreement with ICE. Companies that completed the IMAGE requirements become "IMAGE Certified"—a distinction DHS believes will become an industry standard."[37]

E-Verify is "an Internet-based system that compares information from an employee's Form I-9, Employment Eligibility Verification, to data from U.S. Department of Homeland Security and Social Security Administration records to confirm employment eligibility. E-Verify is fast, free and easy to use—and it's the best way employers can ensure a legal workplace."[38] An I-9 form attests to a worker's eligibility and is completed when a worker is hired. The form requires information such as a Social Security number, but an active counterfeiting business had developed to provide false documentation. Fake driver's licenses were also prevalent.

One concern of ICE was that employers could exploit undocumented workers who were desperate for work. ICE raided 15 Chun's Mesquite Broiler restaurants in Arizona and California and arrested the owners, their bookkeeper, and 40 illegal immigrants. In the criminal indictment against the owners the government alleged that they had maintained two payrolls, one for legal workers and one for illegal workers. The illegal immigrants were paid under the table without taxes being withheld. The owners were alleged to have failed to pay $400,000 in Social Security and Medicare taxes.[39]

CHIPOTLE AND ICE

In 2010 ICE conducted an investigation of Chipotle restaurants leading to the firing of 400 workers. ICE had also investigated 20–25 Chipotle restaurants in Virginia and Washington, D.C., resulting in the firing of 40 workers who had supplied new documentation "that proved to be fraudulent."[40] Chris Arnold, spokesperson for Chipotle, explained, "We found that these workers were not legally authorized to work in this country. Many workers left immediately, but we had to let others go because we can't employ them under the law because they are not legally authorized to work in the United States."[41]

In April 2011 the criminal division of the U.S. Attorney's office in Washington joined the investigation, requesting additional information from the company. Criminal charges could be filed if the U.S. Attorney determined that the company had knowingly hired undocumented workers. Chipotle Co-CEO Monty Moran said that the company was "completely open" and that discussions with the government "seem to be going well."[42] Robert Laskin of Patton Boggs LLP, outside counsel for Chipotle, said, "The company remains fully committed to cooperating with the government's investigations."[43] The *Wall Street Journal* wrote, "the immigration probe has cast a pall over the Wall Street favorite, with some analysts downgrading its share value. The

company's labor costs are likely to rise as it hires new workers who require training to replace undocumented workers."[44]

THE POLITICS OF UNDOCUMENTED WORKERS

The chair of the immigration subcommittee of the House Judiciary Committee, Elton Gallegly (R-CA), argued that the use of E-Verify should be mandatory: "making [E-Verify] universally mandatory would ease the cumbersome and easily manipulated I-9 process employers now used to screen employees. It would also greatly reduce the number of illegal immigrants in the American workplace."[45] Lamar Smith (R-TX), chair of the House Judiciary Committee, said, "With unemployment at 9 percent for 21 months, jobs are scarce and families are worried. According to the Pew Hispanic Center, 7 million people are working in the U.S. illegally. Those jobs should go to legal workers."[46]

The U.S. Chamber of Commerce reported that its members had mixed reactions to making E-Verify mandatory. Some small businesses were concerned about the time and hassle of the system and the possible difficulty of using it in the field. The agriculture industry relied on undocumented workers and opposed the use of E-Verify. Craig J. Regelbrugge, vice-president of the American Nursery & Landscape Association, said, "Simply put, any E-Verify expansion that comes without meaningful immigration reform would be disastrous for the American agricultural economy. It would leave the United States importing food and exporting jobs." He continued, "Every lowly, backbreaking farm-working job sustains three jobs in the non-farm economy. What Congress needs to know is we have 1.6 million dedicated farm workers, and if they go away, we will lose several million American jobs upstream and downstream. We happen to think that is too high a price."[47] Smith countered, "Critics of E-Verify claim illegal immigrants hold jobs that Americans won't do. But even in the agriculture industry, where amnesty supporters insist we need illegal workers, 50 percent of the agricultural jobs are held by U.S. citizens and legal immigrants. And if farmers really need foreign labor, they can get it legally—we have a guest worker program for agricultural workers that has no numerical limit."[48] Brian Stanley of Stanley Farms in Georgia that produces Vidalia onions said, "There's nothing out there to replace hand labor, and we don't have American people applying for these jobs. Using E-Verify would cut our work force and hurt our business."[49]

ETHICS AND UNDOCUMENTED WORKERS

Sahari Uribe of the National Day Labor Organizing Network said, "I saw the workers shortly after they were fired. Some were crying, some had been working for Chipotle for six years and many felt they had been treated like trash."[50] Yeny Portales, one of those fired, said, "We've dedicated so much time to Chipotle, and for them to fire us all of a sudden, and in this way,

---

[37]http://www.ice.gov/image Accessed April 25, 2011.
[38]Ibid.
[39]*Wall Street Journal*, April 21, 2011. In 2010, 180 criminal indictments were filed against company officials.
[40]*Wall Street Journal*, May 4, 2011.
[41]*Washington Post*, March 24, 2011.
[42]*Wall Street Journal*, April 21, 2011.
[43]*Wall Street Journal*, May 4, 2011.

[44]Ibid.
[45]*Washington Post*, February 10, 2011.
[46]Ibid.
[47]Ibid.
[48]Ibid.
[49]*Wall Street Journal*, February 24, 2011.
[50]*Washington Post*, March 24, 2011.

made us feel terrible. We felt like they didn't value our years of service and that we, as their employees, didn't matter to them."[51]

Advocates for undocumented workers argued that firing the workers would simply drive them into the underground economy. The Service Employees International Union (SEUI), the largest U.S. union with 2.2 million members, had grown by enlisting immigrants and advocated an amnesty program for undocumented workers. Javier Morillo, president of the SEIU chapter in the twin cities in Minnesota, said, "You are taking hard-working people in good-paying jobs and moving them to jobs where they are exploited."[52] Referring to the I-9 audits conducted by ICE, Ben Monterroso of the SEIU said, "Silent raids are not helping keep good people employed, and they are not helping the economy."[53]

Chipotle's Code of Ethics for Co-Chief Executive Officer required Steve Ells to "adhere to the following principles and responsibilities," including[54]

• Comply with rules and regulations of all U.S. and non-U.S. governmental entities and other private and

public regulatory agencies to which the company is subject, …

• Act in what I reasonably and independently believe to be in the best interests of the Company.

• Promote ethical behavior among employees under my supervision. ▪

Preparation Questions

1. Is it the higher labor costs that should concern Chipotle? Is it the fate of the workers it has to fire? Is it violations of the law? Is it the possibility of criminal charges?
2. Is ICE forcing the company to take unethical actions?
3. Have the undocumented workers earned certain rights? Have they been fairly compensated at wages higher than they could have earned in their home country?
4. Should Chipotle use E-Verify for new hires? For its present employees?
5. Should Chipotle join the IMAGE program?

Environmental Injustice?

Studies have shown that the poor and minorities are disproportionately represented in locations proximate to toxic emissions sites and hazardous waste facilities. The General Accounting Office (GAO) (1983) and the United Church of Christ (UCC) (1987) conducted studies indicating that hazardous waste landfill and treatment sites disproportionately were located in poor and minority communities, and most subsequent studies reached the same conclusion.[55] In 2007 the UCC commissioned a new study that used 2000 census data to identify the characteristics of communities in which the 413 commercial hazardous waste facilities were located. The study found that "neighborhoods within 3 kilometers of commercial hazardous waste facilities are 56% people of color whereas non-host areas are 30% people of color.… Poverty rates in the host neighborhoods are 1.5 times greater than non-host areas (18% vs. 12%) and mean annual household incomes and mean owner-occupied housing values in host neighborhoods are 15% lower …. Neighborhoods with facilities clustered close together have higher percentages of people of color than those

with non-clustered facilities (69% vs. 51%). Likewise, neighborhoods with clustered facilities have disproportionately high poverty rates."[56] These disparities were present in almost all parts of the country, and the disparities were on average greater for the 343 commercial hazardous waste facilities located in metropolitan areas. Advocates for the poor and minorities conclude that this was clear evidence of environmental injustice.[57] This case addresses two aspects of this situation. The first centers on an explanation for the empirical finding. The second centers on whether the situation is unjust.

What is the explanation for the finding that minorities and those in poverty are disproportionately located proximate to toxic emissions and hazardous waste facilities? One possible explanation is that the firms that construct and operate plants with toxic emissions and hazardous waste facilities seek

---

[51]Ibid.

[52]*Wall Street Journal*, March 29, 2011.

[53]*Wall Street Journal*, February 24, 2011.

[54]www.chipotle.com Accessed, May 3, 2011.

[55]General Accounting Office. 1983, *Siting of Hazardous Waste Landfills and Their Correlation with Racial and Economic Status of Surrounding Communities*, Washington, DC. United Church of Christ. 1987, *Toxic Waste and Race in the United States*, Cleveland, Ohio.

[56]The study was prepared by environmental justice scholars and published as *Toxic Wastes and Race at Twenty 1987–2007*, Cleveland, Ohio, February, 2007. The report was "designed to facilitate renewed grassroots organizing and provide a catalyst for local, regional, and national environmental justice public forums, discussion groups, and policy changes in 2007 and beyond."

[57]Concern that minority populations and/or low-income populations bear a disproportionate amount of adverse health and environmental effects of environmental pollution and hazards led President Clinton to issue Executive Order 12898 in 1994, which directed the attention of federal agencies to this situation. (http://www.epa.gov/oswer/ej/index.html. Accessed July 2, 2009.) The Environmental Protection Agency (EPA) subsequently defined environmental justice as the "fair treatment for people of all races, cultures, and incomes, regarding the development of environmental laws, regulations, and policies."

to impose harm on the poor and minorities. This explanation, however, is farfetched and begs the question of why they would intentionally harm people.

A second possible explanation is that the locations for such facilities are chosen on an economic basis, taking into account land prices, the availability of workers, and where other similar facilities are located. Low land prices indicate an economically attractive location, but low land prices also mean that housing is less expensive in that location and people with low incomes naturally live where housing is less expensive. The poor and minorities are disproportionately represented among low income people, and hence they are disproportionately present in the low-cost locations for the facilities. Firms thus locate their facilities where costs are low understanding that in those locations low income people are disproportionately present.

A third possible explanation is that the locations for toxic emissions and hazardous waste facilities are chosen based on economic considerations and with the intent of avoiding posing a risk to people. That is, sites are chosen where land prices are low and where relatively few people are present. The siting of a facility in a location where there are few people keeps land prices low and may even lower them. These low land prices subsequently attract low cost housing, and low-income people choose to live there despite the presence of the facility and known emissions. That is, they trade off lower housing prices for a greater risk of exposure to toxic emissions. This explanation is thus that firms locating their facilities take into account both economic and human factors, but after they have placed their facility in a low-cost location, low-income people subsequently locate near the facility because of the lower land and housing prices.

The bulk of the empirical studies examining toxic emissions and hazardous waste facilities and the socio-economic characteristics of people who might be exposed to the hazards analyze the data at a point in time at which both the toxic emission site and the people are present. For example, they use 2000 census data and facilities in place in the early 2000s. This provides information about the current situation, but does not differentiate between the second and third explanations. To so differentiate, it is necessary to consider the time at which the facility location was chosen rather than at some later point in time.

Ann Wolverton, an economist at the EPA, conducted such a study.[58] She used data from the time at which the location was chosen for new plants in Texas that were required to report toxic emissions to the EPA's Toxic Releases Inventory (TRI). The toxic emissions of the new plants met regulatory standards and hence did not pose a significant health risk, since otherwise a permit would have been denied.[59] Socio-economic data were then obtained on the characteristics of the community at the time the site was chosen. To capture the choice of a location from among the many where the plant could have been located, she estimated an econometric model of the choice among the many alternative locations. She also controlled for

"the costs of land and labor, the quality of labor, the degree of urbanization, average plant size, and distance to rail-based transportation...," in addition to whether there was already a plant at that location that reported emissions to the TRI; what the 2007 UCC study referred to as clustering. Plant location decisions are also affected by potential or actual protests against the plant, and some communities are better organized for such NIMBY protests than others.[60] She thus took into account the percent of the community who voted in the immediately prior presidential election as a measure of potential community activism, and she also used the percent of the community that was born in the United States as another factor that could affect community activism and the likelihood of protest.

Her empirical study largely confirmed the finding of the other studies that the current plant locations are disproportionately in communities where the poor and minorities live. When matched to the community characteristics at the time of the location decision, however, she found no statistically significant relation between race and location or the percent of the population that was foreign born. The sites were more likely to be located in lower-income communities, but the sites were less likely to be in communities with a higher proportion of people in poverty. Factors such as land and labor prices, the quality of labor and the distance to rail transportation were statistically significant as predicted by economic theory, as was the prior presence of a plant that reported toxic emissions. The potential for community protests was statistically significant, but plants were less likely to be located in neighborhoods with established households and more likely to be located in communities in which a higher percent of the people voted.[61]

Wolverton's study thus supports the third explanation and not the first or second explanations. The firms in the study did not locate their facilities in communities in which minorities and those in poverty were disproportionately represented, but after the passage of time, those communities attracted a disproportionate number of minorities, although not people in poverty. The firms apparently made their siting decisions based on economic considerations, and those decisions did not have a disproportionate impact on minorities and those in poverty at the time the facility was sited.

Although Wolverton's study provides an explanation for how the current situation came to be and suggests no intentional and perhaps no unintentional discrimination by firms, the question remains whether the current situation is unjust. From the perspective of a time slice theory of justice such as that of Rawls the answer could be "yes," since minorities, disadvantaged by the effects of past if not present discrimination and those in poverty are disproportionately present near toxic emissions and hazardous waste facilities. Nozick, however, argued that any time slice theory is inadequate and that

---

[58]Wolverton, Ann. 2009. "Effects of Socio-Economic and Input-Related Factors on Polluting Plants' Location Decisions," *The B.E. Journal of Economic Analysis & Policy*. Vol. 9: Article 14.

[59]If health were harmed by the emissions, the injured person would be able to file a tort lawsuit seeking compensation and damages.

---

[60]Hamilton found that firms take into account in their siting decisions the likelihood of community protests. Hamilton, James. 1995. "Testing for Environmental Racism: Prejudice, Profits, and Political Power?" *Journal of Policy Analysis and Management*. 14: 107–132.

[61]Wolverton speculated that communities with high voter turnout were better organized and might have sought to have the facility located in their communities.

the path along which the current situation came to be must be considered. In particular, people chose whether to locate in a community in which hazards were present, and they benefitted from lower housing prices. ▪

Preparation Questions

1. Should the history of the siting of a facility matter or is the time slice perspective appropriate?

2. Is the current situation in which the poor and minorities are disproportionately located in communities where there are toxic emissions and hazardous waste sites unjust?

3. If so, who has a duty to rectify the injustice?

4. As the owner of a hazardous waste treatment company, should you relocate a facility that has a disproportionate share of minority and poor residents proximate to the facility?

23

BEHAVIORAL ETHICS, INDIVIDUALS, AND MANAGEMENT

INTRODUCTION

Corporate statements of social responsibility and codes of ethics have become commonplace. Many companies have established the position of chief ethics officer, and membership in the Ethics and Compliance Officer Association increased from 12 in 1992 to 1,300 in 2007, including more than half of the Fortune 100 companies. Some codes and statements of responsibility are little more than public relations, whereas others reflect a strong corporate commitment to specific standards of conduct. That commitment increasingly involves not just policies but measurement and accountability. But decisions are made and actions taken by individuals or teams of individuals, and their conduct ultimately determines the ethical conduct of the company and its social performance. In the wake of the series of scandals discussed in Chapter 20, Chuck Prince, the new CEO of Citigroup, said, "I never thought that you had to say to people, 'We want to grow aggressively—and don't forget not to break the law.'"[1] In the Chapter 11 case *Citigroup and Subprime Lending*, Citigroup also failed to anticipate the morally motivated nonmarket action directed against its subprime lending business.

As an example of morally motivated nonmarket action, under Warren Buffett's leadership Berkshire Hathaway allowed shareholders to designate $18 a share of their dividends to three charities of their choice. A woman who had become an independent sales agent for Berkshire's Pampered Chef in part because the company's mission statement encouraged its employees to "develop their God-given talents," learned that some of the profits she would generate would be donated to Planned Parenthood and other pro-choice groups. She launched a private politics campaign over the Internet. Customers complained, some sales agents resigned, and Pampered Chef was pressured to the point that Berkshire ended the dividend contributions program. The company, which had frequently been targeted by pro-life groups, said it ended the program because it was hurting Pampered Chef and its employees.

Using the perspective of behavioral ethics, this chapter focuses on the conduct of individuals and teams in settings where moral concerns are present. Behavioral ethics approaches moral issues not through fundamental moral principles such as Kant's categorical imperative or the utilitarian principle of maximizing aggregate well-being but by trying to understand the behavior of people and the extent to which their behavior reflects moral standards such as altruism, fairness, and reciprocity. How managers and firms actually make decisions on issues such as workers rights, environmental policies, privacy, lending, and so on is difficult to observe directly, and motivation is even more difficult to assess. Researchers thus have turned to laboratory and more recently Internet-based experiments to try to understand how individuals make choices when facing a moral issue. This chapter examines laboratory experiments that identify motivation based on the choices made by participants where incentives are present to serve one's own interests or broader social interests. The focus is on self-interest, altruism, fairness, audience effects, reciprocity, and moral reinforcement. The chapter is positive in its orientation in that it focuses on understanding individual behavior rather than making normative judgments. The chapter draws implications for management practices from the findings of the experiments and considers examples of management approaches to ethical conduct.

The experiments considered address how one person interacts with or treats another person or how in group settings a person makes decisions where individual interests differ from collective interests. The experiments are more informative about consequentialist ethics systems and less informative about deontological factors such as moral rights and motives for actions.

The discussion of the experiments uses a standard terminology. The experiments involve games with participants as players assigned to specific roles. The proposer typically is the participant that takes the first

---

[1] *Fortune*, November 29, 2004.

action, and the responder either receives something from the proposer or takes the second action. The action of a participant is referred to as an allocation or contribution. An experiment is anonymous if the participants do not know or see each other. An experiment is double blind if the experimenters do not know which participants are in which roles. The results of the experiments are referred to as findings, and how convincing the findings are is determined by statistical significance and replication of the findings by other experiments, as well as by theories that provide understandings of the findings. A treatment is an experiment with a specific context and set of instructions. An experiment typically includes several treatments in which the experimenter makes one change in the instructions or context in each treatment so as to isolate an effect. The participants in the experiments were primarily undergraduate students, and they were paid for their participation. The amounts paid were small, but studies have shown that when the amounts were larger behavior was very similar.

BEHAVIORAL ETHICS EXPERIMENTS

Self-Interest, Altruism, and Fairness

This section considers a line of research based on behavior in dictator games. A dictator game involves two participants—a proposer who unilaterally makes a decision about how much of a sum of money, referred to as an endowment, to keep and how much to contribute to a responder, who takes no action and simply receives the contribution. If the dictator is solely self-interested, the rational action is to keep all the money, allocating zero to the responder. In experiments, however, many proposers contribute some of their endowment to the responder. In the initial experiment Kahneman, Knetsch, and Thaler (1986) found that most proposers chose an equal allocation of the endowment rather than a very unequal allocation favoring the proposer. This finding has been confirmed in numerous other experiments.

Researchers have offered alternative explanations for the behavior observed in the dictator experiments. One is that participants in the role of the proposer are not rationally self-interested and instead are altruistic or other regarding. Another explanation is that fairness considerations dictate sharing the endowment. A third is that there are social norms that people follow in considering how to allocate the endowment. The norm could be that the endowment was a gift or windfall and the person in the role of proposer was just as likely to be assigned the role of responder and hence should allocate the endowment evenly.

One factor that could affect behavior in the experiments is the source of the endowment. If the researcher leaves the source of the money unexplained or ambiguous, participants can imagine a variety of scenarios. The endowment could be a windfall; it could be money found on the street; it could have been earned by the proposer; and so on. To explore the effect of the source of the endowment, List (2007) used a treatment in which participants performed a task for 30 minutes to earn their endowment. In this treatment 94 percent of the participants kept the entire endowment and only 6 percent contributed a positive amount to the responder, and the average allocation was small. The moral cost of self-interested behavior was negated by having earned the endowment, or alternatively a different norm applied when it is earned. Cherry, Frykblom, and Shogren (2002) also found that in a double-blind anonymous dictator game 95 percent of the proposers that earned their endowments kept all their earnings.[2] Earning the endowment gives moral authority to the proposer to keep what has been earned.

List and others have explored other treatments that have large effects on the behavior of participants. One was to give the proposers additional choices in a dictator game. In one treatment proposers allocated their endowment between themselves and a responder, but they could also take money from the responder. When the amount that could be taken from the responder was large relative to the endowment, 30 percent of the proposers kept the entire endowment and took nothing from the responder, but more than half kept the entire endowment and took almost the maximum from the responder. Only 10 percent of the proposers contributed a positive amount of their endowment to the responder. List (p. 484) concluded that "By allowing choices that are not entirely selfish in the nonpositive domain, the social norms of the game change, providing the

---

[2]The experimental treatment included a statement that the responder did not have "the opportunity to earn any money" to avoid the interpretation that the responder already had similar earnings. It also included a statement that the proposer was allocating "his or her earnings."

dictator with the 'moral authority' to give nothing."[3] That is, the opportunity to take from a responder gives the proposer moral authority that overcomes the moral cost of self-interested behavior.

An unconditional altruist takes into account the well-being of others independently of their actions. A conditional altruist takes into account the well-being of others conditional on their past actions as well as their current situation. Those actions can determine how "deserving" individuals are perceived to be. Eckel and Grossman (1994) found that proposers contributed more to the responder when the responder was more deserving. They identified the responder as the American Red Cross.

Fong and Oberholzer-Gee (2011) conducted an experiment to determine if individuals would spend part of their endowment to learn about the type of responder with whom they were paired. Responders were poor people who resided in public housing in Pittsburgh[4] and were poor either because they had a disability or because of drug use. Some proposers were given no information about the responder, some were told why the responder was poor, and others were given the opportunity to spend 10 percent of their endowment to obtain information about why the responder was poor. One third of the participants given the opportunity to buy information about the responder chose to do so, indicating that they had a preference for one type of responder over the other. Those proposers who bought information did so not to allocate more to a responder who was poor because of a disability but to avoid allocations to those who were poor because of drug use. Proposers who had no information about the responder allocated a substantial amount to the responder,[5] but the opportunity to buy information resulted in lower overall allocations to responders than when information could not be obtained

In the chapter case *Fresenius Medical Care in China*, the company had to assess the reason patients were coming to its facility for kidney dialysis for short periods of time. Moreover, it had to decide whether to investigate the source of the kidneys being transplanted in the adjacent hospital. The concerns centered on the issues of patient tourism and the possible harvesting of organs from prisoners.

Hoffman, McCabe, and Smith (1996a) considered various degrees of anonymity in dictator games and found that proposers contributed less to responders the more anonymous were the experimental conditions. They interpreted their findings as indicating that proposers were less generous the greater their "social distance" from the responders.

Most of the experiments make the connection between the proposer's action and the consequences for the responder perfectly transparent to the participants. Transparency is not, however, present in many managerial settings where nature as well as other people may affect the connection between actions and outcomes. Dana, Weber, and Kuang (2007) explored the effect of transparency by introducing uncertainty between actions and outcomes. In their experiments proposers were given the choice between an equal allocation of the endowment and an unequal allocation that heavily favored the proposer. In a treatment in which there were two proposers either of whom could make an equal allocation of their endowment, the researchers found that 74 percent of the proposers chose the unequal allocation. The presence of another proposer who could provide an equal allocation gave both proposers some wiggle room to choose the unequal allocation. Dana, Weber, and Kuang also conducted an experiment to determine whether proposers were influenced by whether responders could identify the proposer's action, which in the treatment could have been made by nature.[6] Over half of those who made a choice chose the unequal allocation, but 24 percent allowed nature to make the choice. The authors concluded that

---

[3]See List (2007).

[4]The practice in experiments conducted by economists is not to lie to participants. For example, in a dictator game the responder is passive and does not play a role. The experiment could be conducted by the experimenter telling the proposer that there was a responder in another room even though there was not. Instead, participants in the role of responder are generally present and receive the allocation made by the proposer. In the experiment by Fong and Oberholzer-Gee residents in public housing were surveyed to develop the experimental descriptions of the responders, proposers and residents were matched even though the residents were not physically present in the laboratory, and the allocations made by proposers were paid to the matched residents.

[5]The proposers were given the endowment rather than earning it, so proposers would be expected to be more generous than if they had earned the funds.

[6]In this treatment proposers could choose between an equal or unequal allocation, and if they decided quickly, which was easy to do, their choice would determine the outcome. If they delayed, there was a chance (random) that nature would intervene and impose either the equal allocation or the unequal allocation.

the possible intervention by nature provided the proposers plausible deniability in the sense that the unequal allocation could have been due to nature rather than to the proposer. Obscuring the link between the proposer's action and the consequences for the responder provided wiggle room.

Oberholzer-Gee and Eichenberger (2008) also found that in an anonymous, double-blind dictator game, proposers kept more of the endowment when they could choose to play an unattractive lottery as an alternative to playing the dictator game. In the terminology of Dana, Weber, and Kuang, the lottery allowed the proposer the ultimate wiggle room of not playing the dictator game, and approximately half the proposers choose that alternative even though they were throwing away money. In a similar setting in which proposers could avoid playing the dictator game by purchasing an unfavorable lottery ticket, Lazear, Malmendier, and Weber (2011) found that "the majority of subjects share without really wanting to, as evidenced by their willingness to avoid the dictator game and to even pay for avoiding it."

The results of these experiments can be summarized as follows. In double blind, anonymous experiments most proposers act in a self-interested manner, but proposers that are matched with more deserving responders exhibit a sense of fairness by allocating more of their endowment to the responder. If, however, the proposer earns the endowment rather than it being a windfall provided by the experimenter, self-interested behavior is much more prevalent. Moreover, many proposers choose to avoid being in a situation where they must make an allocation.

Throughout this line of experiments a portion of the participants exhibited altruistic or other regarding preferences. That portion was lower if proposers earned their endowments, the link between actions and outcomes was obscured, the set of alternatives was expanded, or there was wiggle room that allowed proposers to act in their self-interest. The chapter case *Insider Trading* considers a situation in which self-interest and possibly greed led to illegal activity.

Audience Effects, the Self, and Corporate Social Responsibility

Experimenters have studied audience effects to assess whether proposers allocate a portion of the endowment to the responder so as not to appear selfish either to the responder, the experimenter, or one self. Andreoni and Bernheim (2009) conducted a dictator game experiment in which the allocations by proposers to the responders were publicly observable so as "to heighten the effects of social image." Proposers allocated their endowment, but with a publicly known probability nature intervened and allocated all the endowment either to the proposer or the responder with equal probabilities. When nature could not intervene, more than half the proposers chose an equal allocation and less than a third chose to keep the entire endowment, consistent with other experimental findings of an audience effect. When the probability that nature could intervene was high, the percentage of responders choosing the equal allocation decreased substantially and the percent of proposers keeping the entire endowment increased to over 70 percent. Consistent with the finding by Dana, Weber, and Kuang, the weaker the connection between the proposer's actions and the consequences for the responder, the more self-interested was the behavior of the proposer. In other terminology, the audience effect was weaker when the audience could not with certainty attribute an unequal allocation to the proposer. Transparency increases audience costs, and obscurity reduces those costs leading to more self-interested behavior. As considered in Chapter 24, to reduce corruption, companies and activists have campaigned for greater transparency in the disposition of royalties paid to the governments of developing countries from oil and minerals extraction.

Audience effects can have implications for firms considering whether to practice corporate social responsibility (CSR). To the extent that CEOs and firms are subject to audience effects they may adopt CSR to appear to be generous before their peers, other members of their industry, customers, or the public. When it is not clear what the implications are for stakeholders, audience effects can be weaker, and less CSR would then be expected.

Audience effects should be a function of the size and composition of the audience. The larger the audience, the greater should be the effect, and the greater the importance of the audience members, for example, the news media, a firm's customers or employees, or government, the greater the likely effect. The audience effect can also depend on the degree of scrutiny of actions. The greater the anonymity of the decision maker the weaker is the scrutiny, and weaker scrutiny could result in less consideration for stakeholders and the public in the firm's decisions. Audience effects could explain peer group pressure and actions that follow from it. Many companies embraced CSR in the same time period, and this could have resulted from audience effects. Greater scrutiny by NGOs and social activists strengthen the audience effects, giving firms incentives to be more socially responsible. The news media and in the last decade the Internet and social media have increased the scrutiny of business and may have reduced the wiggle room for companies to avoid broader social responsibilities. Scrutiny as a source of social pressure is considered in Chapter 4.

Behavior can also be affected by one's own self-image. Monin and Miller (2001) conducted experiments in which participants were given an opportunity to establish their "ethical credentials" before making a choice that had ethical implications. The only audience in the experiment was the person giving instructions to the participants. In the first part of the experiment participants could establish credentials as not being prejudiced, and in the second part they faced a decision which could reveal their true sentiments. Participants who had the opportunity to establish their moral credential were more likely to make an ethically questionable decision than those with no opportunity to establish moral credentials. Monin and Miller concluded, "moral credentials do not serve solely to make one appear less prejudiced to others; they also serve, at least partially, to reaffirm one's self image as a nonprejudiced person."

Reciprocity

The simplest setting in which to study reciprocity is a variant of a dictator game referred to as an ultimatum game. In an ultimatum game the responder can accept or reject the allocation by the proposer. If the allocation is accepted by the responder, the endowment is allocated as proposed. If it is rejected, both the proposer and the responder receive nothing. If both players are rational and self-interested, the equilibrium is for the proposer to allocate close to zero to the responder and the responder to accept the allocation because it is better than nothing. Even in experiments in which the participants were anonymous and would never see each other, few participants behaved in this manner. Hoffman, McCabe, Shachat, and Smith (1994) found in double-blind experiments that the allocations to the responder in an ultimatum game were greater than those in a dictator game, indicating that strategic considerations were important. Hoffman, McCabe, and Smith (1996) found that there was no effect on behavior of increasing the size of the endowment.[7] In accord with the findings in dictator games, when proposers earned their endowments, they allocated significantly less to responders than when the endowment was not earned.

The proposer in an ultimatum game could believe that the responder would be guided by a reciprocity norm such that a satisfactory allocation would lead the responder to accept and an unsatisfactory allocation would lead the responded to reject. Uncertainty about what is a satisfactory allocation could result in a proposal that would be rejected, but in the experiments the possibility that the responder was following a norm of reciprocity resulted in higher allocations than when the responder was passive, as in a dictator game. To explore reciprocity further, Blount (1995) conducted an ultimatum game experiment in which the proposer was replaced by a computer. Since the computer could not be viewed as anticipating that the responder would be guided by a reciprocity norm, responders accepted significantly lower allocations than they did when the proposer was a person.

Behavior in experiments could depend on culture. Roth, Praenikar, Okuno-Fujiwara, and Zamir (1991) conducted ultimatum game and market game experiments in Pittsburgh, Tokyo, Jerusalem, and Ljubinje in the then Yugoslavia and the present Slovenia. The results in the market games were the same in the four countries with market forces driving behavior to the market equilibrium. The results of the ultimatum game experiments differed significantly, however. Proposers in the United States allocated the most to responders followed by Yugoslavia, Japan, and Israel, and all the differences were statistically significant other than that between the United States and Yugoslavia. The researchers conjectured that the differences in behavior were due to culture, although other factors such as rates of military service could also be important.

In a second variant of a dictator game, referred to as a trust game, the responder has the endowment and moves first. It can trust part or all of the endowment to the proposer, in which case the experimenter doubles the amount given. The proposer then decides how much of the

---

[7]Cameron (1999) studied the effect of the size of the endowment on the behavior of proposers and responders with endowments up to 3 times the monthly expenditures of students in Indonesia. The behavior of proposers was unaffected by the size of the endowment. Camerer and Hogarth (1999) surveyed the literature and found no effect of the size of the endowment on behavior. Carpenter, Verhoogen, and Burks (2005) verified this result and found that it was also true for dictator games.

doubled amount to allocate to the responder and how much to keep for herself. If both players are rational and self-interested, the proposer would keep all the money for herself, and recognizing this, the responder would not entrust any of her endowment to the proposer. In experiments where the participants are anonymous, many responders entrust a portion of their endowment to the proposer, and proposers respond by returning more to the responder than was entrusted. A reciprocity norm was evident in the trust game.

Berg, Dickhaut, and McCabe (1995) found that responders who entrusted their entire endowments to the proposers received more than the amount they had entrusted.[8] When participants were allowed to examine the results of an earlier experiment in which allocating the full endowment was reciprocated, a higher percentage of the proposers entrusted all their endowment to the responder. Socialization in the sense of sharing information on the behavior of others strengthened the reciprocity norm and generated greater trust.

Fehr, Gächter, and Kirchsteiger (1997) studied reciprocity in an employment contracting setting and concluded that when both parties to a transaction could reciprocate, reciprocity was powerful, whereas when only one party to the transaction had the opportunity to reciprocate, reciprocity was less effective. They conducted an experiment in which participants took the roles of firms and workers who interacted in a labor market and a work environment. In the two-sided reciprocity treatment, given their wage workers could reciprocate by working harder, and employers could reciprocate by giving them a bonus if they worked harder, where the bonus was voluntary.[9] In the one-sided reciprocity treatment participants in the role of the firm offered a fixed wage premium above the prevailing wage in the labor market with the hope that this would induce the worker to exert greater effort; the workers were in the position of a dictator and could shirk on the effort expended.

In the one-sided reciprocity treatment, participants in the role of firms consistently attempted to induce greater effort from workers by offering a wage higher than the prevailing wage and calling for greater effort than would be expended at the prevailing wage. The higher the wage offered, the greater was the effort expended by the workers, but workers shirked by expending less effort than called for in the contract. The average effort level was approximately equal to that for the prevailing wage. Workers gained, whereas on average firms did not.[10]

Fehr, Gächter, and Kirchsteiger strengthened the incentives for reciprocity by giving the firm the opportunity to both reward and penalize workers for the effort they expended. In this treatment the firm could reciprocate a high effort by the worker with a reward and could penalize shirking, and both reciprocating and penalizing were costly to the firm. The firm had the last move, so it did not need to reward the worker when they exerted high effort. Both firms and workers could gain if firms offered contracts with higher wages and higher specified effort levels and the workers did not shirk. In the two-sided reciprocity experiment firms offered contracts with sharply higher wages and effort levels than in the one-sided reciprocity treatment, and workers generally expended higher effort. Although there was shirking by workers, on average the shirking was lower than with the one-sided reciprocity treatment. Workers anticipated being rewarded by firms for greater effort and exerted greater effort. On average both firms and workers gained relative to the one-sided reciprocity treatment. Stronger reciprocity induced participants who naturally would not reciprocate to do so.

This and other experiments suggest that relational contracts supported by reciprocity could be effective in improving the performance of workers and firms. The situations of individual firms and industries can differ in important ways, however, and extrapolation from the laboratory to actual settings must be done with care. For example, in intensely competitive industries

---

[8]Endowments were the participation payment given to participants as they arrived at the laboratory, so there was a sense in which they had earned their endowments by participating.

[9]In the one-sided reciprocity treatment, firms offered contracts consisting of a wage, an effort level desired from a worker, and a limited penalty the firm could impose at a cost if the worker shirked on his/her effort. Workers accepted or rejected the contract offers. For the accepted contracts the firm first paid the wage to the worker, and the worker then chose her effort, which was costly to the worker and could be below the effort level specified in the contract; that is, the worker was free to shirk but faced the possibility of a penalty if detected. The incentive to shirk was stronger the higher the effort called for in the contract. The penalty was costly for the firm, and the firm gained nothing by imposing it. With a specified probability, the firm detected whether the worker shirked, and if detected, the penalty could be imposed by the firm. With a complementary probability the firm was unable to observe the effort and hence could not impose a penalty for shirking.

[10]Gains were possible for firms for some contract offers even when taking into account the shirking.

producing relatively homogeneous products, competition could dissipate the gains from relational contracts supported by reciprocity. Nevertheless, it is useful to consider possible implications and applications of reciprocity in managerial settings.

The Chapter 22 case *Chipotle Mexican Grill and Undocumented Workers* considers a company under investigation for employing undocumented workers, most of whom likely were illegal immigrants. Some of the workers had worked loyally for the company for several years. The nature of the relationship between the company and its workers could involve a relationship of trust as in the experiment of Fehr, Gächter, and Kirchsteiger, or it could be analogous to a dictator game in which the company has all the power with respect to the undocumented workers. The company was faced with the issues of complying with the law that prohibited employing undocumented workers, what to do about workers found to be working illegally, and whether to check to determine if workers were working illegally.

Behavior in Groups

Group decisions have been studied using a (linear) public goods game in which all participants in a group have an endowment that they can keep for themselves or they can contribute some portion of it to a public good that benefits all members of the group. A linear public goods game is identical to the free-rider problem considered in Chapter 6, where a participant can contribute c, which yields benefits b to every member of the group where $b < c$. For groups of size n such that $nb > c$, the utilitarian maximum is for every group member to contribute their entire endowment.[11] In the public goods game played only once, however, it is a dominant strategy for a self-interested player to contribute nothing; that is, to free ride on the contributions of others. In laboratory experiments, however, many of the participants contribute a sizeable portion of their endowment to the public good, whereas others contribute nothing. When the game is repeated with the same players, they can develop coordinated behavior in which they contribute because they believe that others will contribute in the future if they do so in the present. Contributions deteriorate over time, however. If the participants in the groups are randomized each round of play so that expectations about future contributions are more uncertain, contributions deteriorate faster over time.

When the players in the public goods game can be punished, the level of contributions typically can be sustained at higher levels, but contributions decline over time if those who are punished for free-riding retaliate and punish the other players for having punished them. Gintis (2011) interprets this "antisocial" behavior as resulting from the perceived right of players to free ride. To study this phenomenon, Herrmann, Thöni, and Gächter (2008) conducted linear public goods games in 15 countries with 16 participant pools all of which were composed of undergraduate students. In some countries antisocial behavior was rare, whereas in others it was common. The amount of antisocial behavior was highly correlated with the World Democracy Audit ratings for democracy and democratic development in the country. In countries with strong democracies, antisocial behavior was rare and the contributions to the public good were high, whereas in countries with poor democracy ratings, antisocial behavior was more prevalent and the contributions to the public good were low.[12] Culture and the development of democratic traditions and institutions can result in behavior that differs across countries.

The punishment of those who disciplined the free riders is an example of a reaction to those who do the right thing. That reaction is often resentment and rejection as in the case of a whistle-blower who exposes illegal or unethical behavior in a company or a government employee who exposes corruption by other employees. In a series of experiments Monin, Snyder, and Marquez (2008) studied the attitudes toward what they referred to as "moral rebels." They concluded (p. 89) "that resentment is a defensive reaction to the perception that

---

[11]For example, suppose that each participant has an endowment of $10 and could contribute to a public good that yields benefits equal to $0.60 for each group member for each dollar contributed. For a group of size 4 with all members contributing $5 each, the aggregate public good would yield benefits of $12 for each group member. A subject who contributed $5 then had the $5 he did not contribute plus the $12 from the public good for a total of $17, compared to $10 if everyone contributed nothing. The utilitarian maximum then is for members to contribute their entire endowments to the public good, in which case the benefits to each member would be $24. If, however, the other members contributed nothing, a contributor of $10 would receive only $6.

[12]There were several outliers. Both Greece and Oman had intermediate democracy scores, but the participants in those countries contributed little to the public good. Both Saudi Arabia and China had low democracy scores, yet participants in Chengdu in Sichuan province contributed near the maximum to the public good and participants in Riyadh contributed near the minimum of the 16 groups.

rebels are implicitly rejecting those who do not question the situation." This is analogous to an audience effect except that it is introspective; participants view the behavior as a criticism of their self. That is, it is the perception that one's self is being rejected by the moral rebel. The researchers concluded (p. 89), "these studies consistently demonstrate that rebels can elicit resentment and rejection in individuals who failed to take such a principled stance and who experience the rebellion as a personal rejection."

Implications for the Application of Ethics Principles

The results of these experiments provide insight into the discourse on ethics principles. Nozick criticized Rawls's theory of justice because it represents a slice in time and ignores how that slice in time was arrived at. In dictator and ultimatum games some participants exhibit altruism, or follow a fairness norm, but if their endowment is earned, most participants act in a self-interested manner. This provides support for Nozick's assertion that the past can (and should) matter.

The actions taken by individuals in the past as well as events beyond their control determine where they are located on the justice frontier. The experiments of Fong and Oberholzer-Gee indicate that many participants take into account past actions (drug use) and events beyond their control (disabilities) in deciding how to allocate an endowment. This suggests that fairness for two people at the same location (poor persons living in public housing) on the justice frontier could depend on how their past actions are evaluated by others. Those evaluations could affect the actions by individuals or the choice of public policies. For example, in the *Chipotle Mexican Grill and Undocumented Workers* case, what does fairness imply for how documented and undocumented workers performing the same tasks should be treated by the company?

The Chapter 22 case *Environmental Injustice?* considers the situation of companies with plants that emit legal quantities of toxic substances and are disproportionately proximate to where low-income people live. The managerial issue is whether the companies should take measures to compensate the low-income residents based on justice considerations. Does it matter whether the companies built the plants in an area where low-income people were already living or if the companies built the plants away from populated areas and low-income people subsequently moved close to the plants because of low land and housing prices?

Monin, Snyder, and Marques concluded that their experiments on moral rebels provided insight into the wisdom of Rawl's veil of ignorance. Their experiment included observers who did not participate in the experiment but observed the contributions made. The observers generally respected rather than resented the moral rebels. Indeed, observers who did not participate in the experiment and who assessed the behavior of the moral rebels a month after the experiment and outside the laboratory had the greatest appreciation for the moral rebels. The researchers noted that the evaluations by those who participated in the experiment were strikingly different from those of the observers who had not participated. They stated (p. 89), "stepping foot in the situation as an unquestioning actor seems to change one's very 'conception of the good,' whereas an observer behind the veil of ignorance sees a brave moral exemplar, an actor down in the trenches sees a self-righteous pest."

A number of the experiments found that ethical behavior was more likely the lower was the cost of acting ethically. For example, greater social difference in the form of anonymity led to lower contributions in dictator games. This behavior is inconsistent with a deontological ethics system that identifies inviolable principles based on reflection and introspection, but it could be consistent with a utilitarian system. The experimental findings that participants failed to contribute all their endowments in a trust game are inconsistent with a rule utilitarian system, since it requires that all the endowment be entrusted, regardless of whether the responder returns money to the proposer.

In the public goods setting, from the perspective of rule utilitarianism all participants should make maximal contributions to the public good. Free riding is unethical. Moreover, rule utilitarianism requires that a person contribute even if others do not contribute, but many participants do not contribute and contributions typically deteriorate with repeated play. Virtuous behavior may not be reciprocated.

Moral Suasion

Behavior can be influenced by moral suasion. To study in the laboratory the significance of moral suasion, Dal Bó and Dal Bó (2009) used a public goods game with two players. Players could keep their endowments or contribute to a public good that provided a multiple of 1.4 times the total contributions, with the resulting amount split evenly between the two players. It is a dominant strategy, however, to free ride. In a baseline experiment Dal Bó and Dal Bó found that when anonymous, randomly matched participants played the game repeatedly, contributions were small on average and declined over the 20 rounds of play. The experimenters then gave each pair of players one of five messages between the 10th and 11th rounds. One message was blank, and a second reminded players that self-interested and rational players would contribute 0, a third urged players to contribute but did not use moral language, and the other two messages used moral language. One was a statement of the Golden Rule, and the other stated that utilitarianism required the maximization of the aggregate payoff for both players. Participants receiving the moral messages and the message urging contributions increased their contributions on average, whereas participants receiving the other two messages did not. Contributions deteriorated over time, but the deterioration was less steep with the moral messages.[13] Moral suasion and suasion more generally had an effect.

Brañas-Garza (2007) studied framing in the context of a dictator game by increasing the "moral cost" of selfish behavior. In the baseline experiment proposers were told nothing about the responder, and in the treatment proposers were given the message: "Note that your recipient relies on you." Those given the message significantly increased their contributions to the responder. In contrast to the experiment by Fong and Oberholzer-Gee the greater contributions were due to a message that did not characterize the responder as more or less deserving but rather identified a duty.

Moral suasion can change the preferences of participants, but it could also serve as a coordination mechanism by increasing the confidence of participants that their partner would contribute and not free ride, in which case they themselves would contribute. To explore the mechanisms through which moral suasion might work, Dal Bó and Dal Bó conducted further experiments and concluded that both mechanisms were evident in the participants' behavior. That is, the moral messages may have changed the preferences of some participants and may have served to coordinate the behavior of others.

Conclusions from the Experiments

The experimental findings discussed suggest a number of conclusions about behavior, each of which should be interpreted with caution and as a tendency rather than a law of human behavior.

1. The higher the cost (moral or otherwise) of acting ethically, the less likely is ethical behavior.
2. Individuals exhibit greater altruism when endowments are windfalls than when they are earned.
3. Greater social distance increases the cost of acting ethically and decreases the likelihood of ethical behavior.
4. History matters. In particular, the more deserving is the responder, the greater is the fairness exhibited, and how deserving the responder is can depend in part on past actions and events. Cultural and social traditions, such as democratic experience and tradition, can also affect behavior.
5. Some behavior consistent with fairness considerations can be due instead to strategic considerations based on self-interested preferences.
6. A norm of reciprocity can foster ethical behavior, and greater opportunities for reciprocity can strengthen ethical behavior.
7. Reciprocity can be based on self-interest. Self-interested individuals can anticipate the reciprocation by partners (e.g., responders in an ultimatum game) and hence may entrust resources to them.
8. Two-sided reciprocity where people have the opportunity to reward and punish partners can sustain higher contributions than one-sided reciprocity. Relational contracts enforced through two-sided reciprocity can be beneficial.
9. Repeated encounters encourage greater contributions to a public good by strengthening a norm of reciprocity or by making others seem more deserving through familiarity. Ethical behavior gives way to self-interest over time, however.
10. Socialization through the sharing of information about how others behave can strengthen a reciprocity norm.
11. Some people choose to avoid choices with moral ramifications.

---

[13]In debriefings after the experiment, a high percentage of the participants remembered the message they had received, so the message likely had a causal effect.

12. Moral rebels can be punished by others who see their behavior as an implicit rejection of their own conduct.
13. Moral suasion can increase ethical behavior as well as serve as a coordination mechanism.

Extrapolation

Care must also be taken in extrapolating from experimental findings to real-world contexts. Levitt and List (pp. 168–169) observed,

> In contrast to the lab, many real-world markets operate in ways that make pro-social behavior much less likely. In financial markets, for instance, the stakes are large, actors are highly anonymous, and little concern seems to exist about future analysis of one's behavior. Individuals with strong social preferences are likely to self-select away from these markets, instead hiring agents who lack such preferences to handle their financial dealings .... It seems highly unlikely, for instance, that at the end of a day's trading, a successful trader would seek out the party that was on the wrong side of a market move and donate a substantial fraction of the day's profits to the person who lost ....

The Chapter 11 case *Goldman Sachs and Its Reputation* considers a financial company that treated its clients as sophisticated investors, but the public and government viewed its conduct as exploitive.

Overconfidence in One's Self

People often overestimate their ability to deal effectively with moral issues. As an example of over-estimation, MBA students in a required ethics course at a leading business school were asked to compare themselves to their fellow students on a number of dimensions. On athletic ability the students on average rated themselves only slightly above their peers, but on "will power" and "independence of mind" they rated themselves at the 63.3 and 65.8 percentiles, respectively. On "ethical standards" the students rated themselves at the 65.4 percentile, meaning that on average they ranked nearly two-thirds of their classmates as having lower ethical standards than they had. The average ranking by senior executives participating in an executive education course was the 75.1 percentile. By defini-tion, the mean and median responses have to be the 50th percentile. These self-reported rankings are subject to a number of interpretations, but what is clear is that neither 65.4 nor 75.1 percent of their classmates can on average be below those levels. The self-serving bias of moral superiority can lead to overconfidence and reduced care when making decisions on issues involving moral concerns.

MANAGERIAL IMPLICATIONS

This section discusses the implications of the experiments for ethical conduct and management in the nonmarket environment, and applications are presented in the following chapter. The most consistent conclusion from the experiments is that people differ in their behavior, preferences, and moral conduct. They also differ in the importance of factors such as the characteristics of those affected by their decisions, the audience for their actions, the scrutiny they face, the social context of their situation, and how they take strategic considerations into account. The implications of the experiments are relevant for two types of situations. One is for firms and their managers when mak-ing decisions that involve moral concerns. The other is for anticipating nonmarket action that may be motivated by the (ethical) conduct of a firm. Different people can have different ethics evalua-tions of a firm's actions, and while some may, for example, view a firm's action on an environmen-tal issue favorably, others may view it unfavorably. This means that in evaluating alternative courses of action in the presence of nonmarket issues with moral dimensions, management must consider multiple perspectives to assess how alternatives will be evaluated. Understanding these evaluations can help predict whether those in the nonmarket environment will take actions individually or col-lectively in response to the firm's decisions. Management must guard against the view that because it has the decision authority, it can choose whichever actions it prefers based only on its own prefer-ences. In the terminology of the experiments, because a dictator's actions have consequences for others, those actions will be evaluated both by those directly affected as well as by those, such as the media, social activists, NGOs, and governments, who scrutinize the behavior of the firm.

An important question in assessing the scrutiny the firm may face is whether the public views the profits of firms as earned or views them in part as unearned windfalls. In the case of oil company profits that increase sharply when world prices jump upwards, as in the case of the 2011 Arab Spring, the public may see those profits as windfalls and demand more of the companies. Moreover, some politicians recognize that criticizing windfall profits can be politically advantageous with some voters.

The experiments by Dal Bó and Dal Bó illustrate the importance of training employees in ethics to address specific issues such as sexual harassment, bribery, privacy protection, and intellectual property protection. The widespread use of codes of conduct is a manifestation of both of the importance to companies and their employees of issues with moral dimensions and the role of reinforcement in improving behavior.

Reciprocity has implications for dealing with direct stakeholders and for the implementation and maintenance of relational contracts. Direct stakeholders are those who have economic transactions with the firm and include employees, customers, suppliers, shareholders, retailers, business partners, and communities. Developing trust and reciprocity may be possible with some stakeholders such as employees, business partners, and communities that have frequent or continuous interactions with the firm and where social distance is small. It may be more difficult to develop trust and reciprocity with stakeholders that have only irregular interactions with the firm. In some cases interactions may be organized through formal contracts, whereas with others, relational contracts that govern interactions through mutual expectations of performance may be used. The social distance to stakeholders, however, can limit what can be accomplished. Shareholders as investors, for example, are distant from the firm and have the alternative of selling their shares.

Transparency can reduce social distance and make it easier to develop trust and reciprocity. Opacity can give a firm wiggle room with respect to its moral obligations. In the 1990s, firms assumed limited responsibility for the practices of their overseas suppliers, and scrutiny of those practices was limited. The activist and union campaigns against Nike and so-called sweatshop conditions in suppliers' factories provided a degree of transparency, and Nike and other firms had little alternative to assuming responsibilities that had previously rested with the suppliers. In addition, the workers in the suppliers' factories had low incomes and may have been viewed by consumers in developed countries as deserving of better treatment by their employer and Nike. The Chapter 4 case *Nike in Southeast Asia* provides more detail.

In addition to their economic transactions with the firm, stakeholders constitute an audience that can provide a degree of scrutiny to the operations and practices of a firm. Monitoring of the firm by stakeholders and other parties such as NGOs tends to increase the moral cost of violating ethics standards or shying away from moral duties. The Nike case is a good example.

Transparency for employees can be provided by internal communication, but transparency with stakeholders outside the boundaries of the firm is a more delicate matter. Many firms are hesitant to reveal information about their operations for fear that strategically important information can be gleaned by competitors. In the absence of transparency, firms may be unable to credibly communicate with stakeholders and may need independent parties to certify their actions. Many firms have partnered with environmental NGOs in cooperative engagements in which the NGO attests to the measures a firm has taken to protect the environment and reduce its footprint.

The experiments on moral rebels have implications for the design of corporate ethics policies and codes of conduct. Effective ethics policies and codes of conduct require not only that employees abide by the policies and codes but also that they report any violations. The experiments as well as anecdotal evidence indicate that an employee who reports a violation by another employee may be subjected to ostracization, or worse, by other employees who had failed to report the violation. This discourages reporting by any employee. Company internal whistle-blowing policies thus must be designed to give respect to the whistle-blower as well as shield the person from harm. As considered in more detail in Chapter 24, to discourage bribery and to encourage ethical behavior, Cummins Engine Inc. has a stated policy that a person who refuses to violate its code of conduct will not be retaliated against.

The experiments suggest that the presence of an audience can significantly affect behavior. The obvious implication is that firms may change their behavior when they are closely scrutinized, but this leaves the question of how strong the audience effects are. The framework for analyzing the effect of the news media in Chapter 3 can be used to guide the assessment of the strength of the audience effect. The audience effect should be stronger the broader is the audience and the more important is the moral issue to members of the audience. The audience effect should also be stronger, the greater the transparency of the situation, as the experiment by Dana, Weber, and Kuang illustrates. The audience effect should also be stronger, the more the audience identifies with those who bear the consequences, as indicated by the experiment of Fong and Oberholzer-Gee. More can be demanded of companies when those affected by its actions are judged to be deserving. The BP oil platform explosion and oil spill in the Gulf of Mexico affected many innocent people both through the oil itself and through the federal government's decision to shut down fishing and other commercial activities in the Gulf. Moral sympathy for the victims created social pressure on the company in addition to that coming from the government and from lawsuits.

Another implication of the experimental evidence regarding audience effects is that firms that have the public and consumers as an audience may undertake activities that firms out of the view of the public and consumers may not undertake. For example, industrial or business-to-business firms may undertake fewer corporate social responsibility (CSR) activities than firms that have consumers as their customers. Similarly, intermediaries such as investment banks that do not have a consumer face may undertake fewer CSR activities than banks that take deposits, have branches, and hence interact directly with consumers and communities.

Legitimacy can also be important in interactions with stakeholders and others in a firm's nonmarket environment. The experiments point to the importance of having earned one's place. When profits have clearly been earned through innovation as in the case of Apple, Facebook, and Google, external parties and stakeholders may view the companies as free to do with their funds as they choose. In other cases the stakeholders and external parties may believe that a firm has obligations to them. During the Arab Spring in 2011 motorists in the United States complained about the soaring gasoline prices, and many blamed the oil companies. Exxon felt compelled to address the complaints by pointing out that its refinery operations had low rates of return and that the high prices were due to the turmoil in the Middle East, rising demand as countries emerged from the recession, the falling U.S. dollar, and continued strong demand in China that was adding 800,000 vehicles to its roadways annually.

THE CHALLENGE OF CORPORATE SOCIAL RESPONSIBILITY

The spread of codes of ethics and statements of social responsibility is due to two factors. The first is a belief by some firms that they should be accountable for conduct beyond profit maximization. The second is a defensive motivation intended to avoid private politics led by activists and other interest groups or to preempt public politics and additional government regulation. Regardless of the motivation, these codes and statements commit firms to particular standards of conduct. The focus in this section is on the first motivation and how the resulting standards are implemented.

The social responsibilities of business are identified by ethics principles and reasoning based on those principles. The reliance on principles, however, may not be sufficient to identify unambiguously the appropriate concept of corporate responsibility. Principles are stated generally, and translating them into rules of behavior and goals is challenging. Ethics systems are not sufficiently precise, for example, to determine how much corporations should contribute to charities. A system of justice might imply that some portion of profits be used for charitable purposes, whereas a rights-based system that emphasizes maximal liberty holds that the firm's owners as principals should choose whether and how much to contribute from their dividends or share price appreciation. On some issues, the actions consistent with a utilitarian standard may differ from the actions consistent with rights or justice standards. From the perspective of utilitarianism, an integrity test is appropriate for a job if the benefits it yields are greater than its costs. An ethics system that holds that individuals have rights to privacy and freedom from arbitrary treatment, however, indicates that the use of the tests should be limited. The challenge for management is to formulate policies that respect these important considerations and resolve conflicts among them.

One approach used to giving standing to corporate social responsibility is the "triple bottom line."[14] The triple bottom line is intended to measure corporate environmental, social, and financial performance. More importantly, it serves as a reminder to management and other employees that profits are not the only relevant measure of corporate performance. It also commits the firm to report on all three dimensions of performance. Much of this reporting could

---

[14]See Elkington (1997).

be done independently of the triple bottom-line perspective, so the value of the triple bottom line may primarily be in terms of motivation and commitment.[15]

An important concern about the triple bottom line is whether the product and capital markets will actually reward environmental and social performance. And, if it is rewarded, is it because it helps reduce social pressure from private and public politics or because consumers, investors, and employees reward socially responsible behavior? As indicated in Chapter 20, the empirical literature is inconclusive on this question. The study by Baron, Harjoto, and Jo discussed in that chapter provides evidence that on average social performance may not be rewarded, whereas social pressure penalizes firms.

Another approach to measuring corporate social performance is the balanced scorecard.[16] The balanced scorecard was proposed as a system for evaluating overall performance by assessing financial performance, customer relationships, internal company processes, and learning and growth. Some companies have extended it to include ethics and social performance. The balanced scorecard has been used to assess corporate performance, business unit performance, and the performance of individual managers. Compensation can then be based on the resulting scores.

As an example, in the late 1990s Citibank introduced a balanced scorecard that broadened performance evaluation to include five components: financial performance, customer/ franchise performance, strategic cost management, risk management, and people management. Its incentive compensation system, including bonuses and stock options, was also broadened to include performance along these five dimensions. One objective was to build teamwork with a focus on the overall performance of the corporation and its businesses. Each of its five businesses—consumer banking, credit cards, private banking, corporate banking, and emerging markets—was evaluated in terms of these five measures. For the chairman and several other top executives, 100 percent of their variable compensation (bonus) was based on corporate scorecard performance. For the next group of 30 executives, 50 percent of their bonus was based on the corporate scorecard performance and 50 percent on individual scorecard performance. The balanced scorecard did not explicitly include corporate social responsibility, but compliance

---

EXAMPLE   Citigroup: Responsibility Under Fire?

Citigroup was one of the most profitable companies in the world with 2003 net earnings of $18 billion, compared to $21.5 billion for ExxonMobil and $15 billion for General Electric. Earnings were up again in 2004. Yet Citigroup's involvement in a series of scandals had continued unabated, and some commentators argued its seeming inability to stop the scandals had depressed its stock price. In addition to the regulatory judgments, settlements of lawsuits, and remaining lawsuits discussed in Chapter 20, which could ultimately cost Citigroup $10 billion, new scandals arose. In London Citigroup traders had dumped $13.3 billion of European government bonds on the market and then repurchased the bonds at depressed prices. The whipsawing of the bond market violated unwritten financial services industry standards and led to an investigation by British and German regulators. In Japan irregularities in Citigroup's private banking operations were identified in 2001 by Japanese regulators, but by 2003 the private banking group had returned to the same practices. The Japanese government ordered Citigroup's private bank to close, and Citigroup did so and also voluntarily closed its trust bank. Several Citigroup bankers in Japan were fired, and CEO Prince publicly apologized in Japan.

Some commentators argued that the source of Citigroup's problems was a culture emphasizing strong earnings growth and aggressive internal competition for performance. Citigroup had a decentralized organizational structure with a matrix overlay.[1] Bonuses were tied to balanced scorecard grades, but financial and earnings performance dominated. High-powered incentives were used in trading, as was standard practice in the industry.

As the scandals began to unfold, Citigroup hired a new chief financial officer from outside the company, and Prince instituted tighter financial controls. He transferred responsibility for compliance with Citigroup's code of conduct from the legal department to the bank's senior risk manager. Citigroup established a new Policy Compliance Assessment Group and required multiple compliance reports to the board of directors. Prince subsequently fired three of the most senior Citigroup executives, all of whom had had some oversight responsibility for private banking in Japan. In a message to employees, Prince said, "We have to have the moral compass to deliver those profits and growth responsibly and honestly.

---

[1]See Baron and Besanko (2001) for an analysis of Citigroup's organization of its global corporate banking business.

---

[15]Norman and MacDonald (2003) provide a scathing criticism of the triple bottom-line concept.

[16]See Kaplan and Norton (1992).

Citigroup's culture must be synonymous with integrity."[2] Prince attempted to embed the message in Citigroup's culture by requiring ethics training of all employees and promoting an internal "ethics hotline." All finance, accounting, treasury, tax, and investor relations professionals worldwide were required to sign Citigroup's code of ethics. Prince also planned to include additional qualitative questions in its balanced score-card evaluation system.

Prince, however, commented, "We want to maintain that aggressive nature. We're not going to turn ourselves into a charity, we're not going to become, you know, a big, bureaucratic government institution."[3] One observer commented, "The constraint on Citi's growth is not its market size, nor its capital. It may well be that Citi can't achieve its growth ambitions because it cannot safeguard itself properly from regulatory and reputation risk."[4] The challenge for Citigroup was whether it could conduct its business with integrity and avoid nonmarket limits to its growth. With 300,000 employees operating in over 100 countries, the challenge was substantial.

Whether a result of culture or bad judgment, Citigroup was embroiled in the financial crisis in 2007–2008, which led to the write-off of $40 billion in subprime mortgage securities with more write-offs likely. CEO Chuck Prince was fired, and the bank faced lawsuits, investor outrage, and new regulations. Citigroup required a bailout from the government.

[2]*BusinessWeek,* October 4, 2004.
[3]*New York Times,* November 7, 2004.

[4]*BusinessWeek,* October 4, 2004.

with the company's code of conduct was implicit in the evaluations. Given the incidents and scandals involving Citigroup listed in Chapter 20 and CEO Prince's comment earlier in the chapter, perhaps compliance with the law should have been explicitly included in the scorecard.

Core Principles and Their Evolution

Johnson & Johnson's "Our Credo" identifies commitments to a set of stakeholders and can be revised as the set of relevant issues it faces evolves. Revisions of guiding principles such as "Our Credo" are based on a set of core principles that provide consistency over time. The relationship between core principles and current policies and practices is illustrated in Figure 23-1.[17] The relationship is based on three components: organizational values, corporate objectives,

FIGURE 23-1 Principles, Objectives, and Strategies

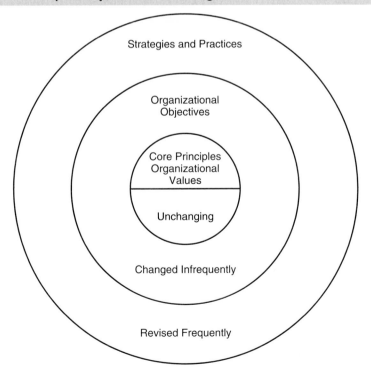

[17]This figure is due to Kirk Hanson.

EXAMPLE   Johnson & Johnson's "Our Credo"

We believe our first responsibility is to the doctors, nurses, and patients, to mothers and fathers and all others who use our products and services. In meeting their needs everything we do must be of high quality. We must constantly strive to reduce our costs in order to maintain reasonable prices. Customers' orders must be serviced promptly and accurately. Our suppliers and distributors must have an opportunity to make a fair profit.

We are responsible to our employees, the men and women who work with us throughout the world. Everyone must be considered as an individual. We must respect their dignity and recognize their merit. They must have a sense of security in their jobs. Compensation must be fair and adequate, and working conditions clean, orderly and safe. We must be mindful of ways to help our employees fulfill their family responsibilities. Employees must feel free to make suggestions and complaints. There must be equal opportunity for employment, development and advancement for those

qualified. We must provide competent management, and their actions must be just and ethical.

We are responsible to the communities in which we live and work and to the world community as well. We must be good citizens—support good works and charities and bear our fair share of taxes. We must encourage civic improvements and better health and education. We must maintain in good order the property we are privileged to use, protecting the environment and natural resources.

Our final responsibility is to our stockholders. Business must make a sound profit. We must experiment with new ideas. Research must be carried on, innovative programs developed and mistakes paid for. New equipment must be purchased, new facilities provided and new products launched. Reserves must be created to provide for adverse times. When we operate according to these principles, the stockholders should realize a fair return.

---

and strategies and practices. Organizational values serve as the core principles that guide the strategies and practices of the company as it strives to achieve its objectives. Core principles can be viewed as unchanging. Organizational objectives are revised when necessary but only infrequently. Strategies and practices are revised frequently as a function of the salience of the issues in the market and nonmarket environments.

Statements such as "Our Credo" serve as commitments to stakeholders and other constituents. Johnson & Johnson's culture, however, appeared to change as top management viewed its operating units as investments generating a portfolio of results. The company appeared to lose its moral compass and experienced a series of serious quality control problems, as considered in the Chapter 5 case, *Johnson & Johnson and its Quality Reputation.*

Statements such as "Our Credo" communicate to employees a set of principles and values that they can follow in their jobs. The chapter case *Denny's and Customer Service* considers a company facing serious allegations about racial discrimination and the challenge of developing a program for eliminating discrimination and changing its culture. Seven years later Advantica Restaurant Group, Inc., the company formed to operate Denny's, Coro's, and Carrows restaurants, was ranked first in *Fortune* magazine's "America's 50 Best Companies for Minorities."

SOURCES OF UNETHICAL BEHAVIOR

Unethical behavior has a number of sources; some are idiosyncratic to the particular individuals involved and others are functions of the managerial practices or the policies of the firm itself. Codes of conduct provide useful guidance, but alone they may be insufficient to prevent unethical behavior and promote ethical behavior. If the culture in the organization encourages or condones questionable behavior or if incentive systems place self-interest before all else, ethical behavior will primarily rest on the personal integrity of employees. Personal integrity may be sufficient for most, but perhaps not all, employees, and for most, but perhaps not all, issues.[18]

Personal weakness and temptation can contribute to unethical behavior in business, as well as in other contexts. This includes situations in which an individual understands what is right but does not have the fortitude to take the right action, perhaps because it involves a degree of personal or career risk. In that case, the policies of the firm should be reexamined to lessen the risks associated with taking the right action. This may require revisions in incentive structures so that employees do not find themselves in positions in which their performance will be evaluated negatively as a result, for example, of a lost sale that could have been obtained only through an unethical act.

---

[18]See Sonnenfeld and Lawrence (1978) for an analysis of the causes of price fixing in the folding-carton industry.

The structure of both explicit and implicit incentives within a firm can be an important obstacle to ethical behavior. In 1990 Eastern Airlines and nine of its maintenance supervisors were indicted for failing to perform required maintenance and for falsifying maintenance records.[19] To improve its on-time performance, Eastern had instituted an incentive system for maintenance supervisors in which bonuses were paid for good on-time performance. Supervisors whose on-time and flight cancellation record was poor were transferred or in some cases fired. Not only did the supervisors face incentives and pressure from upper management, but the unions, which were incensed by layoffs and management's demands for wage reductions, often blocked supervisors' efforts to improve on-time performance. Under pressure from both sides, maintenance supervisors began to falsify records for maintenance that was not performed. The situation deteriorated to the point at which some pilots refused to fly aircraft that had accumulated maintenance problems. Believing that the complaints were part of the unions' struggle with management, Eastern executives reportedly continued to pressure the supervisors.

In another setting charges were brought against Sears for allegedly recommending unneeded repairs, such as brake repairs and front-wheel alignments, in its auto centers. Service advisors reportedly recommended the repairs to earn higher commissions, and in settlements of charges in 41 states and 19 class action lawsuits, Sears agreed to eliminate commissions for its service advisors. After a corporate restructuring, the position of service advisor was eliminated and replaced by the position of service consultant, who was paid on a commission basis. The position of service consultant differed significantly from that of service advisor, however, because the consultants could not recommend repairs, whereas earlier the advisors had inspected cars and recommended repairs. Repairs were now recommended only by mechanics, who did not receive commissions. Because of its past problems, when its new system was announced, Sears received increased scrutiny by state attorneys general.

Unethical behavior can be due to temptation, which can be exacerbated by several factors. First, if there is a belief that others are acting unethically or are succumbing to temptation, an individual may have more difficulty resisting. This is particularly true if employees find themselves in a prisoners' dilemma in which each has a dominant strategy of succumbing to temptation. For example, if a partnership will go to the associate with the highest billings, the competing associates may be induced to take unwarranted actions. What is required is a promotion system that considers factors in addition to billings. Second, succumbing to temptation is more likely if the prevailing attitude in the firm involves either shortcutting ethics analysis, using principles only to justify actions taken on other grounds, or practicing casuistry. For example, the balancing of responsibilities can induce managers to underemphasize rights and principles of justice in favor of lessening stakeholder pressure. Third, temptation may be exacerbated by an aggressive culture of earnings growth, as in the Citigroup example. Fourth, temptation combined with greed can lead to unethical conduct. The Chapter 10 case *Enron Power Marketing, Inc., and the California Market* provides an example.

Unethical behavior can also result from too narrow a focus on the duties imposed by the law. The law identifies actions that an individual or firm must not take, but the set of lawful actions can be considerably larger than the set of ethical actions. The law provides only minimum restraints on behavior.

Another source of unethical behavior is reliance on an ethics framework that gives insufficient attention to important considerations. Relying only on utilitarianism and ignoring intrinsic rights or justice considerations can result in conduct that violates ethics standards that people hold to be important. For this reason, each of the three ethics systems considered in the previous two chapters should be considered in managerial decision making.

SUMMARY

A useful test in situations with moral dimensions is to assess whether an action can be explained both to others in the firm and to the public. This *public disclosure test* has two purposes. First, it forces the manager to articulate the reasons or basis for the action. This should involve an

---

[19]The FAA had frequently cited Eastern for maintenance, safety, and record-keeping violations and fined it $12 million between 1987 and 1989.

articulation of the reasoning used in arriving at the decision and should not be a search among ethics systems for arguments that come closest to justifying the action the manager prefers to take on other grounds. Second, it requires the manager to reflect on how others will evaluate the action. This does not mean that the action is subject to a vote among stakeholders. Instead, it focuses attention on the moral evaluations that others may have of the action.

Reliance on the personal integrity of employees is seldom sufficient to ensure ethical conduct, and employees should not be left to operate in an ethics vacuum. A commitment by top management is essential, and part of top management's responsibilities is to establish an environment in which ethical behavior is encouraged, supported, and rewarded. This requires formal and informal communication about exemplary conduct and leadership by deed as well as by word.

Temptation and pressure are principal causes of unethical behavior. Performance standards should be realistically attainable through means consistent with ethics principles. Incentive systems should be structured in a manner that encourages rather than hinders ethical conduct. In many firms, the selection, retention, and promotion of employees depend on the individual's integrity and record of conduct in addition to more traditional measures of performance.

Individuals must implement the ethics policy adopted by a company, and the experiments conducted by researchers provide insight to how people behave in situations that may have moral dimensions. The experiments identify the extent of self-interest and the limits of altruism. The experiments also show the importance of history, audience effects, opportunities for reciprocity, and the reinforcement of moral standards.

Statements of corporate responsibility and codes of conduct are useful guides for employees. These should identify principles, provide specific guidance for situations that are likely to be encountered, and indicate how to reason about situations and issues. A code should also indicate what an individual is to do when uncertain about whether an action is right. A compliance system is important in the implementation of ethics standards and should be designed to give top management confidence that unethical actions will be deterred or at least detected. A process that encourages and does not unduly punish self-disclosure can be an important component of a compliance system.

CASES

Denny's and Customer Service

Early on the morning of April 1, 1993, 21 members of the U.S. Secret Service arrived in Annapolis, Maryland, to prepare for President Bill Clinton's speech at the U.S. Naval Academy later that day. Before setting up security at the academy, the contingent, in full uniform, went to a local Denny's restaurant for breakfast. The group included six African American agents who sat at a table together, and an African American supervisor who, with the white agents, sat at other tables. After all the agents had ordered, the six black agents realized that the white agents and their supervisor had been served while they had not. Agent Robin Thompson went to ask the waitress about the order, and she said it was on its way. He then asked to talk with the manager and was told that the manager was on the phone. (White agents seated at other tables later reported that the waitress rolled her eyes after turning to leave the black agents' table.) After having waited an hour, the agents stood to leave, and only then, they said, were they offered a single tray of food. They refused the food because there was no time to eat. "We had to go to a Roy Rogers (a local fast-food restaurant) and eat in the van," said one of the African American agents.

Seven weeks after the incident, the six agents filed a lawsuit seeking unspecified monetary and punitive damages. The suit alleged that their civil rights had been violated because Denny's had denied them service because of their race. "It's a classic case of some kind of bias," Thompson said. The lawsuit immediately attracted nationwide media coverage. On the *CBS Evening News* Dan Rather summarized the incident by saying that the agents "put their lives on the line every day, but they can't get served at a Denny's."

Denny's, a unit of Flagstar, Inc., was a nationwide chain operating 1,487 restaurants throughout the United States. Flagstar was formed in 1989 when Coniston Partners headed a leveraged buyout of TW Services. In 1992 Kohlberg, Kravis, Roberts & Company paid $300 million for a 47 percent interest in the highly leveraged Flagstar. Approximately 70 percent of the Denny's restaurants were owned by Flagstar and the rest were owned by franchisees. In contrast to fast-food chains such as McDonald's and Burger King, Denny's operated sit-down restaurants, so when a restaurant became crowded, customers did not wait in lines but instead waited to be seated, order, and served.

In response to the agents' charges, Flagstar ordered an investigation of the incident. After questioning employees at the restaurant the day after the lawsuit was filed, the company fired the manager of the restaurant for failure to report the episode. Flagstar officials also defended their employees' actions. Steve McManus, a senior vice president who had questioned employees at the Annapolis restaurant, said the delay in the agents' service was caused by the size of their party and the complexity of their orders, which caused a backlog in the kitchen. The black agents were most affected by the delay because their table was the last to order. He said, "It's a service issue, not a discriminatory issue." In response, the agents said a group of white customers entered the restaurant after them, ordered, and was served while the agents waited. Flagstar CEO Jerome J. Richardson said, "We had one cook, and either two or three servers to serve the entire restaurant. If they say they were discriminated against, I apologize. But in my opinion, there was not an intent to not serve black people."[20]

The Annapolis incident was neither the beginning nor the end of Denny's troubles. "It's 1993 and certain things should not be happening. I just cannot imagine them not wanting to serve those children," said Randy Shepard, director of the all-black Martin Luther King All Children's Choir of Virginia. Shepard was referring to a June 1993 incident in which 70 children and 54 adults were returning home by bus to Raleigh, North Carolina, after weekend performances in the Washington, D.C., area and were allegedly refused service at two Denny's restaurants. According to Shepard, the group first went to a Shoney's restaurant off Interstate 95 in Woodbridge, Virginia. "The manager there said he would be glad to accommodate us, but there was only 20 minutes before they closed, and service would take a long time," Shepard said. "He suggested we go to Denny's down the street." The three buses then stopped at a Denny's outside Dale City, Virginia, about 11:00 P.M. Shepard said he entered the restaurant and asked a manager if he could accommodate the group. "He said he couldn't accommodate us because he didn't have the staff and recommended a larger Denny's the next exit down." At the second Denny's, Shepard said the manager met him in the parking lot and also told him he could not accommodate the group. "Some of the children had gone in to use the bathroom, so I went to get them," Shepard said. He added that the restaurant did not seem full, and "they seemed like they had ample enough staff around, and it appeared they had already started clearing tables to serve us." Prince William County Supervisor John Jenkins, whose district included one of the two Denny's restaurants, commented: "I feel like they ought to close that chain down. They have an interstate service route and ought to have enough help to serve those customers." Jenkins called for a county investigation of the incident.

Denny's officials and employees disputed many of Shepard's claims. "Our restaurant can't handle that kind of crowd—not with just two cooks and four servers. And I'm not prejudiced," said waitress Kimberly Marshall, who was white. However, her husband Dennis Marshall, an African American, said "If you're open for business, you can't say you can't serve that many people. It doesn't make sense to me."[21] Denny's officials said that the first restaurant was full, the second was half full, and the bus driver had "indicated the group outside was in a hurry." Furthermore, a company spokesman stated that "in both Denny's restaurants, we offered to serve the large group and indicated there would be a lengthy wait," but the group left before the restaurant could serve them. Denny's officials stated that they were not equipped to serve 130 people with a staff appropriate for the off-peak time of 11:00 P.M. The officials acknowledged that the manager at the first Denny's suggested that the group try the other restaurant, but added that "he offered to phone the other restaurant to make the arrangements." Coleman Sullivan, vice president of communications of Flagstar, said, "It was 11:00 P.M. on a Sunday, and our manager told this bus group it would take a while to serve them. There was no discrimination."[22]

Eighteen months before the Annapolis incident, the Department of Justice (DOJ) had initiated an investigation of the Denny's chain in response to complaints from African American customers in California. After the investigation substantiated allegations of bias, Denny's and the DOJ entered into negotiations to settle the complaints. The complainants also took other action. Their lawyers had earlier established a toll-free number to encourage others to report racist episodes so they could qualify a class action suit.[23] On March 24, 1993, a group of 32 African American customers filed a class action civil suit in San Jose alleging several discriminatory practices, including the following:

- A group of 18 African American college students was forced to pay a cover charge of $2 each and pay for their meals in advance at a Denny's restaurant in San Jose, California, while six white students acquainted with one of the African American students were seated at a nearby table and were not required to pay the cover charge or pay in advance for their meals. According to the company, several Denny's restaurants had in the past implemented a "late night policy" requiring all groups of 10 or more to prepay for meals after 10 P.M. as a "security measure" to thwart the rising theft of meals, and the policy had "not been enforced in a discriminatory fashion."
- A racially mixed couple, Danny and Susan Thompson, took their three children to a Denny's restaurant in Vallejo, California, to celebrate their daughter Rachel's 13th birthday. According to the lawsuit, Denny's refused to serve Rachel their famous free birthday meal, despite the fact that she had both her baptismal certificate and school identification. "I felt violated, humiliated, and embarrassed, so we didn't eat there. I can't adequately describe the pain that you feel to see this happen to your child," Mrs. Thompson said.
- Denny's allegedly threatened or forcibly removed African American customers from several California restaurants.
- Denny's employed "a general policy of limiting black customers," using the term "blackout" to signal employees when too many blacks were in a restaurant.

---

[20]*Newsweek,* July 19, 1993.
[21]*Washington Post,* June 7, 1993.
[22]*Fortune,* July 12, 1993.
[23]By early July, they had received over 1,000 calls.

The suit also alleged that one district manager instructed store managers to "start cracking down and get rid of some of those blackouts." Some Denny's managers asked for prepayment of meals or told blacks that the restaurant would be closing soon.

- When an employee at a Denny's restaurant in San Jose, California, told a manager a customer's eggs needed to be recooked, he was told to "take it to the niggers, and if they have a complaint, tell them to come see me."

The class action lawsuit came only 5 months after a $105 million settlement of an employment discrimination suit against Shoney's, Inc., another leading national restaurant chain, that alleged that the company limited the number of African American employees at each location and restricted them to kitchen jobs by blackening the *o* in the word *Shoney's* on the job application to indicate an applicant was an African American. Lawyers for Saperstein, Mayeda, Larkin & Goldstein, the law firm that represented the plaintiffs in the Shoney's case and was currently negotiating for the plaintiffs in the Denny's lawsuit, commented that the Denny's case might be more remarkable because it dealt with mistreatment of the most important element of any business, the customer. "These practices evoke the bald racism of the 1950s," the lawyers said in a statement. Former California Supreme Court Justice Cruz Reynoso, who had been recalled by California voters and was now a law professor at the University of California at Los Angeles, said he believed the Denny's case was the first "pattern and practice" racism case in the past 15 or 20 years involving a major public accommodation.

The service in a restaurant depended on a variety of factors, including Denny's policies, the practices of the restaurant managers, and the individual employees of the restaurant. The problem for Flagstar was twofold. First, although the company encouraged Denny's franchises to end practices that might be discriminatory, there was a limit to the control the company could exercise over the privately owned outlets. Second, the application of existing policies was problematic because policies intended to apply to all customers might instead be applied in a discriminatory fashion at individual locations by individual managers or employees.

While the negotiations with the DOJ were under way, Denny's addressed some of the issues by apologizing to customers, firing or transferring "bad-apple" employees, and creating a cultural diversity team. The "late night policy," which had been instituted to prevent diners from walking out without paying, was discontinued at all the chain's restaurants, both company owned and franchised. Mr. Richardson said, "The managers had problems with customers walking out on checks. Some required prepayment, which can be a problem when it's not applied to everyone."[24] In addition, Flagstar initiated meetings with civil rights groups.

Complicating the situation, Mr. Richardson, a former wide receiver for the Baltimore Colts who had started with a single hamburger restaurant in Spartansburg, South Carolina, had for 6 years been working to obtain one of the two National Football League franchises to be awarded in the fall of 1993. Denny's and Mr. Richardson had been criticized by the Reverend Jesse Jackson and his son, who headed the Rainbow Coalition. The younger Mr. Jackson had asked in a May 27 press release, "Are we seeing the beginning of a racist sports connection and pattern here?"[25]

Preparation Questions

1. What were the causes of the individual incidents at the Denny's restaurants? Were they more than incidents of bad service? What might they reflect? How serious are they?
2. What responsibilities does Flagstar have with regard to the incidents?
3. What roles have the media and plaintiffs' attorneys played in this issue?
4. What should Flagstar do about these incidents and allegations? What should Flagstar do about the lawsuits?
5. What policies should the company adopt for its customer service and its employees, and how should those policies be implemented? How should it deal with independently owned Denny's restaurants?

Insider Trading

INTRODUCTION

On October 13, 2011, billionaire Raj Rajaratnam, head of the Galleon Group hedge fund, was sentenced to 11 years in prison for illegal insider trading, fined $10 million, ordered to disgorge $53.8 million, and subsequently assessed a penalty of $92.8 million in a related civil case brought by the Securities and Exchange Commission (SEC). The government had charged him with making $63 million in illegal profits using information provided by a network of tipsters. He was found guilty on 5 counts of conspiracy to commit securities fraud and 9 counts of securities fraud. One conspiracy charge pertained to a strategy of Galleon to seek non-public information on companies and trade on it. The federal prosecutor called the crimes "brazen, pervasive and egregious" and said, "There is no one who is Mr. Rajaratnam's equal in terms of the breadth and scope of his insider trading crimes."[26] The case had also ensnared people who gave the information to Rajaratnam and Galleon. As of

[24]*Fortune,* July 12, 1993.
[25]*Wall Street Journal,* July 1, 1993.
[26]*New York Times,* October 14, 2011.

October 2011 the federal prosecutors in the Galleon case had charged 55 persons with insider trading and illegally passing on nonpublic information, obtaining 51 guilty pleas and convictions.

INSIDER TRADING

Insider trading can be legal or illegal. Corporate executives frequently buy and sell on their own account shares in the companies that employ them, and those transactions are to be reported to the SEC within 2 days and are made public on a weekly basis. In its weekend edition the *Wall Street Journal* publishes in its Insider-Trading Spotlight the largest trades as compiled by Thomson Financial. For example, on October 25 and 26, 2011, Bill Gates sold 10,000 shares of Microsoft in two transactions for $267 million, and two Jeffries Group executives each bought 1,000 shares for $11.8 million. Many investors view the reported trades by insiders as informative about the prospects of the firms.[27]

Illegal insider trading covers a variety of practices associated with securities transactions. The SEC explained:[28]

Illegal insider trading refers generally to buying or selling a security, in breach of a fiduciary duty or other relationship of trust and confidence, while in possession of material, nonpublic information about the security. Insider trading violations may also include "tipping" such information, securities trading by the person "tipped," and securities trading by those who misappropriate such information.

Examples of insider trading cases that have been brought by the SEC are cases against:

Corporate officers, directors, and employees who traded the corporation's securities after learning of significant, confidential corporate developments;

Friends, business associates, family members, and other "tippees" of such officers, directors, and employees, who traded the securities after receiving such information;

Employees of law, banking, brokerage and printing firms who were given such information to provide services to the corporation whose securities they traded;

Government employees who learned of such information because of their employment by the government; and

Other persons who misappropriated, and took advantage of, confidential information from their employers.

Because insider trading undermines investor confidence in the fairness and integrity of the securities markets, the SEC has treated the detection and prosecution of insider trading violations as one of its enforcement priorities.

Illegal insider trading was difficult to detect, and the Galleon case was by far the most sweeping. At the sentencing of Zvi Goffer, a trader at Galleon, the judge said, "Insider trading is very hard to detect. Because of that, it has to be dealt with harshly."[29] Goffer received a 10-year sentence.[30] Also sentenced at the same time was Winifred Jiau, who worked for Primary Global Research and had provided confidential information to Galleon in exchange for $200,000 in cash and gifts. She was convicted by a jury and received a 4-year sentence.

Insider trading was a controversial issue among lawyers and economists. Insider trading moved the price of a company's stock closer to the post-public disclosure price, making the securities market more efficient. In addition, there were no identifiable victims as there were in many financial fraud cases. Rajaratnam's lawyers had argued for a light sentence, writing that it does not cause "the kinds of measurable losses to identifiable victims that conventional fraud causes."[31] Consistent with the SEC statement about insider trading, the prosecutors and judges said that insider trading reduced confidence in the securities markets.

RAJARATNAM AND THE GALLEON GROUP

Rajaratnam was raised in Sri Lanka and attended college in England and the United States, receiving an MBA from the Wharton School of the University of Pennsylvania. He had worked on Wall Street as a semiconductor industry analyst and developed a set of contacts in the industry with whom he exchanged information. His success led to his promotion to president of Needham & Co. in 1991. In 1996 he founded Galleon, which recorded a peak of $7 billion in funds under management.

In 2003 Rajaratnam expanded his sources of information by offering Anil Kumar, a partner in McKinsey & Company, $500,000 a year for information.[32] Rajaratnam told him, "You have such good knowledge that is worth a lot of money to me."[33] After Kumar passed confidential information on a planned takeover that allowed Galleon to gain $19 million, Rajaratnam said, "Anil, you are a hero."[34] Rajaratnam and Galleon also received information from Danielle Chiesi, who had worked as an analyst at New Castle Funds, an investment management company. She pleaded guilty to criminal charges and was sentenced to 2½ years in prison. The co-founder of New Castle also pleaded guilty and was sentenced to 27 months in prison.

The government had been alerted to Rajaratnam's activities by messages uncovered during an investigation of a hedge fund run by his brother.[35] In one of the messages Roomy Kahn, then an Intel employee, mentioned inside information on a company, and she subsequently cooperated with the government.[36] Other tipsters were identified and cooperated with the government. The government also secretly wiretapped Rajaratnam's phone, which provided information on the insider

---

[27]Gates' sales were likely scheduled and provided no information to the market.
[28]www.sec.gov/answers/insider.htm (November 5, 2011).

[29]*San Jose Mercury News*, September 22, 2011.
[30]Emanuel Goffer, whom his older brother had recruited into the network, was sentenced to 3 years in prison.
[31]*New York Times*, September 20, 2011.
[32]Rajaratnam had paid $1.75 million to Kumar over a nearly 5-year period.
[33]*New York Times*, May 12, 2011.
[34]*Wall Street Journal*, January 8, 2010.
[35]The brother was never charged.
[36]She pleaded guilty to fraud, obstruction of justice, and conspiracy.

trades. The judge in the insider trading case ruled that the information obtained by wiretaps was admissible, and those taped conversations were believed to have convinced the jury to return a guilty verdict.

In a taped telephone conversation, Rajaratnam said to an unidentified contact, "I heard yesterday from somebody who's on the board of Goldman Sachs that they are going to lose $2 per share. The Street has them making $2.50."[37] The board member was not named, but the suspicion was that it was Rajat Gupta, former head of McKinsey, and a director of Goldman Sachs and Procter & Gamble. The SEC said that in 2008 Gupta had given Rajaratnam information obtained at a Goldman board meeting about a $5 billion investment by Warren Buffet's Berkshire Hathaway when Goldman was under financial stress. In October 2011 the U.S. Attorney in Manhattan filed criminal charges against Gupta charging that he had provided information to Rajaratnam. He was alleged to have also passed on information on Procter & Gamble's earnings. Gupta had not received any payments for the information, and federal prosecutors planned to argue that illegal tipping did not require receiving payment for information.[38]

EXPERT NETWORKS

One source of information for Rajarartnam was so-called expert networks. Firms such as Primary Global Research LLC of Mountain View, California, assembled a list of experts to provide information and consulting to clients on a variety of subjects. U.S. Attorney Preet Bharara said of Winifred Jiau, "Winnie Jiau gave new meaning to the concept of social networking. She used and exploited friends at public companies for the purpose of obtaining, and then selling, inside information."[39] The government had taped Primary Global's telephone conversations with clients who were cooperating with the government. Bob Nguyen, a former analyst at Primary Global, described the company to a federal judge, "One of the

goals of [Primary Global] was to recruit current employees of public companies" to "provide current material and nonpublic information about their company, including information about … revenues, suppliers and customers to [Primary Global] clients."[40] Also pleading guilty was Don Ching Trang Chu, a former executive at Primary Global, who received 2 years' probation after agreeing to cooperate with the government.

Primary Global's compliance policy for its experts stated[41]:

> Experts are explicitly instructed to decline to comment on subjects that represent information that is confidential or proprietary to the organizations they are affiliated with. At no point are expert consultants permitted to breach any agreement with their employers and are required to keep in confidence proprietary information acquired by them. They are forbidden to disclose to PGR or to any of its customers or partners any material, non-public, confidential or proprietary information belonging to any previous or current employers or others. ■

Preparation Questions

1. What likely motivated Raj Rajaratnam to develop sources of information about companies? What likely motivated him to buy information from Anil Kumar and Winifred Jiau?
2. Why did Kumar and Jiau agree to solicit nonpublic information and pass it on to Galleon? Is this a matter of temptation and self-interest or greed or …?
3. Is illegal insider trading actually harmful?
4. Was Mr. Gupta likely to have been discussing matters with a friend or was he likely passing on information that he knew his friend could benefit from? Does it matter under the law?
5. Is the experts network business model one that inevitably risks crossing the line to illegal activity?

Fresenius Medical Care in China

Fresenius Medical Care with headquarters in Bad Homburg, Germany, was established in 1996 through the combination of the Dialysis Systems Division of Fresenius AG, a major German pharmaceutical and medical systems producer and distributor, and National Medical Care, a subsidiary of W. R. Grace. Fresenius Medical Care provided dialysis and renal services, dialysis products, and home care. In 1997 it had revenue of $3.3 billion, compared with $3.1 billion in 1996, and profits were $90 million. Fresenius Medical Care's core businesses were dialysis care and sales of dialysis products. Worldwide there were 765,000 dialysis patients, representing

a total market of $29 billion for dialysis treatment and products. Fresenius Medical Products treated 53,400 patients in the United States and 13,800 outside the United States. "As a result of our focused acquisition programs in the U.S., Europe and Latin America we dramatically improved our strategic position during the last year, and enhanced our continued leadership of the dialysis care industry," said CEO Udo Werlé.

Fresenius Medical Care operated or supplied products in 100 countries. The company had worked to strengthen its market position in the rapidly growing Asia-Pacific and Latin American markets by establishing additional subsidiaries and

---

[37]*Wall Street Journal*, October 26, 2011.
[38]Gupta was not caught on any of the wiretaps, and the government reportedly had no direct evidence that he provided information. (*Wall Street Journal*, October 26, 2011.)
[39]*New York Times*, June 21, 2011.

[40]*Wall Street Journal*, January 12, 2011.
[41]http://www.pg-research.com/consultant-compliance-policies.php (Accessed November 9, 2011).

joint ventures. Fresenius Medical Care viewed Southeast Asia as its next major market for investment. China represented a major market opportunity, and Fresenius had a foothold through a joint venture, the Guangzhou Nanfang NMC Hemodialysis Center, established in 1994 between National Medical Care and a military hospital complex in Guangzhou.

Advanced chronic kidney failure was the irreversible loss of kidney function and required either regular dialysis treatment or a kidney transplant. Dialysis had to be continued indefinitely, whereas a transplant was typically a permanent solution. In the United States in 1995, 200,000 patients received regular dialysis treatment, but only 12,000 received kidney transplants. In the absence of a transplant, dialysis was required for the rest of the patient's life. Dialysis had two modes: hemodialysis and peritoneal dialysis. Hemodialysis involved taking the blood outside the body and through a filter or dialyzer to remove waste products and excess water and then returning the blood to the patient. The treatments lasted 3–6 hours each, and three treatments a week were typically required. The treatment was often exhausting and difficult. Peritoneal dialysis used a surgically implanted catheter through which a sterile solution was introduced and used the peritoneal, the membrane in the abdominal cavity covering the intestinal organs, as the dialysis membrane. Peritoneal dialysis involved less disruption of daily life than hemodialysis but required a patient to have some residual renal function. Only 15 percent of the worldwide patient population used peritoneal dialysis.

Human rights groups and activists had regularly charged that China sold human organs harvested from executed prisoners, many of whom were sentenced to death for political crimes or for theft or corruption. In fall 1997 ABC *Primetime Live* broadcasted a report that a Chinese doctor was advertising human organs in a Chinese-language newspaper in New York with a price of $30,000 for a kidney. The organs were believed to have been harvested from executed prisoners. The report included the story of a woman from Thailand who had received a kidney transplant at the military hospital and had received kidney dialysis at the Nanfang dialysis facility.

In February 1998 in New York the FBI arrested two Chinese government officials who were attempting to sell human organs harvested from executed prisoners. The FBI sting was arranged by Harry Wu, a controversial Chinese dissident living in the United States, who had previously exposed a number of human rights violations. In February 1998 the German magazine *Stern* published an article consistent with the information in the *Primetime Live* report. The Chinese embassy in Washington issued a statement that organs were rarely harvested from executed prisoners and only with their written consent.

Fresenius Medical Care's Nanfang facility was operated by Chinese doctors, and Fresenius had one employee in Hong Kong who monitored the facility. The Nanfang dialysis center was located adjacent to a military organ transplant hospital, and Fresenius's investigation revealed that foreign patients were receiving dialysis treatment at Nanfang for relatively short periods. Patients awaiting transplants required ongoing dialysis. *Stern* quoted a Thai kidney specialist to the effect that no consent forms existed and that prisoners were "simply shot in the head and then disemboweled." *Stern* quoted another Thai kidney specialist, who said, "There would be no kidney transplants in Nanfang Hospital without Fresenius." *Stern* also had information on patients in Asia and the United States who were notified about upcoming executions so that they could travel to China. *Stern* referred to this as "patient tourism" and reported that the going price for a kidney transplant was $40,000. ▪

Preparation Questions

1. What should Fresenius Medical Care do with regard to the ABC and *Stern* reports?
2. Suppose that the reports were true. What should Fresenius Medical Care do?
3. Should Fresenius Medical Care and Fresenius AG sell medical equipment and supplies to the transplant hospital complex in Guangzhou?

Source: This case was written by Professor David P. Baron. Copyright © 1998 by the Board of Trustees of the Leland Stanford Junior University. All rights reserved. Reproduced with permission.

24 | ETHICS IN INTERNATIONAL BUSINESS

INTRODUCTION

Ethics issues abound within a country, but they take on added dimensions when a firm operates across national and cultural borders. Countries differ in the institutions that govern their political and economic activity as well as in their customs and culture. Countries also differ in their capacities to address social and ethical issues. The capacities of many countries are limited by poverty, corruption, and political turmoil. Furthermore, their legal, health care, educational, and social services capabilities are often constrained by limited resources. World Bank data revealed that in 2010 per capita gross domestic product was $345 a year in the Democratic Republic of the Congo, $405 in Burundi, and $416 in Liberia, compared to $89,769 in Luxembourg, $57,505 in Norway, and $47,154 in the United States.[1] Life expectancy in 2009 was under 50 years in 10 African countries. In contrast, the life expectancy in China was 73 years, Mexico 76 years, and Japan 83 years.

In contrast to the differences among countries, ethics principles are intended to be universal. Applying those principles in international settings with such differences among countries, however, presents major challenges. Are the costs and benefits resulting from environmental protection in a low-income country the same as in a high-income country? Should a firm maintain the same safety and environmental standards in all countries? Should and do individuals in all countries have the same rights? If practices that are morally unacceptable in one country are acceptable and legal in other countries, which should a company follow? At a more general level, are the Western ethics systems considered in Chapters 21 and 22 applicable in countries that do not have Western intellectual and moral traditions?

Rather than attempt to address the broad range of ethics issues that arise in international business, emphasis here is on five specific issues—culture and moral standards, human rights, operating in developing countries, company compliance programs, and questionable foreign payments made to secure sales. The next section considers international law and institutions, and the following section addresses the perspective of cultural relativism and contrasts it with the universalism perspective. Issues associated with operating in developing countries are then considered, including the development of private institutions to govern operating standards. The issues of corruption and questionable payments are then examined, and principles for reasoning about requests for payments are presented along with individual company and collective efforts to reduce bribery and corruption.

INTERNATIONAL LAW AND INSTITUTIONS

Interactions between nations and foreign firms are governed by the laws of the host nation and by international law. International law consists of national laws that pertain to foreign persons, entities, and other nations; intergovernmental treaties and agreements; rulings by international courts; and actions of international bodies such as the United Nations and the Organization of American States.[2]

National laws include laws pertaining to international trade, official boycotts such as that against Cuba, the Foreign Corrupt Practices Act (FCPA), and required government approval for the acquisition by a foreign firm of a U.S. firm essential to national defense. Treaties and agreements include the North American Free Trade Agreement, the International Monetary Fund, the treaties of the European Union, the Geneva Convention, the Kyoto Protocol on global climate change, reciprocal tax agreements, and accords on technical standards. International court rulings include those of the International Court of Justice, the International Criminal Court, the World Court, the European Court of Justice, and the World Trade

---

[1]GDP is given using the purchasing power parity basis.
[2]See Shaw (2003) for a treatment of international law.

Organization's dispute resolution mechanism. Actions of international bodies include the United Nations' (UN) response to Iraq's invasion of Kuwait, the Law of the Sea, and the UN Convention on Contracts for the International Sale of Goods.

International agreements also provide frameworks within which continuing problems can be addressed. The 1985 Vienna Convention for the Protection of the Ozone Layer provided a framework for addressing ozone depletion and global warming.[3] The 1987 Montreal Protocol on Substances That Deplete the Ozone Layer resulted from this framework and committed the signatories to reduce CFCs to 50 percent of 1986 consumption. This reduction was judged insufficient, and the 1989 Helsinki Declaration committed the parties to eliminate all CFC production as soon as possible and no later than 2000.

The international law pertaining to global climate change began with UN action in 1988 and the 1989 Hague Declaration calling for the establishment of the UN Framework Convention on Climate Change. The convention covered greenhouse gases not covered by the Montreal Protocol. The convention established a Conference of Nations as well as a secretariat and two advisory committees and committed the parties to concluding a more specific agreement by 1997. The result was the Kyoto Protocol on global climate change, which took effect in 2005 and its emissions targets were scheduled to expire in 2012.

International law differs from domestic law because sanctions may not be credible and enforcement is often left to individual nations. Some sanctions have been shown to be credible. Many elements of international law, however, are respected not because of enforcement powers but because of mutual interests in preserving those laws. For example, the Dispute Settlement Body (DSB) of the World Trade Organization (WTO) rules on trade disputes, but it has no real enforcement powers. It can only authorize a country to impose duties on imports of another country that refuses to halt a trade violation. WTO members have generally accepted the DSB decisions.

In 1789 the first U.S. Congress passed the Alien Tort Claims Act (ATCA), which allowed courts to hear "any civil action by any alien for a tort only, committed in violation of the law of nations or a treaty of the United States." In the 1990s activists sought to use ATCA against U.S. corporations for alleged human rights violations abroad. In 1996, 12 refugees from Myanmar, formerly Burma, sued Unocal in the United States for alleged responsibility for murder, rape, forced labor, and torture. The actions were allegedly conducted by soldiers protecting a natural gas pipeline being built by Unocal subsidiaries, the French oil company Total, and the government of Myanmar.

In 2004 the Supreme Court limited the grounds on which lawsuits could be filed under the ATCA but allowed some cases involving serious human rights violations to go forward. A lawsuit against Unocal had been dismissed in federal court, but a California judge allowed the case to proceed. Unocal settled the case before it went to trial. In 2007 Yahoo! settled the case deriving from the arrest of a Chinese dissident discussed in Chapter 16.

A rash of ATCA lawsuits was filed in the 2000s, spurred by U.S. lawyers going abroad to seek clients and large judgments. Twelve Nigerians sued Royal Dutch Shell for aiding the Nigerian government in human rights abuse and environmental damage in the Ogoni region of the country. In 2011 a village in Nigeria sued Royal Dutch Shell for $1 billion under the ATCA. Exxon Mobil was sued under the ATCA for alleged killings and torture by Indonesian troops protecting oil operations in the country. In 2011 Cisco and its top executives were sued by Falun Gong members alleging that the company sold customized equipment to the Chinese government that was used in the "Golden Shield" Firewall to censor the Internet and track dissidents. The company replied, "Cisco does not operate networks in China or elsewhere, nor does Cisco customize our products in any way that would facilitate censorship or repression."[4] Some of the cases filed under the ATCA had proceeded through the courts, and some appeals courts had ruled that corporations could be sued while others had ruled that they could not be sued. The Supreme Court decided in its 2011–2012 session to hear the appeal in the case against Royal Dutch Shell filed by the 12 Nigerians. The appeal centered not on the alleged human rights abuses and environmental damage but instead on whether corporations could be sued in U.S. courts under the ATCA.

---

[3]See Shaw (1997, pp. 610–614).
[4]*New York Times*, May 23, 2011.

The application of domestic laws also resulted in lawsuits against foreign corporations. A court in Ecuador ordered Chevron to pay $8.6 billion for environmental damages in a case that lasted 17 years. Chevron filed a lawsuit against the plaintiff alleging fraud and corruption by the court. The company took its case to U.S. courts and to the International Court of Justice in the Hague. Dole Foods was sued by former workers on banana farms for harm caused by the chemical DBCP that the company stopped using in 1979, and a Nicaraguan court awarded the workers $2.2 billion.[5] A judge in Los Angeles who had awarded the plaintiffs $1.5 million issued a further ruling in 2009 in which she concluded that many of the cases were fake and that lawyers had recruited and trained plaintiffs and faked evidence. She wrote, "An entire industry has developed around DBCP litigation in Nicaragua for the purpose of bringing fraudulent charges." She cited U.S. lawyers as having "actively participated" in "litigation fraud."[6] These cases indicate a risk associated with operations in some international settings.

Firms that operate internationally are subject to the laws of their home country as well as their host countries, and at times those laws may be inconsistent. Moreover, practice and law are often in conflict, as in the case of questionable foreign payments. The FCPA prohibits practices that are not uncommon in some countries. Because of the demands for payments, a number of companies adopted codes of conduct that went beyond the requirements of the law. Increasing and persistent corruption and pressure from the United States and other countries resulted in an international agreement under the OECD to prohibit certain types of bribery, as considered later in the chapter.

Practices within a country pose both legal and ethical concerns. In some countries corruption is a fact (although not an inevitable fact) of life in many sectors of business activity.[7] In the mid-1980s Indonesia concluded that corruption and bribery in its ports were impeding economic growth by delaying imports and exports, at times for substantial periods. One report placed the amount of bribes at $200 million annually. To address the problem, the government ordered half the 13,000 employees in the Customs and Excise Service not to report to work. They continued to be paid their full wages, receive benefits, and even promotions, but they were not in a position to extract payments from importers and exporters.[8] A number of countries, including Indonesia, subsequently hired foreign firms to operate their customs services. In 2009 Mexico replaced all 700 of its customs inspectors with 1,400 better trained agents. The objective was to reduce tax evasion and the smuggling of guns into the country.

CULTURAL RELATIVISM

The Coalition for Justice in the Maquiladoras launched a campaign to improve conditions in the 2,000 U.S.-owned plants (maquiladoras) located in the area near the U.S. border from Tijuana to Matamoros, Mexico. The coalition argued that although the firms met Mexican standards, they should meet the same health, safety, and environmental standards they met in the United States. "Moral behavior knows no borders. What would be wrong in the United States is wrong in Mexico," said Sister Susan Mika of the Interfaith Center on Corporate Responsibility (ICCR). Sister Mika expressed the view that moral standards are universal and that the standards in developed countries are the ones that should apply universally. The former is a rejection of cultural relativism, whereas the latter is a claim about particular standards.

Ethics, requires that firms, as well as individuals, not simply accept existing customs or prevailing standards and practices in a country. Instead, firms and their managers are to evaluate issues of importance in terms of principles and standards that are universal.[9] Universal principles include respect for individual autonomy, improvements in aggregate well-being, and just actions regarding less-advantaged persons. Some cultural differences, such as in the institutions of political representation in democracies, are easily accepted. A democracy with a strong executive and a system of checks and balances, as in the United States, may be morally no better or worse than a parliamentary democracy. Some differences, such as the suppression of political liberties and human rights in countries such as Myanmar and North Korea are not tolerated but are difficult to change.

---

[5]The case was featured in the documentary *Bananas!*
[6]*Business Week,* July 6, 2007.
[7]See Palmier (1989) for examples.
[8]*Far Eastern Economic Review,* June 6, 1990.
[9]See Donaldson (1989, Ch. 2) and Freeman and Gilbert (1988, Ch. 2) for analyses and rejections of cultural relativism. Brandt (1959) provides an extended evaluation of ethical relativism.

In considering countries and cultures, Sen (1997) warned against generalizations that "hide more than they reveal." He advocated the simultaneous recognition of

- The significance of cultural variation
- The need to avoid cultural stereotypes and sweeping generalizations
- The importance of taking a dynamic rather than a static view of cultures
- The necessity of recognizing heterogeneity within given communities

In considering the relevance of differences in cultures and in the positions of peoples and nations in their development, it is useful to identify two concepts—*cultural relativism* and *cultural imperialism*—and to recognize that there is a considerable distance between the two. In its strongest version, cultural relativism holds that appropriate behavior in a country or culture is determined by its own laws and customs.[10] That is, what is moral is defined by the customs within individual countries; when in Rome, do as the Romans do. If corruption is widespread in a country, then a firm should accept the functioning system and act as domestic firms do. At some level cultural differences and local practices surely are important, and it is clear that moral standards differ among cultures. Ethics principles, however, are to be universal rather than culturally determined.

Cultural imperialism in its strongest form means that in operating internationally a firm maintains the standards of its home country and judges others by those standards.[11] Cultural imperialism is surely not universally applicable, since the differences among cultures and countries are both important and difficult to ignore. Donaldson (1996) cites the instance of a U.S. company that caught one of its employees in China stealing and turned the employee over to the authorities—who had the employee executed.

Donaldson identifies two fundamental conflicts between universal principles and local customs and practices. The first is a "conflict of relative development," which requires firms to recognize that countries and their peoples may differ in their capabilities due to their stages of economic development. He advocates that the following question be asked about local practices:

> Would the practice be acceptable at home if my country were in a similar stage of economic development?

As an example, apparel and footwear companies participating in the Fair Labor Association (discussed later in the chapter) use suppliers that pay the prevailing wage and employ children as young as 14, when that is consistent with host country laws. Do these two practices receive an answer of yes to Donaldson's question? The likely answer is that a firm is justified in paying the prevailing wage rate and legally hiring children. But, should it meet only local workplace safety standards? One answer is based on whether local safety standards are unreasonable to the point of jeopardizing a person's human dignity by failing to treat the person as an end as well as a means.

The second conflict is a "conflict of cultural tradition." In many cases, this conflict is more difficult to resolve. Donaldson (1996, p. 60) proposes,

> Managers should deem a practice permissible only if they can answer no to both of the following questions: Is it possible to conduct business successfully in the host country without undertaking the practice? And is the practice a violation of a core human value?

For example, the arbitrary firing of employees is unlikely to be necessary to operate successfully and is a violation of basic principles. A company thus would not be justified in acting in such a manner. Bribery, however, is sufficiently pervasive in some countries that it might be required at times to operate successfully. If it is not a violation of a core human value, a company could be justified in providing "facilitating payments" in certain circumstances, as indicated in the later section on questionable foreign payments. In considering whether it should do business in a country where the answer is persistently no to the first question and yes to the second question, Levi Strauss refused to do business in Myanmar.

---

[10]See Bowie (1990).
[11]De George (1993) argues for an intermediate position in which the goal is not a set of ethics principles on which agreement is unlikely but rather is a set of international guidelines for business practice on which everyone can agree.

Donaldson (1996, pp. 61–62) argues that three general principles should guide companies in their global business activity:

1. Respect for core human values (human dignity, respect for basic rights, and good citizenship), which determine the absolute moral threshold for all business activities
2. Respect for local traditions
3. The belief that context matters when deciding what is right and wrong.

He also offers five guidelines for "ethical leadership": (1) Treat corporate values and formal standards of conduct as absolutes.[12] (2) Design and implement conditions of engagement for suppliers and customers. (3) Allow foreign business units to help formulate ethics standards and interpret ethics issues. (4) In host countries, support efforts to decrease institutional corruption. (5) Exercise moral imagination.

As an example of moral imagination, Levi Strauss faced a dilemma in Bangladesh. It learned that one of its suppliers was employing children younger than 14 years of age. The income earned by the children was important to their impoverished families, yet their working deprived them of the opportunity to attend school. Faced with this dilemma Levi Strauss convinced the supplier to pay the children their wages and benefits while they attended school and guarantee that they could return to their jobs once they completed their schooling.[13] Levi Strauss paid for their tuition, books, and school uniforms.

As indicated in Chapters 21 and 22, ethics frameworks can differ in terms of how the good and the right are conceived, as well as in their methods of analysis and their prescriptions. These differences, coupled with the differences among countries, suggest that at least some differences in practices and standards should be tolerated. Yet there are universal principles that are sufficiently important that firms should work toward their achievement. Donaldson (1989, pp. 81–86) proposes that respect for and promotion of rights should be universal and that all nations, firms, and individuals have a duty to respect a certain minimal set of rights. Those rights are the following:

1. Freedom of physical movement
2. Ownership of property
3. Freedom from torture
4. Fair trial
5. Nondiscriminatory treatment (freedom from discrimination on the basis of such characteristics as race and/or sex)
6. Physical security
7. Speech and association
8. Minimal education
9. Political participation
10. Subsistence

Using a distinction suggested by Shue (1980), Donaldson argued that firms have a duty not to deprive individuals of any of these rights and an affirmative duty to help protect individuals from being deprived of any of the last six. He also argued that the rights to nondiscriminatory treatment, political participation, and ownership of property are subject to cultural interpretation. One might disagree about which rights should be included in these sets, but the concept that respect for and promotion of certain rights constitutes minimal acceptable behavior is important.

Google had to decide whether to operate in China where it would be required to censor its searches and news and where it could be required to turn over to the government information on users. The question Google asked was whether operating in China would benefit the Chinese people sufficiently to justify participating in censorship. The Chapter 16 case *Google in China* considers Google's decision to operate in China with limited offerings intended to avoid putting users in jeopardy. In 2009 Google experienced a cyberattack originating in China that was directed at accessing the gmail accounts of dissidents and critics of Chinese human rights practices. The chapter case *Google Out of China* considers its next decision.

The next section considers two companies' attempts to address human rights issues.

---

[12]For example, do not make exceptions to standards solely for the purpose of improving one's business prospects.

[13]See "Third-World Families at Work: Child Labor or Child Care?" *Harvard Business Review,* January–February, 1993.

HUMAN RIGHTS AND JUSTICE

Some ethics issues arise not from the actions of individuals and firms, but instead from the policies of governments. Particularly in the case of countries that are not democracies, ethics concerns pertaining to human rights and justice can arise. Because of concerns about human rights in the countries in which their suppliers were located, several firms, including Levi Strauss and Reebok, formulated human rights statements pertaining to their business partners. Reebok's "Human Rights Production Standards" covered the following subjects: nondiscrimination, working hours/overtime, fair wages, child labor, freedom of association, and a safe and healthy work environment. Reebok applied its standards at the level of its business partners.

Levi Strauss also developed guidelines for its business partners. In addition, the company applied its standards at the country level. It concluded that it should not do business with even an exemplary supplier if the policies of its home country resulted in pervasive violations of human rights. The development and application of these standards is considered in Chapter 23.

Slave Labor in Saipan?

Shortly after Levi Strauss adopted its guidelines, they underwent their first challenge. The issue involved a supplier based in the U.S. Territory of Saipan that worked for a number of apparel firms, including Liz Claiborne and Eddie Bauer. Levi Strauss learned that the supplier was in legal trouble, and one of its vice presidents met with the contractor in San Francisco. He asked blunt questions about the supplier's legal problems, but the supplier assured him that there were only routine problems and that he need not be concerned.

A few months later the NBC television affiliate in Washington, D.C., broadcast a story about the Saipan supplier, alleging that he was using Chinese workers as "slave labor" and that the merchandise they produced was mislabeled as "Made in the U.S.A." In fact, products produced in Saipan are required to carry that label. The slave labor allegation, however, was more serious. It centered on the common practice in Saipan of bringing young women from China to work in the factories for a few years and then returning them to China. The young women were eager to come because the wages were high compared with wages in China. NBC also reported that the supplier was about to plead no contest to a felony charge of denying workers compensation totaling several million dollars.

A day after the story made the national news, Levi Strauss executives met to begin their own investigation of the Saipan facilities. A group of senior executives visited the factory and found it to be an excellent facility—better than some in the United States. The dormitories where the workers were housed were substandard, but Levi Strauss concluded that the allegations of slave labor were unwarranted. What was clear, however, was that the supplier had consistently misled Levi Strauss. The recently approved Global Sourcing Guidelines called for business partners to maintain standards consistent with the company's standards. Consequently, Levi Strauss canceled its contract with the Saipan supplier and paid several hundred thousand dollars in contract penalties to do so.

To Levi Strauss the Saipan incident indicated why guidelines were needed. In addition to protecting workers, the guidelines would protect the company's integrity and commercial success by preventing it from sourcing with suppliers with questionable practices.

OPERATING IN DEVELOPING COUNTRIES

In developing countries, institutions are not always present to provide guidance to firms and their managers. Also, issues are more complex when people do not have the means to protect their rights and advance their interests. Poverty, lack of education, and inadequate health care create situations in which individuals cannot be expected to make the same decisions that would be made in a developed country. Furthermore, their governments may not have the means to provide the needed information, guidance, or regulation found in developed countries.

In developed countries, for example, the liability system assigns the social cost of injuries to producers and consumers, creating incentives for care and the reduction of hazards. In addition, regulation establishes safety standards and requires information and warnings about hazards. If institutions are not present or function imperfectly in a developing country, business is without an important source of guidance. In such cases, the temptation may be to follow local practice.

The consequences, however, may not be acceptable. Following local practice could lead to the exploitation of the ignorant and disadvantaged or the exposure of consumers or workers to hazards that they may not reasonably be able to avoid.

In such situations, ethics can provide guidance. To understand how a firm might reason in situations in which institutions are imperfect, consider the case of a safety decision about a product marketed in a developing country. Suppose that the product is safe under proper use but that misuse can result in injury. Also, suppose that many of the people who are likely to buy the product are impoverished and have a minimal formal education. There is no functioning liability system, and regulatory agencies are overburdened and cannot be expected to address the safety issue. The firm and its managers must provide their own guidance on appropriate action.

From the perspective of utilitarianism, the Calabresi and Melamed principles considered in Chapters 14 and 21 provide a basis for reasoning about the appropriate level of safety and how the product should be marketed. Those principles are intended to be applied in situations in which institutions are imperfect, entitlements and their protection are unclear, or transactions costs prohibit bargaining to resolve the issue. The principles first ask which party is best positioned to make a cost-benefit analysis of the product and its safety features. In a developed country, the answer is typically that the government is best placed to do so, as reflected in the institutions of liability and regulation. In the absence of those institutions, the responsibility falls on the firm and consumers. In a developing country, many consumers may be poorly positioned to evaluate hazards and exercise proper care.

The Calabresi and Melamed principles also ask which party is best positioned to induce others to take actions that will improve the difference between social benefits and social costs. Consumers are typically not in that position. The firm may be able to induce consumers to use the product properly and can take steps through product design to reduce the hazards from anticipated misuse. In addition, marketing might focus on those market segments in which the product is most likely to be used properly. Similarly, distribution of the product might be restricted to outlets where instruction in proper use can be given. In a number of countries, however, such measures may not be sufficient.

The firm then is faced with the prospect of anticipatable misuse. Depending on the product in question, design and safety features can be effective means of reducing hazards from misuse, but the institutions of liability and regulation are not present to provide information on which safety features to incorporate.[14] The firm then is left with the issue of determining if the social costs of an injury in Bangladesh are the same as in Germany. Compensation for injuries is not the same even among developed countries, and the disparity between developed and developing countries can be considerable. The Calabresi and Melamed principles are incapable of resolving this issue. Utilitarianism evaluates alternatives using the preferences of those affected, which suggests using the trade-offs made in the developing country as the guide for deciding on the safety features to incorporate to reduce the hazards from anticipatable misuse.

Donaldson (1989, p. 116) addressed the issue of risks in developing countries and proposed a modification of Rawls's second principle to guide decisions about risks. He argued that the "difference principle would need to be adjusted to include freedom from risk as one of the primary goods normally covered by the principle." From this perspective a basic level of safety should be assured for all individuals, which could mean that higher standards than those practiced in developing countries should be used.

When misuse can be anticipated, marketing a product to those who are likely to misuse it may constitute deception. This would violate moral rules focusing on treating individuals as ends whose ability to choose should be developed rather than their ignorance exploited. Advertising is frequently viewed as a culprit in such situations. Activists have campaigned for over 30 years against the practices used in marketing infant formula in developing countries. Similarly, critics argue that the promotion and advertising of cigarettes in developing countries not only causes health problems but also puts an economic burden on the poor.

AIDS AND DEVELOPING COUNTRIES

Many developing countries lack the means to provide basic services for their people. Many of these same countries, particularly those in sub-Saharan Africa, have also been devastated by the AIDS pandemic. Some 20 million people worldwide have died from AIDS, and 33 million were

---

[14]See the Chapter 14 case *California Space Heaters, Inc.*

living with HIV/AIDS in 2009, three-quarters of whom are in sub-Saharan Africa. AIDS has led to sharp declines in life expectancy and negative economic growth, since AIDS strikes the most productive age group. This has worsened impoverishment and countries' abilities to address the pandemic.

The treatment of AIDS victims was impeded by the high cost of AIDS drugs, all of which were under patent. Although there is no cure for AIDS, with a strict regimen of drugs AIDS has become a treatable chronic disease in developed countries. Those drugs, however, were priced high, with many costing $10,000 or more a year. With the per capita income in sub-Saharan Africa averaging $1.50 a day, AIDS drugs were beyond the means of almost every country.

With many countries unable to prevent the spread of AIDS and provide care for victims, developed countries belatedly began to fund treatment and prevention programs. Under the leadership of United Nations Secretary General Kofi Annan, the independent Global Fund to Fight AIDS, Tuberculosis, and Malaria was established and financed privately by the developed countries, as well as by philanthropists, businesses, and the public. A number of companies participate through Product (RED) under which they contribute a portion of their revenue to the Global Fund. The Gates Foundation has spent billions of dollars and has emphasized prevention programs.

The Global Fund makes grants to countries based on their ability to make progress in combating AIDS and its spread. The PEFCO program started by President George W. Bush makes grants directly to health care providers to purchase antiretroviral drugs and fund treatment programs.[15] This funding plus the contributions of health care delivery organizations, such as the AIDS Healthcare Foundation and Doctors Without Borders, and the efforts of the afflicted countries have dramatically improved patient care as well as slowed the spread of AIDS. A cure has yet to be found, however.

Some countries threatened to use the "medical emergency" provisions of TRIPS to invoke compulsory licensing of AIDS drugs, and in 2007 Thailand did so, as considered in the Chapter 19 case *Compulsory Licensing, Thailand, and Abbott Laboratories*. In addition, Indian pharmaceutical companies began to produce and export AIDS drugs under India's unique patent system.[16] The pharmaceutical companies argued vigorously that compulsory licensing weakened patent protection and diminished incentives to conduct research and development on new AIDS drugs.[17]

Intense private and public politics were directed at pharmaceutical companies, and after several years they began to lower their prices under preferential pricing programs. Even at cost, however, the drugs were not affordable. The Part V integrative case *GlaxoSmithKline and AIDS Drugs Policy* addresses the challenges faced by the early market leader in AIDS drugs in responding to the pandemic.

Gilead Sciences, which produces the most effective first line drug, Viread, for treating HIV/AIDS, was committed to making its drug accessible throughout the developing world. It launched a major effort to make the drug available in Africa, but after 2 years of work only 35,000 patients in Africa were receiving Viread. The Chapter 21 case *Gilead Sciences (A): The Gilead Access Program for HIV Drugs* describes its efforts and asks if there is a more effective approach to making its drugs available where they are needed.

RESPONSIBILITY FOR WORKING CONDITIONS IN SUPPLIERS' FACTORIES

Sweatshops

In the 1990s concern developed about "sweatshops" in Asia and Latin America that supplied U.S. footwear and apparel companies. The issue was propelled by poignant stories of poverty and abuse; nonmarket action by labor unions and human rights groups; and pressure from the U.S. Department of Labor. The media provided extensive coverage of the issue and advocated higher workplace standards. The pressure reached a crescendo when abuses at a Nike supplier in

---

[15]The antiretroviral drugs reduce the viral content of the blood from millions to fewer than 80 per milliliter.

[16]See Chapter 14. India was forced by World Trade Organization rules to change its patent law.

[17]See Vachani and Smith (2004) for a perspective on AIDS drugs pricing.

Vietnam were reported.[18] Yet, in many of the countries in which the factories in question were located, few concerns were expressed over the working conditions. Moreover, since demand in those industries had grown rapidly as factories in the United States and other developed countries closed, many of the overseas factories were modern, as Levi Strauss had found in Saipan. The fear of many workers in the overseas factories was that higher standards would increase costs, causing purchasers to look elsewhere for lower cost suppliers.

To improve practices in suppliers' factories, President Clinton appointed an 18-member White House Apparel Industry Partnership, which included Nike, Reebok, L.L. Bean, Liz Claiborne, unions, human rights groups, and activist and advocacy representatives.[19] The task force was charged with producing a code and an enforcement mechanism to achieve standards, including a 60-hour workweek, a minimum employment age of 14, and wage guidelines. The task force, however, became embroiled in strong disagreements about implementation details.

The Union of Needletrade, Industrial, and Textile Employees (UNITE) and activists sought a majority on the governing board of any organization the partnership created to audit compliance with the standards. The companies, however, were successful in having the board have an equal representation of companies and the other groups.

The other sources of disagreement proved to be more contentious, and the task force failed to reach an accord by the deadline. The labor and human rights groups pressed for "living wages," rather than the prevailing wages, for suppliers' employees. The labor and human rights groups also sought a provision directed at China requiring that workers have the right to form independent unions and engage in collective bargaining. Such a requirement could force companies not to source products in China, since China did not allow independent unions. Some commentators suggested that the motivation behind these labor provisions was protection of union jobs in the United States.

With the partnership deadlocked a group of committee members, including Liz Claiborne, Nike, Reebok, and a number of human rights groups, reached an agreement on standards and established a private governance organization, the Fair Labor Association (FLA), to ensure compliance. The standards included a 60-hour workweek, a ban on employing children under the age of 15 unless the country explicitly allowed 14-year-olds to work, independent monitoring of suppliers' factories, and a requirement to pay the maximum of the official minimum wage and the prevailing market wage. The U.S. Secretary of Labor praised the agreement: "It is workable for business and creates a credible system that will let consumers know the garments they buy are not produced by exploited workers."[20]

Two members of the partnership, UNITE and an activist group, rejected the agreement. They joined with other activist groups, including the United Students Against Sweatshops, and other labor unions to form the Worker Rights Consortium (WRC) to work for more aggressive monitoring and higher standards including a living wage. Both the FLA and the WRC recruited affiliated members, primarily colleges and universities concerned about their licenses for sports apparel, but the WRC had no companies as members.

Private Governance and Self-Regulation: The Fair Labor Association

The FLA has many of the characteristics of a government institution. The FLA agreement specified representation, decision rights, standards, monitoring, certification, public reporting, and amendment procedures. The FLA has a detailed code of workplace standards, covering forced labor, child labor, harassment or abuse, nondiscrimination, health and safety, freedom of association and collective bargaining, wages and benefits, hours of work, and overtime compensation. The FLA code does not provide for a "living wage," as does the code for the WRC. In 2011 the FLA included 33 apparel and footwear companies and 14 suppliers, more than 200 colleges and universities. The companies, the NGOs, and universities each had six board seats with an independent chair as the 19th member. A supermajority of two-thirds of the companies and

---

[18]One result was the 1997 enactment of the Sanders Amendment, which bans the import of foreign products produced with forced child labor.
[19]See Golodner (2000).
[20]*New York Times,* November 5, 1998.

two-thirds of the labor/NGOs was required to change the standards. This provided assurances to all sides that the standards would not be changed unless there was considerable consensus.

The FLA selected and certified independent third-party monitors to inspect a specified percentage of the factories each year, and the companies chose from the set for the inspections. The FLA has also specified detailed procedures (Monitoring Guidance and Compliance Benchmarks) for the inspections. Any finding of noncompliance by an independent monitor was posted on the FLA Web site. The FLA also had a Third-Party Complaint System that allowed anyone to report "any situation of serious noncompliance" about any FLA member company. The FLA then reviewed the complaint and investigated any verifiable violation of the code.

Company Responses

Nike went beyond the FLA standards by pledging not to hire anyone under the age of 18 in its footwear plants and to meet U.S. air quality standards in the workplace. CEO Phil Knight stated, "The Nike product has become synonymous with slave wages, forced overtime and arbitrary abuse. I truly believe the American consumer doesn't want to buy products made under abusive conditions."[21] Nike began a reporting system, "Transparency 101," under which it publicly released the external monitoring reports conducted by PricewaterhouseCoopers on suppliers' factories. It also posted information on the factories' efforts to implement the action plans developed as a result of the inspections. Nike also opened its contractors' facilities to student monitors and publicly released the reports on 32 contractors that produced college-licensed apparel. In 2005 in its corporate responsibility report Nike released the names of 700 of its suppliers and reviewed the problems remaining. In 2000 Phil Knight spoke at the United Nations about Nike's participation in the UN-sponsored Global Compact along with other companies and NGOs. The companies in the Global Compact pledged to meet global labor and environmental standards.

Nike embarked on an aggressive campaign to ensure that suppliers were complying fully with its code. It conducted its own audits of suppliers' factories in addition to the inspections by the FLA. When violations were found, Nike worked with the supplier to rectify the problem and in the case of recurrent violations it terminated the supply arrangement. Nike turned over its factory inspection data to researchers at the Massachusetts Institute of Technology who sought to understand why some factories had better audit results than others. Part of the difference appeared to be cultural. Factories in the Americas, Europe, Middle East, and Africa regions performed significantly better than those in North Asia and South Asia. Locke, Qin, and Brause (2007) found that firms in countries in which the rule of law was stronger had significantly better performance, and larger factories had significantly worse performance.[22] The authors also found that factories owned by citizens of the country in which they were located had worse performance than those owned by foreigners. Overall, Nike's suppliers showed only modest improvement over time.

Part of the compliance problem rested with the factory owners and their supervisors, who were willing to violate the code to achieve more important goals such as meeting a delivery date. Nike recognized that it needed to identify the root causes of the problems in achieving compliance with its code. Some of the root causes rested with the factory owners and supervisors, who in some cases lacked respect for workers. Most of the suppliers had poor HR practices that made it difficult to respond to the rights of workers. Much of the root cause, however, was found to rest with Nike. Its purchasing agents, for example, would at times set unreasonable delivery schedules and not provide sufficient lead time. Moreover, purchasing made little attempt to smooth its orders over time. These failures forced factory supervisors to schedule excessive overtime and to pressure workers to be more productive, violating Nike's code.

Nike embarked on a process to move beyond compliance. In its 2005–2006 Corporate Social Responsibility Report the company stated, "While monitoring continues to be a cornerstone of our approach, we are taking a broader, more holistic look at our supply chain, focusing on root cause identification and solutions that will drive systemic change." Nike took steps to smooth orders over the year and provide greater lead time.

---

[21]*New York Times,* May 13, 1998.
[22]The Rule of Law index used was from the World Bank's Worldwide Governance Indicator project.

QUESTIONABLE FOREIGN PAYMENTS AND CORRUPTION

Corruption is costly both tangibly and intangibly. Corruption distorts economic activity, resulting in a substantial cost to an economy. Corruption also undermines trust and confidence in government. As international trade and foreign direct investment expanded, the opportunities for corruption increased and more firms were exposed to demands for payments or temptations to offer payments when they believed competitors were likely to be offering payments. Both countries and companies wanted to reduce corruption, and in the 1990s international efforts began. One important development was the establishment of Transparency International, an NGO formed to combat corruption, considered in Chapter 17. Another development was the negotiation of an anti-bribery code under the auspices of the OECD. These developments are considered later in the chapter, after considering frameworks for evaluating the moral concerns about these questionable payments.

In a number of countries, the exchange of gifts and favors is customary, and in some cases favors may extend into the domain of unethical conduct. In a country in which small payments to low-level government employees are necessary to clear administrative hurdles, a firm may be justified in making the payments to avoid a greater injustice. When those payments are recurring and pervasive, however, the question is which is the greater injustice. A firm may decide to forgo sales if those sales necessitate a continuing violation of ethics principles.

When corruption is pervasive, a company may go further and decide to withdraw from a country. A Unilever executive explained the company's decision to leave Bulgaria: "It was impossible for us to do business without getting involved in corruption. So we took the logical step and accepted the consequences. That meant packing our bags."[23]

Questionable Payments and Ethics Principles

The disclosure in 1975 that the Lockheed Corporation had made payments of over $12 million to Japanese business executives and government officials to secure a sale of commercial aircraft led to revelations that over 450 U.S. companies had made similar payments totaling more than $300 million worldwide. The questionable foreign payments ranged from outright bribes to obtain sales to extortion payments made to customs officials to avoid delays in clearing imports. In response, Congress passed the FCPA.

Some payments were made because firms, or their sales representatives, had reason to believe that competitors were offering payments to a customer. In an industry or a country in which such payments are customary, a firm may be unable unilaterally to change the practice, and the payments can be self-perpetuating.[24] This, however, does not provide a moral justification for the practice, and change can occur.[25]

In a situation in which payments are either demanded or likely to be required to obtain a sale, firms and their managers have two sources of guidance—one is ethics and the other is the law. Ethics is considered first, and then the law is presented and interpreted. Corporate codes of conduct are then considered. The ethics analysis focuses on bribery and the question of when, if ever, a firm is morally justified in paying a bribe.

A bribe is a payment to an individual in an organization intended to influence that person's exercise of his or her responsibilities; that is, a bribe is intended to corrupt the behavior of the recipient. Bribery is ethically objectionable on a number of grounds. From a utilitarian perspective, bribery distorts markets and reduces economic efficiency. That is, when bribes replace value and merit as the basis for decisions, competition cannot be as efficient. From a rights perspective, bribery distorts the fair opportunity to compete in markets. Furthermore, bribes induce the recipients to violate a duty to the principals who employ them.

More fundamentally, the bases for Kant's moral rules are violated. First, a rule under which bribes are allowed is not universalizable because there is little reason to believe that in the original position individuals would will competition in bribes rather than competition without bribes. Second, bribery is not reversible. A firm would not want its own purchasing agents to make their decisions based on the bribes they received.

---

[23]*Wall Street Journal,* February 16, 1999.

[24]Getz (2000) provides an overview and analysis of bribery and corruption.

[25]Klitgaard (1988) discusses the steps taken by the U.S. Army to overcome corruption in the construction and supply industries in Korea in the 1970s.

Bribes paid to government officials also undermine the impartiality of government and hence the equality of political rights. A bribe also exploits the position a person occupies in the recipient organization and distorts the fair equality of opportunity to qualify for the position. Furthermore, the recipient may receive too much, having done nothing to deserve it. Bribes would also not be expected to benefit the least advantaged persons, even indirectly.

The remaining issue is whether bribes are justified if there is a greater injustice that can be avoided. This issue is considered next in the context of the Lockheed case.

The Lockheed Case

The Lockheed case was described by Vice Chairman A. Carl Kotchian (1977), who authorized the payments in Japan. The $12 million payments in question represented less than 3 percent of the revenue on the L-1011 aircraft sold to All Nippon Airlines (ANA). The payments were made to the office of the prime minister, seven other politicians and government officials, and the president of ANA. The payments were not illegal under U.S. law at the time, and such payments were not unknown in the aircraft industry.[26] However, the payments were in violation of Japanese law. If Kotchian had been unsure of their legality in Japan, he could have contacted a Japanese lawyer or the commercial attaché at the U.S. embassy. Although it is customary in Japan to give gifts, an individual payment of $1.7 million cannot be viewed as a gift or as a routine political contribution.[27] Similarly, a payment of $50,000 per aircraft to the president of ANA could not be viewed as a part of the functioning system.

Kotchian offered several justifications for making the payments. He argued that the payments were "worthwhile from Lockheed's standpoint" because "they would provide Lockheed workers with jobs, and thus redound to the benefit of their dependents, their communities, and stockholders of the corporation."[28] As considered in Chapter 21, this is casuist reasoning in that an unethical action is said to be justified by the benefits it provides to stakeholders. From a utilitarian perspective, the benefits to Lockheed's stakeholders are likely to be little different from the benefits to Boeing's or McDonnell Douglas's stakeholders if they were to obtain the sale. Furthermore, a market in which a competition in bribes takes place does not function as efficiently as when decisions are made on the basis of merit and value.

The ethics evaluation of this case depends on whether in the absence of payments ANA would have selected Lockheed aircraft. If ANA would have selected another aircraft supplier that did not offer a bribe, Lockheed's payments would be an explicit bribe, which cannot be ethically justified. To obtain the sale, Lockheed could have reduced the price of the aircraft, in which case the benefit would accrue to ANA and not to its executives and government officials.

A second possibility is that ANA would have purchased the L-1011 even if the payments were not made. The ethics issue then is whether Lockheed would be justified in making the payments, which, under this supposition, would be a response to extortion, as Kotchian claimed it was. He wrote: "From a purely ethical and moral standpoint I would have declined such a request [for payments]. However, in that case, I would most certainly have sacrificed commercial success."[29] Extortion involves the use of coercion to extract a payment. Such a payment would be morally justified in the case of ransom paid in a kidnapping, for example. The difference between a ransom payment and the payments that Lockheed made, however, is that if after the fact Lockheed had publicly revealed the payments, the public would have reacted quite differently than it would in the case of a ransom payment. The Lockheed payments thus do not pass Gert's injustice test (Chapter 22) or the public disclosure test discussed in Chapter 23.

---

[26]Lockheed's subsequent legal problems in the United States were due to a failure to disclose the payments as required by U.S. law. See Hay and Gray (1981, pp. 134–138) for a discussion of some of the Lockheed payments. In 1982, the Boeing Company pleaded guilty and paid a $400,000 fine for 40 counts of failure to disclose to the Export-Import Bank that it had paid "irregular commissions" to agents involved in foreign sales. (The Export-Import Bank required such disclosure on any sales it financed.) In 1981 the McDonnell Douglas Corporation pleaded guilty to fraud and making false statements and paid fines of over $1.2 million.

[27]It might be argued that the payments were justified because they were a part of the functioning system in the aircraft industry. This, however, is not a moral justification, even if the competition often involved payments.

[28]Kotchian (1977, p. 12).

[29]Ibid.

TABLE 24-1 Utilities of A, B, and C

		Company B	
		Not Bribe	**Bribe**
Company A	**Not Bribe**	(4, 2, 14)	(0, 5, 9)
	Bribe	(5, 0, 11)	(2, 1, 12)

Gert's test for when an injustice is warranted to avoid a greater injustice requires that a rational observer would understand the reason for the action. That test would surely not be met. As for the public disclosure test, Lockheed would never have been able to justify the payments to the Japanese or American publics.

A third possibility is that the payments were required to match payments offered by other aircraft manufacturers. This situation is considered next.

A Utilitarian Analysis of Bribery

From a utilitarian perspective, bribery is bad because it distorts economic activity away from producing the greatest well-being. To illustrate this, consider two companies, A and B, seeking a contract for a sale to country C. Suppose that company A's product is likely better for country C than is the product of company B and in the absence of bribes would likely be selected by C. If no bribes are offered, the expected utilities of A and B and country C are 4, 2, and 14, respectively, as presented in the upper left cell of Table 24-1. For example, suppose that the profit on the sale would be $6 million, and in the absence of bribery the likelihood that A would be selected is two-thirds and the likelihood that B would be selected is one-third. The expected profits for A and B then are 4 and 2, respectively.

Consider next the possibility that the government officials responsible for selecting the contract winner can be bribed. If one company offers a bribe and the other does not, suppose its probability of winning the contract becomes one. Bribery involves transactions costs because both parties must conceal the payments and take measures to justify the selection. Suppose that the utilities if A does not bribe and B does bribe are 0, 5, and 9, respectively.[30] Suppose also that the utilities if A bribes and B does not are 5, 0, and 11. If both companies pay bribes, assume that the likelihood that A would be selected is unchanged at two-thirds and the utilities are 2, 1, and 12.

Before considering the application of utilitarianism, suppose that the companies were self-interested. Inspection of Table 24-1 indicates that each company has a dominant strategy of paying a bribe. That is, if B were believed to be offering a bribe, then A is better off offering a bribe and obtaining a utility of 2 than not bribing and having a utility of 0. Similarly, if B were believed not to be offering a bribe, A is better off offering a bribe. Utilitarianism, however, requires that each company consider the aggregate utility of all three parties.

Under rule utilitarianism each of the three parties chooses actions for A and B simultaneously based on the greatest aggregate utility. The aggregate utilities are presented in Table 24-2. The moral rule thus is that neither A nor B bribes.

Suppose, however, that company B is not a utilitarian but instead is purely self-interested. Since B has a dominant strategy, it will offer a bribe. Is a matching bribe ethically justified in this

TABLE 24-2 Aggregate Utility

		Company B	
		Not Bribe	**Bribe**
Company A	**Not Bribe**	20	14
	Bribe	16	15

---

[30]Recall that B's product is worse for C than is A's product, so C's utility if B is selected is lower than if A is selected. The well-being of the recipients of the bribes is included in the utility for C.

case? From the perspective of rule utilitarianism, the answer is no. As just demonstrated, the moral rule is that no bribes are offered, and hence B is acting immorally. Act utilitarianism, however, takes B's behavior (offering a bribe) as given and asks whether aggregate utility is higher if A offers a matching bribe. From Table 24-2, if B is offering a bribe, A should offer a bribe because that results in an aggregate utility of 15 compared to 14 if it does not offer a bribe. Such reasoning can perpetuate bribery and is inappropriate.[31] This illustrates the weakness of act utilitarianism. Instead of offering the bribe, A could work for a collective agreement banning bribes.

If one can show that the payment matches a payment that a competitor is offering, would the public approve? In some countries the answer might be yes. In the United States the FCPA requires the answer no. That is, pay no bribes but instead work to convince others not to offer or accept bribes. The OECD Anti-Bribery Convention reflects the success of such an approach.

One reason bribery is difficult to eradicate is that both the offeror and the recipient have strong incentives to conceal it. Also, self-interest and the suspicion that a competitor may be offering a bribe may lead a company to offer a bribe. If both companies harbor such suspicions, the slippery slope can result in a competition in bribes. The chapter case *Siemens: Anatomy of Bribery* considers a company that engaged in widespread bribery.

Another reason not to pay bribes in situations in which there will be repeated encounters was given by an executive of a global company. He said, "If you pay once, you pay forever."

The Foreign Corrupt Practices Act

In the Lockheed case the payments were made both through an official agent, the Marubeni Trading Company, and a confidential consultant. In conducting business in foreign countries, it is often advisable to retain the services of a local representative who is familiar with the system in the country and has contacts that will, at a minimum, save time in arranging appointments and may help speed permits and contracts through the host country's bureaucracy. These agents are often compensated on a fee or commission basis, and the disposition of those monies may be known only to agents. If a portion of the commissions might be passed on to influence the actions of customers or government officials, the firm may be contributing to a corrupt act. Ethically, the firm has an obligation to instruct its agent about which practices are acceptable and which are unacceptable. Moreover, the firm has a duty to monitor the activities of its agents. The FCPA addresses these issues, among others.[32]

The FCPA makes bribery of foreign officials, political parties, candidates for office, and public international organizations a criminal offense. It provides for a fine of up to $2 million for the company and up to $250,000 and imprisonment for not more than 5 years for an individual making a payment or offer covered by the act. It assigns the burden of knowing whether illegal payments are being made to the company and imposes detailed record-keeping requirements. Under the FCPA, it is unlawful to make any "offer, payment, promise to pay, or authorization of the payment of any money, or offer, gift, promise to give, or authorization of anything ..." to influence a decision, omit a required action, or give "any improper advantage" to the company. The term foreign official "does not include any employee of a foreign government or any department, agency, or instrumentality thereof whose duties are essentially ministerial or clerical." The FCPA thus allows small "facilitating payments" to low-level government employees such as customs inspectors, if the payments do not influence a decision.

The use of agents, intermediaries, or third parties is also covered, and they are subject to both criminal and civil penalties. In its original language, the FCPA pertained to "any person, while knowing or having reason to know" about a payment for the purposes previously listed. This imposed a stringent duty on a company to know how fees paid to agents, intermediaries, and third parties were actually used. After the first few years of experience with the FCPA, a poll of 1,200 large businesses indicated that substantial sales had been lost in countries in which bribery was a common practice.[33] Although U.S. firms indicated that they supported the FCPA, 68 percent responded that the record-keeping burden should be reduced and that the law should be more specific about who in a foreign country can receive payments and for what purposes.

---

[31]The same question can be posed regarding whether B should offer a bribe if A is offering a bribe. The answer is no, since the aggregate utility with only A bribing is 16, whereas if both offer bribes, it is 15.

[32]See Pastin and Hooker (1988) and Alpern (1988) for ethics analyses of the FCPA.

[33]*BusinessWeek,* September 19, 1983.

The Omnibus Trade and Competitiveness Act of 1988 amended the FCPA in several ways.[34] First, it altered the language about the use of third parties or intermediaries by eliminating the phrase "or having reason to know." Second, a payment to a foreign individual became illegal under the act if it was illegal in the foreign country. Third, if a payment were legal in the foreign country, the defendant in an action brought under the act could use that legality as a defense. Fourth, the language of the act was clarified to indicate that payments that secured performance of routine government actions, such as signing customs documents and unloading or loading cargoes, were not illegal. Fifth, the amendments provided firms with a number of affirmative defenses, including consistency with host country laws and legitimate business expenses.

The FCPA has had considerable impact on the behavior of the companies, and many companies have compliance departments and provide training to their employees. Companies that discover that questionable payments have been made disclose the payments to the U.S. government. In 2011 Pfizer disclosed "potentially improper payments" made "in conjunction with certain sales activities outside the U.S."[35] Most companies reach settlements with the government, as in the case of Johnson & Johnson which paid $80 million and Alcatel-Lucent which paid $137 million to settle charges. Executives found to have participated in the bribery can be imprisoned.

The FCPA does not prohibit payments to private businesses. The bribery of private businesses, or private-to-private bribery, is believed to be less common than the bribery of government officials. In 2001, however, the Department of Justice obtained guilty pleas from major international construction companies, including ABB and PhillippHoltzman, for kickbacks and the payment of bribes on U.S. Agency for International Development–financed water projects in Egypt. The companies met secretly to arrange for some of the companies to submit inflated bids and others not to bid at all on certain contracts. In exchange the companies received monetary payments from the winning bidder or the remaining bidders.[36]

The UK Bribery Act

The United Kingdom Bribery Act that took effect in July 2011 goes considerably farther than the FCPA. In addition to prohibiting bribery of government officials, it prohibits bribes paid to private companies. Furthermore, the law prohibits "grease payments," or facilitating payments, even if they do not affect decision making by government employees such as those that provide routine services. Under the law an employee can be guilty of bribery even if the person was unaware of it. The effects of the law will depend on its enforcement, and the U.S. Chamber of Commerce said making these payments a criminal act was "troubling."[37]

Company Codes

Most firms have policies or codes to ensure compliance with the FCPA and international conventions and to clarify when foreign payments can be made and how they are to be accounted for. The three principal purposes of these codes are to provide guidance to employees, make it easier for them to say no to demands for payment, and ultimately discourage demands for payments.

The extent to which a firm encounters demands for payments depends on its lines of business, the countries in which it does business, and its organization. Some industries and some countries are characterized by a functioning system in which bribery and facilitating payments are not uncommon. A firm's lines of business and the countries in which it operates thus affect the scope of the problems it faces. That scope is also affected by the organizational structure of the firm. Firms can conduct their foreign business through a wholly owned subsidiary, a joint venture, a sales office that manages local dealers and distributors, or agents with whom the firm deals at arm's length. Controlling and monitoring payments generally becomes more difficult and making questionable payments becomes easier, the more independent is the business unit or agent.

---

[34]The FCPA was also amended in the Anti-Bribery and Fair Competition Act of 1998 to bring it into accord with the OECD Convention considered later in the chapter. The preceding text includes these changes.

[35]*Wall Street Journal,* August 12, 2011.

[36]*New York Times,* April 13, 2001.

[37]*Wall Street Journal,* December 23, 2011.

Corruption in Russia is not uncommon, particularly in the oil industry. Demands for bribes were regularly made, and BP and Shell responded in quite different ways. Shell packed its bags and left the country. BP made a call to the chairman of Gazprom, the giant Russian natural gas producer, and complained about the demands for payments. Corruption in Russia is "organized," and the demands for payments stopped quickly. BP thanked the chairman and said to call if it could be of any help. The son of the chairman subsequently attended a university in the United Kingdom at no expense.

Company codes typically state the principal features of the FCPA; require that the representatives of the firm know the local laws and the functioning system in the country; distinguish between gratuities, facilitating payments, and bribes; and specify record-keeping and reporting requirements. A code may also provide guidance for handling a request for a payment and indicate to whom an employee can turn if a payment's propriety is in question. Firms have also established audit procedures to detect illegal payments. In many firms, managers and sales representatives are required to pledge to abide by the FCPA and company guidelines. The FCPA has had an impact on suppliers and vendors, many of which have established compliance programs so as to qualify for supply contracts with U.S. companies. Trace Internation provides training to suppliers, and its president AlexandraWrage said, "Companies are forcing their anti-bribery standards out through their international supply and marketing chains."[38]

Company policies not only provide guidance to managers and sales representatives, but they also establish a basis for a response when a government official or a customer demands a payment. A response that "company policy does not permit it" may, in some cases, lead to the demand being retracted. Furthermore, knowledge that the firm does not make such payments may eventually decrease the number of demands. For this to be effective, however, the firm must establish a reputation for not making payments.

BP has a policy of not paying bribes and also not making facilitating payments. CEO Lord Browne wrote to employees stating, "We work within the law in every one of the 100 countries in which we operate and we work to our standards, which are often higher than the legal requirement. Those standards are universal in BP. We will not engage in bribery or corruption in any form including facilitating payments."[39]

As a result of the policy BP employees were held "hostage" in Russia, but gradually the requests for facilitating payments decreased. The demands resurfaced from time to time, and BP was forced to add an extensive audit and control staff in Russia to detect whether payments had been made. Some employees were fired for making payments. Lord Browne explained that BP ran "a high-cost operation in Russia."

BP also follows a policy of "publishing what you pay." That is, when contract payments such as royalties are made to foreign governments, the amounts and the recipients are made public. With this information, citizens in the country can hold government officials accountable for the disposition of the funds. Publish what you pay is now practiced by many companies in extractive industries. Sixty large oil, gas, and mining companies participate along with countries in the Extractive Industries Transparency Initiative, which along with PWYP, a coalition of 300 NGOs, promotes publish what you pay.[40]

Cummins's Practice

Cummins Inc.'s policy on questionable foreign payments is striking in its articulation of a principle for reasoning about whether a payment should be made in a particular instance. Cummins stated its "Primary Ethical Guide":

> The key element which distinguishes ethically unacceptable payments is the corruption of [a] relationship of trust. When a company pays an agent of a buyer in order to influence that agent's purchasing decision, and when that payment is not known to the buyer, the company corrupts a relationship of trust between buyer and agent. The buyer's expectation that his agent will act with only the buyer's interest in mind is betrayed. Similarly, when a

---

[38]*Wall Street Journal,* June 24, 2011.

[39]Lord Browne of Madingley, "To Our Employees," August, 2002. In 2003 BP fired 165 people for violating the company's ethics standards.

[40]PWYP (Publish What You Pay) is a coalition of 600 NGOs in 30 countries.

company pays a government agent in order to influence that agent's official decisions, the company corrupts a relationship of trust between the public and that official. The corruption of such a relationship of trust not only violates fundamental principles of fair dealing but also hampers efficient economic development and undermines social cohesion.[41]

Cummins's guide meets both the Kantian standard and the standard of rule utilitarianism. It treats the buyer as an autonomous end, and the rule of not corrupting a relationship of trust is one that people would will to be universal. From the perspective of rule utilitarianism the guide supports efficiency by requiring competition to be on a commercial basis rather than on bribes.

Figure 24-1 displays the framework of this principle. In contrast to Kotchian's analysis, which focuses on the consequences for the firm from making the payment, Cummins's principle focuses on the buyer and its agent. That agent is in a relationship of trust with its principal—shareholders in the case of private firms and citizens in the case of a government agency. In this relationship, the agent is to serve the interests of the principal; accepting a bribe sacrifices the interests of the principal for the interests of the agent. Cummins applies this reasoning in the tests that an employee is to use in determining if a payment is acceptable. "Does this payment undermine a relationship of trust? What expectations does the principal have of his agent in the particular transaction at issue? Is the payment known to the principal or is it not?"

Payments are allowable only if three conditions are met:

a. The payment is required to induce the official to perform a routine act which he is already under a duty to perform.

b. The payment is consistent with local practice. If the payment is consistent with local practice, it is reasonable to assume that it is consistent with public expectations of official behavior, and

c. There is no reasonable alternative available for obtaining the official act or service at issue.

Although the phrase "reasonable alternative" is not precise, condition c requires the company to consider such possibilities as reducing the price or expediting delivery to obtain the sale. Reducing the price to make the sale, rather than paying a bribe, causes the benefit to go to the principal rather than the agent, which is consistent with the relationship of trust. The relevant test is the requirement that the Cummins employee determine whether the principal knows of the payment, since then the principal can determine where the benefit should reside.

In cases in which the employee is uncertain whether a payment is allowed, Cummins states, "Where there is a question as to the propriety of a particular payment in view of the foregoing standards, the payment should not be made." To encourage compliance, Cummins also assures that "no employee is put at a career disadvantage because of his or her willingness to raise a question about a corporate practice or unwillingness to pursue a course of action which seems

FIGURE 24-1 Cummins, Inc.: Questionable Foreign Payments and the Relationship of Trust

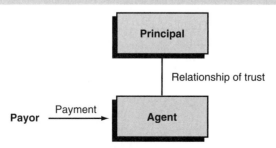

Rule: A payment corrupts when
1. it influences the agent's decision
2. it is not known to the principal

[41]Cummins Practices, October 1, 1980.

inappropriate or morally dubious." Cummins also provides its version of the public disclosure test: "Cummins employees do nothing in search of business that they should not reveal willingly and publicly to any other member of the Cummins family or to any government official in any land."

In addition to providing principles on which to reason and standards for assessing when a payment is allowable, Cummins's standards go beyond the FCPA by prohibiting corrupt payments to private, as well as to public, buyers. Recognizing that in some countries payments that do not satisfy its standards could be necessary to do business, Cummins states that it will "accept the loss of business." If the pattern of questionable payments continues, Cummins states that it will bring the matter to the attention of the host government to determine how the government wants the matter to be handled. If the demands for payments persist, Cummins is prepared to forgo the business.

The OECD Anti-Bribery Convention

For over two decades the FCPA stood alone among the developed countries with its imposition of both criminal penalties and stringent requirements for reporting and monitoring. The United States estimated that its companies lost billions of dollars a year in sales because of bribes paid by companies from other countries. In France, Germany, and many other European countries, bribes and other payments to foreign officials were tax deductible if required to secure a sale. With the growth in foreign direct investment in developing countries and increased trade, the scale of corruption expanded, and more companies became concerned about the effect of corruption not only on business activity but also on the countries where the payments were made. Pressure from the United States and European countries and from organizations such as Transparency International led to negotiations within the OECD. The result was the 1997 Anti-Bribery Convention (Convention on Combating Bribery of Foreign Public Officials in International Business Transactions), signed by the 34 OECD member countries plus Argentina, Brazil, Bulgaria, and South Africa.

The Convention requires signatories to make the act of bribery and the making of other forms of illicit payments to foreign public officials a criminal offense, whether paid directly or indirectly "in order to obtain or retain business or other improper advantage in the conduct of international business."[42] Small "facilitation" payments that are not made "to obtain or retain business" are not viewed as an offense. A foreign public official is defined to include not only those holding elective or appointive office, but also officials of public agencies and public enterprises at least 50 percent owned by the government. The Convention also imposes record-keeping obligations on businesses so that payments can be identified. The Convention does not pertain to private-to-private bribery.

The bargaining on the Convention revealed the complexity of the issue. Since in many developing countries the government owns or controls companies, the United States argued and eventually was successful in including government-controlled companies under the Convention. The United States also successfully obtained inclusion of elected members of parliament in the category of government officials, over the objections of several European countries that allowed payments to their members of parliament provided the payments were not to influence votes. The United States lost, however, in its attempt to include payments to political parties and party officials as an offense.

The European Union enacted a Criminal Law Convention on Corruption in 1999 that made criminal offenses of active bribery and passive bribery (extortion) that gives any "undue advantage" of domestic and foreign public officials and of private sector personnel. The United States signed the OECD Convention in 2000 and changed its laws accordingly. Germany also enacted the Convention, which led in part to the prosecutions in the chapter case *Siemens: Anatomy of Bribery.*

SUMMARY

Countries differ considerably in terms of their history, culture, resources, and institutions, yet fundamental ethics principles are intended to be universal rather than country specific. Cultural relativism, in which one relies solely on host country laws and practices, is inappropriate, and

---

[42]The Convention pertains to "active corruption" committed by the offeror of a bribe rather than to "passive corruption" committed by the recipient of the bribe. Like the FCPA the Convention pertains to the supply side of bribery.

universal relativism, in which one applies the same principles everywhere, ignores relevant differences among countries. The principles underpinning utilitarianism, rights theories, and theories of justice remain useful guides for operating across borders. The application of these principles, however, leaves unresolved issues about trade-offs between costs and benefits, how duties to ensure rights are assigned, and how justice considerations are to be taken into account.

Guidance for managers is provided by international, host country, and home country law and by ethics principles. International law is important, yet its enforcement is often irregular and its application to moral issues is often limited to general, rather than specific, matters. Host country law is an important guide, and when those laws are consistent with universal standards, they are to be respected. If they do not meet those standards, firms must develop policies guided by principles as well as law. Firms also must determine whether they will apply the same standards to their operations in all countries or adapt their policies and practices to the situation of each host country. This is a particular challenge in low-income countries that do not have the capacity to provide guidance through regulation or where people prefer economic growth over the safety and environmental standards of high-income countries.

The working conditions and human rights situation in the factories of overseas suppliers has raised moral concerns, and an innovative approach to addressing those concerns has been undertaken by individual companies and by the apparel and footwear industries. A multi-stakeholder approach has been institutionalized in the form of the Fair Labor Association, which provides for independent monitoring of factories and the public disclosure of results.

Bribery and other forms of corruption are common in some countries. The FCPA and the OECD Convention provide guidance, assign duties, and impose penalties for violations. However, laws can leave a variety of issues, such as payments to private companies, unaddressed. In such cases, principles in addition to host country practices can provide guidance. Utilitarianism concludes that bribery is morally wrong. Some managers argue that bribes are required because of extortion by government officials or bribes offered by competitors. In such cases, the injustice standard is applicable and requires that the manager ask whether, if the payment were publicly disclosed, the publics in the host and home country would agree that it should have been paid.

The approach of Cummins Inc. is useful for guiding managers in their reasoning about such issues, even if one does not reach the same conclusions the company reached. The approach involves a statement of principles, a method for reasoning from those principles to the specifics of a situation, standards that managers are to apply, and protection for employees who raise corruption issues within the firm.

The range of ethics issues that arise in global operations is broader than those in a firm's home country, and in developing countries the institutions found in developed countries may function imperfectly. Furthermore, the facts of the situations encountered internationally may be more difficult to discern. These factors complicate the application of ethics principles and leave managers with the challenge of formulating policies guided by a combination of law, ethics principles, and culture.

CASES

Google Out of China

Perhaps we can return to serving mainland China in the future,

Serge Brin, Google Co-Founder and President, Technology.[43]

INTRODUCTION

Google began serving the Chinese market from servers located in the United States, but service was frequently interrupted by Chinese censors. After lengthy internal debate Google decided to launch Google.cn in 2006 despite concerns

about censorship and putting users in jeopardy (See the Chapter 16 case *Google in China*). Google expressed its reservations, "we will carefully monitor conditions in China, including new laws and other restrictions on our services. If we determine that we are unable to achieve the objectives outlined we will not hesitate to reconsider our approach to China." Google's reservations met with criticism from the Chinese government and its state-controlled newspapers. Google's entry into China was criticized by human rights advocates and NGOs, and in committee hearings members of

[43]*New York Times*, March 24, 2010.

Congress criticized the company for participating in censorship. In 2006 Serge Brin expressed his ambivalence about the decision to operate in China, "We felt that perhaps we could compromise our principles but provide ultimately more information for the Chinese and be a more effective service and perhaps make more of a difference.... Perhaps now the principled approach make more sense."[44] Google's motto was, "Don't be evil."[45]

In December 2009 Google detected an extensive and sophisticated cyber attack that targeted companies and specific employees within the companies. After investigating the attack, Google announced on January 12 that it was changing its approach in China. Senior vice-president David Drummond explained, "we detected a highly sophisticated and targeted attack on our corporate infrastructure originating from China that resulted in the theft of intellectual property from Google... we have discovered that at least twenty other large companies ... have been similarly targeted.... We have evidence to suggest that a primary goal of the attackers was accessing the Gmail accounts of Chinese human rights activists.... we have discovered that the accounts of dozens of U.S.-, China- and Europe-based Gmail users who are advocates of human rights in China have been routinely accessed by third parties."[46] He announced, "We have decided we are no longer willing to continue censoring our results on Google.cn,.... We recognize that this may well mean having to shut down Google.cn, and potentially our offices in China." Drummond acknowledged that "hundreds of millions of Chinese people [have been lifted] out of poverty..." and praised the country, "Indeed, this great nation is at the heart of much economic progress and development in the world today."[47]

Microsoft chairman Bill Gates commented that China's "efforts to censor the Internet have been very limited" and that it was "easy to go around" the controls. He stated, "And so you've got to obey the laws of the countries you're in, or not?"[48] CEO Steve Balmer said, "I think you have to respect sovereign nations to make that decision.... It's important we comply with the laws and conventions in the countries [where] we do business."[49] Microsoft continued to provide Internet services in China, as did Yahoo.[50]

CENSORSHIP AND THE CYBER ATTACKS

Censorship of the Internet in China took two forms. First, the Chinese government blocked Internet sites and used the Great Firewall to block access to foreign sites. Facebook, Twitter, and YouTube were blocked in China, and Chinese equivalents were quickly established: Renren for Facebook, QQ for instant messaging, and Baidu and Li Senhe for Google's YouTube. Second, Internet service providers were expected to self-censor. The Chinese government did not specify what content or links should be censored, and companies developed their own approaches. Google pinged the Great Firewall to see what was blocked, monitored actions taken by the government, and attended weekly "wind blowing" meetings held by the State Council Information Office. Search requests on Google for Tiananmin Square, the Falun Gong, and riots in Tibet and Xinjiang returned only links understood to be satisfactory to the government. A 2008 study by the Citizen Lab at the University of Toronto found that Google.cn was less censored than other search engines.[51]

Brin commented that leading up to the 2008 Beijing Olympics, "I actually felt like things really improved. We were actually able to censor less and less, and our local competitors there also censored less and less." After the Games he said that "there has been a lot more blocking going on."[52] The tighter controls were justified by the government as responses to internal threats that had escalated. Government officials cited the riots in Lhasa, Tibet, protests intended to disrupt the Olympic Games, a human rights petition signed by 10,000 people, and the July 2009 ethnic riots in Xinjiang that resulted in nearly 200 deaths and 1,700 injuries. The government claimed that the Internet was used to recruit Uighur youths to go to Xinjiang and attack ethnic Han citizens.[53] The Communist party's official newspaper, the *People's Daily*, editorialized, "How did the unrest after the Iranian elections come about? It was because online warfare launched by America, via You Tube video and Twitter micro-blogging, spread rumors, created splits, stirred up and sowed discord."[54]

Although Google traced the attacks to China, it did not allege that they were conducted by the government.[55] The attack reportedly targeted Google's Gaia password system that controls access to its Web services, email, and applications.[56] Adobe Systems and Juniper Networks also said they were victims of the attacks. A spokesperson for the Ministry of Industry and Information Technology (MIIT) stated, "Any accusation that the Chinese government participated in cyber attacks, either in an explicit or indirect way, is groundless and aims to discredit China."[57]

The *New York Times* reported that investigators had concluded that the cyber attacks were conducted using computers at Shanghai Jiaotong University and the Lanxiang Vocational School and may have been connected with the Chinese military

[44]*San Jose Mercury News*, June 7, 2006.

[45]Google Code of Conduct, http://investor.google.com/conduct.html

[46]One of those whose Gmail account was accessed was Tenzin Seldon, a sophomore at Stanford University, who was active in the Tibetan human rights movement.

[47]David Drummond, http://googleblog.blogspot.com/2010/01/new-approach-to-china.html, January 12, 2010.

[48]*Wall Street Journal*, January 28, 2010.

[49]*Wall Street Journal*, January 22, 2010.

[50]Yahoo had turned operations of its services in China over to Alibaba, in which it held a 40 percent share.

[51]www.cnn.com/2009/TECH/06/16/cnet.google.tiananmen.square/index/html, June 16, 2009.

[52]*Wall Street Journal*, March 13–14, 2010.

[53]*New York Times*, February 12, 2010.

[54]Ibid.

[55]Google reportedly asked the U.S. National Security Administration for technical assistance in investigating the cyber attacks.

[56]*New York Times*, April 20, 2010. The attackers knew the names of the developers of Gaia and attempted to enter through their computers but failed. They then used other means to access the code, which they then transferred to a computer at Rackspace in Texas, which was unaware of the activity.

[57]*San Jose Mercury News*, January 25, 2010.

or government. Ma Shaoxu, a spokesperson for the foreign ministry, responded angrily to the allegations: "Reports that these attacks came from Chinese schools are groundless, and accusations of Chinese government involvement are irresponsible and out of ulterior motives."[58]

In June 2009 the government had blocked Google's Web site for linking too often to pornography and vulgar content. Google pledged renewed efforts to avoid pornography. In January 2010 China announced that it would scan text messages for "illegal or unhealthy content" as part of its campaign against pornography. Sun Li, a businesswoman in Beijing, said, "This is against the law. You can block Web sites for pornography or violence, but texts are from person to person. It has nothing to do with the public. If this is really so, I can't text anyone anymore, or call anyone."[59] In January 2010 the Foreign Correspondents Club of China reported that the Gmail accounts of some of its members were hacked, and in April 2010 the Club's Web site experienced a denial of service attack.

Censorship was practiced by many countries. Iran had shut down G-mail in February, and Secretary of State Hillary Clinton spoke of a "spike in threats to the free flow of information" in the Middle East and pointed to Egypt, Iran, Saudi Arabia, Tunisia, Uzbekistan, and Vietnam.[60] The United States released its annual report on human rights abuses, which criticized China, and China issued its report on human rights abuses listing what it said were abuses in the United States.

THE DECISION

Google hoped to negotiate with the Chinese government to allow it to remain in China without self-censoring. At the World Economic Forum in Davos CEO Eric Schmidt commented, "We love what the Chinese are doing as a country, in terms of growth, improving the states of lives of people, and using information. We just don't like the censorship, and we said that very publicly. What we hope is that that will change. And we hope that we can apply some form of negotiation or pressure to make things better for the Chinese people."[61]

Although Schmidt said "we're in active negotiations with the Chinese government,...", Miao Wei, China's vice-minister of MIIT said there had been no negotiations.[62] The Minister, Li Yizhong, warned, "If you insist on taking this action that violates Chinese laws, I repeat: You are unfriendly and irresponsible, and you yourself will have to bear the consequences."[63]

On March 22, citing the cyberattacks Drummond announced that Google had stopped censoring its search services—Google Search, Google News, and Google Images— on Google.cn. Google users were now redirected to a new

"entirely legal" service on Google.com.hk for uncensored search in simplified Chinese using servers located in Hong Kong.[64] Google explained that "the Chinese government has been crystal clear throughout our discussions that self-censorship is a non-negotiable legal requirement," and added "we are well aware that it could at any time block access to our services." Hong Kong had a separate Internet and communications infrastructure, and political dissidents operated blogs from there and human rights NGOs located there.[65] The Hong Kong site, however, was outside the Great Firewall, and censoring by the Chinese government replaced Google's self-censoring. On March 30 Google's search site stopped working for several hours, and Google explained, "So what happened to block Google.com.hk must have been as a result of a change in the Great Firewall."[66]

The reaction by the government was swift and harsh. An official of the Internet bureau of the State Council Information Office told the Xinhua news agency that Google had "violated its written promise it made when entering the Chinese market by stopping filtering its searching service and blaming China" and "we're uncompromisingly opposed to the politicization of commercial issues, and express our discontent and indignation to Google for its unreasonable accusations and conducts."[67] A Chinese embassy official in Washington stated, "China's policies of encouraging Internet development will remain unchanged. So will its policies of managing the Internet according to Chinese laws and regulations."[68]

Serge Brin said that the cyber-attack "was the straw that broke the camel's back." He explained, "I think at some point it is appropriate to stand up for your principles, and if more companies, governments, organizations, individuals did that, I do think the world would be a better place."[69] Silicon Valley venture capitalist Mitch Kapor echoed Brin's sentiments, "More businesses ought to follow 'gut principles' and shareholders and customers ought to support and encourage them to do so."[70] Two days after Google's announcement, Go Daddy Group told a congressional committee that it would cut back operations in China because the government had required information about registrants in China.

Commenting on the move to Hong Kong, Brin said, "We got reasonable indications that this was O.K. We can't be completely confident."[71] In its announcement Google also stated that it would continue its R&D work in China, would maintain a sales force on the continent, and would continue in its partnerships. Drummond explained, "We certainly expected that if

[58]*San Jose Mercury News*, February 24, 2010.

[59]*New York Times*, January 20, 2010.

[60]*San Jose Mercury News*, January 25, 2010. The Arabic Network for Human Rights Information provided a report on Internet censorship in 20 Arab countries: "One Social Network With a Rebellious Message," December 2009. www.anhri.net/en

[61]*San Jose Mercury News*, January 30, 2010.

[62]*San Jose Mercury News*, March 11, 2010.

[63]*Wall Street Journal*, March 13–14, 2010.

[64]Simplified Chinese was preferred by Internet users on the mainland, whereas traditional Chinese was preferred by Internet users in Hong Kong. Google continued to offer its uncensored services in traditional Chinese on Google.com.hk.

[65]*San Jose Mercury News*, March 23, 2010. Hong Kong was governed for 50 years under the One China, Two Systems government structure established when the United Kingdom returned Hong Kong to China.

[66]*Wall Street Journal*, March 31, 2010.

[67]*Wall Street Journal*, March 23, 2010.

[68]Ibid.

[69]*Wall Street Journal*, March 25, 2010.

[70]Ibid.

[71]*New York Times*, March 23, 2010.

we take a stand around censorship that the government doesn't like that it would have an impact on our business. We understood that as a possibility."[72] The decision to move its search and news services to Hong Kong risked not only losing mainland users but also jeopardizing its partnering.

Tom.com, an Internet portal located in Hong Kong and controlled by tycoon Li Ka-Shing, quickly switched its default search link from Google.cn to Baidu.com explaining, "As a Chinese company, we adhere to rules and regulations in China where we operate our business."[73] Tianya.cn announced that it was discontinuing cooperation with Google on some projects,[74] and Sina Corporation said that it was considering whether to switch to another search provider. Mobile phone operator China Unicom Ltd. announced that it would not install Google search in its new handsets. China Mobile Ltd. commented that it was working with Microsoft's Bing and other search engines in addition to Google. Motorola said it would provide links to other search engines on its Android system phones in China.

When it made its January 12 announcement, Google postponed the introduction of its smart phone in China, and MIIT stated that Android based applications would not be affected. A spokesperson explained, "As long as it fulfills Chinese laws and regulations and has good communication with telecom operators, I think its application should have no restrictions."[75]

China had over 300 million Internet users in 2009 and was projected to have 800 million users by 2013. Beijing-based Analysys International estimated that for the first quarter 2010 Google's share of Internet advertising revenue fell from 35.6 percent to 30.9 percent and Baidu's share rose from 58.4 percent to 64 percent.[76] Although Google's market share was only half that of Baidu, Google users were better educated and had a higher average income than Baidu users. Google's searches were said to be less biased than those on Baidu, where advertisers paid for placements of their links. China was the second largest traffic generator for Google according to Jeffries & Co. Analysts estimated that Google's revenue in China was between $250 and $500 million, representing 1–2 percent of its $23.6 billion revenue.

Commentators speculated that Google employees in China might defect to Microsoft. Hao Wu of the Chinese subsidiary of TripAdvisor said, "Once Google made the announcement to possibly exit China, many tech companies were interested in poaching their employees."[77]

At the beginning of April 2010 Google started posting the number of requests it received from governments for information about its Web users and the requests to remove content from its services. Drummond stated, "We hope this tool will shine some light on the scale and scope of government requests for censorship and data around the globe."[78] China was not included because it was illegal to identify government requests. During the last half of 2009 Brazil had the most with 3,663 requests for user data and 291 requests that material be removed. The United States was second with 3,580 requests for user data and fourth in removal requests.

"'The Internet is really big,' said Wang Quiya, a 27-year-old worker in Beijing's financial district. 'Something will take [Google's] place, right?'"[79] ■

Preparation Questions

1. How much is Google sacrificing in moving its Web services to Hong Kong?
2. Is Google's move to Hong Kong an appropriate decision or an uncomfortable compromise of principles?
3. Does it matter if Google self-censors or China does the censoring if the result is the same?
4. Why is China so adamant about censoring?
5. Should Google have stayed in China? Use principles of utilitarianism, rights, and justice in answering.

De Beers and Conflict Diamonds (A)

For decades De Beers operated a cartel in the diamond industry in which it controlled nearly 80 percent of the distribution of rough diamonds.[80] De Beers also produced, primarily in South Africa, a large but decreasing share of the world's diamonds. The company founded by Cecile Rhodes and managed by the Oppenheimer family bought under long-term contracts the bulk of the world's diamonds from mining companies, maintained a large inventory, and sold rough diamonds in an orderly manner to maintain high prices. Distribution of the diamonds was through the Central Selling Organization in London, which sold in bulk to diamond cutters.[81] De Beers did not have retail operations.

This system worked well until 1990 when the production of diamonds increased and more began to leak into the market.

---

[72]*New York Times*, March 24, 2010.

[73]*Wall Street Journal*, March 24, 2010.

[74]*Wall Street Journal*, March 26, 2010.

[75]*San Jose Mercury News*, January 28, 2010.

[76]*Wall Street Journal*, April 27, 2010. Baidu's profit for the first quarter 2010 increased by 65 percent to $70.4 million, and sales increased by 60 percent to $189.6 million, compared to a year earlier.

[77]*Wall Street Journal*, February 25, 2010.

[78]*Wall Street Journal*, April 2, 2010.

[79]*New York Times*, January 17, 2010.

[80]See Deborah Spar, *The Cooperative Edge: The Internal Politics of International Cartels*, Ithaca, NY: Cornell University Press, 1994, and Prakaj Ghemawat and Sonia Marciano, "De Beers at the Millennium," Case No. 9-706-518, Harvard Business School, February 5, 2007, for detailed information on De Beers and the diamond industry.

[81]Almost all diamond cutting was done in Amsterdam, Mumbai, New York, and Tel Aviv.

The collapse of the Soviet Union and increased production there and production increases in Western Canada and elsewhere resulted in an increase in the supply of diamonds. Most diamond mining involved capital intensive shaft mining, but alluvial diamonds were found near the surface. Alluvial diamonds were easy to mine and became the source of funding for rebels and guerrillas in parts of Africa. The result was horrific civil wars, killings, torture, and mutilations. These diamonds became known as "conflict diamonds." Killings financed by conflict diamonds were most severe in Sierra Leone, Angola, and Liberia.

The world was incensed by the tragedy accompanying the conflict diamonds. The international diplomatic community and NGOs campaigned to end the killings, but it became clear that as long as conflict diamonds were available to finance the purchase of weapons the killings would continue. NGO activity increased during the 1990s led by Global Witness, which issued reports in 1998 and 1999, blaming companies as well as governments for the atrocities. The United Nations sanctioned the UNITA rebels in Angola and applied sanctions on the diamond trade in Angola and Sierra Leone, but conflict diamonds continued to find their way into the international markets.

De Beers continued its traditional policies during the 1990s but found that its stockpile of rough diamonds was skyrocketing as it bought excess diamonds. In 2000 it was forced to end its control of the diamond supply, focusing instead on the orderly distribution of diamonds. De Beers along with others in the industry was also worried that the image of diamonds could be tarnished. The high price of diamonds was in an important sense artificial, since diamonds had no intrinsic value.[82] De Beers began a consumer marketing campaign to enhance the image of diamonds as symbols of love and marriage and attempted to brand diamonds at retail.

The atrocities and killings in Africa had rallied an array of NGOs that concluded that the only way to stop the killings was to stop the flow of conflict diamonds. The NGOs pressured the United Nations, individual countries in the developed world, and the African countries to stop the flow of conflict diamonds. They also blamed the diamond companies for their role in buying the diamonds. Some of the NGOs began to label them "blood diamonds" and sought to persuade consumers not to buy diamonds. A movie entitled *Blood Diamond* was made, and rapper Kanye West released "Diamonds from Sierra Leone." The campaign posed a threat to the image that gave diamonds their value. ▪

Preparation Questions

1. How serious are the developments centering on conflict diamonds? To what extent is De Beers at risk? To what extent is De Beers responsible?

2. Identify the key actors in the case and their interests and objectives.

3. Is there a mechanism that can stop the supply of conflict diamonds, end the killings, and restore order to the market? Which parties should lead the development of this mechanism? How would the mechanism be enforced?

4. Are there ways to get around the mechanism?

Source: This case was based on public sources, including the paper by Virginia Haulfer, "The Kimberly Process, Club Goods, and Public Enforcement of a Private Regime." Working paper, University of Maryland College Park, 2007. Copyright © 2008 by David P. Baron. All rights reserved. Reprinted with permission.

De Beers and Conflict Diamonds (B)

NGOs, diamond companies, and countries where diamonds were produced and consumed formed the Kimberly Process, a self-regulation organization operating under consensus, to stem the flow of conflict diamonds by providing certification of diamonds and tracking from the diamond fields to consumers. The Kimberly Process was successful in stopping the use of conflict diamonds to fund rebel groups, which contributed to the return of peace to Liberia, Sierra Leone, and other countries.

In 2011, however, the Kimberly Process was threatened. Associated with the development of the Marange diamond mines in Zimbabwe were human rights abuses by government troops and the smuggling of diamonds. As a result of a Kimberly Process decision, diamond exports from Marange were suspended in June 2009, and a work plan was agreed to with the government of Zimbabwe. The work plan was not followed by the country, however. In 2011 Zimbabwe sought to have the suspension lifted, but the Kimberly Process participants were unable to reach a consensus on renewing diamond exports. The NGOs and northern countries refused to agree to end the suspension until the military presence at the diamond mines was reduced, human rights were respected, and independent inspectors were present to certify all diamond shipments. Suddenly, at a Kimberly Process meeting in June 2011 Chairman Matthieu Yamba announced that diamond exports could begin. The NGOs stormed out of the meeting, and Canada, the United States, Israel, and the European Union protested the action.

The Kimberly Process covered conflict diamonds used to fund hostilities against a government, but the Marange issue was different. The concern was that the Zimbabwe government under the control of 86-year old Robert Mugabe would use the diamond exports to fund violence against opposition parties and opponents of the government leading up to elections in 2012. Violence had been rampant before the previous election in which widespread voter fraud was present. International pressure led to a power sharing arrangement with the principal opposition party, but Mugabe retained control over the police

---

[82]The industrial diamond market relied primarily on synthetic diamonds.

and military. Zimbabwe and some other African countries argued that because the Marange diamond mines were owned by the government, diamond exports would not fund violence against the government and hence were not covered by the Kimberly Process.[83]

Arvind Ganesan, business and human rights director of Human Rights Watch, said, "The KP desperately needed to reform to ban the sale of all blood diamond, not just some. But the chairman chose profits over rights and might have ruined the KP in the process. Consumers aren't going to care whether

it is blood shed by governments or rebels since the diamonds are tainted either way."[84] ▣

Preparation Questions

1. Will diamonds be tainted if violence breaks out again in Zimbabwe?
2. Is it likely that the Kimberly Process can be expanded to include all blood diamonds?
3. Is there a way to save the Kimberly Process?

Siemens: Anatomy of Bribery

In November 2006, 200 German police officers raided the headquarters of Siemens AG, Europe's leading engineering company, seeking evidence pertaining to widespread bribery. The raid heightened attention to bribery issues, and at the January 2007 annual meeting CEO Klaus Kleinfeld said he was "shocked" and commented, "I can assure you that we are doing everything that we can to clear up these incidents completely." Supervisory board chairman Heinrich von Pierer said, "I am deeply distressed that these efforts were not successful enough."[85]

The raid followed extensive investigations of Siemens' activities that originated from a bank's internal scrutiny of accounts believed to be used for money laundering. The suspicions broadened, and the company initiated its own internal investigation. Siemens identified €420 million of suspicious transactions in its telecommunications unit and hired a private law firm to conduct an independent internal investigation. The law firm subsequently reported to the management board that it had identified €1.3 billion of suspicious payments since 1999. The law firm subsequently received "important … new information" that could implicate high-ranking executives. The possibility that the bribery investigation would identify high ranking officers caused the Siemens supervisory board to postpone the Entlastung or approval of the actions of the company's management board for the fiscal year 2007, seven of whom had resigned during the year.[86] The vote would have shielded the management board members from liability stemming from the ongoing bribery investigation.

Prior to 1999 German firms were allowed to deduct foreign bribes from their German taxes if those bribes were

necessary to win business. Under pressure from the United States and other countries, the Organization for Economic Cooperation and Development (OECD) adopted strong anti-bribery rules, including making bribes criminal offenses. The member states of the European Union endorsed the OECD agreement and enacted the rules as part of their national laws. The enacted OECD anti-bribery convention pertained only to bribery of public officials, and in 2002 Germany enacted an additional law extending the prohibition of bribes to employees of private firms as well as public officials.

With bribes illegal, companies took additional measures to hide their payments. Greater secrecy was required in the aftermath of September 11, as countries adopted stronger laws against money laundering. Despite the tougher laws, bribery continued as companies sought to secure foreign sales. Companies had used offshore accounts to transfer money, but once countries enacted new laws against money laundering, other routes were needed. One approach was to hire consulting companies to act on behalf of a company. For example, Siemens hired a consulting firm based in Monte Carlo and headed by Tonio Arcaini to assist in deals in the Middle East and Eastern Europe. In fiscal 2007 Siemens' auditor KPMG identified €100 million in questionable payments to more than a dozen consulting firms, including €14.5 million to Arcaini's firm. Siemens paid a total of €36.5 million to Arcaini between 2001 and 2006. Patrick Moulette, head of the anticorruption unit of the OECD observed, "It's much more difficult to detect bribery when funds are channeled through intermediaries. Today it seems this is a prevailing trend in international bribery schemes."[87]

In February 2007 CEO Kleinfeld said, "We are interested in getting to the facts, but getting to all the facts. We are talking about things that are important, that we can't take lightheartedly." In referring to obtaining change in the company's practices, he said, "You need a certain amount of time for adjustment. Don't get me wrong: this is not meant as an excuse." He added, "If you, in your mind, get it wrong and think, 'I just have to beat the competition,' you are fundamentally doing something wrong." He commented that he could make Siemens a model for

---

[83]One of the two mines was wholly-owned by the government, and the other was 50 percent government owned in partnership with a private South African company.

[84]Press Release, Human Rights Watch, June 28, 2011.

[85]*Wall Street Journal*, January 31, 2007.

[86]The German corporate governance system included a two-tiered board arrangement. The management board was responsible for the management of the company. The supervisory board was responsible for overseeing the management board and approving major transactions. The supervisory board was composed of equal representation of shareholders and representatives of workers, including labor unions. A representative of workers was also a member of the management board.

[87]*Wall Street Journal*, April 20, 2007.

corporate ethics and mused that someday this could make "a Harvard Business case on how you do it right."[88]

THE GERMAN COURT

The increased scrutiny of financial transactions after September 11 was directed at detecting money laundering used to finance terrorism. In 2003 LGT Group, the largest bank in Liechtenstein, noticed a flurry of money transfers in the account of Martha Overseas Corporation, based in Panama, and Eagle Invest & Finance AG, based in the British Virgin Islands. Martha Overseas was controlled by a Siemens telecommunications unit executive, Prodromos Mavridis, in Greece, and Eagle was controlled by another Siemens telecommunications unit executive, Reinhard Siekaczek, in Germany. After investigation LGT blocked a transaction by Siemens and notified authorities in Germany and Switzerland, as well as Siemens. Siekaczek subsequently alerted another executive, Michael Kutschenreuter, who said he then notified senior management. Swiss authorities froze €200 million of accounts suspected of belonging to Siemens.

In 2004 Kutschenreuter received a call from the Saudi Arabian consulting firm Beit Al Etisailat, a business partner of Siemens, demanding payment of $910 million for commissions on telecommunications contracts. Kutschenreuter said he reported the demand to Kleinfeld, then head of Siemens' telecommunications unit, and then CEO von Pierer. The management board subsequently approved a settlement of $50 million, according to testimony.

Three years of investigations by prosecutors in several countries revealed many more transfers involving a variety of offshore companies linked to Siemens. Prosecutors began to unravel a series of bribes associated with Siemens' telecommunications unit. In October 2007 a court in Munich ordered Siemens to pay €201 million after tracing €12 million in bribes paid to 77 government officials in Libya, Nigeria, and Russia.[89] The bribes were paid between 2001 and 2004 and were associated with Mr. Siekaczek.[90] The bribes were funneled through outside consulting contracts and Siemens executives. In testimony Siekaczek identified bribes in more than 12 countries, including Greece where payments were said to have been made to gain security systems contracts.[91] In August 2007 German prosecutors again searched the company's facilities in conjunction with alleged bribes in Serbia. Austria began an investigation into €60 million in suspicious payments.

In addition to the civil penalties and criminal charges against some former employees, Siemens risked being barred by countries from bidding on contracts. Nigeria announced that on "moral grounds" Siemens was not worthy of consideration for new contracts.

BRIBERY IN ITALY

In a separate case two Siemens employees went on trial in Darmstadt for paying €6 million to managers in the Italian company Enel to secure contracts for power generation equipment between 1999 and 2002. The two Siemens officials testified that the payments had been demanded by two managers conducting the bidding process and argued that the managers were not public officials because Enel was being privatized. One of the Siemens managers explained before the court the justification for paying the bribes, "The alternative would have been to turn down the project, which would have denied Siemens not only the business but also a foot in the door in the Italian market."[92] In May the court found the two Siemens managers guilty of breach of trust and bribery, ordered the company to forfeit €38 million in profits from the contract, and gave the managers suspended prison sentences. Siemens announced that it would appeal and stated, "The court's decision has no basis in law or in fact."

THE LABOR SCANDAL

In 2006 senior management was scheduled to receive 30 percent raises, and when the raises became public, complaints began to arise, particularly after the handset unit Siemens had sold to a Taiwanese firm went bankrupt. The pressure from workers and the public led the executives to forgo their raises and give the money to workers who had lost their jobs in the bankruptcy.[93]

In March 2007 German authorities in Nuremberg arrested Johannes Feldmayer, a member of Siemens' executive committee, in conjunction with a probe into questionable consulting contracts with the head of an independent union group, the Association of Independent Employees or AUB. The AUB was friendly to the company and offset some of the influence of IG Metall, the principal union representing Siemens employees. The head of AUB had been arrested in February for tax evasion in conjunction with the consulting contracts from Siemens.[94]

In December 2007 Siemens promoted Hannes Apitzsch to chief financial officer. Within a week the company revoked the appointment after a Siemens attorney was allowed to see a preliminary report of the prosecutor in Nuremberg in the AUB case.

MANAGEMENT TURNOVER

In April the supervisory board balked at approving the contract of Chairman von Pierer, who was under pressure as a result of the bribery revelations. He resigned and issued a statement, "Siemens has run into a difficult situation due to the in part apparent and in part alleged misconduct of a number of managers and employees.... I assume that electing a new chairman of the supervisory board will also make a contribution toward taking our company out of the headlines and bringing it back into calmer waters."[95] At the supervisory board meeting the following week the board did not renew CEO Kleinfeld's contract. Kleinfeld then announced he would leave the company when his contract expired in September.[96] He stated, "In times like these the company needs clarity about its leadership. I have therefore decided not to make myself

---

[88]*New York Times*, February 28, 2007.
[89]German law allowed a fine of only €1 million. The rest of the payment was for the profits earned as a result of the bribes.
[90]Siekaczek was indicted in 2007 for embezzling €24 million.
[91]*Wall Street Journal*, November 16, 2007.

[92]*New York Times*, March 14, 2007.
[93]*Wall Street Journal*, April 26, 2007.
[94]*Wall Street Journal*, March 28, 2007.
[95]*New York Times*, April 20, 2007.
[96]Kleinfeld became CEO of Alcoa, on whose board he had served.

available for an extension of my contract."[97] Within a week the top two executives at Siemens had stepped down.[98] In addition to the bribery allegations the resignations were also due to pressure from IG Metall, which held nearly half the seats on the supervisory board and was outraged by the questionable consulting contracts with AUB.

Siemens then hired Peter Loscher from Merck as CEO, the first outsider to head the company in its 160 year history. Gerhard Cromme, chairman of ThyssenKrupp, assumed the chairmanship of the supervisory board.

OTHER DEVELOPMENTS

In January 2007 Siemens was fined €400 million by the European Union for price fixing on electric power switching equipment. Also in 2007 a Siemens subsidiary in the United States pleaded guilty and paid a $2.5 million fine for setting up a sham company with a minority-owned firm to gain a $50 million medical equipment contract.[99]

The U.S. Securities and Exchange Commission (SEC) had begun an informal inquiry, and in April it upgraded the inquiry to a formal investigation. This gave the SEC the authority to issue subpoenas. The SEC had jurisdiction over Siemens because its shares were listed on the New York Stock Exchange. Siemens was also subject to the U.S. Foreign Corrupt Practices Act (FCPA), because it had sales of €22.9 billion and 104,000 employees in the United States. Peter von Blomberg, deputy chair of the German chapter of Transparency International, commented on the possible U.S. actions, "The potential fines are much bigger than what companies have been used to in Germany."[100] Daniel E. Karson, executive managing director of the investigative firm Kroll Associates, said, "The FCPA has now surpassed Sarbanes-Oxley for being at the nerve endings of corporate general counsels and executives."[101]

THE INTERNAL INVESTIGATION

After the November raid CEO Kleinfeld announced a "zero tolerance" for corruption. He hired Michael J. Hershman, a former Senate investigator for Watergate and a founder of Transparency International, to advise the audit committee of the supervisory board and assist in the development of a compliance system. Siemens tightened the requirements on consulting companies requiring an explanation for what the funds would be used for and requiring signatures of the senior executives and the chief compliance officer.[102] In December Kleinfeld hired the U.S. law firm Debevoise & Plimpton LLP to investigate possible wrongdoings.

Debevoise & Plimpton subsequently reported that it had identified €1.6 billion of suspicious payments of which €1.15 billion was in Siemens' telecommunications unit. Most of the rest was believed to be in the power generation unit. Prosecutors were subsequently reported to have found a €140 million slush fund in the health care unit. In January 2008 the company announced that it had found €80 million of suspicious payments in its power transmission unit.

To address employee suspicions about the internal investigations and the use of an American law firm, Siemens prepared a slide show entitled "Rumors vs. Facts." To encourage employees to cooperate in the company's investigation, Siemens established an amnesty program to encourage whistle-blowing on bribery. The amnesty program spurred the investigation and resulted in "significant new information and leads pertaining to individuals who in the past several years served on the managing board," according to a letter from Debevoise & Plimpton. Siemens extended the amnesty program through February 2008.

In January 2008 Debevoise & Plimpton wrote to the company that as a result of the amnesty program it had developed "very substantial leads" that could implicate management board members. Debevosie & Plimpton was investigating activities in 65 countries. The law firm also told the supervisory board that Siemens' long-time auditor, KPMG Germany, had not provided information to the audit committee in a timely manner.

GOING FORWARD

In fiscal 2007 Siemens had sales of €87 billion, net income of €3.9 billion, 475,000 employees, and operations in 190 countries. During fiscal 2007 Siemens spent €347 million on outside advisors including Debevoise & Plimpton. At the annual meeting in January 2008 CEO Loscher heralded a surge in quarterly sales and profits and forecast strong sales and profits for 2008. He also said that Siemens would begin negotiations with the SEC and the U.S. Department of Justice on reaching "a comprehensive and fair settlement" of bribery allegations.

At the end of 2007 Siemens began a worldwide advertising campaign with planned expenditures of over €100 million for each of the next 3 years. The "Siemens answers" campaign emphasized the company's technological prowess. Siemens had dropped from the most respected company in Germany to number 10.

The trial of Mr. Siekaczek on 58 counts of breach of trust began in May 2008. ▪

Preparation Questions

1. What are the causes of the corruption problems within Siemens?
2. What is the likely scope of those problems?
3. How should Siemens clean up its problems?
4. Evaluate the justification given by the Siemens employee in the Italian case.
5. What principles should Siemens use to help its employees avoid bribery and corruption in the future?
6. What management systems should Siemens put in place to prevent bribery and corruption?

---

[97]*New York Times*, April 26, 2007.
[98]The chief compliance officer also resigned after less than a year on the job.
[99]*Wall Street Journal*, April 26, 2007.
[100]*BusinessWeek*, November 26, 2007.
[101]*New York Times*, November 25, 2007.
[102]*Wall Street Journal*, April 20, 2007.

Source: This case was prepared from public sources by Professor David P. Baron. Copyright © 2008 by the Board of Trustees of the Leland Stanford Junior University. David P. Baron. All rights reserved. Reprinted with permission.

PART V

GlaxoSmithKline and AIDS Drugs Policy

In Africa GlaxoSmithKline (GSK) confronted the reality of the AIDS pandemic every day, and its decisions impacted thousands. There were no ready answers to the crisis, but everyone—governments, nongovernmental organizations, the media, shareholders, and others—had an opinion. GSK had to determine how to address the crisis while maintaining business viability in developing countries in the midst of the pressures swirling around it.

Throughout the late 1990s, the CEO of GSK, Stanford Graduate School of Business alumnus Dr. Jean-Pierre Garnier, was at the forefront of the controversy over antiretroviral drug pricing, patent protection, and drug access. Proactive in addressing critics, he was seen as the de facto spokesperson for the pharmaceutical industry in addressing these critical issues.

AZT DISCOVERY: THE SOURCE OF HOPE AND THE ROOT OF CONTROVERSY

The controversy traced back to 1987 when the FDA approved Burroughs Wellcome's compound, zidovudine, commonly known as AZT, as the first antiretroviral (ARV) drug for the treatment of the HIV virus. Burroughs Wellcome, expecting a small market and short life cycle for the drug and hoping to recoup development and clinical trial costs, announced that a year of the treatment would cost patients $8,000 to $10,000. This resulted in an avalanche of criticism for excessive corporate profiteering and united a number of disparate parties against Burroughs Wellcome. Activist groups, the media, and government officials led the charge.

The controversy was further fueled by the assertion of critics that its development was funded by government grants and therefore AZT should enter generic production immediately. In 1991 Barr Laboratories filed for FDA approval to produce a generic version of AZT. Burroughs Wellcome spent 5 years in court fighting to protect its patent, and in the end prevailed. The eventual commercial success of AZT increased the public outcry. Despite Burroughs Wellcome's initial belief that the market for the drug was quite small and its life cycle short due to anticipated new drugs, by 1993 AZT, marketed under the brand name Retrovir, was Burroughs Wellcome's number two product with cumulative sales of over $1 billion.

GLAXOSMITHKLINE AND AIDS DRUGS

Because of the high costs and the risks of research and development, the pharmaceutical industry experienced a wave of mergers and acquisitions in the 1990s. In 1995 Glaxo acquired Burroughs Wellcome and AZT, making the company, now GlaxoWellcome, the leader in AIDS therapy. Glaxo's own AIDS drug, lamivudine (3TC) was expected to soon be approved by the FDA, and the company hoped to combine 3TC

with AZT into a dual-drug combination. During the merger process management carefully evaluated its strategy for AIDS therapies and considered abandoning the market altogether. There were significant risks involved in pursuing new research in the controversial AIDS area, as indicated by Burroughs Wellcome's AZT experience. Some of the company's executives worried that the new company would expose itself to more public inquiry and scrutiny if it continued to pursue a leadership position in AIDS drugs.

The company's competitors were proceeding with their own efforts to develop AIDS therapies. Advanced trials were underway for a new class of protease inhibitors that showed promise when combined with the older AIDS drugs. Concerned about these new offerings and convinced that the market for AIDS therapies would remain sustainable, GlaxoWellcome decided to continue its AIDS research. In 1995 and 1996 the FDA approved four new AIDS drugs from Roche, Merck, Abbott Laboratories, and Agouron. In 1999 GlaxoWellcome added to its AIDS portfolio with amprenavir.

In 2001 GlaxoSmithKline was formed by the merger of GlaxoWellcome and SmithKline Beecham, becoming the world's second-largest pharmaceutical company. In 2002 GSK had net income of $6.941 billion on sales of $31.819 billion. Its return on equity was among the highest in the world. GSK was registered in the United Kingdom, but its top management was located in Philadelphia. GSK had been strategically pieced together through a number of mergers, combining the venerable pharmaceutical companies Glaxo, Wellcome, Burroughs, Beecham, and SmithKline and French and their drug portfolios, including some of the most successful AIDS therapies on the market.[103] In 2002 ARVs and AIDS drugs accounted for 7.9 percent of GSK's total revenues.

COMMITMENT TO DEVELOPING COUNTRIES

After the merger, GSK reaffirmed its corporate commitment to developing countries. For the past 20 years GSK, as one of the leading worldwide producers of vaccines, had offered vaccines to developing markets at preferential prices. As an indication of its continuing pledge to remain in the sub-Saharan Africa market, GSK maintained more registered patents in the countries of that region than any other pharmaceutical company, even though 90 percent of its revenues came from the larger markets of the United States and Europe. It also maintained a presence in a majority of markets in Africa and continued to serve both the public sector and the small emerging private sector. However, despite lowering prices to

---

[103]Rick Mullin, "Pharma M & A Declines, But Financing Picks Up," *Chemical Week,* March 20, 2002.

offer access to a wider population, GSK found that the local sub-Saharan African governments were either uninterested in or financially unable to provide these drugs to their citizens. With each successive drug price decrease, the private market participants benefited, but few additional drugs reached the community at large.

As corporate policy GSK did not sell its drugs below production cost even in sub-Saharan Africa. In February 2002 Garnier announced that GSK would "not profit" from AIDS drugs sold in the poorest countries, including those in sub-Saharan Africa.[104]

THE AIDS DRUG PRICING CONTROVERSY

There was no known cure for AIDS. Nonetheless, the introduction of ARVs as part of HIV clinical care made AIDS a more manageable chronic illness by achieving dramatic reductions in viral load (the level of the HIV virus in the blood), thereby arresting immune system damage. Typically, ARV-based treatment consisted of a "cocktail" of at least three drugs from the various classes of ARV drugs. This three-drug cocktail was called "Highly Active Antiretroviral Therapy" (HAART). Each class of anti-HIV drugs in a cocktail attacked the virus at a different stage of its replication in the human host lymphocyte cell. GSK combined AZT and Epivir to form Combivir, which became the company's largest selling ARV. Combivir was typically used in a combination with a protease inhibitor. As of June 2000 there were 14 FDA-approved HIV/AIDS drugs. GSK held patents on four of them.

The introduction of ARVs widened the discrepancy in the quality of AIDS care between rich and poor countries. In the United States HAART therapy led to a 70 percent decline in deaths attributable to HIV/AIDS. However, most of the 36 million people in the developing world living with HIV/AIDS did not benefit from the therapy. The World Health Organization (WHO) conservatively estimated that in 2002, 6 million people in developing countries were in need of life-sustaining ARV therapy. Yet, fewer than 250,000 had access to these therapies, and half of those were in one country, Brazil.

PRICING PRESSURE FROM MULTIPLE DIRECTIONS

As with other drugs the patents on the ARVs were owned by multinational pharmaceutical companies such as GSK, Bristol Myers Squibb, Pfizer, and Roche. Many observers argued that these patents resulted in high prices and kept needed drugs out of Africa and the rest of the developing world. Since most ARVs had been developed recently, the expiration of the patents would not occur soon. The patent for AZT would expire in 2005, but the patents on many other ARVs extended until 2014. As a result few observers expected AIDS drugs to reach the developing world during the height of the AIDS pandemic.

The first negotiations over global access to AIDS drugs began in Geneva in 1991 when 18 drug companies met with WHO representatives for a series of talks. A key topic in these discussions was the cost of new AIDS drugs—estimated to be $10,000 or more a year. The talks ended in 1993 with no resolution.

The major producers of AIDS drugs steadfastly opposed the idea of lowering prices in poor countries such as in sub-Saharan Africa. The industry maintained that the real obstacles to AIDS treatment in Africa and other low-income regions were not inflated drug prices but social, managerial, and political barriers, such as the absence of roads, shortages of doctors and nurses, the limited use of contraceptive devices, and the lack of resources to provide even basic health care to many citizens. They asserted that treatment should be borne by governments and society and not the companies per se. Moreover, the companies argued that on a continent where nearly half the population lived on less than a dollar a day, there was no price at which AIDS drugs could be commercially distributed to victims. In addition, the companies worried that without the proper infrastructure and health monitoring, the widespread use of AIDS drugs would result in an even more virulent strain of HIV that would be drug-resistant.[105]

GSK and the other pharmaceutical companies believed their pricing policies were justified by the high costs of research and development. Patents were essential to pricing successful drugs, and without patent protection, the economic model of the industry would fail, eliminating the incentive for future innovation in AIDS/HIV treatment. In the early 1990s the industry had lobbied the Clinton administration to extend domestic patent protection worldwide. These efforts were important in the creation of the Trade Related Aspects of Intellectual Property (TRIPS) agreement that was incorporated into the rules of the World Trade Organization (WTO) when it was formed in 1995. GSK and other drug companies were also concerned that if they agreed to price concessions for developing countries, they would face increased price pressures in their core U.S. and European markets. Pressure could arise from the gray market importation of drugs from low-income countries or from activist campaigns that drew attention to the price differentials between developing countries and the U.S. and European markets.

The pressure on the industry continued for much of the 1990s, fueled by the unrelenting spread of HIV. Through agencies such as WHO and UNAIDS, the United Nations and its member countries exerted pressure on the pharmaceutical companies to reduce prices to improve access to drugs for HIV/AIDS victims. Activist groups like the AIDS Coalition to Unleash Power, or ACT UP! (which was formed in response to the initial launch price of AZT), Médecins sans Frontières, and the Consumer Project on Technology led protests and campaigns that charged the industry with profiteering from history's worst pandemic, using slogans like "Pfizer's Greed Kills," "Death Under Patent," and "GlaxoSmithKline! Global Serial Killer." These sentiments were exacerbated by the remarkable

---

[104]"AHF Reports GlaxoSmithKline Head Vows to Make 'No Profit' on AIDS Drugs in Poor Countries; Advocates Ask for Public Disclosure of Costs," *Business Wire*, February 27, 2002.

[105]The distribution of ARVs and supervision of their use was crucial, since if a person did not follow a strict regimen of taking them every day, drug-resistant strains of HIV could develop. Moreover, if a patient stopped taking the ARVs for 2 weeks, resistance to the drug developed, and ARVs were then ineffective.

financial performance the drug industry experienced during this period. In 1999 the industry topped all three of *Fortune* magazine's measures of profitability and had one of the highest rates of return of any industry.

By the end of the decade public criticism had reached a crescendo. AIDS protestors badgered Vice President Gore's presidential campaign and chained themselves to desks in U.S. Trade Representative Charlene Barshefsky's office, demanding that the Clinton administration stop backing the industry against generic competitors. Activists became more aggressive and confrontational toward the drug companies, regularly taking actions such as storming into the offices of companies, including Pfizer and Bristol Myers, to disrupt their corporate events.

The media was also critical of drug companies and their handling of the AIDS drug pricing issue. Mainstream publications such as the *New York Times, Washington Post,* and the *Wall Street Journal* portrayed the pharmaceutical companies and their management as profit-centric and uncaring about the plight of poor countries. This public censure was echoed by journalists in both developed and developing countries and translated into antagonism against the drug companies and their pricing practices, domestically and internationally. The pharmaceutical industry had inadvertently become a primary recipient of the worldwide blame for the growing AIDS epidemic.

PREFERENTIAL PRICING BEGINS

In late 1999 the industry responded to the mounting criticisms. Prompted by the senior management of GSK and Bristol-Myers Squibb, the International Federation of Pharmaceutical Manufacturers Associations organized a meeting to explore solutions to the issue. Six of the major companies participated in a conference call in January 2000 at which executives at Glaxo and Bristol-Myers volunteered to draft a set of principles for an industry-led AIDS treatment initiative. After a series of talks and meetings, the companies agreed on a consensus draft to be presented to the United Nations agencies. By this time the original group of six companies had been reduced to five— Bristol-Myers Squibb, GlaxoSmithKline, Merck, Boehringer Ingelheim, and Roche. Pfizer had withdrawn, citing disagreement with the concept of preferential pricing.

Shortly after Pfizer's withdrawal, eight ACT UP! activists stormed the office of Pfizer CEO William Steere, Jr. They demanded that the company acquiesce to pressure from South African activists in the Treatment Action Campaign (TAC) and drop the price of fluconazole (diflucan) or issue a voluntary license for the importation of generic versions of the drug from a less expensive supplier. Fluconazole was effective in treating crypto-coccal meningitis, the most common AIDS-related systemic fungal infection. Fluconazole was priced at $8.92 per pill in South Africa. In Thailand, where Pfizer did not have exclusive marketing rights, fluconazole cost only $0.29 per pill.[106] The average daily wage in South Africa in 1999 was about $7.00. The activists claimed that it was unacceptable for a corporation to maintain high prices while AIDS patients in poor

countries were dying of treatable diseases. ACT UP! threatened to bring the issue to the attention of politicians and investors and claimed that Pfizer's actions were socially unconscionable. In April 2000 Pfizer announced that instead of lowering the price it would give away fluconazole to 3.6 million victims in South Africa. Two months later Pfizer extended the offer to 50 other less-developed countries.

Pfizer's initiative was applauded by advocacy groups. It immediately shifted the onus to the remaining five companies to follow Pfizer's lead. In particular, TAC called on GSK to make AZT available to pregnant women to reduce the risk of mother-to-child transmission. The five remaining pharmaceutical companies lobbied the U.N. agencies—UNAIDS, WHO, UNICEF, U.N. Development Program—and the World Bank to consider their proposed preferential pricing policy. Finally on May 11, 2000, the five companies and the United Nations issued a joint Statement of Intent for an Accelerating Access initiative as a basis for preferential pricing for HIV/AIDS medicines in developing countries. The concessions were to be made on a country-by-country basis and involved significant restrictions on the resale and use of the drugs. The industry and the United Nations publicly hailed the initiative as a major step forward. Still, critics remained unhappy and charged the drug companies with continuing to maintain high prices by offering discounts selectively. The critics were angry that the language of the initiative was vague and that none of the drug companies, with the exception of GSK, had made firm commitments to exact price reductions.

In 2002 United Nations Secretary General Kofi Annan established the independent Global Fund to Fight AIDS, Tuberculosis and Malaria with $2.1 billion in funding to purchase AIDS drugs and conduct AIDS prevention programs in Africa. The funds came primarily from governments and the Gates Foundation. The Gates Foundation emphasized prevention programs over treatment of AIDS victims as the most cost effective means of addressing the AIDS pandemic.

COMPULSORY LICENSING

Another issue confronting GSK was the decision of countries such as Thailand and Brazil to invoke compulsory licensing under TRIPS and either allow local manufacturers to produce ARVs based on patented formulas or import generic substitutes for the patented drugs. Although not directly affected by the decisions in Thailand and Brazil, GSK watched with great interest the unfolding of negotiations in both countries. Together with other major drug producers, GSK was a strong proponent of intellectual property protection and for many years had lobbied the U.S. government to support patent rights and the TRIPS agreement. However, at the end of 1999 the U.S. government reversed its stance and announced that it would not object to compulsory licensing in situations where a medical emergency justified it.

This represented a potentially serious threat to GSK's ability to protect its patented products from generic competitors in overseas markets. Management feared that many countries might follow the examples of Thailand and Brazil and use the opportunity to import or make cheap imitation drugs at the expense of patent holders. The decision by the U.S. government meant that foreign governments would not face trade sanctions if they used compulsory licensing.

In 1997 the South African parliament granted its Ministry of Health the power to permit parallel importation of drugs produced under license in another country. In February 1998, 39 major drug companies (including GSK), represented by the Pharmaceutical Manufacturers Association of South Africa (PMA), filed a lawsuit against the Government of South Africa to strike down the law on the grounds that it breached international trade agreements such as TRIPS and was unconstitutional, since it gave the health minister arbitrary power to ignore patent rights. The lawsuit and subsequent trial drew strong criticism from the media and advocacy groups, and in April 2001 after the trial had been under way for 6 weeks, the PMA withdrew its lawsuit.

On February 7, 2001, Cipla, an Indian generic drug manufacturer, offered to supply a triple-combination therapy for HIV/AIDS at $350 per patient per year to Médecins sans Frontières, an independent medical and humanitarian aid agency working in Africa. Cipla was able to manufacture these drugs under Indian patent law and export them at a fraction of the price at which the drugs were available from their primary manufacturers. It also offered to sell the therapy for $600 per patient per year to the governments of poor countries on the condition that the recipient governments provide the drugs for free to those with HIV/AIDS. The comparative cost of this regimen in developed nations was $10,000 to $15,000 annually. Cipla's offer put pressure on other pharmaceutical companies to reduce their prices. Cipla also began to produce AZT and by the end of 2002 was producing 10 of the 14 most widely used AIDS drugs. In May Merck announced that it would sell its AIDS drug Crixivan for $600 per patient per year and Stocrin for $500 per patient per year in the developing world. According to the company, it made no profit at these prices. Shortly thereafter, Boehringer Ingelheim, Bristol-Myers Squibb, and Abbott Laboratories followed with similar discount offers.

Preferential pricing and compulsory licensing posed another challenge to the patent holders of AIDS drugs. Corrupt officials could intercept AIDS drugs and smuggle them into European countries and the United States, where they could be sold at market prices. GSK sought to avoid this by providing the preferentially priced drugs directly to health care providers. Nevertheless, corruption and re-exportation posed a problem for its markets in developed countries.

MEDIA COVERAGE

Extremely critical of the pharmaceutical industry on the drug pricing and access issue, the press had been relentless in its pressure on GSK. Beginning with Burroughs Wellcome's initial announcement of the price for AZT, the news media had successfully reframed HIV/AIDS drug pricing as a social justice and moral issue.

Even though GSK had lowered prices and negotiated with sub-Saharan Africa governments to provide the drugs to their citizens, the press reports continued to point to pricing as the primary barrier to drug access. In particular, the media in

socially conscious Western countries faulted GSK and other pharmaceutical companies for not doing enough to ensure that those in sub-Saharan Africa had access to HIV/AIDS medicines. Initially, GSK was reactive in dealing with this pressure, often addressing questions and concerns with complex justifications about differential pricing and the specific positive steps that GSK had taken. Additionally, GSK was hesitant to fault publicly the governments that it had to work with on a regular basis.

ACTIVIST GROUPS

The activist groups were concerned about a broad range of issues, from HIV/AIDS itself to social justice, consumer rights, and humanitarian relief. The challenge for GSK lay in how to address the concerns of these often hostile groups without impairing its business objectives. The power and influence of the advocacy organizations could not be ignored. They were well organized, had access to funds, and possessed considerable leverage in shaping public opinion. Their campaigns drew considerable attention from the media and politicians and were effective in galvanizing support from the public for their cause. GSK management recognized this and was responsive to the major activist groups. Those groups, however, were generally distrustful of major corporations and continued to publicly pressure the drug companies to change their policies.

The AIDS Healthcare Foundation (AHF), an NGO that was the world's largest specialized provider of HIV medical care, launched a multipronged campaign against GSK. First, AHF sought to convince CalPERS, the California state retirement system, which held $1 billion of GSK's shares, to pressure the company to lower ARV prices. Second, AHF filed a lawsuit challenging GSK's patent on AZT, arguing that the research had been financed by public funds. Third, AHF filed a complaint against GSK in South Africa, where AHF operated a clinic, challenging GSK's pricing and other policies in South Africa. Fourth, it filed a false advertising lawsuit in California against GSK. Fifth, it organized protests and demonstrations against GSK.

GSK'S RESPONSE

Social Responsibility Committee

Despite the commitment made to the Accelerating Access initiative in 2000, GSK continued to receive negative press coverage of its response to the AIDS crisis. The company faced unrelenting pressure to cut further its prices and extend its discounts to a broader group of countries and organizations. The intense public scrutiny in turn triggered concern among the company's shareholders about the reputational risks involved in failing to address the issue of access to needed medicines. GSK spent considerable time in discussions with its key institutional shareholders to address these concerns.

In response to the pressure GSK established a corporate social responsibility committee, chaired by Sir Richard Sykes, GSK's new nonexecutive chairman, to review the company's policies on access. Specifically, the committee was charged with crafting a policy response for GSK not only to HIV/AIDS but to the broader issue of access to drugs in the developing world. The committee would also advise the board of directors on issues of significance in the relationship between the company and society and would regularly review the company's policy on health care in the developing world.

On February 21, 2001, GSK announced that it would extend its preferential pricing offer for HIV/AIDS medicines beyond governments to include not-for-profit nongovernmental organizations (NGOs), such as international agencies, aid groups, and churches and charities that had facilities in place to appropriately monitor and treat patients. GSK also offered preferential prices on ARVs to employers in Africa that provided HIV/AIDS care and treatment directly to their employees through workplace clinics. Specifically, the price of Ziagen, which sold for $10.68 a day in the U.S. for the standard two-pill treatment, was reduced to $3.80 a day; Trizivir, a potent, triple-drug combination pill taken twice a day at a cost of $27.92 in the U.S. was priced at $6.60 in low-income countries; and Agenerase, a protease inhibitor that cost $18.50 a day for 16 pills in the U.S., was priced at $8.70 a day under the new preferential pricing plan. In addition to the AIDS drugs, GSK also reduced the price of its malarial pill Malarone from the U.S. list price of $52.71 for a full course of 12 tablets to $19.20 in the developing world.

Nonetheless, Garnier conceded that even with these steep discounts, the new prices would remain out of reach for most patients in the developing world. "We're not naive about the fact that compared to the means in these countries, everything is overpriced, even the generics," he said in an interview.

CORPORATE POLICY: "FACING THE CHALLENGE"

One unexpected result of the criticism of GSK's policies concerning access to ARVs in sub-Saharan Africa was the impact on the morale of employees, shareholders, and partners. In an effort to reassure its internal constituents, in June 2001 GSK published "Facing the Challenge," a report articulating the company's product, pricing, and partnership commitments to increased access to medicines for patients in need in developing countries. Reshaping the role of GSK as a partner in the global fight against AIDS, the report was a turning point for the company and its stakeholders. Garnier said of GSK's new partner role:

> As a leading international research based pharmaceutical company, GlaxoSmithKline can make a real difference to health care in the developing world. We believe this is both an ethical imperative and key to business success. "Facing the Challenge" is a signal of our intention and commitment to making access to medicines a continued priority of our company. We are extending our preferential pricing offers to more products, to more countries and to more customer groups, in an effort to secure greater access for patients to treatment that is

both appropriate and sustainable. Our activities will be undertaken together with organizations that have relevant specialized knowledge, such as governments, international agencies, charities and academic institutions. The pharmaceutical industry can play an important role, but it does not have the mandate, expertise or resources to deliver health care unilaterally to developing countries.

GSK'S CHALLENGE GOING FORWARD

GSK faced an enormous challenge at the beginning of 2003. How could it address the continuing concerns raised by activists, the media, and governments, while simultaneously serving the interests of GSK stakeholders? How should social responsibility be balanced against generating profits? Should it go further than its current commitment and begin to deliver health care in the poorest countries? What should be the cost basis on which it prices its ARVs—for example, the marginal cost of producing the drugs or the average cost, taking into account its research and development costs? Should it make further reductions in its prices for its ARVs? How should GSK deal with the possibility of AIDS drugs supplied to Africa being diverted to Europe and the United States? Should GSK voluntarily license its ARVs to local drug producers in South Africa or other countries? Should it match Cipla's prices? How should it price its next AIDS drug currently in the pipeline? Should it continue to invest in research and development on drug therapies whose prices would likely be driven down by criticism from activists, governments, and the media or by patent infringements by companies in developing countries? GSK participated along with other pharmaceutical companies in TRIPS negotiations regarding compulsory licensing and parallel imports. What should GSK do to protect its intellectual property while providing access to drugs under patent for people and countries in need? More generally, what role should social concerns and societal pressure play in GSK's business strategy? And how could GSK better manage nonmarket considerations, both now and in the future? ▪

Preparation Questions

1. The European Union expressed concern about the availability of pharmaceuticals to poor countries. The Commission of the European Union held an annual meeting of its Health and TRIPS Issue Group on the subject of "Access to Essential Medicines." GSK was an active participant in the meetings, the next of which was scheduled for April 28, 2003. Garnier had agreed to attend the meeting and understood that he would be questioned about GSK's AIDS drugs policy. In the role of CEO Garnier, would you announce any changes in the company's policy? What defense would you give in support of either the current policy or the new policy you plan to announce?

2. What position should Garnier take on TRIPS and compulsory licensing?

REFERENCES

Abegglen, James C., and George Stalk, Jr. (1985). *Kaisha, the Japanese Corporation.* New York: Basic Books.

Aggarwal, Vinod K. (Ed.) (2001). *Winning in Asia, European Style.* New York: Palgrave Macmillan.

Akerlof, George A. (1970). "The Market for 'Lemons': Qualitative Uncertainty and the Market Mechanism." *Quarterly Journal of Economics,* 84, 488–500.

Alesina, Alberto, and Romain Wacziarg. (1999). "'Is Europe Going Too Far?' Carnegie-Rochester Conference on Public Policy." *Journal of Monetary Economics,* 51, 1–42.

Alpern, Kenneth D. (1988). "Moral Dimensions of the Foreign Corrupt Practices Act: Comments on Pastin and Hooker." In Thomas Donaldson and Patricia H. Werhane (Eds.), *Ethical Issues in Business: A Philosophical Approach,* 54–59. Englewood Cliffs, NJ: Prentice Hall.

American Society of Newspaper Editors. (1999). "Examining Our Credibility: Examining Credibility, Explaining Ourselves." Reston, VA. www.asne.org.

Andreoni, James, and B. Douglas Bernheim. (2009). "Social Image and the 50-50 Norm: A Theoretical and Experimental Analysis of Audience Effects." *Econometrica,* 77, 1607–1636.

Ansolabehere, Stephen, John de Figueiredo, and James M. Snyder. (2003). "Why Is There So Little Money in U.S. Politics?" *Journal of Economic Perspectives,* 17, 105–130.

Areeda, Phillip, and Herbert Hovenkamp. (2004). *Fundamentals of Antitrust Law.* New York: Aspen Law & Business.

Areeda, Phillip, and Louis Kaplow. (1997). *Antitrust Analysis: Problems, Text, and Cases* (5th ed.). New York: Aspen Publishers.

Areeda, Phillip, and Donald Turner. (1975, February). "Predatory Pricing and Related Practices under Section 2 of the Sherman Act." *Harvard Law Review,* 88, 697–733.

Argenti, Paul A. (2004). "Collaborating with Activists: How Starbucks Works with NGOs." *California Management Review,* 47, 91–116.

Arrow, Kenneth A. (1963). *Social Choice and Individual Values* (2nd ed.). New York: Wiley.

Banerjee, Abhijit V., and Esther Duflo. (2011). *Poor Economics: A Radical Rethinking of the Way to Fight Global Poverty.* New York: PublicAffairs.

Banerjee, Abhijit V., Esther Duflo, Rachel Glennerster, and Cynthia Kinnan. (2009). "The Miracle of Microfinance? Evidence from a Randomized Evaluation." Working Paper, Massachusetts of Technology, Cambridge, MA.

Baron, David P. (1983). *The Export-Import Bank: An Economic Analysis.* New York: Academic Press.

_____. (1995a). "The Nonmarket Strategy System." *Sloan Management Review,* 37(Fall), 73–85.

_____. (1995b). "Integrated Strategy: Market and Nonmarket Components." *California Management Review,* 37(Winter), 47–65.

_____. (1999). "Integrated Market and Nonmarket Strategies in Client and Interest Group Politics." *Business and Politics,* 1(April), 7–34.

_____. (2000). *Business and Its Environment* (3rd ed.). Upper Saddle River, NJ: Prentice Hall.

_____. (2001). "Private Politics, Corporate Social Responsibility, and Integrated Strategy." *Journal of Economics & Management Strategy,* 10(Spring), 7–45.

_____. (2005). "Competing for the Public Through the News Media." *Journal of Economics and Management Strategy,* 14, 339–376.

_____. (2006). *Business and Its Environment* (5th ed.). Upper Saddle River, NJ: Prentice Hall.

_____. (2007). "Corporate Social Responsibility and Social Entrepreneurship." *Journal of Economics and Management Strategy,* 16, 683–717.

_____. (2008). "Managerial Contracting and Corporate Social Responsibility." *Journal of Public Economics,* 92, 268–288.

_____. (2009). "A Positive Theory of Moral Management, Social Pressure, and Corporate Social Performance." *Journal of Economics and Management Strategy,* 18, 7–43.

Baron, David P., and David Besanko. (2001). "Strategy, Organization, and Incentives: Global Corporate Banking at Citibank." *Industrial and Corporate Change,* 10, 1–36.

Baron, David P., and Daniel Diermeier. (2007). "Strategic Activism and Nonmarket Strategy." *Journal of Economics and Management Strategy,* 16, 599–634.

Baron, David P., Maretno A. Harjoto, and Hoje Jo. (2011). "The Economics and Politics of Corporate Social Responsibility." *Business and Politics,* 13(2), Article 1.

Barone, Michael, and Chuck McCutcheon. (2011). *The Almanac of American Politics 2012.* Washington, DC: National Journal.

Bartlett, Christopher A., and Sumantra Ghoshal. (1989). *Managing Across Borders: The Transnational Solution.* Boston, MA: Harvard Business School.

Baysinger, Barry D., Gerald D. Keim, and Carl P. Zeithaml. (1985). "An Empirical Evaluation of the Potential for Including Shareholders in Corporate Constituency Programs." *Academy of Management Journal,* 28, 180–200.

Becker, Gary S. (1983). "A Theory of Competition and Pressure Groups for Political Influence." *Quarterly Journal of Economics,* 98, 371–400.

Bellis, Jean-Francois. (1989). "The EEC Antidumping System." In John H. Jackson and Edwin A. Vermulst (Eds.), *Antidumping Laws and Practice,* 41–97. Ann Arbor: University of Michigan Press.

Benkard, C. L. (2000). "Learning and Forgetting: The Dynamics of Aircraft Production." *American Economic Review,* 90, 1034–1054.

Benmelech, Efraim, and Jennifer Dlugosz. (2009). "The Alchemy of CDO Credit Ratings." *Journal of Monetary Economics,* 56, 617–634.

——. (2010). "The Credit Rating Crisis." *NBER Macroeconomics Annual,* 24, 161–208.

Bentham, Jeremy. (1789). *An Introduction to the Principles of Morals and Legislation.* Reprint, Buffalo, NY: Prometheus Books (1988).

Berg, Joyce, John Dickhaut, and Kevin McCabe. (1995). "Trust, Reciprocity, and Social History." *Games and Economic Behavior,* 10, 122–142.

Berle, Adolph A., and Gardiner C. Means. (1932). *The Modern Corporation and Private Property.* Reprint, Buffalo, NY: W. S. Wein (1982).

Bernstein, Marver H. (1955). *Regulation by Independent Commission.* Princeton, NJ: Princeton University Press.

Besanko, David, David Dranove, Mark Shanley, and Scott Schaefer. (2009). *The Economics of Strategy* (5th ed.). New York: Wiley.

Binmore, Kenneth M. (1994). *Game Theory and the Social Contract.* Cambridge, MA: MIT Press.

Black, Henry C. (1983). *Black's Law Dictionary* (abridged 5th ed.). St. Paul, MN: West Publishing.

Blount, Sally. (1995). "When Social Outcomes Aren't Fair: The Effect of Causal Attributions on Preferences." *Organization Behavior & Human Decision Processes,* 63, 131–144.

Boardman, Anthony E., David H. Greenberg, Aidan R. Vining, and David L. Weimer. (2006). *Cost-Benefit Analysis: Concepts and Practice* (4th ed.). Upper Saddle River, NJ: Prentice Hall.

Bouchoux, Deborah E. (2001). *Protecting Your Company's Intellectual Property.* New York: AMACOM.

Bowie, Norman E. (1990). "Business Ethics and Cultural Relativism." In Peter Madsen and Jay M. Shafritz (Eds.), *Essentials of Business Ethics,* 366–382. New York: Penguin Books.

Brady, David, and Craig Volden. (1998). *Revolving Gridlock.* Boulder, CO: Westview Press.

Brañas-Garza, Pablo. (2007). "Promoting Helping Behavior with Framing in Dictator Games." *Journal of Economic Psychology,* 28, 477–486.

Brandt, Richard B. (1959). *Ethical Theory.* Upper Saddle River, NJ: Prentice Hall.

——. (1979). *A Theory of the Good and the Right.* Oxford, UK: Clarendon Press.

Brenner, Ian. (2005). "Managing Risk in an Uncertain World." *Harvard Business Review,* June, 51–60.

Breyer, Stephen. (1982). *Regulation and Its Reform.* Cambridge, MA: Harvard University Press.

Brock, William A., and David S. Evans. (1986). *The Economics of Small Business.* New York: Holmes and Meyer.

Brulle, Robert J., and J. Craig Jenkins. (2010). "Civil Society and the Environment: Understanding the Dynamics and Impacts of the U.S. Environmental Movement." In Thomas P. Lyon (Ed.), *Good Cop, Bad Cop: Environmental NGOs and Their Strategies Toward Business,* 73–102. Washington, DC: RFF Press.

Bulow, Jeremy, and Paul Klemperer. (1998). "The Tobacco Deal." *Brookings Papers on Economic Activity.* Washington, DC: Brookings.

Business Roundtable. (1981). "Statement on Corporate Responsibility." New York.

——. (1990). "Corporate Governance and American Competitiveness." New York.

——. (1997). "Statement on Corporate Governance." New York.

Calabresi, Guido, and Douglas A. Melamed. (1972). "Property Rules, Liability Rules and Inalienability: One View of the Cathedral." *Harvard Law Review,* 85, 1089–1128.

Calingaert, Michael. (1993). "Government-Business Relations in the European Community." *California Management Review,* Winter, 118–133.

Camerer, Colin F., and Robin M. Hogarth. (1999). "The Effects of Financial Incentives in Experiments: A Review and Capital-Labor Framework." *Journal of Risk and Uncertainty,* 19, 7–42.

Cameron, Lisa A. (1999). "Raising the Stakes in the Ultimatum Game: Experimental Evidence from Indonesia." *Economic Inquiry,* 37, 47–59.

Campbell, Thomas J., Daniel P. Kessler, and George B. Shepherd. (1998). "The Link Between Liability Reforms and Productivity: Some Empirical Evidence." In *Brookings Papers in Economic Activity: Microeconomics.* Washington, DC: Brookings.

Carp, Robert A., and Ronald Stidham. (2001). *The Federal Courts* (4th ed.). Washington, DC: CQ Press.

Carpenter, Jeffrey, Eric Verhoogen, and Stephen Burks. (2005). "The effects of stakes in distribution experiments." *Economic Letters,* 86, 395–398.

Casadesus-Masanell, Ramon, Michael Crooke, Forest Reinhardt, and Vishal Vasishth. (2009). "Households' Willingness to Pay for 'Green' Goods: Evidence from Patagonia's Introduction of Organic Cotton Sportswear." *Journal of Economics and Management Strategy,* 18, 203–233.

Cater, Douglass. (1959). *The Fourth Branch of Government.* Boston, MA: Houghton Mifflin.

Cecchini, Paolo, with Michel Catinat, and Alexis Jacquemin. (1988). *The European Challenge 1992: The Benefits of a Single Market.* Aldershot, UK: Wildwood.

Chandler, Alfred D. (1977). *The Visible Hand.* Cambridge, MA: Harvard University Press.

Chandler, Alfred D., and Richard S. Tedlow. (1985). *The Coming of Managerial Capitalism: A Casebook on the History of American Economic Institutions.* Homewood, IL: Richard D. Irwin.

Chang, Wejen. (1998). "Confucian Theory of Norms and Human Rights." In Wm. Theodore de Bary and Tu Weiming (Eds.), *Confucianism and Human Rights,* 117–141. New York: Columbia University Press.

Chavis, Larry, and Phillip Leslie. (2008). "Consumer Boycotts: The Impact of the Iraq War on French Wines." *Quantitative Marketing and Economics,* 7, 37–67.

Cheng, Chung-ying. (1998). "Transforming Confucian Virtues into Human Rights: A Study of Human Agency and Potency in

Confucian Ethics." In Wm. Theodore de Bary and Tu Weiming (Eds.), *Confucianism and Human Rights,* 142–153. New York: Columbia University Press.

Cherry, Todd L., Peter Frykblom, and Jason F. Shogren. (2002). "Hardnose the Dictator." *American Economic Review,* 92, 1218–1221.

Chinn, Menzie D., and Jeffry A. Frieden. (2011). *Lost Decades: The Making of America's Debt Crisis and the Long Recovery.* New York: W.W. Norton.

Christiansen, Flemming, and Shirin M. Rai. (1996). *Chinese Politics and Society: An Introduction.* Upper Saddle River, NJ: Prentice Hall.

Cini, Michelle, and Lee McGowan. (1998). *Competition Policy in the European Union.* London, UK: Macmillan.

Clark, Robert C. (1985). "Agency Costs versus Fiduciary Duties." In John W. Pratt and Richard J. Zeckhauser (Eds.), *Principals and Agents: The Structure of Business,* 55–79. Boston, MA: Harvard Business School.

Clarkson, Kenneth W., and Timothy J. Muris (Eds.). (1981). *The Federal Trade Commission Since 1970.* Cambridge, UK: Cambridge University Press.

Coase, Ronald H. (1960). "The Problem of Social Cost." *The Journal of Law and Economics,* 3 (October), 1–44.

Coen, David. (1999). "The Impact of U.S. Lobbying Practice on the European Business-Government Relationship." *California Management Review,* 41, 27–44.

Coffee, John C., Jr., Louis Lowenstein, and Susan Rose-Ackerman. (1988). *Knights, Raiders & Targets: The Impact of the Hostile Takeover.* New York: Oxford University Press.

Cohen, Henry. (1990, November). *Products Liability: A Legal Overview.* Washington, DC: Congressional Research Service, Library of Congress.

Committee for the Study of Economic and Monetary Union. (1989). *Report of Economic and Monetary Union in the European Community.* Brussels, Belgium.

Condorcet, Marquis de. (1785). *Essai sur l'Application de l'Analyse à la Probabilité des Decisions Rendues a la Pluralité des Voix.* Reprint, New York: Chelsea, 1972.

———. (2009). *Federal Regulatory Directory* (14th ed.). Washington, DC: CQ Press.

Conroy, Michael E. (2007). *Branded! How the 'Certification Revolution' is Transforming Global Corporations.* Gabriola Island, British Columbia, Canada: New Society Publications.

Cook, Timothy E. (1989). *Making Laws & Making News: Media Strategies in the U.S. House of Representatives.* Washington, DC: Brookings.

Cooter, Robert, and Thomas Ulen. (1988). *Law and Economics.* Reading, MA: Addison-Wesley.

———. (1997). *Law and Economics* (2nd ed.). Reading, MA: Addison-Wesley.

———. (2004). *Law and Economics* (4th ed.) Boston, MA: Addison-Wesley.

———. (2007). *Law and Economics* (5th ed.). Boston, MA: Addison-Wesley.

Cull, Robert, Asli Demirguç-Kunt, and Jonathan Morduch. (2008). "Microfinance Meets the Market." World Bank Policy Research Working Paper No. 4630, World Bank, Washington, DC.

Cummins Engine Company. (1980, October). *Cummins Practice.* Columbus, IN.

Cutler, David M., Edward L. Glaeser, and Jesse M. Shapiro. (2003). "Why Have Americans Become More Obese?" *Journal of Economic Perspectives,* 17, 93–118.

Dal Bó, Ernesto, and Pedro Dal Bó. (2009). "'Do the Right Thing:' The Effects of Moral Suasion on Cooperation." Working Paper, University of California-Berkeley.

Dalton, D., C. Daily, A. Ellstrand, and J. Johnson. (1998). "Meta-analytic Reviews of Board Composition, Leadership Structure, and Financial Performance." *Strategic Management Review,* 19, 269–290.

Dalton, Dan R., and Michael B. Metzger. (1993). "Integrity Testing for Personnel Selection: An Unsparing Perspective." *Journal of Business Ethics,* 12, 147–156.

Dana, Jason, Roberto A. Weber, and Jason Xi Kuang. (2007). "Exploiting Moral Wiggle Room: Experiments Demonstrating an Illusory Preference for Fairness." *Economic Theory,* 33, 67–80.

Davidson, Wallace N., Dan L. Worrell, and Abuzar El-Jelly. (1995). "Influencing Managers to Change Unpopular Corporate Behavior Through Boycotts and Divestitures." *Business & Society,* 34(August), 171–196.

Davies, Kert. (2010). "Greenpeace." In Thomas P. Lyon (Ed.), *Good Cop, Bad Cop: Environmental NGOs and Their Strategies Toward Business,* 195–207. Washington, DC: RFF Press.

De Bary, William T. (1991). *The Trouble with Confucianism.* Cambridge, MA: Harvard University Press.

deFigueiredo, Rui J. P., Jr., and Geoff Edwards. (2007). "Does Private Money Buy Public Policy? Campaign Contributions and Regulatory Outcomes in Telecommunications." *Journal of Economics and Management Strategy,* 16, 547–576.

De George, Richard T. (1993). "International Business Ethics." *Business Ethics Quarterly,* 4, 1–9.

Delmas, Magali. (2000). "Barriers and Incentives to the Adoption of ISO 14001 in the United States." *Duke Environmental Law and Policy Forum,* Fall, 1–38.

———. (2001). "Stakeholders and Competitive Advantage: The Case of ISO 14001." *Production and Operation Management,* 10, 343–358.

Derthick, Martha, and Paul J. Quirk. (1985). *The Politics of Deregulation.* Washington, DC: Brookings.

Deyo, Frederic C. (Ed.). (1987). *The Political Economy of the New Asian Industrialism.* Ithaca, NY: Cornell University Press.

Diermeier, Daniel. (2011). *Reputation Rules.* New York: McGraw-Hill.

Dollinger, Marc J. (1988). "Confucian Ethics and Japanese Management Practices." *Journal of Business Ethics,* 7, 575–584.

Donaldson, Thomas. (1989). *The Ethics of International Business.* Oxford, UK: Oxford University Press.

———. (1996). "Values in Tension: Ethics Away from Home." *Harvard Business Review,* September–October, 48–49, 52–56, 58, 60, 62.

Durlabhji, Subhash. (1990). "The Influence of Confucianism and Zen on the Japanese Organization." *Akron Business and Economic Review,* 21(2), 31–45.

Easterbrook, Frank H., and Daniel R. Fischel. (1981). "The Proper Role of a Target's Management in Responding to a Tender Offer." *Harvard Law Review,* April, 1161–1204.

Eckel, Catherine C., and Philip J. Grossman. (1994). "Altruism in Anonymous Dictator Games." *Games and Economic Behavior,* 16, 181–191.

Edley, Christopher F., Jr. (1990). *Administrative Law.* New Haven, CT: Yale University Press.

Elfenbein, Daniel W., and Brian McManus. (2010). "A Greater Price for a Greater Good? Evidence that Consumers Pay More for Charity-Linked Products." *American Economic Journal: Economic Policy,* 2, 28–60.

Elkington, John. (1997). *Cannibals with Forks: The Triple Bottom Line of 21st Century Business.* Stony Creek, CT: New Society Publishers.

Ellerman, A. Denny, Paul L. Joskow, and David Harrison, Jr. (2003). *Emissions Trading in the U.S.: Experience, Lessons, and Considerations for Greenhouse Gases.* Arlington, VA: Pew Center for Global Climate Change.

Ellickson, Robert C. (1991). *Order Without Law.* Cambridge, MA: Harvard University Press.

Elzinga, Kenneth G., and William Briet. (1976). *The Antitrust Penalties: A Study in Law and Economics.* New Haven, CT: Yale University Press.

Emerson, Michael, Michael Aujean, Michael Catinat, Phillippe Goybet, and Alexis Jacquemin. (1988). *The Economics of 1992.* Oxford, UK: Oxford University Press.

Epstein, Edward Jay. (1973). *News from Nowhere.* New York: Random House.

Epstein, Marc J., and Karen E. Schnietz. (2002). "Measuring the Cost of Environmental and Labor Protests to Globalization: An Event Study of the Failed 1999 Seattle WTO Talks." *The International Trade Journal,* XVI, 129–160.

Epstein, Richard A. (1980). *A Theory of Strict Liability.* San Francisco: Cato Institute.

Esty, Daniel C. (1994). *Greening the GATT: Trade, Environment, and the Future.* Washington, DC: Institute for International Economics.

_____. (2001). "Bridging the Trade-Environment Divide." *Journal of Economic Perspectives,* 15, 113–130.

European Commission. (1988). "Social Dimensions of the Internal Market." Commission Working Paper, SEC (88) 1148, Brussels, Belgium.

Evans, Fred J. (1987). *Managing the Media.* New York: Quorum Books.

Fairbank, John K. (1992). *China: A New History.* Cambridge, MA: Harvard University Press.

Fama, Eugene F., and Michael C. Jensen. (1983). "Separation of Ownership and Control." *Journal of Law & Economics,* 26(June), 301–325.

Faruqi, Ahmad, and Sanem Sergici. (2008). *Household Response to Dynamic Pricing of Electricity: A Survey of Seventeen Pricing Experiments.* Cambridge, MA: The Brattle Group.

Federal Trade Commission. (1990). "The Hart-Scott-Rodino Antitrust Improvements Act of 1976." Washington, DC.

Fehr, Ernst, Simon Gächter, and Georg Kirchsteiger. (1997). "Reciprocity as a Contract Enforcement Device: Experimental Evidence." *Econometrica,* 65, 833–860.

Feinstein, Alvan R. (1988). "Scientific Standards in Epidemiologic Studies of the Menace of Daily Life." *Science,* 242(December), 1257–1263.

Fink, Steven. (2002). *Crisis Management: Planning for the Inevitable.* Lincoln, NE: Authors Guild Backprint.com Edition.

Fiorino, Daniel J. (2006). *The New Environmental Regulation.* Cambridge, MA: MIT Press.

Fiorina, Morris P. (1989). *Congress: Keystone of the Washington Establishment* (2nd ed.). New Haven, CT: Yale University Press.

Fishwick, Frank. (1993). *Making Sense of Competition Policy.* London, UK: Kogan Page.

Fong, Christina M., and Felix Oberholzer-Gee. (2011). "Truth in giving: Experimental Evidence on the Welfare Effects of Informed Giving to the Poor." *Journal of Public Economics,* 95, 436–444.

Fowler, Linda L., and Ronald G. Shaiko. (1987). "The Grass Roots Connection: Environmental Activists and Senate Roll Calls." *American Journal of Political Science,* 31(August), 484–510.

Francis, John. (1993). *The Politics of Regulation: A Comparative Perspective.* Oxford, UK: Blackwell.

Frank, Reuven. (1991). *Out of Thin Air: The Brief Wonderful Life of Network News.* New York: Simon & Schuster.

Franklin, Marc A., and Robert L. Rabin. (1996). *Cases and Materials on Tort Law and Alternatives* (6th ed.). Mineola, NY: Foundation Press.

Freeman, R. Edward. (1984). *Strategic Management: A Stakeholder Approach.* Boston, MA: Pitman.

Freeman, R. Edward, and Daniel R. Gilbert, Jr. (1988). *Corporate Strategy and the Search for Ethics.* Upper Saddle River, NJ: Prentice Hall.

Friedman, Milton. (1962). *Capitalism and Freedom.* Chicago: University of Chicago Press.

_____. (1970). "The Social Responsibility of Business Is to Increase Its Profits." *New York Times Magazine,* September 13, 32–33, 122, 126.

Friedman, Monroe. (1985). "Consumer Boycotts in the United States, 1970–1980: Contemporary Events in Historical Perspective." *Journal of Consumer Affairs,* 19(Summer), 96–117.

_____. (1999). *Consumer Boycotts.* New York: Routledge.

Gale, Jeffrey, and Rogene A. Buchholz. (1987). "The Political Pursuit of Competitive Advantage: What Business Can Gain from Government." In A. A. Marcus, A. M. Kaufman, and D. R. Beam (Eds.), *Business Strategy and Public Policy Perspectives from Industry and Academia,* 31–42. Westport, CN: Quorum Books.

Galvin, Robert W. (1992, October). *International Business and the Changing Nature of Global Competition.* Oxford, OH: Miami University.

Gauthier, David. (1986). *Morals by Agreement.* Oxford, UK: Clarendon Press.

Gavil, Andrew I., William E. Kovacic, and Jonathan B. Baker. (2004). *Teacher's Update: Summer 2004,* to *Antitrust Law in Perspective.* St. Paul, MN: Thomson/West.

_____. (2008). *Antitrust Law in Perspective: Cases, Concepts and Problems in Competition Policy* (2nd ed.). St. Paul, MN: Thomson/West.

Gert, Bernard. (1988). *Morality: A New Justification of the Moral Rules.* New York: Oxford University Press.

Getz, Kathleen A. (2000). "International Instruments on Bribery and Corruption." In Oliver F. Williams (Ed.), *Global Codes of Conduct: An Idea Whose Time Has Come?* 141–166. Notre Dame, IN: University of Notre Dame Press.

Gintis, Herbert. (2011). "Behavioral Ethics." In Edward Slingerland and Mark Collard (Eds.), *Creating Consilience: Integrating the Sciences and the Humanities,* Oxford University Press (forthcoming).

Gold, T. B. (1996). "Civil Society in Taiwan." In W. M. Tu (Ed.), *Confucian Traditions in East Asian Modernity.* Cambridge, MA: Harvard University Press.

Golodner, Linda F. (2000). "The Apparel Industry Code of Conduct: A Consumer Perspective on Social Responsibility." In Oliver F. Williams (Ed.), *Global Codes of Conduct: An Idea Whose Time Has Come?* 241–252. Notre Dame, IN: University of Notre Dame Press.

Goodman, John B. (1992). *Monetary Sovereignty: The Politics of Central Banking in Western Europe.* Ithaca, NY: Cornell University Press.

Goolsbee, Austan. (2000). "In a World Without Borders: The Impact of Taxes on Internet Commerce." *Quarterly Journal of Economics,* 115(2), 561–576.

Gorton, Gary B., and Andrew Metrick. (2009). "Securitization Banking and the Run on Repo." NBER Working Paper 15223, Cambridge, MA.

Gorton, Gary, and Nicholas S. Souleles. (2006). "Special Purpose Vehicles and Securitization." In Rene Stulz and Mark Carey (Eds.), *The Risks of Financial Institutions.* Chicago, IL: University of Chicago Press.

Graber, Doris A. (Ed.) (2000). *Media Power in Politics.* Washington, DC: CQ Press.

Green, Edward, and Robert Porter. (1984). "Noncooperative Collusion under Imperfect Price Information." *Econometrica,* 52, 87–100.

Greenblat, Alan. (1998). "Growing Ranks of Cigarette Tax Critics Invigorate Big Tobacco's Lobbying Effort." *Congressional Quarterly Weekly Report,* May 16.

Greve, Michael S., and Fred L. Smith, Jr. (1992). *Environmental Politics: Public Costs, Private Politics.* New York: Praeger.

Grieco, Joseph. (1990). *Cooperation Among Nations.* Ithaca, NY: Cornell University Press.

Griffin, J. J., and J. F. Mahon. (1997). "The Corporate Social Performance and Corporate Financial Performance Debate: Twenty-Five Years of Incomparable Research." *Business and Society,* 36, 5–31.

Groarke, Leo. (1990). "Affirmative Action as a Form of Restitution." *Journal of Business Ethics,* 9, 207–213.

Groseclose, Timothy. (1996). "An Examination of the Market for Favors and Votes in Congress." *Economic Inquiry,* 34(April), 1–21.

Groseclose, Timothy, and Jeff Milyo. (2005). "A Measure of Media Bias." *Quarterly Journal of Economics,* 120, 1191–1237.

Groseclose, Timothy, and James M. Snyder, Jr. (1996). "Buying Supermajorities." *American Political Science Review,* 90 (June), 303–315.

Groves, Theodore, Yongmiao Hong, John McMillan, and Barry Naughton. (1994). "Autonomy and Incentives in Chinese State Enterprises." *Quarterly Journal of Economics,* 109 (February), 183–209.

_____. (1995). "China's Evolving Managerial Labor Market." *Journal of Political Economy,* 103(August), 873–892.

Grub, Phillip D., and Jian Hai Lin. (1991). *Foreign Direct Investment in China.* New York: Quorum Books.

Haggard, Stephen. (1990). *Pathways from the Periphery: The Politics of Growth in the Newly Industrializing Countries.* Ithaca, NY: Cornell University Press.

Hall, Richard L., and Frank W. Wayman. (1990). "Buying Time: Moneyed Interests and the Mobilization of Bias in Congressional Committees." *American Political Science Review,* 84, 707–820.

Hamilton, Gary G. (1996). "Overseas Chinese Capitalism." In W. M. Tu (Ed.), *Confucian Traditions in East Asian Modernity.* Cambridge, MA: Harvard University Press, 1996.

Hamilton, James T. (1993). "Politics and Social Costs: Estimating the Impact of Collective Action on Hazardous Waste Facilities." *RAND Journal of Economics,* 24 (Spring), 101–125.

_____. (1995). "Pollution as News: Media and Stock Market Reactions to the Toxics Release Inventory Data." *Journal of Environmental Economics & Management,* 28, 187–206.

_____. (1997). "Taxes, Torts, and the Toxics Release Inventory: Congressional Voting on Instruments to Control Pollution." *Economic Inquiry,* 35(October), 745–762.

_____. (1998). *Channeling Violence: The Economic Market for Violent Television Programming.* Princeton, NJ: Princeton University Press.

Handler, Edward, and John R. Mulkern. (1982). *Business and Politics.* Lexington, MA: Lexington Books.

Hardin, Russell. (1982). *Collective Action,* Resources for the Future. Baltimore, MD: Johns Hopkins University Press.

_____. (1988). *Morality within the Limits of Reason.* Chicago, IL: University of Chicago Press.

Harding, Harry. (1987). *China's Second Revolution: Reform After Mao.* Washington, DC: Brookings.

Harris, Richard A., and Sidney M. Milkis. (1989). *The Politics of Regulatory Change: A Tale of Two Agencies.* Oxford, UK: Oxford University Press.

Harsanyi, John C. (1977). "Rule Utilitarianism and Decision Theory." *Erkenntnis,* 11, 25–53.

_____. (1982). "Morality and the Theory of Rational Behavior." In A. Sen and B. Williams (Eds.), *Utilitarianism and Beyond,* 39–62. Cambridge, UK: Cambridge University Press.

Hawk, Barry E. (1988). "The American Antitrust Revolution: Lessons for the EEC?" *European Competition Law Review,* 9, 53–87.

Hay, Robert D., and Edmund R. Gray. (1981). *Business & Society: Cases and Text.* Cincinnati, OH: South-Western Publishing.

Hayward, K. (2005, April). "Trade Disputes in the Commercial Aircraft Industry: A Background Note." Royal Aeronautical Society Specialist Paper. London, United Kingdom.

Heckathorn, Douglas D., and Steven M. Maser. (1990). "The Contractual Architecture of Public Policy: A Critical Reconstruction of Lowi's Typology." *Journal of Politics,* 52, 1101–1123.

Hendry, J. R. (2006). "Shareholder Influence Strategies: An Empirical Exploration." *Journal of Business Ethics,* 61, 79–99.

Henisz, Witold, and Bennet A. Zelner. (2008). "Managing Policy Risk." Working Paper, University of Pennsylvania, Philadelphia, PA.

Herrmann, Benedikt, Christian Thöni, and Simon Gächter. (2008). "Antisocial Punishment Across Societies." *Science,* 319 (March 7), 1362–1367.

Hewlett-Packard Company. (1984). "How to Deal with the Press." Palo Alto, CA.

_____. (1989). "Standards of Business Conduct." Palo Alto, CA.

Heymann, E. (2007). *Boeing vs. Airbus: The WTO dispute that neither can win.* Deutsche Bank Research.

Hillman, Amy J., Gerald D. Keim, and Rebecca A. Luce. (2001). "Board Composition and Stakeholder Performance: Do Stakeholder Directors Make a Difference." *Business & Society,* 40, 295–314.

Hirschman, Albert O. (1970). *Exit, Voice, and Loyalty.* Cambridge, MA: Harvard University Press.

Hiscox, Michael J., and Nicholas F. B. Smyth. (2006). "Is There Consumer Demand for Improved Labor Standards? Evidence from Field Experiments in Social Product Labeling." Working Paper, Harvard University, Cambridge, MA.

Hix, Simon. (2005). *The Political System of the European Union.* Basingstoke: Palgrave Macmillan, United Kingdom.

Hobbes, Thomas. (1651). *Leviathan.* Edited by C. B. Macpherson. Reprint, London, UK: Pelican Books, 1968.

Hoffman, Elizabeth, Kevin McCabe, Keith Shachat, and Vernon L. Smith. (1994). "Preferences, Property Rights and Anonymity in Bargaining Games." *Games and Economic Behavior,* 7, 346–380.

Hoffman, Elizabeth, Kevin McCabe, and Vernon L. Smith. (1996a). "Social Distance and Other-Regarding Behavior in Dictator Games." *American Economic Review,* 86, 653–660.

_____. (1996b). "On Expectations and the Monetary Stakes in Ultimatum Games." *International Journal of Game Theory,* 25, 289–301.

Holt, Charles A., and David T. Scheffman. (1989). "Strategic Business Behavior and Antitrust." In Robert J. Larner and James W. Meehan, Jr. (Eds.), *Economics and Antitrust Policy,* 39–82. New York: Quorum Books.

Hong, Harrison, and Marcin Kacperczyk. (2007). "The Price of Sin: The Effects of Social Norms on Markets." Working Paper, Princeton University, Princeton, NJ.

Hoscheit, J. M., and W. Wessels (Eds.). (1988). *The European Council 1974–1986: Evaluation and Prospects.* Maastricht, The Netherlands: European Institute of Public Administration.

Huber, Peter, and Robert E. Litan (Eds.). (1991). *The Liability Maze: The Impact of Liability Law on Safety and Innovation.* Washington, DC: Brookings.

Hufbauer, Gary C., and Kimberly A. Elliott. (1994). *Measuring the Costs of Protection in the United States.* Washington, DC: Institute for International Economics.

Ivanhoe, Philip J. (1993). *Confucian Moral Self Cultivation.* New York: Peter Lang.

Iyengar, Shanto, and Donald R. Kinder. (1987). *News That Matters.* Chicago: University of Chicago Press.

Jensen, Michael J. (1988). "Takeovers: Their Causes and Consequences." *Journal of Economic Perspectives,* 2, 21–44.

_____. (2001). "Value Maximization, Stakeholder Theory, and the Corporate Objective Function." *Journal of Applied Corporate Finance,* 14, 8–21.

John, Stefanie, and Daniela Schwarzer. (2006). "Industrial Lobbying within the European Union: Actors, Strategies, and Trends in the Multi-Level System." American Institute for Contemporary German Studies, Johns Hopkins University.

Jonsen, Albert R., and Stephen Toulmin. (1988). *The Abuse of Casuistry.* Berkeley: University of California Press.

Joskow, Paul L., and Richard Schmalensee. (1983). *Markets for Power: An Analysis of Electric Utility Deregulation.* Cambridge, MA: MIT Press.

_____. (1998). "The Political Economy of Market-Based Environmental Policy: The U.S. Acid Rain Program." *Journal of Law and Economics,* 41 (April), 37–84.

Joskow, Paul L., Richard Schmalensee, and Elizabeth M. Bailey. (1998). "The Market for Sulfur Dioxide Emissions." *American Economic Review,* 88 (September), 669–685.

Jury Verdict Research. (2001). *Personal Injury Valuation Handbook: Current Award Trends in Personal Injury, 2001 Edition.* LRP Publications. Palm Beach Gardens, FL.

Kahneman, Danny, J. Knetsch, and Richard Thaler. (1986). "Fairness and the Assumptions of Economics." *Journal of Business,* 59, 285–300.

Kalt, Joseph P. (1981). *The Economics and Politics of Oil Price Regulation.* Cambridge, MA: MIT Press.

Kant, Immanuel. (1785). *Ethical Philosophy, (a) Grounding for the Metaphysics of Morals; (1785) (b) The Metaphysical Principles of Virtue (1797).* Translation by James W. Ellington, introduction by Warner A. Wick. Indianapolis, IN: Hackett, 1983.

Kaplan, Robert, and David Norton. (1992). "The Balanced Scorecard—Measures That Drive Performance." *Harvard Business Review.*

Karlin, Dean, and Janathan Zinnan. (2009). "Expanding Microenterprise Credit Access: Using Randomized Supply Decisions to Estimates the Impact in Manila." Working Paper, Yale University, New Haven, CT.

Karnani, Aneel. (2007). "The Mirage of Marketing to the Bottom of the Pyramid." *California Management Review,* 49, 90–111.

Karpoff, Jonathan M., and Paul H. Malatesta. (1989). "The Wealth Effects of Second-Generation State Take-Over Legislation." *Journal of Financial Economics,* 25, 291–322.

Keim, Gerald D. (1985). "Corporate Grassroots Programs in the 1980s." *California Management Review,* 28(Fall), 110–123.

Kennedy, Scott. (2005). *The Business of Lobbying in China.* Cambridge, MA: Harvard University Press.

Kerwin, Cornelius M. (1994). *Rulemaking: How Government Agencies Write Law and Make Policy.* Washington, DC: CQ Press.

Kerwin, Cornelius M., and Scott R. Furlong. (2010). *Rulemaking: How Government Agencies Write Law and Make Policy* (4th ed.). Washington, DC: CQ Press.

Khanna, Tarun, and Yishay Yafeh. (2007). "Business Groups in Emerging Markets: Paragons or Parasites." *Journal of Economic Literature,* 45, 331–372.

Kimmel, Lisa. (2008). "U.S. Tort Liability Index: 2008 Report." Working Paper, University of California-Berkeley.

King, Andrew A., and Michael J. Lenox. (2000). "Industry Self-Regulation without Sanctions: The Chemical Industry's Responsible Care Program." *Academy of Management Journal,* 43, 698–716.

_____. (2002). "Exploring the Locus of Profitable Pollution Reduction." *Management Science,* 48, 289–299.

King, Brayden G., and Sarah A. Soule. (2007). "Social Movements as Extra-Institutional Entrepreneurs: The Effect of Protests on Stock Price Returns." *Administrative Science Quarterly,* 52, 413–442.

Klitgaard, Robert. (1988). *Controlling Corruption.* Berkeley: University of California Press.

Kneese, Alvin V., and Charles L. Schultze. (1975). *Pollution, Prices, and Public Policy.* Washington, DC: Brookings.

Knorr, A, J. Bellmann, and R. Schomaker, R. (2010). *International Trade Rules and Aircraft Manufacturing: Will the WTO Resolve the Airbus-Boeing Dispute?* Föv Discussion Paper, 60. Speyer, Germany.

Koku, Paul Sergius, Aigbe Akhigbe, and Thomas M. Springer. (1997). "The Financial Impact of Boycotts and Threats of Boycotts." *Journal of Business Research,* 40, 15–20.

Konar, Shameek, and Mark A. Cohen. (1997). "Information as Regulation: The Effect of Community Right to Know Laws on Toxic Emissions." *Journal of Environmental Economics & Management,* 32, 109–124.

Kose, M. Ayhan, and Eswar S. Prasad. (2010). *Emerging Markets: Resilience and Growth Amid Global Turmoil.* Washington, DC: Brookings.

Kotchian, A. Carl. (1977, July 9). "The Payoff: Lockheed's 70-Day Mission to Tokyo." *Saturday Review,* 5–12.

Krehbiel, Keith. (1996). "Institutional and Partisan Sources of Gridlock: A Theory of Divided and Unified Government." *Journal of Theoretical Politics,* 8, 7–40.

_____. (1998). *Pivotal Politics: A Theory of U.S. Lawmaking.* Chicago, IL: University of Chicago Press.

_____. (1999). "Pivotal Politics: A Refinement of Nonmarket Analysis for Voting Institutions." *Business and Politics,* 1 (April).

Kreps, David M. (1990). "Corporate Culture and Economic Theory." In James A. Alt and Kenneth Shepsle (Eds.), *Perspectives on Positive Political Economy,* 90–143. Cambridge, UK: Cambridge University Press

Kreps, David M., and Robert Wilson. (1982). "Reputation and Imperfect Information." *Journal of Economic Theory,* 27, 253–279.

Krill, Jennifer. (2010). "Rainforest Action Network." In Thomas P. Lyon (Ed.), *Good Cop, Bad Cop: Environmental NGOs and Their Strategies Toward Business,* 208–220. Washington, DC: RFF Press.

Kroszner, Randall S., and Thomas Stratmann. (1998). "Interest Group Competition and the Organization of Congress: Theory and Evidence from Financial Services Political Action Committees." *American Economic Review,* 88 (December), 1163–1187.

Krugman, Paul (Ed.). (1986). *Strategic Trade Policy and the New International Economics.* Cambridge, MA: MIT Press.

Krugman, Paul R. (1990). *Rethinking International Trade.* Cambridge, MA: MIT Press.

Küng-Shankleman, Lucy. (2000). *Inside the BBC and CNN: Managing News Organizations.* London: Routledge.

Kupfer, Joseph. (1993). "The Ethics of Genetic Screening in the Workplace." *Business Ethics Quarterly,* 3, 17–25.

Lakdawalla, Darius, and Tomas Philipson. (2009). "The Growth of Obesity and Technological Change: A Theoretical and Empirical Examination." *Economics and Human Biology,* 7, 283–293.

Lande, Stephen L., and Craig Vangrasstek. (1986). *The Trade and Tariff Act of 1984: Trade Policy in the Reagan Administration.* Lexington, MA: Lexington Books.

Lardy, Nicholas R. (1998). *China's Unfinished Economic Revolution.* Washington, DC: Brookings.

Lazear, Edward P., Ulrike Malmendier, and Roberto A. Weber. (2011). "Sorting in Experiments." *American Economic Association: Economic Analysis,* 4, 136–163.

Lenox, Michael, and Charles Eesley. (2008). "Private Environmental Activism and the Selection and Response of Firm Targets." *Journal of Economics and Strategy* 18, 45-73.

Leuz, Christian, and Felix Oberholzer-Gee. (2006). "Political Relationships, Global Financing, and Corporate Transparency: Evidence from Indonesia." *Journal of Financial Economics,* 81, 411–439.

Levine, S. I. (1997). "The United States and China: Managing a Stormy Relationship." In W. A. Joseph (Ed.), *China Briefing 1995–1996.* Armonk, NY: M. E. Sharpe.

Levitt, Steven D., and John A. List. (2007). "What Do Laboratory Experiments Measuring Social Preferences Reveal about the Real World?" *Journal of Economic Perspectives,* 21, 153–174.

Li, Shaomin. (2004). "Why Is Property Right Protection Lacking in China?" *California Management Review,* 46, 99–115.

Lieberthal, Kenneth. (1995). *Governing China.* New York: W.W. Norton.

List, John A. (2007). "On the Interpretation of Giving in Dictator Games." *Journal of Political Economy,* 115, 482–493.

Littlejohn, Stephen E. (1986). "Competition and Cooperation: New Trends in Corporate Public Issue Identification and Resolution." *California Management Review,* 29(Fall), 109–123.

Locke, John. (1690). *The Works of John Locke.* Reprint, Westport, CT: Greenwood, 1989.

Locke, Richard M., Fei Qin, and Alberto Brause. (2007). "Does Monitoring Improve Labor Standards? Lessons from Nike." *Industrial and Labor Relations Review,* 61, 3–31.

Lord, Michael D. (2000). "Constituency-Based Lobbying as Corporate Political Strategy: Testing an Agency Theory Perspective." *Business and Politics,* 2, 289–308.

Lowi, Theodore J. (1964). "American Business, Public Policy, Case-Studies, and Political Theory." *World Politics,* 16 (July), 677–693.

Lukes, Steven. (1973). *Individualism.* Oxford, UK: Basil Blackwell.

Lynn, Leornard H., and Timothy J. McKeown. (1988). *Organizing Business: Trade Associations in America and Japan.* Washington, DC: American Enterprise Institute.

Lyon, Thomas P. (Ed.). (2010). *Good Cop, Bad Cop: Environmental NGOs and Their Strategies Toward Business.* Washington, DC: RFF Press.

Lyon, Thomas P., and Eun-Hee Kim. (2007). "Greenhouse Gas Reductions or Greenwash? The DOE's 1605b Program." Working Paper, University of Michigan, Ann Arbor, MI.

Lyons, David. (1965). *The Forms and Limits of Utilitarianism.* Oxford, UK: Oxford University Press.

MacAvoy, Paul W. (1981, December 20). "The Business Lobby's Wrong Business." *The New York Times.*

Mackey, John. (2005). "Putting Customers Ahead of Investors." *Reason.* October.

Magat, Wesley A., Alan J. Krupnick, and Winston Harrington. (1986). *Rules in the Making: A Statistical Analysis of Regulatory Agency Behavior.* Washington, DC: Resources for the Future.

Magee, Stephen P., William A. Brock, and Leslie Young. (1989). *Black Hole Tariffs and Endogenous Policy Theory: Political Economy in General Equilibrium.* Cambridge, UK: Cambridge University Press.

Mahon, John F., and Jennifer J. Griffin. (1999). "Painting a Portrait." *Business & Society,* 38 (March), 126–133.

Mahoney, Richard J., and Stephen E. Littlejohn. (1989). "Innovation on Trial: Punitive Damages versus New Products." *Science,* 15 (December), 1398.

Manheim, Jarol B. (2001). *The Death of a Thousand Cuts.* Mahwah, NJ: Lawrence Erlbaum.

Margolis, Joshua D., and James P. Walsh. (2001). *People or Profits? The Search for a Link between a Company's Social and Financial Performance.* Mahwah, NJ: Lawrence Erlbaum.

_____. (2003). "Misery Loves Companies: Rethinking Social Initiatives by Business." *Administrative Sciences Quarterly,* 48, 268–305.

Mashaw, Jerry L., and Richard A. Merrill. (1985). *Administrative Law: The American Public Law System: Cases and Materials* (2nd ed.). St. Paul, MN: West Publishing.

Maxwell, John W., Thomas P. Lyon, and Steven C. Hackett. (2000). "Self-Regulation and Social Welfare: The Political Economy of Corporate Environmentalism." *Journal of Law & Economics,* 43 (October), 583–617.

Mayhew, David. (2004). *Congress: The Electoral Connection* (2nd ed.). New Haven, CT: Yale University Press.

McCraw, Thomas K. (Ed.). (1981). *Regulation in Perspective: Historical Essays.* Boston, MA: Harvard Business School.

McDonald's Corporation—Environmental Defense Fund, Waste Reduction Task Force. (1991). "Final Report," April.

McGuire, J. B., T. Schneeweis, and B. Branch. (1990). "Perceptions of Firm Quality: A Cause or Result of Firm Performance." *Journal of Management,* 16, 167–180.

McGuire, Jean B., Alison Sundgren, and Thomas Schneeweis. (1988). "Corporate Social Responsibility and Firm Financial Performance." *Academy of Management Journal,* 31, 854–872.

Milgrom, Paul, and John D. Roberts. (1982). "Limit Pricing and Entry under Incomplete Information." *Econometrica,* 50, 443–459.

Mill, John Stuart. (1859). *On Liberty.* Edited by David Spitz. New York: W.W. Norton. 1975.

_____. (1861). "Utilitarianism." In Alan Ryan (Ed.), *Utilitarianism and Other Essays: J. S. Mill and Jeremy Bentham.* New York: Penguin Books, 1987.

Milyo, Jeffrey, David Primo, and Timothy Groseclose. (2000). "Corporate PAC Campaign Contributions in Perspective." *Business and Politics,* 2, 75–88.

Moe, Terry M. (1980). *The Organization of Interests.* Chicago: University of Chicago Press.

Moore, Barrington. (1966). *Social Origins of Dictatorship and Democracy.* Boston, MA: Beacon Press.

Monin, Benoit, and Dale T. Miller. (2001). "Moral Credentials and the Expression of Prejudice." *Journal of Personality and Social Psychology,* 81, 33–43.

Monin, Benoit, Pamela J. Sawyer, and Matthew J. Marquez. (2008). "The Rejection of Moral Rebels: Resenting Those Who Do the Right Thing." *Journal of Personality and Social Psychology,* 95, 76–93.

Mortgage Asset Research Institute. (2010). "Twelfth Periodic Mortgage Fraud Case Report." April. http://www.lexisnexis.com/risk/fraudreport.

Mukherji, Rahul. (2007). *India's Economic Transition: The Politics of Reforms.* Oxford, UK: Oxford University Press.

Natural Resources Defense Council. (1989). "Intolerable Risk: Pesticides in Our Children's Food." Washington, DC.

Naughton, Barry. (2007). *The Chinese Economy: Transitions and Growth.* Cambridge, MA: MIT Press.

Newman, Edwin. (1984). "A Journalist's Responsibility." In Robert Schumhl (Ed.), *The Responsibilities of Journalism,* 19–38. Notre Dame: University of Notre Dame Press.

Nivison, David S. (1996). *The Ways of Confucianism.* Chicago: Open Court.

Noll, Roger G., and Bruce M. Owen. (1983). *The Political Economy of Deregulation: Interest Groups in the Regulatory Process.* Washington, DC: American Enterprise Institute.

Norman, Wayne, and Chris MacDonald. (2003). "Getting to the Bottom of 'Triple Bottom Line.' " *Business Ethics Quarterly,* 14, 243–262.

North, Douglass C. (1990). *Institutions, Institutional Change and Economic Performance.* Cambridge, UK: Cambridge University Press.

Nozick, Robert. (1974). *Anarchy, State, and Utopia.* New York: Basic Books.

Nugent, Neill. (2003). *The Government and Politics of the European Union* (5th ed.). Durham, NC: Duke University Press.

Nyborg, Karine, and Tao Zhang. (2011). "Is Corporate Social Responsibility Associated with Lower Wages?" Working Paper, University of Oslo, Oslo, Norway.

Oberholzer-Gee, Felix, and Reiner Eichenberger. (2008). "Fairness in Extended Dictator Games." *B.E. Journal of Economic Analysis & Policy,* 8, Article 16.

O'Halloran, Sharyn. (1994). *Politics, Process, and American Foreign Policy.* Ann Arbor: University of Michigan Press.

Olson, Mancur J. (1965). *The Logic of Collective Action.* Cambridge, MA: Harvard University Press.

Ordover, Janusz A., and Robert D. Willig. (1983). "The 1982 Department of Justice Merger Guidelines: An Economic Assessment." *California Law Review,* 71, 535–574.

Orlitsky, Marc, Frank L. Schmidt, and Sara L. Rynes. (2003). "Corporate Social and Financial Performance: A Meta-analysis." *Organization Studies,* 24, 403–411.

Oster, Sharon M. (1999). *Modern Competitive Analysis* (3rd ed.). Oxford, UK: Oxford University Press.

Overturf, Stephen F. (1986). *The Economic Principles of European Integration.* New York: Praeger.

Owen, Bruce M., and Ronald Braeutigam. (1978). *The Regulation Game: Strategic Use of the Administrative Process.* Cambridge, MA: Balinger.

Palmier, Leslie. (1989). "Corruption in the West Pacific." *The Pacific Review,* 2(1), 23.

Panagariya, Arvind. (2008). *India: The Emerging Giant.* Oxford, UK: Oxford University Press.

Pastin, Mark, and Michael Hooker. (1988). "Ethics and the Foreign Corrupt Practices Act." In Thomas Donaldson and Patricia H. Werhane (Eds.), *Ethical Issues in Business: A Philosophical Approach,* 48–53. Englewood Cliffs, NJ: Prentice Hall.

Pavcnik, N. (2002). "Trade Disputes in the Commercial Aircraft Industry." *World Economy,* 25, 733–751.

Pei, M. (1997). "Racing Against Time: Institutional Decay and Renewal in China." In William A. Joseph (Ed.), *China Briefing 1995–1996.* Armonk, NY: M. E. Sharpe.

Peltzman, Sam. (1975). "The Effects of Automobile Safety Regulation." *Journal of Political Economy,* 83(August), 677–725.

_____. (1976). "Toward a More General Theory of Regulation." *Journal of Law and Economics,* 19, 211–240.

Peterson, Steven P., and George E. Hoffer. (1994). "The Impact of Airbag Adoption on Relative Personal Injury and Absolute Collision Insurance Claims." *Journal of Consumer Research,* 20(March), 657–662.

Peters, Glen P., Jan C. Minx, Christopher L. Weber, and Ottmar Edenhofer. (2011). "Growth in Emissions Transfers via International Trade from 1990 to 2008." *Proceedings of the National Academies of Science,* 108, 8903–8908.

Pfeffer, Jeffrey, and Gerald Salancik. (1978). *The External Control of Organizations.* New York: Harper and Row.

Pierson, Paul. (1999). "Social Policy and European Integration." In Andrew Moravcsik (Ed.), *Centralization or Fragmentation: Europe Facing the Challenges of Deepening, Diversity, and Democracy.* New York: Council on Foreign Relations.

Polinsky, A. Mitchell. (2011). *An Introduction to Law and Economics* (4th ed.). New York: Aspen Publications.

Polinsky, A. Mitchell, and Steven Shavell. (2010). "The Uneasy Case for Product Liability." *Harvard Law Review,* 123, 1949–1968.

Popoff, Frank P. (1992). "Going beyond Pollution Prevention." In *Business: Championing the Global Environment,* Report Number 995, The Conference Board, New York.

Porter, Michael E. (1980). *Competitive Strategy: Techniques for Analyzing Industries and Competitions.* New York: Free Press.

_____. (1985). *Competitive Advantage.* New York: Free Press.

Porter, Michael E., and C. van der Linde. (1995). "Toward a New Conception of the Environment-Competitiveness Relationship." *Journal of Economic Perspectives,* 9, 97–118.

Posner, Richard A. (1974). "Theories of Economic Regulation." *Bell Journal of Economics,* 5(Autumn), 335–358.

_____. (1976). *Antitrust Law: An Economic Perspective.* Chicago: University of Chicago Press.

_____. (1981). *The Economics of Justice.* Cambridge, MA: Harvard University Press.

Post, James E., Lee F. Preston, and Sybille Sachs. (2002). "Managing the Extended Enterprise: The New Stakeholder View." *California Management Review,* 45, 6–28.

Poterba, James M. (1991). "Tax Policy to Combat Global Warming: On Designing a Carbon Tax." In Dornbusch, Rudiger, and James M. Poterba (Eds.), *Global Warming: Economic Policy Responses,* 71–98. Cambridge, MA: MIT Press

Potoski, Matthew, and Aseem Prakash. (2005). "Green Clubs and Voluntary Governance: ISO 14001 and Firms' Regulatory Compliance." *American Journal of Political Science,* 49, 235–248.

Povich, Elaine S. (1996). *Partners and Adversaries.* Arlington, TX: The Freedom Forum.

Prahalad, C. K. (2004). *The Fortune at the Bottom of the Pyramid: Eradicating Poverty through Profits.* Philadelphia: Wharton School Press.

Prahalad, C. K., and Gary Hamel. (1990). "The Core Competencies of the Corporation." *Harvard Business Review,* May–June, 79–91.

Prakash, Aseem. (2001). "Beyond Seattle: Globalization, the Nonmarket Environment, and Corporate Strategy." *Review of International Political Economy,* 8.

Prakash, Assem, and Matthew Potoski. (2006). *The Voluntary Environmentalists.* Cambridge, UK: Cambridge University Press.

Priest, George L. (1977). "The Common Law Process and the Selection of Efficient Rules." *Journal of Legal Studies,* 6 (January), 65–82.

Pritchard, D., and MacPherson, A. (2004). "Industrial Subsidies and the Politics of World Trade: The Case of the Boeing 7e7." *The Industrial Geographer,* 1, 57–73.

Pruitt, S. W., and Monroe Friedman. (1986). "Determining the Effectiveness of Consumer Boycotts: A Stock Price Analysis of

Their Impact on Corporate Targets." *Journal of Consumer Policy,* 9, 375–387.

Pruitt, S. W., K. C. John Wei, and Richard E. White. (1988). "The Impact of Union-Sponsored Boycotts on the Stock Prices of Target Firms." *Journal of Labor Research,* 9, 285–289.

Putnam, Todd. (1993). "Boycotts Are Busting Out All Over." *Business and Society Review,* 47–51.

Pye, Lucian W. (1978). *China: An Introduction.* Boston, MA: Little, Brown.

_____. (1985). *Asian Power and Politics: The Cultural Dimensions of Authority.* Boston, MA: Little, Brown.

_____. (1988). *The Mandarin and the Cadre: China's Political Cultures.* Ann Arbor: University of Michigan Press.

Quirk, Paul J. (1981). *Industry Influence in Federal Regulatory Agencies.* Princeton, NJ: Princeton University Press.

Rawls, John. (1971). *A Theory of Justice.* Cambridge, MA: Belknap Press.

_____. (1980). "Kantian Constructivism in Moral Theory." *Journal of Philosophy,* 9(September), 515–572.

_____. (2001). *Justice as Fairness: A Restatement.* Edited by Erin Kelly. Cambridge, MA: Harvard University Press.

Redding, S. Gordon. (1996). "Societal Transformation and the Contribution of Authority Relations and Cooperative Norms in Overseas Chinese Business." In Wei-ming Tu (Ed.), *Confucian Traditions in East Asian Modernity.* Cambridge, MA: Harvard University Press.

Rehbein, K., S. Waddock, and S. B. Graves. (2004). "Understanding Shareholder Activism: Which Corporations Are Targeted?" *Business and Society,* 43, 239–267.

Richter, Brian Kelleher. (2011). " 'Good' and 'Evil': The Relationship between Corporate Social Responsibility and Corporate Political Activist." Working Paper, University of Western Ontario, London, Ontario, Canada.

Rodgers, T. J. (2005). "Put Profits First." *Reason.* October.

Reinhart, Carmen M. and Kenneth S. Rogoff. (2009). *This Time Is Different: Eight Centuries of Financial Folly.* Princeton, NJ: Princeton University Press.

Roman, Ronald M., Sefa Hayibor, and Bradley R. Agle. (1999). "The Relationship between Social and Financial Performance: Repainting a Portrait." *Business & Society,* 38 (March): 109–125.

Rose, Nancy L. (1985). "The Incidence of Regulatory Rents in the Motor Carrier Industry." *RAND Journal of Economics,* 16 (Autumn), 299–318.

_____. (1987). "Labor Rent Sharing and Regulation: Evidence from the Trucking Industry." *Journal of Political Economy,* 95, 1146–1178.

Rosenbaum, Walter A. (2007). *Environmental Politics and Policy* (7th ed.). Washington, DC: Congressional Quarterly.

Rosenthal, Douglas E. (1990). "Competition Policy." In Gary C. Hufbauer (Ed.), *Europe 1992: An American Perspective,* 292–343. Washington, DC: Brookings.

Roth, Alvin E., Vesna Prasnikar, Masahiro Okuno-Fujiwara, and Shmuel Zamir. (1991). "Bargaining and Market Behavior in Jerusalem, Ljubjana, Pittsburgh, and Tokyo: An Experimental Study." *American Economic Review,* 81, 1068–1095.

Rousseau, Jean Jacques. (1762). *On the Social Contract.* Reprint, New York: Harper and Row, 1984.

Rubin, Paul H. (1983). *Business Firms and the Common Law: The Evolution of Efficient Rules.* New York: Praeger.

Ruta, Gwen. (2010). "Environmental Defense Fund." In Thomas P. Lyon (Ed.), *Good Cop, Bad Cop: Environmental NGOs and Their Strategies toward Business,* 184–194. Washington, DC: RFF Press

Sabato, Larry J. (1984). *PAC Power: Inside the World of Political Action Committees.* New York: W.W. Norton.

Sackett, P. R., and M. M. Harris. (1984). "Honesty Testing for Personnel Selection: A Review and Critique." *Personnel Psychology,* 37, 221–245.

Salisbury, Robert H. (1992). *Interests and Institutions.* Pittsburgh: University of Pittsburgh Press.

Saloner, Garth, Andrea Shepard, and Joel M. Podolny. (2001). *Strategic Management.* New York: Wiley.

Salop, Steven C., and Lawrence J. White. (1988). "Private Antitrust Litigation: An Introduction and Framework." In Lawrence J. White (Ed.), *Private Antitrust Litigation: New Evidence, New Learning.* Cambridge, MA: MIT Press.

Sasser, Erika N., Aseem Prakash, Benjamin Cashore, and Graeme Auld. (2006). "Direct Targeting as an NGO Political Strategy: Examining Private Authority Regimes in the Forestry Sector." *Business and Politics,* 8, Article 1.

Schickler, Eric, Frances E. Lee, and George C. Edwards III. (2011). *The Oxford Handbook of the American Congress.* New York: Oxford University Press.

Schmalensee, Richard, Paul L. Joskow, A. Denny Ellerman, Juan Pablo Montero, and Elizabeth M. Bailey. (1998). "An Interim Evaluation of Sulfur Dioxide Emissions Trading." *Journal of Economic Perspectives,* 12(Summer), 53–68.

Schmidt, Benno C., Jr. (1981). "The First Amendment and the Press." In Elie Abel (Ed.), *What's News,* 57–80. San Francisco: Institute for Contemporary Studies.

Schoenberger, Karl. (2000). *Levi's Children: Coming to Terms with Human Rights in the Global Marketplace.* New York: Grove Press.

Schuknecht, Ludger. (1992). *Trade Protection in the European Community.* Chur, Switzerland: Harwood Academic.

Schwartz, Benjamin I. (1985). *The World of Thought in Ancient China.* Cambridge, MA: Harvard University Press.

Sen, Amartya. (1987). *On Ethics & Economics.* Oxford, UK: Basil Blackwell.

_____. (1997). "Economics, Business Principles and Moral Sentiments." *Business Ethics Quarterly,* 7, 5–15.

Sexton, Steven E., and Alison L. Sexton. (2011). "Conspicuous Conservation: The Prius Effect and Willingness to Pay for Environmental Bona Fides." Working Paper, University of California-Berkeley.

Shaffer, Brian, and Daniel T. Ostas. (2001). "Exploring the Political Economy of Consumer Legislation: The Development of Automobile Lemon Laws." *Business and Politics,* 3, 65–76.

Shaw, Malcolm W. (1997). *International Law* (4th ed.). Cambridge, UK: Cambridge University Press.

_____. (2003). *International Law* (5th ed.). Cambridge, UK: Cambridge University Press.

Shepsle, Kenneth A., and Mark S. Bonchek. (1997). *Analyzing Politics: Rationality, Behavior, and Institutions.* New York: W.W. Norton.

Shils, Edward. (1996). "Reflections on Civil Society and Civility in the Chinese Intellectual Tradition." In Wei-ming Tu (Ed.), *Confucian Traditions in East Asian Modernity.* Cambridge, MA: Harvard University Press.

Shipper, Frank, and Marianne M. Jennings. (1984). *Business Strategy for the Political Arena.* Westport, CT: Quorum Books.

Shirk, Susan L. (1993). *The Political Logic of Economic Reform in China.* Berkeley: University of California Press.

Shue, Henry. (1980). *Basic Rights: Subsistence, Affluence, and U.S. Foreign Power.* Princeton, NJ: Princeton University Press.

Shue, Vivienne. (1988). *The Reach of the State.* Stanford, CA: Stanford University Press.

Shugart, William F., II. (1990). *Antitrust Policy and Interest-Group Politics.* New York: Quorum Books.

Siegel, Jordan, and Barbara Zepp Larson. (2007). "Labor Market Institutions and Global Strategic Adaptation: Evidence from Lincoln Electric." Working Paper, Harvard Business School, Boston, MA.

Sigman, Betsy Ann, and Susan-Kathryn McDonald. (1987). "The Issues Manager as Public Opinion and Policy Analyst." In A. A. Marcus, A. M. Kaufman, and D. R. Beam (Eds.), *Business Strategy and Public Policy: Perspectives from Industry and Academia*, 164–194. New York: Quorum Books

Smith, Adam. (1776). *An Inquiry into the Nature and Causes of the Wealth of Nations.* Edited by R. H. Campbell and A. S. Skinner. Oxford, UK: Clarendon Press. 1995.

Smith, Steven S., Jason M. Roberts, and Ryan J. Vander Wielen. (2009). *The American Congress.* New York: Cambridge University Press.

Snyder, James M., Jr. (1991). "On Buying Legislatures." *Economics and Politics,* 3 (July), 93–109.

Sonnenfeld, Jeffrey, and Paul R. Lawrence. (1978). "Why Do Companies Succumb to Price Fixing?" *Harvard Business Review,* 56 (July–August), 145–157.

Sood, Neeraj, and Arkadipta Ghosh. (2007). "The Short and Long Run Effects of Daylight Saving Time on Fatal Automobile Crashes." *B.E. Journal of Economic Analysis & Policy,* 7, Article 11.

Sparrow, Batholomew H. (1999). *Uncertain Guardians: The News Media as a Political Institution.* Baltimore, MD: Johns Hopkins University Press.

Spence, A. Michael. (1973). "Job Market Signaling." *Quarterly Journal of Economics,* 87, 355–374.

Spitzer, Matthew L. (1991). "Justifying Minority Preferences in Broadcasting." *Southern California Law Review,* 293, 334–336.

Spulber, Daniel F. (1989). *Regulation and Markets.* Cambridge, MA: MIT Press.

Stavins, Robert N. (1998). "What Can We Learn from the Grand Policy Experiment? Lessons from SO$_2$ Allowance Trading." *Economic Perspectives,* 12 (Summer), 69–88.

Stigler, George. (1971). "The Theory of Economic Regulation." *Bell Journal of Regulation,* 2 (Spring), 3–21.

Streeck, Wolfgang. (1984). *Industrial Relations in West Germany.* New York: St. Martin's Press.

Taka, Iwao. (1994). "Business Ethics: A Japanese View." *Business Ethics Quarterly,* 4, 53–78.

Teece, David J. (2000). *Managing Intellectual Capital.* Oxford, UK: Oxford University Press.

Teoh, Slew Hong, Ivo Welch, and C. Paul Wazzan. (1999). "The Effect of Socially Activist Investment Policies on the Financial Markets: Evidence from the South African Boycott." *Journal of Business,* 72, 35–89.

Thompson, James. (1967). *Organizations in Action.* New York: McGraw-Hill.

Tirole, Jean. (2005). *The Theory of Corporate Finance.* Princeton, NJ: Princeton University Press.

Tomlinson, R. (1997). "A Chinese Giant Forges a Capitalist Soul." *Fortune* (September 29): 184–192.

Trebilcock, Michael J., and Robert C. York. (1990). *Fair Exchange: Reforming Trade Remedy Laws.* Toronto, Canada: C. D. Howe Institute.

Tu, Wei-ming. (1979). *Humanity and Self-Cultivation.* Berkeley: University of California Press.

Tyler, Lisa. (1997). "Liability Means Never Being Able to Say You're Sorry. Corporate Guilt, Legal Constraints, and Defensiveness in Corporate Communication." *Management Communication Quarterly,* 11, 51–73.

Uhlmann, Eric Luis, George Newman, Victoria Brescoll, Adam Galinsky, and Daniel Diermeier. (2008). "The Sound of Silence: Effects of an Engaged, Defensive, and No Comment Response to a Crisis on Corporate Reputation." Working Paper, Northwestern University, Evanston, IL.

Ungericht, Bernhard, and Christian Hirt. (2010). "CSR as a Political Arena: The Struggle for a European Framework." *Business and Politics,* 12(4), Article 1.

Urata, Shuijiro. (2001). "Europe's Trade and Foreign Direct Investment in Asia." In Vinod K. Aggarwal (Ed), *Winning in Asia, European Style,* 31–58. New York: Palgrave Macmillan.

Vachani, Sushil, and N. Craig Smith. (2004). "Socially Responsible Pricing: Lessons from the Pricing of AIDS Drugs in Developing Countries." *California Management Review,* 47, 117–144.

Van Schendelen, M. P. C. M. (1993). "The Netherlands: Lobby It Yourself." In M. P. C. M. Van Schendelen (Ed.), *National Public and Private EC Lobbying.* Hants, UK: Aldershot.

Vaughn, Jacqueline. (2007). *Environmental Politics: Domestic and Global Dimensions* (5th ed.). Belmont, CA: Wadsworth.

Velasquez, Manuel G. (1998). *Business Ethics: Concepts and Cases* (4th ed.). Upper Saddle River, NJ: Prentice Hall.

Viscusi, W. Kip. (1991). *Reforming Products Liability.* Cambridge, MA: Harvard University Press.

Viscusi, W. Kip, and Michael J. Moore. (1993). "Product Liability, Research and Development, and Innovation." *Journal of Political Economy,* 101, 161–184.

Viscusi, W. Kip, John M. Vernon, and Joseph E. Harrington, Jr. (2000). *Economics of Regulation and Antitrust* (3rd ed.). Cambridge, MA: MIT Press.

———. (2005). *Economics of Regulation and Antitrust* (4th ed.). Cambridge, MA: MIT Press.

Vogel, David. (1978). *Lobbying the Corporation: Citizen Challenges to Business Authority.* New York: Basic Books.

_____. (1986). *National Styles of Regulation: Environmental Policy in Great Britain and the United States.* Ithaca, NY: Cornell University Press.

_____. (1991). "Business Ethics: New Perspectives on Old Problems." *California Business Review,* 33 (Summer), 101–117.

_____. (2005). *Can Corporations Be Made Responsible? The Potential and Limits of Corporate Social Responsibility.* Washington, DC: Brookings.

Waddock, Sandra A., and Samuel B. Graves. (1997). "The Corporate Social Performance–Financial Performance Link." *Strategic Management Journal,* 18, 303–319.

Wartick, Steven L., and Robert E. Rude. (1986). "Issues Management: Corporate Fad or Corporate Function?" *California Management Review,* 29 (Fall), 124–140.

Watkins, Sherron S. (2003). "Ethical Conflicts at Enron: Moral Responsibility in Corporate Capitalism." *California Management Review,* 45, 6–19.

Weaver, Suzanne. (1977). *Decision to Prosecute: Organization and Public Policy in the Antitrust Division.* Cambridge, MA: MIT Press.

Weidenbaum, Murray L. (1996). "The Chinese Family Business Enterprise." *California Management Review,* 38 (Summer), 141–156.

———. (2004). *Business and Government in the Global Marketplace* (7th ed.). Upper Saddle River, NJ: Prentice Hall.

Weingast, Barry M., and Mark Moran. (1983). "Bureaucratic Discretion or Congressional Control? Regulatory Policymaking by the Federal Trade Commission." *Journal of Political Economy,* 91 (October), 765–800.

Weston, J. Fred, Kwang S. Chung, and Susan E. Hoag. (1990). *Mergers, Restructuring, and Corporate Control.* Upper Saddle River, NJ: Prentice Hall.

White, Lawrence J. (Ed.). (1988). *Private Antitrust Litigation: New Evidence, New Learning.* Cambridge, MA: MIT Press.

White, Michelle J. (2004). "Asbestos and the Future of Mass Torts." Working Paper 10308, National Bureau of Economic Research, Cambridge, MA.

White, Matthew W. (1997). "Power Struggles: Explaining Deregulatory Reforms in Electricity Markets." *Brookings Papers on Economic Activity: Micro-Economics,* 201–250.

Williamson, Oliver E. (1975). *Markets and Hierarchies: Analysis and Antitrust Implications.* New York: Free Press.

Wilson, James Q. (1980). *The Politics of Regulation.* New York: Basic Books.

_____. (1989). *Bureaucracy: What Government Agencies Do and Why They Do It.* New York: Basic Books.

Wilson, Robert. (2001). "Architecture of Power Markets." Working Paper, Stanford University, Stanford, CA.

Wise, Mark, and Richard Gibb. (1993). *Single Market to Social Europe.* Essex, UK: Longman Scientific & Technical.

Wiseman, Alan. (2000). *The Internet Economy: Access, Taxes, and Market Structure.* Washington, DC: Brookings.

Wiseman, Alan E., and Jerry Ellig. (2004). "Market and Nonmarket Barriers to Internet Wine Sales: The Case of Virginia." *Business and Politics,* 6, Article 4.

Wolf, Charles, Jr. (1979). "A Theory of Nonmarket Failure." *Journal of Law and Economics,* 22(April), 107–139.

_____. (1988). *Markets or Governments.* Cambridge, MA: MIT Press.

Wu, Abraham H. (1994). "Contributions, Lobbying, and Participation." Working Paper, Stanford University, Stanford, CA.

Yang, C. K. (1959). *Chinese Communist Society: The Family and the Village.* Cambridge, MA: MIT Press.

Yang, M. M. (1994). *Gifts, Favors, and Banquets.* Ithaca, NY: Cornell University Press.

Yoffie, David B. (1987). "Corporate Strategies for Political Action: A Rational Model." In A. A. Marcus, A. M. Kaufman, and D. R. Beam (Eds.), *Business Strategy and Public Policy Perspectives from Industry and Academia.* New York: Quorum Books

_____. (1988). "How an Industry Builds Political Advantage." *Harvard Business Review,* May–June, 82–89.

Young, Louis H. (1978, September 21). "Business and the Media: The Failure to Understand How the Other Operates." Speech delivered at the ITT Key Issues Lecture Series, Columbia, Missouri.

INDEX

7-Eleven, 185, 554
60 Minutes (television program), 53, 64, 67
401(k) plans (Enron), 584

A

Abacus AC1, 309–310
Abatement, 326
ABB Ltd., 695
Abbott Laboratories, 115, 489, 508, 527,
    531, 539, 545–549, 604, 688, 707, 710
ABC, 59, 272
ABN Amro, 340
Abúndez, Alejandra, 494
Accelerated Access Initiative, 618
Access, 168, 199, 435
Access to Capital Coalition, 190
ACCION International, 483
Accountability. *See* Social accountability
Accounting and Auditing Organization for
    Islamic Financial Institutions, 489
Accuracy, in news media, 60–62
Acid rain, cap-and-trade systems for,
    328–329
ACORN, 126, 299, 319
Acres for America, 587
Acrylamide, 21
Act Up–Paris, 115, 548–549
Act utilitarianism, 603–605
Action on Smoking and Health (ASH), 157
Actions, for environmental management and
    stability, 321–322
Activist strategies, 84–87
Ad hoc coalitions, 206
Ad Hoc Committee of AZ-NM-TX-FL
    Producers of Gray Portland Cement, 541
Adams, Cathie, 223, 224
Adani, Gautam, 507
Adarand Constructors v. Peña, 64
Adelphia Communications, 563
Adjusted minimum tax (AMT), 189–192
Administration, 14, 15
Administrative agencies. *See* Institutions;
    specific administrative agencies
Administrative institutions, responsiveness
    of, 180–181
Administrative law judge (ALJ), 334
Administrative Procedures Act (APA),
    267, 268
AdSense, 34, 35
Advanced Technologies Laboratories, Inc.
    case, 517–518
Advantica Restaurant Group, Inc., 673
Adverse selection, 274
Advertising
    children and, 21
    direct-to-consumer, 36–37
    tobacco politics and, 157, 158
Advisory Commission on Electronic
    Commerce, 214

Advocacy groups, 9, 75
Advocacy journalism, 61
Advocacy science, 85–86, 338–339
Affirmative action, 646–647
AFL-CIO, 127
Age Discrimination in Employment
    Act, 634
Agence France-Presse, 26
Agencies. *See* Regulatory agencies
Agenda-setting strategies, 177–178
Aggregate benefits, 134
Aggregate utility, 693
Agouron, 707
Agricultural agreement, 527
Agriculture, international trade
    agreements and, 527
AIDS, 115, 168
    compulsory licensing case, 545–549
    developing countries and, 687–688
    gilead sciences case, 615–619
AIDS Coalition to Unleash Power
    (ACT UP!), 708
AIDS drugs policy case, 707–711
AIDS Healthcare Foundation (AHF), 80,
    546–548, 688, 710
Airbus, 142–144, 148, 179–180, 428,
    523, 549
Airbus and Boeing Trade Disputes
    case, 549
Airline industry, price fixing case, 252–253
Airspace, 157
Alar, 53–54, 57, 61, 65, 67–69, 76
Alarmist media coverage, 61
Albertson's, 124, 128
Alfano, Deborah, 222
Alford, Harry, 354–355
Alien Tort Claims Act (ATCA), 682
Allchin, James, 260
Alliance of Automobile Manufacturers,
    7, 11
Allmark, David, 118
All Nippon Airlines, 692
Alpac corporation, 105
Alstom, 429
Altech, 500
Altruism, 602
Amakudari, 554
Amalgamated Clothing and Textile Workers
    Union, 342
Amazon.com, 39, 167, 168, 169, 207, 217
    Internet taxation, 217
Ambani, Anil, 498
Ambani, Mukesh, 500, 507
AMD, 237
America Online. *See* AOL
American Academy of Neurology, 619
American Academy of Pediatrics, 221,
    224, 279
American Airlines, 27, 206, 432, 604, 609

American Association of Advertising
    Agencies, 158
American Association of Nurserymen, 185
American Association of Retired Persons
    (AARP), 12, 150, 319
American Bankers Association, 159, 204,
    296, 307, 588
American Booksellers Association, 216
American Chamber of Commerce, 434, 436,
    547, 589
American Civil Liberties Union (ACLU),
    227, 593
American College of Obstetricians and
    Gynecologists' Committee on
    Ethics, 518
American Electric Power Company, 326
American Electronics Association,
    215, 217, 218
American Express, 128, 237, 526
American Farm Bureau, 186
American Federation of State, County, and
    Municipal Employees (AFSCME),
    171, 204
American Feed Industry
    Association (AFIA), 68
American Furniture Manufacturers, 339
American Heart Association, 157
American Home Products Corporation,
    165–166, 613
American Humane Association, 22
American Law Institute, 398–399
American League of Lobbyists, 203
American Lung Association, 157
American Medical Association (AMA),
    17–18, 37
American Psychological
    Association (APA), 633
American Red Cross, 387, 661
Americans for Democratic Action, 171
Americans for Nonsmokers' Rights, 157
Americans for Tax Reform, 215
American Society of Newspaper
    Editors (ASNE), 59, 60, 61, 66
Americans with Disabilities Act (ADA),
    21, 171, 564, 653
American Tort Reform Association, 402, 403
American Tuna Boat Association, 569
American Wholesalers Marketers
    Association, 158
American Wind Energy Association, 370
Ames, 266
Amnesty International, 88, 474, 475
Amway, 463, 471
Amway Asia Pacific, 472
Analysis, of nonmarket issues, 43–44
Andean Community, 532
Anderson, Carolyn, 279
Animal Liberation Front (ALF), 23
Animal welfare, 22

Annan, Kofi, 688, 709
Antibiotics Coalition, 22
Anti-Bribery Convention, 694, 698
Antidumping, 528, 540–544
Antiglobalization protests, 42, 85
Antitrust Division of the Department of Justice, 230, 263
Antitrust laws, 231–232
  automobile industry, 6
  compliance with, 250
  enforcement of, 235–238
  European Union, 425
  exemptions, 233–234
  Microsoft, 1, 3, 41, 257–263
  price fixing case, 252–253
  statutes, 231–232
Antitrust policy, 230–231, 250–251
Antitrust Procedures and Penalties Act, 236
Antitrust statutes, 230, 231–232
Antitrust thought, 238–244
  Chicago school, 241–243
  collusion and price fixing, 247–248
  differences in, 244–250
  mergers and merger guidelines, 248–250
  new IO approach, 243–244
  predatory pricing and entry deterrence, 246–247
  structural approach, 239–241
  vertical arrangements, 244–246
AOL, 24, 68, 250, 260
  antitrust laws, 250
  mergers, 428
AOL Time Warner, 250
Aongsomwang, Saree, 547
Apitzsch, Hannes, 705
Apotex, 409–411
Apple Computer, 260, 387
Apple and private politics in China case, 470
Application of Ethics Principals, 666
Applied ethics, 598
Applied rights analysis, 629–631
Appropriability, 382, 383, 384
Arbitration, 378, 391
Arby's, 23
Arcaini, Tonio, 704
Archer Daniels Midland, 236, 427
Argentina, 291, 447, 481, 488, 530, 532
Armstrong, C. Michael, 215
Armstrong, Scott, 66
Arnold, Benedict, 607
Arrow's impossibility theorem, 183
Arthur Andersen, Enron and, 563, 581–582, 584, 585
Ash Grove Cement, 541
Ashcroft, John, 290
Asia-Pacific Economic Cooperation (APEC), 531
Asner, Ed, 66, 101
Assanand, Sashi, 518
Assessment, of activist organizations, 87–88
Assets, nonmarket, 168–169

Assocham, 514
Associates First Capital Corporation, 318, 603
Association of American Publishers, 26
Association of Community Organizations for Reform Now (ACORN), 126, 319
Association of Independent Employees (AUB), 705
Association of the British Pharmaceutical Industry, 621
Association of Trial Lawyers, 402
Assumption of risk, 399
Asymmetric information, 274
AT&T, 24, 25
  antitrust laws, 235, 242
  Citigroup and, 100
  deregulation, 281, 283, 289
  Google and, 34, 35
  Internet taxation case, 215
  judicial actions, 211
  public advocacy, 210
AT&T and T-Mobile Merger case, 253
Audience interest perspective, 55, 56–57
Audits, in crisis management, 107
Auerbach, Alan, 190
Austin v. Michigan Chamber of Commerce, 164
Australia, 221, 328, 620
Authorization committees, 154
Authors Guild, 26
Automobile industry
  lemon laws, 164
  nonmarket environment of, 5–11
  positioning, 41
  safety regulations, 14–15
Aventis Pharmaceutical, 17, 236, 409, 410, 411
Avoidance, in crisis management program, 108
Avon Products, 471
Axios, 618

B

BAA, 431
Baczko, Joseph, 552
BADvertising Institute, 157
Bahrain, 23, 488, 489
Baidu.com, 28, 472, 473, 702
Baker, Howard, Jr., 199
Balance, in media coverage, 58
Bale, Harvey, 547
Ballmer, Steve, 29, 263
Banco Compartamos, 482, 483, 493–494
Bangladesh, 503
Bank of America, 159, 256, 297
Banks, Louis, 55
Banzhaf, John, 19, 21, 411
Barbecue Industry Association, 185
Barclays, 340, 582, 585
Bargaining, 382
Barnard, Neil, 20, 413

Barnesandnoble.com, 216, 217
Barnette, Curtis, 536
Barns, Abraham, 341
Barriers to entry, 239, 241, 242, 258
Barr Laboratories, 707
Barshefsky, Charlene, 472, 709
BASF, 236
Bayer, 18
Baze, Christine, 222
Beard, Mike, 94
Becker, Dan, 8
Becker, George, 536
Beit Al Etisailat, 705
Behavior, Unethical, 673–674
Belgium, 417, 441, 536
Bell, Georgianna, 620
Benda, Ernst, 93
Benetton, 433
Benfield, James A., 185
Bennington College, 141
Benson, Martha, 97
Benson, Medea, 96
Bentham, Jeremy, 600
Bentley, Jeremy, 353
Bentsen, Lloyd, 209
Berardino, Joseph, 585
Berkshire Hathaway, 128, 309, 659, 679
Bernstein, Carl, 59
Bertelsmann AG, 250, 428
Bethlehem Steel, 536
BEUC, 25
Bharti Airtel Ltd., 498
Bias, in news media, 60–61
BidBay, 39
Bidder's Edge, 39
Biden, Joe, 366
Big Doe, 583
Big River Funding, 582
Bilateral Free Trade Agreement, 539
Bills, 152–154
Biomaterials Access Assurance Act, 402
Bipartisan Campaign Reform Act, 203
Bisio, John, 218, 219
Black economy, 505
Black Women's Agenda, 96
Blackstone Group, 189, 313
Blair, Jayson, 60
Blame avoidance, 155
Blank, Paul, 125
Bloomer, Phil, 486
Blue Circle, 434
Blue Cross of California, 17
Bluewater Network, 50
BMW of North America, 405
Boards of directors
  duties of, 577–579
  Enron, 584–585
Bocchini, Joseph A., 224
Bockstein, Mindy, 24

Bodnar, Andrew G., 410
Boehner, John, 171, 172
Boehringer Ingelheim, 620, 709, 710
Boeing, 549, 692
    ethics and, 659
    nonmarket analysis, 134, 135, 140–149
    nonmarket strategies, 180
Bohannon, Mark, 217
Boies, David, 260
Boise Cascade, campaigns against,
        78, 89, 90–91
Bolivia, 483, 532
Bondurant, Stuart, 404
Boofstin, Robert, 212
Book Search Library Project
        (Google), 26
Boone, Pat, 587
Borders.com, 216–217
Boschwitz, Rudy, 204
Boycotts, 76–77, 78–79, 234
BP, 1, 103, 533, 576
    activist organizations and, 90
    cap-and-trade systems, 327
    company codes, 695, 696
    crisis management, 103, 107, 108,
        110, 114
    emissions trading within, 333
    environmental protection issues, 342
    nonmarket issue analysis, 45
    positioning, 40, 41, 42
    reputation of, 43
BPAmoco, 76
BP Conservation program, 40
Brady, Jim, 26
Brazil, 18, 22, 28, 485, 531, 536, 545, 549
Breach of contract, 211, 324, 389, 623
Brent Spar, 92–95
Breyer, Stephen, 210, 406
Bribery, 693–694, 704–706
BrightSource Energy case, 372–375
Brin, Serge, 28, 35, 472, 475, 700, 701
Brink, Scott, 130
Brinton, Louise, 404
Bristol Myers, 165, 210, 709
Bristol-Myers Squibb, 19, 409–411,
        709, 710
Britain, 449, 503, 507
British Airways, 116, 206, 237,
        247, 252–253
British Columbia College of Physicians
        and Surgeons, 518
British East India Company, 449
British Pharmaceutical Industry, 621
Bromberg, Lee, 26
Bromberg & Sustein, 26
Brookins, Howard, Jr., 219
Brooks Eckerd Pharmacy, 128
Brotz, Melissa, 546, 548
Brown, Jamie, 212
Brown, Mark, 219
Brown, Melvin, 125
Brown & Williamson Tobacco
        Corporation, 67

Browne, Lord, 696
Browner, Carol, 85, 354
Brune, Michael, 76, 98, 346
Bubble program, 336
Buche, Tim, 279
Buchholz, Todd, 412
Buckley v. Valeo, 203
Buffalo Rock Company, 106
Buffett, Warren, 191, 309, 315, 316, 659
Bureaucracy
    China, 449, 456–457
Burger King, acrylamide, 21
Burke, Edmund, 52
Burlington Northern Santa Fe Railway
        Company, 653
Burroughs Wellcome, 707, 710
Bush, George W., 59, 155, 160, 269, 635
    campaign financing, 202
    Enron and, 584
    environmental politics, 340, 341
    executive authority, 155
    Kyoto Protocol, 327, 330
    NAFTA, 538
    peak associations, 206
    pharmaceutical industry, 16, 19
    products liability politics, 403
    regulatory rule making, 270
    steel imports, 537
    taxes, 190, 191
Business, nonmarket analysis for. *See*
        Nonmarket analysis, for business
*Business Electronics Corp. v. Sharp
        Electronics Corp.,* 246
Business environment, 2
    news media and, 53
Business Environmental Leadership
        Council, 40
Business ethics, 595
    See also International business ethics
Business grassroots campaigns, 208
Business groups, in underdeveloped
        markets, 481
Business interactions, with news
        media, 62–65
Business judgment rule, 577
Business nonmarket action,
        criticisms of, 163–166
Business objectives, public interest
        versus, 163–164
Business relationships, in China, 457
Business Roundtable, 205, 558, 566–567, 577
Business Software Alliance (BSA), 39, 466
Business versus business case, 158
Buy, Richard, 585
Byrd Amendment, 533

C

Cable, Stephen, 223
Cable Television Act, 279
Café Borders, 486
Calabresi and Melamed principles, 395–396,
        602–603
California electricity market case, 289–290

California Institute of Technology, 336
California Labor Federation, 127
California Proposition 211, 209
California Public Utilities
        Commission (CPUC), 163, 337, 373, 376
California Space Heaters, Inc., 407–409
Callahan, Michael, 474
CalPERS, 80, 190, 315, 578, 582, 710
Camarillo, Lily, 354
Campaign contributions, 204–205
Campaign financing, myths and
        realities of, 202
Campaigns
    grassroots and constituency, 208–209
    steel imports and, 536–537
Canada
    automobile industry and, 532
    environmental activism in, 346
    international trade policy, 527
    mad cow disease, 21
    NAFTA and, 537, 538
    Toys 'Я' Us case, 552
    trade agreements, 531
    trade disputes, 529
    U.S. protectionism and, 536
    Wal-Mart crisis management
        case, 127–128
Canada Dry, 251
Cancer Research and Prevention
        Foundation, 221–222
Cap-and-trade systems, 327–330
Capobianco, Fabrizio, 35
Capture theory, 277
Carbon dioxide emission regulations, 5, 9
Cardoso e Cunha, Antonio, 440
Caricom, 532
Carlyle, Thomas, 52
Carlyle Group, 190, 191
Carr, Janet, 23
Carrefour, 487, 513, 514
Carried interest taxation, 189–192
Carrows, 673
Carson, Rachel, 76
Carter, Jimmy, 251, 268–269
Case, Steve, 215
Casuistry, 597–598
Catalan Institute of Pharmacology, 287
Categorical imperative, 624
Caterpillar, 331, 403, 524, 536
Causey, Richard, 585
Cawthorne, Paul, 547
CBS, 59, 60, 66–68, 675
CEFIC, 433
Celler-Kefauver Act, 248
Cellular Telecommunications Industry
        Association, 25
Cemex, 164, 172
    antidumping case, 540–544
    emerging markets and, 488
Censorship, in China, 472–476
Center for Auto Safety (CAS), 8, 15, 69
Center for Community and
        Corporate Ethics, 126

Center for Democracy and Technology, 352, 590
Center for Digital Democracy, 24, 590
Center for Environmental Leadership, 40
Center for Medical Consumers, 223
Center for Public Integrity, 196
Center for Responsive Politics, 195, 201
Center for Science in the Public Interest (CSPI), 20, 21, 74, 413
Center on Race, Poverty and the Environment, 353
Centers for Disease Control and Prevention (CDC), 19, 412
Centers for Disease Control and Prevention (CDC) Advisory Committee, 221–222, 224
Central American Common Market, 532
Central Committee (China), 459–460
Central Intelligence Agency (CIA), 502
Central Selling Organization, 702
Cessna Aircraft, 402
Chafee, John H., 160
Chamber of Commerce. *See* U.S. Chamber of Commerce
Chambers, M. Susan, 129
Chan, Elisha, 116
Chan-Fishel, Michelle, 341
    Change ethics and, 593–597
    nonmarket environment, 11–13
    nonmarket strategy and, 32
Chaphe, Robert, 499
Chávez, Hugo, 487, 488, 489
Chavez, R. Martin, 290
Cheeseburger bill. *See* Personal Responsibility in Food Consumption Act
Chester, Jeff, 590
Chewco Investments LP, 582
Chiang Kai-shek, 450
Chicago Climate Exchange, 327
Chicago Federation of Labor, 219
Chicago school, 238, 239, 241–243, 244, 246–248
Chicago Workers' Rights Board, 219
Childhood Vaccine Act, 403
Child Online Protection Act, 26, 475
Children, advertising to, 21
Children's Online Privacy Protection Act, 592
Chile, 346, 481, 532
Chin, Wendall, 125
China, 448
    antidumping measures and, 528
    automobile industry and, 5, 6, 7
    business, 462–464
    Confucianism and social explanations, 453–457
    direct selling case, 471–472
    emerging markets and, 489, 490, 491
    environmental global climate change and, 322
    foreign direct investment, 463
    global climate change and, 322
    Google, 27–28, 472–476, 699–702

historical background, 448–453
human rights issues, 686
international trade policy and WTO membership, 463–464
Kyoto Protocol and, 330–331, 491
Levi Strauss & Company, 649–650
most favored nation status, 179
Nike and, 95, 96
nonmarket environment and four I's, 457–462
nonmarket issues, 464–469
protectionism, 535
regulation, 464
state-owned enterprises, 462–463
China Democratic Party, 465
China Labor Watch, 119, 469
Chinese Communist Party (CCP)
    Chinese history and, 448, 450–452, 522
    direct selling case, 471–472
    human rights issues, 465
    intellectual property issues, 466
    nonmarket environment, 457, 458, 459–460, 461
Chinese market, 48
Chipotle Mexican Grill and Undocumented Workers, 648, 654–656
Chirac, Jacques, 179, 180
Chocolate Manufacturers Association, 185
Choi, Francis, 118
Choice. *See* Decision making
Christian Aid, 567
Chrysler, 7, 70, 199, 300, 304
Ciba-Geigy, 249
Cigna Corporation, 209
Cipla, 548, 710
Cisco Systems
    antitrust laws, 250
    China and, 466, 475
    international trade policy, 525
    Internet taxation case, 217
    positioning, 41
Citibank, 45–46
    corporate social responsibility, 671
    private politics and, 99, 100
Citicorp, 318
CitiFinancial, 318
Citigroup, 1, 97
    activist organizations and, 89
    activist strategies, 84
    activist targeting of, 116–117
    boycotts against, 76
    Calabresi and Melamed principles, 602
    corporate social responsibility, 671
    crisis management, 107
    Enron and, 564, 581, 582, 583, 584
    environmental programs, 322
    environmental protection issues, 343
    Equator Principles, 340
    ethics and, 659
    private politics case, 97–100
    subprime lending case, 318–320
Citigroup: Responsibility Under Fire, 671–672

Citizen journalism, 62
Citizens' Clearinghouse for Hazardous Waste, 345
City of Hope Medical Center (COH), 389
Civil Aeronautics Board (CAB), 15
Civil law, 381
Civil Rights Act (1866), 634
Civil Rights Act (1964), 353, 623, 633, 636, 646, 647
Civil Rights Act (1991), 635, 636
Civil war, in China, 450
Claimed rights, 629–630
Clark, Sarah, 127
Class action lawsuits, 7, 12, 157
Clayton, Kenneth, 296
Clayton Act, 230, 231, 232, 233, 234, 235, 250
Clean Air Act, 6, 133, 177, 309, 349–350
Clean Air Act Amendments (1977), 183
Clean Air Act Amendments (1990), 328, 336, 345, 348
    cap-and-trade systems, 327, 328
    distributive politics, 339
    Environmental Defense and, 345
Clean Air Northfield, 342
Clean Air Working Group, 206
Clean Development Mechanism (CDM) program, 332, 469
Cleaner and Greener Green Energy program, 328
Clean Water Act, 129, 334, 335, 336, 338
Cleland, Scott, 24
Cleveland Clinic, 287
Client politics, 138, 139, 177–178, 386, 458, 524
Clinical trial obligations, 644
Clinton, Hillary, 191, 203
Clinton, William Jefferson, 12
    Abbott Laboratories, 546–547
    Btu tax, 337
    China and, 472
    EU carbon tax case, 439–441
    executive authority, 155
    health care reform, 210
    Internet taxation, 216
    Kyoto Protocol, 330–331
    luxury tax repeal and, 160
    market opening, 539
    NAFTA, 537–538
    news media and, 59
    pollution credits trading systems case, 354, 355
    products liability politics, 401–402
    regulation, 269, 270, 278
    steel imports, 536, 537
    Superfund, 337
    sweatshops, 688
    vote recruitment by, 174
Cloture, 152
Cloud, Doyle, 199
CNN, 62, 213, 517
Coalition building, 140, 148, 172, 181, 205–207

Coalition for Justice in the Maquiladoras, 683
Coalition nonmarket strategies, 168
Coalition of Labor Union Women, 96, 222
Coalition of Tri-Lakes Committees, 129
Coalition on Smoking OR Health, 157
Coalitions, consensus in, 206–207
Coase theorem, 324–327
Coca-Cola Company
    antitrust laws, 251
    boycotts against, 76
    European Union and, 425, 426, 438
    Greenpeace and, 93
    judicial actions, 211
Cohen, Ben, 413
Cohen, Jacqueline, 158
Collateralized Debt Obligations (CDOs), 293
Collective action, 140, 150–151, 169
Collevecchio Declaration, 340
Collins, Philip, 252
Collusion, 234
    Chicago school, 241–243
    mergers and, 248–249
    structural approach, 239–241
Colombia, 488, 532
Columbia University, private politics at, 98–99, 118
Comcast, 254, 278
Comer, Clarence, 541
Command-and-control regulation, 324
Commercial Credit Corporation, 318
Commercial law, 381
Commission. *See* Regulatory commissions
Commission of the European Union, 18
Committee of Permanent Representatives (COREPER), 421, 435, 437
Committees, in U.S. Congress, 154
Committee staffs, in U.S. Congress, 154–155
Committee to End Tax-Funded Abortions, 86
Commodities and Futures Trading Commission (CFTC), 303
Common Agriculture Policy (CAP), 428, 527
Common Cause, 58
Common law, 381
Common Market of the European Union, 531
Common-Sense Consumption Act, 20
Communication, in crisis management program, 111–113
Communications Decency Act (CDA), 38, 68
Communist era, in China, 450–452
Communities for a Better Environment, 353–355, 356
Community Reinvestment Act (CRA), 90, 299, 319
Community Research Initiative of New England, 616
Company codes, 695–696

Compaq, 215, 259, 261
Comparative advantage, 520
Comparative damages, 401
Compassion Over Killing, 22
Compatibility, 239, 243
Compensatory damages, 400
Compensatory justice, 639–640
Competition
    Chicago school, 241
    majority-building strategies and, 174
    nonmarket strategy and, 32–33
    pluralism of, 163
    political, 137–140
Competition policy, of European Union, 425–430
Competitive Enterprise Institute (CEI), 20
Competitiveness, in emerging markets, 478–479
Competitive theory, 520–522
Complementary products, 385
Compliance, 250, 563–564
Comptroller of the Currency (OCC), 314, 317, 319
Compulsory licensing, 709–710
CompuServe, 250
Computer and Communications Industry Association (CCIA), 26, 255, 427
Concentration. *See* Industry concentration
Concerned Families for ATV Safety, 279
Condorcet's Paradox and Arrow's impossibility theorem, 183
Conerly, Bill, 487
Confederation of Food and Drink Industries, 433
Confederation of India Industry, 514
Conference of Nations, 682
Conflict diamonds case, 702–704
Confrontational and Cooperative Private Politics, Synergies, 83
Confucianism, 448, 453–457
Confucius, 453, 454, 455
Conglomerate merger, 234
Congo, 498
Congressional Black Caucus, 319, 586
Congressional Support Group, 200
Congress Party (India), 503, 504, 514, 516
Coniston, 675
Conner, Adam, 48
Consensus, in coalitions, 206
Consequential damages, 390
Conservation International (CI), 40, 83, 88, 343, 344
Constituency campaigns, 208–209
Constituency connection, 155
Constituency Power, 304
Constituents, 155
Consultative Group to Assist the Poor, 494
Consumentenbond, 434
Consumer Electronics Association, 416
Consumer Federation of America (CFA), 119, 150, 277, 318
Consumer Financial Protection Bureau (CFPB), 303

Consumer Products Safety Commission (CPSC), 75, 266, 270, 279, 408
    California Space Heaters, Inc. case, 407–409
    crisis management and, 117, 118, 119
Consumer rewards, for corporate social performance, 573
Consumer surplus, 272
Consumers Union, 256
Consuming Trade Action Coalition, 536
Continental TV v. GTE Sylvania, 245
Contractarian framework, 641
Contracts, 388–391
Contractual joint ventures (CJVs), 463
Contributory negligence, 400
Controls, on lobbying, 200–201
Cookies (Internet), 431
Co-op America, 486
Cooperative Private Politics, 81–83
Coordinating Committee for Multilateral Export Controls (CoCom), 172
Coordinating Sphere of Activities Law, 554
Copper Indium Gallium Selenide (CIGS), 365
Copiepresse, 26
Copyrights, 386–387
    See also Intellectual property
Core Financial Partners, 191
Core principles, 672–673
Cornell University, private politics at, 101
Coro's, 673
Coronado, Rodney, 23
Corporate financial performance (CFP), 574, 580
Corporate governance, 564, 576–579
Corporate social performance (CSP), 568–573
Corporate social responsibility (CSR), 557
    audience effects, 662
    challenge of, 670–673
    Citigroup, 671
    core principles and their evolution, 672–673
    corporate governance, 576–579, 580–585
    corporate social performance, 568–570
    Enron case, 580–585
    GlaxoSmithKline case, 710
    Google, 27
    legal compliance, 563–564
    profit maximization and, 558–563
    stakeholder theory, 564–566
    summary, 574
    trust gap, 557–558
    Wal-Mart case, 124–131
Correction of a defect, 400
Corruption, 467–468
Corzine, Jon, 203
Costco, 128, 130
Cost-of-service regulation, 283
Costs
    news media, 61

nonmarket action, 135–136
protectionism, 535
Cotton, Richard, 71
Council of Ministers (EU), 421–422, 428, 435, 437, 439, 441, 443
Countervailing duties, 528
Country assessment, 477–480
CountryWatch, 504
Counts, Alex, 494
Coups, 488
Court of Justice (European Union), 420, 422
Courts. *See* Judiciary; U.S. Supreme Court
Cowell, Lisa, 216
Cox, Christopher, 214
Crandall, Robert L., 206
Cranston, Alan, 204
Credibility, 178, 198–199
Credit Availability, 304–305
Credit cards, 45
Credit claiming, 155
Credit default swap, 294
Credit Lyonnais, 340, 563
Credit rating agencies, 306
Credit Suisse, 340, 369
Criminal Law Convention on Corruption, 698
Crises, nature and causes of, 102–103
Crisis development, pattern of, 103–107
Crisis management, 102
    Mattel case, 116–120
    Merck case, 286–287
    summary, 115–116
    Wal-Mart case, 124–131
Crisis management program, components of, 107–115
Crisis preparedness, 108–110
Croma, 514
Cromme, Gerhard, 706
Crosby, Susan, 222
Cross-subsidization, 280–281
Cruz Azul, 541
Cuisinart, 236
Cultural imperialism, 681
Cultural relativism, 683–685
Culture, in emerging markets, 480
Cummings, Elijah, 120
Cummins Inc.
    corporate social responsibility, 696–698
    questionable foreign payments guide of, 696–697
Customer service case, 675–677
CVS, 128
CV Therapeutics, 644
Cypress Semiconductors, 562

D

Dach, Leslie, 586
Daimler-Chrysler, 128
Dalai Lama, 474, 487
Daley, Richard, 220
Daley-Harris, Sam, 494
Damages, in products liability cases, 400–401

Danel, Carlos, 483, 493, 494
Daoism, 448
Daschle, Thomas A., 186
Data Quality Act, 270
Data Retention Directive (EU), 25
Dateline (television program), 66, 70–71, 170
Davidson, Alan, 212
Davies, Simon, 590
Davis, Gray, 217, 290
Dawson, Don, 126
Daylight Saving Time Coalition, 133, 138, 168, 181–182, 185, 205
Daylight saving time politics, 184–187
Deadweight loss (DWL), 271, 272
Dealing, exclusive, 234
Dean, Howard, 125, 218
De Beers, 702–704
Debevoise & Plimpton LLP, 706
Debrowski, Thomas A., 117, 119
Decision making, 50
    moral transgressions and, 666
    nonmarket strategies, 191–192, 205–206
Defamation, 22, 66–68, 71–88
Defects, 398
Deferred compensation, at Enron, 584
Deficit Reduction Act, 149, 160
Delaney amendment, 338
DeLauro, Rosa, 20
Delegation, 267–269
Delisi, Dianne, 223
Dell, 35, 260, 276
Delors, Jacques, 440
Delta Air Lines, 206
Demand-side increasing returns, 243
Democracy, 52
Democratic revolutions, 488
Deng Xiaoping, 452, 459
Denier, Greg, 126
Denison, Richard, 345
Denmark
    environmental management and stability, 322
    EU carbon tax case, 439, 440
    EU nonmarket issues, 430
    McDonald's in, 22
    Shell case, 92
Denny's, 111, 116, 673, 675–677
    Customer Service case, 675–677
Deontological ethics systems, 622, 623
Department of Justice, 676
Deregulation, 283–285
    California electricity market case, 289–290
Design defects, 399
D'Esposito, Steve, 93
Det Norske Veritas, 94
Deutsche Bank AG, 316
Deutscher Gewerkschaftsbund (DGB), 434
Deutsche Telekom, 253, 255
Developing countries
    AIDS and, 687–688
    GlaxoSmithKline case, 707–708

operations in, 686–687
    See also Emerging markets
Dickenson, Larry S., 179
Diet (Japan), 176
Digene Corporation, 222
Digital Millennium Copyright Act (DMCA), 39
Dingell, John, 114, 157
Directive on Data Protection (EU), 421, 431, 442–444
Direct Marketing Association, 227, 228
Direct-to-consumer advertising, 36–37
Disclaimers, 400
Discovery credit cards, 128
Discretion, 267–269
Discrimination, 27, 130
Disparate impact versus Disparate treatment, 635
Dispute resolution, 528–530
    news media, 65–69
Dispute Settlement Body (DSB), 528–531, 682
Distribution, altruism and, 602
Distribution channels, 248
Distributive consequences, 133, 142–144
Distributive justice, 638–639
Distributive politics, 339
Distributive politics spreadsheet, 136–137, 146, 147
Dixon, Pam, 24
DLC Management, 190
DLF Universal, 515
Dobriansky, Paula, 475
Dr. Miles Medical Co. v. John D. Park & Sons, 244
Doctors Without Borders, 547, 688
Dodd-Frank Wall Street Reform Act, 301–307
Dodson, William, 582
Doerfler, Katrina, 218
Doha Round, 489, 519, 527, 531
Dolan, Peter R., 410, 411
Dole, Elizabeth H., 186
Dole, Robert, 79, 141, 160, 186
Domestic reform, in China, 453
Domino's Pizza, 86, 596
Dongguan Zhongxin Toner Powder Factory, 117
Dongxing New Energy Company, 117
Dorgan, Byron, 216
DotOrg, 28
DoubleClick, 24–25, 29, 207
Douglass, Adele, 22
Dow Chemical, 84, 85, 321, 344–345, 576
Dow Corning Company, 404
Drea, Elizabeth, 219
Dreyer's Grand Ice Cream, 249
Drummond, David, 24, 29, 386
Drunk driving, 6, 13
Drury, Richard, 354
Due process, 267–269
Duke Power, 289

Dun & Bradstreet v. Greenmoss Builders, 67
Dunkin' Donuts, 486, 507
DuPont, 11, 84, 322, 341, 343
Duty
    boards of directors, 577–578
    countervailing, 528
    justice and, 644–645
    utilitarian, 602–603
Duty of care, 577
Duty of loyalty, 577
Duty to warn, 398
Dynamic efficiency, 243, 244
Dynamic Internet Technology (DIT), 474
Dynegy, 284

E

Eagle Invest & Finance AG, 705
Early Light Industrial Company, 118
Earth Island Institute (EII), 50, 76, 569
Earth Liberation Front (ELF), 23
Eastern Airlines, 674
*Eastern Railroad Conference v. Noerr
    Motor Freight,* 164
Eastman Kodak, 579
eBay
    coalitions and consensus, 206–207
    integrated strategy, 38–39, 41
    international strategy, 33
    monopolies and, 233
    news media and, 68
Eckert, Robert A., 117, 118, 119
E-commerce, 506
Economic and Monetary Union (EMU),
    424–425
Economic efficiency, 241, 242
Economic freedom, emerging markets, 478
Economic policy, antitrust policy and, 230
Economic Recovery Tax Act (ERTA), 140,
    141, 144, 148
Economics, international trade policy,
    520–523
Ecuador, 532
Eddie Bauer, 686
Edelman, 586
Editors, 59
E-Fairness Coalition, 216
Effective National Action to Control
    Tobacco (ENACT), 157
Effectiveness, of nonmarket action, 135–136
Eggart, Tim, 93
Egypt, 499
Eichorn, Tom, 354
Eiger, Peter, 478
Eighth International Conference on AIDS in
    Asia and the Pacific, 547
Eizenstat, Stuart, 217
Ekbom Support Group, 621
Elanco Animal Health, 22
Election financing laws, 202–203
Electoral strategies, 202
Electoral support, 202–205
Électricité de France, 63, 442
Electricity market, in California, 289–290

Electric power, deregulation of, 283–284
Electronic Frontier Foundation, 227
Electronic Industries Association, 174
Electronic Privacy Information Center
    (EPIC), 23, 24, 443, 589–590, 592
Eli Lilly & Co., 389, 467
Elise, Kimberly, 221
El Salvador, 66
Emergency Committee for American
    Trade, 537
Emergency Medical Treatment and Active
    Labor Act (EMTALA), 275
Emergency Planning and Community
    Right-to-Know Act, 334
Emerging markets, 477
    Banco Compartamos case, 493–494
    country assessment, 477–480
    Kiva case, 495–496
    MTN Group Limited case, 498–500
    nonmarket environment,
        management in, 492–493
    opportunities, 480–487
    risk assessment, 487–492
    summary, 493
    Tesco PLC case, 512–515
EMI Group, 428
Emission trading systems, 332
Empirical research, on corporate social
    performance, 574–576
Employee rewards, for corporate social
    performance, 573
Empresas Tolteca, 541
Endangered Species Act, 270, 334, 374
Enel, 705
Energy Information Administration, 32
Energy issues, in China, 468–469
Energy Policy Act, 284, 365
Enforceability, of contracts, 388–389
Enforcement, 14, 15, 26
Engineering controls, under EPA, 335
England, 552
Enron, 1
    Citigroup and, 99, 100
    corporate social responsibility case,
        580–585
    ethics and, 595
    manipulation by, 165
Enron Columbia Energy BV, 581
Enron Energy Services, 289
Enron Power Marketing, Inc., 289–290
Entitlements, 394–396
Entrepreneurial politics, 138, 139, 368,
    524, 537
Entry deterrence, 246–247
Environmental Defense, 322
    environmental protection issues,
        343, 344–345
    Equator Principles, 340, 341
    McDonald's and, 21
    Wal-Mart and, 587
Environmental Demonstration Store, 343
Environmental Injustice case, 656
Environmental issues China, 468–469

Google, 27
    McDonald's and, 22
Environmentalist Opposition, 361
Environmentalist versus Environmentalist
    case, 356
Environmental justice case, 353–356
Environmental management and stability, 321
    cap-and-trade systems, 327–330
    emission trading systems, 330–333
    Environmental Protection Agency,
        333–337
    externalities, socially efficient control of,
        324–327
    global climate change, 322, 330–333
    goals and actions, 321–322
    policy, 322–323, 333–337
    political economy of, 338–342
    pollution credits trading systems case,
        353–356
    protection issues, 342–346
    regulation, 333–334
    summary, 347–348
    tradeoffs, 323–324
    voluntary collective programs, 347
Environmental politics, 338
Environmental Protection Agency (EPA), 5
    advocacy science and, 338–339
    automobile industry and, 8
    California Space Heaters, Inc. case, 407
    cap-and-trade systems, 327–328
    crisis management and, 116, 118, 129
    environmental policy, 333–337
    environmental politics, 338, 341
    fuel economy standards case, 5
    pollution credits trading systems case,
        328, 353, 355
    private and public politics, 326
    regulation, 266, 270, 271
    responsiveness of, 180
    restaurant industry, 20
    trade disputes, 529
    utilitarianism and, 669
Environmental protection issues, 342–346
Environmental risks, in emerging
    markets, 491
Epstein, Richard, 548
Equal employment opportunity, 267, 629,
    633–636
Equal Employment Opportunity Commission
    (EEOC), 267, 634–635, 646, 653
Equator Principles, 44, 82, 88, 322, 340–341,
    343, 491
Equity Bank of Kenya, 496
Equity joint ventures (EJVs), 463
Ernst & Young, 16, 96, 97
Escalation stage of crisis life cycle, 103–104
Escola v. Coca Cola Bottling Co., 398
eSolar, Inc., 28
Esso, 40, 86, 92
Ethics, 594
    casuistry, 597–598
    defining, 595
    managerial role of, 594

methodology of, 598–599
moral philosophy and political philosophy, 599–600
Norplant System case, 613–615
personal and business, 595
Pfizer case, 288
politics and change, 596–597
private interests and, 596
summary, 612
See also International business ethics
Ethics analysis process, 599
Ethics, Behavioral, 659–660
altruism, 660–662
audience effect, 662–663
experimental conclusions, 667–668
experiments, 660–668
in groups, 665–666
overconfidence, 668
self-interest, 660–662
Ethics and Compliance Officer Association, 659
Ethics Committee of the American Society for Reproductive Medicine, 518
Ethics in Government Act, 201
Ethics principles
paternalism and, 637
questionable payments and, 691–692
Ethics systems, 659–660
Advanced Technology Laboratories case, 517–518
classification of, 622
corporate social responsibility, challenge of, 670–673
Denny's customer service case, 675–677
Gilead Sciences case, 615–618
higher order standards for, 650
Levi Strauss and global sourcing, 650–651
nonmarket action, moral determinants of, 594
summary, 674–675
unethical behavior, sources of, 673–674
See also Justice; Rights; Utilitarianism
Ethnic conflicts, in emerging markets, 458
ETI, 551
EURATOM, 417
Euro Crisis case, 444
European Agency for the Evaluation of Medicinal Products, 18, 221
European Automobile Manufacturers Association, 6
European Banking Federation, 429
European Central Bank, 419, 424–425
European Chemical Industry Council (CEFIC), 433, 442
European Chemicals Agency, 432
European Coal and Steel Community (ECSC), 417
European Coal and Steel Council Consultative Committee, 442
European Commission, 6, 24, 418, 420, 423, 426–427, 435, 436, 439, 591
European Confederation of Retail Trade, 433

European Council, 421
European Court of Human Rights, 68
European Court of Justice, 681
European Economic and Social Committee (EESC), 423
European Economic Community (EEC), 417
European Environment Agency (EEA), 332
European Federation of Pharmaceutical Industries' Associations, 434
European Information Technology Roundtable, 437
European Monetary System, 417
European Parliament (EP), 6, 119, 177, 419–420, 422, 435–436, 443, 547
European Roundtable of Industrialists, 433
European System of Central Banks, 424
European Trading System (ETS), 332, 434
European Union
agenda setting, 177
antitrust laws, 250
applied rights analysis and, 629
bribery and, 698
cap-and-trade systems, 327
carbon dioxide emission regulations, 10
China and, 463
crisis management and, 119
Doha Round, 531
emissions trading in, 332
fuel economy regulation in, 5–6
GlaxoSmithKline case, 620
Google, 24
international law and, 681
international trade policy, 527, 528, 529
legislative process, 423, 424
lobbying in, 34
McDonald's, 22
Microsoft antitrust case, 257
pharmaceutical industry, 18
pivotal voters and, 176
price fixing case, 252–253
Single European Act, 418–419
trade agreements, 531
trade disputes, 529–530
U.S. protectionism and, 537
value-added tax, 217, 419
European Union Committee of the American Chamber of Commerce (Amcham), 434
European Union political economy, 417–418
carbon tax case, 439–442
Directive on Data Protection case, 442–444
institutions, 420–430
interests and their organization, 433–434
Maastricht Treaty, 418–419
nonmarket issues, 430–433
nonmarket strategies in, 434–438
Single European Act, 417–418
summary, 439
Evans, Daniel, 142
Evans, Donald, 584
Evolution of Private Politics, 76
Exclusive dealing, 234
Executive authority, 155
Executive branch, 155–156

access to, 199
China, 530–531
See also Institutions; Presidency; *specific U.S. presidents*
Executive Order 12291, 269
Exemptions, 233–234
Exon, J. James, 184, 186–187
Expectations damages, 390
Expectations statements, 671–672
Export-Import Bank (Eximbank), 133, 140, 142, 144, 340
Export Trading Company Act, 233
Express warranties, 397
Externalities, 272
network, 239, 243
socially efficient control of, 324–327
Extractive Industries Transparency Initiative, 696
Exxon, 335
crisis management, 103, 104–105, 106, 109, 113
environmental issues, 334
ExxonMobil, 43
activist targeting of, 86
corporate social responsibility, 671
emerging markets and, 492
reputation of, 43
Exxon Valdez oil spill, 3, 102, 103–104, 110, 113–114, 335, 405, 573

F

Facebook in China case, 47
Facebook and Online Privacy case, 588
Fair Labor Association (FLA), 75, 89, 131, 468, 684, 689–690
Fair Labor Standards Act, 270
Fairness
justice as, 640–642
news media, 58, 60–61
regulation, 277
Fair trade, 485–486
Fairtrade Labeling Organization (FLO), 486, 487
Fair trade laws, 236
Families USA, 16
Family Leave Act, 280
Fannie Mae, 301
Farroukh, Ahamad, 499
Fast-food industry, nonmarket environment of, 19–23
Fastow, Andrew, 563, 581, 582, 583, 585
Fay, Christopher, 94
Featherstone, Lisa, 124
Federal Aviation Administration (FAA), 188, 267, 282, 604
Federal Bureau of Investigation (FBI), 72, 91, 106, 236, 372, 410, 680
Federal Communications Commission (FCC), 12, 35, 168, 185, 249, 266
affirmative action and, 647
auctions, 285
· Google, 34, 35
utilitarianism and, 607

Federal Deposit Insurance Corporation (FDIC), 128, 159, 292, 319–320
Federal Election Campaign Act (FECA), 202
Federal Election Commission (FEC), 202, 203
Federal Energy Regulatory Commission, 266, 267, 284, 289, 373, 584
Federal Express, 596
  ad hoc coalitions, 206
  Environmental Defense and, 345
  labor organization and, 188
  lobbying, 200
Federal judiciary, 155
Federal Register, 268
Federal Reserve Board, 319
Federal Reserve System, 295
Federal Trade Commission (FTC)
  antitrust laws, 231, 235–236, 237, 239, 250–251
  Citigroup case, 319
  Google, 23, 24, 26
  news media and, 68
  patents case, 410, 411
  privacy regulations, 24, 25
  responsiveness of, 180
  restaurant industry, 19
Federal Trade Commission Act, 230, 232, 235, 251
Federal Water Pollution Control Act, 334
Federation of Associations of Maharashtra (FAM), 514
Federation of German Employers' Associations (BDA), 433
Federation of German Industry (BDI), 433
FedEx Systems, 321, 345
Feinstein, Dianne, 290
Feist Publications, Inc. v. Rural Telephone Service Co., 39, 387
Felando, August, 569
Feldmayer, Johannes, 705
Fenton, David, 53
Fenton Communications, 53, 404
Fiat, 428
Fifth Amendment, 266, 585, 646
Figueroa, Alfredo Acosta, 374
Fill, Dennis C., 517
Financial Crisis (2007–2009), 296–301
  inquiry Commission, 298–300
  See also The Financial Crisis Inquiry Commission (FCIC)
Financial Crisis Inquiry Commission (FCIC), 298–300
Financial Market, 291
Financial restrictions, in emerging markets, 489
Financial Stability Oversight Council, 302
Finland, 418, 440, 447, 479
Fiorina, Carly, 214
First Amendment, 26, 56, 67, 68, 139, 162–164, 200, 203, 227, 306, 315, 386
First Five Year Plan (China), 451
First-mover advantage, 87, 223
First National Bank of Boston v. Bellotti, 163–164

Fish and Wildlife Foundation, 343, 587
Flagstar, Inc., 675, 676, 677
Flanagan, Brian, 411
Flannery, Mark, 495
Fleischer, Peter, 23, 25
Fleischer, Victor, 189, 191
FLO-Cert Ltd., 486
Focus, 200
Fonovisa, Inc. v. Cherry Auctions, Inc., 39
Food and Drug Administration (FDA), 4
  crisis management and, 105–106, 110, 111, 114, 116, 119, 121
  Gilead Sciences case, 615, 616, 617, 618
  GlaxoSmithKline cases, 619, 620, 707
  lobbying and, 220, 221, 224
  mad cow disease, 21
  patents case, 409
  Pfizer case, 288
  pharmaceutical industry, 16, 17, 18, 19, 36, 37, 38, 165
  pharmaceutical politics and, 207
  preemption, 400, 401
  regulation, 271, 278
  restaurant industry, 20, 21
  tobacco politics, 157
  trade association lobbying and, 206
  utilitarianism and, 609
Food Marketing Institute (FMI), 158
Ford, Wendell, 184
Ford Motor Company
  activist targeting of, 86
  Center for Environmental Leadership, 40–41
  nonmarket strategies, 179
  product liability, 6
  recalls, 6
Foreign Corrupt Practices Act (FCPA), 681, 683, 691, 694–695, 696, 698–699, 706
Foreign direct investment (FDI), 504
  China, 463–464
  India, 512–515
Foreign Investment Promotion Board (India), 508, 513
Foreign payments, questionable, 691–698
Foreign relations, of pre-Republican China, 448–449
Forest and Biodiversity Conservation Alliance, 88
Forest Ethics, 346
Forest Stewardship Council (FSC), 75, 82, 91, 346
Formal and Informal (Shadow) Banking Systems, 291–295
Fourteenth Amendment, 266, 267, 634, 636
Fourth Amendment, 628
"Fourth branch," 52
  See also Journalism; News media
Fourth International North Sea Conference, 93
Fox, 59, 270
France, 428, 429
  EU carbon tax case, 440, 441
  EU nonmarket issues, 430, 432

Google in, 26, 27
  Greenpeace and, 93
  lobbying in, 435
  Mattel crisis management case, 116
  nonmarket strategy, 438
  Shell case, 92
  trade disputes, 529
  U.S. protectionism and, 536
  Yahoo!, 33
Franchisees, of McDonald's, 22
Franchisement, 170
Franchising, in European Union, 438
Frank, Barney, 301
Frank, Reuven, 59
Franklin, Benjamin, 184
Freddie Mac, 318
Free the Grapes, 139
Free trade agreements, 7, 12
  See also specific free trade agreements
Freedom, in emerging markets, 478
Freedom House, 477–478
Free-rider problem, 84, 135–137, 139, 149–151, 163
Fresenius Medical Care (China) case, 679–680
Friedman, Milton, 558–562, 602
Friends of the Earth, 341
Frontline Wireless, 25
Fuel economy regulation, 5
Fujita, Den, 554
Fumento, Michael, 61
Funambol, 35
Future of Music Coalition, 256

G

G-8, antiglobalization protests against, 85
Gallant, Paul, 27
Galloway, Ron, 126
Galson, Steven, 287
Galvin, Robert, 4
Gandhi, Mohandas, 503
Gandhi, Rajiv, 504
Gap Inc., 576
Garnier, Jean-Pierre, 707, 708, 711
Gartner, Michael, 58, 66, 71
Gatch, Mary, 570
Gates, Bill, 257, 258, 260, 263, 495, 678, 700
Gates Foundation, 548, 688, 709
Gateway, 218
Gay and Lesbian Alliance Against Defamation, 254
Gazprom, 696
GE Consumer Finance, 128
Genentech, 388, 389
General Accounting Office (GAO), 214, 216, 656
General Agreement on Tariffs and Trade (GATT), 167, 172, 452, 519, 525, 526, 528, 530, 544, 550
General Agreement on Trade in Services (GATS), 526
General Aviation Revitalization Act, 402

General Electric (GE), 59
  antitrust laws, 250
  campaigns against, 78, 80
  corporate social responsibility, 671
  European Union and, 428
  General Motors (GM), 43
  EU nonmarket issues, 431
  international trade policy, 523
  judicial actions, 211
  market for control, 579
  news media and, 66, 69–71
  nonmarket analysis, 136
  nonmarket strategies, 180
  safety regulations, 14
  steel imports and, 536–537
General Motors, 41, 43, 69–71, 322
General Services Administration (GSA), 14
Generic activist strategies, 86–87
Generic nonmarket strategies, 172–180
Generic Pharmaceutical Industry Association
  (GPIA), 207
Genetically modified organisms (GMOs),
  431, 480, 530, 629
Genetic Information Nondiscrimination
  Act, 653
Genetic testing in workplaces (case),
  652–653
Geneva Convention, 681
Genmar, 207
Gente Nueva, 493
Gephardt, Richard, 218
Gerard, Joe, 339
German Toy Manufacturers Association, 553
Germany, 429, 430
  EU carbon tax case, 440, 441
  EU nonmarket issues, 430, 432
  interests, 433–434
  lobbying in, 34, 435
  nonmarket strategy, 438
  pharmaceutical industry, 18
  Pizza Hut in, 79
  Shell in, 92–94
  Siemens case, 704–705
  Toys 'Я' Us case, 553
  trade disputes, 529
Ghana, 498, 500
Gilding, Paul, 76, 84
Gilead Sciences, 40, 41, 493, 610,
  615–616, 688
Gillen, Michele, 70, 71
Gilmore, James, 215
Ginsburg, Ruth Bader, 386
Girls, missing, 511–512
Glass-Steagal Act, 162, 296, 308
GlaxoSmithKline (GSK), 18, 37
  AIDS drugs pricing case, 707–711
  lobbying case, 221, 222
  private and public politics, 80
  restless leg syndrome case, 619–621
Glaxo Wellcome, 707
Global Alliance, 206
Global Business Dialogue on Electronic
  Commerce, 215

Global capital requirements
  regulation-Basel III, 307
Global climate change, 322, 330–333
Global Crossing, 563
Global Exchange, 42, 86, 96, 486, 572
Global Finance Campaign, 98–101
Global Fund to Fight AIDS, Tuberculosis and
  Malaria, 546, 617, 688, 709
Global Health Program, 548
Global Internet Freedom Act, 475
Global Internet Task Force, 475
Globalization case (Toys 'Я' Us), 552–556
  See also International trade policy
Global market strategies, 32–33
Global sourcing, 649–650
Global Witness, 703
GlobeScan Inc., 557
Goals, for environmental management and
  stability, 321–322
Golden Rule, 455
Goldman Sachs, 103, 112, 116, 290, 292–294
Goldman Sachs Alternative Mortgage
  Products (GSAMP) trust, 293
Goldman Sachs and Its Reputation case, 308
Goldstein, Michael, 554
Goodman, Ellen, 220
Google, 1
  China case, 472–476
  EU nonmarket issues, 430
  integrated strategy, 34–38
  nonmarket capabilities, 212–213
  nonmarket environment of, 23–29
  trade secrets, 387
Google Earth, 23, 28
Google Health, 27
Google in India case, 515–517
Google News, 26
Google Out of China case, 699
Gore, Al, 354, 584, 652
Gorton, Slade, 142, 184
Government, corporate social responsibility
  and, 560–561
Government agencies. *See* Regulatory
  agencies; *specific agencies*
Government allies, 200
Government arenas, nonmarket strategies for.
  See Nonmarket strategy (government
  arenas); Nonmarket strategy
  implementation (government arenas)
Government enforcement, of antitrust laws,
  235–237
Government imperfections, 276–277
Government institutions. *See* Institutions;
  specific government institutions
Government procurement, 528
Government Procurement
  Agreement (GPA), 528
Government regulation. *See* Regulation
Graham, David, 287
Grameen Bank, 482
Grameen Foundation, 494
Gramm-Leach-Bliley Act, 162, 296
Grandin, Temple, 22

Granted rights, 629–630
Grassroots Action Information Network, 206
Grassroots campaigns, 208–209
Great Leap Forward (China), 451
Greece, 441
Greed, Linda, 339
Green Corps, 99
Greenip, Janet, 223
Green Lights Programme (EU), 22
Greenman v. Yuba Power Products, 398
Greenmoss Builders, 67
Greenpeace, 22, 53, 93
  activist strategy, 86, 91
  campaigns, 79
  firm challenges against, 90
  news media and, 53, 68
  nonmarket analysis, 133
  private politics case, 92–94
Greenwald, Robert, 125
Greenwood, James, 580
Griggs v. Duke Power, 635
Gronet, Chris, 366
Gross, Taylor, 587
Grossman, Andy, 126
Grove, Andy, 214, 215, 317
Growth hormones, 21
Grubman, Jack, 100
Grupo Cementos Apasco, S.A. de C.V.
  (Apasco), 541
GTE, 245, 250
Guanxi, 456–457, 459
Guomindang (GMD), 450, 453
Guruswamy, Mohan, 514

H

Habitat for Humanity, 99
Hague Declaration, 682
Haldane, J. B. S., 652
Hallmark Cards, 13
Halvorson, Debbie, 224
Hamied, Yusuf, 548
Hand, Learned, 233
Handelsanstalldas Forbund, 555
Handler, Brent, 55
Hannah, Daryl, 119
*Hanson Trust PLC v. ML SCM
  Acquisition,* 577
Hard money, 203
Hardee's, 185
Harkin, Tom, 20
Harmonization, 418
Harrington, Michael, 548
Harris, William, 260
Hart-Scott-Rodino Antitrust Improvements
  Act, 235
Harvard Vanguard Medical Associates, 616
Hasbro, 277
Hastert, Dennis, 20, 413
Hatteras Yachts, 160
Haupt, Richard M., 220
Hausen, Harald zur, 220
Hausfeld, Michael, 252
Hayes, Randy, 101, 346

Heald v. Engler, 211
Health Care Reform Project, 79, 80
Health Information National Trends Survey
    (HINTS), 224
Health issues
    news media and, 61
    restaurant industry, 19–23
    See also AIDS
Health maintenance organizations
    (HMOs), 637
Hearst Corporation, 235
Heesen, Mark, 191
Helsinki Declaration, 682
Henry, David, 620
Herfindahl-Hirschman index (HH), 249
Heritage Foundation, 478, 490
Herkstroeter, C.A.J., 92
Hershman, Michael J., 706
Hertz Rent-A-Car, 579
Heskjer, Fran, 555
Hewlett-Packard
    antitrust laws, 250, 251
    business grassroots campaigns, 208
    emerging markets and, 484
    Internet taxation case, 214, 216
    media guidelines of, 64
    Microsoft antitrust case, 260
Higgins, Arthur, 546
High Five for Farmers, 486
Hilton international, 579
Hindrey, Leo, Jr., 190
Hindustan Lever Limited, 482
Hirsch, Samuel, 411, 413
HIV drugs case, 615–618
H. J. Heinz, 569
HLL, 514
Hobee's, 569
Hoffmann-La Roche, 616
Hogue, Ilyse, 98, 99, 341, 343
Holderbank Financière, Glaris Ltd., 541
Hollings, Ernest, 215
Holnam, 541
Holwill, Richard, 472
Holzle, Urs, 28
Home Depot
    Chicago public politics case, 219
    environmental activism at, 346
    environmental protection issues, 343
    nonmarket strategy, 168
    products liability politics, 403
    public politics and, 76
    strategy and negotiations, 89
Home Mortgage Disclosure Act
    (HMDA), 90
Honda, 7, 33
Honduras, 529
Honeywell, 174, 250
Honeywell International, 204, 428
Hong Kong, 449, 453, 552
Hong Li Da, 118
Horizontal merger, 234
Horizontal practices, 232, 237, 250
Horizontal price fixing, 234

Horton, Chuck, 412
Household Responsibility
    System (China), 452
House of the People. *See* Lok Sabha
House of States. *See* Rajya Sabha
Huawei Technologies, 466
Huge Group, 500
Hughes, Keith W., 318
Hughes Aircraft, 70
Hu Jia, 465, 487
Hu Jintao, 461
Human Development Report (1999), 217
Human Genome Project, 653
Human rights
    China, 28, 464–466
    justice and, 686
Hume, Ellen, 58
Hundt, Reed, 25
Hustinx, Peter, 25
Huston, Allan S., 79
Hu Yaobang, 452
Hu Yingying, 474
HVB Group, 340
Hyde, Henry, 216
Hynix Semiconductors, 211

I

IBM
    antitrust laws, 235, 242
    business grassroots campaigns, 208
    environmental protection issues, 343
    European Union and, 427
    Internet taxation case, 215
    Microsoft antitrust case, 260
Identification stage of crisis life cycle, 104
IFC, 340
Ifshin, Adam, 190
IG Metall, 705–706
Ikuta, Masaharu, 478
IMD, 478, 479
Immune Deficiency Foundation, 78
Imperial China, 449
Implication, managerial, 668–670
Implied warranties, 397
Imports, steel, 536–537
Incentives, 133
    environmental management and
        stability, 212
    EPA, 335–336
    justice and, 643–644
    property law, 382
Income redistribution, through
    regulation, 280
Independent Community Bankers of
    America, 128
Independent Service Organization (ISO), 289
Index of Economic Freedom, 478, 490
India, 503
    Kyoto Protocol and, 330–331
    MTN Group Limited case, 498
    opportunities in, 480–481
    pharmaceutical industry, 508
    Tesco PLC case, 512–515

trade disputes, 530
Indigenous peoples, 28
Individual freedoms, in emerging markets,
    477–478
Indonesia, Nike and, 95, 96
Industry concentration
    Chicago school, 241–243
    structural approach, 239–241
INFACT, 78
Infiniti Retail, 514
Information, 4, 10–11
    asymmetric, 274
    daylight saving time politics, 186
    incentives and, 382
    news media and, 62
    relevance of, 198–199
    technical and political, 197–198
    utilitarianism and, 609
Informational strategies, 178–179
Information Industry Association (IIA),
    217, 261
Information Technology Association of
    America (ITAA), 215
Insider trading case, 677–678
Injustice, 640
Installed base, 517
Institute of Medicine, 60, 404
Institutional arenas, in nonmarket
    strategy, 167
Institutional change, 11, 15
Institutional officeholders
    nonmarket strategies targeting, 179
    political competition and, 139, 146
    See also Access
Institutions, 4, 9–10
    China, 455–456, 459–460
    European Union, 420–430, 435
    Gilead Sciences case, 615
    international law and, 681–682
    nonmarket strategies and, 180–181
    political competition and, 140, 146
Instrumental rights, 625–627
Insurance, 109, 274
Integrated strategy, 30, 34, 36, 37
    Google, 34–35
    nonmarket environment, 31–34
    nonmarket issues analysis framework,
        43–44
    nonmarket positioning, 38–42
    nonmarket strategy function,
        organization of, 46
    pharmaceutical industry, 36–37
    summary, 46–47
Integrity tests, 610–611, 632, 633–634, 647
Intel, 25, 35
    antitrust laws, 235, 237, 250
    Internet taxation case, 214
    Microsoft antitrust case, 257, 260
    Project XL, 336
Intellectual property
    China and, 466–467
    eBay, 38
    Gilead Sciences case, 615

Google, 26
  pharmaceutical industry, 18
  TRIPS, 527
Intellectual property law, 382–387, 409–411
Interbrand competition, 244
Interest group activity, 11, 14
Interest group formation, 14–15
Interest group politics, 138, 168, 177,
  181–182, 280, 524
Interest groups, 9
  news media and, 52
  nonmarket analysis, 133–134
  See also specific groups
Interests, 4, 9
  Boeing, 144
  European Union, 433–434
  nonmarket analysis, 133–134
  nonmarket strategies and, 180–181
  rights and, 631–632
  tobacco politics, 157–158
Interfaith Center on Corporate Responsibility
  (ICCR), 547, 576, 683
InterFit Health, 128
InterMedia Partners LP, 191
Internal Revenue Service (IRS), 90, 191
International business ethics, 681
  corruption and questionable foreign
    payments, 691–698
  cultural relativism, 683–686
  De Beers case, 702–704
  developing countries, 686–687
  GlaxoSmithKline case, 707–711
  human rights and justice, 686–687
  international law and institutions,
    681–682
  Siemens case, 704–706
  summary, 698–699
  working conditions in suppliers' factories,
    688–690
International Climate Change Partnership, 40
International Coffee Agreement, 485
International Council of Shopping
  Centers, 216
International Court of Justice, 681, 683
International Covenant on Civil and Political
  Rights, 465
International Federation of Pharmaceutical
  Manufacturers Associations, 547, 709
International Finance Corporation (IFC),
  340, 483
International Franchising Association
  (IFA), 438
International institutions. *See* Institutions;
  specific international institutions
International Labor Rights Fund, 130
International law, 681–683
International market strategies, 33–34
International Monetary Fund (IMF), 85, 340,
  445, 458, 463, 681
International Paper, 209
International Trade Administration (ITA),
  167, 532, 535
International trade agreements, 525–532

International Trade Commission (ITC), 167,
  181, 211, 266, 267, 514, 532, 540, 542
International Trade Organization
  (ITO), 525
International trade policy, 519–520
  Abbott Laboratories case, 545–549
  Cemex antidumping case, 540–544
  China, 463
  economics of, 520–523
  international trade agreements, 525–532
  market opening, political economy of,
    537–539
  political economy of, 523–525
  process, 520
  protectionism, political economy of,
    533–537
  summary, 539–540
  Toys '牙' Us case, 552–556
  U.S. trade policy, 532–533
Internet
  citizen journalism on, 62
  crisis management and, 104
Internet Non-Discrimination Act, 214, 215,
  216, 217
Internet privacy, 24, 31, 277, 431
Internet Solutions, 500
Internet taxation case, 214–218
Internet Tax Fairness Coalition (ITFC),
  215, 218
Internet Tax Freedom Act (ITFA), 214, 215
Interpretation, of news messages, 54
Interstate Commerce Act (1887), 230,
  265, 271
Interstate Commerce Commission (ICC),
  15, 188, 265
Intervention stage of crisis life cycle, 104
Interviews, with media, 64
Intrabrand competition, 244
Intrinsic rights, 625–627
Intuit Corporation, 260
Investcom LLC, 498
Investor Responsibility Research Center
  (IRRC), 586
Investor rewards, for corporate social
  performance, 573–574
IO approach. *See* New IO approach
Irancell, 500
Ireland, 441
ISO 14001, 347
Issue identification, 14, 15, 32, 33
Issues, 5–9
  See also Nonmarket issues
iTalk Cellular, 500
Italy
  bribery in, 705
  EU carbon tax case, 441, 442
  trade disputes, 530
  U.S. protectionism and, 536
ITC, 514

J

Jackley, Jessica, 495
Jackson, Brooks, 58

Jackson, Henry, 142
Jackson, Jesse, 677
Jacobson, Michael F., 20
Jacobson, Walter, 67
Jaedicke, Robert K., 584
James, Charles A., 263
Japan, 437
  EU agriculture policy and, 428
  EU carbon tax case, 440
  EU nonmarket issues, 431
  international trade policy, 527
  lobbying in, 34
  Pizza Hut in, 79
  Toys '牙' Us case, 553–554
  U.S. protectionism and, 536
Jarvis, Ron, 346
JEDI, 582, 585
Jenkins, John, 676
Jennings, John, 94
Jiang Zemin, 461
Ji Xiaoyin, 474
Johnson, Bobby Jo, 106
Johnson, Laurie, 353
Johnson & Johnson
  credo of, 673
  crisis management, 102, 108,
    110, 111
  institutional manipulation by, 165
  trademarks, 387
Johnson & Johnson and Its Quality
  Reputation case, 120–123
Joint and several liability, 402–403
Joint Council of Energy and Environment
  Ministers, 439
Jointly determined consequences,
  605–606
Joint venture policy, in China, 463
Jones, Stephanie Tubbs, 319
Jonsson, Gunnar, 555
Jonway UFO, 466
Jordan, Jim, 125
Journalism, 52
  citizen, 62
  news media and, 59–60
  standards versus judgments, 60
  See also News media
Journalists, 52, 63
JPMorgan Chase, 305, 311, 322,
  581, 583
Judicial actions, 211
Judicial branch, in China, 461
Judicial politics, of environmental
  protection, 338
Judiciary
  appointments to, 155
  responsiveness of, 180
  See also U.S. Supreme Court;
    specific cases
Jury Verdict Research, 401
Justice
  human rights and, 686
  principles of, 642–643
Justice, Dwight, 119

Justice theories, 650–651
   categories of, 638–640
   Rawls, John, 640–650

K

Kadrmas, Sarita, 629
Kadrmas v. Dickinson Public Schools, 629
Kahn, Alfred, 15
Kalin-Casey, Mary, 23
Kansas Alliance for U.S.-China Trade, 180
Kantian maxims, 624–629
Karlsson, Therese, 555
Karson, Daniel E., 706
Kassenbaum, Nancy, 79
Keating five, 204
Keidanren, 205
Keller, Rick, 20, 413
Kelly, Craig, 252
Kennedy, Edward, 79, 124
Kenya, 341, 484–485, 490–491, 495–498
Kenyatta, Jomo, 490
Kerry, John, 125, 191, 592
Kessler, David, 404
Khalifa family (Bahrain), 23–24
Khanlou, Homayoon, 546
Kibaki, Mwai, 490
Killino, Jeffrey, 406
Kinder, Lydenberg, Domini Research &
   Analytics (KLD), 575
Kingsford Company, 185
Kinko's, 89
Kiodex, 290
Kitjiwatchakul, Kannikar, 547
Kiva, 495–496
Kleiner Perkins Caufield & Byers, 191,
   255, 375
Kleinfeld, Klaus, 704–706
Klitxman, Robert L., 620
Knight, Douglas John, 106
Knight, Phil, 52, 95, 96, 97, 690
Knight Foundation, 62
Koenkai, 553
Kofinis, Chris, 125
Kohl, Helmut, 94
Kohlberg, Kravis, Roberts &
   Company, 675
Kollar-Kotelly, Colleen, 262, 263
Kongsberg Vaapenfabrik, 173
Kopper, Michael J., 582–583, 585
Kopperud, Steve, 68
Korea
   automobile industry and, 7
   Nike and, 95, 97
Korean Air Lines, 252
Kotchian, A. Carl, 692
Kous, 460
KPMG, 316, 704
KPMG Germany, 706
Kraft, 486
Kravis, Henry, 189
Kravitz, Richard, 37, 619
Kroc, Ray, 106
Kroger, 124

Kroll Associates, 706
Kroszner, Randall S, 205
Krugman, Paul, 189, 316
Krupp, Fred, 340, 345
Kubo, Tatsuko, 554
Kuneva, Maglena, 119
Kutschenreuter, Michael, 705
Kwak, Mary, 263
Kweder, Sandra, 287
Kyoto Protocol, 40, 327, 330–333, 345, 432,
   434, 469, 491, 681–682
   cap-and-trade systems, 327
   China and, 469
   Clinton administration and, 330–333
   Environmental Defense and, 345
   European Union and, 332, 432
   international law and, 681–683
Kyoto Treaty, 5, 10

L

Labarthe, Carlos, 483, 493–494
Labor Contract Law (China), 468, 470
Labor issues, in restaurant industry, 20–21
Labor markets, in European
   Union, 429–430
Labor organization, Federal
   Express and, 188
Labor Research Associates (LRA), 130
Labor unions
   European Union, 433
   free-rider problem, 150
   grassroots campaigns, 208
   See also specific unions
Lacey, Frederick B., 411
Lafarge, 541
Lafarge Coppée, 434, 541
Lambert, Debra, 106
Lamy, Pascal, 531, 537, 550
Landmark Group, 515
Lane, Barry, 353
Lange, Louis G., 644
Lantos, Tom, 28, 475
Large-Scale Retail Store Law (Japan), 554
Larsson, Fredrik, 555
Law, 380–381
   California Space Heaters, Inc. case, 394,
      407–409, 687
   common law, 381
   contracts, 388–391
   entitlements, 394–396
   intellectual property law, 382–387
   international, 681–683
   liability system, imperfections
      in, 403–406
   obesity and McLawsuits case, 411–414
   patents case, 409–411
   product safety problems, 392–394
   products liability law, 396–403
   property law, 382
   regulation versus liability, 395
   social efficiency, 392–395
   summary, 406
   torts, 391

   U.S. trade, 532–533
   See also Antitrust laws
Law of the Sea, 682
Lawsuits, 90
Lay, Kenneth, 581, 583, 584, 585
Lazarus, Charles, 552, 554
League of Conservation Voters, 171, 340
Leahy, Sir Terry, 513
Least-cost avoider, 390, 393
Lederer, Bob, 185
Lee, Kai-fu, 474
Lee Der, 117–118
Legalism, 448
Legal recourse, to news media disputes,
   66–68
Legal space, positioning in, 38–39
Legislation, 14, 15
   carried interest taxation, 189, 191
   daylight saving time, 184–187
   election financing, 202–204
   informational strategies and, 179
   nonmarket strategy and, 168–169
   rights and, 623
   See also specific laws
Legislative arena, responsiveness of, 180
Legislative branch, in China, 460
Legislative process
   European Union, 423–424
   U.S. Congress, 152–154
Legislators, 155
Legislature. *See* Institutions; U.S. Congress;
   specific laws
Lehman, Bruce, 548
Lemon laws, 164–165, 169, 205
Lents, James, 354
Levi Strauss & Company, 566, 649–650
Levin, Carl, 310, 316
Levin, Gerald M., 215
Leyden Corporation, 597, 601
LGT Group, 705
Li, 454
Li, Robin, 48, 473
Liability
   crisis management and, 114
   products, 396–399
   regulation versus, 395
Liability rule, 326, 328, 394–395, 406, 560
Liability system, imperfections in, 403–406
Li & Fung Ltd., 552
Libel, 66–68
Liberal Democratic Party (Japan), 553
Licensing, compulsory, 709–710
Liecha, Harold, 219
Life insurance screening, 611, 631,
   648–649
Lightfoot, Jim, 608
Lin Biao, 451
Lincoln Electric, 480
Liquidated damages, 390, 406
Litigation strategy, 211
Littlejohn, Gail, 46, 405
Little River Funding, 582
Liu Zhengrong, 474

Liz Claiborne, 686, 689
LJM Cayman LP, 582
LJM partnerships, 582–583, 585
Lladro, 513
L.L. Bean, 380, 689
Lobbying, 11, 195–201
    access, 199
    controls on, 200–201
    credibility and relevance of information,
        198–199
    European Union, 435
    government allies, 200
    informational strategies, 178
    multidomestic market strategy and, 33
    nature of, 196–197
    technical and political information,
        197–198
    timing and focus, 200
Lobbying Act (1946), 200, 435
Lobbying case, 220–224
Lobbying Disclosure Act (1995), 200
Local governments, 462
Local protests, in India, 8
Lockheed Corporation, 691
Logue, William, 345
Lok Sabha, 502
Lone Star Industries, 541
Long, Russell, 50
L'Oréal, 39
Lorfelder, Jochen, 93
Los Angeles Economic Development
    Corporation, 586
Loscher, Peter, 706
Louis Vuitton, 27
Louis Vuitton and Moet Hennessey (LVMH)
    Group, 513
Lowell, Roger, 105
Lowenstein, Doug, 189, 191
Lower Mainland Multicultural Family
    Support Services Centre, 518
Lowe's, 76–77, 126, 159, 219, 346
LTV, 536
Lufthansa AG, 252
Lula da Silva, Luiz Inacio, 545, 549
Lustgarten, Karen, 220
Luxembourg, 217, 417, 421, 422, 441,
    479, 488, 681
Luxury tax, repeal of, 133, 134, 139,
    160–161
Lynch, John, 333

M

Maastricht Treaty, 418–419
MacArthur, Kelly Jo, 262
Mackey, John, 562
Mackey, Linda, 318
MacPherson v. Buick Motor Company, 397
MacRobert, Angus, 500
Mad cow disease, 21
Magnuson, Keith, 345
Magnuson-Moss Warranty Act, 397
Mahonia, 581
Major, John, 94

Majoritarian politics, 137, 149, 182,
    210, 524
Majority-building strategies, 174–178
Majority protection, 177
Major League Baseball, 26
Malaysia, 364, 479, 530
Managed Funds Association, 190, 192
Management
    corporate social performance, 572
    ethics and, 594–595
    integrated strategy and, 30
    role of, 3
Managers, nonmarket strategies and,
    166–170
Mandelson, Peter, 119, 547
Manipulation, in business nonmarket action,
    165–166
Mankiw, Greg, 189
Mao Zedong, 450
Marine Mammal Protection Act, 530, 569
Maritz, Paul, 260
Market environment, 1–2
    business, 2–3
    management, 3
    nonmarket environment and, 4
    summary, 16
Market for control, 560, 579
Market forces, 13
Market imperfections, 271–276
Market opening, political economy of,
    537–539
Markets, resource allocation and, 559
Market strategy, 39–41, 124–125
    nonmarket positioning and, 38–42
    nonmarket strategies and, 37–38
    See also Integrated strategy
The Market Threat from China, 364
Markey, Edward J., 184, 580, 589
Märklin, Gebruder, 553
Marlin, 581
Marshall, Dennis, 676
Marshall, Kimberly, 676
Marshall, Thurgood, 164, 631
Martha Overseas Corporation, 705
Martin, Jerome, 548
Martin, John, 616, 618
Martin, Kevin, 278
Martin Luther King All Children's Choir
    of Virginia, 676
Marubeni Trading Company, 694
Mary Kay Cosmetics, 471
MasterCard, 45, 158, 159, 237–238
Mattel, 40, 116–120, 277, 406
Maxims, Kantian, 624–629
McCain, John, 181, 247, 335
McConnell, Mitch, 171
McCrery, Jim, 190
McDonald's, 1, 2, 20
    activist organizations and, 86–89
    campaigns against, 79, 84
    corporate social performance, 568
    crisis management, 106, 109
    Environmental Defense and, 345

    environmental issues, 345
    Japan and, 554
    news media and, 68
    nonmarket environment of, 19–23
    obesity and McLawsuits case, 411–414
    regulation, 277
    strategy and negotiations, 88–90
McDonald v. Santa Fe Trail
    Transportation Co., 634
McDonnell Douglas, 142, 143, 148, 692
M-Cell, 498
McGlynn, Margaret, 224
McGovern, James, 20, 413
McGraw, Ali, 101
McGreevy, Lisa, 190, 192
McGuire, Bill, 45
McGuire Act, 236
MCI, 211, 215, 281, 428
MCI-Worldcom, 215
McKinnell, Henry, 288
McKinsey & Co., 323, 480, 505, 514, 678
McLaughlin, Andrew, 28, 213, 473
McLawsuits case, 411–414
McLibel, 68, 90
McManus, Steve, 573, 676
McMenu bills, 20, 414
McNealy, Scott, 263
Media. *See* News media
Media Access Project, 256
Media coverage
    GlaxoSmithKline case, 710
Media interviews, 64
Median voter theorem, 171, 177–178, 184, 186
Media ownership rules (FCC), 278
Media strategies, 63
Media vacuums, 63–64
Medicaid, 16, 17, 127, 192, 213, 275, 614
Medicare, 17, 19, 136, 218, 220
Medicines Control Agency (Germany), 18
Médecins sans Frontières, 547, 708, 710
Medstory, 27
Melchett, Lord Peter, 94
Menu Education and Labeling Act
    (MEAL), 20, 414
Mercedes-Benz, environmental regulations
    case, 234
Mercer, William W., 252
Mercer Human Resource Consulting, 607
Merchants National Bank & Trust, 90
Merck
    compulsory licensing case, 545–549
    crisis management case, 286–287
    GlaxoSmithKline AIDS drugs, 707
    policy case, 707–711
    lobbying case, 220–224
    Siemens bribery case, 706
    Vioxx case, 286
Mercosur, 7, 10, 532, 540
Mergers
    conglomerate, 234
    EU competition policy and, 427
    horizontal, 232
    merger guidelines and, 248–250

Merkel, Angelika, 93
Merrill Lynch, 128, 256, 300, 563, 583
Meskala, Tadesse, 487
Messages (news), 54
Metro AG, 515
Metro Broadcasting v. F.C.C., 646
Metro Cash & Carry, 514
Metro Group, 513
Metzenbaum, Howard, 141
Mexican Cement Industry, 540–541, 544
Mexico, 489, 537–538, 545
    See also Cemex
Michigan State University, 505
Microcredit Summit Campaign, 482,
    484, 494
Microfinance, 482–485
Micron Technology, 211
Microsoft
    antitrust issues, 1, 4, 41, 233, 247,
        257–263
    China and, 473, 475
    copyrights, 386
    EU competition policy and, 427
    Google and, 24, 26, 27, 35
    Internet taxation case, 216
    Yahoo! and, 29
Mika, Susan, 683
Mill, John Stuart, 600
Millennium Copyright Act, 27, 39
Miller, George, 219
Miller, Ellen, 255
Miller, David, 371
Miller-Tydings Act, 236
Milloy, Steven, 21
Ministry of Commerce and Industry
    (India), 514
Ministry of Finance (China), 461
Ministry of Information Industry (China), 28
Ministry of International Trade and
    Industry (Japan), 173
Ministry of Small-Scale Industries
    (India), 513
Minnesota Family Council, 223
Minnesota Medical Association, 224
Miramax Films, 78
Misener, Paul, 217, 229
Mitchell, George J., 199
Mitsubishi Motors, 79
Mitts, Emma, 128, 219
Mobilization, in grassroots and
    constituency campaigns, 208–209
Moderates and Radicals, 84
Moi, Daniel arap, 490
Monaghan, Thomas S., 86
Monopoly, 231, 232, 233, 271–272
    See also Antitrust laws
Monsanto, 288, 530
Monsanto Co. v. Spray-Rite Service Co., 246
Montreal Protocol on Substances That
    Deplete the Ozone Layer, 682
Moody, Krista, 223
Moore, Debbie, 128
Moral concerns, 11, 13, 44

collective action, 140
    informational strategies and, 179
    nonmarket analysis, 133, 139
    See also Ethics
Moral hazard, 274–275
Moral motivation, for corporate social
    performance, 571
Moral philosophy, 599–600
Moral rules, 624–629
Moral standing, rights and, 630
Moral Suasion, 666–667
Morris, Michael, 263
Mortgage Lending, 296–297
Mortgage loan, 292
Most favored nation (MFN) status,
    for China, 179–180
Mothers Against Drunk Driving
    (MADD), 6, 13
Motivation, corporate social
    performance, 571–572
Motorola, 4, 386, 463, 499, 702
Motor Vehicle Safety Act, 14
Moulette, Patrick, 704
MoveOn.org, 85, 125, 208
Moynihan, Daniel Patrick, 14
Ms. Foundation for Women, 96
MSN, 26, 261, 473, 475
MTN Foundation, 499
MTN Group Limited, 482, 490, 498–501, 526
MTN Holdings, 498
Mudaraba, 489
Mugabe, 489
Multidomestic market strategies, 33–34
Multi-Fiber Arrangement (MFA), 526, 534
Multilateral trade policy, 524
Multilevel lobbying, 197
Munn v. Illinois, 266, 271
Murdock, Rupert, 72–73
Murphy, Brian, 411
Murphy, Matt, 255
Musaraka, 489
Mutual recognition, 418–419
Mwangi, James, 484, 496
Myanmar, 478, 682–684
Myers, Mark, 223

N

Nader, Ralph, 14, 58
Nanya Technology, 211
Napoleonic Code, 381
Napster, 384
Nardelli, Robert, 402
Nath, Kamal, 514
National Academy of Sciences, 10–11,
    98, 198
National Association for the Advancement of
    Colored People (NAACP), 353
National Association of Broadcasters,
    168, 415
National Association of Chain Drug
    Stores, 19
National Association of Convenience Stores,
    128, 158

National Association of Counties, 216
National Association of Home Builders
    (NAHB), 172
National Association of Manufacturers,
    145, 205
National Association of Securities
    Dealers, 100
National Automobile Dealers Association
    (NADA), 304
National Black Chamber of Commerce, 254
National Bureau of Corruption
    (China), 467
National Cancer Institute, 220, 224,
    288, 404
National Candy Brokers Association, 185
National Cattlemen's Beef Association
    (NCBA), 21, 23
National Center for Policy Analysis, 487
National Center for Tobacco-Free Kids, 157
National Chamber Alliance for Politics, 206
National Community Pharmacist
    Association (NCPA), 19
National Confectioners Association, 185
National Conference of State
    Legislatures, 222
National Conference on Public Employee
    Retirement Systems (NCPERS), 190
National Council of State Legislators
    (NCSL), 216
National Democratic Alliance (NDA), 503
National Development and Reform
    Commission (China), 461
National Education Association (NEA), 126
National Federation of Independent Business
    (NFIB), 135, 136, 205, 206, 280, 636
National Federation of Teachers, 126
National Football League (NFL), 677
National Governors Association (NGA), 216
National Grocers Association, 128, 158
National Highway Traffic Safety
    Administration (NHTSA), 6, 10,
    14, 267
    formation of, 14
    General Motors and, 69–71
    regulation, 267–269
National Hispanic Media Coalition, 78, 256
National Industrial Recovery Act, 267
National Institutes of Health (NIH), 288
Nationalization, in emerging markets, 489
National Labor Relations Act (NLRA),
    188, 282
National Labor Relations Board (NLRB),
    128, 266, 267, 281
National League of Cities, 216
Nationally Recognized Statistical Rating
    Organizations (NRSRO), 306
National Marine Manufacturers Association
    (NMMA), 160, 207
National Network for Immunization
    Information, 223
National Party Congress (China), 459, 460
National Population and Family Planning
    Commission (China), 465

National Restaurant Association, 20, 411
National Retail Federation (NRF), 193, 216
National Rifle Association (NRA), 208
National Safety Council, 186
National Small Business Association, 205, 280
National Soft Drink Association, 251
National Telecommunications and Information Administration (NTIA), 415
National Tobacco Policy and Youth Smoking Reduction Act, 157
National Trade Estimate Report (NTER), 539
National Transportation Safety Board (NTSB), 18, 49, 609
National Vaccine Information Center, 223
National Venture Capital Association (NVCA), 191
Natural monopoly, 271–272
Natural Resources Defense Council (NRDC), 53, 322, 343, 586
    activist strategy, 84–87
    environmental politics, 338
    environmental protection issues, 342–346
    news media and, 52–54, 56, 67
    Project XL and, 344
    TRI and, 342
    Wal-Mart and, 586
Nature Conservancy, 83, 88, 92, 328, 346
NatureServe, firm interactions with, 88
NBC, 53, 58, 59, 66, 70–71, 170, 686
Nebbia v. New York, 266
Nebergall, Mark, 215
Negligence, 60, 114, 335, 391, 397–398, 400–401, 403, 406–407
Nehru, Jawaharlal, 503
Neighbor to Neighbor, 66
Neoclassical liberalism, 637–638
Nestlé, 74, 78, 249, 439, 486, 506
NetCoalition.com, 207
Netherlands, 92–94, 104, 417, 419, 430, 434, 440–441, 479, 485, 487, 590
    emerging markets and, 485, 487
    Enron and, 581
    EU carbon tax case, 439–442
    fair trade movement, 485–486
    Shell in, 92–95
NetPAC, 213
Netscape, 247, 258–261, 263
Netscape/AOL, 263
Network Advertising Initiative, 24
Network externalities, 239, 243–244, 251
New IO approach, 239, 243–244, 247
Newman, Edwin, 55, 58
News Corporation, 59, 72–73
News media, 52
    activist strategies, 85
    audience interest perspective, 55
    balance and fairness, 58
    business interactions with, 62–65

coverage and treatment theory, 54–57
coverage costs, 58
crisis management and, 107
dispute resolution with, 65–71
    General Motors case, 69–71
    messages and their interpretation, 54
    nature of, 59–62
    newsworthiness, concept of, 57–58
    nonmarket issues and, 52–54
    societal significance perspective, 55–56
    summary, 69
News organizations, as businesses, 59
News of the World, The, 72
New Source Performance Standards (NSPS), 328
Newsworthiness, concept of, 57–58
New York State Consumer Protection Board, 24
New York State Pension Funds, 28
New York Stock Exchange (NYSE), 563, 706
New York Times v. Sullivan, 67, 69
NGO Good Jobs First, 219
Nguyen, Bob, 679
Nguyen, Thuyen, 96
Nielsen Monitor-Plus, 619
Nielson, Howard C., 184
Nigeria, 498, 499, 500, 558, 682, 705
Nike, 1, 2
    activist strategies, 84
    activist targeting of, 86
    boycotts against, 78
    corporate social responsibility, 671
    ethics issues, 688
    FLA and, 689–690
    news media and, 52
    nonmarket strategy, 32
    positioning, 39–41
    private politics case, 95–97
    reputation of, 43
NIMBY movement, environmental politics and, 338, 341–342, 348
Nissan
    fuel economy exception for, 6
    lobbying by, 11
Nixon, Richard M., 157, 333, 452
Nokia, 35, 385, 500
Nokia Siemens Networks, 500
Nongovernmental organizations (NGOs), 2, 97, 707, 711
    See also specific organizations
Nonmarket action Boeing, 144–145
    criticisms of, 163–166
    free-rider problem and, 150–151
    public politics and, 133
    responsible, 162–166
Nonmarket agenda, of Boeing, 144
Nonmarket analysis, 133–137
    Boeing, 140–142
    for business, 132
    collective action, moral determinants of, 140

free-rider problem and nonmarket action, 150–151
    luxury tax repeal, 160–161
    nonmarket strategy and, 166
    political competition, nature of, 137–140
    public politics, 133–137
    summary, 149
    tobacco politics, 157–158
    U.S. Congress, 152–156
Nonmarket assets, 168–169
Nonmarket capabilities, 42–43, 47, 212–213
Nonmarket environment, 1–2
    analysis of, 5
    anticipation of change, 13
    automobile industry, 5–11
    business, 2–3
    change in, 11–13
    China, 457–462
    Google case, 23–29
    management, 3, 492–493
    market environment and, 5
    McDonald's case, 19–23
    nonmarket issue life cycle, 14–15
    pharmaceutical industry case, 16–19
    regulatory agencies, 269–271
    summary, 15–16
Nonmarket forces, India, 514
Nonmarket issue life cycle, 14–15, 32
Nonmarket issues
    analysis of, 43–46
    anticipation of, 64–65
    China, 464–469
    European Union, 430–433
    news coverage theory on, 56–57
    unanticipated, 65
    See also News media
Nonmarket objectives, of Boeing, 144
Nonmarket portfolio, of PacifiCare, 202
Nonmarket positioning, 38–42
Nonmarket pressure, 124–131, 586–588
Nonmarket strategy, 31–34
    Boeing, 146–147
    European Union, 434–439
    market strategies and, 39–41
    organization of, 46
    Wal-Mart case, 586–588
    See also Integrated strategy
Nonmarket strategy (government arenas), 162
    carried interest taxation, 189–192
    choice of, 180–182
    daylight saving time politics, 184–187
    Federal Express and labor organization, 188
    formulation of, 166–170
    generic, 172–180
    institutions and interests, 180–181
    outcomes, understanding, 171–172
    responsible nonmarket action, 162–166
    summary, 182
    Wal-Mart's urban expansion strategy, 218–220

Nonmarket strategy implementation (government arenas), 195
  coalition building, 205–207
  electoral support, 202–205
  grassroots and constituency campaigns, 208–209
  Internet taxation case, 214–218
  judicial actions, 211
  lobbying, 195–201, 220–224
  nonmarket capabilities, development of, 212–213
  nonmarket effectiveness, organizing for, 212
  public advocacy, 210
  summary, 213
  testimony, 209–210
Nonpecuniary externality, 273
Norplant Foundation, 614
Norplant System, 613–615
Norquist, Grover, 215
Norris-LaGuardia Act, 233
North American Free Trade Agreement (NAFTA), 12, 137, 167, 174, 205, 519, 537, 543, 681
  Cemex and, 453
  international law and, 681
  international trade policy, 519, 523–525, 531
  political economy of, 537–539
  vote recruiting and, 174–175
North, Douglass, 4
Northern Pacific Railroad v. U.S., 238
Norvig, Peter, 475
Norway, 93–94, 332, 417, 479, 573, 681
Notice of Proposed Rule Making (NPRM), 268
Novartis, 249
Novell, Inc., 427

O

Obama, Barack, 191, 201, 281, 362, 365, 375, 415
Obesity, 19–21, 411–414
Objectives
  business objectives versus public interest, 163–164
  nonmarket strategy, 167
Occupational Safety and Health Administration (OSHA), 75, 267, 392
O'Connor, Sandra Day, 405, 630, 632
OECD Anti-Bribery Convention, 694, 698, 704
Officeholders. *See* Institutional officeholders
Office of Economic Analysis (OEA), 323
Office of Fair Trading (UK), 252
Office of Information and Regulatory Affairs (OIRA), 269
Office of Management and Budget (OMB), 156, 269
Office of Pesticide Programs, 334
Office of Thrift Supervision (OTS), 295, 319
Offsets, 336, 356
Ogilvy Government Relations, 190

Okrent, Daniel, 60
O'Leary, Michael, 252
Omnibus Trade and Competitiveness Act, 539, 695
OnBank, 89–91
One-child-per-family policy (China), 458, 465
O'Neill, Paul, 584
Online Privacy, 442, 576, 588–593, 628
Open Handset Alliance (OHA), 35
Opium War, 449
Opportunities
  emerging markets, 480–487, 514–515
  nonmarket strategy and, 31
Oracle, 225, 260, 386, 431
Orange, 497, 499
Orangina, 425
Orascom, 499
O'Reilly, Arthur, 569
O'Reilly, Gavin, 26
Organization for Economic Cooperation and Development (OECD), 217, 323, 340, 429, 440, 517, 526–527, 606, 683, 691, 694, 698–699, 704
Organization of American States, 681
Organizing costs, 135–136
O'Rourke, Dana, 117
Orszag, Peter R., 190
Osprey, 581
Otero, Maria, 494
Ottawa Taxation Framework Conditions, 217
Outcomes, understanding, 171–172
Overstock.com, 225–226, 228
Oxfam America, 527
Oyagbola, Amina, 499

P

Pacific Gas & Electric, 163, 196, 284, 348–353, 373, 376
Pacific Gas & Electric Co. v. Public Utilities Commission of California, 163
Pacific Gas & Electric and the Smart Meter Challenge case, 348–353
Pacific Stock Exchange, 336
Page, Larry, 28, 385
Pakistan, 27, 483, 491, 503–504, 515, 530, 589
Pampered Chef, 659
Pantaloon Retail, 514
Paraguay, 532
Parents Requesting Open Vaccine Education, 223
Parent Teacher Association (PTA), 13, 186
Parker, Dick, 94
Partnership to End Cervical Cancer, 222
Patent law, 507–508
Patents, 384–386, 409–411
  See also Intellectual property
Patent wars, 385
Paternalism, 456, 628, 637
Patillo, Bob, 494
Paulson, Hank, 190

Paxton, Michael, 127
PayPal, 495
Peak associations, 205–206, 433, 436–437, 439
Pearce, Harry, 71
Pecuniary externality, 272–273
Peer-to-peer systems, 384
Pelosi, Nancy, 171
People for the Ethical Treatment of Animals (PETA), 22
PepsiCo
  antitrust laws, 251
  crisis management, 105–106, 109, 111–112, 114
Per capita benefits, 134
Perfect competition, 239, 241–242, 522–523
Performance, Chicago school and, 241
Perrier. *See* Source Perrier S.A., crisis management
Perry, Rick, 223, 227
Per se violations, 238
Personal ethics, 595
Personal injury lawsuits, 401
Personal Responsibility in Food Consumption Act, 20, 413
Personal staffs, in U.S. Congress, 154–155
Personal Watercraft, aka Jet Skis, case, 49
Perspectives, changes in, 11, 12
Peru, 98, 377, 532
Pesterre, Pete, 70
Pettersson, Kenth, 555
Pew Charitable Trusts, 58
Pew Research Center, 62
Pew Trust, 40
Pfizer, 16, 17
  Celebrex case, 288
  ethics case, 288
  GlaxoSmithKline AIDS drugs, 708
  policy case, 707–711
  nonmarket strategy, 168
Pharmaceutical industry
  India's, 508
  integrated strategy, 36–37
  lobbying case, 220–224
  manipulation in, 165
  nonmarket capabilities, 43
  nonmarket environment of, 16–19
  politics of, 207
  positioning, 41–42
Pharmaceutical Manufacturers Association (PMA), 207, 209, 547, 709–710
Pharmaceutical Research and Manufacturers Association (PhRMA), 16, 37, 40, 206, 434
Pharmaceutical Research & Manufacturing Association of Thailand, 546
Pharmacia, 288
Philanthropy, by Google, 28
Philips Electronics, 35, 276, 433, 437
Phillip Holtzman, 695
Physicians Committee for Responsible Medicine, 20, 413

Physicians for Social Responsibility, 78
Pickle, J. J., 140–149
Piracy. *See* Intellectual property
Pivotal voters, 175–178
Pizza Hut, 78–80, 85, 87, 197–198, 200, 438
Planned Parenthood, 220, 614, 659
Plavix case, 409–411
Pluralism, 132, 417, 457–458
Point Carbon, 332
Polenetsky, Jules, 24
Policy jurisdictions, 154
Policymaking, in China, 460
Policy risk, in emerging markets, 489
Politburo (China), 460, 461
Political action committees (PACs), 165, 202–205
Political competition, nature of, 137–139
Political contributions, from Enron, 584
Political corruption, in emerging markets, 490
Political economy
    environmental management and stability, 338–342
    international trade policy, 523–524
    market opening, 537–539
    protectionism, 533–537
    regulation, 276–278, 279
    See also European Union political economy; International trade policy
Political Economy of India, 502–512
    2011 census, 511, 512
    corruption, 509–510
    economic restrictions, 546
    government, 502–503
    history and economic development, 503–504
    market opportunities, 505–507
    poverty and welfare, 510–511
    summary, 512
Political information, 178, 197–198
Political institutions, in China, 455–456
Political megalomania, in emerging markets, 489–490
Political parties, 155
Political philosophy, 599–600
Political recourse, to news media disputes, 68
Political risk, in emerging markets, 479
Political space, positioning in, 41–42
Politics
    Boeing, 140–142
    daylight saving time, 184–187
    ethics and, 596–597
    products liability, 401–403
    tobacco, 157–158
    See also Nonmarket strategy (government arenas); Nonmarket strategy implementation (government arenas); Private politics; Public politics
Pollution credits trading systems case, 353–356
Pope, Carl, 126
Population Council, 613–615

Porras, Carlos, 355
Porsche, 8
Portland General Electric (PGE), 290
Portugal, 441, 447
Positioning
    nonmarket, 38–42
    spaces, 41–42
Posner, Richard, 62, 261
Potgieter, Anton, 500
Powerex, 289
Power
    bureaucratic (China), 449
    business nonmarket action, 163–166
Powers, William, 585
Prahalad, C. K., 481
Prasad, Jageshwar, 514
Predatory pricing, 246–247
Preemption, 278, 400
Preexisting conditions, screening for, 611, 631, 648–649
Pre-Natal Diagnostic Techniques (Regulation and Prevention of Misuses) Act, 517
Pre-Republican China, 448–449
Prescott, Edward, 429
Prescription Access Litigation Project, 18, 37
Prescription Medicines Code of Practice Authority, 621
Presidency, 155–156, 181. *See also* Institutions; *specific U.S. presidents*
Presidential appointments, 155
President's Commission for the Study of Ethical Problems in Medicine and Biomedical and Behavioral Research, 518
President's Emergency Plan for AIDS Relief (PEPFAR), 617
Price-Anderson Act, 403
Price controls, in emerging markets, 489
Price Costco, 130
Price discrimination, 234
Price fixing, 233, 252–253
Price maintenance, resale, 233–234, 236
PricewaterhouseCoopers, 690
Pricing
    AIDS drugs, 708–710
    Norplant System case, 613–615
    predatory, 246–247
    retail electricity, 359
    solar power, 367–368
Prince, Chuck, 659, 672
Prioritization, 632
Privacy
    European Union, 13
    Google, 23–25
    See also Internet privacy
Privacy International, 25, 590
Privacy rights, 24–25, 515
Privacy Rights Clearinghouse, 590
Private enforcement, of antitrust laws, 237–238
Private Equity Council, 189, 190, 191

Private governance, 75, 89, 689–690
Private interests, ethics and, 596
Private politics, 74–75
    activist strategies, 84–87
    campaigns, 96
    environmental protection, 340–342
    Nike case, 95–97
    nonmarket strategy and, 32
    Rainforest Action Network and Citigroup case, 97–100
    Shell and Greenpeace case, 92–95
    summary, 91
Private recourse, to news media disputes, 65–66
Privity of contract, 397
Procedural due process, 268, 356
Procter & Gamble
    business nonmarket action and, 166
    crisis management, 106
    emerging markets and, 486
    ethics, 674
    news media and, 66
Product liability, in automobile industry, 6
Product safety, 392–394, 467
Products liability law, 396–399
Product tampering, 106
Profit maximization, 559–563
Project XL, 335, 336
Pro Mujer, 494
Pronuptia, 438–439
Property law, 382
Property rule, 324, 394
Proposition 211 (California), 209
Protection channels, 535
Protectionism, 523, 524, 533–537
Provincial governments, 461
Proximate cause, 399
PRS Group, 479
Public advocacy, 210
Public Citizen, 16, 17, 199, 402
Public Company Accounting Oversight Board, 578
Public disclosure test, 674
Public goods, 273–274
Public Health Advocacy Institute of Boston, 411
Public interest, business objectives versus, 163–164
Public officeholders, nonmarket strategies targeting, 179
    See also Institutional officeholders
Public politics, 74, 127
    environmental protection, 340–341
    nonmarket action in, 133–137
    See also Nonmarket strategy (government arenas); Nonmarket strategy implementation (government arenas)
Public resources allocation, 276
Public sentiment, positioning for, 42
Public shaming, 84–85
Puget Sound Electric, 289
Punitive damages, 401

Q

Qin Dynasty (China), 449
Qing Dynasty (China), 449–450
Qualified Residential Mortgages
  (QRM), 303
Questionable foreign payments, 691–698
Quill v. North Dakota, 214

R

Rabobank, 340
Railway Labor Act (RLA), 188
Rainbow Coalition, 677
Raines, Franklin, 318
Rainforest Action Network (RAN), 76
  campaigns by, 80
  corporate social performance and, 571
  environmental protection issues, 343
  Equator Principles, 340–341
  firm challenges against, 90–91
  firm interactions with, 87, 88
  first-mover advantage, 87
  Home Depot and, 346
  private politics case, 81, 97–100
  target selection by, 86
Rajya Sabha, 502
Rambus, Inc., 211
Ramsey, Fiona, 495–496
Rangel, Charles, 189, 193
Rao, Muralidhara, 514
Raptors, 581, 583, 585
Rather, Dan, 675
Rathke, Wade, 126
Rawl, Lawrence, 113
Rawls, John, 637, 639, 640–650
RC2 Corporation, 116
REACH, 432
Read, Robert, 71
Read, Russell, 190
Reagan, Ronald, 144, 155
  antitrust laws, 239, 242, 250
  regulation, 269–271
Real Estate Roundtable, 190
RealNetwork, 259, 262, 247
Reason. *See* Rule of reason
Reasoning, principles and, 670
Recalls, in automobile industry, 6
Reciprocal exchange, 553
Reciprocal Trade Agreement Act, 532
Reciprocity, 663–665
Recourse, to news media disputes, 65–70
Red Cross, 110, 387
Redistribution, through regulation, 280–281
Redlining, 611–612, 648
Reebok, 513, 686, 689
Reed, Brian, 27
Reform era, in China, 452–453
Refusals to deal, 233, 234
*Regents of University of California
  v. Bakke,* 646
Regional Clean Air Incentives Market
  (RECLAIM), 336–337
Regional Greenhouse Gas Initiative
  (RGGI), 332

Regulation, 264–265
  China, 464
  credit card, 296
  command-and-control, 324
  constitutional basis for, 266
  Cummins Inc. case, 696–698
  delegation, rule-making, due process, and
    discretion, 267–269
  Enron Power Marketing, Inc. case,
    288–290
  explanations for, 271
  liability versus, 395
  market imperfections, 271–276
  nonmarket theory of, 278–283
  political economy of, 276–283
  securities, 295–296
  summary, 285
  See also Deregulation
Regulatory agencies, 266–267, 269–271
  See also specific agencies
Regulatory Analysis Review Group, 269
Regulatory change, periods of, 265–266
Regulatory commissions, 266–267
Regulatory Flexibility Act, 280
Regulatory Impact Analysis, 269
Regulatory institutions, responsiveness
  of, 180
Regulatory risk, in emerging markets, 489
Reid, Harry, 171–172, 191
Reilly, Thomas F., 262
Relationships, with journalists, 64
Reliance, 388
Reliance Communications, 498, 500
Reliance damages, 390
Reliance Industries LTD., 500
Religious conflicts, in emerging markets,
  490–491
Remedies, for breach of contract, 390–391
Remuda Ranch, 23
Ren, 454
Renault, 428
Renewable Portfolio Standard (RPS), 362
Renewable power and trade
  complaints, 534
Rensi, Ed, 345
Rent chain, 169–170
Rent-seeking theories, 276–277
Reporters Without Borders, 473, 474
Representation strategies, 172
Republican China, 450
Repurchase agreement, 292
Reputation, 42–43
  crisis management and, 107–115
  nonmarket strategy and, 168–169
  Wal-Mart, 75, 80, 124–127,
    192, 343, 586
Resale price maintenance, 233–234, 236
Research, on corporate social performance,
  574–576
Resolution, in crisis management program,
  114–115
Resolution stage of crisis life
  cycle, 114–115

Resource allocation, markets and, 559
Resources, for nonmarket action, 136
Response, in crisis management program, 111
Responsible Care programs, 347
Responsible nonmarket action, 162–166
Responsiveness, in nonmarket strategies,
  180–181
Restaurant industry, nonmarket environment
  of, 20–24
Restless legs syndrome case, 619–621
Restless Legs Syndrome Foundation
  (RLS), 620
Retail Workers Union (Handelsanstalldas
  Forbund), 555
Retaliation, market opening and, 538–539
Reversibility, 624
Revolutionary Alliance (China), 450
Revolutions, democratic, 488
Rewards, for corporate social performance,
  573–574
Rexrodt, Guenther, 94
Reynoso, Cruz, 677
Rhodes, Cecile, 702
Rhone-Poulenc, 236
Rhythms NetConnections, 582
Rice, Paul, 487, 562
Richardson, Brooke, 473
Richardson, Dawn, 223
Richardson, Jerome J., 676
Rickard, Lisa A., 411
Riders, 188
Rights, 651–652
  applied rights analysis, 629–631
  Citigroup subprime lending case,
    318–320
  classes of, 623
  conflicts among, 631–633
  equal employment opportunity, 633–635
  genetic testing in workplaces (case),
    652–653
  GlaxoSmithKline restless legs syndrome
    case, 619–621
  Kantian maxims versus moral rules,
    624–629
  neoclassical liberalism, 637–638
  utilitarianism and, 605–606
  See also Human rights; Workers' rights,
    in China
Rio Earth Summit, 440
Ripa di Meana, Carlo, 440
Risk
  emerging markets, 499–500
  strict liability and, 400
Risk assessment, for emerging markets,
  487–492
Rite-Aid, 128
Rivera, Micaela, 494
R. J. Reynolds, 157
Robert Mondavi, 201
Roberts, John, 400
Roberts, Kenneth, 14
Robinson-Patman Act, 232, 234, 236, 241
Roche Holding AG, 236, 427

Rodgers, T. J., 365, 562
Roe, David, 355
Röhm, Elizabeth, 221
Root cause analysis, 110–111
Rosenbaum, Ruth, 486
Rosenberg, David, 487
Rosenblum, Bruce, 190
Rosston, Gregory L., 35
Rotenberg, Marc, 23, 443, 589, 431
Royal Ahold NV, 487
Royal Bank of Scotland, 310, 340
Royal Dutch/Shell Group. *See* Shell
RP Foundation Fighting Blindness, 133,
    136, 181, 182, 184–185, 205
RPG Group, 514
RT Strategies, 587
Rubenstein, David M., 190
Rubin, Andy, 35
Rubin, Robert, 101, 308, 584
Ruby Tuesday, Inc., 414
Ruckelshaus, William, 341
Rule-making, 267–269
Rule of reason, 238
Rules, moral, 624–629
Rules Committee, 152
Rule utilitarianism, 603–606
Rurka, David, 555
Russia, 47, 291, 300, 330, 471, 477,
    479–480, 491, 506, 526, 532, 536,
    558, 644–645, 696, 705
Rwanda, 498
Rx Partners, 210
Ryanair, 252

S

Safe Drinking Water and Toxic Enforcement
    Act, 21
Safeguards, in international trade
    agreements, 528
Safety regulations and standards, in
    automobile industry, 7, 14–15
Safeway, 106, 124, 158, 218, 247, 249
Saipan, slave labor in, 686
Sakurai, Masao, 554
Salomon Smith Barney, 100
Sam's Club, 130
Samsung, 385–386
Sandhu, Dalip, 518
Sandoz, 249
Sangeorge, Robert, 94
Sanofi-Aventis, 409–411
Saperstein, Mayeda, Larkin & Goldstein, 677
Sara Lee, 471, 486
Sarandon, Susan, 101
Sarbanes-Oxley Act, 91, 578, 706
Saudi Arabia, 10, 491, 499, 516,
    665, 701
Scalia, Antonin, 164, 400, 405
Scandal, July 2011, 72
Schering-Plough, 17, 18–19, 36, 37
Schiemann, Dylan, 35
Schilling, David, 576
Schlein, Ted, 191

Schmidt, Eric, 24, 26, 27, 29, 34, 701
Schmidt, Hans Chr., 22
Schrage, Elliot, 472, 475
Schumer, Charles, 119, 191
Schwartz, Lisa M., 619, 620
Schwartzman, Jay, 256
Schwarzman, Stephen A., 189, 313
Science. *See* Advocacy science
Scientific discovery, 11–12, 15
Scott, H. Lee, 124, 192, 343, 586–587
Screening, 44
Seamen's Union, 555
Sears, 225, 674
Securities and Exchange Commission (SEC),
    85, 103, 168, 266–267, 296, 314, 495,
    564, 579, 581, 588, 677, 706
Sederholm, Pamela, 185
Sefl, Tracy, 125, 127
Seizures, in emerging markets, 489
Self-cultivation, 454–455
Self-interest, 601–602
Self-regulation, 568, 689
Semiconductor Industry Association (SIA),
    200, 538
Sen, Nirupam, 514
Sensenbrenner, James, 20, 413
Service Employees International Union
    (SEIU), 125, 191, 192, 656
    campaign contributions, 204–205
Sethi, S. Prakash, 116
Seven-Up, 251
SHAC, 91
Shadow banking system, 292
Shah, Premil, 495
Shaming, 84
Shantou Institute of Ultrasonic
    Instruments, 517
Shapiro, Paul, 22
Sharav, Vera Hassner, 224
Shareholder rights, 85
Shell
    boycotts against, 76
    company codes, 695
    environmental issues, 324
    private politics case, 81, 91–95
    public politics and, 76
Shendahl, 342
Shepard, Randy, 676
Sherman, Richard, 409
Sherman Antitrust Act, 265, 271
    enforcement of, 235–238, 251
    European Union and, 426
    Microsoft antitrust case, 41, 233, 247,
        257–263
    predatory pricing and entry deterrence,
        246–247
    regulation, 271
Shinawatra, Thaksin, 488
Shi Tao, 465, 473
Shoney's, 634, 676, 677
Shops and Establishments Acts
    (India), 513
Shu, 455

Shuhong, Zhang, 117
Sibal, Kapil, 505
Sidor, 488
Siekaczek, Reinhard, 705, 706
Siemens AG., 704–706
Sierra Club, 83, 126
    activist strategy, 85, 86
    crisis management and, 116
    environmental politics, 340
    environmental protection issues, 343
    nonmarket analysis, 133, 135, 136
    vote recruitment by, 174–175
    Wal-Mart and, 587
Sigma Delta Chi, 66
Silent Spring (Carson), 76
Silver, Jonathan, 191
Silver, Robert S., 410
Silver Spring Networks and the Smart
    Grid case, 375–377
Singapore Airlines, 148
Singhal, Arvind, 514
Single European Act (SEA), 12,
    418–419, 439
SitePen, 35
Sjoblom, Bjorn, 555
Skidmore, Janet, 224
Skilling, Jeffrey, 563, 580, 581, 585
Skype, 25
Slave labor, in Saipan, 686
Small and Medium-Size Business and
    Cooperative Law (Japan), 554
Small and Medium-Size Enterprises Agency
    (Japan), 554
Small Business Administration, 133
Smith, Adam, 559, 565
Smith, Bradford, 24
Smith, Chris, 475
Smith, Gary, 279
Smith, Gordon, 189
Smith, Synthia, 106
Smith, Todd, 402
Smithfield Foods, 338
SmithKline Beecham, 707
Smith v.Van Gorkom, 577
Smoke*Screen, 157
Smoot-Hawley Act, 519
Social accountability, 576–577
Social Charter (EU), 429–430
Social costs, 395–396
Social democracy, 429–430
Social efficiency
    environmental management and
        stability, 324–327
    law and, 392–394, 395–396
Social entrepreneurship cases, 493–496
Social explanations, 453–457
Social harmony, 454, 456
Social policy, antitrust policy and, 230
Social pressure, 571–572
Social responsibility. *See* Corporate social
    responsibility (CSR)
Social value, 325, 326
Societal significance perspective, 55–56

Societal well-being, 601–602
Société Générale, 103, 110
Society of Professional Journalists, 65
Soft Drink Interbrand Competition Act,
   234, 251
Software and Information Industry
   Association, 215, 217
Sohu.com, 473
Solar Power
   implementation, 369–370
   nonmarket risks (China), 370
   opportunities and risks, 366–367
   Solyndra, Inc., 365–372
Solyndra, Inc., 365–372
Songkhla, Mongkol na, 545
Sonny Bono Copyright Term Extension
   Act, 386
Source Perrier S.A., crisis management, 104
Sourcing, global, 649–650
South Africa, 499, 500
Southampton Place LP, 582
Southdown, 541
Southern Baptist Convention, 78
Southern California Edison, 284, 349, 373–374
Southern Wine and Spirits, 139
South Korea, 536, 537
Southland Corporation, 185
Sovereign Default Risk, 479
Soviet Union, 172, 173
SPA Agencies, 513
Spain, 441, 442, 444–445
Special Economic Zones (China),
   452–453, 463
Special interest groups, 9
Specialty Vehicle Institute of America
   (SVIA), 279
Specific performance, 390
Spectrum auction, 25–26, 34–36
Spectrum for Wireless Broadband: Old Media
   Versus New Media case, 415
Spencer's, 515
Spitzer, Eliot, 100
Sporting Goods Manufacturers
   Association, 185
Sprint Communications, 428
Spurlock, Morgan, 20
Staffs, in U.S. Congress, 154–155
Stakeholder theory, 564–566
Standardization, 233, 240, 243–244,
   272, 345, 552
Standards setting, under EPA, 335
Standing Committee of Politburo (China), 40
Stanford Group Company, 37
Stanhill, William D., 191
Staples, 88, 462, 569
Starbucks, 39–40, 42, 47, 86, 487, 506–507,
   572, 575
Stark, Pete, 440
Starkie-Alves, Anne, 119
StarKist Seafood Company, 569
StarKist Tuna, boycotts against, 78
State Administration for Industry and
   Commerce, 471

State Administration of Radio, Film, and
   Television (China), 28–29
State aid, in European union, 428–429
State Council (China), 5, 460–461, 464,
   471–472
State Council Information Office (China),
   473, 474
State Education Commission, 461
State Environmental Protection
   Administration (SEPA), 469
State Food and Drug Administration
   (China), 467
State government environmental policy
   initiatives, 337
   Internet taxation, 216
   nonmarket strategy and, 167
   trade association lobbying and, 205–206
State institutions, in China, 460–461
"State of the News Media, The," 58, 61
State-owned enterprises (China), 448,
   462–464
State Planning Commission (China), 461
Static efficiency, 243, 244
Statute of limitations, 400
Statute of repose, 400
Statutes, antitrust, 230, 231–234
Steel imports, 535–536
Steere, William, Jr., 709
Stein, Sidney, 411
Step Up Women's Network, 221
Stevens, Frank, 619
Stinchfield, Patti, 224
Strategic corporate social
   performance, 572
Strategic trade theory, 522–523
Strategies for Addressing Social
   Pressure, 87
Strategy. See Nonmarket strategy
Street, William, 319
Strict liability, 396–401, 403, 405–407
Structural approach (antitrust thought),
   239–241, 251
Structured pluralism, 132, 134, 417,
   457–458
Students for Environmental and Economic
   Justice (SEEJ), 99
Stupak, Bart, 116
Subprime lending case, 318–320
Subprime Mortgages, 296–297
Subsidization
   cost, 362–363
   economic and political rationales,
   361–365
   renewable power, 361
Subsidization, in European Union, 428
   See also Cross-subsidization
Substantive due process, 268
Substitutes, 134
Sudan, 479, 489, 491, 497–498, 500
Sukuk, 489
Sulfur Dioxide and Nitrogen Oxides, tradable
   permits, 329
Sullivan, Coleman, 676

Sullivan, Nick, 589
Sullivan, Ted, 374
Sun Bank, 611
Sun Microsystems, 258, 260, 263,
   427, 475
   European Union and, 427
   Microsoft antitrust case, 258, 259, 260,
   262, 263
Sun Yat-sen, 450
Super 301, 539
Super Size Me (documentary), 20
Superfund, 334, 337, 342
Suppliers, in restaurant industry, 22
Suppliers' factories, working conditions in,
   688–690
Supply side, in nonmarket analysis, 136,
   145–146
Supreme People's Court (China), 461
Supreme People's Procurator (China), 461
Surui (indigenous tribe), 28
SustainAbility, Ltd., 91
Sustainable Forest Initiative (SFI), 91
Sustainable Forestry Institute (SFI), 82
SUV Owners of America, 3
Swap Sub, 582
Swaziland, 498
Sweatshops, 688–689
Sweden
   EU carbon tax case, 433
   EU nonmarket issues, 430–433
   interests, 433
   Toys 'Я' Us case, 552, 554–555
Sweet, Robert W., 413
Sykes, Sir Richard, 710
Syntex, 166
Syracuse Housing Partnership, 90
Syria, 488, 498, 500

T

Taiwan, 97, 363, 450, 452–453
Talon, 583
Tandy/Radio Shack, 216
Tang Dynasty (China), 449
Tanzania, 491, 495–497
Target
   Chicago public politics case, 219
   crisis management, 128
Target selection
   private politics, 86
   public officeholders, 179–180
Tariff Act (1930), 532
Tariffs, on automobile industry, 7
Tata, 514, 507
Tata, Ratan, 507
Tauke, Thomas J., 26
Taxes
   carried interest, 189–192
   Internet, 214–218
   luxury, 160
   value-added, 217, 419, 500
Tax Reduction and Reform
   Act (2007), 189
Taylor, Bret, 592

Taylor, Gordon, 73
Teamsters Union, 282, 538
Technical information, 178, 197–198
Technological advancement, 11–12
Technology
    dynamic Internet, 474
    ultrasound, 517
    face-recognition, 589–590
    See also Internet
Technopak, 514
Telecom Watchdog, 500
Telecommunications Act (1996), 162
Telecommunications industry, 13, 25,
    31, 415, 503
Teleological ethics systems, 622, 623
Television news, 59, 61–62, 193
    See also News media
Telewest Communications, 427
Tesco PLC, 504, 512–515, 531
    India case, 512–515
Testimony, 209–210
Texaco, 354, 634
Texas Eagle Forum, 223, 224
Texas State Board of Education, 78
Thailand, 98, 115, 481, 488–489, 513, 527–528,
    530–531, 539, 545–549,
    604, 680, 688, 709
Thai Network of People Living with
    AIDS/HIV, 547
Thirteenth Amendment, 634
Thompson, Danny, 676
Thompson, Robin, 675
Thompson, Susan, 676
ThyssenKrupp, 706
TIAA-CREF, 578
Tianya.cn, 28–29, 702
Tibet, 459, 465, 474, 487, 700
Tillinghast-Towers Perrin, 391
Tillman Act, 202
Timberland company, 563
Time Warner, 215, 250, 254
Timing, 200
Tipping, 510, 678–679
Tobacco politics, 133, 135, 157–158
Tobacco Resolution, 157
Tokyo Round, 525
Toomey, Mike, 223
Torts, 391
Toshiba Machine Company, 173
Toshiba, 209
Toxic Substances Control Act (TSCA),
    117, 334
Toxics Release Inventory (TRI), 85, 342
Toyota, 1, 2
    antitrust thought, 244
    carbon dioxide emission regulations, 7
    China and, 466
    intellectual property issues, 8
    media coverage of, 8
    products liability politics, 403
    recalls, 6
    UAW and, 7
Toys 'Я' Us, 119, 552–556

Tradable permits systems. *See* Cap-and-trade
    systems
Trade Act (1974), 532
Trade Adjustment Assistance Act, 533
Trade agreements. *See* International trade
    agreements
Trade associations, 206
Trade disputes, 529–530
Trade liberalization, 205, 523–525,
    531–532, 538–540
    See also Free trade agreements; *specific
    free trade agreements*
Trademarks, 27, 384, 387
    See also Intellectual property
Tradeoffs, 323–324
Trade policy. *See* International
    trade policy
Trade-Related Aspects of Intellectual
    Property Rights (TRIPS), 18, 489, 508,
    526–527, 531, 545–546, 617, 688,
    709–711
Trade secrets, 387
Transaction costs, 327
Transfair USA, 486, 487, 562
Transparency International (TI), 467, 478,
    479, 509, 691, 698, 706
Travelers Group, 296, 318
Treatment Action Campaign
    (TAC), 709
Treatment Action Group, 548
Treaty Establishing the European
    Community, 429
Treaty of Brussels, 417
Treaty of Lisbon, 418–421, 423, 437,
    439, 443, 446
Treaty of Nanjing, 449
Treaty of Paris, 417
Treaty of Rome, 417, 419, 425, 428
Treble damages, 232, 236–237,
    250–251, 384
Trial Lawyers Association, 9
Triplett, Earl, 105
Triplett, Mary, 105
Tropical Forest Foundation, 346
Troubled Asset Relief Program
    (TARP), 300
Trust gap, 75, 85, 557–558, 596
T-Solar and the Solar Power Market
    case, 377–379
Tudou, 29
Tunney Act, 263
Tupperware, 471
TW Services, 675
Twenty-First Amendment, 139
TXU and the Leveraged Buyout, 83
Tying, 234
Tyson Foods, 201

U

UBS, 289
UCB SA, 620
Uganda, 491, 495–498
UK Bribery Act, 695

Umbrella organizations. *See* Peak
    associations
UNAIDS, 546–547, 618, 708–709
Unanimous consent agreements
    (UCAs), 152
Unanticipated consequences, 306–307
Underdeveloped markets, business groups
    in, 481
Understandings, changes in, 12
Unethical behavior, sources of, 673–674
UNICEF, 618, 709
Uniform Standards Coalition, 206
Uniform Time Act, 184
Unilateral nonmarket strategies, 168
Union of Food and Commercial Workers
    (UFCW), 125–126, 128, 131, 218–219
Union of Industrial and Employers
    Confederations of Europe (UNICE), 433
Union of Needletrade, Industrial and Textile
    Employees (UNITE), 95, 689
Unions. *See* Labor unions; *specific unions*
UNITA, 703
United Airlines, 206, 579, 604, 609
United Auto Workers (UAW), 5, 9, 126,
    205, 539
    coalition building, 205
    international trade policy, 525
United Egg Producers (UEP), 22
United Food and Commercial Workers
    (UFCW), 125–126, 128, 131, 218–219
United Kingdom
    China and, 452
    emerging markets and, 512–513
    EU carbon tax case, 440
    GlaxoSmithKline case, 620
    McDonald's libel case, 68
    pharmaceutical industry, 18
    price fixing case, 252
    private politics case, 91
United Methodist Church, 78
United Nations, 23, 75, 96, 179, 217, 321–323,
    332, 432, 518, 527, 546, 558, 568, 617,
    681–682, 688, 690, 703, 708–709
United Nations Convention on Contracts
    for the International Sale of Goods,
    681–682
United Nations Development Program, 709
United Nations Framework Convention on
    Climate Change, 681–682
United Nations International Conference on
    Population and Development, 518
United Progressive Alliance (UPA), 504
U.S. Agency for International Development
    (USAID), 695
United States Association of Importers of
    Textiles and Apparel, 535
U.S. Chamber Institute for Legal Reform,
    411–413
U.S. Chamber of Commerce, 190, 205, 354,
    411–413, 472, 655, 695
U.S. Climate Action Partnership, 322, 331
U.S. Conference of Mayors, 216,
    270, 355

U.S. Congress, 7, 10
  access to, 199
  Boeing and, 141
  Doha Round, 531
  intellectual property law and, 466
  Internet taxation case, 216
  overview of, 152–156
  responsiveness of, 180–181
  tobacco politics, 133
  trade association lobbying and, 205–206
  See also Legislation; Taxes; *specific laws,
    representatives, and senators*
U.S. Constitution, 266, 282
  regulation and, 265–266, 267
  rights and, 623, 628
  See also specific amendments
U.S. Court of International Trade (CIT), 167,
  533, 544
U.S. Department of Agriculture (USDA),
  21–23, 412
U.S. Department of Commerce, 544
U.S. Department of Defense, 173
U.S. Department of Energy, 92, 270, 330,
  347, 360, 365, 371–372, 374
U.S. Department of Health and Human
  Service, 412
U.S. Department of Justice, 236, 252, 263,
  410, 427, 706
  Antitrust Division, 230, 263, 410
  antitrust laws, 211, 235–238, 242, 250,
    251, 252, 263, 463, 563, 589
  Citigroup case, 319
  crisis management and, 129
  Denny's customer service case, 676
  European Union and, 428
  Google and, 26, 475
  judicial actions, 211
  Microsoft and, 29, 257–263
  price fixing case, 252–253
  responsiveness of, 180–181
U.S. Department of Labor, 14, 130, 579, 688
U.S. Department of State, 173
U.S. Department of the Treasury, 146, 199,
  300–301, 358
U.S. Department of Transportation, 10, 184,
  211, 608
U.S. Green Building Council, 323
U.S. Green Lights program, 22
U.S. House of Representatives, 152
U.S. India Business Council (USIBC), 508
U.S. Industry Coordinating Group, 434
U.S. International Trade Commission, 540
U.S. Navy, 408
U.S. Partnership for Renewable Energy
  Finance (US PREF), 369
U.S. Public Interest Research Group, 24
U.S. Secret Service, 675
U.S. Senate, 486, 525
U.S. Supreme Court
  appointments to, 155
  class action lawsuits and, 12
U.S. Surgeon General, 19, 412
U.S. trade policy, 532–533

U.S. Trade Representative (USTR), 146, 174,
  199, 472, 530, 532, 554, 709
U.S. v. Aluminum Co. of America, 233
U.S. v. Arnold Schwinn & Co., 244
U.S. v. Harriss, 200
United Steel Workers (USW), 169, 370,
  523, 534
United Steelworkers of America v. Weber, 646
United Students Against Sweatshops, 689
Universalizability, 624
University of California–Berkeley, 45, 117, 190
University of Tennessee, 216, 225
Unocal Corporation, 682
Upakaew, Kamol, 547
Upjohn, 165
Upsher-Smith Laboratories, 18
Upton, Fred, 371
Urban expansion strategy, of Wal-Mart,
  218–220
Uruguay, 532
Uruguay Round, 525, 526–528, 531, 534,
  545, 617
USAir, 206
Usmani, Muhammad Taqi, 489
Utilitarian duty, 602–603
Utilitarianism, 600–602
  act and rule, 603–606
  application of, 609–612
  bribery and, 693–694
  criticisms of, 606–609
  distribution and altruism, 602
  rights and, 606
  self-interest and societal well-being,
    601–602
  summary, 612
  utilitarian duty and the Calabresi and
    Melamed principles, 602–603
Utility, interpersonal comparisons of, 607
Utz Kapeh, 487

V

Vacharanukulki-eti, Kriengsak, 547
Vallese, Julie, 120
Value-added tax (VAT), 217, 419, 500
Value chain, 76, 88, 112, 169, 172
Van Andel, Steve, 472
Van Eeden, Dirk, 546
Van Etten, W. Thomas, 610
Vegetarian Resource Group, 23
Venezuela, 479, 481, 487–488, 492, 505,
  529, 532, 542
Verispan LLC, 410
Verizon, 25, 34, 35, 253–255,
  415–416, 500
Verizon Business, 500
Vermont Renewal, 223
Vertical arrangements, 231, 236–239, 241,
  243–246, 250–251, 425
Vertical integration, 234, 461
Vertical practices, 233, 244
Veteran Affairs Outcomes Group, 619
Viacom, 59
Video Privacy Protection Act, 591

Vienna Convention for the Protection of the
  Ozone Layer, 682
Vietnam, 95–97, 481, 485, 489, 530,
  689, 701
Vietnam Labor Watch (VLW), 96
Viking Yacht, 160
Vinson and Elkins, 583–585
Virgin Atlantic Airways, price fixing by,
  252–253
Visa, 45, 158–159, 237, 238
Vista (operating system), 29
Vivendi SA, 250, 428
Vodacom, 499–500
Vodafone, 253, 497, 499, 504
Volcker, Paul, 302
Volcker Rule, 302
Volkswagen, 8, 430–431, 464
Voluntary collective programs, for
  environmental management and
  stability, 347
Von Pierer, Heinrich, 704, 705
Vote recruitment, 174–175, 177,
  181, 188

W

Waitt, Theodore, 215
WakeUpWalMart.com, 125, 126, 587
Wako Koeki, 173
Wallerstein, Barry, 354
Wall Street Journal, 478
Wal-Mart
  antitrust laws, 237
  corporate social performance, 570
  corporate social responsibility, 586–588
  crisis management, 102, 109–110,
    124–131
  emerging markets and, 515
  environmental programs, 322
  environmental protection issues, 343
  Internet taxation case, 216, 217
  Michelle Obama, 201
  nonmarket capabilities of, 43
  rent chain and, 170
  reputation and stakeholder management,
    124–131
  urban expansion strategy, 43, 164,
    168–169, 174, 197, 200, 218
Wal-Mart bill (Maryland), 127
Wal-Mart and Its Urban Expansion Strategy
  case, 218
Wal-Mart: The High Cost of Low Price
  (documentary), 125
Wal-Mart Watch, 125, 127–128,
  192, 586
Wal-Mart Workers Association, 126
Walsh, Willie, 252
Walt Disney Company, 59, 78, 215, 591
Walter, Jim, 116, 118
Walton, Sam, 124
Walton Family Foundation, 126
Wang Zhongfu, 471
Warranties, 274, 397, 400
Warranty of merchantability, 397

Warring States Period (China), 449
Waste reduction, by McDonald's, 345
Watchdog groups, 9, 163, 181
    See also specific organizations
Watergate affair, 59
Water Keeper Alliance, 338
Watkins, Sherron, 583
WBBM (Chicago television station), 67–68
Weatherup, Craig A., 105, 106
Webb-Pomerene Act, 233
Weill, Sandy, 86, 99, 101, 318, 564
Weinstein, Michael, 547, 548
Weintraub, Rachel, 119
WellPoint Health Networks, 17
Wendy's, 106–107
Wen Jiabao, 461
West, Kanye, 703
Westco Oil Company, 353
Westerfield, Charles, 494
Westin Hotels, 579
WestLB, 340
Westpac, 340
Weyerhaeuser, 89, 104, 105
Whaley, Soso, 20
WHDH-TV (Boston television station), 66
White, Miles D., 548
White House Apparel Industry
    Partnership, 689
White Spaces Coalition, 35, 276
Whitt, Larry, 200
Whitt, Richard, 35
Whole Foods Market, 249, 486
Wholly foreign-owned enterprise (WFOE), 463
*Why Wal-Mart Works & Why That Makes
    Some People Crazy* (Galloway), 126
Wilderness Society, 133
Wildfeuer, Christian, 259
Wild Oats Markets, 249
Wilkes, Michael, 619
Willett, Walter, 21
Williams, Simon, 252
Wilson-Lowi matrix, 137–138, 144, 158,
    167, 181
Wind and Solar Power environment, 359–361
Wine America, 139
Wine and Spirit Wholesalers of America, 139
Wine Institute (California), 139
Winkelman, John, 619
Winn-Dixie, 128

Woicke, Peter, 340
Woloshin, Steven, 620, 621
Women in Government, 222–224
Women's Environment and Development
    Organization (WEDO), 518
Women's rights, in China, 464–465
Wong, Nicole, 24, 25, 516
Wood, Bob, 97
Wood, Pat, III, 584
Wood Purchasing Policy, 346
Woods, Willie E., Jr., 190
Woodward, Robert, 59
Woolard, Edgar S., Jr., 343
Woolworths, 513–514
Wootan, Margo, 20
Worker Rights Consortium, 689
Workers' rights, in China, 468–469
Working conditions, in suppliers' factories,
    688–690
Working Families for Wal-Mart, 587
Workplace obesity, 21
World Association of Newspapers, 26
World Bank, 340
    antiglobalization protests against, 85
    China and, 463
    emerging markets and, 490
    GlaxoSmithKline AIDS drugs policy case,
        527, 531, 604, 688, 707–711
WorldCom, 1, 215, 306, 314, 428,
    563–564, 578
World Council for Sustainable
    Development, 568
World Court, 681
World Health Organization (WHO), 12, 350,
    412, 546, 548, 617, 708
World Intellectual Property
    Organization, 527
World Privacy Forum, 24
World Trade Organization (WTO), 7, 10,
    18, 708
    antiglobalization protests against, 85
    applied rights analysis and, 629
    China and, 179, 448, 458, 464
    compulsory licensing case, 545
    Dispute Settlement Body, 528, 682
    Doha Round, 519, 531, 545
    emerging markets and, 499
    GlaxoSmithKline AIDS drugs policy
        case, 707
    international trade agreements, 525–526
    international trade policy, 519

Internet taxation, 216, 217
    pharmaceutical industry, 18
    restaurant industry, 20
World War II, China and, 450
World Wildlife Fund, 88, 346
Wright, Robert, 71
Wugang, 451
Wu Yi, 119, 472
Wyatt, Amy, 515
Wyden, Ron, 214, 535, 614
Wyeth-Ayerst Laboratories, 609, 613

X

Xia, Bill, 474
Xingtian Company, 471
Xin Ye, 473
Xitongs, 461
XL Insurance, 109

Y

Yahoo!
    China and, 465, 473, 474
    Google and, 25, 26, 27
    international strategy, 33
    Microsoft and, 29
Yamada, Tadataka, 548
Yamaha Motor Company, 50
Yamoff, Seymour L., 66
Yang, Jerry, 29
Yang, Sam, 95
Yetraeus, Sten, 555
Yi, Wu, 119
Yoffie, David, 263
Youku, 28
Young, Andrew, 96, 97
Young, Louis H., 55, 62
Yousif, Mahmoud al-, 23–24
YouTube, 8, 27, 29, 48, 104, 118, 213,
    488, 491, 517, 700
Yuan Shikai, 450
Yuguang, Xie, 117
Yunus, Muhammad, 482, 494, 495

Z

Zambrano, Lorenzo, 540, 543, 544
Zhao Jing, 473
Zhou Enlai, 452
Zimbabwe, 478–479, 489–490, 499, 703
Zindler, Harald, 93, 95
Zogby International, 127
Zonneveld, Luuk Laurens, 486